Collins

Collins Spanish Dictionary

HarperCollins Publishers
Westerhill Road
Bishopbriggs
Glasgow
G64 2QT
Great Britain

Fifth Edition 2009

Reprint 10 9 8 7 6 5 4 3 2 1 0

ISBN 978-0-00-733151-2

www.collinslanguage.com

A catalogue record for this book is available from the British Library

Art Direction by Mark Thomson
Designed by Wolfgang Homola
Typeset by Davidson Publishing Solutions, Glasgow

Printed in Italy by LEGO Spa, Lavis (Trento)

Acknowledgements
We would like to thank those authors and publishers who kindly gave permission for copyright material to be used in the Collins Word Web. We would also like to thank Times Newspapers Ltd for providing valuable data.

EDITORIAL MANAGEMENT
Gaëlle Amiot-Cadey

EDITORIAL COORDINATION
Susie Beattie

EDITORS
Teresa Álvarez, Jeremy Butterfield, Cordelia Lilly, Fernando León Solís, Gerry Breslin, Malihé Forghani-Nowbari, Jane Horwood, Anna Jené Palat, Lesley Johnston, Victoria Ordóñez Diví, Carol Styles, Eduardo Vallejo, José María Ruiz Vaca

CONCEPT DEVELOPMENT
Michela Clari
Ray Carrick

TECHNICAL SUPPORT
Thomas Callan

SERIES EDITOR
Rob Scriven

Our thanks to the following for their help in researching the project:
Maree Airlie, Teresa Álvarez, Phyllis Gautier, Janet Gough, Sharon Hunter, Mary James, Cordelia Lilly, Carol McCann, Jill McNair, Janet Chalmers

William Collins' dream of knowledge for all began with the publication of his first book in 1819. A self-educated mill worker, he not only enriched millions of lives, but also founded a flourishing publishing house. Today, staying true to this spirit, Collins books are packed with inspiration, innovation, and practical expertise. They place you at the centre of a world of possibility and give you exactly what you need to explore it.

Language is the key to this exploration, and at the heart of Collins Dictionaries is language as it is really used. New words, phrases, and meanings spring up every day, and all of them are captured and analysed by the Collins Word Web. Constantly updated, and with over 2.5 billion entries, this living language resource is unique to our dictionaries.

Words are tools for life. And a Collins Dictionary makes them work for you.

Collins. Do more.

Contents

Introduction

Collins Easy Learning Spanish Dictionary is an innovative dictionary designed specifically for anyone starting to learn Spanish. We are grateful to all those teachers who have contributed to its development by advising us on how to tailor it to the needs of their students. We also gratefully acknowledge the help of the examining boards, whom we have consulted throughout this project, and whose word lists and exam papers we carefully studied when compiling this dictionary in order to ensure appropriate coverage and support for GCSE and other exams of a similar level.

Free downloadable resources are now available for teachers and learners of Spanish at **www.collinslanguage.com**.

Dictionary skills

Using a dictionary is a skill you can improve with practice and by following some basic guidelines. This section gives you a detailed explanation of how to use this dictionary to ensure you get the most out of it.

The answers to the questions in this section are on page 16.

Make sure you look on the right side of the dictionary

The Spanish - English side comes first, followed by the English - Spanish. At the side of the page, you will see a tab with either **Spanish - English** or **English - Spanish**, so you know immediately if you're looking up the side you want.

1 **Which side of the dictionary would you look up to translate 'la bicicleta'?**

Finding the word you want

When looking for a word, for example **feliz**, look at the first letter - **f** - and find the **F** section in the Spanish - English side. At the top of each page, you'll find the first and last words on that page. When you find the page with the words starting with **fe**, scan down the page until you find the word you want. Remember that even if a word has an accent on it, for example **fórmula**, it makes no difference to the alphabetical order. The exception to this rule is **ñ** (*n tilde*), which is treated as a separate letter in Spanish, so that *leña* follows *lento*.

2 **On which page will you find the word - 'hermana'?**
3 **Which comes first - 'francesa' or 'francés'?**

To help you expand your vocabulary, we have also suggested possible alternatives in the WORD POWER features at the most common adjectives in English - try looking up **big** on page 24 and learning some of the words you could use.

Make sure you look at the right entry

An entry is made up of a **word**, its translations and, often, example phrases to show you how to use the translations. Key words which you need to be familiar with for your GCSE or other exams of a similar level are highlighted throughout both sides of the dictionary to help you find and learn them more easily. If there is more than one entry for the same word, then there is a note to tell you so. Look at the following example entries:

flat ADJECTIVE
▷ *see also* **flat** NOUN
llano (FEM llana)
□ a flat surface una superficie llana
■ **flat shoes** zapatos bajos
■ **I've got a flat tyre.** Tengo una rueda desinflada.

flat NOUN
▷ *see also* **flat** ADJECTIVE
el piso (el apartamento *Latin America*)

4 **Which of the two entries above will help you translate the phrase *'My car has a flat tyre'?* Look for the two clues which are there to help you:**
> **an example similar to what you want to say**
> **the word ADJECTIVE**

Look out for information notes which have this symbol on the left-hand side. They will give you guidance on grammatical points, and tell you about differences between Spanish and British life.

Choosing the right translation

The main translation of a word is shown on a new line and is underlined to make it stand out from the rest of the entry. If there is more than one main translation for a word, each one is numbered. On the English - Spanish side, Latin American equivalents are shown in brackets after the main translation, and are labelled *Latin America*.

Often you will see phrases in light blue, preceded by a white square □. These help you to choose the translation you want because they show how the translation they follow can be used.

5 **Use the phrases given at the entry *'hard'* to help you translate: *'This bread is hard'*.**

Words often have more than one meaning and more than one translation. For example, a **pool** can be a puddle, a pond or a swimming pool; **pool** can also be a game. When you are translating from English into Spanish, be careful to choose the Spanish word that has the particular meaning you want. The dictionary offers you a lot of help with this. Look at the following entry:

pool NOUN
1 el estanque *(pond)*
2 la piscina *(swimming pool)*
3 el billar americano *(game)*
■ **a pool table** una mesa de billar
■ **the pools** las quinielas □ I do the pools every week. Juego a las quinielas todas las semanas.

The underlining highlights all the main translations, the numbers tell you that there is more than one possible translation and the words in brackets in *italics* after the translations help you choose the translation you want.

6 **How would you translate *'I like playing pool'?***

Never take the first translation you see without looking at the others. Always look to see if there is more than one translation underlined.

Phrases in **bold type** preceded by a blue or black square ■/■ are phrases which are particularly common or important. Sometimes these phrases have a completely different translation from the main translation; sometimes the translation is the same. For example:

el **acuerdo** NOUN
agreement
□ llegar a un acuerdo to reach an agreement
■ **estar de acuerdo con alguien** to agree with somebody
■ **ponerse de acuerdo** to agree □ Al final no nos pusimos de acuerdo. In the end we couldn't agree. □ Nos pusimos de acuerdo para prepararle una bienvenida. We agreed to organize a welcome for him.
■ **¡De acuerdo!** All right!

When you look up a word, make sure you look beyond the main translations to see if the entry includes any **bold phrases**.

7 **Look up 'ir' to help you translate the sentence 'Voy a casa mañana'?**

Making use of the phrases in the dictionary

Sometimes when you look up a word you will find not only the word, but the exact phrase you want. For example, you might want to say '*What's the date today?*'. Look up **date** and you will find that exact phrase and its translation.

Sometimes you have to adapt what you find in the dictionary. If you want to say '*I ate a sandwich*' and look up **eat** you will find:

to **eat** VERB
comer
□ Would you like something to eat?
¿Quieres comer algo?

You have to substitute **comí** for the infinitive form **comer**. You will often have to adapt the infinitive in this way, adding the correct ending and choosing the present, future or past form. For help with this, look at the verb tables. On the **Spanish - English** side of the dictionary, you will notice that verbs are followed by a number in square brackets, which correspond to verb tables on pages 19-30 in the middle section of this dictionary. **Estudiar** is a verb ending in **-ar** so it follows the same pattern as verb number [25] **hablar**, which is set out in full on page 24.

8 **How would you say *'I don't eat meat'*?**

Phrases containing nouns and adjectives also need to be adapted. You may need to make the noun plural, or the adjective feminine or plural. Remember that some Spanish nouns and adjectives change their spelling in the feminine or plural and that this is shown in the entry.

9 **How would you say *'The boys are Spanish'*?**

Don't overuse the dictionary

It takes time to look up words so try to avoid using the dictionary unnecessarily, especially in exams. Think carefully about what you want to say and see if you can put it another way, using words you already know. To rephrase things you can:

> Use a word with a similar meaning. This is particularly easy with adjectives, as there are a lot of words which mean *good*, *bad*, *big* etc and you're sure to know at least one.

> Use negatives: if the cake you made was a total disaster, you could just say it wasn't very good.

> Use particular examples instead of general terms. If you are asked to describe the sports *facilities* in your area, and time is short, you could say something like *'In our town there is a swimming pool and a football ground.'*

10 **How could you say *'Argentina is huge'* without looking up the word *'huge'*?**

You can also often guess the meaning of a Spanish word by using others to give you a clue. If you see the sentence *'María lee un buen libro'*, you may not know the meaning of the word **lee**, but you know it's a verb because it's preceded by **María**. Therefore it must be something you can do to a book: **read**. So the translation is: *María is reading a good book.*

11 **Try NOT to use your dictionary to work out the meaning of the sentence 'La chica escribe una carta a su amiga en español'.**

Parts of speech

If you look up the word **flat**, you will see that there are two entries for this word as it can be a noun or an adjective. It helps to choose correctly between entries if you know how to recognize these different types of words.

Nouns and pronouns

Nouns often appear with words like *a, the, this, that, my, your* and *his*. They can be singular (abbreviated to SING in the dictionary):

his ***dog*** *her* ***cat*** *a* ***street***

or plural (abbreviated to PL in the dictionary):

the ***facts*** *those* ***people*** *his* ***shoes*** *our* ***holidays***

They can be the subject of a verb:

Vegetables *are good for you*

or the object of a verb:

I play ***tennis***

Words like *I, me, you, he, she, him, her* and *they* are pronouns. They can be used instead of nouns. You can refer to a person as *he* or *she* or to a thing as *it*.

I bought my mother a box of chocolates.

12 **Which three words in this sentence are nouns?**

13 **Which of the nouns is plural?**

14 **Which word is a pronoun?**

Spanish nouns are either masculine or feminine (abbreviated to MASC and FEM). Masculine nouns are shown by **el**:

el *hombre* ***el*** *gato* ***el*** *fútbol*

Feminine nouns are shown by **la**:

la *mujer* ***la*** *economía* ***la*** *fábrica*

The plural forms of **el** and **la** are **los** and **las**. The plural of most Spanish nouns is made by adding **s** if the word ends in a vowel, or **es** if it ends in a consonant:

los *gatos* ***las*** *mujeres*

Adjectives

Flat can be an adjective as well as a noun. Adjectives describe nouns: your tyre can be **flat**, you can have a pair of **flat** shoes.

15 **In which sentence is *'dark'* an adjective?**

I'm afraid of the dark.

The girl has dark hair.

Spanish adjectives can be masculine or feminine, singular or plural, depending on the noun they describe:

un chico **guapo** (MASC SING)
una chica **guapa** (FEM SING: replace -**o** of masculine with -**a**)
unos chicos **guapos** (MASC PL = masculine singular + **s**)
unas chicas **guapas** (FEM PL = feminine singular + **s**)

The masculine and feminine singular forms of regular adjectives are shown on both sides of the dictionary. So if you want to find out what kind of houses **unas casas viejas** are, look under **viejo**.

There are separate masculine and feminine, singular and plural forms for irregular adjectives of nationality, and those ending in -**án**, -**ín**, -**ón**, eg **español** MASCULINE SINGULAR, **española**, FEMININE SINGULAR, **españoles** MASCULINE PLURAL, **españolas** FEMININE PLURAL.

Adjectives ending in -**or** also follow the above pattern unless they are comparatives. The feminine is shown in the dictionary for adjectives of this type.

hablador (FEM **habladora**) ADJECTIVE
1 chatty
2 gossipy

talkative ADJECTIVE
hablador (FEM habladora)

Other adjectives ending in a consonant do not have a separate feminine form, but do change in the plural, eg **azul** MASCULINE and FEMININE SINGULAR, **azules** MASCULINE and FEMININE PLURAL.

feliz (FEM **feliz**, PL **felices**) ADJECTIVE
happy
□ Se la ve muy feliz. She looks very happy.
■ **¡Feliz cumpleaños!** Happy birthday!
■ **¡Feliz Año Nuevo!** Happy New Year!
■ **¡Felices Navidades!** Happy Christmas!

happy ADJECTIVE
feliz (FEM feliz, PL felices)
□ Janet looks happy. Janet parece feliz.
■ **to be happy with something** estar contento con algo □ I'm very happy with your work. Estoy muy contento con tu trabajo.
■ **Happy birthday!** ¡Feliz cumpleaños!
■ **a happy ending** un final feliz

If the masculine form of an adjective ends in **-e** or **-a**, the feminine form is the same, and both the masculine and feminine plurals are formed by adding **-s** to the masculine, eg **verde** MASCULINE and FEMININE SINGULAR, **verdes** MASCULINE and FEMININE PLURAL. Some adjectives remain the same whether they're masculine, feminine or plural. This is also shown in the dictionary:

el **rosa** ADJECTIVE, NOUN
pink
□ Va vestida de rosa. She's wearing pink.
■ **Llevaba unos calcetines rosa.** He was wearing pink socks.

Verbs

She's going to record the programme for me.
His time in the race was a new world record.

Record is a verb in the first sentence. In the second, it is a noun.

One way to recognize a verb is that it frequently comes with a pronoun such as **I**, **you** or **she**, or with somebody's name. Verbs can relate to the present, the past or the future. They have a number of different forms to show this: **I'm going** (present), **he will go** (future), and **Nicola went by herself** (past). Often verbs appear with **to**: **they promised to go**. This basic form of the verb is called the infinitive.

In this dictionary, verbs are preceded by 'to', so you can identify them at a glance. No matter which of the four previous examples you want to translate, you should look up 'to **go**', not '**going**' or '**went**'. If you want to translate '**I thought**', look up 'to **think**'.

16 What would you look up to translate the verbs in these phrases?

*I **came*** *she**'s crying*** *they**'ve done it*** *he**'s** out*

Verbs have different endings in Spanish, depending on whether you are talking about **yo**, **tú**, **nosotros** etc: **yo hablo**, **tú hablas**, **nosotros hablamos** etc. They also have different forms for the present, future, past etc. **Hablamos** (*we speak* = present), **hemos hablado** (*we spoke* = past), **hablaremos** (*we will speak* = future). **Hablar** is the infinitive and is the form that appears in the dictionary.

Sometimes the verb changes completely between the infinitive form and the **yo**, **tú**, **él** etc form. For example, *to give* is **dar**, but *I give* is **doy**, and **digo** comes from **decir** (*to say*).

On pages 24-30 of the middle section of this dictionary, you will find 7 of the most important regular and irregular Spanish verbs shown in full. On pages 19-23, you will find a list of the main forms of other key Spanish verbs. On the **Spanish - English** side of the dictionary, each Spanish verb has a number beside it - if you look this number up in the verb table section on pages 19-30 you will find the verb forms for that type of verb. Irregular Spanish verbs are marked in the dictionary with an asterisk.

to **fulfil** VERB
realizar*
□ He fulfilled his dream to visit China. Realizó su sueño de viajar a China.
■ **to fulfil a promise** cumplir una promesa

ir* VERBO [27]
1 to go
□ Anoche fuimos al cine. We went to the cinema last night. □ ¿A qué colegio vas? What school do you go to?
■ **ir de vacaciones** to go on holiday
■ **ir a por** to go and get

17 Which verb pattern does the verb estudiar follow?

Adverbs

An adverb is a word that describes a verb or an adjective:
*Write **soon**.* *Check your work **carefully**.*
*The film was **very** good.*

In the sentence '*The swimming pool is open daily*', **daily** is an adverb describing the adjective **open**. In the phrase '*my daily routine*', **daily** is an adjective describing the noun **routine**. We use the same word in English for both adjective and adverb forms, but to get the right Spanish translation, it is important to know if it's being used as an adjective or an adverb. When you look up **daily** you find:

daily ADJECTIVE, ADVERB
1 diario
□ daily life la vida diaria □ It's part of my daily routine. Forma parte de mi rutina diaria.
■ **a daily paper** un periódico
2 todos los días
□ The pool is open daily. La piscina abre todos los días.

The examples show you **daily** being used as an adjective and as an adverb and will help you choose the right Spanish translation.

Take the sentence '*The menu changes daily*'.
18 **Is '*daily*' an adverb or an adjective here?**

Prepositions

Prepositions are words like **for**, **with** and **across**, which are followed by nouns or pronouns:
*I've got a present **for** David.* *Come **with** me.* *He ran **across** the road.*

The party's over.
The shop's just over the road.

19 **Which sentence shows a preposition followed by a noun?**

Answers

1 the Spanish side
2 on page 159
3 **francés** comes first
4 the first (ADJECTIVE) entry
5 **Este pan está duro.**
6 **Me gusta jugar al billar americano.**
7 **I'm going home tomorrow.**
8 **No como carne.**
9 **Los niños son españoles.**
10 **Argentina es muy grande.**
11 **The girl is writing a letter to her friend in Spanish.**
12 **mother**, **box** and **chocolates** are nouns
13 **chocolates** is plural
14 **I** is a pronoun
15 in the second sentence
16 to **come**, to **cry**, to **do**, to **be**
17 **hablar**, number [25]
18 daily is an **adverb**
19 the second sentence

Aa

a *(a + el = al)* PREPOSITION
1 to
□ Fueron a Madrid. They went to Madrid.
■ **Me caí al río.** I fell into the river.
■ **Se subieron al tejado.** They climbed onto the roof.
■ **Marta llegó a la oficina.** Marta arrived at the office.
■ **Está a 15 km de aquí.** It's 15 km from here.
2 at
□ a las 10 at 10 o'clock □ a medianoche at midnight □ a los 24 años at the age of 24 □ Íbamos a más de 90 km por hora. We were going at over 90 km an hour.
■ **Estamos a 9 de julio.** It's the 9th of July.
■ **Los huevos están a 1,50 euros la docena.** Eggs are 1.50 euros a dozen.
■ **una vez a la semana** once a week □ Voy a verle. I'm going to see him. □ Vine a decírtelo. I came to tell you. □ Me obligaban a comer. They forced me to eat.
■ **Al verlo, lo reconocí inmediatamente.** When I saw him, I recognized him immediately.
■ **Nos cruzamos al salir.** We bumped into each other as we were going out. □ Se lo di a Ana. I gave it to Ana. □ Le enseñé a Pablo el libro que me dejaste. I showed Pablo the book you lent me.
■ **Se lo compré a él.** I bought it from him.
■ **Vi a Juan.** I saw Juan.
■ **Llamé al médico.** I called the doctor.
■ **Gira a la derecha.** Turn right.
■ **Me voy a casa.** I'm going home.
■ **¡A comer!** Lunch is ready!

la **abadía** NOUN
abbey (PL abbeys)

abajo ADVERB
1 below
□ Los platos y las tazas están abajo. The plates and cups are below. □ La montaña no parece tan alta desde abajo. The mountain doesn't seem so high from below.
■ **Mete las cervezas abajo del todo.** Put the beers at the bottom.
■ **El estante de abajo.** The bottom shelf.
■ **La parte de abajo del contenedor.** The bottom of the container.
2 downstairs
□ Abajo están la cocina y el salón. The kitchen and lounge are downstairs. □ Hay una fiesta en el piso de abajo. There's a party in the flat downstairs.
■ **más abajo** further down
■ **ir calle abajo** to go down the street
■ **Todos los bolsos son de 50 euros para abajo.** All the bags are 50 euros or under.
■ **abajo de** *(Latin America)* under

abandonado (FEM **abandonada**) ADJECTIVE
■ **un pueblo abandonado** a deserted village

abandonar VERB [25]
1 to leave
□ Decidieron abandonar el país. They decided to leave the country.
■ **Abandonó a su familia.** He deserted his family.
■ **Mucha gente abandona a sus perros en Navidad.** A lot of people abandon their dogs at Christmas.
2 to give up
□ Tuve que abandonar la idea de comprarme otro coche. I had to give up the idea of buying another car.

el **abanico** NOUN
fan

abarrotado (FEM **abarrotada**) ADJECTIVE
packed
□ abarrotado de gente packed with people

la **abarrotería** NOUN *(Mexico)*
grocer's (PL grocers' shops)

los **abarrotes** NOUN *(Mexico, Chile)*
groceries

abastecer* VERB [12]
■ **abastecer de algo a alguien** to supply somebody with something
■ **Nos abastecimos bien de comida para el viaje.** We stocked up with food for the trip.

el **abdomen** NOUN
stomach

los **abdominales** NOUN
sit-ups
□ hacer abdominales to do sit-ups

el **abecedario** NOUN
alphabet

la **abeja** NOUN
bee

el **abeto** NOUN
fir

abierto VERB
▷ *see also* **abierto** ADJECTIVE ▷ *see* **abrir**

abierto (FEM **abierta**) ADJECTIVE
▷ *see also* **abierto** VERB
1 open
□ ¿Están abiertas las tiendas? Are the shops open?
2 on
□ No dejes el gas abierto. Don't leave the gas on.

el **abogado**, la **abogada** NOUN
lawyer

abolir VERB [58]
to abolish

abollar VERB [25]
to dent
□ Me han abollado el coche. Someone has dented my car.
■ **abollarse** to get dented

abombarse VERB [25] *(Latin America)*
to go bad

abonar VERB [25]
1 to pay
□ abonar dinero en una cuenta to pay money into an account
2 to fertilize
□ Hay que abonar el terreno antes de sembrar. The land has to be fertilized before sowing.
■ **abonarse a** 1 to take out a subscription to 2 to join

el **abono** NOUN
1 fertilizer
2 season ticket

abortar VERB [25]
1 to have an abortion
2 to miscarry

el **aborto** NOUN
1 abortion
2 miscarriage

abrasar VERB [25]
to burn
□ El fuego le abrasó las manos. The fire burned his hands.
■ **abrasarse** to be burned □ Mucha gente se abrasó viva en el incendio. A lot of people were burned alive in the fire.

abrazar* VERB [13]
to hug
□ Al verme me abrazó. He hugged me when he saw me.
■ **¡Abrázame fuerte!** Give me a big hug!
■ **abrazarse** to hug □ Se abrazaron y se besaron. They hugged and kissed.

el **abrazo** NOUN
hug
□ ¡Dame un abrazo! Give me a hug!
■ **Siempre están dándose besos y abrazos.** They're always hugging and kissing.
■ **'un abrazo'** 'with best wishes'

el **abrebotellas** (PL los **abrebotellas**) NOUN
bottle opener

el **abrelatas** (PL los **abrelatas**) NOUN
tin opener

la **abreviatura** NOUN
abbreviation

el **abridor** NOUN
1 bottle opener
2 tin opener

abrigar* VERB [37]
■ **Esta chaqueta abriga mucho.** This jacket's great for keeping warm.
■ **Ponte algo que te abrigue.** Put something warm on.
■ **Abriga bien al niño, que hace frío.** Wrap the baby up well - it's cold.
■ **abrigarse** to wrap up well

el **abrigo** NOUN
coat
□ un abrigo de pieles a fur coat
■ **ropa de abrigo** warm clothing

abril MASC NOUN
April
□ en abril in April □ Nació el 20 de abril. He was born on 20 April.

abrir* VERB [58, PAST PARTICIPLE **abierto**]
1 to open
□ Las tiendas abren a las diez. The shops open at ten o'clock. □ Abre la ventana. Open the window.
■ **¡Abre, soy yo!** Open the door, it's me!
2 to turn on
□ ¿Has abierto el gas? Have you turned the gas on?
■ **abrirse** to open □ De repente se abrió la puerta. Suddenly the door opened.

abrocharse VERB [25]
to do up
□ Abróchate la camisa. Do your shirt up.
■ **Abróchense los cinturones.** Please fasten your seatbelts.

absoluto (FEM **absoluta**) ADJECTIVE
absolute
□ Nos dio garantía absoluta. He gave us an absolute guarantee.
■ **La operación fue un éxito absoluto.**

The operation was a complete success.
■ **en absoluto** at all □ ¿Te molesta que fume? — En absoluto. Do you mind if I smoke? — Not at all. □ nada en absoluto nothing at all

absorber VERB [8]
to absorb

abstemio (FEM **abstemia**) ADJECTIVE
teetotal
□ Soy abstemio. I'm teetotal.

la **abstención** (PL las **abstenciones**) NOUN
abstention

abstenerse* VERB [53]
to abstain
□ Yo me abstengo. I'm abstaining.
■ **abstenerse de hacer algo** to refrain from doing something

abstracto (FEM **abstracta**) ADJECTIVE
abstract

absurdo (FEM **absurda**) ADJECTIVE
absurd
■ **lo absurdo es que ...** the absurd thing is that ...

la **abuela** NOUN
grandmother
□ mi abuela my grandmother
■ **¿Dónde está la abuela?** Where's Gran?

el **abuelo** NOUN
grandfather
□ mi abuelo my grandfather
■ **¿Dónde está el abuelo?** Where's Grandad?
■ **mis abuelos** my grandparents

abultado (FEM **abultada**) ADJECTIVE
bulky

abultar VERB [25]
to be bulky
□ No abulta mucho. It isn't very bulky.
■ **Tus cosas apenas abultan.** Your things hardly take up any space at all.

abundante (FEM **abundante**) ADJECTIVE
1 plenty of
□ Habrá comida y bebida abundante. There'll be plenty of food and drink.
2 enormous
□ El año pasado tuvimos abundantes pérdidas. We had enormous losses last year.

aburrido (FEM **aburrida**) ADJECTIVE
1 bored
□ Estaba aburrida y me marché. I was bored so I left.
2 boring
□ una película muy aburrida a very boring film □ No seas aburrida y vente al cine. Don't be boring and come to the film.
3 tired
□ Estaba aburrido de esperarte, así que me fui. I was tired of waiting for you, so I left.

el **aburrimiento** NOUN
■ **¡Qué aburrimiento!** What a bore this is!
■ **Estoy muerto de aburrimiento.** I'm bored stiff.

aburrirse VERB [58]
to get bored
□ Me aburro viendo la tele. I get bored watching television.

abusar VERB [25]
■ **abusar de alguien 1** to take advantage of somebody **2** to abuse somebody
■ **Está bien beber de vez en cuando pero sin abusar.** Drinking every so often is fine as long as you don't overdo it.
■ **No conviene abusar del aceite en las comidas.** You shouldn't use too much oil in food.
■ **Abusó de nuestra hospitalidad.** He abused our hospitality.

el **abuso** NOUN
abuse
□ el abuso de las drogas drug abuse
■ **los abusos sexuales** sexual abuse *sing*
■ **Lo que han hecho me parece un abuso.** I think what they've done is outrageous.

acá ADVERB
here
□ ¡Vente para acá! Come over here!
■ **Hay que ponerlo más acá.** You'll have to bring it closer.

acabar VERB [25]
to finish
□ Cuando acabe esta cerveza me voy. When I've finished this beer I'm going. □ Ayer acabé de pintar la valla. Yesterday I finished painting the fence.
■ **acabar con 1** to put an end to □ Hay que acabar con tanto desorden. We must put an end to all this confusion. **2** to finish □ Hemos acabado con todas las provisiones. We've finished all our provisions.
■ **Acabo de ver a tu padre.** I've just seen your father. □ Acababa de entrar cuando sonó el teléfono. I had just come in when the phone rang.
■ **acabarse** to run out □ La impresora te avisa cuando se acaba el papel. The printer tells you when the paper runs out. □ Se me acabó el tabaco. I ran out of cigarettes.

la **academia** NOUN
school
□ una academia de idiomas a language school
■ **una academia militar** a military academy

académico (FEM **académica**) ADJECTIVE
academic

□ el curso académico the academic year

la **acampada** NOUN

■ **ir de acampada** to go camping

acampar VERB [25]

to camp

el **acantilado** NOUN

cliff

acariciar VERB [25]

1 to stroke

2 to caress

acaso ADVERB

■ **¿Acaso tengo yo la culpa?** Is it MY fault?

■ **por si acaso** just in case

■ **No necesito nada; si acaso, un poco de leche.** I don't need anything; well maybe a little milk.

■ **Si acaso lo vieras, dile que me llame.** If you should see him, tell him to call me.

acatarrarse VERB [25]

to catch cold

acceder VERB [8]

■ **acceder a 1** to agree to □ Al final accedió a venir. In the end he agreed to come. **2** to gain access to

accesible (FEM **accesible**) ADJECTIVE

1 accessible

□ Es un lugar sólo accesible por barco. The place is only accessible by boat.

2 approachable

□ Es una persona muy accesible. He's very approachable.

el **acceso** NOUN

access

□ La casa tiene acceso por delante y por detrás. Access to the house is from the front and from the rear. □ Tiene acceso a información confidencial. He has access to confidential information.

■ **Quieren mejorar los accesos al aeropuerto.** They want to improve access to the airport.

■ **las pruebas de acceso a la universidad** university entrance exams

el **accesorio** NOUN

accessories

□ accesorios para el automóvil car accessories

accidentado (FEM **accidentada**) ADJECTIVE

1 rough

2 eventful

el **accidente** NOUN

accident

□ los accidentes de trabajo accidents in the workplace

■ **Han tenido un accidente.** They've had a car accident.

la **acción** (PL las **acciones**) NOUN

1 action

□ una película llena de acción an action-packed film

■ **entrar en acción** to go into action

2 share

□ comprar acciones de una empresa to buy shares in a company

el/la **accionista** NOUN

shareholder

el **aceite** NOUN

oil

■ **el aceite de girasol** sunflower oil

■ **el aceite de oliva** olive oil

aceitoso (FEM **aceitosa**) ADJECTIVE

oily

la **aceituna** NOUN

olive

□ aceitunas rellenas stuffed olives

el **acelerador** NOUN

accelerator

acelerar VERB [25]

to accelerate

□ Aceleré para adelantarlos. I accelerated to overtake them.

■ **¡Acelera, que no llegamos!** Speed up or we'll never get there!

■ **acelerar el paso** to walk faster

las **acelgas** NOUN

spinach beet *sing*

el **acento** NOUN

1 accent

□ 'Té' lleva acento cuando significa 'bebida'. 'Té' has an accent when it means 'drink'.

□ Tiene un acento cerrado del sur. He has a strong southern accent.

2 stress

□ ¿Qué sílaba lleva el acento en 'microphone'? Which syllable is the stress on in 'microphone'?

acentuarse* VERB [1]

to have an accent

□ No se acentúa. It doesn't have an accent.

aceptable (FEM **aceptable**) ADJECTIVE

acceptable

aceptar VERB [25]

to accept

□ Acepté su invitación. I accepted his invitation. □ Cuesta aceptar la derrota. It's hard to accept defeat.

■ **aceptar hacer algo** to agree to do something

la **acequia** NOUN

irrigation channel

la **acera** NOUN

pavement

acerca ADVERB

■ **acerca de** about □ un documental acerca de la fauna africana a documentary about African wildlife

acercar* VERB [48]
1 to pass
□ ¿Me acercas los alicates? Could you pass me the pliers?
2 to bring over
□ Acerca la silla. Bring your chair over here.
■ **¿Acerco más la cama a la ventana?** Shall I put the bed nearer the window?
■ **Nos acercaron al aeropuerto.** They gave us a lift to the airport.
■ **acercarse 1** to come closer □ Acércate, que te vea. Come closer so that I can see you. **2** to go over □ Me acerqué a la ventana. I went over to the window.
□ Acércate a la tienda y trae una botella de agua. Go over to the shop and get a bottle of water.
■ **Ya se acerca la Navidad.** Christmas is getting near.

el **acero** NOUN
steel
□ acero inoxidable stainless steel

acertar* VERB [39]
1 to get...right
□ He acertado todas las respuestas. I got all the answers right.
■ **No acerté.** I got it wrong.
■ **Creo que hemos acertado con estas cortinas.** I think these curtains were a good choice.
2 to guess
□ Si aciertas cuántos caramelos hay, te los regalo todos. If you guess how many sweets there are, I'll give you them all.
■ **Acerté en el blanco.** I hit the target.

ácido (FEM **ácida**) ADJECTIVE
acid

el **ácido** NOUN
acid

acierto VERB ▷ *see* **acertar**

el **acierto** NOUN
1 right answer
□ Tuve más aciertos que fallos en el examen. I got more right answers than wrong ones in the exam.
2 good idea
□ Fue un acierto ir de vacaciones a la montaña. Going to the mountains on holiday was a good idea.

aclarar VERB [25]
1 to rinse
□ Aclara la ropa antes de tenderla. Rinse the washing before hanging it out.
2 to clear up
□ Necesito que me aclares unas dudas. I need you to clear up some doubts for me.
□ No me iré hasta que no se aclare este asunto. I shan't go until this business is cleared up.
■ **Con tantos números no me aclaro.** There are so many numbers that I can't get it straight.

el **acné** NOUN
acne

acobardarse VERB [25]
■ **No se acobarda por nada.** He isn't frightened by anything.

acogedor (FEM **acogedora**) ADJECTIVE
cosy
□ un cuarto muy acogedor a very cosy room

acoger* VERB [7]
to receive
□ La ciudad acoge todos los años a miles de visitantes. The city receives thousands of visitors every year.
■ **Me acogieron muy bien en Estados Unidos.** I was made very welcome in the United States.

la **acogida** NOUN
reception
□ una fría acogida a cold reception
■ **una calurosa acogida** a warm welcome
■ **tener buena acogida** to be well received

acomodado (FEM **acomodada**) ADJECTIVE
well-off

el **acomodador** NOUN
usher

la **acomodadora** NOUN
usherette

acompañar VERB [25]
1 to come with
□ Si vas al centro te acompaño. If you're going to the centre of town I'll come with you.
2 to go with
□ Me pidió que la acompañara a la estación. She asked me to go to the station with her.
■ **¿Quieres que te acompañe a casa?** Would you like me to see you home?
3 to stay with
□ Me acompañó hasta que llegó el autobús. He stayed with me until the bus arrived.

aconsejar VERB [25]
1 to advise
■ **aconsejar a alguien que haga algo** to advise somebody to do something
■ **Te aconsejo que lo hagas.** I'd advise you to do it.
2 to recommend
□ Debe de ser bueno cuando lo aconseja el médico. It must be good if the doctor recommends it.

el **acontecimiento** NOUN
event

acordar* VERB [11]
to agree on

Spanish-English

a

□ Acordamos un precio y unas condiciones. We agreed on a price and terms.
■ **acordar hacer algo** to agree to do something

acordarse* VERB [11]
to remember
□ Ahora mismo no me acuerdo. Right now I can't remember.
■ **acordarse de** to remember □ ¿Te acuerdas de mí? Do you remember me?
□ Acuérdate de cerrar la puerta con llave. Remember to lock the door.
■ **acordarse de haber hecho algo** to remember doing something

el **acordeón** (PL los **acordeones**) NOUN
accordion

acostado (FEM **acostada**) ADJECTIVE
■ **estar acostado** to be in bed

acostarse* VERB [11]
1 to lie down
2 to go to bed
■ **acostarse con alguien** to go to bed with somebody

acostumbrarse VERB [25]
■ **acostumbrarse a** to get used to □ No me acostumbro a la vida en la ciudad. I can't get used to city life.
■ **acostumbrarse a hacer algo** to get used to doing something □ Ya me he acostumbrado a trabajar de noche. I've got used to working at night now.

el/la **acróbata** NOUN
acrobat

la **actitud** NOUN
attitude

la **actividad** NOUN
activity (PL activities)

activo (FEM **activa**) ADJECTIVE
active
□ Es una mujer muy activa. She's a very active woman.

el **acto** NOUN
1 act
□ Romper el carnet fue un acto de rebeldía. Tearing his ID card up was an act of rebellion.
2 ceremony (PL ceremonies)
□ Grandes personalidades acudieron al acto. There were some important people at the ceremony.
■ **acto seguido** immediately afterwards
□ Acto seguido la gente echó a correr. Immediately afterwards people began running.
■ **en el acto** instantly
■ **Te arreglan tus zapatos en el acto.** They will repair your shoes while you wait.

el **actor** NOUN
actor

la **actriz** (PL las **actrices**) NOUN
actress (PL actresses)

la **actuación** (PL las **actuaciones**) NOUN
1 performance
□ Fue una actuación muy buena. It was a very good performance.
2 gig
□ Esta noche tenemos una actuación en el Café del Jazz. Tonight we're doing a gig at the Café del Jazz.

actual (FEM **actual**) ADJECTIVE
present
□ la situación actual del país the country's present situation
■ **uno de los mejores pintores del arte actual** one of the greatest painters of today

LANGUAGE TIP Be careful! The Spanish word **actual** does not mean **actual**.

la **actualidad** NOUN
■ **un repaso a la actualidad nacional** a round-up of the national news
■ **un tema de gran actualidad** a very topical issue
■ **en la actualidad 1** currently □ Hay en la actualidad más de 2 millones de parados. There are currently over 2 million unemployed. **2** nowadays □ Eso ya no ocurre en la actualidad. That doesn't happen nowadays.

actualmente ADVERB
1 nowadays
□ Actualmente apenas se utilizan las máquinas de escribir. Typewriters are hardly used nowadays.
2 currently
□ Soy geólogo, pero actualmente estoy en paro. I'm a geologist but I'm currently out of work.

LANGUAGE TIP Be careful! **actualmente** does not mean **actually**.

actuar* VERB [1]
1 to act
□ Es difícil actuar con naturalidad delante de las cámaras. It's hard to act naturally in front of the cameras.
■ **Hay que actuar con cautela.** We'll have to be cautious.
■ **No comprendo tu forma de actuar.** I can't understand your behaviour.
■ **No actuó en esa película.** He wasn't in that film.
2 to perform
□ Hoy actúan en el Café del Jazz. Today they'll be performing at the Café del Jazz.

la **acuarela** NOUN
watercolour

el **acuario** NOUN
aquarium

Acuario MASC NOUN
Aquarius
■ **Soy acuario.** I'm Aquarius.

acuático (FEM **acuática**) ADJECTIVE
■ **esquí acuático** water skiing
■ **aves acuáticas** waterfowl *pl*

acudir VERB [58]
1 to go
□ Acudieron en su ayuda. They went to her aid. □ Acudió a un amigo en busca de consejo. He went to a friend for advice.
■ **No tengo a quien acudir.** I have no one to turn to.
■ **acudir a una cita** to keep an appointment
2 to come
□ El perro acude cuando lo llamo. The dog comes when I call.

acuerdo VERB ▷ *see* **acordar**

el **acuerdo** NOUN
agreement
□ llegar a un acuerdo to reach an agreement
■ **estar de acuerdo con alguien** to agree with somebody
■ **ponerse de acuerdo** to agree □ Al final no nos pusimos de acuerdo. In the end we couldn't agree. □ Nos pusimos de acuerdo para prepararle una bienvenida. We agreed to organize a welcome for him.
■ **¡De acuerdo!** All right!

la **acupuntura** NOUN
acupuncture

acurrucarse* VERB [25]
to curl up

acusar VERB [25]
1 to accuse
□ Su novia lo acusaba de mentiroso. His girlfriend accused him of being a liar.
■ **Los otros te acusan a ti de haber roto el jarrón.** The others say it was you who broke the vase.
2 to charge
□ Me acusan de homicidio. They're charging me with homicide.

acústico (FEM **acústica**) ADJECTIVE
acoustic
□ una guitarra acústica an acoustic guitar

adaptar VERB [25]
to adapt
□ Es la misma receta pero adaptada. It's the same recipe, but I've adapted it.
■ **adaptarse** to adapt □ No consigo adaptarme a la vida en el campo. I can't seem to adapt to country life.

adecuado (FEM **adecuada**) ADJECTIVE
1 suitable
□ No es la ropa más adecuada para ir de boda. They aren't the most suitable clothes to wear to a wedding.
2 right
□ Has entrado en el momento adecuado. You've arrived at just the right moment.
□ el hombre adecuado para el puesto the right man for the job

a. de J.C. ABBREVIATION *(= antes de Jesucristo)*
B.C. *(= before Christ)*

adelantado (FEM **adelantada**) ADJECTIVE
1 advanced
□ Suecia es un país muy adelantado. Sweden is a very advanced country.
■ **los niños más adelantados de la clase** the children who are doing best in the class
2 fast
□ Este reloj va adelantado. This watch is fast.
■ **pagar por adelantado** to pay in advance

adelantar VERB [25]
1 to bring...forward
□ Tuvimos que adelantar la boda. We had to bring the wedding forward.
2 to overtake
□ Adelanta a ese camión cuando puedas. Overtake that lorry when you can.
3 to put...forward
□ El domingo hay que adelantar los relojes una hora. On Sunday we'll have to put the clocks forward an hour.
■ **Así no adelantas nada.** You won't get anywhere that way.
■ **Tu reloj adelanta.** Your watch gains.

adelantarse VERB [25]
to go on ahead
□ Me adelanté para coger asiento. I went on ahead to get a seat.
■ **adelantarse a alguien** to get ahead of somebody □ Se nos adelantaron los de la competencia. The competition got ahead of us.

adelante ADVERB
▷ *see also* **adelante** EXCLAMATION
forward
□ Se inclinó hacia adelante. He leant forward.
■ **¿Nos vamos adelante para ver mejor?** Shall we sit near the front to get a better view?
■ **más adelante** **1** further on □ El pueblo está más adelante. The village is further on. **2** later □ Más adelante hablaremos de los resultados. Later we'll discuss the results.
■ **adelante de** *(Latin America)* in front of
■ **Hay que seguir adelante.** We must go on.

■ **de ahora en adelante** from now on

adelante EXCLAMATION

▷ *see also* **adelante** ADVERB

1 come on!

2 come in!

el **adelanto** NOUN

advance

□ los adelantos de la ciencia the advances in science □ Le pidió un adelanto a su jefe. He asked his boss for an advance.

adelgazar* VERB [13]

to lose weight

□ ¡Cómo has adelgazado! What a lot of weight you've lost!

■ **He adelgazado cinco kilos.** I've lost five kilos.

además ADVERB

1 as well

□ Es profesor y además carpintero. He's a teacher and a carpenter as well.

2 what's more

□ El baño es demasiado pequeño y, además, no tiene ventana. The bathroom's too small and, what's more, it hasn't got a window.

3 besides

□ Además, no tienes nada que perder. Besides, you've got nothing to lose.

■ **además de** as well as □ El ordenador es, además de rápido, eficaz. The computer is efficient as well as fast.

adentro ADVERB

inside

□ Empezó a llover y se metieron adentro. It began to rain so they went inside.

■ **tierra adentro** inland

■ **adentro de** *(Latin America)* inside

□ desde adentro de la casa from inside the house

adhesivo (FEM **adhesiva**) ADJECTIVE

sticky

□ cinta adhesiva sticky tape

el **adhesivo** NOUN

sticker

la **adicción** (PL las **adicciones**) NOUN

addiction

la **adición** (PL las **adiciones**) NOUN

(River Plate)

bill

adicto (FEM **adicta**) ADJECTIVE

addicted

□ Es adicto a la cafeína. He is addicted to caffeine.

el **adicto**, la **adicta** NOUN

addict

□ un adicto a las drogas a drug addict

adinerado (FEM **adinerada**) ADJECTIVE

wealthy

adiós EXCLAMATION

1 goodbye!

■ **decir adiós a alguien** to say goodbye to somebody

2 hello!

el **aditivo** NOUN

additive

la **adivinanza** NOUN

guess (PL guesses)

adivinar VERB [25]

to guess

□ Adivina quién viene. Guess who's coming.

■ **adivinar el pensamiento a alguien** to read somebody's mind

■ **adivinar el futuro** to see into the future

el **adjetivo** NOUN

adjective

adjunto (FEM **adjunta**) ADJECTIVE

1 enclosed

2 attached

3 deputy

□ el director adjunto the deputy head

la **administración** (PL las **administraciones**) NOUN

1 administration

□ Master de Administración de Empresas Master of Business Administration

2 civil service

□ Carmen trabaja en la administración. Carmen works for the civil service.

el **administrador de Web**, la **administradora de Web** NOUN

webmaster

administrativo (FEM **administrativa**) ADJECTIVE

administrative

□ gastos administrativos administrative expenses

■ **trabajo administrativo** clerical work

el **administrativo**, la **administrativa** NOUN

clerk

la **admiración** NOUN

1 admiration

□ Siento profunda admiración por él. I have great admiration for him.

2 amazement

□ para admiración de todos to everyone's amazement

■ **Su franqueza causó admiración entre los presentes.** His frankness amazed everyone there.

■ **signo de admiración** exclamation mark

admirar VERB [25]

to admire

□ Todos la admiran. Everyone admires her.

■ **Me admira lo poco que gastas en ropa.** I'm amazed at how little you spend on clothes.

admitir VERB [58]
1 to admit
□ Admite que estabas equivocado. Admit you were wrong.
2 to accept
□ La máquina no admite monedas de dos euros. The machine doesn't accept two-euro coins.
■ **Espero que me admitan a la universidad.** I hope I'll get a place at university.
3 to allow in
□ Aquí no admiten perros. Dogs aren't allowed in here.

el/la **adolescente** NOUN
teenager

adonde CONJUNCTION
where
■ **la ciudad adonde nos dirigimos** the city we're going to

adónde ADVERB
where
□ ¿Adónde ibas? Where were you going?

la **adopción** (PL las **adopciones**) NOUN
adoption

adoptar VERB [25]
to adopt

adoptivo (FEM **adoptiva**) ADJECTIVE
■ **un hijo adoptivo** an adopted child
■ **mis padres adoptivos** my adoptive parents

adorar VERB [25]
1 to adore
□ Adora a sus hijos. He adores his children.
2 to worship
□ adorar a Dios to worship God

adornar VERB [25]
to decorate

el **adorno** NOUN
1 ornament
□ Quitó los adornos de la estantería para limpiarla. He took the ornaments off the shelf to clean it.
2 decoration
□ Habían puesto adornos en las calles. Decorations had been put up in the streets.
□ Es sólo de adorno. It's only for decoration.

adosado (FEM **adosada**) ADJECTIVE
■ **un chalet adosado** a terraced house

adquirir* VERB [2]
to acquire
□ adquirir conocimientos de algo to acquire a knowledge of something
■ **adquirir velocidad** to gain speed
■ **adquirir fama** to achieve fame
■ **adquirir una vivienda** to purchase a property
■ **adquirir importancia** to become important
■ **Lo podrá adquirir en tiendas especializadas.** You'll be able to get it from specialist shops.

adrede ADVERB
on purpose

la **aduana** NOUN
customs *sing*

el **aduanero**, la **aduanera** NOUN
customs officer

el **adulto** NOUN
adult
■ **educación de adultos** adult education

el **adverbio** NOUN
adverb

el **adversario**, la **adversaria** NOUN
opponent

la **advertencia** NOUN
warning

advertir* VERB [51]
1 to warn
□ Ya te advertí que no intervinieras. I warned you not to get involved.
■ **advertir a alguien de algo** to warn somebody about something
■ **Te advierto que no va a ser nada fácil.** I must warn you that it won't be at all easy.
2 to notice
□ No advertí nada extraño en su comportamiento. I didn't notice anything strange about his behaviour.

aéreo (FEM **aérea**) ADJECTIVE
air
□ un ataque aéreo an air raid
■ **por vía aérea** by air mail
■ **una fotografía aérea** an aerial photograph

el **aerobic** NOUN
aerobics *sing*

el **aeromozo**, la **aeromoza** NOUN
(Latin America)
flight attendant

el **aeropuerto** NOUN
airport

el **aerosol** NOUN
aerosol

el **afán** (PL los **afanes**) NOUN
1 ambition
□ Todo su afán era ser pintora. Her great ambition was to be a painter.
2 effort
■ **Trabajan con mucho afán.** They put a lot of effort into their work.

afectado (FEM **afectada**) ADJECTIVE
upset
□ Está muy afectado por la noticia. He's very upset at the news.

afectar VERB [25]

Spanish-English

a

to affect
□ Esto a ti no te afecta. This doesn't affect you.
■ **Me afectó mucho la noticia.** The news upset me terribly.

afectivo (FEM **afectiva**) ADJECTIVE
emotional
□ problemas afectivos emotional problems

el **afecto** NOUN
affection
□ Me cuesta demostrar afecto. I find it difficult to show affection.
■ **tener afecto a alguien** to be fond of somebody

afectuoso (FEM **afectuosa**) ADJECTIVE
affectionate
□ Es un chico muy afectuoso. He's a very affectionate boy.
■ **'Un saludo afectuoso'** 'With best wishes'

afeitar VERB [25]
to shave
■ **afeitarse** to shave □ Voy a afeitarme. I'm going to shave.
■ **Me afeité la barba.** I shaved off my beard.

Afganistán MASC NOUN
Afghanistan

el **afiche** NOUN *(Latin America)*
poster

la **afición** (PL las **aficiones**) NOUN
1 hobby (PL hobbies)
□ Mi afición es la filatelia. My hobby is stamp collecting. □ por afición as a hobby
■ **Tengo mucha afición por el ciclismo.** I'm very keen on cycling.
■ **En este país hay poca afición al teatro.** In this country people aren't very interested in the theatre.
2 fans *pl*
□ la afición del Athletic the Athletic fans

aficionado (FEM **aficionada**) ADJECTIVE
1 keen
□ Es muy aficionada a la pintura. She's very keen on painting.
2 amateur
□ un equipo de fútbol aficionado an amateur football team

el **aficionado**, la **aficionada** NOUN
1 enthusiast
□ un libro para los aficionados al bricolaje a book for DIY enthusiasts
2 lover
□ los aficionados al teatro theatre lovers
3 amateur
□ un partido para aficionados a game for amateurs

aficionarse VERB [25]
■ **aficionarse a algo 1** to take up something □ Raúl se aficionó al billar. Raúl took up billiards. **2** to become interested in something □ Me he aficionado al teatro. I've become interested in the theatre.
■ **Me he aficionado al chocolate suizo.** I've developed a taste for Swiss chocolate.

afilado (FEM **afilada**) ADJECTIVE
sharp

afilar VERB [25]
to sharpen

afiliarse VERB [25]
■ **afiliarse a algo** to join something

afinar VERB [25]
to tune
□ afinar un violín to tune a violin

afirmar VERB [25]
■ **afirmar que ...** to say that ... □ Afirmaba que no la conocía. He said that he didn't know her.
■ **Afirma haberla visto aquella noche.** He says that he saw her that night.

afirmativo (FEM **afirmativa**) ADJECTIVE
affirmative

aflojar VERB [25]
to loosen
■ **Tengo que aflojarme la corbata.** I must loosen my tie.
■ **aflojarse** to come loose □ Se ha aflojado un tornillo. A screw has come loose.

el **afluente** NOUN
tributary (PL tributaries)

afónico (FEM **afónica**) ADJECTIVE
■ **Estoy afónico.** I've lost my voice.

el **aforo** NOUN
capacity (PL capacities)
□ El teatro tiene un aforo de 2.000 personas. The theatre has a capacity of 2000 people.

afortunadamente ADVERB
fortunately

afortunado (FEM **afortunada**) ADJECTIVE
lucky
□ Es un tipo afortunado. He's a lucky guy.

África FEM NOUN
Africa

el **africano** (FEM la **africana**) ADJECTIVE, NOUN
African

afrontar VERB [25]
to face up to
□ afrontar un problema to face up to a problem

afuera ADVERB
outside
□ Vámonos afuera. Let's go outside.
■ **afuera de** *(Latin America)* outside

las **afueras** NOUN
outskirts
□ en las afueras de Barcelona on the outskirts of Barcelona

■ **un barrio a las afueras de Londres** a London suburb

agacharse VERB [25]
1 to crouch down
2 to bend down

la **agarradera** NOUN *(Latin America)*
handle

agarrado (FEM **agarrada**) ADJECTIVE
stingy

agarrar VERB [25]
1 to grab
□ Agarró al niño por el hombro. He grabbed the child by the shoulder.
2 to hold
□ Agarra bien la sartén. Hold the frying pan firmly.
3 to catch
□ Ya han agarrado al ladrón. They've already caught the thief. □ He agarrado un buen resfriado. I've caught an awful cold.
4 to take *(Latin America)*
□ Agarré otro pedazo de pastel. I took another piece of cake.
■ **agarrarse** to hold on □ Agárrate a la barandilla. Hold on to the rail.

la **agencia** NOUN
agency (PL agencies)
□ una agencia de noticias a news agency
□ una agencia de publicidad an advertising agency
■ **una agencia inmobiliaria** an estate agent's
■ **una agencia de viajes** a travel agent's

la **agenda** NOUN
1 diary (PL diaries)
2 address book

LANGUAGE TIP Be careful! The Spanish word **agenda** does not mean **agenda**.

el/la **agente** NOUN
agent
■ **un agente de bolsa** a stockbroker
■ **un agente de seguros** an insurance broker
■ **un agente de policía** a police officer

ágil (FEM **ágil**) ADJECTIVE
agile

agitado (FEM **agitada**) ADJECTIVE
hectic

agitar VERB [25]
1 to stir
□ Agitaba su café con una cucharilla. He was stirring his coffee with a teaspoon.
2 to shake
□ Agítese antes de usar. Shake before use.
3 to wave
□ La gente agitaba los pañuelos. People were waving their handkerchiefs.

aglomerarse VERB [25]
■ **La gente se aglomeraba a la entrada.** People were crowding around the entrance.

agobiante (FEM **agobiante**) ADJECTIVE
1 stifling
2 overwhelming
3 exhausting

agobiar VERB [25]
■ **Le agobian sus problemas.** His problems are getting on top of him.
■ **agobiarse** to worry □ No te agobies; ya encontraremos una solución. Don't worry, we'll find a solution.

agosto MASC NOUN
August
□ en agosto in August □ Nació el 8 de agosto. He was born on 8 August.

agotado (FEM **agotada**) ADJECTIVE
1 exhausted
□ Estoy agotado. I'm exhausted.
2 sold out
□ Ese modelo en concreto está agotado. That particular model is sold out.

agotador (FEM **agotadora**) ADJECTIVE
exhausting

agotar VERB [25]
1 to use up
□ Agotamos todas nuestras reservas de combustible. We used up all our fuel supplies.
2 to tire out
□ Me agota tanto ejercicio. All this exercise is tiring me out.
■ **agotarse** to run out □ Se está agotando la leña. The firewood's running out.
■ **Se agotaron todas las entradas.** The tickets sold out.

agradable (FEM **agradable**) ADJECTIVE
nice

agradar VERB [25]
■ **Esto no me agrada.** I don't like this.

agradecer* VERB [12]
■ **agradecer algo a alguien** to thank somebody for something
■ **Te agradezco tu interés.** Thank you for your interest.
■ **Le agradecería me enviara ...** I should be grateful if you would send me ...

agradecido (FEM **agradecida**) ADJECTIVE
■ **estar agradecido a alguien por algo** to be grateful to somebody for something

el **agrado** NOUN
■ **no fue de mi agrado** it was not to my liking

agrario (FEM **agraria**) ADJECTIVE
agricultural
□ la política agraria agricultural policy

agredir VERB [58]

to attack

la **agresión** (PL las **agresiones**) NOUN
1 attack
□ una brutal agresión de dos jóvenes a brutal attack on two young people
2 aggression
□ un acto de agresión an act of aggression

agresivo (FEM **agresiva**) ADJECTIVE
aggressive

agrícola (FEM **agrícola**) ADJECTIVE
agricultural

el **agricultor**, la **agricultora** NOUN
farmer

la **agricultura** NOUN
farming

agridulce (FEM **agridulce**) ADJECTIVE
sweet-and-sour
□ salsa agridulce sweet-and-sour sauce

agrio (FEM **agria**) ADJECTIVE
1 sour
2 tart

la **agrupación** (PL las **agrupaciones**) NOUN
group

agrupar VERB [25]
1 to group
□ agrupados en distintas categorías grouped into different categories □ Los insectos se agrupan en varias categorías. Insects can be grouped into several categories.
2 to bring together
□ una organización que agrupa a varios países an organization which brings several countries together
■ **Los ecologistas se han agrupado en varios partidos.** The ecologists have formed several parties.
■ **Se agruparon en torno a su jefe.** They gathered round their boss.

el **agua** FEM NOUN
water
■ **agua corriente** running water
■ **agua potable** drinking water
■ **agua dulce** fresh water
■ **agua salada** salt water
■ **agua de colonia** cologne
■ **agua oxigenada** peroxide

el **aguacate** NOUN
avocado (PL avocados)

el/la **aguafiestas** (PL los/las **aguafiestas**) NOUN
spoilsport

la **aguanieve** NOUN
sleet

aguantar VERB [25]
1 to stand
□ No aguanto la ópera. I can't stand opera.
□ Su vecina no la aguanta. Her neighbour can't stand her.
2 to take
□ La estantería no va a aguantar el peso. The shelf won't take the weight. □ ¡No aguanto más! I can't take any more!
3 to hold
□ Aguántame el martillo un momento. Can you hold the hammer for me for a moment?
□ Aguanta la respiración. Hold your breath.
4 to last
□ Este abrigo ya no aguanta otro invierno. This coat won't last another winter.
■ **No pude aguantar la risa.** I couldn't help laughing.
■ **Últimamente estás que no hay quien te aguante.** You've been unbearable lately.
■ **¿Puedes aguantarte hasta que lleguemos a casa?** Can you hold out until we get home?
■ **Si no puede venir, que se aguante.** If he can't come, he'll just have to lump it.

el **aguante** NOUN
■ **tener aguante 1** to be patient **2** to have stamina

aguardar VERB [25]
to wait for

agudo (FEM **aguda**) ADJECTIVE
1 sharp
2 high-pitched
3 acute
4 witty

el **aguijón** (PL los **aguijones**) NOUN
sting

el **águila** FEM NOUN
eagle

la **aguja** NOUN
needle
■ **las agujas del reloj** the hands of the clock

el **agujero** NOUN
1 hole
■ **hacer un agujero** to make a hole
2 pocket

la **agujeta** NOUN *(Mexico)*
shoe lace

las **agujetas** NOUN
■ **tener agujetas** to be stiff

ahí ADVERB
there
□ ¡Ahí están! There they are! □ Ahí llega el tren. There's the train.
■ **Ahí está el problema.** That's the problem.
■ **ahí arriba** up there
■ **Están ahí dentro.** They're in there.
■ **Lo tienes ahí mismo.** You've got it right there.
■ **de ahí que** that's why

■ por ahí **1** over there □ Tú busca por ahí. You look over there. **2** somewhere □ Nos iremos por ahí a celebrarlo. We'll go out somewhere to celebrate.

■ ¿Las tijeras? Andarán por ahí. The scissors? They must be somewhere around. **3** thereabouts □ 200 o por ahí 200 or thereabouts

ahogarse* VERB [37]

1 to drown

□ Se ahogó en el río. He drowned in the river.

2 to suffocate

□ Se ahogaron por falta de aire. They suffocated for lack of air.

3 to get breathless

□ Me ahogo subiendo las cuestas. I get breathless going uphill.

ahora ADVERB

now

□ ¿Dónde vamos ahora? Where are we going now?

■ Ahora te lo digo. I'll tell you in a moment.

■ ahora mismo right now □ Ahora mismo está de viaje. He's away on a trip right now.

■ Ahora mismo voy. I'm just coming.

■ de ahora en adelante from now on

■ hasta ahora **1** so far □ Hasta ahora nadie se ha quejado. Nobody has complained so far. **2** till now □ Hasta ahora nadie se había quejado. Nobody had complained till now.

■ ¡Hasta ahora! See you shortly!

■ ahora bien however □ Aceptó las condiciones. Ahora bien, hace falta que las cumpla. He accepted the conditions. However, he now needs to comply with them.

■ por ahora for the moment □ Por ahora no cambies nada. Don't change anything for the moment.

ahorcar* VERB [48]

to hang

■ ahorcarse to hang oneself

ahorita ADVERB *(Latin America)*

now

ahorrar VERB [25]

to save

los **ahorros** NOUN

savings

ahumado (FEM **ahumada**) ADJECTIVE

smoked

el **aire** NOUN

1 air

□ Necesitamos aire para respirar. We need air to breathe.

■ aire acondicionado air conditioning

■ tomar el aire to get some fresh air

2 wind

□ El aire se le llevó el sombrero. The wind blew his hat off.

■ Hace mucho aire. It's very windy.

■ al aire libre **1** outdoors □ Comimos al aire libre. We had lunch outdoors.

2 outdoor □ una fiesta al aire libre an outdoor party

aislado (FEM **aislada**) ADJECTIVE

isolated

□ Es un caso aislado. It's an isolated case.

■ El pueblo estaba aislado por la nieve. The village was cut off by the snow.

el **ajedrez** (PL los **ajedreces**) NOUN

1 chess

□ jugar al ajedrez to play chess

2 chess set

□ Tráete el ajedrez y echamos una partida. Get the chess set and we'll have a game.

ajeno (FEM **ajena**) ADJECTIVE

■ No respeta la opinión ajena. He doesn't respect other people's opinions.

■ por razones ajenas a nuestra voluntad for reasons beyond our control

ajetreado (FEM **ajetreada**) ADJECTIVE

busy

□ Ha sido un día muy ajetreado. It has been a very busy day.

el **ají** NOUN *(River Plate)*

chili sauce

el **ajo** NOUN

garlic

ajustado (FEM **ajustada**) ADJECTIVE

tight

□ Lleva ropa muy ajustada. He wears very tight clothes. □ La falda me queda un poco ajustada. The skirt's a bit tight on me.

ajustar VERB [25]

1 to adjust

□ Hay que ajustar los frenos. The brakes need adjusting.

2 to tighten

□ Ajusté bien todas las tuercas. I tightened up all the nuts.

3 to fit

□ Esta puerta no ajusta bien. This door doesn't fit very well.

■ ajustarse a **1** to fit in with □ Tendremos que ajustarnos al horario previsto. We'll have to fit in with the programme. □ Tu versión no se ajusta a la realidad. Your version doesn't fit in with the facts. **2** to keep to □ Nos ajustaremos al presupuesto. We'll keep to the budget.

al PREPOSITION ▷ *see* **a**

el **ala** FEM NOUN

1 wing

2 brim

alabar VERB [25]
to praise

la **alambrada** NOUN
fence
□ una alambrada eléctrica an electric fence

el **alambre** NOUN
wire

el **álamo** NOUN
poplar

alardear VERB [25]
■ **alardear de algo** to boast about something

el **alargador** NOUN
extension lead

alargar* VERB [37]
1 to lengthen
□ Hay que alargar un poco las mangas. We'll need to lengthen the sleeves a little.
2 to extend
□ Van a alargar esta línea de metro. This underground line is going to be extended.
□ Decidieron alargar las vacaciones. They decided to extend their holidays.
3 to stretch out
□ Alargué el brazo para apagar la luz. I stretched out my arm to put out the light.
4 to pass
□ ¿Me alargas la llave inglesa? Will you pass me the wrench?
■ **alargarse 1** to get longer □ Ya van alargándose los días. The days are getting longer. **2** to go on □ La fiesta se alargó hasta el amanecer. The party went on into the early hours.

la **alarma** NOUN
alarm
□ Saltó la alarma. The alarm went off.
■ **dar la voz de alarma** to raise the alarm
■ **alarma de incendios** fire alarm

el **alba** FEM NOUN
dawn
■ **al alba** at dawn

el/la **albañil** NOUN
1 builder
2 bricklayer

el **albaricoque** NOUN
apricot

la **alberca** NOUN *(Latin America)*
swimming pool

el **albergue** NOUN
1 mountain refuge
2 hostel
■ **un albergue juvenil** a youth hostel

las **albóndigas** NOUN
meatballs

el **albornoz** (PL los **albornoces**) NOUN
bathrobe

el **alboroto** NOUN
racket
□ ¡Vaya alboroto que estaban montando los niños! What a racket the kids were making!

el **álbum** (PL los **álbumes**) NOUN
album

la **alcachofa** NOUN
1 artichoke
2 shower head
3 rose

el **alcalde**, la **alcaldesa** NOUN
mayor

el **alcance** NOUN
1 range
□ misiles de largo alcance long-range missiles
2 scale
□ Se desconoce el alcance de la catástrofe. The scale of the disaster isn't yet known.
■ **Está al alcance de todos.** It's within everybody's reach.

la **alcantarilla** NOUN
1 sewer
2 drain
■ **una boca de alcantarilla** a manhole

alcanzar* VERB [13]
1 to catch up with
□ La alcancé cuando salía por la puerta. I caught up with her just as she was going out of the door.
2 to reach
□ alcanzar la cima de la montaña to reach the top of the mountain
3 to find
□ alcanzar la fama to find fame
4 to pass
□ ¿Me alcanzas las tijeras? Could you pass me the scissors?
■ **Con dos botellas alcanzará para todos.** Two bottles will be enough for all of us.

el **alcaucil** NOUN *(River Plate)*
artichoke

la **alcoba** NOUN
bedroom

LANGUAGE TIP Be careful! **alcoba** does not mean **alcove**.

el **alcohol** NOUN
alcohol
■ **cerveza sin alcohol** non-alcoholic beer

alcohólico (FEM **alcohólica**) ADJECTIVE
alcoholic

la **aldea** NOUN
village

el **aldeano**, la **aldeana** NOUN
villager

alegrar VERB [25]
to cheer up
□ Intenté alegrarlos con unos chistes. I tried to cheer them up with a few jokes.

■ **Me alegra que hayas venido.** I'm glad you've come.
■ **alegrarse** to be glad □ ¿Te gusta? Me alegro. You like it? I'm glad.
■ **alegrarse de algo** to be glad about something □ Me alegro de tu ascenso. I'm glad about your promotion.
■ **Me alegro de oír que estás bien.** I'm glad to hear that you're well.
■ **alegrarse por alguien** to be happy for somebody □ Me alegro por ti. I'm happy for you.

alegre (FEM **alegre**) ADJECTIVE
cheerful
■ **Estoy muy alegre.** I'm feeling very happy.

la **alegría** NOUN
■ **Sentí una gran alegría.** I was really happy.
■ **¡Qué alegría!** How lovely!

alejarse VERB [25]
to move away
□ Aléjate un poco del fuego. Move a bit further away from the fire.
■ **El barco se iba alejando de la costa.** The boat was getting further and further away from the coast.

el **alemán** (FEM la **alemana**) ADJECTIVE, NOUN
German

el **alemán** NOUN
German

Alemania FEM NOUN
Germany

alentador ADJECTIVE (FEM **alentadora**
encouraging

la **alergia** NOUN
allergy (PL allergies)
■ **la alergia al polen** hay fever

la **alerta** ADJECTIVE, NOUN, ADVERB
alert
■ **dar la alerta** to give the alert
■ **estar alerta** to be alert

la **aleta** NOUN
1 fin
2 flipper
3 wing

el **alfabeto** NOUN
alphabet

la **alfarería** NOUN
pottery (PL potteries)

el **alfarero**, la **alfarera** NOUN
potter

el **alféizar** NOUN
sill

el **alfil** NOUN
bishop

el **alfiler** NOUN
pin

la **alfombra** NOUN
1 rug
2 carpet

la **alfombrilla** NOUN
mat

las **algas** NOUN
seaweed *sing*

algo PRONOUN
▷ *see also* **algo** ADVERB
1 something
□ Algo se está quemando. Something is burning. □ ¿Quieres algo de comer? Would you like something to eat? □ ¿Te pasa algo? Is something the matter?
■ **Aún queda algo de café.** There's still some coffee left.
2 anything
□ ¿Algo más? Anything else? □ ¿Has visto algo que te guste? Have you seen anything you like?
■ **algo así como** a bit like □ Es algo así como una nave espacial. It's a bit like a spaceship.
■ **o algo así** or something of the sort
■ **Por algo será.** There must be a reason for it.

algo ADVERB
▷ *see also* **algo** PRONOUN
rather
□ La falda te está algo corta, pero puede valer. The skirt's rather short on you, but it may be all right.

el **algodón** (PL los **algodones**) NOUN
cotton
□ ropa de algodón cotton clothes
■ **Me puse algodones en los oídos.** I put cotton wool in my ears.

alguien PRONOUN
1 somebody
□ Alguien llama a la puerta. There's somebody knocking at the door.
□ ¿Necesitas que te ayude alguien? Do you need somebody to help you?
2 anybody
□ ¿Conoces a alguien aquí? Do you know anybody here?

algún ADJECTIVE (FEM **alguna**, MASC PL **algunos**)
1 some
□ Algún día iré. I'll go there some day.
2 any
□ ¿Compraste algún cuadro? Did you buy any pictures?
■ **¿Quieres alguna cosa más?** Was there anything else?
■ **algún que otro ...** the odd ... □ He leído algún que otro libro sobre el tema. I've read the odd book on the subject.

alguno PRONOUN (FEM **alguna**)
1 somebody

□ Siempre hay alguno que se queja. There's always somebody who complains.
■ **Algunos piensan que no ocurrió así.** Some people think that it didn't happen like that.
2 one
□ Tiene que haber sido alguno de ellos. It must have been one of them. □ Tiene que estar en alguna de estas cajas. It must be in one of these boxes.
3 some
□ Son tantas maletas que alguna siempre se pierde. There are so many suitcases that some inevitably get lost.
■ **Sólo conozco a algunos de los vecinos.** I only know some of the neighbours.
4 any
□ Necesito una aspirina. ¿Te queda alguna? I need an aspirin. Have you got any left? □ Si alguno quiere irse que se vaya. If any of them want to leave, fine. □ ¿Lo sabe alguno de vosotros? Do any of you know?

el **aliado**, la **aliada** NOUN
ally (PL allies)

la **alianza** NOUN
1 alliance
□ formar una alianza to form an alliance
2 wedding ring

aliarse* VERB [21]
■ **aliarse con alguien** to form an alliance with somebody

los **alicates** NOUN
pliers

el **aliento** NOUN
breath
□ Tengo mal aliento. I've got bad breath.
■ **Llegué sin aliento.** I arrived out of breath.

aligerar VERB [25]
to make...lighter
□ aligerar la carga del barco to make the cargo lighter
■ **¡Aligera o llegaremos tarde!** Hurry up or we'll be late!

la **alimentación** NOUN
diet
□ Hay que cuidar la alimentación. You need to be sensible about your diet.
■ **una tienda de alimentación** a grocer's shop

alimentar VERB [25]
to feed
□ alimentar a un niño to feed a child
■ **Esto no alimenta.** That's not very nutritious.
■ **alimentarse de algo** to live on something

el **alimento** NOUN
food
■ **alimentos congelados** frozen food *sing*
■ **Las legumbres tienen mucho alimento.** Pulses are very nutritious.

la **alineación** (PL las **alineaciones**) NOUN
line-up

aliñar VERB [25]
to season

el **aliño** NOUN
dressing

aliviar VERB [25]
to make...better
□ El jarabe te aliviará la tos. The syrup will make your cough better. □ Estas pastillas te aliviarán. These pills will make you better.

el **alivio** NOUN
relief
■ **¡Qué alivio!** What a relief!

allá ADVERB
there
□ allá arriba up there
■ **más allá** further on
■ **Échate un poco más allá.** Move over that way a bit.
■ **más allá de** beyond
■ **¡Allá tú!** That's up to you!
■ **el más allá** the next world

allanar VERB [25]
to level

allí ADVERB
there
□ Allí está. There it is.
■ **Allí viene tu hermana.** Here comes your sister.
■ **allí abajo** down there
■ **allí mismo** right there
■ **Marta es de por allí.** Marta comes from somewhere around there.

el **alma** FEM NOUN
soul
■ **Lo siento en el alma.** I'm really sorry.

el **almacén** (PL los **almacenes**) NOUN
store
■ **unos grandes almacenes** a department store

almacenar VERB [25]
to store

la **almeja** NOUN
clam

la **almendra** NOUN
almond

el **almíbar** NOUN
syrup
■ **en almíbar** in syrup

el **almirante** NOUN
admiral

la **almohada** NOUN
pillow

la **almohadilla** NOUN
cushion

almorzar* VERB [3]
to have lunch
□ No he almorzado todavía. I haven't had lunch yet.
■ **¿Qué has almorzado?** What did you have for lunch?

almuerzo VERB ▷ *see* **almorzar**

el **almuerzo** NOUN
lunch (PL lunches)

aló EXCLAMATION *(Latin America)*
hello!

alocado (FEM **alocada**) ADJECTIVE
crazy
□ una decisión alocada a crazy decision
■ **una chica un poco alocada** a rather silly girl

el **alojamiento** NOUN
accommodation

alojarse VERB [25]
to stay
□ ¿Dónde os alojáis? Where are you staying?

la **alpargata** NOUN
espadrille

los **Alpes** NOUN
the Alps

el **alpinismo** NOUN
mountaineering

el/la **alpinista** NOUN
mountaineer

alquilar VERB [25]
1 to rent
□ Alquilaremos un apartamento en la playa. We'll rent an apartment near the beach.
2 to let
□ Alquilan habitaciones a estudiantes. They let rooms to students.
■ **'se alquila'** 'to let'
3 to hire
□ Alquilamos un coche. We hired a car.

el **alquiler** NOUN
rent
□ pagar el alquiler to pay the rent
■ **un piso de alquiler** a rented flat
■ **un coche de alquiler** a hire car
■ **alquiler de automóviles** car-hire

alrededor ADVERB
■ **alrededor de 1** around □ El satélite gira alrededor de la Tierra. The satellite goes around the Earth. □ A su alrededor todos gritaban. Everybody around him was shouting. **2** about □ Deben de ser alrededor de las dos. It must be about two o'clock.

los **alrededores** NOUN
■ **Ocurrió en los alrededores de Madrid.** It happened near Madrid.
■ **Hay muchas tiendas en los alrededores del museo.** There are a lot of shops in the area around the museum.

el **alta** FEM NOUN
■ **dar de alta a alguien** to discharge somebody
■ **darse de alta** to join

el **altar** NOUN
altar

el **altavoz** (PL los **altavoces**) NOUN
loudspeaker

alterar VERB [25]
to change
□ Alteraron el orden. They changed the order.
■ **alterar el orden público** to cause a breach of the peace
■ **alterarse** to get upset □ ¡No te alteres! Don't get upset!

alternar VERB [25]
■ **alternar algo con algo** to alternate something with something
■ **Alterna con gente del teatro.** He mixes with people from the theatre.

la **alternativa** NOUN
alternative
■ **No tenemos otra alternativa.** We have no alternative.

alterno (FEM **alterna**) ADJECTIVE
alternate
□ en días alternos on alternate days
■ **corriente alterna** alternating current

los **altibajos** NOUN
ups and downs
□ tener altibajos to have ups and downs

la **altitud** NOUN
altitude

alto (FEM **alta**) ADJECTIVE
▷ *see also* **alto** ADVERB, EXCLAMATION
1 tall
□ Es un chico muy alto. He's a very tall boy.
□ un edificio muy alto a very tall building
2 high
□ El Everest es la montaña más alta del mundo. Everest is the highest mountain in the world. □ Sacó notas altas en todos los exámenes. He got high marks in all his exams.
3 loud
□ La música está demasiado alta. The music's too loud.
■ **a altas horas de la noche** in the middle of the night
■ **Celebraron la victoria por todo lo alto.** They celebrated the victory in style.
■ **alta fidelidad** hi-fi
■ **una familia de clase alta** an upper-class family

alto ADVERB

Spanish-English

a

▷ *see also* **alto** ADJECTIVE, EXCLAMATION
high
□ subir muy alto to go up very high
■ **Pepe habla muy alto.** Pepe has got a very loud voice.
■ **¡Más alto, por favor!** Speak up, please!
■ **Pon el volumen más alto.** Turn the volume up.

alto EXCLAMATION
▷ *see also* **alto** ADJECTIVE, ADVERB
stop!

el **alto** NOUN
■ **La pared tiene dos metros de alto.** The wall is two metres high.
■ **en lo alto de** at the top of
■ **hacer un alto** to stop □ A las dos haremos un alto para comer. We'll stop to have lunch at two o'clock.
■ **pasar algo por alto** to overlook something
■ **el alto el fuego** ceasefire

el **altoparlante** NOUN *(Latin America)*
loudspeaker

la **altura** NOUN
height
□ Volamos a una altura de 15.000 pies. We're flying at a height of 15,000 feet.
■ **La pared tiene dos metros de altura.** The wall's two metres high.
■ **cuando llegues a la altura del hospital** when you reach the hospital
■ **a estas alturas** at this stage □ A estas alturas no podemos hacer nada. There's nothing we can do at this stage.

las **alubias** NOUN
beans

alucinar VERB [25]
to be amazed
□ Alucino con las cosas que haces. I'm amazed at the things you do.

el **alud** NOUN
avalanche

aludir VERB [58]
to refer
□ No aludió a lo del otro día. He didn't refer to that business the other day.
■ **No se dio por aludida.** She didn't take the hint.

el **aluminio** NOUN
aluminium

el **alumno**, la **alumna** NOUN
pupil

la **alusión** (PL las **alusiones**) NOUN
■ **hacer alusión a** to refer to

la **alverja** NOUN *(Latin America)*
pea

el **alza** FEM NOUN
rise
□ un alza de los precios a rise in prices
■ **El balonmano es un deporte en alza.** Handball is becoming increasingly popular.

alzar* VERB [13]
to raise
□ alzar la voz to raise one's voice
■ **alzarse** to rise □ Se alzó el telón. The curtain rose.
■ **alzarse en armas** to take up arms

el **ama** FEM NOUN
owner
■ **ama de casa** housewife
LANGUAGE TIP Word for word, **ama de casa** means 'owner of house'.
■ **ama de llaves** housekeeper
LANGUAGE TIP Word for word, **ama de llaves** means 'owner of keys'.

amable (FEM **amable**) ADJECTIVE
kind
■ **Es usted muy amable.** You're very kind.

amamantar VERB [25]
1 to breast-feed
2 to suckle

amanecer* VERB [12]
1 to get light
□ Amanece a las siete. It gets light at seven.
2 to wake up
□ El niño amaneció con fiebre. The boy woke up with a temperature.

el **amanecer** NOUN
dawn

el/la **amante** NOUN
lover
■ **amantes del cine** cinema lovers

la **amapola** NOUN
poppy (PL poppies)

amar VERB [25]
to love

amargado (FEM **amargada**) ADJECTIVE
bitter
■ **estar amargado por algo** to be bitter about something

amargar* VERB [37]
to spoil
□ Ya me habéis amargado la tarde. You've spoilt my evening.
■ **amargar la vida a alguien** to make somebody's life a misery
■ **amargarse** to get upset □ No te amargues por tan poca cosa. It's not worth getting upset about such a little thing.

amargo (FEM **amarga**) ADJECTIVE
bitter

el **amarillo** ADJECTIVE, NOUN
yellow
■ **la prensa amarilla** the gutter press

amarrar VERB [25]
1 to moor

2 to tie up
3 to do up *(Latin America)*
□ Se amarró los zapatos. He did up his shoes.

el/la **amateur** (PL los/las **amateurs**) ADJECTIVE, NOUN
amateur

el **Amazonas** NOUN
the Amazon

el **ámbar** NOUN
amber

la **ambición** (PL las **ambiciones**) NOUN
ambition

ambicioso (FEM **ambiciosa**) ADJECTIVE
ambitious

el **ambientador** NOUN
air freshener

el **ambiente** NOUN
atmosphere
□ Se respira un ambiente tenso. There's a tense atmosphere.
■ **Había un ambiente muy cargado en la habitación.** It was very stuffy in the room.
■ **Necesito cambiar de ambiente.** I need a change of scene.
■ **el medio ambiente** the environment

ambiguo (FEM **ambigua**) ADJECTIVE
ambiguous

el **ámbito** NOUN
scope

ambos (FEM **ambas**) PRONOUN
both
□ Vinieron ambos. They both came.
□ Ambos tenéis los ojos azules. You've both got blue eyes.

la **ambulancia** NOUN
ambulance

el **ambulatorio** NOUN
out-patients' department

amén EXCLAMATION
amen

amenace VERB ▷ *see* **amenazar**

la **amenaza** NOUN
threat

amenazar* VERB [13]
to threaten
■ **amenazar a alguien con hacer algo** to threaten to do something □ Le amenazó con decírselo al profesor. He threatened to tell the teacher.

ameno (FEM **amena**) ADJECTIVE
enjoyable

América FEM NOUN
the Americas
■ **América Central** Central America
■ **América Latina** Latin America
■ **América del Sur** South America
■ **el español de América** Latin American Spanish

la **americana** NOUN
1 jacket
2 American

el **americano** ADJECTIVE, NOUN
American

la **ametralladora** NOUN
machine gun

las **amígdalas** NOUN
tonsils

el **amigo**, la **amiga** NOUN
friend
■ **hacerse amigos** to become friends
■ **ser muy amigos** to be good friends

la **amistad** NOUN
friendship
■ **hacer amistad con alguien** to make friends with somebody
■ **las amistades** friends

amistoso (FEM **amistosa**) ADJECTIVE
friendly

el **amo** NOUN
owner
□ el amo del perro the dog's owner

amontonar VERB [25]
to pile up
■ **Se me amontona el trabajo.** My work's piling up.

el **amor** NOUN
love
■ **hacer el amor** to make love
■ **amor propio** self-esteem

amoratado (FEM **amoratada**) ADJECTIVE
1 blue
2 black and blue

amortiguar* VERB [25, **gu** → **gü** before **e** and **i**]
1 to cushion
2 to muffle

ampliar* VERB [21]
1 to expand
2 to enlarge
3 to extend

el **amplificador** NOUN
amplifier

amplio (FEM **amplia**) ADJECTIVE
1 wide
□ una calle muy amplia a very wide street
2 spacious
□ una habitación amplia a spacious room
3 loose
□ ropa amplia loose clothing

la **ampolla** NOUN
blister

amputar VERB [25]
to amputate

amueblar VERB [25]
to furnish
□ un piso amueblado a furnished flat

■ **un piso sin amueblar** an unfurnished flat

analfabeto (FEM **analfabeta**) ADJECTIVE
illiterate

el **analgésico** NOUN
painkiller

el **análisis** (PL los **análisis**) NOUN
1 analysis (PL analyses)
□ un análisis de la situación an analysis of the situation
2 test
□ un análisis de sangre a blood test

analizar* VERB [13]
to analyse

la **anarquía** NOUN
anarchy

la **anatomía** NOUN
anatomy

ancho (FEM **ancha**) ADJECTIVE
1 wide
□ una calle ancha a wide street
2 loose
□ Le gusta llevar ropa ancha. He likes to wear loose clothing.
■ **Me está ancho el vestido.** The dress is too big for me.
■ **Es ancho de espaldas.** He's broad-shouldered.

el **ancho** NOUN
width
□ el ancho de la tela the width of the cloth
■ **¿Cuánto mide de ancho?** How wide is it?
■ **Mide tres metros de ancho.** It's three metres wide.
■ **Le hice un corte a lo ancho.** I cut it crossways.

la **anchoa** NOUN
anchovy

la **anchura** NOUN
width
□ Midió la anchura de la mesa. He measured the width of the table.
■ **¿Qué anchura tiene?** How wide is it?
■ **Tiene tres metros de anchura.** It's three metres wide.

la **anciana** NOUN
elderly woman

anciano (FEM **anciana**) ADJECTIVE
elderly

el **anciano** NOUN
elderly man
■ **los ancianos** the elderly

el **ancla** FEM NOUN
anchor

anda EXCLAMATION
1 well I never!
□ ¡Anda, un billete de 50 euros! Well I never, a 50-euro note!
2 come on
□ ¡Anda, ponte el abrigo y vámonos! Come on, put your coat on and let's go!
■ **¡Anda ya!** You're not serious!

Andalucía FEM NOUN
Andalusia

el **andaluz** (FEM la **andaluza**, MASC PL **andaluces**) ADJECTIVE, NOUN
Andalusian

el **andamio** NOUN
scaffolding
□ Ya han quitado los andamios. They've taken the scaffolding down now.

andar* VERB [4]
1 to walk
□ Anduvimos varios kilómetros. We walked several kilometres.
■ **Iremos andando a la estación.** We'll walk to the station.
2 to be
□ Últimamente ando muy liado. I've been very busy lately. □ No sé por dónde anda. I don't know where he is. □ ¿Qué tal andas? How are you? □ Ando buscando un socio. I'm looking for a partner.
■ **andar mal de dinero** to be short of money
■ **Anda por los cuarenta.** He's about forty.
■ **Siempre andan a gritos.** They're always shouting.
3 to go
□ Este reloj anda muy bien. This watch goes very well.
■ **¡No andes ahí!** Keep away from there!
■ **Ándate con cuidado.** Take care.

el **andén** (PL los **andenes**) NOUN
platform

los **Andes** NOUN
the Andes

anduve VERB ▷ *see* **andar**

la **anécdota** NOUN
anecdote

la **anemia** NOUN
anaemia

la **anestesia** NOUN
anaesthetic
■ **poner anestesia a alguien** to give somebody an anaesthetic

el **anfiteatro** NOUN
1 amphitheatre
2 lecture theatre

el **ángel** NOUN
angel

las **anginas** NOUN
■ **tener anginas** to have tonsillitis

el **anglosajón** (FEM la **anglosajona**, MASC PL los **anglosajones**) ADJECTIVE, NOUN
Anglo-Saxon

el **anglosajón** NOUN

Anglo-Saxon
el **ángulo** NOUN
angle
■ **en ángulo recto** at right angles
el **anillo** NOUN
ring
■ **un anillo de boda** a wedding ring
animado (FEM **animada**) ADJECTIVE
1 cheerful
□ Últimamente parece que está más animada. She has seemed more cheerful lately.
2 lively
□ Fue una fiesta muy animada. It was a very lively party.
■ **dibujos animados** cartoons
el **animador**, la **animadora** NOUN
1 entertainments officer
2 animator
el **animal** NOUN
animal
■ **los animales domésticos** pets
animar VERB [25]
1 to cheer up
□ Lo ha pasado muy mal y necesita que la animen. She has had a rough time and needs cheering up.
2 to cheer on
□ Estuvimos animando al equipo. We were cheering the team on.
3 to liven up
□ Sus chistes animaron la fiesta. His jokes livened up the party.
■ **animar a alguien a que haga algo** to encourage somebody to do something
■ **animarse** to cheer up □ ¡Vamos, anímate hombre! Come on, cheer up mate!
■ **animarse a hacer algo** to make up one's mind to do something
el **ánimo** NOUN
■ **Está muy mal de ánimo.** He's in very low spirits.
■ **dar ánimos a alguien 1** to cheer somebody up **2** to give somebody moral support
■ **tener ánimos para hacer algo** to feel like doing something
ánimo EXCLAMATION
cheer up!
□ ¡Ánimo, chaval, que no es el fin del mundo! Cheer up mate, it's not the end of the world!
el **anís** (PL los **anises**) NOUN
anisette
el **aniversario** NOUN
anniversary (PL anniversaries)
□ su aniversario de boda their wedding anniversary
anoche ADVERB
last night
■ **antes de anoche** the night before last
anochecer* VERB [12]
to get dark
□ En invierno anochece muy temprano. It gets dark very early in winter.
anónimo (FEM **anónima**) ADJECTIVE
anonymous
el **anónimo** NOUN
anonymous threat
el **anorak** (PL los **anoraks**) NOUN
anorak
anormal (FEM **anormal**) ADJECTIVE
odd
□ Yo no noté nada anormal en su comportamiento. I didn't notice anything odd about his behaviour.
■ **¡Soy anormal!** What a fool I am!
anotar VERB [25]
1 to take a note of
□ Anota mi dirección. Take a note of my address.
2 to score
□ Jones anotó 34 puntos. Jones scored 34 points.
la **ansiedad** NOUN
anxiety
ansioso (FEM **ansiosa**) ADJECTIVE
■ **estar ansioso por hacer algo** to be eager to do something
el **Antártico** NOUN
the Antarctic
ante PREPOSITION
1 before
□ Le da vergüenza aparecer ante tanta gente. She's shy about appearing before so many people.
2 in the face of
□ Mantuvo la calma ante el peligro. He remained calm in the face of danger.
el **ante** NOUN
suede
anteanoche ADVERB
the night before last
anteayer ADVERB
the day before yesterday
los **antecedentes** NOUN
■ **antecedentes penales** criminal record *sing*
la **antelación** NOUN
■ **hacer una reserva con antelación** to make an advance booking
■ **Deben avisarte con un mes de antelación.** They must give you a month's notice.
antemano ADVERB
■ **de antemano** in advance □ Yo lo sabía de

antemano. I knew in advance.

la **antena** NOUN
aerial
■ **una antena parabólica** a satellite dish

los **anteojos** NOUN *(Latin America)*
glasses
■ **los anteojos de sol** sunglasses

los **antepasados** NOUN
ancestors

anterior (FEM **anterior**) ADJECTIVE
1 before
□ La semana anterior llovió mucho. It rained a lot the week before. □ Su boda fue anterior a la nuestra. Their wedding was before ours.
2 front
□ las extremidades anteriores the front limbs

anteriormente ADVERB
previously

antes ADVERB
1 before
□ Esta película ya la he visto antes. I've seen this film before. □ Él estaba aquí antes que yo. He was here before me. □ la noche antes the night before
■ **El supermercado está justo antes del semáforo.** The supermarket is just before the lights.
■ **antes de** before □ antes de la cena before dinner □ antes de ir al teatro before going to the theatre □ antes de que te vayas before you go
2 first
□ Nosotros llegamos antes. We arrived first.
■ **Antes no había tanto desempleo.** There didn't use to be so much unemployment.
■ **cuanto antes mejor** the sooner the better
■ **lo antes posible** as soon as possible
■ **antes de nada** first and foremost
■ **Antes que verle prefiero esperar aquí.** I'd rather wait here than see him.

el **antibiótico** NOUN
antibiotic

anticipado (FEM **anticipada**) ADJECTIVE
early
□ convocar elecciones anticipadas to call early elections
■ **por anticipado** in advance □ pagar por anticipado to pay in advance

anticipar VERB [25]
1 to foresee
□ Es imposible anticipar lo que va a ocurrir. It's impossible to foresee what will happen.
2 to bring...forward
□ Habrá que anticipar la reunión. We'll have to bring the meeting forward.
3 to pay...in advance
□ Tuvimos que anticipar el alquiler de dos meses. We had to pay two months' rent in advance.
■ **anticiparse a alguien** to get in before somebody □ Se me anticipó y pagó la cuenta. He got in before me and paid the bill.
■ **Se anticipó a su tiempo.** He was ahead of his time.

el **anticipo** NOUN
advance
□ pedir un anticipo to ask for an advance
■ **ser un anticipo de algo** to be a foretaste of something

el **anticonceptivo** ADJECTIVE, NOUN
contraceptive

anticuado (FEM **anticuada**) ADJECTIVE
outdated
■ **quedarse anticuado** to become outdated

la **anticuaria** NOUN
antique dealer

el **anticuario** NOUN
1 antique shop
2 antique dealer

el **antifaz** (PL los **antifaces**) NOUN
mask

antiguamente ADVERB
1 in the past
□ Antiguamente no se gastaba tanto. In the past people didn't spend so much money.
2 formerly
□ Antiguamente tenía el nombre de Sociedad de Naciones. Formerly it was called the Society of Nations.

la **antigüedad** NOUN
■ **Es un monumento de gran antigüedad.** It's a very old monument.
■ **en la antigüedad** in ancient times
■ **las antigüedades** antiques
■ **una tienda de antigüedades** an antique shop

antiguo (FEM **antigua**) ADJECTIVE
1 old
□ Este reloj es muy antiguo. This clock is very old.
2 ancient
□ Estudia historia antigua. He studies ancient history.
3 former
□ el antiguo secretario general del partido the former general secretary of the party

las **Antillas** NOUN
the West Indies

antipático (FEM **antipática**) ADJECTIVE
unfriendly

antirrobo (PL **antirrobo**) ADJECTIVE

anti-theft
□ un sistema antirrobo an anti-theft system

el **antiséptico** ADJECTIVE, NOUN
antiseptic

antojarse VERB [25]
to feel like
■ **Siempre hace lo que se le antoja.** He always does what he feels like.
■ **Se me ha antojado un helado.** I really fancy an ice-cream.

la **antorcha** NOUN
torch (PL torches)

la **antropología** NOUN
anthropology

anual (FEM **anual**) ADJECTIVE
annual

anular VERB [25]
1 to call off
□ Anularon el partido por la lluvia. The match was called off owing to the rain.
2 to disallow
□ El árbitro anuló el gol. The referee disallowed the goal.
3 to overturn
□ El Tribunal Supremo anuló la sentencia. The Supreme Court overturned the sentence.

el **anular** NOUN
ring finger

anunciar VERB [25]
1 to advertise
□ anunciar detergente to advertise washing powder
2 to announce
□ anunciar una decisión to announce a decision

el **anuncio** NOUN
1 advertisement
□ Pusieron un anuncio en el periódico. They put an advertisement in the paper.
■ **anuncios por palabras** small ads
2 announcement
□ Tengo que hacer un anuncio importante. I have an important announcement to make.

el **anzuelo** NOUN
hook

la **añadidura** NOUN
■ **por añadidura** in addition

añadir VERB [58]
to add

los **añicos** NOUN
■ **hacer algo añicos** to smash something to pieces
■ **hacerse añicos** to smash to pieces

el **año** NOUN
year
□ Estuve allí el año pasado. I was there last year.
■ **el año que viene** next year
■ **el año escolar** the school year
■ **¡Feliz Año Nuevo!** Happy New Year!
■ **los años 80** the 80s
■ **¿Cuántos años tiene?** How old is he?
■ **Tiene 15 años.** He's 15.

apagado (FEM **apagada**) ADJECTIVE
switched off
□ La tele estaba apagada. The TV was switched off.

apagar* VERB [37]
1 to switch off
□ Apaga la tele. Switch the TV off. □ No apagues la luz. Don't switch the light off.
2 to put out
□ Por favor, apaguen sus cigarrillos. Please put your cigarettes out.
■ **apagar el fuego** to put the fire out

el **apagón** (PL los **apagones**) NOUN
power cut

apañado (FEM **apañada**) ADJECTIVE
resourceful
□ ¡Qué apañada eres! How resourceful you are!

apañarse VERB [25]
to manage
□ ¿Podrás hacerlo solo? — Ya me apañaré. Can you do it on your own? — I'll manage.
■ **apañarse con algo** to make do with something □ Nos apañaremos con la comida que sobró. We can make do with the leftovers.

el **aparador** NOUN
1 sideboard
2 shop window *(Mexico)*

el **aparato** NOUN
■ **No sé manejar este aparato.** I don't know how to operate this.
■ **un aparato de televisión** a television
■ **los aparatos de gimnasia** the apparatus
■ **Fabrican aparatos electrónicos.** They make electronic equipment.
■ **un aparato electrodoméstico** an electrical appliance

el **aparcamiento** NOUN
1 car park
□ un aparcamiento subterráneo an underground car park
2 parking place
□ buscar aparcamiento to look for a parking place

aparcar* VERB [48]
to park
■ **'prohibido aparcar'** 'no parking'

aparecer* VERB [12]
1 to appear
□ De repente apareció la policía. Suddenly

the police appeared.
2 to turn up
□ Aparecieron casi una hora tarde. They turned up nearly an hour late. □ ¿Han aparecido ya las tijeras? Have the scissors turned up yet?
3 to come out
□ Su nueva novela aparecerá el mes próximo. His latest novel will come out next month.

aparentar VERB [25]
to appear
□ Aparentaba no enterarse. He appeared not to understand.
■ **Aparenta más edad de la que tiene.** He looks older than he is.

aparente (FEM **aparente**) ADJECTIVE
apparent

aparentemente ADVERB
apparently

la **apariencia** NOUN
■ **Tiene la apariencia de un profesor de universidad.** He looks like a university lecturer.
■ **En apariencia nada ha cambiado.** On the surface, nothing had changed.
■ **guardar las apariencias** to keep up appearances

apartado (FEM **apartada**) ADJECTIVE
isolated
□ un lugar apartado an isolated place
■ **Vive apartado de todos.** He lives a secluded life.

el **apartado** NOUN
section
□ en el siguiente apartado in the following section
■ **apartado de correos** PO box

el **apartamento** NOUN
apartment

apartar VERB [25]
1 to remove
□ Lo apartaron del equipo. They removed him from the team.
2 to move out of the way
□ Aparta todas las sillas. Move all the chairs out of the way.
■ **¡Aparta!** Stand back!
3 to set aside
□ Hay que apartar algo del sueldo para las vacaciones. You'll have to set aside some of your pay for the holidays.
■ **apartarse** to stand back □ Apártense de la puerta. Stand back from the door.

aparte ADVERB
▷ *see also* **aparte** ADJECTIVE
separately
□ Cada caso será tratado aparte. Each case will be dealt with separately.
■ **La ropa que no valga ponla aparte.** Put the clothes that aren't any use on one side.
■ **aparte de** 1 apart from □ Nadie protestó aparte de ella. Nobody complained apart from her. 2 as well as □ Aparte de los patines, también quería una bici. I'd like a bike as well as the skates.
■ **punto y aparte** full stop, new paragraph

aparte (FEM **aparte**) ADJECTIVE
▷ *see also* **aparte** ADVERB
separate
□ El tuyo es un caso aparte. You're a separate case.

apasionante (FEM **apasionante**) ADJECTIVE
exciting

apasionar VERB [25]
■ **Le apasiona el fútbol.** He's crazy about football.

apdo. ABBREVIATION (*= apartado de correos*)
PO box (*= Post Office box*)

apearse VERB [25]
■ **apearse de** to get off

el **apego** NOUN
■ **tener apego a algo** to be attached to something

apellidarse VERB [25]
■ **Se apellida Pérez.** His surname is Pérez.

el **apellido** NOUN
surname

apenado (FEM **apenada**) ADJECTIVE
1 sad
2 embarrassed (*Latin America*)

apenas ADVERB, CONJUNCTION
1 hardly
□ No tenemos apenas nada de comer. We've got hardly anything to eat. □ Apenas podía levantarse. He could hardly stand up.
2 hardly ever
□ Apenas voy al cine. I hardly ever go to the cinema.
3 barely
□ Hace apenas 10 minutos que hablé con ella. I spoke to her barely 10 minutes ago.
■ **Terminé en apenas dos horas.** It only took me two hours to finish.
4 as soon as
□ Apenas me vio, se puso a llorar. As soon as he saw me he began to cry.

la **apendicitis** NOUN
appendicitis

el **aperitivo** NOUN
aperitif

la **apertura** NOUN
opening
□ el acto de apertura the opening ceremony

apestar VERB [25]
to stink

□ Te apestan los pies. Your feet stink.
■ **apestar a** to stink of

apetecer* VERB [12]
■ **¿Te apetece una tortilla?** Do you fancy an omelette?
■ **No, gracias, ahora no me apetece.** No, thanks, I don't feel like it just now.

el **apetito** NOUN
appetite
□ Eso te va a quitar el apetito. You won't have any appetite left.
■ **No tengo apetito.** I'm not hungry.

apetitoso (FEM **apetitosa**) ADJECTIVE
1 tasty
2 tempting

el **apio** NOUN
celery

aplastante (FEM **aplastante**) ADJECTIVE
overwhelming

aplastar VERB [25]
to squash
□ Me senté encima del regalo y lo aplasté. I sat on the present and squashed it.

aplaudir VERB [58]
to clap
□ Todos aplaudían. Everyone clapped.

el **aplauso** NOUN
applause
■ **Los aplausos duraron varios minutos.** The applause lasted for several minutes.

aplazar* VERB [13]
to postpone

la **aplicación** (PL las **aplicaciones**) NOUN
application
□ un producto con muchas aplicaciones a product with a lot of applications

aplicado (FEM **aplicada**) ADJECTIVE
hard-working
□ un alumno aplicado a hard-working pupil

aplicar* VERB [48]
1 to apply
□ Aplíquese sobre la zona afectada. Apply to the affected area.
2 to enforce
□ No se aplicaron las normas. The rules weren't enforced.

apoderarse VERB [25]
■ **apoderarse de un lugar** to take over a place
■ **Se apoderaron de las joyas.** They went off with the jewels.

el **apodo** NOUN
nickname

el **apogeo** NOUN
height
□ en el apogeo de su poder at the height of his power
■ **La fiesta estaba en su apogeo.** The party was in full swing.

aportar VERB [25]
to provide

aposta ADVERB
on purpose

apostar* VERB [11]
to bet
■ **apostar por algo** to bet on something
■ **¿Qué te apuestas a que ...?** What's the betting that ...?

el **apóstrofo** NOUN
apostrophe

apoyar VERB [25]
1 to lean
□ Apoya el espejo contra la pared. Lean the mirror against the wall.
2 to rest
□ Apoya la espalda en este cojín. Rest your back against this cushion.
3 to support
□ Todos mis compañeros me apoyan. All my colleagues support me.
■ **apoyarse** to lean □ No te apoyes en la mesa. Don't lean on the table.

el **apoyo** NOUN
support

apreciar VERB [25]
■ **apreciar a alguien** to be fond of somebody □ Lo apreciábamos mucho. We were very fond of him.
■ **Aprecio mucho mi tiempo libre.** I really value my free time.

el **aprecio** NOUN
■ **tener aprecio a alguien** to be fond of somebody

aprender VERB [8]
to learn
□ Ya me he aprendido los verbos irregulares. I've already learnt the irregular verbs.
■ **aprender a hacer algo** to learn to do something
■ **aprender algo de memoria** to learn something by heart

el **aprendiz**, la **aprendiza** (MASC PL los **aprendices**) NOUN
trainee
□ Es aprendiz de mecánico. He's a trainee mechanic.
■ **estar de aprendiz** to be doing an apprenticeship

el **aprendizaje** NOUN
learning
□ dificultades de aprendizaje learning difficulties

aprensivo (FEM **aprensiva**) ADJECTIVE
overanxious

apresurado (FEM **apresurada**) ADJECTIVE
hasty

apresurarse VERB [25]
■ **No nos apresuremos.** Let's not be hasty.
■ **Me apresuré a sugerir que ...** I hastily suggested that ...

apretado (FEM **apretada**) ADJECTIVE
1 tight
□ Estos pantalones me están muy apretados. These trousers are very tight on me. □ Tenemos un programa muy apretado. We've got a very tight programme.
2 cramped
□ Íbamos muy apretados en el autobús. We were very cramped on the bus.

apretar* VERB [39]
1 to tighten
□ Aprieta bien los tornillos. Tighten up the screws.
2 to press
□ Aprieta este botón. Press this button.
■ **apretar el gatillo** to press the trigger
■ **Me aprietan los zapatos.** My shoes are too tight.
■ **La apretó contra su pecho.** He clasped her to his bosom.
■ **Apretaos un poco para que me siente yo también.** Move up a bit so I can sit down too.
■ **apretarse el cinturón** to tighten one's belt

el **aprieto** NOUN
■ **estar en un aprieto** to be in a tight spot

aprisa ADVERB
fast
□ No vayas tan aprisa. Don't go so fast.
■ **¡Aprisa!** Hurry up!

aprobar* VERB [11]
1 to pass
□ aprobar un examen to pass an exam
■ **Han aprobado una ley antitabaco.** They've passed an anti-smoking law.
■ **aprobar por los pelos** to scrape through
2 to approve
□ La decisión fue aprobada por mayoría. The decision was approved by a majority.
3 to approve of
□ No apruebo esa conducta. I don't approve of that sort of behaviour.

apropiado (FEM **apropiada**) ADJECTIVE
suitable

aprovechar VERB [25]
1 to make good use of
□ No aprovecha el tiempo. He doesn't make good use of his time. □ Mi madre aprovecha toda la comida que sobra. My mother makes good use of any leftovers.
2 to use
□ Aprovecharé los ratos libres para estudiar. I'll use the free time to study.
■ **aprovecho la ocasión para decirles ...** I'd like to take this opportunity to tell you ...
■ **Aprovecharé ahora que estoy solo para llamarle.** I'll call him now while I'm on my own.
■ **¡Que aproveche!** Enjoy your meal!
■ **aprovecharse de** to take advantage of
□ Me aproveché de la situación. I took advantage of the situation. □ Todos se aprovechan del pobre chico. Everyone takes advantage of the poor boy.

aproximadamente ADVERB
about

aproximado (FEM **aproximada**) ADJECTIVE
approximate

aproximarse VERB [25]
to approach
□ Se aproximaba un barco. A boat was approaching.

apruebo VERB ▷ *see* **aprobar**

la **aptitud** NOUN
1 suitability
2 aptitude

apto (FEM **apta**) ADJECTIVE
■ **ser apto para algo** to be suitable for something □ No es apta para el puesto. She isn't suitable for the job.
■ **una película no apta para niños** an unsuitable film for children

la **apuesta** NOUN
bet
□ Hicimos una apuesta. We had a bet.

apuesto VERB ▷ *see* **apostar**

apuntar VERB [25]
1 to write down
□ Apúntalo o se te olvidará. Write it down or you'll forget.
■ **Apunta mis datos.** Can you take a note of my details?
2 to point
□ Apuntó el arma hacia nosotros. He pointed the gun at us.
■ **Me apuntó con el dedo.** He pointed at me.
■ **Luis me apuntó en el examen.** Luis gave me the answers in the exam.
■ **apuntarse** to put one's name down
□ Nos hemos apuntado para el viaje a Marruecos. We've put our names down for the trip to Morocco.
■ **apuntarse a un curso** to enrol on a course
■ **¡Yo me apunto!** Count me in!

LANGUAGE TIP Be careful! **apuntar** does not mean **to appoint**.

los **apuntes** NOUN
notes

■ **tomar apuntes** to take notes

apuñalar VERB [25]
to stab

apurado (FEM **apurada**) ADJECTIVE
difficult
□ Estábamos en una situación bastante apurada. We were in rather a difficult situation.
■ **Si estás apurado de dinero, dímelo.** If you're short of money, tell me.
■ **estar apurado** to feel embarrassed

apurar VERB [25]
to finish up
□ Apura la cerveza que nos vamos. Finish up your beer and let's go.
■ **apurarse 1** to hurry up □ ¡Apúrate! Hurry up! **2** to worry □ Yo me encargo; no te apures por nada. I'll deal with it – don't you worry about anything.

el **apuro** NOUN
fix
□ El dinero de la herencia los sacó del apuro. The money they inherited got them out of the fix.
■ **Pasé muchos apuros para salir del agua.** I had a lot of trouble getting out of the water.
■ **Me da mucho apuro no llevar ningún regalo.** I feel very embarrassed about not taking a present.
■ **estar en apuros** to be in trouble

aquel (FEM **aquella**) ADJECTIVE
that
□ Me gusta más aquella mesa. I prefer that table.

aquél (FEM **aquélla**) PRONOUN
that one
□ Éste no, aquél. Not this one, that one.
■ **Aquél no era el que yo quería.** That wasn't the one I wanted.

aquello PRONOUN
■ **aquello que hay allí** that thing over there
■ **Me fui; aquello era insoportable.** I left. It was just unbearable.
■ **¿Qué fue de aquello del viaje alrededor del mundo?** What ever happened to that round-the-world trip idea?

aquellos (FEM **aquellas**) PL ADJECTIVE
those
□ ¿Ves aquellas montañas? Can you see those mountains?

aquéllos (FEM **aquéllas**) PL PRONOUN
those ones
□ Aquéllos de allí son mejores. Those ones over there are better.
■ **Aquéllos no eran los que vimos ayer.** Those aren't the ones we saw yesterday.

aquí ADVERB
1 here
□ Aquí está el informe que me pediste. Here's the report you asked me for.
■ **aquí abajo** down here
■ **aquí arriba** up here
■ **aquí mismo** right here
■ **por aquí 1** around here □ Lo tenía por aquí en alguna parte. I had it around here somewhere. **2** this way □ Pasen por aquí, si son tan amables. Please come this way.
2 now
■ **de aquí en adelante** from now on
■ **de aquí a siete días** a week from now
■ **hasta aquí 1** up to here □ Hasta aquí el camino es cuesta abajo. Up to here the path goes downhill. **2** up to now □ Hasta aquí todos han ido pagando. Up to now everyone has paid.

el/la **árabe** ADJECTIVE, NOUN
Arab

el **árabe** NOUN
Arabic

Arabia FEM NOUN
■ **Arabia Saudí** Saudi Arabia

el **arado** NOUN
plough

la **araña** NOUN
spider

arañar VERB [25]
to scratch
□ Me arañó el gato. The cat scratched me.
□ Me arañé la cara con las zarzas. I scratched my face on the brambles.
■ **Pedro se arañó las rodillas al caer.** Pedro grazed his knees when he fell over.

el **arañazo** NOUN
scratch (PL scratches)

arar VERB [25]
to plough

el **árbitro**, la **árbitra** NOUN
referee

el **árbol** NOUN
tree
□ un árbol frutal a fruit tree
■ **el árbol de Navidad** the Christmas tree
■ **un árbol genealógico** a family tree

el **arbusto** NOUN
1 bush (PL bushes)
2 shrub

el **arca** FEM NOUN
chest
■ **el Arca de Noé** Noah's Ark

las **arcadas** NOUN
■ **Me dieron arcadas con el olor.** The smell made me retch.

el **arcén** (PL los **arcenes**) NOUN
hard shoulder

el **archivador** NOUN

1 filing cabinet
2 file

archivar VERB [25]
to file

el **archivo** NOUN
1 archive
2 file
■ **los archivos policiales** police files

la **arcilla** NOUN
clay

el **arco** NOUN
1 bow
2 arch (PL arches)
■ **el arco iris** the rainbow

LANGUAGE TIP Word for word, **arco iris** means 'iris arch'.

arder VERB [8]
to burn
□ Ese tronco no va a arder. That log won't burn.
■ **¡La sopa está ardiendo!** The soup's boiling hot!
■ **El jefe está que arde.** The boss is seething.

la **ardilla** NOUN
squirrel

el **ardor** NOUN
passion
■ **Defiende sus ideas con ardor.** He defends his ideas passionately.
■ **tener ardor de estómago** to have heartburn

el **área** FEM NOUN
1 area
□ el área del triángulo the area of the triangle □ en áreas muy pobladas in heavily populated areas
■ **en distintas áreas del país** in different parts of the country
■ **un área de descanso** a lay-by
■ **un área de servicios** a service area
2 penalty area
□ una falta al borde del área a foul on the edge of the penalty area

la **arena** NOUN
sand
■ **arenas movedizas** quicksand *sing*

LANGUAGE TIP Word for word, **arenas movedizas** means 'moving sands'.

el **arenque** NOUN
herring
■ **arenques ahumados** kippers

Argelia FEM NOUN
Algeria

el **argelino** (FEM la **argelina**) ADJECTIVE, NOUN
Algerian

Argentina FEM NOUN
Argentina

el **argentino** (FEM la **argentina**) ADJECTIVE, NOUN
Argentinian

la **argolla** NOUN
ring

el **argot** (PL los **argots**) NOUN
1 slang
2 jargon

el **argumento** NOUN
1 argument
□ los argumentos a favor del desarme the arguments in favour of disarmament
2 plot
□ el argumento de la película the plot of the film

árido (FEM **árida**) ADJECTIVE
arid

Aries MASC NOUN
Aries
■ **Soy aries.** I'm Aries.

el/la **aristócrata** NOUN
aristocrat

el **arma** FEM NOUN
1 weapon
□ Los guerrilleros entregaron las armas. The guerrillas handed over their weapons. □ Se prohibió el uso de armas químicas. The use of chemical weapons was banned.
■ **un fabricante de armas** an arms manufacturer
2 gun
□ Nos apuntaba con un arma. He pointed a gun at us.
■ **un arma de fuego** a firearm

la **armada** NOUN
navy (PL navies)

la **armadura** NOUN
armour
■ **una armadura medieval** a medieval suit of armour

el **armamento** NOUN
arms *pl*
□ negociaciones para la limitación de armamento talks on arms control

armar VERB [25]
1 to arm
□ No iban armados. They weren't armed.
2 to assemble
□ El armario viene desmontado y luego tú lo armas. The cupboard comes in pieces and you assemble it.
3 to make
□ Los vecinos de arriba arman mucho jaleo. Our upstairs neighbours make a lot of noise.
■ **Si no aceptan voy a armar un escándalo.** If they don't agree I'm going to make a fuss.
■ **armarse un lío** to get in a muddle

■ **armarse de paciencia** to be patient
■ **armarse de valor** to summon up one's courage
■ **Se armó la gorda.** *(colloquial)* All hell broke loose.

el **armario** NOUN
1 cupboard
■ **un armario de cocina** a kitchen cupboard
2 wardrobe
■ **un armario empotrado** a built-in wardrobe

el **armazón** (PL los **armazones**) NOUN
frame

la **armonía** NOUN
harmony

la **armónica** NOUN
mouth organ

el **aro** NOUN
1 ring
□ los aros olímpicos the Olympic rings
2 hoop

el **aroma** NOUN
aroma

la **aromaterapia** NOUN
aromatherapy

el **arpa** FEM NOUN
harp

la **arqueóloga** NOUN
archaeologist

la **arqueología** NOUN
archaeology

el **arqueólogo** NOUN
archaeologist

el **arquero**, la **arquera** NOUN *(Latin America)*
goalkeeper

el **arquitecto**, la **arquitecta** NOUN
architect

la **arquitectura** NOUN
architecture

arrancar* VERB [48]
1 to pull up
□ Estaba arrancando malas hierbas. I was pulling up weeds.
■ **El viento arrancó varios árboles.** Several trees were uprooted by the wind.
■ **arrancar algo de raíz** to pull something up by the roots
2 to pull out
□ Le arranqué una espina del dedo. I pulled a thorn out of his finger.
3 to tear out
□ Arrancó una hoja del cuaderno. He tore a page out of the exercise book.
4 to pull off
□ Me arranqué la tirita. I pulled off the sticking plaster.
5 to snatch
□ Me lo arrancaron de las manos. They snatched it from me.
■ **Arranca y vámonos.** Start the engine and let's get going.
■ **arrancarle información a alguien** to drag information out of somebody

arrasar VERB [25]
1 to sweep away
□ El pueblo fue arrasado por las inundaciones. The village was swept away by the floods.
2 to destroy
□ El fuego arrasó la cosecha. The harvest was destroyed by fire.
■ **Los socialistas arrasaron en las elecciones.** The socialists swept the board in the elections.

arrastrar VERB [25]
1 to drag
□ Arrastraba una enorme maleta. He was dragging an enormous suitcase.
2 to sweep along
□ El aire nos arrastraba. The wind swept us along.
3 to trail on the ground
□ Las cortinas arrastran un poco. The curtains trail on the ground slightly.
□ Llevas la falda arrastrando. Your skirt's trailing on the ground.
■ **arrastrarse** to crawl □ Llegaron hasta la valla arrastrándose. They crawled up to the fence.

arrebatar VERB [25]
snatch
□ Me lo arrebató de las manos. He snatched it from me.

el **arrecife** NOUN
reef
■ **los arrecifes de coral** coral reefs

arreglar VERB [25]
1 to fix
□ ¿Sabrás arreglarme el grifo? Could you fix the tap for me?
■ **Están arreglando las aceras.** The pavements are being repaired.
2 to do up
□ Este verano hemos arreglado la cocina. This summer we did up the kitchen.
3 to sort out
□ Si tienes algún problema, él te lo arregla. If you have any problems, he'll sort them out for you.
■ **Deja tu cuarto arreglado antes de salir.** Leave your room tidy before going out.
■ **arreglarse 1** to get ready □ Se arregló para salir. She got ready to go out. **2** to work out □ Ya verás como todo se arregla. It'll all

Spanish-English

a

work out, you'll see. **3** to manage □ ¿Qué tal te arreglas sin coche? How are you managing without a car?

■ **arreglarse el pelo** to do one's hair

■ **arreglárselas para hacer algo** to manage to do something

el **arreglo** NOUN

1 repair

□ El tostador sólo necesita un pequeño arreglo. The toaster only needs a minor repair.

■ **Esta tele no tiene arreglo.** This TV is unrepairable.

■ **Este problema no tiene arreglo.** There's no solution to this problem.

2 compromise

□ Llegamos a un arreglo. We reached a compromise.

■ **con arreglo a** in accordance with

arrepentirse* VERB [51]

■ **arrepentirse de algo** to regret something

■ **arrepentirse de haber hecho algo** to regret doing something

arrestar VERB [25]

to arrest

el **arresto** NOUN

arrest

□ un arresto domiciliario house arrest

arriba ADVERB

above

□ Los platos y las tazas están arriba. The plates and mugs are above. □ Visto desde arriba parece más pequeño. Seen from above it looks smaller.

■ **Pon esos libros arriba del todo.** Put those books on top.

■ **la parte de arriba del biquini** the bikini top □ Arriba están los dormitorios. The bedrooms are upstairs. □ los vecinos de arriba our upstairs neighbours

■ **allí arriba** up there

■ **más arriba** further up

■ **ir calle arriba** to go up the street

■ **Tenemos bolsos de 20 euros para arriba.** We've got bags from 20 euros upwards.

■ **arriba de 1** *(Latin America)* on top of □ Lo dejé arriba del refrigerador. I left it on top of the fridge. **2** *(Latin America)* above □ Viven en el departamento arriba del mío. They live in the flat above mine.

■ **mirar a alguien de arriba abajo** to look somebody up and down

arriesgado (FEM **arriesgada**) ADJECTIVE

risky

arriesgar* VERB [37]

to risk

□ Carlos arriesgó su vida para salvar a su perro. Carlos risked his life to save his dog.

■ **arriesgarse** to take a risk □ Se arriesgó pero salió ganando. He took a risk but he came out on top.

■ **arriesgarse a hacer algo** to risk doing something □ Me arriesgo a perderlo todo. I risk losing everything.

arrimar VERB [25]

to bring...closer

□ Arrima tu silla a la mía. Bring your chair closer to mine.

■ **Vamos a arrimar la mesa a la pared.** Let's put the table by the wall.

■ **arrimarse** to get close □ Al aparcar procura arrimarte a la acera. Try to get close to the pavement when parking.

■ **Arrímate a mí.** Come closer.

arrodillarse VERB [25]

to kneel down

arrogante (FEM **arrogante**) ADJECTIVE

arrogant

arrojar VERB [25]

1 to throw

□ Arrojaban piedras y palos. They were throwing sticks and stones.

■ **arrojar a alguien de un sitio** to throw somebody out of a place

2 to dump

□ 'Prohibido arrojar basuras' 'No dumping'

■ **arrojarse** to throw oneself □ Un hincha se arrojó al campo. A fan threw himself onto the pitch.

arropar VERB [25]

1 to tuck in

□ Voy a arropar al niño. I'll go and tuck the baby in.

2 to wrap up

□ Arrópala bien. Wrap her up well.

■ **arrópate bien 1** tuck yourself up warmly **2** wrap up well

el **arroyo** NOUN

stream

el **arroz** (PL los **arroces**) NOUN

rice

■ **arroz blanco** white rice

■ **arroz con leche** rice pudding

LANGUAGE TIP Word for word, **arroz con leche** means 'rice with milk'.

la **arruga** NOUN

1 wrinkle

2 crease

arrugarse* VERB [37]

1 to get wrinkled

□ La piel se va arrugando. Skin gets increasingly wrinkled.

2 to get creased

□ Se me han arrugado los pantalones.

My trousers have got creased. □ Procura que no se arrugue el sobre. Try not to let the envelope get creased.

arruinar VERB [25]
to ruin
□ Esto arruinó mis planes. That ruined my plans.
■ **arruinarse** to be ruined □ Con aquel negocio se arruinó. He was ruined thanks to that deal.

el **arte** (PL las **artes**) NOUN
1 art
□ el arte del Renacimiento Renaissance art
■ **el arte abstracto** abstract art
■ **el arte dramático** drama
■ **las artes plásticas** plastic arts
2 flair
□ Tiene arte para la cocina. She has a flair for cooking.
■ **por arte de magia** by magic

el **artefacto** NOUN
device
□ un artefacto explosivo an explosive device

la **arteria** NOUN
artery (PL arteries)

la **artesana** NOUN
craftswoman (PL craftswomen)

la **artesanía** NOUN
■ **la artesanía local** local crafts
■ **objetos de artesanía** hand-crafted goods

el **artesano** NOUN
craftsman (PL craftsmen)

ártico (FEM **ártica**) ADJECTIVE
arctic

la **articulación** (PL las **articulaciones**) NOUN
joint

el **artículo** NOUN
article
□ el artículo determinado the definite article □ el artículo indeterminado the indefinite article
■ **artículos de lujo** luxury goods
■ **artículos de escritorio** stationery
■ **artículos de tocador** toiletries

artificial (FEM **artificial**) ADJECTIVE
artificial

el/la **artista** NOUN
artist
■ **un artista** actor
■ **una artista** actress

la **arveja** NOUN *(Latin America)*
pea

el **arzobispo** NOUN
archbishop

el **as** NOUN
ace
□ el as de picas the ace of spades
■ **ser un as de la cocina** to be a wizard at cooking

el **asa** FEM NOUN
handle

asado (FEM **asada**) ADJECTIVE
roast
□ pollo asado roast chicken

el **asado** NOUN
1 roast
2 barbecue *(Latin America)*

asaltar VERB [25]
1 to storm
□ Los rebeldes asaltaron la embajada. The rebels stormed the embassy.
2 to raid
□ Asaltaron un banco. They raided a bank.
3 to mug
□ Me asaltaron a la salida del banco. I was mugged coming out of the bank.

el **asalto** NOUN
1 raid
□ un asalto a una gasolinera a raid on a petrol station
■ **durante el asalto al parlamento** during the storming of parliament
2 round

la **asamblea** NOUN
1 meeting
□ organizar una asamblea to organize a meeting
2 assembly
□ una asamblea legislativa a legislative assembly

asar VERB [25]
to roast
■ **asar algo a la parrilla** to grill something
■ **Me aso de calor.** I'm boiling.
■ **Aquí se asa uno.** It's boiling in here.

ascender* VERB [20]
1 to rise
□ El globo comenzó a ascender. The balloon began to rise.
2 to be promoted
□ Ascendió a teniente. He was promoted to lieutenant.
■ **ascender a primera división** to go up to the first division

el **ascenso** NOUN
promotion

el **ascensor** NOUN
lift

asciendo VERB ▷ *see* **ascender**

el **asco** NOUN
■ **El ajo me da asco.** I think garlic's revolting.
■ **¡Puaj! ¡Qué asco!** Yuk! How revolting!
■ **La casa está hecha un asco.** The house

is filthy.

asegurar VERB [25]

1 to insure

□ Hemos asegurado la casa. We've insured the house.

2 to assure

□ Te aseguro que es verdad. I assure you it's true.

■ **No he sido yo. Te lo aseguro.** It wasn't me, I assure you.

■ **Ella asegura que no lo conoce.** She says that she doesn't know him.

3 to fasten securely

□ Asegura bien la cuerda. Fasten the rope securely.

■ **asegurarse de** to make sure □ Asegúrate de que los grifos están cerrados. Make sure the taps are turned off.

el **aseo** NOUN

■ **el cuarto de aseo** the toilet

LANGUAGE TIP Word for word, **cuarto de aseo** means 'room of cleanliness'.

■ **el aseo personal** personal hygiene

■ **los aseos** the toilets

asequible (FEM **asequible**) ADJECTIVE

1 affordable

□ un precio asequible an affordable price

2 achievable

□ una meta asequible an achievable goal

la **asesina** NOUN

murderer

asesinar VERB [25]

to murder

el **asesinato** NOUN

murder

el **asesino** NOUN

murderer

el **asesor**, la **asesora** NOUN

consultant

■ **asesor fiscal** tax consultant

■ **asesor de imagen** public relations consultant

el **asfalto** NOUN

tarmac

la **asfixia** NOUN

suffocation

asfixiarse VERB [25]

to suffocate

□ Me asfixio de calor. I'm suffocating in this heat.

así ADVERB

1 like this

□ Se hace así. You do it like this.

2 like that

□ Es así: como lo hace Jorge. It's like that: the way Jorge is doing it. □ ¿Ves aquel abrigo? Quiero algo así. Do you see that coat? I'd like something like that.

■ **un tomate así de grande** a tomato this big

■ **Así es la vida.** That's life.

■ **así, así** so-so □ ¿Te gusta? — Así, así. Do you like it? — So-so.

■ **así es** that's right □ ¿Y ocurrió todo en un día? — Así es. And it all happened the same day? — That's right.

■ **¿No es así?** Isn't that so?

■ **así que ...** so ... □ No me gusta, así que lo tiraré. I don't like it, so I'll throw it away.

■ **... o así** ... or thereabouts □ quince euros o así fifteen euros or thereabouts

■ **y así sucesivamente** and so on

Asia FEM NOUN

Asia

el **asiático** (FEM la **asiática**) ADJECTIVE, NOUN

Asian

el **asiento** NOUN

seat

■ **el asiento delantero** the front seat

■ **el asiento trasero** the back seat

la **asignatura** NOUN

subject

■ **Tiene dos asignaturas pendientes.** He's got two subjects to retake.

el **asilo** NOUN

1 home

■ **un asilo de ancianos** an old people's home

■ **un asilo de pobres** a hostel for the poor

2 asylum

□ asilo político political asylum

asimilar VERB [25]

to assimilate

□ Hay que asimilar lo aprendido. You have to assimilate what you've learnt.

■ **El cambio es grande y cuesta asimilarlo.** It's a big change and it takes getting used to.

la **asistencia** NOUN

■ **asistencia médica 1** medical attention □ Tuvieron que recibir asistencia médica. They needed medical attention. **2** medical care □ El seguro cubre la asistencia médica. The insurance covers medical care.

■ **asistencia técnica** technical support

la **asistenta** NOUN

cleaner

el/la **asistente** NOUN

assistant

■ **asistente social** social worker

■ **los asistentes al acto** those present at the ceremony

asistir VERB [58]

1 to go

□ No asistieron a la ceremonia. They didn't go to the ceremony.

2 to treat
□ Le asistió un médico que había de guardia. He was treated by a duty doctor.

el **asma** FEM NOUN
asthma

la **asociación** (PL las **asociaciones**) NOUN
association
□ por asociación de ideas by an association of ideas

asociar VERB [25]
to associate
□ Asocio la lluvia con Londres. I associate rain with London.
■ **asociarse** to go into partnership □ Los dos empresarios decidieron asociarse. The two businessmen decided to go into partnership.

asolearse VERB [25] *(Latin America)*
to sunbathe

asomar VERB [25]
■ **Te asoma el pañuelo por el bolsillo.** Your handkerchief's sticking out of your pocket.
■ **No asomes la cabeza por la ventanilla.** Don't lean out of the window.
■ **Me asomé a la terraza a ver quién gritaba.** I went out onto the balcony to see who was shouting.
■ **Asómate a la ventana.** Look out of the window.

asombrar VERB [25]
to amaze
□ Me asombra que no lo sepas. I'm amazed you don't know.
■ **Intentaba asombrarnos con sus conocimientos.** He was trying to stun us with his knowledge.
■ **asombrarse** to be amazed □ Se asombró de lo tarde que era. He was amazed at how late it was.

el **asombro** NOUN
amazement
□ La gente la observaba con asombro. People were looking at her in amazement.

asombroso (FEM **asombrosa**) ADJECTIVE
amazing

el **aspecto** NOUN
1 appearance
□ A ver si cuidas más tu aspecto. Try taking a bit more trouble with your appearance.
2 aspect
□ Nos interesa mucho el aspecto económico. We are very interested in the financial aspect.
■ **tener buen aspecto** 1 to look well 2 to look good

áspero (FEM **áspera**) ADJECTIVE
1 rough
2 harsh

la **aspiradora** NOUN
vacuum cleaner

aspirar VERB [25]
1 to breathe in
■ **Aspire profundamente.** Take a deep breath.
■ **aspirar a hacer algo** to hope to do something
2 to hoover *(Latin America)*

la **aspirina** NOUN
aspirin

asqueroso (FEM **asquerosa**) ADJECTIVE
1 disgusting
2 filthy
□ Esta cocina está asquerosa. This kitchen is filthy.
3 horrible
□ Esta gente es asquerosa. They're horrible people.

la **astilla** NOUN
splinter

el **astro** NOUN
star

la **astrología** NOUN
astrology

el/la **astronauta** NOUN
astronaut

la **astronomía** NOUN
astronomy

astuto (FEM **astuta**) ADJECTIVE
clever

asumir VERB [58]
to accept
□ Ya he asumido que no voy a ganar. I've already accepted that I'm not going to win.
■ **Asumo toda la responsabilidad.** I take full responsibility.
■ **No estoy dispuesta a asumir ese riesgo.** I'm not prepared to take that risk.

el **asunto** NOUN
matter
□ Es un asunto muy delicado. It's a very delicate matter.
■ **el ministro de asuntos exteriores** the minister for foreign affairs
■ **No me gusta que se metan en mis asuntos.** I don't like anyone meddling in my affairs.
■ **¡Eso no es asunto tuyo!** That's none of your business!

asustar VERB [25]
1 to frighten
□ No me asustan los fantasmas. I'm not frightened of ghosts.
2 to startle
□ ¡Huy! Me has asustado. Goodness! You startled me.

■ **asustarse** to get frightened ▫ Se asusta por nada. He gets frightened over nothing.
■ **No te asustes.** Don't be frightened.

atacar* VERB [48]
to attack

el **atado** NOUN *(River Plate)*
■ **un atado de cigarrillos** a packet of cigarettes

el **atajo** NOUN
short cut
▫ Cogeremos un atajo. We'll take a short cut.

el **ataque** NOUN
attack
▫ un ataque contra alguien an attack on somebody
■ **un ataque cardíaco** a heart attack
■ **Le dio un ataque de risa.** He burst out laughing.
■ **un ataque de nervios** a fit of panic

atar VERB [25]
to tie
▫ Ata al perro a la farola. Tie the dog to the lamppost.
■ **Átate los cordones.** Tie your shoelaces up.

atardecer* VERB [12]
to get dark
▫ Está atardeciendo. It's getting dark.

el **atardecer** NOUN
dusk
■ **al atardecer** at dusk

atareado (FEM **atareada**) ADJECTIVE
busy

el **atasco** NOUN
traffic jam

el **ataúd** NOUN
coffin

Atenas FEM NOUN
Athens

la **atención** (PL las **atenciones**) NOUN
■ **Hay que poner más atención.** You should pay more attention.
■ **Escucha con atención.** He listens attentively.
■ **Me llamó la atención lo grande que era la casa.** I was struck by how big the house was.
■ **El director del colegio le llamó la atención.** The headmaster gave him a talking-to.
■ **Estás llamando la atención con ese sombrero.** You're attracting attention in that hat.

atención EXCLAMATION
Attention!
■ **¡Atención, por favor!** May I have your attention please?
■ **'¡Atención!'** 'Danger!'

atender* VERB [20]
1 to serve
▫ ¿Le atienden? Are you being served?
2 to attend to
▫ Tengo que atender a un par de clientes. I've got a couple of clients to attend to.
3 to look after
▫ atender a los enfermos to look after the sick
4 to pay attention to
▫ Todos en clase atendían al profesor. Everyone in the class was paying attention to the teacher.
■ **atender los consejos de alguien** to listen to somebody's advice
■ **La recepcionista atiende al teléfono.** The receptionist answers the telephone.
■ **No atendieron nuestra petición.** They didn't take any notice of our petition.

el **atentado** NOUN
attack
▫ un atentado terrorista a terrorist attack
▫ un atentado suicida a suicide attack

atentamente ADVERB
1 Yours sincerely
2 Yours faithfully

atento (FEM **atenta**) ADJECTIVE
thoughtful
▫ Es un chico muy atento. He's a very thoughtful boy.
■ **Estaban atentos a las explicaciones del instructor.** They were listening attentively to the instructor's explanations.

el **aterrizaje** NOUN
landing
■ **un aterrizaje forzoso** an emergency landing

aterrizar* VERB [13]
to land

atestado (FEM **atestada**) ADJECTIVE
packed
▫ El local estaba atestado de gente. The place was packed with people.

atiborrarse VERB [25]
to stuff oneself
▫ Se atiborró de pasteles. He stuffed himself with cakes.

el **ático** NOUN
top-floor flat
■ **un ático de lujo** a luxurious penthouse

atiendo VERB ▷ *see* **atender**

atlántico (FEM **atlántica**) ADJECTIVE
Atlantic
■ **el océano Atlántico** the Atlantic Ocean

el **atlas** (PL los **atlas**) NOUN
atlas (PL atlases)

el/la **atleta** NOUN

athlete

el **atletismo** NOUN
athletics

la **atmósfera** NOUN
atmosphere

atolondrado (FEM **atolondrada**) ADJECTIVE
scatterbrained

atómico (FEM **atómica**) ADJECTIVE
atomic

el **átomo** NOUN
the atom

atónito (FEM **atónita**) ADJECTIVE
amazed
■ **quedarse atónito** to be amazed

el **atracador**, la **atracadora** NOUN
1 robber
□ un atracador de bancos a bank robber
2 mugger
□ Unos atracadores le robaron el bolso. She had her bag stolen by muggers.

atracar* VERB [48]
1 to hold up
□ atracar un banco to hold up a bank
2 to mug
□ La atracaron en la plaza. She was mugged in the square.

la **atracción** (PL las **atracciones**) NOUN
attraction
□ una atracción turística a tourist attraction
■ **sentir atracción por algo** to be attracted to something □ Sentía atracción por él. I was attracted to him.

el **atraco** NOUN
1 hold-up
□ un atraco a un banco a hold-up at a bank
2 mugging
□ un atraco en plena calle a mugging in broad daylight

atractivo (FEM **atractiva**) ADJECTIVE
attractive
□ un hombre muy atractivo a very attractive man

el **atractivo** NOUN
attraction
■ **Es una chica con un atractivo especial.** She's a really charming girl.

atraer* VERB [54]
to attract
□ Si bajamos los precios atraeremos a más clientes. If we put our prices down we'll attract more customers.
■ **Esa chica me atrae mucho.** I find that girl very attractive.
■ **No me atrae mucho lo del viaje a Turquía.** That Turkey trip doesn't appeal to me much.

atrapar VERB [25]
to catch

atrás ADVERB
□ Los niños viajan siempre atrás. The children always travel in the back.
■ **la parte de atrás** the back
■ **el asiento de atrás** the back seat □ Mirar hacia atrás. To look back. □ Está más atrás. It's further back.
■ **Ir para atrás.** To go backwards. □ El coche de atrás va a adelantarnos. The car behind is going to overtake us. □ Yo me quedé atrás porque iba muy cansado. I stayed behind because I was very tired.
■ **años atrás** years ago

atrasado (FEM **atrasada**) ADJECTIVE
1 backward
□ Es un país muy atrasado. It's a very backward country.
2 back
□ números atrasados de una revista back numbers of a magazine □ pagos atrasados back payments
3 behind
□ Va bastante atrasado en la escuela. He's rather behind at school.
■ **Tengo mucho trabajo atrasado.** I'm very behind with my work.
■ **El reloj está atrasado.** The clock's slow.
4 late *(Latin America)*
□ Siempre llega atrasada al trabajo. She's always late for work.

atrasar VERB [25]
1 to delay
□ Tuvimos que atrasar nuestra salida. We had to delay our departure.
2 to put back
□ Acordaos de atrasar una hora vuestros relojes. Remember to put your watches back one hour.
■ **atrasarse** to be late □ El tren se atrasó. The train was late.

atravesar* VERB [39]
1 to cross
□ Atravesamos el río. We crossed the river.
2 to go through
□ La navaja le atravesó el hígado. The blade went through his liver. □ Atravesamos un mal momento. We're going through a bad patch.

atravieso VERB ▹ *see* **atravesar**

atreverse VERB [8]
to dare
□ No me atreví a decírselo. I didn't dare tell him.
■ **No me atrevo.** I daren't.
■ **La gente no se atreve a salir de noche.** People are afraid to go out at night.

atrevido (FEM **atrevida**) ADJECTIVE
1 daring

□ El periodista le hizo preguntas muy atrevidas. The reporter asked him some very daring questions. □ un escote muy atrevido a very daring neckline
2 cheeky
□ No seas tan atrevido con el jefe. Don't be so cheeky to the boss.

atropellar VERB [25]
to run over
□ Un coche atropelló al perro. The dog was run over by a car.

el/la **ATS** ABBREVIATION (= *Ayudante Técnico Sanitario*)
Registered Nurse

el **atún** (PL los **atunes**) NOUN
tuna (PL tuna *o* tunas)

audaz (FEM **audaz**, PL **audaces**) ADJECTIVE
daring

la **audiencia** NOUN
audience
□ Su programa tiene mucha audiencia. His programme has a large audience.

audiovisual (FEM **audiovisual**) ADJECTIVE
audiovisual

el **auditorio** NOUN
1 auditorium
□ El auditorio estaba lleno. The auditorium was full.
2 audience
□ Todo el auditorio aplaudió a la orquesta. The whole audience applauded the orchestra.

el **aula** FEM NOUN
classroom

aumentar VERB [25]
to increase
□ El gobierno ha aumentado el presupuesto de educación. The government has increased the education budget.
■ **aumentar de peso** to put on weight

el **aumento** NOUN
increase
□ Se ha producido un aumento de la productividad. There has been an increase in productivity.
■ **Los precios van en aumento.** Prices are going up.

aun ADVERB
even
□ Aun sentado me duele la pierna. Even when I'm sitting down, my leg hurts.
■ **aun así** even so
■ **aun cuando** even if

aún ADVERB
1 still
□ Aún me queda un poco para terminar. I've still got a little bit left to finish. □ ¿Aún te duele? Is it still hurting?
2 yet
□ Aún no han llegado los periódicos de hoy. Today's papers haven't arrived yet. □ ¿No ha venido aún? Hasn't he got here yet? □ Y aún no me has devuelto el libro. You still haven't given me the book back.
3 even
□ La película es aún más aburrida de lo que creía. The film's even more boring than I thought it would be. □ Aquello nos unió aún más. That brought us even closer together.

aunque CONJUNCTION
1 although
□ Me gusta el francés, aunque prefiero el alemán. I like French, although I prefer German. □ Estoy pensando en ir, aunque no sé cuándo. I'm thinking of going, though I don't know when.
2 even though
□ Seguí andando, aunque me dolía mucho la pierna. I went on walking, even though my leg was hurting badly.
■ **No te lo daré, aunque protestes.** I won't give it to you however much you complain.
3 even if
□ Pienso irme, aunque tenga que salir por la ventana. I shall leave, even if I have to climb out of the window.

el **auricular** NOUN
receiver
■ **los auriculares** headphones

la **ausencia** NOUN
absence

ausente (FEM **ausente**) ADJECTIVE
absent

Australia FEM NOUN
Australia

el **australiano** (FEM la **australiana**) ADJECTIVE, NOUN
Australian

Austria FEM NOUN
Austria

el **austriaco** (FEM la **austriaca**) ADJECTIVE, NOUN
Austrian

auténtico (FEM **auténtica**) ADJECTIVE
1 real
□ Es de cuero auténtico. It's real leather.
2 genuine
□ El cuadro era auténtico. The painting was genuine.
■ **Es un auténtico campeón.** He's a real champion.

el **auto** NOUN
car

la **autobiografía** NOUN
autobiography (PL autobiographies)

el **autobús** (PL los **autobuses**) NOUN

bus (PL buses)
■ **en autobús** by bus
■ **un autobús de línea** a coach

el **autocar** NOUN
coach (PL coaches)

la **autoedición** NOUN
desktop publishing

la **autoescuela** NOUN
driving school

el **autógrafo** NOUN
autograph

automático (FEM **automática**) ADJECTIVE
automatic

el **automóvil** NOUN
car

el/la **automovilista** NOUN
motorist

la **autonomía** NOUN
1 autonomy
□ un estatuto de autonomía a statute of autonomy □ Tengo mucha autonomía en mi trabajo. I have a lot of autonomy in my work.
2 autonomous region
□ Andalucía es una de las autonomías más extensas. Andalusia is one of the biggest autonomous regions.

autonómico (FEM **autonómica**) ADJECTIVE
regional

autónomo (FEM **autónoma**) ADJECTIVE
1 autonomous
□ las comunidades autónomas the autonomous regions
2 self-employed
□ Ser autónomo tiene sus ventajas. Being self-employed has its advantages.

la **autopista** NOUN
motorway
■ **autopista de peaje** toll motorway

el **autor**, la **autora** NOUN
author
□ el autor de la novela the author of the novel
■ **el autor del cuadro** the painter
■ **los presuntos autores del crimen** the suspected killers

la **autoridad** NOUN
authority

autorizado (FEM **autorizada**) ADJECTIVE
authorized

autorizar* VERB [13]
to authorize
□ No le han autorizado la entrada al país. His entry into the country hasn't been authorized.
■ **Eso no te autoriza a tratarlo así.** That doesn't give you the right to treat him this way.

el **autoservicio** NOUN
1 supermarket
□ Sale más económico comprar en el autoservicio. It's cheaper to shop at the supermarket.
2 self-service restaurant
□ Comimos en un autoservicio. We ate at a self-service restaurant.

el **autostop** NOUN
hitch-hiking
■ **hacer autostop** to hitch-hike

el/la **autostopista** NOUN
hitch-hiker

la **autovía** NOUN
dual carriageway

el **auxilio** NOUN
help
□ una llamada de auxilio a call for help
■ **los primeros auxilios** first aid

auxilio EXCLAMATION
help!

avanzar* VERB [13]
to make progress
□ Isabel avanzó mucho el pasado trimestre. Isabel made a lot of progress last term.
■ **¿Qué tal avanza el proyecto?** How's the project coming on?

avaricioso (FEM **avariciosa**) ADJECTIVE
greedy

avaro (FEM **avara**) ADJECTIVE
miserly

Avda. ABBREVIATION *(= Avenida)*
Ave. *(= Avenue)*

el **AVE** ABBREVIATION *(= Alta Velocidad Española)*
high-speed train

el **ave** FEM NOUN
bird
■ **un ave de rapiña** a bird of prey
■ **aves de corral** poultry *sing*

la **avellana** NOUN
hazelnut

la **avena** NOUN
oats *pl*

la **avenida** NOUN
avenue

aventajar VERB [25]
■ **El Salamanca aventaja en tres puntos al Córdoba.** Salamanca has a three-point lead over Córdoba.

aventar* VERB [39] *(Mexico)*
to throw

el **aventón** (PL los **aventones**) NOUN *(Mexico)*
lift
□ Le di un aventón. I gave him a lift.

la **aventura** NOUN
1 adventure

□ Te contaré nuestras aventuras en África. I'll tell you about our adventures in Africa.
2 affair
□ Tuvo una aventura con su vecino. She had an affair with her neighbour.

avergonzar* VERB [13]
to embarrass
□ Me avergonzaste delante de todos. You embarrassed me in front of everyone.
■ **Me avergüenzan estas situaciones.** I find this sort of situation embarrassing.
■ **No me avergüenza nuestra relación.** I'm not ashamed of our relationship.
■ **avergonzarse de algo** to be ashamed of something □ No hay de qué avergonzarse. There's nothing to be ashamed of.
■ **Me avergüenzo de haberme portado tan mal.** I'm ashamed of myself for behaving so badly.

la **avería** NOUN
■ **El coche tiene una avería.** The car has broken down.

averiarse* VERB [21]
to break down

averiguar* VERB [25, gu → gü before e and i]
to find out
□ La policía no ha conseguido averiguar dónde se escondió el arma. The police haven't managed to find out where the weapon was hidden.

el **avestruz** (PL los **avestruces**) NOUN
ostrich (PL ostriches)

la **aviación** (PL las **aviaciones**) NOUN
1 aviation
□ aviación civil civil aviation
2 air force
□ Es oficial de aviación. He's an officer in the air force.

aviento VERB ▷ *see* **aventar**

el **avión** (PL los **aviones**) NOUN
plane
■ **ir en avión** to fly

la **avioneta** NOUN
light aircraft

avisar VERB [25]
1 to warn
□ Ya nos avisaron de que había nieve en la carretera. They had warned us that there was snow on the roads.
2 to let...know
□ Avísanos si hay alguna novedad. Let us know if there's any news.
3 to call
□ avisar al médico to call the doctor
□ Avisaron a una ambulancia. They called an ambulance.

el **aviso** NOUN
1 warning
□ El árbitro le dio un aviso. The referee gave him a warning.
2 notice
□ Había un aviso en la puerta. There was a notice on the door.
■ **hasta nuevo aviso** until further notice

la **avispa** NOUN
wasp

ay EXCLAMATION
1 ow!
□ ¡Ay! ¡Me has pisado! Ow! You've trodden on my toe!
2 oh no!
□ ¡Ay! ¡Creo que nos han engañado! Oh no! I think they've cheated us!

ayer ADVERB
yesterday
■ **antes de ayer** the day before yesterday
■ **ayer por la mañana** yesterday morning
■ **ayer por la tarde** 1 yesterday afternoon 2 yesterday evening
■ **ayer por la noche** last night

la **ayuda** NOUN
help
■ **la ayuda humanitaria** humanitarian aid

el/la **ayudante** NOUN
assistant

ayudar VERB [25]
to help
□ ¿Me ayudas con los ejercicios? Could you help me with these exercises?
■ **ayudar a alguien a hacer algo** to help somebody do something

el **ayuntamiento** NOUN
1 council
□ El ayuntamiento recauda sus propios impuestos. The council collects its own taxes.
2 town hall
□ ¿Dónde está el ayuntamiento? Where's the town hall?
3 city hall
□ ¿Dónde está el ayuntamiento? Where's the city hall?

la **azafata** NOUN
air-hostess
■ **una azafata de congresos** a conference hostess

el **azar** NOUN
chance
□ Nos encontramos por azar. We met by chance.
■ **al azar** at random □ Escoge uno al azar. Pick one at random.

azotar VERB [25]
to whip

la **azotea** NOUN

roof

el/la **azteca** ADJECTIVE, NOUN

Aztec

el **azúcar** NOUN

sugar

■ **azúcar moreno** brown sugar

■ **un caramelo sin azúcar** a sugar-free sweet

el **azul** ADJECTIVE, NOUN

blue

□ una puerta azul **a blue door** □ Yo iba de azul. **I was dressed in blue.**

■ **azul celeste** sky blue

■ **azul marino** navy blue

el **azulejo** NOUN

tile

Bb

el **babero** NOUN
bib

el **babi** NOUN
smock

la **baca** NOUN
roof rack

el **bacalao** NOUN
cod

el **bache** NOUN
1 pothole
2 bump

el **Bachillerato** NOUN

DID YOU KNOW...?
The **Bachillerato** is a two-year secondary school course leading to university.

la **bacteria** NOUN
bacterium (PL bacteria)

el **bafle** NOUN
loudspeaker

la **bahía** NOUN
bay (PL bays)

bailar VERB [25]
to dance
■ **sacar a bailar a alguien** to ask someone to dance

el **bailarín**, la **bailarina** NOUN (MASC PL los **bailarines**
dancer

el **baile** NOUN
dance
□ Me han invitado a un baile. I have been invited to a dance.

la **baja** NOUN
■ **darse de baja** to leave □ Se dieron de baja en el club. They left the club.
■ **estar de baja** to be on sick leave

la **bajada** NOUN
drop
□ Hubo una bajada de las temperaturas. There was a drop in temperature.
■ **Me caí en la bajada de la montaña.** I fell going down the mountain.
■ **La bajada hasta la playa es muy pronunciada.** The road down to the beach is very steep.

bajar VERB [25]
1 to go down
□ Bajó la escalera muy despacio. He went down the stairs very slowly.
2 to come down
□ Baja y ayúdame. Come down and help me. □ Han bajado los precios. Prices have come down.
■ **Los coches han bajado de precio.** Cars have come down in price.
3 to take down
□ ¿Has bajado la basura? Have you taken the rubbish down?
4 to bring down
□ ¿Me bajas el abrigo? Hace frío aquí fuera. Could you bring my coat down, it's cold out here.
5 to get down
□ ¿Me bajas la maleta del armario? Could you get me the suitcase down from the wardrobe?
6 to put down
□ ¿Bajo la persiana? Shall I put the blind down? □ Los comercios han bajado los precios. Businesses have put their prices down.
■ **¡Baja la voz, que no estoy sordo!** Keep your voice down, I'm not deaf!
7 to turn down
□ Baja la radio que no oigo nada. Turn the radio down, I can't hear a thing.
8 to download
■ **bajarse de** **1** to get off □ Se bajó del autobús antes que yo. He got off the bus before me. **2** to get out of □ ¡Bájate del coche! Get out of the car! **3** to get down from □ ¡Bájate de ahí! Get down from there!

bajo (FEM **baja**) ADJECTIVE
▷ *see also* **bajo** PREPOSITION, ADVERB
1 low
□ una silla muy baja a very low chair
■ **la temporada baja** the low season
2 short
□ Mi hermano es muy bajo. My brother is very short.
■ **Viven en la planta baja.** They live on the

ground floor.
■ **Hablaban en voz baja.** They spoke quietly.

bajo PREPOSITION
▷ *see also* **bajo** ADJECTIVE, ADVERB
under
□ bajo el título de ... under the title of ...
□ Juan llevaba un libro bajo el brazo. Juan was carrying a book under his arm.
■ **bajo tierra** underground

bajo ADVERB
▷ *see also* **bajo** ADJECTIVE, PREPOSITION
1 low
□ El avión volaba muy bajo. The plane was flying very low.
2 quietly
□ ¡Habla bajo! Speak quietly!

el **bajo** NOUN
1 bass (PL basses)
□ Elena toca el bajo en un grupo. Elena plays bass in a group.
2 ground floor
□ Vivo en un bajo. I live on the ground floor.

el **bakalao** NOUN
techno

la **bala** NOUN
bullet

el **balcón** (PL los **balcones**) NOUN
balcony (PL balconies)

la **baldosa** NOUN
tile

el **baldosín** (PL los **baldosines**) NOUN
tile

balear (FEM **balear**) ADJECTIVE
Balearic

Baleares FEM PL NOUN
the Balearic Islands

la **ballena** NOUN
whale

el **ballet** (PL los **ballets**) NOUN
ballet

el **balneario** NOUN
spa

el **balón** (PL los **balones**) NOUN
ball

el **baloncesto** NOUN
basketball

el **balonmano** NOUN
handball

el **balonvolea** NOUN
volleyball

la **balsa** NOUN
raft

la **banana** NOUN *(Latin America)*
banana

bancario (FEM **bancaria**) ADJECTIVE
bank

el **banco** NOUN
1 bank
2 bench (PL benches)
3 pew

la **banda** NOUN
1 band
□ Toca la trompeta en la banda del pueblo. He plays the trumpet in the village band.
2 gang
□ La policía ha cogido a toda la banda. The police have caught the whole gang.
3 sash (PL sashes)
□ Las autoridades llevaban una banda azul. The dignitaries were wearing blue sashes.
■ **la banda ancha** broadband
■ **la banda sonora** the soundtrack
LANGUAGE TIP Word for word, **banda sonora** means 'sound band'.

la **bandeja** NOUN
tray (PL trays)

la **bandera** NOUN
flag
■ **la bandera blanca** the white flag

el **bandido** NOUN
bandit

el **bando** NOUN
side
□ Un bando está a favor y el otro en contra. One side is in favour and the other is against.

la **banqueta** NOUN
1 stool
2 pavement *(Mexico)*

el **banquete** NOUN
banquet
■ **el banquete de bodas** the wedding reception

el **banquillo** NOUN
bench (PL benches)
□ El entrenador está en el banquillo. The trainer is sitting on the bench.
■ **el banquillo de los acusados** the dock

el **bañador** NOUN
1 swimming trunks *pl*
2 swimming costume

bañarse VERB [25]
1 to have a bath
□ Me gusta más bañarme que ducharme. I prefer having a bath to having a shower.
2 to go for a swim
□ Estuve en la playa pero no me bañé. I was on the beach but I didn't go for a swim.

la **bañera** NOUN
bath

el **baño** NOUN
bathroom
□ ¿Dónde está el baño, por favor? Where is the bathroom, please?
■ **darse un baño 1** to have a bath **2** to go

for a swim

el **bar** NOUN
bar

la **baraja** NOUN
pack of cards

la **barandilla** NOUN
1 banisters *pl*
2 railing

la **barata** NOUN *(Mexico)*
sale

barato (FEM **barata**) ADJECTIVE
▷ *see also* **barato** ADVERB
cheap
□ Esta marca es más barata que aquélla. This brand is cheaper than that one.

barato ADVERB
▷ *see also* **barato** ADJECTIVE
cheaply
□ Aquí se come muy barato. You can eat really cheaply here.

la **barba** NOUN
beard
■ **dejarse barba** to grow a beard

la **barbacoa** NOUN
barbecue

la **barbaridad** NOUN
atrocity (PL atrocities)
□ Hicieron barbaridades en la guerra. They committed atrocities during the war.
■ **Pablo come una barbaridad.** Pablo eats an awful lot.
■ **decir barbaridades** to talk nonsense
■ **¡Qué barbaridad!** Good grief!

la **barbilla** NOUN
chin

la **barca** NOUN
boat

el **barco** NOUN
1 ship
■ **un barco de guerra** a warship
2 boat
■ **un barco de vela** a sailing boat

la **barda** NOUN *(Mexico)*
fence

el **barniz** (PL los **barnices**) NOUN
varnish (PL varnishes)

barnizar* VERB [13]
to varnish

la **barra** NOUN
bar
□ una barra metálica a metal bar □ Me tomé un café en la barra. I had a coffee at the bar.
■ **una barra de pan** a French loaf
■ **una barra de labios** lipstick
■ **las barras paralelas** the parallel bars

la **barraca** NOUN
small farmhouse
■ **una barraca de feria** a fairground stall

el **barranco** NOUN
ravine

barrer VERB [8]
to sweep

la **barrera** NOUN
barrier
■ **una barrera de seguridad** a safety barrier

la **barriga** NOUN
belly (PL bellies)
□ Estás echando barriga. You're getting a bit of a belly.
■ **Me duele la barriga.** I have a sore stomach.

el **barril** NOUN
barrel

el **barrilete** NOUN *(River Plate)*
kite

el **barrio** NOUN
area
□ Ese chico no es del barrio. That boy's not from this area.
■ **la pescadería del barrio** the local fishmonger's
■ **el barrio chino** the red-light district

el **barro** NOUN
1 mud
□ Me llené los zapatos de barro. My shoes got covered in mud.
2 clay
□ una vasija de barro a clay pot

el **barrote** NOUN
bar
□ los barrotes de la ventana the bars on the window

el **barullo** NOUN
1 racket
■ **armar barullo** to make a racket
2 mess
□ Esta habitación está hecha un barullo. This room is a mess.

basarse VERB [25]
■ **Mi conclusión se basa en los datos.** My conclusion is based on the facts.
■ **¿En qué te basas para decir eso?** What grounds have you got for saying that?
■ **Para la novela me basé en la vida de mi abuela.** I based the novel on the life of my grandmother.

la **báscula** NOUN
scales *pl*

la **base** NOUN
1 base
□ la base de la columna the base of the column
2 basis (PL bases)
□ El esfuerzo es la base del éxito. Effort is

the basis for success.
■ **las bases del concurso** the rules of the competition
■ **Lo consiguió a base de mucho trabajo.** She managed it through hard work.
■ **una base militar** a military base
■ **una base de datos** a database

básico (FEM **básica**) ADJECTIVE
basic

bastante (FEM **bastante**) ADJECTIVE, PRONOUN
▷ *see also* **bastante** ADVERB
1 enough
□ No tengo bastante dinero. I haven't enough money. □ Ya hay bastantes libros en casa. There are enough books in the house. □ ¿Hay bastante? Is there enough?
2 quite a lot of
□ Vino bastante gente. Quite a lot of people came.
■ **Se tarda bastante tiempo en llegar.** It takes quite a while to get there.
■ **Voy a tardar bastante.** I'm going to take quite a while.

bastante ADVERB
▷ *see also* **bastante** ADJECTIVE, PRONOUN
1 quite
□ Son bastante ricos. They are quite rich.
□ Juegas bastante bien. You play quite well.
2 quite a lot
□ Sus padres ganan bastante. Their parents earn quite a lot.

bastar VERB [25]
to be enough
□ Con esto basta. That's enough. □ ¡Basta ya de tonterías! That's enough of your nonsense!
■ **¡Basta!** That's enough!
■ **bastarse** to manage □ Yo me basto solo. I can manage on my own.

basto (FEM **basta**) ADJECTIVE
coarse
□ Esta tela es muy basta. It's a very coarse material.
■ **¡Qué basto eres!** You've got no manners!

el **bastón** (PL los **bastones**) NOUN
stick
■ **un bastón de esquí** a ski stick

los **bastos** NOUN
clubs

DID YOU KNOW...?
Bastos are clubs, one of the suits in the Spanish card deck.

la **basura** NOUN
1 rubbish
□ Eso es basura. That's rubbish.
■ **tirar algo a la basura** to put something in the bin
2 litter
□ Hay mucha basura en la calle. There's a lot of litter in the street.

el **basurero** NOUN
1 dustman (PL dustmen)
2 rubbish dump
3 rubbish bin *(Chile, Mexico)*

la **bata** NOUN
1 dressing gown
2 lab coat

la **batalla** NOUN
battle

la **batería** NOUN
1 battery (PL batteries)
□ Se ha agotado la batería. The battery is flat.
2 drums *pl*
□ ¿Tocas la batería? Do you play the drums?
■ **aparcar en batería** to park at an angle to the kerb
■ **una batería de cocina** a set of kitchen equipment
3 drummer
□ La batería del grupo se llama Amanda. The group's drummer is called Amanda.

el **batería** NOUN
drummer
□ El batería del grupo se llama Juan. The group's drummer is called Juan.

el **batido** NOUN
milkshake
□ un batido de fresa a strawberry milkshake

la **batidora** NOUN
mixer

batir VERB [58]
1 to beat
2 to whip
3 to break

el **baúl** NOUN
1 chest
2 trunk
3 boot *(River Plate)*

el **bautizo** NOUN
christening

la **bayeta** NOUN
cloth
■ **¿Has pasado la bayeta por la mesa?** Have you wiped the table?

el **bebe**, la **beba** NOUN *(River Plate)*
baby (PL babies)

el **bebé** (PL los **bebés**) NOUN
baby (PL babies)

el **bebedero** NOUN *(Chile, Mexico)*
drinking fountain

beber VERB [8]
to drink
■ **Se bebió la leche de un trago.** He drank the milk in one gulp.

la **bebida** NOUN

Spanish-English

b

drink
■ **bebidas alcohólicas** alcoholic drinks

bebido (FEM **bebida**) ADJECTIVE
drunk
■ **estar bebido** to be drunk

la **beca** NOUN
1 grant
2 scholarship

el **béisbol** NOUN
baseball

el **belén** (PL los **belenes**) NOUN
crib

el/la **belga** ADJECTIVE, NOUN
Belgian

Bélgica FEM NOUN
Belgium

la **belleza** NOUN
beauty (PL beauties)

bello (FEM **bella**) ADJECTIVE
beautiful
■ **bellas artes** fine art *sing*

bendecir* VERB [15]
to bless

la **bendición** (PL las **bendiciones**) NOUN
blessing

beneficiar VERB [25]
to benefit
■ **beneficiarse de algo** to benefit from something

el **beneficio** NOUN
profit
□ Obtuvieron un beneficio de un millón de euros. They made a profit of a million euros.
■ **No han tenido beneficios este año.** They didn't make any profit this year.
■ **sacar beneficio de algo** to benefit from something □ Seguro que espera sacar algún beneficio. He definitely expects to benefit from it.
■ **a beneficio de** in aid of □ un concierto a beneficio de las víctimas del terremoto a concert in aid of the earthquake victims

benéfico (FEM **benéfica**) ADJECTIVE
charity (PL charities)
□ un concierto benéfico a charity concert

el **berberecho** NOUN
cockle

la **berenjena** NOUN
aubergine

las **bermudas** NOUN
Bermuda shorts
■ **unas bermudas** a pair of Bermuda shorts

la **berza** NOUN
cabbage

besar VERB [25]
to kiss
■ **Ana y Pepe se besaron.** Ana and Pepe kissed each other.

el **beso** NOUN
kiss (PL kisses)
■ **dar un beso a alguien** to give somebody a kiss

la **bestia** NOUN
beast

bestia (FEM **bestia**) ADJECTIVE
■ **¡Qué bestia eres!** You're so rough!
■ **Tiró de él a lo bestia.** He pulled him roughly.

el **besugo** NOUN
sea bream

el **betún** NOUN
shoe polish

el **biberón** (PL los **biberones**) NOUN
baby's bottle
■ **Voy a dar el biberón al niño.** I'm going to give the baby his bottle.

la **Biblia** NOUN
Bible

la **biblioteca** NOUN
library (PL libraries)

el **bicarbonato** NOUN
bicarbonate

el **bicho** NOUN
insect
□ Me ha picado un bicho. I've been bitten by an insect.
■ **un bicho raro** *(colloquial)* an oddball

la **bici** NOUN
bike

la **bicicleta** NOUN
bicycle
■ **una bicicleta de montaña** a mountain bike

el **bidé** (PL los **bidés**) NOUN
bidet

el **bidón** (PL los **bidones**) NOUN
drum

el **bien** NOUN
good
□ Lo digo por tu bien. I'm telling you for your own good.
■ **los bienes** possessions □ todos los bienes de la familia all the family's possessions

bien ADVERB
1 well
□ Habla bien el español. He speaks Spanish well. □ El traje me está bien. The suit fits me well.
2 good
□ Huele bien. It smells good. □ Sabe bien. It tastes good.
■ **Has contestado bien.** You gave the right answer.

■ **Lo pasamos muy bien.** We had a very good time.
3 very
□ un café bien caliente a very hot coffee
■ **¿Estás bien?** Are you OK?
■ **¡Está bien! Lo haré.** OK! I'll do it.
■ **Ese libro está muy bien.** That's a very good book.
■ **Está muy bien que ahorres dinero.** It's good that you're saving.
■ **¡Eso no está bien!** That's not very nice!
■ **Hiciste bien en decírselo.** You were right to tell him.
■ **¡Ya está bien!** That's enough!
■ **¡Qué bien!** Excellent!

el **bienestar** NOUN
well-being

la **bienvenida** NOUN
■ **dar la bienvenida a alguien** to welcome somebody
■ **una fiesta de bienvenida** a welcome party

bienvenido (FEM **bienvenida**) ADJECTIVE
▷ *see also* **bienvenido** EXCLAMATION
welcome
□ Siempre serás bienvenido aquí. You will always be welcome here.

bienvenido EXCLAMATION
▷ *see also* **bienvenido** ADJECTIVE
welcome!

el **bife** NOUN *(Chile, River Plate)*
steak

la **bifurcación** (PL las **bifurcaciones**) NOUN
fork

el **bigote** NOUN
moustache

el **bikini** NOUN
bikini

bilingüe (FEM **bilingüe**) ADJECTIVE
bilingual

el **billar** NOUN
billiards *sing*
■ **el billar americano** pool

el **billete** NOUN
1 ticket
□ un billete de metro an underground ticket
■ **sacar un billete** to buy a ticket
■ **un billete de ida y vuelta** a return ticket

LANGUAGE TIP Word for word, **billete de ida y vuelta** means 'ticket for going and coming back'.

■ **un billete electrónico** an e-ticket
2 note
□ un billete de veinte euros a twenty-euro note

el **billón** (PL los **billones**) NOUN
■ **un billón** a million millions

DID YOU KNOW...?
La palabra **billion** equivale a mil millones.

el **bingo** NOUN
1 bingo
□ jugar al bingo to play bingo
2 bingo hall
□ Van a abrir un bingo aquí. They're opening a bingo hall here.

biodegradable (FEM **biodegradable**) ADJECTIVE
biodegradable

la **biografía** NOUN
biography (PL biographies)

la **biología** NOUN
biology

biológico (FEM **biológica**) ADJECTIVE
1 organic
2 biological

el **biombo** NOUN
folding screen

el **biquini** NOUN
bikini (PL bikinis)

la **birome** NOUN *(River Plate)*
ballpoint pen

la **birria** NOUN
■ **ser una birria** *(colloquial)* to be rubbish

la **bisabuela** NOUN
great-grandmother

el **bisabuelo** NOUN
great-grandfather
■ **mis bisabuelos** my great-grandparents

la **bisagra** NOUN
hinge

bisiesto (FEM **bisiesta**) ADJECTIVE
■ **un año bisiesto** a leap year

la **bisnieta** NOUN
great-granddaughter

el **bisnieto** NOUN
great-grandson
■ **tus bisnietos** your great-grandchildren

el **bistec** (PL los **bistecs**) NOUN
steak

la **bisutería** NOUN
costume jewellery
■ **Son de bisutería.** They're costume jewellery.

bizco (FEM **bizca**) ADJECTIVE
cross-eyed

el **bizcocho** NOUN
sponge cake

blanco (FEM **blanca**) ADJECTIVE
white
□ un vestido blanco a white dress

el **blanco** NOUN
white
□ Me gusta el blanco. I like white.
■ **dar en el blanco** to hit the target

Spanish-English

b

■ **dejar algo en blanco** to leave something blank
■ **Cuando iba a responder me quedé en blanco.** Just as I was about to reply my mind went blank.

blando (FEM **blanda**) ADJECTIVE
1 soft
□ Este colchón es muy blando. This mattress is very soft.
2 easy
□ Es muy blando con sus alumnos. He's very easy on his pupils.

el **bloc** (PL los **blocs**) NOUN
writing pad
■ **un bloc de dibujo** a drawing pad

el **blog** NOUN
blog

el **bloque** NOUN
block
■ **un bloque de pisos** a block of flats

bloquear VERB [25]
to block
□ La nieve bloqueó las carreteras. The snow blocked the roads.

el **Bluetooth®** NOUN
Bluetooth®

la **blusa** NOUN
blouse

la **bobada** NOUN
■ **hacer bobadas** to do stupid things
■ **Este programa es una bobada.** This programme is stupid.
■ **decir bobadas** to talk nonsense

la **bobina** NOUN
reel

bobo (FEM **boba**) ADJECTIVE
silly

la **boca** NOUN
mouth
□ No debes hablar con la boca llena. You shouldn't talk with your mouth full. □ No abrió la boca en toda la tarde. He didn't open his mouth all afternoon.
■ **boca abajo** face down
■ **boca arriba** face up
■ **Me quedé con la boca abierta.** I was dumbfounded.
■ **la boca del metro** the entrance to the underground

la **bocacalle** NOUN
■ **Es una bocacalle del Paseo Central.** It's a side street off the Paseo Central.
■ **La primera bocacalle a la derecha.** The first road on the right.

el **bocadillo** NOUN
■ **Ya me he comido el bocadillo.** I've already had my roll.
■ **un bocadillo de queso** a cheese baguette

el **bocado** NOUN
1 bite
□ Dame un bocado de tu bocadillo. Let me have a bite of your sandwich.
■ **No he probado bocado desde ayer.** I haven't had a bite to eat since yesterday.
2 mouthful
□ Intentaba hablar entre bocado y bocado. I was trying to talk between mouthfuls.

el **bocata** NOUN = **bocadillo**

el **bochorno** NOUN
■ **Hace bochorno.** It's muggy.

la **bocina** NOUN
1 horn
2 receiver *(Chile, River Plate)*

la **boda** NOUN
wedding
■ **las bodas de oro** golden wedding *sing*
■ **las bodas de plata** silver wedding *sing*

la **bodega** NOUN
1 cellar
2 wine cellar
3 wine shop
4 hold

la **bofetada** NOUN
slap
□ dar una bofetada a alguien to give somebody a slap

el **boicot** (PL los **boicots**) NOUN
boycott
■ **hacer el boicot a algo** to boycott something

la **boina** NOUN
beret

la **bola** NOUN
ball
■ **una bola de nieve** a snowball

la **bolera** NOUN
bowling alley

la **boletería** NOUN *(Latin America)*
ticket office

el **boletín** (PL los **boletines**) NOUN
bulletin
■ **un boletín informativo** a news bulletin

el **boleto** NOUN
ticket
□ un boleto de lotería a lottery ticket
■ **un boleto de quinielas** a pools coupon
■ **un boleto electrónico** an e-ticket

el **boli** NOUN
pen

el **bolígrafo** NOUN
pen

el **bolillo** NOUN *(Mexico)*
bun

Bolivia FEM NOUN
Bolivia

el **boliviano** (FEM la **boliviana**) ADJECTIVE,

NOUN
Bolivian

la **bollería** NOUN
pastries *pl*

el **bollo** NOUN
1 bun
□ Me he comido un bollo para desayunar. I had a bun for breakfast.
2 dent
□ Tengo el coche lleno de bollos. My car is full of dents.

los **bolos** NOUN
1 bowls *sing*
2 tenpin bowling *sing*

la **bolsa** NOUN
1 bag
□ una bolsa de plástico a plastic bag
■ **una bolsa de deportes** a sports bag
■ **una bolsa de viaje** a travel bag
2 handbag *(Mexico)*
■ **la Bolsa** the Stock Exchange

el **bolsillo** NOUN
pocket
□ Sacó las llaves del bolsillo. He took the keys out of his pocket.
■ **un libro de bolsillo** a paperback
LANGUAGE TIP Word for word, **libro de bolsillo** means 'book for the pocket'.

el **bolso** NOUN
bag

la **bomba** NOUN
1 bomb
□ la bomba atómica the atomic bomb
2 pump
□ una bomba de agua a water pump
■ **pasarlo bomba** to have a brilliant time

la **bombacha** NOUN *(River Plate)*
panties *pl*

bombardear VERB [25]
to bombard
■ **bombardear a alguien a preguntas** to bombard somebody with questions

el **bombero** NOUN
fireman (PL firemen)
■ **llamar a los bomberos** to call the fire brigade

la **bombilla** NOUN
lightbulb

la **bombita** NOUN *(River Plate)*
lightbulb

el **bombo** NOUN
bass drum

el **bombón** (PL los **bombones**) NOUN
chocolate

la **bombona** NOUN
gas cylinder

la **bondad** NOUN
kindness
□ un acto de bondad an act of kindness
■ **¿Tendría la bondad de ...?** Would you be so kind as to ...?

el **boniato** NOUN
sweet potato (PL sweet potatoes)

bonito (FEM **bonita**) ADJECTIVE
pretty
□ una casa muy bonita a very pretty house

el **bonito** NOUN
tuna (PL tuna *o* tunas)

el **bonobús** (PL los **bonobuses**) NOUN
bus pass (PL bus passes)

el **boquerón** (PL los **boquerones**) NOUN
anchovy (PL anchovies)

el **boquete** NOUN
hole
□ Abrieron un boquete en el muro. They made a hole in the wall.

la **borda** NOUN
■ **echar algo por la borda** to throw something overboard

bordar VERB [25]
to embroider

el **borde** NOUN
edge
□ al borde de la mesa at the edge of the table
■ **estar al borde de algo** to be on the verge of something

borde (FEM **borde**) ADJECTIVE
■ **¡No seas borde!** Don't be so horrible!

el **bordillo** NOUN
kerb
□ Los coches no pueden subirse al bordillo. Cars are not allowed onto the kerb.

bordo MASC NOUN
■ **subir a bordo** to get on board

la **borrachera** NOUN
■ **coger una borrachera** to get drunk

borracho (FEM **borracha**) ADJECTIVE
drunk
□ Estás borracho. You're drunk.

el **borrador** NOUN
1 rough draft
□ Escribe primero un borrador. First write a rough draft.
2 duster
□ Usó un trapo como borrador. He used a rag as a duster.

borrar VERB [25]
1 to rub out
□ Borra toda la palabra. Rub out the whole word.
2 to clean
□ Borra la pizarra. Clean the blackboard.
3 to wipe
□ No borres esa cinta. Don't wipe that tape.
■ **borrarse de 1** to take one's name off

□ Voy a borrarme de la lista. I'm going to take my name off the list. **2** to leave □ Se borró del club. He left the club.

la **borrasca** NOUN
■ **Viene una borrasca por el Atlántico.** There's low pressure over the Atlantic.

el **borrón** (PL los **borrones**) NOUN
stain

borroso (FEM **borrosa**) ADJECTIVE
blurred
□ Lo veo muy borroso. It looks very blurred.

Bosnia FEM NOUN
Bosnia

el **bosnio** (FEM la **bosnia**) ADJECTIVE, NOUN
Bosnian

el **bosque** NOUN
1 wood
2 forest

bostezar* VERB [13]
to yawn

la **bota** NOUN
boot
■ **unas botas de agua** a pair of wellingtons
LANGUAGE TIP Word for word, **botas de agua** means 'boots of water'.
■ **una bota de vino** a wineskin

la **botana** NOUN *(Mexico)*
snack

la **botánica** NOUN
botany

botánico (FEM **botánica**) ADJECTIVE
botanical

botar VERB [25]
1 to bounce
□ Esta pelota no bota. This ball isn't bouncing.
2 to jump
□ Botar de alegría. To jump with joy.
3 to throw out *(Latin America)*
□ Boté los libros. I threw the books out.

el **bote** NOUN
1 can
2 tin
3 jar
4 boat
■ **un bote salvavidas** a lifeboat
■ **pegar un bote** to jump

la **botella** NOUN
bottle

el **botellín** (PL los **botellines**) NOUN
bottle
□ un botellín de cerveza a bottle of beer

el **botijo** NOUN
DID YOU KNOW...?
A **botijo** is an earthenware water container with spouts.

el **botín** (PL los **botines**) NOUN
1 ankle boot
2 haul

el **botiquín** (PL los **botiquines**) NOUN
1 medicine cupboard
2 first-aid kit
3 sick bay

el **botón** (PL los **botones**) NOUN
button
□ He perdido un botón de la camisa. I've lost a button off my shirt.
■ **pulsar un botón** to press a button

la **bóveda** NOUN
vault

el **boxeador**, la **boxeadora** NOUN
boxer

boxear VERB [25]
to box

el **boxeo** NOUN
boxing

el **bozal** NOUN
muzzle

las **bragas** NOUN
knickers
■ **unas bragas** a pair of knickers

la **bragueta** NOUN
fly (PL flies)

la **brasa** NOUN
■ **carne a la brasa** barbecued meat
■ **las brasas** the embers

el **brasier** NOUN *(Mexico)*
bra

Brasil MASC NOUN
Brazil

el **brasileño** (FEM la **brasileña**) ADJECTIVE, NOUN
Brazilian

el **brasilero** (FEM la **brasilera**) ADJECTIVE, NOUN *(Latin America)* = **brasileño**

bravo (FEM **brava**) ADJECTIVE
▷ *see also* **bravo** EXCLAMATION
■ **un toro bravo** a fighting bull

bravo EXCLAMATION
▷ *see also* **bravo** ADJECTIVE
well done!

la **braza** NOUN
breaststroke
■ **nadar a braza** to do the breaststroke

el **brazalete** NOUN
bracelet

el **brazo** NOUN
arm
□ Me duele el brazo. My arm hurts.
□ Estaba sentada con los brazos cruzados. She was sitting with her arms folded.
■ **ir del brazo** to walk arm-in-arm
■ **un brazo de gitano** a swiss roll

la **brecha** NOUN
opening
■ **Me he hecho una brecha en la cabeza.**

I've split my head open.

breve (FEM **breve**) ADJECTIVE
1 brief
□ por breves momentos for a few brief moments □ Para no aburrirlos seré breve. To avoid boring you I will be brief.
2 short
□ un relato breve a short story
■ **en breve** shortly

el **bricolaje** NOUN
DIY
□ una tienda de bricolaje a DIY shop

brillante (FEM **brillante**) ADJECTIVE
1 shiny
□ Tenía el pelo brillante. Her hair was shiny.
■ **El coche estaba brillante.** The car was shining.
■ **blanco brillante** brilliant white
2 outstanding
□ un alumno brillante an outstanding student

el **brillante** NOUN
diamond

brillar VERB [25]
1 to shine
□ Hoy brilla el sol. The sun is shining today.
2 to sparkle

el **brillo** NOUN
1 shine
2 sparkle
■ **La pantalla tiene mucho brillo.** The screen is too bright.
■ **sacar brillo a algo** to polish something

brincar* VERB [48]
to jump up and down
□ ¡Deja de brincar! Stop jumping up and down!
■ **brincar de alegría** to jump for joy

el **brinco** NOUN
■ **pegar un brinco** to jump
■ **Bajé tres escalones de un brinco.** I jumped down three steps.

brindar VERB [25]
■ **brindar por** to drink a toast to
■ **brindarse a hacer algo** to offer to do something □ Se brindó a ayudarme. He offered to help me.

el **brindis** (PL los **brindis**) NOUN
toast
■ **hacer un brindis** to make a toast

la **brisa** NOUN
breeze

británico (FEM **británica**) ADJECTIVE
British

el **británico**, la **británica** NOUN
British person
■ **los británicos** the British

la **brocha** NOUN
1 paintbrush (PL paintbrushes)
2 shaving brush (PL shaving brushes)

el **broche** NOUN
1 brooch (PL brooches)
2 clasp

la **broma** NOUN
joke
■ **gastar una broma a alguien** to play a joke on someone
■ **decir algo en broma** to say something as a joke
■ **una broma pesada** a practical joke

bromear VERB [25]
to joke

el/la **bromista** NOUN
joker

la **bronca** NOUN
1 row
□ Tuvieron una bronca muy gorda. They had a huge row.
■ **echar una bronca a alguien** to tell somebody off
2 fuss
■ **armar una bronca** to kick up a fuss

el **bronce** NOUN
bronze

bronceado (FEM **bronceada**) ADJECTIVE
tanned

el **bronceado** NOUN
suntan

el **bronceador** NOUN
suntan lotion

la **bronquitis** NOUN
bronchitis

brotar VERB [25]
to sprout

bruces ADVERB
■ **Me caí de bruces.** I fell flat on my face.

la **bruja** NOUN
witch (PL witches)

el **brujo** NOUN
wizard

la **brújula** NOUN
compass (PL compasses)

la **bruma** NOUN
mist

brusco (FEM **brusca**) ADJECTIVE
1 sudden
□ un movimiento brusco a sudden movement
2 abrupt
□ una persona brusca an abrupt person

bruto (FEM **bruta**) ADJECTIVE
gross
□ el salario bruto gross salary
■ **¡No seas bruto!** Don't be so rough!
■ **un diamante en bruto** a rough diamond

bucear VERB [25]
to dive

Spanish-English

b

Spanish-English

b

buen ADJECTIVE = **bueno**
bueno (FEM **buena**) ADJECTIVE
good
□ Es un buen libro. It's a good book.
□ Hace buen tiempo. The weather's good.
□ Tiene buena voz. She has a good voice.
□ Es buena persona. He's a good person.
□ un buen trozo a good slice □ Le eché un buen rapapolvo. I gave him a good telling-off.
■ **ser bueno para** to be good for □ Esta bebida es buena para la salud. This drink is good for your health.
■ **Está muy bueno este bizcocho.** This sponge cake is lovely.
■ **Lo bueno fue que ni siquiera quiso venir.** The best thing was that he didn't even want to come.
■ **¡Bueno!** **1** OK! **2** *(Mexico)* Hello!
■ **Bueno. ¿Y qué?** Well?
■ **¡Buenas!** Hello!
■ **Irás por las buenas o por las malas.** You'll go whether you like it or not.
el **buey** NOUN
ox (PL oxen)
la **bufanda** NOUN
scarf (PL scarves)
el **bufete** NOUN
■ **un bufete de abogados** a legal practice
el **buffet** (PL los **buffets**) NOUN
buffet
■ **buffet libre** free buffet
la **buhardilla** NOUN
attic
el **búho** NOUN
owl
el **buitre** NOUN
vulture
la **bujía** NOUN
spark plug
Bulgaria FEM NOUN
Bulgaria
el **búlgaro** (FEM la **búlgara**) ADJECTIVE, NOUN
Bulgarian
el **búlgaro** NOUN
Bulgarian
el **bulto** NOUN
1 lump
□ Tengo un bulto en la frente. I have a lump on my forehead.
2 figure
□ Sólo vi un bulto. I only saw a figure.
■ **Llevábamos muchos bultos.** We were carrying a lot of bags.
el **buñuelo** NOUN
doughnut
BUP MASC NOUN *(= Bachillerato Unificado Polivalente)*

DID YOU KNOW...?
The **BUP** was a three-year secondary course leading to university.

el **buque** NOUN
ship
■ **un buque de guerra** a warship
la **burbuja** NOUN
bubble
■ **un refresco sin burbujas** a still drink
■ **un refresco con burbujas** a fizzy drink
la **burla** NOUN
■ **hacer burla de alguien** to make fun of someone
burlarse VERB [25]
■ **burlarse de alguien** to make fun of someone
el **buró** (PL los **burós**) NOUN *(Mexico)*
bedside table
la **burocracia** NOUN
bureaucracy (PL bureaucracies)
la **burrada** NOUN *(colloquial)*
■ **hacer burradas** to do stupid things
□ No hagas burradas con el coche. Don't do anything stupid with the car.
el **burro** NOUN
1 donkey (PL donkeys)
2 idiot
□ Eres un burro. You're an idiot.
burro (FEM **burra**) ADJECTIVE
1 thick
2 rough
la **busca** NOUN
■ **en busca de** in search of
el **busca** NOUN
bleeper
el **buscador** NOUN
search engine
buscar* VERB [48]
to look for
□ Estoy buscando las gafas. I'm looking for my glasses. □ Ana busca trabajo. Ana's looking for work.
■ **Te voy a buscar a la estación.** I'll come and get you at the station.
■ **Mi madre siempre me viene a buscar al colegio en coche.** My mother always picks me up from school in the car.
■ **buscar una palabra en el diccionario** to look up a word in the dictionary
■ **Él se lo ha buscado.** He was asking for it.
la **búsqueda** NOUN
search (PL searches)
la **butaca** NOUN
1 armchair
2 seat
el **butano** NOUN
bottled gas
■ **color butano** bright orange

el **buzo** NOUN
diver

el **buzón** (PL los **buzones**) NOUN
1 letterbox (PL letterboxes)
2 postbox (PL postboxes)

■ **echar una carta al buzón** to post a letter
■ **buzón de voz** voice mail

LANGUAGE TIP Word for word, **buzón de voz** means 'box of voice'.

Cc

C/ ABBREVIATION *(= calle)*
St *(= Street)*

el **caballero** NOUN
gentleman (PL gentlemen)
□ damas y caballeros ladies and gentlemen
■ **¿Dónde está la sección de caballeros?** Where is the men's department?
■ **'Caballeros'** 'Gents'

el **caballo** NOUN
1 horse
■ **¿Te gusta montar a caballo?** Do you like riding?
■ **un caballo de carreras** a racehorse
2 knight

la **cabaña** NOUN
hut

el **cabello** NOUN
hair

caber* VERB [47, PRESENT **yo quepo**]
to fit
□ No cabe en mi armario. It won't fit in my cupboard.
■ **En mi coche caben dos maletas más.** There's room for two more suitcases in my car.
■ **No cabe nadie más.** There's no room for anyone else.

la **cabeza** NOUN
head
□ Se rascó la cabeza. He scratched his head.
■ **Al oírlos volví la cabeza.** When I heard them I looked round.
■ **Se tiró al agua de cabeza.** He dived headfirst into the water.
■ **estar a la cabeza de la clasificación** to be at the top of the league

la **cabina** NOUN
1 phone box (PL phone boxes)
2 booth (PL booths)
3 cockpit
4 cubicle

el **cable** NOUN
cable

el **cabo** NOUN
1 cape
■ **Cabo Cañaveral** Cape Canaveral
2 corporal
■ **al cabo de dos días** after two days
■ **llevar algo a cabo** to carry something out

la **cabra** NOUN
goat
■ **¡Estás como una cabra!** *(colloquial)* You're crazy!

cabrá VERB ▷ *see* **caber**

cabreado (FEM **cabreada**) ADJECTIVE
annoyed

cabrear VERB [25]
■ **Lo que más me cabrea es que me mientas.** What really annoys me is when you lie to me.
■ **cabrearse** to get annoyed

la **caca** NOUN
■ **hacer caca 1** to do a poo **2** to go to the loo

el **cacahuate** NOUN *(Mexico)*
peanut

el **cacahuete** NOUN
peanut

el **cacao** NOUN
1 cocoa
2 lipsalve

la **cacerola** NOUN
saucepan

el **cacharro** NOUN
■ **los cacharros** the pots and pans

el **cachondeo** NOUN
■ **Las clases eran un cachondeo.** *(colloquial)* The classes were a joke.
■ **No le hagas caso, está de cachondeo.** *(colloquial)* Don't pay any attention to him, he's having you on.

el **cachorro**, la **cachorra** NOUN
1 puppy (PL puppies)
2 cub

el **cactus** (PL los **cactus**) NOUN
cactus (PL cacti)

cada (FEM **cada**) ADJECTIVE
1 each
□ Cada libro es de un color distinto. Each book is a different colour.
■ **cada uno** each one
2 every

□ cada año every year □ cada vez que la veo every time I see her □ uno de cada diez one out of every ten

■ **Viene cada vez más gente.** More and more people are coming.

■ **Viene cada vez menos.** He comes less and less often.

■ **Cada vez hace más frío.** It's getting colder and colder.

■ **¿Cada cuánto vas al dentista?** How often do you go to the dentist?

el **cadáver** NOUN
corpse

la **cadena** NOUN
1 chain
□ una cadena de oro a gold chain
■ **una reacción en cadena** a chain reaction
■ **tirar de la cadena del wáter** to flush the toilet
■ **la cadena de montaje** the assembly line
2 channel
□ Por la cadena 3 ponen una película. There's a film on channel 3.
■ **cadena perpetua** life imprisonment

la **cadera** NOUN
hip

caducar* VERB [48]
to expire
■ **Esta leche está caducada.** This milk is past its sell-by date.

caer* VERB [5]
to fall
□ Me hice daño al caer. I fell and hurt myself.
■ **El avión cayó al mar.** The plane came down in the sea.
■ **Su cumpleaños cae en viernes.** Her birthday falls on a Friday.
■ **caerse** to fall □ Tropecé y me caí. I tripped and fell.
■ **El niño se cayó de la cama.** The child fell out of bed.
■ **No te vayas a caer del caballo.** Be careful not to fall off the horse.
■ **Se cayó por la ventana.** He fell out of the window.
■ **Se me cayeron las monedas.** I dropped the coins.
■ **¡No caigo!** I don't get it!
■ **Su hermano me cae muy bien.** I really like his brother.

el **café** (PL los **cafés**) NOUN
1 coffee
■ **un café con leche** a white coffee
■ **un café solo** a black coffee

LANGUAGE TIP Word for word, **café solo** means 'cafe alone'.

2 café

DID YOU KNOW...?
En Gran Bretaña no se venden bebidas alcohólicas en los cafés y éstos cierran, por lo general, a las 5.30 p.m.

la **cafetera** NOUN
coffee pot

la **cafetería** NOUN
café

cagar* VERB [37]
to have a crap *(vulgar)*

la **caída** NOUN
fall

caigo VERB ▷ *see* **caer**

el **caimán** (PL los **caimanes**) NOUN
alligator

la **caja** NOUN
1 box (PL boxes)
□ una caja de zapatos a shoe box
2 case
3 crate
4 checkout
5 till
6 cash desk
■ **la caja de ahorros** the savings bank
■ **la caja de cambios** the gearbox
■ **la caja fuerte** the safe

el **cajero** NOUN
■ **un cajero automático** a cash dispenser

el **cajero**, la **cajera** NOUN
■ **Trabajo de cajera en un supermercado.** I work on the checkout in a supermarket.

el **cajón** (PL los **cajones**) NOUN
1 drawer
2 crate
3 coffin *(Latin America)*

la **cajuela** NOUN *(Mexico)*
boot

la **cala** NOUN
cove

el **calabacín** (PL los **calabacines**) NOUN
courgette

la **calabacita** NOUN *(Mexico)*
courgette

la **calabaza** NOUN
pumpkin

calado (FEM **calada**) ADJECTIVE
soaked
□ Estaba calado hasta los huesos. He was soaked to the skin.

el **calamar** NOUN
squid
■ **calamares a la romana** squid fried in batter

el **calambre** NOUN
1 cramp
□ Tengo un calambre en la pierna. I've got cramp in my leg.

Spanish–English

C

2 electric shock
□ Si tocas el cable te dará calambre. If you touch the cable you'll get an electric shock.

calar VERB [25]
to soak
□ La lluvia me caló hasta los huesos. I got soaked to the skin in the rain.
■ **Se le caló el coche.** He stalled the car.

la **calavera** NOUN
skull

calcar* VERB [48]
to trace
■ **Es calcado a su abuelo.** He's the spitting image of his grandfather.

el **calcetín** (PL los **calcetines**) NOUN
sock

el **calcio** NOUN
calcium

la **calculadora** NOUN
calculator

calcular VERB [25]
to calculate
□ Calculé lo que nos costaría. I calculated what it would cost us.
■ **Calculo que nos llevará unos tres días.** I reckon that it will take us around three days.

el **cálculo** NOUN
calculation
■ **según mis cálculos** according to my calculations

el **caldo** NOUN
broth
□ Yo tomaré el caldo de verduras. I'll take the vegetable broth.
■ **una pastilla de caldo** a stock cube

la **calefacción** NOUN
heating
□ calefacción central central heating

el **calendario** NOUN
calendar

el **calentador** NOUN
heater

el **calentamiento** NOUN
■ **el calentamiento del planeta** global warming
■ **ejercicios de calentamiento** warm-up exercises

calentar* VERB [39]
1 to heat up
□ ¿Quieres que te caliente la leche? Do you want me to heat up the milk for you?
2 to warm up
■ **calentarse 1** to heat up □ Espera a que se caliente el agua. Wait for the water to heat up. **2** to warm up □ Deja que se caliente el motor. Let the engine warm up.

la **calentura** NOUN
1 temperature
□ Tiene un poco de calentura. He's got a bit of a temperature.
2 cold sore

la **calidad** NOUN
quality (PL qualities)
□ Lo que importa es la calidad. What matters is quality.

caliente VERB
▷ *see also* **caliente** ADJECTIVE ▷ *see* **calentar**

caliente (FEM **caliente**) ADJECTIVE
▷ *see also* **caliente** VERB
1 hot
□ Esta sopa está muy caliente. This soup is very hot.
2 warm
□ ¡Esta cerveza está caliente! This beer is warm!
■ **Mi habitación está calentita.** My room is nice and warm.

la **calificación** (PL las **calificaciones**) NOUN
mark
□ Obtuvo buenas calificaciones. He got good marks.
■ **boletín de calificaciones** school report

calificar* VERB [48]
to mark
□ El profesor califica los ejercicios. The teacher marks the exercises.
■ **Me calificó con sobresaliente.** He gave me an A.

callado (FEM **callada**) ADJECTIVE
quiet
□ Estuvo callado bastante rato. He was quiet for quite a while. □ una persona muy callada a very quiet person

callar VERB [25]
to be quiet
□ Calla, que no me dejas concentrarme. Be quiet, I can't concentrate.
■ **callarse 1** to keep quiet □ Prefirió callarse. He preferred to keep quiet. **2** to stop talking □ Al entrar el profesor todos se callaron. When the teacher came in, everyone stopped talking.
■ **¡Cállate!** *(colloquial)* Shut up!

la **calle** NOUN
1 street
□ Viven en la calle Peñalver, 13. They live at number 13, Peñalver Street.
■ **Hoy no he salido a la calle.** I haven't been out today.
■ **una calle peatonal** a pedestrian precinct
2 lane

el **callejero** NOUN
street map

el **callejón** (PL los **callejones**) NOUN
alley (PL alleys)

el **callo** NOUN

1 corn
2 callus (PL calluses)
■ **callos** tripe *sing*

la **calma** NOUN
calm
■ **Todo estaba en calma.** Everything was calm.
■ **Logró mantener la calma.** He managed to keep calm.
■ **Piénsalo con calma.** Think about it calmly.
■ **Tómatelo con calma.** Take it easy.

el **calmante** NOUN
1 painkiller
2 tranquillizer

calmar VERB [25]
1 to calm down
□ Intenté calmarla un poco. I tried to calm her down a little. □ ¡Cálmate! Calm down!
2 to relieve

el **calor** NOUN
heat
□ No se puede trabajar con este calor. It's impossible to work in this heat.
■ **Hace calor.** It's hot.
■ **Tengo calor.** I'm hot.
■ **entrar en calor** to get warm

la **caloría** NOUN
calorie

caluroso (FEM **calurosa**) ADJECTIVE
hot

calvo (FEM **calva**) ADJECTIVE
bald
■ **Se está quedando calvo.** He's going bald.

el **calzado** NOUN
footwear

los **calzoncillos** NOUN
underpants
■ **unos calzoncillos** a pair of underpants

los **calzones** NOUN *(Chile)*
panties

la **cama** NOUN
bed
■ **hacer la cama** to make the bed
■ **Está en la cama.** He's in bed.
■ **meterse en la cama** to get into bed

la **cámara** NOUN
1 camera
■ **una cámara digital** a digital camera
■ **a cámara lenta** in slow motion
2 inner tube
■ **la cámara de comercio** the Chamber of Commerce
■ **música de cámara** chamber music

la **camarera** NOUN
1 waitress (PL waitresses)
2 maid

el **camarero** NOUN
1 waiter
2 bellboy

el **camarote** NOUN
cabin

cambiar VERB [25]
1 to change
□ No has cambiado nada. You haven't changed a bit.
■ **Quiero cambiar este abrigo por uno más grande.** I want to change this coat for a larger size.
■ **Tenemos que cambiar de tren en París.** We have to change trains in Paris.
■ **He cambiado de idea.** I've changed my mind.
2 to swap
□ Te cambio mi bolígrafo por tu goma. I'll swap my ballpoint for your rubber.
■ **Me gusta el tuyo, te lo cambio.** I like yours, let's swap.
■ **cambiarse** to get changed □ Voy a cambiarme. I'm going to get changed.
■ **Se han cambiado de coche.** They have changed car.
■ **cambiarse de sitio** to move
■ **cambiarse de casa** to move house

el **cambio** NOUN
1 change
□ un cambio brusco de temperatura a sudden change in temperature □ ¿Tiene cambio de veinte euros? Have you got change of twenty euros? □ ¿Te han dado bien el cambio? Have they given you the right change?
2 small change
□ Necesito cambio. I need small change.
3 exchange
□ ¿A cómo está el cambio? What's the exchange rate?
■ **Me lo regaló a cambio del favor que le hice.** He gave it to me in return for the favour I did him.
■ **en cambio** on the other hand

el **camello** NOUN
1 camel
2 drug pusher

la **camilla** NOUN
1 stretcher
2 couch (PL couches)

caminar VERB [25]
to walk

la **caminata** NOUN
long walk

el **camino** NOUN
1 path
■ **un camino de montaña** a mountain track

2 way
□ ¿Sabes el camino a su casa? Do you know the way to his house?
■ **A medio camino paramos a comer.** Half-way there, we stopped to eat.
■ **La farmacia me queda de camino.** The chemist's is on my way.

el **camión** (PL los **camiones**) NOUN
1 lorry (PL lorries)
■ **un camión cisterna** a tanker
■ **el camión de la basura** the dustcart
2 bus (PL buses) *(Mexico)*

el **camionero**, la **camionera** NOUN
lorry driver

la **camioneta** NOUN
van

la **camisa** NOUN
shirt

la **camiseta** NOUN
1 T-shirt
2 vest
3 shirt

el **camisón** (PL los **camisones**) NOUN
nightdress (PL nightdresses)

el **camote** NOUN *(Mexico)*
sweet potato (PL sweet potatoes)

el **campamento** NOUN
camp
□ un campamento de verano a summer camp

la **campana** NOUN
bell

la **campaña** NOUN
campaign
■ **la campaña electoral** the election campaign
■ **una campaña publicitaria** an advertising campaign

el **campeón**, la **campeona** NOUN
champion

el **campeonato** NOUN
championship

el **campesino**, la **campesina** NOUN
1 country person (PL country people)
2 peasant

el **camping** (PL los **campings**) NOUN
1 camping
□ ir de camping to go camping
2 campsite
□ Estamos en un camping. We're at a campsite.

el **campo** NOUN
1 country
□ Prefiero vivir en el campo. I prefer living in the country.
2 countryside
□ El campo se pone verde en primavera. The countryside turns green in springtime.
■ **Corrían campo a través.** They were running cross-country.
■ **el trabajo del campo** farm work
■ **Ya no se ven bueyes en el campo.** You don't see oxen in the fields any more.
3 pitch (PL pitches)
■ **un campo de deportes** a sports ground
■ **un campo de golf** a golf course
■ **un campo de concentración** a concentration camp

la **cana** NOUN
grey hair
■ **Tiene canas.** He's got grey hair.
■ **Le están saliendo canas.** He's going grey.

Canadá MASC NOUN
Canada

el/la **canadiense** ADJECTIVE, NOUN
Canadian

el **canal** NOUN
1 channel
□ Por el canal 2 ponen una película. They're showing a film on channel 2.
■ **el Canal de la Mancha** the English Channel
2 canal
□ un canal de riego an irrigation canal
■ **el Canal de Panamá** the Panama Canal

el **canapé** (PL los **canapés**) NOUN
canapé

Canarias FEM PL NOUN
the Canaries
■ **las Islas Canarias** the Canary Islands

el **canario** NOUN
canary (PL canaries)

la **canasta** NOUN
basket

cancelar VERB [25]
to cancel

Cáncer MASC NOUN
Cancer
■ **Soy cáncer.** I'm Cancer.

el **cáncer** NOUN
cancer
□ cáncer de mama breast cancer

la **cancha** NOUN
1 court
2 pitch (PL pitches) *(Latin America)*

la **canción** (PL las **canciones**) NOUN
song
■ **una canción de cuna** a lullaby

el **candado** NOUN
padlock
■ **Estaba cerrado con candado.** It was padlocked.

el **candidato**, la **candidata** NOUN
candidate
■ **presentarse como candidato a la**

presidencia to stand for president
la **canela** NOUN
cinnamon
los **canelones** NOUN
cannelloni *sing*
el **cangrejo** NOUN
1 crab
2 crayfish (PL crayfish)
el **canguro** NOUN
kangaroo
el/la **canguro** NOUN
baby-sitter
■ **hacer de canguro** to baby-sit
la **canica** NOUN
marble
■ **jugar a las canicas** to play marbles
la **canilla** NOUN *(River Plate)*
tap
la **canoa** NOUN
canoe
cansado (FEM **cansada**) ADJECTIVE
1 tired
□ Estoy muy cansado. I'm very tired.
■ **Estoy cansado de hacer lo mismo todos los días.** I'm tired of doing the same thing every day.
2 tiring
□ Es un trabajo muy cansado. It's a very tiring job.
el **cansancio** NOUN
■ **¡Qué cansancio!** I'm so tired!
cansar VERB [25]
■ **Es un viaje que cansa.** It's a tiring journey.
■ **cansarse** to get tired □ Está muy débil y enseguida se cansa. He is very weak and gets tired quickly.
■ **Me cansé de esperarlo y me marché.** I got tired of waiting for him and I left.
el/la **cantante** NOUN
singer
cantar VERB [25]
to sing
la **cantidad** NOUN
1 amount
□ una cierta cantidad de dinero a certain amount of money
2 quantity (PL quantities)
□ La calidad es más importante que la cantidad. Quality is more important than quantity.
■ **¡Qué cantidad de gente!** What a lot of people!
■ **Había cantidad de turistas.** There were loads of tourists.
la **cantimplora** NOUN
water bottle
el **canto** NOUN
1 edge
2 singing
□ Mi hermana estudia canto. My sister is studying singing.
3 song
la **caña** NOUN
cane
■ **caña de azúcar** sugar cane
■ **Me tomé dos cañas.** I had two beers.
■ **una caña de pescar** a fishing rod
la **cañería** NOUN
pipe
el **caos** NOUN
chaos
□ Aquello fue un verdadero caos. That was absolute chaos.
la **capa** NOUN
1 layer
■ **la capa de ozono** the ozone layer
2 cloak
la **capacidad** NOUN
1 ability (PL abilities)
□ Nadie duda de tu capacidad. No one doubts your ability.
2 capacity (PL capacities)
□ El teatro tiene capacidad para mil espectadores. The theatre has a seating capacity of a thousand.
capaz (FEM **capaz**, PL **capaces**) ADJECTIVE
capable
□ Es capaz de olvidarse el pasaporte. He's quite capable of forgetting his passport.
■ **Por ella sería capaz de cualquier cosa.** He would do anything for her.
la **capilla** NOUN
chapel
la **capital** NOUN
capital
el **capitán**, la **capitana** NOUN
captain
el **capítulo** NOUN
1 chapter
2 episode
el **capricho** NOUN
whim
□ Hacer un crucero fue un puro capricho. Going on a cruise was just a whim.
■ **Lo compré por capricho.** I bought it on a whim.
■ **Decidí viajar en primera para darme un capricho.** I decided to travel first class to give myself a treat.
Capricornio MASC NOUN
Capricorn
■ **Soy capricornio.** I'm Capricorn.
capturar VERB [25]
to capture
la **capucha** NOUN

Spanish-English

C

Spanish-English

C

1 hood
2 top
caqui (PL **caqui**) ADJECTIVE
khaki
la **cara** NOUN
1 face
□ Tiene la cara alargada. He has a long face.
■ **Tienes mala cara.** You don't look well.
■ **Tenía cara de pocos amigos.** He looked very unfriendly.
■ **No pongas esa cara.** Don't look like that.
2 cheek
□ ¡Qué cara! What a cheek!
3 side
□ un folio escrito por las dos caras a sheet written on both sides
■ **¿Cara o cruz?** Heads or tails?
LANGUAGE TIP Word for word, **¿Cara o cruz?** means 'Face or cross?'
■ **Lo echamos a cara o cruz.** We tossed for it.
el **caracol** NOUN
1 snail
2 winkle
el **carácter** (PL los **caracteres**) NOUN
nature
□ Tiene el carácter de su padre. He has his father's nature.
■ **tener buen carácter** to be good-natured
■ **tener mal carácter** to be bad-tempered
■ **La chica tiene mucho carácter.** The girl has a strong personality.
la **característica** NOUN
characteristic
caramba EXCLAMATION
goodness!
el **caramelo** NOUN
sweet
la **caravana** NOUN
caravan
■ **Había una caravana de dos kilómetros.** There was a two kilometre tailback.
el **carbón** NOUN
coal
■ **carbón de leña** charcoal
la **carcajada** NOUN
■ **soltar una carcajada** to burst out laughing
■ **reírse a carcajadas** to roar with laughter
la **cárcel** NOUN
prison
□ Todavía está en la cárcel. He's still in prison.
el **cardenal** NOUN
1 bruise
2 cardinal
cardiaco (FEM **cardiaca**) ADJECTIVE
cardiac
□ ataque cardiaco cardiac arrest
la **careta** NOUN
mask
la **carga** NOUN
1 load
□ carga máxima maximum load
2 burden
□ No quiero ser una carga para ellos. I don't want to be a burden to them.
3 refill
cargado (FEM **cargada**) ADJECTIVE
1 loaded
2 stuffy
3 strong
■ **Venía cargada de paquetes.** She was laden with parcels.
el **cargamento** NOUN
1 cargo (PL cargoes)
2 load
cargar* VERB [37]
1 to load
□ Cargaron el coche de maletas. They loaded the car with suitcases.
2 to fill
3 to charge
■ **Tuve que cargar con todo.** I had to take responsibility for everything.
■ **cargarse algo** *(colloquial)* to break something □ Te vas a cargar el vídeo. You're going to break the video.
el **cargo** NOUN
post
□ un cargo de mucha responsabilidad a very responsible post
■ **Está a cargo de la contabilidad.** He's in charge of keeping the books.
el **Caribe** NOUN
the Caribbean
el **caribeño** (FEM la **caribeña**) ADJECTIVE, NOUN
Caribbean
la **caricatura** NOUN
caricature
la **caricia** NOUN
caress (PL caresses)
■ **Le hacía caricias al bebé.** She was caressing the baby.
la **caridad** NOUN
charity (PL charities)
la **caries** (PL las **caries**) NOUN
1 tooth decay
□ Es importante prevenir la caries dental. It's important to prevent tooth decay.
2 cavity (PL cavities)
el **cariño** NOUN
affection
□ Lo recuerdo con cariño. I remember him with affection.
■ **Les tengo mucho cariño.** I'm very fond

of them.

■ **Le ha tomado cariño al gato.** He has become fond of the cat.

■ **Ven aquí, cariño.** Come here, darling.

cariñoso (FEM **cariñosa**) ADJECTIVE

affectionate

□ Es muy cariñosa con los niños. She is very affectionate towards the children.

el **carnaval** NOUN

carnival

DID YOU KNOW...?
The **carnaval** is the traditional period of celebrating prior to the start of Lent.

la **carne** NOUN

meat

□ No como carne. I don't eat meat.

■ **carne de cerdo** pork

■ **carne de puerco** *(Mexico)* pork

■ **carne de cordero** lamb

■ **carne molida** *(Latin America)* mince

■ **carne picada** mince

■ **carne de ternera** veal

■ **carne de vaca** beef

■ **carne de res** *(Mexico)* beef

el **carnet** (PL los **carnets**) NOUN

card

■ **el carnet de identidad** identity card

■ **un carnet de conducir** a driving licence

la **carnicería** NOUN

butcher's (PL butchers' shops)

□ Lo compré en la carnicería. I bought it at the butcher's.

el **carnicero**, la **carnicera** NOUN

butcher

caro (FEM **cara**) ADJECTIVE, ADVERB

expensive

□ Las entradas me costaron muy caras. The tickets were very expensive. □ Aquí todo lo venden tan caro. Everything is so expensive here.

la **carpeta** NOUN

folder

la **carpintería** NOUN

1 carpenter's shop

2 carpentry

el **carpintero**, la **carpintera** NOUN

carpenter

la **carrera** NOUN

1 race

□ una carrera de caballos a horse race

■ **Me di una carrera para alcanzar el autobús.** I had to run to catch the bus.

2 degree

□ Está haciendo la carrera de derecho. He's doing a law degree.

3 career

□ Estaba en el mejor momento de su carrera. He was at the height of his career.

4 ladder

□ Tienes una carrera en las medias. You've got a ladder in your tights.

el **carrete** NOUN

1 film

2 reel

la **carretera** NOUN

road

■ **una carretera nacional** an A-road

■ **una carretera de circunvalación** a bypass

la **carretilla** NOUN

wheelbarrow

el **carril** NOUN

1 lane

2 rail

el **carril-bici** NOUN (PL los **carriles-bici**)

cycle lane

el **carrito** NOUN

trolley (PL trolleys)

el **carro** NOUN

1 cart

2 trolley (PL trolleys)

3 car *(Latin America)*

■ **un carro de combate** a tank

la **carroza** NOUN

1 coach (PL coaches)

2 float

la **carta** NOUN

1 letter

□ Le he escrito una carta a Juan. I've written Juan a letter.

■ **echar una carta** to post a letter

2 card

□ jugar a las cartas to play cards

3 menu

□ El camarero nos trajo la carta. The waiter brought us the menu.

■ **la carta de vinos** the wine list

el **cartel** NOUN

1 poster

2 sign

□ Un cartel que pone 'prohibida la entrada'. A sign which says 'no entry'.

la **cartelera** NOUN

1 billboard

2 listings *pl*

■ **Estuvo tres años en la cartelera.** It ran for three years.

la **cartera** NOUN

1 wallet

2 briefcase

3 satchel

4 handbag *(Latin America)*

5 postwoman (PL postwomen)

el **cartero** NOUN

postman (PL postmen)

el **cartón** (PL los **cartones**) NOUN
1 cardboard
□ una caja de cartón a cardboard box
2 carton

el **cartucho** NOUN
cartridge

la **cartulina** NOUN
card

la **casa** NOUN
1 house
□ una casa de dos plantas a two-storey house
2 home
□ Estábamos en casa. We were at home.
□ Le dolía la cabeza y se fue a casa. She had a headache so she went home.
■ **Estábamos en casa de Juan.** We were at Juan's.
■ **una casa de discos** a record company

casado (FEM **casada**) ADJECTIVE
married
□ una mujer casada a married woman
■ **Está casado con una francesa.** He's married to a French woman.

casarse VERB [25]
to get married
□ Quieren casarse. They want to get married.
■ **Se casó con una periodista.** He married a journalist.

el **cascabel** NOUN
small bell

la **cascada** NOUN
waterfall

cascar* VERB [48]
to crack

la **cáscara** NOUN
1 shell
2 skin

el **casco** NOUN
helmet
□ El ciclista llevaba casco. The cyclist was wearing a helmet.
■ **el casco antiguo de la ciudad** the old part of the town
■ **el casco urbano** the town centre
■ **los cascos** headphones

casero (FEM **casera**) ADJECTIVE
homemade
□ mermelada casera homemade jam

la **caseta** NOUN
1 kennel
2 bathing hut
3 stall

el **casete** NOUN
1 cassette player
2 cassette

la **casete** NOUN
cassette

casi ADVERB
almost
□ Casi me ahogo. I almost drowned. □ Son casi las cinco. It's almost five o'clock. □ Casi me ahogo. I nearly drowned. □ Casi no comí. I hardly ate. □ No queda casi nada en la nevera. There's hardly anything left in the refrigerator. □ Casi nunca se equivoca. He hardly ever makes a mistake.

la **casilla** NOUN
1 box (PL boxes)
2 square
■ **Casilla de Correos** *(River Plate)* post-office box number

el **casino** NOUN
casino (PL casinos)

el **caso** NOUN
case
□ En casos así es mejor callarse. In such cases it's better to keep quiet.
■ **en ese caso** in that case
■ **En caso de que llueva, iremos en autobús.** If it rains, we'll go by bus.
■ **El caso es que no me queda dinero.** The thing is, I haven't got any money left.
■ **No le hagas caso.** Don't take any notice of him.
■ **Hazle caso que ella tiene más experiencia.** Listen to her, she has more experience.

la **caspa** NOUN
dandruff

la **cassette** = casete

el **cassette** = casete

la **castaña** NOUN
chestnut

castaño (FEM **castaña**) ADJECTIVE
chestnut
□ Mi hermana tiene el pelo castaño. My sister has chestnut hair.

las **castañuelas** NOUN
castanets

el **castellano** (FEM la **castellana**) ADJECTIVE, NOUN
Castilian

el **castellano** NOUN
Spanish

castigar* VERB [37]
to punish
□ Mi padre me castigó por contestarle. My father punished me for answering him back.

el **castigo** NOUN
punishment
□ Tuve que escribirlo diez veces, como castigo. I had to write it out ten times, as punishment.

Castilla FEM NOUN

Castile

el **castillo** NOUN
castle

la **casualidad** NOUN
coincidence
■ **¡Qué casualidad!** What a coincidence!
■ **Nos encontramos por casualidad.** We met by chance.
■ **Da la casualidad que nacimos el mismo día.** It so happens that we were born on the same day.

el **catalán** (FEM la **catalana**, MASC PL los **catalanes**) ADJECTIVE, NOUN
Catalan

el **catalán** NOUN
Catalan

el **catálogo** NOUN
catalogue

Cataluña FEM NOUN
Catalonia

la **catarata** NOUN
waterfall
■ **las cataratas del Niágara** Niagara Falls

el **catarro** NOUN
cold
□ Vas a pillar un catarro. You're going to catch a cold.

la **catástrofe** NOUN
catastrophe

la **catedral** NOUN
cathedral

el **catedrático**, la **catedrática** NOUN
1 professor
2 principal teacher

la **categoría** NOUN
category (PL categories)
□ Cada grupo está dividido en tres categorías. Each group is divided into three categories.
■ **un hotel de primera categoría** a first-class hotel
■ **un puesto de poca categoría** a low-ranking position

el **católico** (FEM la **católica**) ADJECTIVE, NOUN
Catholic
□ Soy católico. I am a Catholic.

catorce (FEM **catorce**) ADJECTIVE, PRONOUN
fourteen
■ **el catorce de enero** the fourteenth of January

el **caucho** NOUN
rubber

la **causa** NOUN
cause
□ No se sabe la causa del accidente. The cause of the accident is unknown.
■ **a causa de** because of

causar VERB [25]
to cause
□ La lluvia causó muchos daños. The rain caused a lot of damage.
■ **Su visita me causó mucha alegría.** His visit made me very happy.
■ **Rosa me causó buena impresión.** Rosa made a good impression on me.

cavar VERB [25]
to dig
□ cavar un hoyo to dig a hole

la **caverna** NOUN
cave

cayendo VERB ▷ *see* **caer**

la **caza** NOUN
1 hunting
2 shooting

el **cazador** NOUN
hunter

la **cazadora** NOUN
1 jacket
2 hunter

cazar* VERB [13]
1 to hunt
□ Salieron a cazar ciervos. They went deer-hunting.
2 to shoot
□ Cazaron muchas codornices. They shot a lot of quail.

el **cazo** NOUN
1 saucepan
2 ladle

la **cazuela** NOUN
pot

el **CD** (PL los **CDs**) NOUN
CD

el **CD-ROM** (PL los **CD-ROMs**) NOUN
CD-ROM

la **CE** ABBREVIATION *(= Comunidad Europea)*
EC *(= European Community)*

el **cebo** NOUN
bait

la **cebolla** NOUN
onion

la **cebolleta** NOUN
1 spring onion
2 pickled onion

la **cebra** NOUN
zebra
■ **un paso de cebra** a zebra crossing

ceder VERB [8]
1 to give in
□ Al final tuve que ceder. Finally I had to give in.
2 to give way
□ La estantería cedió por el peso de los libros. The shelves gave way under the weight of the books.
■ **'Ceda el paso'** 'Give way'

la **ceguera** NOUN
blindness

la **ceja** NOUN
eyebrow

la **celda** NOUN
cell

la **celebración** (PL las **celebraciones**) NOUN
celebration

celebrar VERB [25]
1 to celebrate
■ **En octubre se celebra el día de la Hispanidad.** Columbus Day is in October.
2 to hold

célebre (FEM **célebre**) ADJECTIVE
famous

el **celo** NOUN
Sellotape®

el **celofán** NOUN
cellophane

los **celos** NOUN
jealousy *sing*
□ Lo hizo por celos. He did it out of jealousy.
■ **Tiene celos de su mejor amiga.** She's jealous of her best friend.
■ **Lo hace para darle celos.** He does it to make her jealous.

celoso (FEM **celosa**) ADJECTIVE
jealous
□ Está celoso de su hermano. He's jealous of his brother.

la **célula** NOUN
cell

la **celulitis** NOUN
cellulite

el **cementerio** NOUN
cemetery (PL cemeteries)
■ **un cementerio de coches** a scrapyard

el **cemento** NOUN
1 cement
■ **el cemento armado** reinforced concrete
2 glue *(Latin America)*

la **cena** NOUN
dinner
□ La cena es a las nueve. Dinner is at nine o'clock.

cenar VERB [25]
to have dinner
□ No he cenado. I haven't had dinner.
■ **¿Qué quieres cenar?** What do you want for dinner?

el **cenicero** NOUN
ashtray (PL ashtrays)

la **ceniza** NOUN
ash (PL ashes)

la **censura** NOUN
censorship

el **centavo** NOUN
cent

la **centésima** NOUN
■ **una centésima de segundo** a hundredth of a second

centígrado (FEM **centígrada**) ADJECTIVE
centigrade
□ veinte grados centígrados twenty degrees centigrade

el **centímetro** NOUN
centimetre

el **céntimo** NOUN
cent

central (FEM **central**) ADJECTIVE
central

la **central** NOUN
head office
■ **una central eléctrica** a power-station
■ **una central nuclear** a nuclear power-station

la **centralita** NOUN
switchboard

céntrico (FEM **céntrica**) ADJECTIVE
central
□ Está en un barrio céntrico. It's in a central area.
■ **Es un piso céntrico.** The flat is in the centre of town.

el **centro** NOUN
centre
□ en pleno centro de la ciudad right in the town centre
■ **Fui al centro a hacer unas compras.** I went into town to do some shopping.
■ **un centro comercial** a shopping centre
■ **un centro de deportes** a sports centre
■ **un centro médico** a hospital

el **centroamericano** (FEM la **centroamericana**) ADJECTIVE, NOUN
Central American

ceñido (FEM **ceñida**) ADJECTIVE
tight
■ **Esta falda me queda muy ceñida.** This skirt's too tight for me.

cepillar VERB [25]
to brush
■ **Se está cepillando los dientes.** He's brushing his teeth.

el **cepillo** NOUN
brush (PL brushes)
■ **un cepillo de dientes** a toothbrush

la **cera** NOUN
wax

la **cerámica** NOUN
pottery
□ Me gusta la cerámica. I like pottery.
■ **una cerámica** a piece of pottery

cerca ADVERB
near
□ El colegio está muy cerca. The school is

very near.
■ **¿Hay algún banco por aquí cerca?** Is there a bank nearby?
■ **cerca de la iglesia** near the church
■ **cerca de dos horas** nearly two hours
■ **Quería verlo de cerca.** I wanted to see it close up.

cercano (FEM **cercana**) ADJECTIVE
nearby
□ Viven en un pueblo cercano. They live in a nearby village.
■ **una de las calles cercanas a la catedral** one of the streets close to the cathedral
■ **el Cercano Oriente** the Near East

el **cerdo** NOUN
1 pig
□ Tienen cerdos. They keep pigs.
2 pork
□ No comemos cerdo. We don't eat pork.

el **cereal** NOUN
cereal
■ **Los niños desayunan cereales.** The children have cereal for breakfast.

el **cerebro** NOUN
brain

la **ceremonia** NOUN
ceremony (PL ceremonies)

la **cereza** NOUN
cherry (PL cherries)

la **cerilla** NOUN
match (PL matches)
□ una caja de cerillas a box of matches

el **cerillo** NOUN *(Mexico)*
match (PL matches)

el **cero** NOUN
zero (PL zeros *o* zeroes)
■ **Estamos a cinco grados bajo cero.** It's five degrees below zero.
■ **cero coma tres** zero point three
■ **Van dos a cero.** The score is two-nil.
■ **Empataron a cero.** It was a no-score draw.
■ **quince a cero** fifteen-love
■ **Tuve que empezar desde cero.** I had to start from scratch.

el **cerquillo** NOUN *(Latin America)*
fringe

cerrado (FEM **cerrada**) ADJECTIVE
closed
□ Las tiendas están cerradas. The shops are closed.
■ **una curva muy cerrada** a very sharp bend

la **cerradura** NOUN
lock

cerrar* VERB [39]
1 to close
□ No cierran al mediodía. They don't close at noon. □ Cerró el libro. He closed the book. □ No puedo cerrar la maleta. I can't shut this suitcase.
2 to turn off
□ Cierra el grifo. Turn off the tap.
■ **Cerré la puerta con llave.** I locked the door.
■ **La puerta se cerró de golpe.** The door slammed shut.
■ **Se me cierran los ojos.** I can't keep my eyes open.

el **cerrojo** NOUN
bolt
■ **echar el cerrojo** to bolt the door

certificado (FEM **certificada**) ADJECTIVE
registered
■ **Mandé el paquete certificado.** I sent the parcel by registered post.

el **certificado** NOUN
certificate

la **cervecería** NOUN
bar

la **cerveza** NOUN
beer
□ Fuimos a tomar unas cervezas. We went to have a few beers.
■ **la cerveza de barril** draught beer

cesar VERB [25]
to stop
■ **No cesa de hablar.** He never stops talking.
■ **No cesaba de repetirlo.** He kept repeating it.

el **césped** NOUN
grass
□ 'no pisar el césped' 'keep off the grass'

la **cesta** NOUN
basket
■ **una cesta de Navidad** a Christmas hamper

el **cesto** NOUN
basket

el **chabacano** NOUN *(Mexico)*
apricot

la **chabola** NOUN
shack
■ **un barrio de chabolas** a shantytown

el **chaleco** NOUN
waistcoat
■ **un chaleco salvavidas** a life-jacket

el **chalet** (PL los **chalets**) NOUN
1 cottage
2 villa
3 house

el **champán** (PL los **champanes**) NOUN
champagne

el **champiñón** (PL los **champiñones**) NOUN
mushroom

Spanish–English

C

el **champú** (PL los **champús**) NOUN
shampoo (PL shampoos)
el **chancho**, la **chancha** NOUN *(River Plate)*
pig
la **chancleta** NOUN
flip-flop
■ **unas chancletas** a pair of flip-flops
el **chándal** (PL los **chándals**) NOUN
tracksuit
el **chantaje** NOUN
blackmail
■ **hacer chantaje a alguien** to blackmail somebody
la **chapa** NOUN
1 badge
2 top
3 sheet
4 panel
5 number plate *(Latin America)*
chapado (FEM **chapada**) ADJECTIVE
■ **chapado en oro** gold-plated
el **chaparrón** (PL los **chaparrones**) NOUN
■ **Anoche cayó un buen chaparrón.** There was a real downpour last night.
■ **Es sólo un chaparrón.** It's just a shower.
chapotear VERB [25]
to splash around
la **chapuza** NOUN
botched job
■ **hacer chapuzas** to do odd jobs
el **chapuzón** (PL los **chapuzones**) NOUN
■ **darse un chapuzón** to go for a dip
la **chaqueta** NOUN
1 cardigan
2 jacket
la **charca** NOUN
pond
el **charco** NOUN
puddle
la **charcutería** NOUN
delicatessen
la **charla** NOUN
1 chat
□ Estuvimos de charla. We had a chat.
2 talk
□ Dio una charla sobre teatro clásico. He gave a talk on classical theatre.
charlar VERB [25]
to chat
el **chasco** NOUN
■ **llevarse un chasco** to be disappointed
el **chat** NOUN
chatroom
la **chatarra** NOUN
scrap metal
la **chava** NOUN *(Mexico)*
girl
el **chavo** NOUN *(Mexico)*
boy
checar* VERB [48] *(Mexico)*
to check
el **checo** (FEM la **checa**) ADJECTIVE, NOUN
Czech
■ **la República Checa** the Czech Republic
el **checo** NOUN
Czech
el **chef** (PL los **chefs**) NOUN
chef (PL chefs)
el **cheque** NOUN
cheque
■ **los cheques de viaje** traveller's cheques
el **chequeo** NOUN
check-up (PL check-ups)
□ hacerse un chequeo to have a check-up
chévere (FEM **chévere**) ADJECTIVE, ADVERB *(Latin America)*
great
la **chica** NOUN
girl
el **chícharo** NOUN *(Mexico)*
pea
el **chichón** (PL los **chichones**) NOUN
bump
□ Me ha salido un chichón en la frente. I've got a bump on my forehead.
el **chicle** NOUN
chewing gum
chico (FEM **chica**) ADJECTIVE
small
el **chico** NOUN
1 boy
□ los chicos de la clase the boys in the class
2 guy
□ Me parece un chico muy guapo. I think he's a cute guy.
Chile MASC NOUN
Chile
el **chileno** (FEM la **chilena**) ADJECTIVE, NOUN
Chilean
chillar VERB [25]
1 to scream
2 to squeak
3 to squeal
4 to screech
la **chimenea** NOUN
1 chimney (PL chimneys)
□ Salía humo de la chimenea. There was smoke coming out of the chimney.
2 fireplace
□ sentado frente a la chimenea sitting in front of the fireplace
■ **Enciende la chimenea.** Light the fire.
el **chimpancé** (PL los **chimpancés**) NOUN
chimpanzee
China FEM NOUN

China
la **china** NOUN
1 China woman
2 stone
□ Se me ha metido una china en el zapato. I've got a stone in my shoe.
la **chinche** NOUN *(Mexico, River Plate)*
drawing pin
la **chincheta** NOUN
drawing pin
chino (FEM **china**) ADJECTIVE
Chinese
el **chino** NOUN
1 Chinese man
■ **los chinos** the Chinese
2 Chinese
Chipre MASC NOUN
Cyprus
la **chirimoya** NOUN
custard apple
chirriar* VERB [21]
to squeak
el **chisme** NOUN
1 thing
2 piece of gossip
chismorrear VERB [25]
to gossip
chismoso (FEM **chismosa**) ADJECTIVE
■ **¡No seas chismoso!** Don't be such a gossip!
el **chiste** NOUN
1 joke
□ contar un chiste to tell a joke
■ **un chiste verde** a dirty joke
LANGUAGE TIP Word for word, **chiste verde** means 'green joke'.
2 cartoon
□ el chiste del periódico the newspaper cartoon
chocar* VERB [48]
■ **chocar contra 1** to hit □ El coche chocó contra un árbol. The car hit a tree. **2** to bump into □ Me choqué contra una farola. I bumped into a lamppost.
■ **chocar con algo** to crash into something
■ **Los trenes chocaron de frente.** The trains crashed head-on.
■ **Me choca que no sepas nada.** I'm shocked that you don't know anything about it.
el **chocolate** NOUN
chocolate
□ chocolate con leche milk chocolate
■ **Nos tomamos un chocolate.** We had a cup of hot chocolate.
la **chocolatina** NOUN
chocolate bar
el/la **chófer** NOUN
1 driver
2 chauffeur
el **chopo** NOUN
black poplar
el **choque** NOUN
1 crash (PL crashes)
2 clash (PL clashes)
el **chorizo** NOUN
DID YOU KNOW...?
Chorizo is a kind of spicy sausage.
el **chorrito** NOUN
dash
□ Échame un chorrito de leche. Just a dash of milk, please.
el **chorro** NOUN
■ **salir a chorros** to gush out
la **choza** NOUN
hut
el **chubasco** NOUN
heavy shower
el **chubasquero** NOUN
cagoule
la **chuleta** NOUN
chop
□ una chuleta de cerdo a pork chop
chulo (FEM **chula**) ADJECTIVE
1 cocky *(colloquial)*
■ **ponerse chulo con alguien** to get cocky with someone
2 neat *(colloquial)*
□ ¡Qué mochila más chula! What a neat rucksack!
chupar VERB [25]
to suck
□ Se chupaba el dedo. He was sucking his thumb.
el **chupete** NOUN
dummy (PL dummies)
el **churro** NOUN
DID YOU KNOW...?
A **Churro** is a type of fritter typically served with a cup of hot chocolate at cafés or **churrerías** (churro stalls/ shops).
el **cíber** ABBREVIATION *(= cibercafé)*
Internet café
el **cibercafé** NOUN
Internet café
el **ciberespacio** NOUN
cyberspace
la **cicatriz** (PL las **cicatrices**) NOUN
scar
□ Me quedó una cicatriz en la cara. I was left with a scar on my face.
el **ciclismo** NOUN
cycling
■ **Mi hermano hace ciclismo.** My brother is a cyclist.

el/la **ciclista** NOUN
cyclist
el **ciclo** NOUN
cycle
la **ciega** NOUN
blind woman (PL blind women)
■ **Avanzábamos a ciegas.** We couldn't see where we were going.
■ **Tomaron la decisión a ciegas.** They took the decision blindly.
ciego (FEM **ciega**) ADJECTIVE
blind
■ **quedarse ciego** to go blind
el **ciego** NOUN
blind man
■ **los ciegos** the blind
el **cielo** NOUN
1 sky (PL skies)
□ No había ni una nube en el cielo. There wasn't a single cloud in the sky.
2 heaven
□ ir al cielo to go to heaven
cien (FEM **cien**) ADJECTIVE, PRONOUN
a hundred
□ Había unos cien invitados en la boda. There were about a hundred guests at the wedding. □ cien mil a hundred thousand
■ **cien por cien** a hundred percent □ Es cien por cien algodón. It's a hundred percent cotton.
la **ciencia** NOUN
science
□ Me gustan mucho las ciencias. I really enjoy science. □ ciencias sociales social sciences
■ **ciencias empresariales** business studies
la **ciencia-ficción** NOUN
science fiction
□ novelas de ciencia-ficción science fiction novels
la **científica** NOUN
scientist
científico (FEM **científica**) ADJECTIVE
scientific
el **científico** NOUN
scientist
ciento (FEM **ciento**) ADJECTIVE, PRONOUN
a hundred
■ **ciento cuarenta y dos libras** a hundred and forty two pounds
■ **Recibimos cientos de cartas.** We received hundreds of letters.
■ **el diez por ciento de la población** ten percent of the population
el **cierre** NOUN
1 clasp
2 closing-down
■ **un cierre relámpago** *(River Plate)* a zip
cierro VERB ▷ *see* **cerrar**
cierto (FEM **cierta**) ADJECTIVE
1 true
□ No, eso no es cierto. No, that's not true.
2 certain
□ Viene ciertos días a la semana. He comes certain days of the week.
■ **por cierto** by the way
el **ciervo** NOUN
deer (PL deer)
la **cifra** NOUN
figure
□ un número de cuatro cifras a four-figure number
el **cigarrillo** NOUN
cigarette
el **cigarro** NOUN
cigarette
la **cigüeña** NOUN
stork
la **cima** NOUN
top
□ Quiere llegar a la cima. He wants to get to the top.
los **cimientos** NOUN
foundations
cinco (FEM **cinco**) ADJECTIVE, PRONOUN
five
■ **Son las cinco.** It's five o'clock.
■ **el cinco de enero** the fifth of January
cincuenta (FEM **cincuenta**) ADJECTIVE, PRONOUN
fifty
□ Tiene cincuenta años. He's fifty.
■ **el cincuenta aniversario** the fiftieth anniversary
el **cine** NOUN
cinema
■ **ir al cine** to go to the cinema
■ **una actriz de cine** a film actress
cínico (FEM **cínica**) ADJECTIVE
cynical
la **cinta** NOUN
1 ribbon
2 tape
■ **una cinta de vídeo** a videotape
■ **cinta aislante** insulating tape
■ **una cinta transportadora** a conveyor belt
la **cintura** NOUN
waist
□ ¿Cuánto mides de cintura? What's your waist size?
el **cinturón** (PL los **cinturones**) NOUN
belt
■ **el cinturón de seguridad** the safety belt
el **ciprés** (PL los **cipreses**) NOUN
cypress

el **circo** NOUN
circus (PL circuses)

el **circuito** NOUN
1 track
□ El corredor dio cuatro vueltas al circuito. The runner ran four laps of the track.
2 circuit
■ **circuito cerrado de televisión** closed-circuit television

la **circulación** NOUN
1 traffic
□ un accidente de circulación a traffic accident
2 circulation

circular VERB [25]
1 to drive
□ En Australia se circula por la derecha. In Australia they drive on the left.
■ **¡Circulen!** Move along please!
2 to circulate
3 to go round
□ Circula el rumor de que se van casar. There's a rumour going round that they're getting married.

el **círculo** NOUN
circle
□ Las sillas estaban puestas en círculo. The chairs were set out in a circle.

la **circunferencia** NOUN
circumference

la **circunstancia** NOUN
circumstance

la **ciruela** NOUN
plum
■ **una ciruela pasa** a prune

la **cirugía** NOUN
surgery (PL surgeries)
■ **hacerse la cirugía plástica** to have plastic surgery

el **cirujano**, la **cirujana** NOUN
surgeon

el **cisne** NOUN
swan

la **cisterna** NOUN
cistern

la **cita** NOUN
1 appointment
□ Tengo cita con el Sr. Pérez. I've got an appointment with Mr. Pérez.
2 date
□ No llegues tarde a la cita. Don't be late for your date.
3 quotation
□ una cita de Quevedo a quotation from Quevedo

citar VERB [25]
1 to quote
□ Siempre está citando a los clásicos. He's always quoting the classics.
2 to mention
□ Citó el caso que ocurrió el otro día. He mentioned as an example what happened the other day.
■ **Nos han citado a las diez.** We've been given an appointment for ten o'clock.
■ **Me he citado con Elena.** I've arranged to meet Elena.

la **ciudad** NOUN
1 city (PL cities)
□ una ciudad como Salamanca a city like Salamanca
2 town
□ una pequeña ciudad al norte de Londres a small town north of London
■ **la ciudad universitaria** the university campus

el **ciudadano**, la **ciudadana** NOUN
citizen
□ ser ciudadano español to be a Spanish citizen

civil (FEM **civil**) ADJECTIVE
civil
□ la guerra civil the Civil War

la **civilización** (PL las **civilizaciones**) NOUN
civilization

civilizado (FEM **civilizada**) ADJECTIVE
civilized

la **clara** NOUN
white

el **clarinete** NOUN
clarinet

claro (FEM **clara**) ADJECTIVE
▷ *see also* **claro** ADVERB
1 clear
□ Lo quiero mañana. ¿Está claro? I want it tomorrow. Is that clear?
■ **Está claro que esconden algo.** It's obvious that they are hiding something.
■ **No tengo muy claro lo que quiero hacer.** I'm not very sure about what I want to do.
2 light
□ una camisa azul claro a light blue shirt

claro ADVERB
▷ *see also* **claro** ADJECTIVE
clearly
□ Lo oí muy claro. I heard it very clearly.
■ **Quiero que me hables claro.** I want you to be frank with me.
■ **No he sacado nada en claro de la reunión.** I'm none the wiser after that meeting.
■ **¡Claro!** **1** Sure! □ ¿Te gusta el fútbol? — ¡Claro! Do you like football? — Sure! **2** Of course! □ ¿Te oyó? — ¡Claro que me oyó! Did he hear you? — Of course he heard me!

la **clase** NOUN
1 class (PL classes)
□ A las diez tengo clase de física. I have a physics class at ten.
■ **Mi hermana da clases de inglés.** My sister teaches English.
■ **Hoy no hay clase.** There's no school today.
■ **clases de conducir** driving lessons
■ **clases particulares** private classes
2 classroom
3 kind
□ Había juguetes de todas clases. There were all kinds of toys.
■ **la clase media** the middle class

clásico (FEM **clásica**) ADJECTIVE
1 classical
□ Me gusta la música clásica. I like classical music.
2 classic
□ Es el clásico ejemplo de malnutrición. It's the classic case of malnutrition.

la **clasificación** (PL las **clasificaciones**) NOUN
classification
■ **estar a la cabeza de la clasificación** to be at the top of the table

clasificar* VERB [48]
to classify
■ **Esperan clasificarse para la final.** They hope to qualify for the final.
■ **Se clasificaron en tercer lugar.** They came third.

clavar VERB [25]
■ **clavar una punta en algo** to hammer a nail into something
■ **Las tablas están mal clavadas.** The boards aren't properly nailed down.
■ **Me he clavado una espina en el dedo.** I got a thorn in my finger.
■ **Aquí te clavan.** You get ripped off in this place.

la **clave** NOUN
1 code
■ **un mensaje en clave** a coded message
2 key
□ la clave del éxito the key to success
■ **la clave de sol** the treble clef

el **clavel** NOUN
carnation

la **clavícula** NOUN
collar bone

el **clavo** NOUN
nail

el **clic** NOUN
click
■ **hacer clic en** to click on

el **cliente**, la **clienta** NOUN
1 customer
2 client
3 guest

el **clima** NOUN
climate
□ Es un país de clima tropical. It's a country with a tropical climate.

climatizado (FEM **climatizada**) ADJECTIVE
1 air-conditioned
2 heated

la **clínica** NOUN
hospital

clínico (FEM **clínica**) ADJECTIVE
clinical

el **clip** (PL los **clips**) NOUN
1 paper clip
2 clip

la **cloaca** NOUN
sewer

el **cloro** NOUN
chlorine

el **club** (PL los **clubs**) NOUN
club
□ el club de tenis the tennis club

cobarde (FEM **cobarde**) ADJECTIVE
cowardly
□ una actitud cobarde a cowardly attitude
■ **¡No seas cobarde!** Don't be such a coward!

el/la **cobarde** NOUN
coward

la **cobaya** NOUN
guinea-pig

la **cobija** NOUN *(Latin America)*
blanket

cobrar VERB [25]
to charge
□ Me cobró treinta euros por la reparación. He charged me thirty euros for the repair.
■ **cuando cobre el sueldo de este mes** when I get my wages this month
■ **¿Me cobra los cafés?** How much do I owe for the coffees?
■ **¡Cóbrese, por favor!** Can I pay, please?
■ **cobrar un cheque** to cash a cheque

el **cobre** NOUN
copper

el **cobro** NOUN
■ **llamar a cobro revertido** to reverse the charges

la **Coca-Cola®** (PL las **Coca-Colas**) NOUN
Coke®

la **cocaína** NOUN
cocaine

cocer* VERB [6]
1 to boil
□ Cocer las verduras durante tres minutos. Boil the vegetables for three minutes.

2 to cook
□ Las zanahorias no están cocidas todavía. The carrots aren't properly cooked yet.
■ **Tarda diez minutos en cocerse.** It takes ten minutes to cook.

el **coche** NOUN
1 car
□ Fuimos a Sevilla en coche. We went to Seville by car.
■ **un coche de carreras** a racing car
■ **los coches de choque** the bumper cars
2 pram
3 carriage
■ **Fuimos en coche cama.** We took the sleeper.
■ **un coche de bomberos** a fire engine

cochino (FEM **cochina**) ADJECTIVE
filthy

el **cochino** NOUN
pig

el **cocido** NOUN
stew

DID YOU KNOW...?
The **cocido madrileño** is a stew of chickpeas, vegetables and meat.

la **cocina** NOUN
1 kitchen
□ Comemos en la cocina. We eat in the kitchen.
2 cooker
□ una cocina de gas a gas cooker
■ **la cocina vasca** Basque cuisine
■ **un libro de cocina** a cookery book

cocinar VERB [25]
to cook
□ No sabe cocinar. He can't cook.
■ **Cocinas muy bien.** You're a very good cook.

el **cocinero**, la **cocinera** NOUN
cook
□ Soy cocinero. I'm a cook.

el **coco** NOUN
coconut

el **cocodrilo** NOUN
crocodile

el **código** NOUN
code
■ **el código de la circulación** the highway code
■ **el código postal** the postcode

el **codo** NOUN
elbow

la **codorniz** (PL las **codornices**) NOUN
quail

coger* VERB [7]
1 to take
□ Coge el que más te guste. Take the one which you like best. □ Coja la primera calle a la derecha. Take the first street on the right.
2 to catch
□ ¡Coge la pelota! Catch the ball! □ La cogieron robando. They caught her stealing.
■ **coger un resfriado** to catch a cold
3 to pick up
□ Coge al niño, que está llorando. Pick up the baby, he's crying.
4 to get
□ ¿Nos coges dos entradas? Would you get us two tickets?
5 to borrow
□ ¿Te puedo coger el bolígrafo? Can I borrow your pen?
■ **Voy a coger el autobús.** I'm going to get the bus.
■ **Le cogió cariño al gato.** He took a liking to the cat.
■ **Iban cogidos de la mano.** They were walking hand in hand.

el **cohete** NOUN
rocket
■ **un cohete espacial** a rocket

cohibido (FEM **cohibida**) ADJECTIVE
inhibited
■ **sentirse cohibido** to feel inhibited

la **coincidencia** NOUN
coincidence
■ **¡Qué coincidencia!** What a coincidence!

coincidir VERB [58]
to match
□ Las huellas dactilares coinciden. The fingerprints match.
■ **Coincidimos en el tren.** We happened to meet on the train.
■ **Es que esas fechas coinciden con mi viaje.** The problem is, those dates clash with my trip.

cojear VERB [25]
1 to limp
□ Todavía cojea un poco. He's still limping a little.
2 to be lame
■ **Cojea del pie izquierdo.** He's lame in his left leg.
3 to wobble

el **cojín** (PL los **cojines**) NOUN
cushion

cojo VERB
▷ *see also* **cojo** ADJECTIVE ▷ *see* **coger**

cojo (FEM **coja**) ADJECTIVE
▷ *see also* **cojo** VERB
1 lame
■ **Está cojo.** He's lame.
■ **Vas un poco cojo.** You're limping a bit.
2 wobbly

la **col** NOUN
cabbage

Spanish-English

C

■ **las coles de Bruselas** Brussels sprouts

la **cola** NOUN
1 tail
2 queue
□ Había mucha cola para el baño. There was a long queue for the toilets.
■ **hacer cola** to queue
3 glue

colaborar VERB [25]
■ **Todo el pueblo colaboró.** Everyone in the village joined in.
■ **Se negó a colaborar con nosotros.** He refused to cooperate with us.

el **colador** NOUN
1 strainer
2 sieve

colar VERB [11]
to strain
■ **colarse** *(colloquial)* to push in □ No te cueles. Don't push in.
■ **Nos colamos en el cine.** We sneaked into the cinema without paying.

la **colcha** NOUN
bedspread

el **colchón** (PL los **colchones**) NOUN
mattress (PL mattresses)
■ **un colchón de aire** an airbed

la **colchoneta** NOUN
1 mat
2 air bed

la **colección** (PL las **colecciones**) NOUN
collection

coleccionar VERB [25]
to collect

la **colecta** NOUN
collection
■ **Hicieron una colecta para comprarle el billete.** They had a collection to buy him the ticket.

el **colectivo** NOUN *(River Plate)*
bus (PL buses)

el/la **colega** NOUN
1 colleague
2 mate *(colloquial)*

el **colegio** NOUN
school
□ Voy al colegio en bicicleta. I cycle to school. □ ¿Todavía vas al colegio? Are you still at school? □ Mi hermano estaba en el colegio. My brother was at school.
■ **un colegio de curas** a Catholic boys' school
■ **un colegio de monjas** a convent school
■ **un colegio público** a state school
■ **un colegio mayor** a hall of residence

el **colesterol** NOUN
cholesterol

la **coleta** NOUN
ponytail
■ **La niña llevaba coletas.** The girl wore her hair in bunches.

colgado (FEM **colgada**) ADJECTIVE
hanging
□ Había varios cuadros colgados en la pared. There were several pictures hanging on the wall.
■ **Debe de tener el teléfono mal colgado.** He must have the telephone off the hook.

el **colgante** NOUN
pendant

colgar* VERB [28]
to hang
□ Colgamos un cuadro en la pared. We hung a picture on the wall.
■ **¡No dejes la chaqueta en la silla, cuélgala!** Don't leave your jacket on the chair, hang it up!
■ **Me colgó el teléfono.** He hung up on me.
■ **¡Cuelga, por favor, que quiero hacer una llamada!** Hang up, please. I want to use the phone!
■ **No cuelgue, por favor.** Please hold.

la **coliflor** NOUN
cauliflower

la **colilla** NOUN
cigarette end

la **colina** NOUN
hill

la **colisión** NOUN
collision

el **collar** NOUN
1 necklace
2 collar

la **colmena** NOUN
beehive

el **colmillo** NOUN
1 canine tooth
2 fang
3 tusk

el **colmo** NOUN
■ **¡Esto ya es el colmo!** This really is the last straw!
■ **Para colmo de males, empezó a llover.** To make matters worse, it started to rain.

colocar* VERB [48]
1 to put
□ Colocamos la mesa en medio del comedor. We put the table in the middle of the dining room.
2 to arrange
□ He colocado los libros por temas. I've arranged the books by subject.
■ **colocarse 1** to get a job □ Se colocó de aprendiz en un taller. He got a job as an apprentice in a workshop. **2** *(colloquial)* to

get plastered **3** *(colloquial)* to get high
■ **¡Colocaos en fila!** Get into a line!
■ **El equipo se ha colocado en quinto lugar.** The team are now in fifth place.

Colombia FEM NOUN
Colombia

el **colombiano** (FEM la **colombiana**) ADJECTIVE, NOUN
Colombian

la **colonia** NOUN
1 perfume
2 colony (PL colonies)
3 district *(Mexico)*
■ **una colonia de verano** a summer camp

colonizar* VERB [13]
to colonize

coloquial (FEM **coloquial**) ADJECTIVE
colloquial

el **color** NOUN
colour
□ ¿De qué color son? What colour are they?
■ **un vestido de color azul** a blue dress
■ **una televisión en color** a colour television

colorado (FEM **colorada**) ADJECTIVE
red
■ **ponerse colorado** to blush

la **columna** NOUN
column
■ **la columna vertebral** the spine

el **columpio** NOUN
swing

la **coma** NOUN
comma
□ palabras separadas por comas words separated by commas
■ **cero coma ocho** zero point eight

el **coma** NOUN
coma
■ **estar en coma** to be in a coma

la **comadrona** NOUN
midwife (PL midwives)

el/la **comandante** NOUN
major
■ **el comandante en jefe** the commander in chief

la **comba** NOUN
skipping rope
■ **saltar a la comba** to skip

el **combate** NOUN
battle
□ entrar en combate to go into battle
■ **un piloto de combate** a fighter pilot
■ **un combate de boxeo** a boxing match

combinar VERB [25]
1 to combine
□ Combina los estudios con el trabajo. He combines his studies with work.
2 to match
□ colores que combinan con el azul colours which match with blue

el **combustible** NOUN
fuel

la **comedia** NOUN
comedy (PL comedies)

el **comedor** NOUN
1 dining room
2 refectory (PL refectories)
3 canteen

comentar VERB [25]
1 to say
□ Comentó que le había parecido muy joven. He said that she had seemed very young.
2 to discuss
□ Comentamos el tema en clase. We discussed the subject in class.
■ **Me han comentado que es una película muy buena.** I've been told that is a very good film.

el **comentario** NOUN
comment
□ No hizo ningún comentario. He made no comment.
■ **Fue un comentario desagradable.** It was an unpleasant remark.

el/la **comentarista** NOUN
commentator

comenzar* VERB [19]
to begin
■ **Comenzó a llover.** It began to rain.

comer VERB [8]
1 to eat
□ ¿Quieres comer algo? Do you want something to eat?
■ **Me comí una manzana.** I had an apple.
2 to have lunch
□ Comimos en el hotel. We had lunch in the hotel.
■ **Hemos comido paella.** We had paella for lunch.
■ **¿Qué hay para comer?** What is there for lunch?
3 to have dinner *(Latin America)*
■ **Le estaba dando de comer a su hijo.** She was feeding her son.
■ **No te comas el coco por eso.** *(colloquial)* Don't worry too much about it.

comercial (FEM **comercial**) ADJECTIVE
1 business
2 trade
3 commercial
□ una película muy comercial a very commercial film

el/la **comerciante** NOUN
shopkeeper

el **comercio** NOUN
1 trade
□ el comercio exterior foreign trade
■ **el comercio electrónico** e-commerce
2 shop
□ ¿A qué hora cierran los comercios? What time do the shops close?

el **cometa** NOUN
comet

la **cometa** NOUN
kite

cometer VERB [8]
1 to commit
2 to make

el **cómic** (PL los **cómics**) NOUN
comic
□ un cómic nuevo a new comic
■ **un personaje de cómic** a comic-book character

cómico (FEM **cómica**) ADJECTIVE
1 comical
□ Fue muy cómico. It was very comical.
2 comic
□ un actor cómico a comic actor

la **comida** NOUN
1 food
□ La comida es muy buena en el hotel. The food in the hotel is very good.
2 lunch (PL lunches)
□ La comida es a la una y media. Lunch is at half past one.
3 supper *(Latin America)*
4 meal
□ Es la comida más importante del día. It's the most important meal of the day.

comienzo VERB ▷ *see* **comenzar**

las **comillas** NOUN
quotation marks
■ **entre comillas** in quotation marks

la **comisaría** NOUN
police station

la **comisión** (PL las **comisiones**) NOUN
1 commission
□ una comisión del 20% a 20% commission
2 committee
□ La comisión organizadora del festival. The festival organizing committee.

el **comité** (PL los **comités**) NOUN
committee

como ADVERB, CONJUNCTION
1 like
□ Tienen un perro como el nuestro. They've got a dog like ours. □ Se portó como un imbécil. He behaved like an idiot.
■ **Sabe como a cebolla.** It tastes a bit like onion.
2 as
□ Lo hice como me habían enseñado. I did it as I had been taught. □ Lo usé como cuchara. I used it as a spoon. □ blanco como la nieve as white as snow □ Como ella no llegaba, me fui. As she didn't arrive, I left.
■ **Hazlo como te dijo ella.** Do it the way she told you.
■ **Es tan alto como tú.** He is as tall as you.
■ **tal como lo había planeado** just as I had planned it
■ **como si** as if □ Siguió leyendo, como si no hubiera oído nada. He kept on reading, as if he had heard nothing.
3 if
□ Como lo vuelvas a hacer se lo digo a tu madre. If you do it again I'll tell your mother.
4 about
□ Vinieron como unas diez personas. About ten people came. □ Llegó como a las cuatro. He arrived about four o'clock.

cómo ADVERB
how
□ ¿Cómo se dice en inglés? How do you say it in English? □ ¿Cómo están tus padres? How are your parents? □ No sé cómo voy a explicárselo. I don't know how I'm going to explain it to him.
■ **¿A cómo están las manzanas?** How much are the apples?
■ **¿Cómo es de grande?** How big is it?
■ **¿Cómo es su novio?** 1 What's her boyfriend like? 2 What does her boyfriend look like?
■ **Perdón, ¿cómo has dicho?** Sorry, what did you say?
■ **¡Cómo! ¿Mañana?** What? Tomorrow?
■ **¡Cómo corría!** Boy, was he running!

la **cómoda** NOUN
chest of drawers (PL chests of drawers)

la **comodidad** NOUN
1 comfort
□ Sólo le interesa su propia comodidad. He's only interested in his own comfort.
2 convenience
□ la comodidad de vivir en el centro the convenience of living in the centre

cómodo (FEM **cómoda**) ADJECTIVE
1 comfortable
□ un sillón cómodo a comfortable chair
□ Me siento cómodo en tu casa. I feel comfortable in your house.
2 convenient
□ Tener un coche es muy cómodo. Having a car is very convenient.

el **compact disc** (PL los **compact discs**) NOUN
1 compact disc

2 compact disc player

compadecer* VERB [12]
to feel sorry for
□ Te compadezco. I feel sorry for you.

el **compañero**, la **compañera** NOUN
1 classmate
2 workmate
3 partner
■ **un compañero de piso** a flatmate

la **compañía** NOUN
company (PL companies)
□ una compañía de seguros an insurance company
■ **El chico andaba en malas compañías.** The boy was keeping bad company.
■ **Ana vino a hacerme compañía.** Ana came to keep me company.
■ **una compañía aérea** an airline

la **comparación** (PL las **comparaciones**) NOUN
comparison
■ **Mi coche no tiene comparación con el tuyo.** There's no comparison between my car and yours.
■ **Mi cuarto es pequeñísimo en comparación con el tuyo.** My room is tiny compared to yours.

comparar VERB [25]
to compare
□ Siempre me comparan con mi hermana. I'm always being compared to my sister.

compartir VERB [58]
to share

el **compás** (PL los **compases**) NOUN
compass (PL compasses)
■ **bailar al compás de la música** to dance in time to the music

compatible (FEM **compatible**) ADJECTIVE
compatible

compensar VERB [25]
1 to make up for
□ Intentan compensar la falta de medios con la imaginación. What they lack in resources they try to make up for in imagination.
2 to compensate
□ Compensarán a los agricultores por las pérdidas. The farmers will be compensated for their losses.
■ **No me compensa con el sueldo que pagan.** It's not worth my while for the salary they pay.
■ **No compensa viajar tan lejos por tan poco tiempo.** It's not worth travelling that far for such a short time.
■ **No sé si compensa.** I don't know if it's worth it.

la **competencia** NOUN
1 rivalry
□ la competencia entre dos hermanos the rivalry between two brothers
2 competition
□ Una campaña para desacreditar a la competencia. A campaign to discredit the competition.
■ **una competencia deportiva** *(Latin America)* a sports competition
■ **No quiere hacerle la competencia a su mejor amigo.** He doesn't want to compete with his best friend.

competente (FEM **competente**) ADJECTIVE
competent

la **competición** (PL las **competiciones**) NOUN
competition

competir* VERB [38]
to compete
■ **Van a competir contra los mejores del mundo.** They're going to compete against the best in the world.
■ **competir por un título** to compete for a title

complacer* VERB [12]
to please

el **complejo** NOUN
complex (PL complexes)
■ **Tiene complejo porque es gordo.** He's got a complex about being fat.
■ **un complejo deportivo** a sports complex

completar VERB [25]
to complete

completo (FEM **completa**) ADJECTIVE
1 complete
□ las obras completas de Lorca the complete works of Lorca
2 full
□ Los hoteles estaban completos. The hotels were full.
■ **Me olvidé por completo.** I completely forgot.

complicado (FEM **complicada**) ADJECTIVE
complicated

complicar* VERB [48]
to complicate
■ **complicarse** to get complicated □ La situación se fue complicando cada día más. The situation was getting more complicated by the day.
■ **No quiero complicarme la vida.** I don't want to make life more difficult for myself.

el/la **cómplice** NOUN
accomplice

componer* VERB [41]
to compose
□ Él compuso la música. He composed the music. □ El comité se compone de seis

miembros. The committee is made up of six members.

el **comportamiento** NOUN
behaviour

comportarse VERB [25]
to behave

la **compra** NOUN
shopping
■ **hacer la compra** to do the shopping
■ **Hice unas compras en el centro.** I did some shopping in the centre.
■ **ir de compras** to go shopping

comprar VERB [25]
to buy
□ Les compré un helado a los niños. I bought an ice-cream for the children.
■ **Le compré el coche a mi amigo.** I bought my friend's car.
■ **Quiero comprarme unos zapatos.** I want to buy a pair of shoes.

comprender VERB [8]
to understand
□ ¡No lo comprendo! I don't understand it!

comprensivo (FEM **comprensiva**) ADJECTIVE
understanding

la **compresa** NOUN
sanitary towel

el **comprimido** NOUN
pill

el **comprobante** NOUN
receipt

comprobar* VERB [11]
to check

comprometerse VERB [8]
□ Me he comprometido a ayudarlos. I have promised to help them.
■ **No quiero comprometerme por si después no puedo ir.** I don't want to commit myself in case I can't go.

el **compromiso** NOUN
engagement
□ El ministro canceló sus compromisos. The minister cancelled his engagements.
□ Se iban a casar pero rompieron el compromiso. They were going to get married but they broke off their engagement.
■ **Puede probarlo sin ningún compromiso.** You can try it with no obligation.
■ **Iba a ir pero sólo por compromiso.** I was going to go but only out of duty.
■ **poner a alguien en un compromiso** to put someone in a difficult situation

compruebo VERB ▷ *see* **comprobar**

compuesto VERB ▷ *see* **componer**

compuesto (FEM **compuesta**) ADJECTIVE
■ **un jurado compuesto de seis miembros** a jury made up of six members

el **computador**, la **computadora** NOUN *(Latin America)*
computer
■ **un computador portátil** a laptop

común (FEM **común**) ADJECTIVE
common
□ un apellido muy común a very common surname
■ **No tenemos nada en común.** We have nothing in common.
■ **Hicimos el trabajo en común.** We did the work between us.
■ **las zonas de uso común** the communal areas

la **comunicación** (PL las **comunicaciones**) NOUN
communication
■ **Se ha cortado la comunicación.** We've been cut off.

comunicar* VERB [48]
to be engaged
□ Siempre está comunicando. The line is always engaged.
■ **comunicarse** to communicate □ Le cuesta comunicarse con los demás. He finds it hard to communicate with others.
■ **Los dos despachos se comunican.** The two offices are connected.

la **comunidad** NOUN
community (PL communities)
■ **la Comunidad Europea** the European Community
■ **una comunidad autónoma** an autonomous region

la **comunión** (PL las **comuniones**) NOUN
communion
■ **Voy a hacer la primera comunión.** I'm going to make my first communion.

el/la **comunista** ADJECTIVE, NOUN
communist

con PREPOSITION
with
□ Vivo con mis padres. I live with my parents. □ ¿Con quién vas a ir? Who are you going with?
■ **Lo he escrito con bolígrafo.** I wrote it in pen.
■ **Voy a hablar con Luis.** I'll talk to Luis.
■ **café con leche** white coffee
■ **Ábrelo con cuidado.** Open it carefully.
■ **Con estudiar un poco apruebas.** With a bit of studying you should pass.
■ **Con que me digas tu teléfono basta.** If you just give me your phone number that'll be enough.
■ **con tal de que no llegues tarde** as long as you don't arrive late

el **concejal**, la **concejala** NOUN
town councillor

concentrarse VERB [25]
1 to concentrate
□ Me cuesta concentrarme. I find it hard to concentrate.
■ **Concéntrate en lo que estás haciendo.** Concentrate on what you're doing.
2 to gather
□ Los manifestantes se concentraron en la plaza. The demonstrators gathered in the square.

concertar* VERB [39]
to arrange

la **concha** NOUN
shell

la **conciencia** NOUN
conscience
□ Tengo la conciencia tranquila. My conscience is clear.
■ **Le remuerde la conciencia.** His conscience is pricking him.
■ **Lo han estudiado a conciencia.** They've studied it thoroughly.

el **concierto** NOUN
1 concert
□ Van a dar varios conciertos en Madrid. They're going to give several concerts in Madrid.
2 concerto (PL concertos)
□ un concierto para violín a violin concerto

la **conclusión** (PL las **conclusiones**) NOUN
conclusion
□ Llegamos a la conclusión de que no valía la pena. We reached the conclusion that it wasn't worthwhile.

concreto (FEM **concreta**) ADJECTIVE
1 specific
□ por poner un ejemplo concreto to take a specific example
■ **No hablo de personas concretas.** I don't mean anyone in particular.
2 definite
□ Todavía no hay fechas concretas. There are no definite dates yet.
■ **este modelo en concreto** this particular model
■ **No me refiero a nadie en concreto.** I don't mean anyone in particular.
■ **Todavía no hemos decidido nada en concreto.** We still haven't decided anything definite.

concurrido (FEM **concurrida**) ADJECTIVE
busy

el/la **concursante** NOUN
competitor

el **concurso** NOUN
1 game show
2 competition
□ un concurso de poesía a poetry competition
■ **un concurso de belleza** a beauty contest

el **conde** NOUN
count

la **condecoración** (PL las **condecoraciones**) NOUN
decoration

la **condena** NOUN
sentence
■ **cumplir una condena** to serve a sentence

condenar VERB [25]
to sentence
□ Lo condenaron a tres años de cárcel. He was sentenced to three years in prison.

la **condesa** NOUN
countess

la **condición** (PL las **condiciones**) NOUN
condition
■ **a condición de que apruebes** on condition that you pass
■ **El piso está en muy malas condiciones.** The flat is in a very bad state.
■ **No está en condiciones de viajar.** He's not fit to travel.

el **condón** (PL los **condones**) NOUN
condom

conducir* VERB [9]
1 to drive
■ **No sé conducir.** I can't drive.
2 to ride
■ **Enfadarse no conduce a nada.** Getting angry won't get you anywhere.

la **conducta** NOUN
behaviour

el **conductor**, la **conductora** NOUN
driver

conduzco VERB ▷ *see* **conducir**

conectar VERB [25]
to connect
□ conectar dos cables to connect two cables
■ **Vamos a conectar ahora con el estadio.** Now we go over to the stadium.
■ **Le cuesta conectar con la gente.** He has trouble relating to people.

el **conejillo** NOUN
■ **un conejillo de Indias** a guinea-pig

el **conejo** NOUN
rabbit

la **conexión** (PL las **conexiones**) NOUN
connection

la **conferencia** NOUN
1 lecture
2 conference
3 long-distance call

Spanish-English

C

confesar* VERB [39]
1 to confess to
□ confesar un crimen to confess to a crime
2 to admit
□ Confesó que había sido él. He admitted that it had been him.
■ **confesarse** to go to confession □ Se confiesa todos los domingos. He goes to confession every Sunday.

el **confeti** NOUN
confetti

la **confianza** NOUN
trust
□ Han puesto toda su confianza en él. They have put all their trust in him.
■ **Tengo confianza en ti.** I trust you.
■ **No tiene confianza en sí mismo.** He has no self-confidence.
■ **un empleado de confianza** a trusted employee
■ **Se lo dije porque tenemos mucha confianza.** I told her about it because we're very close.
■ **Los alumnos se toman muchas confianzas con él.** The pupils take too many liberties with him.

confiar* VERB [21]
to trust
□ No confío en ella. I don't trust her.
■ **Confiaba en que su familia le ayudaría.** He was confident that his family would help him.
■ **No hay que confiarse demasiado.** You mustn't be over-confident.

confidencial (FEM **confidencial**) ADJECTIVE
confidential

confieso VERB ▷ *see* **confesar**

confirmar VERB [25]
to confirm

la **confitería** NOUN
cake shop

el **conflicto** NOUN
conflict

conformarse VERB [25]
■ **conformarse con** to be satisfied with
□ Tengo que conformarme con lo que tengo. I have to be satisfied with what I've got.
■ **Se conforman con poco.** They're easily satisfied.
■ **Tendrás que conformarte con uno más barato.** You'll have to make do with a cheaper one.

conforme (FEM **conforme**) ADJECTIVE
satisfied
□ No se quedó muy conforme con esa explicación. He wasn't very satisfied with that explanation.
■ **estar conforme** to agree □ ¿Estáis todos conformes? Do you all agree?

confortable (FEM **confortable**) ADJECTIVE
comfortable

confundir VERB [58]
1 to mistake
□ confundir la sal con el azúcar to mistake the salt for the sugar □ La gente me confunde con mi hermana. People mistake me for my sister.
2 to confuse
□ Su explicación me confundió todavía más. His explanation confused me even more.
■ **Confundí las fechas.** I got the dates mixed up.
■ **¡Vaya! ¡Me he confundido!** Oh! I've made a mistake!
■ **Me confundí de piso.** I got the wrong flat.

la **confusión** (PL las **confusiones**) NOUN
confusion

confuso (FEM **confusa**) ADJECTIVE
confused

congelado (FEM **congelada**) ADJECTIVE
frozen

el **congelador** NOUN
freezer

congelar VERB [25]
to freeze
■ **Me estoy congelando.** I'm freezing.

congestionado (FEM **congestionada**) ADJECTIVE
1 blocked
2 congested

el **congreso** NOUN
conference
■ **un congreso médico** a medical conference
■ **el Congreso de los Diputados** The Lower Chamber of the Spanish Parliament.

la **conjunción** (PL las **conjunciones**) NOUN
conjunction

el **conjunto** NOUN
1 collection
□ El libro es un conjunto de poemas de amor. The book is a collection of love poems.
2 group
□ un conjunto de música pop a pop group
■ **un conjunto de falda y blusa** a matching skirt and blouse
■ **Hay que estudiar esos países en conjunto.** You have to study these countries as a whole.

conmemorar VERB [25]
to commemorate

conmigo PRONOUN
with me

□ ¿Por qué no vienes conmigo? Why don't you come with me?
■ **Rosa quiere hablar conmigo.** Rosa wants to talk to me.
■ **No estoy satisfecho conmigo mismo.** I'm not proud of myself.

conmovedor (FEM **conmovedora**) ADJECTIVE
moving

conmover* VERB [33]
to move

el **cono** NOUN
cone
■ **el Cono Sur** the Southern Cone

conocer* VERB [12]
1 to know
□ Conozco a todos sus hermanos. I know all his brothers. □ Conozco un buen restaurante. I know a good restaurant.
■ **Nos conocemos desde el colegio.** We know each other from school.
■ **Me encantaría conocer China.** I would love to visit China.
2 to meet
□ La conocí en una fiesta. I met her at a party. □ ¿Dónde os conocisteis? Where did you first meet?

la **conocida** NOUN
acquaintance
□ Es una conocida mía. She's an acquaintance of mine.

conocido (FEM **conocida**) ADJECTIVE
well-known
□ un actor muy conocido a well-known actor

el **conocido** NOUN
acquaintance
□ Son conocidos nuestros. They are acquaintances of ours.

el **conocimiento** NOUN
consciousness
■ **perder el conocimiento** to lose consciousness
■ **Tengo algunos conocimientos de francés.** I have some knowledge of French.

conozco VERB ▷ *see* **conocer**

conque CONJUNCTION
so
□ Hemos terminado, conque podéis iros. We've finished, so you may leave now.

conquistar VERB [25]
1 to conquer
□ los países conquistados por los romanos the countries conquered by the Romans
2 to win...over
□ La conquistó con su sonrisa. He won her over with his smile.

consciente (FEM **consciente**) ADJECTIVE
conscious
□ El enfermo no estaba consciente. The patient wasn't conscious.
■ **Es plenamente consciente de sus limitaciones.** He's fully aware of his shortcomings.

la **consecuencia** NOUN
consequence
□ Todo es una consecuencia de su falta de disciplina. Everything is a consequence of his lack of discipline.
■ **Perdió el conocimiento a consecuencia del golpe.** He lost consciousness as a result of the blow.

consecutivo (FEM **consecutiva**) ADJECTIVE
consecutive
□ tres semanas consecutivas three consecutive weeks

conseguir* VERB [50]
1 to get
□ Él me consiguió el trabajo. He got me the job.
2 to achieve
□ Consiguió las mejores calificaciones de la clase. He achieved the best results in the class.
■ **Nuestro equipo consiguió el triunfo.** Our team won.
■ **Después de muchos intentos, al final lo consiguió.** After many attempts, he finally succeeded.
■ **Finalmente conseguí convencerla.** I finally managed to convince her.
■ **No conseguí que se lo comiera.** I couldn't get him to eat it.

el **consejo** NOUN
advice
□ Fui a pedirle consejo. I went to ask him for advice.
■ **¿Quieres que te dé un consejo?** Would you like me to give you some advice?

consentir* VERB [51]
1 to allow
□ No consiento que me faltes al respeto. I won't allow you to be disrespectful to me.
2 to spoil
□ Su abuela lo consiente demasiado. His grandmother spoils him too much.

el/la **conserje** NOUN
1 caretaker
2 janitor
3 porter

la **conserva** NOUN
■ **No comemos muchas conservas.** We don't eat much tinned food.
■ **atún en conserva** tinned tuna

conservador (FEM **conservadora**) ADJECTIVE
conservative

el **conservante** NOUN

preservative

conservar VERB [25]

1 to keep

□ Debe conservarse en la nevera. It should be kept in the fridge. □ conservar las amistades to keep friends

2 to preserve

□ El frío conserva mejor los alimentos. The cold preserves food better.

■ **Enrique se conserva joven.** Enrique looks good for his age.

el **conservatorio** NOUN

music school

considerable (FEM **considerable**) ADJECTIVE

considerable

considerado (FEM **considerada**) ADJECTIVE

considerate

□ Es muy considerado con su madre. He's very considerate towards his mother.

■ **Está muy bien considerada entre los profesores.** She's very highly regarded among the teachers.

considerar VERB [25]

to consider

□ Lo considero una pérdida de tiempo. I consider it a waste of time.

consiento VERB ▷ *see* **consentir**

la **consigna** NOUN

left-luggage office

consigo VERB

▷ *see also* **consigo** PRONOUN ▷ *see* **conseguir**

consigo PRONOUN

▷ *see also* **consigo** VERB

1 with him

2 with her

3 with you

■ **No está satisfecho consigo mismo.** He is not proud of himself.

consiguiendo VERB ▷ *see* **conseguir**

consiguiente (FEM **consiguiente**) ADJECTIVE

consequent

■ **por consiguiente** therefore

consintiendo VERB ▷ *see* **consentir**

consistir VERB [58]

■ **El menú consiste en tres platos.** The menu consists of three courses.

■ **¿En qué consiste el trabajo?** What does the job involve?

■ **En eso consiste el secreto.** That's the secret.

la **consola** NOUN

console

■ **consola de videojuegos** games console

consolar* VERB [11]

to console

□ No pudimos consolarla. We were unable to console her.

■ **Para consolarme me compré un helado.** I bought an ice cream to cheer myself up.

la **consonante** NOUN

consonant

constante (FEM **constante**) ADJECTIVE

constant

□ el ruido constante de los coches the constant noise of the cars

■ **Tienes que ser más constante.** You should keep working at it.

constantemente ADVERB

constantly

constar VERB [25]

■ **La obra consta de siete relatos.** The work consists of seven stories.

■ **¡Que conste que yo pagué mi parte!** Don't forget that I paid my share!

constipado (FEM **constipada**) ADJECTIVE

■ **estar constipado** to have a cold

LANGUAGE TIP Be careful! **constipado** does not mean **constipated**.

el **constipado** NOUN

cold

□ coger un constipado to catch a cold

la **constitución** (PL las **constituciones**) NOUN

constitution

la **construcción** (PL las **construcciones**) NOUN

construction

□ un edificio en construcción a building under construction

■ **Trabajan en la construcción.** They work in the building industry.

el **constructor**, la **constructora** NOUN

builder

□ Es constructor. He's a builder.

construir* VERB [10]

to build

consuelo VERB ▷ *see* **consolar**

el **consuelo** NOUN

consolation

el/la **cónsul** NOUN

consul

el **consulado** NOUN

consulate

la **consulta** NOUN

surgery (PL **surgeries**)

□ La doctora no tiene consulta los martes. The doctor doesn't hold a surgery on Tuesdays.

■ **horas de consulta** surgery hours

■ **un libro de consulta** a reference book

consultar VERB [25]

to consult

□ consultar a un médico to consult a doctor

■ **Tengo que consultarlo con mi familia.** I must discuss it with my family.

consultorio NOUN
1 surgery
2 problem page
3 phone-in

la **consumición** (PL las **consumiciones**) NOUN
drink
□ Con la entrada tienes una consumición. The admission price includes a drink.

consumir VERB [58]
1 to use
□ Mi coche consume mucha gasolina. My car uses a lot of petrol.
2 to drink
■ **No podemos estar en el bar sin consumir.** We can't stay in the pub without buying a drink.
■ **Sólo piensan en consumir.** Spending money is all they think about.

el **consumo** NOUN
consumption
□ el consumo de bebidas alcohólicas alcohol consumption
■ **una charla sobre el consumo de drogas** a talk on drug use
■ **la sociedad de consumo** the consumer society

la **contabilidad** NOUN
accountancy
□ Estudia contabilidad. He's studying accountancy.
■ **Mi madre lleva la contabilidad.** My mother keeps the books.

el/la **contable** NOUN
accountant

contactar VERB [25]
■ **contactar con alguien** to contact someone

el **contacto** NOUN
1 contact
□ el contacto físico physical contact
2 touch
□ Nos mantenemos en contacto por teléfono. We keep in touch by phone. □ Me puse en contacto con su familia. I got in touch with her family.

contado
■ **al contado** ADVERB
■ **Lo pagué al contado.** I paid cash for it.

el **contador** NOUN
meter
□ el contador de la luz the electricity meter

el **contador**, la **contadora** NOUN *(Latin America)*
accountant

contagiar VERB [25]
■ **No quiero contagiarte.** I don't want to give it to you.
■ **Tiene la gripe y no quiere que los niños se contagien.** He has the flu and doesn't want the children to catch it.

contagioso (FEM **contagiosa**) ADJECTIVE
infectious

la **contaminación** NOUN
pollution
□ la contaminación del aire air pollution

contaminar VERB [25]
to pollute
□ El humo contamina la atmósfera. Smoke pollutes the atmosphere.

contar* VERB [11]
1 to count
□ Sabe contar hasta diez. He can count to ten.
2 to tell
□ Les conté un cuento a los niños. I told the children a story. □ Cuéntame lo que pasó. Tell me what happened.
■ **Cuento contigo.** I'm counting on you.
■ **¿Qué te cuentas?** *(colloquial)* How's things?

contendrá VERB ▷ *see* **contener**

contener* VERB [53]
to contain
□ La caja contenía monedas antiguas. The box contained old coins.
■ **contenerse** to control oneself

el **contenido** NOUN
contents *pl*
□ el contenido de la maleta the contents of the suitcase

contentarse VERB [25]
■ **Se contenta con cualquier juguete.** She is happy with any toy.
■ **Tuve que contentarme con el segundo premio.** I had to be satisfied with second prize.

contento (FEM **contenta**) ADJECTIVE
happy
□ Estaba contento porque era su cumpleaños. He was happy because it was his birthday.
■ **estar contento con algo** to be pleased with something

la **contestación** (PL las **contestaciones**) NOUN
reply (PL replies)
■ **No me des esas contestaciones.** Don't answer back.

el **contestador** NOUN
■ **el contestador automático** the answering machine

contestar VERB [25]
to answer
□ Contesté a todas las preguntas. I answered all the questions.

■ **Les he llamado varias veces y no contestan.** I've phoned them several times and there's no answer.
■ **Me escribieron y tengo que contestarles.** They wrote to me and I have to reply to them.

contigo PRONOUN
with you
□ Quiero ir contigo. I want to go with you.
■ **Necesito hablar contigo.** I need to talk to you.

el **continente** NOUN
continent

continuamente ADVERB
constantly

continuar* VERB [1]
to continue
□ Continuaremos la reunión por la tarde. We will continue the meeting in the afternoon. □ Si continúa así habrá que llevarlo al hospital. If he continues like this, he'll have to be taken to hospital.
■ **Continuó estudiando toda la noche.** He carried on studying right through the night.

continuo (FEM **continua**) ADJECTIVE
1 constant
2 continuous

contra PREPOSITION
against
□ Eran dos contra uno. They were two against one. □ El domingo jugamos contra el Málaga. We play against Malaga on Sunday.
■ **Me choqué contra una farola.** I bumped into a lamppost.
■ **Estoy en contra de la pena de muerte.** I'm against the death penalty.

el **contrabajo** NOUN
double bass (PL double basses)

el **contrabando** NOUN
smuggling
□ el contrabando de drogas drug smuggling
■ **Lo trajeron al país de contrabando.** They smuggled it into the country.

contradecir* VERB [15]
to contradict

la **contradicción** (PL las **contradicciones**) NOUN
contradiction

contradicho VERB ▷ *see* **contradecir**

contradigo VERB ▷ *see* **contradecir**

contradije VERB ▷ *see* **contradecir**

contradiré VERB ▷ *see* **contradecir**

contraer* VERB [54]
1 to tense
2 to contract
■ **contraerse** to contract

la **contraria** NOUN
■ **llevar la contraria a alguien 1** to contradict somebody **2** to do the opposite of what somebody wants

contrario (FEM **contraria**) ADJECTIVE
1 opposing
2 opposite
□ Los dos coches iban en dirección contraria. The two cars were travelling in opposite directions.
■ **Ella opina lo contrario.** She thinks the opposite.
■ **Al contrario, me gusta mucho.** On the contrary, I like it a lot.
■ **De lo contrario, tendré que castigarte.** Otherwise, I will have to punish you.

la **contraseña** NOUN
password

contrastar VERB [25]
to contrast
□ El rojo contrasta con el negro. Red contrasts with black.

el **contraste** NOUN
contrast

contratar VERB [25]
1 to hire
2 to sign up

el **contrato** NOUN
contract

la **contribución** (PL las **contribuciones**) NOUN
1 contribution
□ Le agradecemos su contribución. Thank you for your contribution.
2 tax (PL taxes)
□ la contribución municipal local tax

contribuir* VERB [10]
to contribute
□ Todos contribuyeron al éxito de la fiesta. Everyone contributed to the success of the party. □ Cada uno contribuyó con diez euros para el regalo. Each person contributed ten euros towards the present.

el/la **contribuyente** NOUN
taxpayer

el/la **contrincante** NOUN
opponent

el **control** NOUN
1 control
□ Nunca pierde el control. He never loses control.
2 road-block
□ Hay un control a 3 kilómetros. There's a road-block 3 kilometres further on.
■ **el control de pasaportes** passport control

controlar VERB [25]
to control
■ **Tuve que controlarme para no pegarle.**

I had to control myself, otherwise I would have hit him.
■ **No te preocupes, todo está controlado.** Don't worry, everything is under control.

convencer* VERB [12]
1 to convince
□ Su argumento me convenció. His argument convinced me. □ La convencí de que era necesario. I convinced her that it was necessary.
■ **No me convence nada la idea.** I'm not convinced by the idea.
2 to persuade
□ La convencimos para que nos acompañara. We persuaded her to go with us.

convencional (FEM **convencional**) ADJECTIVE
conventional

conveniente (FEM **conveniente**) ADJECTIVE
convenient
□ Cuando te sea más conveniente. Whenever is more convenient for you.
■ **Sería conveniente que se lo dijeras.** It would be advisable to tell him.

convenir* VERB [56]
to suit
□ el método que más le convenga the method that suits you best
■ **Te conviene descansar un poco.** You ought to get some rest.
■ **Quizá convenga recordar que ...** It might be appropriate to recall that ...

la **conversación** (PL las **conversaciones**) NOUN
conversation
□ Necesito clases de conversación. I need conversation classes.
■ **las conversaciones de paz** peace talks

convertir* VERB [51]
to turn
□ Convirtieron la casa en colegio. They turned the house into a school.
■ **convertirse** to convert □ Se convirtió al cristianismo. He converted to Christianity.
■ **convertirse en 1** to become □ Se convirtió en un hombre rico. He became a rich man. □ El convento se convirtió en hotel. The convent became a hotel. **2** to turn into □ Se convirtió en una pesadilla. It turned into a nightmare. □ La oruga se convierte en mariposa. The caterpillar turns into a butterfly.

convocar* VERB [48]
to call
□ Nos convocaron a una reunión. They called us to a meeting.

el **coñac** (PL los **coñacs**) NOUN
brandy (PL brandies)

la **cooperación** NOUN
cooperation

cooperar VERB [25]
to cooperate
□ Cooperaron con la policía en el caso. They cooperated with the police on the case.

la **copa** NOUN
1 glass (PL glasses)
□ Sólo tomé una copa de champán. I only had one glass of champagne.
2 drink
■ **Fuimos a tomar unas copas.** We went for a few drinks.
3 top
■ **copas**

DID YOU KNOW...?
copas are goblets, one of the suits in the Spanish card deck.

la **copia** NOUN
copy (PL copies)
□ hacer una copia to make a copy
■ **una copia impresa** a printout

copiar VERB [25]
to copy
■ **to copy and paste** copiar y pegar

el **copo** NOUN
■ **un copo de nieve** a snowflake
■ **copos de avena** rolled oats

el **corazón** (PL los **corazones**) NOUN
heart
□ Está mal del corazón. He has heart trouble.
■ **Tiene muy buen corazón.** He is very kind-hearted.

la **corbata** NOUN
tie

el **corcho** NOUN
cork
■ **un tapón de corcho** a cork

el **cordel** NOUN
cord

el **cordero** NOUN
lamb
□ Comimos chuletas de cordero. We had lamb chops.

el **cordón** (PL los **cordones**) NOUN
1 shoelace
2 cable

la **corneta** NOUN
bugle

el **coro** NOUN
1 choir
2 chorus

la **corona** NOUN
crown
■ **una corona de flores** a garland

el **coronel** NOUN

colonel

corporal (FEM **corporal**) ADJECTIVE
1 body
2 corporal
3 personal

el **corral** NOUN
1 farmyard
2 playpen

la **correa** NOUN
1 belt
2 lead
3 strap

correcto (FEM **correcta**) ADJECTIVE
correct
□ Las respuestas eran correctas. The answers were correct.

el **corredor**, la **corredora** NOUN
runner

corregir* VERB [18]
1 to correct
□ Corrígeme si me equivoco. Correct me if I get it wrong.
2 to mark
□ Tengo que corregir los exámenes. I have to mark the exams.

el **correo** NOUN
post
□ Me lo mandó por correo. He sent it to me by post.
■ **Correos** post office □ Fui a Correos a comprar sellos. I went to the post office to buy stamps.
■ **el servicio de correos** the postal service
■ **correo electrónico** email

correr VERB [8]
1 to run
□ Tuve que correr para coger el autobús. I had to run to catch the bus.
■ **El ladrón echó a correr.** The thief started to run.
2 to hurry
□ Corre que llegamos tarde. Hurry or we'll be late.
■ **No corras que te equivocarás.** Don't rush or you'll make a mistake.
3 to go fast
□ No corras tanto, que hay hielo en la carretera. Don't go so fast, the road's icy.
4 to move
□ Corre un poco la silla para allá. Move the chair that way a little. □ Córrete un poco hacia la izquierda. Move a bit to the left.
■ **¿Quieres que corra la cortina?** Do you want me to draw the curtains?

la **correspondencia** NOUN
■ **un curso por correspondencia** a correspondence course

corresponder VERB [8]
■ **Me pagó lo que me correspondía.** He paid me my share.
■ **Estas fotos corresponden a otro álbum.** These photos belong to another album.
■ **No me corresponde a mí hacerlo.** It's not for to me to do it.

correspondiente (FEM **correspondiente**) ADJECTIVE
relevant
□ toda la documentación correspondiente all the relevant documentation
■ **los datos correspondientes al año pasado** the figures for last year

el/la **corresponsal** NOUN
correspondent

la **corrida** NOUN
bullfight

corriente (FEM **corriente**) ADJECTIVE
common
□ Pérez es un apellido muy corriente. Pérez is a very common surname.
■ **Es un caso poco corriente.** It's an unusual case.
■ **Tengo que ponerle al corriente de lo que ha pasado.** I have to let him know what has happened.

la **corriente** NOUN
1 current
■ **Te va a dar corriente.** You'll get an electric shock.
2 draught
■ **Si está de mal humor es mejor seguirle la corriente.** If he's in a bad mood it's best just to humour him.

corrijo VERB ▷ *see* corregir

el **corro** NOUN
ring
□ Los niños hicieron un corro. The children formed a ring.

la **corrupción** NOUN
corruption

cortado (FEM **cortada**) ADJECTIVE
1 sour
2 chapped
3 closed
■ **Juan estaba muy cortado con mis padres.** Juan was very shy with my parents.

el **cortado** NOUN

DID YOU KNOW...?
A **cortado** is a small white coffee with only a little milk.

cortar VERB [25]
1 to cut
□ Corta la manzana por la mitad. Cut the apple in half. □ Me corté el dedo con un cristal. I cut my finger on a piece of broken glass.
■ **Te vas a cortar.** You're going to cut

yourself.
■ **Estas tijeras no cortan.** These scissors are blunt.
2 to cut off
□ Han cortado el gas. The gas has been cut off.
3 to close
■ **Fui a cortarme el pelo.** I went to get my hair cut.
■ **De repente se cortó la comunicación.** Suddenly we were cut off.

el **cortaúñas** (PL los **cortaúñas**) NOUN
nail clippers *pl*

el **corte** NOUN
cut
□ Tenía un corte en la frente. He had a cut on his forehead.
■ **un corte de pelo** a haircut
■ **Me da corte pedírselo.** I'm embarrassed to ask him.

cortés (FEM **cortésa**, MASC PL **corteses**) ADJECTIVE
polite

la **cortesía** NOUN
courtesy
■ **por cortesía** as a courtesy

la **corteza** NOUN
1 crust
2 rind
3 bark

la **cortina** NOUN
curtain

corto (FEM **corta**) ADJECTIVE
short
□ Susana tiene el pelo corto. Susana has short hair.
■ **Las mangas me están cortas.** The sleeves are too short for me.
■ **ser corto de vista** to be short-sighted
■ **¡Carlos es más corto ...!** *(colloquial)* Carlos is so dim!

el **corto** ABBREVIATION *(= cortometraje)*
short film

el **cortocircuito** NOUN
short-circuit

la **cosa** NOUN
thing
□ ¿Qué es esa cosa redonda? What's that round thing? □ Cogí mis cosas y me fui. I picked up my things and left.
■ **cualquier cosa** anything
■ **¿Me puedes decir una cosa?** Can you tell me something?
■ **¡Qué cosa más rara!** How strange!
■ **Son cosas de la edad.** It's just old age.

la **cosecha** NOUN
harvest

cosechar VERB [25]
to harvest

coser VERB [8]
to sew
□ Me estaba cosiendo un botón. I was sewing on a button.

el **cosmético** NOUN
cosmetic

las **cosquillas** NOUN
■ **hacer cosquillas a alguien** to tickle someone
■ **Tiene muchas cosquillas.** He's very ticklish.

la **costa** NOUN
coast
□ Pasamos el verano en la costa. We spend the summer on the coast.
■ **Vive a costa de los demás.** He lives at the expense of others.

el **costado** NOUN
side
■ **Estaba tumbado de costado.** He was lying on his side.

costar* VERB [11]
to cost
□ Cuesta mucho dinero. It costs a lot of money. □ ¿Cuánto cuesta? How much does it cost? □ Me costó diez euros. It cost me ten euros.
■ **Las matemáticas le cuestan mucho.** He finds maths very difficult.
■ **Me cuesta hablarle.** I find it hard to talk to him.

Costa Rica FEM NOUN
Costa Rica

el/la **costarricense** (ADJECTIVE, NOUN
Costa Rican

el **costarriqueño** (FEM la **costarriqueña**) ADJECTIVE, NOUN
Costa Rican

el **coste** NOUN
cost
□ el coste de la vida the cost of living

la **costilla** NOUN
rib

el **costo** NOUN
cost

costoso (FEM **costosa**) ADJECTIVE
expensive

la **costra** NOUN
1 scab
2 crust

la **costumbre** NOUN
1 habit
□ Tiene la mala costumbre de mentir. He has the bad habit of lying.
2 custom
□ una costumbre británica a British custom
■ **Se le olvidó, como de costumbre.** He

forgot, as usual.
■ **Nos sentamos en el sitio de costumbre.** We sat in our usual place.

la **costura** NOUN
1 seam
□ Se te ha descosido la costura de la falda. Your skirt has come apart at the seam.
2 sewing
□ No me gusta la costura. I don't like sewing.

cotidiano (FEM **cotidiana**) ADJECTIVE
everyday
□ la vida cotidiana everyday life

el/la **cotilla** NOUN
gossip

cotillear VERB [25]
to gossip

el **cotilleo** NOUN
gossip

COU ABBREVIATION (= *Curso de Orientación Universitaria*)

DID YOU KNOW...?
This is the former term for the final year at school before university.

el **cráneo** NOUN
skull

la **creación** (PL las **creaciones**) NOUN
creation

crear VERB [25]
to create
■ **No quiero crearme problemas.** I don't want to create problems for myself.
■ **crearse enemigos** to make enemies

creativo (FEM **creativa**) ADJECTIVE
creative

crecer* VERB [12]
1 to grow
□ Me crece mucho el pelo. My hair grows very fast. □ ¡Cómo has crecido! Haven't you grown!
2 to grow up
□ Crecí en Sevilla. I grew up in Seville.

el **crecimiento** NOUN
growth

el **crédito** NOUN
1 loan
□ Pedí un crédito al banco. I asked the bank for a loan.
2 credit
□ comprar algo a crédito to buy something on credit

la **creencia** NOUN
belief

creer* VERB [30]
1 to believe
□ ¿Crees en los fantasmas? Do you believe in ghosts? □ Nadie me cree. Nobody believes me.
■ **Eso no se lo cree nadie.** No one will believe that.
2 to think
□ No creo que pueda ir. I don't think I'll be able to go.
■ **Se cree muy lista.** She thinks she's pretty clever.
■ **Creo que sí.** I think so.
■ **Creo que no.** I don't think so.

creído (FEM **creída**) ADJECTIVE
■ **Es muy creído.** He's so full of himself.

la **crema** NOUN
cream
□ Me pongo crema en las manos. I put cream on my hands.
■ **la crema de afeitar** shaving cream
■ **crema de champiñones** cream of mushroom soup
■ **una blusa de color crema** a cream-coloured blouse

la **cremallera** NOUN
zip
□ Súbete la cremallera. Pull up your zip.

el **crematorio** NOUN
crematorium (PL crematoria)

creyendo VERB ▷ *see* **creer**

el/la **creyente** NOUN
believer

crezco VERB ▷ *see* **crecer**

la **cría** NOUN
1 baby
■ **una cría de cebra** a baby zebra
■ **La leona tuvo dos crías.** The lioness had two cubs.
■ **La hembra es muy protectora de sus crías.** The female is very protective of her young.
2 girl

la **criada** NOUN
maid

el **criado** NOUN
servant

criar* VERB [21]
1 to raise
2 to breed
3 to bring up
□ Me criaron mis abuelos. My grandparents brought me up.
■ **Me crié en Sevilla.** I grew up in Seville.

el **crimen** (PL los **crímenes**) NOUN
1 murder
□ cometer un crimen to commit murder
2 crime
□ los crímenes de guerra war crimes

el/la **criminal** NOUN
criminal

el **crío** NOUN
1 baby

■ **¡No seas crío!** Don't be such a baby!
2 boy
■ **los críos** the children

la **crisis** (PL las **crisis**) NOUN
crisis (PL crises)
□ una crisis política a political crisis
■ **una crisis nerviosa** a nervous breakdown

el **cristal** NOUN
1 glass (PL glasses)
□ una botella de cristal a glass bottle
■ **Me corté con un cristal.** I cut myself on a piece of broken glass.
■ **En el suelo había cristales rotos.** There was some broken glass on the floor.
2 window pane
□ Los niños rompieron el cristal. The children broke the window pane.
■ **limpiar los cristales** to clean the windows
3 crystal
□ una estatuilla de cristal a crystal statuette

el **cristiano** (FEM la **cristiana**) ADJECTIVE, NOUN
Christian

Cristo MASC NOUN
Christ

la **crítica** NOUN
1 criticism
■ **No hagas caso de sus críticas.** Pay no attention to his criticism.
2 review
□ La película ha tenido muy buenas críticas. The film got very good reviews.
3 critic
□ Es crítica de cine. She's a film critic.

criticar* VERB [48]
to criticize
□ Siempre me está criticando. He's always criticizing me.

crítico (FEM **crítica**) ADJECTIVE
critical
□ Llegó en un momento crítico. He arrived at a critical moment.

el **crítico** NOUN
critic
□ Es crítico de cine. He's a film critic.

el **croissant** (PL los **croissants**) NOUN
croissant

el **cromo** NOUN
picture card

crónico (FEM **crónica**) ADJECTIVE
chronic

cronometrar VERB [25]
to time

el **cronómetro** NOUN
stopwatch (PL stopwatches)

la **croqueta** NOUN
croquette
□ croquetas de pollo chicken croquettes

el **cruce** NOUN
crossroads
□ En el cruce hay un semáforo. There are traffic lights at the crossroads.
■ **un cruce de peatones** a pedestrian crossing

crucial (FEM **crucial**) ADJECTIVE
crucial

el **crucifijo** NOUN
crucifix (PL crucifixes)

el **crucigrama** NOUN
crossword

crudo (FEM **cruda**) ADJECTIVE
1 raw
□ las zanahorias crudas raw carrots
2 underdone
□ El filete estaba crudo. The fillet was underdone.

cruel (FEM **cruel**) ADJECTIVE
cruel

la **crueldad** NOUN
cruelty

crujiente (FEM **crujiente**) ADJECTIVE
1 crunchy
2 crusty

crujir VERB [58]
1 to rustle
2 to creak
3 to crunch

la **cruz** (PL las **cruces**) NOUN
cross (PL crosses)
■ **la Cruz Roja** the Red Cross

cruzado (FEM **cruzada**) ADJECTIVE
■ **Había un tronco cruzado en la carretera.** There was a tree trunk lying across the road.

cruzar* VERB [13]
1 to cross
2 to fold
■ **Nos cruzamos en la calle.** We passed each other in the street.

el **cuaderno** NOUN
notebook
■ **un cuaderno de ejercicios** an exercise book

la **cuadra** NOUN
1 stable
2 block *(Latin America)*
□ Está a dos cuadras de aquí. It's two blocks from here.

el **cuadrado** ADJECTIVE, NOUN
square
■ **dos metros cuadrados** two square metres

cuadrar VERB [25]
to tally
□ Las cuentas no cuadran. The accounts

Spanish-English

C

don't tally.
■ **Eso no cuadra con lo que ella nos contó.** That doesn't fit in with what she told us.

cuadriculado (FEM **cuadriculada**) ADJECTIVE
■ **papel cuadriculado** squared paper

el **cuadro** NOUN
1 painting
□ un cuadro de Picasso a painting by Picasso □ ¿Quién pintó ese cuadro? Who did that painting?
2 picture
□ Hay varios cuadros en la pared. There are several pictures on the wall.
■ **un mantel a cuadros** a checked tablecloth

cuajar VERB [25]
1 to set
2 to lie
■ **cuajarse** to curdle

cual PRONOUN (PL **cuales**)
1 who
□ el primo del cual te estuve hablando the cousin who I was speaking to you about
2 which
□ la ventana desde la cual nos observaban the window from which they were watching us
■ **lo cual** which □ Se ofendió, lo cual es comprensible. He took offence, which is understandable.
■ **con lo cual** with the result that
■ **sea cual sea la razón** whatever the reason may be

cuál PRONOUN (PL **cuáles**)
1 what
□ ¿Cuál es la solución? What is the solution?
□ No sé cuál es la solución. I don't know what the solution is.
2 which one
□ ¿Cuál te gusta más? Which one do you like best? □ ¿Cuáles quieres? Which ones do you want?

la **cualidad** NOUN
quality (PL qualities)

cualquier ADJECTIVE ▷ *see* **cualquiera**

cualquiera (FEM **cualquiera**) ADJECTIVE
▷ *see also* **cualquiera** PRONOUN
any
□ en cualquier ciudad española in any Spanish town □ Puedes usar un bolígrafo cualquiera. You can use any pen.
■ **No es un empleo cualquiera.** It's not just any job.
■ **cualquier cosa** anything
■ **cualquier persona** anyone
■ **en cualquier sitio** anywhere

cualquiera PRONOUN
▷ *see also* **cualquiera** ADJECTIVE
1 anyone
□ Cualquiera puede hacer eso. Anyone can do that.
■ **cualquiera que le conozca** anyone who knows him
2 any one
□ Me da igual, cualquiera. It doesn't matter, any one.
■ **en cualquiera de las habitaciones** in any one of the rooms
■ **cualquiera que elijas** whichever one you choose
3 either
□ ¿Cuál de los dos prefieres? — Cualquiera. Which of the two do you prefer? — Either.

cuando CONJUNCTION
when
□ cuando vienen a vernos when they come to see us □ Lo haré cuando tenga tiempo. I'll do it when I have time.
■ **Puedes venir cuando quieras.** You can come whenever you like.

cuándo ADVERB
when
□ ¿Cuándo te va mejor? When suits you?
□ No sabe cuándo ocurrió. He doesn't know when it happened.
■ **¿Desde cuándo trabajas aquí?** Since when have you worked here?

cuanto (FEM **cuanta**) ADJECTIVE, PRONOUN
■ **Termínalo cuanto antes.** Finish it as soon as possible.
■ **Cuanto más lo pienso menos lo entiendo.** The more I think about it, the less I understand it.
■ **Cuantas menos personas haya mejor.** The fewer people the better.
■ **En cuanto oí su voz me eché a llorar.** As soon as I heard his voice I began to cry.
■ **Había sólo unos cuantos invitados.** There were only a few guests.
■ **en cuanto a** as for

cuánto (FEM **cuánta**) ADJECTIVE, PRONOUN
1 how much
□ ¿Cuánto dinero? How much money?
□ ¿Cuánto le debo? How much do I owe you? □ Me dijo cuánto costaba. He told me how much it was.
2 how many
□ ¿Cuántas sillas? How many chairs? □ No sé cuántos necesito. I don't know how many I need.
■ **¿A cuántos estamos?** What's the date?
■ **¡Cuánta gente!** What a lot of people!
■ **¿Cuánto hay de aquí a Bilbao?** How far is it from here to Bilbao?
■ **¿Cuánto tiempo llevas estudiando inglés?** How long have you been studying

English?

cuarenta (FEM **cuarenta**) ADJECTIVE, PRONOUN
forty
□ Tiene cuarenta años. He's forty.
■ **el cuarenta aniversario** the fortieth anniversary

el **cuartel** NOUN
barracks (PL barracks)
■ **el cuartel general** the headquarters

cuarto (FEM **cuarta**) ADJECTIVE, PRONOUN
fourth
□ Vivo en el cuarto piso. I live on the fourth floor.

el **cuarto** NOUN
1 room
□ Los niños jugaban en su cuarto. The children were playing in their room.
■ **el cuarto de estar** the living room
■ **el cuarto de baño** the bathroom
2 quarter
□ un cuarto de hora a quarter of an hour
■ **Son las once y cuarto.** It's a quarter past eleven.
■ **A las diez menos cuarto.** At a quarter to ten.
■ **Es un cuarto para las diez.** *(Latin America)* It's a quarter to ten.

el **cuate** NOUN *(Mexico)*
1 twin brother
2 guy

cuatro (FEM **cuatro**) ADJECTIVE, PRONOUN
four
■ **Son las cuatro.** It's four o'clock.
■ **el cuatro de julio** the fourth of July

cuatrocientos (FEM **cuatrocientas**) ADJECTIVE, PRONOUN
four hundred

Cuba FEM NOUN
Cuba

el **cubano** (FEM la **cubana**) ADJECTIVE, NOUN
Cuban

la **cubertería** NOUN
cutlery

cúbico (FEM **cúbica**) ADJECTIVE
cubic
□ tres metros cúbicos three cubic metres

la **cubierta** NOUN
1 cover
2 tyre
3 deck

cubierto VERB ▷ *see* **cubrir**

cubierto (FEM **cubierta**) ADJECTIVE
covered
□ Estaba todo cubierto de nieve. Everything was covered in snow.
■ **una piscina cubierta** an indoor swimming pool

los **cubiertos** NOUN
cutlery *sing*

el **cubito de hielo** NOUN
ice-cube

el **cubo** NOUN
bucket
■ **el cubo de la basura** the dustbin
■ **tres elevado al cubo** three cubed

cubrir* VERB [58, PAST PARTICIPLE **cubierto**]
to cover
□ Son capaces de cubrir grandes distancias. They can cover great distances.
■ **Las mujeres se cubren la cara con un velo.** The women cover their face with a veil.
■ **El agua casi me cubría.** I was almost out of my depth.

la **cucaracha** NOUN
cockroach

la **cuchara** NOUN
spoon

la **cucharada** NOUN
spoonful
□ una cucharada de jarabe a spoonful of syrup

la **cucharilla** NOUN
teaspoon

el **cucharón** (PL los **cucharones**) NOUN
ladle

cuchichear VERB [25]
to whisper

la **cuchilla** NOUN
blade
■ **una cuchilla de afeitar** a razor blade

el **cuchillo** NOUN
knife (PL knives)

cuclillas
■ **en cuclillas** ADVERB squatting
■ **ponerse en cuclillas** to squat down

el **cucurucho** NOUN
cone

cuelgo VERB ▷ *see* **colgar**

el **cuello** NOUN
1 neck
2 collar

la **cuenta** NOUN
1 bill
□ El camarero nos trajo la cuenta. The waiter brought us the bill.
2 account
■ **una cuenta corriente** a current account
■ **Ahora trabaja por su cuenta.** He's self-employed now.
■ **una cuenta de correo** an email account
■ **darse cuenta 1** to realize □ Perdona, no me daba cuenta de que eras vegetariano. Sorry, I didn't realize you were a vegetarian. **2** to notice □ ¿Te has dado cuenta de que han cortado el árbol? Did you notice they've

cut down that tree?
■ **tener algo en cuenta** to bear something in mind □ También hay que tener en cuenta su edad. You must also bear in mind her age.

cuento VERB ▷ *see* **contar**

el **cuento** NOUN
story (PL stories)
□ La abuela nos contaba cuentos. Grandma used to tell us stories.
■ **un cuento de hadas** a fairy-tale

la **cuerda** NOUN
1 rope
□ Le ataron las manos con una cuerda. They tied his hands together with a rope.
2 string
□ Necesito una cuerda para atar este paquete. I need some string to tie up this parcel. □ La guitarra tiene ocho cuerdas. The guitar has eight strings.
■ **la cuerda floja** the tightrope
■ **dar cuerda a un reloj** to wind up a watch

el **cuerno** NOUN
horn

el **cuero** NOUN
leather
□ una chaqueta de cuero a leather jacket

el **cuerpo** NOUN
body (PL bodies)
□ el cuerpo humano the human body
■ **el cuerpo de bomberos** the fire-brigade

el **cuervo** NOUN
raven

cuesta VERB ▷ *see* **costar**

la **cuesta** NOUN
slope
□ una cuesta muy empinada a very steep slope
■ **ir cuesta abajo** to go downhill
■ **ir cuesta arriba** to go uphill
■ **Llevaba la caja a cuestas.** He was carrying the box on his back.

la **cuestión** (PL las **cuestiones**) NOUN
matter
□ Eso es otra cuestión. That's another matter.
■ **Llegaron en cuestión de minutos.** They arrived in a matter of minutes.

la **cueva** NOUN
cave

cuezo VERB ▷ *see* **cocer**

el **cuidado** NOUN
care
□ Pone mucho cuidado en su trabajo. He takes great care over his work.
■ **Conducía con cuidado.** He was driving carefully.
■ **Debes tener mucho cuidado al cruzar la calle.** You must be very careful crossing the street.
■ **¡Cuidado!** Careful!
■ **Carlos está al cuidado de los niños.** Carlos looks after the children.
■ **cuidados intensivos** intensive care *sing*

cuidadoso (FEM **cuidadosa**) ADJECTIVE
careful

cuidar VERB [25]
to look after
□ Ella cuida de los niños. She looks after the children.
■ **cuidarse** to look after oneself □ Tienes que cuidarte. Make sure you look after yourself.
■ **¡Cuídate!** Take care!

la **culebra** NOUN
snake

el **culebrón** NOUN (PL los **culebrones**
soap(-opera) *(colloquial)*

el **culo** NOUN
bum *(colloquial)*

la **culpa** NOUN
fault
□ La culpa es mía. It's my fault.
■ **Tú tienes la culpa de todo.** It's all your fault.
■ **Siempre me echan la culpa a mí.** They're always blaming me.
■ **por culpa del mal tiempo** because of the bad weather

culpable (FEM **culpable**) ADJECTIVE
guilty
□ Yo no soy culpable. I'm not guilty.
□ Se siente culpable de lo que ha pasado. He feels guilty about what has happened.

el/la **culpable** NOUN
culprit
■ **Ella es la culpable de todo.** She is to blame for everything.

cultivar VERB [25]
1 to grow
2 to farm

culto (FEM **culta**) ADJECTIVE
1 cultured
2 formal

la **cultura** NOUN
culture

el **culturismo** NOUN
body-building

la **cumbre** NOUN
summit

el **cumpleaños** (PL los **cumpleaños**) NOUN
birthday (PL birthdays)
□ Mañana es mi cumpleaños. It's my birthday tomorrow.
■ **¡Feliz cumpleaños!** Happy birthday!

cumplir VERB [58]
1 to carry out
2 to keep
3 to observe
4 to serve
■ **Sólo he cumplido con mi deber.** I have only done my duty.
■ **Mañana cumplo dieciséis años.** I'll be sixteen tomorrow.
■ **El viernes se cumple el plazo para entregar las solicitudes.** Friday is the deadline for handing in applications.

la **cuna** NOUN
cradle

la **cuneta** NOUN
ditch (PL ditches)

la **cuñada** NOUN
sister-in-law (PL sisters-in-law)

el **cuñado** NOUN
brother-in-law (PL brothers-in-law)

la **cuota** NOUN
fee
□ La cuota de socio son veinte euros al mes. The membership fee is 20 euros per year.

cupo VERB ▷ *see* **caber**

el **cupón** (PL los **cupones**) NOUN
1 voucher
2 ticket

la **cura** NOUN
1 cure
□ No tiene cura. There is no cure for it.
2 therapy (PL therapies)
□ una cura de reposo rest therapy

el **cura** NOUN
priest

curar VERB [25]
1 to cure
2 to treat
■ **Espero que te cures pronto.** I hope that you get better soon.
■ **Ya se le ha curado la herida.** His wound has already healed.

la **curiosidad** NOUN
curiosity
■ **Lo pregunté por curiosidad.** I asked out of curiosity.
■ **Tengo curiosidad por saber cuánto gana.** I'm curious to know how much he earns.

curioso (FEM **curiosa**) ADJECTIVE
1 curious
□ Tiene una forma muy curiosa. It's a very curious shape.
■ **¡Qué curioso!** How odd!
2 nosy
□ No seas curioso. Don't be nosy.

la **curita** NOUN *(Latin America)*
sticking plaster

cursi (FEM **cursi**) ADJECTIVE
1 affected
2 twee

el **cursillo** NOUN
course
□ un cursillo de cocina a cookery course
■ **hacer un cursillo de natación** to have swimming lessons

el **curso** NOUN
1 year
□ un chico de mi curso a boy in my year
□ Hago segundo curso. I'm in the second year.
■ **el curso académico** the academic year
2 course
□ Hice un curso de alemán. I did a German course.

la **curva** NOUN
1 bend
□ Hay algunas curvas muy cerradas. There are some very sharp bends.
2 curve
□ dibujar una curva to draw a curve

cuyo (FEM **cuya**) ADJECTIVE
whose
□ El marido, cuyo nombre era Ricardo, estaba jubilado. The husband, whose name was Ricardo, was retired. □ La señora en cuya casa me hospedé. The lady whose house I stayed in.

Dd

el **dado** NOUN
dice (PL dice)
■ **jugar a los dados** to play dice

la **dama** NOUN
lady (PL ladies)
□ Damas y caballeros ... Ladies and gentlemen ...
■ **las damas** draughts □ jugar a las damas to play draughts

el **damasco** NOUN *(Latin America)*
apricot

danés (FEM **danesa**, MASC PL **daneses**) ADJECTIVE
Danish

el **danés**, la **danesa** (MASC PL los **daneses**) NOUN
Dane

el **danés** NOUN
Danish

dañar VERB [25]
1 to damage
2 to hurt
■ **Se dañó la pierna.** She hurt her leg.

el **daño** NOUN
damage
□ El daño producido no es muy grave. The damage isn't very serious.
■ **ocasionar daños** to cause damage
□ La sequía ha ocasionado graves daños. The drought has caused a lot of damage.
■ **hacer daño a alguien** to hurt somebody
■ **hacerse daño** to hurt oneself

dar* VERB [14]
1 to give
□ Le dio un bocadillo a su hijo. He gave his son a sandwich. □ Se lo di a Teresa. I gave it to Teresa.
■ **Me dio mucha alegría verla.** I was very pleased to see her.
■ **Déme 2 kilos.** 2 kilos please.
2 to strike
□ El reloj dio las 6. The clock struck 6.
■ **dar a** to look out onto □ Mi ventana da al jardín. My window looks out onto the garden.
■ **dar con** to find □ Dimos con él dos horas más tarde. We found him two hours later.
■ **Al final di con la solución.** I finally came up with the answer.
■ **El sol me da en la cara.** The sun's shining in my face.
■ **¿Qué más te da?** What does it matter to you?
■ **Se han dado muchos casos.** There have been a lot of cases.
■ **Se me dan bien las ciencias.** I'm good at science.
■ **darse un baño** to have a bath
■ **darse por vencido** to give up

el **dátil** NOUN
date

el **dato** NOUN
■ **Ése es un dato importante.** That's an important piece of information.
■ **Necesito más datos para poder juzgar.** I need more information to be able to judge.
■ **reunir datos para un proyecto de investigación** to gather data for a research project
■ **los datos personales** personal details

de *(de + el = del)* PREPOSITION
1 of
□ un paquete de caramelos a packet of sweets
■ **una copa de vino** 1 a glass of wine 2 a wine glass
■ **la casa de Isabel** Isabel's house
■ **las clases de inglés** English classes
■ **un anillo de oro** a gold ring
■ **una máquina de coser** a sewing machine
■ **es de ellos** it's theirs
■ **a las 8 de la mañana** at 8 o'clock in the morning
2 from
□ Soy de Gijón. I'm from Gijón.
■ **salir del cine** to leave the cinema
3 than
□ Es más difícil de lo que creía. It's more difficult than I thought it would be.
■ **más de 500 personas** over 500 people
■ **De haberlo sabido ...** If I'd known ...

dé VERB ▷ *see* **dar**

debajo ADVERB
underneath
□ Levanta la maceta, la llave está debajo. Lift up the flowerpot, the key's underneath.
■ **debajo de** under □ debajo de la mesa under the table

el **debate** NOUN
debate

debatir VERB [58]
to debate

el **deber** NOUN
duty (PL duties)
□ Sólo cumplí con mi deber. I simply did my duty.
■ **los deberes** homework *sing*

deber VERB [8]
1 must
□ Debo intentar verla. I must try to see her.
□ No debes preocuparte. You mustn't worry.
■ **Debería dejar de fumar.** I should stop smoking.
■ **No deberías haberla dejado sola.** You shouldn't have left her alone.
■ **como debe ser** as it should be
■ **deber de** must □ Debe de ser canadiense. He must be Canadian.
■ **No debe de tener mucho dinero.** He can't have much money.
2 to owe
□ ¿Cuánto le debo? How much do I owe you?
■ **deberse a** to be due to □ El retraso se debió a una huelga. The delay was due to a strike.

debido (FEM **debida**) ADJECTIVE
■ **debido a** owing to □ Debido al mal tiempo, el vuelo se suspendió. Owing to the bad weather, the flight was cancelled.
■ **Habla como es debido.** Speak properly.

débil (FEM **débil**) ADJECTIVE
weak

la **debilidad** NOUN
weakness (PL weaknesses)
■ **tener debilidad por algo** to have a weakness for something
■ **tener debilidad por alguien** to have a soft spot for somebody

debilitar VERB [25]
to weaken

la **década** NOUN
decade

la **decena** NOUN
ten
□ decenas de miles de tens of thousands of
■ **Habrá una decena de libros.** There must be about ten books.

decente (FEM **decente**) ADJECTIVE
decent
□ Exigen un sueldo decente. They are demanding a decent wage.

la **decepción** (PL las **decepciones**) NOUN
disappointment

LANGUAGE TIP Be careful! **decepción** does not mean **deception**.

decepcionar VERB [25]
to disappoint
□ Me has decepcionado de nuevo. You've disappointed me again.
■ **La película me decepcionó.** The film was disappointing.

decidido (FEM **decidida**) ADJECTIVE
determined
□ Estoy decidido a hacerlo. I'm determined to do it. □ Julia es una mujer muy decidida. Julia is a very determined woman.

decidir VERB [58]
to decide
□ Tú decides. You decide.
■ **decidirse a hacer algo** to decide to do something
■ **decidirse por algo** to decide on something
■ **¡Decídete!** Make up your mind!

el **decimal** ADJECTIVE, NOUN
decimal

décimo (FEM **décima**) ADJECTIVE, PRONOUN
tenth
■ **Vivo en el décimo.** I live on the tenth floor.

el **décimo** NOUN
■ **un décimo de lotería** a tenth part of a lottery ticket

DID YOU KNOW...?
In Spain's National Lottery, whole tickets are very expensive so smaller shares such as **décimos** are also sold.

decir* VERB [15]
1 to say
□ ¿Qué dijo? What did he say? □ ¿Cómo se dice 'casa' en inglés? How do you say 'casa' in English?
■ **es decir** that's to say
■ **es un decir** it's a manner of speaking
■ **¡Diga!** Hello?
2 to tell
□ Me dijo que no vendría. He told me that he wouldn't come.
■ **decirle a alguien que haga algo** to tell somebody to do something □ Me dijo que esperara fuera. He told me to wait outside.
■ **¡No me digas!** Really?
■ **querer decir** to mean □ No sé lo que quiere decir. I don't know what it means.

la **decisión** (PL las **decisiones**) NOUN

Spanish-English

d

decision
□ tomar una decisión to take a decision

decisivo (FEM **decisiva**) ADJECTIVE
decisive

la **declaración** (PL las **declaraciones**) NOUN
1 statement
□ El ministro no quiso hacer ninguna declaración. The minister didn't want to make a statement.
2 evidence
□ Prestó declaración ante el juez. He gave evidence before the judge.
■ **una declaración de amor** a declaration of love
■ **la declaración de la renta** the income tax return

declarar VERB [25]
1 to declare
□ ¿Algo que declarar? Anything to declare?
□ El presidente declaró que apoyaría el proyecto. The president declared his support for the project.
2 to give evidence
□ declarar en un juicio to give evidence at a trial
■ **declarar culpable a alguien** to find somebody guilty
■ **declararse 1** to declare oneself □ Se declaró partidario de hacerlo. He declared himself in favour of doing it. **2** to break out □ Se declaró un incendio en el bosque. A fire broke out in the forest.
■ **declararse a alguien** to propose to somebody

el **decorador**, la **decoradora** NOUN
interior decorator

decorar VERB [25]
to decorate

el **decreto** NOUN
decree

el **dedal** NOUN
thimble

dedicar* VERB [48]
1 to devote
□ Dedicó su vida a los demás. He devoted his life to others.
2 to dedicate
□ Dedicó el poema a su padre. He dedicated the poem to his father.
■ **¿A qué se dedica?** What does he do for a living?
■ **Ayer me dediqué a arreglar los armarios.** I spent yesterday tidying the cupboards.

la **dedicatoria** NOUN
dedication

el **dedo** NOUN
1 finger
□ Lleva un anillo en el dedo meñique. She wears a ring on her little finger.
■ **hacer dedo** to hitch a lift
■ **no mover un dedo** not to lift a finger
2 toe
■ **el dedo gordo 1** the thumb **2** the big toe

deducir* VERB [9]
to deduce
□ Deduje que había mentido. I deduced that he'd lied.

el **defecto** NOUN
1 defect
□ El jarrón tiene un pequeño defecto. The vase has a small defect.
2 fault
□ Le encuentra defectos a todo. He finds fault with everything.

defender* VERB [20]
to defend
□ Defendió a su amigo de las críticas. He defended his friend against criticisms.
■ **defenderse** to defend oneself
□ Tenemos que defendernos del enemigo. We have got to defend ourselves against the enemy.
■ **Me defiendo en inglés.** I can get by in English.

la **defensa** NOUN
defence
■ **salir en defensa de alguien** to come to somebody's defence
■ **en defensa propia** in self-defence

el **defensor**, la **defensora** NOUN
defender

deficiente (FEM **deficiente**) ADJECTIVE
poor
□ Su trabajo es muy deficiente. His work is very poor.

la **definición** (PL las **definiciones**) NOUN
definition

definir VERB [58]
to define

definitivo (FEM **definitiva**) ADJECTIVE
definitive
□ Esta solución no es definitiva. This is not a definitive solution.
■ **en definitiva** in short

deformar VERB [25]
1 to deform
■ **No cuelgues el jersey así que lo deformarás.** Don't hang the jersey up like that or you'll pull it out of shape.
2 to distort
■ **deformarse** to become deformed
■ **Si lo lavas en la lavadora, se deformará.** If you wash it in the washing machine, it'll lose its shape.

defraudar VERB [25]

1 to disappoint
□ Su comportamiento la defraudó. His behaviour disappointed her.
2 to defraud
□ Defraudar dinero a Hacienda es delito. It's an offence to defraud the Treasury of money.

dejar VERB [25]
1 to leave
□ He dejado las llaves en la mesa. I've left the keys on the table. □ Su novio la ha dejado. Her fiancé has left her. □ Déjame tranquilo. Leave me alone. □ Dejó todo su dinero a sus hijos. He left all his money to his children.
■ **¡Déjalo ya!** Don't worry about it!
■ **Deja mucho que desear.** It leaves a lot to be desired.
2 to let
□ Mis padres no me dejan salir de noche. My parents won't let me go out at night.
■ **dejar caer** to drop □ Dejó caer la bandeja. She dropped the tray.
3 to lend
□ Le dejé mi libro de matemáticas. I lent him my maths book.
4 to give up
□ Dejó el esquí después del accidente. He gave up skiing after the accident.
■ **dejar de** to stop □ dejar de fumar to stop smoking
■ **dejarse** to leave □ Se dejó el bolso en un taxi. She left her bag in a taxi.

del PREPOSITION *(= de + el)* ▷ *see* **de**

el **delantal** NOUN
apron

delante ADVERB
in front
□ Siéntate delante. You sit in front.
■ **de delante** front □ la rueda de delante the front wheel
■ **la parte de delante** the front
■ **delante de 1** in front of □ No digas nada delante de los niños. Don't say anything in front of the children. **2** opposite □ Mi casa está delante de la escuela. My house is opposite the school.
■ **pasar por delante de** to go past □ Ayer pasé por delante de tu casa. I went past your house yesterday.
■ **hacia delante** forward □ Se inclinó hacia delante. He leaned forward.

delantero (FEM **delantera**) ADJECTIVE
front
□ los asientos delanteros the front seats
■ **la parte delantera del coche** the front of the car

delatar VERB [25]
1 to inform on
□ el hombre que los delató the man who informed on them
■ **Los delató a la policía.** He tipped the police off about them.
2 to give away
□ Tu sonrisa te delata. Your smile gives you away.

la **delegación** (PL las **delegaciones**) NOUN
(Mexico)
police station

el **delegado**, la **delegada** NOUN
delegate
■ **el delegado de clase** the class representative

deletrear VERB [25]
to spell out

el **delfín** (PL los **delfines**) NOUN
dolphin

delgado (FEM **delgada**) ADJECTIVE
1 slim
□ Todas las modelos están delgadas. All models are slim.
2 thin
□ Esta tela es demasiado delgada. This material is too thin.

delicado (FEM **delicada**) ADJECTIVE
1 delicate
□ Estas copas son muy delicadas. These glasses are very delicate. □ Se trata de un asunto muy delicado. It's a very delicate subject.
2 thoughtful
□ Enviarte flores ha sido un gesto muy delicado. Sending you flowers was a very thoughtful gesture.

la **delicia** NOUN
delight
□ ¡Qué delicia! What a delight!
■ **Este guiso es una delicia.** This stew is delicious.

delicioso (FEM **deliciosa**) ADJECTIVE
delicious

el/la **delincuente** NOUN
criminal
□ Es uno de los delincuentes más buscados. He's one of the most wanted criminals.
■ **un delincuente juvenil** a juvenile delinquent

el **delito** NOUN
crime

la **demanda** NOUN
demand
□ la oferta y la demanda supply and demand
■ **Se manifestaron en demanda de un aumento salarial.** They demonstrated for a wage increase.

Spanish-English

d

■ **presentar una demanda contra alguien** to sue somebody

demás (FEM **demás**) ADJECTIVE
▷ *see also* **demás** PRONOUN
other
□ los demás niños the other children

demás PRONOUN
▷ *see also* **demás** ADJECTIVE
■ **los demás** the others
■ **lo demás** the rest □ Yo limpio las ventanas y lo demás lo limpias tú. I'll clean the windows and you clean the rest.
■ **todo lo demás** everything else

demasiado (FEM **demasiada**) ADJECTIVE
▷ *see also* **demasiado** ADVERB
too much (PL too many)
□ demasiado vino too much wine
□ demasiados libros too many books

demasiado ADVERB
▷ *see also* **demasiado** ADJECTIVE
1 too
□ Es demasiado pesado para levantarlo. It's too heavy to lift. □ Caminas demasiado deprisa. You walk too quickly.
2 too much
□ Hablas demasiado. You talk too much.

la **democracia** NOUN
democracy (PL democracies)

democrático (FEM **democrática**) ADJECTIVE
democratic

el **demonio** NOUN
devil
■ **¡Jaime es un auténtico demonio!** Jaime's a real devil!
■ **¡Demonios!** Hell! *(colloquial)*
■ **¿Qué demonios será?** *(colloquial)* What the devil can it be?

la **demostración** (PL las **demostraciones**) NOUN
1 demonstration
2 proof

demostrar* VERB [11]
1 to demonstrate
2 to prove
□ Tendrá que demostrar su inocencia. He will have to prove his innocence.
■ **Así sólo demuestras tu ignorancia.** That way you only show how ignorant you are.

la **densidad** NOUN
density
□ la densidad de población population density

denso (FEM **densa**) ADJECTIVE
1 thick
2 heavy

la **dentadura** NOUN
teeth *pl*
■ **la dentadura postiza** false teeth *pl*

el **dentífrico** NOUN
toothpaste

el/la **dentista** NOUN
dentist

dentro ADVERB
inside
□ ¿Qué hay dentro? What's inside?
■ **por dentro** inside □ Mira bien por dentro. Have a good look inside.
■ **Está aquí dentro.** It's in here.
■ **dentro de** in □ Mételo dentro del sobre. Put it in the envelope. □ dentro de tres meses in three months
■ **dentro de poco** soon
■ **dentro de lo que cabe** as far as it goes

la **denuncia** NOUN
■ **Voy a ponerle una denuncia por hacer tanto ruido.** I'm going to report him for making so much noise.
■ **Le pusieron una denuncia por verter residuos en el río.** He was reported to the authorities for tipping waste into the river.

denunciar VERB [25]
to report

el **departamento** NOUN
1 department
2 compartment
3 flat *(Latin America)*

depender VERB [8]
■ **depender de** to depend on □ El precio depende de la calidad. The price depends on the quality.
■ **Depende.** It depends.
■ **No depende de mí.** It's not up to me.

el **dependiente**, la **dependienta** NOUN
sales assistant

el **deporte** NOUN
sport
□ No hago mucho deporte. I don't do much sport. □ los deportes de invierno winter sports

deportista (FEM **deportista**) ADJECTIVE
sporty
□ Alicia es poco deportista. Alicia is not very sporty.

el **deportista** NOUN
sportsman (PL sportsmen)

la **deportista** NOUN
sportswoman (PL sportswomen)

deportivo (FEM **deportiva**) ADJECTIVE
1 sports
□ un club deportivo a sports club
2 sporting

el **depósito** NOUN
1 tank
2 deposit

la **depresión** (PL las **depresiones**) NOUN

1 depression
■ **tener una depresión** to be suffering from depression
2 hollow

deprimido (FEM **deprimida**) ADJECTIVE
depressed

deprimir VERB [58]
to depress
■ **deprimirse por algo** to get depressed about something

deprisa ADVERB
quickly
□ Acabaron muy deprisa. They finished very quickly.
■ **¡Deprisa!** Hurry up!
■ **Lo hacen todo deprisa y corriendo.** They do everything in a rush.

la **derecha** NOUN
1 right hand
□ Escribo con la derecha. I write with my right hand.
2 right
□ doblar a la derecha to turn right □ La derecha ganó las elecciones. The elections were won by the right.
■ **ser de derechas** to be right-wing □ un partido de derechas a right-wing party
■ **a la derecha** on the right □ la segunda calle a la derecha the second turning on the right
■ **a la derecha del castillo** to the right of the castle
■ **conducir por la derecha** to drive on the right

derecho (FEM **derecha**) ADJECTIVE
▷ *see also* **derecho** ADVERB, NOUN
1 right
□ Me duele el ojo derecho. I've got a pain in my right eye. □ Escribo con la mano derecha. I write with my right hand.
■ **a mano derecha** on the right-hand side
2 straight
□ ¡Ponte derecho! Stand up straight!

derecho ADVERB
▷ *see also* **derecho** ADJECTIVE, NOUN
straight
□ Vino derecho hacia mí. He came straight towards me. □ Siga derecho. Carry straight on.

el **derecho** NOUN
▷ *see also* **derecho** ADVERB, ADJECTIVE
1 right
□ tener derecho a hacer algo to have the right to do something □ No tienes derecho a decir eso. You have no right to say that.
□ los derechos humanos human rights
■ **¡No hay derecho!** It's not fair!
2 law
□ Estudio derecho. I'm studying law.
■ **Ponte la camiseta del derecho.** Put your T-shirt on the right way out.

derramar VERB [25]
to spill
□ Derramó vino sobre el mantel. He spilt wine on the tablecloth.

derrapar VERB [25]
to skid

derretir* VERB [38]
to melt
■ **derretirse** to melt □ El queso se ha derretido. The cheese has melted. □ El hielo se está derritiendo. The ice is melting.
■ **derretirse de calor** to be melting

derribar VERB [25]
1 to demolish
2 to shoot down
3 to overthrow

la **derrota** NOUN
defeat
□ sufrir una derrota to suffer a defeat

derrotar VERB [25]
to defeat

derrumbar VERB [25]
to pull down
□ Han derrumbado el cine. The cinema has been pulled down.
■ **derrumbarse** to collapse □ El edificio se derrumbó. The building collapsed.

desabrochar VERB [25]
to undo
■ **desabrocharse 1** to undo □ Me desabroché la blusa. I undid my blouse.
2 to come undone □ Se te ha desabrochado la cremallera. Your zip has come undone.

el **desacuerdo** NOUN
disagreement

desafiar* VERB [21]
to challenge
□ Mi hermano me desafió a una carrera. My brother challenged me to a race.

desafinar VERB [25]
to go out of tune

el **desafío** NOUN
challenge

desafortunado (FEM **desafortunada**) ADJECTIVE
unfortunate

desagradable (FEM **desagradable**) ADJECTIVE
unpleasant
□ un olor muy desagradable a very unpleasant smell
■ **ser desagradable con alguien** to be unpleasant to somebody

desagradecido (FEM **desagradecida**) ADJECTIVE
ungrateful

el **desagüe** NOUN
1 wastepipe
2 drain

desahogarse* VERB [37]
■ **Se desahogó conmigo.** He poured out his heart to me.
■ **Lloraba para desahogarse.** He was crying to let off steam.

desalojar VERB [25]
to clear
□ La policía desalojó a los manifestantes. The police cleared the demonstrators.
□ Los bomberos desalojaron el edificio. The firemen cleared the building.

desanimado (FEM **desanimada**) ADJECTIVE
1 downhearted
2 dull

desanimar VERB [25]
to discourage
□ Me desanimó su falta de interés. His lack of interest discouraged me.
■ **desanimarse** to lose heart

desaparecer* VERB [12]
to disappear
□ Me han desaparecido las gafas. My glasses have disappeared. □ La mancha ha desaparecido. The stain has disappeared.
■ **¡Desaparece de mi vista!** Get out of my sight!

la **desaparición** (PL las **desapariciones**) NOUN
disappearance

desapercibido (FEM **desapercibida**) ADJECTIVE
■ **pasar desapercibido** to go unnoticed

desaprovechar VERB [25]
to waste
□ Han desaprovechado una gran oportunidad. They've wasted a great opportunity.

el **desarme** NOUN
disarmament
□ el desarme nuclear nuclear disarmament

desarrollar VERB [25]
to develop
□ El estudio desarrolla la mente. Study develops the mind.
■ **La UNICEF desarrolla una labor importante.** UNICEF carries out important work.
■ **desarrollarse** 1 to develop □ La empresa se desarrolla rápidamente. The business is developing rapidly. 2 to take place □ La reunión se desarrolló sin incidentes. The meeting took place without incident.

el **desarrollo** NOUN
development
□ Es importante para el desarrollo del niño. It's important for a child's development.
■ **La industria está en pleno desarrollo.** The industry is expanding steadily.
■ **un país en vías de desarrollo** a developing country

el **desastre** NOUN
disaster
□ un gran desastre económico a major economic disaster □ La función fue un desastre. The show was a disaster.
■ **Soy un desastre para la gimnasia.** I'm hopeless at gymnastics.
■ **Siempre va hecho un desastre.** He always looks a mess.

desastroso (FEM **desastrosa**) ADJECTIVE
disastrous

desatar VERB [25]
1 to undo
2 to untie
■ **desatarse** 1 to come undone 2 to get loose 3 to break

desayunar VERB [25]
1 to have breakfast
□ Nunca desayuno. I never have breakfast.
2 to have...for breakfast
□ Desayuné café con leche y un bollo. I had coffee and a roll for breakfast.

el **desayuno** NOUN
breakfast

descalzarse* VERB [13]
to take one's shoes off

descalzo (FEM **descalza**) ADJECTIVE
barefoot
□ Paseaban descalzos por la playa. They walked barefoot along the beach.
■ **No entres en la cocina descalzo.** Don't come into the kitchen in bare feet.

el **descampado** NOUN
open space

descansar VERB [25]
1 to rest
□ Tienes que descansar. You must rest.
■ **descanse en paz** may he rest in peace
2 to sleep
□ ¡Que descanses! Sleep well!

el **descansillo** NOUN
landing

el **descanso** NOUN
1 rest
□ He caminado mucho, necesito un descanso. I've done a lot of walking, I need a rest.
2 break
□ Cada dos horas me tomo un descanso. I have a break every two hours.
3 relief
□ ¡Qué descanso! What a relief!
4 interval

5 half time
■ **tomarse unos días de descanso** to take a few days off

el **descapotable** NOUN
convertible

descarado (FEM **descarada**) ADJECTIVE
cheeky
□ ¡No seas descarado! Don't be cheeky!

la **descarga** NOUN
1 unloading
2 discharge

descargar* VERB [37]
1 to unload
□ Me ayudó a descargar los muebles de la camioneta. He helped me unload the furniture from the van.
2 to take out
□ Descarga su mal humor sobre mí. He takes his bad moods out on me.
3 to download
■ **descargarse** to go flat

el **descaro** NOUN
nerve
□ ¡Qué descaro! What a nerve!

descender* VERB [20]
to go down
□ Descendieron por la escalinata. They went down the staircase. □ Ha descendido el nivel del pantano. The level of the reservoir has gone down.
■ **descender de** to be descended from
□ Desciende de una familia noble. He is descended from a noble family.
■ **Mi equipo ha descendido de categoría.** My team has been relegated.

el/la **descendiente** NOUN
descendant

el **descenso** NOUN
1 drop
□ Va a haber un descenso de las temperaturas. There's going to be a drop in temperature.
2 descent
□ Los ciclistas iniciaron el descenso del puerto. The cyclists began the descent from the mountain pass.
3 relegation
□ el descenso a segunda división relegation to the second division

descolgar* VERB [28]
1 to take down
□ Descolgó las cortinas para lavarlas. He took down the curtains to wash them.
2 to pick up the phone
□ Descolgó y marcó el número. He picked up the phone and dialled the number.
■ **descolgar el teléfono** to pick up the phone
■ **descolgarse por una pared** to lower oneself down a wall

descomponerse* VERB [41] *(Latin America)*
to break down

desconcertar* VERB [39]
to disconcert
■ **desconcertarse** to be disconcerted
□ Se desconcertó al verla allí. He was disconcerted to see her there.

desconectar VERB [25]
1 to unplug
2 to disconnect

desconfiado (FEM **desconfiada**) ADJECTIVE
distrustful

la **desconfianza** NOUN
distrust

desconfiar* VERB [21]
■ **Desconfío de él.** I don't trust him.
■ **Desconfía siempre de las apariencias.** Always beware of appearances.

descongelar VERB [25]
to defrost
■ **descongelarse** to defrost

el **desconocido**, la **desconocida** NOUN
stranger

desconocido (FEM **desconocida**) ADJECTIVE
unknown
□ un actor desconocido an unknown actor
■ **Está desconocido.** He's unrecognizable.

descontar* VERB [11]
to deduct
□ Me descuentan un parte del sueldo. Part of my salary is deducted.
■ **Descuentan el 5% si se paga en metálico.** They give a 5% discount if you pay cash.
■ **Descontaron cinco euros del precio marcado.** They took five euros off the marked price.

descontento (FEM **descontenta**) ADJECTIVE
unhappy
□ Están descontentos de mis notas. They're unhappy with my marks.

descoser VERB [8]
to unpick
■ **descoserse** to come apart at the seams

descremado (FEM **descremada**) ADJECTIVE
skimmed

describir* VERB [58, PAST PARTICIPLE **descrito**]
to describe

la **descripción** (PL las **descripciones**) NOUN
description

el **descubierto** NOUN
overdraft

el **descubrimiento** NOUN
discovery (PL discoveries)

descubrir* VERB [58, PAST PARTICIPLE **descubierto**]
1 to discover
□ Colón descubrió América en 1492. Columbus discovered America in 1492.
2 to find out
□ ¡Me has descubierto! You've found me out!

el **descuento** NOUN
discount
□ Me hicieron un descuento del 3%. They gave me a 3% discount.
■ **con descuento** at a discount

descuidado (FEM **descuidada**) ADJECTIVE
1 careless
□ Es muy descuidada con sus juguetes. She's very careless with her toys.
2 neglected
□ El jardín estaba descuidado. The garden was neglected.

descuidar VERB [25]
to neglect
□ Descuidó su negocio. He neglected his business.
■ **Descuida, que yo lo haré.** Don't worry, I'll do it.
■ **descuidarse** to let one's attention wander □ Se descuidó un segundo y el niño cruzó la calle. He let his attention wander for a second and the child crossed the road.

el **descuido** NOUN
oversight
□ Me olvidé de invitarla, fue un descuido. I forgot to invite her, it was an oversight.

desde PREPOSITION
1 from
□ Desde Burgos hasta mi casa hay 30 km. It's 30km from Burgos to my house. □ Te llamaré desde la oficina. I'll ring you from the office.
2 since
□ Desde que llegó no ha salido. He hasn't been out since he arrived. □ La conozco desde niño. I've known her since I was a child. □ desde entonces since then
■ **¿Desde cuándo vives aquí?** How long have you been living here?
■ **desde hace tres años** for three years
■ **desde ahora en adelante** from now on
■ **desde luego** of course

desdichado (FEM **desdichada**) ADJECTIVE
1 ill-fated
2 unlucky

desdoblar VERB [25]
to unfold
□ Desdobló el plano. He unfolded the map.

desear VERB [25]
to wish
□ Te deseo mucha suerte. I wish you lots of luck.
■ **Estoy deseando que esto termine.** I'm longing for this to finish.
■ **¿Qué desea?** What can I do for you?
■ **dejar mucho que desear** to leave a lot to be desired

desechable (FEM **desechable**) ADJECTIVE
disposable

los **desechos** NOUN
waste *sing*
□ los desechos nucleares nuclear waste

desembarcar* VERB [48]
1 to disembark
□ Fue el primero en desembarcar. He was the first to disembark.
2 to unload
□ Han desembarcado la mercancía. They've unloaded the goods.

el **desembarco** NOUN
landing

desembocar* VERB [48]
■ **desembocar en 1** to flow into □ El Ebro desemboca en el Mediterráneo. The Ebro flows into the Mediterranean. **2** to lead into □ Este callejón desemboca en la Avenida Pablo Casals. This alley leads into Avenida Pablo Casals.

desempacar* VERB [48] *(Latin America)*
to unpack

el **desempate** NOUN
play-off
■ **el partido de desempate** the deciding match
■ **En el minuto veinte llegó el gol del desempate.** The goal which broke the deadlock came in the twentieth minute.

el **desempleado**, la **desempleada** NOUN
unemployed person
■ **los desempleados** the unemployed

el **desempleo** NOUN
unemployment

desenchufar VERB [25]
to unplug

desengañar VERB [25]
■ **Su traición la desengañó.** His betrayal opened her eyes.
■ **¡Desengáñate! No está interesada en ti.** Stop fooling yourself! She isn't interested in you.

el **desengaño** NOUN
disappointment
□ ¡Qué desengaño! What a disappointment!
■ **llevarse un desengaño** to be disappointed
■ **sufrir un desengaño amoroso** to be disappointed in love

desenredar VERB [25]
1 to untangle
2 to resolve
desenrollar VERB [25]
1 to unwind
2 to unroll
desenroscar* VERB [48]
to unscrew
desenvolver* VERB [59]
to unwrap
□ Desenvolvió todos los paquetes. He unwrapped all the parcels.
■ **desenvolverse** to cope □ Se desenvuelve bien en este tipo de situaciones. He copes well in this sort of situation.
■ **desenvolverse bien** to do well
el **deseo** NOUN
wish (PL wishes)
□ Pide un deseo. Make a wish.
desequilibrado (FEM **desequilibrada**) ADJECTIVE
unbalanced
desértico (FEM **desértica**) ADJECTIVE
desert
□ una región desértica a desert region
desesperado (FEM **desesperada**) ADJECTIVE
desperate
el **desesperado**, la **desesperada** NOUN
■ **Corría como un desesperado.** He was running like mad.
desesperante (FEM **desesperante**) ADJECTIVE
infuriating
desesperar VERB [25]
1 to drive...mad
□ Los atascos me desesperan. Traffic jams drive me mad.
2 to despair
□ No desesperes y sigue intentándolo. Don't despair, just keep trying.
■ **desesperarse** to get exasperated
desfavorable (FEM **desfavorable**) ADJECTIVE
unfavourable
el **desfiladero** NOUN
gorge
desfilar VERB [25]
to parade
el **desfile** NOUN
parade
■ **un desfile de modas** a fashion show
la **desgana** NOUN
1 loss of appetite
2 reluctance
■ **hacer algo con desgana** to do something reluctantly
desganado (FEM **desganada**) ADJECTIVE
■ **estar desganado** 1 to have little appetite 2 to be lethargic
desgarrar VERB [25]
to tear up
□ Desgarró la sábana para hacer trapos. He tore up the sheet to make rags.
■ **desgarrarse** to rip □ La cortina se desgarró. The curtain ripped.
el **desgarrón** (PL los **desgarrones**) NOUN
rip
desgastar VERB [25]
1 to wear out
2 to wear away
■ **desgastarse** to get worn out
el **desgaste** NOUN
1 wear and tear
2 erosion
la **desgracia** NOUN
tragedy (PL tragedies)
□ Su muerte fue una auténtica desgracia. His death was an absolute tragedy.
■ **Ha tenido una vida llena de desgracias.** He's had a lot of misfortune in his life.
■ **por desgracia** 1 sadly □ Por desgracia no se salvó nadie. Sadly there were no survivors. 2 unfortunately □ Por desgracia he vuelto a suspender. Unfortunately I've failed again.
■ **tener la desgracia de** to be unfortunate enough to □ Tuvo la desgracia de perder a su hijo. He was unfortunate enough to lose his son.
■ **No hubo desgracias personales.** There were no casualties.
desgraciado (FEM **desgraciada**) ADJECTIVE
1 unhappy
□ Desde que Ana le dejó ha sido muy desgraciado. He has been very unhappy since Ana left him.
2 tragic
□ Murió en un desgraciado accidente. He died in a tragic accident.
deshabitado (FEM **deshabitada**) ADJECTIVE
1 uninhabited
2 unoccupied
deshacer* VERB [26]
1 to untie
2 to unpack
3 to melt
4 to unpick
■ **deshacerse** 1 to come undone 2 to melt
■ **deshacerse de algo** to get rid of something
deshecho (FEM **deshecha**) ADJECTIVE
1 undone
2 unmade
3 broken
4 melted
■ **Estoy deshecho.** 1 I'm shattered. 2 I'm

devastated.

deshidratarse VERB [25]
to become dehydrated

el **deshielo** NOUN
thaw

deshinchar VERB [25]
to let down
■ **deshincharse** **1** to go down **2** to go flat

desierto (FEM **desierta**) ADJECTIVE
deserted
□ El pueblo parecía desierto. The village seemed deserted.

el **desierto** NOUN
desert

desigual (FEM **desigual**) ADJECTIVE
1 different
2 uneven
3 unequal

la **desilusión** (PL las **desilusiones**) NOUN
disappointment
□ ¡Qué desilusión! What a disappointment!
■ **llevarse una desilusión** to be disappointed

desilusionar VERB [25]
to disappoint
□ No quiero desilusionarte, pero ... I don't want to disappoint you, but ...
■ **Su conferencia me desilusionó.** His lecture was disappointing.
■ **desilusionarse** to be disappointed

el **desinfectante** NOUN
disinfectant

desinfectar VERB [25]
to disinfect

desinflar VERB [25]
to let down
□ Alguien me ha desinflado los neumáticos. Somebody has let my tyres down.

el **desinterés** NOUN
lack of interest
□ Muestra un total desinterés por sus estudios. He shows a total lack of interest in his studies.

deslizarse* VERB [13]
to slide
□ El trineo se deslizaba por la nieve. The sledge slid over the snow.

deslumbrar VERB [25]
to dazzle
□ Las luces del coche me deslumbraron. The car headlights dazzled me. □ Tanta riqueza la deslumbró. She was dazzled by so much wealth.

desmayarse VERB [25]
to faint

el **desmayo** NOUN
faint
■ **sufrir un desmayo** to faint

desmemoriado (FEM **desmemoriada**) ADJECTIVE
forgetful

desmontar VERB [25]
1 to take apart
2 to take down
3 to strip down
4 to dismount

desnatado (FEM **desnatada**) ADJECTIVE
1 skimmed
2 low-fat

desnudar VERB [25]
to undress
■ **desnudarse** to get undressed

desnudo (FEM **desnuda**) ADJECTIVE
1 naked
□ una escultura de un hombre desnudo a sculpture of a naked man
■ **Duerme desnudo.** He sleeps in the nude.
2 bare
□ Sin los cuadros la pared parece desnuda. The wall looks bare without the paintings.

desobedecer* VERB [12]
to disobey

desobediente (FEM **desobediente**) ADJECTIVE
disobedient

el **desodorante** NOUN
deodorant

el **desorden** (PL los **desórdenes**) NOUN
mess
□ Hay mucha desorden en esta casa. This whole house is in a mess.
■ **los desórdenes callejeros** street disturbances

desordenado (FEM **desordenada**) ADJECTIVE
untidy

desordenar VERB [25]
to mess up
□ Los niños han desordenado la habitación. The children have messed up the room.

la **desorganización** NOUN
disorganization

desorientar VERB [25]
to confuse
□ Tus consejos me desorientan más. Your advice confuses me more.
■ **desorientarse** to lose one's way □ Se desorientó al salir del metro. He lost his way when he came out of the underground.

despachar VERB [25]
1 to sell
□ También despachamos sellos. We also sell stamps.
2 to serve
□ Me despachó un dependiente muy educado. I was served by a very polite sales assistant.

3 to dismiss
□ Me despachó sin ninguna explicación. He dismissed me without any explanation.

el **despacho** NOUN
1 office
■ **los muebles de despacho** office furniture
■ **una mesa de despacho** a desk
2 study (PL studies)
□ Está trabajando en su despacho. He's working in his study.
■ **un despacho de billetes** a booking office

despacio ADVERB
slowly
□ Conduce despacio. Drive slowly.
■ **¡Despacio!** Take it easy!

despectivo (FEM **despectiva**) ADJECTIVE
1 contemptuous
□ Me habló en un tono muy despectivo. He spoke to me in a very contemptuous tone.
2 pejorative
□ 'Mujerzuela' es una palabra despectiva. 'Mujerzuela' is a pejorative term.

la **despedida** NOUN
■ **Le hicimos una buena despedida a Marta.** We gave Marta a good send-off.
■ **una fiesta de despedida** a farewell party
■ **una despedida de soltero** a stag party
■ **una despedida de soltera** a hen party

despedir* VERB [38]
1 to say goodbye to
□ Salí a la calle a despedirla. I went out into the street to say goodbye to her.
■ **Fueron a despedirlo al aeropuerto.** They went to the airport to see him off.
2 to dismiss
□ Lo despidieron por llegar tarde. He was dismissed for being late.
■ **despedirse** to say goodbye □ Se despidieron en la estación. They said goodbye at the station. □ despedirse de alguien to say goodbye to somebody

despegar* VERB [37]
to take off
□ Despegó la etiqueta del precio. He took the price label off. □ El avión despegó con retraso. The plane took off late.
■ **despegarse** to come unstuck

el **despegue** NOUN
takeoff

despeinar VERB [25]
■ **despeinar a alguien** to mess somebody's hair up
■ **No me toques el pelo, que me despeinas.** Don't touch my hair, you'll mess it up.
■ **Se despeinó al vestirse.** She messed up her hair getting dressed.

despejado (FEM **despejada**) ADJECTIVE
clear
□ El cielo estaba despejado. The sky was clear.
■ **Por las mañanas tengo la mente más despejada.** My head's clearer in the mornings.

despejar VERB [25]
to clear
□ La policía ha despejado la zona. The police have cleared the area. □ El aire fresco te despejará. The fresh air will clear your head.
■ **¡Despejen!** Move along!
■ **Tomaré un café para despejarme.** I'll have a coffee to wake myself up.

despellejar VERB [25]
to skin

la **despensa** NOUN
larder

desperdiciar VERB [25]
1 to waste
□ Está mal desperdiciar la comida. It's wrong to waste food.
2 to throw away
□ Desperdició la oportunidad de hacerse rico. He threw away the chance to get rich.

el **desperdicio** NOUN
waste
□ Tirar toda esta comida es un desperdicio. It's a waste to throw away all this food.
■ **los desperdicios** scraps □ Le dimos los desperdicios al perro. We gave the dog the scraps.
■ **El libro no tiene desperdicio.** It's an excellent book from beginning to end.

desperezarse* VERB [13]
to stretch

el **desperfecto** NOUN
flaw
■ **El pantalón tenía un pequeño desperfecto.** There was a slight flaw in the trousers.
■ **sufrir desperfectos** to get damaged

el **despertador** NOUN
alarm clock

despertar* VERB [39]
1 to wake up
□ No me despiertes hasta las once. Don't wake me up until eleven o'clock.
2 to arouse
□ El debate despertó un gran interés. The debate aroused a lot of interest.
■ **despertarse** to wake up

el **despido** NOUN
dismissal

despierto (FEM **despierta**) ADJECTIVE
1 awake
□ A las siete ya estaba despierto. He was

Spanish-English

d

already awake by seven o'clock.

2 bright

□ Es un niño muy despierto. He's a very bright boy.

el **despistado**, la **despistada** NOUN

scatterbrain

□ Eres un despistado. You're a scatterbrain.

despistado (FEM **despistada**) ADJECTIVE

absent-minded

□ Es tan despistado que siempre se olvida las llaves. He's so absent-minded that he's always forgetting his keys.

despistar VERB [25]

1 to shake off

□ Despistaron al coche que los seguía. They managed to shake off the car that was following them.

2 to be misleading

□ Estas instrucciones, más que ayudar, despistan. These instructions are more misleading than helpful.

■ **Me despisté y salí de la autopista demasiado tarde.** I wasn't concentrating and I turned off the motorway too late.

el **despiste** NOUN

absent-mindedness

□ Su despiste es conocido por todos. His absent-mindedness is notorious.

■ **¡Vaya despiste que tienes!** How absent-minded can you get!

desplazar VERB [13]

1 to move

2 to take the place of

■ **desplazarse** to commute

desplegar* VERB [34]

1 to unfold

□ Desplegó el mapa. He unfolded the map.

2 to spread

□ El águila desplegó las alas. The eagle spread its wings.

■ **desplegarse** to be deployed □ El ejército se desplegó por la ciudad. The army was deployed throughout the city.

desplomarse VERB [25]

to collapse

□ Se ha desplomado el techo. The roof has collapsed.

despreciar VERB [25]

to despise

el **desprecio** NOUN

contempt

■ **Habló de ellos con desprecio.** He spoke of them contemptuously.

■ **Le hicieron el desprecio de no acudir.** They snubbed him by not turning up.

desprender VERB [8]

to give off

■ **desprenderse** to fall off □ Se desprendió una baldosa. A tile fell off.

■ **desprenderse de algo** to give something up □ No quería desprenderse de la casa. He didn't want to give the house up.

despreocuparse VERB [25]

to stop worrying

□ Despreocúpate porque ya no tiene remedio. Stop worrying because there's nothing we can do about it now.

■ **despreocuparse de todo** to show no concern for anything

desprevenido (FEM **desprevenida**) ADJECTIVE

■ **pillar a alguien desprevenido** to catch somebody unawares

después ADVERB

1 afterwards

□ Después todos estábamos muy cansados. Afterwards we were all very tired.

■ **Primero cenaré y después saldré.** I'll have dinner first and go out after that.

2 later

□ Ellos llegaron después. They arrived later.

□ un año después a year later

3 next

□ ¿Qué viene después? What comes next?

■ **después de** after □ Tu nombre está después del mío. Your name comes after mine. □ Después de comer fuimos de paseo. After lunch we went for a walk.

■ **después de todo** after all

■ **después de que** after □ después de que te acostaras after you had gone to bed

destacar* VERB [48]

1 to stress

□ Me gustaría destacar la importancia de esto. I'd like to stress the importance of this.

2 to stand out

□ Isabel destacaba por su generosidad. Isabel's generosity made her stand out.

el **destapador** NOUN *(Latin America)*

bottle opener

destapar VERB [25]

1 to open

2 to take the lid off

■ **destaparse** to get uncovered □ El niño se destapa por las noches. The child gets uncovered at night.

desteñir* VERB [45]

1 to run

□ Estos pantalones destiñen. These trousers run.

2 to fade

□ El sol ha desteñido las cortinas. The sun has faded the curtains.

■ **desteñirse** to fade □ Se ha desteñido el jersey. This jumper has faded.

desternillarse VERB [25]
■ **desternillarse de risa** *(colloquial)* to split one's sides laughing

destinar VERB [25]
1 to post
□ Lo han destinado a Madrid. He has been posted to Madrid.
2 to earmark
□ Destinaron los fondos a una ONG. The funds were earmarked for an NGO.
■ **El libro está destinado al público infantil.** The book is aimed at children.

el **destinatario**, la **destinataria** NOUN
addressee

el **destino** NOUN
1 destination
□ Por fin llegamos a nuestro destino. We finally arrived at our destination.
■ **el tren con destino a Valencia** the train to Valencia
■ **salir con destino a** to leave for
2 posting
□ Cada dos años me cambian de destino. They give me a new posting every two years.
3 use
□ Quiero saber qué destino tendrá este dinero. I want to know what use will be made of this money.

el **destornillador** NOUN
screwdriver

destornillar VERB [25]
to unscrew

la **destreza** NOUN
skill

destrozar* VERB [13]
to wreck
□ Tu perro ha destrozado la silla. Your dog has wrecked the chair.
■ **La noticia le destrozó el corazón.** The news broke his heart.

los **destrozos** NOUN
damage *sing*
□ La lluvia ocasionó grandes destrozos. The rain caused a lot of damage.

la **destrucción** NOUN
destruction

destruir* VERB [10]
1 to destroy
□ Los huracanes destruyen edificios enteros. Hurricanes can destroy whole buildings.
2 to ruin
□ Aquello destruyó su carrera. That business ruined his career.
3 to demolish
□ Con cuatro palabras destruyó todos mis argumentos. He demolished all my arguments with a few words.

desvalijar VERB [25]
1 to burgle
2 to rob

el **desván** (PL los **desvanes**) NOUN
attic

desvelar VERB [25]
1 to keep...awake
□ El café me desvela. Coffee keeps me awake.
2 to reveal
□ Nos desveló todos sus secretos. He revealed all his secrets to us.
■ **Se desvelan por sus hijos.** They're devoted to their children.

la **desventaja** NOUN
disadvantage
■ **estar en desventaja** to be at a disadvantage

desviar* VERB [21]
to divert
□ Desviaron la circulación. Traffic was diverted.
■ **Quería desviar mi atención.** He wanted to divert my attention.
■ **desviar la mirada** to look away
■ **desviarse** to turn off □ No debes desviarte de la carretera principal. You mustn't turn off the main road. □ Nos estamos desviando del tema. We're getting off the point.

el **desvío** NOUN
1 turning
□ Coge el primer desvío a la derecha. Take the first turning on the right.
2 diversion
□ Hay un desvío por obras. There's a diversion due to roadworks.

el **detalle** NOUN
detail
□ No recuerdo todos los detalles. I don't remember all the details.
■ **No pierde detalle.** He doesn't miss a trick.
■ **Quiero comprarte un detalle.** I want to buy you a little something.
■ **tener un detalle con alguien** to be considerate towards somebody
■ **¡Qué detalle!** How thoughtful!
■ **vender al detalle** to sell retail

detectar VERB [25]
to detect

el/la **detective** NOUN
detective
□ un detective privado a private detective

detener* VERB [53]
1 to stop
□ ¡Detenlos! Stop them!
2 to arrest

□ Han detenido a los ladrones. They've arrested the thieves.
■ **detenerse** to stop □ Nos detuvimos en el semáforo. We stopped at the lights.
■ **¡Deténgase!** Stop!

el **detergente** NOUN
detergent

deteriorar VERB [25]
to damage
□ La lluvia ha deteriorado el tejado. The rain has damaged the roof.
■ **deteriorarse** to deteriorate □ Su salud se ha deteriorado. His health has deteriorated.

la **determinación** NOUN
determination
□ Luchó contra su enfermedad con gran determinación. He fought his illness with great determination.
■ **tomar una determinación** to take a decision

determinado (FEM **determinada**) ADJECTIVE
1 certain
□ En determinadas ocasiones es mejor callarse. There are certain occasions when it's better to say nothing.
■ **No hemos quedado a una hora determinada.** We haven't fixed a definite time.
2 particular
□ ¿Buscas algún libro determinado? Are you looking for a particular book?

determinar VERB [25]
1 to determine
□ Trataron de determinar la causa del accidente. They tried to determine the cause of the accident.
2 to fix
□ determinar la fecha de una reunión to fix the date of a meeting
3 to bring about
□ Aquello determinó la caída del gobierno. That brought about the fall of the government.
4 to state
□ El reglamento determina que ... The rules state that ...

detestar VERB [25]
to detest

detrás ADVERB
behind
□ El resto de los niños vienen detrás. The rest of the children are coming on behind.
■ **detrás de** behind □ Se escondió detrás de un árbol. He hid behind a tree.
■ **uno detrás de otro** one after another
■ **La critican por detrás.** They criticize her behind her back.

la **deuda** NOUN
debt
■ **contraer deudas** to get into debt
■ **estar en deuda con alguien** to be in somebody's debt

la **devolución** (PL las **devoluciones**) NOUN
1 return
2 repayment
■ **No se admiten devoluciones.** Goods cannot be returned.

devolver* VERB [59]
1 to give back
□ ¿Me puedes devolver la cinta que te presté? Could you give me back the tape I lent you?
■ **Me devolvieron mal el cambio.** They gave me the wrong change.
■ **Te devolveré el favor cuando pueda.** I'll return the favour when I can.
2 to take back
□ Devolví la falda porque me iba pequeña. I took the skirt back as it was too small for me.
3 to throw up *(colloquial)*
□ Devolvió toda la cena. He threw up his dinner.

devorar VERB [25]
to devour
□ Los leones devoraron un ciervo. The lions devoured a deer.
■ **devorar un bocadillo** to wolf down a sandwich

di VERB ▷ *see* **decir**

el **día** NOUN
day (PL days)
□ Pasaré dos días en la playa. I'll spend a couple of days at the beach. □ Duerme de día y trabaja de noche. He sleeps during the day and works at night.
■ **Es de día.** It's daylight.
■ **¿Qué día es hoy?** **1** What's the date today? **2** What day is it today?
■ **el día de mañana** tomorrow
■ **al día siguiente** the following day
■ **todos los días** every day
■ **un día de estos** one of these days
■ **un día sí y otro no** every other day
■ **¡Buenos días!** Good morning!
■ **un día de fiesta** a public holiday
■ **un día feriado** *(Latin America)* a public holiday
■ **un día laborable** a working day
■ **pan del día** fresh bread

el **diablo** NOUN
devil
□ No creo en el diablo. I don't believe in the devil. □ Juanito es un verdadero diablo. Juanito's a real little devil.
■ **¿Cómo diablos lo has hecho?** *(colloquial)*

How the devil did you do it?
■ **Hace un frío de mil diablos.** *(colloquial)* It's hellishly cold.

el **diagnóstico** NOUN
diagnosis (PL diagnoses)

la **diagonal** ADJECTIVE, NOUN
diagonal
■ **en diagonal** diagonally

el **dialecto** NOUN
dialect

dialogar* VERB [37]
■ **dialogar con alguien** to hold talks with somebody □ El ministro dialogará con los sindicatos. The minister will hold talks with the unions.

el **diálogo** NOUN
conversation
□ Fue un diálogo interesante. It was an interesting conversation.
■ **No hay diálogo entre los dos bandos.** There's no dialogue between the two sides.

el **diamante** NOUN
diamond
■ **diamantes** diamonds

el **diámetro** NOUN
diameter

la **diana** NOUN
1 bull's-eye
□ dar en la diana to get a bull's-eye
2 dartboard
□ En el bar hay una diana y dardos. There's a dartboard and darts in the bar.

la **diapositiva** NOUN
slide

diario ADJECTIVE
daily
□ la rutina diaria the daily routine
■ **la ropa de diario** everyday clothes
■ **a diario** every day □ Va al gimnasio a diario. He goes to the gym every day.

el **diario** NOUN
1 newspaper
2 diary (PL diaries)

la **diarrea** NOUN
diarrhoea

el/la **dibujante** NOUN
1 artist
2 cartoonist
3 draughtsman (PL draughtsmen)

dibujar VERB [25]
to draw
□ No sé dibujar. I can't draw. □ Dibujó un árbol en la pizarra. He drew a tree on the blackboard.

el **dibujo** NOUN
drawing
□ el dibujo técnico technical drawing
■ **los dibujos animados** cartoons

el **diccionario** NOUN
dictionary (PL dictionaries)

dicho VERB
▷ *see also* **dicho** ADJECTIVE, NOUN ▷ *see* **decir**

dicho (FEM **dicha**) ADJECTIVE
▷ *see also* **dicho** VERB, NOUN
■ **en dichos países** in the countries mentioned above
■ **mejor dicho** or rather □ Vendré el lunes, mejor dicho, el martes. I'll come on Monday, or rather, on Tuesday.
■ **dicho y hecho** no sooner said than done

el **dicho** NOUN
▷ *see also* **dicho** VERB, ADJECTIVE
saying

dichoso (FEM **dichosa**) ADJECTIVE
1 happy
2 lucky
■ **¡Dichoso ruido!** Damned noise! *(colloquial)*

diciembre MASC NOUN
December
□ en diciembre in December □ Llegaron el 6 de diciembre. They arrived on 6 December.

diciendo VERB ▷ *see* **decir**

el **dictado** NOUN
dictation
□ La maestra nos hizo un dictado. The teacher gave us a dictation.

el **dictador**, la **dictadora** NOUN
dictator

la **dictadura** NOUN
dictatorship

dictar VERB [25]
to dictate
□ El maestro nos dictó un párrafo del libro. The teacher dictated a paragraph of the book to us.
■ **dictar sentencia** to pass sentence

diecinueve (FEM **diecinueve**) ADJECTIVE, PRONOUN
nineteen
□ Tengo diecinueve años. I'm nineteen.
■ **el diecinueve de julio** the nineteenth of July
■ **en el siglo diecinueve** in the nineteenth century

dieciocho (FEM **dieciocho**) ADJECTIVE, PRONOUN
eighteen
□ Tengo dieciocho años. I'm eighteen.
■ **el dieciocho de abril** the eighteenth of April
■ **en el siglo dieciocho** in the eighteenth century

dieciséis (FEM **dieciséis**) ADJECTIVE, PRONOUN
sixteen

□ Tengo dieciséis años. I'm sixteen.
■ **el dieciséis de febrero** the sixteenth of February
■ **en el siglo dieciséis** in the sixteenth century

diecisiete (FEM **diecisiete**) ADJECTIVE, PRONOUN
seventeen
□ Tengo diecisiete años. I'm seventeen.
■ **el diecisiete de enero** the seventeenth of January
■ **en el siglo diecisiete** in the seventeenth century

el **diente** NOUN
tooth (PL teeth)
□ lavarse los dientes to clean one's teeth
■ **un diente de leche** a milk tooth
■ **un diente de ajo** a clove of garlic

la **dieta** NOUN
diet
□ una dieta vegetariana a vegetarian diet
■ **estar a dieta** to be on a diet
■ **ponerse a dieta** to go on a diet
■ **dietas** expenses

diez (FEM **diez**) ADJECTIVE, PRONOUN
ten
□ Tengo diez años. I'm ten.
■ **Son las diez.** It's ten o'clock.
■ **el diez de agosto** the tenth of August
■ **el siglo diez** the tenth century

la **diferencia** NOUN
difference
■ **a diferencia de** unlike □ A diferencia de su hermana, a ella le encanta viajar. Unlike her sister, she loves travelling.

diferenciar VERB [25]
■ **¿En qué se diferencian?** What's the difference between them?
■ **Sólo se diferencian en el tamaño.** The only difference between them is their size.
■ **Se diferencia de los demás por su bondad.** His kindness sets him apart from the rest.
■ **No diferencia el color rojo del verde.** He can't tell the difference between red and green.

diferente (FEM **diferente**) ADJECTIVE
different

difícil (FEM **difícil**) ADJECTIVE
difficult
□ Es un problema difícil de entender. It's a difficult problem to understand. □ Resulta difícil concentrarse. It's difficult to concentrate. □ Es un hombre difícil. He's a difficult man.

la **dificultad** NOUN
difficulty (PL difficulties)
□ con dificultad with difficulty
■ **tener dificultades para hacer algo** to have difficulty doing something
■ **Nos pusieron muchas dificultades para obtener el visado.** They made it very difficult for us to get a visa.

dificultar VERB [25]
to make...difficult
□ La niebla dificultaba la visibilidad. The fog made visibility difficult.

digerir* VERB [51]
to digest

la **digestión** NOUN
digestion
■ **hacer la digestión** to digest

digestivo (FEM **digestiva**) ADJECTIVE
digestive

digital (FEM **digital**) ADJECTIVE
digital
□ un reloj digital a digital watch
■ **una huella digital** a fingerprint

la **dignidad** NOUN
dignity
□ Se comportó con gran dignidad. He behaved with great dignity.

digno (FEM **digna**) ADJECTIVE
1 decent
2 honourable
■ **digno de mención** worth mentioning
■ **digno de verse** worth seeing

digo VERB ▷ *see* **decir**

dije VERB ▷ *see* **decir**

diluir* VERB [10]
to dilute

diluviar VERB [25]
■ **Está diluviando.** It's pouring with rain.

el **diluvio** NOUN
downpour
□ Cayó un diluvio. There was a downpour.
■ **un diluvio de cartas** a flood of letters

la **dimensión** (PL las **dimensiones**) NOUN
dimension
□ en tres dimensiones in three dimensions
■ **un cine de grandes dimensiones** a huge cinema

el **diminutivo** NOUN
diminutive

diminuto (FEM **diminuta**) ADJECTIVE
tiny

la **dimisión** (PL las **dimisiones**) NOUN
resignation
□ presentar la dimisión to hand in one's resignation

dimitir VERB [58]
to resign
□ Ha dimitido de su cargo. He has resigned from his post.

Dinamarca FEM NOUN
Denmark

dinámico (FEM **dinámica**) ADJECTIVE
dynamic

el **dinero** NOUN
money
□ No tengo más dinero. I haven't got any more money.
■ **una familia de dinero** a wealthy family
■ **andar mal de dinero** to be short of money
■ **dinero suelto** loose change

el **dinosaurio** NOUN
dinosaur

dio VERB ▷ *see* **dar**

Dios MASC NOUN
God
□ ¡Gracias a Dios! Thank God! □ ¡Dios mío! My God!
■ **¡Por Dios!** For God's sake!
■ **¡Si Dios quiere!** God willing!
■ **No vino ni Dios.** *(colloquial)* Nobody turned up.

el **dios** (PL los **dioses**) NOUN
god

la **diosa** NOUN
goddess (PL goddesses)

el **diploma** NOUN
diploma

la **diplomacia** NOUN
diplomacy

diplomático (FEM **diplomática**) ADJECTIVE
diplomatic

el **diplomático**, la **diplomática** NOUN
diplomat

el **diptongo** NOUN
dipthong

el **diputado**, la **diputada** NOUN
Member of Parliament

dirá VERB ▷ *see* **decir**

la **dirección** (PL las **direcciones**) NOUN
1 direction
□ Íbamos en dirección equivocada. We were going in the wrong direction.
■ **Tienes que ir en esta dirección.** You have to go this way.
■ **una calle de dirección única** a one-way street
■ **'dirección prohibida'** 'no entry'
■ **'todas direcciones'** 'all routes'
2 address (PL addresses)
□ Apúntame tu dirección aquí. Can you write your address down here for me?
3 management
□ la dirección de la empresa the management of the company □ Ha tomado la dirección del proyecto. He's taken over the management of the project.

directo (FEM **directa**) ADJECTIVE
1 direct
□ Hay un tren directo a Valencia. There's a direct train to Valencia. □ una pregunta directa a direct question
2 straight
□ Se fue directa a casa. She went straight home.
■ **transmitir en directo** to broadcast live

el **director**, la **directora** NOUN
1 manager
2 headteacher
3 director
4 conductor
5 editor

el **directorio** NOUN
1 directory (PL directories)
2 phone book *(Latin America)*
3 directory

el/la **dirigente** NOUN
1 leader
2 manager

dirigir* VERB [16]
1 to manage
□ Dirige la empresa desde hace diez años. He has been managing the company for ten years.
2 to lead
□ Dirigirá la expedición. He'll be leading the expedition.
3 to aim at
□ Este anuncio va dirigido a los niños. This advertisement is aimed at children.
■ **no dirigir la palabra a alguien** not to speak to somebody
4 to direct
5 to conduct
■ **dirigirse a 1** to address □ El Rey se dirigió a la nación. The King addressed the nation. **2** to write to □ Me dirijo a ustedes para pedirles más información I am writing to you to ask you for more information. **3** to make one's way to □ Se dirigió a la terminal del aeropuerto. He made his way to the airport terminal.

discapacitado (FEM **discapacitada**) ADJECTIVE
disabled

discar* VERB [48] *(Latin America)*
to dial

la **disciplina** NOUN
discipline

el **disco** NOUN
1 record
2 light
3 discus
■ **un disco compacto** a compact disc
■ **el disco duro** the hard disk

la **discoteca** NOUN
discotheque

Spanish-English

d

la **discreción** NOUN
discretion
■ **Ha actuado con mucha discreción.** He was very discreet.

discreto (FEM **discreta**) ADJECTIVE
discreet
□ No dirá nada porque es muy discreto. He won't say anything because he's very discreet.
■ **un color discreto** a sober colour
■ **un sueldo discreto** a modest salary

la **discriminación** NOUN
□ la discriminación racial racial discrimination

la **disculpa** NOUN
■ **pedir disculpas a alguien por algo** to apologize to somebody for something

disculpar VERB [25]
to excuse
□ Disculpa ¿me dejas pasar? Excuse me, can I go past?
■ **disculparse** to apologize □ Se disculpó por llegar tarde. He apologized for being late.

el **discurso** NOUN
speech (PL speeches)
□ pronunciar un discurso to make a speech

la **discusión** (PL las **discusiones**) NOUN
discussion
□ El tema fue sometido a discusión. The subject came up for discussion.
■ **tener una discusión con alguien** to have an argument with somebody

discutir VERB [58]
1 to quarrel
□ Siempre discuten por dinero. They're always quarrelling about money. □ He discutido con mi hermana. I've quarrelled with my sister.
■ **Discutió con su madre.** He had an argument with his mother.
2 to discuss
□ Tenemos que discutir el nuevo proyecto. We've got to discuss the new project.

diseñar VERB [25]
to design

el **diseño** NOUN
1 design
2 drawing *(arte)*

el **disfraz** (PL los **disfraces**) NOUN
1 disguise
□ Llevaba un disfraz para que no lo reconocieran. He wore a disguise so as not to be recognized.
2 costume
□ un disfraz de vaquero a cowboy costume
■ **una fiesta de disfraces** a fancy-dress party

disfrazarse* VERB [13]
■ **disfrazarse de 1** to disguise oneself as □ Se disfrazó de mujer para escapar. He disguised himself as a woman in order to escape. **2** to dress up as □ Su hija se disfrazó de hada. His daughter dressed up as a fairy.

disfrutar VERB [25]
to enjoy oneself
□ Disfruté mucho en la fiesta. I really enjoyed myself at the party.
■ **Disfruto leyendo.** I enjoy reading.
■ **disfrutar de buena salud** to enjoy good health

disgustado (FEM **disgustada**) ADJECTIVE
upset
LANGUAGE TIP Be careful! **disgustado** does not mean **disgusted**.

disgustar VERB [25]
to upset
□ Me disgustó su tono. His tone upset me.
■ **disgustarse** to get upset □ Me disgusté cuando descubrí que mentía. I got upset when I found out he was lying.
■ **disgustarse con alguien** to fall out with somebody

el **disgusto** NOUN
■ **dar un disgusto a alguien** to upset somebody
■ **llevarse un disgusto** to get upset
■ **hacer algo a disgusto** to do something unwillingly
■ **estar a disgusto** to be ill at ease

disimular VERB [25]
to hide
□ Intentó disimular su enfado. He tried to hide his annoyance.
■ **No disimules, sé que has sido tú.** Don't bother pretending, I know it was you.

la **disminución** (PL las **disminuciones**) NOUN
fall
□ una disminución d en el número de robos a fall in the number of thefts

el **disminuido**, la **disminuida** NOUN
■ **un disminuido mental** a mentally handicapped person
■ **un disminuido físico** a physically handicapped person

disminuir* VERB [10]
to fall
□ Ha disminuido el número de accidentes. The number of accidents has fallen.

disolver* VERB [33]
1 to dissolve
2 to break up
■ **disolverse** to break up

disparar VERB [25]

to shoot
□ Le dispararon en la pierna. They shot him in the leg.
■ **disparar a alguien** to shoot at somebody
■ **Disparó dos tiros.** He fired two shots.
■ **dispararse 1** to go off **2** to shoot up

el **disparate** NOUN
silly thing
□ He hecho muchos disparates en mi vida. I've done a lot of silly things in my life.
■ **decir disparates** to talk nonsense
■ **¡Qué disparate!** How absurd!

el **disparo** NOUN
shot

disponer* VERB [41]
to arrange
□ Dispusieron las sillas en un círculo. They arranged the chairs in a circle.
■ **disponer de** to have □ Disponéis de diez minutos para leer las preguntas. You have ten minutes to read the questions.
■ **disponerse a hacer algo** to get ready to do something

disponible (FEM **disponible**) ADJECTIVE
available
□ El director no estará disponible hasta las 4. The manager won't be available until 4 o'clock.

dispuesto (FEM **dispuesta**) ADJECTIVE
1 prepared
□ estar dispuesto a hacer algo to be prepared to do something
2 ready
□ Todo está dispuesto para la fiesta. Everything's ready for the party.

la **disputa** NOUN
dispute

el **disquete** NOUN
diskette

la **distancia** NOUN
distance
■ **mantenerse a distancia** to keep at a distance
■ **¿Qué distancia hay entre Madrid y Barcelona?** How far is Madrid from Barcelona?
■ **¿A qué distancia está la estación?** How far's the station?
■ **a 20 kilómetros de distancia** 20 kilometres away

la **distinción** (PL las **distinciones**) NOUN
distinction
□ hacer una distinción entre ... to make a distinction between ...
■ **No hace distinciones entre sus alumnos.** He treats all his pupils the same.

distinguido (FEM **distinguida**) ADJECTIVE
distinguished

distinguir* VERB [58, **gu** → **g** before **a** and **o**]
1 to distinguish
□ Resulta difícil distinguir el macho de la hembra. It's difficult to distinguish the male from the female.
■ **No distingue entre el rojo y el verde.** He can't tell the difference between red and green.
■ **No sé distinguir entre un coche u otro.** I can't tell one car from another.
■ **Se parecen tanto que no los distingo.** They're so alike that I can't tell them apart.
2 to make out
□ No pude distinguirla entre tanta gente. I couldn't make her out amongst so many people.
■ **distinguirse** to stand out □ No le gusta distinguirse de los demás. He doesn't like to stand out.

distinto (FEM **distinta**) ADJECTIVE
different
□ Carlos es distinto a los demás. Carlos is different from other people.
■ **distintos** several □ distintas clases de coches several types of car

la **distracción** (PL las **distracciones**) NOUN
pastime
□ Coser es mi distracción favorita. My favourite pastime is sewing.
■ **En el pueblo hay pocas distracciones.** There isn't much to do in the village.

distraer* VERB [54]
1 to keep...entertained
□ Les pondré un vídeo para distraerlos. I'll put a video on to keep them entertained.
2 to distract
□ No me distraigas, que tengo trabajo. Don't distract me. I've got work to do.
■ **Me distrae mucho escuchar música.** I really enjoy listening to music.
■ **Me distraje un momento y me pasé de parada.** I let my mind wander for a minute and missed my stop.

distraído (FEM **distraída**) ADJECTIVE
absent-minded
□ Mi padre es muy distraído. My father is very absent-minded.
■ **Perdona, estaba distraído.** Sorry, I wasn't concentrating.

la **distribución** (PL las **distribuciones**) NOUN
1 layout
□ la distribución de las habitaciones the layout of the rooms
2 distribution
□ la distribución de la riqueza the distribution of wealth

distribuir* VERB [10]

to distribute
□ Ellos distribuyen nuestros productos en el extranjero. They distribute our products abroad.

distribuyendo VERB ▷ *see* **distribuir**

el **distrito** NOUN
district
□ un distrito postal a postal district
■ **un distrito electoral** a constituency

la **diversión** (PL las **diversiones**) NOUN
entertainment
LANGUAGE TIP Be careful! **diversión** does not mean **diversion**.

diverso (FEM **diversa**) ADJECTIVE
different
□ Dieron explicaciones muy diversas del incidente. They gave very different explanations for the incident.
■ **diversos** various □ diversos libros various books

divertido (FEM **divertida**) ADJECTIVE
1 funny
2 enjoyable
■ **Fue muy divertido.** It was great fun.

divertir* VERB [51]
to entertain
□ Nos divirtió con sus anécdotas. He entertained us with his stories.
■ **divertirse** to have a good time

dividir VERB [58]
to divide
□ El libro está dividido en dos partes. The book is divided into two parts. □ Dividió sus tierras entre sus tres hijas. He divided his land between his three daughters. □ Divide cuatro entre dos. Divide four by two.
■ **dividirse 1** to divide □ Nos dividimos el trabajo entre los tres. We divided the work between the three of us. **2** to share □ Se dividieron el dinero de la lotería. They shared the lottery money.

divierto VERB ▷ *see* **divertir**

divino (FEM **divina**) ADJECTIVE
divine

la **división** (PL las **divisiones**) NOUN
division
□ en primera división in the first division
□ Ya sabe hacer divisiones. He already knows how to do division.

divorciarse VERB [25]
to get divorced
■ **Se ha divorciado de su mujer.** He has got divorced from his wife.

el **divorcio** NOUN
divorce

divulgar* VERB [37]
to spread
□ divulgar rumores to spread rumours

el **DNI** ABBREVIATION (= *Documento Nacional de Identidad)*
ID card

doblar VERB [25]
1 to double
□ Le han doblado el sueldo. They've doubled his salary.
2 to fold
□ Dobla los pañuelos y guárdalos. Fold the handkerchiefs and put them away.
3 to turn
□ Cuando llegues al cruce, dobla a la derecha. When you reach the junction, turn right.
4 to dub
□ Doblan todas las películas extranjeras. All foreign films are dubbed.
5 to toll
□ Las campanas de la iglesia estaban doblando. The church bells were tolling.

doble (FEM **doble**) ADJECTIVE
double
□ una frase con doble sentido an expression with a double meaning □ una habitación doble a double room

el **doble** NOUN
twice as much
□ Su sueldo es el doble del mío. His salary's twice as much as mine. □ Comes el doble que yo. You eat twice as much as I do.
■ **Trabaja el doble que tú.** He works twice as hard as you do.
■ **jugar un partido de dobles** to play doubles

doce (FEM **doce**) ADJECTIVE, PRONOUN
twelve
□ Tengo doce años. I'm twelve.
■ **Son las doce.** It's twelve o'clock.
■ **el siglo doce** the twelfth century

la **docena** NOUN
dozen

el **doctor**, la **doctora** NOUN
doctor

la **doctrina** NOUN
doctrine

el **documental** NOUN
documentary (PL documentaries)

el **documento** NOUN
document
□ un documento oficial an official document
■ **el documento nacional de identidad** the identity card
■ **un documento adjunto** an attachment

el **dólar** NOUN
dollar

doler* VERB [33]
to hurt

□ Me duele el brazo. My arm hurts. □ Esta inyección no duele. This injection won't hurt. □ Me dolió que me mintiera. I was hurt that he lied to me.
■ **Me duele la cabeza.** I've got a headache.
■ **Me duele el pecho.** I've got a pain in my chest.
■ **Me duele la garganta.** I've got a sore throat.

el **dolor** NOUN
pain
□ Gritó de dolor. He cried out in pain.
■ **Tengo dolor de cabeza.** I've got a headache.
■ **Tengo dolor de estómago.** I've got stomach ache.
■ **Tengo dolor de muelas.** I've got toothache.
■ **Tengo dolor de oídos.** I've got earache.
■ **Tengo dolor de garganta.** I've got a sore throat.

doméstico (FEM **doméstica**) ADJECTIVE
domestic
□ para uso doméstico for domestic use
■ **las tareas domésticas** the housework
■ **un animal doméstico** a pet

el **domicilio** NOUN
residence
□ su domicilio particular their private residence
■ **servicio a domicilio** home delivery

dominar VERB [25]
1 to dominate
□ El padre dominaba totalmente a los hijos. The father totally dominated his children.
■ **tener dominado a alguien** to have somebody at one's mercy
2 to control
□ No pudo dominar su mal genio. He couldn't control his temper.
3 to be fluent in
□ Mi hermana domina el inglés. My sister is fluent in English.
4 to bring under control
□ Los bomberos tardaron en dominar el incendio. The fire brigade took a long time to bring the fire under control.
■ **dominarse** to control oneself

el **domingo** NOUN
Sunday
□ La vi el domingo. I saw her on Sunday. □ todos los domingos every Sunday □ el domingo pasado last Sunday □ el domingo que viene next Sunday □ Jugamos los domingos. We play on Sundays.

el **dominicano** (FEM la **dominicana**) ADJECTIVE, NOUN
Dominican

el **dominio** NOUN
1 command
□ Tiene un gran dominio del inglés. He has a good command of English.
2 rule
□ Francia estuvo bajo el dominio romano. France was under Roman rule.
3 control
□ Ejerce un dominio absoluto sobre sus seguidores. He exercises absolute control over his followers.
■ **dominio de sí mismo** self-control
■ **ser del dominio público** to be public knowledge

el **dominó** NOUN
1 domino
2 dominoes *sing*
□ jugar al dominó to play dominoes

el **don** NOUN
gift
□ Tiene un don para la música. He has a gift for music.
■ **tener don de gentes** to be good with people
■ **don Juan Gómez** Mr Juan Gómez

DID YOU KNOW...?
cuando **don** va seguido sólo del nombre de pila, se traduce por **Mr** más el apellido.

■ **Es un don nadie.** He's a nobody.

la **dona** NOUN *(Mexico)*
doughnut

el/la **donante** NOUN
donor
□ un donante de órganos an organ donor

el **donativo** NOUN
donation

donde ADVERB
where
□ La nota está donde la dejaste. The note's where you left it.

dónde ADVERB
where
□ ¿Dónde vas? Where are you going? □ Le pregunté dónde estaba la catedral. I asked him where the cathedral was. □ ¿Sabes dónde está? Do you know where he is?
■ **¿De dónde eres?** Where are you from?
■ **¿Por dónde se va al cine?** How do you get to the cinema?

la **doña** NOUN
■ **doña Marta García** Mrs Marta García

DID YOU KNOW...?
cuando **doña** va seguido sólo del nombre de pila, se traduce por **Mrs** más el apellido.

dorado (FEM **dorada**) ADJECTIVE
golden

Spanish-English

d

Spanish-English

d

dormir* VERB [17]
to sleep
□ Antonio durmió 10 horas. Antonio slept for 10 hours.
■ **Se me ha dormido el brazo.** My arm has gone to sleep.
■ **dormir la siesta** to have a nap
■ **dormir como un tronco** to sleep like a log
■ **estar medio dormido** to be half asleep
■ **dormirse** to fall asleep

el **dormitorio** NOUN
1 bedroom
2 dormitory (PL dormitories)

el **dorso** NOUN
back
□ Se apuntó el teléfono en el dorso de la mano. He wrote the telephone number on the back of his hand.
■ **'véase al dorso'** 'see over'

dos ADJECTIVE, PRONOUN
1 two
□ ¿Tienes los dos libros que te dejé? Have you got the two books I lent you? □ Tiene dos años. He's two.
■ **Son las dos.** It's two o'clock.
■ **de dos en dos** in twos
■ **el dos de enero** the second of January
■ **cada dos por tres** every five minutes
2 both
□ Al final vinieron los dos. In the end they both came. □ Nos han suspendido a los dos. We have both failed. □ Mis dos hijos han emigrado. Both of my sons have emigrated. □ Los hemos invitado a los dos. We've invited both of them.

doscientos (FEM **doscientas**) ADJECTIVE, PRONOUN
two hundred
□ doscientos cincuenta two hundred and fifty

la **dosis** (PL las **dosis**) NOUN
dose

doy VERB ▷ *see* **dar**

el **dragón** (PL los **dragones**) NOUN
dragon

el **drama** NOUN
drama

dramático (FEM **dramática**) ADJECTIVE
dramatic

la **droga** NOUN
drug
□ las drogas blandas soft drugs □ las drogas duras hard drugs □ el problema de la droga the drug problem

el **drogadicto**, la **drogadicta** NOUN
drug addict

drogar* VERB [37]
to drug
■ **drogarse** to take drugs

la **droguería** NOUN

DID YOU KNOW...?
This is a shop selling cleaning materials, paint and toiletries.

la **ducha** NOUN
shower
□ darse una ducha to have a shower

ducharse VERB [25]
to have a shower

la **duda** NOUN
doubt
■ **Tengo mis dudas.** I have my doubts.
■ **sin duda** no doubt
■ **sin duda alguna** without a doubt
■ **no cabe duda** there's no doubt about it
■ **Tengo una duda.** I have a query.
■ **poner algo en duda** to call something into question
■ **¿Alguna duda?** Any questions?

dudar VERB [25]
to doubt
□ Lo dudo. I doubt it.
■ **Dudo que sea cierto.** I doubt if it's true.
■ **Dudó si comprarlo o no.** He wasn't sure whether to buy it or not.

dudoso (FEM **dudosa**) ADJECTIVE
1 doubtful
□ Es dudoso que vengan. It's doubtful whether they'll come.
2 dubious
□ un chiste de dudoso gusto a joke in dubious taste

duelo VERB ▷ *see* **doler**

el **dueño**, la **dueña** NOUN
owner
■ **ser dueño de sí mismo** to have self-control

duermo VERB ▷ *see* **dormir**

el **Duero** NOUN
the Douro

dulce (FEM **dulce**) ADJECTIVE
1 sweet
2 gentle

el **dulce** NOUN
sweet

el **dúo** NOUN
duet
■ **cantar a dúo** to sing a duet

la **duración** NOUN
length
□ Depende de la duración de la película. It depends on the length of the film.
■ **una pila de larga duración** a long-life battery

duradero (FEM **duradera**) ADJECTIVE
1 lasting

2 hard-wearing

durante ADVERB
during
□ Tuve que trabajar durante las vacaciones. He had to work during the holidays.
■ **durante toda la noche** all night long
■ **Habló durante una hora.** He spoke for an hour.

durar VERB [25]
to last
□ La película dura dos horas. The film lasts two hours. □ Sólo duró dos meses como director. He only lasted two months as manager. □ Todavía le dura el enfado. He's still angry.

el **durazno** NOUN *(Latin America)*
peach (PL peaches)

la **dureza** NOUN
1 hardness
□ la dureza del acero the hardness of steel
2 harshness
□ la dureza de sus palabras the harshness of his words
3 callus (PL calluses)
□ Tiene una dureza en la planta del pie. He has a callus on the sole of his foot.

durmiendo VERB ▷ *see* **dormir**

duro (FEM **dura**) ADJECTIVE
▷ *see also* **duro** ADVERB, NOUN
1 hard
□ Los diamantes son muy duros. Diamonds are very hard.
2 tough
□ Esta carne está dura. This meat's tough.
3 harsh
□ El clima es muy duro. The climate is very harsh.
■ **a duras penas** with great difficulty
■ **ser duro con alguien** to be hard on somebody
■ **ser duro de oído** to be hard of hearing

duro ADVERB
▷ *see also* **duro** ADJECTIVE, NOUN
hard
□ trabajar duro to work hard

el **duro** NOUN
▷ *see also* **duro** ADJECTIVE, ADVERB
five-peseta coin
■ **estar sin un duro** to be broke *(colloquial)*

el **DVD** ABBREVIATION *(= Disco de Vídeo Digital)*
DVD

Ee

e CONJUNCTION

> **LANGUAGE TIP** **e** is used instead of **y** in front of words beginning with **i** and **hi**, but not **hie**.

and
□ Pablo e Inés. Pablo and Inés.

echar VERB [25]
1 to throw
□ Échame las llaves. Throw me the keys over.
■ **Eché la carta en el buzón.** I posted the letter.
2 to put
□ Tengo que echar gasolina. I need to put petrol in the car.
■ **¿Te echo más whisky?** Shall I pour you some more whisky?
3 to throw out
□ Me echó de su casa. He threw me out of the house.
4 to expel
□ Lo han echado del colegio. He's been expelled from school.
■ **La echaron del trabajo.** They sacked her.
■ **La chimenea echa humo.** Smoke is coming out of the chimney.
■ **¿Qué echan hoy en la tele?** What's on TV today?
■ **echar de menos a alguien** to miss somebody □ Echo de menos a mi familia. I miss my family.
■ **¿Cuántos años me echas?** How old do you think I am?
■ **echar una ojeada (a)** to browse
■ **echarse 1** to lie down □ Me eché en el sofá y me dormí. I lay down on the sofa and slept. **2** to jump □ Los niños se echaron al agua. The children jumped into the water.

el **eco** NOUN
echo (PL echoes)

la **ecología** NOUN
ecology

ecológico (FEM **ecológica**) ADJECTIVE
ecological
□ un desastre ecológico an ecological disaster
■ **un producto ecológico** an environmentally friendly product

ecologista (FEM **ecologista**) ADJECTIVE
environmental
□ un grupo ecologista an environmental group

el/la **ecologista** NOUN
environmentalist

la **economía** NOUN
1 economy (PL economies)
□ Un país de economía capitalista. A country with a capitalist economy.
2 economics *sing*
□ Quiero estudiar economía. I want to study economics.

económico (FEM **económica**) ADJECTIVE
1 economic
□ una profunda crisis económica a deep economic crisis
2 economical
■ **un motor económico** an economical engine
3 inexpensive
□ Ese restaurante es muy económico. That restaurant's very inexpensive.

el/la **economista** NOUN
economist

economizar* VERB [13]
to economize
□ Economiza en la comida para gastarlo en joyas. She economizes on food to spend money on jewels.

Ecuador MASC NOUN
Ecuador

el **ecuatoriano** (FEM la **ecuatoriana**) ADJECTIVE, NOUN
Ecuadorean

la **edad** NOUN
age
□ Tenemos la misma edad. We're the same age.
■ **¿Qué edad tienen?** How old are they?
■ **No tiene edad para votar.** She isn't old enough to vote.
■ **Está en la edad del pavo.** She's at that difficult age.

la **edición** (PL las **ediciones**) NOUN
edition
□ una edición de bolsillo a pocket edition

edificar* VERB [48]
to build
□ Están edificando un centro deportivo. They're building a sports centre.

el **edificio** NOUN
building

Edimburgo MASC NOUN
Edinburgh

editar VERB [25]
to publish

el **editor**, la **editora** NOUN
publisher

la **editorial** NOUN
publisher

el **edredón** (PL los **edredones**) NOUN
1 eiderdown
2 duvet

la **educación** NOUN
1 education
□ Han aumentado el presupuesto de educación. They've increased the education budget.
■ **educación física** PE
2 upbringing
□ Rosa recibió una educación muy estricta. Rosa had a very strict upbringing.
■ **Señalar es de mala educación.** It's rude to point.
■ **Se lo pedí con educación.** I asked her politely.
■ **Es una falta de educación hablar con la boca llena.** It's bad manners to speak with your mouth full.

educado (FEM **educada**) ADJECTIVE
polite
■ **Me contestó de forma educada.** He answered me politely.
■ **Es un chico bien educado.** He's a well-mannered boy.

educar* VERB [48]
1 to educate
□ Se educó en un colegio alemán. He was educated at a German school.
2 to bring up
□ Educaron a sus hijos de una manera muy estricta. They brought their children up very strictly.

educativo (FEM **educativa**) ADJECTIVE
educational

EE.UU. ABBREVIATION *(= Estados Unidos)*
USA

efectivamente ADVERB
□ Efectivamente, estaba donde tú decías. You were right, he was where you said.
□ Entonces, ¿Es usted su padre? — Efectivamente. So, are you his father? — That's right.

efectivo (FEM **efectiva**) ADJECTIVE
effective
□ un medicamento muy efectivo a very effective medicine
■ **pagar en efectivo** to pay in cash

el **efecto** NOUN
effect
■ **efectos especiales** special effects
■ **hacer efecto** to take effect □ La aspirina enseguida me hizo efecto. The aspirin took effect on me immediately.
■ **en efecto** indeed □ En efecto, fue como tú dijiste. Indeed, it was just as you said.
■ **Devolvió la pelota con efecto.** He put some spin on the ball.

efectuar* VERB [1]
to carry out

eficaz (FEM **eficaz**) ADJECTIVE
1 effective
□ un remedio eficaz an effective remedy
2 efficient
□ un funcionario eficaz an efficient civil servant

eficiente (FEM **eficiente**) ADJECTIVE
efficient

el **egipcio** (FEM la **egipcia**) ADJECTIVE, NOUN
Egyptian

Egipto MASC NOUN
Egypt

el **egoísmo** NOUN
selfishness

egoísta (FEM **egoísta**) ADJECTIVE
selfish

el/la **egoísta** NOUN
□ María es una egoísta. Maria's very selfish.

Eire MASC NOUN
Eire

el **eje** NOUN
1 axle
2 axis

la **ejecución** (PL las **ejecuciones**) NOUN
execution

ejecutar VERB [25]
1 to carry out
□ Ejecutaron el proyecto según lo previsto. They carried out the project according to plan.
2 to execute
□ La ejecutaron al amanecer. They executed her at dawn.

el **ejecutivo**, la **ejecutiva** NOUN
executive

el **ejemplar** NOUN
copy (PL copies)

el **ejemplo** NOUN
example

□ ¿Puedes ponerme un ejemplo? Can you give me an example?
■ **por ejemplo** for example
■ **Debes dar ejemplo a tu hermano pequeño.** You must set your younger brother an example.

ejercer* VERB [6, no vowel change]
■ **Ejerce de abogado.** He's a practising lawyer.
■ **Ejerce mucha influencia sobre sus hermanos.** He has a lot of influence on his brothers.

el **ejercicio** NOUN
exercise
□ La maestra nos puso varios ejercicios. The teacher gave us several exercises to do.
■ **hacer ejercicio** to exercise

el **ejército** NOUN
army (PL armies)

el **ejote** NOUN *(Mexico)*
green bean

el (FEM SING **la**, MASC PL **los**, FEM PL **las**) ARTICLE
the
□ Perdí el autobús. I missed the bus.
■ **el del sombrero rojo** the one with the red hat
■ **Yo fui el que lo encontró.** I was the one who found it. □ Ayer me lavé la cabeza. I washed my hair yesterday. □ Me puse el abrigo. I put my coat on. □ Tiene un coche bonito, pero prefiero el de Juan. He's got a nice car, but I prefer Juan's. □ No me gusta el pescado. I don't like fish. □ Vendrá el lunes que viene. He's coming next Monday. □ Ha llamado el Sr. Sendra. Mr Sendra called.

él PRONOUN
1 he
□ Me lo dijo él. He told me.
2 him
□ Se lo di a él. I gave it to him. □ Su mujer es más alta que él. His wife is taller than him.
■ **él mismo** himself □ No lo sabe ni él mismo. He doesn't even know himself.
■ **de él** his □ El coche es de él. The car's his.

elaborar VERB [25]
to produce

elástico (FEM **elástica**) ADJECTIVE
■ **un tejido elástico** a stretchy material
■ **una goma elástica** an elastic band

la **elección** (PL las **elecciones**) NOUN
1 election
□ Han convocado elecciones generales. General elections have been called.
2 choice
□ Ésa es una buena elección. That's a good choice. □ No tuve elección. I had no choice.

electoral (FEM **electoral**) ADJECTIVE
■ **la campaña electoral** the election campaign

la **electricidad** NOUN
electricity

el/la **electricista** NOUN
electrician
□ Mi primo es electricista. My cousin's an electrician.

eléctrico (FEM **eléctrica**) ADJECTIVE
1 electric
□ una guitarra eléctrica an electric guitar
2 electrical
□ a causa de un fallo eléctrico due to an electrical fault

el **electrodoméstico** NOUN
domestic appliance

la **electrónica** NOUN
electronics *sing*

electrónico (FEM **electrónica**) ADJECTIVE
electronic
■ **el correo electrónico** email

el **elefante** NOUN
elephant

elegante (FEM **elegante**) ADJECTIVE
smart

elegir* VERB [18]
1 to choose
□ No sabía qué color elegir. I didn't know what colour to choose.
■ **Te dan a elegir entre dos modelos.** You're given a choice of two models.
2 to elect
□ Me eligieron delegado de curso. I was elected class representative.

el **elemento** NOUN
element

elevado (FEM **elevada**) ADJECTIVE
high

elevar VERB [25]
to raise

eligiendo VERB ▷ *see* **elegir**

elijo VERB ▷ *see* **elegir**

eliminar VERB [25]
1 to remove
□ un detergente que elimina las manchas a washing powder that removes the stains
2 to eliminate
□ Fueron eliminados de la competición. They were eliminated from the competition.

el **elixir bucal** NOUN
mouthwash

ella PRONOUN
1 she
□ Ella no estaba en casa. She was not at home.
2 her

□ El regalo es para ella. The present's for her. □ Él estaba más nervioso que ella. He was more nervous than her.
■ **ella misma** herself □ Me lo dijo ella misma. She told me herself.
■ **de ella** hers □ Este abrigo es de ella. This coat's hers.

ellos (FEM **ellas**) PL PRONOUN
1 they
□ Ellos todavía no lo saben. They don't know yet.
2 them
□ Yo me iré con ellas. I'll leave with them.
□ Somos mejores que ellos. We're better than them.
■ **ellos mismos** themselves □ Me lo dijeron ellos mismos. They told me themselves.
■ **de ellos** theirs □ El coche era de ellos. The car was theirs.

elogiar VERB [25]
to praise

el **elote** NOUN *(Mexico)*
1 corncob
2 sweetcorn

e-mail NOUN
1 email
2 email address (PL email addresses)

la **embajada** NOUN
embassy (PL embassies)

el **embajador**, la **embajadora** NOUN
ambassador

embalar VERB [25]
to pack

el **embalse** NOUN
reservoir

embarazada (FEM **embarazada**) ADJECTIVE
pregnant
□ Estaba embarazada de cuatro meses. She was four months pregnant.
■ **quedarse embarazada** to get pregnant

LANGUAGE TIP Be careful! **embarazada** does not mean **embarrassed**.

embarazoso (FEM **embarazosa**) ADJECTIVE
embarrassing

embarcar* VERB [48]
to board
□ Los pasajeros ya estaban embarcando. The passengers were already boarding.

el **embargo** NOUN
embargo
■ **sin embargo** nevertheless

embobado (FEM **embobada**) ADJECTIVE
■ **Se quedaron mirándola embobados.** They watched her in fascination.
■ **Está embobado con su novia.** His girlfriend has got him under her spell.

emborracharse VERB [25]
to get drunk

embotellado (FEM **embotellada**) ADJECTIVE
bottled

el **embotellamiento** NOUN
traffic jam

el **embrague** NOUN
clutch

embrollarse VERB [25]
1 to get tangled up
□ Las cuerdas se embrollaron. The ropes got tangled up.
2 to get muddled up
□ Me embrollé con tanta información. With so much information, I got muddled up.

el **embrollo** NOUN
tangle

embrujado (FEM **embrujada**) ADJECTIVE
haunted
□ una casa embrujada a haunted house

el **embudo** NOUN
spout

el **embustero**, la **embustera** NOUN
fibber

el **embutido** NOUN
cold meats
□ No comemos mucho embutido. We don't eat a lot of cold meats.

la **emergencia** NOUN
emergency (PL emergencies)
■ **la salida de emergencia** the emergency exit
■ **en caso de emergencia** in case of emergency

emigrar VERB [25]
1 to emigrate
2 to migrate

la **emisión** (PL las **emisiones**) NOUN
1 broadcast
2 emission

emitir VERB [58]
1 to broadcast
2 to give off

la **emoción** (PL las **emociones**) NOUN
emotion
□ Me temblaba la voz de emoción. My voice was trembling with emotion.
■ **Su carta me produjo gran emoción.** I was very moved by his letter.
■ **¡Qué emoción!** How exciting!

emocionado (FEM **emocionada**) ADJECTIVE
1 moved
2 excited

emocionante (FEM **emocionante**) ADJECTIVE
1 moving
□ La despedida fue muy emocionante. The farewell was very moving.
2 exciting

□ El partido fue muy emocionante. The match was very exciting.

emocionarse VERB [25]
to be moved
□ Me emocioné mucho con la película. I was very moved by the film.
■ **Se emocionó al volver a ver a su padre.** She got emotional when she saw her father again.

emotivo (FEM **emotiva**) ADJECTIVE
1 moving
2 emotional
□ La vuelta a casa fue muy emotiva. It was a very emotional homecoming.

empacharse VERB [25]
to get a tummy upset
□ Me empaché por comer tanto chocolate. I got a tummy upset through eating so much chocolate.

empalagoso (FEM **empalagosa**) ADJECTIVE
sickly

empalmar VERB [25]
1 to connect
□ Empalma los dos cables. Connect the two wires.
2 to join
□ Esta carretera empalma con la autopista. This road joins the motorway.

la **empanada** NOUN
pasty (PL pasties)

empañarse VERB [25]
to get steamed up
□ Se me empañaron las gafas al entrar en el museo. My glasses got steamed up when I went into the museum.
■ **Los cristales del dormitorio estaban empañados.** There was condensation on the bedroom windows.

empapar VERB [25]
to soak
□ Cierra la ducha que me estás empapando. Can you turn the shower off, you're soaking me.
■ **Se me empaparon los calcetines.** My socks got soaked.
■ **estar empapado hasta los huesos** to be soaked to the skin

empapelar VERB [25]
to paper

empaquetar VERB [25]
to pack
□ Empaqueta todos tus libros. Pack all your books.

el **emparedado** NOUN *(Latin America)*
sandwich (PL sandwiches)

emparejar VERB [25]
to pair up *(objetos, personas)*

empastar VERB [25]
■ **Me han empastado dos muelas.** I've had two fillings.

el **empaste** NOUN
filling

empatar VERB [25]
to draw
□ Empatamos a uno. We drew one-all.
□ Los dos candidatos empataron en la votación. The two candidates got the same number of votes.

el **empate** NOUN
1 draw
□ un empate a cero a goalless draw
2 tie

empedernido (FEM **empedernida**) ADJECTIVE
■ **un fumador empedernido** a chronic smoker
■ **Es un lector empedernido.** He's a compulsive reader.

empeñado (FEM **empeñada**) ADJECTIVE
determined
□ Está empeñado en aprobar el curso. He's determined to get through the course.
■ **Está empeñada en que yo soy mayor que ella.** She insists that I'm older than she is.

empeñarse VERB [25]
■ **empeñarse en hacer algo** **1** to be determined to do something □ Se había empeñado en irse con él. She was determined to go with him. **2** to insist on doing something □ Se empeñó en que nos quedáramos a cenar. He insisted that we should stay for dinner.

empeorar VERB [25]
1 to get worse
□ Empeoró tras la operación. He got worse after the operation.
2 to make...worse
□ Tu comentario sólo emperorará las cosas. Your comment will only make matters worse.

empezar* VERB [19]
to start
□ Las vacaciones empiezan el día 1. The holidays start on the first.
■ **empezar a hacer algo** to start doing something □ Ha empezado a nevar. It's started snowing.
■ **volver a empezar** to start again

empinado (FEM **empinada**) ADJECTIVE
steep

el **empleado**, la **empleada** NOUN
1 employee
2 shop assistant *(Latin America)*
■ **una empleada del hogar** a servant

emplear VERB [25]

1 to use
□ Puedes emplear cualquier jabón. You can use any soap.
2 to employ
□ La fábrica emplea a veinte trabajadores. The factory employs twenty workers.
■ **Le está bien empleado.** It serves her right.

el **empleo** NOUN
job
□ Ha encontrado empleo en un restaurante. He has found a job in a restaurant.
■ **estar sin empleo** to be unemployed
■ **'modo de empleo'** 'how to use'

empollar VERB [25]
to swot
□ Me pasé la noche empollando. I spent the whole night swotting.

el **empollón**, la **empollona** (MASC PL los **empollones**) NOUN
swot

la **empresa** NOUN
firm
□ Trabaja en una empresa de informática. He works in a computer firm.

la **empresaria** NOUN
businesswoman (PL businesswomen)

el **empresario** NOUN
businessman (PL businessmen)

empujar VERB [25]
to push
□ Tuvimos que empujarle al coche. We had to push the car.

el **empujón** (PL los **empujones**) NOUN
□ Me dieron un empujón y me caí. They pushed me and I fell.
■ **abrirse paso a empujones** to shove one's way through

en PREPOSITION
1 in
□ en el armario in the wardrobe □ Viven en Granada. They live in Granada. □ Nació en invierno. He was born in winter. □ Lo hice en dos días. I did it in two days. □ Hablamos en inglés. We speak in English. □ Está en el hospital. She's in hospital.
2 into
□ Entré en el banco. I went into the bank.
□ Me metí en la cama a las diez. I got into bed at ten o'clock.
3 on
□ Las llaves están en la mesa. The keys are on the table. □ Lo encontré tirado en el suelo. I found it lying on the floor. □ La librería está en la calle Pelayo. The bookshop is on Pelayo street. □ La oficina está en el quinto piso. The office is on the fifth floor.
■ **Mi cumpleaños cae en viernes.** My birthday falls on a Friday.
4 at
□ Yo estaba en casa. I was at home.
□ Te veo en el cine. See you at the cinema.
□ Vivía en el número 17. I was living at number 17. □ en ese momento at that moment □ en Navidades at Christmas
5 by
□ Vinimos en avión. We came by plane.
■ **ser el primero en llegar** to be the first to arrive

enamorado (FEM **enamorada**) ADJECTIVE
■ **estar enamorado de alguien** to be in love with somebody

enamorarse VERB [25]
to fall in love
□ Se ha enamorado de Yolanda. He's fallen in love with Yolanda. □ Se enamoraron nada más verse. They fell in love at first sight.

el **enano**, la **enana** NOUN
dwarf (PL dwarves)

encabezar* VERB [13]
to head
□ El Betis encabeza la clasificación de la liga. Betis are heading the League. □ la cita que encabeza el artículo the quote heading the article

encajar VERB [25]
1 to fit
□ Las piezas no encajan. The pieces don't fit.
2 to cope with
□ Ha encajado muy bien la muerte de su madre. She's coped very well with her mother's death.

encaminarse VERB [25]
■ **Nos encaminamos hacia el pueblo.** We headed towards the village.

encantado (FEM **encantada**) ADJECTIVE
1 delighted
□ Está encantada con su nuevo coche. She's delighted with her new car.
2 enchanted
□ un castillo encantado an enchanted castle
■ **¡Encantado de conocerle!** Pleased to meet you!

encantador (FEM **encantadora**) ADJECTIVE
charming

encantar VERB [25]
to love
□ Me encantan los animales. I love animals.
□ Les encanta esquiar. They love skiing.
□ Me encantaría que vinieras. I'd love you to come.

el **encanto** NOUN
charm

■ **Eugenia es un encanto.** Eugenia is charming.

encarcelar VERB [25]
to imprison

el **encargado**, la **encargada** NOUN
manager
□ Quiero hablar con el encargado. I'd like to talk to the manager.

encargar* VERB [37]
1 to order
□ Encargamos dos pizzas. We ordered two pizzas.
2 to ask
□ Le encargó que le recogiera los documentos. She asked him to fetch the documents for her.
■ **Yo me encargaré de avisar a los demás.** I'll take care of letting the others know.
■ **Estoy encargada de vender las entradas.** I'm in charge of selling the tickets.

encariñarse VERB [25]
■ **encariñarse con** to grow fond of

el **encendedor** NOUN
lighter

encender* VERB [20]
1 to light
2 to switch on

encendido (FEM **encendida**) ADJECTIVE
1 on
□ La tele estaba encendida. The telly was on.
2 lit
□ El cigarro no está bien encendido. Your cigarette isn't properly lit.

el **encerado** NOUN
blackboard

encerrar* VERB [39]
1 to shut up
□ Encerré el gato en la cocina. I shut the cat up in the kitchen. □ Me encerré en mi cuarto para estudiar. I shut myself up in my room to study.
2 to lock up
□ Lo encerraron en un calabozo. They locked him up in a cell.
■ **Los manifestantes se encerraron en el ayuntamiento.** The demonstrators held a sit-in in the town hall.

la **enchilada** NOUN *(Mexico)*
stuffed tortilla

el **enchufado**, la **enchufada** NOUN
■ **Amelia es la enchufada del profesor.** *(colloquial)* Amelia's the teacher's pet.

enchufar VERB [25]
to plug in
□ Enchufa la tele. Plug the TV in.

el **enchufe** NOUN
1 plug
2 socket
■ **Consiguió ese puesto por enchufe.** He got that job through pulling strings.

la **encía** NOUN
gum

la **enciclopedia** NOUN
encyclopaedia

enciendo VERB ▷ *see* **encender**

encierro VERB ▷ *see* **encerrar**

encima ADVERB
on
□ Pon el cenicero aquí encima. Put the ashtray on there. □ No llevo dinero encima. I haven't got any money on me.
■ **encima de 1** on □ Ponlo encima de la mesa. Put it on the table. **2** on top of □ Mi maleta está encima del armario. My case is on top of the wardrobe.
■ **Lo leí por encima.** I glanced at it.
■ **por encima de 1** above □ Los helicópteros volaban por encima de nuestras cabezas. The helicopters were flying above our heads. □ Las temperaturas han subido por encima de lo normal. Temperatures have been above average. **2** over □ Tuve que saltar por encima de la mesa. I had to jump over the table.
■ **¡Y encima no te da ni las gracias!** And on top of it he doesn't even thank you!

la **encina** NOUN
oak tree

encoger* VERB [7]
to shrink
□ Este jersey ha encogido. This jumper has shrunk.
■ **Antonio se encogió de hombros.** Antonio shrugged his shoulders.

encontrar* VERB [11]
to find
□ Mi hermano ha encontrado trabajo. My brother has found a job. □ Lo encuentro un poco arrogante. I find him a bit arrogant.
■ **No encuentro las llaves.** I can't find the keys.
■ **encontrarse 1** to feel □ Ahora se encuentra mejor. Now she's feeling better. **2** to meet □ Nos encontramos en el cine. We met at the cinema.
■ **Me encontré con Manolo en la calle.** I bumped into Manolo in the street.

el **encuentro** NOUN
1 meeting
■ **punto de encuentro** meeting point
2 match (PL matches)

la **encuesta** NOUN
survey

enderezar* VERB [13]

to straigthen

endulzar* VERB [13]

to sweeten

endurecer* VERB [12]

to tone up

el **enemigo** (FEM la **enemiga**) ADJECTIVE, NOUN

enemy (PL enemies)

□ el ejército enemigo the enemy army

enemistarse VERB [25]

to fall out

□ Se enemistó con sus primos. He fell out with his cousins.

la **energía** NOUN

energy

□ ahorrar energía to save energy

■ **la energía solar** solar power

■ **la energía eléctrica** electricity

enérgico (FEM **enérgica**) ADJECTIVE

energetic

□ Es una persona muy enérgica. She's very energetic.

enero MASC NOUN

January

□ en enero in January □ Nació el 6 de enero. He was born on 6 January.

enfadado (FEM **enfadada**) ADJECTIVE

angry

□ Mi padre estaba muy enfadado conmigo. My father was very angry with me.

■ **Ana y su novio están enfadados.** Ana and her boyfriend have fallen out.

enfadarse VERB [25]

to be angry

□ Papá se va a enfadar mucho contigo. Dad will be very angry with you.

■ **Mi hermana y su novio se han enfadado.** My brother and his girlfriend have fallen out.

el **enfado** NOUN

■ **Ya se le ha pasado el enfado.** He isn't angry anymore.

enfermarse VERB [25] *(Latin America)*

to fall ill

la **enfermedad** NOUN

1 illness (PL illnesses)

□ Adelgazó mucho durante su enfermedad. He lost a lot of weight during his illness.

2 disease

□ Tiene una enfermedad contagiosa. He's got an infectious disease.

la **enfermería** NOUN

sick bay

el **enfermero**, la **enfermera** NOUN

nurse

□ Mi madre es enfermera. My mother's a nurse.

enfermo (FEM **enferma**) ADJECTIVE

ill

□ He estado enferma toda la semana. I've been ill all week.

■ **¿Cuándo te pusiste enfermo?** When did you get ill?

■ **¡Me pones enfermo!** You make me sick!

el **enfermo**, la **enferma** NOUN

patient

■ **Los enfermos deben tomar precauciones especiales.** Sick people need to take special precautions.

enfocar* VERB [48]

1 to focus on

□ El fotógrafo enfocó el ciervo. The photographer focussed on the deer.

2 to approach

□ Depende de cómo enfoques el problema. It depends on how you approach the problem.

enfrentarse VERB [25]

■ **enfrentarse a algo** to face something

□ Tienes que enfrentarte al problema. You have to face the problem.

enfrente ADVERB

opposite

□ Luisa estaba sentada enfrente. Luisa was sitting opposite.

■ **La panadería está enfrente.** The baker's is across the street.

■ **de enfrente** opposite □ la casa de enfrente the house opposite

■ **enfrente de** opposite □ Mi casa está enfrente del colegio. My house is opposite the school.

enfriarse* VERB [21]

1 to get cold

□ La sopa se ha enfriado. The soup has got cold.

2 to cool down

□ Hay que dejar que se enfríe el motor. We must let the engine cool down.

3 to catch cold

□ Ponte el abrigo que te vas a enfriar. Put your coat on or you'll catch cold.

enganchar VERB [25]

to hook

□ Enganché la correa al collar del perro. I hooked the lead onto the dog's collar.

■ **engancharse** to get caught □ Se me enganchó el jersey en la valla. My jumper got caught on a rosebush.

engañar VERB [25]

1 to cheat

□ Te han engañado: no es de oro. You've been cheated. It's not gold.

2 to lie

□ No me engañes y dime quién lo hizo. Don't lie to me and tell me who did it.

3 to cheat on

□ Su novio la engaña. Her boyfriend is cheating on her.
■ **Las apariencias engañan.** Appearances can be deceptive.

el **engaño** NOUN
1 con
□ Fue un engaño. It was a con.
2 deception
□ Carmen siguió manteniendo el engaño. Carmen continued to keep up the deception.

engordar VERB [25]
1 to put on weight
□ No quiero engordar. I don't want to put on weight.
■ **He engordado dos kilos.** I've put on two kilos.
2 to be fattening
□ Los caramelos engordan mucho. Sweets are very fattening.

engreído (FEM **engreída**) ADJECTIVE
conceited

la **enhorabuena** NOUN
■ **¡Enhorabuena!** Congratulations!
■ **Me dieron la enhorabuena por el premio.** They congratulated me on winning the prize.

el **enlace** NOUN
1 connection
■ **Perdí el enlace con Buenos Aires.** I missed the connecting flight to Buenos Aires.
2 link

enlatado (FEM **enlatada**) ADJECTIVE
tinned

enlazar* VERB [13]
to connect
□ Este vuelo enlaza con el de Moscú. This flight connects with the Moscow flight.

enloquecer* VERB [12]
to be crazy about
□ Le enloquecen las motos. He's crazy about motorbikes.

enmarcar* VERB [48]
to frame

enmoquetado (FEM **enmoquetada**) ADJECTIVE
carpeted

enojado (FEM **enojada**) ADJECTIVE
angry
□ Mi padre estaba muy enojado conmigo. My father was very angry with me.
■ **Ana y su novio están enojados.** Ana and her boyfriend have fallen out.

enojarse VERB [25]
to be angry
□ Mi madre se va a enojar. My mother will be angry. □ Manolo y Luis se han enojado. Manolo and Luis have fallen out.

enorme (FEM **enorme**) ADJECTIVE
enormous
□ Tienen una casa enorme. They have an enormous house.

la **enredadera** NOUN
creeper

enredarse VERB [25]
1 to get tangled up
□ Se me ha enredado el pelo. My hair's got all tangled up.
2 to get into a tangle
□ Me enredé haciendo las cuentas. I got into a tangle with the accounts.

enrevesado (FEM **enrevesada**) ADJECTIVE
difficult

enriquecerse* VERB [12]
to get rich
□ Se enriquecieron tratando con armas. They got rich dealing in arms.

enrollar VERB [25]
to roll up
□ No dobles el póster, enróllalo. Don't fold the poster, roll it up. □ Enrolla la cuerda en este palo. Roll the rope round the stick.
■ **Se enrolló con Juan en la discoteca.** *(colloquial)* She got off with Juan in the disco.

enroscar* VERB [48]
1 to screw in
■ **Enrosca bien la tapa.** Screw the top on tight.
2 to coil
□ La manguera se le enroscó en la pierna. The hose coiled round his leg.

la **ensalada** NOUN
salad

la **ensaladilla** NOUN
■ **una ensaladilla rusa** a Russian salad

ensanchar VERB [25]
to widen
□ Están ensanchando la carretera. They're widening the road.
■ **ensancharse** to stretch □ Mi jersey se ha ensanchado. My jumper has stretched.

ensayar VERB [25]
to rehearse

el **ensayo** NOUN
reharsal
□ Esta tarde tenemos ensayo. We've got a rehearsal this afternoon.

enseguida ADVERB
straight away
□ La ambulancia llegó enseguida. The ambulance arrived straight away.
■ **Enseguida te atiendo.** I'll be with you in a minute.

la **enseñanza** NOUN
1 teaching

□ la enseñanza de lenguas extranjeras the teaching of foreign languages
2 education
□ Debería invertirse más dinero en la enseñanza. More money should be invested in education.
■ **la enseñanza primaria** primary education

enseñar VERB [25]
1 to teach
□ Ricardo enseña inglés en un colegio. Ricardo teaches English in a school. □ Mi padre me enseñó a nadar. My father taught me to swim.
2 to show
□ Ana me enseñó todos sus videojuegos. Ana showed me all her video games.
■ **Les enseñé el colegio.** I showed them round the school.

ensuciar VERB [25]
to get...dirty
□ Vas a ensuciar el sofá. You'll get the sofa dirty.
■ **ensuciarse** to get dirty □ No toques la pintura que te vas a ensuciar. Don't touch the paint or you'll get dirty. □ Me he ensuciado las manos. I've got my hands dirty.
■ **Te has ensuciado de barro los pantalones.** You've got mud on your trousers.

entender* VERB [20]
to understand
□ No entiendo el francés. I don't understand French. □ ¿Lo entiendes? Do you understand?
■ **¿Entiendes lo que quiero decir?** Do you know what I mean?
■ **Creo que lo he entendido mal.** I think I've misunderstood.
■ **Mi primo entiende mucho de coches.** My cousin knows a lot about cars.
■ **entenderse 1** to get on □ Mi hermana y yo no nos entendemos. My sister and I don't get on. **2** to communicate □ Se entienden por gestos. They communicate through sign language.
■ **Dio a entender que no le gustaba.** He implied that he didn't like it.

el **entendido**, la **entendida** NOUN
expert
□ No soy un entendido en el tema. I'm not an expert on the subject.

enterarse VERB [25]
1 to find out
□ Me enteré por Manolo. I found out from Manolo. □ Entérate bien de todos los detalles. Make sure you find out about all the details.
■ **Se enteraron del accidente por la tele.** They heard about the accident on the TV.
■ **Me sacaron una muela y ni me enteré.** They took out a tooth and I didn't notice a thing.
2 to understand
□ No me hables en francés que no me entero. Don't talk to me in French - I won't understand.

entero (FEM **entera**) ADJECTIVE
whole
□ Se comió el paquete entero de galletas. He ate the whole packet of biscuits. □ Se pasó la noche entera estudiando. He spent the whole night studying.
■ **la leche entera** full-cream milk

enterrar* VERB [39]
to bury

entiendo VERB ▷ *see* **entender**

entierro VERB ▷ *see* **enterrar**

el **entierro** NOUN
funeral

entonces ADVERB
1 then
□ Si no es tu padre, ¿entonces quién es? If he isn't your father, then who is he? □ Me recogió y entonces fuimos al cine. He picked me up and then we went to the cinema. □ Iban andando porque entonces no tenían coche. They would walk because they didn't have a car then.
2 so
□ ¿Entonces, vienes o te quedas? So, are you coming or staying?
■ **desde entonces** since then
■ **para entonces** by then

el **entorno** NOUN
surroundings *pl*

la **entrada** NOUN
1 entrance
□ Nos vemos en la entrada. I'll see you at the entrance.
■ **'entrada libre'** 'free admission'
2 ticket
□ Tengo entradas para el teatro. I've got tickets for the theatre.
3 entry (PL entries)
□ la entrada de España en el conflicto Spain's entry into the conflict
■ **'prohibida la entrada'** 'no entry'
4 deposit
□ Dimos una entrada de diez mil euros. We paid a ten-thousand-euro deposit.

el **entrante** NOUN
starter

entrar VERB [25]
1 to go in

□ Abrí la puerta y entré. I opened the door and went in. □ Mi amiga entró al banco. My friend went into the bank.

■ **Pedro entra a trabajar a las 8.** Pedro starts work at 8 o'clock.

■ **No me dejaron entrar por ser menor de 16 años.** They wouldn't let me in because I was under 16.

2 to come in

□ ¿Se puede? — Sí, entra. May I? — Yes, come in. □ Entraron en mi cuarto mientras yo dormía. They came into my room while I was asleep.

3 to fit

□ Estos zapatos no me entran. These shoes don't fit me. □ La maleta no entra en el maletero. The case won't fit in the boot.

■ **El vino no entra en el precio.** The wine is not included in the price.

■ **Le entraron ganas de reír.** She wanted to laugh.

■ **De repente le entró sueño.** He suddenly felt sleepy.

■ **Me ha entrado hambre al verte comer.** Watching you eat has made me hungry.

entre PREPOSITION

1 between

□ Lo terminamos entre los dos. Between the two of us we finished it. □ Vendrá entre las diez y las once. He'll be coming between ten and eleven.

2 among

□ Había un baúl entre las maletas. There was a trunk in among the cases. □ Las mujeres hablaban entre sí. The women were talking among themselves.

■ **Le compraremos un regalo entre todos.** We'll buy her a present between all of us.

3 by

□ 15 dividido entre 3 es 5. 15 divided by 3 is 5

entreabierto (FEM **entreabierta**) ADJECTIVE

ajar

entregar* VERB [37]

1 to hand in

□ Marta entregó el examen. Marta handed her exam paper in.

2 to deliver

□ El cartero entregó el paquete. The postman delivered the parcel.

3 to present with

□ El director le entregó la medalla. The director presented him with the medal.

■ **El ladrón se entregó a la policía.** The thief gave himself up.

los **entremeses** NOUN

appetizers

el **entrenador**, la **entrenadora** NOUN

coach (PL coaches)

el **entrenamiento** NOUN

training

entrenarse VERB [25]

to train

entretanto ADVERB

meanwhile

entretener* VERB [53]

1 to entertain

■ **La tele entretiene mucho.** TV is very entertaining.

2 to keep

□ Una vecina me entretuvo hablando en las escaleras. A neighbour kept me talking on the stairs.

■ **entretenerse** to amuse oneself □ Se entretienen viendo los dibujos animados. They amuse themselves by watching cartoons.

■ **No os entretengáis jugando.** Don't hang about playing.

entretenido (FEM **entretenida**) ADJECTIVE

entertaining

□ La película es muy entretenida. The film is very entertaining.

la **entrevista** NOUN

interview

■ **hacer una entrevista a alguien** to interview somebody □ Le hicieron una entrevista por la radio. They interviewed her on the radio.

el **entrevistador**, la **entrevistadora** NOUN

interviewer

entrevistar VERB [25]

to interview

entrometerse VERB [8]

to meddle

□ No te entrometas en mis asuntos. Don't meddle in my affairs.

entusiasmado (FEM **entusiasmada**) ADJECTIVE

excited

□ Estaba entusiasmado con su fiesta de cumpleaños. He was excited about his birthday party.

entusiasmarse VERB [25]

to get excited

□ Se entusiasmó con la idea de hacer una fiesta. He got very excited about the idea of having a party.

el **entusiasmo** NOUN

enthusiasm

■ **con entusiasmo** enthusiastically

enumerar VERB [25]

to list

el **envase** NOUN

container

□ Viene en envases de plástico. It comes in a plastic container.
■ **'envase no retornable'** 'non-returnable bottle'

envejecer* VERB [12]
to age
□ Sus padres han envejecido mucho. His parents have aged a lot.

enviar* VERB [21]
to send
□ Envíame las fotos. Send me the photos.
■ **Juan me envió el regalo por correo.** Juan posted me the present.

la **envidia** NOUN
envy
■ **¡Qué envidia!** I'm so jealous!
■ **Le tiene envidia a Ana.** She's jealous of Ana.
■ **Le da envidia que mi coche sea mejor.** He's jealous that my car is better.

envidiar VERB [25]
to envy
□ ¡No te envidio! I don't envy you!

envidioso (FEM **envidiosa**) ADJECTIVE
envious

envolver* VERB [59]
to wrap up
□ Llevaba al niño envuelto en una manta. She carried the baby wrapped up in a blanket.
■ **¿Desea que se lo envuelva para regalo?** Would you like it gift-wrapped?

envuelto VERB ▷ *see* **envolver**

la **epidemia** NOUN
epidemic

el **episodio** NOUN
episode

la **época** NOUN
time
□ En aquella época vivíamos en Alicante. At that time we were living in Alicante.
□ en esta época del año at this time of year

equilibrado (FEM **equilibrada**) ADJECTIVE
balanced

el **equilibrio** NOUN
balance
□ Perdí el equilibrio y me caí. I lost my balance and fell over. □ Luis podía mantener el equilibrio en la cuerda floja. Luis managed to keep his balance on the tightrope.

el **equipaje** NOUN
luggage
■ **equipaje de mano** hand luggage

el **equipo** NOUN
1 team
□ un equipo de baloncesto a basketball team
2 equipment
□ Me robaron todo el equipo de esquí. They stole all my skiing equipment.
■ **el equipo de música** the stereo

LANGUAGE TIP Word for word, **equipo de música** means 'music equipment'.

la **equitación** NOUN
riding

equivaler* VERB [55]
■ **equivaler a algo** to be equivalent to something

la **equivocación** (PL las **equivocaciones**) NOUN
mistake
■ **He marcado otro número por equivocación.** I dialled another number by mistake.

equivocado (FEM **equivocada**) ADJECTIVE
wrong
□ Estás equivocada. You're wrong. □ Elena me dio el número equivocado. Elena gave me the wrong number.

equivocarse* VERB [48]
1 to make a mistake
□ Me equivoqué muchas veces en el examen. I made a lot of mistakes in the exam.
2 to be wrong
□ Si crees que voy a dejarte ir, te equivocas. If you think I'm going to let you go, you're wrong.
■ **Perdone, me he equivocado de número.** Sorry, wrong number.
■ **Se equivocaron de tren.** They caught the wrong train.

era VERB ▷ *see* **ser**

eres VERB ▷ *see* **ser**

el **erizo** NOUN
hedgehog
■ **un erizo de mar** a sea urchin

el **error** NOUN
mistake
□ Fue un error contárselo a Luisa. Telling Luisa about it was a mistake. □ Cometí muchos errores en el examen. I made a lot of mistakes in the exam.

eructar VERB [25]
to burp

el **eructo** NOUN
burp

es VERB ▷ *see* **ser**

esa ADJECTIVE ▷ *see* **ese**

ésa PRONOUN ▷ *see* **ése**

esbelto (FEM **esbelta**) ADJECTIVE
slender

escabullirse* VERB [45]
1 to slip away
□ Se escabulló de la fiesta. He managed to

slip away from the party.

2 to wriggle out of

□ No debes escabullirte de tus obligaciones. You mustn't try to wriggle out of your responsibilities.

la **escala** NOUN

1 scale

□ a escala nacional on a national scale

2 stopover

□ Tenemos una escala de tres horas en Bruselas. We've got a three-hour stopover in Brussels.

■ **Hicimos escala en Roma.** We stopped over in Rome.

escalar VERB [25]

to climb

la **escalera** NOUN

stairs *pl*

□ bajar las escaleras to go down the stairs

■ **una escalera de mármol** a marble staircase

■ **una escalera de mano** a ladder

LANGUAGE TIP Word for word, **escalera de mano** means 'hand stairs'.

■ **la escalera de incendios** the fire escape

■ **una escalera mecánica** an escalator

el **escalofrío** NOUN

■ **Tengo escalofríos.** I'm shivering.

■ **La escena te produce escalofríos.** The scene makes you shudder.

el **escalón** (PL los **escalones**) NOUN

step

la **escama** NOUN

scale

escandalizarse* VERB [13]

to shock

□ Mi abuela se escandalizó. My grandmother was shocked.

el **escándalo** NOUN

1 scandal

■ **La boda produjo un gran escándalo.** The wedding caused a huge scandal.

2 racket

□ ¿Qué escándalo es éste? What's all this racket?

escandaloso (FEM **escandalosa**) ADJECTIVE

noisy

el **escandinavo** ADJECTIVE, NOUN

Scandinavian

■ **un escandinavo** a Scandinavian

■ **una escandinava** a Scandinavian

■ **los escandinavos** the Scandinavians

el **escáner** NOUN

1 scanner

2 scan

□ hacerse un escáner to have a scan

escapar VERB [25]

to escape

□ Conseguí escapar de la fiesta. I managed to escape from the party.

■ **No quiero dejar escapar esta oportunidad.** I don't want to let this opportunity slip.

■ **escaparse** to escape □ El ladrón se escapó de la cárcel. The thief escaped from prison. □ El calor se escapa por esta rendija. The heat escapes through this grill.

■ **Se me escapó un eructo.** I let out a burp.

el **escaparate** NOUN

shop window

■ **ir de escaparates** to go window-shopping

el **escape** NOUN

leak

□ Había un escape de gas. There was a gas leak.

escaquearse VERB [25]

■ **escaquearse de clase** to skip school

el **escarabajo** NOUN

beetle

escarbar VERB [25]

to dig

□ Los niños escarbaban en la arena. The children were digging in the sand.

la **escarcha** NOUN

frost

la **escasez** NOUN

shortage

□ Hay escasez de agua. There is a shortage of water.

escaso (FEM **escasa**) ADJECTIVE

scarce

□ Los alimentos eran muy escasos. Food was scarce.

■ **Habrá escasa visibilidad en las carreteras.** Visibility on the roads will be poor.

■ **Duró una hora escasa.** It lasted barely an hour.

la **escayola** NOUN

plaster

□ Mañana me quitan la escayola. I'm getting my plaster taken off tomorrow.

escayolar VERB [25]

■ **Le escayolaron la pierna.** They put his leg in plaster.

la **escena** NOUN

scene

el **escenario** NOUN

stage

escéptico (FEM **escéptica**) ADJECTIVE

sceptical

el **esclavo**, la **esclava** NOUN

slave

la **escoba** NOUN

broom

escocer* VERB [6]
to sting
□ Me escuecen los ojos. My eyes are stinging.

escocés (FEM **escocesa**, MASC PL **escoceses**) ADJECTIVE
Scottish
■ **el whisky escocés** Scotch whisky
■ **una falda escocesa** a kilt

el **escocés** (PL los **escoceses**) NOUN
Scotsman (PL Scotsmen)
□ los escoceses Scottish people

la **escocesa** NOUN
Scotswoman (PL Scotswomen)

Escocia FEM NOUN
Scotland

escoger* VERB [7]
to choose
□ Yo escogí el azul. I chose the blue one.

escolar (FEM **escolar**) ADJECTIVE
school
□ el uniforme escolar school uniform

los **escombros** NOUN
rubble *sing*

esconder VERB [8]
to hide
□ Lo escondí en el cajón. I hid it in the box.
■ **Me escondí debajo de la cama.** I hid under the bed.

las **escondidas** NOUN
■ **jugar a las escondidas** *(Latin America)* to play hide-and-seek
■ **a escondidas** in secret □ Fuman a escondidas. They smoke in secret.

el **escondite** NOUN
■ **jugar al escondite** to play hide-and-seek

la **escopeta** NOUN
shotgun

Escorpio MASC NOUN
Scorpio
■ **Soy escorpio.** I'm Scorpio.

el **escorpión** (PL los **escorpiones**) NOUN
scorpion

escribir* VERB [58, PAST PARTICIPLE **escrito**]
to write
□ Les escribí una carta. I wrote them a letter. □ Escribe pronto. Write soon.
■ **Nos escribimos de vez en cuando.** We write to each other from time to time.
■ **¿Cómo se escribe tu nombre?** How do you spell your name?
■ **escribir a máquina** to type

escrito (FEM **escrita**) ADJECTIVE
written
□ un examen escrito a written exam

el **escritor**, la **escritora** NOUN
writer
□ Pablo es escritor. Pablo's a writer.

el **escritorio** NOUN
1 desk
2 office *(Latin America)*

la **escritura** NOUN
writing

escrupuloso (FEM **escrupulosa**) ADJECTIVE
fussy
□ Es muy escrupuloso con la comida. He's very fussy about food.

escuchar VERB [25]
to listen
□ Juan escuchaba con atención. Juan was listening attentively. □ Escucha el consejo de tus padres. Listen to your parents' advice. □ Me gusta escuchar música. I like listening to music.

el **escudo** NOUN
1 shield
2 badge

la **escuela** NOUN
school
□ Hoy no tengo que ir a la escuela. I don't have to go to school today.
■ **la escuela primaria** primary school
■ **Escuela Oficial de Idiomas**

> **DID YOU KNOW...?**
> The **Escuelas Oficiales** are state-run language schools where you can study a wide range of foreign languages. The qualification obtained is highly regarded.

esculcar* VERB [48] *(Mexico)*
to search

la **escultura** NOUN
sculpture

escupir VERB [58]
to spit

escurridizo (FEM **escurridiza**) ADJECTIVE
slippery

el **escurridor** NOUN
1 colander
2 plate rack

escurrir VERB [58]
1 to wring
2 to drain

ese (FEM **esa**) ADJECTIVE
that
□ Dame ese libro. Give me that book.
■ **A partir de ese momento empezó a mejorar.** From then on it began to get better.

ése (FEM **ésa**) PRONOUN
that one
□ Prefiero ésa. I prefer that one.
■ **¿Quién es ése?** Who's that?

esencial (FEM **esencial**) ADJECTIVE
essential

He entendido lo esencial de la conversación. I understood the main points of the conversation.

esforzarse* VERB [3]
to make an effort
□ Tienes que esforzarte si quieres ganar. You have to make an effort if you want to win.
■ **Se esforzó todo lo que pudo por aprobar el examen.** He did all he could to pass the exam.

el **esfuerzo** NOUN
effort
□ Tuve que hacer un esfuerzo para comer. I had to make an effort to eat.

esfumarse VERB [25]
to vanish

la **esgrima** NOUN
fencing

el **esguince** NOUN
sprain
■ **Me hice un esguince en el tobillo.** I've sprained my ankle.

el **esmalte** NOUN
■ **el esmalte de uñas** nail varnish

esmerarse VERB [25]
■ **Se esmeró para que todo saliera bien.** He did his best so that everything came out right.
■ **No necesitas esmerarte tanto en la presentación.** You don't need to make such an effort with the presentation.

esnob (FEM **esnob**, PL **esnobs**) ADJECTIVE
snobbish

la **ESO** ABBREVIATION *(= Enseñanza Secundaria obligatoria)*

DID YOU KNOW...?
ESO is the compulsory secondary education course done by 12 to 16 year-olds.

eso PRONOUN
that
□ Eso es mentira. That's a lie. □ ¡Eso es! That's it!
■ **a eso de las cinco** at about five
■ **En eso llamaron a la puerta.** Just then there was a ring at the door.
■ **Por eso te lo dije.** That's why I told you.
■ **¡Y eso que estaba lloviendo!** And it was raining and everything!

esos (FEM **esas**) PL ADJECTIVE
those
□ Trae esas sillas aquí. Bring those chairs over here.

ésos (FEM **ésas**) PL PRONOUN
those ones
□ Ésos de ahí son mejores. Those ones over there are better.
■ **Ésos no son los que vimos ayer.** Those aren't the ones we saw yesterday.

espabilar VERB [25] = **despabilar**

el **espacio** NOUN
1 room
□ No hay espacio para tantas sillas. There isn't room for so many chairs. □ El piano ocupa mucho espacio. The piano takes up a lot of room.
2 space
□ Deja más espacio entre las líneas. Leave more space between the lines.
■ **un espacio en blanco** a gap
■ **viajar por el espacio** to travel in space

la **espada** NOUN
sword
■ **espadas**

DID YOU KNOW...?
Espadas are swords, one of the suits in the Spanish card deck.

LANGUAGE TIP Be careful! **espada** does not mean **spade**.

los **espaguetis** NOUN
spaghetti *sing*

la **espalda** NOUN
back
□ Me duele la espalda. My back aches.
■ **Estaba tumbada de espaldas.** She was lying on her back.
■ **Ana estaba de espaldas a mí.** Ana had her back to me.
■ **Le dispararon por la espalda.** They shot him from behind.
■ **Me encanta nadar a espalda.** I love swimming backstroke.

el **espantapájaros** (PL los **espantapájaros**) NOUN
scarecrow

espantar VERB [25]
1 to frighten
2 to frighten off
3 to horrify
□ Me espantan los zapatos de tacón. I hate high heels.
■ **espantarse** to get frightened

espantoso (FEM **espantosa**) ADJECTIVE
awful
□ un monstruo espantoso an awful monster □ Los niños hacían un ruido espantoso. The children were making an awful noise.
■ **Hacía un frío espantoso.** It was awfully cold.

España FEM NOUN
Spain

español (FEM **española**) ADJECTIVE
Spanish

el **español**, la **española** NOUN

Spaniard
■ **los españoles** the Spanish
el **español** NOUN
Spanish
el **esparadrapo** NOUN
plaster
□ Me puse un esparadrapo en la herida. I put a plaster on the wound.
el **espárrago** NOUN
asparagus
□ ¿Te gustan los espárragos? Do you like asparagus?
■ **La mandé a freir espárragos.** I told her to buzz off.
la **especia** NOUN
spice
especial (FEM **especial**) ADJECTIVE
special
□ Fue un día muy especial. It was a very special day.
■ **en especial** particularly □ ¿Desea ver a alguien en especial? Is there anybody you particularly want to see?
la **especialidad** NOUN
speciality (PL specialities)
□ la especialidad de la casa the speciality of the house
el/la **especialista** NOUN
specialist
especializarse* VERB [13]
■ **Rosario se especializó en pediatría.** Rosario specialized in paediatrics.
especialmente ADVERB
1 especially
□ Me gusta mucho el pan, especialmente el integral. I love bread, especially wholemeal bread.
2 specially
□ un vestido diseñado especialmente para ella a dress designed specially for her
la **especie** NOUN
species
específico (FEM **específica**) ADJECTIVE
specific
espectacular (FEM **espectaculara**) ADJECTIVE
spectacular
el **espectáculo** NOUN
performance
□ El espectáculo empieza a las ocho. The performance starts at eight.
■ **Dio el espectáculo delante de todo el mundo.** He made a spectacle of himself in front of everyone.
el **espectador**, la **espectadora** NOUN
spectator
■ **los espectadores** the audience
el **espejo** NOUN
mirror
□ Me miré en el espejo. I looked at myself in the mirror.
■ **el espejo retrovisor** rearview mirror
espeluznante (FEM **espeluznante**) ADJECTIVE
hair-raising
la **espera** NOUN
wait
□ tras una espera de tres horas after a three-hour wait
■ **estar a la espera de algo** to be expecting something
la **esperanza** NOUN
hope
■ **No tengo esperanzas de aprobar.** I have no hope of passing.
■ **No pierdas las esperanzas.** Don't give up hope.
esperar VERB [25]
1 to wait
□ Espera en la puerta, ahora mismo voy. Wait at the door. I'm just coming.
■ **Espera un momento, por favor.** Hang on a moment, please.
2 to wait for
□ No me esperéis. Don't wait for me.
■ **Me hizo esperar una hora.** He kept me waiting for an hour.
3 to expect
□ Llegaron antes de lo que yo esperaba. They arrived sooner than I expected.
□ Esperaban que Juan les pidiera perdón. They were expecting Juan to apologize.
□ Llamará cuando menos lo esperes. He'll call when you're least expecting it. □ No esperes que venga a ayudarte. Don't expect him to come and help you.
■ **esperar un bebé** to be expecting a baby
■ **Me espera un largo día de trabajo.** I've got a long day of work ahead of me.
■ **Era de esperar que no viniera.** He was bound not to come.
4 to hope
□ Espero que no sea nada grave. I hope it isn't anything serious.
■ **¿Vendrás a la fiesta? — Espero que sí.** Are you coming to the party? — I hope so.
■ **¿Crees que Carmen se enfadará? — Espero que no.** Do you think Carmen will be angry? — I hope not.
■ **Fuimos a esperarla a la estación.** We went to the station to meet her.
espeso (FEM **espesa**) ADJECTIVE
thick
el/la **espía** NOUN
spy (PL spies)
espiar* VERB [21]

Spanish-English

e

to spy on
□ Los vecinos nos espiaban. The neighbours were spying on us.

la **espina** NOUN
1 thorn
2 bone
■ **espina dorsal** backbone

la **espinaca** NOUN
spinach
□ No me gustan las espinacas. I don't like spinach.

la **espinilla** NOUN
1 shin
2 blackhead

el **espionaje** NOUN
spying
■ **una novela de espionaje** a spy story

espirar VERB [25]
to breathe out

el **espíritu** NOUN
spirit

espiritual (FEM **espiritual**) ADJECTIVE
spiritual

espléndido (FEM **espléndida**) ADJECTIVE
splendid

la **esponja** NOUN
sponge

esponjoso (FEM **esponjosa**) ADJECTIVE
spongy

espontáneo (FEM **espontánea**) ADJECTIVE
spontaneous
□ Fue una reacción espontánea. It was a spontaneous reaction.
■ **de manera espontánea** spontaneously

la **esposa** NOUN
wife (PL wives)
■ **las esposas** handcuffs

el **esposo** NOUN
husband

la **espuma** NOUN
1 foam
2 head
■ **la espuma de afeitar** shaving cream

espumoso (FEM **espumosa**) ADJECTIVE
■ **vino espumoso** sparkling wine

el **esqueleto** NOUN
skeleton

el **esquema** NOUN
1 outline
2 diagram

el **esquí** (PL los **esquís**) NOUN
1 skiing
□ Me gusta mucho el esquí. I enjoy skiing a lot.
■ **el esquí acuático** water skiing
■ **una pista de esquí** a ski slope
2 ski (PL skis)

esquiar* VERB [21]
to ski
□ ¿Sabes esquiar? Can you ski?

el/la **esquimal** ADJECTIVE, NOUN
Inuit (PL Inuit)

la **esquina** NOUN
corner
■ **doblar la esquina** to turn the corner

esquivar VERB [25]
to dodge

esta (FEM **esta**) ADJECTIVE ▷ *see* **este**

ésta PRONOUN ▷ *see* **éste**

está VERB ▷ *see* **estar**

estable (FEM **estable**) ADJECTIVE
stable

establecer* VERB [12]
to establish
□ Se ha establecido una buena relación entre los dos países. A good relationship has been established between the two countries.
■ **Han logrado establecer contacto con el barco.** They've managed to make contact with the boat.
■ **La familia se estableció en Madrid.** The family settled in Madrid.

el **establecimiento** NOUN
establishment
■ **un establecimiento comercial** a commercial establishment

el **establo** NOUN
stable

la **estación** (PL las **estaciones**) NOUN
1 station
□ la estación de autobuses the bus station
□ la estación de ferrocarril the railway station
2 season
□ las cuatro estaciones del año the four seasons of the year
■ **una estación de esquí** a ski resort
■ **una estación de servicio** a service station

estacionar VERB [25]
to park

estacionarse VERB [25] *(Chile, River Plate, Mexico)*
to park

la **estadía** NOUN *(Latin America)*
stay

el **estadio** NOUN
stadium

el **estado** NOUN
state
□ La carretera está en mal estado. The road is in a bad state.
■ **El Estado Español** The Spanish State
■ **estado civil** marital status
■ **María está en estado.** María is

expecting.

los **Estados Unidos** NOUN
the United States
□ en Estados Unidos in the United States

el/la **estadounidense** ADJECTIVE, NOUN
American

estafar VERB [25]
to swindle
□ Les estafaron mil euros. They swindled a thousand euros out of them.

estallar VERB [25]
1 to explode
2 to burst
3 to break out

la **estampilla** NOUN *(Latin America)*
stamp

estancado (FEM **estancada**) ADJECTIVE
stagnant

la **estancia** NOUN
1 stay
2 ranch (PL ranches)

el **estanco** NOUN
tobacconist's

estándar (FEM **estándar**) ADJECTIVE
standard
□ Éstos son los modelos estándar. These are the standard models.

el **estanque** NOUN
pond

el **estante** NOUN
shelf (PL shelves)
□ Puse los libros en el estante. I put the books on the shelf.

la **estantería** NOUN
1 shelves *pl*
□ la estantería de la cocina the kitchen shelves
2 bookshelves *pl*
3 shelf unit

el **estaño** NOUN
tin

estar* VERB [22]
1 to be
□ En la cama se está muy bien. It's nice being in bed. □ ¿Dónde estabas? Where were you? □ Madrid está en el centro de España. Madrid is in the centre of Spain.
■ **¿Está Mónica?** Is Mónica there? □ ¿Cómo estás? How are you? □ Estoy muy cansada. I'm very tired. □ ¿Estás casado o soltero? Are you married or single? □ Estamos de vacaciones. We're on holiday.
■ **Hoy no estoy para bromas.** I'm not in the mood for jokes today.
2 to look
□ ¡Qué guapa estás esta noche! You look really pretty tonight! □ Ese vestido te está muy bien. That dress looks very good on you. □ ¿A cuánto está el kilo de naranjas? What price are oranges per kilo? □ Estamos a 30 de enero. It's 30 January. □ Estábamos a 30°C. The temperature was 30°C.
□ Estamos esperando a Manolo. We're waiting for Manolo. □ María estaba sentada en la arena. María was sitting on the sand.
□ La radio está rota. The radio's broken.
■ **¡Ya está! Ya sé lo que podemos hacer.** That's it! I know what we can do.
■ **estarse** to be □ ¡Estáte quieto! Keep still!

estas PL ADJECTIVE ▷ *see* **estos**

éstas PL PRONOUN ▷ *see* **éstos**

estatal (FEM **estatal**) ADJECTIVE
state
□ un colegio estatal a state school

la **estatua** NOUN
statue

la **estatura** NOUN
height
□ ¿Cuál es tu estatura? What height are you? □ Tiene casi dos metros de estatura. He's over six and half feet tall.

el **este** NOUN, ADJECTIVE
east
□ el este del país the east of the country
□ en la costa este on the east coast □ en el este de España in the East of Spain
■ **vientos del este** easterly winds
■ **los países del Este** the Eastern bloc countries

este (FEM **esta**) ADJECTIVE
this
□ este libro this book

éste (FEM **ésta**) PRONOUN
this one
□ Ésta me gusta más. I prefer this one.
■ **Éste no es el que vi ayer.** This is not the one I saw yesterday.

esté VERB ▷ *see* **estar**

la **estera** NOUN
mat

el **estéreo** (PL los **estéreos**) NOUN
stereo (PL stereos)

esterlina (FEM **esterlina**) ADJECTIVE
■ **diez libras esterlinas** ten pounds sterling

estético (FEM **estética**) ADJECTIVE
■ **Se ha hecho la cirugía estética.** He's had plastic surgery.

el **estiércol** NOUN
manure

el **estilo** NOUN
style
□ Ése no es mi estilo. That's not my style.
■ **un estilo de vida similar al nuestro** a similar lifestyle to ours
■ **Tiene mucho estilo vistiendo.** He dresses very stylishly.

Spanish-English

e

la **estima** NOUN
■ **Lo tengo en gran estima.** I think very highly of him.
estimado (FEM **estimada**) ADJECTIVE
■ **Estimado señor Pérez** Dear Mr Pérez
estimulante (FEM **estimulante**) ADJECTIVE
stimulating
estimular VERB [25]
1 to encourage
□ Es una forma de estimular a los jugadores. It's a way of encouraging the players.
2 to stimulate
estirar VERB [25]
to stretch
□ Voy a salir a estirar las piernas. I'm going to go out and stretch my legs.
esto PRONOUN
this
□ ¿Para qué es esto? What's this for?
■ **En esto llegó Juan.** Just then Juan arrived.
el **estofado** NOUN
stew
el **estómago** NOUN
stomach
□ Me dolía el estómago. I had stomach ache.
estorbar VERB [25]
to be in the way
□ Las maletas estorban aquí. The cases are in the way here.
estornudar VERB [25]
to sneeze
estos (FEM **estas**) PL ADJECTIVE
these
■ **estas maletas** these cases
éstos (FEM **éstas**) PL PRONOUN
these ones
□ Éstos son los míos. These ones are mine.
■ **Éstos no son los que vimos ayer.** These are not the ones we saw yesterday.
■ **un día de éstos** one of these days
estoy VERB ▷ *see* **estar**
estrafalario (FEM **estrafalaria**) ADJECTIVE
1 eccentric
2 outlandish
estrangular VERB [25]
to strangle
estratégico (FEM **estratégica**) ADJECTIVE
strategic
estrechar VERB [25]
to take in
□ ¿Me puedes estrechar esta falda? Can you take in this skirt for me?
■ **La carretera se estrecha en el puente.** The road gets narrower over the bridge.
■ **Se estrecharon la mano.** They shook hands.
estrecho (FEM **estrecha**) ADJECTIVE
1 narrow
2 tight
□ La falda me va muy estrecha. The skirt is very tight on me.
el **estrecho** NOUN
strait
■ **el estrecho de Gibraltar** the straits of Gibraltar
la **estrella** NOUN
star
■ **una estrella de cine** a film star
■ **una estrella de mar** a starfish
LANGUAGE TIP Word for word, **estrella de mar** means 'sea star'.
estrellarse VERB [25]
to smash
□ El camión se estrelló contra un árbol. The lorry smashed into a tree.
estrenar VERB [25]
to premiere
□ La película se estrenó en junio. The film was premiered in June.
■ **Mañana estrenaré el vestido.** I'll wear the dress for the first time tomorrow.
el **estreno** NOUN
premiere
estreñido (FEM **estreñida**) ADJECTIVE
constipated
el **estrés** NOUN
stress
estricto (FEM **estricta**) ADJECTIVE
strict
estridente (FEM **estridente**) ADJECTIVE
loud
el **estropajo** NOUN
scourer
estropeado (FEM **estropeada**) ADJECTIVE
1 broken
2 broken down
estropear VERB [25]
1 to break
2 to ruin
□ Ese jabón me estropeó la ropa. That soap ruined my clothes. □ La lluvia nos estropeó las vacaciones. The rain ruined our holidays.
■ **estropearse** to break □ Se nos ha estropeado la tele. The TV's broken.
■ **Se me estropeó el coche en la autopista.** My car broke down on the motorway.
■ **La fruta se está estropeando con este calor.** The fruit's going off in this heat.
la **estructura** NOUN
structure
estrujar VERB [25]
1 to squeeze
2 to wring
el **estuche** NOUN

case

el/la **estudiante** NOUN
student

estudiar VERB [25]
1 to study
□ Quiere estudiar medicina. She wants to study medicine.
2 to learn
□ Tengo que estudiar cuatro lecciones para el examen. I have to learn four lessons for the exam.

el **estudio** NOUN
1 studio
2 studio flat
■ **Ha dejado los estudios.** He's given up his studies.

estudioso (FEM **estudiosa**) ADJECTIVE
studious

la **estufa** NOUN
1 heater
□ una estufa de gas a gas heater □ una estufa eléctrica an electric heater
2 stove *(Mexico)*

estupendamente ADVERB
■ **Me encuentro estupendamente.** I feel great.
■ **Nos lo pasamos estupendamente.** We had a great time.

estupendo (FEM **estupenda**) ADJECTIVE
great
□ Pasamos unas Navidades estupendas. We had a great Christmas.
■ **¡Estupendo!** Great!

la **estupidez** (PL las **estupideces**) NOUN
■ **No dice más que estupideces.** He just talks rubbish.
■ **Lo que hizo fue una estupidez.** What he did was stupid.

estúpido (FEM **estúpida**) ADJECTIVE
stupid

el **estúpido**, la **estúpida** NOUN
idiot
□ Ese tío es un estúpido. That guy's an idiot.

estuve VERB ▷ *see* **estar**

la **etapa** NOUN
stage
□ Lo hicimos por etapas. We did it in stages.

etc. ABBREVIATION (= *etcétera)*
etc.

eterno (FEM **eterna**) ADJECTIVE
eternal

la **ética** NOUN
1 ethics
2 ethics *pl*

ético (FEM **ética**) ADJECTIVE
ethical

Etiopía FEM NOUN
Ethiopia

la **etiqueta** NOUN
label
■ **traje de etiqueta** formal dress

étnico (FEM **étnica**) ADJECTIVE
ethnic

ETT ABBREVIATION *(= Empresa de Trabajo Temporal)*
temp agency

eufórico (FEM **eufórica**) ADJECTIVE
ecstatic

el **euro** NOUN
euro

Europa FEM NOUN
Europe

el **europeo** (FEM la **europea**) ADJECTIVE, NOUN
European

Euskadi NOUN
the Basque Country

el **euskera** NOUN
Basque

DID YOU KNOW...?
Basque is one of Spain's four official languages, and there is Basque-language radio and television. It is not from the same family of languages as Spanish.

evacuar* VERB [25]
to evacuate

evadir VERB [58]
1 to avoid
2 to evade

la **evaluación** (PL las **evaluaciones**) NOUN
assessment
□ evaluación continua continuous assessment

evaluar* VERB [1]
to assess

el **evangelio** NOUN
gospel

evaporarse VERB [25]
to evaporate

evasivo (FEM **evasiva**) ADJECTIVE
evasive

eventual (FEM **eventual**) ADJECTIVE
■ **un trabajo eventual** a temporary job

la **evidencia** NOUN
evidence
■ **Ante la evidencia de las hechos, se confesó culpable.** Faced with the evidence, he pleaded guilty.
■ **Carlos la puso en evidencia delante de todos.** Carlos showed her up in front of everyone.

evidente (FEM **evidente**) ADJECTIVE
obvious
■ **Era evidente que estaba agotada.** She was obviously exhausted.

evidentemente ADVERB

obviously

evitar VERB [25]
1 to avoid
□ Quiero evitar ese riesgo. I want to avoid that risk. □ Intento evitar a Luisa. I'm trying to avoid Luisa.
■ **No pude evitarlo.** I couldn't help it.
2 to save
□ Esto nos evitará muchos problemas. This will save us a lot of problems.

la **evolución** (PL las **evoluciones**) NOUN
progress
□ Seguimos de cerca la evolución del paciente. We are keeping a close watch on the patient's progress.
■ **la teoría de la evolución** the theory of evolution

evolucionar VERB [25]
1 to develop
□ Este país no ha evolucionado en la última década. This country hasn't developed in the last decade.
■ **El enfermo evoluciona favorablemente.** The patient is making good progress.
2 to evolve

ex PREFIX
ex
■ **su ex-marido** her ex-husband

exactamente ADVERB
exactly

la **exactitud** NOUN
■ **No lo sabemos con exactitud.** We don't know exactly.

exacto (FEM **exacta**) ADJECTIVE
1 exact
□ el precio exacto the exact price
■ **El tren salió a la hora exacta.** The train left bang on time.
2 accurate
□ Tus conclusiones no son muy exactas. Your conclusions aren't very accurate.
■ **Tenemos que defender nuestros derechos. — ¡Exacto!** We have to stand up for our rights. — Exactly!

la **exageración** (PL las **exageraciones**) NOUN
exaggeration

exagerado (FEM **exagerada**) ADJECTIVE
exaggerated
■ **¡No seas exagerada, no era tan alto!** Don't exaggerate! He wasn't that tall.
■ **El precio me parece exagerado.** I think the price is excessive.

exagerar VERB [25]
to exaggerate

el **examen** (PL los **exámenes**) NOUN
exam
■ **el examen de conducir** driving test

examinar VERB [25]
to examine
□ El médico la examinó. The doctor examined her. □ Nos examinaron dos profesores. We were examined by two teachers.
■ **Mañana me examino de inglés.** Tomorrow I've got an English exam.

la **excavadora** NOUN
digger

excavar VERB [25]
to dig
□ Los niños estaban excavando en la arena. The children were digging in the sand.
□ Están excavando un túnel. They're digging a tunnel.

excelente (FEM **excelente**) ADJECTIVE
excellent

excéntrico (FEM **excéntrica**) ADJECTIVE
excentric

la **excepción** (PL las **excepciones**) NOUN
exception
■ **a excepción de** except for

excepcional (FEM **excepcional**) ADJECTIVE
exceptional

excepto PREPOSITION
except for
□ todos, excepto Juan everyone, except for Juan

excesivo (FEM **excesiva**) ADJECTIVE
excessive

el **exceso** NOUN
■ **Anoche bebí en exceso.** Last night I drank to excess.
■ **exceso de equipaje** excess luggage
■ **Me multaron por exceso de velocidad.** They fined me for speeding.

excitarse VERB [25]
□ Se excitó mucho en la discusión. He got very worked up in the argument.

exclamar VERB [25]
to exclaim

excluir* VERB [10]
to exclude
□ Me excluyeron de la lista. They excluded me from the list.

exclusivo (FEM **exclusiva**) ADJECTIVE
exclusive

excluyendo VERB ▷ *see* **excluir**

la **excursión** (PL las **excursiones**) NOUN
trip
□ Mañana vamos de excursión con el colegio. Tomorrow we're going on a school trip.

la **excusa** NOUN
excuse

la **exhibición** (PL las **exhibiciones**) NOUN
exhibition

Spanish-English
e

exhibir VERB [58]
to exhibit
▪ **Le gusta mucho exhibirse.** He likes drawing attention to himself.

exigente (FEM **exigente**) ADJECTIVE
demanding
□ El jefe es muy exigente con nosotros. The boss is very demanding with us.

exigir* VERB [16]
1 to demand
□ Exigió hablar con el encargado. He demanded to speak to the manager.
▪ **La maestra nos exige demasiado.** Our teacher is too demanding.
2 to require
□ Ese puesto exige mucha paciencia. This job requires a lot of patience.
▪ **Exigen tres años de experiencia para el puesto.** They're asking for three years' experience for the job.

el **exiliado**, la **exiliada** NOUN
exile

existir VERB [58]
to exist
□ ¿Existen los fantasmas? Do ghosts exist?
▪ **Existen dos maneras de hacerlo.** There are two ways of doing it.

el **éxito** NOUN
success (PL successes)
□ Esa novela será un gran éxito. That novel will be a great success.
▪ **Su película tuvo mucho éxito.** His film was very successful.
▪ **Acabaron con éxito el proyecto.** They completed the project successfully.

LANGUAGE TIP Be careful! **éxito** does not mean **exit**.

exótico (FEM **exótica**) ADJECTIVE
exotic

la **expansión** (PL las **expansiones**) NOUN
expansion

la **expedición** (PL las **expediciones**) NOUN
expedition

el **expediente** NOUN
file
▪ **expediente académico** student record
▪ **Le han abierto expediente por mala conducta.** He has been disciplined for bad behaviour.

el **expendio** NOUN *(Latin America)*
shop

expensas FEM PL NOUN
▪ **a expensas de su salud** at the cost of her health
▪ **vivir a expensas de alguien** to live at somebody's expense

la **experiencia** NOUN
experience
□ 'Se requiere experiencia laboral' 'Work experience required'
▪ **con experiencia** experienced
▪ **sin experiencia** inexperienced

experimental (FEM **experimental**) ADJECTIVE
experimental

experimentar VERB [25]
1 to experiment
□ experimentar con animales to experiment on animals
2 to experience

el **experimento** NOUN
experiment

el **experto**, la **experta** NOUN
expert
▪ **Es un experto en informática.** He's a computer expert.

la **explanada** NOUN
open area

la **explicación** (PL las **explicaciones**) NOUN
explanation

explicar* VERB [48]
to explain
□ Le expliqué cómo se hacía una paella. I explained to her how to make a paella.
▪ **Antonio se explica muy bien.** Antonio is very good at expressing himself.
▪ **¿Me explico?** Do I make myself clear?
▪ **No me lo explico.** I can't understand it.

el **explorador**, la **exploradora** NOUN
explorer

explorar VERB [25]
to explore

la **explosión** (PL las **explosiones**) NOUN
explosion
▪ **El artefacto hizo explosión.** The device exploded.

el **explosivo** NOUN
explosive

la **explotación** (PL las **explotaciones**) NOUN
exploitation

explotar VERB [25]
1 to exploit
□ Sabe explotar sus posibilidades. He knows how to exploit his potential.
2 to explode
□ La caldera explotó. The boiler exploded.

exponer* VERB [41]
1 to display
2 to present

la **exportación** (PL las **exportaciones**) NOUN
export

exportar VERB [25]
to export

la **exposición** (PL las **exposiciones**) NOUN

exhibition
□ montar una exposición to put on an exhibition

expresamente ADVERB
1 specifically
□ Mencioné expresamente tu nombre. I specifically mentioned your name.
2 specially
□ Fui expresamente a devolvérselo. I went specially to give it back to him.

expresar VERB [25]
to express
□ No sabe expresarse. He doesn't know how to express himself.

la **expresión** (PL las **expresiones**) NOUN
expression

expresivo (FEM **expresiva**) ADJECTIVE
expressive

el **expreso** NOUN
1 express
2 espresso

exprimir VERB [58]
to squeeze

expuesto VERB ▷ *see* **exponer**

expulsar VERB [25]
1 to expel
□ La expulsaron del colegio. They expelled her from school.
2 to send off
□ El árbitro lo expulsó del campo. The referee sent him off the pitch.

la **expulsión** (PL las **expulsiones**) NOUN
expulsion
■ **La expulsión del jugador fue injusta.** Sending the player off was unfair.

exquisito (FEM **exquisita**) ADJECTIVE
delicious
□ El postre estaba exquisito. The dessert was delicious.

el **éxtasis** NOUN
ecstasy

extender* VERB [20]
to spread
□ Extendí la toalla sobre la arena. I spread the towel out on the sand. □ El fuego se extendió rápidamente. The fire spread quickly.
■ **extender los brazos** to stretch one's arms out

extendido (FEM **extendida**) ADJECTIVE
oustretched

la **extensión** (PL las **extensiones**) NOUN
area
□ una enorme extensión de tierra an enormous area of land
■ **¿Me pone con la extensión 212, por favor?** Can you put me through to extension 212, please?

extenso (FEM **extensa**) ADJECTIVE
extensive

exterior (FEM **exterior**) ADJECTIVE
1 outside
2 foreign

el **exterior** NOUN
outside
■ **Salimos al exterior para ver qué pasaba.** We went outside to see what was going on.

externo (FEM **externa**) ADJECTIVE
1 outside
2 outer

extiendo VERB ▷ *see* **extender**

la **extinción** NOUN
putting out
■ **una especie en vías de extinción** an endangered species

el **extinguidor** NOUN *(Latin America)*
fire extinguisher

extinguir* VERB [58, **gu** → **g** before **a** and **o**]
to put out
■ **extinguirse** to become extinct
■ **El fuego se fue extinguiendo lentamente.** The fire was slowly going out.

extinto (FEM **extinta**) ADJECTIVE
extinct

el **extintor** NOUN
fire extinguisher

extra (FEM **extra**) ADJECTIVE
extra
□ una manta extra an extra blanket
■ **chocolate de calidad extra** top quality chocolate

el/la **extra** NOUN
extra

el **extractor** NOUN
extractor fan
□ un extractor de humos a smoke extractor

extraer* VERB [54]
1 to extract
□ El dentista me ha extraído la muela. The dentist has extracted my tooth.
2 to draw

extraescolar (FEM **extraescolara**) ADJECTIVE
■ **actividades extraescolares** extracurricular activities

extraigo VERB ▷ *see* **extraer**

extranjero (FEM **extranjera**) ADJECTIVE
foreign

el **extranjero**, la **extranjera** NOUN
foreigner
■ **vivir en el extranjero** to live abroad
■ **viajar al extranjero** to travel abroad

extrañar VERB [25]
to miss
□ Extraña mucho a sus padres. He misses his parents a lot.

■ **Me extraña que no haya llegado.** I'm surprised he hasn't arrived.
■ **¡Ya me extrañaba a mí!** I thought it was strange!
■ **extrañarse de algo** to be surprised at something □ Se extrañó de vernos juntos. He was surprised to see us together.

la **extrañeza** NOUN
■ **Nos miró con extrañeza.** He looked at us in surprise.

extraño (FEM **extraña**) ADJECTIVE
strange
■ **¡Qué extraño!** How strange!

extraordinario (FEM **extraordinaria**) ADJECTIVE
extraordinary

extravagante (FEM **extravagante**) ADJECTIVE
extravagant

extraviado (FEM **extraviada**) ADJECTIVE
1 lost
2 missing

extraviar* VERB [21]
to mislay
□ Me extraviaron el equipaje en el aeropuerto. They mislaid my luggage at the airport.

el/la **extremista** ADJECTIVE, NOUN
extremist

extremo (FEM **extrema**) ADJECTIVE
extreme
□ Ése es un caso extremo. That's an extreme case.
■ **la extrema derecha** the far Right
■ **extremo derecho** right winger
■ **el Extremo Oriente** the Far East

el **extremo** NOUN
end
□ Cogí la cuerda por un extremo. I took hold of one end of the rope.
■ **pasar de un extremo a otro** to go from one extreme to the other
■ **en último extremo** as a last resort

extrovertido (FEM **extrovertida**) ADJECTIVE
outgoing
□ José es muy extrovertido. José is very outgoing.

exuberante (FEM **exuberante**) ADJECTIVE
lush

Spanish-English

e

Ff

la **fábrica** NOUN
factory (PL factories)
■ **una fábrica de cerveza** a brewery
LANGUAGE TIP Be careful! **fábrica** does not mean **fabric**.
el/la **fabricante** NOUN
manufacturer
fabricar* VERB [48]
to make
■ **'fabricado en China'** 'made in China'
la **fachada** NOUN
■ **la fachada del edificio** the front of the building
fácil (FEM **fácil**) ADJECTIVE
easy
□ El examen fue muy fácil. The exam was very easy.
■ **Es fácil de entender.** It's easy to understand.
■ **Es fácil que se le haya perdido.** He may have lost it.
la **facilidad** NOUN
■ **Se me rompen las uñas con facilidad.** My nails break easily.
■ **Pepe tiene facilidad para los idiomas.** Pepe has a gift for languages.
■ **Te dan facilidades de pago.** They offer credit facilities.
facilitar VERB [25]
to make...easier
□ Un ordenador facilita mucho el trabajo. A computer makes work much easier.
■ **El banco me facilitó la información.** The bank provided me with the information.
el **factor** NOUN
factor
□ La edad del paciente es un factor importante. The age of the patient is an important factor.
la **factura** NOUN
bill
□ la factura del gas the gas bill
facturar VERB [25]
to check in
la **facultad** NOUN
1 faculty (PL faculties)
□ Mi abuela está perdiendo facultades. My grandmother is losing her faculties.
■ **la Facultad de Derecho** the Law Faculty
2 university
■ **ir a la facultad** to go to university
la **faena** NOUN
work
■ **las faenas domésticas** the housework
la **falda** NOUN
skirt
fallar VERB [25]
to fail
□ Le falla la memoria. His memory is failing.
■ **Fallé el tiro.** I missed.
fallecer* VERB [12]
to die
el **fallo** NOUN
1 fault
□ un pequeño fallo eléctrico a small electrical fault
2 failure
□ debido a un fallo de motor due to engine failure
3 mistake
□ ¡Qué fallo! What a stupid mistake!
■ **Fue un fallo humano.** It was human error.
falsificar* VERB [48]
to forge
falso (FEM **falsa**) ADJECTIVE
1 false
2 forged
■ **Los diamantes eran falsos.** The diamonds were fakes.
■ **Eso es falso.** That's not true.
la **falta** NOUN
1 lack
□ la falta de dinero lack of money
2 foul
□ Ha sido falta. It was a foul.
■ **Tiene cinco faltas de asistencia.** He has been absent five times.
■ **Eso es una falta de educación.** That's bad manners.
■ **una falta de ortografía** a spelling mistake

■ **Me hace falta un ordenador.** I need a computer.
■ **No hace falta que vengáis.** You don't need to come.

faltar VERB [25]
to be missing
□ Me falta un bolígrafo. One of my pens is missing.
■ **Faltan varios libros del estante.** There are several books missing from the shelf.
■ **No podemos irnos. Falta Manolo.** We can't go. Manolo isn't here yet.
■ **A la sopa le falta sal.** There isn't enough salt in the soup.
■ **Falta media hora para comer.** There's half an hour to go before lunch.
■ **¿Te falta mucho?** Will you be long?
■ **faltar al colegio** to miss school

la **fama** NOUN
fame
■ **llegar a la fama** to become famous
■ **tener mala fama** to have a bad reputation
■ **Tiene fama de mujeriego.** He has a reputation for being a womanizer.

la **familia** NOUN
family (PL families)
■ **una familia numerosa** a large family

familiar (FEM **familiar**) ADJECTIVE
1 family
□ la vida familiar family life
2 familiar
□ Su cara me es familiar. Your face is familiar.

el/la **familiar** NOUN
relative
□ un familiar mío a relative of mine

famoso (FEM **famosa**) ADJECTIVE
famous

el/la **fan** (PL los **fans**) NOUN
fan

la **fantasía** NOUN
fantasy (PL fantasies)
□ un mundo de fantasía a fantasy world
□ Son fantasías infantiles. They're just children's fantasies.
■ **las joyas de fantasía** costume jewellery *sing*

el **fantasma** NOUN
ghost

fantástico (FEM **fantástica**) ADJECTIVE
fantastic

el **farmacéutico**, la **farmacéutica** NOUN
chemist

la **farmacia** NOUN
chemist's (PL chemists' shops)
□ Lo compré en la farmacia. I bought it at the chemist's.
■ **una farmacia de guardia** a duty chemist's

el **faro** NOUN
1 lighthouse
2 headlight
3 lamp
■ **los faros antiniebla** foglamps

el **farol** NOUN
1 streetlamp
2 lantern

la **farola** NOUN
1 streetlamp
□ a la luz de la farola by the light of the streetlamp
2 lamppost
□ El coche chocó contra una farola. The car hit a lamppost.

el **fascículo** NOUN
part
□ el primer fascículo del libro the first part of the book

fascinante (FEM **fascinante**) ADJECTIVE
fascinating

el/la **fascista** ADJECTIVE, NOUN
fascist

la **fase** NOUN
phase

fastidiar VERB [25]
1 to annoy
□ Lo que más me fastidia es tener que decírselo. What annoys me most is having to tell him.
■ **Esa actitud me fastidia mucho.** I find this attitude very annoying.
2 to pester
□ ¡Deja ya de fastidiarme! Will you stop pestering me!
3 to spoil
□ El accidente nos fastidió las vacaciones. The accident spoilt our holidays.

el **fastidio** NOUN
■ **¡Qué fastidio!** What a nuisance!

fatal (FEM **fatal**) ADJECTIVE
▷ *see also* **fatal** ADVERB
awful
□ Nos hizo un tiempo fatal. We had awful weather. □ Me siento fatal. I feel awful.
□ La obra estuvo fatal. The play was awful.
■ **Me parece fatal que le trates así.** I think it's rotten of you to treat him like that.

fatal ADVERB
▷ *see also* **fatal** ADJECTIVE
■ **Lo pasé fatal.** I had an awful time.
■ **Lo hice fatal.** I made a mess of it.

el **favor** NOUN
favour
□ ¿Puedes hacerme un favor? Can you do

me a favour?
■ **por favor** please
■ **¡Haced el favor de callaros!** Will you please be quiet!
■ **estar a favor de algo** to be in favour of something

favorecer* VERB [12]
to suit
□ Esa chaqueta te favorece mucho. That jacket really suits you.

favorito (FEM **favorita**) ADJECTIVE
favourite
□ ¿Cuál es tu color favorito? What's your favourite colour?

el **fax** (PL los **fax**) NOUN
fax (PL faxes)
■ **mandar algo por fax** to fax something

la **fe** NOUN
faith
■ **tener fe en algo** to have faith in something

febrero MASC NOUN
February
□ en febrero in February □ Ella nació el 28 de febrero. She was born on 28 February.

la **fecha** NOUN
date
□ ¿En qué fecha estamos? What's the date today?
■ **La carta tiene fecha del 21 de enero.** The letter is dated the 21st of January.
■ **la fecha de caducidad** the use-by date
■ **la fecha límite** the closing date
■ **la fecha tope** the deadline
■ **su fecha de nacimiento** his date of birth

la **felicidad** NOUN
happiness
□ Carmen lloraba de felicidad. Carmen was crying with happiness.
■ **¡Felicidades! 1** Happy birthday! **2** Congratulations!

la **felicitación** (PL las **felicitaciones**) NOUN
congratulations *pl*
□ Mi felicitación al ganador. My congratulations to the winner.
■ **He recibido muchas felicitaciones.** Lots of people have congratulated me.

felicitar VERB [25]
to congratulate
□ La felicité por sus notas. I congratulated her on her exam results.
■ **¡Te felicito!** Congratulations!
■ **felicitar a alguien por su cumpleaños** to wish somebody a happy birthday

feliz (FEM **feliz**, PL **felices**) ADJECTIVE
happy
□ Se la ve muy feliz. She looks very happy.
■ **¡Feliz cumpleaños!** Happy birthday!
■ **¡Feliz Año Nuevo!** Happy New Year!
■ **¡Felices Navidades!** Happy Christmas!

el **felpudo** NOUN
doormat

femenino (FEM **femenina**) ADJECTIVE
1 feminine
□ una chica muy femenina a very feminine girl
2 female
□ el sexo femenino the female sex
3 women's
□ el tenis femenino women's tennis

el **femenino** NOUN
feminine
□ El femenino de 'lobo' es 'loba'. The feminine of 'lobo' is 'loba'.

fenomenal (FEM **fenomenal**) ADJECTIVE, ADVERB
great
□ Nos hizo un tiempo fenomenal. We had great weather.
■ **Lo pasé fenomenal.** I had a great time.

feo (FEM **fea**) ADJECTIVE
ugly
□ un edificio muy feo a very ugly building

el **féretro** NOUN
coffin

la **feria** NOUN
1 fair
■ **una feria de muestras** a trade fair
2 small change *(Mexico)*
3 street market *(Chile, River Plate)*

la **ferretería** NOUN
ironmonger's (PL ironmongers' shops)
□ Lo compré en la ferretería. I bought it at the ironmonger's.

el **ferrocarril** NOUN
railway

fértil (FEM **fértil**) ADJECTIVE
fertile

el **fertilizante** NOUN
fertilizer

festejar VERB [25] *(Latin America)*
to celebrate

el **festival** NOUN
festival

festivo (FEM **festiva**) ADJECTIVE
festive
■ **un día festivo** a holiday

el **feto** NOUN
foetus (PL foetuses)

fiable (FEM **fiable**) ADJECTIVE
reliable

los **fiambres** NOUN
cold meats

la **fianza** NOUN
deposit
□ Dejé una fianza de 20 euros. I left a

20-euro deposit.

fiar* VERB [21]

■ **Es un hombre de fiar.** He's completely trustworthy.

■ **fiarse de alguien** to trust somebody

□ No me fío de él. I don't trust him.

la **fibra** NOUN

fibre

□ fibras artificiales man-made fibres

la **ficha** NOUN

1 index card

2 counter

■ **una ficha de dominó** a domino (PL dominoes)

fichar VERB [25]

1 to clock in

2 to clock out

3 to sign up

el **fichero** NOUN

1 filing cabinet

2 card index

3 file

los **fideos** NOUN

1 noodles

2 pasta *sing (River Plate)*

la **fiebre** NOUN

1 temperature

□ Le bajó la fiebre. His temperature came down.

■ **tener fiebre** to have a temperature

2 fever

□ la fiebre amarilla yellow fever

fiel (FEM **fiel**) ADJECTIVE

faithful

■ **ser fiel a alguien** to be faithful to somebody

la **fiera** NOUN

wild animal

la **fiesta** NOUN

1 party (PL parties)

□ Voy a dar una fiesta para celebrarlo. I'm going to have a party to celebrate.

■ **una fiesta de cumpleaños** a birthday party

2 holiday

□ El lunes es fiesta. Monday is a holiday.

■ **El pueblo está en fiestas.** There's a fiesta on in the town.

la **figura** NOUN

figure

□ una figura de porcelana a porcelain figure

figurar VERB [25]

to appear

□ Su nombre no figura en la lista. His name doesn't appear on the list.

■ **figurarse** to imagine □ Figúrate lo que debió sufrir. Just imagine how he must have suffered.

■ **¡Ya me lo figuraba!** I thought as much!

fijar VERB [25]

to fix

□ Tienes que fijar la fecha. You must fix the date.

■ **fijarse 1** to pay attention □ Tienes que fijarte más en lo que haces. You must pay more attention to what you're doing. **2** to notice □ No me fijé en la ropa que llevaba. I didn't notice what she was wearing.

■ **¡Fíjate en esos dos!** Just look at those two!

fijo (FEM **fija**) ADJECTIVE

1 fixed

□ Gano un sueldo fijo. I earn a fixed salary.

2 permanent

■ **Está fija en la empresa.** She's got a permanent job in the company.

la **fila** NOUN

1 row

□ Estábamos sentados en segunda fila. We were sitting in the second row.

2 line

□ Los niños se pusieron en fila. The children got into line.

el **filete** NOUN

1 steak

□ un filete con patatas fritas steak and chips

2 fillet

□ un filete de merluza a hake fillet

Filipinas FEM PL NOUN

the Philippines

filmar VERB [25]

to film

□ Mi hermano filmó nuestra boda. My brother filmed our wedding.

■ **filmar una película** to shoot a film

el **filo** NOUN

■ **Tiene poco filo.** It isn't very sharp.

filoso (FEM **filosa**) ADJECTIVE *(Latin America)*

sharp

la **filosofía** NOUN

philosophy

filtrar VERB [25]

to filter

□ Hay que filtrar el agua. The water needs filtering.

■ **filtrarse 1** to seep □ El agua se filtraba por las paredes. Water was seeping in through the walls. **2** to filter □ La luz se filtraba por las rendijas. Light was filtering in through the cracks.

el **filtro** NOUN

filter

el **fin** NOUN

end

□ el fin de una era the end of an era

■ **a fines de** at the end of □ a fines de abril

at the end of April
■ **al fin** finally ▫ Al fin llegaron a un acuerdo. They finally reached an agreement.
■ **al fin y al cabo** after all
■ **En fin, ¡qué le vamos a hacer!** Oh well, what can we do about it!
■ **por fin** at last ▫ ¡Por fin hemos llegado! We've got here at last!
■ **el fin de año** New Year's Eve
■ **el fin de semana** the weekend

final (FEM **final**) ADJECTIVE
final
▫ el resultado final the final result

el **final** NOUN
end
▫ Al final de la calle hay un colegio. At the end of the street there's a school.
■ **a finales de mayo** at the end of May
■ **al final** in the end ▫ Al final tuve que darle la razón. In the end I had to admit that he was right.
■ **un final feliz** a happy ending

la **final** NOUN
final
▫ la final de la copa the cup final

la **finca** NOUN
country house

fingir* VERB [16]
to pretend
▫ Fingió no haberme oído. He pretended not to have heard me.

finlandés (FEM **finlandesa**, MASC PL **finlandeses**) ADJECTIVE
Finnish

el **finlandés**, la **finlandesa** (MASC PL los **finlandeses**) NOUN
Finn

el **finlandés** NOUN
Finnish

Finlandia FEM NOUN
Finland

fino (FEM **fina**) ADJECTIVE
1 thin
2 fine
3 slender

la **firma** NOUN
signature

firmar VERB [25]
to sign

firme (FEM **firme**) ADJECTIVE
1 steady
▫ Mantén la escalera firme. Can you hold the ladder steady?
2 firm
▫ Se mostró muy firme con ella. He was very firm with her.

el/la **fiscal** NOUN
public prosecutor

fisgar* VERB [37]
to snoop
▫ La encontré fisgando en mi bolso. I found her snooping in my bag.

la **física** NOUN
1 physics *sing*
2 physicist

físico (FEM **física**) ADJECTIVE
physical

el **físico** NOUN
physicist

flaco (FEM **flaca**) ADJECTIVE
thin

la **flama** NOUN *(Mexico)*
flame

el **flamenco** NOUN
flamenco

el **flan** NOUN
crème caramel

el **flash** (PL los **flashes**) NOUN
flash (PL flashes)

la **flauta** NOUN
1 recorder
2 flute

la **flecha** NOUN
arrow

el **flechazo** NOUN
■ **Fue un flechazo.** It was love at first sight.

los **flecos** NOUN
fringe *sing*
▫ los flecos de la cortina the curtain fringe

el **flequillo** NOUN
fringe

flexible (FEM **flexible**) ADJECTIVE
flexible

flojo (FEM **floja**) ADJECTIVE
1 loose
2 slack
3 weak
4 lazy *(Latin America)*
■ **Todavía tengo las piernas muy flojas.** My legs are still very weak.
■ **Está flojo en matemáticas.** He's weak at maths.

la **flor** NOUN
flower
▫ un ramo de flores a bunch of flowers

el **florero** NOUN
vase

la **floristería** NOUN
florist's (PL florists' shops)
▫ Las compré en la floristería. I bought them at the florist's.

el **flotador** NOUN
1 rubber ring
2 armband

flotar VERB [25]

to float

flote ADVERB
■ **a flote** afloat □ La barca se mantuvo a flote. The boat stayed afloat.

fluir* VERB [10]
to flow

fluorescente (FEM **fluorescente**) ADJECTIVE
fluorescent

fluyendo VERB ▷ *see* **fluir**

la **foca** NOUN
seal

el **foco** NOUN
1 spotlight
2 floodlight
3 headlight *(Latin America)*
4 light bulb *(Mexico)*
■ **el foco de atención** the focus of attention

el **folio** NOUN
sheet of paper (PL sheets of paper)
■ **un documento de 20 folios** a 20-page document
■ **un sobre de tamaño folio** an A4-size envelope

el **folklore** NOUN
folklore

el **folleto** NOUN
1 brochure
2 leaflet

fomentar VERB [25]
to promote

la **fonda** NOUN
1 boarding house
2 restaurant

el **fondo** NOUN
1 bottom
□ el fondo de la cazuela the bottom of the pan
■ **en el fondo del mar** at the bottom of the sea
2 end
□ Mi habitación está al fondo del pasillo. My room's at the end of the corridor.
■ **estudiar una materia a fondo** to study a subject in depth
■ **un corredor de fondo** a long-distance runner
■ **en el fondo** deep down
■ **recaudar fondos** to raise funds

el **fontanero**, la **fontanera** NOUN
plumber

el **footing** NOUN
jogging
□ Hago footing todas las mañanas. I go jogging every morning.

forestal (FEM **forestal**) ADJECTIVE
forest
□ un incendio forestal a forest fire

la **forma** NOUN
1 shape
□ Me gusta la forma de esa mesa. I like the shape of that table.
■ **en forma de pera** pear-shaped
2 way
□ Me miraba de una forma extraña. She was looking at me in a strange way.
■ **de todas formas** anyway
■ **estar en forma** to be fit

la **formación** (PL las **formaciones**) NOUN
training
■ **formación profesional** vocational training

formal (FEM **formal**) ADJECTIVE
responsible
□ un chico muy formal a very responsible boy
■ **Sé formal y pórtate bien.** Be good and behave yourself.

formar VERB [25]
to start
□ Quieren formar una orquesta. They want to start an orchestra.
■ **Se formó una cola enorme en la puerta.** A huge queue formed at the door.
■ **estar formado por** to be made up of
■ **formar parte de algo** to be part of something

formidable (FEM **formidable**) ADJECTIVE
fantastic
□ Pedro tiene un coche formidable. Pedro has got a fantastic car. □ Desde aquí hay una vista formidable. There's a fantastic view from here.

la **fórmula** NOUN
formula
□ una fórmula mágica a magic formula
■ **coches de Fórmula 1** Formula 1 cars

el **formulario** NOUN
form
□ Hay que rellenar un formulario. You have to fill in a form.

forrar VERB [25]
1 to line
2 to cover

el **forro** NOUN
1 lining
2 cover

la **fortuna** NOUN
fortune
□ Vale una fortuna. It's worth a fortune.
■ **por fortuna** luckily

forzar* VERB [3]
to force
■ **Estás forzando la vista.** You're straining your eyes.

la **fosa** NOUN

Spanish-English

1 ditch (PL ditches)
2 grave

el **fósforo** NOUN
match

la **foto** NOUN
photo (PL photos)
□ Les hice una foto a los niños. I took a photo of the children.

la **fotocopia** NOUN
photocopy (PL photocopies)
□ Hice dos fotocopias del recibo. I made two photocopies of the receipt.

la **fotocopiadora** NOUN
photocopier

fotocopiar VERB [25]
to photocopy

la **fotógrafa** NOUN
photographer

la **fotografía** NOUN
1 photograph
□ una fotografía de mis padres a photograph of my parents
2 photography
□ un curso de fotografía a photography course

el **fotógrafo** NOUN
photographer

fracasar VERB [25]
to fail

el **fracaso** NOUN
failure

la **fracción** (PL las **fracciones**) NOUN
fraction

la **fractura** NOUN
fracture

frágil (FEM **frágil**) ADJECTIVE
fragile

el **fraile** NOUN
friar

la **frambuesa** NOUN
raspberry (PL raspberries)

francés (FEM **francesa**, MASC PL **franceses**) ADJECTIVE
French

el **francés** (PL los **franceses**) NOUN
1 Frenchman (PL Frenchmen)
■ **los franceses** the French
2 French

la **francesa** NOUN
Frenchwoman (PL Frenchwomen)

Francia FEM NOUN
France

franco (FEM **franca**) ADJECTIVE
frank
■ **para serte franco ...** to be frank with you ...

el **franco** NOUN
franc

el **franqueo** NOUN
postage

el **frasco** NOUN
bottle
□ un frasco de perfume a bottle of perfume

la **frase** NOUN
sentence
■ **una frase hecha** a set phrase

el **fraude** NOUN
fraud

la **frazada** NOUN *(Latin America)*
blanket

la **frecuencia** NOUN
frequency (PL frequencies)
□ ¿En qué frecuencia está? What frequency is it on?
■ **Nos vemos con frecuencia.** We often see each other.
■ **¿Con qué frecuencia tienen estos síntomas?** How often do they get these symptoms?

frecuente (FEM **frecuente**) ADJECTIVE
1 common
□ un error bastante frecuente a fairly common mistake
2 frequent
□ sus frecuentes viajes al extranjero his frequent trips abroad

el **fregadero** NOUN
sink

fregar* VERB [34]
to wash
□ Tengo que fregar la cazuela. I've got to wash the pan.
■ **fregar los platos** to wash the dishes
■ **Yo estaba en la cocina fregando.** I was in the kitchen washing the dishes.
■ **fregar el suelo** to mop the floor

la **fregona** NOUN
mop

freír* VERB [23]
to fry
□ No sabe ni freír un huevo. He can't even fry an egg.

frenar VERB [25]
to brake

el **frenazo** NOUN
■ **Tuve que dar un frenazo.** I had to brake suddenly.

el **freno** NOUN
brake
□ Me quedé sin frenos. My brakes failed.
■ **el freno de mano** the handbrake

la **frente** NOUN
forehead
□ Tiene una cicatriz en la frente. He has a scar on his forehead.

el **frente** NOUN

front
□ un frente frío a cold front □ un frente común a united front
■ **frente a** opposite □ Frente al hotel hay un banco. There's a bank opposite the hotel.
■ **Los coches chocaron de frente.** The cars collided head on.
■ **Viene un coche de frente.** There's a car coming straight for us.
■ **hacer frente a algo** to face up to something

la **fresa** NOUN
strawberry (PL strawberries)

fresco (FEM **fresca**) ADJECTIVE
1 cool
2 fresh
■ **hace fresco 1** it's chilly **2** it's cool

el **fresco** NOUN
■ **Hace fresco.** It's a bit chilly.

friego VERB ▷ *see* **fregar**

el **frigorífico** NOUN
fridge

el **frijol** NOUN *(Latin America)*
bean

frío VERB
▷ *see also* **frío** ADJECTIVE, NOUN ▷ *see* **freír**

frío (FEM **fría**) ADJECTIVE
▷ *see also* **frío** VERB, NOUN
cold
□ Tengo las manos frías. My hands are cold.
■ **Estuvo muy frío conmigo.** He was very cold towards me.

el **frío** NOUN
▷ *see also* **frío** VERB, ADJECTIVE
■ **Hace frío.** It's cold.
■ **Tengo mucho frío.** I'm very cold.

frito VERB
▷ *see also* **frito** VERB ▷ *see* **freír**

frito (FEM **frita**) ADJECTIVE
▷ *see also* **frito** ADJECTIVE
fried
□ huevos fritos fried eggs

la **frontera** NOUN
border
□ Nos pararon en la frontera. We were stopped at the border.

el **frontón** (PL los **frontones**) NOUN
1 pelota court
2 pelota

frotar VERB [25]
to rub
□ ¿Te froto la espalda? Shall I rub your back for you?
■ **El niño se frotaba las manos para calentarse.** The child was rubbing his hands to get warm.

fruncir* VERB [58, **c** → **z** before **a** and **o**]
■ **fruncir el ceño** to frown

frustrado (FEM **frustrada**) ADJECTIVE
frustrated
□ Se siente frustrado. He feels frustrated.

la **fruta** NOUN
fruit
□ La fruta está muy cara. Fruit is very expensive.

la **frutería** NOUN
greengrocer's (PL greengrocers' shops)
□ Lo compré en la frutería. I bought it at the greengrocer's.

la **frutilla** NOUN *(River Plate)*
strawberry (PL strawberries)

el **fruto** NOUN
fruit
□ el fruto de nuestro trabajo the fruit of our labours
■ **los frutos secos** nuts

fue VERB ▷ *see* **ir, ser**

el **fuego** NOUN
fire
□ encender el fuego to light the fire
■ **prender fuego a algo** to set fire to something
■ **Puse la cazuela al fuego.** I put the pot on to heat.
■ **cocinar algo a fuego lento** to cook something on a low heat
■ **¿Tiene fuego, por favor?** Have you got a light, please?
■ **fuegos artificiales** fireworks
LANGUAGE TIP Word for word, **fuegos artificiales** means 'artificial fires'.

la **fuente** NOUN
1 fountain
2 dish (PL dishes)

fuera VERB
▷ *see also* **fuera** ADVERB ▷ *see* **ir, ser**

fuera ADVERB
▷ *see also* **fuera** VERB
1 outside
□ Los niños estaban jugando fuera. The children were playing outside. □ Por fuera es blanco. It is white on the outside.
■ **¡Estamos aquí fuera!** We are out here!
■ **Hoy vamos a cenar fuera.** We're going out for dinner tonight.
2 away
□ Mis padres llevan varios días fuera. My parents have been away for several days.
■ **El enfermo está fuera de peligro.** The patient is out of danger.
■ **fuera de mi casa** outside my house

fuerte (FEM **fuerte**) ADJECTIVE
▷ *see also* **fuerte** ADVERB
1 strong
2 loud

3 hard
4 bad
■ **'un beso muy fuerte'** 'lots of love'

fuerte ADVERB
▷ *see also* **fuerte** ADJECTIVE
loudly
□ Hablaba fuerte. He was talking loudly.
■ **Agárrate fuerte.** Hold on tight.
■ **No le pegues tan fuerte.** Don't hit him so hard.

la **fuerza** NOUN
strength
□ No le quedaban fuerzas. He had no strength left.
■ **tener mucha fuerza** to be very strong
■ **Sólo lo conseguirás a fuerza de practicar.** You'll only manage it by practising.
■ **No te lo comas a la fuerza.** Don't force yourself to eat it.
■ **la fuerza de gravedad** the force of gravity
■ **la fuerza de voluntad** willpower

fuerzo VERB ▷ *see* **forzar**

fugarse* VERB [25]
to escape

fui VERB ▷ *see* **ir, ser**

el **fumador**, la **fumadora** NOUN
smoker
■ **sección para no fumadores** non-smoking section

fumar VERB [25]
to smoke
□ Quiero dejar de fumar. I want to give up smoking.

la **función** (PL las **funciones**) NOUN
1 function
□ Los insectos desempeñan una función muy importante. Insects perform a very useful function.
2 role
□ la función de la policía en la sociedad the role of the police in society
3 show
□ Los niños representan una función en el colegio. The children are putting on a show at school.

funcionar VERB [25]
to work
□ El ascensor no funciona. The lift isn't working.
■ **'No funciona.'** 'Out of order.'
■ **Funciona con pilas.** It runs on batteries.

el **funcionario**, la **funcionaria** NOUN
civil servant

la **funda** NOUN
cover
■ **una funda de almohada** a pillowcase

fundamental (FEM **fundamental**) ADJECTIVE
basic
□ Hay dos tipos fundamentales de personas. There are two basic types of people.
■ **Es fundamental que entendamos el problema.** It is essential that we understand the problem.

fundar VERB [25]
to found

fundirse VERB [58]
to melt
□ La nieve se está fundiendo. The snow's melting.
■ **Se han fundido los fusibles.** The fuses have blown.

el **funeral** NOUN
funeral

la **funeraria** NOUN
undertaker's

la **furgoneta** NOUN
van

la **furia** NOUN
fury

furioso (FEM **furiosa**) ADJECTIVE
furious
□ Mi padre estaba furioso conmigo. My father was furious with me.

furtivo (FEM **furtiva**) ADJECTIVE
■ **la pesca furtiva** poaching
■ **un cazador furtivo** a poacher

el **fusible** NOUN
fuse
□ Han saltado los fusibles. The fuses have blown.

el **fusil** NOUN
rifle

el **fútbol** NOUN
football
□ jugar al fútbol to play football

el **futbolín** (PL los **futbolines**) NOUN
table football

el/la **futbolista** NOUN
footballer
□ Quiere ser futbolista. He wants to be a footballer.

el **futuro** ADJECTIVE, NOUN
future
□ su futuro marido your future husband
■ **El futuro de 'comes' es 'comerás'.** The future of 'comes' is 'comerás'.
■ **la futura madre** the mother-to-be

Gg

la **gabardina** NOUN
raincoat

el **gabinete** NOUN
1 office
■ **el gabinete de prensa** press office
2 cabinet

las **gafas** NOUN
1 glasses
□ Tengo que llevar gafas. I have to wear glasses.
■ **Había unas gafas encima de la mesa.** There was a pair of glasses on the table.
2 goggles
■ **las gafas de sol** sunglasses

la **gaita** NOUN
bagpipes *pl*
□ tocar la gaita to play the bagpipes
■ **¡Menuda gaita!** What a pain!

los **gajes** NOUN
■ **Son gajes del oficio.** They're occupational hazards.

el **gajo** NOUN
segment

la **galaxia** NOUN
galaxy (PL galaxies)

la **galería** NOUN
gallery (PL galleries)
□ una galería de arte an art gallery
■ **una galería comercial** a shopping centre

Gales MASC NOUN
Wales
■ **el País de Gales** Wales

galés (FEM **galesa**, MASC PL **galeses**) ADJECTIVE
Welsh

el **galés** (PL los **galeses**) NOUN
1 Welshman (PL Welshmen)
□ los galeses the Welsh
2 Welsh

la **galesa** NOUN
Welshwoman (PL Welshwomen)

el **galgo** NOUN
greyhound
□ una carrera de galgos a greyhound race

Galicia FEM NOUN
Galicia

el **gallego** (FEM la **gallega**) ADJECTIVE, NOUN
Galician

el **gallego** NOUN
Galician

la **galleta** NOUN
biscuit
■ **una galleta salada** a cracker

la **gallina** NOUN
hen
■ **Sólo pensarlo me pone la carne de gallina.** It gives me goosepimples just thinking about it.
■ **jugar a la gallinita ciega** to play blind man's buff

el/la **gallina** NOUN
■ **¡Eres un gallina!** *(colloquial)* You're chicken!

el **gallinero** NOUN
1 henhouse
2 madhouse *(colloquial)*
□ La clase era un gallinero. The class was a madhouse.

el **gallo** NOUN
cock
■ **en menos que canta un gallo** in an instant

LANGUAGE TIP Word for word, **en menos que canta un gallo** means 'in less than a cock crows'.

galopar VERB [25]
to gallop

la **gama** NOUN
range
□ una amplia gama de ordenadores a wide range of computers

la **gamba** NOUN
prawn

el **gamberro**, la **gamberra** NOUN
hooligan

la **gana** NOUN
■ **Me visto como me da la gana.** I dress the way I want to.
■ **¡No me da la gana!** I don't want to!
■ **Hazlo como te dé la gana.** Do it however you like.
■ **hacer algo de mala gana** to do something reluctantly

tener ganas de hacer algo to feel like doing something
Tengo ganas de que llegue el sábado. I'm looking forward to Saturday.

la **ganadería** NOUN
Se dedican a la ganadería. They raise cattle.

el **ganado** NOUN
livestock
□ alimento para el ganado livestock feed
el ganado vacuno cattle

ganador (FEM **ganadora**) ADJECTIVE
winning
□ el equipo ganador the winning team

el **ganador**, la **ganadora** NOUN
winner

la **ganancia** NOUN
profit
□ las pérdidas y las ganancias profits and losses

ganar VERB [25]
1 to earn
□ Gana un buen sueldo. He earns a good wage.
ganarse la vida to earn a living
2 to win
□ ¿Quién ganó la carrera? Who won the race? □ Lo importante no es ganar. Winning isn't the most important thing.
3 to beat
□ Ganamos al Olimpic tres a cero. We beat Olimpic three-nil.
Con eso no ganas nada. You won't achieve anything by doing that.
ganar tiempo to save time
¡Te lo has ganado! You deserve it!
salir ganando to do well □ Salí ganando con la venta del coche. I did well out of the sale of the car.

el **ganchillo** NOUN
crochet
□ una aguja de ganchillo a crochet hook
hacer ganchillo to crochet

el **gancho** NOUN
1 hook
□ Colgué el abrigo de un gancho. I hung the coat on a hook.
Maradona tiene gancho. Maradona is a crowd-puller.
2 hanger *(Latin America)*

gandul (FEM **gandula**) ADJECTIVE
lazy

el **gandul**, la **gandula** NOUN
good-for-nothing
□ Su marido es un gandul. Her husband is a good-for-nothing.

la **ganga** NOUN
bargain
□ A ese precio es una ganga. It's a real bargain at that price.

el **gángster** (PL los **gángsters**) NOUN
gangster

el **ganso**, la **gansa** NOUN
goose (PL geese)

el **garabato** NOUN
1 doodle
□ una página llena de garabatos a page full of doodles
Me pasé la clase haciendo garabatos. I spent the whole class doodling.
2 scribble
□ Los garabatos eran ininteligibles. The scribbles were unintelligible.
Mientras pensaba iba haciendo garabatos en una libreta. As I was thinking I scribbled away in my notebook.

el **garaje** NOUN
garage
□ Metí el coche en el garaje. I put the car in the garage.
una plaza de garaje a parking space

la **garantía** NOUN
guarantee
□ La lavadora está todavía en garantía. The washing machine is still under guarantee.

garantizar* VERB [13]
to guarantee
□ No te lo puedo garantizar. I can't guarantee it.

el **garbanzo** NOUN
chick pea

la **garganta** NOUN
throat
□ Me duele la garganta. I've got a sore throat.

la **gargantilla** NOUN
necklace

las **gárgaras** NOUN
hacer gárgaras to gargle

la **garita** NOUN
sentry box (PL sentry boxes)

la **garra** NOUN
1 claw
2 talon

la **garrafa** NOUN
carafe

DID YOU KNOW...?
A **garrafa** is also a large bottle with handles.

vino de garrafa cheap wine

la **garúa** NOUN *(Latin America)*
drizzle

el **gas** (PL los **gases**) NOUN
gas
□ ¿No hueles a gas? Can you smell gas?
agua mineral sin gas still mineral water

■ **una bebida sin gas** a still drink
■ **agua mineral con gas** sparkling mineral water
■ **los gases del tubo de escape** exhaust fumes
■ **gases lacrimógenos** tear gas *sing*
■ **El niño tiene muchos gases.** The baby's got a lot of wind.
■ **Pasó una moto a todo gas.** A motorbike shot past at full speed.

la **gasa** NOUN
gauze

la **gaseosa** NOUN
DID YOU KNOW...?
A **gaseosa** is a drink of sweet fizzy water.

el **gasoil** NOUN
diesel oil

el **gasóleo** NOUN
diesel oil

la **gasolina** NOUN
petrol
□ Tengo que echar gasolina. I have to fill up with petrol.
■ **gasolina súper** four-star petrol
■ **gasolina sin plomo** unleaded petrol

la **gasolinera** NOUN
petrol station

gastado (FEM **gastada**) ADJECTIVE
worn
□ La moqueta está muy gastada. The carpet is very worn.

gastar VERB [25]
1 to spend
■ **Javier gasta mucho en ropa.** Javier spends a lot of money on clothes.
2 to use
□ Gastamos mucha agua. We use a lot of water.
■ **Gasté toda una caja de cerillas.** I used up a whole box of matches.
■ **¿Qué numero de zapato gastas?** What size shoes do you take?
■ **Le gastamos una broma a Juan.** We played a joke on Juan.
■ **Se han gastado las pilas.** The batteries have run out.
■ **Se me han gastado las suelas.** The soles of my shoes have worn out.

el **gasto** NOUN
expense
□ Es un gasto tremendo. It's a horrendous expense. □ Este año hemos tenido muchos gastos. We've had a lot of expenses this year.
■ **gastos de envío** postage and packing *sing*
LANGUAGE TIP Word for word, **gastos de envío** means 'sending expenses'.
■ **el gasto público** public spending

la **gata** NOUN
cat
■ **andar a gatas** to crawl □ El niño todavía anda a gatas. The baby is still crawling.
■ **Tienes que subir las escaleras a gatas.** You have to go up the stairs on all fours.

gatear VERB [25]
to crawl

el **gato** NOUN
1 cat
2 jack

la **gaviota** NOUN
seagull

el **gay** (PL los **gays**) ADJECTIVE, NOUN
gay

el **gazpacho** NOUN
DID YOU KNOW...?
Gazpacho is a refreshing soup made from tomatoes, cucumber, garlic, peppers, oil and vinegar and served cold.

el **gel** NOUN
gel
□ gel de baño bath gel

la **gelatina** NOUN
jelly (PL jellies)

el **gemelo** (FEM la **gemela**) ADJECTIVE, NOUN
identical twin
□ Son gemelos. They're identical twins.
□ mi hermano gemelo my identical twin

los **gemelos** NOUN
1 binoculars
2 cufflinks

Géminis MASC NOUN
Gemini
■ **Soy géminis.** I'm Gemini.

el **gen** NOUN
gene

la **generación** (PL las **generaciones**) NOUN
generation

general (FEM **general**) ADJECTIVE
general
□ medicina general general medicine
■ **en general** in general
■ **por lo general** generally □ Por lo general me acuesto temprano. I generally go to bed early.

el/la **general** NOUN
general

generalizar* VERB [13]
to generalize
□ No se puede generalizar. You can't generalize.

generalmente ADVERB
generally

generar VERB [25]
to generate

Spanish-English

g

el **género** NOUN
1 gender
2 kind
□ ¿Qué género de música prefieres? What kind of music do you prefer?
3 material
□ Para las cortinas necesitamos un género más grueso. We need a thicker material for the curtains.
■ **el género humano** the human race

la **generosidad** NOUN
generosity

generoso (FEM **generosa**) ADJECTIVE
generous

genial (FEM **genial**) ADJECTIVE
brilliant
□ Antonio tuvo una idea genial. Antonio had a brilliant idea. □ El concierto estuvo genial. It was a brilliant concert.

el **genio** NOUN
1 temper
□ ¡Menudo genio tiene tu padre! Your father has got such a temper!
■ **tener mal genio** to have a bad temper
2 genius (PL geniuses)
□ ¡Eres un genio! You're a genius!
3 genie

los **genitales** NOUN
genitals

el **genoma** NOUN
genome

la **gente** NOUN
people
□ Había poca gente en la sala. There were few people in the room. □ La gente está cansada de promesas. People are tired of promises.
■ **Son buena gente.** They're good people.
■ **Óscar es buena gente.** Óscar's a good sort.
■ **la gente de la calle** the people in the street

la **geografía** NOUN
geography

la **geología** NOUN
geology

la **geometría** NOUN
geometry

el **geranio** NOUN
geranium

el/la **gerente** NOUN
manager
□ Isabel es gerente de ventas. Isabel is a sales manager.

el **germen** (PL los **gérmenes**) NOUN
germ

germinar VERB [25]
to germinate

el **gesto** NOUN
■ **Hizo un gesto de alivio.** He looked relieved.
■ **Me hizo un gesto para que me sentara.** He made a sign for me to sit down.

la **gestoría** NOUN

> **DID YOU KNOW...?**
> A **gestoría** is a private agency which deals with government departments on behalf of its clients.

Gibraltar MASC NOUN
Gibraltar

el **gibraltareño** (FEM la **gibraltareña**) ADJECTIVE, NOUN
Gibraltarian

el/la **gigante** NOUN
giant

gigantesco (FEM **gigantesca**) ADJECTIVE
gigantic

la **gimnasia** NOUN
gymnastics *sing*
□ Después del recreo tenemos gimnasia. After break we have gymnastics.
■ **Mi madre hace gimnasia todas las mañanas.** My mother does exercises every morning.

el **gimnasio** NOUN
gym

el/la **gimnasta** NOUN
gymnast

la **ginebra** NOUN
gin

el **ginecólogo**, la **ginecóloga** NOUN
gynaecologist
□ Soy ginecóloga. I'm a gynaecologist.

la **gira** NOUN
tour
□ Hicimos una gira por toda Europa. We did a tour all round Europe.
■ **estar de gira** to be on tour

girar VERB [25]
1 to turn
□ Al llegar al semáforo gira a la derecha. When you get to the lights turn right. □ Giré la cabeza para ver quién era. I turned my head to see who it was.
2 to rotate
□ La Tierra gira alrededor de su eje. The Earth rotates on its axis.
■ **La Luna gira alrededor de la Tierra.** The moon revolves around the Earth.

el **girasol** NOUN
sunflower

el **giro** NOUN
1 turn
□ El avión dio un giro de 90 grados. The plane did a 90 degree turn.
2 postal order

□ Voy a mandarte un giro de 100 euros. I'll send you a 100-euro postal order.

el **gitano**, la **gitana** NOUN
gypsy (PL gypsies)

la **glándula** NOUN
gland

global (FEM **global**) ADJECTIVE
global
□ una solución global a global solution

el **globo** NOUN
balloon
■ **un globo terráqueo** a globe

la **glorieta** NOUN
roundabout

glotón (FEM **glotona**, MASC PL **glotones**) ADJECTIVE
greedy

gobernar* VERB [39]
to govern

el **gobierno** NOUN
government

el **gol** NOUN
goal
■ **meter un gol** to score a goal

el **golf** NOUN
golf
■ **jugar al golf** to play golf

el **golfo** NOUN
gulf
□ el Golfo pérsico the Persian Gulf

la **golondrina** NOUN
swallow

la **golosina** NOUN
sweet

goloso (FEM **golosa**) ADJECTIVE
■ **ser goloso** to have a sweet tooth □ Soy muy golosa. I've got a very sweet tooth.

el **golpe** NOUN
■ **Me he dado un golpe en el codo.** I banged my elbow.
■ **Se dio un golpe contra la pared.** He hit the wall.
■ **El coche de atrás nos dio un golpe.** The car behind ran into us.
knock
□ Oímos un golpe en la puerta. We heard a knock at the door.
■ **Di unos golpecitos a la puerta antes de entrar.** I tapped on the door before going in.
■ **de golpe** suddenly □ De golpe decidió dejar el trabajo. He suddenly decided to give up work.
■ **La puerta se cerró de golpe.** The door slammed shut.
■ **no dar golpe** to be bone idle

golpear VERB [25]
1 to hit
□ Me golpeó en la cara con su raqueta. He hit me in the face with his racquet.
2 to bang
□ El maestro golpeó el pupitre con la mano. The teacher banged the desk with his hand.
■ **Me golpeé la cabeza contra el armario.** I banged my head on the cupboard.

la **goma** NOUN
1 eraser
□ ¿Me prestas la goma? Can you lend me your eraser?
■ **una goma de borrar** an eraser □ unos guantes de goma a pair of rubber gloves
2 elastic band
□ Necesito una goma para el pelo. I need an elastic band for my hair.

gordo (FEM **gorda**) ADJECTIVE
1 fat
□ Estoy muy gordo. I'm very fat.
2 thick
3 big
□ Debe de ser algo bastante gordo. It must be something pretty big.
■ **Su mujer me cae gorda.** I can't stand his wife.

el **gorila** NOUN
gorilla

la **gorra** NOUN
cap
■ **de gorra** for free □ Entramos de gorra. We got in for free.

el **gorrión** (PL los **gorriones**) NOUN
sparrow

el **gorro** NOUN
hat
□ Llevaba un gorro de lana. He wore a woollen hat.
■ **un gorro de baño** a swimming cap
■ **Ya estoy hasta el gorro.** I'm absolutely fed up.

el **gorrón**, la **gorrona** (MASC PL los **gorrones**) NOUN
scrounger

la **gota** NOUN
drop
□ Sólo bebí una gota de vino. I only had a drop of wine.
■ **Están cayendo cuatro gotas.** It's spitting.

gotear VERB [25]
1 to drip
2 to leak

la **gotera** NOUN
leak
□ Tenemos goteras en la cocina. We've got some leaks in the kitchen.

gozar* VERB [13]
■ **gozar de algo** to enjoy something

Spanish-English

g

□ Quiere gozar de la vida. He wants to enjoy life. □ Mis abuelos gozan de buena salud. My grandparents enjoy good health.

la **grabación** (PL las **grabaciones**) NOUN
recording

la **grabadora** NOUN
recorder

grabar VERB [25]
1 to tape
□ Quiero grabar esta película. I want to tape this film.
2 to record
□ Lo grabaron en vivo. It was recorded live.
3 to engrave
□ Grabó sus iniciales en la medalla. He engraved his initials on the medal.
■ **Lo tengo grabado en la memoria.** It's etched on my memory.

la **gracia** NOUN
■ **tener gracia** to be funny □ Sus chistes tienen mucha gracia. His jokes are very funny.
■ **Yo no le veo la gracia.** I don't see what's so funny.
■ **Me hizo mucha gracia.** It was so funny.
■ **No me hace gracia tener que salir con este tiempo.** I'm not too pleased about having to go out in this weather.
■ **¡Muchas gracias!** Thanks very much!
■ **dar las gracias a alguien por algo** to thank somebody for something □ Vino a darme las gracias por las flores. He came to thank me for the flowers.
■ **Ni siquiera me dio las gracias.** He didn't even say thank you.
■ **gracias a** thanks to □ Gracias a él me encuentro con vida. Thanks to him I'm still alive.

gracioso (FEM **graciosa**) ADJECTIVE
funny
□ ¡Qué gracioso! How funny!

las **gradas** NOUN
terraces

el **grado** NOUN
degree
□ Estaban a diez grados bajo cero. It was ten degrees below zero. □ quemaduras de primer grado first-degree burns

graduado (FEM **graduada**) ADJECTIVE
■ **gafas graduadas** prescription glasses

gradual (FEM **gradual**) ADJECTIVE
gradual

graduar* VERB [1]
to adjust
■ **Tengo que graduarme la vista.** I've got to have my eyes tested.
■ **Se graduó en Medicina hace dos años.** He graduated in Medicine two years ago.

la **gráfica** NOUN
graph

gráfico (FEM **gráfica**) ADJECTIVE
graphic

el **gráfico** NOUN
table

la **gramática** NOUN
grammar
□ un libro de gramática inglesa a book on English grammar

el **gramo** NOUN
gram

DID YOU KNOW...?
En los países anglosajones el peso a menudo se expresa en onzas **ounces**. Una onza equivale a 28.35 gramos.

gran ADJECTIVE ▷ *see* **grande**

la **granada** NOUN
pomegranate
■ **una granada de mano** a hand grenade

granate (FEM **granate**) ADJECTIVE
maroon
□ una bufanda granate a maroon scarf

Gran Bretaña FEM NOUN
Great Britain

grande (FEM **grande**) ADJECTIVE
1 big
□ Viven en una casa muy grande. They live in a very big house.
■ **¿Cómo es de grande?** How big is it?
■ **La camisa me está grande.** The shirt is too big for me.
2 large
□ un gran número de visitantes a large number of visitors □ grandes sumas de dinero large sums of money
3 great
□ un gran pintor a great painter □ Es una ventaja muy grande. It's a great advantage.
■ **Me llevé una alegría muy grande.** I felt very happy.
■ **Lo pasamos en grande.** We had a great time.
■ **unos grandes almacenes** a department store

LANGUAGE TIP Word for word, **grandes almacenes** means 'big warehouses'.

granel ADVERB
■ **a granel** in bulk □ Venden las aceitunas a granel. They sell olives in bulk.

el **granero** NOUN
barn

el **granizado** NOUN

DID YOU KNOW...?
A **granizado** is a crushed ice drink.

granizar* VERB [13]
to hail
□ Está granizando. It's hailing.

el **granizo** NOUN
hail

la **granja** NOUN
farm
■ **una granja avícola** a poultry farm

el **granjero**, la **granjera** NOUN
farmer

el **grano** NOUN
1 grain
2 bean
3 spot
□ Me ha salido un grano en la frente. I've got a spot on my forehead.
■ **ir al grano** to get to the point

la **grapa** NOUN
staple

la **grapadora** NOUN
stapler

la **grasa** NOUN
1 fat
□ No me va bien tanta grasa. So much fat isn't good for me.
2 grease
■ **La cocina está llena de grasa.** The cooker's really greasy.

grasiento (FEM **grasienta**) ADJECTIVE
greasy

graso (FEM **grasa**) ADJECTIVE
greasy
□ Tengo el cutis graso. I've got greasy skin.

gratis (PL **gratis**) ADJECTIVE, ADVERB
1 free
□ La entrada es gratis. Entry is free.
2 for free
□ Te lo arreglan gratis. They'll fix it for free.

gratuito (FEM **gratuita**) ADJECTIVE
free

la **grava** NOUN
gravel

grave (FEM **grave**) ADJECTIVE
1 serious
□ Tenemos un problema grave. We've got a serious problem.
■ **Su padre está grave.** His father is seriously ill.
2 low

la **gravedad** NOUN
gravity
□ la ley de la gravedad the law of gravity
■ **estar herido de gravedad** to be seriously injured

gravemente ADVERB
seriously
■ **estar gravemente enfermo** to be seriously ill

Grecia FEM NOUN
Greece

el **griego** (FEM la **griega**) ADJECTIVE, NOUN
Greek

el **griego** NOUN
Greek

la **grieta** NOUN
crack

el **grifo** NOUN
tap
□ abrir el grifo to turn on the tap □ cerrar el grifo to turn off the tap

el **grillo** NOUN
cricket

la **gripe** NOUN
flu
□ tener la gripe to have the flu

el **gris** ADJECTIVE, NOUN
grey
□ una puerta gris a grey door

gritar VERB [25]
1 to shout
■ **El público le gritaba al árbitro.** The crowd were shouting at the referee.
■ **Niños, no gritéis tanto.** Children, stop shouting so much.
2 to scream
□ El enfermo no podía dejar de gritar. The patient couldn't stop screaming.

el **grito** NOUN
1 shout
□ gritos de protesta shouts of protest
■ **¡No des esos gritos!** Stop shouting like that!
2 scream
□ Oímos un grito en la calle. We heard a scream outside.
■ **dando gritos a viva voz** screaming at the top of his voice
■ **Es el último grito.** It's all the rage.

la **grosella** NOUN
redcurrant

grosero (FEM **grosera**) ADJECTIVE
rude

el **grosor** NOUN
thickness
■ **La pared tiene 30cm de grosor.** The wall is 30cm thick.

la **grúa** NOUN
crane
■ **La grúa se ha llevado el coche.** My car was towed away.

grueso (FEM **gruesa**) ADJECTIVE
1 thick
2 stout

el **grumo** NOUN
lump

gruñir* VERB [45]
to grumble
□ El abuelo siempre está gruñendo. Grandad is always grumbling.

el **grupo** NOUN
1 group
□ Se dividieron en grupos. They divided into groups.
■ **el grupo sanguíneo** blood group
■ **Los alumnos trabajan en grupo.** The students work in groups.
2 band
□ un grupo de rock a rock band

el **guacho**, la **guacha** NOUN *(Andes, River Plate)*
homeless child

el **guajolote** NOUN *(Mexico)*
turkey

el **guante** NOUN
glove
□ Uso guantes de goma. I use rubber gloves.
■ **unos guantes** a pair of gloves

la **guantera** NOUN
glove compartment

guapo (FEM **guapa**) ADJECTIVE
1 handsome
2 pretty
3 beautiful
■ **¡Ven, guapo!** Come here, love!

el/la **guarda** NOUN
keeper
■ **guarda jurado** armed security guard

el **guardabarros** (PL los **guardabarros**) NOUN
mudguard

el/la **guardaespaldas** (MASC PL los/las **guardaespaldas**) NOUN
bodyguard

guardar VERB [25]
1 to put away
□ Los niños guardaron los juguetes. The children put away their toys. □ Guardé los documentos en el cajón. I put the documents away in the drawer.
■ **Raúl se guardó el pañuelo en el bolsillo.** Raúl put the handkerchief in his pocket.
2 to keep
□ Guarda el recibo. Keep the receipt. □ No sabe guardar un secreto. He can't keep a secret.
■ **No les guardo rencor.** I don't bear them a grudge.
■ **guardar las apariencias** to keep up appearances
■ **guardar un fichero** to save a file

el **guardarropa** NOUN
cloakroom

la **guardería** NOUN
nursery (PL nurseries)

la **guardia** NOUN
■ **de guardia** on duty □ Me atendió el médico de guardia. I was seen by the doctor on duty. □ Estoy de guardia. I'm on duty.
■ **la Guardia Civil** the Civil Guard

el/la **guardia** NOUN
police officer

el **guarro**, la **guarra** NOUN *(colloquial)*
■ **¡Eres un guarro!** You're disgusting!

guay (FEM **guay**) ADJECTIVE
cool *(colloquial)*
□ ¡Qué moto más guay! What a cool bike!

güero (FEM **güera**) ADJECTIVE *(Mexico)*
blonde

la **guerra** NOUN
war
□ la Segunda Guerra Mundial the Second World War
■ **declarar la guerra a un país** to declare war on a country
■ **estar en guerra** to be at war

el/la **guía** NOUN
guide
□ El guía vino a recogernos al aeropuerto. The guide came to pick us up at the airport.

la **guía** NOUN
guidebook
□ Compré una guía turística de Londres. I bought a tourist guidebook of London.
■ **una guía de hoteles** a hotel guide
■ **una guía telefónica** a telephone directory

guiar* VERB [21]
to guide
□ Mi amigo nos guió a la estación. My friend guided us to the station.
■ **Nos guiamos por un mapa que teníamos.** We found our way using a map that we had.

el **guijarro** NOUN
pebble

la **guinda** NOUN
cherry (PL cherries)

la **guindilla** NOUN
chilli pepper

guiñar VERB [25]
to wink
■ **Me guiñó el ojo.** He winked at me.

el **guión** (PL los **guiones**) NOUN
1 hyphen
■ **La palabra 'self-defence' lleva guión.** The word 'self-defence' is hyphenated.
2 dash
3 script

el **guisante** NOUN
pea

guisar VERB [25]
to cook

la **guitarra** NOUN
guitar

el **gusano** NOUN
1 worm
■ **un gusano de seda** a silk worm
2 maggot
3 caterpillar

gustar VERB [25]
■ **Me gustan las uvas.** I like grapes.
■ **¿Te gusta viajar?** Do you like travelling?
■ **Me gustó como hablaba.** I liked the way he spoke.
■ **Me gustaría conocerla.** I would like to meet her.
■ **Me gusta su hermana.** I fancy his sister.
■ **Le gusta más llevar pantalones.** She prefers to wear trousers.

el **gusto** NOUN
taste
□ No tiene gusto para vestirse. He has no taste in clothes. □ He decorado la habitación a mi gusto. I've decorated the room to my taste.
■ **un comentario de mal gusto** a tasteless remark
■ **Le noto un gusto a almendras.** It tastes of almonds.
■ **¡Con mucho gusto!** With pleasure!
■ **¡Mucho gusto en conocerle!** I'm very pleased to meet you!
■ **sentirse a gusto** to feel at ease

Spanish-English

g

Hh

ha VERB ▷ *see* **haber**

el **haba** NOUN
broad bean

Habana NOUN
■ **La Habana** Havana

haber* VERB [24]
to have
□ He comido. I've eaten. □ Hemos comido. We've eaten. □ Había comido. I'd eaten. □ Se ha sentado. She's sat down.
■ **De haberlo sabido, habría ido.** If I'd known, I would have gone.
■ **¡Haberlo dicho antes!** You should have said so before!
■ **hay**
□ Hay una iglesia en la esquina. There's a church on the corner. □ Hubo una guerra. There was a war. □ Hay treinta alumnos en mi clase. There are thirty pupils in my class. □ ¿Hay entradas? Are there any tickets?
■ **¡No hay de qué!** Don't mention it!
■ **¿Qué hay?** *(colloquial)* How are things?
■ **¿Qué hubo?** *(Mexico: colloquial)* How are things?
■ **hay que ...**
■ **Hay que ser respetuoso.** You must be respectful.
■ **¡Habrá que decírselo!** We'll have to tell him!

hábil (FEM **hábil**) ADJECTIVE
skilful
□ Es un jugador muy hábil. He's a very skilful player.
■ **Es muy hábil con las manos.** He's very good with his hands.
■ **Es muy hábil para los negocios.** He's a very able businessman.

la **habilidad** NOUN
skill
□ Ha demostrado una gran habilidad para los negocios. He's shown great business skill.
■ **Tiene mucha habilidad para los idiomas.** She's very good at languages.

la **habitación** (PL las **habitaciones**) NOUN
1 bedroom
2 room
■ **una habitación doble** a double room
■ **una habitación individual** a single room

el/la **habitante** NOUN
inhabitant
■ **los habitantes de la zona** people living in the area

habitar VERB [25]
to live in
□ los que habitaban en la zona those who lived in the area
■ **La casa está todavía sin habitar.** The house is still unoccupied.

el **hábito** NOUN
habit
□ Fumar es un mal hábito. Smoking is a bad habit.

habitual (FEM **habitual**) ADJECTIVE
usual
□ No es habitual verlos juntos. It's not usual to see them together.
■ **un cliente habitual** a regular customer

el **habla** NOUN
speech
■ **Ha perdido el habla.** He's lost the power of speech.
■ **países de habla inglesa** English-speaking countries
■ **¿Señor López? — Al habla.** Señor López? — Speaking.

hablador (FEM **habladora**) ADJECTIVE
1 chatty
2 gossipy

las **habladurías** NOUN
gossip *sing*

el/la **hablante** NOUN
speaker

hablar VERB [25]
1 to speak
□ ¿Hablas español? Do you speak Spanish?
■ **¿Quién habla?** Who's calling?
2 to talk
□ Estuvimos hablando toda la tarde. We were talking all afternoon.
■ **hablar con alguien 1** to speak to someone □ ¿Has hablado ya con el

profesor? Have you spoken to the teacher yet? **2** to talk to someone □ Necesito hablar contigo. I need to talk to you.
■ **hablar de algo** to talk about something
■ **¿Vas a ayudarle en la mudanza? — ¡Ni hablar!** Are you going to help him with the move? — No way!

habré VERB ▷ *see* **haber**

hacer* VERB [26]
1 to make
□ Tengo que hacer la cama. I've got to make the bed. □ Voy a hacer una tortilla. I'm going to make an omelette. □ Están haciendo mucho ruido. They're making a lot of noise.
2 to do
□ ¿Qué haces? What are you doing? □ Estoy haciendo los deberes. I'm doing my homework. □ Hago mucho deporte. I do a lot of sport. □ ¿Qué hace tu padre? What does your father do?
3 to be
□ Hace calor. It's hot. □ Ojalá haga buen tiempo. I hope the weather's nice. □ Hizo dos grados bajo cero. It was two degrees below zero.
■ **hace ... 1** ago □ Terminé hace una hora. I finished an hour ago. □ Ha estado aquí hasta hace poco. He was here a few minutes ago. **2** for □ Hace un mes que voy. I've been going for a month.
■ **¿Hace mucho que esperas?** Have you been waiting long?
■ **hacer hacer algo** to have something done □ Hicieron pintar la fachada del colegio. They had the front of the school painted.
■ **hacer a alguien hacer algo** to make someone do something □ Hace estudiar a los alumnos. He makes the pupils study.
■ **hacer clic en** to click on
■ **hacerse** to become □ Quiere hacerse famoso. He wants to become famous. □ Se hicieron amigos. They became friends.
■ **Ya se está haciendo viejo.** He's getting old now.

el **hacha** FEM NOUN
axe

hacia PREPOSITION
1 towards
□ Venía hacia mí. He was coming towards me. □ su actitud hacia sus padres his attitude towards his parents
2 at about
□ Volveremos hacia las tres. We'll be back at about three.
■ **hacia adelante** forwards
■ **hacia atrás** backwards
■ **hacia dentro** inside
■ **hacia fuera** outside
■ **hacia abajo** down
■ **hacia arriba** up

el **hada** NOUN
fairy (PL fairies)
■ **un hada madrina** a fairy godmother
■ **un cuento de hadas** a fairy tale

hago VERB ▷ *see* **hacer**

hala EXCLAMATION
come on!

halagar* VERB [37]
to flatter

hallar VERB [25]
to find
■ **hallarse** to be □ Se halla fuera del país. He's out of the country.

la **hamaca** NOUN
1 hammock
2 deckchair
3 swing *(River Plate)*

el **hambre** NOUN
hunger
■ **tener hambre** to be hungry □ Tengo mucha hambre. I'm very hungry.

la **hamburguesa** NOUN
hamburger

el **hámster** (PL los **hámsters**) NOUN
hamster

el **hardware** NOUN
hardware

haré VERB ▷ *see* **hacer**

la **harina** NOUN
flour
■ **harina de trigo** wheat flour

hartar VERB [25]
■ **hartarse** to get fed up □ Me harté de estudiar. I got fed up with studying.
■ **Me harté de pasteles.** I stuffed myself with cakes.
■ **¡Me estás hartando!** You're getting on my nerves!

harto (FEM **harta**) ADJECTIVE
▷ *see also* **harto** ADVERB
1 fed up
■ **estar harto de algo** to be fed up with something □ Estábamos hartos de repetirlo. We were fed up with repeating it. □ ¡Me tienes harto! I'm fed up with you!
2 a lot of *(Latin America)*
□ Había harta comida. There was a lot of food.

harto ADVERB
▷ *see also* **harto** ADJECTIVE *(Latin America)*
1 very
□ Es un idioma harto difícil. It's a very difficult language.
2 a lot

□ Tenemos harto que estudiar. We've got a lot to study.

hasta ADVERB
▹ *see also* **hasta** PREPOSITION, CONJUNCTION
even
□ Estudia hasta cuando está de vacaciones. He even studies when he's on holiday.

hasta PREPOSITION, CONJUNCTION
▹ *see also* **hasta** ADVERB
1 till
□ Está abierto hasta las cuatro. It's open till four o'clock.
■ **¿Hasta cuándo?** How long? □ ¿Hasta cuándo te quedas? — Hasta la semana que viene. How long are you staying? — Till next week.
■ **Hasta ahora no ha llamado nadie.** No one has called up to now.
■ **hasta que** until □ Espera aquí hasta que te llamen. Wait here until you're called.
2 up to
□ Caminamos hasta la puerta. We walked up to the door.
3 as far as
□ Desde aquí se ve hasta el pueblo de al lado. From here you can see as far as the next town.
■ **¡Hasta luego!** See you!
■ **¡Hasta el sábado!** See you on Saturday!

hay VERB ▹ *see* **haber**

haz VERB ▹ *see* **hacer**

he VERB
▹ *see also* **he** ADVERB ▹ *see* **haber**

he ADVERB
▹ *see also* **he** VERB
■ **He aquí un ejemplo.** Here's an example.
■ **He aquí unos ejemplos.** Here are some examples.
■ **he aquí por qué ...** that's why ...

la **hebilla** NOUN
buckle

el **hebreo** (FEM la **hebrea**) ADJECTIVE, NOUN
Hebrew

el **hebreo** NOUN
Hebrew

el **hechizo** NOUN
spell

hecho VERB
▹ *see also* **hecho** ADJECTIVE, NOUN ▹ *see* **hacer**

hecho (FEM **hecha**) ADJECTIVE
▹ *see also* **hecho** VERB, NOUN
made
□ ¿De qué está hecho? What's it made of?
■ **hecho a mano** handmade
■ **hecho a máquina** machine-made
■ **Me gusta la carne bien hecha.** I like my meat well done.
■ **un filete poco hecho** a rare steak
■ **¡Bien hecho!** Well done!
■ **un hombre hecho y derecho** a fully grown man

el **hecho** NOUN ADJECTIVE, VERB
1 fact
□ el hecho de que ... the fact that ...
■ **el hecho es que ...** the fact is that ...
2 event
□ un hecho histórico an historic event
■ **de hecho** in fact

la **helada** NOUN
frost

la **heladera** NOUN *(River Plate)*
refrigerator

la **heladería** NOUN
ice-cream parlour

helado (FEM **helada**) ADJECTIVE
1 frozen
□ El lago está helado. The lake's frozen over.
2 freezing
□ Este cuarto está helado. This room's freezing. □ ¡Estoy helado! I'm freezing!

el **helado** NOUN
ice cream
□ un helado de chocolate a chocolate ice cream

helar* VERB [39]
to freeze
□ El frío ha helado las tuberías. The cold has frozen the pipes. □ Esta noche va a helar. It's going to freeze tonight.
■ **helarse** to freeze □ Me estoy helando. I'm freezing.
■ **Anoche heló.** There was a frost last night.

el **helecho** NOUN
fern

el **helicóptero** NOUN
helicopter

la **hembra** ADJECTIVE, NOUN
female
□ un elefante hembra a female elephant

hemos VERB ▹ *see* **haber**

heredar VERB [25]
to inherit

la **heredera** NOUN
heiress (PL heiresses)

el **heredero** NOUN
heir

la **herencia** NOUN
inheritance

la **herida** NOUN
1 wound
□ una herida de bala a bullet wound □ una herida de cuchillo a stab wound
2 injury (PL injuries)
□ Murió a causa de las heridas del accidente. He died from injuries received in the accident.

herido (FEM **herida**) ADJECTIVE
1 wounded
2 injured
herir* VERB [51]
1 to wound
□ Lo hirieron en el pecho. He was wounded in the chest.
2 to injure
□ Resultó gravemente herido en la caída. He was seriously injured in the fall.
la **hermana** NOUN
sister
la **hermanastra** NOUN
stepsister
el **hermanastro** NOUN
stepbrother
■ **mis hermanastros** 1 my stepbrothers 2 my stepbrothers and sisters
el **hermano** NOUN
brother
■ **mis hermanos** 1 my brothers 2 my brothers and sisters
hermético (FEM **hermética**) ADJECTIVE
airtight
hermoso (FEM **hermosa**) ADJECTIVE
beautiful
la **hermosura** NOUN
beauty
□ el secreto de su hermosura the secret of her beauty
■ **¡Qué hermosura de paisaje!** What a beautiful landscape!
el **héroe** NOUN
hero (PL heroes)
la **heroína** NOUN
heroine
el **heroinómano**, la **heroinómana** NOUN
heroin addict
la **herradura** NOUN
horseshoe
la **herramienta** NOUN
tool
el **herrero** NOUN
blacksmith
hervir* VERB [51]
to boil
□ El agua está hirviendo. The water's boiling.
■ **hervir agua** to boil water
el/la **heterosexual** ADJECTIVE, NOUN
heterosexual
hice VERB ▷ *see* **hacer**
hielo VERB ▷ *see* **helar**
el **hielo** NOUN
ice
la **hierba** NOUN
1 grass
2 herb
■ **una mala hierba** a weed
LANGUAGE TIP Word for word, **mala hierba** means 'bad grass'.
la **hierbabuena** NOUN
mint
el **hierbajo** NOUN
weed
el **hierro** NOUN
iron
□ una caja de hierro an iron box
el **hígado** NOUN
liver
la **higiene** NOUN
hygiene
higiénico (FEM **higiénica**) ADJECTIVE
hygienic
■ **poco higiénico** unhygienic
el **higo** NOUN
fig
■ **un higo chumbo** a prickly pear
la **higuera** NOUN
fig tree
la **hija** NOUN
daughter
■ **Soy hija única.** I'm an only child.
■ **Sí, hija mía, tienes razón.** Yes, my dear, you're right.
la **hijastra** NOUN
stepdaughter
el **hijastro** NOUN
stepson
■ **mis hijastros** 1 my stepsons 2 my stepchildren
el **hijo** NOUN
son
□ su hijo mayor his oldest son
■ **mis hijos** 1 my sons 2 my children
■ **Soy hijo único.** I'm an only child.
la **hilera** NOUN
1 row
□ una hilera de casas a row of houses
2 line
□ ponerse en hilera to get into a line
el **hilo** NOUN
1 thread
□ hilo de coser sewing thread
2 linen
□ un traje de hilo a linen suit
■ **los hilos del teléfono** the telephone wires
el **himno** NOUN
hymn
■ **el himno nacional** the national anthem
el/la **hincha** NOUN
fan
□ los hinchas del fútbol football fans
hinchado (FEM **hinchada**) ADJECTIVE

swollen

el **hipermercado** NOUN
hypermarket

el **hipo** NOUN
hiccups
□ Tengo hipo. I've got hiccups. □ Me ha dado hipo. It's given me hiccups.

hipócrita (FEM **hipócrita**) ADJECTIVE
hypocritical
■ **¡No seas hipócrita!** Don't be such a hypocrite!

el/la **hipócrita** NOUN
hypocrite

el **hipódromo** NOUN
racecourse

el **hipopótamo** NOUN
hippo (PL hippos)

la **hipoteca** NOUN
mortgage

hiriendo VERB ▷ *see* **herir**

hirviendo VERB ▷ *see* **hervir**

hispanohablante (FEM **hispanohablante**) ADJECTIVE
Spanish-speaking
□ los países hispanohablantes Spanish-speaking countries

el/la **hispanohablante** NOUN
Spanish-speaker

la **historia** NOUN
1 history
□ la historia de España Spanish history
2 story (PL stories)
□ El libro cuenta la historia de dos niños. The book tells the story of two children.
■ **la misma historia de siempre** the same old story

el **historial** NOUN
record

histórico (FEM **histórica**) ADJECTIVE
1 historic
□ una ciudad histórica a historic city
2 historical
□ un personaje histórico a historical character

la **historieta** NOUN
comic strip

hizo VERB ▷ *see* **hacer**

el **hobby** NOUN
hobby (PL hobbies)
■ **Lo hago por hobby.** I do it as a hobby.

el **hockey** NOUN
hockey
■ **el hockey sobre hielo** ice hockey

el **hogar** NOUN
home
□ en todos los hogares españoles in every Spanish home
■ **productos para el hogar** household products

la **hoguera** NOUN
bonfire

la **hoja** NOUN
1 leaf (PL leaves)
2 sheet
□ una hoja de papel a sheet of paper
■ **una hoja de cálculo** a spreadsheet
■ **una hoja de solicitud** an application form
3 page
□ las hojas de un libro the pages of a book
■ **una hoja de afeitar** a razor blade

el **hojaldre** NOUN
puff pastry

hojear VERB [25]
to leaf through

hola EXCLAMATION
hello!

Holanda FEM NOUN
Holland

holandés (FEM **holandesa**, MASC PL **holandeses**) ADJECTIVE
Dutch

el **holandés** (PL los **holandeses**) NOUN
1 Dutchman (PL Dutchmen)
■ **los holandeses** the Dutch
2 Dutch

la **holandesa** NOUN
Dutchwoman (PL Dutchwomen)

holgazán (FEM **holgazana**, MASC PL **holgazanes**) ADJECTIVE
lazy

el **hollín** NOUN
soot

el **hombre** NOUN
man (PL men)
■ **un hombre de negocios** a businessman
■ **la historia del hombre sobre la tierra** the history of mankind on earth

el **hombro** NOUN
shoulder
■ **encogerse de hombros** to shrug one's shoulders

el **homenaje** NOUN
tribute
■ **en homenaje a** in honour of

el/la **homosexual** ADJECTIVE, NOUN
homosexual

hondo (FEM **honda**) ADJECTIVE
deep
□ un pozo muy hondo a very deep well □ Se ha tirado por la parte honda de la piscina. He dived into the deep end of the pool.

Honduras FEM NOUN
Honduras

el **hondureño** (FEM la **hondureña**) ADJECTIVE, NOUN

Honduran

la **honestidad** NOUN
1 honesty
2 decency

honesto (FEM **honesta**) ADJECTIVE
honest
□ un vendedor honesto an honest salesman

el **hongo** NOUN
1 fungus
2 mushroom *(Latin America)*

el **honor** NOUN
honour

la **honradez** NOUN
honesty

honrado (FEM **honrada**) ADJECTIVE
honest
□ Es una persona muy honrada. He's a very honest person.

la **hora** NOUN
1 hour
□ El viaje dura una hora. The journey lasts an hour.
2 time
□ ¿Qué hora es? What's the time? □ ¿Tienes hora? Have you got the time?
■ **¿A qué hora llega?** What time is he arriving?
■ **llegar a la hora** to arrive on time
■ **la hora de cenar** dinner time
■ **a última hora** at the last minute
3 period
■ **Después de inglés tenemos una hora libre.** After English we have a free period.
4 appointment
□ Tengo hora para el dentista. I've got an appointment at the dentist's.
■ **horas extras** overtime *sing*
■ **en mis horas libres** in my spare time

el **horario** NOUN
timetable
■ **el horario de trenes** the train timetable
■ **horario de visitas** visiting hours *pl*

la **horchata** NOUN

DID YOU KNOW...?
Horchata is a milky looking drink made from tiger nuts and served with ice.

horizontal (FEM **horizontal**) ADJECTIVE
horizontal

el **horizonte** NOUN
horizon
□ en el horizonte on the horizon

la **hormiga** NOUN
ant

el **hormigón** NOUN
concrete

el **hormigueo** NOUN
pins and needles
□ Tengo hormigueo en la pierna. I've got pins and needles in my leg.

el **horno** NOUN
oven
□ ¡Este lugar es un horno! This place is like an oven!
■ **pescado al horno** baked fish
■ **pollo al horno** roast chicken
■ **un horno microondas** a microwave oven

el **horóscopo** NOUN
horoscope

la **horquilla** NOUN
hairgrip

horrible (FEM **horrible**) ADJECTIVE
awful
□ El tiempo ha estado horrible. The weather has been awful.

el **horror** NOUN
horror
□ los horrores de la guerra the horrors of war
■ **tener horror a algo** to be terrified of something □ Les tengo horror a las arañas. I'm terrified of spiders.
■ **¡Qué horror!** How awful!

horroroso (FEM **horrorosa**) ADJECTIVE
1 horrific
□ un accidente horroroso a horrific accident
2 hideous
□ ¡Qué camisa mas horrorosa! What a hideous shirt!

la **hortaliza** NOUN
vegetable

hortera (FEM **hortera**) ADJECTIVE
naff *(colloquial)*
□ Tiene un gusto muy hortera. He's got really naff taste.

hospedarse VERB [25]
to stay
□ Se hospedaron en un hotel. They stayed in a hotel.

el **hospital** NOUN
hospital
□ La tuvieron que llevar al hospital. She had to be taken to hospital.

la **hospitalidad** NOUN
hospitality

el **hostal** NOUN
small hotel

la **hostia** NOUN
host

el **hotel** NOUN
hotel

hoy ADVERB
today
□ Hoy no tenemos clases. We haven't got any classes today. □ el periódico de hoy today's paper □ los jóvenes de hoy young

people today
■ **desde hoy en adelante** from now on
■ **hoy en día** nowadays
■ **hoy por la mañana** this morning

el **hoyo** NOUN
hole

hube VERB ▷ *see* **haber**

la **hucha** NOUN
moneybox

hueco (FEM **hueca**) ADJECTIVE
hollow

el **hueco** NOUN
1 space
□ Deja un hueco para la respuesta. Leave a space for the answer.
■ **Hazme un hueco para sentarme.** Make a bit of room so that I can sit down.
2 free period
□ Los lunes tengo un hueco entre clase y clase. I have a free period between classes on Mondays.
■ **Entró por un hueco que había en la valla.** He got in through a gap in the fence.

la **huelga** NOUN
strike
□ una huelga general a general strike
■ **estar en huelga** to be on strike
■ **declararse en huelga** to go on strike

el/la **huelguista** NOUN
striker

la **huella** NOUN
footprint
■ **huellas** tracks
■ **Desapareció sin dejar huella.** He disappeared without trace.
■ **huella digital** fingerprint

huelo VERB ▷ *see* **oler**

huérfano (FEM **huérfana**) ADJECTIVE
■ **un niño huérfano** an orphan
■ **ser huérfano** to be an orphan
■ **es huérfano de padre** he's lost his father
■ **quedarse huérfano** to be orphaned

el **huérfano**, la **huérfana** NOUN
orphan

la **huerta** NOUN
1 vegetable garden
2 orchard

el **huerto** NOUN
1 kitchen garden
2 orchard

el **hueso** NOUN
1 bone
2 stone
■ **aceitunas sin hueso** pitted olives
■ **La profesora de francés es un hueso.** *(colloquial)* The French teacher's a real dragon.

el/la **huésped** NOUN
guest

el **huevo** NOUN
egg
■ **un huevo duro** a hard-boiled egg
■ **un huevo escalfado** a poached egg
■ **un huevo frito** a fried egg
■ **huevos revueltos** scrambled eggs
■ **un huevo pasado por agua** a soft-boiled egg

la **huida** NOUN
escape

huir* VERB [10]
to escape
□ Huyó de la cárcel. He escaped from prison.
■ **Huyeron del país.** They fled the country.
■ **salir huyendo** to run away

el **hule** NOUN
1 oilcloth
2 rubber *(Mexico)*
□ una liga de hule a rubber band

la **humanidad** NOUN
humanity

humano (FEM **humana**) ADJECTIVE
human
□ el cuerpo humano the human body
■ **los seres humanos** human beings

el **humano** NOUN
human being

la **humareda** NOUN
cloud of smoke

la **humedad** NOUN
1 dampness
2 humidity

húmedo (FEM **húmeda**) ADJECTIVE
1 damp
□ La ropa está húmeda todavía. The clothes are still damp.
2 humid
□ El día estaba muy húmedo. It was a very humid day.

humilde (FEM **humilde**) ADJECTIVE
humble
□ Era de familia humilde. She was from a humble background.

el **humo** NOUN
smoke
□ El humo de la chimenea. The smoke from the chimney.
■ **darse humos** to brag
■ **bajar los humos a alguien** to take someone down a peg or two
■ **Estaba que echaba humo.** She was absolutely fuming.

el **humor** NOUN
mood
□ No está de humor para bromas. He's not in the mood for jokes.

■ **estar de buen humor** to be in a good mood
■ **estar de mal humor** to be in a bad mood
■ **Tiene un gran sentido del humor.** He has got a good sense of humour.
■ **humor negro** black humour

hundirse VERB [58]
1 to sink
□ El barco se hundió durante la tormenta. The boat sank during the storm.
2 to collapse
□ El techo se hundió con el peso. The ceiling collapsed under the weight.

el **húngaro** (FEM la **húngara**) ADJECTIVE, NOUN
Hungarian

el **húngaro** NOUN
Hungarian

Hungría FEM NOUN
Hungary

el **huracán** NOUN
hurricane

hurgar* VERB [37]
to rummage
□ La encontré hurgando en los cajones. I found her rummaging through the drawers. □ Hurgó en sus bolsillos buscando las llaves. He rummaged in his pockets for the keys.
■ **hurgarse la nariz** to pick one's nose

huyendo VERB ▷ *see* **huir**

Ii

I.B. ABBREVIATION *(= Instituto de Bachillerato)*

DID YOU KNOW...?
In Spain the **Institutos de Bachillerato** are state secondary schools for 12- to 18-year-olds.

iba VERB ▷ *see* **ir**

el **iberoamericano** (FEM la **iberoamericana**) ADJECTIVE, NOUN
Latin American

el **iceberg** (PL los **icebergs**) NOUN
iceberg

el **icono** NOUN
icon

la **ictericia** NOUN
jaundice

la **ida** NOUN
single
□ ¿Cuánto cuesta la ida? How much does a single cost?
■ **¿Me da uno de ida y vuelta para Londres, por favor?** A return to London please.
■ **un billete de ida y vuelta** a return ticket
■ **un boleto de ida y vuelta** *(Latin America)* a return ticket
■ **a la ida** on the way there
■ **El viaje de ida duró dos horas.** The journey there took two hours.

la **idea** NOUN
idea
□ ¡Qué buena idea! What a good idea! □ No tengo ni idea. I haven't the faintest idea.
■ **Mi idea era que nos juntáramos en mi casa.** I thought that we could meet at my house.
■ **Ya me voy haciendo a la idea.** I'm beginning to get used to the idea.
■ **cambiar de idea** to change one's mind
□ He cambiado de idea. I've changed my mind.

ideal (FEM **ideal**) ADJECTIVE
ideal
□ el lugar ideal para las vacaciones the ideal place for the holidays

el **ideal** NOUN
ideal
□ los ideales democráticos democratic ideals □ Mi ideal sería trabajar cuatro horas diarias. My ideal would be to work four hours a day.

idear VERB [25]
to devise
□ Idearon un nuevo sistema. They devised a new system.

idéntico (FEM **idéntica**) ADJECTIVE
identical
□ Tiene una falda idéntica a la mía. She has an identical skirt to mine.
■ **Es idéntica a su padre.** She's the spitting image of her father.

identificar* VERB [48]
to identify
□ Ya han identificado a la víctima. They've already identified the victim.
■ **identificarse con alguien** to identify with somebody

el **idioma** NOUN
language
□ Habla tres idiomas a la perfección. He speaks three languages perfectly.

idiota (FEM **idiota**) ADJECTIVE
stupid
□ ¡No seas tan idiota! Don't be so stupid!

el/la **idiota** NOUN
idiot

la **idiotez** (PL las **idioteces**) NOUN
■ **Deja de decir idioteces.** Stop talking nonsense.

el **ídolo** NOUN
idol

la **iglesia** NOUN
church (PL churches)
□ Voy a la iglesia todos los domingos. I go to church every Sunday.
■ **la Iglesia católica** the Catholic Church

ignorante (FEM **ignorante**) ADJECTIVE
ignorant

ignorar VERB [25]
1 not to know
□ Ignoramos su paradero. We don't know his whereabouts.
2 to ignore

□ Es mejor ignorarla. It's best to ignore her.

igual (FEM **igual**) ADJECTIVE
▷ *see also* **igual** ADVERB
1 equal
□ Se repartieron el dinero en partes iguales. They divided the money into equal shares.
■ **X es igual a Y.** X is equal to Y.
2 the same
□ Todas las casas son iguales. All the houses are the same.
■ **Es igual a su madre.** 1 She looks just like her mother. 2 She's just like her mother.
■ **Tengo una falda igual que la tuya.** I've got a skirt just like yours.
■ **ir iguales** to be even
■ **Van quince iguales.** It's fifteen all.
■ **Es igual hoy que mañana.** Today or tomorrow, it doesn't matter.
■ **Me da igual.** I don't mind.

igual ADVERB
▷ *see also* **igual** ADJECTIVE
1 the same
□ Se visten igual. They dress the same.
2 maybe
□ Igual no lo saben todavía. Maybe they don't know yet.
3 anyway
□ No hizo nada pero la castigaron igual. She didn't do anything but they punished her anyway.

la **igualdad** NOUN
equality
□ la igualdad racial racial equality
■ **la igualdad de oportunidades** equal opportunities

igualmente ADVERB
the same to you
□ ¡Feliz Navidad! — Gracias, igualmente. Happy Christmas! — Thanks, the same to you.

ilegal (FEM **ilegal**) ADJECTIVE
illegal

ilegible (FEM **ilegible**) ADJECTIVE
illegible
□ Tiene una letra ilegible. His handwriting's illegible.

ileso (FEM **ilesa**) ADJECTIVE
unhurt
□ Salió ileso del accidente. He escaped unhurt from the accident.
■ **Todos resultaron ilesos.** No one was hurt.

la **iluminación** NOUN
lighting
□ La iluminación de las calles es insuficiente. The street lighting is poor.
■ **Se cortó la iluminación del estadio.** The stadium floodlighting went out.

iluminar VERB [25]
to light
□ las farolas que iluminan la calle the streetlamps that light the street □ Unas velas iluminaban la habitación. The room was lit by candles.
■ **El flash le iluminó el rostro.** The flash lit up his face.
■ **Esta lámpara ilumina muy poco.** This lamp gives out very little light.
■ **Se le iluminó la cara.** His face lit up.

la **ilusión** (PL las **ilusiones**) NOUN
1 hope
□ Llegó aquí con muchísima ilusión. He arrived here full of hope. □ No te hagas muchas ilusiones. Don't build your hopes up.
2 dream
□ Mi mayor ilusión es llegar a ser médico. My dream is to become a doctor.
3 illusion
□ una ilusión óptica an optical illusion
■ **Le hace mucha ilusión que vengas.** He's really looking forward to you coming.
■ **Tu regalo me hizo mucha ilusión.** I was delighted to get your present.
■ **¡Qué ilusión!** How wonderful!

ilusionado (FEM **ilusionada**) ADJECTIVE
excited

ilusionar VERB [25]
■ **Me ilusiona mucho la idea.** I'm really excited about the idea.
■ **ilusionarse** to build up one's hopes □ No te ilusiones demasiado. Don't build up your hopes too much.
■ **ilusionarse con algo** to get really excited about something

la **ilustración** (PL las **ilustraciones**) NOUN
illustration

la **imagen** (PL las **imágenes**) NOUN
1 image
□ Han decidido cambiar de imagen. They've decided to change their image.
■ **ser la viva imagen de alguien** to be the spitting image of somebody
2 picture
□ Las películas dan una imagen falsa de América. Films give a false picture of America.

la **imaginación** (PL las **imaginaciones**) NOUN
imagination
□ Tiene mucha imaginación. He has a vivid imagination.
■ **Esas son imaginaciones tuyas.** You're imagining things.
■ **Ni se me pasó por la imaginación.** It never even occurred to me.

imaginarse VERB [25]
to imagine
□ No te imaginas lo mal que me sentí. You can't imagine how bad I felt. □ Me imagino que seguirá en Madrid. I imagine that he's still in Madrid.
■ **Me imagino que sí.** I imagine so.
■ **Me imagino que no.** I wouldn't think so.
■ **¿Se enfadó mucho? — ¡Imagínate!** Was he very angry? — What do you think!

el **imán** (PL los **imanes**) NOUN
magnet

imbécil (FEM **imbécil**) ADJECTIVE
stupid
□ ¡No seas imbécil! Don't be stupid!

la **imitación** (PL las **imitaciones**) NOUN
1 impression
□ Es muy buena haciendo imitaciones. She's very good at doing impressions.
2 imitation
□ Aprendemos a hablar por imitación. We learn to speak by imitation. □ los diamantes de imitación imitation diamonds □ Es imitación de cuero. It's imitation leather.

imitar VERB [25]
to copy
□ Imita todo lo que hace su hermano. He copies everything his brother does.
■ **imitar a alguien** to do an impression of somebody □ Imita muy bien a la directora. She does a very good impression of the headmistress.
■ **imitar un acento** to imitate an accent

impaciente (FEM **impaciente**) ADJECTIVE
impatient
□ Se estaba empezando a poner impaciente. He was beginning to get impatient.
□ Estarás impaciente por saberlo. You'll be impatient to know.

impar (FEM **impar**) ADJECTIVE
odd
□ un número impar an odd number

el **impar** NOUN
odd number

imparcial (FEM **imparcial**) ADJECTIVE
impartial

impecable (FEM **impecable**) ADJECTIVE
impeccable
□ Su comportamiento siempre ha sido impecable. His behaviour has always been impeccable.
■ **Siempre va impecable.** He is always impeccably dressed.

impedir* VERB [38]
1 to prevent
□ Trataron de impedir la huida de los presos. They tried to prevent the prisoners' escape.
□ impedir que alguien haga algo to prevent somebody from doing something
2 to stop
□ A mí nadie me lo va a impedir. Nobody is going to stop me.
3 to block
□ Un camión nos impedía el paso. A lorry was blocking our way.

el **imperdible** NOUN
safety pin

el **imperio** NOUN
empire

impermeable (FEM **impermeable**) ADJECTIVE
waterproof
□ una tela impermeable waterproof material

el **impermeable** NOUN
raincoat

impersonal (FEM **impersonal**) ADJECTIVE
impersonal

impertinente (FEM **impertinente**) ADJECTIVE
impertinent

impidiendo VERB ▷ *see* **impedir**

impido VERB ▷ *see* **impedir**

imponer* VERB [41]
to impose
□ Le impusieron una multa de 50 euros. They imposed a 50-euro fine on him.
■ **imponerse** 1 to triumph □ El corredor nigeriano se impuso en la segunda carrera. The Nigerian runner triumphed in the second race. 2 to assert oneself □ Sabe imponerse. He knows how to assert himself.

la **importación** (PL las **importaciones**) NOUN
import
□ una empresa de importación/exportación an import-export business
■ **los artículos de importación** imported goods
■ **Está prohibida su importación.** There's a ban on importing it.

la **importancia** NOUN
importance
□ un asunto de suma importancia a matter of great importance
■ **dar importancia a algo** to attach importance to something □ Les da demasiada importancia a los detalles. He attaches too much importance to details.
■ **darse importancia** to give oneself airs
■ **La educación tiene mucha importancia.** Education is very important.
■ **¡Me he olvidado tu libro! — No tiene importancia.** I've forgotten your book! — It doesn't matter.

■ **cuestiones sin importancia** unimportant matters

importante (FEM **importante**) ADJECTIVE
important
■ **lo importante** the important thing □ Lo importante es que vengas. The important thing is that you come.

importar VERB [25]
1 to import
□ Importa especias de la India. He imports spices from India.
2 to matter
□ ¿Y eso qué importa? And what does that matter?
■ **no importa** 1 it doesn't matter □ No importa lo que piensen los demás. It doesn't matter what other people think.
2 never mind □ No importa, podemos hacerlo mañana. Never mind, we can do it tomorrow.
■ **No me importa levantarme temprano.** I don't mind getting up early. □ ¿Le importa que fume? Do you mind if I smoke?
■ **¿Y a ti qué te importa?** What's it to you?
■ **Me importan mucho mis estudios.** My studies are very important to me.
■ **Me importa un bledo.** I couldn't care less.

imposible (FEM **imposible**) ADJECTIVE
impossible
□ Es imposible predecir quién ganará. It's impossible to predict who will win. □ Es imposible de saber por anticipado. It's impossible to predict. □ El abuelo está imposible hoy. Granddad is being impossible today.
■ **Me es imposible comprenderla.** I can't understand her.
■ **Es imposible que lo sepan.** They can't possibly know.

el **impostor**, la **impostora** NOUN
impostor

imprescindible (FEM **imprescindible**) ADJECTIVE
essential

la **impresión** (PL las **impresiones**) NOUN
impression
□ Le causó muy buena impresión a mis padres. He made a very good impression on my parents.
■ **Tengo la impresión de que no va a venir.** I have a feeling that he won't come.
■ **Me dio mucha impresión verlo tan delgado.** I was shocked to see him looking so thin.

impresionante (FEM **impresionante**) ADJECTIVE
1 impressive
□ una colección de sellos impresionante an impressive stamp collection
2 amazing
□ una cantidad impresionante de coches an amazing number of cars
3 striking
□ El parecido es impresionante. The likeness is striking.
■ **paisajes de una belleza impresionante** strikingly beautiful landscapes

impresionar VERB [25]
1 to shock
□ Me impresionó mucho su palidez. I was really shocked at how pale he was.
2 to impress
□ Unos poemas me impresionaron más que otros. Some poems impressed me more than others.
■ **Impresiona lo rápido que es.** His speed is impressive.
■ **impresionarse** to be impressed □ Se impresiona con facilidad. He's easily impressed.

el **impreso** NOUN
form
□ un impreso de solicitud an application form

la **impresora** NOUN
printer
□ una impresora láser a laser printer

imprevisible (FEM **imprevisible**) ADJECTIVE
1 unforeseeable
□ acontecimientos imprevisibles unforeseeable events
2 unpredictable
□ Sus reacciones son imprevisibles. His reactions are unpredictable.

imprevisto (FEM **imprevista**) ADJECTIVE
unexpected

el **imprevisto** NOUN
■ **si no surge algún imprevisto** if nothing unexpected comes up

imprimir* VERB [58]
to print

improvisar VERB [25]
to improvise

la **imprudencia** NOUN
■ **Saltar la tapia fue una imprudencia.** It was unwise to jump over the wall.
■ **El accidente fue debido a una imprudencia del conductor.** The accident was caused by reckless driving.

imprudente (FEM **imprudente**) ADJECTIVE
unwise
□ Sería imprudente nadar aquí. It would be unwise to go swimming here.
■ **conductores imprudentes** reckless drivers

impuesto VERB ▷ *see* **imponer**

el **impuesto** NOUN
tax (PL taxes)
■ **el impuesto sobre la renta** income tax
■ **el impuesto sobre el valor añadido** value-added tax
■ **el impuesto sobre el valor agregado** *(Latin America)* value-added tax
■ **libre de impuestos** duty-free □ Lo compré en la tienda libre de impuestos. I bought it at the duty-free shop.

impulsar VERB [25]
to drive
□ Está impulsado por un motor eléctrico. It's driven by an electric motor. □ La ambición la impulsó a mentir. Ambition drove her to lie.
■ **una política destinada a impulsar el comercio** a policy designed to boost trade

el **impulso** NOUN
impulse
□ Actué por impulso. I acted on impulse.
■ **Mi primer impulso fue salir corriendo.** My first instinct was to run away.
■ **Tomó impulso antes de saltar.** He took a run up before jumping.

inaceptable (FEM **inaceptable**) ADJECTIVE
unacceptable

inadecuado (FEM **inadecuada**) ADJECTIVE
unsuitable

inadvertido (FEM **inadvertida**) ADJECTIVE
■ **pasar inadvertido** to go unnoticed □ Tu ausencia no pasó inadvertida. Your absence didn't go unnoticed.

inapropiado (FEM **inapropiada**) ADJECTIVE
unsuitable
□ Esos zapatos son inapropiados para ir al campo. Those shoes are unsuitable for the country.

la **inauguración** (PL las **inauguraciones**) NOUN
opening
□ Había mucha gente en la inauguración. There were a lot of people at the opening.
□ la ceremonia de inauguración the opening ceremony

inaugurar VERB [25]
to open
□ Mañana inauguran el nuevo hospital. The new hospital is being opened tomorrow.

el/la **inca** ADJECTIVE, NOUN
Inca

la **incapacidad** NOUN
inability
□ debido a su incapacidad para concentrarse owing to his inability to concentrate
■ **la incapacidad física** physical disability
■ **la incapacidad mental** mental disability

incapaz (FEM **incapaz**, PL **incapaces**) ADJECTIVE
incapable
□ Es incapaz de estarse callado. He is incapable of keeping quiet.
■ **Hoy soy incapaz de concentrarme.** I can't concentrate today.

incendiarse VERB [25]
to catch fire
□ Se le incendió el coche. His car caught fire.

el **incendio** NOUN
fire
□ Se declaró un incendio en el hotel. A fire broke out in the hotel.

el **incentivo** NOUN
incentive
□ No tengo incentivo para estudiar. I have no incentive to study.

el **incidente** NOUN
incident
□ La reunión transcurrió sin incidentes. The meeting passed off without incident.

incierto (FEM **incierta**) ADJECTIVE
uncertain
□ un porvenir incierto an uncertain future

inclinar VERB [25]
to tilt
□ Inclina un poco más la sombrilla. Can you tilt the sun umbrella a bit more?
■ **inclinar la cabeza** to nod
■ **inclinarse 1** to bend down □ Se inclinó para besarlo. She bent down to kiss him. **2** to lean □ inclinarse sobre algo to lean over something □ inclinarse hacia delante to lean forward □ inclinarse hacia atrás to lean back **3** to bow □ inclinarse ante alguien to bow to somebody

incluido (FEM **incluida**) ADJECTIVE
included
□ El servicio no está incluido en el precio. Service is not included.

incluir* VERB [10]
to include
□ El precio incluye las comidas. The price includes meals.
■ **El examen no incluye este tema.** This topic doesn't come into the exam.

inclusive ADVERB
1 inclusive
□ Está abierto de lunes a sábado inclusive. It's open from Monday to Saturday inclusive.
2 including
□ hasta el capítulo diez inclusive up to and including chapter ten

incluso ADVERB
even
□ He tenido que estudiar incluso los domingos. I've even had to study on Sundays.

incluyendo VERB ▷*see* **incluir**

incómodo (FEM **incómoda**) ADJECTIVE
uncomfortable
□ Este asiento es muy incómodo. This seat is very uncomfortable. □ Se siente muy incómoda cuando está con él. She feels very uncomfortable with him.

incompetente (FEM **incompetente**) ADJECTIVE
incompetent

incompleto (FEM **incompleta**) ADJECTIVE
incomplete

incomprensible (FEM **incomprensible**) ADJECTIVE
incomprehensible

inconsciente (FEM **inconsciente**) ADJECTIVE
1 unconscious
□ estar inconsciente to be unconscious
□ Quedó inconsciente con el golpe. The force of the blow left him unconscious.
□ un deseo inconsciente an unconscious desire
2 thoughtless
□ ¡Qué inconsciente eres! How thoughtless you are!

inconveniente (FEM **inconveniente**) ADJECTIVE
inconvenient
□ a una hora inconveniente at an inconvenient time

el **inconveniente** NOUN
1 problem
□ Ha surgido un inconveniente. A problem has come up.
2 drawback
□ El plan tiene sus inconvenientes. The plan has its drawbacks.
■ **No tengo ningún inconveniente.** I have no objection.
■ **No tengo inconveniente en preguntárselo.** I don't mind asking him.
■ **¿Tienes algún inconveniente en que le dé tu teléfono?** Do you mind if I give him your telephone number?

incorrecto (FEM **incorrecta**) ADJECTIVE
1 incorrect
□ una respuesta incorrecta an incorrect answer
2 impolite
□ Has estado muy incorrecto. You were very impolite.

increíble (FEM **increíble**) ADJECTIVE
incredible

inculto (FEM **inculta**) ADJECTIVE
ignorant

incurable (FEM **incurable**) ADJECTIVE
incurable

indeciso (FEM **indecisa**) ADJECTIVE
indecisive
□ Es una persona muy indecisa. She's very indecisive.
■ **Estoy indecisa, no sé cuál comprar.** I can't make up my mind, I don't know which to buy.

indefenso (FEM **indefensa**) ADJECTIVE
defenceless

la **indemnización** (PL las **indemnizaciones**) NOUN
compensation
□ Recibieron mil dólares de indemnización. They received a thousand dollars compensation.
■ **la indemnización por daños y perjuicios** damages *pl*

indemnizar* VERB [13]
to compensate
□ El gobierno indemnizará a las víctimas. The government will compensate the victims.
■ **Nos tienen que indemnizar.** They've got to pay us compensation.

la **independencia** NOUN
independence

independiente (FEM **independiente**) ADJECTIVE
1 independent
□ Es una chica muy independiente. She's a very independent girl.
2 self-contained
□ Son apartamentos independientes. They are self-contained flats.

independientemente ADVERB
independently
□ Los dos motores funcionan independientemente. The two engines work independently.
■ **Iremos, independientemente de lo que hayan decidido.** We'll go, regardless of what they have decided.

independizarse* VERB [13]
to become independent
□ Quiero independizarme. I want to become independent.

la **india** NOUN
Indian

India FEM NOUN
■ **La India** India

la **indicación** (PL las **indicaciones**) NOUN
sign
■ **Nos hizo una indicación para que siguiéramos.** He signalled to us to go on.
■ **indicaciones 1** instructions □ Hay que seguir las indicaciones del manual. You'll need to follow the instructions in the manual. **2** directions □ Me dio indicaciones de cómo llegar. He gave me directions for getting there.

Spanish-English

i

indicar* VERB [48]
1 to indicate
□ El termómetro indicaba treinta grados. The thermometer indicated thirty degrees. □ Todo indica que ... Everything indicates that ...
2 to tell
□ ¿Puede indicarme dónde hay una gasolinera? Please can you tell where there's a petrol station? □ Un guardia me indicó el camino. A policeman told me the way.
3 to advise
□ El médico me indicó que no fumara. The doctor advised me not to smoke.

el **índice** NOUN
1 index (PL indexes *o* indices)
□ un índice alfabético an alphabetical index
■ **el índice de materias** the table of contents
■ **el índice de natalidad** the birth rate
2 index finger

la **indiferencia** NOUN
indifference

indiferente (FEM **indiferente**) ADJECTIVE
indifferent
□ Parece indiferente al cariño. She seems indifferent to affection.
■ **Es indiferente que viva en Glasgow o Edimburgo.** It makes no difference whether he lives in Glasgow or Edinburgh.
■ **Me es indiferente hacerlo hoy o mañana.** I don't mind whether I do it today or tomorrow.

indígena (FEM **indígena**) ADJECTIVE
indigenous
□ la población indígena the indigenous population

el/la **indígena** NOUN
native

la **indigestión** NOUN
indigestion

indignado (FEM **indignada**) ADJECTIVE
angry
□ Están muy indignados con ella. They're very angry with her.

indignar VERB [25]
to infuriate
□ Su comportamiento los indignó. His behaviour infuriated them.
■ **indignarse por algo** to get angry about something
■ **indignarse con alguien** to be furious with somebody

el **indio** ADJECTIVE, NOUN
Indian

la **indirecta** NOUN
hint
□ lanzar una indirecta to drop a hint

indirecto (FEM **indirecta**) ADJECTIVE
indirect

indispensable (FEM **indispensable**) ADJECTIVE
essential
□ Es indispensable saber inglés. It's essential to know English.
■ **Llevaba sólo lo indispensable.** He was carrying only the essentials.

individual (FEM **individual**) ADJECTIVE
1 individual
□ Los venden en paquetes individuales. They're sold in individual packets.
2 single
□ Quisiera una habitación individual. I'd like a single room.

el **individual** NOUN
singles *pl*
□ la final del individual femenino the ladies' singles final

el **individuo** NOUN
individual

la **industria** NOUN
industry (PL industries)
□ la industria pesada heavy industry □ la industria petrolífera the oil industry

industrial (FEM **industrial**) ADJECTIVE
industrial

el/la **industrial** NOUN
industrialist

ineficiente (FEM **ineficiente**) ADJECTIVE
inefficient

inesperado (FEM **inesperada**) ADJECTIVE
unexpected
□ una visita inesperada an unexpected visit

inestable (FEM **inestable**) ADJECTIVE
1 unsteady
2 changeable

inevitable (FEM **inevitable**) ADJECTIVE
inevitable

inexacto (FEM **inexacta**) ADJECTIVE
inaccurate
□ La biografía contiene muchos datos inexactos. The biography contains a lot of inaccurate details.

inexperto (FEM **inexperta**) ADJECTIVE
inexperienced

inexplicable (FEM **inexplicable**) ADJECTIVE
inexplicable

infantil (FEM **infantil**) ADJECTIVE
1 children's
□ un programa infantil a children's programme
2 childish
□ ¡No seas tan infantil! Don't be so childish!

el **infarto** NOUN
heart attack

□ Le dio un infarto. He had a heart attack.

la **infección** (PL las **infecciones**) NOUN
infection
□ tener una infección to have an infection
□ Tiene una infección de oídos. He has got an ear infection.

infeliz (FEM **infeliz**, PL **infelices**) ADJECTIVE
unhappy

inferior (FEM **inferior**) ADJECTIVE
1 lower
□ Tenía el labio inferior hinchado. His lower lip was swollen. □ Las temperaturas han sido inferiores a lo normal. Temperatures have been lower than normal.
2 inferior
□ de calidad inferior of inferior quality
■ **un número inferior a nueve** a number below nine

el **infiernillo** NOUN
stove

el **infierno** NOUN
hell

el **infinitivo** NOUN
infinitive

inflable (FEM **inflable**) ADJECTIVE
inflatable

la **inflación** NOUN
inflation
□ Hay que reducir la inflación. Inflation has to be reduced.

inflamable (FEM **inflamable**) ADJECTIVE
inflammable

inflar VERB [25]
1 to blow up
2 to inflate

la **influencia** NOUN
influence
□ Mi abuelo tuvo una gran influencia en mí. My grandfather had a great influence on me.

influenciar VERB [25]
to influence

influir* VERB [10]
■ **dos hombres que influyeron en su vida** two men who influenced his life
■ **Mis padres influyeron mucho en mí.** My parents had a great influence on me.
■ **El cansancio ha influido en su rendimiento.** Tiredness has affected his work.

la **información** (PL las **informaciones**) NOUN
1 information
□ Quisiera información sobre los cursos de inglés. I'd like some information on English courses.
■ **una información muy importante** a very important piece of information
2 news *sing*
□ Este canal tiene mucha información deportiva. There's a lot of sports news on this channel.
3 directory enquiries
□ Llama a información y pide que te den el número. Call directory enquiries and ask them for the number.
■ **Pregunta en información de dónde sale el tren.** Ask at the information desk which platform the train leaves from.

informal (FEM **informal**) ADJECTIVE
1 informal
□ un ambiente muy informal a very informal atmosphere
■ **Prefiero la ropa informal.** I prefer casual clothes.
2 unreliable
□ Es una persona muy informal. He's a very unreliable person.

informar VERB [25]
to inform
□ Nos informaron de que venía con retraso. They informed us that it was going to be late.
■ **Les han informado mal.** You've been misinformed.
■ **¿Me podría informar sobre los cursos de inglés?** Could you give me some information about English courses?
■ **informarse de algo** to find out about something

la **informática** NOUN
computing
□ los avances de la informática advances in computing
■ **Quiere estudiar informática.** He wants to study computer science.

informático (FEM **informática**) ADJECTIVE
computer
□ un programa informático a computer program

el **informático** NOUN
computer expert

el **informe** NOUN
report
□ Presentó un informe detallado sobre lo ocurrido. He gave a detailed report about what had happened.
■ **según mis informes** according to my information
■ **pedir informes** to ask for references

la **infusión** (PL las **infusiones**) NOUN
herbal tea
■ **una infusión de manzanilla** a camomile tea

ingeniar VERB [25]
to devise
□ Habían ingeniado un sistema para evadir impuestos. They had devised a system for

evading taxes.
■ **ingeniárselas** to manage □ No sé cómo se las ingenió para conseguir el dinero. I don't know how he managed to get the money.

la **ingeniera** NOUN
engineer
□ Quiere ser ingeniera. She wants to be an engineer.

la **ingeniería** NOUN
engineering

el **ingeniero** NOUN
engineer
□ Quiere ser ingeniero. He wants to be an engineer.
■ **un ingeniero agrónomo** an agriculturist

el **ingenio** NOUN
1 ingenuity
2 wit
■ **un ingenio azucarero** *(Latin America)* a sugar refinery

ingenioso (FEM **ingeniosa**) ADJECTIVE
1 ingenious
□ ¡Qué idea más ingeniosa! What an ingenious idea!
2 witty
□ un comentario ingenioso a witty comment

ingenuo (FEM **ingenua**) ADJECTIVE
naïve

Inglaterra FEM NOUN
England

inglés (FEM **inglesa**, MASC PL **ingleses**) ADJECTIVE
English
□ la comida inglesa English food

el **inglés** (PL los **ingleses**) NOUN
1 Englishman (PL Englishmen)
■ **los ingleses** the English
2 English
□ El inglés le resulta difícil. He finds English difficult.

la **inglesa** NOUN
Englishwoman (PL Englishwomen)

el **ingrediente** NOUN
ingredient

ingresar VERB [25]
to pay in
□ ingresar un cheque en una cuenta to pay a cheque into an account
■ **ingresar en el hospital** to go into hospital
■ **Han vuelto a ingresar a mi abuela.** They've taken my grandmother into hospital again.
■ **ingresar en un club** to join a club

el **ingreso** NOUN
admission
■ **un examen de ingreso** an entrance exam
■ **los ingresos** income *sing* □ Tiene unos ingresos muy bajos. He has a very low income.

la **inicial** NOUN
initial

la **iniciativa** NOUN
initiative
□ Lo hizo por iniciativa propia. He did it on his own initiative.

la **injusticia** NOUN
injustice
□ Lucharon contra las injusticias sociales. They fought against social injustices.
■ **Es una injusticia que lo hayan expulsado.** It was unfair of them to expel him.

injusto (FEM **injusta**) ADJECTIVE
unfair

inmaduro (FEM **inmadura**) ADJECTIVE
1 immature
2 unripe

inmediatamente ADVERB
immediately

inmediato (FEM **inmediata**) ADJECTIVE
immediate
■ **inmediato a algo** next to something
□ en el edificio inmediato a la embajada in the building next to the embassy
■ **de inmediato** immediately

inmenso (FEM **inmensa**) ADJECTIVE
immense
■ **la inmensa mayoría** the vast majority

la **inmigración** NOUN
immigration

el/la **inmigrante** NOUN
immigrant

inmoral (FEM **inmoral**) ADJECTIVE
immoral

inmortal (FEM **inmortal**) ADJECTIVE
immortal

inmóvil (FEM **inmóvil**) ADJECTIVE
motionless
□ Se quedó inmóvil. He remained motionless.

innecesario (FEM **innecesaria**) ADJECTIVE
unnecessary

inocente (FEM **inocente**) ADJECTIVE
innocent
□ Es inocente. He's innocent.
■ **El jurado la declaró inocente.** The jury found her not guilty.

inofensivo (FEM **inofensiva**) ADJECTIVE
harmless

inolvidable (FEM **inolvidable**) ADJECTIVE
unforgettable

inquietante (FEM **inquietante**) ADJECTIVE
worrying

inquietar VERB [25]

to worry
■ **inquietarse** to worry □ ¡No te inquietes! Don't worry!

inquieto (FEM **inquieta**) ADJECTIVE
1 worried
□ Estaba inquieta porque su hijo no había llegado. She was worried because her son hadn't come home.
2 restless
□ Es un niño muy inquieto y le cuesta dormirse. He's a very restless boy and finds it hard to get to sleep.

el **inquilino**, la **inquilina** NOUN
1 tenant
2 lodger

insatisfecho (FEM **insatisfecha**) ADJECTIVE
dissatisfied

inscribirse* VERB [58, PAST PARTICIPLE **inscrito**]
to enrol
□ Se inscribió en un curso de idiomas. He enrolled on a language course.

la **inscripción** (PL las **inscripciones**) NOUN
1 enrolment
□ Mañana se cierra la inscripción. Tomorrow is the last day for enrollment.
2 inscription
□ Sobre la puerta hay una inscripción con el año. Above the door there's an inscription with the year on it.

inscrito VERB ▷ *see* **inscribirse**

el **insecto** NOUN
insect

la **inseguridad** NOUN
insecurity
□ la inseguridad en el trabajo job insecurity
■ **la inseguridad ciudadana** the lack of safety on the streets

inseguro (FEM **insegura**) ADJECTIVE
1 insecure
2 unsafe

insensato (FEM **insensata**) ADJECTIVE
foolish

insensible (FEM **insensible**) ADJECTIVE
insensitive
□ Se han vuelto insensibles al frío. They have become insensitive to the cold.
■ **Es insensible al sufrimiento ajeno.** He is blind to the suffering of others.

la **insignia** NOUN
badge

insignificante (FEM **insignificante**) ADJECTIVE
insignificant

insinuar* VERB [1]
to hint at
□ No lo dijo pero lo insinuó. He didn't say it but he hinted at it.
■ **¿Insinúas que miento?** Are you insinuating that I'm lying?

insípido (FEM **insípida**) ADJECTIVE
insipid

insistir VERB [58]
to insist
□ insistir en hacer algo to insist on doing something □ Insiste en que vea a un médico. He's insisting that I see a doctor.

la **insolación** NOUN
sunstroke

insolente (FEM **insolente**) ADJECTIVE
insolent

insoportable (FEM **insoportable**) ADJECTIVE
unbearable

el **inspector**, la **inspectora** NOUN
inspector

las **instalaciones** NOUN
facilities
□ El hotel tiene unas estupendas instalaciones deportivas. The hotel has excellent sports facilities.

instalar VERB [25]
1 to install
□ Instaló una alarma en el coche. He installed an alarm in the car.
2 to set up
□ Aquí van a instalar unas oficinas. They're going to set up offices here.
■ **instalarse** to settle □ Decidieron instalarse en el centro. They decided to settle in the town centre.

instantáneo (FEM **instantánea**) ADJECTIVE
instantaneous
■ **el café instantáneo** instant coffee

el **instante** NOUN
moment
□ por un instante for a moment
■ **A cada instante suena el teléfono.** The phone rings all the time.
■ **al instante** right away

el **instinto** NOUN
instinct

la **institución** (PL las **instituciones**) NOUN
institution

el **instituto** NOUN
institute
□ el Instituto Británico the British Institute
■ **un instituto de enseñanza secundaria** a secondary school

las **instrucciones** NOUN
instructions

instructivo (FEM **instructiva**) ADJECTIVE
educational

el **instructor**, la **instructora** NOUN
instructor
□ un instructor de esquí a ski instructor
□ un instructor de autoescuela a driving instructor

el **instrumento** NOUN
instrument

insuficiente (FEM **insuficiente**) ADJECTIVE
insufficient
□ una cantidad insuficiente de dinero an insufficient amount of money

el **insuficiente** NOUN
■ **Sacó un insuficiente en francés.** He got an F in French.

la **insulina** NOUN
insulin

insultar VERB [25]
to insult

el **insulto** NOUN
insult

el/la **intelectual** ADJECTIVE, NOUN
intellectual

la **inteligencia** NOUN
intelligence

inteligente (FEM **inteligente**) ADJECTIVE
intelligent

la **intención** (PL las **intenciones**) NOUN
intention
□ No tengo la más mínima intención de hacerlo. I haven't got the slightest intention of doing it.
■ **tener intención de hacer algo** to intend to do something □ Tenía intención de descansar un rato. He intended to rest for a while.
■ **Lo que cuenta es la intención.** It's the thought that counts.

intencionado (FEM **intencionada**) ADJECTIVE
deliberate
□ La patada fue intencionada. It was a deliberate kick.
■ **bien intencionado** well-meaning
■ **mal intencionado** malicious

intensivo (FEM **intensiva**) ADJECTIVE
intensive
□ un curso intensivo de inglés an intensive English course

intenso (FEM **intensa**) ADJECTIVE
intense

intentar VERB [25]
to try
□ ¿Por qué no lo intentas otra vez? Why don't you try again? □ intentar hacer algo to try to do something

el **intento** NOUN
attempt
□ Aprobó al primer intento. He passed at the first attempt.

intercambiar VERB [25]
1 to exchange
2 to swap

el **intercambio** NOUN
exchange

el **interés** (PL los **intereses**) NOUN
interest
□ Tienes que poner más interés en tus estudios. You must take more of an interest in your studies. □ El banco da un interés del 5%. The bank gives 5% interest.
■ **tener interés en hacer algo** to be keen to do something
■ **Todo lo hace por interés.** Everything he does is out of self-interest.

interesante (FEM **interesante**) ADJECTIVE
interesting

interesar VERB [25]
to interest
□ Eso es algo que siempre me ha interesado. That's something that has always interested me.
■ **Me interesa mucho la física.** I'm very interested in physics.
■ **interesarse por algo** to ask about something

el **interfono** NOUN
intercom

interior (FEM **interior**) ADJECTIVE
1 inside
2 inner

el **interior** NOUN
■ **El tren se detuvo en el interior del túnel.** The train stopped inside the tunnel.

el/la **interiorista** NOUN
interior designer

intermedio (FEM **intermedia**) ADJECTIVE
1 intermediate
2 medium

el **intermedio** NOUN
interval

interminable (FEM **interminable**) ADJECTIVE
endless

intermitente (FEM **intermitente**) ADJECTIVE
1 intermittent
2 flashing

el **intermitente** NOUN
indicator

internacional (FEM **internacional**) ADJECTIVE
international

el **internado** NOUN
boarding school

el/la **internauta** NOUN
internet user

el/la **Internet** NOUN
the internet
□ en Internet on the internet

interno (FEM **interna**) ADJECTIVE
■ **estar interno en un colegio** to be a boarder at a school

el **interno**, la **interna** NOUN

1 boarder
2 houseman (PL housemen)

la **interpretación** (PL las **interpretaciones**) NOUN
interpretation
■ **la interpretación simultánea** simultaneous interpreting
■ **Todo fue producto de una mala interpretación.** It was all the result of a misunderstanding.

interpretar VERB [25]
1 to interpret
□ Sabe interpretar los sueños. He knows how to interpret dreams.
2 to play
□ Interpreta el papel de Victoria. She plays the part of Victoria.
3 to perform
□ Interpretó una pieza de Mozart. He performed a piece by Mozart.
■ **No me interpretes mal.** Don't misunderstand me.

el/la **intérprete** NOUN
interpreter
□ Quiere ser intérprete. She wants to be an interpreter.

interrogar* VERB [37]
to question
□ Fue interrogado por la policía. He was questioned by the police.

interrumpir VERB [58]
1 to interrupt
2 to cut short
3 to block
□ Estás interrumpiendo el paso. You're blocking the way.

la **interrupción** (PL las **interrupciones**) NOUN
interruption

el **interruptor** NOUN
switch (PL switches)

interurbano (FEM **interurbana**) ADJECTIVE
long-distance

el **intervalo** NOUN
interval

intervenir* VERB [56]
1 to take part
□ No intervino en el debate. He did not take part in the debate.
2 to intervene
□ La policía intervino para separarlos. The police intervened to separate them.

la **intimidad** NOUN
1 private life
□ Protege mucho su intimidad. He's very protective of his private life.
2 privacy
□ En esta casa no tengo ninguna intimidad. I have no privacy in this house.
■ **La boda se celebró en la intimidad.** It was a private wedding.

intimidar VERB [25]
to intimidate

íntimo (FEM **íntima**) ADJECTIVE
intimate
□ mis secretos íntimos my intimate secrets
■ **Es un amigo íntimo.** He's a close friend.

la **introducción** (PL las **introducciones**) NOUN
introduction

introducir* VERB [9]
1 to insert
□ Introdujo la moneda en la ranura. He inserted the coin in the slot.
2 to bring in
□ Quieren introducir un nuevo sistema de trabajo. They want to bring in new working methods.
■ **Han introducido cambios en el horario.** They've made changes to the timetable.

introvertido (FEM **introvertida**) ADJECTIVE
introverted

el **intruso**, la **intrusa** NOUN
intruder

la **intuición** NOUN
intuition
□ la intuición femenina feminine intuition
■ **por intuición** intuitively

la **inundación** (PL las **inundaciones**) NOUN
flood

inundar VERB [25]
to flood
□ El río inundó el pueblo. The river flooded the village.
■ **inundarse** to be flooded □ Se nos inundó el baño. Our bathroom was flooded.

inútil (FEM **inútil**) ADJECTIVE
useless
□ La oficina está llena de trastos inútiles. The office is full of useless rubbish. □ Es inútil tratar de hacerle entender. It's useless trying to make him understand.
■ **Es inútil que esperes.** There's no point in your waiting.

el/la **inútil** (PL los/las **inútiles**) NOUN
■ **¡Es un inútil!** He's useless!

invadir VERB [58]
to invade

la **inválida** NOUN
disabled woman (PL disabled women)

inválido (FEM **inválida**) ADJECTIVE
disabled
□ Quedó inválida después del accidente. She was left disabled following the accident.

el **inválido** NOUN
disabled man (PL disabled men)

■ **los inválidos** the disabled

la **invasión** (PL las **invasiones**) NOUN
invasion

inventar VERB [25]
1 to invent
□ Inventaron un nuevo sistema. They invented a new system.
2 to make up
□ Inventó toda la historia. He made up the whole story.

el **invento** NOUN
invention

el **inventor**, la **inventora** NOUN
inventor

el **invernadero** NOUN
greenhouse
■ **el efecto invernadero** the greenhouse effect

invernar VERB [39]
to hibernate

inverosímil (FEM **inverosímil**) ADJECTIVE
unlikely

la **inversión** (PL las **inversiones**) NOUN
investment

inverso (FEM **inversa**) ADJECTIVE
reverse
□ en orden inverso in reverse order
■ **a la inversa** the other way round

invertir* VERB [51]
1 to invest
□ He invertido mucho dinero en esto. I've invested a lot of money in this.
2 to spend
□ Hemos invertido muchas horas en el proyecto. We've spent a lot of time on this project.
3 to reverse

la **investigación** (PL las **investigaciones**) NOUN
1 research
□ Está haciendo una investigación sobre Internet. He's doing some research on the Internet.
2 investigation
3 inquiry (PL inquiries)
□ Se hará una investigación pública. There will be a public inquiry.

el **invierno** NOUN
winter
□ en invierno in winter □ el invierno pasado last winter

invisible (FEM **invisible**) ADJECTIVE
invisible

la **invitación** (PL las **invitaciones**) NOUN
invitation

el **invitado**, la **invitada** NOUN
guest
□ Es el invitado de honor. He's the guest of honour.

invitar VERB [25]
to invite
□ Me invitó a una fiesta. He invited me to a party. □ Me gustaría invitarla a cenar. I'd like to invite her to dinner.
■ **Te invito a un café.** I'll buy you a coffee.
■ **Esta vez invito yo.** This time it's on me.

la **inyección** (PL las **inyecciones**) NOUN
injection
□ ponerle una inyección a alguien to give someone an injection

inyectar VERB [25]
■ **Le tuvieron que inyectar insulina.** They had to give him insulin injections.
■ **inyectarse algo** to inject oneself with something □ Se había inyectado heroína. He had injected himself with heroin.

ir* VERB [27]
1 to go
□ Anoche fuimos al cine. We went to the cinema last night. □ ¿A qué colegio vas? What school do you go to?
■ **ir de vacaciones** to go on holiday
■ **ir a por** to go and get □ Voy a por el paraguas. I'll go and get the umbrella. □ Ha ido a por el médico. She has gone to get the doctor.
■ **Voy a hacerlo mañana.** I'm going to do it tomorrow.
■ **vamos** let's go □ Vamos a casa. Let's go home.
■ **¡Vamos!** Come on! □ ¡Vamos! ¡Di algo! Come on! Say something!
■ **¡Vamos a ver!** Let's see!
2 to be
□ Iba muy bien vestido. He was very well dressed. □ Iba con su madre. He was with his mother. □ como iba diciendo as I was saying □ Va a ser difícil. It will be difficult.
3 to come
□ ¡Ahora voy! I'm just coming!
■ **¿Puedo ir contigo?** Can I come with you?
■ **ir a pie** to walk
■ **ir en avión** to fly
■ **¿Cómo te va?** How are things?
■ **¿Cómo te va en los estudios?** How are you getting on with your studies?
■ **¡Que te vaya bien!** Take care of yourself!
■ **¡Qué va!** What are you talking about!
■ **¡Vaya! ¿Qué haces tú por aquí?** Well, what a surprise! What are you doing here?
■ **¡Vaya coche!** What a car!
■ **irse 1** to leave □ Acaba de irse. He has just left. **2** to go out □ Se ha ido la luz. The lights have gone out.
■ **¡Vámonos!** Let's go!
■ **¡Vete!** Go away!

■ **Vete a hacer los deberes.** Go and do your homework.

Irak MASC NOUN
Iraq

Irán MASC NOUN
Iran

el/la **iraní** (PL los/las **iraníes**) ADJECTIVE, NOUN
Iranian

el/la **iraquí** (PL los/las **iraquíes**) ADJECTIVE, NOUN
Iraqui

Irlanda FEM NOUN
Ireland
□ Irlanda del Norte Northern Ireland

irlandés (FEM **irlandesa**, MASC PL **irlandeses**) ADJECTIVE
Irish
□ un café irlandés an Irish coffee

el **irlandés** (PL los **irlandeses**) NOUN
1 Irishman (PL Irishmen)
■ **los irlandeses** the Irish
2 Irish

la **irlandesa** NOUN
Irishwoman (PL Irishwomen)

irónico (FEM **irónica**) ADJECTIVE
ironic

irracional (FEM **irracional**) ADJECTIVE
irrational

irrelevante (FEM **irrelevante**) ADJECTIVE
irrelevant

irresistible (FEM **irresistible**) ADJECTIVE
irresistible

irresponsable (FEM **irresponsable**) ADJECTIVE
irresponsible

irritante (FEM **irritante**) ADJECTIVE
irritating

irritar VERB [25]
to irritate

irrompible (FEM **irrompible**) ADJECTIVE
unbreakable

la **isla** NOUN
island
□ una isla desierta a desert island
■ **la Isla de Pascua** Easter Island

el **Islam** NOUN
Islam

islámico (FEM **islámica**) ADJECTIVE
Islamic

islandés (FEM **islandesa**, MASC PL **islandeses**) ADJECTIVE
Icelandic

el **islandés**, la **islandesa** (MASC PL los **islandeses**) NOUN
Icelander

el **islandés** NOUN
Icelandic

Islandia FEM NOUN
Iceland

el **isleño** NOUN
islander

Israel MASC NOUN
Israel

el/la **israelí** (PL los/las **israelíes**) ADJECTIVE, NOUN
Israeli

Italia FEM NOUN
Italy

el **italiano** (FEM la **italiana**) ADJECTIVE, NOUN
Italian

el **italiano** NOUN
Italian

el **itinerario** NOUN
1 route
□ Hicimos el itinerario de costumbre. We took the usual route.
2 itinerary (PL itineraries)
□ Me gustaría incluir Roma en el itinerario. I'd like to include Rome on our itinerary.

el **IVA** ABBREVIATION
▷ *see also* **IVA** ABBREVIATION (= *Impuesto sobre el Valor Añadido*)
VAT (= *Value Added Tax*)

el **IVA** ABBREVIATION
▷ *see also* **IVA** ABBREVIATION (= *Impuesto sobre el Valor Agregado*) (*Latin America*)
VAT (= *Value Added Tax*)

izar* VERB [13]
to hoist
□ Izaron la bandera a media asta. They hoisted the flag to half mast.

la **izquierda** NOUN
1 left hand
■ **Escribo con la izquierda.** I write with my left hand.
2 left
□ doblar a la izquierda to turn left □ La izquierda ganó las elecciones. The elections were won by the left.
■ **ser de izquierdas** to be left-wing □ un partido de izquierdas a left-wing party
■ **a la izquierda** on the left □ la segunda calle a la izquierda the second turning on the left
■ **a la izquierda del edificio** to the left of the building
■ **conducir por la izquierda** to drive on the left

izquierdo (FEM **izquierda**) ADJECTIVE
left
□ Levanta la mano izquierda. Raise your left hand.
■ **Escribo con la mano izquierda.** I write with my left hand.
■ **el lado izquierdo** the left side
■ **a mano izquierda** on the left-hand side

Jj

el **jabón** (PL los **jabones**) NOUN
soap
la **jaiba** NOUN *(Latin America)*
crab
jalar VERB [25] *(Latin America)*
1 to pull
□ No le jales el pelo. Don't pull his hair.
2 to take
□ Jaló un folleto de la mesa. He took a leaflet from the table.
jamás ADVERB
never
□ Jamás he visto nada parecido. I've never seen anything like it.
el **jamón** (PL los **jamones**) NOUN
ham
□ un bocadillo de jamón a ham sandwich
■ **jamón serrano** cured ham
■ **jamón de York** boiled ham
Japón MASC NOUN
Japan
el **japonés** (FEM la **japonesa**, MASC PL los **japoneses**) ADJECTIVE, NOUN
Japanese
el **japonés** NOUN
Japanese
el **jarabe** NOUN
syrup
■ **jarabe para la tos** cough syrup
el **jardín** (PL los **jardines**) NOUN
garden
■ **el jardín de infancia** nursery school
la **jardinera** NOUN
1 gardener
2 window box
la **jardinería** NOUN
gardening
el **jardinero** NOUN
gardener
la **jarra** NOUN
1 jug
2 beer glass
el **jarro** NOUN
jug
el **jarrón** (PL los **jarrones**) NOUN
vase

la **jaula** NOUN
cage
el **jefe**, la **jefa** NOUN
1 boss (PL bosses)
□ Carlos es mi jefe. Carlos is my boss.
2 head
□ El jefe de la empresa dimitió. The head of the company resigned.
■ **el jefe del departamento** the head of department
■ **jefe de estado** head of state
■ **el jefe del grupo guerrillero** the leader of the guerrilla group
el **jerez** NOUN
sherry
la **jeringuilla** NOUN
syringe
el **jersey** (PL los **jerséis**) NOUN
jumper
Jesús EXCLAMATION
1 Bless you!
2 Good God!
el **jinete** NOUN
jockey (PL jockeys)
la **jirafa** NOUN
giraffe
el **jitomate** NOUN *(Mexico)*
tomato (PL tomatoes)
la **jornada** NOUN
■ **jornada de trabajo** working day
■ **trabajar a jornada completa** to work full-time
■ **trabajar a media jornada** to work part-time
joven (FEM **joven**, PL **jóvenes**) ADJECTIVE
young
□ un chico joven a young boy
el/la **joven** (PL los/las **jóvenes**) NOUN
■ **un joven** a young man
■ **una joven** a young woman
■ **los jóvenes** young people
la **joya** NOUN
jewel
■ **Me han robado mis joyas.** My jewellery has been stolen.
la **joyera** NOUN

jeweller
la **joyería** NOUN
jeweller's
el **joyero** NOUN
1 jeweller
2 jewellery box
la **jubilación** (PL las **jubilaciones**) NOUN
1 retirement
□ La edad de jubilación es a los 65 años. The retirement age is 65.
2 pension
□ cobrar la jubilación to get one's pension
jubilado (FEM **jubilada**) ADJECTIVE
retired
■ **estar jubilado** to be retired
el **jubilado**, la **jubilada** NOUN
pensioner
jubilarse VERB [25]
to retire
la **judía** NOUN
Jew
■ **judía blanca** haricot bean
■ **judía verde** green bean
judío (FEM **judía**) ADJECTIVE
Jewish
el **judío** NOUN
Jew
el **judo** NOUN
judo
juego VERB ▷ *see* **jugar**
el **juego** NOUN
1 game
□ un juego de ordenador a computer game
■ **juegos de cartas** card games
■ **juegos de mesa** board games
2 gambling
□ Lo perdió todo en el juego. He lost everything through gambling.
3 set
□ un juego de café a coffee set
■ **Las cortinas hacen juego con el sofá.** The curtains go with the sofa.
la **juerga** NOUN
■ **irse de juerga** to go out on the town
el **jueves** (PL los **jueves**) NOUN
Thursday
□ La vi el jueves. I saw her on Thursday. □ todos los jueves every Thursday □ el jueves pasado last Thursday □ el jueves que viene next Thursday □ Jugamos los jueves. We play on Thursdays.
el **juez**, la **jueza** (MASC PL los **jueces**) NOUN
judge
■ **juez de línea** linesman (PL linesmen)
el **jugador**, la **jugadora** NOUN
player
jugar* VERB [28]
1 to play
□ ¿Jugamos una partida de dominó? Shall we have a game of dominoes?
■ **jugar al fútbol** to play football
2 to gamble
□ Perdió un dineral jugando en el casino. He lost a fortune gambling at the casino.
■ **jugar a la lotería** to do the lottery
el **jugo** NOUN
1 juice
2 gravy
el **juguete** NOUN
toy (PL toys)
■ **un avión de juguete** a toy plane
la **juguetería** NOUN
toy shop
el **juicio** NOUN
trial
□ El juicio empieza mañana. The trial starts tomorrow.
■ **llevar a alguien a juicio** to take someone to court
julio MASC NOUN
July
□ en julio in July □ Nació el 4 de julio. He was born on 4 July.
la **jungla** NOUN
jungle
junio MASC NOUN
June
□ en junio in June □ Nací el 20 de junio. I was born on 20 June.
la **junta** NOUN
committee
■ **La junta directiva tiene la última palabra.** The board of management has the final say.
juntar VERB [25]
1 to put together
□ Vamos a juntar los pupitres. Let's put the desks together.
2 to gather together
□ Consiguieron juntar a mil personas. They managed to gather together one thousand people.
■ **juntarse 1** to move closer together □ Si os juntáis más, cabremos todos. If you move closer together we'll all fit in. **2** to meet up □ Nos juntamos los domingos para comer. We meet up for dinner on Sundays.
junto (FEM **junta**) ADJECTIVE
▷ *see also* **junto** ADVERB
1 close together
□ Los muebles están demasiado juntos. The furniture is too close together.
2 together
□ Cuando estamos juntos apenas hablamos. We hardly talk when we're together.
■ **todo junto** all together □ Ponlo todo

junto en una sola bolsa. Put it all together in one bag.

junto ADVERB

▷ *see also* **junto** ADJECTIVE

■ **junto a** by □ Hay una mesa junto a la ventana. There's a table by the window.

■ **junto con** together with

■ **Mi apellido se escribe todo junto.** My surname is all in one word.

el **jurado** NOUN

1 jury (PL juries)

2 panel

jurar VERB [25]

to swear

la **justicia** NOUN

justice

justificar* VERB [48]

to justify

justo (FEM **justa**) ADJECTIVE

▷ *see also* **justo** ADVERB

1 fair

□ Tuvo un juicio justo. He had a fair trial.

2 right

■ **Este reloj siempre da la hora justa.** This watch always tells the right time.

□ Apareció en el momento justo. He appeared at the right time.

3 tight

□ Me están muy justos estos pantalones. These trousers are tight on me.

4 just enough

□ Tengo el dinero justo para el billete. I have just enough money for the ticket.

justo ADVERB

▷ *see also* **justo** ADJECTIVE

just

□ El supermercado está justo al doblar la esquina. The supermarket is just round the corner. □ La vi justo cuando entrábamos. I saw her just as we came in.

■ **Me dio un puñetazo justo en la nariz.** He punched me right on the nose.

juvenil (FEM **juvenil**) ADJECTIVE

1 youth

2 junior

■ **la literatura juvenil** young people's literature

la **juventud** NOUN

1 youth

□ Fue soldado en su juventud. He was a soldier in his youth.

2 youngsters *pl*

□ La juventud viene aquí a divertirse. Youngsters come here to have fun.

el **juzgado** NOUN

court

juzgar* VERB [37]

to try

□ Lo juzgaron por un delito menor. He was tried on a minor charge.

Kk

el **kárate** NOUN
karate

el **kilo** NOUN
kilo
□ un kilo de tomates a kilo of tomatoes

el **kilogramo** NOUN
kilogramme

el **kilómetro** NOUN
kilometre
□ Está a tres kilómetros de aquí. It's three kilometres from here. □ a 90 kilómetros por hora at 90 kilometres per hour
■ **¡Caminamos kilómetros y kilómetros!** We walked for miles!

el **kiosco** NOUN
news stand

Ll

la ARTICLE
▷ *see also* **la** PRONOUN
the
□ la pared the wall
■ **la del sombrero rojo** the girl in the red hat
■ **Yo fui la que te despertó.** It was I who woke you up.
■ **Ayer me lavé la cabeza.** I washed my hair yesterday.
■ **Abróchate la camisa.** Do your shirt up.
■ **Tiene una casa bonita, pero prefiero la de Juan.** He's got a lovely house, but I prefer Juan's.
■ **No me gusta la fruta.** I don't like fruit.
■ **Vendrá la semana que viene.** He'll come next week.
■ **Me he encontrado a la Sra. Sendra.** I met Mrs Sendra.

la PRONOUN
▷ *see also* **la** ARTICLE
1 her
□ La quiero. I love her.
■ **La han despedido.** She has been sacked.
2 you
□ La acompaño hasta la puerta. I'll see you out.
3 it
□ No la toques. Don't touch it.

el **labio** NOUN
lip

la **labor** NOUN
work
□ Mi labor consiste en regar las plantas. My work is watering the plants.
■ **las labores domésticas** the housework

laborable (FEM **laborable**) ADJECTIVE
■ **día laborable** working day

laboral (FEM **laboral**) ADJECTIVE
1 working
2 labour
3 industrial

el **laboratorio** NOUN
laboratory (PL laboratories)

la **laca** NOUN
1 hairspray
2 lacquer
■ **la laca de uñas** nail varnish

lácteo (FEM **láctea**) ADJECTIVE
■ **los productos lácteos** dairy products

la **ladera** NOUN
hillside

el **lado** NOUN
side
□ a los dos lados de la carretera on both sides of the road □ Hay gente por todos lados. There are people everywhere.
□ Tiene que estar en otro lado. It must be somewhere else.
■ **Mi casa está aquí al lado.** My house is right nearby.
■ **la mesa de al lado** the next table
■ **al lado de** beside □ La silla que está al lado del armario. The chair beside the wardrobe.
■ **Felipe se sentó a mi lado.** Felipe sat beside me.
■ **por un lado ..., por otro lado ...** on the one hand ..., on the other hand ...

ladrar VERB [25]
to bark
□ El perro les ladró. The dog barked at them.

el **ladrillo** NOUN
brick

el **ladrón**, la **ladrona** NOUN
1 thief (PL thieves)
□ Un ladrón me quitó el bolso. A thief took my bag.
2 burglar
□ Los ladrones entraron en la casa. The burglars broke into the house.
3 robber
□ Tres ladrones atracaron el banco. Three robbers raided the bank.

el **lagarto** NOUN
lizard

el **lago** NOUN
lake

la **lágrima** NOUN
tear

la **laguna** NOUN
lake

lamentar VERB [25]
■ **Lamento lo ocurrido.** I am sorry about what happened.
■ **lamentarse** to complain □ De nada vale lamentarse. There's no use complaining.

lamer VERB [8]
to lick

la **lámina** NOUN
1 sheet
2 plate

la **lámpara** NOUN
lamp

la **lana** NOUN
wool
■ **una bufanda de lana** a woollen scarf

la **lancha** NOUN
motorboat
■ **una lancha de salvamento** a lifeboat

la **langosta** NOUN
1 lobster
2 locust

el **langostino** NOUN
king prawn

lanzar* VERB [13]
1 to throw
□ Lanzó una piedra al río. He threw a stone into the river.
2 to launch
□ Han lanzado dos satélites al espacio. They have launched two satellites into space.
■ **lanzarse** to dive □ Los niños se lanzaron a la piscina. The children dived into the swimming pool.

el **lapicero** NOUN
pencil

la **lápida** NOUN
gravestone

el **lápiz** (PL los **lápices**) NOUN
pencil
□ Escribió mi dirección a lápiz. He wrote my address in pencil.
■ **los lápices de colores** crayons
■ **un lápiz de labios** lipstick
■ **un lápiz de ojos** an eyeliner

largo (FEM **larga**) ADJECTIVE
long
□ Fue una conferencia muy larga. It was a very long conference. □ Esta cuerda es demasiado larga. This piece of string is too long.

el **largo** NOUN
length
□ Nadé cuatro largos de la piscina. I swam four lengths of the pool.
■ **¿Cuánto mide de largo?** How long is it?
■ **Tiene nueve metros de largo.** It's nine metres long.
■ **a lo largo del río** along the river
■ **a lo largo de la semana** throughout the week
■ **Pasó de largo sin saludar.** He passed by without saying hello.
LANGUAGE TIP Be careful! **largo** does not mean **large**.

las ARTICLE
▷ *see also* **las** PRONOUN
the
□ las paredes the walls
■ **las del estante de arriba** the ones on the top shelf
■ **Me duelen las piernas.** My legs hurt.
■ **Poneos las bufandas.** Put on your scarves.
■ **Estas fotos son bonitas, pero prefiero las de Pedro.** These photos are nice, but I prefer Pedro's.
■ **No me gustan las arañas.** I don't like spiders.
■ **Vino a las seis de la tarde.** He came at six in the evening.

las PRONOUN
▷ *see also* **las** ARTICLE
1 them
□ Las vi por la calle. I saw them in the street.
■ **Las han despedido.** They've been sacked.
2 you
□ Las acompañaré hasta la puerta, señoras. I'll see you out, ladies.

el **láser** NOUN
laser

la **lástima** NOUN
■ **Me da lástima de ella.** I feel sorry for her.
■ **Es una lástima que no puedas venir.** It's a shame you can't come.
■ **¡Qué lástima!** What a shame!

la **lata** NOUN
1 tin
2 can
■ **Deja de dar la lata.** Stop being a pain.

lateral (FEM **lateral**) ADJECTIVE
side
□ la puerta lateral the side door

el **latido** NOUN
beat

el **látigo** NOUN
whip

el **latín** NOUN
Latin

Latinoamérica FEM NOUN
Latin America

el **latinoamericano** (FEM la **latinoamericana**) ADJECTIVE, NOUN
Latin American

latir VERB [58]
to beat

Spanish-English

l

el **laurel** NOUN
laurel
■ **una hoja de laurel** a bay leaf
el **lavabo** NOUN
1 sink
□ Llené el lavabo de agua. I filled the sink with water.
2 toilet
□ Voy al lavabo. I'm going to the toilet.
el **lavado** NOUN
wash
■ **el lavado en seco** dry cleaning
la **lavadora** NOUN
washing machine
la **lavandería** NOUN
launderette
el **lavaplatos** (PL los **lavaplatos**) NOUN
1 dishwasher
2 sink *(Mexico)*
lavar VERB [25]
to wash
□ Lava estos vasos. Wash these glasses.
■ **lavar la ropa** to do the washing
■ **lavarse** to wash □ Me lavo todos los días. I wash every day.
■ **Ayer me lavé la cabeza.** I washed my hair yesterday.
■ **Lávate los dientes.** Brush your teeth.
el **lavarropas** (PL los **lavarropas**) NOUN *(Mexico)*
washing machine

el **lavavajillas** (PL los **lavavajillas**) NOUN
1 dishwasher
2 washing-up liquid
el **lazo** NOUN
1 bow
2 ribbon
le PRONOUN
1 him
□ Le mandé una carta. I sent him a letter.
□ Le miré con atención. I watched him carefully.
■ **Le abrí la puerta.** I opened the door for him.
2 her
□ Le mandé una carta. I sent her a letter.
■ **No le hablé de ti.** I didn't speak to her about you.
■ **Le busqué el libro.** I looked out the book for her.
3 you
□ Le presento a la Señora Gutiérrez. Let me introduce you to Mrs. Gutiérrez.
■ **Le he arreglado el ordenador.** I've fixed the computer for you. □ Le huelen los pies. His feet smell. □ Le arrastra la falda. Her skirt is trailing on the floor.
la **lealtad** NOUN
loyalty (PL loyalties)
la **lección** (PL las **lecciones**) NOUN
lesson
la **leche** NOUN
milk
■ **la leche desnatada** skimmed milk
■ **la leche en polvo** powdered milk
la **lechuga** NOUN
lettuce
la **lechuza** NOUN
owl
el **lector**, la **lectora** NOUN
1 reader
□ Varios lectores se quejaron del artículo. Several readers complained about the article.
2 language assistant
□ Es la lectora de francés. She's the French language assistant.
el **lector** NOUN
■ **un lector de CD** a CD player
la **lectura** NOUN
reading
□ Me encanta la lectura. I love reading.
leer* VERB [30]
to read
legal (FEM **legal**) ADJECTIVE
legal
la **legaña** NOUN
■ **tener legañas** to have sleep in one's eyes
la **legumbre** NOUN
pulse
lejano (FEM **lejana**) ADJECTIVE
distant
□ un sitio muy lejano a very distant place
la **lejía** NOUN
bleach
lejos ADVERB
far
□ ¿Está lejos? Is it far? □ No está lejos de aquí. It's not far from here.
■ **De lejos parecía un avión.** From a distance it looked like a plane.
la **lencería** NOUN
lingerie
la **lengua** NOUN
1 tongue
□ Me he mordido la lengua. I've bitten my tongue.
2 language
□ Habla varias lenguas. He speaks several languages.
■ **mi lengua materna** my mother tongue
el **lenguado** NOUN
sole
el **lenguaje** NOUN
language
la **lente** NOUN

lense
■ **las lentes de contacto** contact lenses

la **lenteja** NOUN
lentil

los **lentes** NOUN *(Latin America)*
glasses
■ **los lentes de sol** sunglasses

la **lentilla** NOUN
contact lens

lento (FEM **lenta**) ADJECTIVE
▷ *see also* **lento** ADVERB
slow
□ un proceso lento a slow progress

lento ADVERB
▷ *see also* **lento** ADJECTIVE
slowly
□ Vas un poco lento. You're going a bit slowly.

la **leña** NOUN
firewood

Leo MASC NOUN
Leo
■ **Soy leo.** I'm Leo.

el **león** (PL los **leones**) NOUN
lion

la **leona** NOUN
lioness (PL lionesses)

el **leopardo** NOUN
leopard

los **leotardos** NOUN
woolly tights

les PRONOUN
1 them
□ Les mandé una carta. I sent them a letter.
□ Les miré con atención. I watched them carefully.
■ **Les abrí la puerta.** I opened the door for them.
■ **Les eché de comer a los gatos.** I gave the cats something to eat.
2 you
□ Les presento a la Señora Gutiérrez. Let me introduce you to Mrs. Gutiérrez.
■ **Les he arreglado el ordenador.** I've fixed the computer for you. □ Les huelen los pies. Their feet smell. □ Les arrastraban los abrigos. Their coats were trailing on the floor.

la **lesbiana** NOUN
lesbian

la **lesión** (PL las **lesiones**) NOUN
injury (PL injuries)

lesionado (FEM **lesionada**) ADJECTIVE
injured
□ Está lesionado. He's injured.

la **letra** NOUN
1 letter
□ la letra 'a' the letter 'a'
2 handwriting
□ Tengo muy mala letra. My handwriting's very poor.
3 lyrics *pl*
□ Él escribe la letra de sus canciones. He writes the lyrics for his songs.

el **letrero** NOUN
sign

levantar VERB [25]
to lift
□ Levanta la tapa. Lift the lid.
■ **Levantad la mano si tenéis alguna duda.** Raise your hand if you are unclear.
■ **levantarse** to get up □ Hoy me he levantado temprano. I got up early this morning. □ Me levanté y seguí caminando. I got up and carried on walking.

leve (FEM **leve**) ADJECTIVE
minor
□ Sólo tiene heridas leves. He only has minor injuries. □ Cometió una falta leve. He committed a minor mistake.

la **ley** (PL las **leyes**) NOUN
law
□ la ley de la gravedad the law of gravity

leyendo VERB ▷ *see* **leer**

liar* VERB [21]
1 to tie up
□ Lía este paquete con una cuerda. Tie up this parcel with some string.
2 to confuse
□ Me liaron con tantas explicaciones. They confused me with all their explanations.
■ **A mí no me líes en esto.** Don't get me mixed up in this.
■ **liarse** to get muddled up □ Me estoy liando, empezaré otra vez. I'm getting muddled up, I'll start again.
■ **Se lió a tortas con su hermano.** He got into a fight with his brother.
■ **Nos liamos a hablar y se nos pasó la hora.** We got talking and we forgot the time.

Líbano MASC NOUN
Lebanon

el/la **liberal** ADJECTIVE, NOUN
liberal

liberar VERB [25]
to free

la **libertad** NOUN
freedom
□ libertad de expresión freedom of expression
■ **No tengo libertad para hacer lo que quiera.** I'm not free to do what I want.
■ **El rehén está en libertad.** The hostage is free.
■ **poner a alguien en libertad** to release

somebody

la **libra** NOUN
pound

DID YOU KNOW...?
En los países anglosajones el peso a menudo se expresa en libras **pounds**. Un kilogramo equivale a 2.2 libras aproximadamente.

■ **libra esterlina** pound sterling

Libra MASC NOUN
Libra
■ **Soy libra.** I'm Libra.

librarse VERB [25]
■ **librarse de 1** to get out of □ ¡No te librarás de fregar los platos! You're not going to get out of doing the washing-up! **2** to get rid of □ Logré librarme de mi hermana. I managed to get rid of my sister.
■ **Se libró del castigo por pura suerte.** He got away with it by pure good luck.

libre (FEM **libre**) ADJECTIVE
free
□ ¿Está libre este asiento? Is this seat free?
□ El martes estoy libre, así que podemos quedar. I'm free on Tuesday so we can meet up.
■ **los 100 metros libres** the 100 metres freestyle

la **librería** NOUN
1 bookshop
2 bookshelf (PL bookshelves)

LANGUAGE TIP Be careful! **librería** does not mean **library**.

el **librero** NOUN *(Chile, Mexico)*
bookcase

la **libreta** NOUN
notebook
■ **una libreta de ahorros** a savings book

el **libro** NOUN
book
■ **un libro de bolsillo** a paperback
■ **un libro de texto** a text book

la **licencia** NOUN
licence
□ una licencia de armas a gun licence
■ **la licencia de obras** planning permission
■ **estar de licencia** *(Latin America)* to be on leave

el **licenciado**, la **licenciada** NOUN
graduate
□ un licenciado en historia a history graduate

la **licenciatura** NOUN
degree

el **licor** NOUN
liqueur
□ un licor de pera a pear liqueur
■ **Bebimos cerveza y licores.** We drank beer and spirits.

el/la **líder** NOUN
leader

la **liebre** NOUN
hare

la **liga** NOUN
1 league
2 garter

ligar* VERB [37]
■ **Ayer ligué con una chica.** *(colloquial)* I got off with a girl yesterday.

ligero (FEM **ligera**) ADJECTIVE
1 light
□ Me gusta llevar ropa ligera. I like to wear light clothing. □ Comimos algo ligero. We ate something light.
2 slight
□ Tengo un ligero dolor de cabeza. I have a slight headache.
■ **Andaba a paso ligero.** He walked quickly.

la **lila** NOUN
lilac

la **lima** NOUN
1 file
□ una lima de uñas a nail file
2 lime

limitar VERB [25]
to limit
□ Limitaron el tiempo del examen a dos horas. The exam time was limited to two hours.
■ **España limita con Francia.** Spain has a border with France.
■ **Yo me limité a observar.** I just watched.

el **límite** NOUN
1 limit
□ el límite de velocidad the speed limit
■ **fecha límite** deadline
2 boundary (PL boundaries)
□ Está dentro de los límites de la finca. It's within the boundaries of the estate.

el **limón** (PL los **limones**) NOUN
lemon

la **limonada** NOUN
lemonade

la **limosna** NOUN
■ **pedir limosna** to beg

el **limpiaparabrisas** (PL los **limpiaparabrisas**) NOUN
windscreen-wiper

limpiar VERB [25]
1 to clean
□ El sábado voy a limpiar la casa. I'm going to clean the house on Saturday.
2 to wipe
□ ¿Has limpiado la mesa? Have you wiped the table? □ Límpiate la nariz. Wipe your nose.

la **limpieza** NOUN
cleaning
□ Yo hago la limpieza los sábados. I do the cleaning on Saturdays.
■ **limpieza en seco** dry cleaning

limpio (FEM **limpia**) ADJECTIVE
clean
□ El baño está muy limpio. The bathroom's very clean.
■ **Voy a pasar esto a limpio.** I'm going to write this out neat.

lindo (FEM **linda**) ADJECTIVE
1 pretty
□ sus lindos ojos her pretty eyes
2 nice *(Latin America)*
□ un día muy lindo a very nice day

la **línea** NOUN
line
□ Dibujó una línea recta. He drew a straight line.
■ **Vaya en línea recta.** Go straight ahead.
■ **una línea aérea** an airline
■ **en línea** online

el **lino** NOUN
linen

la **linterna** NOUN
torch (PL torches)

el **lío** NOUN
■ **En mi mesa hay un lío enorme de papeles.** My desk is in a real muddle with all these papers.
■ **hacerse un lío** to get muddled up □ Se hizo un lío con tantos nombres. He got muddled up with all the names.
■ **Esta ecuación es un lío.** This equation is a real headache.
■ **Si sigues así te vas a meter en un lío.** If you carry on like that you'll get yourself into a real mess.

la **liquidación** NOUN
sale

el **líquido** ADJECTIVE, NOUN
liquid

Lisboa FEM NOUN
Lisbon

liso (FEM **lisa**) ADJECTIVE
1 smooth
2 straight
3 plain

la **lista** NOUN
list
□ la lista de espera the waiting list
■ **pasar lista** to call the register
■ **la lista de correo** mailing list

listo (FEM **lista**) ADJECTIVE
1 clever
□ Es una chica muy lista. She's a very clever girl.
2 ready
□ ¿Estás listo? Are you ready?

la **litera** NOUN
1 bunk bed
2 berth

la **literatura** NOUN
literature

el **litro** NOUN
litre

liviano (FEM **liviana**) ADJECTIVE
light

la **llaga** NOUN
sore

la **llama** NOUN
flame

la **llamada** NOUN
call
■ **hacer una llamada telefónica** to make a phone call

llamar VERB [25]
1 to call
□ Me llamaron mentiroso. They called me a liar. □ llamar a la policía to call the police
2 to ring
3 to knock
■ **llamar por teléfono a alguien** to phone somebody
■ **¿Cómo te llamas?** What's your name?
■ **Me llamo Adela.** My name's Adela.

llano (FEM **llana**) ADJECTIVE
flat

la **llanta** NOUN
1 wheel rim
2 tyre *(Latin America)*

la **llave** NOUN
1 key
□ las llaves del coche the car keys
■ **Echa la llave de la puerta cuando salgas.** Lock the door when you go out.
■ **una llave inglesa** a spanner
LANGUAGE TIP Word for word, **llave inglesa** means 'English key'.
2 tap *(Latin America)*

el **llavero** NOUN
keyring

la **llegada** NOUN
1 arrival
2 finish

llegar* VERB [37]
1 to get to
□ Estaba lloviendo cuando llegamos a Granada. It was raining when we got to Granada.
■ **¿A qué hora llegaste a casa?** What time did you get home?
2 to arrive
□ Carmen no ha llegado todavía. Carmen hasn't arrived yet.

■ **No llegues tarde.** Don't be late.
■ **Con tres euros no me llega.** Three euros isn't enough.
3 to reach
□ No llego al estante de arriba. I can't reach the top shelf.
■ **El agua me llegaba hasta las rodillas.** The water came up to my knees.
■ **llegar a ser** to become

llenar VERB [25]
to fill
□ Llena la jarra de agua. Fill the jug with water.

lleno (FEM **llena**) ADJECTIVE
full
□ Todos los hoteles están llenos. All the hotels are full. □ El restaurante estaba lleno de gente. The restaurant was full of people.

llevar VERB [25]
1 to take
□ ¿Llevas los vasos a la cocina? Can you take the glasses to the kitchen? □ No llevará mucho tiempo. It won't take long.
2 to wear
□ María llevaba un abrigo muy bonito. María was wearing a nice coat.
3 to give a lift
□ Sofía nos llevó a casa. Sofía gave us a lift home.
4 to carry
□ Yo te llevo la maleta. I'll carry your case.
■ **Sólo llevo diez euros.** I've only got ten euros on me.
■ **¿Cuánto tiempo llevas aquí?** How long have you been here?
■ **Llevo horas esperando aquí.** I've been waiting here for hours.
■ **Mi hermana mayor me lleva ocho años.** My elder sister is eight years older than me.
■ **llevarse algo** to take something
□ Llévatelo. Take it with you. □ ¿Le gusta? — Sí, me lo llevo. Do you like it? — Yes, I'll take it!
■ **Me llevo bien con mi hermano.** I get on well with my brother.
■ **Nos llevamos muy mal.** We get on very badly.

llorar VERB [25]
to cry

llover* VERB [31]
to rain
■ **llover a cántaros** to pour down

lloviznar VERB [25]
to drizzle

llueve VERB ▹ *see* **llover**

la **lluvia** NOUN
rain
□ bajo la lluvia in the rain
■ **la lluvia ácida** acid rain

lluvioso (FEM **lluviosa**) ADJECTIVE
rainy

lo ARTICLE
▹ *see also* **lo** PRONOUN
■ **Lo peor fue que no pudimos entrar.** The worst thing was we couldn't get in.
■ **No me gusta lo picante.** I don't like spicy things.
■ **Pon en mi habitación lo de Pedro.** Put Pedro's things in my room.
■ **Lo mío son las matemáticas.** Maths is my thing.
■ **Lo de vender la casa no me parece bien.** I don't like this idea of selling the house.
■ **Olvida lo de ayer.** Forget what happened yesterday.
■ **¡No sabes lo aburrido que es!** You don't know how boring he is!
■ **lo que 1** what □ Lo que más me gusta es nadar. What I like most is swimming.
2 whatever □ Ponte lo que quieras. Wear whatever you like.
■ **más de lo que** more than □ Cuesta más de lo que crees. It costs more than you think.

lo PRONOUN
▹ *see also* **lo** ARTICLE
1 him
□ No lo conozco. I don't know him.
■ **Lo han despedido.** He's been sacked.
2 you
□ Yo a usted lo conozco. I know you.
3 it
□ No lo veo. I can't see it. □ Voy a pensarlo. I'll think about it.
■ **No lo sabía.** I didn't know.
■ **No parece lista pero lo es.** She doesn't seem clever but she is.

el **lobo** NOUN
wolf (PL wolves)

la **loca** NOUN
madwoman (PL madwomen)

local (FEM **local**) ADJECTIVE
local
□ un producto local a local product

el **local** NOUN
premises *pl*
□ Lo echaron del local. They threw him off the premises.
■ **Ensayan en un local cerca de aquí.** They rehearse in a place near here.

la **localidad** NOUN
1 town
□ una localidad al sur de Madrid a town south of Madrid
2 seat
□ Reserve sus localidades con antelación.

Book your seats in advance.

localizar* VERB [13]
1 to reach
□ Me puedes localizar en este teléfono. You can reach me at this number.
2 to locate
□ No han conseguido localizar a las víctimas. They have been unable to locate the victims.

la **loción** (PL las **lociones**) NOUN
lotion

loco (FEM **loca**) ADJECTIVE
1 mad
□ volverse loco to go mad
■ **volver loco a alguien** to drive somebody mad
2 crazy
□ ¿Estás loco? Are you crazy? □ Está loco con su moto nueva. He's crazy about his new motorbike.
■ **Me vuelve loco el marisco.** I'm crazy about seafood.

el **loco** NOUN
madman (PL madmen)

la **locura** NOUN
madness
□ Es una locura ir solo. It's madness to go on your own.

el **locutor**, la **locutora** NOUN
newsreader

lógico (FEM **lógica**) ADJECTIVE
1 logical
□ No es un razonamiento lógico. It's not logical reasoning.
2 natural
□ Es una reacción lógica. It's a natural reaction.
■ **Es lógico que no quiera venir.** It's only natural he doesn't want to come.

lograr VERB [25]
1 to get
□ Lograron lo que se proponían. They got what they wanted.
2 to manage
□ Logré que me concediera una entrevista. I managed to get an interview with him.

la **lombriz** (PL las **lombrices**) NOUN
worm

el **lomo** NOUN
1 back
2 loin
3 spine

la **lona** NOUN
canvas (PL canvases)

la **loncha** NOUN
slice

Londres MASC NOUN
London

la **longitud** NOUN
length
■ **Tiene tres metros de longitud.** It's three metres long.

el **loro** NOUN
parrot

los ARTICLE
▷ *see also* **los** PRONOUN
the
□ los barcos the boats
■ **los de las bufandas rojas** the people in the red scarves
■ **Se lavaron los pies en el río.** They washed their feet in the river.
■ **Abrochaos los abrigos.** Button your coats.
■ **Me gustan sus cuadros, pero prefiero los de Ana.** I like his paintings, but I prefer Ana's.
■ **No me gustan los melocotones.** I don't like peaches.
■ **Sólo vienen los lunes.** They only come on Mondays.

los PRONOUN
▷ *see also* **los** ARTICLE
1 them
□ Los vi por la calle. I saw them in the street.
■ **Los han despedido.** They've been sacked.
2 you
□ Los acompaño hasta la puerta, señores. I'll see you to the door, gentlemen.

la **lotería** NOUN
lottery (PL lotteries)
□ Le tocó la lotería. He won the lottery.

la **lucha** NOUN
fight
■ **lucha libre** wrestling
LANGUAGE TIP Word for word, **lucha libre** means 'free fight'.

luchar VERB [25]
to fight

lucir* VERB [9]
to shine
□ Lucían las estrellas. The stars were shining.
■ **Carlos se lució en el examen.** Carlos performed brilliantly in the exam.

luego ADVERB
▷ *see also* **luego** CONJUNCTION
1 then
□ Primero se puso de pie y luego habló. First he stood up and then he spoke.
2 later
□ Mi mujer viene luego. My wife's coming later.
■ **desde luego** of course □ ¡Desde luego que me gusta! Of course I like it!
■ **¡Hasta luego!** See you!

3 soon *(Chile, Mexico)*
□ Vuelvo luego. I'll be back soon.

luego CONJUNCTION
▷ *see also* **luego** ADVERB
therefore
□ Yo he pagado, luego tengo derecho a verlo. I have paid, therefore I have a right to see it.

el **lugar** NOUN
place
□ Este lugar es muy bonito. This is a lovely place.
■ **Llegó en último lugar.** He came last.
■ **en lugar de** instead of
■ **tener lugar** to take place

el **lujo** NOUN
luxury (PL luxuries)
■ **un coche de lujo** a luxury car

lujoso (FEM **lujosa**) ADJECTIVE
luxurious

la **luna** NOUN
1 moon
2 window pane
3 window
■ **la luna de miel** honeymoon

el **lunar** NOUN
mole
■ **una corbata de lunares** a spotted tie

el **lunes** (PL los **lunes**) NOUN
Monday
□ La vi el lunes. I saw her on Monday.
□ todos los lunes every Monday □ el lunes pasado last Monday □ el lunes que viene next Monday □ Jugamos los lunes. We play on Mondays.

la **lupa** NOUN
magnifying glass

el **luto** NOUN
■ **estar de luto por alguien** to be in mourning for somebody

Luxemburgo MASC NOUN
Luxembourg

la **luz** (PL las **luces**) NOUN
1 light
□ Enciende la luz, por favor. Put on the light please.
2 electricity
□ No hay luz en todo el edificio. There's no electricity in the whole building.
■ **dar a luz** to give birth

Spanish-English

l

Mm

los **macarrones** NOUN
macaroni *sing*
□ Me gustan los macarrones. I like macaroni.
la **macedonia** NOUN
fruit salad
la **maceta** NOUN
flowerpot
machacar* VERB [48]
1 to crush
□ Machacó los ajos en el mortero. He crushed the garlic in the mortar.
2 to thrash
□ El equipo visitante los machacó. The visiting team thrashed them.
el **macho** ADJECTIVE, NOUN
male
□ un conejo macho a male rabbit
la **madera** NOUN
wood
□ Está hecho de madera. It's made of wood.
■ **un juguete de madera** a wooden toy
■ **Dame esa madera.** Give me that piece of wood.
■ **Tiene madera de profesor.** He's got the makings of a teacher.
la **madrastra** NOUN
stepmother
la **madre** NOUN
mother
■ **¡Madre mía!** Goodness!
Madrid MASC NOUN
Madrid
madrileño (FEM **madrileña**) ADJECTIVE
from Madrid
□ Soy madrileño. I'm from Madrid.
la **madrina** NOUN
1 godmother
2 matron of honour (PL matrons of honour)
la **madrugada** NOUN
early morning
■ **levantarse de madrugada** 1 to get up early 2 to get up at daybreak
■ **a las 4 de la madrugada** at 4 o'clock in the morning
madrugar* VERB [37]
to get up early
maduro (FEM **madura**) ADJECTIVE
1 mature
2 ripe
el **maestro**, la **maestra** NOUN
teacher
□ Mi tía es maestra. My aunt's a teacher.
■ **un maestro de escuela** a schoolteacher
la **magia** NOUN
magic
mágico (FEM **mágica**) ADJECTIVE
magic
□ una varita mágica a magic wand
el **magisterio** NOUN
■ **Estudia magisterio.** He's training to be a teacher.
magnífico (FEM **magnífica**) ADJECTIVE
splendid
el **mago**, la **maga** NOUN
magician
■ **los Reyes Magos** the Three Wise Men
el **maíz** (PL los **maíces**) NOUN
1 maize
2 sweetcorn
■ **una mazorca de maíz** a corn cob
la **majestad** NOUN
■ **Su Majestad** 1 His Majesty 2 Her Majesty
majo (FEM **maja**) ADJECTIVE
1 nice
2 pretty
mal ADJECTIVE
▷ *see also* **mal** ADVERB, NOUN = **malo**
mal ADVERB
▷ *see also* **mal** ADJECTIVE, NOUN
1 badly
□ Toca la guitarra muy mal. He plays the guitar very badly. □ un trabajo mal pagado a badly paid job
■ **Esta habitación huele mal.** This room smells bad.
■ **Lo pasé muy mal.** I had a very bad time.
■ **Me entendió mal.** He misunderstood me.
■ **hablar mal de alguien** to speak ill of someone
2 wrong

□ Han escrito mal mi apellido. They've spelt my surname wrong. □ Está mal mentir. It's wrong to tell lies.

el **mal** NOUN ADJECTIVE, NOUN
evil
□ el bien y el mal good and evil

la **mala** NOUN
■ **la mala de la película** the villain in the film

malcriado (FEM **malcriada**) ADJECTIVE
badly brought up

maldito (FEM **maldita**) ADJECTIVE
damned
□ ¡Malditos vecinos! Damned neighbours!
■ **¡Malditas las ganas que tengo de verle!** I really don't feel like seeing him!
■ **¡Maldita sea!** Damn it!

maleducado (FEM **maleducada**) ADJECTIVE
bad-mannered

el **malentendido** NOUN
misunderstanding

el **malestar** NOUN
discomfort

la **maleta** NOUN
suitcase
■ **hacer la maleta** to pack

el **maletero** NOUN
boot

el **maletín** (PL los **maletines**) NOUN
briefcase

malgastar VERB [25]
to waste

malhumorado (FEM **malhumorada**) ADJECTIVE
bad-tempered
■ **Hoy parece malhumorado.** He appears to be in a bad mood today.

la **malicia** NOUN
1 malice
2 mischief

malicioso (FEM **maliciosa**) ADJECTIVE
malicious

la **malla** NOUN
1 mesh
2 leotard
■ **una malla de baño** *(River Plate)* a swimsuit
■ **mallas** **1** tights **2** leggings

Mallorca FEM NOUN
Majorca

el **malo** NOUN
■ **el malo de la película** the villain in the film

malo (FEM **mala**) ADJECTIVE
1 bad
□ un mal día a bad day □ Este programa es muy malo. This is a very bad programme. □ Soy muy mala para las matemáticas. I'm very bad at maths.
■ **Hace malo.** The weather's bad.
■ **Lo malo es que ...** the trouble is that ...
2 naughty
□ ¿Por qué eres tan malo? Why are you so naughty?
3 off
□ Esta carne está mala. This meat's off.
4 ill
□ Mi hija está mala. My daughter's ill. □ Se puso malo después de comer. He started to feel ill after lunch.

maltratar VERB [25]
to ill-treat
□ Maltrata a su perro. He ill-treats his dog.
■ **los niños maltratados** abused children

malvado (FEM **malvada**) ADJECTIVE
evil

la **mama** NOUN
1 breast
2 mum

la **mamá** (PL las **mamás**) NOUN
mum
□ tu mamá your mum □ ¡Hola, mamá! Hi Mum!

mamar VERB [25]
to suckle
□ El cordero aún mama. The lamb is still suckling.
■ **El bebé mama cada cuatro horas.** The baby has a feed every four hours.
■ **dar de mamar** to breastfeed

el **mamífero** NOUN
mammal

el **manantial** NOUN
spring

la **mancha** NOUN
stain

manchar VERB [25]
to stain
□ La cerveza no mancha. Beer doesn't stain.
■ **mancharse** to get dirty □ No te manches la camisa. Don't get your shirt dirty.
■ **Me he manchado el vestido de tinta.** I've got ink stains on my dress.

mandar VERB [25]
1 to order
□ El sargento le mandó barrer el patio. The sergeant ordered him to sweep the yard.
■ **Nos mandó callar.** He told us to be quiet.
■ **Aquí mando yo.** I'm the boss here.
2 to send
□ Se lo mandaremos por correo. We'll send it to you by post. □ Me mandaron a hacer un recado. They sent me on an errand.
■ **mandar llamar a alguien** *(Latin America)* to send for someone
■ **mandar a arreglar algo** *(Latin America)*

to have something repaired
■ **¿Mande?** *(Mexico)* Pardon?
■ **El médico me mandó un jarabe.** The doctor gave me a prescription for syrup.

la **mandarina** NOUN
tangerine

la **mandíbula** NOUN
jaw

el **mando** NOUN
■ **un alto mando** a high-ranking officer
■ **Está al mando del proyecto.** He's in charge of the project.
■ **el mando a distancia** the remote control
■ **los mandos** the controls

la **manecilla** NOUN
hand
□ las manecillas del reloj the hands of the clock

manejable (FEM **manejable**) ADJECTIVE
1 manoeuvrable
□ un coche muy manejable a very manoeuvrable car
2 easy to use
□ Este taladro es muy manejable. This drill is very easy to use.

manejar VERB [25]
1 to operate
2 to manage
3 to drive *(Latin America)*
■ **un examen de manejar** *(Latin America)* a driving test

la **manera** NOUN
way
□ Lo hice a mi manera. I did it my way.
■ **de todas maneras** anyway
■ **No hay manera de convencerla.** There's nothing one can do to convince her.
■ **de manera que 1** so □ No has hecho los deberes, de manera que no hay tele. You haven't done your homework so there's no TV. **2** so that □ Lo puse de manera que pudieran verlo. I put it so that they could see it.
■ **¡De ninguna manera!** Certainly not!

la **manga** NOUN
sleeve
□ Súbete las mangas. Roll your sleeves up.
■ **de manga corta** short-sleeved
■ **de manga larga** long-sleeved

el **mango** NOUN
1 handle
2 mango

la **manguera** NOUN
hose

la **manía** NOUN
■ **Tiene la manía de repetir todo lo que digo.** He has an irritating habit of repeating everything I say.
■ **El profesor me tiene manía.** *(colloquial)* The teacher has it in for me.

maniático (FEM **maniática**) ADJECTIVE
■ **Es muy maniático para comer.** He's very fussy about eating.
■ **Es una maniática del orden.** She's obsessed with keeping things tidy.

la **manifestación** (PL las **manifestaciones**) NOUN
demonstration
□ Convocaron una manifestación contra el terrorismo. They held a demonstration against terrorism.

el/la **manifestante** NOUN
demonstrator

manifestarse* VERB [39]
to demonstrate

el **manillar** NOUN
handlebars *pl*

la **maniobra** NOUN
manoeuvre
□ una maniobra política a political manoeuvre
■ **hacer maniobras** to manoeuvre

manipular VERB [25]
1 to handle
□ La higiene es imprescindible para manipular alimentos. Hygiene is essential when handling food.
2 to manipulate
□ La publicidad manipula a la opinión pública. Advertising manipulates public opinion.

el/la **maniquí** (PL los/las **maniquíes**) NOUN
model

el **maniquí** (PL los **maniquíes**) NOUN
dummy (PL dummies)

la **manivela** NOUN
crank

la **mano** NOUN
hand
□ Dame la mano. Give me your hand.
■ **tener algo a mano** to have something to hand
■ **hecho a mano** handmade
■ **de segunda mano** secondhand
■ **echar una mano** to lend a hand
■ **estrechar la mano a alguien** to shake somebody's hand
■ **la mano de obra** labour
LANGUAGE TIP Word for word, **mano de obra** means 'hand of work'.
■ **una mano de pintura** a coat of paint

el **manojo** NOUN
bunch (PL bunches)
□ un manojo de llaves a bunch of keys

la **manopla** NOUN
mitten

□ El niño llevaba manoplas. The child was wearing mittens.
■ **una manopla de cocina** an oven-glove

manso (FEM **mansa**) ADJECTIVE
tame

la **manta** NOUN
blanket

la **manteca** NOUN
butter *(River Plate)*
■ **manteca de cerdo** lard

el **mantel** NOUN
tablecloth

mantener* VERB [53]
1 to keep
□ Les mantendremos informados. We'll keep you informed. □ mantener la calma to keep calm
2 to support
□ Mantiene a su familia. He supports his family.
■ **mantener una conversación** to have a conversation
■ **mantenerse** to support oneself
■ **mantenerse en forma** to keep fit
■ **mantenerse en pie** to remain standing

el **mantenimiento** NOUN
maintenance
□ el encargado de mantenimiento the person in charge of maintenance
■ **ejercicios de mantenimiento** keep-fit exercises

la **mantequilla** NOUN
butter

mantuve VERB ▷ *see* **mantener**

el **manual** ADJECTIVE, NOUN
manual

el **manubrio** NOUN *(Latin America)*
handlebars *pl*

el **manuscrito** NOUN
manuscript

la **manzana** NOUN
1 apple
2 block

el **manzano** NOUN
apple tree

la **maña** NOUN
■ **Tiene mucha maña para hacer arreglos caseros.** She's a dab hand at mending things around the house.

la **mañana** NOUN
morning
□ Llegó a las nueve de la mañana. He arrived at nine o'clock in the morning.
■ **Por la mañana voy al gimnasio.** In the mornings I go to the gym.
■ **a media mañana** mid-morning

mañana ADVERB
tomorrow
□ ¡Hasta mañana! See you tomorrow!
■ **pasado mañana** the day after tomorrow
■ **mañana por la mañana** tomorrow morning
■ **mañana por la noche** tomorrow night

el **mapa** NOUN
map
□ El pueblo no está en el mapa. The village isn't on the map. □ un mapa de carreteras a road map

la **maqueta** NOUN
model

el **maquillaje** NOUN
make-up *sing*

maquillarse VERB [25]
to put one's make-up on

la **máquina** NOUN
machine
□ una máquina de coser a sewing machine
□ una máquina expendedora a vending machine □ una máquina tragaperras a fruit machine
■ **una máquina de afeitar** an electric razor
■ **una máquina de escribir** a typewriter
■ **escrito a máquina** typed
■ **una máquina fotográfica** a camera

la **maquinilla** NOUN
razor
□ una maquinilla eléctrica an electric razor

el **mar** NOUN
sea
■ **por mar** by sea
■ **en alta mar** on the high seas
■ **Lo hizo la mar de bien.** He did it really well.

el **maratón** (PL los **maratones**) NOUN
marathon

la **maravilla** NOUN
■ **¡Qué maravilla de casa!** What a wonderful house!
■ **ser una maravilla** to be wonderful
■ **Se llevan de maravilla.** They get on wonderfully well together.

maravilloso (FEM **maravillosa**) ADJECTIVE
marvellous

la **marca** NOUN
1 mark
□ Había marcas de neumático en la arena. There were tyre marks in the sand.
2 make
□ ¿De qué marca es tu coche? What make's your car?
3 brand
□ una conocida marca de cigarrillos a well-known brand of cigarettes
■ **la ropa de marca** designer clothes

el **marcador** NOUN
1 scoreboard

2 bookmark

marcar* VERB [48]

1 to mark
2 to brand
3 to dial
4 to score
5 to set

■ **Mi reloj marca las 2.** It's 2 o'clock according to my watch.

■ **marcar algo con una equis** to put a cross on something

la **marcha** NOUN

1 departure

□ Su marcha les dejó muy tristes. His departure left them feeling very sad.

2 gear

□ cambiar de marcha to change gear

■ **salir de marcha** to go out on the town

■ **a toda marcha** at full speed

■ **estar en marcha** 1 to be running 2 to be underway

■ **dar marcha atrás** to reverse

■ **No te subas nunca a un tren en marcha.** Never get onto a moving train.

marcharse VERB [25]

to leave

el **marco** NOUN

frame

la **marea** NOUN

tide

■ **una marea negra** an oil slick

LANGUAGE TIP Word for word, **marea negra** means 'black tide'.

mareado (FEM **mareada**) ADJECTIVE

■ **Estoy mareado.** 1 I feel dizzy. 2 I feel sick.

marear VERB [25]

to make...feel sick

□ Ese olor me marea. That smell makes me feel sick.

■ **marearse** 1 to get dizzy □ Te marearás si das tantas vueltas. You'll get dizzy going round and round like that. 2 to get seasick □ ¿Te mareas cuando vas en barco? Do you get seasick when you travel by boat? 3 to get carsick □ Siempre me mareo en coche. I always get carsick.

■ **¡No me marees!** Stop going on at me!

el **mareo** NOUN

1 sea sickness
2 car sickness

■ **Le dio un mareo a causa del calor.** The heat made her feel ill.

el **marfil** NOUN

ivory

la **margarina** NOUN

margarine

la **margarita** NOUN

daisy (PL daisies)

el **margen** (PL los **márgenes**) NOUN

margin

□ Escribe las notas al margen. Write your notes in the margin.

el **marido** NOUN

husband

el **marinero** NOUN

sailor

la **mariposa** NOUN

butterfly (PL butterflies)

el **marisco** NOUN

shellfish (PL shellfish)

□ No me gusta el marisco. I don't like shellfish.

el **mármol** NOUN

marble

marrón (FEM **marrón**, PL **marrones**) ADJECTIVE

brown

□ un traje marrón a brown suit

Marruecos MASC NOUN

Morocco

el **martes** (PL los **martes**) NOUN

Tuesday

□ La vi el martes. I saw her on Tuesday. □ todos los martes every Tuesday □ el martes pasado last Tuesday □ el martes que viene next Tuesday □ Jugamos los martes. We play on Tuesdays.

el **martillo** NOUN

hammer

marzo MASC NOUN

March

□ en marzo in March □ Nací el 17 de marzo. I was born on 17 March.

más ADJECTIVE, ADVERB

more

□ Ahora salgo más. I go out more these days.

■ **Últimamente nos vemos más.** We've been seeing more of each other lately.

■ **¿Quieres más?** Would you like some more?

■ **No tengo más dinero.** I haven't any more money. □ barato – más barato cheap – cheaper □ joven – más joven young – younger □ largo – más largo long – longer □ grande – más grande big – bigger □ contento – más contento happy – happier □ rápido – más rápido fast – faster □ temprano – más temprano early – earlier

■ **lejos – más lejos** far – further □ hermoso – más hermoso beautiful – more beautiful □ guapo – más guapo handsome – more handsome □ deprisa – más deprisa quickly – more quickly □ Es más grande que el tuyo. It's bigger than yours. □ Corre más rápido que yo. He runs faster than I do.

■ **Trabaja más que yo.** He works harder than I do.

■ **más de mil libros** more than a thousand books
■ **No tiene más de dieciséis años.** He isn't more than sixteen.
■ **más de lo que yo creía** more than I thought □ el bolígrafo más barato the cheapest pen □ el niño más joven the youngest child □ el coche más grande the biggest car □ la persona más feliz the happiest person □ el más inteligente de todos the most intelligent of all of them
■ **su película más innovadora** his most innovative film
■ **Paco es el que come más.** Paco's the one who eats the most.
■ **Fue el que más trabajó.** He was the one who worked the hardest.
■ **el punto más lejano** the furthest point
■ **¿Qué más?** What else?
■ **¡Qué perro más sucio!** What a filthy dog!
■ **Tenemos uno de más.** We have one too many.
■ **Por más que estudio no apruebo.** However hard I study I don't pass.
■ **más o menos** more or less
■ **2 más 2 son 4** 2 and 2 are 4
■ **14 más 20 menos 12 es igual a 22** 14 plus 20 minus 12 equals 22

la **masa** NOUN
1 dough
□ la masa de pan bread dough
2 mass (PL masses)
■ **las masas** the masses
■ **en masa** 1 mass □ la producción en masa mass production 2 en masse
□ Fueron en masa a recibir al futbolista. They went en masse to greet the footballer.

el **masaje** NOUN
massage

la **máscara** NOUN
mask

masculino (FEM **masculina**) ADJECTIVE
1 male
□ el sexo masculino the male sex
2 men's
□ la ropa masculina men's clothing
3 masculine
□ el pronombre masculino 'él' the masculine pronoun 'él'

masticar* VERB [48]
to chew

matar VERB [25]
to kill
□ El jefe me va a matar. The boss will kill me.
■ **matarse** to be killed □ Se mataron en un accidente de coche. They were killed in a car accident.

el **matasellos** (PL los **matasellos**) NOUN
postmark

mate (FEM **mate**) ADJECTIVE
matt

el **mate** NOUN
1 checkmate
2 maté

las **matemáticas** NOUN
mathematics *sing*

la **materia** NOUN
1 matter
□ materia orgánica organic matter
2 material
□ la materia prima raw material
3 subject
□ Es un experto en la materia. He's an expert on the subject.
■ **entrar en materia** to get to the point

el **material** ADJECTIVE, NOUN
material
□ los materiales de desecho waste material

materno (FEM **materna**) ADJECTIVE
maternal
□ mi abuela materna my maternal grandmother
■ **mi lengua materna** my mother tongue

el **matiz** (PL los **matices**) NOUN
shade

el **matorral** NOUN
bushes *pl*

la **matrícula** NOUN
registration
■ **la matrícula del coche** 1 the registration number of the car 2 the number plate of the car

matricular VERB [25]
to register
■ **matricularse** to enrol

el **matrimonio** NOUN
1 marriage
□ El matrimonio se celebró en la iglesia del pueblo. The marriage took place in the village church.
2 couple
□ Eran un matrimonio feliz. They were a happy couple.

maullar VERB [25]
to miaow

máximo (FEM **máxima**) ADJECTIVE
maximum
□ la velocidad máxima the maximum speed

el **máximo** NOUN
maximum
□ un máximo de 50 euros a maximum of 50 euros
■ **como máximo** 1 at the most □ Te costará 5.000 libras como máximo. It'll cost you £5,000 at the most. 2 at the latest
□ Llegaré a las diez como máximo. I'll be

there by ten o'clock at the latest.

mayo MASC NOUN
May
□ en mayo in May □ Nací el 28 de mayo. I was born on 28 May.

la **mayonesa** NOUN
mayonnaise

mayor (FEM **mayor**) ADJECTIVE, PRONOUN
1 older
□ Paco es mayor que Nacho. Paco is older than Nacho. □ Es tres años mayor que yo. He is three years older than me.
■ **el hermano mayor** 1 the older brother 2 the oldest brother
■ **Soy el mayor.** 1 I'm the older. 2 I'm the oldest.
■ **Nuestros hijos ya son mayores.** Our children are grown-up now.
■ **la gente mayor** the elderly
2 bigger
□ Necesitamos una casa mayor. We need a bigger house.
■ **la mayor iglesia del mundo.** the biggest church in the world

el/la **mayor** NOUN
■ **un mayor de edad** an adult
■ **los mayores** grown-ups

la **mayoría** NOUN
majority (PL majorities)
■ **Somos mayoría.** We are in the majority.
■ **La mayoría de los estudiantes son pobres.** Most students are poor.
■ **la mayoría de nosotros** most of us

la **mayúscula** NOUN
capital letter
□ Empieza cada frase con mayúscula. Start each sentence with a capital letter.
■ **Escríbelo con mayúsculas.** Write it in capitals.
■ **una M mayúscula** a capital M

el **mazapán** (PL los **mazapanes**) NOUN
marzipan

me PRONOUN
1 me
□ Me quiere. He loves me. □ Me regaló una pulsera. He gave me a bracelet.
■ **Me lo dio.** He gave it to me.
■ **¿Me echas esta carta?** Will you post this letter for me?
2 myself
□ No me hice daño. I didn't hurt myself.
■ **me dije a mí mismo** I said to myself
□ Me duelen los pies. My feet hurt. □ Me puse el abrigo. I put my coat on.

mear VERB [25]
to piss *(vulgar)*
■ **mearse** to wet oneself
■ **mearse de risa** *(vulgar)* to piss oneself laughing

la **mecánica** NOUN
1 mechanic
□ Quiere ser mecánica. She wants to be a mechanic.
2 mechanics *sing*

mecánico (FEM **mecánica**) ADJECTIVE
mechanical

el **mecánico** NOUN
mechanic
□ Es mecánico. He's a mechanic.

el **mecanismo** NOUN
mechanism

la **mecanografía** NOUN
typing

la **mecha** NOUN
1 wick
2 fuse

el **mechero** NOUN
cigarette lighter

la **medalla** NOUN
medal

la **media** NOUN
1 average
□ Trabajo una media de seis horas diarias. I work an average of six hours a day.
2 sock *(Latin America)*
■ **medias** 1 stockings 2 tights
■ **medias bombachas** *(River Plate)* tights
■ **a las cuatro y media** at half past four

mediados PL NOUN
■ **a mediados de** around the middle of

mediano (FEM **mediana**) ADJECTIVE
medium
□ de mediana estatura of medium height
■ **de tamaño mediano** medium-sized
■ **el hijo mediano** the middle son

la **medianoche** NOUN
midnight
□ a medianoche at midnight

mediante PREPOSITION
■ **Izaron las cajas mediante una polea.** They lifted the crates using a pulley.

mediático (FEM **mediática**) ADJECTIVE
media

el **medicamento** NOUN
medicine

la **medicina** NOUN
medicine
□ Estudia medicina en la universidad. He's studying medicine at university. □ ¿Te has tomado ya la medicina? Have you taken your medicine yet?

el **médico**, la **médica** NOUN
doctor
□ Quiere ser médica. She wants to be a doctor. □ el médico de cabecera the family doctor

Spanish-English

m

Spanish-English

■ **ir al médico** to go to the doctor's

la **medida** NOUN
measure
□ medidas de seguridad security measures
□ tomar medidas contra la inflación to take measures against inflation
■ **El sastre le tomó las medidas.** The tailor took his measurements.
■ **un traje a medida** a made-to-measure suit
■ **a medida que ...** as ... □ Saludaba a los invitados a medida que iban llegando. He greeted the guests as they arrived.

medio (FEM **media**) ADJECTIVE
▷ *see also* **medio** ADVERB, NOUN
1 half
□ medio litro half a litre □ Nos queda media botella de leche. We've got half a bottle of milk left. □ media hora half an hour □ una hora y media an hour and a half
■ **Son las ocho y media.** It's half past eight.
2 average
□ la temperatura media the average temperature

medio ADVERB
▷ *see also* **medio** ADJECTIVE, NOUN
half
□ Estaba medio dormido. He was half asleep. □ una manzana a medio comer a half eaten apple

el **medio** NOUN
▷ *see also* **medio** ADJECTIVE, ADVERB
1 middle
□ Está en el medio. It's in the middle.
■ **en medio de** in the middle of
2 means
□ un medio de transporte a means of transport
■ **por medio de** by means of
■ **medios** means □ por medios pacíficos by peaceful means
■ **los medios de comunicación** the media
■ **el medio ambiente** the environment

el **mediodía** NOUN
■ **al mediodía 1** at midday **2** at lunchtime

medir* VERB [38]
to measure
□ ¿Has medido la ventana? Have you measured the window?
■ **¿Cuánto mides? — Mido 1.50 m.** How tall are you? — I'm 1.5 m tall.
■ **¿Cuánto mide esta habitación? — Mide 3 m por 4.** How big is this room? — It measures 3 m by 4.

el **Mediterráneo** NOUN
the Mediterranean

mediterráneo (FEM **mediterránea**) ADJECTIVE
Mediterranean

la **medusa** NOUN
jellyfish (PL jellyfish)

la **mejilla** NOUN
cheek

el **mejillón** (PL los **mejillones**) NOUN
mussel

mejor (FEM **mejor**) ADJECTIVE
1 better
□ Éste es mejor que el otro. This one is better than the other one.
■ **Es el mejor de los dos.** He's the better of the two.
2 best
□ mi mejor amiga my best friend □ el mejor de la clase the best in the class □ Es el mejor de todos. He's the best of the lot.

mejor ADVERB
1 better
□ La conozco mejor que tú. I know her better than you do.
2 best
□ ¿Quién lo hace mejor? Who does it best?
■ **a lo mejor** probably
■ **Mejor nos vamos.** We had better go.

la **mejora** NOUN
improvement

mejorar VERB [25]
to improve
□ El tiempo está mejorando. The weather's improving. □ Han mejorado el servicio. They have improved the service.
■ **¡Que te mejores!** Get well soon!

la **mejoría** NOUN
improvement

la **melena** NOUN
1 long hair
□ Lleva una melena rubia. She has long blond hair.
2 mane

el **mellizo** (FEM la **melliza**) ADJECTIVE, NOUN
twin
□ Son mellizos. They're twins.

el **melocotón** (PL los **melocotones**) NOUN
peach (PL peaches)

la **melodía** NOUN
tune
□ tararear una melodía to hum a tune

el **melón** (PL los **melones**) NOUN
melon

la **memoria** NOUN
memory (PL memories)
□ tener mala memoria to have a bad memory
■ **aprender algo de memoria** to learn something by heart

memorizar* VERB [13]
to memorize

m

mencionar VERB [25]
to mention

el **mendigo**, la **mendiga** NOUN
beggar

menor (FEM **menor**) ADJECTIVE, PRONOUN
1 younger
□ Es tres años menor que yo. He's three years younger than me. □ Juanito es menor que Pepe. Juanito is younger than Pepe.
■ **el hermano menor** 1 the younger brother 2 the youngest brother
■ **Yo soy el menor.** 1 I'm the younger. 2 I'm the youngest.
2 smaller
□ una talla menor a smaller size
■ **No tiene la menor importancia.** It's not in the least important.

el/la **menor** NOUN
■ **un menor de edad** a minor
■ **los menores** the under-18s

Menorca FEM NOUN
Minorca

menos ADJECTIVE, ADVERB
1 less
□ Fernando está menos deprimido. Fernando is less depressed. □ Ahora salgo menos. I go out less these days.
■ **Últimamente nos vemos menos.** We've been seeing less of each other recently.
□ menos harina less flour □ menos gatos fewer cats □ menos gente fewer people
■ **menos...que** less...than □ Me gusta menos que el otro. I like it less than the other one. □ Lo hizo menos cuidadosamente que ayer. He did it less carefully than yesterday.
■ **Trabaja menos que yo.** He doesn't work as hard as I do.
■ **menos de 50 cajas** fewer than 50 boxes
■ **Tiene menos de dieciocho años.** He's under eighteen.
2 least
□ el chico menos desobediente de la clase the least disobedient boy in the class
■ **Fue el que menos trabajó.** He was the one who worked the least hard. □ el método que lleva menos tiempo the method which takes the least time □ el examen con menos errores the exam paper with the fewest mistakes
■ **No quiero verle y menos visitarle.** I don't want to see him, let alone visit him.
■ **¡Menos mal!** Thank goodness!
■ **al menos** at least
■ **por lo menos** at least
■ **¡Ni mucho menos!** No way!

menos PREPOSITION
except
□ todos menos él everyone except him
■ **5 menos 2 son tres** 5 minus 2 is three
■ **a menos que** unless

el **mensaje** NOUN
message
■ **un mensaje de texto** a text message
■ **el envío de mensajes con foto** picture messaging

el **mensajero**, la **mensajera** NOUN
messenger

mensual (FEM **mensual**) ADJECTIVE
monthly
■ **50 dólares mensuales** 50 dollars a month

la **menta** NOUN
mint
□ un caramelo de menta a mint sweet

la **mentalidad** NOUN
mentality (PL mentalities)
□ Tiene mentalidad de burócrata. He has a bureaucratic mentality.
■ **Tiene una mentalidad muy abierta.** He has a very open mind.

la **mente** NOUN
mind
□ No me lo puedo quitar de la mente. I can't get it out of my mind.
■ **tener en mente hacer algo** to be thinking of doing something □ Tiene en mente cambiar de empleo. He's thinking of changing jobs.

mentir* VERB [51]
to lie
□ No me mientas. Don't lie to me.

la **mentira** NOUN
lie
□ No digas mentiras. Don't tell lies.
■ **Parece mentira que aún no te haya pagado.** It's incredible that he still hasn't paid you.
■ **una pistola de mentira** a toy pistol

el **mentiroso**, la **mentirosa** NOUN
liar

el **menú** (PL los **menús**) NOUN
menu
■ **el menú del día** the set meal

menudo (FEM **menuda**) ADJECTIVE
slight
□ Es una chica muy menuda. She's a very slight girl.
■ **¡Menudo lío!** What a mess!
■ **a menudo** often

el **meñique** NOUN
little finger

el **mercado** NOUN
market

la **mercancía** NOUN
commodity (PL commodities)

la **mercería** NOUN

haberdasher's (PL haberdashers' shops)

merecer* VERB [12]
to deserve
□ Mereces que te castiguen. You deserve to be punished.
■ **merece la pena** it's worthwhile

merendar* VERB [39]
to have tea

el **merengue** NOUN
meringue

la **merienda** NOUN
tea

el **mérito** NOUN
merit
□ una obra de gran mérito artístico a work of great artistic merit
■ **Eso tiene mucho mérito.** That's very commendable.
■ **El mérito es todo suyo.** The credit is all his.

la **merluza** NOUN
hake

la **mermelada** NOUN
jam

mero ADVERB *(Mexico)*
almost
□ Ya mero no vengo. I almost didn't come.

el **mes** (PL los **meses**) NOUN
month
□ el mes que viene next month □ a final de mes at the end of the month

la **mesa** NOUN
table
■ **poner la mesa** to lay the table
■ **quitar la mesa** to clear the table

la **mesera** NOUN *(Latin America)*
waitress (PL waitresses)

el **mesero** NOUN *(Latin America)*
waiter

la **mesilla** NOUN
■ **una mesilla de noche** a bedside table

la **meta** NOUN
1 aim
2 finishing line
3 goal

el **metal** NOUN
metal

metálico (FEM **metálica**) ADJECTIVE
metal
□ un objeto metálico a metal object
■ **en metálico** in cash

LANGUAGE TIP Word for word, **en metálico** means 'in metallic'.

meter VERB [8]
to put
□ ¿Dónde has metido las llaves? Where have you put the keys?
■ **meterse en** to go into □ Se metió en la cueva. He went into the cave.
■ **meterse en política** to go into politics
■ **No te metas donde no te llaman.** Don't poke your nose in where it doesn't belong.
■ **meterse con alguien** to pick on somebody

el **método** NOUN
method

el **metro** NOUN
1 underground
□ coger el metro to take the underground
2 metre
□ Mide tres metros de largo. It's three metres long.

el **mexicano** (FEM la **mexicana**) ADJECTIVE, NOUN
Mexican

México MASC NOUN
Mexico

la **mezcla** NOUN
mixture

mezclar VERB [25]
to mix
□ Hay que mezclar el azúcar y la harina. You have to mix the sugar and the flour.
■ **mezclarse en algo** to get mixed up in something

mezquino (FEM **mezquina**) ADJECTIVE
mean

la **mezquita** NOUN
mosque

mi (FEM **mi**, PL **mis**) ADJECTIVE
my
□ mis hermanas my sisters

mí PRONOUN
me
□ para mí for me
■ **Para mí que ...** I think that ...
■ **Por mí no hay problema.** There's no problem as far as I'm concerned.

el **microbio** NOUN
microbe

el **micrófono** NOUN
microphone

el **microondas** (PL los **microondas**) NOUN
microwave
□ un horno microondas a microwave oven

el **microscopio** NOUN
microscope

midiendo VERB ▷ *see* **medir**

el **miedo** NOUN
fear
□ el miedo a la oscuridad fear of the dark
■ **tener miedo** to be afraid □ Le tenía miedo a su padre. He was afraid of his father.
□ Tengo miedo a morir. I'm afraid of dying.
□ Tenemos miedo de que nos ataquen. We're afraid that they may attack us.

■ **dar miedo a** to scare □ Me daba miedo hacerlo. I was scared of doing it.
■ **pasarlo de miedo** to have a fantastic time *(colloquial)*

miedoso (FEM **miedosa**) ADJECTIVE
■ **¡No seas tan miedoso!** Don't be such a coward!
■ **Mi hijo es muy miedoso.** My son gets frightened very easily.

la **miel** NOUN
honey

el **miembro** NOUN
limb

el/la **miembro** NOUN
member

mientras ADVERB, CONJUNCTION
while
□ Lava tú mientras yo seco. You wash while I dry.
■ **Seguiré conduciendo mientras pueda.** I'll carry on driving for as long as I can.
■ **mientras que** while
■ **mientras tanto** meanwhile

el **miércoles** (PL los **miércoles**) NOUN
Wednesday
□ La vi el miércoles. I saw her on Wednesday. □ todos los miércoles every Wednesday □ el miércoles pasado last Wednesday □ el miércoles que viene next Wednesday □ Jugamos los miércoles. We play on Wednesdays.

la **mierda** NOUN
shit
■ **Esta película es una mierda.** *(vulgar)* This film's a load of crap.
■ **¡Vete a la mierda!** *(colloquial)* Go to hell!

la **miga** NOUN
crumb
■ **hacer buenas migas** *(colloquial)* to hit it off

LANGUAGE TIP Word for word, **hacer buenas migas** means 'to make good breadcrumbs'.

mil (FEM **mil**) ADJECTIVE, PRONOUN
thousand
□ miles de personas thousands of people
□ dos mil euros two thousand euros
■ **miles de veces** hundreds of times

el **milagro** NOUN
miracle
□ No nos hemos matado de milagro. It was a miracle we weren't killed.

la **mili** NOUN
military service
□ hacer la mili to do one's military service

el **milímetro** NOUN
millimetre

el/la **militar** NOUN
soldier
■ **los militares** the military

militar (FEM **militar**) ADJECTIVE
military

la **milla** NOUN
mile

el **millón** (PL los **millones**) NOUN
million
□ millones de personas millions of people
■ **mil millones** a billion

el **millonario**, la **millonaria** NOUN
millionaire

mimado (FEM **mimada**) ADJECTIVE
spoiled

la **mina** NOUN
mine

el **mineral** ADJECTIVE, NOUN
mineral

el **minero**, la **minera** NOUN
miner

la **miniatura** NOUN
miniature
■ **una casa en miniatura** a miniature house

el **minidisco** NOUN
Minidisc®

la **minifalda** NOUN
miniskirt

mínimo (FEM **mínima**) ADJECTIVE
minimum
□ el salario mínimo the minimum wage
■ **No tienes ni la más mínima idea.** You haven't the faintest idea.

el **mínimo** NOUN
minimum
□ un mínimo de 10 euros a minimum of 10 euros
■ **lo mínimo que puede hacer** the least he can do
■ **Como mínimo podrías haber llamado.** You could at least have called.

el **ministerio** NOUN
ministry (PL ministries)

el **ministro**, la **ministra** NOUN
minister

la **minoría** NOUN
minority (PL minorities)
□ las minorías étnicas ethnic minorities

minucioso (FEM **minuciosa**) ADJECTIVE
thorough

la **minúscula** NOUN
small letter

la **minusválida** NOUN
disabled woman (PL disabled women)

el **minusválido** NOUN
disabled man (PL disabled men)
■ **los minusválidos** the disabled

el **minuto** NOUN
minute

Spanish-English

m

▫ Espera un minuto. Wait a minute.

mío (FEM **mía**) ADJECTIVE, PRONOUN
mine
▫ Estos caballos son míos. Those horses are mine. ▫ ¿De quién es esta bufanda? — Es mía. Whose scarf is this? — It's mine. ▫ El mío está en el armario. Mine's in the cupboard. ▫ Éste es el mío. This one's mine.
■ **un amigo mío** a friend of mine

miope (FEM **miope**) ADJECTIVE
short-sighted

la **mirada** NOUN
look
▫ con una mirada de odio with a look of hatred
■ **echar una mirada a algo** to have a look at something ▫ ¿Le has echado una mirada a mi informe? Have you had a look at my report?

mirar VERB [25]
to look
▫ ¡Mira! Un ratón. Look! A mouse. ▫ Mira a ver si está ahí. Look and see if he is there.
■ **mirar algo** to look at something ▫ Mira esta foto. Look at this photo.
■ **mirar por la ventana** to look out of the window
■ **mirar algo fijamente** to stare at something
■ **¡Mira que es tonto!** What an idiot!
■ **mirarse al espejo** to look at oneself in the mirror
■ **Se miraron asombrados.** They looked at each other in amazement.

la **misa** NOUN
mass (PL masses)
▫ la misa del gallo midnight mass ▫ ir a misa to go to mass

la **miseria** NOUN
1 poverty
▫ estar en la miseria to be living in poverty
2 pittance
▫ Gano una miseria. I earn a pittance.

la **misión** (PL las **misiones**) NOUN
mission

el **misionero**, la **misionera** NOUN
missionary (PL missionaries)

mismo (FEM **misma**) ADJECTIVE
▹ *see also* **mismo** ADVERB, PRONOUN
same
▫ Nos gustan los mismos libros. We like the same books. ▫ Vivo en su misma calle. I live in the same street as him.
■ **yo mismo** myself ▫ Lo hice yo mismo. I did it myself.

mismo ADVERB
▹ *see also* **mismo** ADJECTIVE, PRONOUN
■ **Hoy mismo le escribiré.** I'll write to him today.
■ **Nos podemos encontrar aquí mismo.** We can meet right here.
■ **enfrente mismo del colegio** right opposite the school

mismo PRONOUN
▹ *see also* **mismo** ADJECTIVE, ADVERB
■ **lo mismo** the same ▫ Yo tomaré lo mismo. I'll have the same.
■ **Da lo mismo.** It doesn't matter.
■ **No ha llamado pero lo mismo viene.** He hasn't phoned but he may well come.

el **misterio** NOUN
mystery (PL mysteries)

misterioso (FEM **misteriosa**) ADJECTIVE
mysterious

la **mitad** NOUN
half (PL halves)
▫ Se comió la mitad del pastel. He ate half the cake. ▫ más de la mitad de los trabajadores more than half the workers
■ **La mitad son chicas.** Half of them are girls.
■ **a mitad de precio** half-price
■ **a mitad de camino** halfway there
■ **Corta el pan por la mitad.** Cut the loaf in half.

el **mito** NOUN
myth

mixto (FEM **mixta**) ADJECTIVE
mixed
▫ una escuela mixta a mixed school

el **mobiliario** NOUN
furniture

la **mochila** NOUN
rucksack

el **moco** NOUN
■ **Límpiate los mocos.** Wipe your nose.
■ **tener mocos** to have a runny nose

la **moda** NOUN
fashion
■ **estar de moda** to be in fashion
■ **pasado de moda** old-fashioned

los **modales** NOUN
manners
▫ buenos modales good manners

el/la **modelo** ADJECTIVE, NOUN
model
▫ una niña modelo a model child ▫ Quiero ser modelo. I want to be a model.

moderado (FEM **moderada**) ADJECTIVE
moderate

modernizar* VERB [13]
to modernize
■ **modernizarse** to get up to date

moderno (FEM **moderna**) ADJECTIVE
modern

la **modestia** NOUN

modesty

modesto (FEM **modesta**) ADJECTIVE
modest

modificar* VERB [48]
to modify

el **modisto**, la **modista** NOUN
dressmaker
□ Es modista. She's a dressmaker.

el **modo** NOUN
way
□ Le gusta hacerlo todo a su modo. She likes to do everything her own way.
■ **de todos modos** anyway
■ **de modo que 1** so □ No has hecho los deberes, de modo que no puedes salir. You haven't done your homework so you can't go out. **2** so that □ Mueve la tele de modo que todos la podamos ver. Move the TV so that we can all see it.
■ **los buenos modos** good manners
■ **los malos modos** bad manners
■ **'modo de empleo'** 'instructions for use'

el **moho** NOUN
1 mould
2 rust

mojado (FEM **mojada**) ADJECTIVE
wet

mojar VERB [25]
to get...wet
□ ¡No mojes la alfombra! Don't get the carpet wet! □ Me he mojado las mangas. I got my sleeves wet.
■ **Moja el pan en la salsa.** Dip the bread into the sauce.
■ **mojarse** to get wet

el **molde** NOUN
mould

moler* VERB [33]
to grind
■ **Estoy molido.** *(colloquial)* I'm knackered.

molestar VERB [25]
1 to bother
□ ¿Te molesta la radio? Is the radio bothering you? □ Siento molestarle. I'm sorry to bother you.
2 to disturb
□ No me molestes, que estoy trabajando. Don't disturb me, I'm working.
■ **molestarse** to get upset □ Se molestó por algo que dije. She got upset because of something I said.
■ **molestarse en hacer algo** to bother to do something

la **molestia** NOUN
■ **tomarse la molestia de hacer algo** to take the trouble to do something
■ **'perdonen las molestias'** 'we apologize for any inconvenience'
■ **Aún tengo molestias en el hombro.** My shoulder still bothers me.

molesto (FEM **molesta**) ADJECTIVE
annoying
■ **estar molesto** to be annoyed

el **molinillo** NOUN
■ **un molinillo de café** a coffee grinder

el **molino** NOUN
mill
□ un molino de viento a windmill

el **momento** NOUN
moment
□ Espera un momento. Wait a moment.
□ en un momento in a moment
■ **en este momento** at the moment
□ Tenemos mucho trabajo en este momento. We've got a lot of work at the moment.
■ **de un momento a otro** any moment now
□ Llegarán de un momento a otro. They'll be here any moment now.
■ **por el momento** for the moment
■ **Llegó el momento de irnos.** The time came for us to go.

la **momia** NOUN
mummy (PL mummies)

el/la **monarca** NOUN
monarch

la **monarquía** NOUN
monarchy (PL monarchies)

el **monasterio** NOUN
monastery (PL monasteries)

la **moneda** NOUN
coin
□ una moneda de dos euros a two-euro coin
■ **la moneda extranjera** foreign currency

el **monedero** NOUN
purse

el **monitor**, la **monitora** NOUN
instructor
□ un monitor de esquí a skiing instructor

el **monitor** NOUN
monitor

la **monja** NOUN
nun

el **monje** NOUN
monk

mono (FEM **mona**) ADJECTIVE
pretty
□ ¡Qué piso tan mono! What a pretty flat!
■ **¡Qué niña tan mona!** What a sweet little girl!

el **mono** NOUN
1 monkey
2 overalls *pl*
3 dungarees *pl*

el **monopatín** (PL los **monopatines**) NOUN
skateboard

Spanish-English

m

Spanish-English

monótono (FEM **monótona**) ADJECTIVE
monotonous

el **monstruo** NOUN
monster

la **montaña** NOUN
mountain
□ Fuimos de vacaciones a la montaña. We went to the mountains on holiday.
■ **la montaña rusa** the roller coaster
LANGUAGE TIP Word for word, **montaña rusa** means 'Russian mountain'.

montañoso (FEM **montañosa**) ADJECTIVE
mountainous

montar VERB [25]
1 to assemble
2 to set up
■ **montar una tienda** to put up a tent
■ **montar a caballo** to ride a horse
■ **montar en bici** to ride a bike
■ **montarse** to get on □ Se montó en el autobús. He got on the bus.

el **monte** NOUN
mountain

el **montón** (PL los **montones**) NOUN
pile
□ Puso el montón de libros sobre la mesa. He put the pile of books on the table.
■ **un montón de ...** loads of ...
□ un montón de gente loads of people
□ un montón de dinero loads of money

el **monumento** NOUN
monument

el **moño** NOUN
bun
□ Mi abuela siempre lleva moño. My grandmother always wears her hair in a bun.

la **moqueta** NOUN
carpet

la **mora** NOUN
1 blackberry (PL blackberries)
2 mulberry (PL mulberries)

morado (FEM **morada**) ADJECTIVE
purple
□ un vestido morado a purple dress

moral (FEM **moral**) ADJECTIVE
moral

la **moral** NOUN
1 morale
■ **levantar la moral a alguien** to cheer somebody up
■ **estar bajo de moral** to be down
2 morals *pl*
□ No tienen moral. They have no morals.

la **moraleja** NOUN
moral

la **morcilla** NOUN
black pudding

morder* VERB [33]
to bite
■ **morderse las uñas** to bite one's nails

el **mordisco** NOUN
bite
□ Dame un mordisco de tu bocadillo. Let me have a bite of your sandwich.
■ **dar un mordisco** to bite □ Me dio un mordisco. He bit me.

moreno (FEM **morena**) ADJECTIVE
1 dark
■ **Es moreno.** 1 He has dark hair. 2 He is dark-skinned.
■ **ponerse moreno** to get brown
2 brown

morir* VERB [32]
to die
□ Murió de cáncer. He died of cancer.
■ **morirse de hambre** to starve □ ¡Me muero de hambre! I'm starving!
■ **morirse de vergüenza** to die of shame
■ **Me muero de ganas de ir a nadar.** I'm dying to go for a swim.

la **mortadela** NOUN
mortadella

mortal (FEM **mortal**) ADJECTIVE
1 fatal
2 mortal

la **mosca** NOUN
fly (PL flies)
■ **por si las moscas** just in case
LANGUAGE TIP Word for word, **por si las moscas** means 'for if the flies'.

el **mosquito** NOUN
mosquito (PL mosquitoes)

la **mostaza** NOUN
mustard

el **mostrador** NOUN
counter

mostrar* VERB [11]
to show
□ Nos mostró el camino. He showed us the way.
■ **mostrarse amable** to be kind

el **mote** NOUN
nickname

el **motivo** NOUN
1 reason
□ Dejó el trabajo por motivos personales. He left the job for personal reasons.
■ **sin motivo** for no reason
2 motive
□ ¿Cuál fue el motivo del crimen? What was the motive for the crime?

la **moto** NOUN
motorbike

la **motocicleta** NOUN
motorbike

m

el **motor** NOUN
motor
el/la **motorista** NOUN
motorcyclist
mover* VERB [33]
to move
□ Mueve un poco las cajas para que podamos pasar. Move the boxes a bit so that we can get past.
■ **moverse** to move □ ¡No te muevas! Don't move!
móvil (FEM **móvil**) ADJECTIVE
mobile
el **móvil** NOUN
1 mobile
2 motive
el **movimiento** NOUN
movement
la **moza** NOUN
girl
el **mozo** NOUN
1 youth
2 waiter
■ **un mozo de estación** a porter
el **MP3** NOUN
MP3
□ un reproductor de MP3 an MP3 player
la **muchacha** NOUN
1 girl
2 maid
el **muchacho** NOUN
boy
la **muchedumbre** NOUN
crowd
mucho (FEM **mucha**) ADJECTIVE
▷ *see also* **mucho** PRONOUN, ADVERB
1 a lot of
□ Había mucha gente. There were a lot of people. □ Tiene muchas plantas. He has got a lot of plants.
2 much (PL many)
□ No tenemos mucho tiempo. We haven't got much time. □ ¿Conoces a mucha gente? Do you know many people? □ Muchas personas creen que ... Many people think that ...
■ **no hace mucho tiempo** not long ago
■ **Hace mucho calor.** It's very hot.
■ **Tengo mucho frío.** I'm very cold.
■ **Tengo mucha hambre.** I'm very hungry.
■ **Tengo mucha sed.** I'm very thirsty.
mucho PRONOUN
▷ *see also* **mucho** ADJECTIVE, ADVERB
1 a lot
□ Tengo mucho que hacer. I've got a lot to do. □ ¿Cuántos había? — Muchos. How many were there? — A lot.
2 much (PL many)
□ No tengo mucho que hacer. I haven't got much to do. □ ¿Hay manzanas? — Sí, pero no muchas. Are there any apples? — Yes, but not many.
■ **¿Vinieron muchos?** Did many people come?
■ **Muchos dicen que ...** Many people say that ...
mucho ADVERB
▷ *see also* **mucho** ADJECTIVE, PRONOUN
1 very much
□ Te quiero mucho. I love you very much. □ No me gusta mucho la carne. I don't like meat very much. □ Me gusta mucho el jazz. I really like jazz.
2 a lot
□ Come mucho. He eats a lot.
■ **mucho más** a lot more
■ **mucho antes** long before
■ **No tardes mucho.** Don't be long.
■ **Como mucho leo un libro al mes.** At most I read one book a month.
■ **Fue, con mucho, el mejor.** He was by far the best.
■ **Por mucho que lo quieras no debes mimarlo.** No matter how much you love him, you shouldn't spoil him.
la **mudanza** NOUN
move
mudarse VERB [25]
to move
■ **mudarse de casa** to move house
mudo (FEM **muda**) ADJECTIVE
dumb
■ **quedarse mudo de asombro** to be dumbfounded
el **mueble** NOUN
■ **un mueble** a piece of furniture
■ **los muebles** furniture *sing*
■ **seis muebles** six pieces of furniture
la **muela** NOUN
tooth (PL teeth)
■ **una muela del juicio** a wisdom tooth
el **muelle** NOUN
1 spring
2 quay
muelo VERB ▷ *see* **moler**
muerdo VERB ▷ *see* **morder**
la **muerta** NOUN
dead woman (PL dead women)
la **muerte** NOUN
death
□ Lo condenaron a muerte. He was sentenced to death.
■ **Nos dio un susto de muerte.** He nearly frightened us to death.
■ **un hotel de mala muerte** a grotty hotel
muerto VERB ▷ *see* **morir**

Spanish-English

m

Spanish-English

muerto (FEM **muerta**) ADJECTIVE
dead
■ **Está muerto de cansancio.** *(colloquial)* He's dead tired.

el **muerto** NOUN
dead man (PL dead men)
■ **los muertos** the dead
■ **Hubo tres muertos.** Three people were killed.
■ **hacer el muerto** to float

la **muestra** NOUN
1 sample
□ una muestra gratuita a free sample
2 sign
□ dar muestras de to show signs of
3 token
□ Me lo regaló como muestra de afecto. She gave it to me as a token of affection.

muestro VERB ▷ *see* **mostrar**

muevo VERB ▷ *see* **mover**

la **mujer** NOUN
1 woman (PL women)
□ Vino a verte una mujer. A woman came to see you.
2 wife (PL wives)
□ la mujer del médico the doctor's wife

la **muleta** NOUN
crutch (PL crutches)

DID YOU KNOW...?
In bullfighting, the **muleta** is a special stick with a red cloth attached to it that the matador uses.

la **multa** NOUN
fine
□ una multa de 50 euros a 50-euro fine
■ **poner una multa a alguien** to fine somebody

múltiple (FEM **múltiple**) ADJECTIVE
■ **múltiples** many □ un sistema con múltiples inconvenientes a system with many drawbacks

multiplicar* VERB [48]
to multiply
□ Hay que multiplicarlo por cinco. You have to multiply it by five.
■ **la tabla de multiplicar** the multiplication tables *pl*

la **multitud** NOUN
crowd
■ **multitud de** lots of

mundial (FEM **mundial**) ADJECTIVE
1 world
2 worldwide

el **mundial** NOUN
world championship

el **mundo** NOUN
world
■ **todo el mundo** everybody □ Se lo ha dicho a todo el mundo. He has told everybody.
■ **No lo cambiaría por nada del mundo.** I wouldn't change it for anything in the world.

municipal (FEM **municipal**) ADJECTIVE
1 council
2 local
3 public

el **municipio** NOUN
1 municipality (PL municipalities)
2 town council

la **muñeca** NOUN
1 wrist
2 doll

el **muñeco** NOUN
1 doll
■ **un muñeco de peluche** a soft toy
2 figure

la **muralla** NOUN
city wall

el **murciélago** NOUN
bat

el **murmullo** NOUN
murmur

la **murmuración** (PL las **murmuraciones**) NOUN
gossip *sing*

el **muro** NOUN
wall

el **músculo** NOUN
muscle

el **museo** NOUN
museum
■ **un mueso de arte** an art gallery

la **música** NOUN
1 music
□ la música pop pop music
2 musician

el **músico** NOUN
musician

el **muslo** NOUN
thigh

el **musulmán** (FEM la **musulmana**, MASC PL los **musulmanes**) ADJECTIVE, NOUN
Moslem

mutuo (FEM **mutua**) ADJECTIVE
mutual
□ de mutuo acuerdo by mutual agreement

muy ADVERB
very
□ muy bonito very pretty
■ **Eso es muy español.** That's typically Spanish.
■ **No me gusta por muy guapa que sea.** However pretty she is, I still don't like her.

m

Nn

el **nabo** NOUN
turnip
nacer* VERB [12]
to be born
□ Nació en 1964. He was born in 1964.
el **nacimiento** NOUN
1 birth
2 crib
la **nación** (PL las **naciones**) NOUN
nation
■ **las Naciones Unidas** the United Nations
nacional (FEM **nacional**) ADJECTIVE
1 national
2 home
■ **vuelos nacionales** domestic flights
la **nacionalidad** NOUN
nationality (PL nationalities)
el **nacionalismo** NOUN
nationalism
el/la **nacionalista** ADJECTIVE, NOUN
nationalist
nada PRONOUN
▷ *see also* **nada** ADVERB
1 nothing
□ ¿Qué has comprado? — Nada. What have you bought? — Nothing. □ No dijo nada. He said nothing.
2 anything
□ No quiero nada. I don't want anything.
■ **No dijo nada más.** He didn't say anything else.
■ **Quiero uno nada más.** I only want one, that's all.
■ **Encendió la tele nada más llegar.** He turned on the TV as soon as he came in.
■ **¡Gracias! — De nada.** Thanks! — Don't mention it.
■ **Se lo advertí, pero como si nada.** I warned him but he paid no attention.
■ **No sabe nada de español.** He knows no Spanish at all.
■ **No me dio nada de nada.** He gave me absolutely nothing.
nada ADVERB
▷ *see also* **nada** PRONOUN
at all
□ Esto no me gusta nada. I don't like this at all. □ No está nada triste. He isn't sad at all.
nadar VERB [25]
to swim
nadie PRONOUN
1 nobody
□ Nadie habló. Nobody spoke. □ No había nadie. There was nobody there.
2 anybody
□ No quiere ver a nadie. He doesn't want to see anybody.
la **nafta** NOUN *(River Plate)*
petrol
el **naipe** NOUN
playing card
las **nalgas** NOUN
buttocks
la **nana** NOUN
lullaby (PL lullabies)
naranja ADJECTIVE
orange
□ un anorak naranja an orange anorak
el **naranja** NOUN
orange
la **naranja** NOUN
orange
el **narcotráfico** NOUN
drug trafficking
la **nariz** (PL las **narices**) NOUN
nose
■ **No metas las narices en mis asuntos.** Don't poke your nose into my business.
■ **estar hasta las narices de algo** to be totally fed up with something
la **narración** (PL las **narraciones**) NOUN
story (PL stories)
narrar VERB [25]
to tell
la **narrativa** NOUN
fiction
la **nata** NOUN
1 cream
2 skin
■ **la nata líquida** single cream
■ **la nata montada** whipped cream
la **natación** NOUN

swimming

natal (FEM **natal**) ADJECTIVE
home
□ su pueblo natal his home town

las **natillas** NOUN
custard *sing*

nato (FEM **nata**) ADJECTIVE
■ **un actor nato** a born actor

natural (FEM **natural**) ADJECTIVE
natural
□ con ingredientes naturales with natural ingredients □ Comes mucho y es natural que estés gordo. You eat a lot, so it's only natural you're fat.
■ **Es natural de Alicante.** He's from Alicante.

la **naturaleza** NOUN
nature
■ **Es despistado por naturaleza.** He's naturally absent-minded.

el **naufragio** NOUN
shipwreck

las **náuseas** NOUN
■ **tener náuseas** to feel sick

náutico (FEM **náutica**) ADJECTIVE
■ **club náutico** yacht club

la **navaja** NOUN
clasp knife (PL clasp knives)
■ **una navaja de afeitar** a razor

Navarra FEM NOUN
Navarre

la **nave** NOUN
ship
■ **una nave espacial** a spaceship

el **navegador** NOUN
browser
■ **un navegador de Web** a web browser

navegar* VERB [37]
to sail
■ **navegar por Internet** to surf the Net

la **Navidad** NOUN
Christmas
■ **¡Feliz Navidad!** Happy Christmas!

la **neblina** NOUN
mist

necesario (FEM **necesaria**) ADJECTIVE
necessary
□ No estudié más de lo necesario. I didn't study any more than necessary.
■ **Ya tengo el dinero necesario para el billete.** I've now got the money I need for the ticket.
■ **Llamaré al médico si es necesario.** I'll call the doctor if need be.
■ **No es necesario que vengas.** You don't have to come.

la **necesidad** NOUN
1 need
□ No hay necesidad de hacerlo. There is no need to do it.
2 necessity (PL necessities)
□ Comer bien es una necesidad, no un lujo. Eating well is a necessity, not a luxury.
■ **Hizo sus necesidades.** He did his business.

necesitar VERB [25]
to need
□ Necesito cien euros. I need a hundred euros. □ Necesito sacar un notable en el examen. I need to get a good mark in the exam. □ Necesito que me ayudes. I need you to help me.
■ **'Se necesita camarero'** 'Waiter wanted'

negar* VERB [34]
1 to deny
□ Decían que era el ladrón, pero él lo negaba. They said that he was the thief, but he denied it.
■ **negar con la cabeza** to shake one's head
2 to refuse
□ Me negaron el permiso para entrar en el bar. They refused me permission to go into the bar.
■ **Se negó a pagar la multa.** He refused to pay the fine.

negativo (FEM **negativa**) ADJECTIVE
negative

el **negativo** NOUN
negative

la **negociación** NOUN
negotiation

negociar VERB [25]
■ **Su empresa negocia con armas.** His company deals in arms.
■ **Los dos gobiernos están negociando un acuerdo.** The two governments are negotiating an agreement.

el **negocio** NOUN
business (PL businesses)
□ Hemos montado un negocio de videojuegos. We set up a video games business.
■ **el mundo de los negocios** the business world

la **negra** NOUN
black woman (PL black women)
■ **tener la negra** to be out of luck

negro (FEM **negra**) ADJECTIVE
black

el **negro** NOUN
1 black
2 black man (PL black men)
■ **los negros** Blacks

el **nervio** NOUN
nerve
■ **Me pone de los nervios.** He gets on my

nerves.

el **nerviosismo** NOUN

■ **Me entra nerviosismo cuando la veo.** I get nervous when I see her.

nervioso (FEM **nerviosa**) ADJECTIVE

nervous

□ Me pongo muy nervioso en los exámenes. I get very nervous during exams.

■ **¡Me pone nervioso!** He gets on my nerves!

el **neumático** NOUN

tyre

neutral (FEM **neutral**) ADJECTIVE

neutral

la **nevada** NOUN

snowfall

nevar* VERB [39]

to snow

la **nevera** NOUN

refrigerator

ni CONJUNCTION

1 or

□ No bebe ni fuma. He doesn't drink or smoke.

2 neither

□ Ella no fue, ni yo tampoco. She didn't go and neither did I.

■ **ni ... ni** neither ... nor □ No vinieron ni Carlos ni Sofía. Neither Carlos nor Sofía came.

■ **No me gustan ni el bacalao ni el hígado.** I don't like either cod or liver.

■ **No compré ni uno ni otro.** I didn't buy either of them.

■ **Ni siquiera me saludó.** He didn't even say hello.

Nicaragua FEM NOUN

Nicaragua

el/la **nicaragüense** ADJECTIVE, NOUN

Nicaraguan

la **nicotina** NOUN

nicotine

el **nido** NOUN

nest

la **niebla** NOUN

fog

■ **Hay niebla.** It's foggy.

niego VERB ▷ *see* **negar**

la **nieta** NOUN

granddaughter

el **nieto** NOUN

grandson

■ **los nietos** grandchildren

nieva VERB ▷ *see* **nevar**

la **nieve** NOUN

snow

NIF ABBREVIATION (= *número de identificación fiscal*)

DID YOU KNOW...?

This is an ID number used for tax purposes in Spain.

ningún PRONOUN ▷ *see* **ninguno**

ninguno (FEM **ninguna**) ADJECTIVE, PRONOUN

1 no

□ No tengo ningún interés en ir. I have no interest in going.

2 any

□ No vimos ninguna serpiente en el río. We didn't see any snakes in the river.

3 none

□ ¿Cuál eliges? — Ninguno. Which do you want? — None of them. □ No me queda ninguno. I have none left. □ Ninguno de nosotros va a ir a la fiesta. None of us are going to the party.

■ **No lo encuentro por ningún sitio.** I can't find it anywhere.

■ **ninguno de los dos 1** neither of them □ A ninguna de las dos les gusta el café. Neither of them likes coffee. **2** either of them □ No me gusta ninguno de los dos. I don't like either of them.

la **niña** NOUN

girl

la **niñera** NOUN

nursemaid

la **niñez** NOUN

childhood

niño (FEM **niña**) ADJECTIVE

young

□ Es todavía muy niño. He's still very young.

el **niño** NOUN

boy

■ **de niño** as a child

■ **los niños** the children

el **nitrógeno** NOUN

nitrogen

el **nivel** NOUN

1 level

□ el nivel del agua the water level

2 standard

□ Pretenden aumentar el nivel educativo. They are trying to raise the standard of education.

■ **el nivel de vida** the standard of living

no ADVERB

no

□ ¿Quieres venir? — No. Do you want to come? — No.

■ **¿Te gusta? — No mucho.** Do you like it? — Not really. □ No me gusta. I don't like it. □ María no habla inglés. María doesn't speak English. □ No puedo venir esta noche. I can't come tonight. □ No tengo tiempo. I haven't got time. □ No debes preocuparte. You mustn't worry. □ No hace

frío. It isn't cold. ◻ No conozco a nadie. I don't know anyone. ◻ Esto es tuyo, ¿no? This is yours, isn't it? ◻ Fueron al cine, ¿no? They went to the cinema, didn't they?
■ **¿Puedo salir esta noche? — ¡Que no!** Can I go out tonight? — I said no!
■ **los no fumadores** non-smokers

noble (FEM **noble**) ADJECTIVE
noble

la **noche** NOUN
night
◻ Pasó la noche sin dormir. He had a sleepless night.
■ **¡Buenas noches!** 1 Good evening! 2 Goodnight!
■ **esta noche** tonight
■ **hoy por la noche** tonight
■ **por la noche** at night ◻ Estudia por la noche. He studies at night. ◻ el sábado por la noche on Saturday night
■ **Era de noche cuando llegamos a casa.** It was night time when we got back home.
■ **No me gusta conducir de noche.** I don't like driving at night.

la **Nochebuena** NOUN
Christmas Eve

la **Nochevieja** NOUN
New Year's Eve

las **nociones** NOUN
■ **Tengo nociones de informática.** I know a little about computers.

nocturno (FEM **nocturna**) ADJECTIVE
1 night
2 evening

nomás ADVERB *(Latin America)*
just
◻ Está ahí nomás. It's just there.
■ **así nomás** just like that

nombrar VERB [25]
1 to appoint
◻ Lo han nombrado director del colegio. He was appointed Head of the school.
2 to mention
◻ Me nombró en su discurso. He mentioned me in his speech.

el **nombre** NOUN
1 name
■ **nombre de pila** first name
■ **nombre y apellidos** full name
2 noun

la **nómina** NOUN
pay slip
■ **estar en nómina** to be on the payroll

el **nordeste** NOUN
northeast

el **noreste** NOUN
northeast

la **noria** NOUN
big wheel

la **norma** NOUN
rule

normal (FEM **normal**) ADJECTIVE
1 normal
◻ una persona normal a normal person
◻ Es normal que quiera divertirse. It's only normal that he wants to enjoy himself.
2 ordinary
◻ ¿Es guapo? — No, normal. Is he handsome? — No, just ordinary.

normalmente ADVERB
normally

el **noroeste** NOUN
northwest

el **norte** NOUN
north

el **norteamericano** (FEM la **norteamericana**) ADJECTIVE, NOUN
American

Noruega FEM NOUN
Norway

el **noruego** (FEM la **noruega**) ADJECTIVE, NOUN
Norwegian

el **noruego** NOUN
Norwegian

nos PRONOUN
1 us
◻ Nos vinieron a ver. They came to see us.
◻ Nos dio un consejo. He gave us some advice.
■ **Nos lo dio.** He gave it to us.
■ **Nos tienen que arreglar el ordenador.** They have to fix the computer for us.
2 ourselves
◻ Tenemos que defendernos. We must defend ourselves.
■ **Nos levantamos a las ocho.** We got up at eight o'clock.
3 each other
◻ No nos hablamos desde hace tiempo. We haven't spoken to each other for a long time. ◻ Nos dolían los pies. Our feet were hurting. ◻ Nos pusimos los abrigos. We put our coats on.

nosotros (FEM **nosotras**) PRONOUN
1 we
◻ Nosotros no somos italianos. We are not Italian.
2 us
◻ ¿Quién es? — Somos nosotros. Who is it? — It's us. ◻ Tu hermano vino con nosotros. Your brother came with us. ◻ Llegaron antes que nosotros. They arrived before us.
■ **nosotros mismos** ourselves

la **nota** NOUN
1 mark
◻ Saca muy malas notas. He gets very bad

marks.
2 note
□ Tomó muchas notas en la conferencia. He took a lot of notes during the lecture.
□ Te he dejado una nota en la nevera. I've left you a note on the fridge.

notar VERB [25]
1 to notice
□ Notó que le seguían. He noticed they were following him.
2 to feel
□ Con este abrigo no noto el frío. I don't feel the cold with this coat on.
■ **Se nota que has estudiado mucho este trimestre.** You can tell that you've studied a lot this term.

el **notario**, la **notaria** NOUN
notary (PL notaries)

la **noticia** NOUN
news *sing*
□ Tengo una buena noticia que darte. I've got some good news for you.
■ **Fue una noticia excelente para la economía.** It was an excellent piece of news for the economy.
■ **Vi las noticias de las nueve.** I watched the nine o'clock news.
■ **No tengo noticias de Juan.** I haven't heard from Juan.

LANGUAGE TIP Be careful! **noticia** does not mean **notice**.

notificar* VERB [48]
to notify

el **novato**, la **novata** NOUN
beginner

novecientos (FEM **novecientas**) ADJECTIVE, PRONOUN
nine hundred

la **novedad** NOUN
■ **Las últimas novedades en moda infantil.** The latest in children's fashions.
■ **¿Cómo sigue tu hijo? — Sin novedad.** How's your son? — There's no change.

la **novela** NOUN
novel
■ **una novela policíaca** a detective story

noveno (FEM **novena**) ADJECTIVE, PRONOUN
ninth
■ **Vivo en el noveno.** I live on the ninth floor.

noventa (FEM **noventa**) ADJECTIVE, PRONOUN
ninety
■ **el noventa aniversario** the ninetieth anniversary

la **novia** NOUN
1 girlfriend
2 fiancée
3 bride

el **noviazgo** NOUN
relationship
□ Su noviazgo duró muy poco. Their relationship didn't last very long.

noviembre MASC NOUN
November
□ en noviembre in November □ Llegará el 30 de noviembre. He'll arrive on 30 November.

los **novillos** NOUN
■ **hacer novillos** to play truant

el **novio** NOUN
1 boyfriend
2 fiancé
3 bridegroom
■ **los novios** the bride and groom

la **nube** NOUN
cloud

nublado (FEM **nublada**) ADJECTIVE
cloudy

nublarse VERB [25]
to cloud over

nuboso (FEM **nubosa**) ADJECTIVE
cloudy

la **nuca** NOUN
nape

nuclear ADJECTIVE
nuclear
■ **una central nuclear** a nuclear power station

el **núcleo** NOUN
■ **el núcleo urbano** the city centre

el **nudo** NOUN
knot
■ **atar con un nudo** to tie in a knot

la **nuera** NOUN
daughter-in-law (PL daughters-in-law)

nuestro (FEM **nuestra**) ADJECTIVE, PRONOUN
1 our
□ nuestro perro our dog □ nuestras bicicletas our bicycles
2 ours
□ ¿De quién es esto? — Es nuestro. Whose is this? — It's ours. □ Esta casa es la nuestra. This house is ours.
■ **un amigo nuestro** a friend of ours

nueve (FEM **nueve**) ADJECTIVE, PRONOUN
nine
■ **Son las nueve.** It's nine o'clock.
■ **el nueve de marzo** the ninth of March

nuevo (FEM **nueva**) ADJECTIVE
new
□ Necesito un ordenador nuevo. I need a new computer. □ Soy nuevo en el colegio. I'm new at the school.
■ **El mecánico me dejó el coche como nuevo.** The mechanic left my car like new.

Spanish-English

n

■ Tuve que leer el libro de nuevo. I had to read the book again.

la **nuez** (PL las **nueces**) NOUN

1 nut

■ la nuez moscada nutmeg

2 Adam's apple

el **número** NOUN

1 number

2 size

3 issue

■ Calle Aribau, sin número. Aribau street, no number.

■ número de teléfono telephone number

■ montar un número to make a scene

nunca ADVERB

1 never

□ No viene nunca. He never comes.

■ No le veré nunca más. I'll never see him again.

2 ever

□ Ninguno de nosotros había esquiado nunca. Neither of us had ever skied before.

□ Casi nunca me escribe. He hardly ever writes to me.

la **nutria** NOUN

otter

el **nylon** NOUN

nylon

Ññ

ñoño (FEM **ñoña**) ADJETIVO
soppy

el **ñu** SUSTANTIVO
gnu (PL gnus)

Oo

o CONJUNCTION
or
□ ¿Quieres té o café? Would you like tea or coffee? □ ¿Vas a ayudarme o no? Are you going to help me or not?
■ **o ... o ...** either ... or ... □ O ha salido o no coge el teléfono. Either he's out or he's not answering the phone.
■ **O te callas o no sigo hablando.** If you're not quiet I won't go on.

obedecer* VERB [12]
to obey
■ **obedecer a alguien** to obey someone

obediente (FEM **obediente**) ADJECTIVE
obedient

obeso (FEM **obesa**) ADJECTIVE
obese

el **obispo** NOUN
bishop

la **objeción** (PL las **objeciones**) NOUN
objection
■ **No puso ninguna objeción.** He didn't object.

el **objetivo** NOUN
objective
□ un objetivo militar a military objective
■ **Nuestro principal objetivo es ganar las elecciones.** Our main aim is to win the elections.

el **objeto** NOUN
object
□ un objeto metálico a metal object
■ **¿Cuál es el objeto de su visita?** What's the reason for your visit?
■ **con objeto de hacer algo** in order to do something
■ **los objetos de valor** valuables

la **obligación** (PL **obligaciones**) NOUN
obligation
■ **Obedecer a tus padres es tu obligación.** It's your duty to obey your parents.

obligado (FEM **obligada**) ADJECTIVE
■ **verse obligado a hacer algo** to be forced to do something □ Se vieron obligados a vender su casa. They were forced to sell their house.
■ **No estás obligado a venir si no quieres.** You don't have to come if you don't want to.

obligar* VERB [37]
1 to force
□ Nadie te obliga a aceptar este empleo. Nobody's forcing you to accept this job.
2 to make
□ No puedes obligarme a ir. You can't make me go.

obligatorio (FEM **obligatoria**) ADJECTIVE
compulsory

la **obra** NOUN
1 work
■ **una obra de arte** a work of art
■ **la obra completa de Neruda** the complete works of Neruda
■ **una obra de teatro** a play
■ **una obra maestra** a masterpiece
2 building site
■ **'obras'** 'roadworks'

el **obrero**, la **obrera** NOUN
worker
□ Mi primo es obrero de la construcción. My cousin works on a building site.

el **obsequio** NOUN
gift
□ como obsequio as a gift

la **observación** (PL las **observaciones**) NOUN
1 observation
□ El paciente está en observación. The patient is under observation.
2 comment
□ hacer una observación to make a comment

observador (FEM **observadora**) ADJECTIVE
observant

observar VERB [25]
1 to observe
2 to remark

la **obsesión** (PL las **obsesiones**) NOUN
obsession
□ su obsesión por la limpieza his obsession with cleanliness

obsesionar VERB [25]
■ **Es un tema que le obsesiona.**

He's obsessed by the subject.

el **obstáculo** NOUN
obstacle
□ Nos puso muchos obstáculos. He put many obstacles in our way.

obstante ADVERB
■ **no obstante** nevertheless

obstinado (FEM **obstinada**) ADJECTIVE
obstinate

obstinarse VERB [25]
to insist
□ ¿Por qué te obstinas en hacerlo? Why do you insist on doing it?

obtener* VERB [53]
to obtain

obvio (FEM **obvia**) ADJECTIVE
obvious

la **oca** NOUN
goose (PL geese)

la **ocasión** (PL las **ocasiones**) NOUN
1 opportunity (PL opportunities)
□ Ésta es la ocasión que esperábamos. This is the opportunity we've been waiting for.
2 occasion
□ en varias ocasiones on several occasions
■ **un libro de ocasión** a secondhand book

ocasionar VERB [25]
to cause

occidental (FEM **occidental**) ADJECTIVE
western
■ **los países occidentales** the West

el **occidente** NOUN
■ **el Occidente** the West

el **océano** NOUN
ocean
□ el océano Atlantico the Atlantic Ocean

ochenta (FEM **ochenta**) ADJECTIVE, PRONOUN
eighty
□ Tiene ochenta años. He's eighty.
■ **el ochenta aniversario** the eightieth anniversary

ocho (FEM **ocho**) ADJECTIVE, PRONOUN
eight
■ **Son las ocho.** It's eight o'clock.
■ **el ocho de agosto** the eighth of August

ochocientos (FEM **ochocientas**) ADJECTIVE, PRONOUN
eight hundred

el **ocio** NOUN
■ **en mis ratos de ocio** in my spare time

octavo (FEM **octava**) ADJECTIVE, PRONOUN
eighth
■ **Vivo en el octavo.** I live on the eighth floor.

octubre MASC NOUN
October
□ en octubre in October □ Llegaré el 3 de octubre. I'll arrive on 3 October.

el/la **oculista** NOUN
eye specialist
□ Es oculista. He's an eye specialist.

ocultar VERB [25]
to conceal
□ Nos ocultó su edad. He concealed his age from us.
■ **No nos ocultes la verdad.** Don't try to hide the truth from us.
■ **ocultarse** to hide

la **ocupación** (PL las **ocupaciones**) NOUN
1 activity (PL activities)
□ Tiene muchas ocupaciones. He's involved in many activities.
2 occupation
□ ¿Qué ocupación tiene? What's his occupation? □ la ocupación de la embajada por parte de los guerrilleros the occupation of the embassy by the guerrillas

ocupado (FEM **ocupada**) ADJECTIVE
1 busy
□ Estoy muy ocupado. I'm very busy.
2 engaged
□ La línea está ocupada. The line's engaged.
■ **'ocupado'** 'engaged'
■ **¿Está ocupado este asiento?** Is this seat taken?

ocupar VERB [25]
1 to occupy
□ Los obreros han ocupado la fábrica. The workers have occupied the factory. □ El edifico ocupa todo el solar. The building occupies the whole site.
2 to take up
□ Ocupa casi todo mi tiempo. It takes up almost all my time.
■ **Los espectadores ocuparon sus asientos.** The spectators took their seats.
■ **ocuparse de algo** to look after something
■ **Yo me ocuparé de decírselo.** I'll tell him.

la **ocurrencia** NOUN
■ **Juan tuvo la ocurrencia de decírselo a la cara.** Juan had the bright idea to tell her to her face.
■ **¡Qué ocurrencia!** Him and his crazy ideas!

ocurrir VERB [58]
to happen
□ Lo que ocurrió podría haberse evitado. What happened could have been avoided.
■ **¿Qué te ocurre?** What's the matter?
■ **Se nos ocurrió una idea brillante.** We had a brilliant idea.

odiar VERB [25]
to hate
□ Odio tener que levantarme pronto. I hate having to get up early.

el **odio** NOUN

hate

el **oeste** NOUN, ADJECTIVE
west
□ el oeste del país the west of the country
□ en la costa oeste on the west coast
■ **al oeste de la ciudad** west of the city
■ **Viajábamos hacia el oeste.** We were travelling west.
■ **una película del oeste** a western
■ **vientos del oeste** westerly winds

ofender VERB [8]
offend
■ **ofenderse** to take offence

la **ofensa** NOUN
insult

la **oferta** NOUN
offer
■ **una oferta especial** a special offer
■ **estar de oferta** to be on special offer
■ **'ofertas de trabajo'** 'situations vacant'

oficial (FEM **oficial**) ADJECTIVE
official

el/la **oficial** NOUN
officer
□ Es oficial de marina. He's an officer in the navy.

la **oficina** NOUN
office
■ **la oficina de turismo** the tourist office
■ **la oficina de empleo** the job centre
■ **la oficina de correos** the post office
■ **la oficina de objetos perdidos** the lost property office

el **oficio** NOUN
trade
□ Es carpintero de oficio. He's a carpenter by trade.

ofrecer* VERB [12]
to offer
□ Nos ofrecieron tabaco. They offered us cigarettes.
■ **ofrecerse para hacer algo** to offer to do something
■ **¿Qué se le ofrece?** What can I get you?

el **ofrecimiento** NOUN
offer

el **oído** NOUN
1 hearing
2 ear
■ **tener buen oído** to have a good ear

oír* VERB [35]
1 to hear
□ He oído un ruido. I heard a noise. □ ¿Me oyes bien desde ahí? Can you hear me all right from there?
2 to listen to
□ Óyeme bien, no vuelvas a hacerlo. Now listen to what I'm telling you, don't do it again.
■ **oír la radio** to listen to the radio
■ **¡Oye!** Hey!
■ **¡Oiga, por favor!** Excuse me!

el **ojal** NOUN
buttonhole

ojalá EXCLAMATION
1 I hope
□ ¡Ojalá Toni venga hoy! I hope Toni comes today!
2 if only
■ **¡Ojalá pudiera!** If only I could!

las **ojeras** NOUN
■ **tener ojeras** to have bags under one's eyes

el **ojo** NOUN
eye
□ Tengo algo en el ojo. I've got something in my eye.
■ **ir con ojo** to keep one's eyes open for trouble
■ **costar un ojo de la cara** to cost an arm and a leg
■ **¡Ojo! Es muy mentiroso.** Be careful! He's an awful liar.

la **ola** NOUN
wave

oler* VERB [36]
to smell
□ Me gusta oler las flores. I like smelling the flowers.
■ **Huele a tabaco.** It smells of cigarette smoke.
■ **oler bien** to smell nice □ Esta salsa huele muy bien. This sauce smells very good.
■ **oler mal** to smell awful □ ¡Qué mal huelen estos zapatos! These shoes smell awful!

el **olfato** NOUN
sense of smell

las **Olimpiadas** NOUN
the Olympics

olímpico (FEM **olímpica**) ADJECTIVE
Olympic
■ **los Juegos Olímpicos** the Olympic Games

la **oliva** NOUN
olive
■ **el aceite de oliva** olive oil

el **olivo** NOUN
olive tree

la **olla** NOUN
pot
■ **una olla a presión** a pressure cooker

el **olor** NOUN
smell
□ un olor a tabaco a smell of cigarette smoke

■ **¡Qué mal olor!** What a horrible smell!

olvidar VERB [25]

1 to forget

□ No olvides comprar el pan. Don't forget to buy the bread.

■ **olvidarse de hacer algo** to forget to do something

■ **Se me olvidó por completo.** I completely forgot.

2 to leave

□ Olvidé las llaves en la mesa. I left the keys on the table.

el **olvido** NOUN

■ **Ha sido un olvido imperdonable.** It was an unforgivable oversight.

el **ombligo** NOUN

navel

omitir VERB [58]

to leave out

□ Han omitido varios nombres de la lista. They've left several names out of the list.

once (FEM **once**) ADJECTIVE, PRONOUN

eleven

□ Tengo once años. I'm eleven.

■ **Son las once.** It's eleven o'clock.

■ **el once de agosto** the eleventh of August

la **onda** NOUN

wave

■ **onda corta** short wave

ondear VERB [25]

to fly

ondulado (FEM **ondulada**) ADJECTIVE

wavy

□ un chico con el pelo ondulado a boy with wavy hair

ONG ABBREVIATION *(= Organización no gubernamental)*

NGO *(= non-governmental organization)*

la **ONU** NOUN *(= Organización de las Naciones Unidas)*

UN *(= United Nations)*

opaco (FEM **opaca**) ADJECTIVE

1 opaque

2 dull

la **opción** (PL las **opciones**) NOUN

option

□ No tienes otra opción. You have no option.

la **ópera** NOUN

opera

la **operación** (PL **operaciones**) NOUN

operation

□ una operación de cataratas a cataract operation

operar VERB [25]

to operate on

□ Lo tienen que operar. They have to operate on him.

■ **Me van a operar del corazón.** I'm going to have a heart operation.

■ **operarse** to have an operation □ Me tengo que operar de la rodilla. I have to have a knee operation.

opinar VERB [25]

to think

□ ¿Y tú qué opinas de la propuesta? So what do you think about the proposal?

la **opinión** (PL las **opiniones**) NOUN

opinion

■ **en mi opinión** in my opinion

oponerse* VERB [41]

to oppose

□ Se opuso al proyecto. He opposed the project.

■ **No me opongo.** I don't object.

la **oportunidad** NOUN

chance

□ No tuvo la oportunidad de hacerlo. He didn't have a chance to do it.

■ **dar otra oportunidad a alguien** to give someone another chance

oportuno (FEM **oportuna**) ADJECTIVE

■ **en el momento oportuno** at the right time

la **oposición** (PL las **oposiciones**) NOUN

opposition

■ **las oposiciones** public examinations

optar VERB [25]

■ **optar por hacer algo** to choose to do something □ Al final, optó por ir. In the end, she chose to go.

optativo (FEM **optativa**) ADJECTIVE

optional

□ las asignaturas optativas optional subjects

la **óptica** NOUN

optician's

□ Me he comprado unas gafas de sol en la óptica. I bought a pair of sunglasses at the optician's.

el **optimismo** NOUN

optimism

optimista (FEM **optimista**) ADJECTIVE

optimistic

el/la **optimista** NOUN

optimist

óptimo (FEM **óptima**) ADJECTIVE

optimum

opuesto (FEM **opuesta**) ADJECTIVE

1 conflicting

2 opposite

opuse VERB ▷ *see* **oponer**

la **oración** (PL las **oraciones**) NOUN

1 prayer

2 sentence

el **orador**, la **oradora** NOUN

speaker

oral (FEM **oral**) ADJECTIVE
oral
■ **por vía oral** orally
■ **un examen oral** an oral exam

la **órbita** NOUN
1 orbit
2 eye socket

el **orden** NOUN
order
■ **por orden alfabético** in alphabetical order
■ **La casa está en orden.** The house is tidy.

la **orden** (PL las **órdenes**) NOUN
order
■ **¡Deja de darme órdenes!** Stop bossing me about!

ordenado (FEM **ordenada**) ADJECTIVE
tidy
□ Siempre tiene la habitación muy ordenada. He always keeps his room very tidy.

el **ordenador** NOUN
computer
■ **un ordenador portátil** a laptop

ordenar VERB [25]
1 to tidy up
□ ¿Por qué no ordenas tu habitación? Why don't you tidy your room up?
2 to order
□ El policía nos ordenó que saliéramos del edificio. The policeman ordered us to get out of the building.

ordeñar VERB [25]
to milk

ordinario (FEM **ordinaria**) ADJECTIVE
1 common
□ Es una mujer muy ordinaria. She's a very common woman.
2 ordinary
□ los acontecimientos ordinarios ordinary events
■ **de ordinario** usually □ De ordinario coge el autobús para ir a trabajar. He usually takes the bus to work.

la **oreja** NOUN
ear

orgánico (FEM **orgánica**) ADJECTIVE
organic

el **organismo** NOUN
organization
□ un organismo internacional an international organization

la **organización** (PL las **organizaciones**) NOUN
organization

organizar* VERB [13]
to organize
■ **organizarse** to organize oneself □ Te tienes que organizar mejor. You need to organize yourself better.

el **órgano** NOUN
organ

el **orgullo** NOUN
pride

orgulloso (FEM **orgullosa**) ADJECTIVE
proud

la **orientación** (PL las **orientaciones**) NOUN
■ **tener sentido de la orientación** to have a good sense of direction
■ **la orientación profesional** careers advice

el **oriente** NOUN
■ **el Oriente** the East

el **origen** (PL los **orígenes**) NOUN
origin

original (FEM **original**) ADJECTIVE
original

la **originalidad** NOUN
originality

la **orilla** NOUN
1 shore
2 bank
■ **a orillas de 1** on the shores of **2** on the banks of
■ **un paseo a la orilla del mar** a walk along the seashore

la **orina** NOUN
urine

orinar VERB [25]
to urinate

el **oro** NOUN
gold
□ un collar de oro a gold necklace
■ **oros**

DID YOU KNOW...?
Oros are 'golden coins', one of the suits in the Spanish card deck.

la **orquesta** NOUN
orchestra
■ **una orquesta de jazz** a jazz band

ortodoxo (FEM **ortodoxa**) ADJECTIVE
orthodox

la **ortografía** NOUN
spelling

la **oruga** NOUN
caterpillar

os PRONOUN
1 you
□ No os oigo. I can't hear you. □ Os he comprado un libro a cada uno. I've bought each of you a book.
■ **Os lo doy.** I'll give it to you.
■ **¿Os han arreglado ya el ordenador?** Have they fixed the computer for you yet?
2 yourselves

□ ¿Os habéis hecho daño? Did you hurt yourselves?
■ **Os tenéis que levantar antes de las ocho.** You have to get up before eight.
3 each other
□ Quiero que os pidáis perdón. I want you to say sorry to each other. □ No hace falta que os quitéis el abrigo. You don't need to take your coats off. □ Lavaos las manos. Wash your hands.

oscilar VERB [25]
to range
□ Las máximas han oscilado entre los 15 y los 20 grados. Maximum temperatures have ranged from 15 to 20 degrees.

oscurecer* VERB [12]
to get dark

la **oscuridad** NOUN
darkness
■ **Estaban hablando en la oscuridad.** They were talking in the dark.

oscuro (FEM **oscura**) ADJECTIVE
dark
□ una habitación muy oscura a very dark room
■ **azul oscuro** dark blue
■ **a oscuras** in darkness

el **oso**, la **osa** NOUN
bear
■ **un oso de peluche** a teddy bear

el **ostión** (PL los **ostiones**) NOUN
oyster *(Mexico)*

la **ostra** NOUN
oyster
■ **¡Ostras!** Good grief!

la **OTAN** NOUN *(= Organización del Tratado del Atlántico Norte)*
NATO *(= North Atlantic Treaty Organization)*

el **otoño** NOUN
autumn
□ en otoño in autumn □ el otoño pasado last autumn

otro (FEM **otra**) ADJECTIVE, PRONOUN
1 another
□ otro coche another car □ ¿Me das otra manzana, por favor? Can you give me another apple, please?
■ **¿Has perdido el lápiz? — No importa, tengo otro.** Have you lost your pencil? — It doesn't matter, I've got another one.
■ **¿Hay alguna otra manera de hacerlo?** Is there any other way of doing it?
■ **No quiero éste, quiero el otro.** I don't want this one, I want the other one.
2 other
□ Tengo otros planes. I have other plans.
■ **Quiero otra cosa.** I want something else.
■ **otra vez** again
■ **otros tres libros** another three books
■ **Que lo haga otro.** Let someone else do it.
■ **Están enamorados el uno del otro.** They're in love with each other.

ovalado (FEM **ovalada**) ADJECTIVE
oval

la **oveja** NOUN
sheep (PL sheep)

el **ovillo** NOUN
ball
□ un ovillo de lana a ball of wool

el **OVNI** NOUN *(= objeto volador no identificado)*
UFO *(= unidentified flying object)*

oxidado (FEM **oxidada**) ADJECTIVE
rusty

oxidarse VERB [25]
to rust
□ Se ha oxidado la barandilla. The rail has rusted.

el **oxígeno** NOUN
oxygen

oyendo VERB ▷ *see* **oír**

el/la **oyente** NOUN
1 listener
2 occasional student

Pp

la **paciencia** NOUN
patience
□ No tengo paciencia. I have very little patience. □ Perdí la paciencia y le grité. I lost my patience and I shouted at him.
■ **¡Ten paciencia!** Be patient!

el/la **paciente** ADJECTIVE, NOUN
patient

el **Pacífico** NOUN
the Pacific

pacífico (FEM **pacífica**) ADJECTIVE
peaceful

el/la **pacifista** ADJECTIVE, NOUN
pacifist
■ **el movimiento pacifista** the peace movement

el **pacto** NOUN
agreement
□ hacer un pacto to make an agreement

padecer* VERB [12]
1 to suffer from
□ Padece de una enfermedad grave. He suffers from a serious illness.
■ **Padece del corazón.** He has heart trouble.
2 to suffer
□ El pobrecito ha padecido mucho. The poor man has suffered a lot.

el **padrastro** NOUN
stepfather

el **padre** NOUN
father
■ **Es padre de familia.** He's a family man.
■ **mis padres** my parents
■ **rezar el Padre Nuestro** to say the Lord's Prayer

el **padrino** NOUN
godfather
■ **mis padrinos** my godparents

DID YOU KNOW...?
At a wedding, the **padrino** is the person who escorts the bride down the aisle and gives her away, usually her father.

la **paella** NOUN
paella

la **paga** NOUN
1 pocket money
□ Me dan la paga los domingos. I get my pocket money on Sundays.
2 pay
■ **la paga extra**

DID YOU KNOW...?
In Spain, most employees receive two extra payments **pagas extras** a year, each equivalent to a month's salary.

pagar* VERB [37]
1 to pay
□ No han pagado el alquiler. They haven't paid the rent. □ Me pagan muy poco. I get paid very little.
■ **Se puede pagar con tarjeta de crédito.** You can pay by credit card.
2 to pay for
□ Tengo que pagar las entradas. I have to pay for the tickets.

la **página** NOUN
page
□ Está en la página 17. It's on page 17.
■ **una página web** a Web page
■ **las páginas amarillas** the yellow pages

el **pago** NOUN
payment

el **país** (PL los **países**) NOUN
country (PL countries)
■ **el País Vasco** the Basque Country
■ **los Países Bajos** the Netherlands

el **paisaje** NOUN
1 landscape
□ el paisaje de Castilla the Castilian landscape □ pintar un paisaje to paint a landscape
2 scenery
□ Estaba contemplando el paisaje. I was looking at the scenery.

la **paja** NOUN
1 straw
□ un sombrero de paja a straw hat
2 padding
□ El resto del texto es sólo paja. The rest of the text is just padding.

la **pajarita** NOUN

bow tie

el **pájaro** NOUN
bird

la **pajita** NOUN
drinking straw

la **pala** NOUN
1 spade
2 shovel
3 bat
4 blade

la **palabra** NOUN
word
□ un título de dos palabras a two-word title □ Cumplió su palabra. He was true to his word. □ sin decir palabra without a word
■ **No me dirige la palabra.** He doesn't speak to me.

la **palabrota** NOUN
swearword
■ **soltar palabrotas** to swear

el **palacio** NOUN
palace

el **paladar** NOUN
palate

la **palanca** NOUN
lever
■ **la palanca de cambio** gear lever

la **palangana** NOUN
washbasin

el **palco** NOUN
box (PL boxes)

Palestina FEM NOUN
Palestine

el **palestino** (FEM la **palestina**) ADJECTIVE, NOUN
Palestinian

la **paleta** NOUN
1 trowel
2 palette

pálido (FEM **pálida**) ADJECTIVE
pale
□ Se puso pálida. She turned pale.

el **palillo** NOUN
1 toothpick
2 chopstick

la **paliza** NOUN
1 beating
□ Los ladrones le dieron una paliza. The burglars gave him a beating.
2 thrashing
□ Si mi padre se entera me va a dar una paliza. If my father finds out he'll give me a thrashing.
■ **Sus clases son una paliza.** His classes are a real pain.
■ **¡No me des la paliza!** Don't be such a pain!

la **palma** NOUN
palm
■ **dar palmas** to clap

la **palmera** NOUN
palm tree

el **palmo** NOUN
■ **Mide un palmo.** It's several inches long.
■ **Se conoce el lugar de palmo a palmo.** He knows every inch of the place.

el **palo** NOUN
1 stick
□ Le pegó con un palo. He hit him with a stick.
2 club *(golf)*
3 suit *(cards)*
■ **una cuchara de palo** a wooden spoon

la **paloma** NOUN
pigeon
□ una paloma mensajera a carrier pigeon
□ la paloma de la paz the dove of peace

las **palomitas** NOUN
■ **las palomitas de maíz** popcorn *sing*

LANGUAGE TIP Word for word, **palomitas de maíz** means 'little pigeons of corn'.

palpar VERB [25]
to feel

la **palpitación** (PL las **palpitaciones**) NOUN
palpitation

palpitar VERB [25]
1 to pound
□ El corazón me palpitaba de miedo. My heart was pounding with fear.
2 to beat
□ Su corazón dejó de palpitar. His heart stopped beating.

la **palta** NOUN *(Chile, River Plate)*
avocado (PL avocados)

el **pan** NOUN
1 bread
□ pan con mantequilla bread and butter
□ pan integral wholemeal bread □ pan de molde sliced bread □ una barra de pan a loaf of bread
■ **pan rallado** breadcrumbs *pl*
■ **pan tostado** toast
2 loaf (PL loaves)
□ Compré dos panes. I bought two loaves.

la **pana** NOUN
corduroy

la **panadera** NOUN
baker
□ Es panadera. She's a baker.

la **panadería** NOUN
bakery (PL bakeries)

el **panadero** NOUN
baker
□ Es panadero. He's a baker.

Panamá MASC NOUN

Spanish–English

P

Panama

el **panameño** (FEM la **panameña**) ADJECTIVE, NOUN

Panamanian

la **pancarta** NOUN

banner

el **pancito** NOUN *(Latin America)*

bread roll

el **panda** NOUN

panda (PL pandas)

la **pandereta** NOUN

tambourine

la **pandilla** NOUN

gang

el **panfleto** NOUN

pamphlet

el **pánico** NOUN

panic

□ en un momento de pánico in a moment of panic

■ **Me entró pánico.** I panicked.

■ **Les tengo pánico a las arañas.** I'm terrified of spiders.

las **pantaletas** NOUN *(Mexico)*

panties

□ unas pantaletas a pair of panties

la **pantalla** NOUN

1 screen

■ **una pantalla plana** a flat screen

2 lampshade

los **pantalones** NOUN

trousers

■ **unos pantalones** a pair of trousers

■ **pantalones cortos** shorts

■ **pantalones vaqueros** jeans

el **pantano** NOUN

reservoir

la **pantera** NOUN

panther

las **pantimedias** NOUN *(Mexico)*

tights

□ unas pantimedias a pair of tights

los **pantis** NOUN

tights

□ unos pantis a pair of tights

la **pantorrilla** NOUN

calf (PL calves)

los **pants** NOUN *(Mexico)*

tracksuit *sing*

el **pañal** NOUN

nappy (PL nappies)

el **paño** NOUN

cloth

■ **un paño de cocina** a dishcloth

el **pañuelo** NOUN

1 handkerchief (PL handkerchiefs)

2 scarf (PL scarves)

3 headscarf (PL headscarves)

el **papa** NOUN

pope

■ **el Papa** the Pope

la **papa** NOUN *(Latin America)*

potato (PL potatoes)

■ **pescado frito con papas fritas** fish and chips

■ **un paquete de papas fritas** a packet of crisps

el **papá** (PL los **papás**) NOUN

dad

■ **mis papás** my mum and dad

■ **Papá Noel** Father Christmas

el **papalote** NOUN *(Mexico)*

kite

□ volar un papalote to fly a kite

el **papel** NOUN

1 paper

□ una bolsa de papel a paper bag

2 piece of paper

□ Lo escribí en un papel. I wrote it on a piece of paper.

■ **papel de aluminio** tinfoil

■ **papel higiénico** toilet paper

LANGUAGE TIP Word for word, **papel higiénico** means 'hygienic paper'.

■ **papel pintado** wallpaper

LANGUAGE TIP Word for word, **papel pintado** means 'painted paper'.

3 role

□ Le han dado el papel principal. They gave her the leading role. □ Jugó un papel muy importante en las negociaciones. He played a very important part in the negotiations.

■ **¿Qué papeles te piden para sacar el pasaporte?** What documents do you need to get a passport?

el **papeleo** NOUN

paperwork

la **papelera** NOUN

1 wastepaper bin

2 litter bin

la **papelería** NOUN

stationer's (PL stationers' shops)

la **papeleta** NOUN

1 results slip

2 ballot paper

3 raffle ticket

las **paperas** NOUN

mumps

□ tener paperas to have the mumps

la **papilla** NOUN

1 baby food

2 pap

el **paquete** NOUN

1 packet

2 parcel

□ Me mandaron un paquete por correo.

I got a parcel in the post.

Paquistán MASC NOUN
Pakistan

el/la **paquistaní** (PL los/las **paquistaníes**) ADJECTIVE, NOUN
Pakistani

par (FEM **par**) ADJECTIVE
■ **número par** even number

el **par** NOUN
1 couple
□ un par de horas al día a couple of hours a day
2 pair
□ un par de calcetines a pair of socks
■ **Abrió la ventana de par en par.** He opened the window wide.

para PREPOSITION
1 for
□ Es para ti. It's for you. □ Tengo muchos deberes para mañana. I have a lot of homework to do for tomorrow. □ el autobús para Marbella the bus for Marbella
■ **¿Para qué lo quieres?** What do you want it for?
■ **¿Para qué sirve?** What's it for?
■ **para siempre** forever
■ **Para entonces ya era tarde.** It was already too late by then.
2 to
□ Estoy ahorrando para comprarme una moto. I'm saving up to buy a motorbike.
□ Tengo bastante para vivir. I have enough to live on. □ Son cinco para las ocho. *(Latin America)* It's five to eight.
■ **Entré despacito para no despertarla.** I went in slowly so as not to wake her.
■ **para que te acuerdes de mí** so that you remember me

la **parabólica** NOUN
satellite dish

el **parabrisas** (PL los **parabrisas**) NOUN
windscreen

el **paracaídas** (PL los **paracaídas**) NOUN
parachute

el/la **paracaidista** NOUN
1 paratrooper
2 parachutist

el **parachoques** (PL los **parachoques**) NOUN
bumper

la **parada** NOUN
stop
□ Hicimos una parada corta para descansar. We made a short stop to rest.
■ **una parada de autobús** a bus stop
■ **una parada de taxis** a taxi rank

el **paradero** NOUN *(Latin America)*
bus stop

parado (FEM **parada**) ADJECTIVE
unemployed
□ Hace seis meses que está parada. She's been unemployed for six months.
■ **No te quedes ahí parado.** Don't just stand there.
■ **Estuve toda la mañana parado.** *(Latin America)* I was standing all morning.

el **parador** NOUN

> **DID YOU KNOW...?**
> The **paradores** are a group of luxury Spanish hotels occupying castles, monasteries and other historical buildings and sited in scenic areas.

el **paraguas** (PL los **paraguas**) NOUN
umbrella

Paraguay MASC NOUN
Paraguay

el **paraguayo** (FEM la **paraguaya**) ADJECTIVE, NOUN
Paraguayan

el **paraíso** NOUN
paradise

el **paralelo** ADJECTIVE, NOUN
parallel

la **parálisis** (PL las **parálisis**) NOUN
paralysis (PL paralyses)
■ **parálisis cerebral** cerebral palsy

paralítico (FEM **paralítica**) ADJECTIVE
■ **Está paralítico.** He's paralyzed.

el **parapente** NOUN
1 paragliding
2 paraglider

parar VERB [25]
to stop
□ Paramos a poner gasolina. We stopped to get some petrol. □ No paró de llover en toda la noche. It didn't stop raining all night.
■ **Nos equivocamos de tren y fuimos a parar a Manchester.** We got on the wrong train and ended up in Manchester.
■ **pararse 1** to stop □ El reloj se ha parado. The clock has stopped. **2** *(Latin America)* to stand up
■ **hablar sin parar** to talk non-stop

el **pararrayos** (PL los **pararrayos**) NOUN
lightning conductor

la **parcela** NOUN
plot of land

el **parche** NOUN
patch (PL patches)

el **parchís** NOUN
Spanish version of ludo

parcial (FEM **parcial**) ADJECTIVE
1 partial
□ un eclipse parcial a partial eclipse
■ **a tiempo parcial** part time
2 biased

Spanish-English

P

el **parcial** NOUN
mid-term exam

pareado (FEM **pareada**) ADJECTIVE
■ **un chalet pareado** a semi-detached house

parecer* VERB [12]
1 to seem
□ Parece muy simpática. She seems very nice. □ Todo parecía indicar que estaba muy interesado. It all seemed to indicate that he was interested.
■ **Parece mentira que ya haya pasado tanto tiempo.** I can't believe it has been so long.
2 to look
□ Parece más joven. He looks younger.
■ **Parece una modelo.** She looks like a model.
■ **Parece que va a llover.** It looks as if it's going to rain.
3 to think
■ **¿Qué te pareció la película?** What did you think of the film? □ Me parece bien que los multen. I think it's right that they should be fined.
■ **Me parece que sí.** I think so.
■ **Me parece que no.** I don't think so.
■ **si te parece bien** if that's all right with you
■ **parecerse** to look alike □ María y Ana se parecen mucho. María and Ana look very much alike.
■ **parecerse a** to look like □ Te pareces mucho a tu madre. You look very much like your mother.

parecido (FEM **parecida**) ADJECTIVE
similar
□ Las casas son todas parecidas. The houses are all similar. □ Tu blusa es parecida a la mía. Your blouse is similar to mine.
■ **o algo parecido** or something like that

P

la **pared** NOUN
wall

la **pareja** NOUN
1 couple
□ Había varias parejas bailando. There were several couples dancing.
2 pair
□ En este juego hay que formar parejas. For this game you have to get into pairs.
3 partner
□ Vino con su pareja. He came with his partner.

parejo (FEM **pareja**) ADJECTIVE *(Latin America)*
even

el **paréntesis** (PL los **paréntesis**) NOUN
bracket
□ entre paréntesis in brackets

el/la **pariente** NOUN
relative
□ Es pariente mío. He's a relative of mine.
LANGUAGE TIP Be careful! **pariente** does not mean **parent**.

París MASC NOUN
Paris

el/la **parisiense** ADJECTIVE, NOUN
Parisian

el **parisino** (FEM la **parisina**) ADJECTIVE, NOUN
Parisian

el **parking** (PL los **parkings**) NOUN
car park

el **parlamento** NOUN
parliament

parlanchín (FEM **parlanchina**, MASC PL **parlanchines**) ADJECTIVE
chatty

el **parlante** NOUN *(Latin America)*
loudspeaker

el **paro** NOUN
1 unemployment
□ Ha bajado el paro. Unemployment has come down.
■ **Mi hermano está en paro.** My brother is on the dole.
■ **cobrar el paro** to get the dole
2 strike
□ un paro de tres días a three-day strike

parpadear VERB [25]
to blink

el **párpado** NOUN
eyelid

el **parque** NOUN
park
□ un parque nacional a national park
■ **un parque de atracciones** an amusement park
■ **un parque infantil** a children's playground
■ **un parque temático** a theme park
■ **un parque zoológico** a zoo

el **parquímetro** NOUN
parking meter

la **parra** NOUN
vine

el **párrafo** NOUN
paragraph

la **parrilla** NOUN
grill
■ **carne a la parrilla** grilled meat

la **parrillada** NOUN
grill

el **párroco** NOUN
parish priest

la **parroquia** NOUN
parish (PL parishes)

la **parte** NOUN
1 part
□ El examen consta de dos partes. The exam consists of two parts. □ ¿De qué parte de Inglaterra eres? What part of England are you from?
2 share
□ mi parte de la herencia my share of the inheritance □ Tengo que haberlo dejado en alguna parte. I must have left it somewhere.
□ por todas partes everywhere
■ **en parte** partly □ Se debe en parte a su falta de experiencia. It's partly due to his lack of experience.
■ **la mayor parte de los españoles** most Spanish people
■ **la parte delantera** the front
■ **la parte de atrás** the back
■ **la parte de arriba** the top
■ **la parte de abajo** the bottom
■ **por una parte ..., por otra ...** on the one hand ..., on the other hand ...
■ **Llamo de parte de Juan.** I'm calling on behalf of Juan.
■ **¿De parte de quién?** Who's calling please?
■ **Estoy de tu parte.** I'm on your side.

participar VERB [25]
to take part
■ **participar en un concurso** to take part in a competition

el **participio** NOUN
participle

particular (FEM **particular**) ADJECTIVE
private
□ clases particulares private classes
■ **El vestido no tiene nada de particular.** The dress is nothing special.
■ **en particular** in particular

la **partida** NOUN
1 game
□ echar una partida de cartas to have a game of cards
2 certificate
□ partida de nacimiento birth certificate

partidario (FEM **partidaria**) ADJECTIVE
■ **ser partidario de algo** to be in favour of something

el **partidario**, la **partidaria** NOUN
supporter

el **partido** NOUN
1 party (PL parties) *(political)*
2 match (PL matches) *(football, tennis)*
3 game *(Latin America)*
□ un partido de ajedrez a game of chess
■ **Sabe sacarle partido a todo.** He knows how to make the most out of everything.

partir VERB [58]
1 to cut
2 to crack
3 to break off
4 to leave
□ La expedición partirá mañana de París. The expedition is to leave from Paris tomorrow.
■ **a partir de enero** from January □ a partir de ahora from now on
■ **partirse** to break □ El remo se partió en dos. The oar broke in two.
■ **partirse de risa** to split one's sides laughing

la **partitura** NOUN
score

el **parto** NOUN
birth
■ **estar de parto** to be in labour

la **pasa** NOUN
raisin

la **pasada** NOUN
■ **¡Ese coche es una pasada!** This car is amazing!
■ **¿Has visto cómo ha saltado? ¡Qué pasada!** Did you see him jump? Amazing!

pasado (FEM **pasada**) ADJECTIVE
1 last
□ el verano pasado last summer
2 after
□ Pasado el semáforo, verás un cine. After the traffic lights you'll see a cinema.
□ Volvió pasadas las tres de la mañana. He returned after three in the morning.
■ **pasado mañana** the day after tomorrow
■ **un sombrero pasado de moda** an old-fashioned hat

el **pasado** NOUN
past
□ en el pasado in the past

el **pasador** NOUN
1 hair slide
2 tiepin

el **pasaje** NOUN
1 ticket
■ **un pasaje electrónico** an e-ticket
2 passage

pasajero (FEM **pasajera**) ADJECTIVE
1 temporary
2 passing

el **pasajero**, la **pasajera** NOUN
passenger

el **pasamanos** (PL los **pasamanos**) NOUN
banister

el **pasaporte** NOUN
passport

pasar VERB [25]
1 to pass
□ ¿Me pasas la sal, por favor? Can you pass

me the salt, please?
■ **Cuando termines pásasela a Isabel.** When you've finished pass it on to Isabel.
■ **La foto fue pasando de mano en mano.** The photo was passed around.
■ **Cuando muera la empresa pasará al hijo.** When he dies the company will go to his son.
■ **Un momento, te paso con Pedro.** Just a moment, I'll put you on to Pedro.

2 to go past
□ Pasaron varios coches. A number of cars went past. □ El autobús pasó de largo. The bus went past.
■ **¡Pase, por favor!** Please come in.
■ **El tiempo pasa deprisa.** Time goes so quickly.
■ **Pasaron cinco años.** Five years went by.
■ **Ya ha pasado una hora.** It's been an hour already.

3 to spend
□ Voy a pasar unos días con ella. I'm going to spend a few days with her. □ Me pasé el fin de semana estudiando. I spent the weekend studying.

4 to happen
□ Por suerte no le pasó nada. Luckily nothing happened to him. □ pase lo que pase whatever happens
■ **¿Qué pasa? 1** What's the matter? **2** What's happening?
■ **¿Qué le pasa a Juan?** What's the matter with Juan?
■ **pasar la aspiradora** to do the vacuuming
■ **pasarlo bien** to have a good time
■ **pasarlo mal** to have a bad time
■ **Hemos pasado mucho frío.** We were very cold.
■ **Están pasando hambre.** They are starving.
■ **pasar algo a máquina** to type something
■ **¡Paso de todo!** I couldn't care less!
■ **pasar por 1** to go though □ Pasamos por un túnel muy largo. We went through a very long tunnel. □ No creo que el sofá pase por esa puerta. I don't think the settee will go through the door. □ pasar por la aduana to go through customs □ Está pasando por un mal momento. He's going through a bad patch. □ No pasamos por la ciudad. We don't go through the city. **2** to go past □ Ese autobús pasa por mi colegio. That bus goes past my school.
■ **Podrían perfectamente pasar por gemelos.** They could easily pass for twins.
■ **No puedo pasar sin teléfono.** I can't get by without a telephone.
■ **Está bien hacer ejercicio pero no hay que pasarse.** It's OK to exercise but there's no point in overdoing it.
■ **pasarse de moda** to go out of fashion

el **pasatiempo** NOUN
hobby (PL hobbies)

la **Pascua** NOUN
Easter
■ **¡Felices Pascuas!** Happy Christmas!

el **pase** NOUN
pass (PL passes)
□ un pase gratis a free pass
■ **un pase de modelos** a fashion show

pasear VERB [25]
to walk
■ **ir a pasear** to go for a walk

el **paseo** NOUN
walk
□ Salimos a dar un paseo. We went out for a walk.
■ **ir de paseo** to go for a walk
■ **un paseo en barco** a boat trip
■ **un paseo en bicicleta** a bike ride
■ **el paseo marítimo** the promenade
LANGUAGE TIP Word for word, **paseo marítimo** means 'maritime walk'.

el **pasillo** NOUN
1 corridor
2 aisle

la **pasión** (PL las **pasiones**) NOUN
passion

pasivo (FEM **pasiva**) ADJECTIVE
passive

pasmado (FEM **pasmada**) ADJECTIVE
amazed
□ Cuando me enteré, me quedé pasmado. I was amazed when I found out.

el **paso** NOUN
1 step
□ Dio un paso hacia atrás. He took a step backwards. □ paso a paso step by step
■ **He oído pasos.** I heard footsteps.
■ **Vive a un paso de aquí.** He lives right near here.
■ **A ese paso no terminarán nunca.** At this rate they'll never finish.
2 way
□ Han cerrado el paso. They've blocked the way. □ La policía le abría paso. The police made way for him.
■ **'Ceda el paso'** 'Give way'
■ **'Prohibido el paso'** 'No entry'
■ **El banco me pilla de paso.** The bank is on my way.
■ **Están de paso por Barcelona.** They're just passing through Barcelona.
■ **un paso de peatones** a pedestrian crossing
■ **un paso de cebra** a zebra crossing

■ **un paso a nivel** a level crossing
la **pasta** NOUN
1 pasta
2 dosh
■ **pastas de té** biscuits
■ **pasta de dientes** toothpaste
pastar VERB [25]
to graze
el **pastel** NOUN
cake
la **pastelería** NOUN
patisserie
la **pastilla** NOUN
1 pill
■ **pastillas para la tos** cough sweets
2 bar
3 piece
■ **pastillas de caldo** stock cubes
el **pasto** NOUN *(Latin America)*
grass
el **pastor** NOUN
shepherd
■ **un pastor alemán** an Alsatian
■ **un perro pastor** a sheepdog
la **pastora** NOUN
shepherdess
la **pata** NOUN
leg
□ las patas de la silla the chair legs
■ **saltar a la pata coja** to hop
■ **Encontramos la casa patas arriba.** We found the house in a right mess.
■ **¡He vuelto a meter la pata!** I've gone and put my foot in it again!
■ **Me parece que he metido la pata en el examen de física.** I think I messed up my physics exam.
la **patada** NOUN
■ **Me dio una patada.** He kicked me.
Patagonia FEM NOUN
Patagonia
la **patata** NOUN
potato (PL potatoes)
■ **un filete con patatas fritas** steak and chips
■ **una bolsa de patatas fritas** a bag of crisps
el **paté** (PL los **patés**) NOUN
pâté
la **patera** NOUN
small boat
paterno (FEM **paterna**) ADJECTIVE
paternal
la **patilla** NOUN
1 sideburn
□ dejarse patillas to grow sideburns
2 arm *(of glasses)*
el **patín** (PL los **patines**) NOUN
1 roller skate
2 skate
3 pedal boat
el **patinaje** NOUN
1 roller skating
2 ice skating
■ **patinaje artístico** figure skating
patinar VERB [25]
1 to roller-skate
2 to skate
3 to skid
el **patinete** NOUN
scooter
el **patio** NOUN
1 playground
2 courtyard
■ **el patio de butacas** the stalls *pl*
el **pato** NOUN
duck
patoso (FEM **patosa**) ADJECTIVE
clumsy
la **patria** NOUN
homeland
patriota (FEM **patriota**) ADJECTIVE
patriotic
el **patrocinador**, la **patrocinadora** NOUN
sponsor
patrocinar VERB [25]
to sponsor
el **patrón** (PL los **patrones**) NOUN
1 patron saint
2 boss (PL bosses)
la **patrona** NOUN
1 patron saint
2 landlady (PL landladies)
la **patrulla** NOUN
patrol
□ estar de patrulla to be on patrol
la **pausa** NOUN
1 pause
2 break
el **pavimento** NOUN
1 paving
2 surface
el **pavo** NOUN
turkey
■ **un pavo real** a peacock
el **payaso**, la **payasa** NOUN
clown
■ **Deja de hacer el payaso.** Stop clowning around.
la **paz** (PL las **paces**) NOUN
peace
■ **¡Déjame en paz!** Leave me alone!
■ **Ha hecho las paces con su novio.** She's made it up with her boyfriend.
el **PC** ABBREVIATION

Spanish-English

p

PC (PL PCs)

P.D. ABBREVIATION *(= posdata)*
P.S.

el **peaje** NOUN
toll

el **peatón** (PL los **peatones**) NOUN
pedestrian

la **peca** NOUN
freckle

el **pecado** NOUN
sin

pecar* VERB [48]
to sin

el **pecho** NOUN
1 chest
2 breast
■ **dar el pecho a un niño** to breastfeed a baby
■ **¡No te lo tomes a pecho! Era una broma.** Don't take it to heart. I was only joking.

la **pechuga** NOUN
breast

el **pedal** NOUN
pedal
□ el pedal del freno the brake pedal

pedalear VERB [25]
to pedal

pedante (FEM **pedante**) ADJECTIVE
pedantic

el **pedazo** NOUN
piece
□ un pedazo de pan a piece of bread
■ **hacer pedazos** **1** to smash **2** to tear up

el/la **pediatra** NOUN
paediatrician

el **pedido** NOUN
order
□ hacer un pedido to place an order

pedir* VERB [38]
1 to ask for
□ Le pedí dinero a mi padre. I asked my father for some money. □ He pedido hora para el médico. I've asked for a doctor's appointment.
2 to ask
□ ¿Te puedo pedir un favor? Can I ask you a favour? □ ¿Cuánto pide por el coche? How much is he asking for the car?
■ **Pedí que me enviaran la información por correo.** I asked them to mail me the information.
3 to order
□ Yo pedí paella. I ordered paella.
■ **Le pedí disculpas.** I apologized to him.
■ **Tuve que pedir dinero prestado.** I had to borrow some money.

el **pedo** NOUN
fart *(vulgar)*
■ **tirarse un pedo** *(vulgar)* to fart

la **pega** NOUN
snag
□ La única pega es que la oficina me queda lejos. The only snag is that the office is a long way away.
■ **Me pusieron muchas pegas.** They made things very difficult for me.

pegadizo (FEM **pegadiza**) ADJECTIVE
catchy

pegajoso (FEM **pegajosa**) ADJECTIVE
1 sticky
2 catchy *(Latin America)*

el **pegamento** NOUN
glue

pegar* VERB [37]
1 to hit
□ Andrés me ha pegado. Andrés hit me.
□ La pelota pegó en el árbol. The ball hit the tree.
2 to stick
□ Lo puedes pegar con celo. You can stick it on with sellotape. □ Tengo que pegar las fotos en el álbum. I have to stick the photos in the album.
■ **Se te va a pegar el arroz.** Be careful or the rice will stick.
3 to give
□ Le pegaron un tremendo empujón. They gave him a great push. □ Le pegó una bofetada. He gave him a slap. □ Me has pegado la gripe. You've given me the flu.
□ ¡Qué susto me has pegado! What a fright you gave me!
■ **Pegó un grito.** He shouted.
■ **Le pegaron un tiro.** They shot him.
4 to look right
□ Ese jarrón no pega aquí. This vase doesn't look right here.
■ **Esta camisa no pega con el traje.** This shirt doesn't look right with the suit.
■ **El niño se pegó a su madre.** The boy clung to his mother.

la **pegatina** NOUN
sticker

el **peinado** NOUN
hairstyle

peinar VERB [25]
1 to comb
□ Péinate antes de salir. Comb your hair before you go out.
2 to brush
□ Su madre la estaba peinando. Her mother was brushing her hair.
■ **Mañana voy a peinarme.** I'm going to have my hair done tomorrow.

el **peine** NOUN
comb

p.ej. ABBREVIATION (= *por ejemplo*)
e.g.
pelar VERB [25]
1 to peel
2 to shell
■ **Se me está pelando la espalda.** My back is peeling.
■ **Hace un frío que pela.** It's bitterly cold.
el **peldaño** NOUN
1 step
2 rung
la **pelea** NOUN
1 fight
□ Hubo una pelea en la discoteca. There was a fight at the disco.
2 argument
□ Tuvo una pelea con su novio. She had an argument with her boyfriend.
peleado (FEM **peleada**) ADJECTIVE
■ **Están peleados.** They've fallen out.
pelear VERB [25]
1 to fight
□ ¡Deja de pelear con tu hermano! Stop fighting with your brother! □ Dos niños se están peleando en el patio. There are two children fighting in the playground.
2 to argue
□ Pelean por cualquier tontería. They argue over the slightest thing.
el **pelícano** NOUN
pelican
la **película** NOUN
film
□ A las ocho ponen una película. There's a film on at eight.
■ **una película de dibujos animados** a cartoon
■ **una película del oeste** a western
■ **una película de suspense** a thriller
el **peligro** NOUN
danger
□ Está fuera de peligro. He's out of danger.
peligroso (FEM **peligrosa**) ADJECTIVE
dangerous
pelirrojo (FEM **pelirroja**) ADJECTIVE
■ **es pelirrojo** he has red hair
el **pellejo** NOUN
skin
■ **No me gustaría estar en su pellejo.** I wouldn't like to be in his shoes.
■ **arriesgar el pellejo** to risk one's neck
pellizcar* VERB [48]
to pinch
□ Me pellizcó el brazo. He pinched my arm.
el **pellizco** NOUN
pinch
□ un pellizco de sal a pinch of salt
el **pelmazo**, la **pelmaza** NOUN
bore
el **pelo** NOUN
hair
□ Tiene el pelo rizado. He has curly hair.
■ **No perdí el avión por un pelo.** I only just caught the plane.
■ **Se me pusieron los pelos de punta.** It made my hair stand on end.
■ **Me estás tomando el pelo.** You're pulling my leg.
la **pelota** NOUN
ball
□ jugar a la pelota to play ball
■ **hacer la pelota a alguien** to suck up to someone
el/la **pelota** NOUN
creep *(colloquial)*
la **peluca** NOUN
wig
peludo (FEM **peluda**) ADJECTIVE
hairy
la **peluquera** NOUN
hairdresser
la **peluquería** NOUN
hairdresser's
el **peluquero** NOUN
hairdresser
la **pena** NOUN
shame
□ Es una pena que no puedas venir. It's a shame you can't come. □ ¡Qué pena! What a shame!
■ **Me dio tanta pena el pobre animal.** I felt so sorry for the poor animal.
■ **Me da pena tener que marcharme.** I'm so sad to have to go away.
■ **No tengas pena.** *(Latin America)* Don't be embarrassed.
■ **Vale la pena.** It's worth it.
■ **No vale la pena gastarse tanto dinero.** It's not worth spending so much money.
■ **la pena de muerte** the death penalty
el **penalty** (PL los **penaltys**) NOUN
penalty (PL penalties)
□ pitar penalty to award a penalty
el **pendejo**, la **pendeja** NOUN *(Latin America)*
nerd
pendiente (FEM **pendiente**) ADJECTIVE
■ **Tenemos un par de asuntos pendientes.** We have a couple of matters to sort out.
■ **Tiene una asignatura pendiente.** He has to resit one subject.
■ **Estaban pendientes de ella.** They were watching her intently.
el **pendiente** NOUN
earring

la **pendiente** NOUN
slope

el **pene** NOUN
penis (PL penises)

penetrar VERB [25]
■ **penetrar en** to find one's way into □ La luz apenas penetra en la cueva. The light hardly finds its way into the cave.

la **penicilina** NOUN
penicillin

la **península** NOUN
peninsula
■ **la Península Ibérica** the Iberian Peninsula

el **penique** NOUN
penny (PL pence)

el **pensamiento** NOUN
1 thought
2 pansy (PL pansies)

pensar* VERB [39]
1 to think
□ Piénsalo bien antes de contestar. Think carefully before you answer. □ ¿Piensas que vale la pena? Do you think it's worth it? □ ¿Qué piensas de Manolo? What do you think of Manolo?
■ **¿Qué piensas del aborto?** What do you think about abortion?
2 to think about
□ Tengo que pensarlo. I'll have to think about it.
■ **Sólo piensa en pasarlo bien.** All he thinks about is having a good time.
■ **Estaba pensando en ir al cine esta tarde.** I was thinking of going to the cinema this evening.
■ **¡Ni pensarlo!** *(colloquial)* No way!
■ **pensándolo bien ...** on second thoughts ...
■ **Piénsatelo.** Think it over.

pensativo (FEM **pensativa**) ADJECTIVE
thoughtful

la **pensión** (PL las **pensiones**) NOUN
1 pension
2 guest house
■ **pensión completa** full board
■ **media pensión** half board

el/la **pensionista** NOUN
pensioner

penúltimo (FEM **penúltima**) ADJECTIVE
■ **la penúltima estación** the last station but one

el **penúltimo**, la **penúltima** NOUN
■ **Soy el penúltimo.** I'm second to last.

el **peñón** (PL los **peñones**) NOUN
■ **el Peñón de Gibraltar** the Rock of Gibraltar

el **peón** (PL los **peones**) NOUN
1 labourer
2 pawn

la **peonza** NOUN
spinning top

peor (FEM **peor**) ADJECTIVE, ADVERB
1 worse
□ Su caso es peor que el nuestro. His case is worse than ours. □ Hoy me siento peor. I feel worse today.
2 worst
□ el peor día de mi vida the worst day of my life □ Sacó la peor nota de toda la clase. He got the worst mark in the whole class.
■ **el restaurante donde peor se come** the restaurant with the worst food
■ **y lo peor es que ...** and the worst thing is that ...
■ **Si no viene, peor para ella.** If she doesn't come, too bad for her.

el **pepinillo** NOUN
gherkin

el **pepino** NOUN
cucumber
■ **Me importa un pepino lo que piense.** I couldn't care less what he thinks.

la **pepita** NOUN
1 pip
2 nugget

pequeño (FEM **pequeña**) ADJECTIVE
small
□ Prefiero los coches pequeños. I prefer small cars. □ Estos zapatos me quedan pequeños. These shoes are too small for me.
■ **¿Cuál prefieres? — El pequeño.** Which one do you prefer? — The small one.
■ **mi hermana pequeña** my younger sister
■ **La pequeña estudia medicina.** The youngest is studying medicine.
■ **Tuvimos un pequeño problema.** We had a slight problem.

el **pequinés** NOUN
Pekinese

la **pera** NOUN
pear

percatarse VERB [25]
■ **percatarse de algo** to notice something

la **percha** NOUN
1 coat hanger
2 coat hook

el **perchero** NOUN
1 coat rack
2 coat stand

percibir VERB [58]
1 to notice
2 to see
3 to sense

la **percusión** NOUN

percussion

perdedor (FEM **perdedora**) ADJECTIVE
losing
□ la pareja perdedora the losing pair

el **perdedor**, la **perdedora** NOUN
loser
□ Eres mal perdedor. You're a bad loser.

perder* VERB [20]
1 to lose
□ He perdido el monedero. I've lost my purse. □ Está intentando perder peso. He's trying to lose weight. □ perder el conocimiento to lose consciousness
□ Perdimos dos a cero. We lost two nil.
■ **Se le perdieron las llaves.** He lost his keys.
2 to miss
□ Date prisa o perderás el tren. Hurry up or you'll miss the train. □ No quiero perder esta oportunidad. I don't want to miss this opportunity.
■ **¡No te lo pierdas!** Don't miss it!
■ **¡Me estás haciendo perder el tiempo!** You're wasting my time!
■ **Has echado a perder la sorpresa.** You've ruined the surprise.
■ **Ana es la que saldrá perdiendo.** Ana is the one who will lose out.
■ **Tenía miedo de perderme.** I was afraid of getting lost.

la **perdición** NOUN
ruin

la **pérdida** NOUN
1 loss (PL losses)
2 leak
■ **Fue una pérdida de tiempo.** It was a waste of time.

perdido (FEM **perdida**) ADJECTIVE
1 lost
□ la oficina de objetos perdidos the lost property office
2 remote
□ un pueblecito perdido en la montaña a remote little village in the mountains
■ **Es tonto perdido.** He's a complete idiot.

el **perdigón** (PL los **perdigones**) NOUN
pellet

la **perdiz** (PL las **perdices**) NOUN
partridge

el **perdón** NOUN
■ **Le pedí perdón.** I apologized to him.
■ **¡Perdón!** **1** Sorry! **2** Excuse me!

perdonar VERB [25]
to forgive
□ ¿Me perdonas? Do you forgive me?
□ No perdona que me haya olvidara de su cumpleaños. He hasn't forgiven me for forgetting his birthday.
■ **¡Perdona! ¿Tienes hora?** Excuse me, do you have the time?
■ **¡Perdona! ¿Te he hecho daño?** I'm so sorry. Did I hurt you?

el **peregrino**, la **peregrina** NOUN
pilgrim

el **perejil** NOUN
parsley

la **pereza** NOUN
laziness
■ **¡Qué pereza tengo!** I feel so lazy!
■ **Me da pereza levantarme.** I can't be bothered to get up.

perezoso (FEM **perezosa**) ADJECTIVE
lazy

perfeccionar VERB [25]
to improve
□ Fue a Inglaterra para perfeccionar el inglés. He went to England to improve his English.

perfectamente ADVERB
perfectly

perfecto (FEM **perfecta**) ADJECTIVE
perfect

el **perfil** NOUN
profile
□ un retrato de perfil a profile portrait
■ **ponerse de perfil** to stand side on

el **perfume** NOUN
perfume

la **perfumería** NOUN
perfume shop

periódico (FEM **periódica**) ADJECTIVE
periodic

el **periódico** NOUN
newspaper

el **periodismo** NOUN
journalism

el/la **periodista** NOUN
journalist
□ Mi tío es periodista. My uncle is a journalist.

el **periodo** NOUN
period
□ un periodo de tres meses a three-month period
■ **Tiene el periodo.** She has her period.

el **periquito** NOUN
budgerigar

perjudicar* VERB [48]
1 to damage
2 to be harmful to
□ Esta ley puede perjudicarnos. This law could be harmful to our interests.
■ **El cambio ha perjudicado sus estudios.** The change has had an adverse effect on his studies.

perjudicial (FEM **perjudicial**) ADJECTIVE

damaging
■ **El tabaco es perjudicial para la salud.** Smoking damages your health.

la **perla** NOUN
pearl

permanecer* VERB [12]
to remain

permanente (FEM **permanente**) ADJECTIVE
permanent

la **permanente** NOUN
perm
■ **hacerse la permanente** to have a perm

el **permiso** NOUN
1 permission
□ Tengo que pedirles permiso a mis padres. I have to ask my parents' permission.
■ **¡Con permiso!** Excuse me.
2 leave
□ Pidió cinco días de permiso. He requested five days' leave. □ Mi hermano está de permiso. My brother is on leave.
3 permit
□ Necesitas un permiso de trabajo. You need a work permit.
■ **un permiso de conducir** a driving licence

permitir VERB [58]
to allow
□ No nos permiten fumar aquí. We're not allowed to smoke here.
■ **No me lo puedo permitir.** I can't afford it.
■ **¿Me permite?** May I?

pero CONJUNCTION
but
□ Me gustaría, pero no puedo. I'd like to, but I can't.

perpendicular (FEM **perpendicular**) ADJECTIVE
at right angles
□ una pared perpendicular a otra one wall at right angles to another

perplejo (FEM **perpleja**) ADJECTIVE
puzzled

la **perra** NOUN
dog
□ Es una perra muy buena. She's a very good dog.
■ **¿Es perra o perro?** Is it a bitch or a dog?

la **perrera** NOUN
dog's home

el **perrito** NOUN
■ **un perrito caliente** a hot dog

el **perro** NOUN
dog
■ **un perro callejero** a stray dog
■ **un perro guardián** a guard dog
■ **un perro pastor** a sheepdog
■ **un perro policía** a police dog
■ **un perro salchicha** a dachshund

el/la **persa** ADJECTIVE, NOUN
Persian

perseguir* VERB [50]
1 to chase
□ Me persigue la policía. The police are chasing me.
2 to persecute
□ Se siente perseguido por su ideología. He feels persecuted for his ideology.

la **persiana** NOUN
blind

persiguiendo VERB ▷ *see* **perseguir**

la **persona** NOUN
person
□ Es una persona encantadora. He's a charming person.
■ **en persona** in person
■ **personas** people □ Había unas diez personas en la sala. There were about ten people in the hall.

el **personaje** NOUN
1 character
□ los personajes de la novela the characters in the novel
2 figure
□ un personaje público a public figure

personal (FEM **personal**) ADJECTIVE
personal

el **personal** NOUN
staff

la **personalidad** NOUN
personality (PL personalities)

personalmente ADVERB
personally

la **perspectiva** NOUN
perspective
□ en perspectiva in perspective
■ **perspectivas** prospects □ buenas perspectivas económicas good economic prospects

persuadir VERB [58]
to persuade
□ Me persuadió para que la acompañara. She persuaded me to go with her.

pertenecer* VERB [12]
■ **pertenecer a** to belong to □ Este reloj perteneció a su abuelo. This watch belonged to his grandfather. □ No pertenezco a ningún partido político. I don't belong to any political party.

las **pertenencias** NOUN
belongings

la **pértiga** NOUN
pole
■ **el salto con pértiga** the pole vault

Perú MASC NOUN
Peru

el **peruano** (FEM la **peruana**) ADJECTIVE, NOUN
Peruvian

perverso (FEM **perversa**) ADJECTIVE
wicked

el **pervertido**, la **pervertida** NOUN
pervert

la **pesa** NOUN
weight
■ **hacer pesas** to do weight training

la **pesadez** NOUN
■ **Es una pesadez tener que madrugar.** *(colloquial)* It's such a pain having to get up early.
■ **¡Qué pesadez de película!** What a boring film!

la **pesadilla** NOUN
nightmare

pesado (FEM **pesada**) ADJECTIVE
1 heavy
2 tiring
3 boring
■ **¡No seas pesado!** Don't be a pain in the neck!

el **pesado**, la **pesada** NOUN
■ **Mi primo es un pesado.** My cousin is a pain in the neck.

el **pésame** NOUN
condolences *pl*
□ Fuimos a darle el pésame. We went to offer our condolences.

pesar VERB [25]
1 to weigh
□ El paquete pesaba 2 kilos. The package weighed 2 kilos. □ ¿Cuánto pesas? How much do you weigh? □ Tengo que pesarme. I must weigh myself.
2 to be heavy
□ Esta maleta pesa mucho. This suitcase is very heavy. □ ¡No pesa nada! It's not heavy at all!
■ **pesar poco** to be very light
■ **Me pesa haberlo hecho.** I regret having done it.
■ **a pesar del mal tiempo** in spite of the bad weather
■ **a pesar de que la quiero** even though I love her

la **pesca** NOUN
fishing
□ ir de pesca to go fishing

la **pescadería** NOUN
fishmonger's (PL fishmongers' shops)

la **pescadilla** NOUN
whiting (PL whiting)

el **pescado** NOUN
fish (PL fish)
□ Quiero comprar pescado. I want to buy some fish.

el **pescador** NOUN
fisherman (PL fishermen)
□ Mi tío es pescador. My uncle is a fisherman.

pescar* VERB [48]
1 to fish
□ Los domingos íbamos a pescar. On Sundays we used to go fishing.
2 to catch
□ Pescamos varias truchas. We caught several trout. □ Me pescaron fumando. I got caught smoking.

el **pesero** NOUN *(Mexico)*
minibus (PL minibuses)

la **peseta** NOUN
peseta

pesimista (FEM **pesimista**) ADJECTIVE
pessimistic
□ una visión pesimista a pessimistic view
■ **No seas pesimista.** Don't be a pessimist.

el/la **pesimista** NOUN
pessimist

pésimo (FEM **pésima**) ADJECTIVE
terrible
□ La comida era pésima. The food was terrible.

el **peso** NOUN
1 weight
□ ganar peso to gain weight □ Ha perdido mucho peso. He's lost a lot of weight.
■ **La fruta se vende a peso.** Fruit is sold by weight.
2 scales *pl*
3 peso

pesquero (FEM **pesquera**) ADJECTIVE
fishing
□ un pueblecito pesquero a fishing village

la **pestaña** NOUN
eyelash (PL eyelashes)

pestañear VERB [25]
to blink

la **peste** NOUN
1 plague
2 stink
□ ¡Qué peste hay aquí! There's a real stink in here!

el **pesticida** NOUN
pesticide

el **pestillo** NOUN
1 bolt
2 latch (PL latches)

la **petaca** NOUN
hip flask

el **pétalo** NOUN
petal

el **petardo** NOUN
firecracker

la **petición** (PL las **peticiones**) NOUN

1 request
□ Hicieron una petición al gobierno. They made a request to the government. □ a petición de la pareja at the request of the couple
2 petition
□ firmar una petición to sign a petition

el **petirrojo** NOUN
robin

el **petróleo** NOUN
oil

el **petrolero** NOUN
oil tanker

el **pez** (PL los **peces**) NOUN
fish (PL fish)
□ Cogimos tres peces. We caught three fish.
■ **un pez de colores** a goldfish
LANGUAGE TIP Word for word, **pez de colores** means 'fish of colours'.
■ **Se sentía como el pez en el agua.** He felt in his element.

la **pezuña** NOUN
hoof (PL hooves)

el/la **pianista** NOUN
pianist
□ Soy pianista. I'm a pianist.

el **piano** NOUN
piano
■ **un piano de cola** a grand piano

piar* VERB [21]
to chirp

el **pibe**, la **piba** NOUN *(River Plate)*
kid *(colloquial)*

la **picada** NOUN *(Latin America)*
■ **El avión cayó en picada.** The plane nose-dived.

picado (FEM **picada**) ADJECTIVE
1 bad
2 choppy
■ **El avión cayó en picado.** The plane nose-dived.

la **picadura** NOUN
1 bite
2 sting

picante (FEM **picante**) ADJECTIVE
hot

el **picaporte** NOUN
door handle

picar* VERB [48]
1 to bite
□ Me han picado los mosquitos. I've been bitten by mosquitoes.
2 to sting
3 to chop up
□ Luego picas un poquito de jamón. Then you chop up a bit of ham.
4 to mince
■ **La salsa pica bastante.** The sauce is quite hot.
■ **Saqué algunas cosas para picar.** I put out some nibbles.
■ **Me pica la espalda.** I've got an itchy back.
■ **Me pica la garganta.** My throat tickles.

el **pichi** NOUN
pinafore

el **picnic** (PL los **picnics**) NOUN
picnic

el **pico** NOUN
1 beak
2 peak
3 pick
■ **Eran las tres y pico.** It was just after three.
■ **doscientos y pico euros** just over two hundred euros
■ **cuello de pico** V-neck
■ **la hora pico** *(Latin America)* the rush hour

picoso (FEM **picosa**) ADJECTIVE *(Mexico)*
hot *(food)*

pidiendo VERB ▷ *see* **pedir**

el **pie** NOUN
foot (PL feet)
□ Fuimos a pie. We went on foot. □ Al pie de la página hay una explicación. There's an explanation at the foot of the page.
■ **Estaba de pie junto a mi cama.** He was standing next to my bed.
■ **ponerse de pie** to stand up
■ **de pies a cabeza** from head to foot

la **piedad** NOUN
mercy
□ tener piedad de alguien to have mercy on someone

la **piedra** NOUN
stone
□ Nos tiraban piedras. They were throwing stones at us.
■ **una piedra preciosa** a precious stone
■ **Cuando me lo dijeron me quedé de piedra.** I was stunned when they told me.

la **piel** NOUN
1 skin
□ Tengo la piel grasa. I have greasy skin.
2 fur
□ un abrigo de pieles a fur coat
3 leather
□ un bolso de piel a leather bag
4 peel

pienso VERB ▷ *see* **pensar**

pierdo VERB ▷ *see* **perder**

la **pierna** NOUN
leg
■ **una pierna de cordero** a leg of lamb

la **pieza** NOUN
piece

□ una pieza del rompecabezas a piece of the jigsaw puzzle □ una pieza de recambio a spare part

el **pijama** NOUN
pyjamas *pl*

pijo (FEM **pija**) ADJECTIVE
posh

la **pila** NOUN
1 battery (PL batteries)
□ Funciona con pilas. It goes on batteries.
2 pile
□ una pila de revistas a pile of magazines
3 sink

el **pilar** NOUN
pillar

la **píldora** NOUN
pill
□ ¿Tomas la píldora? Are you on the pill?

la **pileta** NOUN *(River Plate)*
sink

pillar VERB [25]
1 to catch
□ pillar a un ladrón to catch a thief □ ¡Vaya catarro que has pillado! That's a nasty cold you've caught. □ Lo pillé fumando. I caught him smoking.
■ **Se pilló los dedos en la puerta.** He caught his fingers in the door.
2 to hit
□ La pilló una moto. She was hit by a motorbike.
■ **La estación nos pilla cerca de casa.** The station is pretty close to our house.

pillo (FEM **pilla**) ADJECTIVE
1 crafty
2 naughty

el/la **piloto** NOUN
1 pilot
2 driver
■ **piloto de carreras** racing driver

el **pimentón** NOUN
paprika

la **pimienta** NOUN
pepper
□ pimienta negra black pepper

el **pimiento** NOUN
pepper
□ un pimiento morrón a red pepper

el **pin** (PL los **pins**) NOUN
badge

el **pincel** NOUN
paintbrush (PL paintbrushes)

el/la **pinchadiscos** (PL los/las **pinchadiscos**) NOUN
disc jockey (PL disc jockeys)

pinchar VERB [25]
1 to prick
□ Me pinché con un alfiler. I pricked myself on a pin.
2 to burst
□ El clavo pinchó la pelota. The nail burst the ball.
■ **Me pincharon en el brazo.** They gave me an injection in the arm.
■ **Se me pinchó una rueda.** I had a puncture.
■ **Los cactus pinchan.** Cactuses are prickly.

el **pinchazo** NOUN
1 puncture
□ Tuve un pinchazo en la autopista. I got a puncture on the motorway.
2 sharp pain

el **pincho** NOUN
1 thorn
2 snack
□ Tomamos unos pinchos en el bar. We had some snacks in the bar.
■ **un pincho moruno** a kebab

el **ping-pong** NOUN
table tennis
□ jugar al ping-pong to play table tennis

el **pingüino** NOUN
penguin

el **pino** NOUN
pine tree
■ **hacer el pino** to do a headstand
LANGUAGE TIP Word for word, **hacer el pino** means 'to do the pine tree'.

la **pinta** NOUN
■ **tener buena pinta** to look good □ La paella tiene muy buena pinta. The paella looks delicious.
■ **Con esas gafas tienes pinta de maestra.** You look like a teacher with those glasses on.

las **pintadas** NOUN
graffiti

el **pintalabios** NOUN (PL los **pintalabios**)
lipstick

pintar VERB [25]
1 to paint
□ Quiero pintar la habitación de azul. I want to paint the room blue.
2 to colour in
□ Dibujó un árbol y lo pintó. He drew a tree and coloured it in.
■ **Nunca me pinto.** I never wear makeup.
■ **pintarse los labios** to put on lipstick
■ **pintarse las uñas** to paint one's nails

el **pintor**, la **pintora** NOUN
painter
□ Soy pintor. I'm a painter.

pintoresco (FEM **pintoresca**) ADJECTIVE
picturesque

la **pintura** NOUN
1 paint

□ Tengo que comprar más pintura. I've got to buy some more paint.
2 painting
□ Me gusta la pintura abstracta. I like abstract painting. □ varias pinturas al óleo several oil paintings

la **pinza** NOUN
1 clothes peg
2 hairgrip
3 pincer
■ **unas pinzas** a pair of tweezers

la **piña** NOUN
1 pine cone
2 pineapple

el **piñón** (PL los **piñones**) NOUN
1 pine nut
2 sprocket

el **piojo** NOUN
louse (PL lice)

la **pipa** NOUN
1 pipe
□ Fuma en pipa. He smokes a pipe.
2 seed
■ **comer pipas** to eat sunflower seeds

el **pipí** NOUN
wee
□ hacer pipí to have a wee

la **piragua** NOUN
canoe (PL canoes)

el **piragüismo** NOUN
canoeing

la **pirámide** NOUN
pyramid

pirata (FEM **pirata**) ADJECTIVE
pirate

el/la **pirata** NOUN
pirate
■ **un pirata informático** a hacker

piratear VERB [25]
to hack into a system

los **Pirineos** NOUN
the Pyrenees

el **piropo** NOUN
compliment
□ echar piropos a alguien to make compliments to someone

el **pirulí** (PL los **pirulís**) NOUN
lollipop

la **pisada** NOUN
1 footprint
2 footstep

el **pisapapeles** (PL los **pisapapeles**) NOUN
paperweight

pisar VERB [25]
1 to walk on
■ **¿Se puede pisar el suelo de la cocina?** Can I walk on the kitchen floor?
2 to tread on
□ Perdona, te he pisado. Sorry, I trod on your foot.
■ **Pisé el acelerador a fondo.** I put my foot down.

la **piscina** NOUN
swimming pool

Piscis MASC NOUN
Pisces
■ **Soy piscis.** I'm Pisces.

el **piso** NOUN
1 flat
□ Vivimos en un piso céntrico. We live in a flat in the town centre.
2 floor
□ Su oficina está en el segundo piso. His office is on the second floor. □ El piso estaba lleno de papeles. The floor was covered in pieces of paper.

la **pista** NOUN
1 clue
□ ¿Te doy una pista? Shall I give you a clue?
2 track
□ Los cazadores siguen las pistas del animal. The hunters follow the animal's tracks.
3 court *(sport)*
■ **la pista de aterrizaje** the runway
■ **la pista de baile** the dance floor
■ **la pista de carreras** the racetrack
■ **la pista de esquí** the ski slope
■ **la pista de patinaje** the ice rink

la **pistola** NOUN
pistol

pitar VERB [25]
1 to blow one's whistle
□ El policía nos pitó. The policeman blew his whistle at us.
2 to hoot
□ No sé por qué me pita. I don't know why he's hooting at me.
■ **Salió pitando.** He was off like a shot.

pitear VERB [25] *(Latin America)*
to whistle

el **pito** NOUN
whistle
■ **Me importa un pito.** I don't care a hoot.

el **piyama** NOUN *(Latin America)*
pyjamas *pl*

la **pizarra** NOUN
1 blackboard
2 slate

la **pizca** NOUN
pinch
□ una pizca de sal a pinch of salt

la **pizza** NOUN
pizza

la **placa** NOUN
1 plaque
□ una placa conmemorativa a

commemorative plaque
2 badge
3 hotplate
■ **una placa de matrícula** a number plate

el **placer** NOUN
pleasure

la **plaga** NOUN
1 pest
□ una plaga que estropea los cultivos a pest that damages the crops
2 plague
□ las plagas de Egipto the plagues of Egypt
■ **la plaga del terrorismo** the scourge of terrorism

el **plan** NOUN
plan
□ ¿Qué planes tienes para este verano? What are your plans for the summer?
■ **viajar en plan económico** to travel cheap
■ **Lo dije en plan de broma.** I said it as a joke.
■ **el plan de estudios** the syllabus

la **plancha** NOUN
iron
■ **pescado a la plancha** grilled fish

planchar VERB [25]
1 to iron
□ Tengo que planchar esta camisa. I've got to iron this shirt.
2 to do the ironing
□ ¿Quieres que planche? Do you want me to do the ironing?

el **planeador** NOUN
glider

planear VERB [25]
1 to plan
2 to glide

el **planeta** NOUN
planet

la **planificación** NOUN
planning
■ **planificación familiar** family planning

planificar* VERB [48]
to plan

plano (FEM **plana**) ADJECTIVE
flat

el **plano** NOUN
1 street plan
2 plan
■ **en primer plano** in close-up

la **planta** NOUN
1 plant
□ regar las plantas to water the plants
2 floor
□ El edificio tiene tres plantas. The building has three floors. □ la planta baja the ground floor
■ **la planta del pie** the sole of the foot

plantado (FEM **plantada**) ADJECTIVE
■ **dejar a alguien plantado** to stand someone up

plantar VERB [25]
to plant

plantear VERB [25]
to bring up
□ Se lo plantearé al jefe. I'll bring it up with the boss.
■ **Incluso me planteé dejar los estudios.** I even thought of giving up my studies.

la **plantilla** NOUN
1 insole
2 staff

el **plástico** NOUN
plastic
□ cubiertos de plástico plastic cutlery

la **Plastilina®** NOUN
Plasticine®

la **plata** NOUN
1 silver
2 money *(Latin America)*

la **plataforma** NOUN
platform
□ zapatos de plataforma platform shoes
■ **una plataforma petrolífera** an oil rig

el **plátano** NOUN
banana

platicar* VERB [48] *(Mexico)*
1 to talk
□ Estuve platicando con Manuel. I was talking to Manuel.
2 to tell
□ ¿Qué te platicaron? What did they tell you?

el **platillo** NOUN
■ **un platillo volante** a flying saucer
■ **los platillos** the cymbals

el **platino** NOUN
platinum

el **plato** NOUN
1 plate
□ ¿Me pasas un plato? Could you pass me a plate?
2 dish (PL dishes)
□ un plato típico de Galicia a typical Galician dish
■ **el plato del día** the dish of the day
3 course
□ ¿Qué hay de segundo plato? What's for the main course?
■ **un plato combinado** a main course with vegetables included
4 saucer

la **playa** NOUN
1 beach (PL beaches)
□ Los niños jugaban en la playa. The

Spanish-English

P

children were playing on the beach.
2 seaside
□ Prefiero la playa a la montaña. I prefer the seaside to the mountains.
la **playera** NOUN
1 canvas shoe
2 T-shirt *(Mexico)*
la **plaza** NOUN
1 square
□ la plaza del pueblo the town square
■ **la plaza mayor** the main square
2 market
□ No había pescado en la plaza. There was no fish at the market.
3 place
□ Todavía quedan plazas. There are still some places left.
■ **una plaza de toros** a bullring
el **plazo** NOUN
1 period
□ en un plazo de diez días within a period of ten days
■ **El viernes se cumple el plazo.** Friday is the deadline.
2 instalment
□ pagar a plazos to pay in instalments
□ comprar a plazos to buy on instalments
■ **una solución a corto plazo** a short-term solution
plegable (FEM **plegable**) ADJECTIVE
folding
plegar* VERB [34]
to fold
pleno (FEM **plena**) ADJECTIVE
■ **en pleno verano** in the middle of summer
■ **a plena luz del día** in broad daylight
la **pletina** NOUN
tape deck
pliegue VERB ▷ *see* **plegar**
el **pliegue** NOUN
1 fold
2 pleat
el **plomero**, la **plomera** NOUN *(Latin America)*
plumber
el **plomo** NOUN
lead
■ **gasolina sin plomo** unleaded petrol
■ **Se han fundido los plomos.** The fuses have blown.
la **pluma** NOUN
1 feather
2 pen
■ **una pluma atómica** *(Latin America)* a ballpoint pen
■ **una pluma estilográfica** a fountain pen
el **plural** ADJECTIVE, NOUN
plural
la **población** (PL las **poblaciones**) NOUN
1 population
2 town
pobre (FEM **pobre**) ADJECTIVE
poor
□ Somos pobres. We're poor.
■ **¡Pobre Pedro!** Poor Pedro!
■ **los pobres** the poor
la **pobreza** NOUN
poverty
poco (FEM **poca**) ADJECTIVE, ADVERB, PRONOUN
not much
□ Hay poca leche. There isn't much milk.
□ Tenemos muy poco tiempo. We have very little time.
■ **Sus libros son poco conocidos aquí.** His books are not very well known here.
■ **un poco** a bit □ ¿Tienes frío? — Un poco. Are you cold? — A bit. □ ¿Me das un poco? Can I have a bit? □ He bebido un poco, pero no estoy borracho. I had a bit to drink, but I'm not drunk.
■ **Tomé un poco de vino.** I had a little wine.
■ **pocos** not many □ Tiene pocos amigos. He hasn't got many friends.
■ **unos pocos** a few □ Me llevé unos pocos. I took a few with me.
■ **poco a poco** little by little
■ **poco después** shortly after
■ **dentro de poco** in a short time
■ **hace poco** not long ago
■ **por poco** nearly □ Por poco me caigo. I nearly fell.
podar VERB [25]
to prune
el **poder** NOUN
power
□ estar en el poder to be in power
poder* VERB [40]
1 can
□ Yo puedo ayudarte. I can help you. □ ¡No puede ser! That can't be true! □ ¿Puedo usar tu teléfono? Can I use your phone? □ Pudiste haberte hecho daño. You could have hurt yourself. □ ¡Me lo podías haber dicho! You could have told me! □ Aquí no se puede fumar. You can't smoke here.
2 to be able to
□ Creo que mañana no voy a poder ir. I don't think I'll be able to come tomorrow.
■ **¿Se puede?** May I?
■ **Puede que llegue mañana.** He might arrive tomorrow.
■ **Puede ser.** It's possible.
■ **No puedo con tanto trabajo.** I can't cope with so much work.
poderoso (FEM **poderosa**) ADJECTIVE

powerful
el **podólogo**, la **podóloga** NOUN
chiropodist
podrido (FEM **podrida**) ADJECTIVE
rotten
podrirse VERB [58] = **pudrirse**
el **poema** NOUN
poem
la **poesía** NOUN
1 poetry
□ Me gusta la poesía. I like poetry.
2 poem
□ una poesía de Machado a poem by Machado
el/la **poeta** NOUN
poet
el **póker** NOUN
poker
polaco (FEM **polaca**) ADJECTIVE
Polish
el **polaco**, la **polaca** NOUN
Pole
■ **los polacos** the Poles
el **polaco** NOUN
Polish
la **polémica** NOUN
controversy (PL controversies)
polémico (FEM **polémica**) ADJECTIVE
controversial
el **polen** NOUN
pollen
■ **alergia al polen** hay fever
el **policía** NOUN
policeman (PL policemen)
□ Es policía. He's a policeman.
la **policía** NOUN
1 police
□ Llamamos a la policía. We called the police.
2 policewoman (PL policewomen)
□ Soy policía. I'm a policewoman.
policíaco (FEM **policíaca**) ADJECTIVE
■ **una novela policíaca** a detective novel
el **polideportivo** NOUN
sports centre
la **polilla** NOUN
moth (PL moths)
la **polio** NOUN
polio
la **política** NOUN
1 politics *sing*
□ Hablaban de política. They were talking about politics.
2 policy (PL policies)
□ política exterior foreign policy
3 politician
□ Soy política. I'm a politician.
político (FEM **política**) ADJECTIVE
political
el **político** NOUN
politician
el **pollo** NOUN
chicken
■ **pollo asado** roast chicken
el **polluelo** NOUN
chick
el **polo** NOUN
1 ice lolly (PL ice lollies)
2 polo shirt
■ **el Polo Norte** the North Pole
■ **el Polo Sur** the South Pole
Polonia FEM NOUN
Poland
el **polvo** NOUN
dust
■ **limpiar el polvo** to dust
■ **quitar el polvo** to do the dusting
■ **quitar el polvo a algo** to dust something
■ **en polvo** powdered □ leche en polvo powdered milk
■ **polvos de talco** talcum powder
■ **Estoy hecho polvo.** I'm shattered.
■ **echar un polvo** *(vulgar)* to have a shag
la **pólvora** NOUN
gunpowder
la **pomada** NOUN
ointment
el **pomelo** NOUN
grapefruit (PL grapefruit)
el **pomo** NOUN
handle
la **pompa** NOUN
1 bubble
□ pompas de jabón soap bubbles
2 pomp
el **pómulo** NOUN
cheekbone
ponchar VERB [25] *(Mexico)*
■ **Se nos ponchó una llanta.** We had a puncture.
el **ponche** NOUN
punch (PL punches)
el **poncho** NOUN
poncho (PL ponchos)
pondrá VERB ▷ *see* **poner**
poner* VERB [41]
1 to put
□ ¿Dónde pongo mis cosas? Where shall I put my things?
2 to put on
□ Me puse el abrigo. I put on my coat. □ Voy a poner las patatas. I'm going to put the potatoes on. □ ¿Pongo música? Shall I put some music on? □ Pon el radiador. Put the heater on.
■ **No sé que ponerme.** I don't know what

to wear.
■ **Ponlo más alto.** Turn it up.
■ **¿Ponen alguna película esta noche?** Is there a film on tonight?
3 to set
□ La maestra nos puso un examen. Our teacher set us an exam. □ Puse el despertador para las siete. I set the alarm for seven o'clock. □ poner la mesa to set the table
4 to put in
□ Queremos poner calefacción. We want to put in central heating.
■ **¿Me pone con el Sr. García, por favor?** Could you put me through to Mr. Garcia, please?
■ **Le pusieron Mónica.** They called her Monica.
■ **¿Qué te pongo?** What can I get you?
■ **Cuando se lo dije se puso muy triste.** He was very sad when I told him.
■ **¡Qué guapa te has puesto!** You look beautiful!
■ **Se puso a mi lado en clase.** He sat down beside me in class.
■ **ponerse a hacer algo** to start doing something

el **poney** (PL los **poneys**) NOUN
pony (PL ponies)

pongo VERB ▷ *see* **poner**

pop (FEM **pop**, PL **pop**) ADJECTIVE
pop
□ música pop pop music

el **popote** NOUN *(Mexico)*
straw

popular (FEM **popular**) ADJECTIVE
popular

por PREPOSITION
1 for
□ Lo hice por mis padres. I did it for my parents. □ Lo vendió por 100 euros. He sold it for 100 euros. □ Me castigaron por mentir. I was punished for lying.
2 through
□ La conozco por mi hermano. I know her through my brother. □ por la ventana through the window □ Pasamos por Valencia. We went through Valencia.
3 by
□ Fueron apresados por la policía. They were captured by the police. □ por correo by post □ Me agarró por el brazo. He grabbed me by the arm.
4 along
□ Paseábamos por la playa. We were walking along the beach.
5 around
□ viajar por el mundo to travel around the world □ Viven por esta zona. They live around this area.
6 because of
□ Tuvo que suspenderse por el mal tiempo. It had to be cancelled because of bad weather.
7 per
□ 100 kilómetros por hora 100 kilometres per hour □ diez euros por persona ten euros per person
■ **por aquí cerca** near here
■ **por escrito** in writing
■ **por la mañana** in the morning
■ **por la noche** at night
■ **por mí ...** as far as I'm concerned ...
■ **¿Por qué?** Why?

la **porcelana** NOUN
porcelain

el **porcentaje** NOUN
percentage

el **porche** NOUN
porch (PL porches)

la **porción** (PL las **porciones**) NOUN
portion

porno (FEM **porno**, PL **porno**) ADJECTIVE
porn
□ una película porno a porn film

la **pornografía** NOUN
pornography

pornográfico (FEM **pornográfica**) ADJECTIVE
pornographic

el **poro** NOUN
1 pore
2 leek *(Mexico)*

el **poroto** NOUN *(Chile, River Plate)*
bean

porque CONJUNCTION
because
□ No fuimos porque llovía. We didn't go because it was raining.

la **porquería** NOUN
■ **Este CD es una porquería.** This CD's rubbish.

la **porra** NOUN
truncheon
■ **mandar a alguien a la porra** to send someone packing

el **porrazo** NOUN
■ **Me di un porrazo en la rodilla.** I banged my knee.
■ **Daba porrazos en la puerta.** He was banging on the door.

el **porro** NOUN
joint *(colloquial)*

la **portada** NOUN
1 front page
2 cover

el **portal** NOUN

1 hallway
□ Los buzones están en el portal. The letterboxes are in the hallway.
2 portal
■ **el portal de Belén** the nativity scene

portarse VERB [25]
■ **portarse bien** to behave well
■ **portarse mal** to behave badly
■ **Se portó muy bien conmigo.** He treated me very well.

portátil (FEM **portátil**) ADJECTIVE
portable

el **portavoz** (PL los **portavoces**) NOUN
spokesman (PL spokesmen)

la **portavoz** (PL las **portavoces**) NOUN
spokeswoman (PL spokeswomen)

el **portazo** NOUN
■ **Dio un portazo.** He slammed the door.

la **portera** NOUN
1 caretaker
2 goalkeeper

la **portería** NOUN
goal
□ El balón entró en la portería. The ball went into the goal.

el **portero** NOUN
1 caretaker
2 goalkeeper
■ **un portero automático** an entryphone

LANGUAGE TIP Word for word, **portero automático** means 'automatic doorman'.

el **portorriqueño** (FEM la **portorriqueña**) ADJECTIVE, NOUN
Puerto Rican

Portugal MASC NOUN
Portugal

el **portugués** (FEM la **portuguesa**, MASC PL los **portugueses**) ADJECTIVE, NOUN
Portuguese

el **portugués** NOUN
Portuguese

el **porvenir** NOUN
future

posar VERB [25]
to pose
□ Posó para los fotógrafos. He posed for photographs.
■ **posarse** to land □ El pájaro se posó en la rama. The bird landed on the brach.

la **posdata** NOUN
postscript

poseer* VERB [30]
to possess

la **posguerra** NOUN
■ **durante la posguerra** during the postwar period
■ **los años de posguerra** the years after the war

la **posibilidad** NOUN
1 possibility (PL possibilities)
□ Es una posibilidad. It's a possibility.
2 chance
□ Tendrás la posibilidad de viajar. You'll have the chance to travel.
■ **Tiene muchas posibilidades de ganar.** He has a good chance of winning.

posible (FEM **posible**) ADJECTIVE
possible
□ Es posible. It's possible.
■ **hacer todo lo posible** to do everything possible
■ **Es posible que ganen.** They might win.

la **posición** (PL las **posiciones**) NOUN
position
□ una posición estratégica a strategic position
■ **Está en primera posición.** He's in first place.

positivo (FEM **positiva**) ADJECTIVE
positive
■ **El test dio positivo.** The test was positive.

posponer* VERB [41]
to postpone

posta
■ **a posta** ADVERB on purpose

la **postal** NOUN
postcard

el **poste** NOUN
1 post
2 pole

el **póster** (PL los **pósters**) NOUN
poster

posterior (FEM **posterior**) ADJECTIVE
rear
□ los asientos posteriores the rear seats
■ **la parte posterior** the rear

postizo (FEM **postiza**) ADJECTIVE
false

el **postizo** NOUN
hairpiece

el **postre** NOUN
dessert
□ De postre tomé un helado. I had ice cream for dessert. □ ¿Qué hay de postre? What's for dessert?

la **postura** NOUN
position

potable (FEM **potable**) ADJECTIVE
■ **agua potable** drinking water

el **potaje** NOUN
stew
□ potaje de garbanzos chickpea stew

la **potencia** NOUN
power
□ la potencia del motor the power of the

engine

■ **Es un artista en potencia.** He has the makings of an artist.

potencial (FEM **potencial**) ADJECTIVE
potential

potente (FEM **potente**) ADJECTIVE
powerful

el **potro** NOUN
1 colt
2 horse

el **pozo** NOUN
well

la **práctica** NOUN
practice
□ No tengo mucha práctica. I haven't had much practice.
■ **en la práctica** in practice
■ **poner algo en práctica** to put something into practice

prácticamente ADVERB
practically

practicante (FEM **practicante**) ADJECTIVE
practising
□ Es una católica practicante. She is a practising Catholic.

el/la **practicante** NOUN
nurse

practicar* VERB [48]
to practise
□ Tengo que practicar un poco más. I need to practise a bit more.
■ **No practico ningún deporte.** I don't do any sports.

práctico (FEM **práctica**) ADJECTIVE
practical
□ Es una mujer muy práctica. She is a very practical woman.

el **prado** NOUN
meadow

la **precaución** (PL las **precauciones**) NOUN
precaution
□ tomar precauciones to take precautions
■ **con precaución** with caution

precavido (FEM **precavida**) ADJECTIVE
■ **Es muy precavida.** She's always very well-prepared.

el **precinto** NOUN
seal

el **precio** NOUN
price
□ Han subido los precios. Prices have gone up.
■ **¿Qué precio tiene?** How much is it?

la **preciosidad** NOUN
■ **La casa es una preciosidad.** The house is beautiful.

precioso (FEM **preciosa**) ADJECTIVE
beautiful
□ ¡Es precioso! It's beautiful!

el **precipicio** NOUN
precipice

precipitarse VERB [25]
■ **No hay que precipitarse.** There's no need to rush into anything.
■ **Reconozco que me precipité al tomar esa decisión.** I admit I rushed into the decision.

precisamente ADVERB
precisely

precisar VERB [25]
■ **¿Puedes precisar un poco más?** Can you be a little more specific?
■ **Precisó que no se trataba de un virus.** He said specifically that it was not a virus.

preciso (FEM **precisa**) ADJECTIVE
1 precise
□ Recibió instrucciones precisas. He received precise instructions. □ en ese preciso momento at that precise moment
2 accurate
□ un reloj muy preciso a very accurate watch
■ **si es preciso** if necessary
■ **No es preciso que vengas.** There's no need for you to come.

precoz (FEM **precoz**, PL **precoces**) ADJECTIVE
precocious

predecir* VERB [15]
to predict

predicar* VERB [48]
to preach

la **predicción** (PL las **predicciones**) NOUN
prediction

predicho VERB ▷ *see* **predecir**

preescolar (FEM **preescolara**) ADJECTIVE
pre-school

prefabricado (FEM **prefabricada**) ADJECTIVE
prefabricated

la **preferencia** NOUN
1 preference
□ No tengo ninguna preferencia. I have no preference.
2 priority
□ Tienen preferencia los coches que vienen por la derecha. Cars coming from the right have priority.

preferido (FEM **preferida**) ADJECTIVE
favourite

preferir* VERB [51]
to prefer
□ Prefiero un buen libro a una película. I prefer a good book to a film.
■ **Prefiero ir mañana.** I'd rather go tomorrow.

prefiero VERB ▷ *see* **preferir**

el **prefijo** NOUN

code

□ ¿Cuál es el prefijo de Andorra? What is the code for Andorra?

la **pregunta** NOUN

question

□ hacer una pregunta to ask a question

preguntar VERB [25]

to ask

□ Siempre me preguntas lo mismo. You're always asking me the same question.

■ **Me preguntó por ti.** He asked after you.

■ **Me pregunto si estará enterado.** I wonder if he's heard yet.

prehistórico (FEM **prehistórica**) ADJECTIVE

prehistoric

el **prejuicio** NOUN

prejudice

■ **Yo no tengo prejuicios.** I'm not prejudiced.

prematuro (FEM **prematura**) ADJECTIVE

premature

premiar VERB [25]

1 to award a prize to

□ Han premiado su película. His film has been awarded a prize.

■ **el director premiado** the award-winning director

2 to reward

□ premiar los esfuerzos de un niño to reward a child's efforts

el **premio** NOUN

1 prize

□ llevarse un premio to get a prize

2 reward

□ como premio a tu sacrificio as a reward for your sacrifice

■ **el premio gordo** the jackpot

la **prenda** NOUN

garment

prender VERB [8]

1 to light

2 to switch on *(Latin America)*

■ **prender fuego a algo** to set fire to something

la **prensa** NOUN

press

□ una rueda de prensa a press conference

la **preocupación** (PL las **preocupaciones**) NOUN

worry (PL worries)

preocupado (FEM **preocupada**) ADJECTIVE

worried

■ **estar preocupado por algo** to be worried about something

preocupar VERB [25]

to worry

□ No te preocupes. Don't worry. □ Me preocupa su salud. I'm worried about his health.

■ **preocuparse por algo** to worry about something

■ **Si llego un poco tarde se preocupa.** If I arrive a bit late he gets worried.

■ **Yo me preocupo de comprar las entradas.** I'll see to buying the tickets.

preparar VERB [25]

1 to prepare

□ No he preparado el discurso. I haven't prepared my speech.

2 to prepare for

□ ¿Te has preparado el examen? Have you prepared for the exam?

3 to cook

□ Mi madre estaba preparando la cena. My mother was cooking dinner.

■ **Me estaba preparando para salir.** I was getting ready to go out.

los **preparativos** NOUN

preparations

la **presa** NOUN

1 dam

2 prey

3 prisoner

prescindir VERB [58]

■ **prescindir de** to do without □ No puede prescindir de su secretaria. He can't do without his secretary.

la **presencia** NOUN

presence

□ en presencia de un sacerdote in the presence of a priest

■ **El puesto requiere buena presencia.** A smart appearance is required for the position.

presenciar VERB [25]

to witness

el **presentador**, la **presentadora** NOUN

1 presenter

2 newsreader

presentar VERB [25]

1 to introduce

□ Me presentó a sus padres. He introduced me to his parents.

2 to hand in

□ Mañana tengo que presentar un trabajo. I have to hand in an essay tomorrow.

□ Presentó la dimisión. He handed in his resignation.

3 to present

□ J. Pérez presenta el programa. The programme is presented by J. Pérez.

■ **presentarse 1** to turn up □ Se presentó en mi casa sin avisar. He turned up at my house without warning. **2** to introduce oneself □ Me voy a presentar. Let me

introduce myself.
■ **presentarse a un examen** to sit an exam

el **presente** ADJECTIVE, NOUN
present
□ Juan no estaba presente en la reunión. Juan was not present at the meeting.
■ **el presente** the present
■ **los presentes** those present
■ **¡Presente!** Present!

el **presentimiento** NOUN
premonition

el **preservativo** NOUN
condom

la **presidenta** NOUN
1 president
2 chairperson

el **presidente** NOUN
1 president
2 chairman (PL chairmen)

la **presión** (PL las **presiones**) NOUN
pressure
■ **la presión sanguínea** blood pressure

presionar VERB [25]
1 to put pressure on
□ El casero lo está presionando para que se mude. The landlord is putting pressure on him to move.
2 to press

preso (FEM **presa**) ADJECTIVE
■ **Estuvo tres años preso.** He was in prison for three years.
■ **llevarse a alguien preso** to take someone prisoner

el **preso** NOUN
prisoner

prestado (FEM **prestada**) ADJECTIVE
■ **La cinta no es mía, es prestada.** It's not my tape, someone lent it to me.
■ **Le pedí prestada la bicicleta.** I asked if I could borrow his bicycle.
■ **Me dejó el coche prestado.** He lent me his car.

el **préstamo** NOUN
loan
□ Pidieron un préstamo al banco. They asked the bank for a loan.

prestar VERB [25]
to lend
□ Un amigo me prestó el traje. A friend lent me the suit.
■ **¿Me prestas el boli?** Can I borrow your pen?
■ **Tienes que prestar atención.** You must pay attention.
■ **Se negó a prestar ayuda.** He refused to help.

el **prestigio** NOUN
prestige
■ **una marca de prestigio** a prestigious brand

presumido (FEM **presumida**) ADJECTIVE
vain

presumir VERB [58]
to show off
□ Lleva ropa cara para presumir. He dresses expensively just to show off.
■ **Luis presume de guapo.** Luis thinks he's really handsome.

el **presupuesto** NOUN
1 budget
□ No puedo salirme del presupuesto. I can't go over the budget.
2 estimate
□ Le he pedido un presupuesto al carpintero. I've asked the joiner for an estimate.

pretender VERB [8]
1 to intend
□ Pretendo sacar al menos un notable. I intend to get at least a B.
■ **¿Qué pretendes decir con eso?** What do you mean by that?
2 to expect
□ ¡No pretenderás que te pague la comida! You're not expecting me to pay for your meal, are you?

LANGUAGE TIP Be careful! **pretender** does not mean **to pretend**.

el **pretexto** NOUN
excuse
□ Era sólo un pretexto. It was only an excuse.
■ **Vino con el pretexto de ver al abuelo.** He came in order to see Granddad, or so he said.

la **prevención** NOUN
prevention
□ prevención de incendios fire prevention
■ **las medidas de prevención** preventive measures

prevenir* VERB [56]
1 to prevent
□ prevenir un accidente to prevent an accident
2 to warn
□ Mi madre ya me había prevenido. My mother had already warned me.

prever* VERB [57]
1 to foresee
□ Nadie había previsto esta tragedia. Nobody had foreseen this tragedy.
■ **Han previsto nevadas en el norte.** Snow is forecast for the north.
2 to plan
■ **Tienen previsto acabar el metro para el 2003.** They plan to finish the metro by the

year 2003.
previo (FEM **previa**) ADJECTIVE
previous
□ No tengo experiencia previa en ese campo. I have no previous experience in the field.
previsible (FEM **previsible**) ADJECTIVE
foreseeable
previsto VERB
▷ *see also* **previsto** ADJECTIVE ▷ *see* **prever**
previsto (FEM **prevista**) ADJECTIVE
▷ *see also* **previsto** VERB
■ **Tengo previsto volver mañana.** I plan to return tomorrow.
■ **El avión tiene prevista su llegada a las dos.** The plane is due in at two o'clock.
■ **Como estaba previsto, ganó él.** As expected, he was the winner.
la **prima** NOUN
1 cousin
2 bonus
primario (FEM **primaria**) ADJECTIVE
primary
□ la educación primaria primary education
la **primavera** NOUN
spring
□ en primavera in spring
primer ▷ *see* **primero**
primero (FEM **primera**) ADJECTIVE, PRONOUN
first
□ el primer día the first day □ Primer plato: sopa. First course: soup. □ Primero vamos a comer. Let's eat first.
■ **en primera fila** in the front row
■ **En primer lugar, veamos los datos.** Firstly, let's look at the facts.
■ **primer ministro** prime minister
■ **Vivo en el primero.** I live on the first floor.
■ **Fui la primera en llegar.** I was the first to arrive.
■ **Juan es el primero de la clase.** Juan is top of the class.
■ **Lo primero es la salud.** The most important thing is your health.
■ **El examen será a primeros de mayo.** The exam will be at the beginning of May.
primitivo (FEM **primitiva**) ADJECTIVE
primitive
el **primo** NOUN
cousin
■ **primo segundo** second cousin
la **princesa** NOUN
princess (PL princesses)
principal (FEM **principal**) ADJECTIVE
main
□ el personaje principal the main character
■ **Lo principal es estar sano.** The main thing is to stay healthy.
principalmente ADVERB
mainly
el **príncipe** NOUN
prince
el/la **principiante** NOUN
beginner
el **principio** NOUN
1 beginning
□ El principio me gustó. I liked the beginning.
■ **Al principio parecía fácil.** It seemed easy at first.
■ **a principios de año** at the beginning of the year
2 principle
□ No tiene principios. He has no principles.
■ **En principio me parece una buena idea.** On the face of it, it's a good idea.
la **prioridad** NOUN
priority (PL priorities)
la **prisa** NOUN
rush
■ **Con las prisas me olvidé el paraguas.** In the rush I forgot my umbrella.
■ **¡Date prisa!** Hurry up!
■ **Tengo prisa.** I'm in a hurry.
la **prisión** (PL las **prisiones**) NOUN
prison
□ Lo condenaron a seis años de prisión. He was sentenced to six years in prison.
el **prisionero**, la **prisionera** NOUN
prisoner
los **prismáticos** NOUN
binoculars
privado (FEM **privada**) ADJECTIVE
private
□ un colegio privado a private school
privarse VERB [25]
■ **En vacaciones no me privo de nada.** When I'm on holiday I really spoil myself.
privatizar* VERB [13]
to privatize
el **privilegio** NOUN
privilege
el **pro** NOUN
■ **los pros y contras** the pros and cons
las **probabilidades** NOUN
■ **Tiene muchas probabilidades de ganar.** He has a very good chance of winning.
■ **No tengo muchas probabilidades de aprobar.** I don't have much chance of passing.
probable (FEM **probable**) ADJECTIVE
likely
□ Es muy probable. It's very likely.
■ **Es probable que llegue tarde.** He'll probably arrive late.

probablemente ADVERB
probably

el **probador** NOUN
changing room

probar* VERB [11]
1 to prove
□ La policía no pudo probarlo. The police could not prove it.
2 to taste
□ Probé la sopa para ver si le faltaba sal. I tasted the soup to see if it needed more salt.
3 to try
□ Prueba estas patatas a ver si te gustan. Try these potatoes and see if you like them.
□ Pruébalo antes para ver si funciona bien. Try it first and see if it works properly.
■ **Me probé un vestido.** I tried on a dress.

la **probeta** NOUN
test tube
■ **un niño probeta** a test-tube baby

el **problema** NOUN
problem
□ Tengo que resolver este problema. I have to solve this problem.
■ **Este coche nunca me ha dado problemas.** This car has never given me any trouble.
■ **tener problemas de estómago** to have stomach trouble

procedente (FEM **procedente**) ADJECTIVE
■ **procedente de** from □ el tren procedente de Barcelona the train from Barcelona

el **procesador** NOUN
processor
■ **un procesador de textos** a word processor

el **procesamiento** NOUN
■ **el procesamiento de textos** word processing

la **procesión** (PL las **procesiones**) NOUN
procession

el **proceso** NOUN
process (PL processes)
□ Será un proceso muy largo. It will be a long process.
■ **el proceso de datos** data processing

proclamar VERB [25]
to proclaim

procurar VERB [25]
to try
■ **Procura terminarlo mañana.** Try to finish it tomorrow.

la **producción** (PL las **producciones**) NOUN
production
■ **la producción en serie** mass production

producir* VERB [9]
1 to produce
□ La película fue producida por Juan Pérez. The film was produced by Juan Pérez. □ No producimos lo suficiente. We are not producing enough.
2 to cause
□ Puede producir efectos secundarios. It can cause side-effects.
■ **¿Cómo se produjo el accidente?** How did the accident happen?

productivo (FEM **productiva**) ADJECTIVE
productive

el **producto** NOUN
product
□ productos de limpieza cleaning products
□ productos lácteos dairy products
■ **los productos del campo** farm produce

el **productor**, la **productora** NOUN
producer

la **profesión** (PL las **profesiones**) NOUN
profession

el/la **profesional** ADJECTIVE, NOUN
professional

el **profesor**, la **profesora** NOUN
teacher
□ Amelia es profesora de inglés. Amelia is an English teacher.
■ **mi profesor particular** my private tutor
■ **un profesor universitario** a university lecturer

LANGUAGE TIP Be careful! The Spanish word **profesor** does not mean **professor**.

profundamente ADVERB
1 deeply
2 soundly

la **profundidad** NOUN
depth (PL depths)
□ la profundidad de la piscina the depth of the pool □ analizar un texto en profundidad to analyze a text in depth
■ **Tiene dos metros de profundidad.** It's two metres deep.

profundo (FEM **profunda**) ADJECTIVE
deep
■ **una piscina poco profunda** a shallow pool

el **programa** NOUN
1 programme
□ un programa de televisión a television programme
■ **un programa-concurso** a quiz show
■ **el programa de estudios** the syllabus
2 program

la **programación** NOUN
1 programmes *pl*
2 programming

el **programador**, la **programadora** NOUN

programmer
□ Balbino es programador. Balbino is a programmer.

programar VERB [25]
to programme
□ Programé el vídeo para grabar el partido. I programmed the video to tape the match.

progresar VERB [25]
to progress

el **progreso** NOUN
progress
□ progreso tecnológico technological progress
■ **Carmen ha hecho muchos progresos este trimestre.** Carmen has made great progress this term.

prohibir* VERB [42]
to ban
□ Le prohibieron la entrada en el edificio. He was banned from entering the building. □ Han prohibido las armas de fuego. Firearms have been banned.
■ **queda terminantemente prohibido** it is strictly forbidden
■ **Te prohíbo que toques mi ordenador.** I won't allow you to touch my computer.
■ **'prohibido fumar'** 'no smoking'

prolijo (FEM **prolija**) ADJECTIVE *(River Plate)*
neat

el **prólogo** NOUN
prologue

prolongar* VERB [37]
to extend

el **promedio** NOUN
average

la **promesa** NOUN
promise

prometer VERB [8]
to promise
□ Prometió llevarnos al cine. He promised to take us to the cinema.
■ **¡Te lo prometo!** I promise!

la **promoción** (PL **promociones**) NOUN
promotion
■ **Está en promoción.** It's on offer.

el **pronombre** NOUN
pronoun

pronosticar* VERB [48]
to forecast

el **pronóstico** NOUN
■ **el pronóstico del tiempo** the weather forecast

pronto ADVERB
1 soon
□ Los invitados llegarán pronto. The guests will be here soon.
■ **lo más pronto posible** as soon as possible
■ **¡Hasta pronto!** See you soon!
2 early
□ ¿Por qué has llegado tan pronto? Why have you arrived so early? □ Hoy me he levantado muy pronto. I got up very early today.
■ **De pronto, empezó a nevar.** All of a sudden it began to snow.

pronunciar VERB [25]
to pronounce
□ ¿Cómo se pronuncia esta palabra? How do you pronounce that word?

la **propaganda** NOUN
1 advertising
□ Las revistas están llenas de propaganda. Magazines are full of advertising.
■ **Han hecho mucha propaganda del concierto.** The concert has been well-advertised.
2 junk mail
□ Los buzones están llenos de propaganda. The letterboxes are full of junk mail.

propagarse* VERB [37]
to spread

la **propiedad** NOUN
property (PL properties)

el **propietario**, la **propietaria** NOUN
owner

la **propina** NOUN
tip
□ ¿Vamos a dejar propina? Shall we leave a tip?
■ **Siempre doy propina a los camareros.** I always tip waiters.

propio (FEM **propia**) ADJECTIVE
1 own
□ Tengo mi propia habitación. I have my own room.
2 himself (FEM herself)
□ Lo anunció el propio ministro. It was announced by the minister himself.
3 typical
□ Eso es muy propio de los países mediterráneos. That's very typical of the Mediterranean countries.
■ **un nombre propio** a proper noun

proponer* VERB [41]
1 to suggest
□ Nos propuso pagar la cena a medias. He suggested that we should share the cost of the meal.
■ **Me propuso un trato.** He made me a proposition.
2 to nominate
□ Propusieron a Manuel para alcalde. Manuel was nominated for mayor.
■ **Se ha propuesto adelgazar.** He's decided to lose some weight.

la **proporción** (PL las **proporciones**) NOUN
proportion

proporcional (FEM **proporcional**) ADJECTIVE
proportional

proporcionar VERB [25]
to provide
□ Ellos me proporcionaron la información. They provided me with the information.

el **propósito** NOUN
purpose
□ ¿Cuál es el propósito de su visita? What is the purpose of your visit?
■ **A propósito, ya tengo los billetes.** By the way, I've got the tickets.
■ **Lo hizo a propósito.** He did it deliberately.

la **propuesta** NOUN
proposal

propuesto VERB ▷ *see* **proponer**

la **prórroga** NOUN
1 extension
2 extra time

el **prospecto** NOUN
leaflet

prosperar VERB [25]
to do well

próspero (FEM **próspera**) ADJECTIVE
■ **¡Próspero Año Nuevo!** A prosperous New Year!

la **prostituta** NOUN
prostitute

el/la **protagonista** NOUN
main character
□ El protagonista no muere en la película. The main character doesn't die in the film.
■ **El protagonista es Tom Cruise.** Tom Cruise plays the lead.

la **protección** NOUN
protection

protector (FEM **protectora**) ADJECTIVE
protective
□ una funda protectora a protective cover

proteger* VERB [7]
to protect
□ El muro le protegió de las balas. The wall protected him from the bullets.
■ **Nos protegimos de la lluvia en la cabaña.** We sheltered from the rain in the hut.

la **proteína** NOUN
protein

la **protesta** NOUN
protest
□ como protesta por los despidos as a protest against redundancies

el/la **protestante** ADJECTIVE, NOUN
Protestant

protestar VERB [25]
1 to protest
□ Protestaron contra la subida de la gasolina. They protested against the rise in the price of petrol.
2 to complain
□ Cómete la verdura y no protestes. Eat your vegetables and don't complain.

el **provecho** NOUN
■ **¡Buen provecho!** Enjoy your meal!
■ **Sacó mucho provecho del curso.** He got a lot out of the course.

el **proverbio** NOUN
proverb

la **provincia** NOUN
province

provisional (FEM **provisional**) ADJECTIVE
provisional

las **provisiones** NOUN
provisions

provocar* VERB [48]
1 to provoke
□ No quería pegarle pero me provocó. I didn't mean to hit him but he provoked me.
2 to cause
□ La lluvia ha provocado graves inundaciones. The rain caused serious flooding.
■ **El incendio fue provocado.** The fire was started deliberately.

provocativo (FEM **provocativa**) ADJECTIVE
provocative

próximo (FEM **próxima**) ADJECTIVE
next
□ Lo haremos la próxima semana. We'll do it next week. □ la próxima vez next time
□ la próxima calle a la izquierda the next street on the left

proyectar VERB [25]
1 to show
2 to cast
■ **la imagen que un país proyecta al extranjero** the image a country projects abroad

el **proyectil** NOUN
missile

el **proyecto** NOUN
1 plan
□ ¿Tienes algún proyecto a la vista? Have you got any plans?
2 project
□ el proyecto en el que estamos trabajando the project we are working on
■ **un proyecto de ley** a bill

el **proyector** NOUN
projector

prudente (FEM **prudente**) ADJECTIVE
wise
□ Lo más prudente sería esperar. It would

be wisest to wait.
■ **Debería ser más prudente.** He should be more careful.
prueba VERB ▷ *see* **probar**
la **prueba** NOUN
1 test
□ El médico me hizo más pruebas. The doctor did some more tests.
■ **pruebas nucleares** nuclear tests
2 proof
□ Eso es la prueba de que lo hizo él. This is the proof that he did it.
■ **El fiscal presentó nuevas pruebas.** The prosecutor presented new evidence.
3 heat
□ la prueba de los cien metros valla the hundred metres hurdles heat
■ **a prueba de balas** bullet-proof
pruebo VERB ▷ *see* **probar**
la **psicóloga** NOUN
psychologist
la **psicología** NOUN
psychology
psicológico (FEM **psicológica**) ADJECTIVE
psychological
el **psicólogo** NOUN
psychologist
el/la **psiquiatra** NOUN
psychiatrist
psiquiátrico (FEM **psiquiátrica**) ADJECTIVE
psychiatric
ptas. ABBREVIATION *(= pesetas)*
pesetas
la **púa** NOUN
1 plectrum
2 tooth (PL teeth) *(of comb)*
el **pub** (PL los **pubs**) NOUN
bar
publicar* VERB [48]
to publish
la **publicidad** NOUN
1 advertising
□ una campaña de publicidad an advertising campaign
2 publicity
□ La conferencia tuvo poca publicidad. The conference received little publicity.
público (FEM **pública**) ADJECTIVE
public
el **público** NOUN
1 public
□ cerrado al público closed to the public
2 audience
3 spectators *pl*
pude VERB ▷ *see* **poder**
pudrirse VERB [58]
to rot
el **pueblo** NOUN
1 village
2 town
3 people *pl*
□ El pueblo está a favor de la democracia. The people are in favour of democracy.
puedo VERB ▷ *see* **poder**
el **puente** NOUN
bridge
■ **el puente aéreo** the shuttle service
LANGUAGE TIP Word for word, **puente aéreo** means 'air bridge'.
■ **hacer puente** to make a long weekend of it
DID YOU KNOW...?
When a public holiday falls on a Tuesday or Thursday people often take off Monday or Friday as well to give themselves a long weekend.
el **puerco** NOUN
1 pig
2 pork *(Mexico)*
el **puerro** NOUN
leek
la **puerta** NOUN
1 door
■ **un coche de cuatro puertas** a four-door car
2 gate
■ **Llaman a la puerta.** Somebody's at the door.
■ **Susana me acompañó a la puerta.** Susana saw me out.
■ **la puerta de embarque** boarding gate
el **puerto** NOUN
port
□ un puerto pesquero a fishing port
■ **un puerto deportivo** a marina
■ **un puerto de montaña** a mountain pass
Puerto Rico MASC NOUN
Puerto Rico
el **puertorriqueño** (FEM la **puertorriqueña**) ADJECTIVE, NOUN
Puerto Rican
pues CONJUNCTION
1 then
□ Tengo sueño. — ¡Pues vete a la cama! I'm tired. — Then go to bed!
2 well
□ Pues, como te iba contando ... Well, as I was saying ... □ ¡Pues no lo sabía! Well I didn't know!
■ **¡Pues claro!** Yes, of course!
la **puesta** NOUN
■ **la puesta de sol** sunset
■ **la puesta en libertad de dos presos** the release of two prisoners
puesto VERB ▷ *see* **poner**
el **puesto** NOUN

1 place
□ Acabé la carrera en primer puesto. I finished in first place.
2 stall
□ un puesto de verduras a vegetable stall
■ **un puesto de trabajo** a job
■ **un puesto de socorro** a first aid station
■ **puesto que** since □ Puesto que no lo querías, se lo di a Pedro. Since you didn't want it, I gave it to Pedro.

la **pulga** NOUN
flea

la **pulgada** NOUN
inch (PL inches)

el **pulgar** NOUN
thumb

pulir VERB [58]
to polish

el **pulmón** (PL los **pulmones**) NOUN
lung

la **pulpería** NOUN *(Latin America)*
shop

el **púlpito** NOUN
pulpit

el **pulpo** NOUN
octopus (PL octopuses)
□ Me gusta el pulpo. I like octopus.

pulsar VERB [25]
to press

la **pulsera** NOUN
bracelet
■ **un reloj de pulsera** a wrist watch

el **pulso** NOUN
pulse
□ El doctor le tomó el pulso. The doctor took his pulse.
■ **Tengo muy mal pulso.** My hand is very unsteady.
■ **Echamos un pulso y le gané.** We had an arm-wrestling match and I won.
■ **Lo levantó a pulso.** He lifted it with his bare hands.

el **pulverizador** NOUN
spray

el/la **punk** ADJECTIVE, NOUN
punk

la **punta** NOUN
1 nail *(metal)*
2 tip *(of finger, tongue)*
3 point *(of pen, knife)*
■ **Sácale punta al lápiz.** Sharpen your pencil.
■ **Vivo en la otra punta del pueblo.** I live at the other end of the town.
■ **la hora punta** the rush hour

el **puntapié** (PL los **puntapiés**) NOUN
■ **Le dio un puntapié a la piedra.** He kicked the stone.

la **puntería** NOUN
■ **tener buena puntería** to be a good shot

puntiagudo (FEM **puntiaguda**) ADJECTIVE
pointed

la **puntilla** NOUN
lace edging
■ **andar de puntillas** to tiptoe
■ **ponerse de puntillas** to stand on tiptoe

el **punto** NOUN
1 point
□ Perdieron por tres puntos. They lost by three points. □ Ése es un punto importante. That's an important point. □ desde ese punto de vista from that point of view
2 stitch (PL stitches)
3 dot
4 full stop
■ **punto y seguido** full stop, new sentence
■ **punto y aparte** full stop, new paragraph
■ **punto y coma** semi-colon
■ **dos puntos** colon
■ **puntos suspensivos** dot, dot, dot
■ **Estábamos a punto de salir cuando llamaste.** We were about to go out when you phoned.
■ **Mila estaba a punto de llorar.** Mila was on the verge of tears.
■ **Estuve a punto de perder el tren.** I very nearly missed the train.
■ **a la una en punto** at one o'clock sharp
■ **Me gusta hacer punto.** I like knitting.

la **puntuación** (PL las **puntuaciones**) NOUN
1 punctuation
□ los signos de puntuación punctuation marks
2 score
□ Recibió una alta puntuación. He got a high score.

puntual (FEM **puntual**) ADJECTIVE
1 punctual
□ Sé puntual. Be punctual.
■ **Jamás llega puntual.** He never arrives on time.
2 specific
□ Sólo trató aspectos puntuales del tema. He only dealt with specific aspects of the subject.

la **puntualidad** NOUN
punctuality

puntuar* VERB [1]
■ **Este trabajo no puntúa para la nota final.** This essay doesn't count towards the final mark.
■ **un profesor que puntúa muy bajo** a teacher who gives very low marks

el **puñado** NOUN
handful
□ un puñado de arena a handful of sand

el **puñal** NOUN
dagger

la **puñalada** NOUN
■ **Le dieron una puñalada.** He was stabbed.

el **puñetazo** NOUN
punch (PL punches)
□ un puñetazo en la cara a punch in the face
■ **Le pegó un puñetazo.** He punched him.

el **puño** NOUN
1 fist
2 cuff

la **pupa** NOUN
■ **¿Te has hecho pupa?** Did you hurt yourself?

el **pupitre** NOUN
desk

el **puré** (PL los **purés**) NOUN
■ **puré de verduras** puréed vegetables
■ **puré de patatas** mashed potato

puro (FEM **pura**) ADJECTIVE
pure
□ pura lana pure wool □ por pura casualidad by pure chance
■ **Es la pura verdad.** That's the absolute truth.
■ **Son puras mentiras.** *(Latin America)* It's all lies.

el **puro** NOUN
cigar

el **pus** NOUN
pus

puse VERB ▷ *see* **poner**

Qq

que CONJUNCTION
▷ *see also* **que** PRONOUN
1 than
□ Es más alto que tú. He's taller than you.
■ **Yo que tú, iría.** I'd go if I were you.
2 that
□ José sabe que estás aquí. José knows that you're here. □ Dijo que vendría. He said he'd come.
■ **Dile a Rosa que me llame.** Ask Rosa to call me.
■ **¡Que te mejores!** Get well soon!
■ **¿De verdad que te gusta? — ¡Que sí!** Do you really like it? — Of course I do!

que PRONOUN
▷ *see also* **que** CONJUNCTION
1 which
□ la película que ganó el premio the film which won the award □ el sombrero que te compraste the hat you bought □ el libro del que te hablé the book I spoke to you about
2 who
□ el hombre que vino ayer the man who came yesterday □ la chica que conocí the girl I met

qué ADJECTIVE, ADVERB, PRONOUN
1 what
□ ¿Qué fecha es hoy? What's today's date? □ No sabe qué es. He doesn't know what it is. □ No sé qué hacer. I don't know what to do.
■ **¿qué?** what?
2 which
□ ¿Qué película quieres ver? Which film do you want to see?
■ **¡Qué asco!** How revolting!
■ **¡Qué día más bonito!** What a glorious day!
■ **¿Qué tal?** How are things?
■ **¿Qué tal está tu madre?** How's your mother?
■ **No lo he hecho. ¿Y qué?** I haven't done it. So what?

el **quebrado** NOUN
fraction

quebrar* VERB [39]
to go bankrupt
■ **quebrarse** *(Latin America)* to break
□ Alberto se quebró una pierna. Alberto broke his leg.

quedar VERB [25]
1 to be left
□ No queda ninguno. There are none left.
■ **Me quedan quince euros.** I've got 15 euros left.
2 to be
□ Eso queda muy lejos de aquí. That's a long way from here.
3 to arrange to meet
□ He quedado con ella en el cine. I've arranged to meet her at the cinema.
■ **¿Quedamos en la parada?** Shall we meet at the bus stop?
4 to suit
□ No te queda bien ese vestido. That dress doesn't suit you.
■ **quedarse** to stay □ Ve tú, yo me quedo. You go, I'll stay.
■ **quedarse atrás** to fall behind
■ **quedarse sordo** to go deaf
■ **quedarse con algo** to keep something
□ Quédate con el cambio. Keep the change.

los **quehaceres** NOUN
■ **los quehaceres de la casa** the household chores

la **queja** NOUN
complaint

quejarse VERB [25]
to complain
■ **quejarse de algo** to complain about something
■ **quejarse de que ...** to complain that ...
□ Pablo se quejó de que nadie lo escuchaba. Pablo complained that nobody listened to him.

el **quejido** NOUN
1 moan
2 whine

quemado (FEM **quemada**) ADJECTIVE
burnt

la **quemadura** NOUN
burn

■ **quemaduras de sol** sunburn *sing*

quemar VERB [25]
1 to burn
□ Un incendio quemó todo el bosque. A fire burned the entire forest.
2 to be burning hot
□ Esta sopa quema. This soup's burning hot.
■ **quemarse** to burn oneself □ Me quemé con una cerilla. I burned myself with a match.

quepa VERB ▷ *see* **caber**

querer* VERB [43]
1 to want
□ No quiero ir. I don't want to go.
■ **Quiero que vayas.** I want you to go.
■ **¿Quieres un café?** Would you like some coffee?
2 to love
□ Ana quiere mucho a sus hijos. Ana loves her children dearly.
3 to mean
□ No quería hacerte daño. I didn't mean to hurt you. □ Lo hice sin querer. I didn't mean to do it.
■ **querer decir** to mean □ ¿Qué quieres decir? What do you mean?

querido (FEM **querida**) ADJECTIVE
dear

querré VERB ▷ *see* **querer**

el **queso** NOUN
cheese

el **quicio** NOUN
■ **sacar a alguien de quicio** to drive somebody up the wall

la **quiebra** NOUN
■ **ir a la quiebra** to go bankrupt

quien PRONOUN
who
□ Fue Juan quien nos lo dijo. It was Juan who told us. □ Vi al chico con quien sales. I saw the boy you're going out with.

quién PRONOUN
who
□ ¿Quién es ésa? Who's that? □ ¿A quién viste? Who did you see? □ No sé quién es. I don't know who he is.
■ **¿De quién es ...?** Whose is ...? □ ¿De quién es este libro? Whose is this book?
■ **¿Quién es?** **1** Who's there? **2** Who's calling?

quiero VERB ▷ *see* **querer**

quieto (FEM **quieta**) ADJECTIVE
still
■ **¡Estáte quieto!** Keep still!

la **química** NOUN
1 chemistry
□ clase de química chemistry class
2 chemist
□ Es química. She's a chemist.

el **químico** NOUN
chemist
□ Es químico. He's a chemist.

quince (FEM **quince**) ADJECTIVE, PRONOUN
fifteen
■ **el quince de enero** the fifteenth of January
■ **quince días** a fortnight

el **quinceañero**, la **quinceañera** NOUN
teenager

la **quincena** NOUN
fortnight

quincenal (FEM **quincenal**) ADJECTIVE
fortnightly

la **quiniela** NOUN
football pools *pl*

quinientos (FEM **quinientas**) ADJECTIVE, PRONOUN
five hundred

quinto (FEM **quinta**) ADJECTIVE, PRONOUN
fifth
■ **Vivo en el quinto.** I live on the fifth floor.

el **quiosco** NOUN
1 news stand
2 drinks stand
3 flower stall
4 bandstand

el **quirófano** NOUN
operating theatre

quirúrgico (FEM **quirúrgica**) ADJECTIVE
surgical
■ **una intervención quirúrgica** an operation

quise VERB ▷ *see* **querer**

quisquilloso (FEM **quisquillosa**) ADJECTIVE
1 fussy
□ No soy quisquillosa con la comida. I'm not fussy about what I eat.
2 touchy
□ Está muy quisquilloso últimamente. He's been very touchy lately.

el **quitaesmalte** NOUN
nail polish remover

el **quitamanchas** (PL los **quitamanchas**) NOUN
stain remover

la **quitanieves** (PL las **quitanieves**) NOUN
snowplough

quitar VERB [25]
1 to remove
□ Tardaron dos días en quitar los escombros. It took two days to remove the rubble. □ Este producto quita todo tipo de manchas. This product removes all types of stain.
2 to take away

□ Su hermana le quitó la pelota. His sister took the ball away from him.
■ **Me han quitado la cartera.** I've had my wallet stolen.
■ **Esto te quitará el dolor.** This will relieve the pain.
■ **quitarse** to take off □ Juan se quitó la chaqueta. Juan took his jacket off.
■ **¡Quítate de en medio!** Get out of the way!

quizá ADVERB = **quizás**

quizás ADVERB
perhaps

Rr

el **rábano** NOUN
radish (PL radishes)
■ **¡Me importa un rábano!** I don't give a monkey's!
la **rabia** NOUN
1 rage
□ Lo hizo por rabia. He did it out of rage.
■ **Me da mucha rabia.** It's really annoying.
2 rabies *sing*
□ Vacunamos al perro contra la rabia. We had the dog vaccinated against rabies.
la **rabieta** NOUN
tantrum
■ **agarrarse una rabieta** to throw a tantrum
el **rabo** NOUN
tail
la **racha** NOUN
■ **una racha de buen tiempo** a spell of good weather
■ **una racha de viento** a gust of wind
■ **pasar una mala racha** to go through a bad patch
racial (FEM **racial**) ADJECTIVE
racial
el **racimo** NOUN
bunch (PL bunches)
la **ración** (PL las **raciones**) NOUN
portion
el **racismo** NOUN
racism
el/la **racista** ADJECTIVE, NOUN
racist
el **radar** NOUN
radar
■ **'velocidad controlada por radar'** 'radar speed checks in operation'
la **radiación** NOUN
radiation
la **radiactividad** NOUN
radioactivity
radiactivo (FEM **radiactiva**) ADJECTIVE
radioactive
el **radiador** NOUN
radiator
la **radio** NOUN
radio
□ Por la mañana escucho la radio. In the morning I listen to the radio.
■ **Lo oí por la radio.** I heard it on the radio.
el **radio** NOUN
1 radius (PL radii *o* radiuses)
□ La explosión se oyó en un radio de 50 kilómetros. The explosion could be heard within a 50-kilometre radius.
2 radio *(Latin America)*
3 spoke
el **radiocasete** NOUN
radio cassette player
la **radiografía** NOUN
X-ray
■ **Tengo que hacerme una radiografía.** I've got to have an X-ray.
el **radiotaxi** NOUN
radio taxi
el **raíl** NOUN
rail
la **raíz** (PL las **raíces**) NOUN
root
■ **La planta está echando raíces.** The plant's taking root.
■ **a raíz de** as a result of
la **raja** NOUN
1 crack
2 tear *(in fabric)*
3 slice
rajarse VERB [25]
1 to crack
2 to split
rallar VERB [25]
to grate
el **rally** (PL los **rallys**) NOUN
rally (PL rallies)
la **rama** NOUN
branch (PL branches)
el **ramo** NOUN
bunch (PL bunches)
□ un ramo de claveles a bunch of carnations
■ **el ramo textil** the textile industry
la **rampa** NOUN
ramp
la **rana** NOUN

frog

la **ranchera** NOUN
1 Mexican folk song
2 estate car

el **rancho** NOUN
ranch (PL ranches)

rancio (FEM **rancia**) ADJECTIVE
rancid

el **rango** NOUN
rank
■ **políticos de alto rango** high-ranking politicians

la **ranura** NOUN
slot
□ Introduzca la moneda en la ranura. Put the coin in the slot.

rapar VERB [25]
1 to crop
2 to shave

el **rape** NOUN
monkfish (PL monkfish)

rápidamente ADVERB
quickly

la **rapidez** NOUN
speed
■ **con rapidez** quickly

rápido (FEM **rápida**) ADJECTIVE
▷ *see also* **rápido** ADVERB
1 fast
□ un coche muy rápido a very fast car
2 quick
□ Fue una visita muy rápida. It was a very quick visit.

rápido ADVERB
▷ *see also* **rápido** ADJECTIVE
fast
□ Conduces demasiado rápido. You drive too fast.
■ **Lo hice tan rápido como pude.** I did it as quickly as I could.
■ **¡Rápido!** Hurry up!

raptar VERB [25]
to kidnap

el **rapto** NOUN
kidnapping

la **raqueta** NOUN
1 racket
2 bat

raramente ADVERB
rarely

raro (FEM **rara**) ADJECTIVE
1 strange
□ Tiene unas costumbres muy raras. He has some very strange habits.
■ **¡Qué raro!** How strange!
■ **Sabe un poco raro.** It tastes a bit funny.
2 rare
□ una especie muy rara a very rare species
■ **Es raro que haga tan buen tiempo.** It's unusual to have such good weather.
■ **rara vez** seldom

el **rascacielos** (PL los **rascacielos**) NOUN
skyscraper

rascar* VERB [48]
1 to scratch
□ ¿Me rascas la espalda? Could you scratch my back for me?
2 to scrape
□ Tuvimos que rascar la pintura de la puerta. We had to scrape the paint off the door.
■ **rascarse** to scratch □ No deja de rascarse. He can't stop scratching.

rasgar* VERB [37]
to rip

el **rasgo** NOUN
feature
□ Tiene unos rasgos muy delicados. He has very fine features.

el **rasguño** NOUN
scratch (PL scratches)
■ **Me he hecho un rasguño.** I've scratched myself.

el **rastrillo** NOUN
1 rake
2 razor *(Mexico)*

el **rastro** NOUN
1 trail
□ seguir el rastro de alguien to follow somebody's trail
2 trace
□ Desaparecieron sin dejar rastro. They vanished without trace.
3 fleamarket

rasurarse VERB [25] *(Latin America)*
to shave

la **rata** NOUN
rat

el **rato** NOUN
while
□ después de un rato after a while
■ **Estaba aquí hace un rato.** He was here a few minutes ago.
■ **al poco rato** shortly after
■ **pasar el rato** to while away the time
■ **pasar un buen rato** to have a good time
■ **Pasamos un mal rato.** We had a dreadful time.
■ **en mis ratos libres** in my free time
■ **Tengo para rato con esta redacción.** I've got a way to go yet with this essay.
■ **Tenemos para rato; el avión tiene retraso.** We'll be here for a while yet; the plane has been delayed.

el **ratón** (PL los **ratones**) NOUN
mouse (PL mice)

la **raya** NOUN

1 line
□ trazar una raya to draw a line
■ **pasarse de la raya** to overstep the mark
2 stripe
■ **un jersey a rayas** a striped jumper
3 parting
□ Me hago la raya en medio. I have my parting in the middle.
4 crease (PL creases)
5 dash (PL dashes)

rayar VERB [25]
to scratch

el **rayo** NOUN
1 lightning
□ Cayó un rayo en la torre de la iglesia. The church tower was struck by lightning.
2 ray
□ un rayo de luz a ray of light □ los rayos del sol the sun's rays
■ **los rayos X** X-rays
■ **los rayos láser** laser beams

la **raza** NOUN
1 race
□ la raza humana the human race
2 breed
□ ¿De qué raza es tu gato? What breed's your cat?
■ **un perro de raza** a pedigree dog

la **razón** (PL las **razones**) NOUN
reason
□ ¿Cuál era la razón de su visita? What was the reason for his visit?
■ **tener razón** to be right
■ **dar la razón a alguien** to agree that somebody is right
■ **no tener razón** to be wrong

razonable (FEM **razonable**) ADJECTIVE
reasonable

la **reacción** (PL las **reacciones**) NOUN
reaction

reaccionar VERB [25]
to react

el **reactor** NOUN
1 jet plane
2 jet engine
■ **un reactor nuclear** a nuclear reactor

real (FEM **real**) ADJECTIVE
1 real
□ Esta vez el dolor era real. This time the pain was real.
■ **La película está basada en hechos reales.** The film is based on actual events.
2 royal
□ la familia real the royal family

la **realidad** NOUN
reality (PL realities)
■ **en la realidad** in real life
■ **en realidad** actually □ Parece mayor, pero en realidad es más joven que yo. He looks older but actually he's younger than I am.
■ **Mi sueño se hizo realidad.** My dream came true.
■ **realidad virtual** virtual reality

realista (FEM **realista**) ADJECTIVE
realistic

el **reality** (PL los **realitys**) NOUN
reality show

realizar* VERB [13]
1 to carry out
□ realizar una investigación to carry out an investigation
■ **Has realizado un buen trabajo.** You've done a good job.
2 to realize
□ Nunca realizó su sueño de dar la vuelta al mundo. He never realized his dream of going round the world.
■ **realizarse** to come true □ Su sueño nunca llegó a realizarse. His dream never came true.

realmente ADVERB
1 really
□ Fue una época realmente difícil. It was a really difficult period.
2 actually
□ No creí que realmente ganara. I didn't think he would actually win.

la **rebaja** NOUN
1 discount
□ Me hizo una rebaja por pagar al contado. He gave me a discount for paying cash.
2 reduction
□ La blusa tenía una mancha y pedí una rebaja. There was a mark on the blouse so I asked for a reduction.
■ **las rebajas** the sales □ las rebajas de enero the January sales
■ **Todos los grandes almacenes están de rebajas.** There are sales on in all the department stores.

rebajar VERB [25]
to reduce
□ Han rebajado los abrigos. Coats have been reduced. □ Cada fin de temporada rebajan los precios. Prices are reduced at the end of every season.
■ **rebajarse** to demean oneself □ No quiere rebajarse a pedirme perdón. He won't demean himself by apologizing to me.

la **rebanada** NOUN
slice
□ Cortó el pan en rebanadas. He cut the bread into slices.

el **rebaño** NOUN
flock

□ un rebaño de ovejas a flock of sheep

la **rebeca** NOUN
cardigan

rebelarse VERB [25]
to rebel
□ rebelarse contra alguien to rebel against somebody

rebelde (FEM **rebelde**) ADJECTIVE
rebellious

el/la **rebelde** NOUN
rebel

la **rebelión** (PL las **rebeliones**) NOUN
rebellion

rebobinar VERB [25]
to rewind

rebotar VERB [25]
to bounce
■ **La pelota rebotó en el poste.** The ball bounced off the post.

rebozado (FEM **rebozada**) ADJECTIVE
1 breaded
2 battered

el **recado** NOUN
1 message
□ Dejé recado de que me llamara. I left a message for him to call me.
2 errand
□ Fui a hacer unos recados. I went to do some errands.

la **recaída** NOUN
relapse
□ sufrir una recaída to have a relapse

recalcar* VERB [48]
to stress
□ Me gustaría recalcar que ... I'd like to stress that ...

la **recámara** NOUN *(Mexico)*
bedroom

el **recambio** NOUN
1 spare
□ la rueda de recambio the spare wheel
■ **una pieza de recambio** a spare part
2 refill

recargar* VERB [37]
1 to recharge
2 to fill up

el **recargo** NOUN
■ **El taxista me cobró un recargo por el equipaje.** The taxi driver charged me extra for my luggage.

recaudar VERB [25]
to collect
□ Recaudó dinero para una ONG. He collected money for an NGO.

la **recepción** (PL las **recepciones**) NOUN
reception

el/la **recepcionista** NOUN
receptionist

el **receptor** NOUN
receiver

la **recesión** (PL las **recesiones**) NOUN
recession

la **receta** NOUN
1 recipe
□ Me dio la receta de los raviolis. He gave me the recipe for the ravioli.
2 prescription
□ Los antibióticos sólo se venden con receta. Antibiotics are only available on prescription.

LANGUAGE TIP Be careful! **receta** does not mean **receipt**.

recetar VERB [25]
to prescribe
□ Las enfermeras no pueden recetar medicamentos. Nurses can't prescribe drugs.
■ **El médico me recetó un jarabe.** The doctor gave me a prescription for cough syrup.

rechazar* VERB [13]
1 to reject
□ El director rechazó mi propuesta. The manager rejected my proposal.
2 to turn down
□ Tuve que rechazar su oferta. I had to turn down his offer.

rechoncho (FEM **rechoncha**) ADJECTIVE
stocky

el **recibidor** NOUN
entrance hall

recibir VERB [58]
1 to receive
□ No he recibido tu carta. I haven't received your letter.
■ **Recibí muchos regalos.** I got a lot of presents.
2 to meet
□ Vinieron a recibirnos al aeropuerto. They came and met us at the airport.
■ **El director me recibió en su despacho.** The manager saw me in his office.

el **recibo** NOUN
1 receipt
□ No se admiten devoluciones sin recibo. No refunds will be given without a receipt.
2 bill
□ pagar el recibo del teléfono to pay the telephone bill

el **reciclaje** NOUN
recycling

reciclar VERB [25]
to recycle

recién ADVERB
just
□ El comedor está recién pintado. The

dining room has just been painted.
■ **Recién se fueron.** *(Latin America)* They've just left.
■ **los recién casados** the newly-weds
■ **un recién nacido** a newborn baby
■ **'recién pintado'** 'wet paint'

reciente (FEM **reciente**) ADJECTIVE
recent
■ **pan reciente** fresh bread

recientemente ADVERB
recently

el **recipiente** NOUN
container

el **recital** NOUN
recital
□ dar un recital de piano to give a piano recital

recitar VERB [25]
to recite

la **reclamación** (PL las **reclamaciones**) NOUN
complaint
□ presentar una reclamación to make a complaint
■ **el libro de reclamaciones** the complaints' book

reclamar VERB [25]
1 to complain
□ Fui a reclamar al director. I went and complained to the manager.
2 to demand
□ Reclaman mejores condiciones de trabajo. They're demanding better working conditions.

el **reclamo** NOUN *(Latin America)*
complaint

el/la **recluta** NOUN
recruit

el **recogedor** NOUN
dustpan

recoger* VERB [7]
1 to pick up
□ Se agachó para recoger la cuchara. He bent down to pick up the spoon. □ Recogí el papel del suelo. I picked the paper up off the floor. □ Me recogieron en la estación. They picked me up at the station.
■ **recoger fruta** to pick fruit
2 to collect
□ A las diez recogen la basura. The rubbish gets collected at ten o'clock.
3 to clear up
□ Recógelo todo antes de marcharte. Clear up everything before you leave.
■ **Recogí los platos y los puse en el fregadero.** I cleared away the plates and put them in the sink.
■ **recoger la mesa** to clear the table

la **recogida** NOUN
collection
□ la recogida de basuras the refuse collection □ el horario de recogida del correo the mail collection times
■ **recogida de equipajes** baggage reclaim

la **recomendación** (PL las **recomendaciones**) NOUN
1 recommendation
□ Fuimos a ese restaurante por recomendación de un amigo. We went to that restaurant on the recommendation of a friend.
■ **una carta de recomendación** a letter of recommendation
2 advice
□ Hago régimen por recomendación del médico. I'm on a diet on my doctor's advice.

recomendar* VERB [39]
to recommend

la **recompensa** NOUN
reward
□ Ofrecen una recompensa de mil euros. They're offering a thousand-euro reward.

reconciliarse VERB [25]
■ **reconciliarse con alguien** to make it up with somebody □ Riñeron, pero ya se han reconciliado. They had a row but they've made it up again.

reconocer* VERB [12]
1 to recognize
□ No te había reconocido con ese sombrero. I didn't recognize you in that hat.
2 to admit
□ Reconócelo, ha sido culpa tuya. Admit it, it was your fault.

el **reconocimiento** NOUN
checkup
□ hacerse un reconocimiento médico to have a checkup

la **reconquista** NOUN
reconquest

reconstruir* VERB [10]
to rebuild

el **récord** (PL los **récords**) NOUN
record
□ Posee el récord mundial de salto de altura. He holds the world record in the high jump.
■ **batir el récord** to break the record
■ **establecer un récord** to set a record

recordar* VERB [25]
1 to remember
□ No recuerdo dónde lo puse. I can't remember where I put it.
2 to remind
□ Recuérdame que hable con Daniel. Remind me to speak to Daniel. □ Me

recuerda a su padre. He reminds me of his father.

LANGUAGE TIP Be careful! **recordar** does not mean **to record**.

recorrer VERB [8]

1 to travel around

□ Recorrimos Francia en moto. We travelled around France on a motorbike.

2 to do

□ Ese día recorrimos 100 kilómetros. We did 100 kilometres that day.

el **recorrido** NOUN

■ **¿Qué recorrido hace este autobús?** Which route does this bus take?

■ **un recorrido turístico** a tour

■ **un tren de largo recorrido** an inter-city train

recortar VERB [25]

to cut out

□ Recorté el artículo para enseñárselo a Pedro. I cut the article out to show it to Pedro.

■ **recortar gastos** to cut costs

el **recorte** NOUN

■ **recortes de prensa** press cuttings

■ **recortes de personal** staff cutbacks

recostarse* VERB [11]

to lie down

□ Se recostó en el sofá. He lay down on the settee.

el **recreo** NOUN

break

□ Tenemos 20 minutos de recreo. We have a 20-minute break.

■ **Salimos al recreo a las 11.** We have a break at 11 o'clock.

■ **la hora del recreo** playtime

la **recta** NOUN

straight line

■ **la recta final** the home straight

rectangular (FEM **rectangular**) ADJECTIVE

rectangular

el **rectángulo** NOUN

rectangle

recto (FEM **recta**) ADJECTIVE, ADVERB

straight

□ una línea recta a straight line □ Mantén la espalda recta. Keep your back straight.

■ **todo recto** straight on □ Siga todo recto. Go straight on.

el **recuadro** NOUN

box (PL boxes)

recuerdo VERB ▷ *see* **recordar**

el **recuerdo** NOUN

1 memory (PL memories)

□ Me trae buenos recuerdos. It brings back happy memories.

2 souvenir

□ una tienda de recuerdos a souvenir shop

■ **un recuerdo de familia** a family heirloom

■ **¡Recuerdos a tu madre!** Give my regards to your mother!

■ **Dale recuerdos de mi parte.** Give him my regards.

la **recuperación** (PL las **recuperaciones**) NOUN

1 recovery

2 resit

recuperar VERB [25]

to get back

□ Tardé unos minutos en recuperar el aliento. It took me a few minutes to get my breath back.

■ **recuperar fuerzas** to get one's strength back

■ **recuperarse de 1** to get over □ Tardé una semana en recuperarme de la gripe. It took me a week to get over my flu. **2** to recover from □ Se está recuperando de la operación. He's recovering from the operation.

■ **recuperar el tiempo perdido** to make up for lost time

recurrir VERB [58]

■ **recurrir a algo** to resort to something

□ Hay que evitar recurrir a la violencia. We must avoid resorting to violence.

■ **recurrir a alguien** to turn to somebody

□ ¿A quién puedo recurrir? Who can I turn to?

el **recurso** NOUN

■ **como último recurso** as a last resort

■ **recursos** resources □ recursos naturales natural resources

la **red** NOUN

1 net

□ una red de pesca a fishing net □ La pelota dio contra la red. The ball went into the net.

2 network

□ una red informática a computer network

■ **la Red** the Net

■ **una red de tiendas** a chain of shops

la **redacción** (PL las **redacciones**) NOUN

essay (PL essays)

■ **hacer una redacción sobre algo** to do an essay on something

■ **el equipo de redacción** the editorial staff

redactar VERB [25]

to write

□ redactar un artículo de periódico to write a newspaper article

el **redactor**, la **redactora** NOUN

editor

□ el redactor deportivo the sports editor

□ la redactora jefe the editor in chief

la **redada** NOUN
raid
□ Fue detenido en una redada policial. He was arrested during a police raid.
■ **La policía hizo una redada en el club.** The police raided the club.

redondo (FEM **redonda**) ADJECTIVE
round
□ una mesa redonda a round table
■ **Todo salió redondo.** Everything worked out perfectly.

la **reducción** (PL las **reducciones**) NOUN
reduction

reducir* VERB [9]
1 to reduce
□ Reduzca la velocidad. Reduce speed.
2 to cut
□ Van a reducir personal. They're going to cut staff.

reembolsar VERB [25]
to refund

el **reembolso** NOUN
refund
□ Cancelaron la excursión y nos hicieron un reembolso. They cancelled the trip and gave us a refund.
■ **enviar algo contra reembolso** to send something cash on delivery

reemplazar* VERB [13]
to replace

la **referencia** NOUN
reference
□ un punto de referencia a point of reference
■ **con referencia a** with reference to
■ **hacer referencia a** to refer to
■ **referencias** references □ La niñera traía muy buenas referencias. The nanny had very good references.

el **referéndum** (PL los **referéndums**) NOUN
referendum (PL referenda *o* referendums)

referente (FEM **referente**) ADJECTIVE
■ **referente a** concerning □ el párrafo referente al uniforme escolar the paragraph concerning school uniform

referirse* VERB [51]
■ **referirse a** to refer to □ ¿Te refieres a mí? Are you referring to me?
■ **¿A qué te refieres?** **1** What exactly do you mean? **2** What are you referring to?

la **refinería** NOUN
refinery (PL refineries)

refiriendo VERB ▷ *see* **referir**

reflejar VERB [25]
to reflect

el **reflejo** NOUN
reflection
□ el reflejo de la luna en el lago the reflection of the moon in the lake
■ **reflejos** reflexes □ Estás bien de reflejos. You have good reflexes.

la **reflexión** (PL las **reflexiones**) NOUN
reflection

reflexionar VERB [25]
to think
□ Hace las cosas sin reflexionar. He does things without thinking. □ reflexionar sobre algo to think about something
■ **Reflexiona bien antes de tomar una decisión.** Think it over carefully before taking a decision.

reflexivo (FEM **reflexiva**) ADJECTIVE
reflexive

la **reforma** NOUN
1 reform
□ la reforma educativa the education reforms *pl*
2 alteration
□ Estamos haciendo reformas en el piso. We're having alterations made to the flat.
■ **'Cerrado por reformas'** 'Closed for refurbishment'

reformar VERB [25]
1 to reform
2 to do up

el **refrán** (PL los **refranes**) NOUN
saying

refrescante (FEM **refrescante**) ADJECTIVE
refreshing

refrescar* VERB [48]
to get cooler
■ **refrescarse** to freshen up

el **refresco** NOUN
soft drink

el **refrigerador** NOUN
fridge

el **refugiado**, la **refugiada** NOUN
refugee

refugiarse VERB [25]
1 to shelter
□ Nos refugiamos de la lluvia en un portal. We sheltered from the rain in a doorway.
2 to take refuge
□ La gente se refugiaba en los sótanos. People took refuge in the cellars.

el **refugio** NOUN
refuge
□ un refugio de montaña a mountain refuge
■ **Los montañeros buscaron refugio en una cueva.** The climbers sheltered in a cave.
■ **un refugio antiaéreo** an air-raid shelter

la **regadera** NOUN
1 watering can
2 shower *(Mexico)*
■ **estar como una regadera** to be as mad

as a hatter

regalar VERB [25]

1 to give

□ ¿Y si le regalamos un libro? What about giving him a book?

■ **Ayer fue mi cumpleaños. — ¿Qué te regalaron?** It was my birthday yesterday. — What did you get?

2 to give away

□ La tele vieja la vamos a regalar. We're going to give the old TV away.

el **regaliz** NOUN

liquorice

el **regalo** NOUN

present

□ hacer un regalo a alguien to give somebody a present

■ **una tienda de regalos** a gift shop

■ **papel de regalo** wrapping paper

■ **de regalo** free □ Te dan un CD de regalo. They give you a free CD.

regañadientes

■ **a regañadientes** ADVERB reluctantly

regañar VERB [25]

to tell off

□ La maestra me regañó por llegar tarde. The teacher told me off for being late.

regar* VERB [34]

to water

la **regata** NOUN

yacht race

regatear VERB [25]

1 to haggle

□ Regateaban por el precio de la alfombra. They were haggling over the price of the carpet.

2 to dodge past

□ Regateó a varios defensas. He dodged past several defenders.

el **régimen** (PL los **regímenes**) NOUN

1 diet

■ **estar a régimen** to be on a diet

■ **ponerse a régimen** to go on a diet

2 regime

□ un régimen comunista a communist regime

el **regimiento** NOUN

regiment

la **región** (PL las **regiones**) NOUN

region

regional (FEM **regional**) ADJECTIVE

regional

registrar VERB [25]

1 to search

□ Estuvieron registrando la casa. They were searching the house. □ Me registraron. They searched me.

2 to register

□ Tienes que registrarte en el consulado. You have to register at the consulate.

3 to check in

□ Fui a recepción a registrarme. I went to reception to check in.

■ **Me registré en el hotel.** I checked into the hotel.

el **registro** NOUN

1 search (PL searches)

■ **realizar un registro en un lugar** to carry out a search of a place

2 register

■ **el registro civil** the registry office

la **regla** NOUN

1 rule

□ saltarse las reglas to break the rules

2 period

□ Estoy con la regla. I've got my period.

3 ruler

□ Trazó la línea con una regla. He drew the line with a ruler.

■ **por regla general** generally

■ **tener todo en regla** to have everything in order

el **reglamento** NOUN

regulations *pl*

□ El reglamento no lo permite. The regulations don't allow it.

regresar VERB [25]

1 to go back

□ Paco regresó a casa por el paraguas. Paco went back home for his umbrella.

2 to come back

□ Regresaré sobre las ocho. I'll come back at about eight.

■ **Regresamos tarde.** We got back late.

3 to give back *(Latin America)*

■ **regresarse 1** *(Latin America)* to go back **2** *(Latin America)* to come back

el **regreso** NOUN

return

■ **a nuestro regreso** on our return

■ **de regreso** on the way back □ De regreso paramos a comer en Ávila. On the way back we stopped to have lunch in Ávila.

regulable (FEM **regulable**) ADJECTIVE

adjustable

regular (FEM **regular**) ADJECTIVE

▷ *see also* **regular** ADVERB

regular

□ un verbo regular a regular verb □ a intervalos regulares at regular intervals

■ **La obra estuvo regular.** The play was pretty ordinary.

regular ADVERB

▷ *see also* **regular** ADJECTIVE

■ **El examen me fue regular.** My exam didn't go brilliantly.

■ **¿Cómo te encuentras? — Regular.** How are you? — Not too bad.

rehacer* VERB [26]
to redo

el/la **rehén** (PL los/las **rehenes**) NOUN
hostage

la **reina** NOUN
queen

el **reinado** NOUN
reign

el **reino** NOUN
kingdom

el **Reino Unido** NOUN
the United Kingdom

reír* VERB [44]
to laugh
□ No te rías. Don't laugh.
■ **echarse a reír** to burst out laughing
■ **Siempre nos reímos con él.** We always have a good laugh with him.
■ **reírse** to laugh
■ **reírse de** to laugh at □ ¿De qué te ríes? What are you laughing at?

la **reivindicación** (PL las **reivindicaciones**) NOUN
claim
□ reivindicaciones salariales wage claims

la **reja** NOUN
grille
□ La puerta de la joyería está protegida con una reja. The door to the jeweller's is protected with a grille.
■ **estar entre rejas** to be behind bars

la **relación** (PL las **relaciones**) NOUN
1 link
□ la relación entre el tabaco y el cáncer the link between smoking and cancer
2 relationship
□ Tenemos una relación de amistad. We have a friendly relationship.
■ **las relaciones entre empresarios y trabajadores** the relationship between employers and workers
■ **con relación a** in relation to
■ **relaciones públicas** public relations
■ **relaciones sexuales** sexual relations

relacionar VERB [25]
to link
□ Los expertos relacionan el tabaco con el cáncer. The experts link smoking with cancer.
■ **Le gusta relacionarse con niños mayores que él.** He likes mixing with older children.
■ **No se relaciona mucho con la gente.** He doesn't mix much.

relajado (FEM **relajada**) ADJECTIVE
1 relaxed
□ ¿Estás relajado? Are you feeling relaxed?
2 laid-back
□ Es un tipo muy relajado. He's a very laid-back guy.

relajante (FEM **relajante**) ADJECTIVE
relaxing

relajar VERB [25]
to relax
□ Relaja los músculos. Relax your muscles.
□ ¡Relájate! Relax!
■ **La música clásica me relaja mucho.** I find classical music really relaxing.

el **relámpago** NOUN
flash of lightning (PL flashes of lightning)
□ Vimos varios relámpagos. We saw several flashes of lightning.
■ **No me gustan los relámpagos.** I don't like lightning.

relativamente ADVERB
relatively

relativo (FEM **relativa**) ADJECTIVE
relative
□ un pronombre relativo a relative pronoun
□ Eso es muy relativo. That's all relative.
■ **en lo relativo a** concerning

el **relato** NOUN
story

el **relevo** NOUN
■ **una carrera de relevos** a relay race
■ **tomar el relevo a alguien** to take over from somebody

la **religión** (PL las **religiones**) NOUN
religion

religioso (FEM **religiosa**) ADJECTIVE
religious

el **rellano** NOUN
landing

rellenar VERB [25]
1 to stuff
□ Rellene los pimientos con el arroz. Stuff the peppers with the rice.
2 to fill in
□ Rellene este impreso, por favor. Can you fill in this form please.

relleno (FEM **rellena**) ADJECTIVE
stuffed
□ aceitunas rellenas stuffed olives
■ **relleno de algo** filled with something

el **reloj** NOUN
1 clock
□ El reloj de la cocina va atrasado. The kitchen clock's slow.
■ **un reloj despertador** an alarm clock
■ **un reloj de cuco** a cuckoo clock
■ **contra reloj** against the clock
2 watch (PL watches)
□ Se me ha parado el reloj. My watch has stopped.

■ **un reloj digital** a digital watch
■ **un reloj sumergible** a waterproof watch
■ **El horno tiene un reloj automático.** The cooker has an automatic timer.
■ **un reloj de sol** a sundial

la **relojera** NOUN
watchmaker

la **relojería** NOUN
watchmaker's (PL watchmakers' shops)

el **relojero** NOUN
watchmaker

relucir* VERB [9]
to shine

remar VERB [25]
1 to paddle
2 to row

remediar VERB [25]
to solve
□ Con llorar no vas a remediar nada. You're not going to solve anything by crying.
■ **Me eché a reír, no lo pude remediar.** I began to laugh, I couldn't help it.

el **remedio** NOUN
remedy (PL remedies)
□ un remedio contra la tos a cough remedy
□ un remedio casero a household remedy
■ **No tuve más remedio que hacerlo.** I had no choice but to do it.

el **remite** NOUN
name and address of sender

el/la **remitente** NOUN
sender

el **remo** NOUN
1 oar
2 rowing

remojar VERB [25]
to soak

el **remojo** NOUN
■ **poner algo en remojo** to leave something to soak

la **remolacha** NOUN
beetroot

remolcar* VERB [48]
to tow

el **remolque** NOUN
trailer

el **remordimiento** NOUN
remorse *sing*
□ No siente remordimientos por lo que ha hecho. He feels no remorse for what he has done.

remoto (FEM **remota**) ADJECTIVE
remote

remover* VERB [33]
1 to stir
2 to toss
3 to turn over

el **renacuajo** NOUN
tadpole

el **rencor** NOUN
ill-feeling
□ Existe mucho rencor entre los dos. There's a lot of ill-feeling between the two of them.
■ **guardar rencor a alguien** to bear a grudge against somebody □ No le guardo rencor. I don't bear him a grudge.

rencoroso (FEM **rencorosa**) ADJECTIVE
■ **No soy rencoroso.** I don't bear grudges.

rendido (FEM **rendida**) ADJECTIVE
worn out
□ Estaba rendido de tanto andar. I was worn out after so much walking.

la **rendija** NOUN
1 crack
2 gap

el **rendimiento** NOUN
performance

rendir* VERB [38]
■ **Este negocio no rinde.** This business doesn't pay.
■ **El dinero rinde poco en una cuenta corriente.** You don't get much interest on your money in a current account.
■ **rendirse 1** to give up □ No sé la respuesta; me rindo. I don't know the answer; I give up. **2** to surrender □ El enemigo se rindió. The enemy surrendered.

el **renglón** (PL los **renglones**) NOUN
line

el **reno** NOUN
reindeer (PL reindeer *o* reindeers)

renovable (FEM **renovable**) ADJECTIVE
renewable

renovar* VERB [11]
1 to renew
□ Tengo que renovarme el pasaporte. I must renew my passport.
2 to renovate
□ Van a renovar la fachada del edificio. They're going to renovate the front of the building.
3 to change
□ Han renovado el mobiliario de la casa. They've changed the furniture in the house.

la **renta** NOUN
1 income
2 rent

rentable (FEM **rentable**) ADJECTIVE
profitable
□ No es rentable hacer el viaje en coche. It isn't profitable to make the journey by car.
■ **una fábrica poco rentable** an uneconomic factory

rentar VERB [25] *(Mexico)*

to rent

reñido (FEM **reñida**) ADJECTIVE
hard-fought

reñir* VERB [45]
1 to tell somebody off
□ No le riñas, la culpa no es suya. Don't tell her off, it's not her fault.
2 to quarrel
□ Mi hermana y yo siempre estábamos riñendo. My sister and I were always quarrelling.
3 to fall out
□ Ángeles y Manolo han reñido. Ángeles and Manolo have fallen out. □ Ha reñido con su novio. She has fallen out with her boyfriend.

la **reparación** (PL las **reparaciones**) NOUN
repair
■ **'reparaciones en el acto'** 'repairs while you wait'

reparar VERB [25]
to repair

repartir VERB [58]
1 to hand out
□ El profesor repartió los exámenes. The teacher handed out the examination papers.
2 to share out
□ Nos repartimos el dinero. We shared out the money.
3 to deliver
□ Repartimos pizzas a domicilio. We deliver pizzas.
4 to deal

el **reparto** NOUN
1 delivery (PL deliveries)
■ **reparto a domicilio** home delivery service
2 cast
□ un reparto estelar a star cast

repasar VERB [25]
1 to check
□ Repasé la declaración antes de firmarla. I checked the statement before signing it.
2 to revise
■ **repasar para un examen** to revise for an exam

el **repaso** NOUN
revision
■ **Tengo que darles un repaso a los apuntes.** I must revise my notes.

el **repelente** NOUN
repellent

el/la **repelente** NOUN
know-all

repente ADVERB
■ **de repente** suddenly

repentino (FEM **repentina**) ADJECTIVE
sudden

el **repertorio** NOUN
repertoire

la **repetición** (PL las **repeticiones**) NOUN
repetition

repetidamente ADVERB
repeatedly

repetir* VERB [38]
1 to repeat
□ ¿Podría repetirlo, por favor? Could you repeat that, please?
2 to have a second helping
□ El arroz está tan bueno que voy a repetir. The rice is so good that I'm going to have a second helping.

repetitivo (FEM **repetitiva**) ADJECTIVE
repetitive

la **repisa** NOUN
shelf (PL shelves)
■ **la repisa de la chimenea** the mantelpiece

LANGUAGE TIP Word for word, **repisa de la chimenea** means 'shelf of the chimney'.

repitiendo VERB ▷ *see* **repetir**

el **repollo** NOUN
cabbage

el **reportaje** NOUN
1 documentary (PL documentaries)
2 article

el **reposacabezas** (PL los **reposacabezas**) NOUN
headrest

la **reposición** (PL las **reposiciones**) NOUN
1 repeat *(in television)*
2 revival *(in theatre)*

repostar VERB [25]
to refuel

la **repostería** NOUN
confectionery

la **representación** (PL las **representaciones**) NOUN
performance

el/la **representante** NOUN
1 representative
2 agent

representar VERB [25]
1 to represent
□ La representaba su abogado. Her lawyer was representing her.
2 to put on
□ Los niños van a representar una obra de teatro. The children are going to put on a play.
3 to play
□ Representa el papel de Don Juan. He's playing the part of Don Juan.
■ **Tiene cuarenta años pero no los**

representa. He's forty but he doesn't look it.

representativo (FEM **representativa**) ADJECTIVE
representative

el **reprimido** (FEM la **reprimida**) ADJECTIVE, NOUN
■ **Es una reprimida.** She's repressed.

reprobar* VERB [11] *(Latin America)*
to fail
□ Le reprobaron en matemáticas. He failed maths.

reprochar VERB [25]
■ **Me reprochó que no la hubiera invitado.** He reproached me for not having invited her.

la **reproducción** (PL las **reproducciones**) NOUN
reproduction

reproducirse* VERB [9]
to reproduce

el **reproductor** NOUN
■ **un reproductor de CD** a CD player

el **reptil** NOUN
reptile

la **república** NOUN
republic

la **República Dominicana** NOUN
the Dominican Republic

el **republicano** (FEM la **republicana**) ADJECTIVE, NOUN
republican

el **repuesto** NOUN
spare part
■ **de repuesto** spare □ la rueda de repuesto the spare wheel

repugnante (FEM **repugnante**) ADJECTIVE
revolting

la **reputación** (PL las **reputaciones**) NOUN
reputation
■ **tener buena reputación** to have a good reputation

el **requesón** NOUN
cottage cheese

el **requisito** NOUN
requirement
□ Cumple todos los requisitos para el puesto. He satisfies all the requirements for the job.

la **resaca** NOUN
hangover
■ **tener resaca** to have a hangover

resaltar VERB [25]
1 to stand out
□ Lo escribí en mayúsculas para que resaltara. I wrote it in capitals to make it stand out.
2 to highlight
□ El conferenciante resaltó el problema del paro. The speaker highlighted the problem of unemployment.

resbaladizo (FEM **resbaladiza**) ADJECTIVE
slippery

resbalar VERB [25]
1 to be slippery
□ Ten cuidado que este suelo resbala. Be careful, this floor's slippery.
2 to skid
□ El coche resbaló y casi nos estrellamos. The car skidded and we almost crashed.
■ **resbalarse** to slip □ Me resbalé con el hielo de la acera. I slipped on the icy pavement.

rescatar VERB [25]
to rescue

el **rescate** NOUN
1 rescue
□ un equipo de rescate a rescue team
2 ransom
■ **pedir un rescate por alguien** to hold somebody to ransom

el/la **reserva** NOUN
reserve

la **reserva** NOUN
1 reservation
□ He hecho una reserva en el Hilton para dos noches. I've made a reservation at the Hilton for two nights.
■ **Tengo mis reservas al respecto.** I've got reservations about it.
2 reserve
□ una reserva natural a nature reserve
□ El país tiene abundantes reservas de trigo. The country has got plentiful reserves of wheat.

reservado (FEM **reservada**) ADJECTIVE
reserved

reservar VERB [25]
to reserve

resfriado (FEM **resfriada**) ADJECTIVE
■ **estar resfriado** to have a cold □ No fui porque estaba muy resfriado. I didn't go because I had a bad cold.

el **resfriado** NOUN
cold
■ **agarrarse un resfriado** to catch a cold

resfriarse* VERB [21]
to catch a cold

el **resguardo** NOUN
1 ticket
2 receipt

la **residencia** NOUN
residence
□ un permiso de residencia a residence permit □ La reunión tuvo lugar en la residencia del primer ministro. The

meeting took place at the prime minister's residence.
■ **una residencia de ancianos** an old people's home
■ **una residencia de estudiantes** a hall of residence
■ **una residencia sanitaria** a hospital

residencial (FEM **residencial**) ADJECTIVE
residential
□ una zona residencial a residential area

los **residuos** NOUN
waste *sing*
□ residuos radiactivos radioactive waste

la **resistencia** NOUN
resistance
□ Los manifestantes no ofrecieron resistencia. The demonstrators didn't offer any resistance.
■ **resistencia física** stamina

resistente (FEM **resistente**) ADJECTIVE
tough
□ El diamante es una piedra muy resistente. Diamond is a very tough stone.
■ **resistente al calor** heat-resistant

resistir VERB [58]
1 to resist
□ No pude resistir la tentación. I couldn't resist the temptation.
2 to take
□ Esta caja no va a resistir tanto peso. This box won't take so much weight.
3 to stand
□ No puedo resistir este frío. I can't stand this cold.
■ **Se resisten a cooperar.** They are refusing to cooperate.

resolver* VERB [33]
to solve

respaldar VERB [25]
to back up
□ Mis hermanos me respaldaron. My brothers and sisters backed me up.

el **respaldo** NOUN
back

respectivamente ADVERB
respectively

respecto NOUN
■ **con respecto a** with regard to

respetable (FEM **respetable**) ADJECTIVE
respectable

respetar VERB [25]
1 to respect
2 to obey
□ No se respetan las normas de seguridad. The safety regulations aren't being obeyed.

el **respeto** NOUN
respect
□ el respeto a los animales respect for animals
■ **tener respeto a alguien** to respect somebody
■ **No le faltes al respeto.** Don't be disrespectful to him.

la **respiración** NOUN
breathing
□ Tenía la respiración irregular. His breathing was irregular.
■ **quedarse sin respiración** to be out of breath
■ **la respiración boca a boca** the kiss of life
□ Le hicieron la respiración boca a boca. They gave him the kiss of life.
■ **la respiración artificial** artificial respiration

respirar VERB [25]
to breathe

responder VERB [8]
1 to answer
□ Eso no responde a mi pregunta. That doesn't answer my question.
2 to reply
□ No han respondido a mi carta. They haven't replied to my letter. □ Respondió que ya habían salido. He replied that they had already gone out.
3 to respond
□ No responde al tratamiento. He's not responding to the treatment.

la **responsabilidad** NOUN
responsibility (PL responsibilities)

responsable (FEM **responsable**) ADJECTIVE
responsible
□ Cada cual es responsable de sus acciones. Everybody is responsible for their own actions.

el/la **responsable** NOUN
■ **Tú eres la responsable de lo ocurrido.** You're responsible for what happened.
■ **Los responsables serán castigados.** Those responsible will be punished.
■ **Juan es el responsable de la cocina.** Juan is in charge of the kitchen.

la **respuesta** NOUN
answer

resquebrajarse VERB [25]
to crack

la **resta** NOUN
subtraction

restante (FEM **restante**) ADJECTIVE
remaining

restar VERB [25]
to subtract
□ Está aprendiendo a restar. He's learning to subtract.
■ **Tienes que restar 16 de 36.** You have to take 16 away from 36.

la **restauración** (PL las **restauraciones**) NOUN
restoration

el **restaurante** NOUN
restaurant

restaurar VERB [25]
to restore

el **resto** NOUN
rest
□ Yo haré el resto. I'll do the rest.
■ **los restos** **1** the leftovers **2** the wreckage *sing*

restregar* VERB [37]
to rub
□ Cuando tiene sueño se restriega los ojos. He rubs his eyes when he's sleepy.

la **restricción** (PL las **restricciones**) NOUN
restriction

resuelto VERB ▷ *see* **resolver**

resuelvo VERB ▷ *see* **resolver**

el **resultado** NOUN
1 result
2 score
■ **dar resultado** to work □ Nuestro plan no dio resultado. Our plan didn't work.

resultar VERB [25]
to turn out
□ Al final resultó que él tenía razón. In the end it turned out that he was right.
■ **Me resultó violento decírselo.** I found it embarrassing to tell him.

el **resumen** (PL los **resúmenes**) NOUN
summary (PL summaries)
□ un resumen de las noticias a news summary
■ **hacer un resumen de algo** to summarize something
■ **en resumen** in short

resumir VERB [58]
to summarize
■ **Dijo, resumiendo, que el viaje había sido un desastre.** He said, in short, that the trip had been a disaster.

retar VERB [25]
1 to challenge
2 to tell off *(Chile, River Plate)*

retirar VERB [25]
1 to take away
□ La camarera retiró las copas. The waitress took the glasses away. □ Le han retirado el permiso de conducir. He's had his driving licence taken away.
2 to withdraw
□ Fui a retirar dinero de la cuenta. I went to withdraw some money from my account.
□ Se retiraron del torneo. They withdrew from the tournament.
■ **retirarse** to retire □ Mi padre se retira el año que viene. My father will be retiring next year.

el **reto** NOUN
challenge

retorcer* VERB [6]
to twist
□ Me retorció el brazo. He twisted my arm.
■ **retorcerse de risa** to double up with laughter

la **retransmisión** (PL las **retransmisiones**) NOUN
broadcast
□ una retransmisión en directo a live broadcast

retransmitir VERB [58]
to broadcast

retrasado (FEM **retrasada**) ADJECTIVE
1 behind
□ Voy retrasado con este trabajo. I'm behind with this work.
2 slow
□ Este reloj va retrasado veinte minutos. This clock is twenty minutes slow.
■ **Tienen un hijo un poco retrasado.** They've got a son with learning difficulties.

retrasar VERB [25]
1 to postpone
□ Retrasaron la boda al quince. They postponed the wedding until the fifteenth.
2 to delay
□ El mal tiempo retrasó nuestro vuelo. Our flight was delayed due to bad weather.
3 to put back
□ A las dos hay que retrasar los relojes una hora. At two o'clock the clocks have to be put back one hour.
■ **retrasarse** to be late □ El tren de las nueve se retrasó. The nine o'clock train was late.
■ **Tu reloj se retrasa.** Your watch is slow.

el **retraso** NOUN
delay (PL delays)
□ La niebla causó algunos retrasos. The fog caused some delays.
■ **Perdonad por el retraso.** Sorry I'm late.
■ **ir con retraso** to be running late
■ **llegar con retraso** to be late □ El vuelo llegó con una hora de retraso. The flight was an hour late.

el **retrato** NOUN
portrait
■ **hacer un retrato a alguien** to paint somebody's portrait

el **retrete** NOUN
toilet

retroceder VERB [8]
to go back

el **retrovisor** NOUN

rear-view mirror

retuerzo VERB ▷ *see* **retorcer**

el **reúma** NOUN
rheumatism

la **reunión** (PL las **reuniones**) NOUN
1 meeting
□ Mañana tenemos una reunión. We've got a meeting tomorrow.
2 gathering
□ una reunión familiar a family gathering

reunir* VERB [46]
1 to gather together
□ La maestra reunió a los niños en el patio. The teacher gathered the children together in the playground.
2 to satisfy
□ Paula reúne los requisitos para el puesto. Paula satisfies all the requirements for the job.
3 to raise
□ Estamos reuniendo dinero para el viaje. We're raising money for the trip.
■ **reunirse** 1 to gather □ Miles de personas se reunieron en la plaza. Thousands of people gathered in the square. 2 to get together □ En Navidad nos reunimos toda la familia. The whole family gets together at Christmas. 3 to meet □ El comité se reúne una vez al mes. The committee meets once a month.

revelar VERB [25]
1 to develop
□ Luis revela sus propias fotos. Luis develops his own photos.
■ **Todavía no hemos revelado las fotos.** We haven't had the photos developed yet.
■ **Llevé los carretes a revelar.** I took the films to be developed.
2 to reveal
□ No quería revelar su identidad. He didn't want to reveal his identity.

reventar* VERB [39]
to burst
■ **Me revienta tener que ponerme corbata.** I hate having to wear a tie.

el **revés** (PL los **reveses**) NOUN
backhand
■ **al revés** 1 the other way round □ ¿Tres, tres, dos? — No, al revés: dos, dos, tres. Three, three, two? — No, the other way round: two, two, three. 2 inside out □ Te has puesto los calcetines al revés. You've put your socks on inside out. 3 back to front □ Miré el cuello y vi que llevaba el jersey al revés. I looked at the collar and realized that I had my jumper on back to front. 4 upside down □ El dibujo está al revés. The picture's upside down.

reviento VERB ▷ *see* **reventar**

revisar VERB [25]
1 to check
□ Un electricista me revisó la instalación. An electrician checked the wiring for me.
■ **Tengo que ir a que me revisen el coche.** I must take my car for a service.
2 to search *(Latin America)*

la **revisión** (PL las **revisiones**) NOUN
service
□ He llevado el coche a revisión. I've taken the car for a service.
■ **una revisión médica** a checkup

el **revisor**, la **revisora** NOUN
ticket inspector

la **revista** NOUN
magazine
■ **una revista electrónica** a webzine

revoltoso (FEM **revoltosa**) ADJECTIVE
naughty

la **revolución** (PL las **revoluciones**) NOUN
revolution

el **revolucionario**, la **revolucionaria** NOUN
revolutionary (PL revolutionaries)

revolver* VERB [59]
1 to mess up
□ Los niños han revuelto la habitación otra vez. The children have messed the room up again.
■ **No revuelvas mis papeles.** Don't muddle my papers up.
2 to turn upside down
□ Los ladrones revolvieron toda la casa. The burglars turned the whole house upside down.
3 to rummage in
□ No me gusta que me revuelvas el bolso. I don't like you rummaging in my bag.

el **revólver** (PL los **revólveres**) NOUN
revolver

revuelto VERB
▷ *see also* **revuelto** ADJECTIVE ▷ *see* **revolver**

revuelto (FEM **revuelta**) ADJECTIVE
▷ *see also* **revuelto** VERB
in a mess
□ Todo estaba revuelto. Everything was in a mess.
■ **Las fotos están revueltas.** The photos are muddled up.
■ **El tiempo está muy revuelto.** The weather's very unsettled.
■ **Tengo el estómago revuelto.** I've got an upset stomach.

el **rey** (PL los **reyes**) NOUN
king
■ **Los reyes visitaron China.** The King and Queen visited China.

■ **los Reyes Magos** the Three Wise Men

DID YOU KNOW...?
As part of the Christmas festivities, the Spanish celebrate **el día de Reyes** (Epiphany) on 6th of January, when the Three Wise Men bring presents to children.

LANGUAGE TIP Word for word, **Reyes Magos** means 'Magician Kings'.

rezar* VERB [13]
to pray
□ rezar por algo to pray for something
■ **rezar el Padrenuestro** to say the Lord's Prayer

la **ría** NOUN
estuary (PL estuaries)

el **riachuelo** NOUN
stream

la **ribera** NOUN
bank

la **rica** NOUN
rich woman (PL rich women)

el **rico** NOUN
rich man (PL rich men)
■ **los ricos** the rich

rico (FEM **rica**) ADJECTIVE
1 rich
□ Son muy ricos. They're very rich.
2 delicious
□ ¡Qué rico! How delicious!

ridiculizar* VERB [13]
to ridicule

ridículo (FEM **ridícula**) ADJECTIVE
ridiculous
□ ¿A que suena ridículo? Doesn't it sound ridiculous?
■ **hacer el ridículo** to make a fool of oneself
■ **poner a alguien en ridículo** to make a fool of somebody

el **riel** NOUN
rail

las **riendas** NOUN
reins

riendo VERB ▷ *see* **reír**

el **riesgo** NOUN
risk
■ **correr riesgos** to take risks □ No quiero correr ese riesgo. I'd rather not take that risk.
■ **Corres el riesgo de que te despidan.** You run the risk of being dismissed.
■ **un seguro a todo riesgo** a fully comprehensive insurance policy

la **rifa** NOUN
raffle

el **rifle** NOUN
rifle

rígido (FEM **rígida**) ADJECTIVE
1 stiff
2 strict

riguroso (FEM **rigurosa**) ADJECTIVE
1 strict
2 severe

la **rima** NOUN
rhyme

el **rímel** NOUN
mascara
□ No me he puesto rímel. I haven't put any mascara on.

el **rincón** (PL los **rincones**) NOUN
corner

el **rinoceronte** NOUN
rhinoceros (PL rhinoceroses *o* rhinoceros)

la **riña** NOUN
1 row
2 brawl

riñendo VERB ▷ *see* **reñir**

el **riñón** (PL los **riñones**) NOUN
kidney (PL kidneys)
□ un transplante de riñón a kidney transplant
■ **Me duelen los riñones.** I've got a pain in my lower back.

la **riñonera** NOUN
bum bag

río VERB ▷ *see* **reír**

el **río** NOUN
river
□ el río Támesis the River Thames

la **riqueza** NOUN
1 wealth
□ la distribución de la riqueza the distribution of wealth
2 richness
□ la riqueza de su lenguaje the richness of his language

la **risa** NOUN
laugh
□ una risa contagiosa an infectious laugh
■ **Me da risa.** It makes me laugh.
■ **Daba risa la manera en que lo explicaba.** It was so funny the way he told it.
■ **¡Qué risa!** What a laugh!
■ **partirse de risa** to split one's sides laughing

el **ritmo** NOUN
1 rhythm
□ No tiene sentido del ritmo. He has no sense of rhythm.
■ **Daban palmas al ritmo de la música.** They were clapping in time to the music.
2 pace
□ el ritmo de vida the pace of life

el **ritual** NOUN

ritual

el/la **rival** ADJECTIVE, NOUN
rival

la **rivalidad** NOUN
rivalry (PL rivalries)

rizado (FEM **rizada**) ADJECTIVE
curly
□ Tiene el pelo rizado. He has curly hair.

rizar* VERB [13]
1 to curl
□ Me rizo las pestañas. I curl my eyelashes.
2 to perm
■ **Se ha rizado el pelo.** She has had her hair permed.

el **rizo** NOUN
curl

robar VERB [25]
1 to steal
□ Me han robado la cartera. My wallet has been stolen. □ Les robaba dinero a sus compañeros de clase. He was stealing money from his classmates.
2 to rob
□ ¡Nos han robado! We've been robbed!
3 to break into
□ Entraron a robar en mi casa. They broke into my house.

el **roble** NOUN
oak

el **robo** NOUN
1 theft
2 robbery (PL robberies)
3 burglary (PL burglaries)
■ **¡Estos precios son un robo!** This is daylight robbery!

el **robot** (PL los **robots**) NOUN
robot
■ **el robot de cocina** the food processor

robusto (FEM **robusta**) ADJECTIVE
strong

la **roca** NOUN
rock

rociar* VERB [21]
to spray

el **rocío** NOUN
dew

la **rodaja** NOUN
slice
□ cortar algo en rodajas to cut something into slices

el **rodaje** NOUN
shooting
■ **El coche está en rodaje.** The car's running in.

rodar* VERB [11]
1 to roll
□ La pelota bajó rodando por la cuesta. The ball rolled down the slope.
2 to shoot
□ rodar una película to shoot a film

rodear VERB [25]
to surround
□ el bosque que rodea el palacio the forest that surrounds the palace
■ **rodeado de** surrounded by

la **rodilla** NOUN
knee
■ **ponerse de rodillas** to kneel down

el **rodillo** NOUN
1 rolling pin
2 roller

rogar* VERB [28]
1 to beg
□ Me rogó que le perdonara. He begged me to forgive him.
2 to pray
□ Le rogué a Dios que se curara. I prayed to God to make him better.
■ **'Se ruega no fumar'** 'Please do not smoke'

el **rojo** ADJECTIVE, NOUN
red
□ Va vestida de rojo. She's wearing red.
■ **ponerse rojo** to go red □ Se puso rojo de vergüenza. He went red with embarrassment.

el **rollo** NOUN
roll
□ un rollo de papel higiénico a roll of toilet paper
■ **La conferencia fue un rollo.** The lecture was really boring.
■ **¡Qué rollo de película!** What a boring film.
■ **Nos soltó el rollo de siempre.** He gave us the same old lecture.

Roma FEM NOUN
Rome

el **romano** (FEM la **romana**) ADJECTIVE, NOUN
Roman
□ los números romanos Roman numerals
■ **Es romano.** He's from Rome.
■ **los romanos 1** the Romans **2** Romans

el **romántico** (FEM la **romántica**) ADJECTIVE, NOUN
romantic

el **rombo** NOUN
rhombus (PL rhombuses *o* rhombi)

el **rompecabezas** (PL los **rompecabezas**) NOUN
1 jigsaw
2 puzzle

romper* VERB [8, PAST PARTICIPLE **roto**]
1 to break
□ Me rompí el brazo. I broke my arm. □ Se ha roto una taza. A cup has got broken.

□ romper una promesa to break a promise

2 to tear up

□ Rompí la foto de mi novia. I tore up the photo of my girlfriend. □ Rompió la carta a pedazos. He tore the letter up.

■ **Se ha roto una sábana.** A sheet has got torn.

■ **Se me han roto los pantalones.** I've torn my trousers.

■ **romper con alguien** to finish with somebody □ Ha roto con el novio. She has finished with her boyfriend.

el **ron** NOUN
rum

roncar* VERB [48]
to snore

ronco (FEM **ronca**) ADJECTIVE
hoarse

■ **quedarse ronco** to go hoarse

la **ronda** NOUN
round

□ Esta ronda la pago yo. I'll get this round.

■ **hacer la ronda** to be on patrol

el **ronquido** NOUN
snore

ronronear VERB [25]
to purr

la **ropa** NOUN
clothes *pl*

□ Voy a cambiarme de ropa. I'm going to change my clothes.

■ **la ropa interior** underwear

LANGUAGE TIP Word for word, **ropa interior** means 'interior clothes'.

■ **ropa de deporte** sportswear

■ **la ropa de cama** bed linen

■ **la ropa lavada** the washing

■ **la ropa sucia** the dirty washing

el **rosa** ADJECTIVE, NOUN
pink

□ Va vestida de rosa. She's wearing pink.

■ **Llevaba unos calcetines rosa.** He was wearing pink socks.

la **rosa** NOUN
rose

rosado (FEM **rosada**) ADJECTIVE
rosé

el **rosal** NOUN
rosebush (PL rosebushes)

el **rostro** NOUN
face

roto VERB ▷ *see* **romper**

roto (FEM **rota**) ADJECTIVE

1 broken

2 torn

3 worn out

el **roto** NOUN
hole

la **rotonda** NOUN
roundabout

el **rotulador** NOUN

1 felt-tip pen

2 highlighter pen

el **rótulo** NOUN
sign

rozar* VERB [13]
to rub against

□ El sofá roza la pared. The sofa's rubbing against the wall. □ Las botas me rozan el tobillo. My boots are rubbing against my ankle.

■ **La rocé al pasar.** I brushed past her.

rubio (FEM **rubia**) ADJECTIVE
fair

□ Luis tiene el pelo rubio. Luis has got fair hair. □ Yo soy morena pero mi hermana es rubia. I'm dark but my sister is fair.

■ **Es rubia con los ojos azules.** She has got fair hair and blue eyes. □ Quiero teñirme el pelo de rubio. I want to dye my hair blond.

ruborizarse* VERB [13]
to blush

rudimentario (FEM **rudimentaria**) ADJECTIVE
basic

la **rueda** NOUN
wheel

□ la rueda delantera the front wheel □ la rueda trasera the back wheel

■ **Se te ha pinchado la rueda.** You've got a puncture.

■ **una rueda de prensa** a press conference

ruedo VERB ▷ *see* **rodar**

ruego VERB ▷ *see* **rogar**

el **rugby** NOUN
rugby

□ jugar al rugby to play rugby

rugir* VERB [16]
to roar

el **ruido** NOUN
noise

□ ¿Has oído ese ruido? Did you hear that noise? □ No hagáis tanto ruido. Don't make so much noise.

ruidoso (FEM **ruidosa**) ADJECTIVE
noisy

la **ruina** NOUN

■ **Su socio lo llevó a la ruina.** His business partner ruined him financially.

■ **las ruinas** the ruins □ El castillo está en ruinas. The castle is in ruins.

el **rulo** NOUN
roller

la **rulot** (PL las **rulots**) NOUN
caravan

la **rumana** NOUN

Romanian

Rumanía FEM NOUN
Romania

el **rumano** ADJECTIVE, NOUN
Romanian

la **rumba** NOUN
rumba

el **rumor** NOUN
1 rumour
□ Corre el rumor de que se retira. There's a rumour going round that he's retiring.
2 murmur
□ el rumor de las olas the murmur of the waves

rural (FEM **rural**) ADJECTIVE
rural

la **rusa** NOUN
Russian

Rusia FEM NOUN
Russia

el **ruso** ADJECTIVE, NOUN
Russian

la **ruta** NOUN
route

la **rutina** NOUN
routine
□ la rutina diaria the daily routine
■ **un chequeo de rutina** a routine check-up

Ss

el **sábado** NOUN
Saturday
□ La vi el sábado. I saw her on Saturday. □ todos los sábados every Saturday □ el sábado pasado last Saturday □ el sábado que viene next Saturday □ Jugamos los sábados. We play on Saturdays.

la **sábana** NOUN
sheet

saber* VERB [47]
1 to know
□ No lo sé. I don't know. □ Sabe mucho de ordenadores. He knows a lot about computers.
■ **Lo dudo, pero nunca se sabe.** I doubt it, but you never know. □ ¡Y yo que sé! How should I know?
2 to find out
□ En cuanto lo supimos fuimos a ayudarle. As soon as we found out, we went to help him.
■ **No sé nada de ella.** I haven't heard from her.
■ **que yo sepa** as far as I know
3 can
□ No sabe nadar. She can't swim. □ ¿Sabes inglés? Can you speak English?
4 to taste
□ Sabe a pescado. It tastes of fish.
■ **saberse** to know □ Se sabe la lista de memoria. He knows the list off by heart.

sabio (FEM **sabia**) ADJECTIVE
wise

el **sabor** NOUN
1 taste
□ Tiene un sabor muy raro. It's got a very strange taste.
2 flavour
□ ¿De qué sabor lo quieres? What flavour do you want?

el **sabotaje** NOUN
sabotage

sabré VERB ▷ *see* **saber**

sabroso (FEM **sabrosa**) ADJECTIVE
tasty

el **sacacorchos** (PL los **sacacorchos**) NOUN
corkscrew

el **sacapuntas** (PL los **sacapuntas**) NOUN
pencil sharpener

sacar* VERB [48]
1 to take out
□ Voy a sacar dinero del cajero. I'm going to take some money out of the machine. □ Se sacó las llaves del bolsillo. He took the keys out of his pocket. □ sacar la basura to take the rubbish out
■ **Me han sacado una muela.** I've had a tooth taken out.
■ **sacar a pasear al perro** to take the dog out for a walk
■ **sacar a alguien a bailar** to get somebody up for a dance
2 to get
□ Yo sacaré las entradas. I'll get the tickets. □ sacar buenas notas to get good marks
3 to release
□ Han sacado un nuevo disco. They've released a new record.
■ **sacar algo adelante** to conclude
■ **sacar una foto a alguien** to take a photo of somebody
■ **sacar la lengua a alguien** to stick your tongue out at somebody
■ **sacarse el carnet de conducir** to pass one's driving test
■ **sacarse el título de abogado** to qualify as a lawyer
■ **sacarse las botas** to take off one's boots

la **sacarina** NOUN
saccharin

el **sacerdote** NOUN
priest

el **saco** NOUN
1 sack
□ un saco de harina a sack of flour
■ **un saco de dormir** a sleeping bag
2 jacket *(Latin America)*

el **sacrificio** NOUN
sacrifice

sacudir VERB [58]
to shake
□ Hay que sacudir la alfombra. The carpet

needs shaking. □ Un terremoto sacudió la ciudad. An earthquake shook the city.

Sagitario MASC NOUN
Sagittarius
■ **Soy sagitario.** I'm Sagittarius.

sagrado (FEM **sagrada**) ADJECTIVE
1 sacred
2 holy

la **sal** NOUN
salt

la **sala** NOUN
1 room
2 ward
3 hall
■ **sala de embarque** departure lounge
■ **sala de espera** waiting room
■ **sala de estar** living room
■ **sala de fiestas** nightclub
■ **sala de juegos recreativos** amusement arcade
■ **sala de profesores** staffroom

salado (FEM **salada**) ADJECTIVE
1 salty
□ La carne está muy salada. The meat's very salty.
2 savoury
□ ¿Es dulce o salado? Is it sweet or savoury?

el **salario** NOUN
pay
■ **el salario mínimo** the minimum wage

la **salchicha** NOUN
sausage

el **salchichón** (PL los **salchichones**) NOUN
spiced salami sausage

el **saldo** NOUN
balance
■ **saldos** sales

saldré VERB ▷ *see* **salir**

el **salero** NOUN
salt cellar

salgo VERB ▷ *see* **salir**

la **salida** NOUN
1 exit
□ salida de emergencia emergency exit
□ salida de incendios fire exit
■ **a la salida del teatro** on the way out of the theatre
2 departure
□ la terminal de salidas nacionales the domestic departures terminal
■ **El tren de Londres efectuará su salida por el andén número dos.** The London train will depart from platform two.
3 start
■ **El juez dio la salida a la carrera.** The referee started the race.
■ **la salida del sol** sunrise

salir* VERB [49]
1 to come out
□ cuando salimos del cine when we came out of the cinema □ Acaba de salir un disco suyo. A record of his has just come out. □ Nos levantamos antes de que saliera el sol. We got up before the sun came out.
2 to go out
□ ¿Vas a salir esta noche? Are you going out tonight?
■ **Ha salido.** She's out.
■ **salir con alguien** to go out with somebody □ Está saliendo con un compañero de clase. She's going out with one of her classmates.
3 to get out
□ ¡Sal de ahí ahora mismo! Get out of here right now!
4 to leave
□ El autocar sale a las ocho. The coach leaves at eight. □ Quiere salir del país. She wants to leave the country.
5 to appear
□ Su foto salió en todos los periódicos. Her picture appeared in all the newspapers.
■ **Sale a 15 euros por persona.** It works out at 15 euros each.
■ **Me está saliendo una muela del juicio.** One of my wisdom teeth is coming through.
■ **No sé cómo vamos a salir adelante.** I don't know how we're going to go on.
■ **salir bien** to work out well □ El plan salió bien. The plan worked out well.
■ **Espero que todo salga bien.** I hope everything works out all right.
■ **Les salió mal el proyecto.** Their plan didn't work out.
■ **¡Qué mal me ha salido el dibujo!** My drawing hasn't come out very well, has it!
■ **salirse 1** to boil over □ Se ha salido la leche. The milk's boiled over. **2** to leak □ Se salía el aceite del motor. Oil was leaking out of the engine. **3** to come off □ Nos salimos de la carretera. We came off the road. **4** to come out □ Se ha salido el enchufe. The plug has come out.

la **saliva** NOUN
saliva

el **salmón** (PL los **salmones**) NOUN
salmon
■ **rosa salmón** salmon pink

el **salón** (PL los **salones**) NOUN
1 living room
■ **salón de actos** meeting hall
■ **salón de belleza** beauty salon
■ **salón de juegos recreativos** amusement arcade

Spanish-English

2 classroom *(Mexico)*
la **salpicadera** NOUN
mudguard *(Mexico)*
el **salpicadero** NOUN
dashboard
salpicar* VERB [48]
to splash
la **salsa** NOUN
1 sauce
□ salsa de tomate tomato sauce
2 salsa
el **saltamontes** (PL los **saltamontes**) NOUN
grasshopper
saltar VERB [25]
to jump
□ El caballo saltó la valla. The horse jumped over the wall. □ saltar por la ventana to jump out of the window
■ **hacer saltar algo por los aires** to blow something up
■ **saltarse** to skip □ Te has saltado una página. You've skipped a page.
■ **saltarse un semáforo en rojo** to go through a red light
el **salto** NOUN
1 jump
2 dive
■ **dar un salto** to jump
■ **salto de altura** high jump
■ **salto de longitud** long jump
■ **salto mortal** somersault
LANGUAGE TIP Word for word, **salto mortal** means 'mortal jump'.
■ **salto con pértiga** pole vault
■ **salto de trampolín** springboard diving
la **salud** NOUN
health
salud EXCLAMATION
1 cheers!
2 bless you!
saludable (FEM **saludable**) ADJECTIVE
healthy
saludar VERB [25]
1 to say hello
□ Entré a saludarla. I went in to say hello to her.
2 to greet
□ Me saludó dándome un beso. He greeted me with a kiss.
■ **Lo saludé desde la otra acera.** I waved to him from the other side of the street.
3 to salute
el **saludo** NOUN
1 greeting
□ No contestó a mi saludo. He didn't respond to my greeting.
2 regards
□ Carolina te manda un saludo. Carolina sends her regards. □ Saludos cordiales. Kind regards.
■ **¡Saludos a Teresa de mi parte!** Say hello to Teresa for me!
salvaje (FEM **salvaje**) ADJECTIVE
wild
el **salvapantallas** NOUN
screensaver
salvar VERB [25]
to save
□ Pocos se salvaron del naufragio. Few were saved from the shipwreck.
el **salvavidas** (PL los **salvavidas**) NOUN
lifebelt
salvo PREPOSITION
except
□ todos salvo yo everyone except me
■ **salvo que** unless
■ **estar a salvo** to be safe
■ **Consiguieron ponerse a salvo.** They managed to reach safety.
San ADJECTIVE
Saint
□ San Pedro Saint Peter
la **sandalia** NOUN
sandal
■ **unas sandalias** a pair of sandals
la **sandía** NOUN
watermelon
el **sandwich** (PL los **sandwiches**) NOUN
1 sandwich (PL sandwiches)
2 toasted sandwich
sangrar VERB [25]
to bleed
□ Me sangra la nariz. My nose is bleeding.
la **sangre** NOUN
blood
■ **echar sangre** to bleed
la **sangría** NOUN
sangria
la **sanidad** NOUN
public health
□ una reforma de la sanidad pública a reform in public health
sano (FEM **sana**) ADJECTIVE
healthy
□ una dieta sana a healthy diet
■ **sano y salvo** safe and sound
LANGUAGE TIP Be careful! **sano** does not mean **sane**.
la **santa** NOUN
saint
□ Santa Clara Saint Clara
santo (FEM **santa**) ADJECTIVE
holy
el **santo** NOUN
1 saint
□ Santo Domingo Saint Dominic

S

2 name day

DID YOU KNOW...?
Besides birthdays, some Spaniards also celebrate the feast day of the saint they are named after.

el **sapo** NOUN
toad

el **saque** NOUN
service
■ **saque de esquina** corner
■ **saque inicial** kick-off

el **sarampión** (PL los **sarampiones**) NOUN
measles *sing*

sarcástico (FEM **sarcástica**) ADJECTIVE
sarcastic

la **sardina** NOUN
sardine

el/la **sargento** NOUN
sergeant

el **sarpullido** NOUN
rash (PL rashes)
□ Le ha salido un sarpullido en la cara. His face has come out in a rash.

el **sarro** NOUN
tartar

la **sarta** NOUN
■ **Nos contó una sarta de mentiras.** He told us a pack of lies.

la **sartén** (PL las **sartenes**) NOUN
frying pan

el **sartén** (PL los **sartenes**) NOUN *(Latin America)*
frying pan

el **sastre** NOUN
tailor

el **satélite** NOUN
satellite
□ la televisión vía satélite satellite television

la **satisfacción** (PL las **satisfacciones**) NOUN
satisfaction
□ Expresó su satisfacción por la victoria. She expressed her satisfaction at the victory.
■ **Recibió la noticia con satisfacción.** He was pleased to hear the news.

satisfacer* VERB [26]
to satisfy

satisfactorio (FEM **satisfactoria**) ADJECTIVE
satisfactory

satisfecho (FEM **satisfecha**) ADJECTIVE
satisfied
□ No estoy satisfecho con el resultado. I'm not satisfied with the result.

la **sauna** NOUN
sauna

el **saxofón** (PL los **saxofones**) NOUN
saxophone

sazonar VERB [25]
to season

se PRONOUN
□ Pedro necesitaba la calculadora y se la dejé. Pedro needed the calculator and I lent it to him. □ No quiero que Rosa lo sepa. No se lo digas. I don't want Rosa to know. Don't tell her. □ He hablado con mis padres y se lo he explicado. I've talked to my parents and explained it to them. □ Aquí tiene el libro. ¿Se lo envuelvo, señor? Here's your book. Shall I wrap it for you, sir? □ Dáselo a Enrique. Give it to Enrique. □ No se lo digas a Susana. Don't tell Susana. □ ¿Se lo has preguntado a tus padres? Have you asked your parents about it? □ Marcos se ha cortado con un cristal. Marcos cut himself on a piece of broken glass. □ Margarita se estaba preparando para salir. Margarita was getting herself ready to go out. □ La calefacción se apaga sola. The heating turns itself off automatically. □ ¿Se ha hecho usted daño? Have you hurt yourself?
■ **Se está afeitando.** He's shaving.
■ **Mi hermana nunca se queja.** My sister never complains. □ Pablo se lavó los dientes. Pablo brushed his teeth. □ Carmen no podía abrocharse el vestido. Carmen couldn't do up her dress. □ Se dieron un beso. They gave each other a kiss. □ Se cree que el tabaco produce cáncer. It is believed that smoking causes cancer. □ Es lo que pasa cuando se come tan deprisa. That's what happens when you eat so fast.
■ **'se vende'** 'for sale'

sé VERB ▷ *see* **saber**

sea VERB ▷ *see* **ser**

el **secador** NOUN
hair dryer

la **secadora** NOUN
1 tumble dryer
2 hair dryer *(Mexico)*

secar* VERB [48]
to dry
□ Voy a secarme el pelo. I'm going to dry my hair.
■ **secarse** to dry □ Sécate con la toalla. Dry yourself with the towel.
■ **¿Se ha secado ya la ropa?** Is the washing dry yet?
■ **Se han secado las plantas.** The plants have dried up.

la **sección** (PL las **secciones**) NOUN
1 section
□ la sección de deportes del periódico the sports section of the newspaper
2 department
□ la sección de perfumería the perfumery department

seco (FEM **seca**) ADJECTIVE
1 dry
□ El suelo ya está seco. The floor's dry now.
□ Tiene una tos muy seca. He's got a very dry cough.
2 dried
□ flores secas dried flowers

el **secretario**, la **secretaria** NOUN
secretary (PL secretaries)
■ **una secretaria de dirección** a PA (*= personal assistant*)

el **secreto** NOUN
secret
□ Te voy a contar un secreto. I'm going to tell you a secret.
■ **en secreto** in secret

secreto (FEM **secreta**) ADJECTIVE
secret

la **secta** NOUN
sect

el **sector** NOUN
sector
□ el sector de la minería the mining sector

la **secuencia** NOUN
sequence

el **secuestrador**, la **secuestradora** NOUN
1 kidnapper
2 hijacker

secuestrar VERB [25]
1 to kidnap
2 to hijack

el **secuestro** NOUN
1 kidnapping
2 hijack

secundario (FEM **secundaria**) ADJECTIVE
secondary

la **sed** NOUN
thirst
■ **tener sed** to be thirsty

la **seda** NOUN
silk
□ una camisa de seda a silk shirt

el **sedal** NOUN
fishing line

el **sedante** NOUN
sedative

la **sede** NOUN
1 headquarters *pl*
□ la sede de la ONU the UN headquarters
2 venue
□ Barcelona fue la sede de los Juegos Olímpicos del 92. Barcelona was the venue for the 1992 Olympics.

sediento (FEM **sedienta**) ADJECTIVE
thirsty

segar* VERB [34]
1 to reap
2 to mow

seguido (FEM **seguida**) ADJECTIVE
in a row
□ La he visto tres días seguidos. I've seen her three days in a row.
■ **en seguida** straight away □ En seguida estoy con usted. I'll be with you straight away.
■ **En seguida termino.** I'm just about to finish.
■ **todo seguido** straight on □ Vaya todo seguido hasta la plaza y luego ... Go straight on until the square and then ...

seguir* VERB [50]
1 to carry on
□ ¡Sigue, por favor! Carry on, please! □ El ordenador seguía funcionando. The computer carried on working.
■ **El ascensor sigue estropeado.** The lift's still not working.
■ **Sigo sin comprender.** I still don't understand.
■ **Sigue lloviendo.** It's still raining.
2 to follow
□ Tú ve primero que yo te sigo. You go first and I'll follow you.
■ **seguir adelante** to go ahead □ Los Juegos Olímpicos siguieron adelante a pesar del atentado. The Olympics went ahead despite the attack.

según PREPOSITION
1 according to
□ Según tú, no habrá problemas de entradas. According to you there won't be any problems with the tickets.
2 depending on
□ Iremos o no, según esté el tiempo. We might go, depending on the weather.

segundo (FEM **segunda**) ADJECTIVE, PRONOUN
second
■ **el segundo plato** the second course
■ **Vive en el segundo.** He lives on the second floor.

el **segundo** NOUN
second
□ Es un segundo nada más. It'll only take a second.

seguramente ADVERB
probably
□ Seguramente llegarán mañana. They'll probably arrive tomorrow.
■ **¿Lo va a comprar? — Seguramente.** Are you going to buy it? — Almost certainly.

la **seguridad** NOUN
1 safety
□ Hay que mejorar la seguridad en los autocares. Safety on coaches must be improved.

2 security
□ Las medidas de seguridad son muy estrictas. The security measures are very strict.
3 certainty
□ con toda seguridad with complete certainty
■ **seguridad en uno mismo** self-confidence □ Le falta seguridad en sí mismo. He lacks self-confidence.
■ **la seguridad social** social security

seguro (FEM **segura**) ADJECTIVE
1 safe
□ Este avión es muy seguro. This plane is very safe. □ Aquí estaremos seguros. We'll be safe here.
2 sure
□ Estoy segura de que ganaremos. I'm sure we'll win. □ Está muy seguro de sí mismo. He's very sure of himself.
3 certain
□ No es seguro que vayan a venir. It's not certain that they're going to come.

el **seguro** NOUN
insurance
□ el seguro del coche car insurance
■ **seguro de vida** life assurance

seis (FEM **seis**) ADJECTIVE, PRONOUN
six
■ **Son las seis.** It's six o'clock.
■ **el seis de enero** the sixth of January

seiscientos (FEM **seiscientas**) ADJECTIVE, PRONOUN
six hundred

la **selección** (PL las **selecciones**) NOUN
1 selection
□ una selección de los mejores vídeos a selection of the finest videos
2 team
□ la selección nacional the national team

seleccionar VERB [25]
to pick
□ Lo seleccionaron para jugar en su equipo. He was picked to play in the team.

la **selectividad** NOUN
university entrance exam

sellar VERB [25]
1 to seal
2 to stamp
3 to sign on

el **sello** NOUN
1 stamp
□ Colecciona sellos. He collects stamps.
2 seal
□ El producto lleva un sello de calidad. The product bears a seal of quality.

la **selva** NOUN
jungle
■ **la selva tropical** the rainforest

el **semáforo** NOUN
traffic lights *pl*
■ **un semáforo en rojo** a red light

la **semana** NOUN
week
□ dentro de una semana in a week's time
□ una vez a la semana once a week
■ **entre semana** during the week
■ **Semana Santa** Holy Week

semanal (FEM **semanal**) ADJECTIVE
weekly

sembrar* VERB [39]
1 to plant
2 to sow

semejante (FEM **semejante**) ADJECTIVE
1 similar
□ Tenemos unos rasgos muy semejantes. We have very similar features.
2 such
□ Nunca he dicho semejante cosa. I've never said such a thing.

el **semicírculo** NOUN
semicircle

la **semifinal** NOUN
semi-final

la **semilla** NOUN
seed

el **senado** NOUN
senate

el **senador**, la **senadora** NOUN
senator

sencillamente ADVERB
simply
□ Es sencillamente imposible. It's simply impossible.

sencillo (FEM **sencilla**) ADJECTIVE
1 simple
□ Es muy sencillo. It's really simple. □ un vestido sencillo a simple dress
2 modest
□ Es muy sencillo en el trato. He has a very modest manner.

el **sencillo** NOUN
1 single *(record)*
2 small change *(Latin America)*

el **senderismo** NOUN
trekking

el **sendero** NOUN
path

la **sensación** (PL las **sensaciones**) NOUN
feeling
□ Tengo la sensación de que mienten. I get the feeling they're lying. □ una sensación de escozor a burning feeling

sensacional (FEM **sensacional**) ADJECTIVE
sensational

sensato (FEM **sensata**) ADJECTIVE

sensible
□ Lo sensato sería no moverse de aquí. The sensible thing would be not to move from here.

sensible (FEM **sensible**) ADJECTIVE
sensitive
□ Es un chico muy sensible. He's a very sensitive boy. □ Tengo los ojos muy sensibles. My eyes are very sensitive.
LANGUAGE TIP Be careful! The Spanish word **sensible** does not mean **sensible**.

sensual (FEM **sensual**) ADJECTIVE
sensuous

sentado (FEM **sentada**) ADJECTIVE
■ **estar sentado** to be sitting down

sentar* VERB [39]
1 to suit
□ Ese vestido te sienta muy bien. That dress really suits you.
2 to agree with
□ No me sienta bien cenar tanto. Having so much dinner doesn't agree with me.
■ **Le ha sentado mal que no lo invitaras a la boda.** He was put out that you didn't invite him to the wedding.
■ **sentarse** to sit down □ Por favor, siéntese. Please sit down.

la **sentencia** NOUN
sentence

el **sentido** NOUN
1 sense
□ No tiene sentido. It doesn't make sense.
2 meaning
□ palabras con doble sentido words with a double meaning
■ **sentido común** common sense
■ **sentido del humor** sense of humour
■ **una calle de sentido único** a one-way street
■ **en algún sentido** in some respects
■ **en cierto sentido** in a certain sense

sentimental (FEM **sentimental**) ADJECTIVE
sentimental

el **sentimiento** NOUN
feeling

sentir* VERB [51]
1 to feel
□ Sentí un dolor en la pierna. I felt a pain in my leg.
■ **De pronto sentí un poco de frío.** Suddenly I felt a bit cold.
2 to hear
□ No la sentí entrar. I didn't hear her come in.
3 to be sorry
□ Lo siento mucho. I'm very sorry. □ Siento llegar tarde. I'm sorry I'm late.
■ **sentirse** to feel □ No me siento nada bien. I don't feel at all well.

la **seña** NOUN
sign
□ Les hice una seña. I made a sign to them.
□ Nos comunicábamos por señas. We communicated by signs.
■ **señas** address

la **señal** NOUN
1 sign
■ **señal de tráfico** road sign
■ **señal indicadora** signpost
■ **señal de llamada** dialling tone
2 signal
□ Yo daré la señal. I'll give the signal.
■ **Les hice una señal para que se fueran.** I signalled to them to go.
3 deposit
□ Dimos una señal de 30 euros. We paid a deposit of 30 euros.

señalar VERB [25]
to mark
□ Señálalo con un bolígrafo rojo. Mark it with a red pen.
■ **señalar con el dedo** to point

señalizar* VERB [13]
1 to indicate
2 to signpost

el **señor** NOUN
1 man (PL men)
□ Este señor ha llegado antes que yo. This man was before me.
■ **¿Le ocurre algo, señor?** Is there something the matter?
■ **¿Qué le pongo, señor?** What would you like, sir?
2 Mr
□ el señor Delgado Mr Delgado
3 lord
□ un señor feudal a feudal lord
■ **Muy señor mío ...** Dear Sir ...
■ **el señor alcalde** the mayor

la **señora** NOUN
1 lady (PL ladies)
□ Deja pasar a esta señora. Let the lady past.
■ **¿Le ocurre algo, señora?** Is there something the matter?
■ **¿Qué le pongo, señora?** What would you like, madam?
2 Mrs
□ la señora Delgado Mrs Delgado
3 wife
□ Vino con su señora. He came with his wife.

la **señorita** NOUN
young lady
□ Deja pasar a esta señorita. Let the young

lady past. □ la señorita Delgado Miss Delgado

sepa VERB ▷ *see* **saber**

la **separación** (PL las **separaciones**) NOUN

1 separation

2 gap

□ Había una gran separación entre el andén y la vía. There was a large gap between the platform and the rails.

separado (FEM **separada**) ADJECTIVE

1 separate

□ Duermen en camas separadas. They sleep in separate beds.

■ **por separado** separately

2 separated

□ Está separado de su mujer. He's separated from his wife.

separar VERB [25]

to separate

■ **separarse 1** to separate **2** to split up

septiembre MASC NOUN

September

□ en septiembre in September □ Ella nació el 11 de septiembre. She was born on 11 September.

séptimo (FEM **séptima**) ADJECTIVE, PRONOUN

seventh

■ **Vivo en el séptimo.** I live on the seventh floor.

la **sequía** NOUN

drought

ser* VERB [52]

to be

□ Es muy alto. He's very tall. □ Es médico. He's a doctor. □ La fiesta va a ser en su casa. The party's going to be in her house. □ Fue construido en 1960. It was built in 1960. □ Era de noche. It was night.

■ **Soy Lucía.** It's Lucía.

■ **Son las seis y media.** It's half past six.

■ **Éramos cinco en el coche.** There were five of us in the car.

■ **¡Es cierto!** That's right!

■ **Me es imposible asistir.** It's impossible for me to attend.

■ **ser de 1**

■ **Es de Joaquín.** It's Joaquín's. **2** to be from □ ¿De dónde eres? Where are you from? **3** to be made of □ Es de piedra. It's made of stone.

■ **a no ser que ...** unless ... □ a no ser que salgamos mañana unless we leave tomorrow

■ **O sea, que no vienes.** So you're not coming.

■ **mis hijos, o sea, Juan y Pedro** my children, that is, Juan and Pedro

el **ser** NOUN

being

■ **un ser humano** a human being

■ **un ser vivo** a living being

la **serie** NOUN

series

□ Tuvimos una serie de reuniones. We had a series of meetings. □ una serie policíaca a police series

serio (FEM **seria**) ADJECTIVE

serious

■ **en serio** seriously □ No hablaba en serio. I wasn't speaking seriously.

■ **¿Lo dices en serio?** Do you really mean it?

el **sermón** (PL los **sermones**) NOUN

sermon

la **serpiente** NOUN

snake

■ **una serpiente de cascabel** a rattlesnake

serrar* VERB [39]

to saw

el **serrucho** NOUN

saw

servicial (FEM **servicial**) ADJECTIVE

helpful

el **servicio** NOUN

1 service

□ el servicio militar national service □ El servicio no va incluido. Service is not included.

■ **Tenemos servicio a domicilio.** We have a home delivery service.

■ **estar de servicio** to be on duty

■ **estar fuera de servicio 1** to be out of service **2** to be off duty

2 toilet

□ Está en el servicio. He's in the toilet.

■ **el servicio de caballeros** the gents'

■ **el servicio de señoras** the ladies'

■ **Al servicio, Costa.** Costa to serve.

el **servidor** NOUN

server

la **servilleta** NOUN

napkin

servir* VERB [38]

1 to be useful for

□ Estas bolsas sirven para guardar alimentos. These bags are useful for storing food.

■ **¿Para qué sirve esto?** What's this for?

■ **Esta radio aún sirve.** This radio still works.

2 to serve

□ Yo serviré la cena. I'll serve supper.

■ **Sírveme un poco más de vino.** Give me a little bit more wine.

■ **Trabaja sirviendo mesas.** She works as a waitress.

■ **no servir para nada** to be useless
■ **¿En qué puedo servirlo?** How can I help you?

sesenta (FEM **sesenta**) ADJECTIVE, PRONOUN
sixty
□ Tiene sesenta años. He's sixty.
■ **el sesenta aniversario** the sixtieth anniversary

la **sesión** (PL las **sesiones**) NOUN
1 session
□ una sesión parlamentaria a parliamentary session
2 showing
□ Fuimos a la última sesión del sábado. We went to the last showing on Saturday night.

la **seta** NOUN
mushroom
■ **seta venenosa** toadstool

setecientos (FEM **setecientas**) ADJECTIVE, PRONOUN
seven hundred

setenta (FEM **setenta**) ADJECTIVE, PRONOUN
seventy
□ Tiene setenta años. He's seventy.
■ **el setenta aniversario** the seventieth anniversary

el **seto** NOUN
hedge

el **seudónimo** NOUN
pseudonym

severo (FEM **severa**) ADJECTIVE
1 strict
2 harsh

Sevilla FEM NOUN
Seville

el/la **sexista** ADJECTIVE, NOUN
sexist

el **sexo** NOUN
sex

sexto (FEM **sexta**) ADJECTIVE, PRONOUN
sixth
■ **Vivo en el sexto.** I live on the sixth floor.

sexual (FEM **sexual**) ADJECTIVE
sexual
□ acoso sexual sexual harassment
■ **educación sexual** sex education

la **sexualidad** NOUN
sexuality

si CONJUNCTION
1 if
□ Si quieres, te dejo el coche. I'll lend you the car if you like. □ ¿Sabes si hemos cobrado ya? Do you know if we've been paid yet?
■ **¿Y si llueve?** And what if it rains?
■ **Si me hubiera tocado la lotería ...** If only I had won the lottery ...
2 whether
□ No sé si ir o no. I don't know whether to go or not.
■ **si no 1** otherwise □ Ponte crema. Si no, te quemarás. Put some cream on, otherwise you'll get sunburned. **2** if...not
□ Avisadme si no podéis venir. Let me know if you can't come.

sí ADVERB
▷ *see also* **sí** PRONOUN
yes
□ ¿Te apetece un café? — Sí, gracias. Do you fancy a coffee? — Yes, please.
■ **¿Te gusta? — Sí.** Do you like it? — Yes, I do.
■ **Creo que sí.** I think so.
■ **Él no quiere pero yo sí.** He doesn't want to but I do.

sí PRONOUN
▷ *see also* **sí** ADVERB
□ Sólo habla de sí mismo. He only talks about himself. □ Se perjudica a sí misma. She's harming herself. □ Pregúntese a sí mismo el motivo. Ask yourself the reason. □ La pregunta en sí no era difícil. The question itself wasn't difficult. □ Hablaban entre sí. They were talking among themselves.
■ **La Tierra gira sobre sí misma.** The Earth turns on its own axis. □ Es mejor aprender las cosas por sí mismo. It's better to learn things by yourself.

Sicilia FEM NOUN
Sicily

el **sida** NOUN
AIDS

la **sidra** NOUN
cider

siego VERB ▷ *see* **segar**

siembro VERB ▷ *see* **sembrar**

siempre ADVERB
always
□ Siempre llega tarde. She always arrives late.
■ **como siempre** as usual
■ **para siempre** forever
■ **siempre y cuando** provided □ siempre y cuando acepte nuestras condiciones provided he accepts our conditions

siendo VERB ▷ *see* **ser**

siento VERB ▷ *see* **sentir**

la **sierra** NOUN
1 saw
2 mountain range
■ **Tenemos una casa en la sierra.** We have a house in the mountains.

la **siesta** NOUN
nap
■ **echarse la siesta** to have a nap

■ **la hora de la siesta** siesta time

siete (FEM **siete**) ADJECTIVE, PRONOUN
seven
■ **Son las siete.** It's seven o'clock.
■ **el siete de marzo** the seventh of March

las **siglas** NOUN
abbreviation *sing*

el **siglo** NOUN
century (PL centuries)
□ el siglo XX the 20th century

el **significado** NOUN
meaning

significar* VERB [48]
1 to mean
□ ¿Qué significa 'wild'? What does 'wild' mean? □ No sé lo que significa. I don't know what it means.
2 to stand for
□ 'B.C.' significa 'before Christ'. 'B.C.' stands for 'before Christ'.

significativo (FEM **significativa**) ADJECTIVE
significant

el **signo** NOUN
sign
□ Ese apetito es signo de buena salud. Such an appetite is a sign of good health.
■ **¿De qué signo del zodíaco eres?** What star sign are you?
■ **signo de admiración** exclamation mark
■ **signo de interrogación** question mark

siguiendo VERB ▷ *see* **seguir**

siguiente (FEM **siguiente**) ADJECTIVE
next
□ el siguiente vuelo the next flight □ Al día siguiente visitamos Toledo. The next day we visited Toledo.
■ **¡Que pase el siguiente, por favor!** Next please!

la **sílaba** NOUN
syllable

silbar VERB [25]
to whistle

el **silbato** NOUN
whistle

el **silbido** NOUN
whistle

el **silencio** NOUN
silence
■ **guardar silencio** to keep quiet
■ **¡Silencio!** Quiet!

silencioso (FEM **silenciosa**) ADJECTIVE
silent

la **silla** NOUN
chair
■ **silla de montar** saddle
■ **silla de paseo** pushchair
■ **silla de ruedas** wheelchair

el **sillín** (PL los **sillines**) NOUN
saddle

el **sillón** (PL los **sillones**) NOUN
armchair

la **silueta** NOUN
outline
■ **Tiene una silueta perfecta.** She has a perfect figure.

el **símbolo** NOUN
symbol

la **simpatía** NOUN
1 kindness
2 friendly nature
■ **Les tengo simpatía.** I like them.

simpático (FEM **simpática**) ADJECTIVE
nice
□ Estuvo muy simpática con todos. She was very nice to everybody. □ Los cubanos son muy simpáticos. Cubans are very nice people.
■ **Me cae simpático.** I think he's really nice.

LANGUAGE TIP Be careful! **simpático** does not mean **sympathetic**.

simple (FEM **simple**) ADJECTIVE
simple

simplemente ADVERB
simply

simultáneo (FEM **simultánea**) ADJECTIVE
simultaneous

sin PREPOSITION
without
□ Es peligroso ir en moto sin casco. It's dangerous to ride a motorbike without a helmet. □ Salió sin hacer ruido. She went out without making a noise. □ sin que él se diera cuenta without him realising
■ **He dejado el crucigrama sin terminar.** I left the crossword unfinished.
■ **Me quedé sin habla.** I was speechless.
■ **la gente sin hogar** the homeless

sincero (FEM **sincera**) ADJECTIVE
honest
□ Fui sincera con él. I was honest with him.

el/la **sindicalista** NOUN
trade unionist

el **sindicato** NOUN
trade union

la **sinfonía** NOUN
symphony (PL symphonies)

el **singular** ADJECTIVE, NOUN
singular
■ **en singular** in the singular

siniestro (FEM **siniestra**) ADJECTIVE
sinister

sino CONJUNCTION
but
□ No son ingleses sino galeses. They're not English, but Welsh.

Spanish-English

■ **No hace sino pedirnos dinero.** All he does is ask us for money.
■ **No solo nos ayudó, sino que también nos invitó a cenar.** He didn't just help us, he also bought us dinner.

sintético (FEM **sintética**) ADJECTIVE
synthetic

sintiendo VERB ▷ *see* **sentir**

el **síntoma** NOUN
symptom

el/la **sinvergüenza** NOUN
crook
■ **Es una sinvergüenza.** She's shameless.

siquiera ADVERB
■ **ni siquiera** not even □ Ni siquiera me dirigió la palabra. She didn't even acknowledge me.

la **sirena** NOUN
1 siren
2 mermaid

sirviendo VERB ▷ *see* **servir**

la **sirvienta** NOUN
maid

el **sirviente** NOUN
servant

el **sistema** NOUN
system

el **sitio** NOUN
1 place
□ un sitio tranquilo a peaceful place
■ **cambiar algo de sitio** to move something around
■ **en cualquier sitio** anywhere
■ **en algún sitio** somewhere
■ **en ningún sitio** nowhere
2 room
□ Hay sitio de sobra. There's room to spare.
■ **Hemos hecho sitio para ti en el coche.** We've made room for you in the car.
■ **un sitio web** website

la **situación** (PL las **situaciones**) NOUN
situation

situado (FEM **situada**) ADJECTIVE
■ **está situado en ...** it's situated in ...

el **SMS** (PL los **SMS**) NOUN
text message

el **sobaco** NOUN
armpit

el **soborno** NOUN
1 bribery
2 bribe
■ **Denunció un intento de soborno.** He reported an attempted bribe.

sobra FEM NOUN
■ **Tenemos comida de sobra.** We've got more than enough food.
■ **Sabes de sobra que yo no he sido.** You know full well that it wasn't me.
■ **las sobras** the leftovers

sobrar VERB [25]
1 to be left over
□ Ha sobrado mucha comida. There's plenty of food left over.
2 to be spare
□ Esta pieza sobra. This piece is spare.
■ **Este ejemplo sobra.** This example is unnecessary.
■ **Con este dinero sobrará.** This money will be more than enough.

sobre PREPOSITION
1 on
□ Dejó el dinero sobre la mesa. He left the money on the table.
2 about
□ información sobre vuelos information about flights
■ **sobre las seis** at about six o'clock
■ **sobre todo** above all

el **sobre** NOUN
envelope

la **sobredosis** (PL las **sobredosis**) NOUN
overdose

sobrenatural (FEM **sobrenatural**) ADJECTIVE
supernatural

el **sobresaliente** NOUN
distinction

sobrevivir VERB [58]
to survive

la **sobrina** NOUN
niece

el **sobrino** NOUN
nephew
■ **mis sobrinos** 1 my nephews 2 my nieces and nephews

sobrio (FEM **sobria**) ADJECTIVE
sober

la **socia** NOUN
1 partner
2 member

social (FEM **social**) ADJECTIVE
social

el **socialismo** NOUN
socialism

el/la **socialista** ADJECTIVE, NOUN
socialist

la **sociedad** NOUN
society (PL societies)
■ **una sociedad anónima** a limited company

el **socio** NOUN
1 partner
2 member

la **sociología** NOUN
sociology

el/la **socorrista** NOUN
lifeguard

S

el **socorro** NOUN
help
■ **pedir socorro** to ask for help
■ **Acudió en su socorro.** She went to his aid.

socorro EXCLAMATION
help!

la **soda** NOUN
soda

el **sofá** (PL los **sofás**) NOUN
sofa
■ **un sofá-cama** a sofa bed

sofisticado (FEM **sofisticada**) ADJECTIVE
sophisticated

el **software** NOUN
software

sois VERB ▷ *see* **ser**

la **soja** NOUN
soya

el **sol** NOUN
sun
■ **estar al sol** to be in the sun
■ **Hace sol.** It's sunny.
■ **tomar el sol** to sunbathe

solamente ADVERB
only

el **soldado** NOUN
soldier

soleado (FEM **soleada**) ADJECTIVE
sunny

la **soledad** NOUN
loneliness

soler* VERB [33]
□ Suele salir a las ocho. He usually leaves at eight. □ Solíamos ir todos los años a la playa. We used to go to the beach every year.

solicitar VERB [25]
1 to ask for
2 to apply for

la **solicitud** NOUN
1 application
■ **presentar una solicitud** to submit an application
2 request

sólido (FEM **sólida**) ADJECTIVE
solid

solitario (FEM **solitaria**) ADJECTIVE
solitary

sollozar* VERB [13]
to sob

solo (FEM **sola**) ADJECTIVE
1 alone
□ ¡Déjame solo! Leave me alone! □ Me quedé solo. I was left alone.
■ **¿Estás solo?** Are you on your own?
■ **Lo hice solo.** I did it on my own.
2 lonely
□ A veces me siento solo. Sometimes I feel lonely.
3 single
□ No hubo una sola queja. There wasn't a single complaint.
■ **Había un solo problema.** There was just one problem.
■ **Habla solo.** He talks to himself.
■ **un café solo** a black coffee

el **solo** NOUN
solo
□ un solo de guitarra a guitar solo

sólo ADVERB
only
□ Sólo cuesta diez libras. It only costs ten pounds. □ Era sólo una idea. It was only an idea. □ Yo también fumo, sólo que en pipa. I smoke as well, only a pipe.
■ **no sólo ... sino ...** not only ... but ... □ No sólo es barato, sino también de buena calidad. It's not only cheap, but it's good quality too.

el **solomillo** NOUN
sirloin

soltar* VERB [11]
1 to let go of
□ No sueltes la cuerda. Don't let go of the rope.
■ **¡Suéltame!** Let me go!
2 to put down
□ Soltó la bolsa de la compra en un banco. She put her shopping bag down on a bench.
3 to release
□ Han soltado a los rehenes. They've released the hostages.
4 to let out
□ Solté un suspiro de alivio. I let out a sigh of relief.

la **soltera** NOUN
single woman

soltero (FEM **soltera**) ADJECTIVE
single
□ Es soltero. He's single.

el **soltero** NOUN
bachelor

la **solución** (PL las **soluciones**) NOUN
1 solution
2 answer

solucionar VERB [25]
to solve
■ **un problema sin solucionar** an unsolved problem

la **sombra** NOUN
1 shade
□ Prefiero quedarme a la sombra. I prefer to stay in the shade.
2 shadow
□ Sólo vi una sombra. I only saw a shadow.

Spanish-English

■ **sombra de ojos** eye shadow

el **sombrero** NOUN
hat

la **sombrilla** NOUN
1 parasol
2 sunshade

el **somier** NOUN
mattress base

el **somnífero** NOUN
sleeping pill

el **sonajero** NOUN
rattle

sonar* VERB [11]
1 to sound
□ Sonabas un poco triste por teléfono. You sounded a bit sad on the phone.
■ **Escríbelo tal y como suena.** Write it down just the way it sounds.
2 to play
□ Sonaba una canción de Madonna por la radio. They were playing a Madonna song on the radio.
3 to ring
4 to go off
■ **Me suena esa cara.** That face rings a bell.
■ **sonarse la nariz** to blow one's nose

el **sondeo** NOUN
■ **un sondeo de opinión** an opinion poll

el **sonido** NOUN
sound

sonreír* VERB [44]
to smile
□ Me sonrió. She smiled at me.

la **sonrisa** NOUN
smile

sonrojarse VERB [25]
to blush

soñar* VERB [11]
to dream
□ Ayer soñé con él. I dreamed about him yesterday.

la **sopa** NOUN
soup
□ sopa de pescado fish soup

soplar VERB [25]
to blow
□ ¡Sopla con fuerza! Blow hard! □ Soplaba un viento fuerte. A strong wind was blowing.

soportar VERB [25]
to stand
□ No lo soporto. I can't stand him. □ No soporta que la critiquen. She can't stand being criticised.

LANGUAGE TIP Be careful! **soportar** does not mean **to support**.

la **soprano** NOUN
soprano

sorber VERB [8]
to sip

sordo (FEM **sorda**) ADJECTIVE
deaf
■ **quedarse sordo** to go deaf

sordomudo (FEM **sordomuda**) ADJECTIVE
deaf and dumb

sorprendente (FEM **sorprendente**) ADJECTIVE
surprising

sorprender VERB [8]
to surprise
□ No me sorprende. It doesn't surprise me.
■ **Me sorprendí al verlo allí.** I was surprised to see him there.

la **sorpresa** NOUN
surprise
□ ¡Qué sorpresa! What a surprise!
■ **coger a alguien de sorpresa** to take somebody by surprise

el **sorteo** NOUN
draw

la **sortija** NOUN
ring

soso (FEM **sosa**) ADJECTIVE
1 dull
2 bland
■ **Estas patatas fritas están sosas.** These chips need more salt.

la **sospecha** NOUN
suspicion

sospechar VERB [25]
to suspect
■ **Sospechan de él.** They suspect him.

el **sospechoso**, la **sospechosa** NOUN
suspect

sospechoso (FEM **sospechosa**) ADJECTIVE
suspicious

el **sostén** (PL los **sostenes**) NOUN
bra

sostener* VERB [53]
1 to support
□ Está sostenido por cuatro columnas. It is supported by four columns.
2 to hold
□ Sostuvieron la caja entre los dos. They held the box between the two of them.
■ **¿Puedes sostener la puerta un momento?** Can you hold the door open for a moment?
■ **La sombrilla no se sostiene con el viento.** The sunshade won't stay up in the wind.

la **sota** NOUN
jack

el **sótano** NOUN
1 basement
2 cellar

S

soy VERB ▷ *see* **ser**

el **spot** NOUN
■ **un spot publicitario** a commercial

Sr. ABBREVIATION
Mr

Sra. ABBREVIATION
Mrs

Sres. ABBREVIATION
Messrs

Srta. ABBREVIATION
Miss

su ADJECTIVE
1 his
□ su máquina de afeitar his razor □ sus padres his parents
2 her
□ su falda her skirt □ sus amigas her friends
3 its
□ un oso y su cachorro a bear and its cub □ el coche y sus accesorios the car and its fittings
4 their
□ su equipo favorito their favourite team □ sus amigos their friends
5 your
□ Su abrigo, señora. Your coat, madam. □ No olviden sus paraguas. Don't forget your umbrellas.

suave (FEM **suave**) ADJECTIVE
1 smooth
2 soft
3 gentle
4 mild

el **suavizante** NOUN
1 conditioner
2 fabric conditioner

la **subasta** NOUN
auction

el **subcampeón**, la **subcampeona** (MASC PL los **subcampeones**) NOUN
runner-up (PL runners-up)

subdesarrollado (FEM **subdesarrollada**) ADJECTIVE
underdeveloped

el **subdirector**, la **subdirectora** NOUN
1 deputy head
2 deputy director
3 deputy manager deputy manageress)

la **subida** NOUN
1 rise
□ una subida de los precios a rise in prices
2 ascent
□ una subida muy empinada a very steep ascent

subir VERB [58]
1 to go up
□ Subimos la cuesta. We went up the hill. □ La gasolina ha vuelto a subir. Petrol's gone up again.
2 to come up
□ Sube, que te voy a enseñar unos discos. Come up, I've got some records to show you.
3 to climb
□ subir una montaña to climb a mountain
4 to take up
□ ¿Me puedes ayudar a subir las maletas? Can you help me to take up the cases?
5 to put up
□ Los taxistas han subido sus tarifas. Taxi drivers have put their fares up.
6 to raise
□ Sube los brazos. Raise your arms.
7 to turn up
□ Sube la radio, que no se oye. Turn the radio up, I can't hear it.
■ **subirse a 1** to get into **2** to get onto **3** to get on
■ **subirse a un árbol** to climb a tree

el **subjuntivo** NOUN
subjunctive

el **submarino** NOUN
submarine

subrayar VERB [25]
to underline

el **subsidio** NOUN
subsidy (PL subsidies)
□ subsidio de paro unemployment benefit

el **subte** NOUN *(River Plate)*
underground

subterráneo (FEM **subterránea**) ADJECTIVE
underground

subtitulado (FEM **subtitulada**) ADJECTIVE
subtitled

los **subtítulos** NOUN
subtitles

el **suburbio** NOUN
slum area

la **subvención** (PL las **subvenciones**) NOUN
subsidy (PL subsidies)

subvencionar VERB [25]
to subsidize

suceder VERB [8]
to happen
□ ¿Les ha sucedido algo? Has something happened to them?

el **suceso** NOUN
1 event
□ los sucesos de la última decada the events of the last decade □ sucesos históricos historical events
2 incident
□ El suceso ocurrió sobre las tres de la tarde. The incident happened at around three in the afternoon.

■ **Acudieron rápidamente al lugar del suceso.** They rushed to the scene.

LANGUAGE TIP Be careful! **suceso** does not mean **success**.

la **suciedad** NOUN
dirt

sucio (FEM **sucia**) ADJECTIVE
dirty
□ Tienes las manos sucias. You've got dirty hands.

la **sucursal** NOUN
branch (PL branches)

la **sudadera** NOUN
sweatshirt

Sudáfrica FEM NOUN
South Africa

Sudamérica FEM NOUN
South America

el **sudamericano** (FEM la **sudamericana**) ADJECTIVE, NOUN
South American

sudar VERB [25]
to sweat

el **sudeste** NOUN
southeast

el **sudoeste** NOUN
southwest

el **sudor** NOUN
sweat

sudoroso (FEM **sudorosa**) ADJECTIVE
sweaty

la **sueca** NOUN
Swede

Suecia FEM NOUN
Sweden

sueco (FEM **sueca**) ADJECTIVE
Swedish

el **sueco** NOUN
1 Swede
2 Swedish

la **suegra** NOUN
mother-in-law (PL mothers-in-law)

el **suegro** NOUN
father-in-law (PL fathers-in-law)

los **suegros** NOUN
in-laws

la **suela** NOUN
sole

el **sueldo** NOUN
1 salary (PL salaries)
2 wages *pl*

el **suelo** NOUN
1 floor
□ un suelo de mármol a marble floor
2 ground
■ **Me caí al suelo.** I fell over.

suelo VERB ▷ *see* **soler**

suelto VERB
▷ *see also* **suelto** ADJECTIVE, NOUN ▷ *see* **soltar**

suelto (FEM **suelta**) ADJECTIVE
▷ *see also* **suelto** VERB, NOUN
loose
□ Tiene varias hojas sueltas. Some of the pages are loose. □ Lleva el pelo suelto. She wears her hair loose. □ No dejes al perro suelto. Don't let the dog loose.

el **suelto** NOUN
▷ *see also* **suelto** VERB, ADJECTIVE
change

sueno VERB ▷ *see* **sonar**

sueño VERB ▷ *see* **soñar**

el **sueño** NOUN
1 dream
□ Anoche tuve un mal sueño. I had a bad dream last night.
2 sleep
□ un sueño profundo a deep sleep
■ **Tengo sueño.** I'm sleepy.

la **suerte** NOUN
luck
□ No ha tenido mucha suerte. She hasn't had much luck.
■ **por suerte** luckily
■ **Tuvo suerte.** She was lucky.
■ **¡Qué suerte!** How lucky!
■ **¡Qué mala suerte!** What bad luck!

el **suéter** NOUN
sweater

suficiente (FEM **suficiente**) ADJECTIVE
enough
□ No tenía dinero suficiente. I didn't have enough money.

suficientemente ADVERB
sufficiently

sufrir VERB [58]
1 to have
□ Sufrió un ataque al corazón. He had a heart attack.
2 to suffer
□ Sufre de artritis. He suffers from arthritis.
■ **sufrir un colapso** to collapse

la **sugerencia** NOUN
suggestion
■ **hacer una sugerencia** to make a suggestion

sugerir* VERB [51]
to suggest
□ Sugirió que fuéramos al cinea. She suggested going to the cinema.

sugiero VERB ▷ *see* **sugerir**

el **suicidio** NOUN
suicide

Suiza FEM NOUN
Switzerland

el **suizo** (FEM la **suiza**) ADJECTIVE, NOUN
Swiss

■ **los suizos** the Swiss

el **sujetador** NOUN
bra

sujetar VERB [25]
1 to hold
□ Sujétame estos libros un momento. Hold these books for me a moment.
2 to fasten
□ Lo sujetó con un clip. He fastened it with a paper clip.
■ **Sujeta al perro, que no se escape.** Hold on to the dog so it doesn't get away.

el **sujeto** NOUN
subject

la **suma** NOUN
sum
□ una suma de dinero a sum of money
■ **¿Cuánto es la suma de todos los gastos?** What are the total expenses?
■ **hacer una suma** to do a sum

sumar VERB [25]
to add up

suministrar VERB [25]
to supply

el **suministro** NOUN
supply (PL supplies)

supe VERB ▷ *see* **saber**

súper (FEM **súper**) ADJECTIVE
■ **gasolina súper** four-star petrol

superar VERB [25]
1 to get over *(illness, crisis)*
2 to beat *(record)*
3 to pass *(test)*
■ **Las ventas han superado nuestras expectativas.** Sales have exceeded our expectations.

la **superficie** NOUN
1 surface
□ en la superficie terrestre on the Earth's surface
2 area
□ una superficie de 100 metros cuadrados an area of 100 square metres

superior (FEM **superior**) ADJECTIVE
1 upper
■ **el labio superior** the upper lip
2 top
□ el piso superior the top floor
■ **superior a** superior to
■ **Su inteligencia es superior a la media.** He has above-average intelligence.
■ **un curso de inglés de nivel superior** an advanced level English course

el **supermercado** NOUN
supermarket

el/la **superviviente** NOUN
survivor

el **suplemento** NOUN
supplement
□ el suplemento dominical the Sunday supplement

el/la **suplente** NOUN
1 reserve
2 supply teacher
3 locum

suplicar* VERB [48]
to beg

suponer* VERB [41]
1 to suppose
□ Supongo que vendrá. I suppose she'll come.
■ **Supongo que sí.** I suppose so.
2 to think
□ Te suponía más alto. I thought you'd be taller. □ Supusimos que no vendrías. We didn't think you would be coming.
3 to involve
□ Tener un coche supone más gastos. Having a car involves more expenses.

el **supositorio** NOUN
suppository

suprimir VERB [58]
to delete

supuesto VERB ▷ *see* **suponer**

el **supuesto** NOUN
■ **¿Y en el supuesto de que no venga?** And supposing he doesn't come?
■ **por supuesto** of course
■ **¡Por supuesto que no!** Of course not!

supuse VERB ▷ *see* **suponer**

el **sur** NOUN, ADJECTIVE
south
□ el sur del país the south of the country
□ en la costa sur on the south coast
■ **vientos del sur** southerly winds

sureño (FEM **sureña**) ADJECTIVE
southern

el **sureste** NOUN
southeast

el **surf** NOUN
surfing
■ **surf a vela** windsurfing
■ **practicar el surf** to surf

surgir* VERB [16]
to come up
□ Ha surgido un problema. A problem has come up.

el **suroeste** NOUN
southwest

surtido (FEM **surtida**) ADJECTIVE
assorted
□ pasteles surtidos assorted cakes
■ **estar bien surtido** to have a good selection

el **surtido** NOUN
selection

el **surtidor** NOUN
petrol pump
susceptible (FEM **susceptible**) ADJECTIVE
touchy
la **suscripción** (PL las **suscripciones**) NOUN
subscription
suspender VERB [8]
1 to call off
□ Han suspendido la boda. They've called the wedding off.
2 to postpone
□ Ha suspendido su visita hasta la semana que viene. He's postponed his visit until next week.
■ **El partido se suspendió a causa de la lluvia.** The game was rained off.
3 to fail
□ He suspendido Matemáticas. I've failed maths.
el **suspense** NOUN
suspense
□ una película de suspense a thriller
el **suspenso** NOUN
suspense *(Latin America)*
□ una película de suspenso a thriller
■ **Tengo un suspenso en inglés.** I failed English.
suspicaz (FEM **suspicaz**, PL **suspicaces**) ADJECTIVE
suspicious
suspirar VERB [25]
to sigh
el **suspiro** NOUN
sigh
la **sustancia** NOUN
substance
■ **una sustancia química** a chemical
el **sustantivo** NOUN
noun
sustituir* VERB [10]
1 to replace
□ Lo sustituí como secretario del club. I replaced him as club secretary.
2 to stand in for
□ ¿Me puedes sustituir un par de semanas? Can you stand in for me for a couple of weeks?
el **sustituto**, la **sustituta** NOUN
1 replacement
2 substitute
■ **Soy el sustituto del profesor de inglés.** I'm standing in for the English teacher.
sustituyendo VERB ▷ *see* **sustituir**
el **susto** NOUN
fright
□ ¡Qué susto! What a fright!
■ **dar un susto a alguien** to give somebody a fright
susurrar VERB [25]
to whisper
□ Me susurró su nombre al oído. He whispered his name in my ear.
sutil (FEM **sutil**) ADJECTIVE
subtle
suyo (FEM **suya**) PRONOUN, ADJECTIVE
1 his
□ Todas estas tierras son suyas. All this land is his. □ ¿Es éste su cuarto? — No, el suyo está abajo. Is this his room? — No, his is downstairs.
■ **un amigo suyo** a friend of his
2 hers
□ Es suyo. It's hers. □ ¿Es éste su abrigo? — No, el suyo es marrón. Is this her coat? — No, hers is brown.
■ **un amigo suyo** a friend of hers
3 theirs
□ Es suyo. It's theirs. □ ¿Es ésta su casa? — No, la suya está más adelante. Is this their house? — No, theirs is further on.
■ **un amigo suyo** a friend of theirs
4 yours
□ Todos estos libros son suyos. All these books are yours. □ ¿Es ésta nuestra habitación? — No, la suya está arriba. Is this our room? — No, yours is upstairs.
■ **un amigo suyo** a friend of yours

Tt

el **tabaco** NOUN
1 tobacco
■ **tabaco negro** dark tobacco
■ **tabaco rubio** Virginia tobacco
2 cigarettes *pl*

la **taberna** NOUN
bar

el **tabique** NOUN
partition

la **tabla** NOUN
plank
□ El agujero estaba cubierto con tablas. The hole was covered with planks.
■ **la tabla de multiplicar** the multiplication table
■ **una tabla de cocina** a chopping board
■ **la tabla de planchar** the ironing board
■ **la tabla de surf** the surfboard
■ **quedar en tablas** to draw

el **tablero** NOUN
board
■ **el tablero de ajedrez** the chessboard
■ **el tablero de mandos** the dashboard

la **tableta** NOUN
1 bar
2 tablet

el **tablón** (PL los **tablones**) NOUN
plank
□ los tablones del andamio the scaffolding planks
■ **el tablón de anuncios** the notice board

el **tabú** (PL los **tabúes**) NOUN
taboo (PL taboos)

el **taburete** NOUN
stool

tacaño (FEM **tacaña**) ADJECTIVE
mean

el **tacaño**, la **tacaña** NOUN
skinflint

tachar VERB [25]
to cross out
□ No lo taches, bórralo. Don't cross it out, erase it.
■ **La tacharon de mentirosa.** They accused her of being a liar.

el **taco** NOUN
1 rawlplug
2 stud
3 cube
4 cue
5 swearword
■ **soltar tacos** to swear
6 heel *(Chile, River Plate)*

el **tacón** (PL los **tacones**) NOUN
heel
■ **zapatos de tacón** high-heeled shoes

la **táctica** NOUN
tactics *pl*
□ El equipo cambió de táctica. The team changed tactics.

el **tacto** NOUN
1 touch
□ suave al tacto smooth to the touch
2 tact
■ **Lo dijo con mucho tacto.** He said it very tactfully.

la **tajada** NOUN
slice

tajante (FEM **tajante**) ADJECTIVE
1 emphatic
2 sharp
□ Lo dijo de manera tajante. He said it sharply.

tal (FEM **tal**) ADJECTIVE, PRONOUN
such
□ En tales casos es mejor consultar con un médico. In such cases it's better to see a doctor. □ ¡En el aeropuerto había tal confusión! There was such confusion at the airport!
■ **Lo dejé tal como estaba.** I left it just as it was.
■ **con tal de que** as long as □ con tal de que regreséis antes de las once as long as you get back before eleven
■ **¿Qué tal?** How are things?
■ **¿Qué tal has dormido?** How did you sleep?
■ **tal vez** perhaps

la **taladradora** NOUN
1 pneumatic drill
2 punch (PL punches)

Spanish-English

taladrar VERB [25]
to drill
el **taladro** NOUN
drill
el **talento** NOUN
talent
□ Sus hijos tienen talento para la música. Their children have a talent for music.
la **talla** NOUN
size
□ ¿Tienen esta camisa en la talla cuatro? Do you have this shirt in a size four?
tallar VERB [25]
1 to carve
2 to sculpt
3 to scrub *(Chile, River Plate)*
los **tallarines** NOUN
noodles
el **taller** NOUN
1 garage
□ Tengo el coche en el taller. My car is in the garage.
2 workshop
■ **un taller de teatro** a theatre workshop
el **tallo** NOUN
stem
el **talón** (PL los **talones**) NOUN
1 heel
2 cheque
□ cobrar un talón to cash a cheque
el **talonario** NOUN
1 chequebook
2 book of tickets
3 receipt book
el **tamaño** NOUN
size
■ **¿Qué tamaño tiene?** What size is it?
tambalearse VERB [25]
1 to wobble
2 to stagger
también ADVERB
also
□ Canta flamenco y también baila. He sings flamenco and also dances.
■ **Tengo hambre. — Yo también.** I'm hungry. — So am I.
■ **Yo estoy de acuerdo. — Nosotros también.** I agree. — So do we.
el **tambor** NOUN
drum
el **Támesis** NOUN
the Thames
el **tamiz** (PL los **tamices**) NOUN
sieve
tampoco ADVERB
1 either
□ Yo tampoco lo compré. I didn't buy it either.
2 neither
□ Yo no la vi. — Yo tampoco. I didn't see her. — Neither did I. □ Nunca he estado en París. — Yo tampoco. I've never been to Paris. — Neither have I.
el **tampón** (PL los **tampones**) NOUN
tampon
tan ADVERB
1 so
□ No creí que fueras a venir tan pronto. I didn't think you'd come so soon. □ ¡No es tan difícil! It's not so difficult!
■ **¡Qué hombre tan amable!** What a kind man!
■ **tan ... que ...** so ... that ... □ Habla tan deprisa que no la entiendo. She talks so fast that I can't understand her.
2 such
□ No era una idea tan buena. It wasn't such a good idea. □ ¡Tiene unos amigos tan simpáticos! He has such nice friends!
■ **tan ... como ...** as ... as ... □ No es tan guapa como su madre. She's not as pretty as her mother. □ Vine tan pronto como pude. I came as soon as I could.
el **tanque** NOUN
tank
tantear VERB [25]
to weigh up
tanto (FEM **tanta**) ADJECTIVE, ADVERB, PRONOUN
1 so much (PL so many)
□ Ahora no bebo tanta leche. I don't drink so much milk now. □ Se preocupa tanto que no puede dormir. He worries so much that he can't sleep. □ ¡Tengo tantas cosas que hacer hoy! I have so many things to do today! □ No necesitamos tantas. We don't need so many.
■ **Vinieron tantos que no cabían en la sala.** So many people came that they couldn't fit into the room.
■ **No recibe tantas llamadas como yo.** He doesn't get as many calls as I do.
■ **Gano tanto como tú.** I earn as much as you.
2 so often
□ Ahora no la veo tanto. Now I don't see her so often.
■ **¡No corras tanto!** Don't run so fast!
■ **tanto tú como yo** both you and I
■ **tanto si viene como si no** whether he comes or not
■ **¡Tanto gusto!** How do you do?
■ **entre tanto** meanwhile
■ **por lo tanto** therefore
el **tanto** NOUN
1 goal
□ Juárez marcó el segundo tanto. Juárez

t

scored the second goal.
2 amount
□ Me paga un tanto fijo cada semana. He pays me a fixed amount each week.
■ **un tanto por ciento** a percentage
■ **Había cuarenta y tantos invitados.** There were forty-odd guests.
■ **Manténme al tanto.** Keep me informed.

la **tapa** NOUN
1 lid
2 top
3 cover
4 tapa
□ Pedimos unas tapas en el bar. We ordered some tapas in the bar.

la **tapadera** NOUN
lid

el **tapado** NOUN *(River Plate)*
coat

tapar VERB [25]
to cover
□ La tapé con una manta. I covered her with a blanket.
■ **Tapa la olla.** Put the lid on the pan.
■ **Me estás tapando el sol.** You're keeping the sun off me.
■ **Tápate bien que hace frío.** Wrap up well as it's cold.

el **tapete** NOUN
1 embroidered tablecloth
2 rug *(Mexico)*

la **tapia** NOUN
wall
□ la tapia del jardín the garden wall

la **tapicería** NOUN
1 upholstery
2 upholsterer's

el **tapiz** (PL los **tapices**) NOUN
tapestry (PL tapestries)

tapizar* VERB [13]
to upholster

el **tapón** (PL los **tapones**) NOUN
1 plug
2 top
3 cork
■ **tapón de rosca** screw top

la **taquigrafía** NOUN
shorthand

la **taquilla** NOUN
1 box office
2 ticket office
3 locker

tararear VERB [25]
to hum

tardar VERB [25]
to be late
□ Te espero a las ocho. No tardes. I expect you at eight. Don't be late.
■ **Tardaron una semana en contestar.** They took a week to reply. □ El arroz tarda media hora en hacerse. Rice takes half an hour to cook.
■ **En avión se tarda dos horas.** The plane takes two hours.

la **tarde** NOUN
1 afternoon
□ a las tres de la tarde at three in the afternoon □ ¡Buenas tardes! Good afternoon! □ por la tarde in the afternoon □ hoy por la tarde this afternoon
2 evening
□ a las ocho de la tarde at eight in the evening □ ¡Buenas tardes! Good evening! □ por la tarde in the evening □ hoy por la tarde this evening

tarde ADVERB
late
□ Se está haciendo tarde. It's getting late.
■ **más tarde** later
■ **tarde o temprano** sooner or later
■ **Llegaré a las nueve como muy tarde.** I'll arrive at nine at the latest.

la **tarea** NOUN
task
□ Una de sus tareas es repartir la correspondencia. One of his tasks is to hand out the mail.
■ **las tareas domésticas** the chores
■ **las tareas** *(Latin America)* homework

la **tarifa** NOUN
1 rate
□ tarifa plana flat rate
2 fare
■ **tarifa de precios** price list

la **tarima** NOUN
platform

la **tarjeta** NOUN
card
□ Me mandó una tarjeta de Navidad. He sent me a Christmas card.
■ **una tarjeta de cajero automático** a cash card
■ **una tarjeta de crédito** a credit card
■ **una tarjeta de visita** a visiting card
■ **una tarjeta telefónica** a phonecard
■ **una tarjeta de embarque** a boarding pass

el **tarro** NOUN
1 jar
2 mug *(Mexico)*

la **tarta** NOUN
1 cake
□ una tarta de cumpleaños a birthday cake
2 tart

tartamudear VERB [25]
to stammer

tartamudo (FEM **tartamuda**) ADJECTIVE
■ **ser tartamudo** to stutter

la **tasa** NOUN
rate
□ la tasa de natalidad the birth rate

tasar VERB [25]
to value

la **tasca** NOUN
tavern

el **tata** NOUN *(Latin America)*
1 daddy
2 grandpa

el **tatuaje** NOUN
tattoo (PL tattoos)

tatuar* VERB [1]
to tattoo

Tauro MASC NOUN
Taurus
■ **Soy tauro.** I'm Taurus.

el **taxi** NOUN
taxi
□ tomar un taxi to take a taxi

el **taxímetro** NOUN
taximeter

el/la **taxista** NOUN
taxi driver

la **taza** NOUN
1 cup
□ Tomamos una taza de café. We had a cup of coffee.
2 cupful
□ una taza de arroz a cupful of rice
3 bowl

el **tazón** (PL los **tazones**) NOUN
bowl

TDT ABBREVIATION *(= televisión digital terrestre)*
DTT *(= digital terrestrial television)*

te PRONOUN
1 you
□ Te quiero. I love you. □ Te voy a dar un consejo. I'm going to give you some advice.
■ **Me gustaría comprártelo.** I'd like to buy it for you.
2 yourself
□ ¿Te has hecho daño? Have you hurt yourself? □ ¿Te duelen los pies? Do your feet hurt? □ Te tienes que poner el abrigo. You should put your coat on.

el **té** (PL los **tés**) NOUN
tea
■ **Me hice un té.** I made myself a cup of tea.

el **teatro** NOUN
theatre
□ Por la noche fuimos al teatro. At night we went to the theatre.
■ **una obra de teatro** a play

el **tebeo** NOUN
comic

el **techo** NOUN
1 ceiling
□ El techo está pintado de blanco. The ceiling is painted white.
2 roof *(Latin America)*

la **tecla** NOUN
key (PL keys)
■ **pulsar una tecla** to press a key

el **teclado** NOUN
keyboard

teclear VERB [25]
to type

la **técnica** NOUN
1 technique
2 technology (PL technologies)
3 technician
□ Mi hermana es técnica de laboratorio. My sister is a laboratory technician.

técnico (FEM **técnica**) ADJECTIVE
technical

el **técnico** NOUN
1 technician
□ un técnico de laboratorio a laboratory technician
2 repairman (PL repairmen)
□ El técnico me arregló la lavadora. The repairman fixed my washing machine.

el **tecno** NOUN
techno

la **tecnología** NOUN
technology (PL technologies)
■ **tecnología punta** state-of-the-art technology

tecnológico (FEM **tecnológica**) ADJECTIVE
technological

la **teja** NOUN
tile

el **tejado** NOUN
roof (PL roofs)

los **tejanos** NOUN
jeans

tejer VERB [8]
1 to weave
2 to knit

el **tejido** NOUN
1 fabric
2 tissue

tel. ABBREVIATION *(= teléfono)*
tel.

la **tela** NOUN
fabric
■ **tela metálica** wire netting

la **telaraña** NOUN
cobweb

la **tele** NOUN
TV
□ Estábamos viendo la tele. We were

watching TV.

las **telecomunicaciones** NOUN
telecommunications

el **telediario** NOUN
news *sing*
□ el telediario de las nueve the nine o'clock news

teledirigido (FEM **teledirigida**) ADJECTIVE
remote-controlled

el **teleférico** NOUN
cable car

telefonear VERB [25]
to phone
□ Tengo que telefonear a mis padres. I have to phone my parents.

telefónico (FEM **telefónica**) ADJECTIVE
telephone
■ **la guía telefónica** the telephone directory

el/la **telefonista** NOUN
telephonist

el **teléfono** NOUN
telephone
■ **No tengo teléfono.** I don't have a telephone.
■ **Hablamos por teléfono.** We spoke on the phone.
■ **Está hablando por teléfono.** He's on the phone.
■ **colgar el teléfono a alguien** to hang up the phone on somebody
■ **un teléfono de tarjeta** a card phone
■ **un teléfono con cámara** a camera phone
■ **un teléfono fijo** a landline (phone)
■ **un teléfono móvil** a mobile phone

el **telegrama** NOUN
telegram

la **telenovela** NOUN
soap opera (PL soap operas)

la **telepatía** NOUN
telepathy

la **telerrealidad** NOUN
reality TV

el **telescopio** NOUN
telescope

el **telesilla** NOUN
chairlift

el **telespectador**, la **telespectadora** NOUN
viewer

el **telesquí** (PL los **telesquís**) NOUN
ski-lift

el **teletexto** NOUN
Teletext®

las **televentas** NOUN
telesales

televisar VERB [25]
to televise

la **televisión** (PL las **televisiones**) NOUN
television
■ **Dieron la noticia por la televisión.** They gave the news on the television.
■ **¿Qué ponen en la televisión esta noche?** What's on the television tonight?
■ **la televisión por cable** cable television
■ **la televisión digital** digital TV

el **televisor** NOUN
television set

el **telón** (PL los **telones**) NOUN
curtain
□ Subió el telón. The curtain rose.

el **tema** NOUN
1 topic
□ El tema de la redacción era 'Las vacaciones'. The topic of the essay was 'The holidays'.
2 subject
□ Luego hablaremos de ese tema. We'll talk about that subject later.
■ **cambiar de tema** to change the subject
■ **temas de actualidad** current affairs
■ **el tema de conversación** the talking point

temblar* VERB [39]
to tremble
□ Me temblaban las manos. My hands were trembling.
■ **temblar de miedo** to tremble with fear
■ **temblar de frío** to shiver

el **temblor de tierra** NOUN
earthquake

tembloroso (FEM **temblorosa**) ADJECTIVE
trembling

temer VERB [8]
1 to be afraid
□ No temas. Don't be afraid.
2 to be afraid of
□ Le teme al profesor. He's afraid of the teacher. □ Temo ofenderles. I'm afraid of offending them.

temible (FEM **temible**) ADJECTIVE
fearsome

el **temor** NOUN
fear
□ el temor a la oscuridad fear of the dark
□ por temor a equivocarme for fear of making a mistake

temperamental (FEM **temperamental**) ADJECTIVE
temperamental

el **temperamento** NOUN
temperament

la **temperatura** NOUN
temperature
□ El médico le tomó la temperatura.

The doctor took his temperature.

la **tempestad** NOUN
storm

templado (FEM **templada**) ADJECTIVE
1 lukewarm
2 mild

el **templo** NOUN
temple

la **temporada** NOUN
season
□ la temporada de esquí the ski season
□ la temporada alta the high season
□ la temporada baja the low season

temporal (FEM **temporal**) ADJECTIVE
temporary

el **temporal** NOUN
storm

temporario (FEM **temporaria**) ADJECTIVE
(Latin America)
temporary

temprano ADVERB
early
■ **por la mañana temprano** early in the morning

ten VERB ▷ *see* **tener**

tenaz (FEM **tenaz**, PL **tenaces**) ADJECTIVE
tenacious

las **tenazas** NOUN
pliers

el **tendedero** NOUN
1 clothes line
2 clothes horse

la **tendencia** NOUN
tendency (PL tendencies)
■ **Tengo tendencia a engordar.** I tend to put on weight.

tender* VERB [20]
1 to hang out
□ Marta estaba tendiendo la ropa. Marta was hanging out the washing.
2 to lay out
□ Tendí la toalla sobre la arena. I laid the towel out on the sand.
■ **Me tendió la mano.** He stretched out his hand to me.
■ **tender a hacer algo** to tend to do something
■ **tender una trampa** to set a trap
■ **tenderse en el sofá** to lie down on the sofa
■ **tender la cama** *(Latin America)* to make the bed
■ **tender la mesa** *(Latin America)* to lay the table

el **tendero**, la **tendera** NOUN
shopkeeper

tendido (FEM **tendida**) ADJECTIVE
■ **La ropa estaba tendida.** The washing was hanging out.
■ **Lo encontré tendido en el suelo.** I found him lying on the floor.

el **tendón** (PL los **tendones**) NOUN
tendon

tendrá VERB ▷ *see* **tener**

el **tenedor** NOUN
fork

tener* VERB [53]
1 to have
□ Tengo dos hermanas. I have two sisters.
□ ¿Tienes dinero? Do you have any money?
□ Tiene el pelo rubio. He has blond hair.
□ Va a tener un niño. She's going to have a baby. □ Luis tiene la gripe. Luis has the flu.
■ **¿Cuántos años tienes?** How old are you?
■ **Tiene cinco metros de largo.** It's five metres long.
■ **Ten cuidado.** Be careful.
■ **No tengas miedo.** Don't be afraid.
■ **Tenía el pelo mojado.** His hair was wet.
2 to hold
□ Tenía el pasaporte en la mano. He was holding his passport in his hand.
■ **tener que hacer algo** to have to do something
■ **Tendrías que comer más.** You should eat more.
■ **No tienes por qué ir.** There's no reason why you should go.
■ **Eso no tiene nada que ver.** That's got nothing to do with it.
■ **¡Tenga!** Here you are!
■ **tenerse en pie** to stand

tenga VERB ▷ *see* **tener**

el/la **teniente** NOUN
lieutenant

el **tenis** NOUN
tennis
■ **¿Juegas al tenis?** Do you play tennis?
■ **tenis de mesa** table tennis

el/la **tenista** NOUN
tennis player

el **tenor** NOUN
tenor

tensar VERB [25]
to tighten

la **tensión** (PL las **tensiones**) NOUN
1 tension
□ Hubo mucha tensión durante la reunión. There was a lot of tension during the meeting.
2 blood pressure
□ El médico me tomó la tensión. The doctor took my blood pressure.
■ **un cable de alta tensión** a high-voltage cable

tenso (FEM **tensa**) ADJECTIVE

1 tense
2 taut

la **tentación** (PL las **tentaciones**) NOUN
temptation
■ **caer en la tentación** to give in to temptation

tentador (FEM **tentadora**) ADJECTIVE
tempting

tentar* VERB [39]
to tempt
□ Estuve tentado de marcharme. I was tempted to leave.
■ **No me tienta la idea.** The idea isn't very tempting.

la **tentativa** NOUN
attempt

el **tentempié** (PL los **tentempiés**) NOUN
snack

tenue (FEM **tenue**) ADJECTIVE
faint

teñir* VERB [45]
to dye
□ Se ha teñido el pelo. He's dyed his hair.

la **teología** NOUN
theology

la **teoría** NOUN
theory (PL theories)
□ En teoría es fácil. In theory it's easy.

teórico (FEM **teórica**) ADJECTIVE
theoretical
□ Ése es un caso teórico. It's a theoretical case.
■ **un examen teórico** a theory exam

terapéutico (FEM **terapéutica**) ADJECTIVE
therapeutic

la **terapia** NOUN
therapy (PL therapies)

tercer ▷ *see* **tercero**

tercero (FEM **tercera**) ADJECTIVE, PRONOUN
third
□ la tercera vez the third time □ Llegué el tercero. I arrived third.
■ **una tercera parte de la población** a third of the population
■ **Vivo en el tercero.** I live on the third floor.
■ **el Tercer Mundo** the Third World

el **tercio** NOUN
third

el **terciopelo** NOUN
velvet

terco (FEM **terca**) ADJECTIVE
obstinate

tergiversar VERB [25]
to distort

el **terminal** NOUN
terminal

la **terminal** NOUN
terminal

terminante (FEM **terminante**) ADJECTIVE
1 categorical
2 strict

terminantemente ADVERB
strictly

terminar VERB [25]
1 to finish
□ He terminado el libro. I've finished the book.
■ **cuando terminó de hablar** when he finished talking
2 to end
□ ¿A qué hora termina la clase? At what time does the class end?
■ **Terminé rendido.** I ended up exhausted.
■ **Terminaron peleándose.** They ended up fighting.
■ **Se nos ha terminado el café.** We've run out of coffee.
■ **He terminado con Andrés.** I've broken up with Andrés.

el **término** NOUN
term
□ un término médico a medical term
■ **por término medio** on average

la **termita** NOUN
termite

el **termo®** NOUN
Thermos flask®

el **termómetro** NOUN
thermometer
■ **Le puse el termómetro.** I took his temperature.

el **termostato** NOUN
thermostat

la **ternera** NOUN
1 calf (PL calves) *(animal)*
2 veal

el **ternero** NOUN
calf (PL calves) *(animal)*

la **ternura** NOUN
tenderness
■ **con ternura** tenderly

el/la **terrateniente** NOUN
landowner

la **terraza** NOUN
1 balcony (PL balconies)
2 roof terrace
■ **Salimos a la terraza del bar a tomar algo.** We went out to the beer garden for a drink.

el **terremoto** NOUN
earthquake

el **terreno** NOUN
1 land
□ una granja con mucho terreno a farm with a lot of land

Spanish-English

t

■ **un terreno** a piece of land □ Hemos comprado un terreno. We've bought a piece of land.
2 field
□ terrenos plantados de naranjos fields planted with orange trees □ en el terreno de la informática in the field of computing science
■ **el terreno de juego** the pitch
■ **Lo decidiremos sobre el terreno.** We'll decide as we go along.

terrestre (FEM **terrestre**) ADJECTIVE
land

terrible (FEM **terrible**) ADJECTIVE
terrible
□ Fue una experiencia terrible. It was a terrible experience.
■ **Tenía un cansancio terrible.** I was awfully tired.

el **terrier** (PL los **terriers**) NOUN
terrier

el **territorio** NOUN
territory (PL territories)

el **terrón** (PL los **terrones**) NOUN
lump

el **terror** NOUN
terror
□ Fuimos víctimas de una campaña de terror. We were the victims of a terror campaign.
■ **Les tiene terror a los perros.** He's terrified of dogs.
■ **una película de terror** a horror film

el **terrorismo** NOUN
terrorism

el/la **terrorista** ADJECTIVE, NOUN
terrorist
■ **un terrorista suicida** a suicide bomber

la **tesis** (PL las **tesis**) NOUN
thesis (PL theses)

el **tesón** NOUN
determination

el **tesorero**, la **tesorera** NOUN
treasurer

el **tesoro** NOUN
treasure
■ **Ven aquí, tesoro.** Come here, darling.

el **test** (PL los **tests**) NOUN
test
□ Hoy nos han hecho un test. We had a test today.

el **testamento** NOUN
will
■ **hacer testamento** to make one's will
■ **el Antiguo Testamento** the Old Testament
■ **el Nuevo Testamento** the New Testament

testarudo (FEM **testaruda**) ADJECTIVE
stubborn

el/la **testigo** NOUN
witness (PL witnesses)
■ **un Testigo de Jehová** a Jehovah's Witness
■ **Fui testigo del accidente.** I witnessed the accident.

el **testimonio** NOUN
evidence

el **tétanos** NOUN
tetanus

la **tetera** NOUN
1 teapot
2 kettle *(Chile, Mexico)*
3 baby's bottle *(Mexico)*

la **tetina** NOUN
teat

el **textil** (FEM el **textil**) ADJECTIVE, NOUN
textile

el **texto** NOUN
text
■ **un libro de texto** a textbook

la **textura** NOUN
texture

la **tez** NOUN
complexion

ti PRONOUN
you
□ una llamada para ti a call for you
■ **Sólo piensas en ti mismo.** You only think of yourself.

la **tía** NOUN
1 aunt
□ mi tía my aunt
2 girl
□ Es una tía majísima. She's a really nice girl.

tibio (FEM **tibia**) ADJECTIVE
lukewarm

el **tiburón** (PL los **tiburones**) NOUN
shark

el **tic** NOUN
tic
□ un tic nervioso a nervous tic

el **tictac** NOUN
tick-tock

tiemblo VERB ▷ *see* **temblar**

el **tiempo** NOUN
1 time
□ No tengo tiempo. I don't have time.
□ ¿Qué haces en tu tiempo libre? What do you do in your spare time? □ Me llevó bastante tiempo. It took me quite a long time.
■ **¿Cuánto tiempo hace que vives aquí?** How long have you been living here?
■ **Hace mucho tiempo que no la veo.**

I haven't seen her for a long time.
■ **al mismo tiempo** at the same time
■ **perder el tiempo** to waste time
■ **al poco tiempo** soon after
■ **a tiempo** in time □ Llegamos a tiempo de ver la película. We got there in time to see the film.
■ **¿Qué tiempo tiene el niño?** How old is the baby?
2 weather
■ **¿Qué tiempo hace ahí?** What's the weather like there?
■ **hizo buen tiempo** the weather was fine
■ **Hace mal tiempo.** The weather's bad.
3 half
■ **Metieron el gol durante el segundo tiempo.** They scored the goal during the second half.

la **tienda** NOUN
shop
■ **una tienda de comestibles** a grocer's shop (PL grocers' shops)
■ **una tienda de discos** a record shop
■ **ir de tiendas** to go shopping
■ **una tienda de campaña** a tent

tiendo VERB ▷ *see* **tender**

tiene VERB ▷ *see* **tener**

tiento VERB ▷ *see* **tentar**

tierno (FEM **tierna**) ADJECTIVE
1 tender
2 fresh

la **tierra** NOUN
1 land
□ Trabajan la tierra. They work the land.
■ **la Tierra Santa** the Holy Land
■ **tierra adentro** inland
2 soil
■ **echar algo por tierra** to ruin something
□ Echó por tierra todos nuestros planes. It ruined all our plans.
■ **la Tierra** the Earth

tieso (FEM **tiesa**) ADJECTIVE
1 stiff
■ **quedarse tieso de frío** to be frozen stiff
2 straight
□ Ponte tiesa. Stand up straight.

el **tiesto** NOUN
flowerpot

el **tigre** NOUN
tiger

las **tijeras** NOUN
scissors
□ Es más fácil cortarlo con las tijeras. It's easier to cut with scissors.
■ **¿Tienes unas tijeras?** Do you have a pair of scissors?
■ **unas tijeras de podar** a pair of secateurs

timar VERB [25]
1 to con
2 to rip off
□ Te han timado con ese coche. They've ripped you off with that car.

el **timbrazo** NOUN
ring

el **timbre** NOUN
1 bell
□ Ya ha sonado el timbre. The bell has already gone.
■ **llamar al timbre** to ring the bell
2 stamp *(Mexico)*

la **timidez** NOUN
shyness

tímido (FEM **tímida**) ADJECTIVE
shy

el **timo** NOUN
1 con
2 rip off
■ **¡Vaya timo!** What a rip-off!

la **tinaja** NOUN
large earthenware vat

la **tinta** NOUN
ink
□ escrito con tinta written in ink
■ **tinta China** Indian ink

LANGUAGE TIP Word for word, **tinta china** means 'Chinese ink'.

■ **sudar tinta** to sweat blood

el **tinte** NOUN
dye

el **tintero** NOUN
inkwell

el **tinto** NOUN
red wine

la **tintorería** NOUN
dry cleaner's

tiñendo VERB ▷ *see* **teñir**

el **tío** NOUN
1 uncle
■ **mis tíos** my uncle and aunt
2 guy
□ Es un tío muy simpático. He's a really nice guy.
■ **Oye, tío, me alegro de verte.** Hey, man, nice to see you.

el **tiovivo** NOUN
merry-go-round (PL merry-go-rounds)

típicamente ADVERB
typically

típico (FEM **típica**) ADJECTIVE
typical
■ **Eso es muy típico de ella.** That's very typical of her.

el **tipo** NOUN
1 kind
□ No me gusta este tipo de fiestas. I don't like this kind of party.

■ **todo tipo de ...** all sorts of ...
2 figure
□ Marisa tiene un tipo muy bonito. Marisa has a lovely figure.
3 bloke
□ un tipo de aspecto sospechoso a suspicious-looking bloke

el **tíquet** (PL los **tíquets**) NOUN
1 ticket
2 receipt

la **tira** NOUN
strip
□ una tira de papel a strip of paper □ una tira cómica a comic strip
■ **Tiene la tira de libros.** He has lots of books.
■ **Hace la tira de tiempo que no la veo.** I haven't seen her for ages.

la **tirada** NOUN
1 print run
□ La tirada inicial fue de 50.000 ejemplares. The initial print run was 50,000 copies.
2 circulation
□ La revista tiene una tirada semanal de 200.000 ejemplares. The magazine has a weekly circulation of 200,000 copies.
■ **de una tirada** in one go

tirado (FEM **tirada**) ADJECTIVE
1 dirt-cheap
2 dead easy

el **tirador** NOUN
handle

la **tirana** NOUN
tyrant

tiránico (FEM **tiránica**) ADJECTIVE
tyrannical

el **tirano** NOUN
tyrant

tirante (FEM **tirante**) ADJECTIVE
1 tight
2 tense

el **tirante** NOUN
strap
■ **tirantes** braces

tirar VERB [25]
1 to throw
□ Tírame la pelota. Throw me the ball.
□ Les tiraban piedras a los soldados. They were throwing stones at the soldiers. □ Se tiró al suelo. He threw himself to the ground.
2 to throw away
□ No tires la comida. Don't throw away the food.
■ **tirar algo a la basura** to throw something out
■ **tirar al suelo** to knock over □ La moto la tiró al suelo. The motorbike knocked her over.
■ **Tropezó con la maceta y la tiró al suelo.** He tripped on the flowerpot and knocked it to the ground.
3 to knock down
□ Queremos tirar esta pared. We want to knock this wall down.
4 to drop
■ **tirar a la derecha** to turn right
■ **tirar de algo** to pull something
■ **tirar la cadena** *(Latin America)* to pull the chain
■ **Vamos tirando.** We're getting by.
■ **tirarse al agua** to plunge into the water
■ **tirarse de cabeza** to dive in head first
■ **tirarse en el sofá** *(Latin America)* to lie down on the sofa
■ **Se tiró toda la mañana estudiando.** He spent the whole morning studying.

la **tirita** NOUN
plaster

tiritar VERB [25]
to shiver
■ **tiritar de frío** to shiver with cold

el **tiro** NOUN
shot
□ Oímos un tiro. We heard a shot.
■ **Lo mataron de un tiro.** They shot him dead.
■ **Me salió el tiro por la culata.** It backfired on me.
■ **tiro al blanco** target practice
■ **un tiro libre** a free kick

el **tiroteo** NOUN
shoot-out

el **títere** NOUN
puppet

titubear VERB [25]
to hesitate
□ Respondí sin titubear. I answered without hesitating.

titulado (FEM **titulada**) ADJECTIVE
qualified
□ una enfermera titulada a qualified nurse

el **titular** NOUN
headline

el/la **titular** NOUN
1 holder
2 owner

titular VERB [25]
to call
□ La novela se titula 'Marcianos'. The novel is called 'Marcianos'.
■ **¿Cómo vas a titular el trabajo?** What title are you going to give the essay?

el **título** NOUN
1 title
□ Necesito un título para el poema. I need a

title for the poem.
2 qualification
□ Tiene el título de enfermera. She has a nursing qualification.
3 certificate
□ Tenía los títulos colgados en la pared. His certificates were hanging on the wall.

la **tiza** NOUN
chalk
■ **una tiza** a piece of chalk

la **toalla** NOUN
towel
□ una toalla de baño a bath towel

el **tobillo** NOUN
ankle
□ Me he torcido el tobillo. I've twisted my ankle.

el **tobogán** (PL los **toboganes**) NOUN
1 slide
2 toboggan

el **tocadiscos** (PL los **tocadiscos**) NOUN
record player

el **tocador** NOUN
dressing table

tocar* VERB [48]
1 to touch
□ Si lo tocas te quemarás. If you touch it you'll burn yourself.
2 to play
□ Toca el violín. He plays the violin.
3 to ring
4 to blow
■ **tocar a la puerta** *(Latin America)* to knock on the door
■ **Te toca fregar los platos.** It's your turn to do the dishes.
■ **Le tocó la lotería.** He won the lottery.

el **tocino** NOUN
pork fat

todavía ADVERB
1 still
□ ¿Todavía estás en la cama? Are you still in bed? □ ¡Y todavía se queja! And he still complains!
2 yet
□ Todavía no han llegado. They haven't arrived yet. □ ¿Todavía no has comido? Have you not eaten yet? □ Todavía no. Not yet.

todo (FEM **toda**) ADJECTIVE, PRONOUN
1 all
□ todos los niños all the children □ Todos son caros. They're all expensive. □ el más bonito de todos the prettiest of all
■ **toda la noche** all night
■ **todos vosotros** all of you
■ **todos los que quieran venir** all those who want to come
2 every
□ todos los días every day
3 the whole
□ He limpiado toda la casa. I've cleaned the whole house.
■ **Ha viajado por todo el mundo.** He has travelled throughout the world.
■ **Todo el mundo lo sabe.** Everybody knows.
4 everything
□ Lo sabemos todo. We know everything.
□ todo lo que me dijeron everything they told me
5 everybody
□ Todos estaban de acuerdo. Everybody agreed.
■ **Vaya todo seguido.** Keep straight on.
■ **todo lo contrario** quite the opposite

el **toldo** NOUN
1 sun blind
2 awning
3 sunshade

tolerante (FEM **tolerante**) ADJECTIVE
tolerant

tolerar VERB [25]
to tolerate
□ No voy a tolerar ese comportamiento. I won't tolerate that behaviour.
■ **Sus padres le toleran demasiado.** His parents let him get away with too much.

tomar VERB [25]
1 to take
□ En clase tomamos apuntes. We take notes in class. □ Se lo ha tomado muy en serio. He's taken it very seriously.
□ Se tomó la molestia de acompañarnos. He took the trouble to accompany us.
■ **tomar a alguien de la mano** to take somebody by the hand
■ **tomarse algo a mal** to take something badly
2 to have
□ ¿Qué quieres tomar? What are you going to have? □ De postre tomé un helado. I had an ice cream for dessert.
■ **Toma, esto es tuyo.** Here, this is yours.
■ **tomar cariño a alguien** to become fond of somebody
■ **tomar el pelo a alguien** to pull somebody's leg
■ **tomar el aire** to get some fresh air
■ **tomar el sol** to sunbathe
■ **tomar nota de algo** to note something down

el **tomate** NOUN
tomato (PL tomatoes)
■ **ponerse como un tomate** to turn as red as a beetroot

Spanish-English

el **tomillo** NOUN
thyme
el **tomo** NOUN
volume
el **tonel** NOUN
barrel
la **tonelada** NOUN
ton
la **tónica** NOUN
tonic
el **tono** NOUN
1 tone
□ Lo dijo en tono cariñoso. He said it in an affectionate tone.
■ **un tono de llamada** a ringtone
2 shade
□ un tono un poco más oscuro a slightly darker shade
la **tonta** NOUN
fool
■ **hacerse la tonta** to act dumb
la **tontería** NOUN
silly thing
□ Se pelearon por una tontería. They fell out over a silly thing.
■ **tonterías** nonsense □ ¡Eso son tonterías! That's nonsense! □ ¡No digas tonterías! Don't talk nonsense!
tonto (FEM **tonta**) ADJECTIVE
silly
□ ¡Qué error más tonto! What a silly mistake!
el **tonto** NOUN
fool
■ **hacer el tonto** to act the fool
■ **hacerse el tonto** to act dumb
toparse VERB [25]
■ **toparse con alguien** to bump into somebody
los **topes** NOUN
■ **El autobús iba hasta los topes.** The bus was packed.
el **tópico** NOUN
cliché (PL clichés)
topless (FEM + PL **topless**) ADJECTIVE
topless
el **topo** NOUN
mole
el **toque** NOUN
■ **dar los últimos toques a algo** to put the finishing touches to something
■ **el toque de queda** the curfew
el **tórax** NOUN
thorax
la **torcedura** NOUN
■ **una torcedura de tobillo** a sprained ankle
torcer* VERB [6]
1 to twist
□ ¡Me estás torciendo el brazo! You're twisting my arm!
■ **torcerse el tobillo** to sprain one's ankle
2 to turn
□ torcer a la derecha to turn right □ torcer la esquina to turn the corner
torcido (FEM **torcida**) ADJECTIVE
1 crooked
□ Tiene la boca un poco torcida. His mouth's a bit crooked.
2 bent
□ El tronco está torcido. The trunk is bent.
■ **Ese cuadro está torcido.** That picture isn't straight.
torear VERB [25]
to fight
□ No volverá a torear. He will never fight again.
el **toreo** NOUN
bullfighting
el **torero**, la **torera** NOUN
bullfighter
la **tormenta** NOUN
storm
■ **Hubo tormenta.** There was a storm.
■ **un día de tormenta** a stormy day
el **torneo** NOUN
tournament
el **tornillo** NOUN
1 screw
■ **A tu hermana le falta un tornillo.** Your sister's got a screw loose.
2 bolt
el **toro** NOUN
bull
■ **los toros** bullfighting
■ **ir a los toros** to go to a bullfight
la **toronja** NOUN *(Latin America)*
grapefruit (PL grapefruit)
torpe (FEM **torpe**) ADJECTIVE
1 clumsy
2 dim
la **torre** NOUN
1 tower
□ la torre de control the control tower
2 pylon
3 rook
la **torta** NOUN
1 small flat cake
2 pie *(Latin America)*
3 filled roll *(Mexico)*
■ **pegar una torta a alguien** to give somebody a slap
■ **No entiendo ni torta.** I don't understand a thing.
■ **No ve ni torta.** He's as blind as a bat.

t

la **tortilla** NOUN
1 omelette
■ **una tortilla de patatas** a Spanish omelette
2 tortilla

la **tortuga** NOUN
1 tortoise
2 turtle

la **tortura** NOUN
torture

torturar VERB [25]
to torture

la **tos** (PL las **toses**) NOUN
cough (PL coughs)
■ **Tengo mucha tos.** I have a bad cough.

toser VERB [8]
to cough

la **tostada** NOUN
1 piece of toast
□ ¿Quieres una tostada? Do you want a piece of toast?
■ **tostadas** toast □ Tomé café con tostadas. I had coffee and toast.
2 fried corn tortilla *(Mexico)*

tostado (FEM **tostada**) ADJECTIVE
1 toasted
2 roasted
3 tanned

el **tostador** NOUN
toaster

tostar* VERB [11]
1 to toast
2 to roast

el **total** (FEM el **total**) ADJECTIVE, NOUN
total
□ Fue un fracaso total. It was a total failure.
□ El total son 45,75 euros. The total is 45.75 euros.
■ **un cambio total** a complete change
■ **En total éramos catorce.** There were fourteen of us altogether.

total ADVERB
■ **Total, que perdí mi trabajo.** So, in the end, I lost my job.

totalitario (FEM **totalitaria**) ADJECTIVE
totalitarian

totalmente ADVERB
1 totally
□ Mario es totalmente distinto a Luis. Mario is totally different from Luis.
2 completely
□ Estoy totalmente de acuerdo. I completely agree.
■ **¿Estás seguro? — Totalmente.** Are you sure? — Absolutely.

tóxico (FEM **tóxica**) ADJECTIVE
toxic

el **toxicómano**, la **toxicómana** NOUN
drug addict (PL drug addicts)

la **toxina** NOUN
toxin

tozudo (FEM **tozuda**) ADJECTIVE
obstinate

trabajador (FEM **trabajadora**) ADJECTIVE
hard-working
□ un chico muy trabajador a very hard-working boy

el **trabajador**, la **trabajadora** NOUN
worker
□ trabajadores no cualificados unskilled workers

trabajar VERB [25]
to work
□ No trabajes tanto. Don't work so hard.
■ **¿En qué trabajas?** What's your job?
■ **Trabajo de camarero.** I work as a waiter.
■ **trabajar jornada completa** to work full-time
■ **trabajar media jornada** to work part-time

el **trabajo** NOUN
1 work
□ Tengo mucho trabajo. I have a lot of work.
□ Me puedes llamar al trabajo. You can call me at work.
■ **estar sin trabajo** to be unemployed
■ **trabajo en equipo** teamwork
■ **el trabajo de la casa** the housework
■ **trabajos manuales** handicrafts
2 job
□ Le han ofrecido un trabajo en el banco. He's been offered a job in the bank. □ No encuentro trabajo. I can't find a job.
■ **quedarse sin trabajo** to find oneself out of work
3 essay (PL essays)
□ Tengo que entregar dos trabajos mañana. I have to hand in two essays tomorrow.

el **tractor** NOUN
tractor

la **tradición** (PL las **tradiciones**) NOUN
tradition

tradicional (FEM **tradicional**) ADJECTIVE
traditional

la **traducción** (PL las **traducciones**) NOUN
translation
□ Una traducción del italiano al inglés. A translation from Italian into English.

traducir* VERB [9]
to translate
□ traducir del inglés al francés to translate from English into French

el **traductor**, la **traductora** NOUN
translator

traer* VERB [54]
1 to bring

□ He traído el paraguas por si acaso. I've brought the umbrella just in case.
2 to carry
□ El periódico trae un artículo sobre eso. The newspaper carries an article on this.
3 to wear
□ Traía un vestido nuevo. She was wearing a new dress.

el/la **traficante** NOUN
dealer
□ traficantes de armas arms dealers

el **tráfico** NOUN
traffic
■ **un accidente de tráfico** a road accident
■ **tráfico de drogas** drug-trafficking

tragar* VERB [37]
to swallow
■ **Nadie se va a tragar esa historia.** Nobody is going to swallow that story.
■ **No la trago.** I can't stand her.

la **tragedia** NOUN
tragedy (PL tragedies)

trágico (FEM **trágica**) ADJECTIVE
tragic

el **trago** NOUN
drink
□ ¿Te apetece un trago? Do you fancy a drink?
■ **de un trago** in one gulp

la **traición** (PL las **traiciones**) NOUN
1 betrayal
2 treason

traicionar VERB [25]
to betray

traicionero (FEM **traicionera**) ADJECTIVE
treacherous

el **traidor**, la **traidora** NOUN
traitor

traigo VERB ▷ *see* **traer**

el **tráiler** (PL los **tráilers**) NOUN
1 trailer
2 articulated lorry

el **traje** NOUN
1 suit
□ Luis llevaba un traje negro. Luis was wearing a black suit.
■ **un traje de chaqueta** a suit
■ **un traje de buzo** a diving suit
2 dress (PL dresses)
□ un traje de noche an evening dress
■ **el traje de novia** the bridal gown
■ **un traje de baño 1** a pair of swimming trunks **2** a swimsuit

la **trama** NOUN
plot

tramitar VERB [25]
■ **Estoy tramitando un préstamo con el banco.** I'm negotiating a loan with the bank.
■ **Estamos tramitando el divorcio.** We are going through the divorce proceedings.

el **tramo** NOUN
1 section *(of road)*
2 flight *(of stairs)*

la **trampa** NOUN
trap
□ caer en la trampa to fall into the trap
■ **Les tendió una trampa.** He set a trap for them.
■ **hacer trampa** to cheat

el **trampolín** (PL los **trampolines**) NOUN
1 diving board
□ Se tiró desde el trampolín. He plunged from the diving board.
2 trampoline

el **tramposo**, la **tramposa** NOUN
cheat

tranquilamente ADVERB
calmly
□ Háblale tranquilamente. Speak to him calmly.
■ **Yo estaba sentado tranquilamente viendo la tele.** I was sitting peacefully watching TV.

la **tranquilidad** NOUN
peace and quiet
□ Necesito un poco de tranquilidad. I need a little peace and quiet.
■ **Respondió con tranquilidad.** He answered calmly.
■ **Llévatelo a casa y léelo con tranquilidad.** Take it home with you and read it at your leisure.
■ **¡Qué tranquilidad! ¡Ya se han acabado los exámenes!** What a relief! The exams are over at last!

tranquilizar* VERB [13]
to calm down
□ ¡Tranquilízate! Calm down!
■ **Las palabras del médico me tranquilizaron.** The doctor's words reassured me.

tranquilo (FEM **tranquila**) ADJECTIVE
1 calm
□ El día del examen estaba bastante tranquilo. On the day of the exam I was quite calm.
2 peaceful

el **transatlántico** NOUN
ocean liner

el **transbordador** NOUN
ferry (PL ferries)
■ **el transbordador espacial** the space shuttle

el **transbordo** NOUN
■ **Hay que hacer transbordo en París.**

You have to change trains in Paris.
transcurrir VERB [58]
to pass
□ Transcurrieron dos años. Two years passed.
el/la **transeúnte** NOUN
passer-by (PL passers-by)
la **transferencia** NOUN
transfer
□ transferencia bancaria bank transfer
la **transformación** (PL las **transformaciones**) NOUN
transformation
transformar VERB [25]
to transform
□ La cirugía estética lo ha transformado completamente. Plastic surgery has completely transformed him.
■ **Hemos transformado el garaje en sala de estar.** We've converted the garage into a living room.
■ **El príncipe se transformó en un monstruo.** The prince turned into a monster.
la **transfusión** (PL las **transfusiones**) NOUN
■ **Me hicieron una transfusión de sangre.** They gave me a blood transfusion.
transgénico (FEM **transgénica**) ADJECTIVE
genetically modified
la **transición** NOUN
transition
el **transistor** NOUN
transistor
transitivo (FEM **transitiva**) ADJECTIVE
transitive
el **tránsito** NOUN
traffic
■ **los pasajeros en tránsito para Moscú** transfer passengers to Moscow
la **transmisión** (PL las **transmisiones**) NOUN
broadcast
□ una transmisión en directo a live broadcast
transmitir VERB [58]
1 to transmit
2 to broadcast
transparente (FEM **transparente**) ADJECTIVE
transparent
la **transpiración** NOUN
perspiration
transportar VERB [25]
to carry
□ El camión transportaba medicamentos. The lorry was carrying medicines.
el **transporte** NOUN
transport
■ **el transporte público** public transport
el/la **transportista** NOUN
carrier
el **tranvía** NOUN
tram
el **trapo** NOUN
cloth
□ Lo limpié con un trapo. I wiped it with a cloth.
■ **un trapo de cocina** a dishcloth
■ **Pásale un trapo al espejo.** Give the mirror a wipe over.
■ **el trapo del polvo** the duster
la **tráquea** NOUN
windpipe
tras PREPOSITION
after
□ Salimos corriendo tras ella. We ran out after her. □ semana tras semana week after week
trasero (FEM **trasera**) ADJECTIVE
back
□ la rueda trasera de la bici the back wheel of the bike
el **trasero** NOUN
bottom
trasladar VERB [25]
1 to move
□ Mañana nos trasladamos al piso. We're moving to the flat tomorrow.
2 to transfer
□ Me quieren trasladar a otra sucursal. They want to transfer me to another branch.
el **traslado** NOUN
move
■ **He pedido traslado a Barcelona.** I've asked for a transfer to Barcelona.
■ **los gastos de traslado de la oficina** the office's relocation expenses
el **trasluz** NOUN
■ **al trasluz** against the light
trasnochar VERB [25]
to stay up late
traspapelarse VERB [25]
to get mislaid
traspasar VERB [25]
1 to go through
□ La bala traspasó el sofá. The bullet went through the sofa.
2 to transfer
3 to sell
el **traspié** (PL los **traspiés**) NOUN
■ **dar un traspié** to trip
trasplantar VERB [25]
to transplant
el **trasplante** NOUN
transplant
el **trastero** NOUN

Spanish-English

t

storage room

los **trastes** NOUN *(Mexico)*
pots and pans
■ **lavar los trastes** to do the dishes

el **trasto** NOUN
piece of junk
□ El coche es un trasto. The car's a piece of junk.
■ **El desván está lleno de trastos.** The loft is full of junk.

trastornado (FEM **trastornada**) ADJECTIVE
disturbed

el **trastorno** NOUN
disruption
□ La huelga ha causado muchos trastornos. The strike has caused a lot of disruption.
■ **trastornos mentales** mental disorders

el **tratado** NOUN
treaty (PL treaties)

el **tratamiento** NOUN
treatment
■ **Está en tratamiento médico.** He's having medical treatment.
■ **tratamiento de datos** data processing
■ **tratamiento de textos** word processing

tratar VERB [25]
1 to treat
□ Su novio la trata muy mal. Her boyfriend treats her very badly.
2 to deal with
□ Trataremos este tema en la reunión. We'll deal with this subject in the meeting.
■ **Trato con todo tipo de gente.** I deal with all sorts of people.
■ **tratar de hacer algo** to try to do something
■ **¿De qué se trata?** What's it about?
■ **La película trata de un adolescente en Nueva York.** The film is about a teenager in New York.

el **trato** NOUN
deal
□ hacer un trato to make a deal
■ **¡Trato hecho!** It's a deal!
■ **No tengo mucho trato con él.** I don't have much to do with him.
■ **recibir malos tratos de alguien** to be treated badly by somebody

el **trauma** NOUN
trauma

través PREPOSITION
■ **a través de 1** across □ Nadó a través del río. He swam across the river. **2** through □ Se enteraron a través de un amigo. They found out through a friend.

la **travesía** NOUN
1 crossing
2 side-street

la **travesura** NOUN
prank
■ **hacer travesuras** to get up to mischief

travieso (FEM **traviesa**) ADJECTIVE
naughty

el **trayecto** NOUN
1 journey (PL journeys)
2 way (PL ways)
■ **¿Qué trayecto hace el 34?** What way does the 34 go?

trazar* VERB [13]
1 to draw
2 to draw up

el **trébol** NOUN
clover
■ **tréboles** clubs

trece (FEM **trece**) ADJECTIVE, PRONOUN
thirteen
□ Tengo trece años. I'm thirteen.
■ **el trece de enero** the thirteenth of January

treinta (FEM **treinta**) ADJECTIVE, PRONOUN
thirty
□ Tiene treinta años. He's thirty.
■ **el treinta aniversario** the thirtieth anniversary

tremendo (FEM **tremenda**) ADJECTIVE
1 terrible
□ Tenía un tremendo dolor de cabeza. I had a terrible headache.
■ **Hacía un frío tremendo.** It was terribly cold.
2 tremendous
□ La película tuvo un éxito tremendo. The film was a tremendous success.

el **tren** NOUN
train
■ **viajar en tren** to travel by train
■ **Tomé un tren directo.** I took a through train.
■ **con este tren de vida** with such a hectic life

la **trenza** NOUN
plait
■ **Le hice una trenza.** I plaited her hair.

la **trepadora** NOUN
climber

trepar VERB [25]
to climb
■ **trepar a un árbol** to climb a tree

tres (FEM **tres**) ADJECTIVE, PRONOUN
three
■ **Son las tres.** It's three o'clock.
■ **el tres de febrero** the third of February

trescientos (FEM **trescientas**) ADJECTIVE, PRONOUN
three hundred

el **tresillo** NOUN

three-seater sofa
el **triángulo** NOUN
triangle
la **tribu** NOUN
tribe
la **tribuna** NOUN
1 platform
2 stand
el **tribunal** NOUN
1 court
2 board of examiners
el **triciclo** NOUN
tricycle
tridimensional (FEM **tridimensional**) ADJECTIVE
three-dimensional
el **trigo** NOUN
wheat
trillar VERB [25]
to thresh
los **trillizos**, las **trillizas** NOUN
triplets
trimestral (FEM **trimestral**) ADJECTIVE
quarterly
■ **los exámenes trimestrales** the end-of-term exams
el **trimestre** NOUN
term
trinchar VERB [25]
to carve
la **trinchera** NOUN
trench
el **trineo** NOUN
1 sledge
2 sleigh
la **Trinidad** NOUN
the Trinity
el **trío** NOUN
trio
la **tripa** NOUN
gut
el **triple** NOUN
■ **Esta habitación es el triple de grande.** This room is three times as big.
■ **Gastan el triple que nosotros.** They spend three times as much as we do.
triplicar* VERB [48]
to treble
la **tripulación** (PL las **tripulaciones**) NOUN
crew
triste (FEM **triste**) ADJECTIVE
1 sad
□ Me puse muy triste cuando me enteré. I was very sad when I heard.
■ **El invierno me pone triste.** Winter makes me miserable.
2 gloomy
la **tristeza** NOUN
sadness
triturar VERB [25]
1 to crush
2 to grind
triunfar VERB [25]
to triumph
□ Los socialistas triunfaron en las elecciones. The socialists triumphed in the elections.
■ **triunfar en la vida** to succeed in life
el **triunfo** NOUN
triumph
trivial (FEM **trivial**) ADJECTIVE
trivial
las **trizas** NOUN
■ **hacer algo trizas** to tear something to shreds
trocear VERB [25]
to cut up
□ trocear las zanahorias to cut up the carrots
el **trofeo** NOUN
trophy (PL trophies)
el **trombón** (PL los **trombones**) NOUN
trombone
la **trompa** NOUN
1 trunk *(of elephant)*
2 horn *(musical instrument)*
■ **coger una trompa** to get plastered
la **trompeta** NOUN
trumpet
tronar* VERB [11]
to thunder
□ Ha estado tronando toda la noche. It has been thundering all night.
troncharse VERB [25]
■ **Yo me tronchaba de risa.** I was killing myself laughing.
el **tronco** NOUN
1 trunk
2 log
■ **dormir como un tronco** to sleep like a log
el **trono** NOUN
throne
las **tropas** NOUN
troops
tropezar* VERB [19]
to trip
□ Tropecé y me caí. I tripped and fell.
■ **tropezar con una piedra** to trip on a stone
■ **tropezar contra un árbol** to bump into a tree
■ **Me tropecé con Juan en el banco.** I bumped into Juan in the bank.
el **tropezón** (PL los **tropezones**) NOUN
trip
■ **dar un tropezón** to trip

Spanish-English

tropical (FEM **tropical**) ADJECTIVE
tropical

el **trópico** NOUN
tropic

tropiece VERB ▷ *see* **tropezar**

trotar VERB [25]
to trot

el **trote** NOUN
■ **El abuelo ya no está para estos trotes.** Grandad is not up to that sort of thing any more.

el **trozo** NOUN
piece
□ un trozo de madera a piece of wood
□ Dame un trocito sólo. Just give me a small piece.
■ **Vi la película a trozos.** I saw bits of the film.

la **trucha** NOUN
trout

el **truco** NOUN
trick
■ **Ya le he cogido el truco.** I've got the hang of it already.

truena VERB ▷ *see* **tronar**

el **trueno** NOUN
■ **Oímos un trueno.** We heard a clap of thunder.
■ **Me despertaron los truenos.** The thunder woke me up.

la **trufa** NOUN
truffle

tu ADJECTIVE
your
□ tu coche your car □ tus familiares your relations

tú PRONOUN
you
□ Cuando tú quieras. Whenever you like.
□ Llegamos antes que tú. We arrived before you.

la **tuberculosis** NOUN
tuberculosis

la **tubería** NOUN
pipe
□ Ha reventado una tubería. A pipe has burst.

el **tubo** NOUN
1 pipe
□ el tubo de escape the exhaust pipe
■ **el tubo de desagüe** the drainpipe
2 tube
□ un tubo de crema para las manos a tube of hand cream

la **tuerca** NOUN
nut

tuerto (FEM **tuerta**) ADJECTIVE
■ **Es tuerto.** He's blind in one eye.

tuerzo VERB ▷ *see* **torcer**

el **tuétano** NOUN
marrow

el **tufo** NOUN
stench

el **tulipán** (PL los **tulipanes**) NOUN
tulip

la **tumba** NOUN
1 grave
2 tomb
□ una tumba egipcia an Egyptian tomb

tumbar VERB [25]
to knock down
□ El perro me tumbó. The dog knocked me down.
■ **tumbarse** to lie down □ Me tumbé en el sofá. I lay down on the sofa.

el **tumbo** NOUN
■ **El borracho iba dando tumbos.** The drunk staggered along.

la **tumbona** NOUN
deck chair

el **tumor** NOUN
tumour

el **túnel** NOUN
tunnel
■ **un túnel de lavado** a car wash
LANGUAGE TIP Word for word, **túnel de lavado** means 'washing tunnel'.

Túnez MASC NOUN
1 Tunisia
2 Tunis

tupido (FEM **tupida**) ADJECTIVE
1 dense
2 close-woven
3 bushy

el **turbante** NOUN
turban

la **turbina** NOUN
turbine

turbio (FEM **turbia**) ADJECTIVE
cloudy

turbulento (FEM **turbulenta**) ADJECTIVE
turbulent

turco (FEM **turca**) ADJECTIVE
Turkish

el **turco**, la **turca** NOUN
Turk

el **turco** NOUN
Turkish

el **turismo** NOUN
1 tourism
□ El turismo es importante para nuestra economía. Tourism is important for our economy.
■ **turismo rural** tourism in rural areas
■ **casas de turismo rural** holiday cottages
■ **la oficina de turismo** the tourist office

t

2 tourists *pl*
□ En verano hay mucho turismo.
In summer there are a lot of tourists.
3 car

el/la **turista** NOUN
tourist

turístico (FEM **turística**) ADJECTIVE
tourist

turnarse VERB [25]
to take it in turns
□ Nos turnamos para fregar los platos.
We take it in turns to do the washing-up.

el **turno** NOUN
1 turn
□ cuando me tocó el turno when it was my turn
2 shift
□ Hago el turno de tarde. I do the afternoon shift.

la **turquesa** ADJECTIVE, NOUN
turquoise
□ un anorak turquesa a turquoise anorak

Turquía FEM NOUN
Turkey

el **turrón** (PL los **turrones**) NOUN
nougat

tutear VERB [25]
DID YOU KNOW...?
to address somebody using the familiar **tú** form rather than the more formal **usted** form.
□ Se tutean con el jefe. They address the boss in familiar terms.

el **tutor**, la **tutora** NOUN
1 tutor
2 guardian

tuve VERB ▷ *see* **tener**

tuyo (FEM **tuya**) ADJECTIVE, PRONOUN
yours
□ ¿Es tuyo este abrigo? Is this coat yours?
□ La tuya está en el armario. Yours is in the cupboard. □ mis amigos y los tuyos my friends and yours
■ **un amigo tuyo** a friend of yours

Uu

u CONJUNCTION
or
□ ¿Minutos u horas? Minutes or hours?

ubicado (FEM **ubicada**) ADJECTIVE
situated
□ bien ubicado well situated

Ud. ABBREVIATION = **usted**

Uds. ABBREVIATION = **ustedes**

la **UE** ABBREVIATION (= *Unión Europea*)
EU

uf INTERJECTION
1 phew!
2 ugh!

la **úlcera** NOUN
ulcer

últimamente ADVERB
recently

el **ultimátum** (PL los **ultimátums**) NOUN
ultimatum (PL ultimatums)

último (FEM **última**) ADJECTIVE
1 last
□ la última vez que hablé con ella the last time I spoke to her
2 top
□ No llego al último estante. I can't reach the top shelf.
3 back
□ Nos sentamos en la última fila. We sat in the back row.
■ **la última moda** the latest fashion
■ **a última hora** at the last minute □ A última hora decidió acompañarme. He decided to come with me at the last minute.
■ **llegar en último lugar** to arrive last

el **último**, la **última** NOUN
the last one
■ **a últimos de mes** towards the end of the month
■ **por último** lastly

el/la **ultra** NOUN
right-wing extremist

ultrasónico (FEM **ultrasónica**) ADJECTIVE
ultrasonic

ultravioleta (FEM **ultravioleta**) ADJECTIVE
ultraviolet

un, **una** ARTICLE
1 a
□ una silla a chair
2 an
□ un paraguas an umbrella
3 some
□ Fui con unos amigos. I went with some friends.
■ **Tiene unas uñas muy largas.** He has very long nails.
■ **Había unas 20 personas.** There were about 20 people.
■ **Me he comprado unos zapatos de tacón.** I have bought a pair of high-heels.

unánime (FEM **unánime**) ADJECTIVE
unanimous

undécimo (FEM **undécima**) ADJECTIVE, PRONOUN
eleventh
□ Vivo en el undécimo piso. I live on the eleventh floor.

únicamente ADVERB
only
□ Me encargo únicamente del teléfono. I'm only in charge of the telephone.

el **único** (FEM la **única**) ADJECTIVE, NOUN
only
□ el único día que tengo libre the only day I have free
■ **Soy hija única.** I'm an only child.
■ **el único que me queda** the only one I've got left
■ **Lo único que no me gusta ...** The only thing I don't like ...
■ **una colección de sellos única** a unique stamp collection

la **unidad** NOUN
1 unit
□ una unidad de peso a unit of weight
■ **unidad de cuidados intensivos** intensive care unit
2 unity
□ falta de unidad en la familia lack of family unity

unido (FEM **unida**) ADJECTIVE
close
□ una familia muy unida a very close family

uniforme (FEM **uniforme**) ADJECTIVE
even
□ una superficie uniforme an even surface
el **uniforme** NOUN
uniform
□ Llevaba el uniforme del colegio. He was wearing his school uniform.
la **unión** (PL las **uniones**) NOUN
union
■ **la Unión Europea** the European Union
unir VERB [58]
1 to link
□ Este pasaje une los dos edificios. This passage links the two buildings.
2 to join
□ Unió los dos extremos con una cuerda. He joined the two ends with some string.
3 to unite
□ Los unió en matrimonio. He united them in marriage.
4 to bring together
□ La enfermedad de la madre ha unido a los hijos. The mother's illness has brought the children together.
■ **unirse a algo** to join something □ Andrés se unió a la expedición. Andrés joined the expedition.
■ **Más adelante los dos caminos se unen.** The two paths join further on.
■ **Los dos bancos se han unido.** The two banks have merged.
universal (FEM **universal**) ADJECTIVE
universal
la **universidad** NOUN
university (PL universities)
□ El año que viene voy a la universidad. I'm going to university next year.
■ **Universidad a Distancia** Open University

DID YOU KNOW...?
La **Open University** imparte cursos a distancia con el apoyo de programas de radio y televisión emitidos por la BBC.

universitario (FEM **universitaria**) ADJECTIVE
university
□ estudiantes universitarios university students
el **universitario**, la **universitaria** NOUN
1 university student
2 graduate
el **universo** NOUN
universe
uno (FEM **una**) ADJECTIVE, PRONOUN
one
□ Vivo en el número uno. I live at number one. □ Uno de ellos era mío. One of them was mine.
■ **unos pocos** a few
■ **uno mismo** oneself
■ **Entraron uno a uno.** They came in one by one.
■ **unas diez personas** about ten people
■ **el uno de abril** the first of April
■ **Es la una.** It's one o'clock.
■ **Unos querían ir, otros no.** Some of them wanted to go, others didn't.
■ **Se miraron uno al otro.** They looked at each other.
untar VERB [25]
■ **untar algo con algo** to spread something on something □ Primero hay que untar el pan con mantequilla. First you have to spread the butter on the bread.
■ **Te has untado las manos de chocolate.** You've got chocolate all over your hands.
■ **unta el molde con aceite** grease the baking dish with oil
la **uña** NOUN
1 nail
2 claw
el **uranio** NOUN
uranium
la **urbanización** (PL las **urbanizaciones**) NOUN
housing estate
la **urgencia** NOUN
emergency (PL emergencies)
□ en caso de urgencia in an emergency
□ los servicios de urgencia the emergency services
■ **urgencias** accident and emergency
■ **Tuvimos que ir a urgencias.** We had to go to casualty.
■ **con urgencia** urgently
urgente (FEM **urgente**) ADJECTIVE
urgent
■ **Lo mandé por correo urgente.** I sent it express.
la **urna** NOUN
ballot box
Uruguay MASC NOUN
Uruguay
el **uruguayo** (FEM la **uruguaya**) ADJECTIVE, NOUN
Uruguayan
usado (FEM **usada**) ADJECTIVE
1 secondhand
□ una tienda de ropa usada a secondhand clothes shop
2 worn
□ Estas zapatillas están ya muy usadas. These slippers are very worn now.
usar VERB [25]
1 to use

□ Uso una maquinilla eléctrica. I use an electric razor.

2 to wear

□ ¿Qué número de zapato usas? What size shoe do you take?

el **uso** NOUN

use

□ instrucciones de uso instructions for use

usted PRONOUN

you

□ Quisiera hablar con usted en privado. I'd like to speak to you in private.

ustedes PL PRONOUN

you

□ Quisiera hablar con ustedes en privado. I'd like to speak to you in private.

usual (FEM **usual**) ADJECTIVE

usual

el **usuario**, la **usuaria** NOUN

user

el **utensilio** NOUN

utensil

□ utensilios de cocina kitchen utensils

el **útero** NOUN

uterus

útil (FEM **útil**) ADJECTIVE

useful

utilizar* VERB [13]

to use

la **uva** NOUN

grape

■ **estar de mala uva** to be in a bad mood

Spanish-English

u

Vv

va VERB ▷*see* **ir**

la **vaca** NOUN
1 cow
2 beef
□ No como carne de vaca. I don't eat beef.

las **vacaciones** NOUN
holidays
■ **las vacaciones de Navidad** the Christmas holidays
■ **La secretaria está de vacaciones.** The secretary is on holiday.
■ **En agosto me voy de vacaciones.** I'm going on holiday in August.

vacante (FEM **vacante**) ADJECTIVE
1 vacant
2 unoccupied

la **vacante** NOUN
vacancy (PL vacancies)

vaciar* VERB [21]
to empty
□ Vacié la nevera para limpiarla. I emptied the fridge to clean it.

vacilar VERB [25]
to hesitate
□ Vaciló unos instantes antes de responder. He hesitated for a moment or two before answering.
■ **sin vacilar** without hesitating

vacío (FEM **vacía**) ADJECTIVE
empty

el **vacío** NOUN
void
□ Se arrojó al vacío. He hurled himself into the void.
■ **envasado al vacío** vacuum-packed

la **vacuna** NOUN
vaccine
□ la vacuna de la hepatitis the hepatitis vaccine
■ **¿Te has puesto la vacuna?** Have they given you the vaccination?

vacunar VERB [25]
to vaccinate
■ **Mi abuelo se vacuna contra la gripe.** My grandfather has flu vaccinations.

el **vado** NOUN
■ **'vado permanente'** 'no parking – in constant use'

la **vaga** NOUN
layabout

la **vagabunda** NOUN
tramp

vagabundo (FEM **vagabunda**) ADJECTIVE
stray

el **vagabundo** NOUN
tramp

vagar* VERB [37]
to wander

la **vagina** NOUN
vagina

vago (FEM **vaga**) ADJECTIVE
1 lazy
2 vague

el **vago** NOUN
layabout
■ **hacer el vago** to laze around

el **vagón** (PL los **vagones**) NOUN
carriage
■ **vagón cama** sleeper
■ **vagón restaurante** restaurant car

el **vaho** NOUN
steam

la **vainilla** NOUN
vanilla
□ un helado de vainilla a vanilla ice cream

la **vajilla** NOUN
dishes *pl*
□ La vajilla está en el lavaplatos. The dishes are in the dishwasher.
■ **Me regaló una vajilla de porcelana.** She gave me a china dinner service.

el **vale** NOUN
1 voucher
□ un vale de regalo a gift voucher
■ **un vale de descuento** a money-off coupon
2 credit note

la **valenciana** NOUN
Valencian

el **valenciano** ADJECTIVE, NOUN
Valencian
■ **Hablan valenciano.** They speak

Valencian.

la **valentía** NOUN
bravery
■ **con valentía** bravely

valer* VERB [55]
1 to cost
□ ¿Cuánto vale? How much does it cost?
2 to be worth
□ El terreno vale más que la casa. The land is worth more than the house.
■ **No vale mirar.** You're not allowed to look.
■ **¡Eso no vale!** That's not fair!
■ **vale la pena** it's worth it
■ **Vale la pena hacer el esfuerzo.** It's worth the effort.
■ **no vale la pena** it's not worth it
■ **No vale la pena gastar tanto dinero.** It's not worth spending that much money.
■ **Este cuchillo no vale para nada.** This knife is useless.
■ **Yo no valdría para enfermera.** I'd make a hopeless nurse.
■ **¿Vale?** OK?
■ **¿Vamos a tomar algo? — ¡Vale!** Shall we go for a drink? — OK!
■ **Más vale que te lleves el abrigo.** You'd better take your coat.
■ **No puede valerse por sí mismo.** He can't look after himself.

válido (FEM **válida**) ADJECTIVE
valid

valiente (FEM **valiente**) ADJECTIVE
brave

la **valija** NOUN
suitcase *(River Plate)*
■ **valija diplomática** diplomatic bag

valioso (FEM **valiosa**) ADJECTIVE
valuable

la **valla** NOUN
fence
■ **valla publicitaria** hoarding
■ **los cien metros vallas** the hundred metre hurdles

el **valle** NOUN
valley (PL valleys)

el **valor** NOUN
1 value
□ valor sentimental sentimental value
■ **una pulsera de gran valor** an extremely valuable bracelet
2 courage
□ armarse de valor to pluck up courage
■ **objetos de valor** valuables
■ **valor adquisitivo** purchasing power

valorar VERB [25]
to value

el **vals** NOUN
waltz
■ **bailar un vals** to waltz

la **válvula** NOUN
valve

el **vampiro**, la **vampira** NOUN
vampire

el **vandalismo** NOUN
vandalism

la **vanguardia** NOUN
avant-garde
■ **de vanguardia** avant-garde

la **vanidad** NOUN
vanity

vanidoso (FEM **vanidosa**) ADJECTIVE
vain

vano (FEM **vana**) ADJECTIVE
vain
□ un intento vano a vain attempt
■ **en vano** in vain

el **vapor** NOUN
steam
■ **plancha de vapor** steam iron
■ **al vapor** steamed

vaquero (FEM **vaquera**) ADJECTIVE
denim
□ una falda vaquera a denim skirt

el **vaquero** NOUN
cowboy (PL cowboys)
■ **una película de vaqueros** a western
■ **vaqueros** jeans □ Llevaba unos vaqueros negros. He was wearing black jeans.

variable (FEM **variable**) ADJECTIVE
variable
■ **El tiempo es muy variable.** The weather is very changeable.

variado (FEM **variada**) ADJECTIVE
varied
□ Prefiero un trabajo más variado. I prefer a more varied job.

variar* VERB [21]
to vary
□ Los precios varían según las tallas. Prices vary according to size.
■ **Decidí ir en tren, para variar.** I decided to go by train for a change.

la **varicela** NOUN
chickenpox
□ Yo no he pasado la varicela. I've never had chickenpox.

la **variedad** NOUN
variety (PL varieties)
□ una nueva variedad de clavel a new variety of carnation

la **varilla** NOUN
rod
■ **la varilla del aceite** the dipstick

varios (FEM **varias**) ADJECTIVE, PRONOUN
several
□ Estuve enfermo varios días. I was ill for

several days. □ Le hicimos un regalo entre varios. Several of us clubbed together to get him a present.

la **variz** (PL las **varices**) NOUN
varicose vein

varón (PL **varones**) ADJECTIVE
male
□ los herederos varones the male heirs

el **varón** (PL los **varones**) NOUN
□ Tiene dos hembras y un varón. She has two girls and a boy.
■ **Sexo: varón.** Sex: male.

Varsovia FEM NOUN
Warsaw

la **vasca** NOUN
Basque

el **vasco** ADJECTIVE, NOUN
Basque
■ **Hablamos vasco.** We speak Basque.
■ **el País Vasco** the Basque Country

la **vasija** NOUN
vessel
□ una vasija fenicia a Phoenician vessel

el **vaso** NOUN
glass (PL glasses)
□ Bebí un vaso de leche. I drank a glass of milk.
■ **un vaso de plástico** a plastic cup
■ **un vaso sanguíneo** a blood vessel

el **váter** NOUN
loo *(colloquial)*

el **Vaticano** NOUN
Vatican

el **vatio** NOUN
watt

vaya VERB ▷ *see* **ir**

Vd. ABBREVIATION = **usted**

Vds. ABBREVIATION = **ustedes**

ve VERB ▷ *see* **ir, ver**

la **vecina** NOUN
1 neighbour
2 inhabitant

el **vecindario** NOUN
neighbourhood

vecino (FEM **vecina**) ADJECTIVE
neighbouring
□ las ciudades vecinas the neighbouring towns

el **vecino** NOUN
1 neighbour
□ los vecinos de al lado the next door neighbours
2 inhabitant
□ todos los vecinos de Torrevieja all the inhabitants of Torrevieja

la **vegetación** (PL las **vegetaciones**) NOUN
vegetation
■ **vegetaciones** adenoids

el **vegetal** ADJECTIVE, NOUN
vegetable
□ aceite vegetal vegetable oil

el **vegetariano** (FEM la **vegetariana**) ADJECTIVE, NOUN
vegetarian
□ Es vegetariano. He's vegetarian.

el **vehículo** NOUN
vehicle

veinte (FEM **veinte**) ADJECTIVE, PRONOUN
twenty
□ Tiene veinte años. He's twenty.
■ **el veinte de enero** the twentieth of January
■ **el siglo veinte** the twentieth century

la **vejez** NOUN
old age

la **vejiga** NOUN
bladder

la **vela** NOUN
1 candle
□ Encendimos una vela. We lit a candle.
2 sail
3 sailing
■ **un barco de vela** a yacht
■ **Pasé la noche en vela.** I had a sleepless night.
■ **estar a dos velas** to be broke

velarse VERB [25]
■ **Se han velado las fotos.** The photos got exposed by accident.

el **velero** NOUN
yacht

el **vello** NOUN
1 hair
□ Tiene mucho vello. He's very hairy.
2 down

el **velo** NOUN
veil

la **velocidad** NOUN
1 speed
□ Pasó una moto a toda velocidad. A motorbike went past at full speed.
■ **¿A qué velocidad ibas?** How fast were you going?
2 gear
□ cambiar de velocidad to change gear

el **velocímetro** NOUN
speedometer

el/la **velocista** NOUN
sprinter

el **velódromo** NOUN
cycle track

veloz (FEM **veloz**, PL **veloces**) ADJECTIVE
swift

ven VERB ▷ *see* **ir, ver**

la **vena** NOUN
vein

vencedor (FEM **vencedora**) ADJECTIVE
winning
□ el equipo vencedor the winning team
el **vencedor**, la **vencedora** NOUN
winner
vencer* VERB [6, no vowel change]
1 to defeat
2 to overcome
3 to expire
□ El pasaporte me vence mañana. My passport expires tomorrow.
vencido (FEM **vencida**) ADJECTIVE
■ **darse por vencido** to give up
la **venda** NOUN
1 bandage
■ **Me pusieron una venda en el brazo.** They bandaged my arm.
2 blindfold
■ **poner una venda en los ojos a alguien** to blindfold someone
vendar VERB [25]
to bandage
□ Me vendaron el codo. They bandaged my elbow.
■ **vendar los ojos a alguien** to blindfold someone
el **vendedor** NOUN
salesman (PL salesmen)
■ **vendedor ambulante** pedlar
■ **vendedor de periódicos** newspaper seller
la **vendedora** NOUN
saleswoman (PL saleswomen)
vender VERB [8]
to sell
□ He vendido el coche. I've sold the car.
■ **Venden la oficina de arriba.** The office upstairs is for sale.
■ **'se vende'** 'for sale'
■ **venderse por** to sell for □ El cuadro se vendió por treinta mil euros. The painting sold for thirty thousand euros.
la **vendimia** NOUN
grape harvest
vendré VERB ▷ *see* **venir**
el **veneno** NOUN
1 poison
2 venom
venenoso (FEM **venenosa**) ADJECTIVE
poisonous
el **venezolano** (FEM la **venezolana**) ADJECTIVE, NOUN
Venezuelan
Venezuela FEM NOUN
Venezuela
la **venganza** NOUN
revenge
vengarse* VERB [37]
to take revenge
■ **vengarse de alguien** to take revenge on someone
■ **vengarse de algo** to avenge something
vengo VERB ▷ *see* **venir**
la **venida** NOUN
arrival
■ **La venida la hicimos en autobús.** We came by bus on the way here.
venir* VERB [56]
1 to come
□ Vino en taxi. He came by taxi. □ Vinieron a verme al hospital. They came to see me in hospital. □ Viene en varios colores. It comes in several colours. □ ¡Ven aquí! Come here!
■ **Enseguida vengo.** I'll be back in a minute.
2 to be
□ La noticia venía en el periódico. The news was in the paper.
■ **¡Venga, vámonos!** Come on, let's go!
■ **La casa se está viniendo abajo.** The house is falling apart.
■ **Mañana me viene mal.** Tomorrow isn't good for me.
■ **¿Te viene bien el sábado?** Is Saturday alright for you?
■ **el año que viene** next year
■ **¡Venga ya!** Come off it!
la **venta** NOUN
sale
■ **estar en venta** to be for sale
la **ventaja** NOUN
advantage
□ Tiene la ventaja de que está cerca de casa. It has the advantage of being close to home.
■ **llevar ventaja a alguien** to have an advantage over someone
■ **jugar con ventaja** to be at an advantage
la **ventana** NOUN
window
la **ventanilla** NOUN
1 window
□ Baja la ventanilla. Open the window.
2 box office
la **ventilación** NOUN
ventilation
■ **El sótano tiene poca ventilación.** The basement is poorly ventilated.
ventilar VERB [25]
to air
la **ventisca** NOUN
1 gale force winds
2 blizzard
ver* VERB [57]
1 to see
□ Te vi en el parque. I saw you in the park.

□ ¡Cuánto tiempo sin verte! I haven't seen you for ages! □ No he visto esa película. I haven't seen that film. □ El médico todavía no la ha visto. The doctor hasn't seen her yet. □ ¿Ves? Ya te lo dije. See? I told you so.
■ **Voy a ver si está en su despacho.** I'll see if he's in his office.
■ **Quedamos en vernos en la estación.** We arranged to meet at the station.
■ **¡Luego nos vemos!** See you later!
■ **Eso no tiene nada que ver.** That has nothing to do with it.
■ **¡No la puede ver!** He can't stand her!
■ **A ver ...** Let's see ...
■ **Se ve que no tiene idea de informática.** It's clear he's got no idea about computers.
2 to watch

veranear VERB [25]
to spend the summer holidays
□ Veraneamos en Calpe. We spend our summer holidays in Calpe.

el **veraneo** NOUN
■ **lugar de veraneo** summer resort
■ **No pudimos ir de veraneo el año pasado.** We couldn't go on holiday last summer.

el **verano** NOUN
summer
□ En verano hace mucho calor. It's very hot in summer. □ las vacaciones de verano the summer holidays

veras FEM PL NOUN
■ **de veras** really

veraz (FEM **veraz**, PL **veraces**) ADJECTIVE
truthful

la **verbena** NOUN
open-air dance
■ **la verbena de San Roque** the festival of San Roque

el **verbo** NOUN
verb

la **verdad** NOUN
truth
□ Les dije la verdad. I told them the truth.
■ **¡Es verdad!** It's true!
■ **La verdad es que no tengo ganas.** I don't really feel like it.
■ **¿De verdad?** Really?
■ **De verdad que yo no dije eso.** I didn't say that, honestly.
■ **No era un policía de verdad.** He wasn't a real policeman.
■ **Es bonito, ¿verdad?** It's pretty, isn't it?
■ **No te gusta, ¿verdad?** You don't like it, do you?

verdadero (FEM **verdadera**) ADJECTIVE
real
□ Su apellido verdadero es Rodríguez. His real surname is Rodríguez. □ Es un verdadero caballero. He's a real gentleman.

el **verde** ADJECTIVE, NOUN
1 green
□ Tiene los ojos verdes. She has green eyes.
□ Estos plátanos están todavía verdes. These bananas are still green.
2 dirty
□ un chiste verde a dirty joke
■ **los verdes** the Green Party

el **verdugo** NOUN
1 executioner
2 hangman

la **verdulería** NOUN
greengrocer's (PL greengrocers' shops)

la **verdura** NOUN
vegetables *pl*
□ Comemos mucha verdura. We eat a lot of vegetables.

la **vereda** NOUN
1 path
2 pavement *(Chile, River Plate)*

vergonzoso (FEM **vergonzosa**) ADJECTIVE
1 shy
□ Es muy vergonzosa. She is very shy.
2 disgraceful
□ Es vergonzoso cómo los trataron. It's disgraceful the way they were treated.

la **vergüenza** NOUN
1 embarrassment
□ Casi me muero de vergüenza. I almost died of embarrassment.
2 shame
□ No tienen vergüenza. They have no shame.
■ **¡Qué vergüenza!** How embarrassing!
■ **Le da vergüenza pedírselo.** He's embarrassed to ask her.
■ **¡Es una vergüenza!** It's disgraceful!

verídico (FEM **verídica**) ADJECTIVE
true

verificar* VERB [48]
to check

la **verja** NOUN
1 railings *pl*
2 gate

el **vermut** NOUN
vermouth

la **verruga** NOUN
1 wart
2 verruca

la **versión** (PL las **versiones**) NOUN
version
■ **una película francesa en versión original** a film in the original French version

el **verso** NOUN
1 line
2 verse

la **vértebra** NOUN
vertebra (PL vertebrae)

el **vertedero** NOUN
rubbish tip

verter* VERB [20]
1 to pour
□ Vertió un poco de leche en el cazo. He poured a little milk into the saucepan.
2 to dump

vertical (FEM **vertical**) ADJECTIVE
vertical
■ **Ponlo vertical.** Put it upright.

el **vértigo** NOUN
vertigo
■ **Me da vértigo.** It makes me dizzy.

la **Vespa®** NOUN
scooter

vespertino (FEM **vespertina**) ADJECTIVE
evening
□ un diario vespertino an evening paper

el **vestíbulo** NOUN
1 hall
2 foyer

vestido (FEM **vestida**) ADJECTIVE
■ **Iba vestida de negro.** She was dressed in black.
■ **Yo iba vestido de payaso.** I was dressed as a clown.
■ **un hombre bien vestido** a well-dressed man

el **vestido** NOUN
dress (PL dresses)
■ **el vestido de novia** the bridal gown

vestir* VERB [38]
to wear
□ Vestía pantalones vaqueros y una camiseta. He was wearing jeans and a T-shirt.
■ **vestir a alguien** to dress someone □ Estaba vistiendo a los niños. I was dressing the children.
■ **vestir bien** to dress well
■ **vestirse** to get dressed □ Se está vistiendo. He's getting dressed.
■ **Se vistió de princesa.** She dressed up as a princess.
■ **ropa de vestir** smart clothes *pl*

el **vestón** (PL los **vestones**) NOUN
jacket *(Chile, River Plate)*

el **vestuario** NOUN
1 changing room
2 wardrobe

el **veterinario**, la **veterinaria** NOUN
vet

la **vez** (PL las **veces**) NOUN
time
□ la próxima vez next time □ ¿Cuántas veces al año? How many times a year?
■ **a la vez** at the same time
■ **a veces** sometimes
■ **algunas veces** sometimes
■ **muchas veces** often
■ **cada vez más** more and more
■ **cada vez menos** less and less
■ **de una vez** once and for all
■ **de vez en cuando** from time to time
■ **en vez de** instead of
■ **¿La has visto alguna vez?** Have you ever seen her?
■ **otra vez** again
■ **tal vez** maybe
■ **una vez** once □ La veo una vez a la semana. I see her once a week.
■ **dos veces** twice
■ **una y otra vez** again and again

vi VERB ▷ *see* **ver**

la **vía** NOUN
1 track
2 platform
□ Nuestro tren sale por la vía dos. Our train leaves from platform two.
■ **por vía aérea** by airmail
■ **Madrid-Berlín vía París** Madrid-Berlin via Paris

viajar VERB [25]
to travel
□ viajar en autocar to travel by coach

el **viaje** NOUN
1 trip
■ **¡Buen viaje!** Have a good trip!
■ **un viaje de negocios** a business trip
2 journey
□ Es un viaje muy largo. It's a very long journey.
■ **estar de viaje** to be away
■ **salir de viaje** to go away
■ **una agencia de viajes** a travel agency
■ **el viaje de novios** honeymoon

el **viajero**, la **viajera** NOUN
passenger

la **víbora** NOUN
viper

la **vibración** (PL las **vibraciones**) NOUN
vibration

vibrar VERB [25]
to vibrate

la **vicepresidenta** NOUN
1 vice president
2 chairwoman (PL chairwomen)

el **vicepresidente** NOUN
1 vice president
2 chairman (PL chairmen)

viceversa ADVERB
vice versa

viciarse VERB [25]
to deteriorate

■ **viciarse con las drogas** to become addicted to drugs

el **vicio** NOUN
vice
□ El tabaco es mi único vicio. Smoking is my only vice.
■ **Tengo el vicio de morderme las uñas.** I bite my nails; I know it's a bad habit.

la **víctima** NOUN
victim

la **victoria** NOUN
victory (PL victories)
□ la victoria del partido conservador the conservative party victory
■ **su primera victoria fuera de casa** their first away win

la **vid** NOUN
vine

la **vida** NOUN
life (PL lives)
□ He vivido aquí toda mi vida. I've lived here all my life. □ Llevan una vida muy tranquila. They lead a very quiet life. □ ¡Esto sí que es vida! This is the life!
■ **la media de vida de un televisor** the average life span of a television set
■ **vida nocturna** nightlife
■ **estar con vida** to be alive
■ **salir con vida** to escape alive
■ **Se gana la vida haciendo traducciones.** He earns his living by translating.
■ **¡Vida mía!** My darling!

el **video** NOUN *(Latin America)*
video

el **vídeo** NOUN
video
□ Tengo la película en vídeo. I've got the film on video.
■ **cinta de vídeo** videotape

la **videocámara** NOUN
video camera

el **videojuego** NOUN
video game

la **videollamada** NOUN
video call

el **videoteléfono** NOUN
videophone

la **vidriera** NOUN
1 stained glass window
2 shop window *(Latin America)*

el **vidrio** NOUN
1 glass
□ botellas de vidrio glass bottles
■ **Me corté el dedo con un vidrio.** I cut my finger on a piece of glass.
2 windowpane

la **vieja** NOUN
old woman (PL old women)
□ Había una viejecita sentada a mi lado. There was an old woman sitting next to me.

viejo (FEM **vieja**) ADJECTIVE
old
□ un viejo amigo mío an old friend of mine □ Estos zapatos ya están muy viejos. These shoes are very old now.
■ **hacerse viejo** to get old

el **viejo** NOUN
old man (PL old men)
■ **los viejos** old people
■ **llegar a viejo** to reach old age

viene VERB ▷ *see* **venir**

el **viento** NOUN
wind
■ **Hace mucho viento.** It's very windy.

el **vientre** NOUN
stomach
■ **hacer de vientre** to go to the toilet

el **viernes** (PL los **viernes**) NOUN
Friday
□ La vi el viernes. I saw her on Friday. □ todos los viernes every Friday □ el viernes pasado last Friday □ el viernes que viene next Friday □ Jugamos los viernes. We play on Fridays.
■ **Viernes Santo** Good Friday
LANGUAGE TIP Word for word, **Viernes Santo** means 'Holy Friday'.

vierta VERB ▷ *see* **verter**

el/la **vietnamita** ADJECTIVE, NOUN
Vietnamese
■ **los vietnamitas** the Vietnamese

la **viga** NOUN
1 beam
2 girder

la **vigilancia** NOUN
1 surveillance
□ bajo vigilancia policial under police surveillance
2 vigilance
□ El paciente necesita vigilancia constante. The patient needs constant vigilance.
■ **patrulla de vigilancia** security patrol

el/la **vigilante** NOUN
1 security guard
2 store detective
■ **vigilante jurado** security guard
■ **vigilante nocturno** night watchman (PL night watchmen)

vigilar VERB [25]
1 to guard
□ Un policía vigilaba al preso. A policeman was guarding the prisoner.
2 to watch
□ Nos vigilan. They're watching us.
3 to keep an eye on
□ ¿Me vigilas el bolso un momento?

Can you keep an eye on my bag for a minute?

VIH ABBREVIATION *(= virus de inmunodeficiencia humana)*
HIV

la **villa** NOUN
1 town
2 villa

el **villancico** NOUN
carol

el **vinagre** NOUN
vinegar

el **vínculo** NOUN
bond

vine VERB ▷ *see* **venir**

viniendo VERB ▷ *see* **venir**

el **vino** NOUN
wine
■ **vino blanco** white wine
■ **vino tinto** red wine
■ **vino de la casa** house wine

la **viña** NOUN
vineyard

el **viñedo** NOUN
vineyard

la **violación** (PL las **violaciones**) NOUN
1 rape
2 violation

el **violador**, la **violadora** NOUN
rapist

violar VERB [25]
1 to rape
2 to violate

la **violencia** NOUN
violence

violento (FEM **violenta**) ADJECTIVE
1 violent
□ La película contiene algunas escenas violentas. The film contains some violent scenes.
2 embarrassing
□ Era una situación violenta. It was an embarrassing situation.
■ **Me resulta violento decírselo.** I'm embarrassed to tell him.

el **violeta** ADJECTIVE, NOUN
purple
□ unas cortinas violeta purple curtains

la **violeta** NOUN
violet

el **violín** (PL los **violines**) NOUN
violin

el/la **violinista** NOUN
violinist

el **violón** (PL los **violones**) NOUN
double bass (PL double basses)

el/la **violonchelista** NOUN
cellist

el **violonchelo** NOUN
cello (PL cellos)

virgen (FEM **virgen**, PL **vírgenes**) ADJECTIVE
1 virgin
■ **ser virgen** to be a virgin
2 blank *(tape)*

la **virgen** (PL las **vírgenes**) NOUN
virgin
■ **la Virgen** the Virgin

Virgo MASC NOUN
Virgo
■ **Soy virgo.** I'm Virgo.

viril (FEM **viril**) ADJECTIVE
virile

la **virilidad** NOUN
virility

virtual ADJECTIVE
virtual

la **virtud** NOUN
virtue

la **viruela** NOUN
smallpox
□ Tiene la viruela. He has smallpox.

el **virus** (PL los **virus**) NOUN
virus (PL viruses)

la **visa** NOUN *(Latin America)*
visa

el **visado** NOUN
visa

la **visera** NOUN
1 peak
2 visor

la **visibilidad** NOUN
visibility
□ Había muy poca visibilidad. Visibility was very poor.

visible (FEM **visible**) ADJECTIVE
visible

el **visillo** NOUN
net curtain

la **visión** (PL las **visiones**) NOUN
1 vision
□ la visión nocturna night vision
2 view
□ una visión pesimista de la vida a pessimistic view of life
■ **Tú estás viendo visiones.** You're seeing things.

la **visita** NOUN
1 visit
■ **hacer una visita a alguien** to visit someone
2 visitor
□ Tienes visita. You've got visitors.
■ **horario de visita** visiting hours *pl*
■ **tarjeta de visita** business card

el/la **visitante** NOUN
visitor

visitar VERB [25]

to visit
□ 5.000 personas han visitado ya la exposición. 5000 people have already visited the exhibition.

el **viso** NOUN
slip *(clothes)*
■ **visos** signs □ La situación no tiene visos de mejorar. The situation shows no signs of improving.
■ **esta tela hace visos** this material is two-tone

el **visón** (PL los **visones**) NOUN
mink
■ **un abrigo de visón** a mink coat

la **víspera** NOUN
the day before
□ la víspera de la boda the day before the wedding
■ **la víspera de Navidad** Christmas Eve

la **vista** NOUN
1 sight
2 view
□ una habitación con vistas al mar a room with a sea view
■ **a primera vista** at first glance
■ **alzar la vista** to look up
■ **bajar la vista** to look down
■ **perder la vista** to lose one's sight
■ **volver la vista** to look back
■ **conocer a alguien de vista** to know someone by sight
■ **hacer la vista gorda** to turn a blind eye
■ **¡Hasta la vista!** See you!

el **vistazo** NOUN
■ **echar un vistazo a algo** to have a look at something

vistiendo VERB ▷ *see* **vestir**

visto VERB
▷ *see also* **visto** ADJECTIVE ▷ *see* **ver**

visto (FEM **vista**) ADJECTIVE
▷ *see also* **visto** VERB
■ **Está visto que ...** It's clear that ...
■ **Hurgarse la nariz está mal visto.** Picking your nose is frowned upon.
■ **por lo visto** apparently
■ **dar el visto bueno a algo** to give something one's approval

vistoso (FEM **vistosa**) ADJECTIVE
showy

vital (FEM **vital**) ADJECTIVE
vital

la **vitalidad** NOUN
vitality

la **vitamina** NOUN
vitamin

vitorear VERB [25]
to cheer

la **vitrina** NOUN
1 glass cabinet
2 shop window *(Latin America)*

viuda ADJECTIVE
■ **Es viuda.** She's a widow.
■ **quedarse viuda** to be widowed

la **viuda** NOUN
widow

viudo ADJECTIVE
■ **Es viudo.** He's a widower.
■ **Se quedó viudo a los 50 años.** He was widowed at 50.

el **viudo** NOUN
widower

vivaracho (FEM **vivaracha**) ADJECTIVE
lively

los **víveres** NOUN
provisions *pl*

el **vivero** NOUN
nursery (PL nurseries)

la **vivienda** NOUN
1 house
2 flat
3 housing
□ la escasez de la vivienda the housing shortage

vivir VERB [58]
1 to live
□ ¿Dónde vives? Where do you live?
2 to be alive
□ ¿Todavía vive? Is he still alive?
■ **vivir de algo** to live on something
□ Viven de su pensión. They live on his pension.
■ **¡Viva!** Hurray!

vivo (FEM **viva**) ADJECTIVE
1 alive
□ Estaba vivo. He was alive.
2 bright
■ **en vivo** live □ una retransmisión en vivo a live broadcast

el **vocabulario** NOUN
vocabulary

la **vocación** (PL las **vocaciones**) NOUN
vocation

la **vocal** NOUN
vowel

el **vodka** NOUN
vodka

el **volante** NOUN
1 steering wheel
2 shuttlecock
3 referral note
■ **volantes** flounce *sing*

volar* VERB [11]
1 to fly
□ El helicóptero volaba muy bajo. The helicopter was flying very low. □ Se me pasó la semana volando. The week just flew by.

2 to blow up
□ Volaron el puente. They blew up the bridge.
■ **Tuvimos que ir volando al hospital.** We had to rush to the hospital.

el **volcán** (PL los **volcanes**) NOUN
volcano (PL volcanoes)

volcar* VERB [59, **c** → **qu** before **e** and **i**]
1 to knock over
□ El perro volcó el cubo de la basura. The dog knocked the dustbin over.
2 to capsize
3 to overturn

el **voleibol** NOUN
volleyball

el **voltaje** NOUN
voltage

la **voltereta** NOUN
1 forward roll
■ **dar una voltereta** to do a forward roll
2 somersault

el **voltio** NOUN
volt

el **volumen** (PL los **volúmenes**) NOUN
volume
■ **bajar el volumen** to turn the volume down
■ **subir el volumen** to turn the volume up

la **voluntad** NOUN
1 will
□ Lo hizo contra mi voluntad. He did it against my will.
2 willpower
□ Le cuesta, pero tiene mucha voluntad. It's difficult for him, but he has a lot of willpower.

la **voluntaria** NOUN
volunteer

voluntario (FEM **voluntaria**) ADJECTIVE
voluntary
■ **ofrecerse voluntario para algo** to volunteer for something

el **voluntario** NOUN
volunteer

volver* VERB [59]
1 to come back
2 to go back
3 to turn
□ Me volvió la espalda. He turned away from me.
■ **Me volví para ver quién era.** I turned round to see who it was.
4 to become
■ **Se ha vuelto muy cariñoso.** He's become very affectionate.
■ **volver a hacer algo** to do something again
■ **volver en sí** to come round

vomitar VERB [25]
to be sick
□ Ha vomitado dos veces. He's been sick twice.
■ **Vomitó todo lo que había comido.** He threw up everything he'd eaten.

vos PRONOUN *(River Plate)*
you

vosotros (FEM **vosotras**) PL PRONOUN
you
□ Vosotros vendréis conmigo. You'll come with me.
■ **Hacedlo vosotros mismos.** Do it yourselves.

la **votación** (PL las **votaciones**) NOUN
■ **Hicimos una votación.** We took a vote.
■ **Salió elegida por votación.** She was voted in.

votar VERB [25]
to vote
□ Voté por Alcántara. I voted for Alcántara.
■ **Votaron a los socialistas.** They voted for the Socialists.

voy VERB ▷ *see* **ir**

la **voz** (PL las **voces**) NOUN
voice
□ No tengo buena voz. I don't have a very good voice.
■ **hablar en voz alta** to speak loudly
■ **dar voces** to shout

vuelco VERB ▷ *see* **volcar**

el **vuelco** NOUN
■ **dar un vuelco** to overturn
to capsize
■ **Me dio un vuelco el corazón.** My heart missed a beat.

vuelo VERB ▷ *see* **volar**

el **vuelo** NOUN
flight
■ **vuelo de bajo coste** low cost flight
■ **vuelo chárter** charter flight
■ **vuelo regular** scheduled flight
■ **Las gaviotas levantaron el vuelo.** The seagulls flew away.

la **vuelta** NOUN
1 return
□ un billete de ida y vuelta a return ticket
2 lap
□ Di tres vueltas a la pista. I did three laps of the track.
3 change
□ Quédese con la vuelta. Keep the change.
■ **a vuelta de correo** by return of post
■ **Vive a la vuelta de la esquina.** He lives round the corner.
■ **El coche dio la vuelta.** The car turned round.
■ **Dimos una vuelta de campana.**

We overturned completely.
■ **dar la vuelta a la página** to turn the page
■ **dar la vuelta al mundo** to go round the world
■ **No le des más vueltas a lo que dijo.** Stop worrying about what he said.
■ **dar una vuelta** **1** to go for a walk **2** to go for a drive
■ **dar media vuelta** to turn round
■ **estar de vuelta** to be back
■ **vuelta ciclista** cycle race

vuelto VERB ▷ *see* **volver**

el **vuelto** NOUN *(Latin America)*
change

vuelvo VERB ▷ *see* **volver**

vuestro (FEM **vuestra**) ADJECTIVE, PRONOUN

1 your
□ vuestra casa your house □ vuestros amigos your friends
■ **un amigo vuestro** a friend of yours

2 yours
□ ¿Son vuestros? Are they yours?
■ **¿Es ésta la vuestra?** Is this one yours?
■ **¿Y los bocadillos? — Los vuestros están aquí.** Where are the sandwiches? — Yours are over here.

vulgar (FEM **vulgar**) ADJECTIVE
vulgar

Ww

el **walkie-talkie** (PL los **walkie-talkies**) NOUN
walkie-talkie

el **walkman®** (PL los **walkmans**) NOUN
Walkman®

el **wáter** NOUN
loo

la **web** NOUN
1 website
2 (World Wide) Web

el **western** (PL los **westerns**) NOUN
western

el **whisky** (PL los **whiskys**) NOUN
whisky (PL whiskies)

el **windsurf** NOUN
1 windsurfing
2 windsurf

Xx

xenófobo (FEM **xenófoba**) ADJECTIVE
xenophobic

el **xilófono** NOUN
xylophone

Yy

y CONJUNCTION
and
□ Andrés y su novia. Andrés and his girlfriend.
■ **Yo quiero una ensalada. ¿Y tú?** I'd like a salad. What about you?
■ **¡Y yo!** Me too!
■ **¿Y qué?** So what?
■ **Son las tres y cinco.** It's five minutes past three.

ya ADVERB
already
□ Ya se han ido. They've already left.
□ ¿Ya has terminado? Have you finished already?
■ **ya no** any more □ Ya no salimos juntos. We're not going out any more.
■ **Estos zapatos ya me están pequeños.** These shoes are too small for me now.
■ **ya que** since
■ **Ya lo sé.** I know.
■ **Ya veremos.** We'll see.
■ **Rellena el impreso y ya está.** Fill in the form and that's it.
■ **¡Ya voy!** I'm coming!

el **yacimiento** NOUN
site
■ **un yacimiento petrolífero** an oilfield

el/la **yanqui** (PL los/las **yanquis**) ADJECTIVE, NOUN
Yank

el **yate** NOUN
1 pleasure cruiser
2 yacht

la **yedra** NOUN
ivy

la **yegua** NOUN
mare

la **yema** NOUN
1 yolk
2 fingertip

yendo VERB ▷ *see* **ir**

el **yerno** NOUN
son-in-law (PL sons-in-law)

el **yeso** NOUN
plaster

yo PRONOUN
1 I
□ Carlos y yo no fuimos. Carlos and I didn't go.
2 me
□ ¿Quién ha visto la película? — Ana y yo. Who's seen the film? — Ana and me.
□ Es más alta que yo. She's taller than me.
□ Soy yo, María. It's me, María.
■ **¡Yo también!** Me too!
■ **yo mismo** myself □ Lo hice yo misma. I did it myself.
■ **yo que tú** if I were you

el **yoga** NOUN
yoga

el **yogur** NOUN
yoghurt

el **yudo** NOUN
judo

Yugoslavia FEM NOUN
Yugoslavia
□ en la antigua Yugoslavia in the former Yugoslavia

Zz

el **zafiro** NOUN
sapphire
zambullirse* VERB [45]
to dive underwater
zamparse VERB [25]
to wolf down *(colloquial)*
□ Se zampó todas las galletas. He wolfed down all the biscuits.
la **zanahoria** NOUN
carrot
la **zancadilla** NOUN
■ **poner la zancadilla a alguien** to trip someone up
el **zancudo** NOUN *(Latin America)*
mosquito (PL mosquitos)
la **zanja** NOUN
ditch (PL ditches)
zanjar VERB [25]
to settle
la **zapatera** NOUN
shoemaker
la **zapatería** NOUN
1 shoe shop
2 shoe repairer's
el **zapatero** NOUN
shoemaker
la **zapatilla** NOUN
slipper
■ **zapatillas de ballet** ballet shoes
■ **zapatillas de deporte** training shoes
el **zapato** NOUN
shoe
■ **zapatos de tacón** high-heeled shoes
■ **zapatos planos** flat shoes
la **zarpa** NOUN
paw
zarpar VERB [25]
to set sail
la **zarza** NOUN
bramble
la **zarzamora** NOUN
blackberry bush
el **zigzag** NOUN
zigzag
■ **una carretera en zigzag** a winding road

Zimbabue MASC NOUN
Zimbabwe
el **zinc** NOUN
zinc
el **zíper** (PL los **zípers**) NOUN *(Latin America)*
zip
el **zócalo** NOUN
1 skirting board
2 main square *(Latin America)*
el **zodíaco** NOUN
zodiac
□ los signos del zodíaco the signs of the zodiac
la **zona** NOUN
area
□ Viven en una zona muy tranquila. They live in a very quiet area.
■ **Fue declarada zona neutral.** It was declared a neutral zone.
■ **una zona azul** a pay-and-display area
■ **una zona industrial** an industrial park
■ **una zona peatonal** a pedestrian precinct
■ **una zona verde** a green space
el **zoo** NOUN
zoo
la **zoóloga** NOUN
zoologist
la **zoología** NOUN
zoology
el **zoológico** NOUN
zoo
el **zoólogo** NOUN
zoologist
el **zoom** (PL los **zooms**) NOUN
zoom lens (PL zoom lenses)
zoquete (FEM **zoquete**) ADJECTIVE
dim *(colloquial)*
el/la **zoquete** NOUN
blockhead
el **zorro** NOUN
fox (PL foxes)
□ piel de zorro fox fur
el **zueco** NOUN
clog
zumbar VERB [25]
to buzz

□ Me zumban los oídos. My ears are buzzing.

■ **salir zumbando** *(colloquial)* to whizz off

el **zumo** NOUN

juice

□ zumo de naranja orange juice

zurcir* VERB [58, **c** → **z** before **a** and **o**]

to darn

zurdo (FEM **zurda**) ADJECTIVE

1 left-handed

2 left-footed

zurrar VERB [25]

to thrash

Spanish in Action

Map of Spain

- Spain is the second biggest country by area in Western Europe, covering 504 800 km^2 (well over twice the size of the UK).
- The River Ebro is around 910 km long, rising in the Cantabrian Mountains and flowing into the Mediterranean.
- Spain's highest mountain is in the Canary Islands: Teide (3 718m), in Tenerife.
- 40.8 million people live in Spain. The population is one of the slowest-growing in the world.

Relationships and feelings

Some useful phrases

Esta es mi hermana, Elena.	This is my sister, Elena.
Ella se casa el verano que viene.	She's getting married next summer.
Tengo un hermano gemelo.	I have a twin brother.
Tengo una hermana gemela.	I have a twin sister.
Tengo un hermanastro.	I have a half-brother.
Yo soy hijo único.	I'm an only child. (boy)
Yo soy hija única.	I'm an only child. (girl)
Mis padres están separados/divorciados.	My parents are separated/divorced.
Mi abuelo murió el año pasado.	My grandfather died last year.
Mi madre se ha vuelto a casar.	My mother has got married again.

Las relaciones	Relationships
Me llevo bien con mi hermana.	I get on well with my sister.
No me llevo nada bien con mi hermano.	I don't get on at all with my brother.
Mi mejor amigo se llama Tamir.	My best friend is called Tamir.
Tengo tres mejores amigas.	I've got three best friends.
Somos inseparables.	We're always together.
Me he peleado con Rachida.	I've had a quarrel with Rachida.
Ya no me hablo con Jessica.	I'm not talking to Jessica any more.

Los miembros de la familia	Members of the family
mi padre	my father, my dad
mi madre	my mother, my mum
mi hermano	my brother
mi hermana	my sister
mi tío	my uncle
mi tía	my aunt
mi primo	my cousin (male)
mi prima	my cousin (female)
mi abuelo	my grandfather, my granddad
mi abuela	my grandmother, my gran
mis abuelos	my grandparents
mi hermano mayor	my big brother
mi hermana pequeña	my little sister
el novio de mi hermana	my sister's boyfriend
la novia de mi hermano	my brother's girlfriend
el novio de mi hermana	my sister's fiancé
la novia de mi hermano	my brother's fiancée

Las emociones	Emotions
estar ...	**to be ...**
triste	sad
contento/contenta	pleased
feliz	happy
enfadado/enfadada	angry
enamorado/enamorada	in love
dolido/dolida	hurt
Estoy enamorada de Ruth.	I'm in love with Ruth.
Bruno y yo nos hemos separado.	Bruno and I have split up.
Estoy contenta de que vengas.	I'm pleased you're coming.
Estoy triste por irme.	I'm sad to be leaving.
Espero que no estés demasiado enfadado.	I hope you're not too angry.
Ella se molestó por no haber sido invitada.	She was hurt that she wasn't invited.

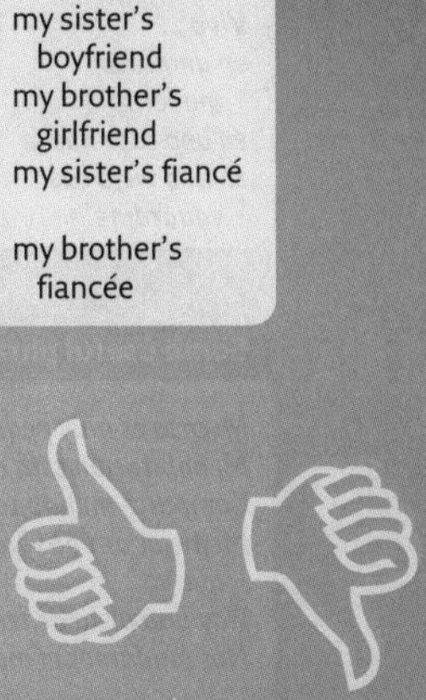

At home

¿Dónde vives?	Where do you live?
Vivo ...	**I live ...**
en un pueblo	in a village
en una ciudad pequeña	in a small town
en el centro	in the town centre
en las afueras de Londres	in the suburbs of London
en el campo	in the countryside
en la playa	at the seaside
al lado de un riachuelo	beside a small river
a 100 km de Manchester	100 km from Manchester
al norte de Birmingham	north of Birmingham
en una casa individual	in a detached house
en una casa adosada	in a semi-detached house
en una casa de dos plantas	in a two-storey house
en un bloque de pisos	in a block of flats
en un piso	in a flat
en una urbanización	on a housing estate
Vivo en un piso ...	**I live in a flat ...**
en la planta baja	on the ground floor
en la primera planta	on the first floor
en la segunda planta	on the second floor
en la última planta	on the top floor
Vivo ...	**I live ...**
en una casa moderna	in a modern house
en una casa nueva	in a new house
en una vieja casa eduardina	in an old Edwardian house

De casa al colegio	From home to school
El colegio está bastante lejos de mi casa.	School is quite a long way from my house
Vivo a cinco minutos andando del colegio.	I live five minutes' walk from school.
Mi padre me lleva al colegio en coche.	My father takes me to school in the car.
Voy al colegio en autobús.	I go to school by bus.

En casa	At home
En la planta baja está ...	**On the ground floor there is ...**
la cocina	the kitchen
la sala de estar	the living room
el comedor	the dining room
el salón	the lounge
En la primera planta, está ...	**Upstairs there is ...**
mi habitación	my bedroom
la habitación de mi hermano	my brother's bedroom
la habitación de mis padres	my parents' room
la habitación de invitados	the spare bedroom
el cuarto de baño	the bathroom
un despacho	a study
un jardín	a garden
un campo de fútbol	a football pitch
una pista de tenis	a tennis court
un vecino	a neighbour
los vecinos de enfrente	the people opposite
los vecinos de al lado	the next-door neighbours

Some useful phrases	
Mi casa es muy pequeña.	My house is very small.
Mi habitación está ordenada.	My room is tidy.
Comparto mi habitación con mi hermano.	I share my bedroom with my brother.
Mi mejor amigo vive en la misma calle que yo.	My best friend lives in the same street as me
Hay una pista de tenis al lado de mi casa.	There's a tennis court next to my house.
Nos mudamos el mes que viene.	We're moving next month.

In town

Algunos sitios importantes	**A few landmarks**
un cine	a cinema
un teatro	a theatre
un museo	a museum
una plaza	public gardens
un cajero automático	a cash dispenser
la oficina de turismo	the tourist office
una catedral	a cathedral
una iglesia	a church
una mezquita	a mosque
una calle peatonal	a pedestrian street
un banco	a bank
la piscina	the swimming pool
la pista de patinaje sobre hielo	the ice rink
la biblioteca	the library
el ayuntamiento	the town hall
el mercado	the market square

Los medios de transporte	**Means of transport**
un autobús	a bus
un autocar	a coach
el metro	the underground
el tranvía	the tram
el tren	the train
la estación	the station
la estación de autobuses	the bus station
una estación de metro	an underground station
¿A qué hora es el próximo tren para Madrid?	What time is the next train to Madrid?
Querría un billete de ida para Sevilla.	I'd like a single to Seville.
Un billete de ida y vuelta para Valencia, por favour.	A return to Valencia, please.
¿Dónde está el andén 10?	Where is platform 10?
¿Dónde está la estación de metro más cercana?	Where is the nearest underground station?

Las direcciones	**Directions**
enfrente de	opposite
al lado de	next to
cerca de	near
entre ... y ...	between ... and ...
¿Dónde se encuentra la estación de autobuses?	Where's the bus station?
Estoy buscando la oficina de turismo.	I'm looking for the tourist office.
Vaya hasta el final de la calle.	Go right to the end of the street.
Gire a la derecha.	Turn right.
Cruce el puente.	Cross the bridge.
Tome la primera calle a la izquierda.	Take the first street on the left.
Está a su derecha.	It's on your right.
Está enfrente del cine.	It's opposite the cinema.
Está al lado de correos.	It's next to the post office.

My plans for the future

El trabajo	Work
Me gustaría estudiar ...	**I'd like to study ...**
medicina	medicine
ingeniería	engineering
derecho	law
sociología	sociology
psicología	psychology
idiomas	languages
arquitectura	architecture
Me gustaría ...	**I'd like to ...**
ganar mucho dinero	earn lots of money
trabajar en una tienda	work in a shop
trabajar en un banco	work in a bank
trabajar en el turismo	work in tourism
hacer prácticas	do an apprenticeship
conseguir un título	do a qualification
Me gustaría ser ...	**I'd like to be ...**
abogado	a solicitor
profesor	a teacher
dentista	a dentist
actriz	an actress
cantante	a singer
peluquero	a hairdresser
periodista	a journalist
actor	an actor
jugador de fútbol profesional	a professional footballer
músico	a musician
político	a politician
Pienso que es ...	**I think it's ...**
interesante	interesting
cansado	tiring
gratificante	rewarding
estresante	stressful
Pienso que está ...	**I think it's ...**
bien pagado	well paid
mal pagado	badly paid

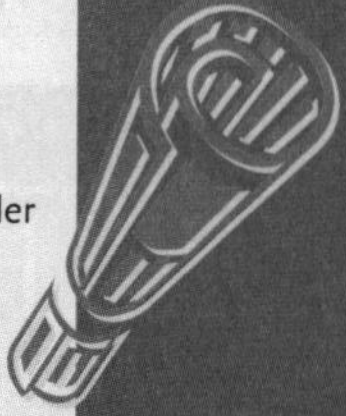

Las ambiciones	Ambitions
Tengo la intención de ir a la universidad.	I'm planning to go to university.
Después me gustaría irme al extranjero.	Afterwards I'd like to go abroad.
Me gustaría casarme y tener muchos hijos.	I'd like to get married and have lots of children.
No sé todavía lo que quiero hacer.	I don't know yet what I want to do.

Los exámenes	Exams
un examen	an exam
un simulacro de examen	a mock exam
las notas	the results
Este año preparo el GCSE.	I'm doing my GCSEs this year.
Hago mi primer simulacro de examen el lunes que viene.	I'm going to do my first mock exam next Monday.
Espero aprobar los exámenes.	I hope I'll pass my exams.
Creo que he suspendido el examen de matemáticas.	I think I've failed my maths exam.
Me darán los resultados en el mes de agosto.	I'll get the results in August.
Me han salido bien los exámenes.	I've done well in my exams.
El año que viene voy a preparar ocho exámenes.	I'm going to do eight exams next year.

Los deportes	Sports
Juego …	**I play …**
al fútbol	football
al baloncesto	basketball
al rugby	rugby
al tennis	tennis
al ping-pong	table tennis
Hago …	**I …**
esquí	ski
kayak	canoe
gimnasia	do gymnastics
natación	swim
equitación	go horse riding
vela	go sailing
Este verano voy a hacer un cursillo de vela.	I'm going to do a sailing course this summer.
Nunca he hecho esquí.	I've never been skiing.
Voy a aprender a hacer kayak.	I'm going to learn how to canoe.

Trabajo	Jobs
un currículum o CV	a CV
una entrevista	an interview
Yo trabajo …	**I work …**
en la farmacia el sábado	at the chemist's on Saturdays
en el supermercado en vacaciones	at the supermarket in the holidays
en una tienda de ropa el fin de semana	in a clothes shop at the weekend
Soy canguro.	I do baby-sitting.
Hago la compra para una señora mayor.	I do an old lady's shopping for her.
Reparto los periódicos.	I deliver papers.
Gano 7,50 euros por hora.	I earn 7.50 euros an hour.
Nunca he trabajado.	I've never had a job.
Voy a buscar un trabajo para este verano.	I'm going to look for a job for this summer.

Los instrumentos musicales	Musical instruments
Yo toco …	**I play the …**
el violín	violin
el piano	piano
la guitarra	guitar
la flauta	flute
Toco el violín desde hace ocho años.	I've been playing the violin since I was eight.
Toco en la orquesta del colegio.	I play in the school orchestra.
Me gustaría aprender a tocar la guitarra.	I'd like to learn to play the guitar.

Cocinar en casa	Cooking at home
Me gusta cocinar.	I like cooking
No sé cocinar.	I can't cook.
Hago muy bien los pasteles.	I'm very good at making cakes.

Mis pasatiempos preferidos	My favourite hobbies
Me gusta leer libros.	I like reading novels.
Me encanta escuchar música en mi habitación.	I love listening to music in my room.
Me gusta mucho ir a la ciudad con mis amigas.	I love going into town with my friends.
Mi pasatiempo preferido es la equitación.	My favourite hobby is riding.
Prefiero salir con mis amigos.	I'd rather go out with my friends.

Describing someone

La personalidad	Personality
Él/Ella es ...	**He/She is ...**
divertido/divertida	funny
simpático/simpática	nice
tímido/tímida	shy
reservado/reservada	quiet
exasperante	annoying
generoso/generosa	generous
hablador/habladora	talkative
inteligente	intelligent
tonto/tonta	stupid
avaro	stingy
raro	strange

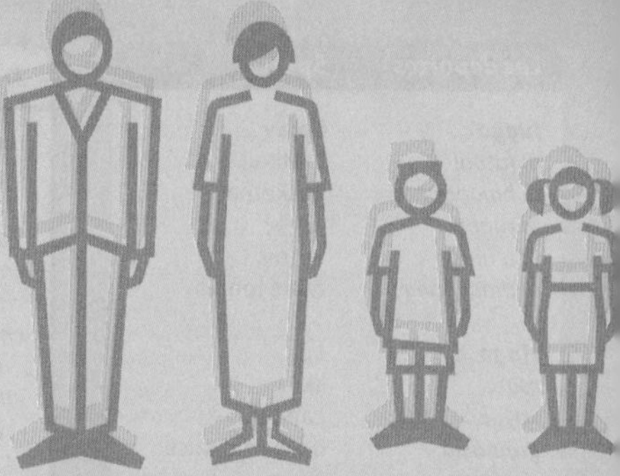

Los colores	Colours
amarillo, amarilla	yellow
naranja	orange
rojo, roja	red
rosa	pink
violeta	purple
azul	blue
verde	green
marrón	brown
gris	grey
negro, negra	black
blanco, blanca	white
burdeos (masc, fem, pl)	maroon
azul marino (masc, fem, pl)	navy (blue)
turquesa (masc, fem, pl)	turquoise
beige	beige
crema (masc, fem, pl)	cream
también para los ojos:	**For eyes:**
avellana (masc, fem, pl)	hazel
también para el pelo:	**For hair:**
caoba	auburn
rubio, rubia	blonde
castaño	brown
castaño claro	light brown
moreno, morena	dark brown
pelirrojo, pelirroja	red
Tengo los ojos color avellana.	I've got hazel eyes.
Tiene el pelo castaño.	He's got brown hair.
Tiene el pelo corto y gris.	She's got short grey hair.
Ella es pelirroja.	She's got red hair.
Él es calvo.	He's bald.
Ella tiene el pelo rubio, largo y rizado.	She's got long curly blonde hair.

Las características	**Characteristics**
Él/Ella es ...	**He/She is ...**
alto/alta	tall
bajo/baja	small
delgado/delgada	slim
gordo/gorda	fat
guapo/guapa	good-looking
joven	young
viejo/vieja	old
Tiene unos treinta años.	He's about thirty.
Ella es alta, delgada y bastante guapa.	She's tall, slim and quite nice-looking.
Se parece a Cameron Diaz.	She looks like Cameron Diaz.

La ropa	**Clothes**
un jersey	a jumper
un pantalón	trousers
una blusa	a blouse
una camiseta	a T-shirt
un abrigo	a coat
una chaqueta	a jacket
un chaleco	a cardigan
un vestido	a dress
une falda	a skirt
une corbata	a tie
una chaqueta	a jacket
una camisa	a shirt
zapatos	shoes
zapatillas de deporte	trainers
botas	boots
Ella lleva una camiseta azul claro.	She's wearing a light blue T-shirt.
Él lleva un traje gris oscuro.	He's wearing a dark grey suit.
Mi uniforme se compone de una falda azul marino, una blusa blanca, una corbata a rayas burdeos y gris, calcetines grises, una americana burdeos y zapatos negros.	My uniform consists of a navy blue skirt, a white blouse, a tie with maroon and grey stripes, grey socks, a maroon blazer and black shoes.

Keeping fit and healthy

Las comidas	**Meals**
el desayuno	breakfast
el almuerzo	lunch
la merienda	afternoon snack
la cena	dinner
Me encanta …	**I love …**
el chocolate	chocolate
la ensalada	salad
Me encantan …	**I love …**
las fresas	strawberries
Me gusta …	**I like …**
el pescado	fish
la limonada	lemonade
Me gustan …	**I like …**
las verduras	vegetables
No me gusta …	**I don't like …**
el zumo de naranja	orange juice
el agua gaseosa	sparkling water
No me gustan …	**I don't like …**
los plátanos	bananas
No como cerdo.	I don't eat pork.
Como mucha fruta.	I eat a lot of fruit.
No como guarrerías entre comidas.	I don't eat junk food between meals.
Evito las bebidas gaseosas.	I avoid fizzy drinks.
Soy vegetariano/a.	I'm a vegetarian.
Soy alérgico/a a los cacahuetes.	I'm allergic to peanuts.

Las enfermedades	**Ailments**
Me duele …	**I have a sore …**
la barriga	stomach
la espalda	back
la rodilla	knee
el pie	foot
el cuello	neck
la cabeza	head
la garganta	throat
la pierna	leg
Me duelen los dientes.	I've got toothache.
Me duelen las orejas.	I've got earache.
Me duelen los ojos.	My eyes are hurting.
Estoy resfriado.	I've got a cold.
Tengo la gripe.	I've got flu.
Tengo ganas de vomitar.	I feel sick.
Estoy cansado.	I'm tired.
Estoy enfermo.	I'm ill.
tener …	**to be …**
frío	cold
calor	hot
miedo	scared
sed	thirsty
hambre	hungry

Me temo que voy a suspender el examen.
I'm afraid that I'm going to fail the exam.

Para estar en forma …	**To be fit …**
Hago mucho deporte.	I do a lot of sport.
Yo no fumo.	I don't smoke.
Me acuesto temprano.	I go to bed early.
Voy al colegio andando.	I walk to school.
Es bueno para la salud.	It's good for your health.
El alcohol es malo para la salud.	Alcohol is bad for your health.

When your number answers

Hola, ¿está Susana?	Hello! Could I speak to Susana, please?
Le puede decir que me llame, por favor?	Would you ask him/her to call me back, please?
Le vuelvo a llamar dentro de media hora.	I'll call back in half an hour.

Answering the telephone

¿Diga? Soy Marcos.	Hello! It's Marcos speaking.
Sí, soy yo.	Speaking.
¿Con quién hablo?	Who's speaking?

When the switchboard answers

¿De parte de quién?	Who shall I say is calling?
Le paso.	I'm putting you through.
No cuelgue.	Please hold.
¿Quiere dejar un mensaje?	Would you like to leave a message?

Difficulties

No hay línea.	I can't get through.
Perdone, me he equivocado de número.	I'm sorry, I've got the wrong number.
Se oye muy mal.	This is a very bad line.
No les funciona el teléfono.	Their phone is out of order.

Letter

Writing a letter

Note colon

Date

Valencia, 5 de junio de 2007

Queridos abuelos:

Muchas gracias a los dos por la preciosa pulsera que me mandásteis por mi cumpleaños, que me ha gustado muchísimo. Voy a disfrutar de verdad poniéndomela para mi fiesta del sábado, y estoy segura de que a Cristina le va a dar una envidia tremenda.

En realidad no hay demasiadas cosas nuevas que contaros, ya que últimamente parece que no hago otra cosa que estudiar para los exámenes, que ya están a la vuelta de la esquina. No sabéis las ganas que tengo de terminarlos todos y poder empezar a pensar en las vacaciones.

Paloma me encarga que os dé recuerdos de su parte.

Muchos besos de

Ana

Writing a personal letter
Just the name of the town/city you are writing from, and the date

Alternatively
Un abrazo (a un amigo o un familiar)
Con cariño

Starting a personal letter

Gracias por tu carta.	Thank you for your letter.
Me alegró mucho tener noticias tuyas.	It was lovely to hear from you.
Perdona que no te haya escrito antes.	I'm sorry I didn't write earlier.

Ending a personal letter

¡Escríbeme pronto!	Write soon!
Dale un beso a Vanesa de mi parte.	Give my love to Vanesa.
Samuel te manda recuerdos.	Samuel sends his best wishes.

Writing an email

Archivo **Edición** **Ver** **Herramientas** **Correo** **Ayuda** **Enviar**

Correo
- **Nuevo mensaje**
- **Responder al autor**
- **Responder a todos**
- **Reenviar**
- **Archivo adjunto**

A: belen.huertas@glnet.es
Cc:
Copia oculta:
Asunto: Concierto

Hola, ¿qué tal el fin de semana?

Me sobran dos entradas para el concierto de mañana, de unos amigos que no pueden venir. Si te interesa, o conoces a alguien que quiera ir, avísame en cuanto puedas.

Un beso,

E.

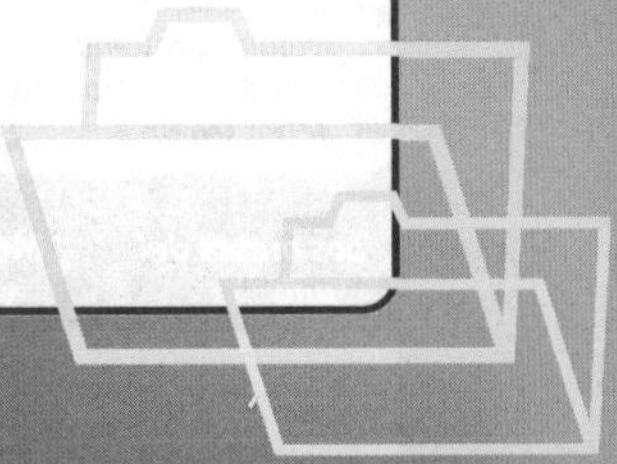

Saying your email address
To give your email address to someone in Spanish, say:
"belen punto huertas arroba globanet punto es"

Spanish	English
nuevo mensaje (m)	new message
A	to
de	from
asunto	subject
CC	cc (carbon copy)
copia oculta	bcc (blind carbon copy)
archivo adjunto	attachment
enviar	send
archivo	file
edición (f)	edit
ver	view
herramientas (fpl)	tools
correo	mail
ayuda	help
responder al autor	reply to sender
responder a todos	reply to all
reenviar	forward
fecha	sent

Abbrev.	Spanish	English
+trd	*más tarde*	later
2	*tú*	you
a2	*adiós*	goodbye
bboo	*besos*	love (from)
find	*fin de semana*	weekend
gnl	*genial*	wonderful
h lgo HL	*hasta luego*	see you later
LAP	*lo antes posible*	asap (as soon as possible)
msj	*mensaje*	message
NLS	*no lo sé*	I don't know
q acc? q hcs?	*¿qué haces?*	what are you doing?
QT1BD	*¡que tengas un buen día!*	have a good day!
q tl?	*¿qué tal?*	how are you?
salu2	*saludos*	best wishes
tq	*te quiero*	I love you
x	*por*	for, by etc
xdon	*perdón*	sorry
xq	*porque*	because
xq?	*¿por qué?*	why?

Días de la semana	Days of the week
lunes	Monday
martes	Tuesday
miércoles	Wednesday
jueves	Thursday
viernes	Friday
sábado	Saturday
domingo	Sunday
el lunes	on Monday
los lunes	on Mondays
todos los lunes	every Monday
el martes pasado	last Tuesday
el próximo viernes	next Friday
el sábado de la semana que viene	a week on Saturday
el sábado de dentro de dos semanas	two weeks on Saturday

Los meses del año	Months of the year
enero	January
febrero	February
marzo	March
abril	April
mayo	May
junio	June
julio	July
agosto	August
septiembre	September
octubre	October
noviembre	November
diciembre	December
¿A qué fecha estamos hoy?	What date is it today?
Estamos a 16 de junio.	It's 16th of June.
¿Cuál es la fecha de tu cumpleaños?	What date is your birthday?
Es el 22 de mayo.	It's the 22nd of May.

Las fiestas	Festivals
Navidad (fem)	Christmas
el día de Navidad	Christmas Day
Nochebuena	Christmas Eve
la cena de Nochebuena	Christmas Eve celebrations
el día después de Navidad	Boxing Day
la Nochevieja	New Year's Eve
Año Nuevo	New Year's Day
San Valentín	Valentine's Day
martes de ceniza	Pancake Day
el día de los Santos Inocentes (28 de diciembre)	April Fool's Day
Semana Santa (fem)	Easter
el día de la madre	Mother's Day
el día del padre	Father's Day
el día de todos los santos	All Saints' Day
el 11 de noviembre	Remembrance Day
el Ramadán	Ramadan
¡Feliz navidad!	Happy Christmas!
¡Inocente!	April fool!
en Semana Santa	at Easter
celebrar Año Nuevo	to celebrate New Year
¿Qué haces el día de Navidad?	What do you do on Christmas Day?
Pasamos el día después de Navidad en casa.	We spend Boxing Day at home.
Vamos a casa de mis primos el día de Año Nuevo.	We go to my cousins' for New Year.

Las vacaciones	Holidays
las vacaciones de verano	the summer holidays
el puente de todos los santos	the autumn half-term
las vacaciones de Navidad	the Christmas holidays
la semana blanca	the spring half-term
las vacaciones de Semana Santa	the Easter holidays
la playa	the seaside
la montaña	the mountains
¿Qué vas a hacer durante las vacaciones?	What are you going to do in the holidays?
Este verano nos vamos una semana a Italia.	We're going to Italy for a week this summer.
Este año no nos vamos de vacaciones.	We're not going on holiday this year.
Siempre vamos a esquiar en febrero.	We always go skiing in February.
El verano que viene voy a pasar una semana en casa de mi correspondiente en Francia.	I'm going to stay with my pen-friend in France for a week next year.
El verano pasado fui a Estados Unidos.	Last summer I went to the United States.

¿Qué hora es? — What time is it? It's...

es la una

es la una y diez

es la una y cuarto

es la una y media

son las dos menos veinte

son las dos menos cuarto

¿A qué hora? — At what time?

a medianoche

al mediodía

a la una (de la tarde)

a las once (de la noche)

las 11:15 or *las once quince*

las 20:45 or *las veinte cuarenta y cinco*

In Spanish times are often given in the twenty-four hour clock.

Numbers

Numbers

1	*uno*
2	*dos*
3	*tres*
4	*cuatro*
5	*cinco*
6	*seis*
7	*siete*
8	*ocho*
9	*nueve*
10	*diez*
11	*once*
12	*doce*
13	*trece*
14	*catorce*
15	*quince*
16	*dieciséis*
17	*diecisiete*
18	*dieciocho*
19	*diecinueve*
20	*veinte*
21	*veintiuno*
30	*treinta*
31	*treinta y uno*
40	*cuarenta*
41	*cuarenta y uno*
50	*cincuenta*
60	*sesenta*
70	*setenta*
80	*ochenta*
90	*noventa*
100	*cien*
101	*ciento uno*
200	*doscientos*
201	*doscientos uno*
1000	*mil*
1001	*mil uno*
1,000,000	*un millón*

Examples

en la página diecinueve – on page nineteen

en el capítulo siete – in chapter seven

en una escala del uno al quince – on a scale of one to fifteen

Fractions etc

1/2	*un medio*
1/3	*un tercio*
1/4	*un cuarto*
1/5	*un quinto*
0,5	*cero coma cinco*
3,4	*tres coma cuatro*
6,89	*seis coma ochenta y nueve*
10%	*diez por ciento*
100%	*cien por cien*

1°	*primero*
2°	*segundo*
3°	*tercero*
4°	*cuarto*
5°	*quinto*
6°	*sexto*
7°	*séptimo*
8°	*octavo*
9°	*noveno*
10°	*décimo*
11°	*decimoprimero*
12°	*decimosegundo*
13°	*decimotercero*
14°	*decimocuarto*
15°	*decimoquinto*
16°	*decimosexto*
17°	*decimoséptimo*
18°	*decimoctavo*
19°	*decimonoveno*
20°	*vigésimo*
21°	*vigésimo primero*
30°	*trigésimo*
100°	*centésimo*
101°	*centésimo primero*
1000°	*milésimo*

Examples

vive en el quinto piso – he lives on the fifth floor

llegó el tercero – he came in third

un cuarto del pastel – a quarter of the cake

Contents

Spanish verb tables

This section is designed to help you find all the verb forms you need in Spanish. From pages 19–23 you will find a list of 59 regular and irregular verbs with a summary of their main forms, followed on pages 24-30 by 7 very common regular and irregular verbs shown in full, with example phrases.

How to find the verb you need

All the verbs on the **Spanish - English** side of the dictionary are followed by a number in square brackets. Each of these numbers corresponds to a verb in this section.

limpiar VERBO [25]
1 to clean

In this example, the number [25] after the verb **limpiar** means that **limpiar** follows the same pattern as verb number [25] in the list, which is **hablar**. In this instance, **hablar** is given in full on page 24.

introducir* VERBO [9]
1 to insert

For other verbs, a summary of the main forms is given. In the example above, **introducir** follows the same pattern as verb number [9] in the list, which is **conducir**. On page 19 of this section, you can see that the main forms of **conducir** are given to show you how this verb (and others like it) works.

In the full verb tables, you will find examples of regular verbs: a regular **-ar** verb (**hablar**), a regular **-er** verb (**comer**) and a regular **-ir** verb (**vivir**). Regular verbs follow one of three set patterns. When you have learnt these patterns, you will be able to form any regular verb.

You will also find **tener** (to have), **ser** (to be) and **estar** (to be) in the full verb tables. These are the most important irregular verbs and should be learnt. You use them when you want to say 'I have' *etc* or 'I am' *etc*. However, to form the **perfect tense** of any Spanish verb you use the present tense of **haber** (to have) + the past participle. **Haber** is verb number 24 in the list.

Finally, for more information on the various tenses of Spanish verbs, as well as additional verb tables, remember to visit **www.collinslanguage.com**

Spanish verb forms

INFINITIVE	PRESENT	PERFECT	PRETERITE	FUTURE	PRESENT SUBJUNCTIVE
1 **actuar**	yo actúo	he actuado	actué	actuaré	actúe
	tú actúas				
	él/ella/usted actúa				
	nosotros/as actuamos				
	vosotros/as actuáis				
	ellos/ellas/ustedes actúan				
2 **adquirir**	yo adquiero	he adquirido	adquirí	adquiriré	adquiera
-**ir** verb with	tú adquieres				
a spelling	él/ella/usted adquiere				
change	nosotros/as adquirimos				adquiramos
	vosotros/as adquirís				adquiráis
	ellos/ellas/ustedes adquieren				
3 **almorzar**	yo almuerzo	he almorzado	almorcé	almorzaré	almuerce
-**ar** verb with	tú almuerzas		almorzaste		
a spelling	él/ella/usted almuerza				
change	nosotros/as almorzamos				almorcemos
	vosotros/as almorzáis				almorcéis
	ellos/ellas/ustedes almuerzan				
4 **andar**	yo ando	he andado	anduve	andaré	ande
-**ar** verb with	tú andas		anduviste		
a spelling	él/ella/usted anda		anduvo		
change	nosotros/as andamos		anduvimos		
	vosotros/as andáis		anduvisteis		
	ellos/ellas/ustedes andan		anduvieron		
5 **caer**	yo caigo	he caído	caí	caeré	caiga
-**er** verb with	tú caes		caíste		
a spelling	él/ella/usted cae		cayó		
change	nosotros/as caemos		caímos		
	vosotros/as caéis		caísteis		
	ellos/ellas/ustedes caen		cayeron		
6 **cocer**	yo cuezo	he cocido	cocí	coceré	cueza
-**er** verb with	tú cueces				
a spelling	él/ella/usted cuece				
change	nosotros/as cocemos				cozamos
	vosotros/as cocéis				cozáis
	ellos/ellas/ustedes cuecen				
7 **coger**	yo cojo	he cogido	cogí	cogeré	coja
-**er** verb with	tú coges				
a spelling	él/ella/usted coge				
change	nosotros/as cogemos				
	vosotros/as cogéis				
	ellos/ellas/ustedes cogen				
8 **comer**	see full verb table page 25				
9 **conducir**	yo conduzco	he conducido	conduje	conduciré	conduzca
-**ir** verb with	tú conduces		condujiste		
a spelling	él/ella/usted conduce		condujo		
change	nosotros/as conducimos		condujimos		
	vosotros/as conducís		condujisteis		
	ellos/ellas/ustedes conducen		condujeron		
10 **construir**	yo construyo	he construido	construí	construiré	construya
-**ir** verb with	tú construyes				
a spelling	él/ella/usted construye		construyó		
change	nosotros/as construimos				
	vosotros/as construís				
	ellos/ellas/ustedes construyen		construyeron		
11 **contar**	yo cuento	he contado	conté	contaré	cuente
-**ar** verb with	tú cuentas				
a spelling	él/ella/usted cuenta				
change	nosotros/as contamos				contemos
	vosotros/as contáis				contéis
	ellos/ellas/ustedes cuentan				

INFINITIVE	PRESENT	PERFECT	PRETERITE	FUTURE	PRESENT SUBJUNCTIVE
12 **crecer**	yo crezco	he crecido	crecí	creceré	crezca
similar to	tú creces				
cocer [6]					
13 **cruzar**	yo cruzo	he cruzado	crucé	cruzaré	cruce
-ar verb with	tú cruzas				
a spelling	él/ella/usted cruza				
change	nosotros/as cruzamos				crucemos
	vosotros/as cruzasteis				crucéis
	ellos/ellas/ustedes cruzan				
14 **dar**	yo doy	he dado	di	daré	dé
	tú das		diste		des
	él/ella/usted da		dio		dé
	nosotros/as damos		dimos		demos
	vosotros/as dais		disteis		deis
	ellos/ellas/ustedes dan		dieron		den
15 **decir**	yo digo	he dicho	dije	diré	diga
	tú dices		dijiste		
	él/ella/usted dice		dijo		
	nosotros/as decimos		dijimos		
	vosotros/as decís		dijisteis		
	ellos/ellas/ustedes dicen		dijeron		
16 **dirigir**	yo dirijo	he dirigido	dirigí	dirigiré	dirija
-ir verb with	tú diriges				
a spelling	él/ella/usted dirige				
change	nosotros/as dirigimos				
	vosotros/as dirigís				
	ellos/ellas/ustedes dirigen				
17 **dormir**	yo duermo	he dormido	dormí	dormiré	duerma
-ir verb with	tú duermes				
a spelling	él/ella/usted duerme		durmió		
change	nosotros/as dormimos				durmamos
	vosotros/as dormís				durmáis
	ellos/ellas/ustedes duermen		durmieron		
18 **elegir**	yo elijo	he elegido	elegí	elegiré	elija
similar to					
dirigir [16]					
19 **empezar**	yo empiezo	he empezado	empecé	empezaré	empiece
similar to	tú empiezas		empezaste		
almorzar [3]	él/ella/usted empieza		empezó		
	nosotros/as empezamos		empezamos		empecemos
	vosotros/as empezáis		empezasteis		empecéis
	ellos/ellas/ustedes empiezan		empezaron		
20 **entender**	yo entiendo	he entendido	entendí	entenderé	entienda
-er verb with	tú entiendes				
a spelling	él/ella/usted entiende				
change	nosotros/as entendemos				entendamos
	vosotros/as entendéis				entendáis
	ellos/ellas/ustedes entienden				
21 **enviar**	yo envío	he enviado	envié	enviaré	envíe
similar to	tú envías				
actuar [1]					
22 **estar**	see full verb table page 27				
23 **freír**	yo frío	he frito	freí	freiré	fría
-ir verb with	tú fríes		freíste		
a spelling	él/ella/usted fríe		frió		
change	nosotros/as freímos		freímos		
	vosotros/as freís		freísteis		
	ellos/ellas/ustedes fríen		frieron		
24 **haber**	yo he	he habido	hube	habré	haya
	tú has		hubiste		
	él/ella/usted ha		hubo		
	nosotros/as hemos		hubimos		
	vosotros/as habéis		hubisteis		
	ellos/ellas/ustedes han		hubieron		

INFINITIVE	PRESENT	PERFECT	PRETERITE	FUTURE	PRESENT SUBJUNCTIVE
25 **hablar**	see full verb table page 24				
26 **hacer**	yo hago	he hecho	hice	haré	haga
	tú haces		hiciste		
	él/ella/usted hace		hizo		
	nosotros/as hacemos		hicimos		
	vosotros/as hacéis		hicisteis		
	ellos/ellas/ustedes hacen		hicieron		
27 **ir**	see full verb table page 28				
28 **jugar**	yo juego	he jugado	jugué	jugaré	juegue
-ar verb with	tú juegas		jugaste		
a spelling	él/ella/usted juega				
change	nosotros/as jugamos				juguemos
	vosotros/as jugáis				juguéis
	ellos/ellas/ustedes juegan				
29 **lavarse**	yo me lavo	me ha lavado	me lavé	me lavaré	me lave
	tu te lavas				
	él/ella/usted se lava				
	nosotros/as nos lavamos				
	vosotros/as os laváis				
	ellos/ellas/ustedes se lavan				
30 **leer**	yo leo	he leído	leí	leeré	lea
-er verb with	tú lees		leíste		
a spelling	él/ella/usted lee		leyó		
change	nosotros/as leemos		leímos		
	vosotros/as leéis		leísteis		
	ellos/ellas/ustedes leen		leyeron		
31 **llover**	llueve	ha llovido	llovió	lloverá	llueva
impersonal verb					
32 **morir**	yo muero	he muerto	morí	moriré	muera
-ir verb with	tú mueres				
a spelling	él/ella/usted muere		murió		
change	nosotros/as morimos				muramos
	vosotros/as morís				muráis
	ellos/ellas/ustedes mueren		murieron		
33 **mover**	yo muevo	he movido	moví	moveré	mueva
-er verb with	tú mueves				
a spelling	él/ella/usted mueve				
change	nosotros/as movemos				movamos
	vosotros/as movéis				mováis
	ellos/ellas/ustedes mueven				
34 **negar**	yo niego	he negado	negué	negaré	niegue
-ar verb with	tú niegas		negaste		
a spelling	él/ella/usted niega				
change	nosotros/as negamos				neguemos
	vosotros/as negáis				neguéis
	ellos/ellas/ustedes niegan				
35 **oír**	yo oigo	he oído	oí	oiré	oiga
-ir verb with	tú oyes		oíste		
a spelling	él/ella/usted oye		oyó		
change	nosotros/as oímos		oímos		
	vosotros/as oís		oísteis		
	ellos/ellas/ustedes oyen		oyeron		
36 **oler**	yo huelo	he olido	olí	oleré	huela
-er verb with	tú hueles				
a spelling	él/ella/usted huele				
change	nosotros/as olemos				olamos
	vosotros/as oléis				oláis
	ellos/ellas/ustedes huelan				

INFINITIVE	PRESENT	PERFECT	PRETERITE	FUTURE	PRESENT SUBJUNCTIVE
37 **pagar**	yo pago	he pagado	pagué	pagaré	pague
-ar verb with	tú pagas		pagaste		
a spelling	él/ella/usted paga				
change	nosotros/as pagamos				
	vosotros/as pagáis				
	ellos/ellas/ustedes pagan				
38 **pedir**	yo pido	he pedido	pedí	pediré	pida
-ir verb with	tú pides				
a spelling	él/ella/usted pide		pidió		
change	nosotros/as pedimos				
	vosotros/as pedís				
	ellos/ellas/ustedes piden		pidieron		
39 **pensar**	yo pienso	he pensado	pensé	pensaré	piense
-ar verb with	tú piensas				
a spelling	él/ella/usted piensa				
change	nosotros/as pensamos				pensemos
	vosotros/as pensáis				penséis
	ellos/ellas/ustedes piensan				
40 **poder**	yo puedo	he podido	pude	podré	pueda
-er verb with	tú puedes		pudiste		
a spelling	él/ella/usted puede		pudo		
change	nosotros/as podemos		pudimos		podamos
	vosotros/as podéis		pudisteis		podáis
	ellos/ellas/ustedes pueden		pudieron		
41 **poner**	yo pongo	he puesto	puse	pondré	ponga
	tú pones		pusiste		pongas
	él/ella/usted pone		puso		
	nosotros/as ponemos		pusimos		pongamos
	vosotros/as ponéis		pusisteis		pongáis
	ellos/ellas/ustedes ponen		pusieron		
42 **prohibir**	yo prohíbo	he prohibido	prohibí	prohibiré	prohíba
similar to	tú prohíbes				
adquirir [2]	él/ella/usted prohíbe				
	ellos/ellas/ustedes prohíben				
43 **querer**	yo quiero	he querido	quise	querré	quiera
	tú quieres		quisiste		
	él/ella/usted quiere		quiso		
	nosotros/as queremos		quisimos		
	vosotros/as queréis		quisisteis		
	ellos/ellas/ustedes quieren		quisieron		
44 **reír**	yo río	he reído	reí	reiré	ría
similar to	tú ríes		reíste		
freír [23],	él/ella/usted ríe		rió		
except for the	nosotros/as reímos		reímos		
perfect tense	vosotros/as reís		reísteis		
	ellos/ellas/ustedes ríen		rieron		
45 **reñir**	yo riño	he reñido	reñí	reñiré	riña
-ir verb with	tú riñes		reñiste		
a spelling	él/ella/usted riñe		riñó		
change	nosotros/as reñimos		reñimos		
	vosotros/as reñís		reñisteis		
	ellos/ellas/ustedes riñen		riñeron		
46 **reunir**	yo reúno	he reunido	reuní	reuniré	reúna
-ir verb with	tú reúnes				
a spelling	él/ella/usted reúne				
change	nosotros/as reunimos				
	vosotros/as reunís				
	ellos/ellas/ustedes reúnen				
47 **saber**	yo sé	he sabido	supe	sabré	sepa
	tú sabes		supiste		
	él/ella/usted sabe		supo		
	nosotros/as sabemos		supimos		
	vosotros/as sabéis		supisteis		
	ellos/ellas/ustedes saben		supieron		

INFINITIVE	PRESENT	PERFECT	PRETERITE	FUTURE	PRESENT SUBJUNCTIVE
48 **sacar** **-ar** verb with a spelling change	yo saco tú sacas él/ella/usted saca nosotros/as sacamos vosotros/as sacáis ellos/ellas/ustedes sacan	he sacado	saqué sacaste	sacaré	saque
49 **salir** similar to **decir** [15] except for the perfect and future tenses	yo salgo	he salido	salí	saldré	salga
50 **seguir** **-ir** verb with a spelling change	yo sigo tú sigues él/ella/usted sigue nosotros/as seguimos vosotros/as seguís ellos/ellas/ustedes siguen	he seguido	seguí siguió siguieron	seguiré	siga
51 **sentir** **-ir** verb with a spelling change	yo siento tú sientes él/ella/usted siente nosotros/as sentimos vosotros/as sentís ellos/ellas/ustedes sienten	he sentido	sentí sintió sintieron	sentiré	sienta sintamos sintáis
52 **ser**	see full verb table page 29				
53 **tener**	see full verb table page 30				
54 **traer** **-er** verb with a spelling change	yo traigo tú traes él/ella/usted trae nosotros/as traemos vosotros/as traéis ellos/ellas/ustedes traen	he traído	traje trajiste trajo trajimos trajisteis trajeron	traeré	traiga traigas traiga traigamos traigáis traigan
55 **valer** **-er** verb with a spelling change	yo valgo tú vales él/ella/usted vale nosotros/as valemos vosotros/as valéis ellos/ellas/ustedes valen	he valido	valí	valdré	valga
56 **venir**	yo vengo tú vienes él/ella/usted viene nosotros/as venimos vosotros/as venís ellos/ellas/ustedes vienen	he venido	vine viniste vino vinimos vinisteis vinieron	vendré	venga
57 **ver** similar to **comer** [8] except for the perfect tense	yo veo tú ves él/ella/usted ve nosotros/as vemos vosotros/as veis ellos/ellas/ustedes ven	he visto	vi viste vio vimos visteis vieron	veré	vea
58 **vivir**	see full verb table page 26				
59 **volver** **-er** verb with a spelling change	yo vuelvo tú vuelves él/ella/usted vuelve nosotros/as volvemos vosotros/as volvéis ellos/ellas/ustedes vuelven	he vuelto	volví	volveré	vuelva volvamos volváis

hablar (to speak, to talk)

	PRESENT		PRESENT SUBJUNCTIVE
yo	**hablo**	yo	**hable**
tú	**hablas**	tú	**hables**
él/ella/usted	**habla**	él/ella/usted	**hable**
nosotros/as	**hablamos**	nosotros/as	**hablemos**
vosotros/as	**habláis**	vosotros/as	**habléis**
ellos/ellas/ustedes	**hablan**	ellos/ellas/ustedes	**hablen**

	PRETERITE		IMPERFECT
yo	**hablé**	yo	**hablaba**
tú	**hablaste**	tú	**hablabas**
él/ella/usted	**habló**	él/ella/usted	**hablaba**
nosotros/as	**hablamos**	nosotros/as	**hablábamos**
vosotros/as	**hablasteis**	vosotros/as	**hablabais**
ellos/ellas/ustedes	**hablaron**	ellos/ellas/ustedes	**hablaban**

	FUTURE		CONDITIONAL
yo	**hablaré**	yo	**hablaría**
tú	**hablarás**	tú	**hablarías**
él/ella/usted	**hablará**	él/ella/usted	**hablaría**
nosotros/as	**hablaremos**	nosotros/as	**hablaríamos**
vosotros/as	**hablaréis**	vosotros/as	**hablaríais**
ellos/ellas/ustedes	**hablarán**	ellos/ellas/ustedes	**hablarían**

IMPERATIVE

habla / hablad

PAST PARTICIPLE

hablado

GERUND

hablando

EXAMPLE PHRASES

Hoy **he hablado** con mi hermana. I've spoken to my sister today.
No **hables** tan alto. Don't talk so loud.
No **se hablan**. They don't talk to each other.

Remember that subject pronouns are not used very often in Spanish.

comer (to eat)

	PRESENT		PRESENT SUBJUNCTIVE
yo	**como**	yo	**coma**
tú	**comes**	tú	**comas**
él/ella/usted	**come**	él/ella/usted	**coma**
nosotros/as	**comemos**	nosotros/as	**comamos**
vosotros/as	**coméis**	vosotros/as	**comáis**
ellos/ellas/ustedes	**comen**	ellos/ellas/ustedes	**coman**

	PRETERITE		IMPERFECT
yo	**comí**	yo	**comía**
tú	**comiste**	tú	**comías**
él/ella/usted	**comió**	él/ella/usted	**comía**
nosotros/as	**comimos**	nosotros/as	**comíamos**
vosotros/as	**comisteis**	vosotros/as	**comíais**
ellos/ellas/ustedes	**comieron**	ellos/ellas/ustedes	**comían**

	FUTURE		CONDITIONAL
yo	**comeré**	yo	**comería**
tú	**comerás**	tú	**comerías**
él/ella/usted	**comerá**	él/ella/usted	**comería**
nosotros/as	**comeremos**	nosotros/as	**comeríamos**
vosotros/as	**comeréis**	vosotros/as	**comeríais**
ellos/ellas/ustedes	**comerán**	ellos/ellas/ustedes	**comerían**

IMPERATIVE

come / comed

PAST PARTICIPLE

comido

GERUND

comiendo

EXAMPLE PHRASES

No **come** carne. He doesn't eat meat.
No **comas** tan deprisa. Don't eat so fast.
Se lo ha comido todo. He's eaten it all.

Remember that subject pronouns are not used very often in Spanish.

vivir (to live)

PRESENT

yo	**vivo**
tú	**vives**
él/ella/usted	**vive**
nosotros/as	**vivimos**
vosotros/as	**vivís**
ellos/ellas/ustedes	**viven**

PRESENT SUBJUNCTIVE

yo	**viva**
tú	**vivas**
él/ella/usted	**viva**
nosotros/as	**vivamos**
vosotros/as	**viváis**
ellos/ellas/ustedes	**vivan**

PRETERITE

yo	**viví**
tú	**viviste**
él/ella/usted	**vivió**
nosotros/as	**vivimos**
vosotros/as	**vivisteis**
ellos/ellas/ustedes	**vivieron**

IMPERFECT

yo	**vivía**
tú	**vivías**
él/ella/usted	**vivía**
nosotros/as	**vivíamos**
vosotros/as	**vivíais**
ellos/ellas/ustedes	**vivían**

FUTURE

yo	**viviré**
tú	**vivirás**
él/ella/usted	**vivirá**
nosotros/as	**viviremos**
vosotros/as	**viviréis**
ellos/ellas/ustedes	**vivirán**

CONDITIONAL

yo	**viviría**
tú	**vivirías**
él/ella/usted	**viviría**
nosotros/as	**viviríamos**
vosotros/as	**viviríais**
ellos/ellas/ustedes	**vivirían**

IMPERATIVE

vive / vivid

PAST PARTICIPLE

vivido

GERUND

viviendo

EXAMPLE PHRASES

Vivo en Valencia. I live in Valencia.
Vivieron juntos dos años. They lived together for two years.
Hemos vivido momentos difíciles. We've had some difficult times.

Remember that subject pronouns are not used very often in Spanish.

estar (to be)

	PRESENT		**PRESENT SUBJUNCTIVE**
yo	**estoy**	yo	**esté**
tú	**estás**	tú	**estés**
él/ella/usted	**está**	él/ella/usted	**esté**
nosotros/as	**estamos**	nosotros/as	**estemos**
vosotros/as	**estáis**	vosotros/as	**estéis**
ellos/ellas/ustedes	**están**	ellos/ellas/ustedes	**estén**

	PRETERITE		**IMPERFECT**
yo	**estuve**	yo	**estaba**
tú	**estuviste**	tú	**estabas**
él/ella/usted	**estuvo**	él/ella/usted	**estaba**
nosotros/as	**estuvimos**	nosotros/as	**estábamos**
vosotros/as	**estuvisteis**	vosotros/as	**estabais**
ellos/ellas/ustedes	**estuvieron**	ellos/ellas/ustedes	**estaban**

	FUTURE		**CONDITIONAL**
yo	**estaré**	yo	**estaría**
tú	**estarás**	tú	**estarías**
él/ella/usted	**estará**	él/ella/usted	**estaría**
nosotros/as	**estaremos**	nosotros/as	**estaríamos**
vosotros/as	**estaréis**	vosotros/as	**estaríais**
ellos/ellas/ustedes	**estarán**	ellos/ellas/ustedes	**estarían**

IMPERATIVE

está / estad

PAST PARTICIPLE

estado

GERUND

estando

EXAMPLE PHRASES

Estoy cansado. I'm tired.
Estuvimos en casa de mis padres. We went to my parents'.
¿A qué hora **estarás** en casa? What time will you be home?

Remember that subject pronouns are not used very often in Spanish.

ir (to go)

PRESENT		PRESENT SUBJUNCTIVE	
yo	**voy**	yo	**vaya**
tú	**vas**	tú	**vayas**
él/ella/usted	**va**	él/ella/usted	**vaya**
nosotros/as	**vamos**	nosotros/as	**vayamos**
vosotros/as	**vais**	vosotros/as	**vayáis**
ellos/ellas/ustedes	**van**	ellos/ellas/ustedes	**vayan**

PRETERITE		IMPERFECT	
yo	**fui**	yo	**iba**
tú	**fuiste**	tú	**ibas**
él/ella/usted	**fue**	él/ella/usted	**iba**
nosotros/as	**fuimos**	nosotros/as	**íbamos**
vosotros/as	**fuisteis**	vosotros/as	**ibais**
ellos/ellas/ustedes	**fueron**	ellos/ellas/ustedes	**iban**

FUTURE		CONDITIONAL	
yo	**iré**	yo	**iría**
tú	**irás**	tú	**irías**
él/ella/usted	**irá**	él/ella/usted	**iría**
nosotros/as	**iremos**	nosotros/as	**iríamos**
vosotros/as	**iréis**	vosotros/as	**iríais**
ellos/ellas/ustedes	**irán**	ellos/ellas/ustedes	**irían**

IMPERATIVE

ve / id

PAST PARTICIPLE

ido

GERUND

yendo

EXAMPLE PHRASES

¿**Vamos** a comer al campo? Shall we have a picnic in the country?
El domingo **iré** a Edimburgo. I'll go to Edinburgh on Sunday.
Yo no **voy** con ellos. I'm not going with them.

Remember that subject pronouns are not used very often in Spanish.

ser (to be)

	PRESENT		PRESENT SUBJUNCTIVE
yo	**soy**	yo	**sea**
tú	**eres**	tú	**seas**
él/ella/usted	**es**	él/ella/usted	**sea**
nosotros/as	**somos**	nosotros/as	**seamos**
vosotros/as	**sois**	vosotros/as	**seáis**
ellos/ellas/ustedes	**son**	ellos/ellas/ustedes	**sean**

	PRETERITE		IMPERFECT
yo	**fui**	yo	**era**
tú	**fuiste**	tú	**eras**
él/ella/usted	**fue**	él/ella/usted	**era**
nosotros/as	**fuimos**	nosotros/as	**éramos**
vosotros/as	**fuisteis**	vosotros/as	**erais**
ellos/ellas/ustedes	**fueron**	ellos/ellas/ustedes	**eran**

	FUTURE		CONDITIONAL
yo	**seré**	yo	**sería**
tú	**serás**	tú	**serías**
él/ella/usted	**será**	él/ella/usted	**sería**
nosotros/as	**seremos**	nosotros/as	**seríamos**
vosotros/as	**seréis**	vosotros/as	**seríais**
ellos/ellas/ustedes	**serán**	ellos/ellas/ustedes	**serían**

IMPERATIVE

sé / sed

PAST PARTICIPLE

sido

GERUND

siendo

EXAMPLE PHRASES

Soy español. I'm Spanish.
¿**Fuiste** tú el que llamó? Was it you who phoned?
Era de noche. It was dark.

Remember that subject pronouns are not used very often in Spanish.

tener (to have)

PRESENT

yo	**tengo**
tú	**tienes**
él/ella/usted	**tiene**
nosotros/as	**tenemos**
vosotros/as	**tenéis**
ellos/ellas/ustedes	**tienen**

PRESENT SUBJUNCTIVE

yo	**tenga**
tú	**tengas**
él/ella/usted	**tenga**
nosotros/as	**tengamos**
vosotros/as	**tengáis**
ellos/ellas/ustedes	**tengan**

PRETERITE

yo	**tuve**
tú	**tuviste**
él/ella/usted	**tuvo**
nosotros/as	**tuvimos**
vosotros/as	**tuvisteis**
ellos/ellas/ustedes	**tuvieron**

IMPERFECT

yo	**tenía**
tú	**tenías**
él/ella/usted	**tenía**
nosotros/as	**teníamos**
vosotros/as	**teníais**
ellos/ellas/ustedes	**tenían**

FUTURE

yo	**tendré**
tú	**tendrás**
él/ella/usted	**tendrá**
nosotros/as	**tendremos**
vosotros/as	**tendréis**
ellos/ellas/ustedes	**tendrán**

CONDITIONAL

yo	**tendría**
tú	**tendrías**
él/ella/usted	**tendría**
nosotros/as	**tendríamos**
vosotros/as	**tendríais**
ellos/ellas/ustedes	**tendrían**

IMPERATIVE

ten / tened

PAST PARTICIPLE

tenido

GERUND

teniendo

EXAMPLE PHRASES

Tengo sed. I'm thirsty.
No **tenía** suficiente dinero. She didn't have enough money.
Tuvimos que irnos. We had to leave.

Remember that subject pronouns are not used very often in Spanish.

Aa

a INDEFINITE ARTICLE

LANGUAGE TIP Use **un** for masculine nouns, **una** for feminine nouns.

1 un *masc*

□ a book un libro

2 una *fem*

□ an apple una manzana

LANGUAGE TIP Sometimes 'a' is not translated, particularly if referring to professions.

□ He's a butcher. Es carnicero. □ I haven't got a car. No tengo coche. □ a year ago hace un año

■ **a hundred pounds** cien libras

■ **once a week** una vez a la semana

■ **70 kilometres an hour** 70 kilómetros por hora

■ **30 pence a kilo** 30 peniques el kilo

to **abandon** VERB

abandonar

abbey NOUN

la abadía

abbreviation NOUN

la abreviatura

ability NOUN

la capacidad

■ **to have the ability to do something** tener la capacidad de hacer algo

able ADJECTIVE

■ **to be able to do something** poder hacer algo □ Will you be able to come on Saturday? ¿Puedes venir el sábado?

to **abolish** VERB

abolir*

abortion NOUN

el aborto

■ **to have an abortion** abortar

about PREPOSITION, ADVERB

1 sobre

□ a book about London un libro sobre Londres □ I don't know anything about it. No sé nada sobre eso.

■ **I'm phoning you about tomorrow's meeting.** Te llamo por lo de la reunión de mañana.

■ **What's it about?** ¿De qué trata?

2 unos (FEM unas) *(approximately)*

□ It takes about 10 hours. Se tarda unas 10 horas.

■ **at about 11 o'clock** sobre las 11

3 por

□ to walk about the town caminar por la ciudad

■ **What about me?** ¿Y yo?

■ **to be about to do something** estar a punto de hacer algo □ I was about to go out. Estaba a punto de salir.

■ **How about going to the cinema?** ¿Qué tal si vamos al cine?

above PREPOSITION, ADVERB

LANGUAGE TIP When something is located above something, use **encima de**. When there is movement involved, use **por encima de**.

1 encima de

□ There was a picture above the fireplace. Había un cuadro encima de la chimenea.

2 por encima de

□ He put his hands above his head. Puso las manos por encima de la cabeza.

■ **the flat above** el piso de arriba

■ **above all** sobre todo

3 más de *(more than)*

□ above 40 degrees más de 40 grados

abroad ADVERB

■ **to go abroad** ir al extranjero

■ **to live abroad** vivir en el extranjero

abrupt ADJECTIVE

1 brusco (FEM brusca)

□ He was a bit abrupt with me. Fue un poco brusco conmigo.

2 repentino (FEM repentina)

□ His abrupt departure aroused suspicion. Su repentina marcha levantó sospechas.

abruptly ADVERB

de repente

□ He got up abruptly. Se levantó de repente.

absence NOUN

1 la ausencia *(of people)*

2 la falta *(of things)*

■ **absence from school** la falta de asistencia a clase

absent ADJECTIVE
ausente (FEM ausente)

absent-minded ADJECTIVE
distraído (FEM distraída)

absolutely ADVERB
totalmente
□ I absolutely refuse to do it. Me niego totalmente a hacerlo.
■ **Jill's absolutely right.** Jill tiene toda la razón.
■ **It's absolutely delicious!** ¡Está riquísimo!
■ **They did absolutely nothing to help him.** No hicieron absolutamente nada para ayudarle.
■ **Do you think it's a good idea? — Absolutely!** ¿Te parece una buena idea? — ¡Desde luego!

absorbed ADJECTIVE
■ **to be absorbed in something** estar absorto en algo

absurd ADJECTIVE
absurdo (FEM absurda)

abuse NOUN
▷ *see also* **abuse** VERB
el abuso *(of power)*
■ **to shout abuse at somebody** insultar a alguien

to **abuse** VERB
▷ *see also* **abuse** NOUN
maltratar
□ abused children niños maltratados

abusive ADJECTIVE
■ **He became abusive.** Se puso a insultar.

academic ADJECTIVE
académico (FEM académica)
□ the academic year el año académico

academy NOUN
la academia
□ a military academy una academia militar
■ **an academy of music** un conservatorio

to **accelerate** VERB
acelerar

accelerator NOUN
el acelerador

accent NOUN
el acento
□ He's got a Spanish accent. Tiene acento español.

to **accept** VERB
aceptar
□ She accepted the offer. Aceptó la oferta.
■ **to accept responsibility for something** asumir la responsabilidad de algo
■ **This telephone accepts 20 pence coins only.** Este teléfono sólo admite monedas de 20 peniques.

acceptable ADJECTIVE
aceptable (FEM aceptable)

access NOUN
el acceso
□ He has access to confidential information. Tiene acceso a información reservada.
■ **Her ex-husband has access to the children.** Su ex marido puede ver a los niños.

accessible ADJECTIVE
accesible (FEM accesible)

accessory NOUN
el accesorio
□ fashion accessories los accesorios de moda

accident NOUN
el accidente
□ to have an accident sufrir un accidente
■ **by accident 1** por casualidad □ They made the discovery by accident. Lo descubrieron por casualidad. **2** sin querer □ The burglar killed him by accident. El ladrón lo mató sin querer.

accidental ADJECTIVE
■ **I didn't do it deliberately, it was accidental.** No lo hice adrede, fue sin querer.
■ **accidental death** la muerte por accidente

to **accommodate** VERB
alojar

accommodation NOUN
el alojamiento

to **accompany** VERB
acompañar

accord NOUN
■ **of his own accord** por su cuenta

accordingly ADVERB
en consecuencia *(consequently)*

according to PREPOSITION
según
□ According to him, everyone had gone. Según él, todos se habían ido.

account NOUN
1 la cuenta
□ a bank account una cuenta bancaria
■ **to do the accounts** llevar la contabilidad
2 el informe
□ He gave a detailed account of what happened. Dio un informe detallado de lo ocurrido.
■ **to take something into account** tener algo en cuenta
■ **by all accounts** a decir de todos
■ **on account of** a causa de □ We couldn't go out on account of the bad weather. No pudimos salir a causa del mal tiempo.

accountable ADJECTIVE
■ **to be accountable to someone** responder ante alguien

accountancy NOUN
la contabilidad

accountant NOUN
el/la contable (el contador, la contadora *Latin America*)
□ She's an accountant. Es contable.

to **account for** VERB
explicar*
□ If she was ill, that would account for her poor results. Si estuviera enferma, se explicarían sus malos resultados.

accuracy NOUN
la exactitud

accurate ADJECTIVE
exacto (FEM exacta)

accurately ADVERB
con exactitud

accusation NOUN
la acusación (PL las acusaciones)

to **accuse** VERB
■ **to accuse somebody of something** acusar a alguien de algo □ The police are accusing her of murder. La policía la acusa de asesinato.

ace NOUN
el as
□ the ace of hearts el as de corazones

ache NOUN
▹ *see also* **ache** VERB
el dolor
□ stomach ache dolor de estómago

to **ache** VERB
▹ *see also* **ache** NOUN
■ **My leg's aching.** Me duele la pierna.

to **achieve** VERB
conseguir*

achievement NOUN
el logro
□ That was quite an achievement. Aquello fue todo un logro.

acid NOUN
el ácido

acid rain NOUN
la lluvia ácida

acne NOUN
el acné

acre NOUN
el acre

acrobat NOUN
el/la acróbata

across PREPOSITION, ADVERB
1 al otro lado de
□ He lives across the river. Vive al otro lado del río.
2 a través de
□ an expedition across the Sahara una expedición a través del Sahara
■ **the shop across the road** la tienda en la acera de enfrente
■ **to run across the road** cruzar la calle corriendo
■ **across from** frente a □ He sat down across from her. Se sentó frente a ella.

to **act** VERB
▹ *see also* **act** NOUN
actuar*
□ The police acted quickly. La policía actuó con rapidez. □ He acts really well. Actúa muy bien.
■ **She's acting the part of Juliet.** Interpreta el papel de Julieta.
■ **She acts as his interpreter.** Ella le hace de intérprete.

act NOUN
▹ *see also* **act** VERB
el acto
□ in the first act en el primer acto
■ **It was all an act.** Era todo un cuento.
■ **an Act of Parliament** una ley parlamentaria

action NOUN
la acción (PL las acciones)
□ The film was full of action. Era una película con mucha acción.
■ **to take firm action against** tomar severas medidas contra

active ADJECTIVE
activo (FEM activa)
□ He's a very active person. Es una persona muy activa.
■ **an active volcano** un volcán en actividad

activity NOUN
la actividad
□ outdoor activities actividades al aire libre

actor NOUN
el actor

actress NOUN
la actriz (PL las actrices)

actual ADJECTIVE
real (FEM real)
□ The film is based on actual events. La película está basada en hechos reales.

LANGUAGE TIP Be careful not to translate **actual** by the Spanish word **actual**.

actually ADVERB
1 realmente
□ Did it actually happen? ¿Ocurrió realmente?
■ **You only pay for the electricity you actually use.** Sólo pagas la electricidad que consumes.
2 de hecho
□ I was so bored I actually fell asleep! ¡Me aburría tanto que de hecho me quedé dormido!

■ **Fiona's awful, isn't she? — Actually, I quite like her.** Fiona es una antipática, ¿verdad? — Pues a mí me cae bien.
■ **Actually, I don't know him at all.** La verdad es que no lo conozco de nada.

acupuncture NOUN
la acupuntura

AD ABBREVIATION *(= Anno Domini)*
d.C. *(= después de Cristo)*
□ in 800 AD en el año 800 d.C.

ad NOUN
el anuncio

to **adapt** VERB
adaptar
□ His novel was adapted for television. Su novela fue adaptada para la televisión.
■ **to adapt to something** adaptarse a algo
□ He adapted to his new school very quickly. Se adaptó a su nuevo colegio muy rápidamente.

adaptor NOUN
1 el ladrón (PL los ladrones) *(for several plugs)*
2 el adaptador *(for different types of plugs)*

to **add** VERB
añadir
□ Add more flour to the dough. Añada más harina a la masa.

to **add up** VERB
sumar
□ Add up the figures. Suma las cifras.

addict NOUN
el adicto
la adicta
■ **a drug addict** un drogadicto □ She's a drug addict. Es drogadicta.
■ **Martin's a football addict.** Martin es un fanático del fútbol.

addicted ADJECTIVE
■ **to be addicted to drugs** ser drogadicto
■ **She's addicted to heroin.** Es heroinómana.
■ **She's addicted to soaps.** Es una apasionada de las telenovelas.

addition NOUN
■ **in addition** además □ He's bought a new car and, in addition, a motorbike. Se ha comprado un coche nuevo y además una moto.
■ **in addition to** además de □ There's a postage fee in addition to the repair charge Hay que pagar el envío, además de los gastos de reparación.

address NOUN
la dirección (PL las direcciones)

adjective NOUN
el adjetivo

to **adjust** VERB
1 regular *(temperature, height)*
□ You can adjust the height of the chair. Se puede regular la altura de la silla.
2 ajustar *(mechanism)*
□ It can be easily adjusted using a screwdriver. Se ajusta fácilmente con un destornillador.
■ **to adjust to something** adaptarse a algo
□ He adjusted to his new school very quickly. Se adaptó a su nuevo colegio muy rápidamente.

adjustable ADJECTIVE
regulable (FEM regulable)

administration NOUN
la administración

admiral NOUN
el almirante

to **admire** VERB
admirar

admission NOUN
la entrada
■ **'admission free'** 'entrada gratuita'

to **admit** VERB
reconocer*
□ I must admit that I've never heard of him. Tengo que reconocer que nunca he oído hablar de él. □ He admitted that he'd done it. Reconoció que lo había hecho.

adolescent NOUN
el/la adolescente

to **adopt** VERB
adoptar

adopted ADJECTIVE
adoptivo (FEM adoptiva)

adoption NOUN
la adopción (PL las adopciones)

to **adore** VERB
adorar

adult NOUN
el adulto
la adulta
■ **adult education** la educación de adultos

to **advance** VERB
▷ *see also* **advance** NOUN
avanzar*
□ The troops are advancing. Las tropas avanzan. □ Technology has advanced a lot. La tecnología ha avanzado mucho.

advance NOUN
▷ *see also* **advance** VERB
■ **in advance** con antelación □ They bought the tickets a month in advance. Compraron los billetes con un mes de antelación.

advance booking NOUN
■ **Advance booking is essential.** Es indispensable reservar con antelación.

advanced ADJECTIVE
avanzado (FEM avanzada)

advantage NOUN
la ventaja
□ Going to university has many advantages. Ir a la universidad tiene muchas ventajas.
■ **to take advantage of something** aprovechar algo □ He took advantage of his day off to have a rest. Aprovechó su día libre para descansar.
■ **to take advantage of somebody** aprovecharse de alguien □ The company was taking advantage of its employees. La compañía se aprovechaba de sus empleados.

adventure NOUN
la aventura

adverb NOUN
el adverbio

to advertise VERB
anunciar
□ Jobs are advertised in the papers. Las ofertas de empleo se anuncian en los periódicos.

advertising NOUN
la publicidad

advice NOUN
el consejo
□ to ask for advice pedir consejo □ I'd like to ask your advice. Quería pedirte consejo.
■ **to give somebody advice** aconsejar a alguien
■ **a piece of advice** un consejo □ He gave me a good piece of advice. Me ha dado un buen consejo.

to advise VERB
aconsejar
LANGUAGE TIP **aconsejar que** has to be followed by a verb in the subjunctive.
□ He advised me to wait. Me aconsejó que esperara. □ He advised me not to go there. Me aconsejó que no fuera.

aerial NOUN
la antena

aerobics NOUN
aerobic *masc*
□ I do aerobics. Hago aerobic.

aeroplane NOUN
el avión (PL los aviones)

aerosol NOUN
el aerosol

affair NOUN
1 la aventura
□ to have an affair with somebody tener una aventura con alguien
2 el asunto
□ The government has mishandled the affair. El gobierno ha llevado mal el asunto.

to affect VERB
afectar

affectionate ADJECTIVE
cariñoso (FEM cariñosa)

to afford VERB
permitirse
□ I can't afford a new pair of jeans. No puedo permitirme comprar otros vaqueros.
■ **We can't afford to go on holiday.** No podemos permitirnos el lujo de ir de vacaciones.

afraid ADJECTIVE
■ **to be afraid of something** tener miedo de algo □ I'm afraid of spiders. Tengo miedo de las arañas.
■ **I'm afraid I can't come.** Me temo que no puedo ir.
■ **I'm afraid so.** Me temo que sí.
■ **I'm afraid not.** Me temo que no.

Africa NOUN
África *fem*

African ADJECTIVE
▷ *see also* **African** NOUN
africano (FEM africana)

African NOUN
▷ *see also* **African** ADJECTIVE
el africano
la africana

after PREPOSITION, CONJUNCTION, ADVERB
1 después de
□ after the match después del partido
□ After watching television I went to bed. Después de ver la televisión me fui a la cama. □ After I'd had a rest I went for a walk. Después de descansar me fui a dar un paseo.
2 después de que
LANGUAGE TIP When there's a change of subject in an 'after' clause, use **después de que** with a verb in an appropriate tense instead of **después de** + infinitive.
□ I met her after she had left the company. La conocí después de que dejó la empresa.
LANGUAGE TIP **después de que** has to be followed by a verb in the subjunctive when referring to an event in the future.
□ I'll help you after we've finished this. Te ayudaré después de que terminemos esto.
□ She said she'd phone after her mother had gone out. Dijo que me llamaría después de que se marchara su madre.
■ **after dinner** después de cenar
■ **He ran after me.** Corrió detrás de mí.
■ **after all** después de todo
■ **soon after** poco después

afternoon NOUN
la tarde
□ in the afternoon por la tarde □ 3 o'clock

in the afternoon las 3 de la tarde □ on Saturday afternoon el sábado por la tarde

afters NOUN
el postre
□ What's for afters? ¿Qué hay de postre?

aftershave NOUN
el after shave

afterwards ADVERB
después
□ She left not long afterwards. Se marchó poco después.

again ADVERB
otra vez
□ They're friends again. Ya son amigos otra vez. □ I'd like to hear it again. Me gustaría escucharlo otra vez.

LANGUAGE TIP In Spanish you often use the verb **volver a** and an infinitive to talk about doing something 'again'.

□ I'd like to hear it again. Me gustaría volver a escucharlo. □ I won't tell you again! ¡No te lo vuelvo a repetir!
■ **Can you tell me again?** ¿Me lo puedes repetir?
■ **not...again** no...más □ I won't go there again. No volveré más por allí.
■ **Do it again!** ¡Vuelve a hacerlo!
■ **again and again** una y otra vez

against PREPOSITION
1 contra
□ He leant against the wall. Se apoyó contra la pared.
2 en contra de
□ I'm against nuclear testing. Estoy en contra de las pruebas nucleares.

age NOUN
la edad
□ an age limit un límite de edad
■ **at the age of sixteen** a los dieciséis años
■ **I haven't been to the cinema for ages.** Hace siglos que no voy al cine.

aged ADJECTIVE
■ **aged 10** de 10 años

agenda NOUN
el orden del día

LANGUAGE TIP Be careful not to translate **agenda** by the Spanish word **agenda**.

agent NOUN
el/la agente
□ an estate agent un agente inmobiliario
■ **She's a travel agent.** Es empleada de una agencia de viajes.

aggressive ADJECTIVE
agresivo (FEM agresiva)

ago ADVERB
■ **two days ago** hace dos días
■ **not long ago** no hace mucho
■ **How long ago did it happen?** ¿Cuánto hace que ocurrió?

agony NOUN
■ **to be in agony** sufrir mucho dolor
■ **It was agony!** ¡Fue un suplicio!

to **agree** VERB
estar* de acuerdo
□ I don't agree! ¡No estoy de acuerdo!
□ I agree with Carol. Estoy de acuerdo con Carol.
■ **to agree to do something 1** *(when someone requests)* aceptar hacer algo □ He agreed to go with her. Aceptó acompañarla. **2** *(arrange)* acordar hacer algo □ They agreed to meet again next week. Acordaron volver a reunirse la semana próxima.
■ **to agree that...** reconocer que... □ I agree it's difficult. Reconozco que es difícil.
■ **Garlic doesn't agree with me.** El ajo no me sienta bien.

agreed ADJECTIVE
acordado (FEM acordada)
□ at the agreed time a la hora acordada

agreement NOUN
el acuerdo
■ **to be in agreement** estar de acuerdo

agricultural ADJECTIVE
agrícola (FEM agrícola)

agriculture NOUN
la agricultura

ahead ADVERB
delante
□ She looked straight ahead. Miró hacia delante.
■ **ahead of time** con antelación
■ **to plan ahead** hacer planes con antelación
■ **The Spanish are five points ahead.** Los españoles llevan cinco puntos de ventaja.
■ **Go ahead! Help yourself!** ¡Venga! ¡Sírvete!

aid NOUN
la ayuda
■ **in aid of sick children** a beneficio de los niños enfermos

AIDS NOUN
el sida

to **aim** VERB
▷ *see also* **aim** NOUN
■ **to aim at** apuntar a □ He aimed a gun at me. Me apuntó con una pistola.
■ **The film is aimed at children.** La película está dirigida a los niños.
■ **to aim to do something** pretender hacer algo

aim NOUN
▷ *see also* **aim** VERB
el propósito

air NOUN
el aire
□ to get some fresh air tomar un poco el aire
■ **by air** en avión

air-conditioned ADJECTIVE
con aire acondicionado

air conditioning NOUN
el aire acondicionado

Air Force NOUN
el ejército del aire

air hostess NOUN
la azafata
□ She's an air hostess. Es azafata.

airline NOUN
la línea aérea

airmail NOUN
■ **by airmail** por correo aéreo

airplane NOUN (US)
el avión (PL los aviones)

airport NOUN
el aeropuerto

aisle NOUN
el pasillo *(in plane, cinema)*

alarm NOUN
la alarma
■ **a fire alarm** una alarma contra incendios

alarm clock NOUN
el despertador

album NOUN
el álbum

alcohol NOUN
el alcohol

alcoholic NOUN
▷ *see also* **alcoholic** ADJECTIVE
el alcohólico
la alcohólica

alcoholic ADJECTIVE
▷ *see also* **alcoholic** NOUN
alcohólico (FEM alcohólica)
□ alcoholic drinks bebidas alcohólicas

alert ADJECTIVE
1 despierto (FEM despierta)
□ He's a very alert baby. Es un bebé muy despierto.
2 atento (FEM atenta)
□ We must stay alert. Hay que estar atentos.

A levels PL NOUN

DID YOU KNOW...?
Under the reformed Spanish Educational System, if students stay on at school after the age of 16, they can do a two-year course – **bachillerato**. In order to get in to university, they sit an entrance exam – **la selectividad** – in the subjects they have been studying for the **bachillerato**.

Algeria NOUN
Argelia *fem*

alike ADVERB
■ **to look alike** parecerse □ The two sisters look alike. Las dos hermanas se parecen.

alive ADJECTIVE
vivo (FEM viva)

all ADJECTIVE, PRONOUN, ADVERB
todo (FEM toda)
□ That's all I can remember. Eso es todo lo que recuerdo. □ I ate all of it. Me lo comí todo. □ all day todo el día □ all the apples todas las manzanas
■ **All of us went.** Fuimos todos.
■ **all alone** completamente solo
■ **not at all** en absoluto □ I'm not at all tired. No estoy en absoluto cansado.
■ **Thank you. — Not at all.** Gracias. — De nada.
■ **She talks all the time.** No para de hablar.
■ **The score is five all.** El marcador es de empate a cinco.

allergic ADJECTIVE
alérgico (FEM alérgica)
□ to be allergic to something ser alérgico a algo

alley NOUN
la callejuela

to allow VERB
■ **to allow somebody to do something** dejar a alguien hacer algo □ His mum allowed him to go out. Su madre le dejó salir. □ He's not allowed to go out at night. No le dejan salir por la noche.
■ **Smoking is not allowed.** Está prohibido fumar.

all right ADVERB, ADJECTIVE
bien
□ Everything turned out all right. Todo salió bien. □ Are you all right? ¿Estás bien?
■ **Is that all right with you?** ¿Te parece bien?
■ **The film was all right.** La película no estuvo mal.
■ **We'll talk about it later. — All right.** Lo hablamos después. — Vale.

almond NOUN
la almendra

almost ADVERB
casi
□ I've almost finished. Ya casi he terminado.

alone ADJECTIVE, ADVERB
solo (FEM sola)
□ She lives alone. Vive sola.
■ **to leave somebody alone** dejar en paz a alguien □ Leave her alone! ¡Déjala en paz!
■ **to leave something alone** no tocar algo □ Leave my things alone! ¡No toques mis cosas!

along PREPOSITION, ADVERB
por
□ Chris was walking along the beach. Chris paseaba por la playa.
■ **all along** **1** a lo largo de □ There were bars all along the street. Había bares a lo largo de toda la calle. **2** desde el principio □ He was lying to me all along. Me había mentido desde el principio.

aloud ADVERB
en voz alta

alphabet NOUN
el alfabeto

Alps PL NOUN
los Alpes

already ADVERB
ya
□ Liz had already gone. Liz ya se había ido.

also ADVERB
también

altar NOUN
el altar

to **alter** VERB
cambiar

alternate ADJECTIVE
■ **on alternate days** en días alternos

alternative NOUN
▹ *see also* **alternative** ADJECTIVE
la alternativa
□ You have no alternative. No tienes otra alternativa.
■ **Fruit is a healthy alternative to chocolate.** La fruta es una opción más sana que el chocolate.
■ **There are several alternatives.** Hay varias posibilidades.

alternatively ADVERB
■ **Alternatively, we could just stay at home.** Si no, podemos simplemente quedarnos en casa.

although CONJUNCTION
aunque
□ Although she was tired, she stayed up late. Aunque estaba cansada, se quedó levantada hasta tarde.

altogether ADVERB
1 en total *(in total)*
□ You owe me £20 altogether. En total me debes 20 libras.
2 del todo *(completely)*
□ I'm not altogether happy with your work. No estoy del todo satisfecho con tu trabajo.

aluminium (US **aluminum**) NOUN
el aluminio

always ADVERB
siempre
□ He's always moaning. Siempre está quejándose.

am VERB ▹ *see* **be**

a.m. ABBREVIATION
de la mañana
□ at 4 a.m. a las 4 de la mañana

amateur NOUN
el/la amateur (PL los/las amateurs)

amazed ADJECTIVE
asombrado (FEM asombrada)
□ I was amazed that I managed to do it. Estaba asombrado de haberlo conseguido.

amazing ADJECTIVE
1 asombroso (FEM asombrosa)
□ That's amazing news! ¡Es una noticia asombrosa!
2 extraordinario (FEM extraordinaria)
□ Vivian's an amazing cook. Vivian es una cocinera extraordinaria.

ambassador NOUN
el embajador
la embajadora

amber ADJECTIVE
■ **an amber light** *(when driving)* un semáforo en ámbar

ambition NOUN
la ambición (PL las ambiciones)

ambitious ADJECTIVE
ambicioso (FEM ambiciosa)

ambulance NOUN
la ambulancia

amenities PL NOUN
■ **The hotel has very good amenities.** El hotel tiene excelentes servicios e instalaciones.
■ **The town has many amenities.** La ciudad ofrece gran variedad de servicios.

America NOUN
1 los Estados Unidos *masc pl (United States)*
2 América *fem (continent)*

American ADJECTIVE
▹ *see also* **American** NOUN
norteamericano (FEM norteamericana)

American NOUN
▹ *see also* **American** ADJECTIVE
el norteamericano
la norteamericana
□ the Americans los norteamericanos

among PREPOSITION
entre

amount NOUN
la cantidad
□ a huge amount of rice una cantidad enorme de arroz
■ **a large amount of money** una alta suma de dinero

amp NOUN
1 el amplificador *(amplifier)*
2 el amperio *(ampere)*

amplifier NOUN
el amplificador

to **amuse** VERB *(make laugh)*
divertir*
□ The thought seemed to amuse him. La idea parecía divertirle.

amusement arcade NOUN
el salón de juegos

an INDEFINITE ARTICLE ▷*see* **a**

to **analyse** VERB
analizar*

analysis NOUN
el análisis (PL los análisis)

to **analyze** VERB (US)
analizar*

ancestor NOUN
el antepasado

anchor NOUN
el ancla *fem*

LANGUAGE TIP Although it's a feminine noun, remember that you use **el** and **un** with **ancla**.

ancient ADJECTIVE
antiguo (FEM antigua)
□ ancient Greece la antigua Grecia
■ **an ancient monument** un monumento histórico

and CONJUNCTION
y
□ Mary and Jane Mary y Jane

LANGUAGE TIP Use **e** to translate 'and' before words beginning with **i** or **hi** but not **hie**.

□ Miguel and Ignacio Miguel e Ignacio

LANGUAGE TIP 'and' is not translated when linking numbers.

□ two hundred and fifty doscientos cincuenta
■ **Please try and come!** ¡Procura venir!
■ **He talked and talked.** No paraba de hablar.
■ **better and better** cada vez mejor

angel NOUN
el ángel

anger NOUN
el enfado (el enojo *Latin America*)

angle NOUN
el ángulo

angler NOUN
el pescador
la pescadora

angling NOUN
■ **His hobby is angling.** Su hobby es la pesca.

angry ADJECTIVE
enfadado (FEM enfadada) (enojado *Latin America*)
□ to be angry with somebody estar enfadado con alguien □ Your father looks very angry. Tu padre parece estar muy enfadado.
■ **to get angry** enfadarse (enojarse *Latin America*)

animal NOUN
el animal

ankle NOUN
el tobillo
□ I've twisted my ankle. Me he torcido el tobillo.

anniversary NOUN
el aniversario
□ wedding anniversary aniversario de bodas

to **announce** VERB
anunciar

announcement NOUN
el anuncio

to **annoy** VERB
molestar
□ Make a note of the things that annoy you. Haz una lista de las cosas que te molestan.
■ **He's really annoying me.** Me está fastidiando de verdad.
■ **to be annoyed with somebody** estar molesto con alguien
■ **to get annoyed** enfadarse (enojarse *Latin America*)
□ Don't get annoyed! ¡No te enfades!

annoying ADJECTIVE
molesto (FEM molesta)
□ the most annoying problem el problema más molesto
■ **I find it very annoying.** Me molesta mucho.

annual ADJECTIVE
anual (FEM anual)

anorak NOUN
el anorak (PL los anoraks)

another ADJECTIVE, PRONOUN
otro (FEM otra)
□ Have you got another skirt? ¿Tienes otra falda?
■ **another two kilometres** dos kilómetros más

to **answer** VERB
▷*see also* **answer** NOUN
responder
□ Can you answer my question? ¿Puedes responder a mi pregunta?
■ **to answer the phone** contestar al teléfono
■ **to answer the door** abrir la puerta □ Can you answer the door please? ¿Puedes ir a abrir la puerta?

answer NOUN
▷*see also* **answer** VERB
1 la respuesta *(to question)*

English-Spanish a

2 la solución (PL las soluciones) *(to problem)*

answering machine NOUN
el contestador automático

ant NOUN
la hormiga

Antarctic NOUN
■ **the Antarctic** el Antártico

anthem NOUN
■ **the national anthem** el himno nacional

antibiotic NOUN
el antibiótico

antidepressant NOUN
el antidepresivo

antique NOUN
la antigüedad

antique shop NOUN
la tienda de antigüedades

antiseptic NOUN
el antiséptico

any ADJECTIVE, ADVERB
▷ *see also* **any** PRONOUN

LANGUAGE TIP In questions and negative sentences 'any' is usually not translated.

□ Have you got any change? ¿Tienes cambio? □ Are there any beans left? ¿Quedan alubias? □ He hasn't got any friends. No tiene amigos.

LANGUAGE TIP Use **algún/alguna** + singular noun in questions and **ningún/ninguna** + singular noun in negatives where 'any' is used with plural nouns and the number of items is important.

□ Do you speak any foreign languages? ¿Hablas algún idioma extranjero? □ I haven't got any books by Cervantes. No tengo ningún libro de Cervantes.

LANGUAGE TIP Use **cualquier** in affirmative sentences.

□ Any teacher will tell you. Cualquier profesor te lo dirá.
■ **Come any time you like.** Ven cuando quieras.
■ **Would you like any more coffee?** ¿Quieres más café?
■ **I don't love him any more.** Ya no le quiero.

any PRONOUN
▷ *see also* **any** ADJECTIVE, ADVERB

1 alguno (FEM alguna) *(in questions)*
□ I need a stamp. Have you got any left? Necesito un sello. ¿Te queda alguno?

LANGUAGE TIP Only use **alguno/alguna** if 'any' refers to a countable noun. Otherwise don't translate it.

□ I fancy some soup. Have we got any? Me apetece sopa. ¿Tenemos?

2 ninguno (FEM ninguna) *(in negatives)*
□ I don't like any of them. No me gusta ninguno.

LANGUAGE TIP Only use **ninguno/ninguna** if 'any' refers to a countable noun. Otherwise don't translate it.

□ Did you buy the oranges? — No, there weren't any. ¿Compraste las naranjas? — No, no había.

anybody PRONOUN

1 alguien

LANGUAGE TIP Use **alguien** in questions.

□ Has anybody got a pen? ¿Tiene alguien un bolígrafo?

2 nadie

LANGUAGE TIP Use **nadie** in negative sentences.

□ I can't see anybody. No veo a nadie.

3 cualquiera

LANGUAGE TIP Use **cualquiera** in affirmative sentences.

□ Anybody can learn to swim. Cualquiera puede aprender a nadar.

anyhow ADVERB
de todas maneras
□ He doesn't want to go out and anyhow he's not allowed. No quiere salir y de todas maneras no le dejan.

anyone PRONOUN

1 alguien

LANGUAGE TIP Use **alguien** in questions.

□ Has anyone got a pen? ¿Tiene alguien un bolígrafo?

2 nadie

LANGUAGE TIP Use **nadie** in negative sentences.

□ I can't see anyone. No veo a nadie.

3 cualquiera

LANGUAGE TIP Use **cualquiera** in affirmative sentences.

□ Anyone can learn to swim. Cualquiera puede aprender a nadar.

anything PRONOUN

1 algo

LANGUAGE TIP Use **algo** in questions.

□ Do you need anything? ¿Necesitas algo? □ Would you like anything to eat? ¿Quieres algo de comer?

2 nada

LANGUAGE TIP Use **nada** in negative sentences.

□ I can't hear anything. No oigo nada.

3 cualquier cosa

LANGUAGE TIP Use **cualquier cosa** in affirmative sentences.

□ Anything could happen. Puede pasar cualquier cosa.

anyway ADVERB
de todas maneras
□ He doesn't want to go out and anyway he's not allowed. No quiere salir y de todas maneras no le dejan.

anywhere ADVERB
1 en algún sitio
LANGUAGE TIP Use **en** or **a algún sitio** in questions.
□ Have you seen my coat anywhere? ¿Has visto mi abrigo en algún sitio? □ Are we going anywhere? ¿Vamos a algún sitio?
2 en ningún sitio
LANGUAGE TIP Use **en** or **a ningún sitio** in negative sentences.
□ I can't find it anywhere. No lo encuentro en ningún sitio. □ I can't go anywhere. No puedo ir a ningún sitio.
3 en cualquier sitio
LANGUAGE TIP Use **en cualquier sitio** in affirmative sentences.
□ You can buy stamps almost anywhere. Se pueden comprar sellos casi en cualquier sitio.
■ **You can sit anywhere you like.** Siéntate donde quieras.

apart ADVERB
■ **The two towns are 10 kilometres apart.** Los dos pueblos están a 10 kilómetros el uno del otro.
■ **It was the first time we had been apart.** Era la primera vez que estábamos separados.
■ **apart from** aparte de □ Apart from that, everything's fine. Aparte de eso, todo va bien.

apartment NOUN
el piso (el apartamento *Latin America*)

to **apologize** VERB
disculparse
□ He apologized for being late. Se disculpó por llegar tarde.
■ **I apologize!** ¡Lo siento!

apology NOUN
la disculpa
□ I owe you an apology. Te debo una disculpa.

apostrophe NOUN
el apóstrofo

apparatus NOUN
los aparatos

apparent ADJECTIVE
1 aparente (FEM aparente)
□ for no apparent reason sin razón aparente
2 claro (FEM clara)
□ It was apparent that he disliked me. Estaba claro que no le caigo bien.

apparently ADVERB
por lo visto (dizque *Latin America*)
□ Apparently he was abroad when it happened. Por lo visto estaba en el extranjero cuando ocurrió.

to **appeal** VERB
▷ *see also* **appeal** NOUN
1 hacer* un llamamiento
□ They appealed for help. Hicieron un llamamiento de ayuda.
2 atraer*
□ Greece doesn't appeal to me. Grecia no me atrae.

appeal NOUN
▷ *see also* **appeal** VERB
el llamamiento
□ They have launched an appeal for unity. Han hecho un llamamiento a la unidad.

to **appear** VERB
1 aparecer*
□ The bus appeared around the corner. El autobús apareció por la esquina.
■ **to appear on TV** salir en la tele
2 parecer*
□ She appeared to be asleep. Parecía estar dormida.

appearance NOUN
el aspecto
□ She takes great care over her appearance. Cuida mucho su aspecto.
■ **to make an appearance** aparecer

appendicitis NOUN
la apendicitis
□ She's got appendicitis. Tiene apendicitis.

appetite NOUN
el apetito

to **applaud** VERB
aplaudir

applause NOUN
los aplausos

apple NOUN
la manzana
■ **an apple tree** un manzano

applicant NOUN
el candidato
la candidata

application NOUN
■ **a job application** una solicitud de empleo

application form NOUN
el impreso de solicitud

to **apply** VERB
■ **to apply for a job** solicitar un empleo
■ **to apply to** afectar a □ This rule doesn't apply to us. Esta norma no nos afecta.

appointment NOUN
la cita

□ to make an appointment with someone concertar una cita con alguien

■ **I've got a dental appointment.** Tengo hora con el dentista.

to **appreciate** VERB

agradecer*

□ I really appreciate your help. Agradezco de veras tu ayuda.

apprentice NOUN

el aprendiz (PL los aprendices)

la aprendiza

to **approach** VERB

1 acercarse* a

□ He approached the house. Se acercó a la casa.

2 abordar

□ to approach a problem abordar un problema

appropriate ADJECTIVE

apropiado (FEM apropiada)

□ That dress isn't very appropriate for an interview. Ese vestido no es muy apropiado para una entrevista.

■ **Tick the appropriate box.** Marque la casilla que corresponda.

approval NOUN

la aprobación

to **approve** VERB

■ **I don't approve of his choice.** No me parece bien su elección.

■ **They didn't approve of his girlfriend.** No veían con buenos ojos a su novia.

approximate ADJECTIVE

aproximado (FEM aproximada)

apricot NOUN

el albaricoque

April NOUN

abril *masc*

□ in April en abril □ on 4 April el 4 de abril

■ **April Fool's Day** el día de los Santos Inocentes *(1 de abril)*

DID YOU KNOW...?

In Spanish-speaking countries **el día de los Santos Inocentes** falls on the 28th of December. People play practical jokes in the same way as they do on April Fool's Day.

apron NOUN

el delantal

Aquarius NOUN

el Acuario *(sign)*

■ **I'm Aquarius.** Soy acuario.

Arab ADJECTIVE

▷ *see also* **Arab** NOUN

árabe (FEM árabe)

Arab NOUN

▷ *see also* **Arab** ADJECTIVE

el/la árabe

□ the Arabs los árabes

Arabic ADJECTIVE

árabe (FEM árabe)

arch NOUN

el arco

archaeologist NOUN

el arqueólogo

la arqueóloga

□ He's an archaeologist. Es arqueólogo.

archaeology NOUN

la arqueología

archbishop NOUN

el arzobispo

archeologist NOUN (US)

el arqueólogo

la arqueóloga

archeology NOUN (US)

la arqueología

architect NOUN

el arquitecto

la arquitecta

□ She's an architect. Es arquitecta.

architecture NOUN

la arquitectura

Arctic NOUN

■ **the Arctic** el Ártico

are VERB ▷ *see* **be**

area NOUN

1 la zona

□ a mountainous area of Spain una zona montañosa de España

2 la superficie

□ The field has an area of 1500 m². El terreno tiene una superficie de 1500 m².

3 el área *fem (in football)*

LANGUAGE TIP Although it's a feminine noun, remember that you use **el** and **un** with **área**.

Argentina NOUN

Argentina *fem*

Argentinian ADJECTIVE

▷ *see also* **Argentinian** NOUN

argentino (FEM argentina)

Argentinian NOUN

▷ *see also* **Argentinian** ADJECTIVE

el argentino

la argentina

to **argue** VERB

discutir

□ They never stop arguing. Siempre están discutiendo.

argument NOUN

la discusión (PL las discusiones)

□ to have an argument discutir

Aries NOUN

el Aries *(sign)*

■ **I'm Aries.** Soy aries.

arm NOUN

el brazo

□ I burnt my arm. Me quemé el brazo.

armchair NOUN
el sillón (PL los sillones)

armour (US **armor**) NOUN
la armadura

army NOUN
el ejército

around PREPOSITION, ADVERB
1 alrededor de
□ She wore a scarf around her neck. Llevaba una bufanda alrededor del cuello. □ It costs around £100. Cuesta alrededor de 100 libras.
■ **She ignored the people around her.** Ignoró a la gente que estaba a su alrededor.
■ **Shall we meet at around 8 o'clock?** ¿Quedamos sobre las 8?
2 por
□ I've been walking around the town. He estado paseando por la ciudad.
■ **We walked around for a while.** Paseamos por ahí durante un rato.
■ **around here** por aquí □ Is there a chemist's around here? ¿Hay alguna farmacia por aquí?

to **arrange** VERB
organizar*
□ to arrange a party organizar una fiesta
■ **to arrange to do something** quedar en hacer algo □ They arranged to go out together on Friday. Quedaron en salir juntos el viernes.

arrangement NOUN
■ **to make an arrangement to do something** quedar en hacer algo
■ **a flower arrangement** un arreglo floral
■ **arrangements** los preparativos
□ Pamela is in charge of the travel arrangements. Pamela se encarga de los preparativos para el viaje.
■ **They made arrangements to go out on Friday night.** Hicieron planes de salir el viernes por la noche.

to **arrest** VERB
▷ *see also* **arrest** NOUN
detener*

arrest NOUN
▷ *see also* **arrest** VERB
la detención (PL las detenciones)
■ **You're under arrest!** ¡Queda detenido!

arrival NOUN
la llegada
□ the airport arrivals hall la sala de llegadas del aeropuerto

to **arrive** VERB
llegar*
□ I arrived at 5 o'clock. Llegué a las 5.

arrow NOUN
la flecha

art NOUN
el arte
■ **works of art** las obras de arte
■ **art school** la escuela de Bellas Artes

artery NOUN
la arteria

art gallery NOUN
1 el museo *(state-owned)*
2 la galería de arte *(private)*

article NOUN
el artículo

artificial ADJECTIVE
artificial (FEM artificial)

artist NOUN
el/la artista
□ She's an artist. Es artista.

artistic ADJECTIVE
artístico (FEM artística)

as CONJUNCTION, ADVERB
1 cuando
□ He came in as I was leaving. Entró cuando yo me iba.
2 mientras
□ Everyone looked at him as he stood up. Todos lo miraron mientras se levantaba.
3 como
□ As it's Sunday, you can have a lie-in. Como es domingo, puedes quedarte en la cama hasta tarde.
4 de
□ He works as a waiter in the holidays. En vacaciones trabaja de camarero.
■ **as...as** tan...como □ Peter's as tall as Michael. Peter es tan alto como Michael.
■ **as much...as** tanto...como □ I haven't got as much energy as you. No tengo tanta energía como tú.
■ **Her coat cost twice as much as mine.** Su abrigo costó el doble que el mío.
■ **as soon as possible** cuanto antes
■ **as from tomorrow** a partir de mañana
■ **as if** como si
LANGUAGE TIP **como si** has to be followed by a verb in the subjunctive.
□ She acted as if she hadn't seen me. Hizo como si no me hubiese visto.
■ **as though** como si □ She acted as though she hadn't seen me. Hizo como si no me hubiese visto.

asap ABBREVIATION *(= as soon as possible)*
cuanto antes

ash NOUN
1 la ceniza *(from fire, cigarette)*
2 el fresno *(tree, wood)*

ashamed ADJECTIVE
■ **to be ashamed** estar avergonzado □ I'm ashamed of myself for shouting at you.

English-Spanish

a

Estoy avergonzado de gritarte.
■ **You should be ashamed of yourself!** ¡Debería darte vergüenza!

ashtray NOUN
el cenicero

Asia NOUN
Ásia *fem*

Asian ADJECTIVE
▷ *see also* **Asian** NOUN
asiático (FEM asiática)

Asian NOUN
▷ *see also* **Asian** ADJECTIVE
el asiático
la asiática

to **ask** VERB
1 preguntar
□ 'Have you finished?' she asked. '¿Has terminado?' preguntó.
■ **to ask somebody something** preguntar algo a alguien
■ **to ask about something** preguntar por algo □ I asked about train times to Leeds. Pregunté por el horario de trenes a Leeds.
■ **to ask somebody a question** hacer una pregunta a alguien
2 pedir*
LANGUAGE TIP **pedir que** has to be followed by a verb in the subjunctive.
□ She asked him to do the shopping. Le pidió que hiciera la compra.
■ **to ask for something** pedir algo □ He asked for a cup of tea. Pidió una taza de té.
■ **Peter asked her out.** Peter le pidió que saliera con él.
3 invitar
□ Have you asked Matthew to the party? ¿Has invitado a Matthew a la fiesta?

asleep ADJECTIVE
■ **to be asleep** estar dormido
■ **to fall asleep** quedarse dormido

asparagus NOUN
los espárragos

aspect NOUN
el aspecto

aspirin NOUN
la aspirina

asset NOUN
la ventaja
□ Her experience will be an asset to the firm. Su experiencia supondrá una ventaja para la empresa.

assignment NOUN
la tarea *(at school)*

assistance NOUN
la ayuda

assistant NOUN
1 el dependiente
la dependienta *(in shop)*
2 el/la ayudante *(helper)*

association NOUN
la asociación (PL las asociaciones)

assortment NOUN
el surtido

to **assume** VERB
suponer*
□ I assume she won't be coming. Supongo que no vendrá.

to **assure** VERB
asegurar
□ He assured me he was coming. Me aseguró que venía.

asthma NOUN
el asma *fem*
□ He's got asthma. Tiene asma.
LANGUAGE TIP Although it's a feminine noun, remember that you use **el** with **asma**.

to **astonish** VERB
pasmar

astrology NOUN
la astrología

astronaut NOUN
el/la astronauta

astronomy NOUN
la astronomía

asylum seeker NOUN
el/la solicitante de asilo

at PREPOSITION
1 en
□ at home en casa □ at school en la escuela □ at the office en la oficina □ at work en el trabajo
2 a
□ at 50 km/h a 50 km/h
■ **two at a time** de dos en dos
■ **at 4 o'clock** a las 4
■ **at night** por la noche
■ **at Christmas** en Navidad
■ **What are you doing at the weekend?** ¿Qué haces este fin de semana?

ate VERB ▷ *see* **eat**

Athens NOUN
Atenas *fem*

athlete NOUN
el/la atleta

athletic ADJECTIVE
atlético (FEM atlética)

athletics NOUN
el atletismo
□ I enjoy watching the athletics on television. Me gusta ver el atletismo en la televisión.

Atlantic NOUN
el Atlántico

atlas NOUN
el atlas (PL los atlas)

atmosphere NOUN
la atmósfera

atom NOUN
el átomo

atomic ADJECTIVE
atómico (FEM atómica)

to **attach** VERB
atar
□ They attached a rope to the car. Ataron una cuerda al coche.
■ **Please find attached a cheque for £10.** Se adjunta cheque de 10 libras.

attached ADJECTIVE
■ **to be attached to somebody** tener cariño a alguien

attachment NOUN
el documento adjunto *(to email)*

to **attack** VERB
▷ *see also* **attack** NOUN
atacar*

attack NOUN
▷ *see also* **attack** VERB
el ataque
■ **to be under attack** ser atacado

attempt NOUN
▷ *see also* **attempt** VERB
el intento

to **attempt** VERB
▷ *see also* **attempt** NOUN
■ **to attempt to do something** intentar hacer algo □ I attempted to write a song. Intenté escribir una canción.

to **attend** VERB
asistir a
□ to attend a meeting asistir a una reunión

attention NOUN
la atención
■ **to pay attention to** prestar atención a □ He didn't pay attention to what I was saying. No prestó atención a lo que estaba diciendo.
■ **Don't pay any attention to him!** ¡No le hagas caso!
■ **Pay attention, please!** ¡Atención por favor!

attic NOUN
el desván (PL los desvanes) (el altillo *Latin America*)

attitude NOUN
la actitud

attorney NOUN (US)
el abogado
la abogada

to **attract** VERB
atraer*
□ The Lake District attracts lots of tourists. La Región de los Lagos atrae a muchos turistas.

attraction NOUN
la atracción (PL las atracciones)
□ a tourist attraction una atracción turística

attractive ADJECTIVE
atractivo (FEM atractiva)

aubergine NOUN
la berenjena

auction NOUN
la subasta

audience NOUN
el público

audition NOUN
la prueba

August NOUN
agosto *masc*
□ in August en agosto □ on 13 August el 13 agosto

aunt NOUN
la tía
■ **my aunt and uncle** mis tíos

aunty NOUN
la tía

au pair NOUN
la au pair (PL las au pairs)

Australia NOUN
Australia *fem*

Australian ADJECTIVE
▷ *see also* **Australian** NOUN
australiano (FEM australiana)

Australian NOUN
▷ *see also* **Australian** ADJECTIVE
el australiano
la australiana
□ the Australians los australianos

Austria NOUN
Austria *fem*

Austrian ADJECTIVE
▷ *see also* **Austrian** NOUN
austríaco (FEM austríaca)

Austrian NOUN
▷ *see also* **Austrian** ADJECTIVE
el austríaco
la austríaca
□ the Austrians los austríacos

author NOUN
el autor
la autora
□ the author of the book el autor del libro
■ **a famous author** un escritor famoso

autobiography NOUN
la autobiografía

autograph NOUN
el autógrafo

automatic ADJECTIVE
automático (FEM automática)

automatically ADVERB
automáticamente

autumn NOUN
el otoño
□ in autumn en el otoño

availability NOUN
la disponibilidad

available ADJECTIVE
disponible (FEM disponible)
□ There is very little available information. Hay muy poca información disponible.
■ **Free brochures are available on request.** Disponemos de folletos gratuitos para quien los solicite.
■ **Is Mr Cooke available today?** ¿Está libre el señor Cooke hoy?

avalanche NOUN
el alud

avenue NOUN
la avenida

average NOUN
▹ *see also* **average** ADJECTIVE
la media
□ on average de media

average ADJECTIVE
▹ *see also* **average** NOUN
medio (FEM media)
□ the average price el precio medio

avocado NOUN
el aguacate

to **avoid** VERB
evitar
□ Avoid going out on your own at night. Evite salir solo por la noche.

awake ADJECTIVE
■ **to be awake** estar despierto

award NOUN
el premio
□ the award for the best actor el premio al mejor actor

aware ADJECTIVE
■ **to be aware that** saber que
■ **to be aware of something** ser consciente de algo □ We are aware of what is happening. Somos conscientes de lo que ocurre.
■ **not that I am aware of** que yo sepa, no

away ADJECTIVE, ADVERB
■ **It's two kilometres away.** Está a dos kilómetros de distancia.
■ **The coast is two hours away by car.** La costa está a dos horas en coche.
■ **The holiday was two weeks away.** Faltaban dos semanas para las vacaciones.
■ **to be away** estar fuera □ Jason was away on a business trip. Jason estaba fuera en viaje de negocios.
■ **He's away for a week.** Se ha ido una semana.
■ **Go away!** ¡Vete!
■ **away from** lejos de □ away from family and friends lejos de la familia y los amigos
■ **It's 30 miles away from town.** Está a 30 millas de la ciudad.
■ **He was still working away in the library.** Seguía trabajando sin parar en la biblioteca.

away match NOUN
■ **It is their last away match.** Es el último partido que juegan fuera.

awful ADJECTIVE
horrible (FEM horrible)
□ The weather's awful. Hace un tiempo horrible.
■ **I feel awful.** Me siento fatal.
■ **We met and I thought he was awful.** Nos conocimos y me cayó fatal.
■ **an awful lot of work** un montón de trabajo

awfully ADVERB
■ **I'm awfully sorry.** Lo siento muchísimo.

awkward ADJECTIVE
1 incómodo (FEM incómoda)
□ It was awkward to carry. Era incómodo de llevar. □ an awkward situation una situación incómoda
■ **Mike's being awkward about letting me have the car.** Mike no hace más que ponerme pegas para dejarme el coche.
■ **It's a bit awkward for me to come and see you.** Me viene un poco mal pasar a verte.
2 torpe (FEM torpe)
□ an awkward gesture un gesto torpe

axe NOUN
el hacha *fem*

LANGUAGE TIP Although it's a feminine noun, remember that you use **el** and **un** with **hacha**.

Bb

BA ABBREVIATION *(= Bachelor of Arts)*
la licenciatura en Letras
■ **a BA in French** una licenciatura en Filología Francesa
■ **She's got a BA in History.** Es licenciada en Historia.

baby NOUN
el/la bebé (PL los/las bebés)

baby carriage NOUN (US)
el cochecito de niño

to **babysit** VERB
hacer* de canguro

babysitter NOUN
el/la canguro

babysitting NOUN
■ **I don't like babysitting.** No me gusta hacer de canguro.

bachelor NOUN
el soltero

back NOUN
▷ *see also* **back** ADJECTIVE, ADVERB, VERB
1 la espalda *(of person)*
□ He's got a bad back. Tiene problemas de espalda.
2 el lomo *(of animal)*
■ **the back of a chair** el respaldo de una silla
■ **on the back of the cheque** al dorso del cheque
■ **at the back of the house** en la parte de atrás de la casa
■ **in the back of the car** en la parte trasera del coche
■ **at the back of the class** al fondo de la clase

back ADJECTIVE, ADVERB
▷ *see also* **back** NOUN, VERB
trasero (FEM trasera)
□ the back seat el asiento trasero
■ **the back door** la puerta de atrás
■ **He's not back yet.** Todavía no ha vuelto.
■ **to get back** volver □ What time did you get back? ¿A qué hora volviste? □ We went there by bus and walked back. Fuimos allí en autobús y volvimos a pie.
■ **to call somebody back** volver a llamar a alguien
■ **I'll call back later.** Volveré a llamar más tarde.

to **back** VERB
▷ *see also* **back** NOUN, ADJECTIVE
respaldar
□ The union is backing his claim for compensation. El sindicato respalda su demanda de compensación.
■ **to back a horse** apostar por un caballo
■ **She backed into the parking space.** Aparcó dando marcha atrás.

to **back out** VERB
echarse para atrás
□ They promised to help us and then backed out. Prometieron ayudarnos y luego se echaron para atrás.

to **back up** VERB
respaldar
□ She complained, and her colleagues backed her up. Presentó una queja y sus colegas la respaldaron.

backache NOUN
el dolor de espalda
□ to have backache tener dolor de espalda

backbone NOUN
la columna vertebral

to **backfire** VERB
tener* el efecto contrario *(go wrong)*

background NOUN
el fondo *(of picture)*
□ a house in the background una casa en el fondo
■ **background noise** ruido de fondo
■ **his family background** su historial familiar

backhand NOUN
el revés (PL los reveses)

backing NOUN
el apoyo
□ They promised their backing. Prometieron su apoyo.

backpack NOUN
la mochila

backpacker NOUN
el mochilero
la mochilera

English-Spanish

b

backside NOUN
el trasero
backstroke NOUN
la espalda
backup NOUN
el apoyo
□ We have extensive computer backup. Tenemos amplio apoyo informático.
■ **They've got a generator as an emergency backup.** Tienen un generador de reserva para emergencias.
■ **a backup file** una copia de seguridad
backwards ADVERB
hacia atrás
□ to take a step backwards dar un paso hacia atrás
■ **to fall backwards** caerse de espaldas
back yard NOUN
el patio trasero
bacon NOUN
el bacon (el tocino *Latin America*)
□ bacon and eggs los huevos fritos con bacon
bad ADJECTIVE
1 malo (FEM mala)
□ You bad boy! ¡Malo!
LANGUAGE TIP Use **mal** before a masculine singular noun.
□ bad weather mal tiempo

WORD POWER
You can use a number of other words instead of **bad** to mean 'terrible':
awful horrible
□ awful weather un tiempo horrible
dreadful terrible
□ a dreadful mistake un terrible error
terrible espantoso
□ a terrible book un libro espantoso

■ **to be in a bad mood** estar de mal humor
■ **to be bad at something** ser malo para algo □ I'm really bad at maths. Soy muy malo para las matemáticas.
2 grave (FEM grave) *(serious)*
□ a bad accident un accidente grave
■ **to go bad** *(food)* echarse a perder
■ **I feel bad about it.** *(guilty)* Me siento un poco culpable.
■ **How are you? — Not bad.** ¿Cómo estás? — Bien.
■ **That's not bad at all.** No está nada mal.
■ **bad language** las palabrotas
badge NOUN
1 la chapa *(metal, plastic)*
2 el escudo *(cloth)*
badly ADVERB
mal
□ badly paid mal pagado
■ **badly wounded** gravemente herido
■ **He badly needs a rest.** Le hace muchísima falta un descanso.
badminton NOUN
el bádminton
□ to play badminton jugar al bádminton
bad-tempered ADJECTIVE
■ **to be bad-tempered** **1** *(by nature)* tener mal genio □ He's a really bad-tempered person. Es una persona con muy mal genio. **2** *(temporarily)* estar de mal humor □ He was really bad-tempered yesterday. Ayer estaba de muy mal humor.
bag NOUN
la bolsa
baggage NOUN
el equipaje
baggage reclaim NOUN
la recogida de equipajes
baggy ADJECTIVE
ancho (FEM ancha) *(trousers)*
bagpipes PL NOUN
la gaita
to **bake** VERB
■ **to bake bread** hacer pan
■ **She loves to bake.** Le gusta cocinar al horno.
baked beans PL NOUN
las alubias blancas en salsa de tomate
baked potato NOUN
la patata asada
baker NOUN
el panadero
la panadera
□ He's a baker. Es panadero.
■ **at the baker's** en la panadería
bakery NOUN
la panadería
baking ADJECTIVE
■ **It's baking in here!** ¡Aquí hace un calor insoportable!
balance NOUN
el equilibrio
□ to lose one's balance perder el equilibrio
balanced ADJECTIVE
equilibrado (FEM equilibrada)
balcony NOUN
el balcón (PL los balcones)
bald ADJECTIVE
calvo (FEM calva)
ball NOUN
1 la pelota *(for tennis, basketball, rugby)*
2 el balón (PL los balones) *(for football)*
□ a golf ball una pelota de golf
ballet NOUN
el ballet (PL los ballets)
□ We went to a ballet. Fuimos a ver un ballet.
■ **ballet lessons** las clases de ballet

ballet dancer NOUN
el bailarín (PL los bailarines)
la bailarina
ballet shoes PL NOUN
las zapatillas de ballet
balloon NOUN
el globo
■ **a hot-air balloon** un globo aerostático
ballpoint pen NOUN
el bolígrafo
ballroom dancing NOUN
el baile de salón
ban NOUN
▷ *see also* **ban** VERB
la prohibición (PL las prohibiciones)
to **ban** VERB
▷ *see also* **ban** NOUN
prohibir*
banana NOUN
el plátano
□ a banana skin una piel de plátano
band NOUN
1 el grupo *(pop, rock)*
2 la banda *(military)*
3 la orquesta *(at a dance)*
bandage NOUN
▷ *see also* **bandage** VERB
la venda
to **bandage** VERB
▷ *see also* **bandage** NOUN
vendar
□ The nurse bandaged his arm. La enfermera le vendó el brazo.
Band-Aid® NOUN (US)
la tirita
bandit NOUN
el bandido
bang NOUN
▷ *see also* **bang** VERB
1 el estallido *(noise)*
□ I heard a loud bang. Oí un fuerte estallido.
2 el golpe *(blow)*
□ a bang on the head un golpe en la cabeza
to **bang** VERB
▷ *see also* **bang** NOUN
golpear
□ I banged my head. Me golpeé la cabeza.
■ **to bang on the door** aporrear la puerta
■ **to bang the door** dar un portazo
banger NOUN
la salchicha *(informal)*
□ bangers and mash las salchichas con puré de patatas
bank NOUN
1 el banco *(financial)*
2 la orilla *(of river, lake)*
bank account NOUN
la cuenta bancaria
banker NOUN
el banquero
la banquera
□ He's a banker. Es banquero.
bank holiday NOUN
el día festivo
banknote NOUN
el billete de banco
bar NOUN
1 el bar *(pub)*
2 la barra *(counter)*
■ **a bar of chocolate** 1 *(large)* una tableta de chocolate 2 *(small)* una chocolatina
■ **a bar of soap** una pastilla de jabón
barbaric ADJECTIVE
bárbaro (FEM bárbara)
barbecue NOUN
la barbacoa
□ to have a barbecue hacer una barbacoa
barber NOUN
el barbero
□ He's a barber. Es barbero.
■ **at the barber's** en la barbería
bare ADJECTIVE
desnudo (FEM desnuda)
barefoot ADJECTIVE, ADVERB
descalzo (FEM descalza)
□ The children go around barefoot. Los niños van descalzos.
barely ADVERB
apenas
□ I could barely hear what she was saying. Apenas oía lo que estaba diciendo.
bargain NOUN
la ganga
□ It was a bargain! ¡Era una ganga!
barge NOUN
la barcaza
to **bark** VERB
ladrar
barmaid NOUN
la camarera
□ She's a barmaid. Es camarera.
barman NOUN
el barman (PL los barmans)
□ He's a barman. Es barman.
barn NOUN
el granero
barrel NOUN
1 el barril *(container)*
2 el cañón (PL los cañones) *(of gun)*
barrier NOUN
la barrera
bartender NOUN (US)
el barman (PL los barmans)
□ He's a bartender. Es barman.
base NOUN
la base

baseball NOUN
el béisbol
□ to play baseball jugar al béisbol
■ **a baseball cap** una gorra de béisbol

based ADJECTIVE
■ **based on** basado en

basement NOUN
el sótano
□ a basement flat un apartamento en el sótano

to **bash** VERB
▷ *see also* **bash** NOUN
golpear con fuerza

bash NOUN
▷ *see also* **bash** VERB
■ **I'll have a bash at it.** Lo intentaré.

basic ADJECTIVE
básico (FEM básica)
□ It's a basic model. Es un modelo básico.
■ **The accommodation was pretty basic.** El alojamiento tenía sólo lo imprescindible.

basically ADVERB
básicamente
□ They are basically the same thing. Son básicamente lo mismo.
■ **Basically, I just don't like him.** Simplemente, no me gusta.

basics PL NOUN
los principios básicos

basil NOUN
la albahaca

basin NOUN
1 el lavabo *(washbasin)*
2 el cuenco *(for cooking, mixing food)*

basis NOUN
la base
□ On the basis of what you've said. En base a lo que has dicho.
■ **on a daily basis** diariamente
■ **on a regular basis** regularmente

basket NOUN
el cesto

basketball NOUN
el baloncesto
□ to play basketball jugar al baloncesto

bass NOUN
el bajo *(voice)*
■ **a bass guitar** un bajo
■ **a double bass** un contrabajo

bass drum NOUN
el bombo

bassoon NOUN
el fagot (PL los fagots)

bat NOUN
1 el bate *(for baseball, cricket)*
2 la raqueta *(for table tennis)*
3 el murciélago *(animal)*

bath NOUN
1 el baño
□ a hot bath un baño caliente
■ **to have a bath** bañarse
2 la bañera *(bathtub)*

to **bathe** VERB
bañarse

bathing suit NOUN (US)
el traje de baño

bathroom NOUN
el cuarto de baño

baths PL NOUN
■ **swimming baths** la piscina
■ **Turkish baths** los baños turcos

bath towel NOUN
la toalla de baño

batter NOUN
la masa para rebozar

battery NOUN
1 la pila *(for torch, toy)*
2 la batería *(for car)*

battle NOUN
la batalla
□ the Battle of Hastings la batalla de Hastings
■ **It was a battle, but we managed in the end.** Fue muy difícil, pero al final lo conseguimos.

battleship NOUN
el acorazado

bay NOUN
la bahía

BC ABBREVIATION *(= before Christ)*
a.C. *(= antes de Cristo)*

to **be** VERB

> LANGUAGE TIP There are two basic verbs to translate 'be' into Spanish: **estar** and **ser**. **estar** is used to form continuous tenses; to talk about where something is; and with adjectives describing a temporary state. It is also used with past participles used adjectivally even if these describe a permanent state.

1 estar*
□ What are you doing? ¿Qué estás haciendo? □ Edinburgh is in Scotland. Edimburgo está en Escocia. □ I've never been to Madrid. No he estado nunca en Madrid. □ I'm very happy. Estoy muy contento. □ The window is broken. La ventana está rota. □ Is he hurt? ¿Está herido? □ He's dead. Está muerto.
■ **You're late.** Llegas tarde.

> LANGUAGE TIP **ser** is used to talk about the time and date; with adjectives describing permanent or inherent states such as nationality and colour; with nouns to say what somebody or something is; and to form the passive.

2 ser*
□ It's four o'clock. Son las cuatro. □ It's the 28th of October today. Hoy es 28 de octubre. □ She's English. Es inglesa. □ He's a doctor. Es médico. □ Paris is the capital of France. París es la capital de Francia. □ He's very tall. Es muy alto. □ The house was destroyed by an earthquake. La casa fue destruida por un terremoto.

LANGUAGE TIP Passive constructions are not as common in Spanish as in English. Either the active or a reflexive construction are preferred.

□ He was killed by a terrorist. Lo mató un terrorista. □ These cars are produced in Spain. Estos coches se fabrican en España.

LANGUAGE TIP When referring to the weather, use **hacer**.

□ It's a nice day, isn't it? Hace buen día, ¿verdad? □ It's cold. Hace frío. □ It's too hot. Hace demasiado calor.

LANGUAGE TIP With certain adjectives, such as 'cold', 'hot', 'hungry', and 'thirsty', use **tener*** with a noun.

□ I'm cold. Tengo frío. □ I'm hungry. Tengo hambre.

LANGUAGE TIP When saying how old somebody is, use **tener***.

□ I'm fourteen. Tengo catorce años. □ How old are you? ¿Cuántos años tienes?

beach NOUN
la playa

bead NOUN
la cuenta

beak NOUN
el pico

beam NOUN
el rayo *(of light)*

beans PL NOUN
las alubias
■ **beans on toast** las alubias blancas en salsa de tomate sobre una tostada

bear NOUN
▷ *see also* **bear** VERB
el oso

to **bear** VERB
▷ *see also* **bear** NOUN
aguantar
□ I can't bear it! ¡No lo aguanto!

beard NOUN
la barba
□ a man with a beard un hombre con barba
■ **He's got a beard.** Lleva barba.

bearded ADJECTIVE
con barba (FEM con barba)

beat NOUN
▷ *see also* **beat** VERB
el ritmo

to **beat** VERB
▷ *see also* **beat** NOUN
ganar
□ We beat them three-nil. Les ganamos tres a cero.
■ **Beat it!** ¡Lárgate! *(informal)*

beautiful ADJECTIVE
precioso (FEM preciosa)

beauty NOUN
la belleza

beauty spot NOUN
el lugar pintoresco *(place)*

became VERB ▷ *see* **become**

because CONJUNCTION
porque
■ **because of** a causa de □ because of the weather por culpa del mal tiempo

to **become** VERB
llegar* a ser

bed NOUN
la cama
■ **to go to bed** acostarse
■ **to go to bed with somebody** irse a la cama con alguien

bed and breakfast NOUN
la pensión (PL las pensiones)
□ We stayed in a bed and breakfast. Nos quedamos en una pensión.
■ **How much is it for bed and breakfast?** ¿Cuánto es la habitación con desayuno?

bedclothes PL NOUN
la ropa de cama

bedding NOUN
la ropa de cama

bedroom NOUN
el dormitorio
■ **a three-bedroom house** una casa de tres dormitorios

bedsit NOUN
el cuarto de alquiler

bedspread NOUN
la colcha

bedtime NOUN
■ **Ten o'clock is my usual bedtime.** Normalmente me voy a la cama a las diez.
■ **Bedtime!** ¡A la cama!

bee NOUN
la abeja

beef NOUN
la carne de vaca
■ **roast beef** el rosbif

beefburger NOUN
la hamburguesa

been VERB ▷ *see* **be**

beer NOUN
la cerveza

beetle NOUN
el escarabajo

English-Spanish

b

beetroot NOUN
la remolacha

before PREPOSITION, CONJUNCTION, ADVERB
1 antes de
□ before Tuesday antes del martes □ Before opening the packet, read the instructions. Antes de abrir el paquete, lea las instrucciones. □ I'll phone before I leave. Llamaré antes de salir.
2 antes de que
LANGUAGE TIP **antes de que** has to be followed by a verb in the subjunctive.
□ I'll call her before she leaves. La llamaré antes de que se vaya.
■ **I've seen this film before.** Esta película ya la he visto.
■ **the week before** la semana anterior

beforehand ADVERB
con antelación

to **beg** VERB
1 mendigar* *(for money, food)*
2 suplicar*
LANGUAGE TIP **suplicar que** has to be followed by a verb in the subjunctive.
□ He begged me to stop. Me suplicó que parara.

began VERB ▷ *see* **begin**

beggar NOUN
el mendigo
la mendiga

to **begin** VERB
empezar*
■ **to begin doing something** empezar a hacer algo

beginner NOUN
el/la principiante

beginning NOUN
el comienzo
■ **in the beginning** al principio

begun VERB ▷ *see* **begin**

behalf NOUN
■ **on behalf of somebody** de parte de alguien

to **behave** VERB
comportarse
□ He behaved like an idiot. Se comportó como un idiota.
■ **to behave oneself** portarse bien □ Did the children behave themselves? ¿Se portaron bien los niños?
■ **Behave!** ¡Compórtate!

behaviour (US **behavior**) NOUN
el comportamiento

behind PREPOSITION, ADVERB
▷ *see also* **behind** NOUN
detrás de
□ behind the television detrás de la televisión
■ **to be behind** *(late)* ir atrasado □ I'm behind with my work. Voy atrasado con mi trabajo.

behind NOUN
▷ *see also* **behind** PREPOSITION, ADVERB
el trasero

beige ADJECTIVE
beige (FEM + PL beige)
LANGUAGE TIP Pronounce this word like the English word 'base'.

Belgian ADJECTIVE
▷ *see also* **Belgian** NOUN
belga (FEM belga)
□ He's Belgian. Es belga.

Belgian NOUN
▷ *see also* **Belgian** ADJECTIVE
el/la belga
□ the Belgians los belgas

Belgium NOUN
Bélgica *fem*

to **believe** VERB
creer*
□ I don't believe you. No te creo.
■ **I don't believe it!** ¡No me lo creo!
■ **to believe in something** creer en algo
□ Do you believe in ghosts? ¿Crees en los fantasmas?

bell NOUN
1 el timbre *(of door, in school)*
□ The bell goes at half past three. El timbre suena a las tres y media.
2 la campana *(of church)*
□ the church bell la campana de la iglesia
3 el cascabel *(of toy, on animal)*
□ Our cat has a bell on its collar. Nuestro gato lleva un cascabel en el collar.

belly NOUN
la barriga

to **belong** VERB
■ **to belong to somebody** pertenecer a alguien □ This ring belonged to my grandmother. Este anillo pertenecía a mi abuela.
■ **Who does it belong to?** ¿De quién es?
■ **That belongs to me.** Eso es mío.
■ **Do you belong to any clubs?** ¿Eres miembro de algún club?
■ **Where does this belong?** ¿Dónde va esto?

belongings PL NOUN
■ **I collected my belongings.** Recogí mis cosas.
■ **personal belongings** los efectos personales

below PREPOSITION, ADVERB
1 debajo de
□ the apartment directly below ours el apartamento que está justo debajo del nuestro

2 abajo
□ seen from below visto desde abajo □ on the floor below en el piso de abajo
■ **ten degrees below freezing** diez grados bajo cero

belt NOUN
el cinturón (PL los cinturones)

beltway NOUN (US)
la carretera de circunvalación

bench NOUN
el banco

bend NOUN
▷ *see also* **bend** VERB
la curva

to **bend** VERB
▷ *see also* **bend** NOUN
1 doblar
□ I can't bend my arm. No puedo doblar el brazo.
2 torcerse*
□ It bends easily. Se tuerce fácilmente.

to **bend down** VERB
agacharse

to **bend over** VERB
inclinarse

beneath PREPOSITION
bajo

benefit NOUN
▷ *see also* **benefit** VERB
el beneficio
■ **state benefits** los subsidios estatales

to **benefit** VERB
▷ *see also* **benefit** NOUN
beneficiar
□ This will benefit us all. Esto nos beneficiará a todos.
■ **He'll benefit from the change.** Se beneficiará con el cambio.

bent VERB ▷ *see* **bend**

bent ADJECTIVE
torcido (FEM torcida)
□ a bent fork un tenedor torcido
■ **to be bent on doing something** estar empeñado en hacer algo

beret NOUN
la boina

berserk ADJECTIVE
■ **to go berserk** ponerse hecho una fiera

berth NOUN
la litera *(bunk)*

beside PREPOSITION
al lado de
□ beside the television al lado de la televisión
■ **He was beside himself.** Estaba fuera de sí.
■ **That's beside the point.** Eso no viene al caso.

besides ADVERB
además
□ Besides, it's too expensive. Además, es demasiado caro.
■ **... and much more besides.** ... y mucho más todavía.

best ADJECTIVE, ADVERB
mejor (FEM mejor)
□ He's the best player in the team. Es el mejor jugador del equipo. □ Janet's the best at maths. Janet es la mejor en matemáticas. □ Emma sings best. Emma es la que canta mejor.
■ **That's the best I can do.** No puedo hacer más.
■ **to do one's best** hacer todo lo posible
□ It's not perfect, but I did my best. No es perfecto, pero he hecho todo lo posible.
■ **You'll just have to make the best of it.** Tendrás que arreglártelas con lo que hay.

best man NOUN
el padrino de boda

bet NOUN
▷ *see also* **bet** VERB
la apuesta

to **bet** VERB
▷ *see also* **bet** NOUN
apostar*
□ I bet you he won't come. Te apuesto a que no viene.

to **betray** VERB
traicionar

better ADJECTIVE, ADVERB
mejor (FEM mejor)
□ This one's better than that one. Éste es mejor que aquél. □ Are you feeling better now? ¿Te sientes mejor ahora?
■ **That's better!** ¡Así está mejor!
■ **better still** mejor todavía
■ **to get better 1** *(improve)* mejorar □ I hope the weather gets better soon. Espero que el tiempo mejore pronto. **2** *(from illness)* mejorarse □ I hope you get better soon. Espero que te mejores pronto.
■ **You'd better do it straight away.** Más vale hacerlo enseguida.
■ **I'd better go home.** Tengo que irme a casa.

betting shop NOUN
la casa de apuestas

between PREPOSITION
entre
□ between 15 and 20 minutes entre 15 y 20 minutos

bewildered ADJECTIVE
desconcertado (FEM desconcertada)

beyond PREPOSITION, ADVERB
al otro lado de

English-Spanish

b

□ There is a lake beyond the mountains. Hay un lago al otro lado de las montañas.
■ **We have no plans beyond the year 2009.** No tenemos planes para después del año 2009.
■ **the wheat fields and the mountains beyond** los campos de trigo y las montañas al fondo
■ **It's beyond me.** No lo entiendo.
■ **beyond belief** increíble
■ **beyond repair** irreparable

biased ADJECTIVE
parcial (FEM parcial)

Bible NOUN
la Biblia

bicycle NOUN
la bicicleta

bifocals PL NOUN
las gafas bifocales

big ADJECTIVE
grande (FEM grande)
□ a big house una casa grande □ a big car un coche grande

LANGUAGE TIP Use **gran** before a singular noun.

□ It's a big business. Es un gran negocio.

WORD POWER
You can use a number of other words instead of **big** to mean 'large':
enormous enorme
□ an enormous cake un pastel enorme
gigantic gigantesco
□ a gigantic house una casa gigantesca
huge enorme
□ a huge garden un jardín enorme
immense inmenso
□ an immense room una habitación inmensa

■ **my big brother** mi hermano mayor
■ **He's a big guy.** Es un tipo grandote.
■ **Big deal!** ¡Vaya cosa!

bigheaded ADJECTIVE
■ **to be bigheaded** ser engreído

bike NOUN
1 la bici *(bicycle)*
□ by bike en bici
2 la moto *(motorbike)*

LANGUAGE TIP Although **moto** ends in **-o**, it is actually a feminine noun.

bikini NOUN
el bikini

bilingual ADJECTIVE
bilingüe (FEM bilingüe)

bill NOUN
1 la cuenta *(in restaurant)*
□ Can we have the bill, please? ¿Nos trae la cuenta, por favor?
2 la factura *(for gas, electricity, telephone)*
□ the gas bill la factura del gas
3 el billete (US)
□ a five-dollar bill un billete de cinco dólares

billiards NOUN
el billar
□ to play billiards jugar al billar

billion NOUN
los mil millones
□ two billion dollars dos mil millones de dólares

bin NOUN
1 el cubo de la basura *(in kitchen)*
2 la papelera *(for paper)*

bingo NOUN
el bingo

binoculars PL NOUN
los prismáticos
□ a pair of binoculars unos prismáticos

biochemistry NOUN
la bioquímica

biography NOUN
la biografía

biology NOUN
la biología

bird NOUN
el pájaro

birdwatching NOUN
■ **He likes to go birdwatching on Sundays.** Los domingos le gusta ir a ver pájaros.

Biro® NOUN
el bolígrafo

birth NOUN
el nacimiento
□ date of birth la fecha de nacimiento

birth certificate NOUN
la partida de nacimiento

birth control NOUN
el control de natalidad

birthday NOUN
el cumpleaños (PL los cumpleaños)
□ a birthday cake un pastel de cumpleaños
□ a birthday card una tarjeta de cumpleaños
□ a birthday party una fiesta de cumpleaños
□ When's your birthday? ¿Cuándo es tu cumpleaños?

biscuit NOUN
la galleta

bishop NOUN
el obispo

bit VERB ▷ *see* **bite**

bit NOUN
el trozo
□ Would you like another bit? ¿Quieres otro trozo?
■ **a bit** un poco □ He's a bit mad. Está un poco loco. □ Wait a bit! ¡Espera un poco!

■ **a bit of 1** un trozo de □ a bit of cake un trozo de pastel **2** un poco de □ a bit of music un poco de música
■ **It's a bit of a nuisance.** Es un poco fastidioso.
■ **to fall to bits** caerse a pedazos
■ **to take something to bits** desmontar algo
■ **bit by bit** poco a poco

bitch NOUN
1 la perra *(female dog)*
2 la bruja *(rude: woman)*

to **bite** VERB
▷ *see also* **bite** NOUN
1 morder* *(person, dog)*
□ My dog's never bitten anyone. Mi perro nunca ha mordido a nadie.
2 picar* *(insect)*
□ I got bitten by mosquitoes. Me picaron los mosquitos.
■ **to bite one's nails** morderse las uñas

bite NOUN
▷ *see also* **bite** VERB
1 la picadura *(insect bite)*
2 el mordisco *(animal bite)*
■ **to have a bite to eat** comer alguna cosa

bitter ADJECTIVE
1 amargo (FEM amarga)
□ It tastes bitter. Sabe amargo.
2 glacial (FEM glacial)
□ It's bitter today. Hoy hace un frío glacial.

black ADJECTIVE
negro (FEM negra)
□ a black jacket una chaqueta negra
□ She's black. Es negra.
■ **black and white** blanco y negro

blackberry NOUN
la mora

blackbird NOUN
el mirlo

blackboard NOUN
la pizarra

black coffee NOUN
el café solo

blackcurrant NOUN
la grosella negra

blackmail NOUN
▷ *see also* **blackmail** VERB
el chantaje

to **blackmail** VERB
▷ *see also* **blackmail** NOUN
chantajear

blackout NOUN
el apagón (PL los apagones) *(power cut)*
■ **to have a blackout** *(faint)* sufrir un desvanecimiento

black pudding NOUN
la morcilla

blade NOUN
la hoja

to **blame** VERB
echar la culpa a
□ Don't blame me! ¡No me eches la culpa a mí! □ He blamed it on my sister. Le echó la culpa a mi hermana.

blank ADJECTIVE
▷ *see also* **blank** NOUN
en blanco *(sheet of paper)*
■ **My mind went blank.** Me quedé en blanco.

blank cheque NOUN
el cheque en blanco

blanket NOUN
la manta

blast NOUN
■ **a bomb blast** una explosión

blatant ADJECTIVE
flagrante (FEM flagrante)

blaze NOUN
el incendio

blazer NOUN
el blazer (PL los blazers)

bleach NOUN
la lejía

bleak ADJECTIVE
poco prometedor (FEM poco prometedora)
□ The future looks bleak. Se presenta un futuro poco prometedor.

to **bleed** VERB
sangrar
■ **to bleed to death** morir desangrado
■ **My nose is bleeding.** Me sangra la nariz.

bleeper NOUN
el busca
LANGUAGE TIP Although **busca** ends in **-a**, it is actually a masculine noun.

blender NOUN
la licuadora

to **bless** VERB
bendecir*
■ **Bless you!** *(after sneezing)* ¡Jesús! (¡Salud! *Latin America*)

blew VERB ▷ *see* **blow**

blind ADJECTIVE
▷ *see also* **blind** NOUN
ciego (FEM ciega)

blind NOUN
▷ *see also* **blind** ADJECTIVE
la persiana *(for window)*

blindfold NOUN
▷ *see also* **blindfold** VERB
la venda

to **blindfold** VERB
▷ *see also* **blindfold** NOUN
■ **to blindfold somebody** vendar los ojos a alguien

to **blink** VERB
parpadear

bliss NOUN
■ **It was bliss!** ¡Era la gloria!

blister NOUN
la ampolla

blizzard NOUN
la ventisca de nieve

blob NOUN
la gota
□ a blob of glue una gota de pegamento

block NOUN
▹ *see also* **block** VERB
el bloque
□ He lives in our block. Vive en nuestro bloque. □ a block of flats un bloque de apartamentos

to **block** VERB
▹ *see also* **block** NOUN
bloquear

blockage NOUN
la obstrucción (PL las obstrucciones)

bloke NOUN
el tío *(informal)*

blonde ADJECTIVE
rubio (FEM rubia)
□ She's got blonde hair. Tiene el pelo rubio.

blood NOUN
la sangre

blood pressure NOUN
la presión sanguínea
■ **to have high blood pressure** tener la tensión alta

blood sports PL NOUN
los deportes sangrientos

blood test NOUN
el análisis de sangre (PL los análisis de sangre)

bloody ADJECTIVE
■ **that bloody television** esa maldita televisión
■ **Bloody hell!** ¡Me cago en la mar!
■ **The exam was bloody difficult.** El examen fue difícil con ganas.

blouse NOUN
la blusa

blow NOUN
▹ *see also* **blow** VERB
el golpe

to **blow** VERB
▹ *see also* **blow** NOUN
soplar
□ A cold wind was blowing. Soplaba un viento frío. □ He blew on his fingers. Se sopló los dedos.
■ **They were one-all when the whistle blew.** Iban uno a uno cuando sonó el pito.
■ **to blow one's nose** sonarse la nariz

to **blow up** VERB
1 volar*
□ They blew up a plane. Volaron un avión.
2 inflar
□ We've blown up the balloons. Hemos inflado los globos.
3 saltar por los aires
□ The house blew up. La casa saltó por los aires.

blow-dry NOUN
el secado con secador de mano
■ **A cut and blow-dry, please.** Un corte y un secado a mano, por favor.

blue ADJECTIVE
azul (FEM azul)
□ a blue dress un vestido azul
■ **a blue movie** una película porno
■ **out of the blue** en el momento menos pensado

blues PL NOUN
el blues (PL los blues) *(music)*

to **bluff** VERB
▹ *see also* **bluff** NOUN
farolear

bluff NOUN
▹ *see also* **bluff** VERB
el farol

blunder NOUN
la metedura de pata

blunt ADJECTIVE
1 directo (FEM directa) *(person)*
2 desafilado (FEM desafilada) *(knife)*

to **blush** VERB
ruborizarse*

board NOUN
1 la tabla *(plank)*
2 la pizarra *(blackboard)*
3 el tablón de anuncios (PL los tablones de anuncios) *(noticeboard)*
4 el trampolín (PL los trampolines) *(for diving)*
5 el tablero *(for games)*
■ **on board** a bordo
■ **'full board'** 'pensión completa'

boarder NOUN
el interno
la interna

board game NOUN
el juego de mesa

boarding card NOUN
la tarjeta de embarque

boarding school NOUN
el internado

to **boast** VERB
alardear
□ to boast about something alardear de algo
■ **Stop boasting!** ¡Deja ya de presumir!

boat NOUN
el barco

body NOUN
1 el cuerpo
□ the human body el cuerpo humano
2 el cadáver *(corpse)*
bodybuilding NOUN
el culturismo
bodyguard NOUN
el guardaespaldas (PL los guardaespaldas)
□ He's a bodyguard. Es guardaespaldas.
bog NOUN
la ciénaga *(marsh)*
boil NOUN
▷ *see also* **boil** VERB
el furúnculo
to **boil** VERB
▷ *see also* **boil** NOUN
hervir*
□ to boil some water hervir un poco de agua
□ The water's boiling. El agua está hirviendo.
■ **to boil an egg** cocer un huevo
to **boil over** VERB
salirse*
boiled ADJECTIVE
hervido (FEM hervida)
■ **a boiled egg** un huevo pasado por agua
boiling ADJECTIVE
■ **It's boiling in here!** ¡Aquí dentro se asa uno!
■ **a boiling hot day** un día asfixiante de calor
bolt NOUN
1 el cerrojo *(on door, window)*
2 el tornillo *(type of screw)*
bomb NOUN
▷ *see also* **bomb** VERB
la bomba
to **bomb** VERB
▷ *see also* **bomb** NOUN
bombardear
bomber NOUN
el bombardero *(plane)*
bombing NOUN
el bombardeo
bond NOUN
el vínculo
□ the bond between mother and child el vínculo entre la madre y el hijo
bone NOUN
1 el hueso *(of human, animal)*
2 la espina *(of fish)*
bone dry ADJECTIVE
completamente seco (FEM completamente seca)
bonfire NOUN
la hoguera
bonnet NOUN
el capó *(of car)*
bonus NOUN
1 el plus *(extra payment)*
2 la ventaja *(added advantage)*
book NOUN
▷ *see also* **book** VERB
el libro
to **book** VERB
▷ *see also* **book** NOUN
reservar
■ **We haven't booked.** No hemos hecho reserva.
bookcase NOUN
la librería
booklet NOUN
el folleto
bookmark NOUN
el marcador *(book, computer)*
bookshelf NOUN
la estantería
bookshop NOUN
la librería
to **boost** VERB
■ **The win boosted the team's morale.** La victoria levantó la moral del equipo.
■ **They're trying to boost the economy.** Intentan dar un empuje a la economía.
boot NOUN
1 el maletero *(of car)*
2 la bota *(fashion boots)*
3 el borceguí (PL los borceguíes) *(for hiking)*
booze NOUN
la bebida
border NOUN
la frontera
bore VERB ▷ *see* **bear**
bored ADJECTIVE
aburrido (FEM aburrida)
□ to be bored estar aburrido
■ **to get bored** aburrirse
boredom NOUN
el aburrimiento
boring ADJECTIVE
aburrido (FEM aburrida)
□ It's boring. Es aburrido.
born ADJECTIVE
■ **to be born** nacer □ I was born in 1992. Nací en 1992.
to **borrow** VERB
pedir* prestado
■ **to borrow something from somebody** pedir algo prestado a alguien □ I borrowed some money from a friend. Le pedí dinero prestado a un amigo.
■ **Can I borrow your pen?** ¿Me prestas el bolígrafo?
Bosnia NOUN
la Bosnia
Bosnian ADJECTIVE
bosnio (FEM bosnia)

boss NOUN
el jefe
la jefa

to **boss around** VERB
■ **to boss somebody around** mandonear a alguien

bossy ADJECTIVE
mandón (FEM mandona, PL mandones)

both ADJECTIVE, PRONOUN, ADVERB
los dos (FEM los dosa)
□ We both went. Fuimos los dos. □ Both of your answers are wrong. Tus respuestas están las dos mal. □ Both of them play the piano. Los dos tocan el piano.
■ **Both Emma and Jane went.** Fueron Emma y Jane.
■ **He has houses in both France and in Spain.** Tiene casas tanto en Francia como en España.

to **bother** VERB
1 preocupar *(worry)*
□ What's bothering you? ¿Qué es lo que te preocupa?
2 molestar *(disturb)*
□ I'm sorry to bother you. Siento molestarle.
■ **Don't bother!** ¡No te preocupes!
■ **to bother to do something** tomarse la molestia de hacer algo □ He didn't bother to tell me about it. Ni se tomó la molestia de decírmelo.

bottle NOUN
la botella

bottle bank NOUN
el contenedor del vidrio

bottle-opener NOUN
el abrebotellas (PL los abrebotellas)

bottom NOUN
▹ *see also* **bottom** ADJECTIVE
1 el fondo *(of container, bag, sea)*
■ **at the bottom of the page** al final de la página
■ **He was always bottom of the class.** Siempre era el último de la clase.
2 el trasero *(buttocks)*

bottom ADJECTIVE
▹ *see also* **bottom** NOUN
de abajo
□ the bottom shelf el estante de abajo

bought VERB ▹ *see* **buy**

to **bounce** VERB
rebotar

bouncer NOUN
el gorila

LANGUAGE TIP Although **gorila** ends in **-a**, it is actually a masculine noun.

bound ADJECTIVE
■ **He's bound to fail.** Seguro que suspende.
■ **She's bound to come.** Es seguro que vendrá.

boundary NOUN
el límite

bow NOUN
▹ *see also* **bow** VERB
1 el lazo *(knot)*
□ to tie a bow hacer un lazo
2 el arco
□ a bow and arrow un arco y flecha

to **bow** VERB
▹ *see also* **bow** NOUN
hacer* una reverencia

bowels PL NOUN
los intestinos

bowl NOUN
▹ *see also* **bowl** VERB
1 el tazón (PL los tazones) *(for soup, cereals)*
2 el cuenco *(for cooking, mixing food)*

to **bowl** VERB
▹ *see also* **bowl** NOUN
lanzar* la pelota

bowler NOUN
el lanzador
la lanzadora

bowling NOUN
los bolos
■ **to go bowling** jugar a los bolos
■ **a bowling alley** una bolera

bowls PL NOUN
los bolos

bow tie NOUN
la pajarita

box NOUN
1 la caja
□ a box of matches una caja de cerillas
■ **a cardboard box** una caja de cartón
2 la casilla *(on form)*

boxer NOUN
el boxeador

boxer shorts PL NOUN
los bóxers
□ a pair of boxer shorts unos bóxers

boxing NOUN
el boxeo

Boxing Day NOUN
el 26 de diciembre

boy NOUN
1 el muchacho *(young man)*
□ a boy of fifteen un muchacho de quince años
2 el niño *(child)*
□ a boy of seven un niño de siete años
■ **She has two boys and a girl.** Tiene dos niños y una niña.
■ **a baby boy** un niño

boyfriend NOUN
el novio

□ Have you got a boyfriend? ¿Tienes novio?

bra NOUN
el sostén (PL los sostenes)

brace NOUN
el aparato *(on teeth)*
□ Richard wears a brace. Richard lleva un aparato.

bracelet NOUN
la pulsera

brackets PL NOUN
■ **in brackets** entre paréntesis

brain NOUN
el cerebro

brainy ADJECTIVE
inteligente (FEM inteligente)

brake NOUN
▹ *see also* **brake** VERB
el freno

to **brake** VERB
▹ *see also* **brake** NOUN
frenar

branch NOUN
1 la rama *(of tree)*
2 la sucursal *(of bank)*

brand NOUN
la marca
□ a well-known brand of coffee una marca de café muy conocida

brand name NOUN
la marca

brand-new ADJECTIVE
flamante (FEM flamante)

brandy NOUN
el coñac (PL los coñacs)

brass NOUN
el latón *(metal)*
■ **the brass section** los bronces

brass band NOUN
la banda de música

brat NOUN
el mocoso
la mocosa
□ He's a spoiled brat. Es un mocoso consentido.

brave ADJECTIVE
valiente (FEM valiente)

Brazil NOUN
el Brasil

bread NOUN
el pan
□ bread and butter el pan con mantequilla

break NOUN
▹ *see also* **break** VERB
1 la pausa *(rest)*
□ to take a break hacer una pausa
2 el recreo *(at school)*
■ **the Christmas break** las vacaciones de Navidad
■ **Give me a break!** ¡Déjame en paz!

to **break** VERB
▹ *see also* **break** NOUN
1 romper*
□ Careful, you'll break something! ¡Cuidado, que vas a romper algo!
■ **I broke my leg.** Me rompí la pierna.
2 romperse*
□ Careful, it'll break! ¡Ten cuidado, que se va a romper!
■ **to break a promise** faltar a una promesa
■ **to break a record** batir un récord

to **break down** VERB
averiarse*
■ **The car broke down.** El coche se averió.

to **break in** VERB
■ **The thief had broken in through a window.** El ladrón había entrado por una ventana.

to **break off** VERB
desprenderse *(come free)*

to **break out** VERB
1 estallar *(war)*
2 desencadenarse *(fire, fighting)*
3 escaparse *(prisoner)*
■ **He broke out in a rash.** Le salió un sarpullido.

to **break up** VERB
1 disolver*
□ Police broke up the demonstration. La policía disolvió la demostración.
2 dispersarse *(crowd)*
3 fracasar *(marriage)*
□ More and more marriages break up. Cada día fracasan más matrimonios.
4 romper* *(two lovers)*
□ Richard and Marie have broken up. Richard y Marie han roto.
■ **to break up a fight** poner fin a una pelea
■ **We break up next Wednesday.** El miércoles que viene empezamos las vacaciones.
■ **You're breaking up.** *(mobile phone)* No hay cobertura.

breakdown NOUN
1 la crisis nerviosa (PL las crisis nerviosas)
□ He had a breakdown because of the stress. Sufrió una crisis nerviosa debida al estrés.
2 la avería *(in vehicle)*
□ to have a breakdown tener una avería

breakdown van NOUN
la grúa

breakfast NOUN
el desayuno
■ **to have breakfast** desayunar

break-in NOUN
■ **There have been a lot of break-ins in**

my area. Han entrado a robar en muchas casas de mi barrio.

breast NOUN
el pecho
■ **chicken breast** la pechuga de pollo

to **breast-feed** VERB
amamantar

breaststroke NOUN
la braza

breath NOUN
el aliento
□ He's got bad breath. Tiene mal aliento.
■ **I'm out of breath.** Estoy sin aliento.
■ **to get one's breath back** recobrar el aliento

to **breathe** VERB
respirar

to **breathe in** VERB
aspirar

to **breathe out** VERB
espirar

to **breed** VERB
▹ *see also* **breed** NOUN
reproducirse* *(reproduce)*
■ **to breed dogs** criar perros

breed NOUN
▹ *see also* **breed** VERB
la raza

breeze NOUN
la brisa

brewery NOUN
la fábrica de cerveza

to **bribe** VERB
sobornar

brick NOUN
el ladrillo

bricklayer NOUN
el albañil
□ He's a bricklayer. Es albañil.

bride NOUN
la novia

bridegroom NOUN
el novio

bridesmaid NOUN
la dama de honor

bridge NOUN
1 el puente
2 el bridge *(card game)*
□ to play bridge jugar al bridge

brief ADJECTIVE
breve (FEM breve)

briefcase NOUN
el maletín (PL los maletines)

briefly ADVERB
brevemente

briefs PL NOUN
los calzoncillos
□ a pair of briefs unos calzoncillos

bright ADJECTIVE
1 vivo (FEM viva)
□ a bright colour un color vivo □ bright red rojo vivo
2 brillante (FEM brillante) *(light)*
3 listo (FEM lista)
□ He's not very bright. No es muy listo.

brilliant ADJECTIVE
1 estupendo (FEM estupenda)
■ **We had a brilliant time!** ¡Lo pasamos estupendo!
2 genial (FEM genial)
□ a brilliant scientist un científico genial

to **bring** VERB
traer*
□ Bring warm clothes. Trae ropa de abrigo.
□ Can I bring a friend? ¿Puedo traer a un amigo?

to **bring back** VERB
devolver* *(book)*
■ **That song brings back memories.** Esa canción me trae recuerdos.

to **bring forward** VERB
adelantar
□ The meeting was brought forward. La reunión se adelantó.

to **bring up** VERB
criar*
□ She brought up five children on her own. Crió a cinco hijos ella sola.

Britain NOUN
la Gran Bretaña

British ADJECTIVE
británico (FEM británica)
■ **the British** los británicos
■ **the British Isles** las Islas Británicas
■ **She's British.** Es británica.

broad ADJECTIVE
ancho (FEM ancha)
■ **in broad daylight** a plena luz del día

broadband NOUN
la banda ancha

broadcast NOUN
▹ *see also* **broadcast** VERB
la emisión (PL las emisiones)

to **broadcast** VERB
▹ *see also* **broadcast** NOUN
emitir
□ The interview was broadcast all over the world. La entrevista se emitió a todo el mundo.
■ **to broadcast live** emitir en directo

broad-minded ADJECTIVE
■ **He's very broad-minded.** Tiene una mentalidad muy abierta.

broccoli NOUN
el brécol

brochure NOUN
el folleto

to **broil** VERB (US)
1 hacer* al grill *(in cooker)*
2 asar a la parrilla *(barbecue)*
broke VERB ▷ *see* **break**
broke ADJECTIVE
■ **to be broke** estar sin blanca *(informal)*
broken ADJECTIVE
roto (FEM rota)
□ It's broken. Está roto. □ He's got a broken arm. Tiene un brazo roto.
bronchitis NOUN
la bronquitis
bronze NOUN
el bronce
□ the bronze medal la medalla de bronce
brooch NOUN
el broche
broom NOUN
la escoba
brother NOUN
el hermano
brother-in-law NOUN
el cuñado
brought VERB ▷ *see* **bring**
brown ADJECTIVE
1 marrón (FEM marrón, PL marrones) *(clothes)*
2 castaño (FEM castaña) *(hair, eyes)*
3 moreno (FEM morena) *(tanned)*
■ **brown bread** el pan integral
Brownie NOUN
la guía
to **browse** VERB
navegar *(on internet)*
browser NOUN
el navegador
bruise NOUN
el moretón (PL los moretones)
brush NOUN
▷ *see also* **brush** VERB
1 el cepillo *(for hair, teeth)*
2 el pincel *(paintbrush)*
to **brush** VERB
▷ *see also* **brush** NOUN
cepillar
■ **to brush one's hair** cepillarse el pelo
■ **to brush one's teeth** cepillarse los dientes □ I brush my teeth every night. Me cepillo los dientes todas las noches.
Brussels NOUN
la Bruselas
Brussels sprouts PL NOUN
las coles de Bruselas
brutal ADJECTIVE
brutal (FEM brutal)
BSc ABBREVIATION (= *Bachelor of Science*)
la licenciatura en Ciencias
■ **a BSc in Mathematics** una licenciatura en Matemáticas
■ **She's got a BSc in Chemistry.** Es licenciada en Química.
bubble NOUN
1 la pompa *(of soap)*
2 la burbuja *(of air, gas)*
bubble bath NOUN
el baño de espuma
bubble gum NOUN
el chicle
bucket NOUN
el cubo
buckle NOUN
la hebilla *(on belt, watch, shoe)*
Buddhism NOUN
el budismo
Buddhist ADJECTIVE
budista (FEM budista)
buddy NOUN (US)
el amiguete
la amigueta
budget NOUN
el presupuesto
budgie NOUN
el periquito
buffet NOUN
el buffet
buffet car NOUN
el coche restaurante
bug NOUN
1 el insecto *(insect)*
2 el virus (PL los virus) *(illness, in computer)*
□ There's a bug going round. Hay un virus en el ambiente.
■ **a stomach bug** una gastroenteritis
bugged ADJECTIVE
■ **The phone was bugged.** El teléfono estaba pinchado.
to **build** VERB
construir*
□ They're going to build houses here. Van a construir viviendas aquí.
to **build up** VERB
1 acumular
□ He has built up a huge collection of stamps. Ha ido acumulando una gran colección de sellos.
2 acumularse
□ Our debts are building up. Nuestras deudas se están acumulando.
builder NOUN
1 el/la contratista *(contractor)*
2 el albañil *(worker)*
building NOUN
el edificio
built VERB ▷ *see* **build**
bulb NOUN
1 la bombilla *(electric)*
2 el bulbo *(of flower)*

English-Spanish

b

bull NOUN
el toro

bullet NOUN
la bala

bulletin board NOUN
el tablón de noticias

bullfighting NOUN
■ **Do you like bullfighting?** ¿Te gustan los toros?

bully NOUN
▹ *see also* **bully** VERB
el matón (PL los matones)
□ He's a bully. Es un matón.

to **bully** VERB
▹ *see also* **bully** NOUN
intimidar

bum NOUN
el culo *(informal)*

bum bag NOUN
la riñonera

bump NOUN
▹ *see also* **bump** VERB
1 el chichón (PL los chichones) *(on head)*
2 el bulto *(on surface)*
3 el bache *(on road)*
4 el golpe *(minor accident)*
□ We had a bump. Nos dimos un golpe.

to **bump** VERB
▹ *see also* **bump** NOUN
□ I bumped my head on the wall. Me di con la cabeza en la pared.

bumper NOUN
el parachoques (PL los parachoques)

bumpy ADJECTIVE
lleno de baches (FEM llena de baches) *(road)*

bun NOUN
el bollo *(bread)*

bunch NOUN
■ **a bunch of flowers** un ramo de flores
■ **a bunch of grapes** un racimo de uvas
■ **a bunch of keys** un manojo de llaves

bunches PL NOUN
las coletas
□ She has her hair in bunches. Lleva coletas.

bungalow NOUN
el bungalow

bunk NOUN
la litera

burger NOUN
la hamburguesa

burglar NOUN
el ladrón (PL los ladrones)
la ladrona

to **burglarize** VERB (US)
entrar a robar en

burglary NOUN
el robo *(con allanamiento de morada)*

to **burgle** VERB
entrar a robar en
□ Her house was burgled. Le entraron a robar en casa.

burn NOUN
▹ *see also* **burn** VERB
la quemadura

to **burn** VERB
▹ *see also* **burn** NOUN
quemar *(rubbish, documents)*
□ I burned the rubbish. Quemé la basura.
■ **I burned the cake.** Se me quemó el pastel.
■ **to burn oneself** quemarse
■ **I've burned my hand.** Me quemé la mano.

to **burn down** VERB
quedar reducido a cenizas
□ The factory burned down. La fábrica quedó reducida a cenizas.

to **burst** VERB
reventarse*
□ The balloon burst. El globo se reventó.
■ **to burst a balloon** reventar un globo
■ **to burst out laughing** echarse a reír
■ **to burst into tears** romper a llorar
■ **to burst into flames** incendiarse

to **bury** VERB
enterrar*

bus NOUN
el autobús (PL los autobuses)
□ by bus en autobús
■ **the school bus** el autocar escolar
■ **a bus ticket** un billete de autobús

bush NOUN
el arbusto

business NOUN
1 el negocio *(firm)*
□ He's got his own business. Tiene su propio negocio.
2 los negocios
□ He's away on business. Está en un viaje de negocios.
■ **a business trip** un viaje de negocios
■ **It's none of my business.** No es asunto mío.

businessman NOUN
el hombre de negocios

businesswoman NOUN
la mujer de negocios

busker NOUN
el músico callejero
la música callejera

bus station NOUN
la estación de autobuses (PL las estaciones de autobuses)

bus stop NOUN
la parada de autobús

bust NOUN
el busto

busy ADJECTIVE
1 ocupado (FEM ocupada) *(person, telephone line)*
□ She's a very busy woman. Es una mujer muy ocupada.
2 ajetreado (FEM ajetreada) *(day, week)*
□ It's been a very busy day. Ha sido un día muy ajetreado.
3 concurrido (FEM concurrida) *(street, shop)*

busy signal NOUN (US)
la señal de comunicando

but PREPOSITION, CONJUNCTION
1 pero
□ I'd like to come, but I'm busy. Me gustaría venir, pero tengo trabajo.
2 sino
LANGUAGE TIP Use **sino** when you want to correct a previous negative statement.
□ He's not English but French. No es inglés sino francés.
3 menos
□ They won all but two of their matches. Ganaron todos los partidos menos dos.
■ **the last but one** el penúltimo

butcher NOUN
el carnicero
la carnicera
□ He's a butcher. Es carnicero.
■ **at the butcher's** en la carnicería

butter NOUN
la mantequilla

butterfly NOUN
la mariposa *(insect, swimming)*
□ Her favourite stroke is the butterfly. Su estilo favorito es mariposa.

buttocks PL NOUN
las nalgas

button NOUN
1 el botón (PL los botones)
2 la chapa (US: *metal, plastic)*

to **buy** VERB
▷ *see also* **buy** NOUN
comprar
□ He bought me an ice cream. Me compró un helado.
■ **to buy something from somebody** comprar algo a alguien □ I bought a watch from him. Le compré un reloj.

buy NOUN
▷ *see also* **buy** VERB
■ **It was a good buy.** Fue una buena compra.

by PREPOSITION
1 por
□ The thieves were caught by the police. Los ladrones fueron capturados por la policía.
2 de
□ a painting by Picasso un cuadro de Picasso
3 en
□ by car en coche
■ **by train** en tren
■ **by bus** en autobús
4 junto a
□ Where's the bank? — It's by the post office. ¿Dónde está el banco? — Está junto a la oficina de correos.
5 para
□ We have to be there by 4 o'clock. Tenemos que estar allí para las cuatro.
■ **by the time...** cuando □ By the time I got there it was too late. Cuando llegué allí ya era demasiado tarde. □ It'll be ready by the time you get back. Estará listo para cuando regreses.
■ **That's fine by me.** Por mí no hay problema.
■ **all by himself** él solo
■ **I did it all by myself.** Lo hice yo solo.
■ **by the way** a propósito

bye EXCLAMATION
¡adiós!

bypass NOUN
la carretera de circunvalación *(road)*

Cc

cab NOUN
el taxi
□ I'll go by cab. Iré en taxi.

cabbage NOUN
la berza

cabin NOUN
1 el camarote *(on ship)*
2 la cabina *(on aeroplane)*

cabinet NOUN
■ **a bathroom cabinet** un armario de cuarto de baño
■ **a drinks cabinet** un mueble-bar

cable NOUN
el cable

cable car NOUN
el teleférico

cable television NOUN
la televisión por cable

cadet NOUN
el/la cadete
□ a police cadet un cadete de policía

café NOUN
la cafetería

cage NOUN
la jaula

cagoule NOUN
el canguro *(chubasquero)*

cake NOUN
el pastel

to **calculate** VERB
calcular

calculation NOUN
el cálculo

calculator NOUN
la calculadora

calendar NOUN
el calendario

calf NOUN
1 el ternero *(of cow)*
2 la pantorrilla *(of leg)*

call NOUN
▷ *see also* **call** VERB
la llamada
□ Thanks for your call. Gracias por su llamada. □ a phone call una llamada telefónica
■ **to be on call** *(doctor)* estar de guardia

to **call** VERB
▷ *see also* **call** NOUN
llamar
□ We called the police. Llamamos a la policía. □ I'll tell him you called. Le diré que has llamado.
■ **to be called** llamarse □ He's called Fluffy. Se llama Fluffy. □ What's she called? ¿Cómo se llama?

to **call back** VERB
volver* a llamar
□ I'll call back later. Volveré a llamar más tarde.
■ **Can I call you back later?** ¿Puedo llamarte más tarde?

to **call for** VERB
1 pasar a recoger
□ Shall I call for you at seven thirty? ¿Paso a recogerte a las siete y media?
2 requerir*
□ This calls for strong nerves. Esto require unos nervios de acero.
■ **This calls for a drink!** ¡Esto hay que celebrarlo!

to **call off** VERB
suspender
□ The match was called off. El partido se suspendió.

call box NOUN
la cabina telefónica

call centre NOUN
el centro de atención al cliente

calm ADJECTIVE
tranquilo (FEM tranquila)

to **calm down** VERB
calmarse
□ Calm down! ¡Cálmate!

Calor gas® NOUN
el butano

calorie NOUN
la caloría

calves PL NOUN ▷ *see* **calf**

camcorder NOUN
la videocámara

came VERB ▷ *see* **come**

camel NOUN
el camello
camera NOUN
la cámara
cameraman NOUN
el cámara
camera phone NOUN
el teléfono con cámara
to camp VERB
▹ *see also* **camp** NOUN
acampar
camp NOUN
▹ *see also* **camp** VERB
el campamento
□ a summer camp un campamento de verano
■ **a refugee camp** un campo de refugiados
campaign NOUN
la campaña
camper NOUN
el/la campista
■ **a camper van** una caravana
camping NOUN
■ **to go camping** ir de camping
camping gas® NOUN
el camping gas®
campsite NOUN
el camping (PL los campings)
campus NOUN
el campus (PL los campus)
can NOUN
▹ *see also* **can** VERB
la lata
□ a can of peas una lata de guisantes
□ a can of beer una lata de cerveza
■ **a can of petrol** un bidón de gasolina
can VERB
▹ *see also* **can** NOUN
1 poder* *(be able to, be allowed to)*
□ Can I use your phone? ¿Puedo usar el teléfono? □ I can't do that. No puedo hacer eso. □ I'll do it as soon as I can. Lo haré tan pronto como pueda. □ That can't be true! ¡No puede ser cierto! □ You could hire a bike. Podrías alquilar una bici. □ He couldn't concentrate because of the noise. No se podía concentrar a causa del ruido.
2 saber* *(know how to)*
□ I can swim. Sé nadar. □ He can't drive. No sabe conducir.
LANGUAGE TIP 'can' is sometimes not translated.
□ I can't hear you. No te oigo. □ I can't remember. No me acuerdo. □ Can you speak French? ¿Hablas francés?
■ **You could be right.** Es posible que tengas razón.

Canada NOUN
el Canadá
Canadian ADJECTIVE
▹ *see also* **Canadian** NOUN
canadiense (FEM canadiense)
Canadian NOUN
▹ *see also* **Canadian** ADJECTIVE
el/la canadiense
canal NOUN
el canal
Canaries NOUN
■ **the Canaries** las Canarias
canary NOUN
el canario
■ **the Canary Islands** las islas Canarias
to cancel VERB
cancelar
□ I had to cancel my appointment. Tuve que cancelar la cita. □ Our flight was cancelled. Cancelaron nuestro vuelo.
cancellation NOUN
la cancelación (PL las cancelaciones)
Cancer NOUN
el Cáncer *(sign)*
■ I'm Cancer. Soy cáncer.
cancer NOUN
el cáncer
□ He's got cancer. Tiene cáncer.
candidate NOUN
el candidato
la candidata
candle NOUN
1 la vela
2 el cirio *(in church)*
candy NOUN (US)
los dulces
□ I love candy. Me encantan los dulces.
■ **a candy** un caramelo
candyfloss NOUN
el algodón de azúcar
cannabis NOUN
el canabis
canned ADJECTIVE
en lata *(food)*
cannot VERB = **can not**
canoe NOUN
la canoa
canoeing NOUN
■ **to go canoeing** hacer piragüismo □ We went canoeing. Fuimos a hacer piragüismo.
can-opener NOUN
el abrelatas (PL los abrelatas)
can't VERB = **can not**
canteen NOUN
la cantina
canvas NOUN
la lona
cap NOUN

1 el tapón (PL los tapones) *(of bottle, tube)*
2 la gorra *(hat)*

capable ADJECTIVE
capaz (FEM capaz)
■ **to be capable of doing something** ser capaz de hacer algo □ She's capable of doing much more. Es capaz de hacer mucho más.

capacity NOUN
la capacidad
□ The tank has a 40-litre capacity. El depósito tiene una capacidad de 40 litros.
□ He has a capacity for hard work. Tiene mucha capacidad de trabajo.

capital NOUN
1 la capital
□ Cardiff is the capital of Wales. Cardiff es la capital del país de Gales.
2 la mayúscula *(letter)*
□ in capitals en mayúsculas

capitalism NOUN
el capitalismo

capital punishment NOUN
la pena capital

Capricorn NOUN
el Capricornio *(sign)*
■ **I'm Capricorn.** Soy capricornio.

to **capsize** VERB
volcar*

captain NOUN
el capitán (PL los capitanes)
la capitana

caption NOUN
la leyenda

to **capture** VERB
capturar

car NOUN
el coche
■ **to go by car** ir en coche □ We went by car. Fuimos en coche.
■ **a car crash** un accidente de coche

caramel NOUN
el caramelo
□ a box of caramels una caja de caramelos

caravan NOUN
la caravana
□ a caravan site un cámping de caravanas

card NOUN
1 la tarjeta
□ I got lots of cards and presents on my birthday. Recibí muchas tarjetas y regalos para mi cumpleaños.
2 la carta
■ **a card game** un juego de cartas

cardboard NOUN
el cartón
□ a cardboard box una caja de cartón

cardigan NOUN
la chaqueta de punto

cardphone NOUN
el teléfono de tarjeta

care NOUN
▹ *see also* **care** VERB
el cuidado
□ with care con cuidado
■ **to take care of** cuidar a □ I take care of the children on Saturdays. Yo cuido a los niños los sábados.
■ **Take care! 1** *(be careful!)* ¡Ten cuidado! **2** *(look after yourself!)* ¡Cuídate!

to **care** VERB
▹ *see also* **care** NOUN
■ **to care about** preocuparse por □ a company that cares about the environment una empresa que se preocupa por el medio ambiente □ They don't care about their image. No se preocupan por su imagen.
■ **I don't care!** ¡No me importa!
■ **Who cares?** ¿Y a quién le importa?

career NOUN
la carrera

careful ADJECTIVE
■ **Be careful!** ¡Ten cuidado!

carefully ADVERB
con cuidado *(cautiously)*
□ Drive carefully! ¡Conduce con cuidado!
■ **Think carefully!** ¡Piénsalo bien!
■ **She carefully avoided talking about it.** Tuvo mucho cuidado de no hablar del tema.

careless ADJECTIVE
1 poco cuidado (FEM poco cuidada) *(work)*
■ **a careless mistake** un error de descuido
2 poco cuidadoso (FEM poco cuidadosa) *(person)*
□ She's very careless. Es muy poco cuidadosa.
■ **a careless driver** un conductor imprudente

caretaker NOUN
el/la conserje
■ **school caretaker** el bedel

cargo NOUN
el cargamento

car hire NOUN
el alquiler de coches

Caribbean ADJECTIVE
▹ *see also* **Caribbean** NOUN
caribeño (FEM caribeña)

Caribbean NOUN
▹ *see also* **Caribbean** ADJECTIVE
■ **We're going to the Caribbean.** Vamos al Caribe.
■ **the Caribbean** *(sea)* el mar Caribe

caring ADJECTIVE
bondadoso (FEM bondadosa)
■ **the caring professions** las profesiones de vocación social

carnation NOUN
el clavel
carnival NOUN
el carnaval
carol NOUN
■ **a Christmas carol** un villancico
car park NOUN
el aparcamiento
carpenter NOUN
el carpintero
la carpintera
□ He's a carpenter. Es carpintero.
carpet NOUN
1 la moqueta *(fitted)*
2 la alfombra
□ a Persian carpet una alfombra persa
car rental NOUN (US)
el alquiler de coches
carriage NOUN
el vagón (PL los vagones) *(of train)*
carrier bag NOUN
la bolsa de plástico
carrot NOUN
la zanahoria
to **carry** VERB
1 llevar
□ I'll carry your bag. Te llevo la bolsa.
2 transportar
□ a plane carrying 100 passengers un avión que transporta 100 pasajeros
to **carry on** VERB
seguir*
□ She carried on talking. Siguió hablando.
■ **Carry on!** ¡Sigue! □ Am I boring you? — No, carry on! ¿Te estoy aburriendo? — ¡No, sigue!
to **carry out** VERB
1 cumplir *(orders)*
2 llevar a cabo *(threat, task, instructions)*
carrycot NOUN
el moisés (PL los moisés)
cart NOUN
el carro
carton NOUN
el cartón (PL los cartones) *(of milk, fruit juice)*
cartoon NOUN
1 los dibujos animados *(film)*
2 el chiste *(in newspaper)*
■ **a strip cartoon** una tira cómica
cartridge NOUN
el cartucho
to **carve** VERB
trinchar
□ Dad carved the roast. Papá trinchó el asado.
■ **a carved oak chair** una silla de roble tallado
case NOUN
1 la maleta
□ I've packed my case. He hecho mi maleta.
2 el caso
□ in some cases en algunos casos □ The police are investigating the case. La policía está investigando el caso.
■ **in case it rains** por si llueve
■ **just in case** por si acaso □ Take some money with you, just in case. Llévate algo de dinero por si acaso.
cash NOUN
el dinero
□ I'm a bit short of cash. Ando un poco justo de dinero.
■ **in cash** en efectivo □ £200 in cash 200 libras esterlinas en efectivo
■ **to pay cash** pagar al contado
cash dispenser NOUN
el cajero automático
cashew nut NOUN
el anacardo
cashier NOUN
el cajero
la cajera
cashmere NOUN
el cachemir
□ a cashmere sweater un suéter de cachemir
casino NOUN
el casino
casserole NOUN
el guiso
□ to make a casserole hacer un guiso
■ **a casserole dish** una cazuela
cast NOUN
el reparto
□ There is a very famous actor in the cast. Hay un actor muy famoso en el reparto.
■ **After the play, we met the cast.** Cuando terminó la obra charlamos con los actores.
castle NOUN
el castillo
casual ADJECTIVE
1 informal (FEM informal)
□ I prefer casual clothes. Prefiero la ropa informal.
2 despreocupado (FEM despreocupada)
□ a casual attitude una actitud despreocupada
3 eventual (FEM eventual)
□ It's just a casual job. Es sólo un trabajo eventual.
■ **a casual remark** un comentario hecho de pasada
casually ADVERB
■ **to dress casually** vestir informal
casualty NOUN
1 urgencias *fem pl (hospital department)*

□ He was taken to casualty after the accident. Lo llevaron a urgencias después del accidente.

2 la víctima

□ The casualties include a young boy. Entre las víctimas se encuentra un niño.

cat NOUN
el gato
la gata

catalogue NOUN
el catálogo

catalytic converter NOUN
el catalizador

catarrh NOUN
el catarro

catastrophe NOUN
la catástrofe

to **catch** VERB

1 coger* *(Spain)* (agarrar *Latin America*)

LANGUAGE TIP Be very careful with the verb **coger**: in most of Latin America this is an extremely rude word that should be avoided. However, in Spain this verb is common and not rude at all.

□ They caught the thief. Cogieron al ladrón.
□ We caught the last train. Cogimos el último tren.
■ **My cat catches birds.** Mi gato caza pájaros.

2 agarrar

□ He caught her arm. La agarró del brazo.
■ **to catch a cold** resfriarse
■ **I didn't catch his name.** No me enteré de su nombre.
■ **He caught her stealing.** La pilló robando.
■ **If they catch you smoking you'll be in trouble.** Si te pillan fumando te la vas a cargar.

to **catch up** VERB

1 ponerse* al día

□ I've got to catch up on my work. Tengo que ponerme al día con el trabajo.

2 alcanzar*

□ She caught me up. Me alcanzó.

catching ADJECTIVE
contagioso (FEM contagiosa)
□ Don't worry, it's not catching! ¡No te preocupes, no es contagioso!

catering NOUN
■ **The hotel did all the catering for the wedding.** El hotel se encargó de organizar el banquete de bodas.

cathedral NOUN
la catedral

Catholic ADJECTIVE
▷ *see also* **Catholic** NOUN
católico (FEM católica)

Catholic NOUN
▷ *see also* **Catholic** ADJECTIVE
el católico
la católica
□ I'm a Catholic. Soy católico.

cattle PL NOUN
el ganado

caught VERB ▷ *see* **catch**

cauliflower NOUN
la coliflor

cause NOUN
▷ *see also* **cause** VERB
la causa

to **cause** VERB
▷ *see also* **cause** NOUN
causar

cautious ADJECTIVE
prudente (FEM prudente)

cautiously ADVERB
con cautela

cave NOUN
la cueva

CCTV NOUN *(= closed-circuit television)*
el circuito cerrado de televisión

CD NOUN
el CD (PL los CDs)

CD player NOUN
el reproductor de CD

CD-ROM NOUN
el CD-ROM

ceasefire NOUN
el alto el fuego

ceiling NOUN
el techo

to **celebrate** VERB
celebrar

celebration NOUN
la celebración

celebrity NOUN
la celebridad

celery NOUN
el apio

cell NOUN

1 la celda

□ Prisoners spend many hours in their cells. Los prisioneros pasan muchas horas en sus celdas.

2 la célula *(in biology)*

cellar NOUN
el sótano

cello NOUN
el violonchelo

cell phone NOUN
el móvil

cement NOUN
el cemento

cemetery NOUN
el cementerio

cent NOUN
1 el centavo *(division of dollar)*
2 el céntimo *(division of euro)*

centenary NOUN
el centenario

center NOUN (US)
el centro

centigrade ADJECTIVE
centígrado (FEM centígrada)
□ 20 degrees centigrade 20 grados centígrados

centimetre (US **centimeter**) NOUN
el centímetro

central ADJECTIVE
central (FEM central)

central heating NOUN
la calefacción central

centre NOUN
el centro

century NOUN
el siglo
□ the twentieth century el siglo veinte

cereal NOUN
los cereales
□ I have cereal for breakfast. Desayuno cereales.

ceremony NOUN
la ceremonia

certain ADJECTIVE
1 cierto (FEM cierta) *(particular)*
□ a certain person cierta persona
2 seguro (FEM segura) *(definite)*
□ I am certain he's not coming. Estoy seguro de que no viene.
■ **for certain** con certeza
■ **to make certain** cerciorarse □ I made certain the door was locked. Me cercioré de que la puerta estaba cerrada con llave.

certainly ADVERB
por supuesto
□ I shall certainly be there. Por supuesto que estaré allí. □ Certainly not! ¡Por supuesto que no!
■ **So it was a surprise? — It certainly was!** ¿Así que fue una sorpresa? — ¡Ya lo creo!

certificate NOUN
el certificado

chain NOUN
la cadena
□ a gold chain una cadena de oro

chair NOUN
1 la silla
□ a table and four chairs una mesa y cuatro sillas
2 el sillón (PL los sillones) *(armchair)*

chairlift NOUN
el telesilla

LANGUAGE TIP Although **telesilla** ends in **-a**, it is actually a masculine noun.

chairman NOUN
el presidente
la presidenta

chalet NOUN
el chalet (PL los chalets)

chalk NOUN
la tiza
■ **a piece of chalk** una tiza

challenge NOUN
▷ *see also* **challenge** VERB
el reto

to **challenge** VERB
▷ *see also* **challenge** NOUN
retar
□ She challenged me to a race. Me retó a echar una carrera.

challenging ADJECTIVE
estimulante (FEM estimulante)
□ a challenging job un trabajo estimulante

chambermaid NOUN
la camarera

champagne NOUN
el champán

champion NOUN
el campeón (PL los campeones)
la campeona

championship NOUN
el campeonato

chance NOUN
1 la posibilidad
□ The team's chances of winning are very good. El equipo tiene muchas posibilidades de ganar.
2 la oportunidad
□ I had the chance of working in Brazil. Tuve la oportunidad de trabajar en Brasil.
■ **I'll write when I get the chance.** Te escribiré cuando tenga un momento.
■ **by chance** por casualidad
■ **No chance!** ¡Ni en broma!
■ **to take a chance** arriesgarse □ I'm taking no chances! ¡No me quiero arriesgar!

Chancellor of the Exchequer NOUN
el Ministro de Economía y Hacienda
la Ministra de Economía y Hacienda

to **change** VERB
▷ *see also* **change** NOUN
1 cambiar
□ The town has changed a lot. La ciudad ha cambiado mucho. □ I'd like to change £50. Quisiera cambiar 50 libras esterlinas. □ I'd like to change this jumper, it's too small. Me gustaría cambiar este jersey, es demasiado pequeño.
2 cambiar de
□ He wants to change his job. Quiere cambiar de trabajo. □ I'm going to change my shoes. Voy a cambiarme de zapatos.

■ **to get changed** cambiarse
■ **to change one's mind** cambiar de idea

change NOUN
▹ *see also* **change** VERB
1 el cambio
□ There's been a change of plan. Ha habido un cambio de planes.
■ **a change of clothes** una muda
■ **for a change** para variar
2 el dinero suelto
□ I haven't got any change. No tengo dinero suelto.
■ **Can you give me change for a pound?** ¿Me puede cambiar una libra?
■ **There's your change.** Aquí tiene el cambio.

changeable ADJECTIVE
variable (FEM variable)

changing room NOUN
1 el probador *(in shop)*
2 el vestuario *(for sport)*

channel NOUN
el canal *(TV)*
■ **the English Channel** el Canal de la Mancha
■ **the Channel Islands** las islas del Canal de la Mancha
■ **the Channel Tunnel** el túnel del Canal de la Mancha

chaos NOUN
el caos

chap NOUN
el tipo *(informal)*

chapel NOUN
la capilla

chapter NOUN
el capítulo

character NOUN
1 el carácter (PL los caracteres)
□ Can you describe his character? ¿Puede describirme cómo es su carácter?
2 el personaje *(in film, book)*
■ **She's quite a character.** Es todo un personaje.

characteristic NOUN
la característica

charcoal NOUN
1 el carbón vegetal *(for barbecue)*
2 el carboncillo *(for drawing)*

charge NOUN
▹ *see also* **charge** VERB
■ **Is there a charge for delivery?** ¿Cobran por el envío?
■ **an extra charge** un suplemento
■ **free of charge** gratuito
■ **I'd like to reverse the charges.** Quisiera llamar a cobro revertido.
■ **to be in charge** ser el responsable □ She was in charge of the group. Ella era la responsable del grupo.

to charge VERB
▹ *see also* **charge** NOUN
1 cobrar
□ How much did he charge you? ¿Cuánto te cobró?
2 acusar *(with crime)*
□ The police have charged him with murder. La policía lo ha acusado de asesinato.

charity NOUN
la organización benéfica (PL las organizaciones benéficas) *(organization)*
□ He gave the money to charity. Donó el dinero a una organización benéfica.
■ **to collect for charity** recaudar dinero para obras benéficas

charm NOUN
el encanto

charming ADJECTIVE
encantador (FEM encantadora)

chart NOUN
el gráfico
□ The chart shows the rise of unemployment. El gráfico muestra el aumento del desempleo.
■ **the charts** la lista de éxitos □ The album is still in the charts. El disco está todavía en la lista de éxitos.

charter flight NOUN
el vuelo chárter

to chase VERB
▹ *see also* **chase** NOUN
1 perseguir*
□ The policeman chased the thief along the road. El policía persiguió al ladrón a lo largo de la calle.
2 ir* detrás de
□ He's always chasing the girls. Siempre va detrás de las chicas.

chase NOUN
▹ *see also* **chase** VERB
la persecución (PL las persecuciones)
□ a car chase una persecución en coche

chat NOUN
la charla
■ **to have a chat** charlar

chatroom NOUN
el chat

chat show NOUN
el programa de entrevistas

LANGUAGE TIP Although **programa** ends in **-a**, it is actually a masculine noun.

cheap ADJECTIVE
barato (FEM barata)
□ a cheap T-shirt una camiseta barata □ It's cheaper by bus. Es más barato en autobús.
■ **a cheap flight** un vuelo económico

to **cheat** VERB
▷ *see also* **cheat** NOUN
1 hacer* trampa *(at cards)*
□ You're cheating! ¡Estás haciendo trampa!
2 copiar *(in exam)*

cheat NOUN
▷ *see also* **cheat** VERB
el tramposo
la tramposa

check NOUN
▷ *see also* **check** VERB
1 el control
□ a security check un control de seguridad
2 el cheque (US)
□ to write a check extender un cheque
3 la cuenta (US)
□ The waiter brought us the check. El camarero nos trajo la cuenta.

to **check** VERB
▷ *see also* **check** NOUN
comprobar*
□ Could you check the oil, please? ¿Podría comprobar el aceite, por favor?
■ **to check with somebody** preguntarle a alguien □ I'll check with the driver what time the bus leaves. Le preguntaré al conductor a qué hora sale el autobús.

to **check in** VERB
1 facturar *(at airport)*
2 registrarse *(in hotel)*

to **check out** VERB
dejar el hotel

checked ADJECTIVE
a cuadros

checkers NOUN (US)
las damas
□ to play checkers jugar a las damas

check-in NOUN
la facturación de equipajes

checking account NOUN (US)
la cuenta corriente

checkout NOUN
la caja

check-up NOUN
el reconocimiento

cheek NOUN
la mejilla
□ He kissed her on the cheek. La besó en la mejilla.
■ **What a cheek!** ¡Qué cara!

cheeky ADJECTIVE
descarado (FEM descarada)
□ Don't be cheeky! ¡No seas descarado!
■ **a cheeky smile** una sonrisilla maliciosa

cheer NOUN
▷ *see also* **cheer** VERB
■ **Three cheers for the winner!** ¡Viva el ganador!
■ **Cheers!** 1 *(when drinking)* ¡Salud! 2 *(thank you)* ¡Gracias!

to **cheer** VERB
▷ *see also* **cheer** NOUN
vitorear
■ **to cheer somebody up** levantar el ánimo a alguien □ I was trying to cheer him up. Estaba intentando levantarle el ánimo.
■ **Cheer up!** ¡Anímate!

cheerful ADJECTIVE
alegre (FEM alegre)

cheerio EXCLAMATION
¡hasta luego!

cheese NOUN
el queso

chef NOUN
el/la chef (PL los/las chefs)

chemical NOUN
la sustancia química

chemist NOUN
1 el farmacéutico
la farmacéutica *(dispenser)*
□ She's a chemist. Es farmacéutica
2 la farmacia *(shop)*
□ You get it from the chemist. Se compra en la farmacia.

DID YOU KNOW...?
Chemist's shops in Spain are identified by a green cross outside the shop.

3 el químico
la química *(scientist)*

chemistry NOUN
la química
□ the chemistry lab el laboratorio de química

cheque NOUN
el cheque
□ to write a cheque extender un cheque
□ to pay by cheque pagar con cheque

chequebook NOUN
el talonario de cheques

cherry NOUN
la cereza

chess NOUN
el ajedrez
□ He likes playing chess. Le gusta jugar al ajedrez.

chessboard NOUN
el tablero de ajedrez

chest NOUN
el pecho
□ I've got a pain in my chest. Tengo un dolor en el pecho.

chestnut NOUN
la castaña

chest of drawers NOUN
la cómoda

English-Spanish

C

to **chew** VERB
masticar*
chewing gum NOUN
el chicle
■ **a piece of chewing gum** un chicle
chick NOUN
el polluelo
□ a hen and her chicks una gallina y sus polluelos
chicken NOUN
1 la gallina *(animal)*
2 el pollo *(food)*
chickenpox NOUN
la varicela
□ I've got chickenpox. Tengo la varicela.
chickpeas PL NOUN
los garbanzos
chief NOUN
▷ *see also* **chief** ADJECTIVE
el jefe
la jefa
□ the chief of security el jefe de seguridad
chief ADJECTIVE
▷ *see also* **chief** NOUN
principal (FEM principal)
□ His chief reason for resigning was the low pay. El motivo principal de su dimisión fue el sueldo bajo.
child NOUN
1 el niño
la niña
□ a child of six un niño de seis años
2 el hijo
la hija
□ Susan is our eldest child. Susan es nuestra hija mayor. □ They've got three children. Tienen tres hijos.
childish ADJECTIVE
infantil (FEM infantil)
child minder NOUN
la niñera
children PL NOUN ▷ *see* **child**
Chile NOUN
Chile *masc*
to **chill** VERB
poner* a enfriar *(drink, food)*
■ **Serve chilled.** Sírvase bien frío.
chilli NOUN
el chile
■ **chilli con carne** el chile con carne
chilly ADJECTIVE
frío (FEM fría)
chimney NOUN
la chimenea
chin NOUN
la barbilla
■ **Keep your chin up!** ¡No pierdas el ánimo!

china NOUN
la porcelana
□ a china plate un plato de porcelana
China NOUN
China *fem*
Chinese ADJECTIVE
▷ *see also* **Chinese** NOUN
chino (FEM china)
■ **a Chinese man** un chino
■ **a Chinese woman** una china
Chinese NOUN
▷ *see also* **Chinese** ADJECTIVE
el chino *(language)*
■ **the Chinese** los chinos
chip NOUN
1 la patata frita (la papa frita *Latin America*) *(food)*
2 el chip (PL los chips) *(in computer)*
chiropodist NOUN
el podólogo
la podóloga
□ He's a chiropodist. Es podólogo.
chives PL NOUN
los cebollinos
chocolate NOUN
1 el chocolate
□ a chocolate cake un pastel de chocolate
2 el bombón (PL los bombones)
□ a box of chocolates una caja de bombones
choice NOUN
la elección (PL las elecciones)
■ **I had no choice.** No tenía otro remedio.
choir NOUN
el coro
to **choke** VERB
atragantarse *(on food)*
to **choose** VERB
elegir*
to **chop** VERB
▷ *see also* **chop** NOUN
1 picar* *(onion, herbs)*
2 cortar en trozos pequeños *(meat)*
chop NOUN
▷ *see also* **chop** VERB
la chuleta
□ a pork chop una chuleta de cerdo
chopsticks PL NOUN
los palillos
chose, chosen VERB ▷ *see* **choose**
Christ NOUN
Cristo *masc*
christening NOUN
el bautismo
Christian NOUN
▷ *see also* **Christian** ADJECTIVE
el cristiano
la cristiana

Christian ADJECTIVE
▷ *see also* **Christian** NOUN
cristiano (FEM cristiana)

Christian name NOUN
el nombre de pila

Christmas NOUN
la Navidad
□ Happy Christmas! ¡Feliz Navidad!
■ **Christmas Day** el día de Navidad
■ **on Christmas Day** el día de Navidad
■ **Christmas Eve** Nochebuena
■ **a Christmas tree** un árbol de Navidad
■ **Christmas dinner** la comida de Navidad

DID YOU KNOW...?
As well as lunch on Christmas Day, Spaniards also have a special supper on Christmas Eve.

■ **a Christmas present** un regalo de Navidad

DID YOU KNOW...?
In Spain Christmas presents are traditionally given on 6th January although more and more people are exchanging gifts on Christmas Eve.

■ **Christmas pudding** el pudin de Navidad
■ **Christmas card** la tarjeta de Navidad
■ **at Christmas** en Navidad

chunk NOUN
el pedazo
□ Cut the meat into chunks. Córtese la carne en pedazos.

church NOUN
la iglesia
■ **the Church of England** la Iglesia Anglicana

cider NOUN
la sidra

cigar NOUN
el puro

cigarette NOUN
el cigarrillo

cigarette lighter NOUN
el mechero

cinema NOUN
el cine

cinnamon NOUN
la canela

circle NOUN
el círculo

circular ADJECTIVE
circular

circulation NOUN
1 la circulación
□ She has poor circulation. Tiene mala circulación.
2 la tirada
□ The newspaper has a circulation of around 8000. El periódico tiene una tirada de unos 8.000 ejemplares.

circumstances PL NOUN
las circunstancias
□ in the circumstances dadas las circunstancias
■ **under no circumstances** bajo ningún concepto

circus NOUN
el circo

citizen NOUN
el ciudadano
la ciudadana

City NOUN
■ **the City** la City de Londres

city NOUN
la ciudad
□ the city centre el centro de la ciudad

city technology college NOUN
el centro de formación profesional

civilization NOUN
la civilización (PL las civilizaciones)

civil servant NOUN
el funcionario
la funcionaria
□ He's a civil servant. Es funcionario.

civil war NOUN
la guerra civil

to **claim** VERB
▷ *see also* **claim** NOUN
1 asegurar
□ He claims he found the money. Asegura haber encontrado el dinero.
2 reclamar
□ He's claiming compensation from the company. Reclama una indemnización por parte de la empresa.
3 cobrar
□ She's claiming unemployment benefit. Cobra subsidio de desempleo.
■ **We claimed on our insurance.** Reclamamos al seguro.

claim NOUN
▷ *see also* **claim** VERB
1 la reclamación (PL las reclamaciones) *(on insurance policy)*
■ **to make a claim** reclamar al seguro
2 la afirmación (PL las afirmaciones)
□ The manufacturer's claims are obviously untrue. Las afirmaciones del fabricante son obviamente falsas.

to **clap** VERB
aplaudir
■ **to clap one's hands** dar palmadas

clarinet NOUN
el clarinete

to **clash** VERB
1 desentonar *(colours)*
□ Red clashes with orange. El rojo desentona con el naranja.

2 coincidir *(events)*
□ The party clashes with the meeting. La fiesta coincide con la reunión.

clasp NOUN
el cierre *(of necklace, handbag)*

class NOUN
la clase
□ We're in the same class. Estamos en la misma clase. □ I go to dancing classes. Voy a clases de baile.

classic ADJECTIVE
▹ *see also* **classic** NOUN
clásico (FEM clásica)
□ a classic example un ejemplo clásico

classic NOUN
▹ *see also* **classic** ADJECTIVE
el clásico

classical ADJECTIVE
clásico (FEM clásica)
□ classical music la música clásica

classmate NOUN
el compañero de clase
la compañera de clase

classroom NOUN
la clase

claw NOUN
1 la garra *(of lion, eagle)*
2 la uña *(of cat, parrot)*
3 la pinza *(of crab, lobster)*

clean ADJECTIVE
▹ *see also* **clean** VERB
limpio (FEM limpia)

to **clean** VERB
▹ *see also* **clean** ADJECTIVE
limpiar

cleaner NOUN
1 el hombre de la limpieza
la mujer de la limpieza *(person)*
2 el producto de limpieza *(substance)*

cleaner's NOUN
la tintorería
□ He took his coat to the cleaner's. Llevó el abrigo a la tintorería.

cleaning lady NOUN
la mujer de la limpieza

cleansing lotion NOUN
la leche limpiadora

clear ADJECTIVE
▹ *see also* **clear** VERB
1 claro (FEM clara)
□ a clear explanation una explicación clara
□ It's clear you don't believe me. Está claro que no me crees.
■ **Have I made myself clear?** ¿Me explico?
2 despejado (FEM despejada)
□ Wait till the road is clear. Espera hasta que la carretera esté despejada. □ a clear day un día despejado
3 transparente (FEM transparente)
□ It comes in a clear plastic bottle. Viene en una botella de plástico transparente.

to **clear** VERB
▹ *see also* **clear** ADJECTIVE
1 despejar
□ They are clearing the road. Están despejando la carretera.
■ **She was cleared of murder.** La absolvieron del cargo de asesinato.
■ **to clear the table** quitar la mesa
2 despejarse *(fog, mist)*

to **clear off** VERB
largarse*
□ Clear off and leave me alone! ¡Lárgate y déjame en paz!

to **clear up** VERB
1 ordenar
□ Who's going to clear all this up? ¿Quién va a ordenar todo esto?
2 resolver*
□ Let's try to clear up this problem. Intentemos resolver este problema.
■ **I think it's going to clear up.** *(weather)* Creo que va a despejar.

clearly ADVERB
claramente
□ to speak clearly hablar claramente
■ **Clearly this project will cost money.** Evidentemente este proyecto costará dinero.

clementine NOUN
la clementina

clever ADJECTIVE
1 listo (FEM lista)
□ She's very clever. Es muy lista.
2 ingenioso (FEM ingeniosa)
□ a clever system un sistema ingenioso
■ **What a clever idea!** ¡Qué idea más genial!

to **click on** VERB
hacer* clic en *(computing)*
□ to click on an icon hacer clic en un icono
■ **to click on the mouse** hacer clic con el ratón

client NOUN
el cliente
la clienta

cliff NOUN
el acantilado

climate NOUN
el clima

LANGUAGE TIP Although **clima** ends in **-a**, it is actually a masculine noun.

to **climb** VERB
1 escalar
□ Her ambition is to climb Mount Everest. Su ambición es escalar el Monte Everest.

2 trepar a
□ They climbed a tree. Treparon a un árbol.
■ **to climb the stairs** subir las escaleras

climber NOUN
el escalador
la escaladora

climbing NOUN
el montañismo
■ **to go climbing** hacer montañismo
□ We're going climbing in Scotland. Vamos a hacer montañismo en Escocia.

clinic NOUN
1 el consultorio *(in NHS hospital)*
2 la clínica *(private hospital)*

clip NOUN
1 la horquilla *(for hair)*
2 la secuencia
□ some clips from Scarlett Johansson's latest film unas secuencias de la última película de Scarlett Johansson

clippers PL NOUN
■ **nail clippers** el cortauñas (PL los cortauñas)

cloakroom NOUN
1 el guardarropa *(for coats)*
LANGUAGE TIP Although **guardarropa** ends in **-a**, it is actually a masculine noun.
2 los servicios *(toilet)*

clock NOUN
el reloj
■ **an alarm clock** un despertador
■ **a clock radio** un radio-despertador

clockwork NOUN
■ **to go like clockwork** ir sobre ruedas

clone NOUN
▹ *see also* **clone** VERB
el clon

to **clone** VERB
▹ *see also* **clone** NOUN
clonar
□ to clone a sheep clonar una oveja
■ **a cloned sheep** una oveja clónica

close ADJECTIVE, ADVERB
▹ *see also* **close** VERB
1 cerca (FEM cerca)
□ The shops are very close. Las tiendas están muy cerca. □ The hotel is close to the station. El hotel está cerca de la estación.
■ **Come closer.** Acércate más.
■ **She was close to tears.** Estaba a punto de llorar.
2 cercano (FEM cercana)
□ We have only invited close relations. Sólo hemos invitado a parientes cercanos.
3 íntimo (FEM íntima)
□ She's a close friend of mine. Es amiga íntima mía.
■ **I'm very close to my sister.** Estoy muy unida a mi hermana.
4 reñido (FEM reñida)
□ It was a very close contest. Fue un concurso muy reñido.
■ **It's close this afternoon.** Hace bochorno esta tarde.

to **close** VERB
▹ *see also* **close** ADJECTIVE
1 cerrar*
□ The shops close at five thirty. Las tiendas cierran a las cinco y media. □ Please close the door. Cierra la puerta, por favor.
2 cerrarse*
□ The doors close automatically. Las puertas se cierran automáticamente.

closed ADJECTIVE
cerrado (FEM cerrada)

closely ADVERB
de cerca *(look, examine)*
■ **This will be a closely fought race.** Será una carrera muy reñida.

cloth NOUN
la tela
□ I would like five metres of this cloth, please. Quisiera cinco metros de esta tela, por favor.
■ **a cloth** un trapo □ Wipe it with a damp cloth. Límpialo con un trapo húmedo.

clothes PL NOUN
la ropa
■ **clothes horse** el tendedero plegable
■ **clothes line** la cuerda de tender
■ **clothes peg** la pinza para tender la ropa

cloud NOUN
la nube

cloudy ADJECTIVE
nublado (FEM nublada)

clove NOUN
■ **a clove of garlic** un diente de ajo

clown NOUN
el payaso

club NOUN
1 el club
□ a golf club un club de golf □ the youth club el club juvenil
2 la discoteca
□ We had dinner and went on to a club. Cenamos y fuimos a una discoteca.
■ **clubs** *(at cards)* los tréboles □ the ace of clubs el as de tréboles

clubbing NOUN
■ **to go clubbing** ir de discotecas

to **club together** VERB
hacer* una colecta
□ We clubbed together to buy her a present. Hicimos una colecta para comprarle un regalo.

clue NOUN
la pista
□ an important clue una pista clave
■ **I haven't a clue.** No tengo ni idea.

clumsy ADJECTIVE
torpe (FEM torpe)

clutch NOUN
el embrague *(of car)*

coach NOUN
1 el autobús
□ by coach en autobús □ the coach station la estación de autobuses □ a coach trip una excursión en autobús
2 el entrenador
la entrenadora *(trainer)*
■ **the Spanish coach** el entrenador del equipo español

coal NOUN
el carbón
■ **a coal mine** una mina de carbón
■ **a coal miner** un minero de carbón

coarse ADJECTIVE
1 basto (FEM basta)
□ The bag was made of coarse black cloth. La bolsa estaba hecha de una tela basta de color negro.
2 grueso (FEM gruesa)
□ The sand is very coarse on that beach. La arena es muy gruesa en esa playa.

coast NOUN
la costa
□ It's on the west coast of Scotland. Está en la costa oeste de Escocia.

coastguard NOUN
el guardacostas (PL los guardacostas)

coat NOUN
el abrigo
□ a woollen coat un abrigo de lana
■ **a coat of paint** una mano de pintura

coat hanger NOUN
la percha

cobweb NOUN
la telaraña

cocaine NOUN
la cocaína

cockerel NOUN
el gallo

cocoa NOUN
el cacao
■ **a cup of cocoa** una taza de chocolate

coconut NOUN
el coco

cod NOUN
el bacalao

code NOUN
1 la clave
□ It's written in code. Está escrito en clave.
2 el prefijo *(for telephone)*
□ What is the code for London? ¿Cuál es el prefijo de Londres?

coffee NOUN
el café (PL los cafés)
□ a cup of coffee una taza de café
■ **A cup of coffee, please.** Un café, por favor.

coffeepot NOUN
la cafetera

coffee table NOUN
la mesa de centro

coffin NOUN
el ataúd

coin NOUN
la moneda
□ a 20p coin una moneda de 20 peniques

coincidence NOUN
la coincidencia

Coke® NOUN
la Coca-Cola®

colander NOUN
el colador

cold ADJECTIVE
▷ *see also* **cold** NOUN
frío (FEM fría)
□ The water's cold. El agua está fría.
□ It's cold. Hace frío. □ Are you cold? ¿Tienes frío?

cold NOUN
▷ *see also* **cold** ADJECTIVE
1 el frío
□ I can't stand the cold. No soporto el frío.
2 el resfriado *(illness)*
■ **to catch a cold** resfriarse
■ **to have a cold** estar resfriado

coleslaw NOUN
la ensalada de col

to **collapse** VERB
1 venirse* abajo
□ The bridge collapsed during the storm. El puente se vino abajo en medio de la tormenta.
2 sufrir un colapso
□ He collapsed while playing tennis. Sufrió un colapso mientras jugaba al tenis.

collar NOUN
1 el cuello *(of coat, shirt)*
2 el collar *(for animal)*

collarbone NOUN
la clavícula

colleague NOUN
el/la colega

to **collect** VERB
1 recoger*
□ The teacher collected the exercise books. El maestro recogió los cuadernos. □ Their mother collects them from school. Su madre los recoge del colegio.

2 coleccionar
□ He collects stamps. Colecciona sellos.
3 hacer* una colecta
□ I'm collecting for UNICEF. Estoy haciendo una colecta para la UNICEF.

collect call NOUN (US)
la llamada a cobro revertido

collection NOUN
1 la colección (PL las colecciones)
□ my CD collection mi colección de CDs
2 la colecta
□ a collection for charity una colecta para obras benéficas

collector NOUN
el/la coleccionista

college NOUN
la universidad *(university)*

to **collide** VERB
chocar*

collision NOUN
la colisión (PL las colisiones)

colon NOUN
dos puntos *(punctuation mark)*

colonel NOUN
el/la coronel

colour (US **color**) NOUN
el color
□ What colour is it? ¿De qué color es?
■ **a colour TV** una televisión en color

colourful (US **colorful**) ADJECTIVE
de colores muy vistosos

colouring (US **coloring**) NOUN
el colorante *(for food)*

comb NOUN
▷ *see also* **comb** VERB
el peine

to **comb** VERB
▷ *see also* **comb** NOUN
■ **You haven't combed your hair.** No te has peinado.

combination NOUN
la combinación (PL las combinaciones)

to **combine** VERB
1 combinar
□ The film combines humour with suspense. La película combina el humor con el suspense.
2 compaginar
□ It's difficult to combine a career with a family. Es difícil compaginar la profesión con la vida familiar.

to **come** VERB
1 venir*
□ Helen came with me. Helen vino conmigo. □ Come home. Ven a casa.
□ Come and see us soon. Ven a vernos pronto.
■ **Where do you come from?** ¿De dónde eres?
2 llegar*
□ They came late. Llegaron tarde. □ The letter came this morning. La carta llegó esta mañana.
■ **I'm coming!** ¡Ya voy!

to **come back** VERB
volver*
□ My brother is coming back tomorrow. Mi hermano vuelve mañana.

to **come down** VERB
bajar

to **come in** VERB
entrar
□ Come in! ¡Entra!

to **come on** VERB
■ **Come on!** **1** *(expressing encouragement, urging haste)* ¡Venga! **2** *(expressing disbelief)* ¡Venga ya!

to **come out** VERB
1 salir*
□ We came out of the cinema at 10. Salimos del cine a las 10. □ Her book comes out in May. Su libro sale en mayo.
■ **None of my photos came out.** No salió ninguna de mis fotos.
2 irse*
□ I don't think this stain will come out. No creo que esta mancha se vaya a quitar.

to **come round** VERB
volver* en sí *(after faint, operation)*
□ He came round after about 10 minutes. Volvió en sí después de unos 10 minutos.

to **come up** VERB
1 subir
□ Come up here! ¡Sube aquí!
2 surgir*
□ Something's come up so I'll be late home. Ha surgido algo, así es que llegaré tarde a casa.
■ **to come up to somebody** acercarse a alguien □ She came up to me and kissed me. Se me acercó y me besó.

comedian NOUN
el cómico
la cómica

comedy NOUN
la comedia

comfortable ADJECTIVE
1 cómodo (FEM cómoda)
□ comfortable shoes zapatos cómodos
□ Make yourself comfortable! ¡Ponte cómodo!
2 confortable (FEM confortable) *(house, room)*
□ Their house is small but comfortable. Su casa es pequeña pero confortable.

comic NOUN
el comic (PL los comics)

comic strip NOUN
la tira cómica

coming ADJECTIVE
próximo (FEM próxima)
□ In the coming weeks, we will all have to work hard. En las próximas semanas todos tendremos que trabajar duro.

comma NOUN
la coma

command NOUN
la orden (PL las órdenes)

comment NOUN
▷ *see also* **comment** VERB
el comentario
□ He made no comment. No hizo ningún comentario.
■ **No comment!** ¡Sin comentarios!

to **comment** VERB
▷ *see also* **comment** NOUN
hacer* comentarios
□ The police have not commented on these rumours. La policía no ha hecho comentarios sobre estos rumores.

commentary NOUN
la crónica

commentator NOUN
el/la comentarista

commercial ADJECTIVE
comercial (FEM comercial)

commission NOUN
la comisión (PL las comisiones)
□ The bank charges 1% commission. El banco cobra un 1% de comisión. □ to work on commission trabajar a comisión

to **commit** VERB
■ **to commit a crime** cometer un crimen
■ **to commit suicide** suicidarse
■ **I don't want to commit myself.** No quiero comprometerme.

committee NOUN
el comité

common ADJECTIVE
▷ *see also* **common** NOUN
común (FEM común, PL comunes)
□ 'Smith' is a very common surname. 'Smith' es un apellido muy común.
■ **in common** en común □ We've got a lot in common. Tenemos mucho en común.

common NOUN
▷ *see also* **common** ADJECTIVE
el campo comunal
□ We went for a walk on the common. un paseo por el campo comunal

Commons PL NOUN
■ **the House of Commons** la Cámara de los Comunes

common sense NOUN
el sentido común

to **communicate** VERB
comunicar*

communication NOUN
la comunicación (PL las comunicaciones)

communion NOUN
la comunión (PL las comuniones)

communism NOUN
el comunismo

communist NOUN
▷ *see also* **communist** ADJECTIVE
el/la comunista

communist ADJECTIVE
▷ *see also* **communist** NOUN
comunista (FEM comunista)

community NOUN
la comunidad
■ **the local community** el vecindario
■ **community service** el trabajo comunitario

to **commute** VERB
□ She commutes between Oxford and London. Para ir al trabajo se desplaza diariamente de Oxford a Londres.

compact disc NOUN
el disco compacto
■ **compact disc player** el lector de discos compactos

companion NOUN
el compañero
la compañera

company NOUN
1 la empresa
□ He works for a big company. Trabaja para una empresa grande.
2 la compañía
□ an insurance company una compañía de seguros □ a theatre company una compañía de teatro
■ **to keep somebody company** hacerle compañía a alguien

comparatively ADVERB
relativamente

to **compare** VERB
comparar
□ They compared his work to that of Joyce. Compararon su obra a la de Joyce. □ People always compare him with his brother. La gente siempre lo compara con su hermano.
■ **compared with** en comparación a
□ Oxford is small compared with London. Oxford es pequeño en comparación a Londres.

comparison NOUN
la comparación (PL las comparaciones)

compartment NOUN
el compartimento

compass NOUN
la brújula

compensation NOUN
la indemnización

□ They got £2000 compensation. Recibieron 2.000 libras esterlinas de indemnización.

compere NOUN
el presentador
la presentadora

to **compete** VERB
■ **to compete in** competir en □ I'm competing in the marathon. Compito en el maratón.
■ **to compete for something** competir por algo □ There are 50 students competing for 6 places. Hay 50 estudiantes compitiendo por 6 puestos.

competent ADJECTIVE
competente (FEM competente)

competition NOUN
1 el concurso
□ a singing competition un concurso de canto
2 la competencia
□ Competition in the computer sector is fierce. La competencia en el sector de la informática es muy intensa.

competitive ADJECTIVE
competitivo (FEM competitiva)

competitor NOUN
1 el/la concursante *(contestant)*
2 el/la rival

to **complain** VERB
1 reclamar
□ We're going to complain to the manager. Vamos a reclamar al director.
2 quejarse
□ She's always complaining about her husband. Siempre se está quejando de su marido.

complaint NOUN
la queja

complete ADJECTIVE
completo (FEM completa)

completely ADVERB
completamente

complexion NOUN
el cutis (PL los cutis)

complicated ADJECTIVE
complicado (FEM complicada)

compliment NOUN
▷ *see also* **compliment** VERB
el cumplido
□ to pay somebody a compliment hacerle un cumplido a alguien

to **compliment** VERB
▷ *see also* **compliment** NOUN
felicitar
■ **They complimented me on my Spanish.** Me felicitaron por mi español.

complimentary ADJECTIVE
■ **complimentary ticket** entrada de regalo

composer NOUN
el compositor
la compositora

comprehension NOUN
el ejercicio de comprensión *(school exercise)*

comprehensive school NOUN
el instituto

compromise NOUN
▷ *see also* **compromise** VERB
el arreglo
□ We reached a compromise. Llegamos a un arreglo.

to **compromise** VERB
▷ *see also* **compromise** NOUN
llegar* a un acuerdo

compulsory ADJECTIVE
obligatorio (FEM obligatoria)

computer NOUN
el ordenador (el computador, la computadora *Latin America*)

computer game NOUN
el juego de ordenador

computer programmer NOUN
el programador
la programadora

computer science NOUN
la informática

computing NOUN
la informática

to **concentrate** VERB
concentrarse
□ I couldn't concentrate. No me podía concentrar. □ I was concentrating on my homework. Me estaba concentrando en los deberes.

concentration NOUN
la concentración

concerned ADJECTIVE
preocupado (FEM preocupada)
□ His mother is concerned about him. Su madre está preocupada por él.
■ **As far as the new project is concerned** ... En lo que respecta al nuevo proyecto ...
■ **As far as I'm concerned, you can come any time you like.** Por mí, puedes venir cuando quieras.
■ **It's a stressful situation for everyone concerned.** Es una situación estresante para todos los involucrados.

concert NOUN
el concierto

concrete NOUN
el hormigón

to **condemn** VERB
condenar

condition NOUN
la condición (PL las condiciones)

□ I'll do it, on one condition. Lo haré, con una condición.

■ **in good condition** en buen estado

conditional NOUN
el condicional

conditioner NOUN
el suavizante (el enjuague *Latin America*) *(for hair)*

condom NOUN
el preservativo

to **conduct** VERB
dirigir* *(orchestra)*

conductor NOUN
1 el director de orquesta
la directora de orquesta *(of orchestra)*
2 el cobrador
la cobradora *(on bus)*

cone NOUN
1 el cucurucho
□ an ice cream cone un cucurucho
2 el cono *(geometric shape)*
■ **a traffic cone** un cono para señalizar el tráfico

conference NOUN
la conferencia

to **confess** VERB
confesar*
□ He confessed to the murder. Confesó haber cometido el asesinato.

confession NOUN
la confesión (PL las confesiones)

confidence NOUN
1 la confianza
□ I've got a lot of confidence in him. Tengo mucha confianza en él.
2 la confianza en sí mismo
□ She lacks confidence. Le falta confianza en sí misma.
■ **I told you that story in confidence.** Te conté esa historia de manera confidencial.

confident ADJECTIVE
1 seguro (FEM segura) *(sure of something)*
□ I'm confident everything will be okay. Estoy seguro de que todo saldrá bien.
2 seguro de sí mismo (FEM segura de sí misma) *(self-assured)*
□ She seems quite confident. Parece muy segura de sí misma.

confidential ADJECTIVE
confidencial (FEM confidencial)

to **confirm** VERB
confirmar

confirmation NOUN
la confirmación (PL las confirmaciones)

conflict NOUN
el conflicto

to **confuse** VERB
confundir

confused ADJECTIVE
confuso (FEM confusa) *(person)*

confusing ADJECTIVE
poco claro (FEM poco clara)
□ The traffic signs are confusing. Las señales de tráfico están poco claras.

confusion NOUN
la confusión

to **congratulate** VERB
felicitar
□ My friends congratulated me on passing my test. Mis amigos me felicitaron por aprobar el examen.

congratulations PL NOUN
la enhorabuena
□ Congratulations on your new job! ¡Enhorabuena por tu nuevo empleo!

conjunction NOUN
la conjunción

conjurer NOUN
el prestidigitador
la prestidigitadora

connection NOUN
1 la conexión (PL las conexiones)
□ There's no connection between the two events. No hay ninguna conexión entre los dos sucesos.
2 el enlace
□ We missed our connection. Perdimos el enlace.
■ **There's a loose connection.** Hay un hilo suelto.

to **conquer** VERB
1 conquistar *(country)*
2 vencer* *(enemy, fear)*

conscience NOUN
la conciencia
■ **to have a guilty conscience** tener remordimientos de conciencia

conscious ADJECTIVE
consciente (FEM consciente)
□ He was still conscious when the doctor arrived. Estaba todavía consciente cuando llegó el médico. □ She was conscious of Max looking at her. Era consciente de que Max la miraba.
■ **He made a conscious decision to tell nobody.** Tomó la firme decisión de no decírselo a nadie.

consciousness NOUN
el conocimiento
□ I lost consciousness. Perdí el conocimiento.

consequence NOUN
la consecuencia

consequently ADVERB
por consiguiente

conservation NOUN
la conservación

■ **energy conservation** la conservación de la energía

conservative ADJECTIVE
▷ *see also* **conservative** NOUN
conservador (FEM conservadora)
■ **the Conservative Party** el partido Conservador

Conservative NOUN
▷ *see also* **conservative** ADJECTIVE
el conservador
la conservadora
■ **to vote Conservative** votar a favor del partido Conservador

conservatory NOUN
el invernadero

to **consider** VERB
1 considerar
□ He considers it a waste of time. Lo considera una pérdida de tiempo.
2 pensar* en
■ **We considered cancelling our holiday.** Pensamos en cancelar nuestras vacaciones.

considerate ADJECTIVE
considerado (FEM considerada)

considering PREPOSITION
1 teniendo en cuenta
□ Considering he was ill, he ate well. Teniendo en cuenta que estaba enfermo, comío bien.
2 después de todo
□ I got a good mark, considering. Saqué buena nota, después de todo.

to **consist** VERB
■ **to consist of** consistir en

consonant NOUN
la consonante

constant ADJECTIVE
constante (FEM constante)

constantly ADVERB
constantemente

constipated ADJECTIVE
estreñido (FEM estreñida)
□ I'm constipated. Estoy estreñido.
LANGUAGE TIP Be careful not to translate **constipated** by **constipado**.

to **construct** VERB
construir*

construction NOUN
la construcción (PL las construcciones)

to **consult** VERB
consultar

consumer NOUN
el consumidor
la consumidora

contact NOUN
▷ *see also* **contact** VERB
el contacto
□ I'm in contact with her. Estoy en contacto con ella.

to **contact** VERB
▷ *see also* **contact** NOUN
ponerse* en contacto con
□ Where can we contact you? ¿Dónde podemos ponernos en contacto contigo?

contact lenses PL NOUN
las lentillas (los lentes de contacto *Latin America*)

to **contain** VERB
contener*

container NOUN
el recipiente

contempt NOUN
el desprecio

contents PL NOUN
el contenido

contest NOUN
la competición (PL las competiciones)
□ a fishing contest una competición de pesca
■ **a beauty contest** un concurso de belleza

contestant NOUN
el/la concursante

context NOUN
el contexto

continent NOUN
el continente
■ **the Continent** el continente europeo

continental breakfast NOUN
el desayuno continental

to **continue** VERB
continuar*
□ She continued talking to her friend. Continuó hablando con su amiga. □ We continued working after lunch. Continuamos trabajando después de la comida.

continuous ADJECTIVE
continuo (FEM continua)
■ **continuous assessment** la evaluación continua

contraceptive NOUN
el anticonceptivo

contract NOUN
el contrato

to **contradict** VERB
contradecir*

contrary NOUN
■ **on the contrary** al contrario

contrast NOUN
el contraste

to **contribute** VERB
■ **to contribute to** contribuir a □ Everyone contributed to the success of the play. Todos contribuyeron al éxito de la obra.
□ She contributed £10 to the collection. Contribuyó 10 libras esterlinas a la colecta.

contribution NOUN
la contribución (PL las contribuciones)

control NOUN
▷ *see also* **control** VERB
el control
■ **to lose control** *(of vehicle)* perder el control
■ **the controls** *(of machine)* los mandos
■ **He always seems to be in control.** Parece que siempre está en control la situación.
■ **She can't keep control of the class.** No sabe controlar a la clase.
■ **out of control** fuera de control □ That boy is out of control. Ese muchacho está fuera de control.

to **control** VERB
▷ *see also* **control** NOUN
controlar
□ He can't control the class. No sabe controlar a la clase. □ I couldn't control the horse. No pude controlar al caballo.
□ Please control yourself, everyone's looking at us. Por favor contrólate, todos nos están mirando.

controversial ADJECTIVE
polémico (FEM polémica)
□ Euthanasia is a controversial subject. La eutanasia es un tema polémico.

convenient ADJECTIVE
bien situado (FEM bien situada) *(place)*
□ The hotel's convenient for the airport. El hotel está bien situado con respecto al aeropuerto.
■ **It's not a convenient time for me.** A esa hora no me va bien.
■ **Would Monday be convenient for you?** ¿Te iría bien el lunes?

conventional ADJECTIVE
convencional (FEM convencional)

convent school NOUN
el colegio de monjas

conversation NOUN
las conversación (PL las conversaciones)
□ We had a long conversation. Tuvimos una larga conversación.

to **convert** VERB
convertir*
□ We've converted the loft into a bedroom. Hemos convertido el desván en un dormitorio.

to **convict** VERB
declarar culpable
□ He was convicted of the murder. Fue declarado culpable del asesinato.

to **convince** VERB
convencer*
□ I'm not convinced. No me convence.

to **cook** VERB
▷ *see also* **cook** NOUN
1 cocinar
□ I can't cook. No sé cocinar.
■ **The chicken isn't cooked.** El pollo no está hecho.
2 preparar
□ She's cooking lunch. Está preparando el almuerzo.

cook NOUN
▷ *see also* **cook** VERB
el cocinero
la cocinera
□ She is a cook in a hotel. Es cocinera en un hotel. □ Maria's an excellent cook. María es una cocinera excelente.

cookbook NOUN
el libro de cocina

cooker NOUN
la cocina *(aparato)*
□ a gas cooker una cocina de gas

cookery NOUN
la cocina *(gastronomía)*

cookie NOUN (US)
la galleta

cooking NOUN
la cocina *(gastronomía)*
□ French cooking la cocina francesa
■ **I like cooking.** Me gusta cocinar.

cool ADJECTIVE
fresco (FEM fresca)
□ a cool place un lugar fresco
■ **to stay cool** *(keep calm)* mantenerse en calma □ He stayed cool throughout the crisis. Se mantuvo en calma durante toda la crisis.

cooperation NOUN
la cooperación

cop NOUN
el/la poli *(informal)*

to **cope** VERB
arreglárselas
□ It was hard, but we coped. Fue difícil, pero nos las arreglamos.
■ **She's got a lot of problems to cope with.** Tiene muchos problemas a los que hacer frente.

copper NOUN
1 el cobre
□ a copper bracelet un brazalete de cobre
2 el/la poli *(informal: policeman)*

copy NOUN
▷ *see also* **copy** VERB
1 la copia *(of letter, document)*
2 el ejemplar *(of book)*

to **copy** VERB
▷ *see also* **copy** NOUN
copiar

■ **to copy and paste** *(computing)* copiar y pegar

core NOUN
el corazón (PL los corazones) *(of fruit)*

cork NOUN
el corcho

corkscrew NOUN
el sacacorchos (PL los sacacorchos)

corn NOUN
1 el trigo *(wheat)*
2 el maíz *(sweetcorn)*
■ **corn on the cob** la mazorca de maíz

corner NOUN
1 la esquina
□ the shop on the corner la tienda de la esquina □ He lives just round the corner. Vive a la vuelta de la esquina.
2 el rincón (PL los rincones)
□ in a corner of the room en un rincón de la habitación
3 el saque de esquina *(in football)*

cornet NOUN
1 la corneta *(instrument)*
2 el cucurucho *(ice cream)*

cornflakes PL NOUN
los copos de maíz

cornstarch NOUN (US)
la harina de maíz

Cornwall NOUN
el Cornualles

corporal NOUN
el cabo

corporal punishment NOUN
el castigo corporal

corpse NOUN
el cadáver

correct ADJECTIVE
▷ *see also* **correct** VERB
correcto (FEM correcta)
□ That's correct! ¡Correcto! □ the correct answer la respuesta correcta
■ **You're absolutely correct.** Tienes toda la razón.

to **correct** VERB
▷ *see also* **correct** ADJECTIVE
corregir*

correction NOUN
la corrección (PL las correcciones)

correctly ADVERB
correctamente

correspondent NOUN
el/la corresponsal

corridor NOUN
el pasillo

corruption NOUN
la corrupción

cosmetics PL NOUN
los productos de belleza

to **cost** VERB
▷ *see also* **cost** NOUN
costar*
□ The meal cost £20. La comida costó 20 libras esterlinas. □ How much does it cost? ¿Cuánto cuesta?

cost NOUN
▷ *see also* **cost** VERB
el coste (el costo *Latin America*)
□ the cost of living el coste de vida
■ **at all costs** a toda costa

costume NOUN
el traje

cosy ADJECTIVE
acogedor (FEM acogedora)
□ a cosy room una habitación acogedora

cot NOUN
la cuna

cottage NOUN
el chalet (PL los chalets)

cottage cheese NOUN
el requesón

cotton NOUN
el algodón
□ a cotton shirt una camisa de algodón

cotton wool NOUN
el algodón

couch NOUN
el sofá (PL los sofás)

couchette NOUN
la litera

to **cough** VERB
▷ *see also* **cough** NOUN
toser

cough NOUN
▷ *see also* **cough** VERB
la tos
□ I've got a cough. Tengo tos.
■ **cough mixture** el jarabe para la tos

could VERB ▷ *see* **can**

council NOUN
el ayuntamiento *(in town)*
□ He's on the council. Es concejal del ayuntamiento.
■ **a council estate** un barrio de viviendas de protección oficial
■ **a council house** una casa de protección oficial

councillor NOUN
el concejal
la concejala

to **count** VERB
contar*

to **count on** VERB
contar* con
□ You can count on me. Puedes contar conmigo.

counter NOUN
1 el mostrador *(in shop)*
2 la ventanilla *(in bank, post office)*
3 la ficha *(in game)*

country NOUN
1 el país
□ the border between the two countries la frontera entre los dos países
2 el campo
□ I live in the country. Vivo en el campo.
■ **country dancing** la danza folklórica

countryside NOUN
el campo

county NOUN
el condado

DID YOU KNOW...?
The nearest Spanish equivalent of a county would be a **provincia**.

■ **county council** una corporación administrativa que gobierna un condado

DID YOU KNOW...?
The nearest Spanish equivalent of a county council would be a **diputación provincial**.

couple NOUN
1 la pareja
□ the couple who live next door la pareja que vive al lado
2 el par
□ a couple of hours un par de horas

courage NOUN
el valor

courgette NOUN
el calabacín (PL los calabacines)

courier NOUN
1 el/la guía *(for tourists)*
2 el servicio de mensajero *(delivery service)*
□ They sent it by courier. Lo enviaron por servicio de mensajero.

course NOUN
1 el curso
□ a Spanish course un curso de español
□ to go on a course hacer un curso
2 el plato
□ the main course el segundo plato □ the first course el primer plato
3 el campo
□ a golf course un campo de golf
■ **of course** por supuesto □ Do you love me? — Of course I do! ¿Me quieres? — ¡Por supuesto que te quiero!

court NOUN
el tribunal *(of law)*
■ **a tennis court** una pista de tenis (una cancha de tenis *Latin America*)

courtyard NOUN
el patio

cousin NOUN
el primo
la prima

cover NOUN
▷ *see also* **cover** VERB
1 la tapa *(of book)*
2 la funda *(of duvet)*

to **cover** VERB
▷ *see also* **cover** NOUN
cubrir*
□ My face was covered with mosquito bites. Tenía la cara cubierta de picaduras de mosquito. □ Our insurance didn't cover it. Nuestro seguro no lo cubría.

cow NOUN
la vaca

coward NOUN
el/la cobarde

cowardly ADJECTIVE
cobarde (FEM cobarde)

cowboy NOUN
el vaquero

crab NOUN
el cangrejo

crack NOUN
▷ *see also* **crack** VERB
1 la grieta *(in wall)*
2 la raja *(in cup, window)*
3 el crack *(drug)*
■ **He opened the door a crack.** Abrió la puerta un poquito.
■ **I'll have a crack at it.** Lo intentaré.

to **crack** VERB
▷ *see also* **crack** NOUN
cascar* *(nut, egg)*
■ **He cracked his head on the pavement.** Se dio con la cabeza en la acera.
■ **I think we've cracked it!** ¡Creo que lo hemos resuelto!
■ **to crack a joke** contar un chiste

to **crack down on** VERB
tomar medidas severas contra
□ The police are cracking down on drink-drivers. La policía está tomando medidas severas contra los conductores que beben.

cracked ADJECTIVE
1 rajado (FEM rajada) *(cup, window)*
2 resquebrajado (FEM resquebrajada) *(wall)*

cracker NOUN
la galleta salada *(biscuit)*
■ **Christmas cracker** el petardo sorpresa

cradle NOUN
la cuna

craft NOUN
la artesanía
■ **a craft shop** una tienda de objetos de artesanía

craftsman NOUN
el artesano

to **cram** VERB
■ **We crammed our stuff into the boot.** Apretamos nuestras cosas dentro del maletero.
■ **She crammed her bag with books.** Abarrotó su bolso de libros.
■ **to cram for an exam** empollar a última hora para un examen *(informal)*

crane NOUN
la grúa *(machine)*

to **crash** VERB
▷ *see also* **crash** NOUN
chocar*
□ The two cars crashed. Los dos coches chocaron.
■ **to crash into something** chocar con algo
■ **He's crashed his car.** Ha tenido un accidente con el coche.
■ **The plane crashed.** El avión se estrelló.

crash NOUN
▷ *see also* **crash** VERB
el accidente
■ **a crash helmet** un casco protector
■ **a crash course** un curso intensivo

to **crawl** VERB
▷ *see also* **crawl** NOUN
gatear *(baby)*

crawl NOUN
▷ *see also* **crawl** VERB
el crol
■ **to do the crawl** nadar estilo crol

crazy ADJECTIVE
loco (FEM loca)

cream ADJECTIVE
▷ *see also* **cream** NOUN
de color crema (FEM + PL de color crema)
□ a cream silk blouse una blusa de seda de color crema

cream NOUN
▷ *see also* **cream** ADJECTIVE
1 la nata (la crema de leche *Latin America*)
□ strawberries and cream fresas con nata
□ a cream cake un pastel de nata
■ **cream cheese** el queso cremoso
2 la crema *(for skin)*

crease NOUN
1 la arruga *(in clothes, paper)*
2 la raya *(in trousers)*

creased ADJECTIVE
arrugado (FEM arrugada)

to **create** VERB
crear

creation NOUN
la creación (PL las creaciones)

creative ADJECTIVE
creativo (FEM creativa)

creature NOUN
la criatura

crèche NOUN
la guardería infantil

credit NOUN
el crédito
□ on credit a crédito
■ **He's a credit to his family.** Hace honor a su familia.

credit card NOUN
la tarjeta de crédito

to **creep up** VERB
■ **to creep up on somebody** acercarse sigilosamente a alguien

crept VERB ▷ *see* **creep up**

cress NOUN
el berro

crew NOUN
la tripulación (PL las tripulaciones) *(of plane, boat)*
■ **a film crew** un equipo de rodaje

crew cut NOUN
el pelo cortado al rape

cricket NOUN
1 el críquet
□ I play cricket. Juego al críquet.
2 el grillo *(insect)*

crime NOUN
1 el delito *(offence)*
□ He committed a crime. Cometió un delito. □ the scene of the crime el lugar del delito
2 el crimen (PL los crímenes) *(very serious)*
□ a crime against humanity un crimen contra la humanidad
3 la delincuencia *(activity)*
□ Crime is rising. La delincuencia va en aumento.

criminal NOUN
▷ *see also* **criminal** ADJECTIVE
el/la delincuente

criminal ADJECTIVE
▷ *see also* **criminal** NOUN
■ **It's a criminal offence.** Constituye un delito.
■ **to have a criminal record** tener antecedentes penales

crisis NOUN
la crisis (PL las crisis)

crisp ADJECTIVE
crujiente (FEM crujiente) *(food)*

crisps PL NOUN
las patatas fritas (las papas fritas *Latin America*)
□ a bag of crisps una bolsa de patatas fritas

criterion NOUN
el criterio
□ the selection criteria los criterios de selección
■ **Only one candidate met all the criteria.**

Sólo uno de los candidatos cumplía todos los requisitos.

critic NOUN
el crítico
la crítica

critical ADJECTIVE
crítico (FEM crítica)

criticism NOUN
la crítica

to **criticize** VERB
criticar*

Croatia NOUN
Croacia *fem*

to **crochet** VERB
1 hacer* ganchillo
□ She enjoys crocheting. Le gusta hacer ganchillo.
2 a ganchillo
□ I crocheted a hat. Un gorro a ganchillo.

crocodile NOUN
el cocodrilo

crook NOUN
el/la sinvergüenza

crop NOUN
la cosecha
□ a good crop of apples una buena cosecha de manzanas

cross NOUN
▷ *see also* **cross** ADJECTIVE, VERB
la cruz (PL las cruces)

cross ADJECTIVE
▷ *see also* **cross** NOUN, VERB
enfadado (FEM enfadada) (enojado *Latin America*)
□ He was cross about something. Estaba enfadado por algo.

to **cross** VERB
▷ *see also* **cross** NOUN, ADJECTIVE
cruzar* *(road, river)*

to **cross out** VERB
tachar

cross-country NOUN
■ **a cross-country race** un cross
■ **cross-country skiing** el esquí de fondo

crossing NOUN
1 la travesía
□ a 10-hour crossing una travesía de 10 horas
2 el paso de peatones *(for pedestrians)*

crossroads NOUN
el cruce

crossword NOUN
el crucigrama

LANGUAGE TIP Although **crucigrama** ends in **-a**, it is actually a masculine noun.

to **crouch down** VERB
agacharse

crow NOUN
el cuervo

crowd NOUN
1 la muchedumbre
2 el público *(at sports match)*

crowded ADJECTIVE
abarrotado de gente (FEM abarrotada de gente)

crown NOUN
la corona

crucifix NOUN
el crucifijo

crude ADJECTIVE
vulgar (FEM vulgara)
□ crude language lenguaje vulgar
■ **crude oil** el petróleo en crudo

cruel ADJECTIVE
cruel (FEM cruel)

cruise NOUN
el crucero

crumb NOUN
la miga

to **crush** VERB
1 aplastar *(box, fingers)*
2 machacar*
□ Crush two cloves of garlic. Machacar dos dientes de ajo.

crutch NOUN
la muleta

cry NOUN
▷ *see also* **cry** VERB
el grito
□ He gave a cry of pain. Dio un grito de dolor.
■ **She had a good cry.** Se dio una buena de llorar.

to **cry** VERB
▷ *see also* **cry** NOUN
1 llorar
□ The baby's crying. El bebé está llorando.
2 gritar
□ 'You're wrong', he cried. 'No es cierto', gritó.

crystal NOUN
el cristal

CTC NOUN *(= city technology college)*
el centro de formación profesional

cub NOUN
1 el cachorro *(animal)*
2 el lobato *(scout)*

cube NOUN
1 el cubo *(geometric shape)*
2 el dado
□ Cut the meat into cubes. Cortar la carne en dados.
3 el terrón (PL los terrones) *(of sugar)*

cubic ADJECTIVE
■ **a cubic metre** un metro cúbico

cucumber NOUN
el pepino
to **cuddle** VERB
abrazar*
cue NOUN
el taco *(for snooker, pool)*
culottes PL NOUN
la falda pantalón (PL las faldas pantalón)
culture NOUN
la cultura
cunning ADJECTIVE
1 astuto (FEM astuta) *(person)*
2 ingenioso (FEM ingeniosa)
□ a cunning plan un plan ingenioso
cup NOUN
1 la taza
□ a china cup una taza de porcelana
■ **a cup of coffee** un café
2 la copa *(trophy)*
cupboard NOUN
el armario
to **cure** VERB
▷ *see also* **cure** NOUN
curar
cure NOUN
▷ *see also* **cure** VERB
la cura
□ There is no simple cure for the common cold. No hay una cura sencilla para el catarro común.
curious ADJECTIVE
curioso (FEM curiosa)
■ **to be curious about something** sentir curiosidad por algo
curl NOUN
el rizo
curly ADJECTIVE
rizado (FEM rizada)
currant NOUN
la pasa
currency NOUN
la moneda
□ foreign currency la moneda extranjera
current NOUN
▷ *see also* **current** ADJECTIVE
la corriente
□ The current is very strong. La corriente es muy fuerte.
current ADJECTIVE
▷ *see also* **current** NOUN
1 actual (FEM actual)
□ the current situation la situación actual
2 presente (FEM presente)
□ the current financial year el presente año financiero
current account NOUN
la cuenta corriente
current affairs PL NOUN
los temas de actualidad
curriculum NOUN
el plan de estudios
curriculum vitae NOUN
el currículum vitae
curry NOUN
el curry (PL los curries)
curse NOUN
la maldición (PL las maldiciones)
curtain NOUN
la cortina
cushion NOUN
el cojín (PL los cojines)
custard NOUN
las natillas
custody NOUN
la custodia
□ The mother has custody of the children. La madre tiene la custodia de los hijos.
■ **to be remanded in custody** estar detenido
custom NOUN
la costumbre
□ It's an old custom. Es una vieja costumbre.
customer NOUN
el cliente
la clienta
customs PL NOUN
la aduana
■ **to go through customs** pasar por la aduana
customs officer NOUN
el oficial de aduanas
la oficial de aduanas
cut NOUN
▷ *see also* **cut** VERB
1 el corte
□ He's got a cut on his forehead. Tiene un corte en la frente.
2 la reducción (PL las reducciones) *(in price, spending)*
to **cut** VERB
▷ *see also* **cut** NOUN
1 cortar
□ I'll cut some bread. Voy a cortar pan.
□ I cut my foot on a piece of glass. Me corté el pie con un cristal.
■ **to cut oneself** cortarse
2 reducir* *(price, spending)*
to **cut down** VERB
cortar
■ **She cut down the elm tree.** Cortó el olmo.
to **cut off** VERB
cortar

English-Spanish

C

□ The electricity has been cut off. Han cortado la electricidad. □ We've been cut off. Se ha cortado la comunicación.

to **cut up** VERB
picar* *(vegetables, meat)*

cutback NOUN
el recorte
□ There have been cutbacks in public services. Ha habido recortes en los servicios públicos.

cute ADJECTIVE
mono (FEM mona) *(baby, pet)*
□ Isn't he cute! ¡Qué mono es!

cutlery NOUN
la cubertería

CV NOUN
el currículum vitae

cybercafé NOUN
el cibercafé

to **cycle** VERB
▷ *see also* **cycle** NOUN
ir* en bicicleta
□ I cycle to school. Voy al colegio en bicicleta.

cycle NOUN
▷ *see also* **cycle** VERB
la bicicleta
□ a cycle ride un paseo en bicicleta

cycle lane NOUN
el carril-bibi

cycling NOUN
el ciclismo
■ **The roads round here are ideal for cycling.** Las carreteras de por aquí son ideales para ir en bicicleta.

cyclist NOUN
el/la ciclista

cylinder NOUN
el cilindro

Cyprus NOUN
Chipre *fem*

Czech NOUN
▷ *see also* **Czech** ADJECTIVE
1 el checo
la checa *(person)*
□ the Czechs los checos
2 el checo *(language)*

Czech ADJECTIVE
▷ *see also* **Czech** NOUN
checo (FEM checa)
■ **the Czech Republic** la República Checa

Dd

dad NOUN
1 el padre
□ my dad mi padre
2 papá
□ I'll ask Dad. Se lo preguntaré a papá.

daddy NOUN
papá

daffodil NOUN
el narciso

daft ADJECTIVE
estúpido (FEM estúpida)

daily ADJECTIVE, ADVERB
1 diario
□ daily life la vida diaria □ It's part of my daily routine. Forma parte de mi rutina diaria.
■ **a daily paper** un periódico
2 todos los días
□ The pool is open daily. La piscina abre todos los días.

dairy NOUN
la lechería

dairy products PL NOUN
los productos lácteos

daisy NOUN
la margarita

dam NOUN
la presa

damage NOUN
▷ *see also* **damage** VERB
los daños
□ The storm did a lot of damage. La tormenta provocó muchos daños.

to **damage** VERB
▷ *see also* **damage** NOUN
dañar

damn NOUN
▷ *see also* **damn** ADJECTIVE
■ **I don't give a damn!** *(informal)* ¡Me importa un rábano!
■ **Damn!** *(informal)* ¡Maldita sea!

damn ADJECTIVE
▷ *see also* **damn** NOUN
■ **It's a damn nuisance!** *(informal)* ¡Es una verdadera lata!

damp ADJECTIVE
húmedo (FEM húmeda)

dance NOUN
▷ *see also* **dance** VERB
el baile

to **dance** VERB
▷ *see also* **dance** NOUN
bailar

dancer NOUN
1 el bailador
la bailadora
■ **He is not a very good dancer.** No baila muy bien.
2 el bailarín (PL los bailarines)
la bailarina *(professional)*

dandruff NOUN
la caspa

Dane NOUN
el danés (PL los daneses)
la danesa
□ the Danes los daneses

danger NOUN
el peligro
■ **in danger** en peligro
■ **We were in danger of missing the plane.** Corríamos el riesgo de perder el avión.

dangerous ADJECTIVE
peligroso (FEM peligrosa)

Danish ADJECTIVE
▷ *see also* **Danish** NOUN
danés (FEM danesa)

Danish NOUN
▷ *see also* **Danish** ADJECTIVE
el danés *(language)*

to **dare** VERB
atreverse
□ I didn't dare to tell my parents. No me atreví a decírselo a mis padres.
■ **I dare say it'll be okay.** Yo diría que va a salir bien.
■ **Don't you dare!** ¡Ni se te ocurra!
■ **I dare you!** ¡A que no te atreves!

daring ADJECTIVE
atrevido (FEM atrevida)

dark ADJECTIVE
▷ *see also* **dark** NOUN
oscuro (FEM oscura)
□ a dark green sweater un jersey verde oscuro

□ It's dark in here. Está oscuro aquí dentro.
■ **She's got dark hair.** Tiene el pelo oscuro.
■ **He's got dark skin.** Tiene la piel morena.
■ **It's getting dark.** Está oscureciendo.

dark NOUN
▷ *see also* **dark** ADJECTIVE
la oscuridad
□ I'm afraid of the dark. Me da miedo la oscuridad.
■ **after dark** después del anochecer

darkness NOUN
la oscuridad
□ in the darkness en la oscuridad
■ **The room was in darkness.** La habitación estaba a oscuras.

darling NOUN
cariño
□ Thank you, darling. Gracias, cariño.

dart NOUN
el dardo
□ to play darts jugar a los dardos

to **dash** VERB
▷ *see also* **dash** NOUN
ir* corriendo
□ Everyone dashed to the window. Todos fueron corriendo a la ventana.
■ **I've got to dash!** ¡Tengo que salir pitando!

dash NOUN
▷ *see also* **dash** VERB
1 el chorrito
□ a dash of vinegar un chorrito de vinagre
2 la raya *(punctuation mark)*

data PL NOUN
los datos

database NOUN
la base de datos

date NOUN
1 la fecha
□ my date of birth mi fecha de nacimiento
■ **What's the date today?** ¿A qué estamos hoy?
■ **He's got a date with his girlfriend.** Ha quedado con su novia.
■ **out of date 1** *(document)* caducado □ My passport's out of date. Tengo el pasaporte caducado. **2** *(technology, idea)* anticuado
2 el dátil *(fruit)*

daughter NOUN
la hija

daughter-in-law NOUN
la nuera

dawn NOUN
el amanecer
□ at dawn al amanecer

day NOUN
el día

LANGUAGE TIP Although **día** ends in **-a**, it is actually a masculine noun.

□ during the day por el día □ It's a lovely day. Hace un día precioso. □ every day todos los días
■ **the day after tomorrow** pasado mañana
■ **the day before yesterday** anteayer
■ **a day off** un día libre
■ **a day return** un billete de ida y vuelta para el día

dead ADJECTIVE
▷ *see also* **dead** ADVERB
muerto (FEM muerta)
□ He was dead. Estaba muerto.
■ **He was shot dead.** Lo mataron de un tiro.

dead ADVERB
▷ *see also* **dead** ADJECTIVE
■ **You're dead right!** ¡Tienes toda la razón!
■ **It was dead easy.** Fue facilísimo.
■ **dead centre** justo en el centro
■ **dead on time** a la hora exacta

dead end NOUN
el callejón sin salida

deadline NOUN
■ **October is the deadline for applications.** El plazo para presentar las solicitudes se acaba en octubre.
■ **We're going to miss the deadline.** No vamos a poder cumplir con el plazo.

deaf ADJECTIVE
sordo (FEM sorda)

deafening ADJECTIVE
ensordecedor (FEM ensordecedora)

deal NOUN
▷ *see also* **deal** VERB
el trato
□ It's a good deal. Es un buen trato. □ He made a deal with the kidnappers. Hizo un trato con los secuestradores.
■ **It's a deal!** ¡Trato hecho!
■ **Big deal!** ¡Vaya cosa!
■ **It's no big deal.** No pasa nada.
■ **a great deal** mucho □ a great deal of money mucho dinero

to **deal** VERB
▷ *see also* **deal** NOUN
dar* cartas
□ It's your turn to deal. Te toca dar cartas.

dealer NOUN
■ **a drug dealer** un traficante de drogas (FEM una traficante de drogas)
■ **an antique dealer** un anticuario (FEM una anticuario)

dealt VERB ▷ *see* **deal**

dear ADJECTIVE
1 querido (FEM querida)
□ Dear Paul Querido Paul
■ **Dear Mrs Smith** Estimada señora Smith
■ **Dear Sir** Muy señor mío
■ **Dear Madam** Estimada señora

■ **Dear Sir/Madam** *(in a circular)* Estimados Sres.
■ **Oh dear! I've spilled my coffee.** ¡Oh, no! He derramado el café.
2 caro (FEM cara) *(expensive)*
□ These shoes are too dear. Estos zapatos son demasiado caros.

death NOUN
la muerte
□ after his death después de su muerte
■ **I was bored to death.** Estaba aburrido como una ostra.

debate NOUN
▷ *see also* **debate** VERB
el debate

to **debate** VERB
▷ *see also* **debate** NOUN
discutir

debt NOUN
la deuda
□ heavy debts grandes deudas
■ **to be in debt** estar endeudado

decade NOUN
la década

decaffeinated ADJECTIVE
descafeinado (FEM descafeinada)

to **deceive** VERB
engañar

December NOUN
diciembre *masc*
■ **in December** en diciembre
■ **on 22 December** el 22 de diciembre

decent ADJECTIVE
decente (FEM decente)

to **decide** VERB
1 decidir
□ I decided to write to her. Decidí escribirle.
□ I decided not to go. Decidí no ir.
2 decidirse
□ Haven't you decided yet? ¿Aún no te has decidido?

decimal ADJECTIVE
decimal (FEM decimal)
□ the decimal system el sistema decimal
■ **decimal point** la coma decimal

decision NOUN
la decisión (PL las decisiones)
■ **to make a decision** tomar una decisión

decisive ADJECTIVE
decidido (FEM decidida) *(person)*

deck NOUN
1 la cubierta *(of ship)*
■ **on deck** en cubierta
2 el piso *(of bus)*
■ **a deck of cards** una baraja

deckchair NOUN
la tumbona

to **declare** VERB
declarar

to **decorate** VERB
1 decorar
□ I decorated the cake with glacé cherries. Decoré el pastel con guindas confitadas.
2 pintar *(paint)*
3 empapelar *(wallpaper)*

decrease NOUN
▷ *see also* **decrease** VERB
la disminución (PL las disminuciones)
□ There has been a decrease in the school roll. Ha habido una disminución en el número de alumnos.

to **decrease** VERB
▷ *see also* **decrease** NOUN
disminuir*

dedicated ADJECTIVE
■ **a very dedicated teacher** un maestro totalmente entregado a su trabajo
■ **dedicated followers of classical music** devotos seguidores de la música clásica

to **deduct** VERB
descontar*

deep ADJECTIVE
1 profundo (FEM profunda)
■ **a hole four metres deep** un agujero de cuatro metros de profundidad
■ **How deep is the lake?** ¿Qué profundidad tiene el lago?
2 espeso (FEM espesa)
□ a deep layer of snow una espesa capa de nieve
3 grave (FEM grave)
□ He's got a deep voice. Tiene la voz grave.
■ **to take a deep breath** respirar hondo
■ **to be deep in debt** estar hasta el cuello de deudas

deeply ADVERB
profundamente
□ deeply grateful profundamente agradecido

deer NOUN
el ciervo

defeat NOUN
▷ *see also* **defeat** VERB
la derrota

to **defeat** VERB
▷ *see also* **defeat** NOUN
derrotar

defect NOUN
el defecto

defence NOUN
la defensa

to **defend** VERB
defender*

defender NOUN
1 el defensor
la defensora *(of person, ideas)*

2 el/la defensa *(in sports)*

to **define** VERB
definir

definite ADJECTIVE
1 concreto (FEM concreta)
□ I haven't got any definite plans. No tengo planes concretos.
2 definitivo (FEM definitiva)
□ It's too soon to give a definite answer. Es pronto aún para dar una respuesta definitiva.
3 seguro (FEM segura)
□ Maybe we'll go to Spain, but it's not definite. Quizá vayamos a España, pero no es seguro.
■ **He was definite about it.** Fue rotundo acerca de esto.
4 claro (FEM clara)
□ It's a definite improvement. Es una clara mejoría.

definitely ADVERB
sin duda
□ He's definitely the best player. Es sin duda el mejor jugador.
■ **He's the best player. — Definitely!** Es el mejor jugador. — ¡Desde luego!
■ **Are you going out with him? — Definitely not!** ¿Vas a salir con él? — ¡En absoluto!

definition NOUN
la definición (PL las definiciones)

degree NOUN
1 el grado
□ a temperature of 30 degrees una temperatura de 30 grados
2 la licenciatura
□ a degree in English una licenciatura en filología inglesa
■ **She's got a degree in English.** Es licenciada en filología inglesa.

to **delay** VERB
▷ *see also* **delay** NOUN
retrasar
□ We decided to delay our departure. Decidimos retrasar la salida.
■ **Don't delay!** ¡No pierdas tiempo!
■ **to be delayed** retrasarse □ Our flight was delayed. Nuestro vuelo se retrasó.

delay NOUN
▷ *see also* **delay** VERB
el retraso
□ The tests have caused some delay. Las pruebas han ocasionado algún retraso.
■ **without delay** enseguida

to **delete** VERB
suprimir

deliberate ADJECTIVE
intencionado (FEM intencionada)

deliberately ADVERB
a propósito

delicate ADJECTIVE
delicado (FEM delicada)

delicatessen NOUN
la charcutería

delicious ADJECTIVE
delicioso (FEM deliciosa)

delight NOUN
el placer

delighted ADJECTIVE
encantado (FEM encantada)
□ He'll be delighted to see you. Estará encantado de verte.

delightful ADJECTIVE
encantador (FEM encantadora)

to **deliver** VERB
1 repartir
□ I deliver newspapers. Reparto periódicos.
2 entregar*
□ The package was delivered in the morning. Entregaron el paquete por la mañana.
■ **Doctor Hamilton delivered the twins.** El Doctor Hamilton asistió en el parto de los gemelos.

delivery NOUN
1 la entrega
□ Allow 28 days for delivery. La entrega se realizará en un plazo de 28 días.
2 el parto *(of baby)*

to **demand** VERB
▷ *see also* **demand** NOUN
exigir*
□ I demand an explanation. Exijo una explicación.

demand NOUN
▷ *see also* **demand** VERB
1 la petición (PL las peticiones) *(firm request)*
□ His demand for compensation was rejected. Rechazaron su petición de indemnización.
2 la reivindicación (PL las reivindicaciones) *(of trade union)*
□ They met to discuss the union's demands. Se reunieron para discutir las reivindicaciones del sindicato.
3 la demanda
□ Demand for coal is down. Ha bajado la demanda de carbón.

demanding ADJECTIVE
■ **It's a very demanding job.** Es un trabajo que exige mucho.
■ **a demanding child** un niño exigente

demo NOUN
la manifestación (PL las manifestaciones)

democracy NOUN
la democracia

democratic ADJECTIVE
democrático (FEM democrática)

to **demolish** VERB
derribar

to **demonstrate** VERB
1 demostrar*
□ You have to demonstrate that you are reliable. Tienes que demostrar que se puede confiar en ti.
■ **She demonstrated the technique.** Hizo una demostración de la técnica.
2 manifestarse*
□ They demonstrated outside the court. Se manifestaron a las puertas del tribunal.

demonstration NOUN
1 la demostración (PL las demostraciones) *(of method, product)*
2 la manifestación (PL las manifestaciones) *(protest)*

demonstrator NOUN
el/la manifestante

denim NOUN
■ **a denim jacket** una cazadora vaquera

denims PL NOUN
los vaqueros

Denmark NOUN
Dinamarca *fem*

dense ADJECTIVE
1 denso (FEM densa) *(smoke, fog)*
2 espeso (FEM espesa) *(vegetation)*
■ **He's so dense!** ¡Mira que es corto! *(informal)*

dent NOUN
▷ *see also* **dent** VERB
la abolladura

to **dent** VERB
▷ *see also* **dent** NOUN
abollar

dental ADJECTIVE
dental (FEM dental)
□ dental treatment el tratamiento dental
■ **a dental appointment** una cita con el dentista
■ **dental floss** la seda dental

dentist NOUN
el/la dentista
□ Catherine is a dentist. Catherine es dentista. □ at the dentist's en el dentista

to **deny** VERB
negar*
□ She denied everything. Lo negó todo.

deodorant NOUN
el desodorante

to **depart** VERB
1 partir* *(person)*
□ He departed at three o'clock precisely. Partió a las tres en punto.
2 salir*
□ Trains depart for the airport every half hour. Los trenes salen para el aeropuerto cada media hora.

department NOUN
1 la sección (PL las secciones)
□ the toy department la sección de juguetes
2 el departamento
□ the English department el departamento de inglés

department store NOUN
los grandes almacenes

departure NOUN
la salida
□ The departure of this flight has been delayed. Se ha retrasado la salida de este vuelo.
■ **His sudden departure worried us.** Su marcha repentina nos dejó preocupados.

departure lounge NOUN
la sala de embarque

to **depend** VERB
■ **to depend on** depender de □ The price depends on the quality. El precio depende de la calidad.
■ **You can depend on him.** Puedes confiar en él.
■ **depending on** según
LANGUAGE TIP **según** has to be followed by a verb in the subjunctive.
□ depending on the weather según el tiempo que haga
■ **It depends.** Depende.

to **deport** VERB
deportar

deposit NOUN
1 el depósito *(on hired goods)*
□ You get the deposit back when you return the bike. Al devolver la bici te devuelven el depósito.
2 la señal *(advance payment)*
□ You have to pay a deposit when you book. Se paga una señal al hacer la reserva.
3 la entrada *(in house buying)*
□ He paid a £2000 deposit on the house. Dio una entrada de 2.000 libras para la casa.

depressed ADJECTIVE
deprimido (FEM deprimida)
□ I'm feeling depressed. Estoy deprimido.

depressing ADJECTIVE
deprimente (FEM deprimente)

depth NOUN
la profundidad
□ 14 feet in depth 14 pies de profundidad
■ **to deal with a subject in depth** tratar un tema a fondo

deputy head NOUN
el subdirector
la subdirectora

to **descend** VERB
descender*
□ They descended from the roof slowly. Descendieron con cuidado del tejado.
to **describe** VERB
describir*
description NOUN
la descripción (PL las descripciones)
desert NOUN
el desierto
desert island NOUN
la isla desierta
to **deserve** VERB
merecer*
design NOUN
▹ *see also* **design** VERB
1 el diseño
□ The design of the plane makes it safer. El diseño del avión lo hace más seguro.
□ a design fault un fallo en el diseño
2 el motivo
□ a geometric design un motivo geométrico
■ **fashion design** diseño de modas
to **design** VERB
▹ *see also* **design** NOUN
1 diseñar
□ She designed the dress herself. Ella misma diseñó el vestido.
2 elaborar
□ We will design an exercise plan specially for you. Elaboraremos un programa de ejercicios especial para ti.
designer NOUN
el/la modista *(of clothes)*
■ **designer clothes** la ropa de diseño
desire NOUN
▹ *see also* **desire** VERB
el deseo
to **desire** VERB
▹ *see also* **desire** NOUN
desear
desk NOUN
1 el escritorio *(in office)*
2 el pupitre *(for pupil)*
3 el mostrador *(in hotel, at airport)*
despair NOUN
la desesperación
□ a feeling of despair un sentimiento de desesperación
■ **to be in despair** estar desesperado
desperate ADJECTIVE
desesperado (FEM desesperada)
□ a desperate situation una situación desesperada
■ **I was starting to get desperate.** Estaba empezando a desesperarme.
desperately ADVERB
1 tremendamente
□ We're desperately worried. Estamos tremendamente preocupados.
2 desesperadamente
□ He was desperately trying to persuade her. Intentaba desesperadamente convencerla.
to **despise** VERB
despreciar
despite PREPOSITION
a pesar de
dessert NOUN
el postre
□ for dessert de postre
destination NOUN
el destino
to **destroy** VERB
destruir*
destruction NOUN
la destrucción
detached house NOUN
la casa no adosada
detail NOUN
el detalle
□ I can't remember the details. No recuerdo los detalles.
■ **in detail** detalladamente
detailed ADJECTIVE
detallado (FEM detallada)
detective NOUN
el/la detective
□ He's a detective. Es detective. □ a private detective un detective privado
■ **a detective story** una novela policíaca
detention NOUN
■ **to get a detention** quedarse castigado después de clase
detergent NOUN
el detergente
determined ADJECTIVE
decidido (FEM decidida)
□ She's determined to succeed. Está decidida a triunfar.
detour NOUN
el desvío
devaluation NOUN
la devaluación
devastated ADJECTIVE
deshecho (FEM deshecha)
□ I was devastated when they told me. Cuando me lo dijeron me quedé deshecho.
devastating ADJECTIVE
devastador (FEM devastadora) *(flood, storm)*
□ Unemployment has a devastating effect on people. El desempleo tiene efectos devastadores en la gente.
■ **She received some devastating news.** Recibió unas noticias desoladoras.
to **develop** VERB
1 desarrollar *(idea, quality)*

□ I developed his original idea. Yo desarrollé su idea original.
2 desarrollarse
□ Girls develop faster than boys. Las chicas se desarrollan más rápido que los chicos.
3 revelar
□ to get a film developed revelar un carrete
■ **to develop into** convertirse en □ The argument developed into a fight. La discusión se convirtió en una pelea.

development NOUN
el desarrollo
□ economic development in Pakistan el desarrollo económico de Pakistán
■ **the latest developments** los últimos acontecimientos

device NOUN
el dispositivo

devil NOUN
el diablo

to **devise** VERB
idear

devoted ADJECTIVE
leal (FEM leal) *(friend)*
■ **a devoted wife** una abnegada esposa
■ **He's completely devoted to her.** Está totalmente entregado a ella.

diabetes NOUN
la diabetes

diabetic ADJECTIVE
diabético (FEM diabética)
□ I'm diabetic. Soy diabético.
■ **diabetic chocolate** el chocolate para diabéticos

diagonal ADJECTIVE
diagonal (FEM diagonal)

diagram NOUN
el diagrama
LANGUAGE TIP Although **diagrama** ends in **-a**, it is actually a masculine noun.

to **dial** VERB
marcar* (discar* *Latin America*)

dialling tone NOUN
la señal de marcar

dialogue NOUN
el diálogo

diamond NOUN
el diamante
□ a diamond ring un anillo de diamantes
■ **diamonds** *(at cards)* los diamantes □ the ace of diamonds el as de diamantes

diaper NOUN (US)
el pañal

diarrhoea NOUN
la diarrea
□ to have diarrhoea tener diarrea

diary NOUN
1 la agenda
□ I've got her phone number in my diary. Tengo su número de teléfono en la agenda.
2 el diario
□ I keep a diary. Estoy escribiendo un diario.

dice NOUN
el dado

dictation NOUN
el dictado

dictionary NOUN
el diccionario

did VERB ▷ *see* **do**

to **die** VERB
morir*
□ He died last year. Murió el año pasado.
□ She's dying. Se está muriendo.
■ **to be dying to do something** morirse de ganas de hacer algo

diesel NOUN
1 el gasoil *(fuel)*
2 el coche diesel *(car)*

diet NOUN
▷ *see also* **diet** VERB
1 la dieta
□ a healthy diet una dieta sana
2 el régimen (PL los regímenes)
□ I'm on a diet. Estoy a régimen.
■ **a diet Coke®** una Coca-Cola® light

to **diet** VERB
▷ *see also* **diet** NOUN
hacer* régimen
□ I've been dieting for two months. Llevo dos meses haciendo régimen.

difference NOUN
la diferencia
□ There's not much difference in age between us. No hay mucha diferencia de edad entre nosotros.
■ **Good weather makes all the difference.** Con buen tiempo la cosa cambia mucho.
■ **It makes no difference.** Da lo mismo.

different ADJECTIVE
distinto (FEM distinta)

difficult ADJECTIVE
difícil (FEM difícil)
□ It was difficult to choose. Era difícil escoger. □ It was a difficult decision to make. Era una decisión difícil de tomar.

difficulty NOUN
la dificultad
□ What's the difficulty? ¿Cuál es la dificultad?
■ **to have difficulty doing something** tener dificultades para hacer algo

to **dig** VERB
1 cavar
□ They're digging a hole in the road. Están cavando un hoyo en la calle. □ Dad's out

digging the garden. Papá está fuera cavando en el jardín.
2 escarbar
□ The dog dug a hole in the sand. El perro escarbó un agujero en la arena.

digestion NOUN
la digestión

digger NOUN
la excavadora

digital camera NOUN
la cámara digital

digital radio NOUN
la radio digital

digital television NOUN
la televisión digital

digital watch NOUN
el reloj digital (PL los relojes digitales)

dim ADJECTIVE
1 tenue (FEM tenue) *(light)*
2 lerdo (FEM lerda) *(person)*

dimension NOUN
la dimensión (PL las dimensiones)

to **diminish** VERB
disminuir*

din NOUN
1 el estruendo *(of traffic, machinery)*
2 el jaleo *(of crowd, voices)*

diner NOUN (US)
el restaurante barato

dinghy NOUN
■ **a rubber dinghy** una lancha neumática
■ **a sailing dinghy** una embarcación de vela ligera

dining car NOUN
el vagón restaurante (PL los vagones restaurante)

dining room NOUN
el comedor

dinner NOUN
1 la comida *(at midday)*
2 la cena (la comida *Latin America*) *(in the evening)*
■ **The children have dinner at school.** Los niños comen en la escuela.

dinner jacket NOUN
el esmoquin (PL los esmóquines)

dinner party NOUN
la cena

dinner time NOUN
1 la hora de la comida *(at midday)*
2 la hora de la cena *(in the evening)*

dinosaur NOUN
el dinosaurio

dip
▷ *see also* **dip** VERB NOUN
la salsa
□ a spicy dip una salsa picante
■ **to go for a dip** ir a darse un chapuzón

to **dip** VERB
▷ *see also* **dip** NOUN
mojar
□ He dipped a biscuit into his tea. Mojó una galleta en el té.

diploma NOUN
el diploma
LANGUAGE TIP Although **diploma** ends in **-a**, it is actually a masculine noun.

diplomat NOUN
el diplomático
la diplomática

diplomatic ADJECTIVE
diplomático (FEM diplomática)

direct ADJECTIVE, ADVERB
▷ *see also* **direct** VERB
directo (FEM directa)
□ the most direct route el camino más directo
■ **You can't fly to Manchester direct from Seville.** No hay vuelos directos a Manchester desde Sevilla.

to **direct** VERB
▷ *see also* **direct** ADJECTIVE
dirigir*

direction NOUN
la dirección (PL las direcciones)
□ We're going in the wrong direction. Vamos en la dirección equivocada.
■ **to ask somebody for directions** preguntar el camino a alguien

director NOUN
el director
la directora

directory NOUN
1 la guía telefónica *(telephone)*
■ **directory enquiries** información telefónica
2 el directorio *(in computing)*

dirt NOUN
la suciedad

dirty ADJECTIVE
sucio (FEM sucia)
□ It's dirty. Está sucio.
■ **to get dirty** ensuciarse
■ **to get something dirty** ensuciarse algo
□ He got his hands dirty. Se ensució las manos.
■ **a dirty joke** un chiste verde (un chiste colorado *Latin America*)

disabled ADJECTIVE, NOUN
minusválido (FEM minusválida)
■ **disabled people** los minusválidos

disadvantage NOUN
la desventaja
■ **to be at a disadvantage** estar en desventaja

to **disagree** VERB

■ **We always disagree.** Nunca estamos de acuerdo.
■ **He disagrees with me.** No está de acuerdo conmigo.

disagreement NOUN
el desacuerdo

to **disappear** VERB
desaparecer*

disappearance NOUN
la desaparición (PL las desapariciones)

disappointed ADJECTIVE
decepcionado (FEM decepcionada)
□ I'm disappointed. Estoy decepcionado.

disappointing ADJECTIVE
decepcionante (FEM decepcionante)
□ It's disappointing. Es decepcionante.

disappointment NOUN
la decepción (PL las decepciones)

disaster NOUN
el desastre

disastrous ADJECTIVE
desastroso (FEM desastrosa)

disc NOUN
el disco

discipline NOUN
la disciplina

disc jockey NOUN
el/la discjockey (PL los/las discjockeys)
□ He's a disc jockey. Es discjockey.

disco NOUN
1 la discoteca *(place)*
2 el baile
□ There's a disco at school tonight. Esta noche hay baile en la escuela.

to **disconnect** VERB
desconectar *(appliance)*
■ **to disconnect the water supply** cortar el agua

discount NOUN
el descuento
□ a 20% discount un descuento del 20 por ciento

to **discourage** VERB
desanimar
■ **to get discouraged** desanimarse

to **discover** VERB
descubrir*

discrimination NOUN
la discriminación
□ racial discrimination la discriminación racial

to **discuss** VERB
1 discutir
□ I'll discuss it with my parents. Lo discutiré con mis padres.
2 discutir sobre *(topic)*
□ We discussed the topic at length. Discutimos sobre el tema largo y tendido.

discussion NOUN
la discusión (PL las discusiones)

disease NOUN
la enfermedad

disgraceful ADJECTIVE
vergonzoso (FEM vergonzosa)

disgusted ADJECTIVE
indignado (FEM indignada)
□ I was completely disgusted. Estaba totalmente indignado.

LANGUAGE TIP Be careful not to translate **disgusted** by **disgustado**.

disgusting ADJECTIVE
1 asqueroso (FEM asquerosa) *(food, smell)*
□ It looks disgusting. Tiene un aspecto asqueroso.
2 indignante (FEM indignante) *(disgraceful)*
□ That's disgusting! ¡Es indignante!

dish NOUN
el plato
□ a china dish un plato de porcelana
□ a vegetarian dish un plato vegetariano
■ **to do the dishes** fregar los platos
■ **a satellite dish** una antena parabólica

dishonest ADJECTIVE
poco honrado (FEM poco honrada)

dish soap NOUN (US)
el lavavajillas (PL los lavavajillas)

dish towel NOUN (US)
el paño de cocina

dishwasher NOUN
el lavaplatos (PL los lavaplatos)

disinfectant NOUN
el desinfectante

disk NOUN
el disco
■ **the hard disk** el disco duro
■ **disk drive** la unidad de disco

diskette NOUN
el disquete

to **dislike** VERB
▷ *see also* **dislike** NOUN
■ **I dislike it.** No me gusta.

dislike NOUN
▷ *see also* **dislike** VERB
■ **to take a dislike to somebody** coger antipatía a alguien (agarrar antipatía a alguien *Latin America*)

LANGUAGE TIP Be very careful with the verb **coger**: in most of Latin America this is an extremely rude word that should be avoided. However, in Spain this verb is common and not rude at all.

■ **my likes and dislikes** lo que me gusta y lo que no

to **dismiss** VERB
despedir* *(employee)*

English-Spanish

d

disobedient ADJECTIVE
desobediente (FEM desobediente)

display NOUN
▷ *see also* **display** VERB
■ **The assistant took the watch out of the display.** El dependiente sacó el reloj de la vitrina.
■ **There was a lovely display of fruit in the window.** Había un estupendo surtido de fruta en el escaparate.
■ **to be on display** estar expuesto
■ **a firework display** fuegos artificiales

to **display** VERB
▷ *see also* **display** NOUN
1 mostrar*
□ She proudly displayed her medal. Mostró con orgullo su medalla.
2 exponer* *(in shop window)*

disposable ADJECTIVE
desechable (FEM desechable)
■ **a disposable razor** una maquinilla desechable

to **disqualify** VERB
descalificar*
■ **to be disqualified** ser descalificado
□ They were disqualified from the competition. Fueron descalificados del campeonato.
■ **He was disqualified from driving.** Le retiraron el carnet de conducir.

to **disrupt** VERB
interrumpir
□ The meeting was disrupted by protesters. La reunión fue interrumpida por unos manifestantes.
■ **Train services are being disrupted by the strike.** El servicio ferroviario se está viendo alterado por la huelga.

dissatisfied ADJECTIVE
insatisfecho (FEM insatisfecha)
□ We were dissatisfied with the service. Estábamos insatisfechos con el servicio.

to **dissolve** VERB
disolver*

distance NOUN
la distancia
□ a distance of forty kilometres una distancia de cuarenta kilómetros
■ **It's within walking distance.** Se puede ir andando.
■ **in the distance** a lo lejos

distant ADJECTIVE
lejano (FEM lejana)
□ in the distant future en un futuro lejano

distinction NOUN
1 la distinción (PL las distinciones)
□ to make a distinction between two things hacer una distinción entre dos cosas
2 la matrícula de honor
□ I got a distinction in Spanish. Saqué una matrícula de honor en lengua española.

distinctive ADJECTIVE
característico (FEM característica)

to **distract** VERB
distraer*

to **distribute** VERB
distribuir*

district NOUN
1 el barrio *(of town)*
2 la región (PL las regiones) *(of country)*

to **disturb** VERB
molestar
□ I'm sorry to disturb you. Siento molestarte.

ditch NOUN
▷ *see also* **ditch** VERB
la zanja

to **ditch** VERB
▷ *see also* **ditch** NOUN
dejar
□ She's just ditched her boyfriend. Acaba de dejar al novio.

dive NOUN
▷ *see also* **dive** VERB
1 el salto de cabeza *(into water)*
2 el buceo *(under water)*

to **dive** VERB
▷ *see also* **dive** NOUN
1 tirarse de cabeza *(into water)*
2 bucear *(under water)*

diver NOUN
el/la buzo

diversion NOUN
el desvío *(for traffic)*

LANGUAGE TIP Be careful not to translate **diversion** by **diversión**.

to **divide** VERB
1 dividir
□ Divide the pastry in half. Divide la masa en dos.
■ **12 divided by 3 is 4.** 12 dividido entre 3 es 4.
2 dividirse
□ We divided into two groups. Nos dividimos en dos grupos.

diving NOUN
1 el buceo
□ diving equipment equipo de buceo
2 el salto de trampolín
□ a diving competition una competición de saltos de trampolín

division NOUN
la división (PL las divisiones)

divorce NOUN
el divorcio

divorced ADJECTIVE

divorciado (FEM divorciada)
□ My parents are divorced. Mis padres están divorciados.
■ **to get divorced** divorciarse

DIY NOUN
el bricolaje
□ to do DIY hacer bricolaje □ a DIY shop una tienda de bricolaje

dizzy ADJECTIVE
■ **I feel dizzy.** Estoy mareado.

DJ NOUN
el/la discjockey (PL los/las discjockeys)
□ He's a DJ. Es discjockey.

to **do** VERB
1 hacer*
□ What are you doing this evening? ¿Qué vas a hacer esta noche? □ She did it by herself. Lo hizo ella sola. □ I'll do my best. Haré todo lo que pueda. □ I want to do physics at university. Quiero hacer física en la universidad.
■ **What does your father do?** ¿A qué se dedica tu padre?
2 ir*
□ She's doing well at school. Va bien en el colegio.
■ **How are you doing?** ¿Qué tal?
■ **How do you do?** Mucho gusto.
3 valer*
□ It's not very good, but it'll do. No es muy bueno, pero valdrá. □ Will £10 do? ¿Valdrá con diez libras?
■ **That'll do, thanks.** Así está bien, gracias.
LANGUAGE TIP 'do' is not translated when used to form questions.
□ Do you speak English? ¿Hablas inglés? □ Do you like reading? ¿Te gusta leer? □ Where does he live? ¿Dónde vive? □ Where did you go for your holidays? ¿Dónde te fuiste de vacaciones?
LANGUAGE TIP Use 'no' in negative sentences for 'don't'.
□ I don't understand. No entiendo. □ You didn't tell me anything. No me dijiste nada. □ He didn't come. No vino. □ Why didn't you come? ¿Por qué no viniste?
LANGUAGE TIP 'do' is not translated when it is used in place of another verb.
□ I hate maths. — So do I. Odio las matemáticas. — Yo también. □ I didn't like the film. — Neither did I. No me gustó la película. — A mí tampoco. □ Do you speak English? — Yes, I do. ¿Hablas inglés? — Sí. □ Do you like horses? — No, I don't. ¿Te gustan los caballos? — No.
LANGUAGE TIP Use **¿no?** or **¿verdad?** to check information.
□ You go swimming on Fridays, don't you? Los viernes vas a nadar, ¿no? □ It doesn't matter, does it? No importa, ¿verdad?

to **do up** VERB
1 atarse *(shoes)*
□ Do up your shoes! ¡Átate los zapatos!
2 abrocharse *(shirt, cardigan, coat)*
□ Do your coat up. Abróchate el abrigo.
■ **Do up your zip!** ¡Súbete la cremallera!
3 reformar *(house, room)*

to **do without** VERB
pasar sin
□ I can't do without my computer. Yo no puedo pasar sin el ordenador.

dock NOUN
el muelle

doctor NOUN
el médico
la médica
□ He's a doctor. Es médico. □ at the doctor's en el médico

document NOUN
el documento

documentary NOUN
el documental

to **dodge** VERB
esquivar *(attacker, blow)*

dodgems PL NOUN
los coches de choque

does VERB ▷ *see* **do**

doesn't = **does not**

dog NOUN
el perro
□ Have you got a dog? ¿Tienes perro?

do-it-yourself NOUN
el bricolaje

dole NOUN
el subsidio de paro
■ **He's on the dole.** Está parado.
■ **to go on the dole** quedarse parado

doll NOUN
la muñeca

dollar NOUN
el dólar

dolphin NOUN
el delfín (PL los delfines)

domestic ADJECTIVE
■ **a domestic flight** un vuelo nacional

dominoes PL NOUN
■ **to have a game of dominoes** echar una partida al dominó

to **donate** VERB
donar

done ADJECTIVE
listo (FEM lista)
□ Is the pasta done? ¿Está lista la pasta?
■ **How do you like your steak? — Well done.** ¿Cómo quieres el filete? — Muy hecho.

English-Spanish

d

donkey NOUN
el burro
donor NOUN
el/la donante
don't = **do not**
door NOUN
la puerta
doorbell NOUN
el timbre
doorman NOUN
el portero
doorstep NOUN
el peldaño de la puerta
■ **on my doorstep** en mi puerta
dormitory NOUN
el dormitorio
dose NOUN
la dosis (PL las dosis)

dosh NOUN
la pasta (la lana *Latin America*) *(informal)*
dot NOUN
el punto
■ **on the dot** en punto □ He arrived at nine on the dot. Llegó a las nueve en punto.
to **double** VERB
▹ *see also* **double** ADJECTIVE, ADVERB
1 doblar
□ They doubled their prices. Doblaron los precios.
2 doblarse
□ The number of attacks has doubled. El número de agresiones se ha doblado.
double ADJECTIVE, ADVERB
▹ *see also* **double** VERB
doble (FEM doble)
□ a double helping una ración doble
□ to cost double costar el doble
■ **double bed** la cama de matrimonio
■ **a double room** una habitación doble
double bass NOUN
el contrabajo
to **double-click** VERB
hacer* doble clic
□ to double-click on an icon hacer doble clic en un icono
double-decker bus NOUN
el autobús de dos pisos
double glazing NOUN
el doble acristalamiento
doubles PL NOUN
dobles *masc pl (in tennis)*
□ to play mixed doubles jugar un partido de dobles mixtos
doubt NOUN
▹ *see also* **doubt** VERB
la duda
□ I have my doubts. Tengo mis dudas.
■ **no doubt** sin duda □ as you no doubt know como sin duda sabrá
to **doubt** VERB
▹ *see also* **doubt** NOUN
dudar
□ I doubt it. Lo dudo.
LANGUAGE TIP Use the subjunctive after **dudar que**.
□ I doubt that he'll agree. Dudo que vaya a estar de acuerdo.
doubtful ADJECTIVE
dudoso (FEM dudosa)
□ It's doubtful. Es dudoso.
■ **to be doubtful about doing something** no estar seguro de hacer algo □ I'm doubtful about going by myself. No estoy seguro de ir solo.
■ **You sound doubtful.** No pareces muy convencido.
dough NOUN
la masa
doughnut NOUN
el buñuelo
□ a jam doughnut un buñuelo de mermelada
down ADJECTIVE, ADVERB, PREPOSITION
1 abajo
□ His office is down on the first floor. Su despacho está abajo en el primer piso.
□ It's down there. Está allí abajo.
2 al suelo
□ He threw down his racket. Tiró la raqueta al suelo.
■ **They live just down the road.** Viven más adelante en esta calle.
■ **to feel down** estar desanimado
■ **The computer's down.** El ordenador no funciona.
to **download** VERB
bajarse
□ to download sth from the Internet bajarse algo de Internet
downpour NOUN
el chaparrón (PL los chaparrones)
downstairs ADVERB, ADJECTIVE
1 abajo
□ The bathroom's downstairs. El baño está abajo.
■ **to go downstairs** bajar
2 de abajo
□ the downstairs bathroom el baño de abajo
■ **the neighbours downstairs** los vecinos de abajo
downtown ADVERB (US)
1 al centro de la ciudad *(go, come)*
2 en el centro de la ciudad *(live, be)*
to **doze** VERB
dormitar

to **doze off** VERB
quedarse dormido
dozen NOUN
la docena
□ a dozen eggs una docena de huevos
□ two dozen dos docenas
■ **I've told you that dozens of times.** Te lo he dicho cientos de veces.
drab ADJECTIVE
triste (FEM triste) *(clothes)*
draft NOUN (US)
la corriente de aire
to **drag** VERB
▷ *see also* **drag** NOUN
arrastrar *(thing, person)*
■ **to drag and drop** arrastrar y soltar
drag NOUN
▷ *see also* **drag** VERB
■ **It's a real drag!** ¡Es una verdadera lata! *(informal)*
dragon NOUN
el dragón (PL los dragones)
drain NOUN
▷ *see also* **drain** VERB
1 el desagüe *(of house)*
2 la alcantarilla *(in street)*
to **drain** VERB
▷ *see also* **drain** NOUN
escurrir *(vegetables, pasta)*
draining board NOUN
el escurridero
drainpipe NOUN
el tubo de desagüe
drama NOUN
1 el drama
LANGUAGE TIP Although **drama** ends in **-a**, it is actually a masculine noun.
□ a TV drama un drama para televisión
2 el teatro
□ Greek drama el teatro griego □ Drama is my favourite subject. Mi asignatura favorita es teatro.
■ **drama school** la escuela de arte dramático
dramatic ADJECTIVE
espectacular (FEM espectacular)
□ a dramatic improvement una espectacular mejoría
■ **dramatic news** noticias sensacionales
drank VERB ▷ *see* **drink**
drapes PL NOUN (US)
las cortinas
drastic ADJECTIVE
drástico (FEM drástica)
□ to take drastic action tomar medidas drásticas
draught NOUN
la corriente de aire
□ There's a draught from the window. Entra corriente por la ventana.
■ **draught beer** la cerveza de barril
draughts NOUN
las damas
□ to play draughts jugar a las damas
draw NOUN
▷ *see also* **draw** VERB
1 el empate
□ The game ended in a draw. El partido terminó en empate.
2 el sorteo
□ The draw takes place on Saturday. El sorteo es el sábado.
to **draw** VERB
▷ *see also* **draw** NOUN
1 dibujar *(a scene, a person)*
■ **to draw a picture** hacer un dibujo
■ **to draw a picture of somebody** hacer un retrato de alguien
■ **to draw a line** trazar una línea
2 empatar
□ We drew two all. Empatamos a dos.
■ **to draw the curtains 1** *(open)* descorrer las cortinas **2** *(close)* correr las cortinas
drawback NOUN
el inconveniente
drawer NOUN
el cajón (PL los cajones)
drawing NOUN
el dibujo
■ **He's good at drawing.** Se le da bien dibujar.
drawing pin NOUN
la chincheta
drawn VERB ▷ *see* **draw**
dreadful ADJECTIVE
1 terrible (FEM terrible)
□ a dreadful mistake un terrible error
2 horrible (FEM horrible)
□ The weather was dreadful. Hizo un tiempo horrible.
■ **You look dreadful.** Tienes muy mal aspecto.
■ **I feel dreadful about not having phoned.** Me siento muy mal por no haber llamado.
to **dream** VERB
▷ *see also* **dream** NOUN
soñar*
□ Do you dream every night? ¿Sueñas todas las noches? □ She dreamt about her baby. Soñó con su bebé.
dream NOUN
▷ *see also* **dream** VERB
el sueño
to **drench** VERB
■ **I got drenched.** Me puse empapado.

dress NOUN
▷ *see also* **dress** VERB
el vestido

to **dress** VERB
▷ *see also* **dress** NOUN
vestirse*
□ I got up, dressed, and went downstairs. Me levanté, me vestí y bajé.
■ **to dress somebody** vestir a alguien
■ **to get dressed** vestirse

to **dress up** VERB
disfrazarse*
□ I dressed up as a ghost. Me disfracé de fantasma.

dressed ADJECTIVE
vestido (FEM vestida)
□ I'm not dressed yet. Aún no estoy vestido.
□ How was she dressed? ¿Cómo iba vestida?
□ She was dressed in white. Iba vestida de blanco.
■ **She was dressed in a green sweater and jeans.** Llevaba un jersey verde y vaqueros.

dresser NOUN
el aparador *(furniture)*

dressing gown NOUN
la bata

dressing table NOUN
el tocador

drew VERB ▷ *see* **draw**

dried ADJECTIVE
seco (FEM seca)
■ **dried milk** la leche en polvo
■ **dried fruits** las frutas pasas

drier = **dryer**

drift NOUN
▷ *see also* **drift** VERB
■ **a snow drift** el ventisquero

to **drift** VERB
▷ *see also* **drift** NOUN
1 ir* a la deriva *(boat)*
2 amontonarse *(snow)*

drill NOUN
▷ *see also* **drill** VERB
la taladradora

to **drill** VERB
▷ *see also* **drill** NOUN
taladrar
■ **He drilled a hole in the wall.** Hizo un agujero en la pared.

to **drink** VERB
▷ *see also* **drink** NOUN
beber (tomar *Latin America*)
□ What would you like to drink? ¿Qué te apetece beber? □ She drank three cups of tea. Se bebió tres tazas de té. □ He had been drinking. Había bebido.

drink NOUN
▷ *see also* **drink** VERB
1 la bebida
□ a cold drink una bebida fría
2 la copa *(alcoholic)*
□ They've gone out for a drink. Han salido a tomar una copa.
■ **to have a drink** tomar algo □ Would you like a drink? ¿Quieres tomar algo?

drinking water NOUN
el agua potable *fem*

LANGUAGE TIP Although it's a feminine noun, remember that you use **el** with **agua**.

drive NOUN
▷ *see also* **drive** VERB
1 el paseo en coche
□ to go for a drive ir a dar un paseo en coche
■ **We've got a long drive tomorrow.** Mañana nos espera un largo viaje en coche.
2 el camino de entrada a la casa
□ He parked his car in the drive. Aparcó el coche en el camino de entrada a la casa.

to **drive** VERB
▷ *see also* **drive** NOUN
1 conducir* (manejar *Latin America*) *(a car)*
□ Can you drive? ¿Sabes conducir?
2 ir* en coche *(go by car)*
□ We never drive into the town centre. Nunca vamos en coche al centro.
3 llevar en coche *(transport)*
□ My mother drives me to school. Mi madre me lleva al colegio en coche.
■ **to drive somebody home** acercar a alguien a su casa en coche
■ **to drive somebody mad** volver loco a alguien □ He drives her mad. La vuelve loca.

driver NOUN
el conductor
la conductora
□ He's a bus driver. Es conductor de autobús.
■ **She's an excellent driver.** Conduce muy bien.

driver's license NOUN (US)
el permiso de conducir

driving instructor NOUN
el profesor de autoescuela
la profesora de autoescuela
□ He's a driving instructor. Es profesor de autoescuela.

driving lesson NOUN
la clase de conducir

driving licence NOUN
el permiso de conducir

driving test NOUN
■ **to take one's driving test** hacer el examen de conducir
■ **She's just passed her driving test.** Acaba de sacarse el carnet de conducir.

drizzle NOUN
la llovizna

drop NOUN
▷ *see also* **drop** VERB
1 la gota *(of liquid)*
□ Would you like some milk? — Just a drop. ¿Quieres leche? — Una gota nada más.
2 la bajada
□ a drop in temperature una bajada de las temperaturas

to **drop** VERB
▷ *see also* **drop** NOUN
1 bajar
□ The temperature will drop tonight. La temperatura bajará esta noche.
2 soltar*
□ The cat dropped the mouse at my feet. El gato soltó al ratón junto a mis pies.
■ **I dropped the glass.** Se me cayó el vaso.
3 dejar
□ Could you drop me at the station? ¿Me puedes dejar en la estación?
■ **I'm going to drop chemistry.** No voy a dar más química.

drought NOUN
la sequía

drove VERB ▷ *see* **drive**

to **drown** VERB
ahogarse*
□ A boy drowned here yesterday. Un chico se ahogó ayer aquí.

drug NOUN
1 el medicamento
□ They need food and drugs. Necesitan comida y medicamentos.
2 la droga
□ hard drugs drogas duras □ soft drugs drogas blandas
■ **to take drugs** drogarse
■ **a drug addict** un drogadicto
■ **a drug pusher** un camello *(informal)*
■ **a drug smuggler** un narcotraficante
■ **the drugs squad** la brigada antidroga

drugstore NOUN (US)
la farmacia

drum NOUN
el tambor
□ an African drum un tambor africano
■ **a drum kit** una batería
■ **to play the drums** tocar la batería

drummer NOUN
el/la batería *(in rock group)*

drunk VERB ▷ *see* **drink**

drunk ADJECTIVE
▷ *see also* **drunk** NOUN
borracho (FEM borracha)
□ He was drunk. Estaba borracho.
■ **to get drunk** emborracharse

drunk NOUN
▷ *see also* **drunk** ADJECTIVE
el borracho
la borracha

dry ADJECTIVE
▷ *see also* **dry** VERB
seco (FEM seca)
□ The paint isn't dry yet. Aún no está seca la pintura. □ It's been exceptionally dry this spring. Esta primavera ha sido extraordinariamente seca.
■ **a long dry period** un largo periodo sin lluvia

to **dry** VERB
▷ *see also* **dry** ADJECTIVE
1 secar*
□ to dry the dishes secar los platos
□ There's nowhere to dry clothes here. Aquí no hay un sitio para poner a secar la ropa.
2 secarse*
□ The washing will dry quickly in the sun. La colada se secará rápido al sol.
■ **to dry one's hair** secarse el pelo

dry-cleaner's NOUN
la tintorería

dryer NOUN
■ **a tumble dryer** una secadora
■ **a hair dryer** un secador

DTP NOUN *(= desktop publishing)*
la autoedición

dubbed ADJECTIVE
doblado (FEM doblada)
□ The film was dubbed into Spanish. La película estaba doblada al español.

dubious ADJECTIVE
■ **My parents were a bit dubious about it.** Mis padres tenían sus dudas sobre el tema.

duck NOUN
el pato

due ADJECTIVE, ADVERB
■ **He's due to arrive tomorrow.** Debe llegar mañana.
■ **The plane's due in half an hour.** El avión llegará en media hora.
■ **When's the baby due?** ¿Para cuándo nacerá el niño?
■ **due to** debido a □ The trip was cancelled due to bad weather. El viaje se suspendió debido al mal tiempo.

dug VERB ▷ *see* **dig**

dull ADJECTIVE
1 soso (FEM sosa)
□ He's nice, but a bit dull. Es simpático, pero un poco soso.
2 gris (FEM grisa)
□ It's always dull and wet. El tiempo está siempre gris y lluvioso.

dumb ADJECTIVE
1 mudo (FEM muda)
2 bobo (FEM boba)
□ Don't be so dumb! ¡No seas bobo!
■ **That was a really dumb thing I did!** ¡Lo que hice fue una verdadera bobada!

dummy NOUN
el chupete *(for baby)*

dump NOUN
▷ *see also* **dump** VERB
■ **It's a real dump!** ¡Es una auténtica pocilga!
■ **a rubbish dump** un vertedero

to **dump** VERB
▷ *see also* **dump** NOUN
verter* *(waste)*
□ 'No dumping.' 'Prohibido verter basuras.'

dungarees PL NOUN
el mono (el overol *Latin America*)

dungeon NOUN
la mazmorra

duration NOUN
la duración
□ Courses are of two years' duration. Los cursos tienen una duración de dos años.
■ **for the duration of the trial** durante todo el juicio

during PREPOSITION
durante

dusk NOUN
el anochecer
■ **at dusk** al anochecer

dust NOUN
▷ *see also* **dust** VERB
el polvo

to **dust** VERB
▷ *see also* **dust** NOUN
limpiar el polvo de
□ I dusted the shelves. Limpié el polvo de las estanterías.

dustbin NOUN
el cubo de la basura (el balde *Latin America*)

dustman NOUN
el basurero

dusty ADJECTIVE
polvoriento (FEM polvorienta)

Dutch ADJECTIVE
▷ *see also* **Dutch** NOUN
holandés (FEM holandesa)
□ She's Dutch. Es holandesa.

Dutch NOUN
▷ *see also* **Dutch** ADJECTIVE
el holandés *(language)*
■ **the Dutch** los holandeses

Dutchman NOUN
el holandés

Dutchwoman NOUN
la holandesa

duty NOUN
el deber
□ It was his duty to tell the police. Su deber era decírselo a la policía.
■ **to be on duty 1** *(policeman)* estar de servicio **2** *(doctor, nurse)* estar de guardia

duty-free ADJECTIVE
libre de impuestos (FEM libre de impuestos)

duvet NOUN
el edredón (PL los edredones)

DVD NOUN
el DVD
■ **a DVD player** un lector de DVD

dwarf NOUN
el enano
la enana

dying VERB ▷ *see* **die**

dynamic ADJECTIVE
dinámico (FEM dinámica)

dyslexia NOUN
la dislexia

Ee

each ADJECTIVE, PRONOUN
1 cada (FEM cada)
□ each day cada día
■ **Each house has its own garden.** Todas las casas tienen jardín.
2 cada uno (FEM cada una)
□ They have 10 points each. Tienen 10 puntos cada uno. □ The plates cost £5 each. Los platos cuestan 5 libras cada uno. □ He gave each of us £10. Nos dio 10 libras a cada uno.

LANGUAGE TIP Use a reflexive verb to translate 'each other'.

□ They hate each other. Se odian. □ We write to each other. Nos escribimos. □ They don't know each other. No se conocen.

eager ADJECTIVE
■ **He was eager to tell us about his experiences.** Estaba impaciente por contarnos sus experiencias.

eagle NOUN
el águila *fem*

LANGUAGE TIP Although it's a feminine noun, remember that you use **el** and **un** with **águila**.

ear NOUN
la oreja

earache NOUN
■ **to have earache** tener dolor de oídos

earlier ADVERB
1 antes
□ I saw him earlier. Lo vi antes.
2 más temprano *(in the morning)*
□ I ought to get up earlier. Debería levantarme más temprano.

early ADVERB, ADJECTIVE
1 temprano
□ I have to get up early. Tengo que levantarme temprano.
■ **to have an early night** irse a la cama temprano
2 pronto *(ahead of time)*
□ I came early to avoid the heavy traffic. Vine pronto para evitar el tráfico denso.

to **earn** VERB
ganar
□ She earns £5 an hour. Gana 5 libras esterlinas a la hora.

earnings PL NOUN
los ingresos
□ Her earnings exceed £100,000 per year. Sus ingresos superan las 100.000 libras anuales.

earring NOUN
el pendiente (el arete *Latin America*)

earth NOUN
la tierra
■ **What on earth are you doing here?** ¿Qué diablos haces aquí?

earthquake NOUN
el terremoto

easily ADVERB
fácilmente

east ADJECTIVE, ADVERB
▷ *see also* **east** NOUN
■ **an east wind** un viento del este
■ **the east coast** la costa oriental
■ **east of** al este de □ It's east of London. Está al este de Londres.
hacia el este
□ We were travelling east. Viajábamos hacia el este.

east NOUN
▷ *see also* **east** ADJECTIVE, ADVERB
el este *(direction, region)*
□ in the east of the country al este del país

Easter NOUN
la Pascua
■ **Easter egg** el huevo de Pascua
■ **the Easter holidays** las vacaciones de Semana Santa

eastern ADJECTIVE
oriental (FEM oriental)
□ the eastern part of the island la parte oriental de la isla
■ **Eastern Europe** la Europa del Este

easy ADJECTIVE
fácil (FEM fácil)

easy chair NOUN
el sillón (PL los sillones)

easy-going ADJECTIVE
■ **to be easy-going** ser una persona de

trato fácil □ She's very easy-going. Es una persona de trato fácil.

to **eat** VERB
comer
□ Would you like something to eat? ¿Quieres comer algo?

EC NOUN *(= European Community)*
la CE *(= la Comunidad Europea)*

eccentric ADJECTIVE
excéntrico (FEM excéntrica)

echo NOUN
el eco

ecology NOUN
la ecología

e-commerce NOUN
el comercio electrónico

economic ADJECTIVE
1 económico (FEM económica) *(growth, development, policy)*
2 rentable (FEM rentable) *(profitable)*

economical ADJECTIVE
económico (FEM económica)
□ My car is very economical to run. Mi coche me sale muy económico.

economics NOUN
la economía
□ the economics of the third world countries la economía de los países tercermundistas
■ **He's doing economics at university.** Estudia económicas en la universidad.

to **economize** VERB
economizar*
■ **to economize on something** economizar en algo

economy NOUN
la economía

ecstasy NOUN
el éxtasis *(drug)*
■ **to be in ecstasy** estar en éxtasis

eczema NOUN
el eczema
LANGUAGE TIP Although **eczema** ends in **-a**, it is actually a masculine noun.
□ She's got eczema. Tiene eczema.

edge NOUN
1 el borde
□ on the edge of the desk en el borde del escritorio
■ **They live on the edge of the town.** Viven en los límites de la ciudad.
2 la orilla *(of lake)*
■ **to be on the edge of tears** estar a punto de llorar

edgy ADJECTIVE
nervioso (FEM nerviosa)

Edinburgh NOUN
Edimburgo *masc*

editor NOUN
1 el director
la directora *(of newspaper, magazine)*
2 el redactor
la redactora
□ the sports editor el redactor de la sección de deportes

educated ADJECTIVE
culto (FEM culta)

education NOUN
1 la educación
□ There should be more investment in education. Debería invertirse más dinero en educación.
2 la enseñanza *(teaching)*
□ She works in education. Trabaja en la enseñanza.

educational ADJECTIVE
1 educativo (FEM educativa) *(toy)*
2 instructivo (FEM instructiva) *(experience, film)*

effect NOUN
el efecto
□ special effects los efectos especiales

effective ADJECTIVE
eficaz (PL eficaces)

efficient ADJECTIVE
1 eficiente (FEM eficiente)
□ His secretary is very efficient. Su secretaria es muy eficiente.
2 eficaz (FEM eficaz, PL eficaces)
□ It's a very efficient system. Es un sistema muy eficaz.

effort NOUN
el esfuerzo
■ **to make an effort to do something** esforzarse en hacer algo

e.g. ABBREVIATION
p.ej.

egg NOUN
el huevo
□ a hard-boiled egg un huevo duro □ a soft-boiled egg un huevo pasado por agua □ a fried egg un huevo frito □ scrambled eggs los huevos revueltos

egg cup NOUN
la huevera

eggplant NOUN (US)
la berenjena

Egypt NOUN
Egipto *masc*

eight NUMERAL
ocho
□ She's eight. Tiene ocho años.

eighteen NUMERAL
dieciocho
□ She's eighteen. Tiene dieciocho años.

eighteenth ADJECTIVE
decimoctavo (FEM decimoctava)

■ **the eighteenth floor** la planta dieciocho
■ **the eighteenth of August** el dieciocho de agosto

eighth ADJECTIVE
octavo (FEM octava)
□ the eighth floor el octavo piso
■ **the eighth of August** el ocho de agosto

eighty NUMERAL
ochenta
□ He's eighty. Tiene ochenta años.

Eire NOUN
Eire *masc*

either ADJECTIVE, CONJUNCTION, PRONOUN, ADVERB
tampoco
□ I don't like milk, and I don't like eggs either. No me gusta la leche, y tampoco me gustan los huevos. □ I've never been to Spain. — I haven't either. No he estado nunca en España. — Yo tampoco.
■ **either...or...** o...o... □ You can have either ice cream or yoghurt. Puedes tomar o helado o yogur.
■ **either of them** uno u otro □ Choose either of them. Tienes que elegir entre uno u otro.
■ **I don't like either of them.** No me gusta cualquiera de los dos.
■ **on either side of the road** a ambos lados de la carretera

elastic NOUN
el elástico

elastic band NOUN
la goma elástica

elbow NOUN
el codo

elder ADJECTIVE
mayor (FEM mayor)
□ my elder sister mi hermana mayor

elderly ADJECTIVE
anciano (FEM anciana)
■ **an elderly man** un anciano
■ **the elderly** los ancianos

eldest ADJECTIVE, NOUN
mayor (FEM mayor)
□ my eldest sister mi hermana mayor
■ **He's the eldest.** Él es el mayor.

to **elect** VERB
elegir*

election NOUN
la elección (PL las elecciones)

electric ADJECTIVE
eléctrico (FEM eléctrica)
□ an electric fire una estufa eléctrica
□ an electric guitar una guitarra eléctrica
□ an electric blanket una manta eléctrica

electrical ADJECTIVE
eléctrico (FEM eléctrica)
□ electrical engineering la ingeniería eléctrica
■ **an electrical engineer** un ingeniero en electrónica

electrician NOUN
el/la electricista
□ He's an electrician. Es electricista.

electricity NOUN
la electricidad

electronic ADJECTIVE
electrónico (FEM electrónica)

electronics NOUN
la electrónica

elegant ADJECTIVE
elegante (FEM elegante)

elementary school NOUN (US)
la escuela primaria

elephant NOUN
el elefante

elevator NOUN (US)
el ascensor

eleven NUMERAL
once
□ She's eleven. Tiene once años.

eleventh ADJECTIVE
undécimo (FEM undécima)
■ **the eleventh floor** el piso once
■ **the eleventh of August** el once de agosto

else ADVERB
■ **somebody else** otra persona
■ **nobody else** nadie más
■ **something else** otra cosa
■ **nothing else** nada más
■ **somewhere else** en algún otro sitio
■ **Did you look anywhere else?** ¿Miraste en otro sitio?
■ **I would be happy anywhere else.** Estaría contento en cualquier otro sitio.
■ **I didn't look anywhere else.** No miré en ningún otro sitio.
■ **Would you like anything else?** ¿Desea alguna otra cosa?
■ **I don't want anything else.** No quiero nada más.
■ **Arrive on time or else!** ¡Llega a tiempo o si no...!

email NOUN
▷ *see also* **email** VERB
el e-mail

to **email** VERB
▷ *see also* **email** NOUN
■ **to email somebody** enviar un e-mail a alguien
■ **I'll email you the details.** Te mandaré la información por e-mail.

email address NOUN
la dirección de e-mail
□ My email address is jones at collins dot uk. Mi dirección de e-mail es jones arroba collins punto uk.

English-Spanish

e

embankment NOUN
el terraplén (PL los terraplenes) *(of railway)*

embarrassed ADJECTIVE
■ **I was really embarrassed.** Me dio mucha vergüenza.

LANGUAGE TIP Be careful not to translate **embarrassed** by **embarazada.**

embarrassing ADJECTIVE
embarazoso (FEM embarazosa) *(mistake, situation)*
■ **It was so embarrassing.** Fue una situación muy violenta.
■ **How embarrassing!** ¡Qué vergüenza!

embassy NOUN
la embajada

to **embroider** VERB
bordar

embroidery NOUN
el bordado
■ **I do embroidery in the afternoon.** Bordo por las tardes.

emergency NOUN
la emergencia
□ This is an emergency! ¡Es una emergencia!
■ **in an emergency** en caso de emergencia
■ **an emergency exit** una salida de emergencia
■ **an emergency landing** un aterrizaje forzoso
■ **the emergency services** los servicios de urgencia

to **emigrate** VERB
emigrar

emotion NOUN
la emoción (PL las emociones)

emotional ADJECTIVE
emotivo (FEM emotiva)
□ She's very emotional. Es una persona muy emotiva.
■ **He got very emotional at the farewell party.** Se emocionó mucho en la fiesta de despedida.

emperor NOUN
el emperador

to **emphasize** VERB
recalcar*
□ He emphasized the importance of the issue. Recalcó la importancia de la cuestión.
■ **to emphasize that** subrayar que

empire NOUN
el imperio

to **employ** VERB
emplear
□ The factory employs 600 people. La fábrica emplea a 600 trabajadores.
■ **Thousands of people are employed in tourism.** Miles de personas trabajan en el sector de turismo.

employee NOUN
el empleado
la empleada

employer NOUN
el empresario
la empresaria

employment NOUN
el empleo

empty ADJECTIVE
▷ *see also* **empty** VERB
vacío (FEM vacía)

to **empty** VERB
▷ *see also* **empty** ADJECTIVE
vaciar*
■ **to empty something out** vaciar algo

to **encourage** VERB
animar
□ to encourage somebody to do something animar a alguien a hacer algo

encouragement NOUN
el estímulo

encyclopedia NOUN
la enciclopedia

end NOUN
▷ *see also* **end** VERB
1 el final
□ the end of the film el final de la película
□ the end of the holidays el final de las vacaciones
■ **in the end** al final □ In the end I decided to stay at home. Al final decidí quedarme en casa. □ It turned out all right in the end. Al final resultó bien.
2 el extremo
□ at the other end of the table al otro extremo de la mesa
■ **at the end of the street** al final de la calle
■ **for hours on end** durante horas enteras

to **end** VERB
▷ *see also* **end** NOUN
terminar
□ What time does the film end? ¿A qué hora termina la película?
■ **to end up doing something** terminar haciendo algo □ I ended up walking home. Terminé yendo a casa andando.

ending NOUN
el final
□ a happy ending un final feliz

endless ADJECTIVE
interminable (FEM interminable)
□ The journey seemed endless. El viaje parecía interminable.

enemy NOUN
el enemigo
la enemiga

energetic ADJECTIVE
activo (FEM activa)
□ She's very energetic. Es muy activa.

energy NOUN
la energía

engaged ADJECTIVE
1 ocupado (FEM ocupada) *(telephone, toilet)*
2 prometido (FEM prometida)
□ Brian and Mary are engaged. Brian y Mary están prometidos.
■ **to get engaged** prometerse

engaged tone NOUN
la señal de comunicando

engagement NOUN
compromiso
□ They announced their engagement yesterday. Anunciaron su compromiso ayer.
■ **The engagement lasted 10 months.** El noviazgo duró 10 meses.
■ **engagement ring** anillo de compromiso

engine NOUN
1 el motor *(of vehicle)*
2 la locomotora *(of train)*

engineer NOUN
el ingeniero
la ingeniera
□ He's an engineer. Es ingeniero.
■ **service engineer** el técnico

engineering NOUN
la ingeniería

England NOUN
Inglaterra *fem*

English ADJECTIVE
▷ *see also* **English** NOUN
inglés (FEM inglesa, PL ingleses)

English NOUN
▷ *see also* **English** ADJECTIVE
el inglés *(language)*
□ the English teacher el profesor de inglés
■ **the English** *(people)* los ingleses

Englishman NOUN
el inglés (PL los ingleses)

Englishwoman NOUN
la inglesa

to **enjoy** VERB
■ **Did you enjoy the film?** ¿Te gustó la película?
■ **to enjoy oneself** divertirse □ Did you enjoy yourselves at the party? ¿Os divertisteis en la fiesta?

enjoyable ADJECTIVE
agradable (FEM agradable)

enlargement NOUN
la ampliación (PL las ampliaciones) *(of photo)*

enormous ADJECTIVE
enorme (FEM enorme)

enough ADJECTIVE, PRONOUN, ADVERB
bastante (FEM bastante)
□ I didn't have enough money. No tenía bastante dinero. □ Have you got enough? ¿Tienes bastante?
■ **big enough** suficientemente grande
■ **I've had enough!** ¡Ya estoy harto!
■ **That's enough!** ¡Ya basta!

to **enquire** VERB
■ **to enquire about something** informarse acerca de algo

enquiry NOUN
la investigación (PL las investigaciones) *(official investigation)*

to **enter** VERB
entrar en
□ He entered the room and sat down. Entró en la habitación y se sentó.
■ **to enter a competition** presentarse a un concurso

to **entertain** VERB
recibir *(guests)*

entertainer NOUN
el animador
la animadora

entertaining ADJECTIVE
entretenido (FEM entretenida) *(book, movie)*

enthusiasm NOUN
el entusiasmo

enthusiast NOUN
el/la entusiasta
□ She's a DIY enthusiast. Es una entusiasta del bricolaje.

enthusiastic ADJECTIVE
entusiasta (FEM entusiasta) *(response, welcome)*
■ **She didn't seem very enthusiastic about your idea.** No pareció muy entusiasmada con tu idea.

entire ADJECTIVE
entero (FEM entera)
□ the entire world el mundo entero

entirely ADVERB
completamente
□ an entirely new approach un enfoque completamente nuevo
■ **I agree entirely.** Estoy totalmente de acuerdo.

entrance NOUN
la entrada
■ **an entrance exam** un examen de ingreso
■ **entrance fee** la cuota de entrada

entry NOUN
la entrada
■ **'no entry'** **1** *(on door)* 'prohibido el paso' **2** *(on road sign)* 'dirección prohibida'
■ **an entry form** un impreso de inscripción

entry phone NOUN
el portero automático

envelope NOUN
el sobre

envious ADJECTIVE
envidioso (FEM envidiosa)

environment NOUN
el entorno *(surroundings)*
□ She adjusted quickly to her new environment. Se adaptó rápidamente a su nuevo entorno.
■ **the environment** el medio ambiente
□ We are committed to protecting the environment. Estamos comprometidos con la protección del medio ambiente.

environmental ADJECTIVE
medioambiental (FEM medioambiental)
□ environmental pollution contaminación ambiental
■ **environmental groups** grupos ecologistas

environment-friendly ADJECTIVE
ecológico (FEM ecológica)

envy NOUN
▷ *see also* **envy** VERB
la envidia

to **envy** VERB
▷ *see also* **envy** NOUN
envidiar

epileptic NOUN
el epiléptico
la epiléptica

episode NOUN
el episodio

equal ADJECTIVE
igual (FEM igual)
□ The cake was divided into 12 equal parts. El pastel se dividió en 12 partes iguales.
■ **Women demand equal rights at work.** Las mujeres exigen igualdad de derechos en el trabajo.

equality NOUN
la igualdad

to **equalize** VERB
empatar *(in sport)*

equator NOUN
el ecuador

equipment NOUN
el equipo
□ skiing equipment el equipo de esquí

equipped ADJECTIVE
equipado (FEM equipada)
□ This caravan is equipped for four people. Esta caravana está equipada para cuatro personas.
■ **equipped with** provisto de □ All rooms are equipped with phones, computers and faxes. Todas las habitaciones están provistas de teléfonos, ordenadores y fax.
■ **He was well equipped for the job.** Estaba bien preparado para el puesto.

equivalent NOUN
el equivalente

error NOUN
el error

escalator NOUN
la escalera mecánica

escape NOUN
▷ *see also* **escape** VERB
la fuga *(from prison)*
■ **We had a narrow escape.** Nos salvamos por muy poco.

to **escape** VERB
▷ *see also* **escape** NOUN
escaparse
□ A lion has escaped. Se ha escapado un león.
■ **The passengers escaped unhurt.** Los pasajeros salieron ilesos.
■ **to escape from prison** fugarse de la cárcel

escort NOUN
la escolta
□ a police escort una escolta policial

especially ADVERB
especialmente
□ It's very hot there, especially in the summer. Allí hace mucho calor, especialmente en verano.

essay NOUN
el trabajo
□ a history essay un trabajo de historia

essential ADJECTIVE
esencial (FEM esencial)
□ It's essential to bring warm clothes. Es esencial traer ropa de abrigo.

estate NOUN
1 la urbanización (PL las urbanizaciones)
□ I live on an estate. Vivo en una urbanización.
2 la finca
□ He's got a large estate in the country. Tiene una finca grande en el campo.

estate agent NOUN
el agente inmobiliario
la agente inmobiliaria
□ She's an estate agent. Es agente inmobiliaria.

estate agent's NOUN
la agencia inmobiliaria

estate car NOUN
la ranchera

to **estimate** VERB
calcular
□ They estimated it would take three weeks. Calcularon que llevaría tres semanas.

etc ABBREVIATION *(= et cetera)*
etc.

Ethiopia NOUN
Etiopía *fem*

ethnic ADJECTIVE
1 étnico (FEM étnica)

□ an ethnic minority una minoría étnica
■ **ethnic cleansing** la limpieza étnica
2 exótico (FEM exótica) *(restaurant, food)*

e-ticket NOUN
el billete electrónico (el boleto electrónico *Latin America*)

EU NOUN *(= European Union)*
la UE

euro NOUN
el euro

Europe NOUN
Europa *fem*

European ADJECTIVE
▷ *see also* **European** NOUN
europeo (FEM europea)

European NOUN
▷ *see also* **European** ADJECTIVE
el europeo
la europea

to **evacuate** VERB
evacuar*

eve NOUN
■ **Christmas Eve** la Nochebuena
■ **New Year's Eve** la Nochevieja

even ADVERB
▷ *see also* **even** ADJECTIVE
incluso
□ I like all animals, even snakes. Me gustan todos los animales, incluso las serpientes.
■ **not even** ni siquiera □ He didn't even say hello. Ni siquiera saludó.
■ **even if** aunque
LANGUAGE TIP Use the subjunctive after **aunque** when translating 'even if'.
□ I'd never do that, even if you asked me. Nunca haría eso, aunque me lo pidieras.
■ **even though** aunque □ She's a successful writer, even though she's still only 25. Es una escritora de éxito, aunque todavía tiene sólo 25 años.
■ **even more** aún más □ I liked Granada even more than Seville. Me gustó Granada aún más que Sevilla.

even ADJECTIVE
▷ *see also* **even** ADVERB
uniforme (FEM uniforme)
□ an even layer of snow una capa de nieve uniforme
■ **an even surface** una superficie lisa
■ **an even number** un número par
■ **to get even with somebody** vengarse en alguien

evening NOUN
1 la tarde *(before dark)*
2 la noche *(after dark)*
□ in the evening por la tarde/noche
■ **Good evening!** ¡Buenas tardes/noches!
■ **evening class** la clase nocturna

event NOUN
1 el acontecimiento
□ It was one of the most important events in his life. Fue uno de los acontecimientos más importantes de su vida.
■ **a sporting event** un acontecimiento deportivo
2 la prueba
□ She took part in two events at the last Olympic Games. Participó en dos pruebas en los últimos Juegos Olímpicos.
■ **in the event of** en caso de □ in the event of an accident en caso de accidente

eventful ADJECTIVE
lleno de incidentes (FEM llena de incidentes) *(race, journey)*

eventually ADVERB
finalmente

ever ADVERB
■ **Have you ever been to Portugal?** ¿Has estado alguna vez en Portugal?
■ **Have you ever seen her?** ¿La has visto alguna vez?
■ **the best I've ever seen** el mejor que he visto
■ **I haven't ever done that.** Jamás he hecho eso.
■ **It will become ever more complex.** Irá siendo cada vez más complicado.
■ **for the first time ever** por primera vez
■ **ever since** desde que □ ever since I met him desde que lo conozco
■ **ever since then** desde entonces
■ **It's ever so kind of you.** Es muy amable de su parte.

every ADJECTIVE
cada (FEM cada)
□ every pupil cada alumno □ every time cada vez
■ **every day** todos los días
■ **every now and then** de vez en cuando

everybody PRONOUN
todo el mundo
□ Everybody makes mistakes. Todo el mundo se equivoca.
■ **Everybody had a good time.** Todos se lo pasaron bien.

everyone PRONOUN
todo el mundo
□ Everyone makes mistakes. Todo el mundo se equivoca.
■ **Everyone had a good time.** Todos se lo pasaron bien.

everything PRONOUN
todo
□ You've thought of everything! ¡Has pensado en todo! □ Money isn't everything. El dinero no lo es todo.

English-Spanish

e

everywhere ADVERB
en todas partes
□ I looked everywhere, but I couldn't find it. Miré en todas partes, pero no lo encontré.
LANGUAGE TIP **dondequiera** has to be followed by a verb in the subjunctive.
■ **I see him everywhere I go.** Lo veo dondequiera que vaya.

evil ADJECTIVE
1 malvado (FEM malvada) *(person)*
2 maligno (FEM maligna) *(plan, spirit)*

ex- PREFIX
ex-
□ his ex-wife su ex-esposa

exact ADJECTIVE
exacto (FEM exacta)

exactly ADVERB
exactamente
□ exactly the same exactamente igual
■ **It's exactly 10 o'clock.** Son las 10 en punto.

to **exaggerate** VERB
exagerar

exaggeration NOUN
la exageración (PL las exageraciones)

exam NOUN
el examen (PL los exámenes)
□ a French exam un examen de francés
□ the exam results los resultados de los exámenes

examination NOUN
el examen (PL los exámenes)

to **examine** VERB
examinar
□ He examined her passport. Le examinó el pasaporte. □ The doctor examined him. El médico lo examinó.

examiner NOUN
el examinador
la examinadora

example NOUN
el ejemplo
□ for example por ejemplo

excellent ADJECTIVE
excelente (FEM excelente)

except PREPOSITION
excepto
□ everyone except me todos excepto yo
■ **except for** excepto
LANGUAGE TIP **salvo que** may be followed by a verb in subjunctive.
■ **except that** salvo que □ The weather was great, except that it was a bit cold. El tiempo fue estupendo, salvo que hizo un poco de frío.

exception NOUN
la excepción (PL las excepciones)
□ to make an exception hacer una excepción

exceptional ADJECTIVE
excepcional (FEM excepcional)

excess baggage NOUN
el exceso de equipaje

exchange NOUN
▷ *see also* **exchange** VERB
el intercambio
□ I'd like to do an exchange with an English student. Me gustaría hacer un intercambio con un estudiante inglés.
■ **in exchange for** a cambio de

to **exchange** VERB
▷ *see also* **exchange** NOUN
cambiar
□ I exchanged the book for a CD. Cambié el libro por un CD.

exchange rate NOUN
el tipo de cambio

excited ADJECTIVE
entusiasmado (FEM entusiasmada)

exciting ADJECTIVE
emocionante (FEM emocionante)

exclamation mark NOUN
el signo de admiración

excuse NOUN
▷ *see also* **excuse** VERB
la excusa

to **excuse** VERB
▷ *see also* **excuse** NOUN
■ **Excuse me! 1** *(to attract attention, apologize)* ¡Perdón! **2** *(when you want to get past)* ¡Con permiso!

ex-directory ADJECTIVE
■ **She's ex-directory.** Su nombre no aparece en la guía.

to **execute** VERB
ejecutar

execution NOUN
la ejecución (PL las ejecuciones)

executive NOUN
el ejecutivo
la ejecutiva
□ He's an executive. Es ejecutivo.

exercise NOUN
el ejercicio
□ page ten, exercise three página diez, ejercicio tres □ to take some exercise hacer un poco de ejercicio
■ **exercise book** el cuaderno
■ **an exercise bike** una bicicleta estática

exhaust NOUN
el tubo de escape

exhausted ADJECTIVE
agotado (FEM agotada)

exhaust fumes PL NOUN
los gases de escape

exhaust pipe NOUN
el tubo de escape

exhibition NOUN
la exposición (PL las exposiciones)

to **exist** VERB
existir

exit NOUN
la salida

LANGUAGE TIP Be careful not to translate **exit** by **éxito**.

exotic ADJECTIVE
exótico (FEM exótica)

to **expect** VERB
1 esperar
□ I'm expecting him for dinner. Lo espero para cenar. □ She's expecting a baby. Está esperando un bebé. □ I didn't expect that from him. No me esperaba eso de él.
2 imaginarse
□ I expect he'll be late. Me imagino que llegará tarde.
■ **I expect so.** Me imagino que sí.

expedition NOUN
la expedición (PL las expediciones)

to **expel** VERB
■ **to get expelled** *(from school)* ser expulsado

expenses PL NOUN
los gastos

expensive ADJECTIVE
caro (FEM cara)

experience NOUN
la experiencia

experienced ADJECTIVE
■ **an experienced teacher** un maestro con experiencia
■ **She's very experienced in looking after children.** Tiene mucha experiencia en cuidar niños.

experiment NOUN
el experimento

expert ADJECTIVE
experto (FEM experta)
■ **He's an expert cook.** Es un experto cocinero.

to **expire** VERB
caducar
□ My passport has expired. Mi pasaporte ha caducado.

to **explain** VERB
explicar*

explanation NOUN
la explicación (PL las explicaciones)

to **explode** VERB
estallar

to **exploit** VERB
explotar

exploitation NOUN
la explotación

to **explore** VERB
explorar *(place)*

explorer NOUN
el explorador
la exploradora

explosion NOUN
la explosión (PL las explosiones)

explosive ADJECTIVE
▷ *see also* **explosive** NOUN
explosivo (FEM explosiva)

explosive NOUN
▷ *see also* **explosive** ADJECTIVE
el explosivo

to **express** VERB
expresar
■ **to express oneself** expresarse □ It's not easy to express oneself in a foreign language. No es fácil expresarse en un idioma extranjero.

expression NOUN
la expresión (PL las expresiones)
□ It's an English expression. Es una expresión inglesa.

expressway NOUN (US)
la autopista

extension NOUN
1 la ampliación (PL las ampliaciones) *(of building)*
2 la extensión (PL las extensiones) *(telephone)*
□ Extension three one three seven, please. Con la extensión tres uno tres siete, por favor.

extensive ADJECTIVE
1 extenso (FEM extensa)
□ The hotel is situated in extensive grounds. El hotel está situado en medio de extensos jardines.
2 amplio (FEM amplia)
□ My brother has an extensive knowledge of this subject. Mi hermano tiene amplio conocimiento sobre esta materia.
■ **extensive damage** daños de consideración

extent NOUN
■ **to some extent** hasta cierto punto

exterior ADJECTIVE
exterior (FEM exteriora)

extinct ADJECTIVE
extinto (FEM extinta)
□ to be extinct estar extinto □ Dinosaurs are extinct. Los dinosaurios están extintos.
■ **to become extinct** extinguirse

extinguisher NOUN
el extintor (el extinguidor *Latin America*)

extortionate ADJECTIVE
exorbitante (FEM exorbitante)

extra ADJECTIVE, ADVERB
■ **He gave me an extra blanket.** Me dio una manta más.
■ **to pay extra** pagar un suplemento
■ **Breakfast is extra.** El desayuno no está incluido.

■ **Be extra careful!** ¡Ten muchísimo cuidado!

extraordinary ADJECTIVE
extraordinario (FEM extraordinaria)

extravagant ADJECTIVE
derrochador (FEM derrochadora) *(person)*

extreme ADJECTIVE
extremo (FEM extrema)
■ **with extreme caution** con sumo cuidado

extremely ADVERB
sumamente

extremist NOUN
el/la extremista

eye NOUN
el ojo
□ I've got green eyes. Tengo los ojos verdes.
■ **to keep an eye on something** vigilar algo

eyebrow NOUN
la ceja

eyelash NOUN
la pestaña

eyelid NOUN
el párpado

eyeliner NOUN
el lápiz de ojos (PL los lápices de ojos)

eye shadow NOUN
la sombra de ojos

eyesight NOUN
la vista
□ to have good eyesight tener buena vista

Ff

fabric NOUN
la tela
LANGUAGE TIP Be careful not to translate **fabric** by **fábrica**.

fabulous ADJECTIVE
fabuloso (FEM fabulosa)

face NOUN
▷ *see also* **face** VERB
1 la cara
□ He was red in the face. Tenía la cara colorada. □ the north face of the mountain la cara norte de la montaña
■ **face to face** cara a cara
2 la esfera *(of clock)*
■ **on the face of it** a primera vista
■ **in the face of these difficulties** en vista de estas dificultades

to **face** VERB
▷ *see also* **face** NOUN
1 estar* frente a
□ They stood facing each other. Estaban de pie el uno frente al otro.
■ **The garden faces south.** El jardín da al sur.
2 enfrentarse a
□ They face serious problems. Se enfrentan a graves problemas.
■ **Let's face it, we're lost.** Tenemos que admitirlo, estamos perdidos.

face cloth NOUN
la toallita para lavarse

facilities PL NOUN
las instalaciones
□ This school has excellent facilities. Esta escuela tiene unas instalaciones magníficas.
■ **The youth hostel has cooking facilities.** El albergue juvenil dispone de cocina.

fact NOUN
LANGUAGE TIP Use the subjunctive after **el hecho de que**.
■ **the fact that ...** el hecho de que ... □ The fact that you are very busy is of no interest to me. El hecho de que estés muy ocupado no me interesa.
■ **facts and figures** datos y cifras
■ **in fact** de hecho

factory NOUN
la fábrica

to **fade** VERB
1 desteñirse*
□ My jeans have faded. Se me han desteñido los vaqueros.
2 apagarse*
□ The light was fading fast. La luz se apagaba con rapidez. □ The noise gradually faded. El ruido se fue apagando.

fag NOUN
el cigarro

to **fail** VERB
▷ *see also* **fail** NOUN
1 suspender
□ He failed his driving test. Suspendió el examen de conducir.
2 fallar
□ The lorry's brakes failed. Al camión le fallaron los frenos.
3 fracasar
□ The plan failed. El plan fracasó.
■ **to fail to do something** no lograr hacer algo □ They failed to reach the quarter finals. No lograron llegar a los cuartos de final.
■ **The bomb failed to explode.** La bomba no llegó a estallar.

fail NOUN
▷ *see also* **fail** VERB
el suspenso
□ D is a pass, E is a fail. D es un aprobado, E es un suspenso.
■ **without fail** sin falta

failure NOUN
1 el fracaso
□ The attempt was a complete failure. El intento fue un completo fracaso.
2 el fallo
□ a mechanical failure un fallo mecánico
■ **I feel a failure.** Me siento un fracasado.

faint ADJECTIVE
▷ *see also* **faint** VERB
débil (FEM débil)
□ His voice was very faint. Tenía la voz muy débil.
■ **to feel faint** sentirse mareado

to faint VERB
▷ *see also* **faint** ADJECTIVE
desmayarse

fair ADJECTIVE
▷ *see also* **fair** NOUN
1 justo (FEM justa)
□ That's not fair. Eso no es justo.
■ **I paid more than my fair share.** Pagué más de lo que me correspondía.
2 rubio (FEM rubia)
□ He's got fair hair. Tiene el pelo rubio.
3 blanco (FEM blanca)
□ people with fair skin la gente con la piel blanca
4 considerable (FEM considerable)
□ That's a fair distance. Esa es una distancia considerable.
■ **I have a fair chance of winning.** Tengo bastantes posibilidades de ganar.
5 bueno (FEM buena) *(weather)*
□ The weather was fair. El tiempo era bueno.

LANGUAGE TIP Use **buen** before a masculine singular noun.

fair NOUN
▷ *see also* **fair** ADJECTIVE
1 la feria *(travelling funfair)*
2 el parque de atracciones *(on permanent site)*
■ **a trade fair** una feria de muestras

fair-haired ADJECTIVE
rubio (FEM rubia)

fairly ADVERB
1 equitativamente
□ The cake was divided fairly. La tarta se repartió equitativamente.
2 bastante
□ My car is fairly new. Mi coche es bastante nuevo. □ The weather was fairly good. El tiempo fue bastante bueno.

fairy NOUN
el hada *fem*

LANGUAGE TIP Although it's a feminine noun, remember that you use **el** and **un** with **hada**.

fairy tale NOUN
el cuento de hadas

faith NOUN
1 la confianza
□ People have lost faith in the government. La gente ha perdido la confianza en el gobierno.
2 la fe
□ the Catholic faith la fe católica

faithful ADJECTIVE
fiel (FEM fiel)

faithfully ADVERB
■ **Yours faithfully...** *(in letter)* Le saluda atentamente...

fake NOUN
▷ *see also* **fake** ADJECTIVE
la falsificación (PL las falsificaciones)
□ The painting was a fake. El cuadro era una falsificación.

fake ADJECTIVE
▷ *see also* **fake** NOUN
falso (FEM falsa)
□ a fake banknote un billete falso
■ **a fake fur coat** un abrigo de piel sintética

fall NOUN
▷ *see also* **fall** VERB
1 la caída
□ She had a nasty fall. Tuvo una mala caída.
■ **a fall of snow** una nevada
■ **Niagara Falls** las cataratas del Niágara
2 el otoño (US: *autumn)*

to fall VERB
▷ *see also* **fall** NOUN
1 caer*
□ Bombs fell on the town. Las bombas caían sobre la ciudad.

LANGUAGE TIP When the action of falling is not deliberate, use **caerse**.

□ He tripped and fell. Tropezó y se cayó.
□ The book fell off the shelf. El libro se cayó de la estantería.
■ **to fall in love with someone** enamorarse de alguien
2 bajar
□ Prices are falling. Están bajando los precios.

to fall down VERB
caerse*
□ She's fallen down. Se ha caído. □ The house is slowly falling down. La casa se está cayendo poco a poco.

to fall for VERB
1 tragarse*
□ They fell for it! ¡Se lo tragaron!
2 enamorarse de
□ She fell for him immediately. Se enamoró de él en el acto.

to fall out VERB
reñir*
□ Sarah's fallen out with her boyfriend. Sarah ha reñido con su novio.

to fall through VERB
fracasar
□ Our plans have fallen through. Nuestros planes han fracasado.

false ADJECTIVE
falso (FEM falsa)
■ **a false alarm** una falsa alarma
■ **false teeth** la dentadura postiza

fame NOUN
la fama

familiar ADJECTIVE
familiar (FEM familiar)

□ The name sounded familiar to me. El nombre me sonaba familiar.
■ **a familiar face** un rostro conocido
■ **to be familiar with something** conocer bien algo □ I'm familiar with his work. Conozco bien su obra.

family NOUN
la familia
□ the Cooke family la familia Cooke
■ **family planning** la planificación familiar

famine NOUN
la hambruna

famous ADJECTIVE
famoso (FEM famosa)

fan NOUN
1 el/la hincha
□ the England fans los hinchas ingleses
2 el/la fan (PL los/las fans)
□ the Oasis fan club el club de fans de Oasis
■ **I'm one of his greatest fans.** Soy uno de sus mayores admiradores.
3 el aficionado
la aficionada
□ a rap music fan un aficionado al rap
4 el abanico
□ a silk fan un abanico de seda
■ **an electric fan** un ventilador

fanatic NOUN
el fanático
la fanática

to **fancy** VERB
apetecer*
□ I fancy an ice cream. Me apetece un helado. □ What do you fancy doing? ¿Qué te apetece hacer?
LANGUAGE TIP **apetecer que** has to be followed by a verb in the subjunctive.
□ Do you fancy going to the cinema sometime? ¿Te apetece que vayamos al cine algún día?
■ **He fancies her.** Le gusta ella.

fancy dress NOUN
el disfraz (PL los disfraces)
■ **a fancy dress ball** un baile de disfraces

fantastic ADJECTIVE
fantástico (FEM fantástica)

far ADJECTIVE, ADVERB
lejos
□ Is it far? ¿Está lejos? □ It's not far from London. No está lejos de Londres.
■ **How far is it to Madrid?** ¿A qué distancia está Madrid?
■ **It's far from easy.** No es nada fácil.
■ **How far have you got?** ¿Hasta dónde has llegado?
■ **at the far end of the swimming pool** al otro extremo de la piscina
■ **far better** mucho mejor
■ **as far as I know** por lo que yo sé
■ **so far** hasta ahora

fare NOUN
la tarifa
□ Rail fares are very high in Britain. Las tarifas de tren son muy altas en Gran Bretaña. □ The air fare was very reasonable. La tarifa del vuelo fue bastante razonable.
■ **He didn't have the bus fare, so he had to walk.** No tenía dinero para el autobús, así que tuvo que ir andando.
■ **full fare** el precio del billete completo
■ **Children pay half fare on the bus.** Los niños pagan la mitad en el autobús.

Far East NOUN
■ **the Far East** el Extremo Oriente

farm NOUN
la granja (la estancia *Latin America*)

farmer NOUN
el granjero
la granjera (el estanciero, la estanciera *Latin America*)
□ He's a farmer. Es granjero.

farmhouse NOUN
el caserío

farming NOUN
la agricultura
□ organic farming agricultura biológica
■ **dairy farming** la ganadería *(especializada en la producción de leche)*

fascinating ADJECTIVE
fascinante (FEM fascinante)

fashion NOUN
la moda
■ **to be in fashion** estar de moda
■ **to go out of fashion** pasar de moda

fashionable ADJECTIVE
de moda
□ That colour is very fashionable. Ese color está muy de moda.
■ **Jane wears fashionable clothes.** Jane viste a la moda.

fast ADJECTIVE, ADVERB
rápido (FEM rápida)
□ a fast car un coche rápido □ They work very fast. Trabajan muy rápido.
■ **That clock's fast.** Ese reloj va adelantado.
■ **He's fast asleep.** Está profundamente dormido.

fat ADJECTIVE
▷ *see also* **fat** NOUN
gordo (FEM gorda)
□ She thinks she's too fat. Piensa que está demasiado gorda.

fat NOUN
▷ *see also* **fat** ADJECTIVE
1 la grasa *(on meat, in food)*
□ It's very high in fat. Es muy rico en grasas.

2 la manteca *(used for cooking)*

fatal ADJECTIVE
1 mortal (FEM mortal)
□ a fatal accident un accidente mortal
2 fatal (FEM fatal)
□ a fatal mistake un error fatal

father NOUN
el padre
■ **my father and mother** mis padres
■ **Father Christmas** Papá Noel

father-in-law NOUN
el suegro

faucet NOUN (US)
el grifo

fault NOUN
1 la culpa
□ It wasn't my fault. No fue culpa mía.
2 el defecto
□ He has his faults, but I still like him. Tiene sus defectos, pero aun así me gusta.
■ **a mechanical fault** un fallo mecánico

faulty ADJECTIVE
defectuoso (FEM defectuosa)

favour (US **favor**) NOUN
el favor (PL los favores)
□ Could you do me a favour? ¿Me harías un favor?
■ **to be in favour of something** estar a favor de algo

favourite (US **favorite**) ADJECTIVE
▷ *see also* **favourite** NOUN
favorito (FEM favorita)
□ Blue's my favourite colour. El azul es mi color favorito.

favourite (US **favorite**) NOUN
▷ *see also* **favourite** ADJECTIVE
el favorito
la favorita
□ Liverpool are favourites to win the Cup. El Liverpool es el favorito para ganar la Copa.

fax NOUN
▷ *see also* **fax** VERB
el fax (PL los faxes)

to **fax** VERB
▷ *see also* **fax** NOUN
mandar por fax
□ I'll fax you the details. Te mandaré la información por fax.

fear NOUN
▷ *see also* **fear** VERB
el miedo

to **fear** VERB
▷ *see also* **fear** NOUN
temer
□ You have nothing to fear. No tienes nada que temer.

feather NOUN
la pluma

feature NOUN
la característica
□ an important feature una característica importante

February NOUN
febrero *masc*
□ in February en febrero □ on 18 February el 18 de febrero

fed VERB ▷ *see* **feed**

fed up ADJECTIVE
■ **to be fed up with something** estar harto de algo

to **feed** VERB
dar* de comer a
□ Have you fed the cat? ¿Le has dado de comer al gato? □ He worked hard to feed his family. Trabajaba mucho para dar de comer a su familia.

to **feel** VERB
1 sentir*
□ I didn't feel much pain. No sentí mucho dolor.
2 sentirse*
□ I don't feel well. No me siento bien.
□ I felt lonely. Me sentía solo.
■ **I was feeling hungry.** Tenía hambre.
■ **I was feeling cold, so I went inside.** Tenía frío, así que entré.
3 tocar*
□ The doctor felt his forehead. El médico le tocó la frente.
■ **to feel like doing something** tener ganas de hacer algo □ I don't feel like going out tonight. No tengo ganas de salir esta noche.
■ **Do you feel like an ice cream?** ¿Te apetece un helado?

feeling NOUN
1 la sensación (PL las sensaciones)
□ a burning feeling una sensación de escozor
2 el sentimiento
□ He was afraid of hurting my feelings. Tenía miedo de herir mis sentimientos.
■ **What are your feelings about it?** ¿Tú qué opinas de ello?

feet PL NOUN ▷ *see* **foot**

fell VERB ▷ *see* **fall**

felt VERB ▷ *see* **feel**

felt-tip pen NOUN
el rotulador

female ADJECTIVE
▷ *see also* **female** NOUN
1 hembra (FEM + PL hembra)
□ a female bat un murciélago hembra
2 femenino (FEM femenina)
□ the female sex el sexo femenino

female NOUN
▷ *see also* **female** ADJECTIVE
la hembra *(animal)*

feminine ADJECTIVE
femenino (FEM femenina)

feminist NOUN
el/la feminista

fence NOUN
la valla

fern NOUN
el helecho

ferry NOUN
el ferry

fertile ADJECTIVE
fértil (FEM fértil)

fertilizer NOUN
el abono

festival NOUN
el festival
□ a jazz festival un festival de jazz

to **fetch** VERB
1 ir* a por
□ Fetch the bucket. Ve a por el cubo.
■ **to fetch something for someone** traer algo a alguien □ Fetch me a glass of water. Tráeme un vaso de agua.
2 venderse por
□ His painting fetched £5000. Su cuadro se vendió por 5.000 libras esterlinas.

fever NOUN
la fiebre

few ADJECTIVE, PRONOUN
1 pocos (FEM pocas)
□ He has few friends. Tiene pocos amigos.
■ **a few** unos □ She was silent for a few seconds. Se quedó callada unos segundos.
2 algunos (FEM algunas)
□ a few of them algunos de ellos
■ **quite a few people** bastante gente

fewer ADJECTIVE
menos
□ There were fewer people than yesterday. Había menos gente que ayer.

fiancé NOUN
el novio *(prometido)*

fiancée NOUN
la novia *(prometida)*

fiction NOUN
la narrativa *(novels)*

field NOUN
el campo
□ a field of wheat un campo de trigo □ a football field un campo de fútbol (una cancha de fútbol *Latin America*)
□ He's an expert in his field. Es un experto en su campo.

fierce ADJECTIVE
1 feroz (FEM feroz, PL feroces)
□ a fierce Alsatian un pastor alemán feroz
2 encarnizado (FEM encarnizada)
□ There's fierce competition between the companies. Existe una encarnizada competencia entre las empresas.
3 violento (FEM violenta)
□ a fierce attack un violento ataque

fifteen NUMERAL
quince
□ I'm fifteen. Tengo quince años.

fifteenth ADJECTIVE
decimoquinto (FEM decimoquinta)
■ **the fifteenth floor** la planta quince
■ **the fifteenth of August** el quince de agosto

fifth ADJECTIVE
quinto (FEM quinta)
□ the fifth floor el quinto piso
■ **the fifth of August** el cinco de agosto

fifty NUMERAL
cincuenta
□ He's fifty. Tiene cincuenta años.

fifty-fifty ADJECTIVE, ADVERB
a medias
□ They split the prize money fifty-fifty. Se repartieron a medias el dinero del premio.
■ **a fifty-fifty chance** un cincuenta por ciento de posibilidades

fight NOUN
▷ *see also* **fight** VERB
1 la pelea
□ There was a fight in the pub. Hubo una pelea en el pub.
■ **She had a fight with her best friend.** Se peleó con su mejor amiga.
2 la lucha
□ the fight against cancer la lucha contra el cáncer

to **fight** VERB
▷ *see also* **fight** NOUN
1 pelearse
□ The fans started fighting. Los hinchas empezaron a pelearse.
2 luchar
□ She has fought against racism all her life. Ha luchado toda su vida contra el racismo.
□ The demonstrators fought with the police. Los manifestantes lucharon con la policía.
■ **The doctors tried to fight the disease.** Los médicos intentaron combatir la enfermedad.

fighting NOUN
1 la pelea
□ Fighting broke out outside the pub. Se desató una pelea a las puertas del pub.
2 los combates
□ Many people have died in the fighting. Ha muerto mucha gente en los combates.

figure NOUN
1 la cifra
□ Can you give me the exact figures? ¿Me puedes dar las cifras exactas?

English-Spanish

f

2 la silueta
□ Helen saw the figure of a man on the bridge. Helen vio la silueta de un hombre en el puente.
■ **She's got a good figure.** Tiene buen tipo.
■ **I have to watch my figure.** Tengo que mantener la línea.
3 la figura
□ She's an important political figure. Es una importante figura política.

to **figure out** VERB
1 calcular
□ I'll try to figure out how much it'll cost. Intentaré calcular lo que va a costar.
2 llegar* a comprender
□ I couldn't figure out what it meant. No llegué a comprender lo que significaba.

file NOUN
▷ *see also* **file** VERB
1 el expediente
□ There was stuff in that file that was private. Había cosas privadas en ese expediente.
■ **The police have a file on him.** Está fichado por la policía.
2 la carpeta
□ She put the photocopy into her file. Metió la fotocopia en su carpeta.
3 la lima
□ a nail file una lima de uñas
4 el fichero *(on computer)*

to **file** VERB
▷ *see also* **file** NOUN
1 archivar
□ You have to file all these documents. Tienes que archivar todos estos documentos.
2 limarse
□ She was filing her nails. Se estaba limando las uñas.

to **fill** VERB
llenar
□ She filled the glass with water. Llenó el vaso de agua.

to **fill in** VERB
1 rellenar
□ Can you fill in this form, please? Rellene este impreso, por favor.
2 llenar
□ He filled the hole in with soil. Llenó el agujero de tierra.

to **fill up** VERB
llenar
□ He filled the cup up to the brim. Llenó la taza hasta el borde.
■ **Fill it up, please.** *(at petrol station)* Lleno, por favor.

film NOUN
1 la película *(movie)*
2 el carrete
□ I need a 36 exposure film. Quería un carrete de 36.

film star NOUN
la estrella de cine

filthy ADJECTIVE
mugriento (FEM mugrienta)

final ADJECTIVE
▷ *see also* **final** NOUN
1 último (FEM última)
□ a final attempt un último intento
2 definitivo (FEM definitiva)
□ a final decision una decisión definitiva
■ **I'm not going and that's final.** He dicho que no voy y se acabó.

final NOUN
▷ *see also* **final** ADJECTIVE
la final
□ Andy Murray is in the final. Andy Murray ha llegado a la final.

finally ADVERB
1 por último
□ Finally, I would like to say thank you to all of you. Por último me gustaría darles las gracias a todos.
2 al final
□ They finally decided to leave on Saturday. Al final decidieron salir el sábado.

to **find** VERB
encontrar*
□ I can't find the exit. No encuentro la salida.

to **find out** VERB
averiguar*
□ I found out what happened. Averigüé lo que ocurrió.
■ **to find out about** enterarse de □ Try to find out about the cost of a hotel. Intenta enterarte de lo que costaría un hotel. □ Find out as much as possible about the town. Entérate de todo lo que puedas sobre la ciudad.

fine ADJECTIVE, ADVERB
▷ *see also* **fine** NOUN
1 estupendo (FEM estupenda)
□ He's a fine musician. Es un músico estupendo.
■ **How are you? — I'm fine.** ¿Qué tal estás? — Bien.
■ **I feel fine.** Me siento bien.
■ **It'll be ready tomorrow. — That's fine, thanks.** Mañana estará listo. — Muy bien, gracias.
■ **The weather is fine today.** Hoy hace muy buen tiempo.
2 fino (FEM fina)
□ She's got very fine hair. Tiene el pelo muy fino.

fine NOUN
▷ *see also* **fine** ADJECTIVE

la multita

□ I got a fine for driving through a red light. Me pusieron una multa por saltarme un semáforo en rojo.

finger NOUN
el dedo
■ **my little finger** el meñique □ I hurt my little finger. Me hice daño en el meñique.

fingernail NOUN
la uña

finish NOUN
▷ *see also* **finish** VERB
1 el fin
□ from start to finish de principio a fin
2 la llegada
□ We saw the finish of the London Marathon. Vimos la llegada del maratón de Londres.

to **finish** VERB
▷ *see also* **finish** NOUN
terminar
□ I've finished! ¡Ya he terminado!
■ **to finish doing something** terminar de hacer algo □ Have you finished eating? ¿Has terminado de comer?

Finland NOUN
Finlandia *fem*

Finn NOUN
el finlandés (PL los finlandeses)
la finlandesa
□ the Finns los finlandeses

Finnish ADJECTIVE
▷ *see also* **Finnish** NOUN
finlandés (FEM finlandesa, PL finlandeses)

Finnish NOUN
▷ *see also* **Finnish** ADJECTIVE
el finlandés *(language)*

fire NOUN
▷ *see also* **fire** VERB
1 el fuego *(flames)*
□ The fire spread quickly. El fuego se extendió rápidamente.
2 el incendio *(blaze)*
□ The house was destroyed by a fire. La casa fue destruida por un incendio.
3 la hoguera
□ He made a fire to warm himself up. Encendió una hoguera para calentarse.
4 la estufa
□ an electric fire una estufa eléctrica
■ **to be on fire** estar ardiendo

to **fire** VERB
▷ *see also* **fire** NOUN
disparar
□ She fired at him. Le disparó.
■ **to fire a gun** disparar
■ **to fire somebody** despedir a alguien
□ He was fired from his job. Le despidieron del trabajo.

fire alarm NOUN
la alarma contra incendios

fire brigade NOUN
el cuerpo de bomberos

fire engine NOUN
el coche de bomberos

fire escape NOUN
la escalera de incendios

fire extinguisher NOUN
el extintor

fireman NOUN
el bombero
□ He's a fireman. Es bombero.

fireplace NOUN
la chimenea

fire station NOUN
el parque de bomberos

fireworks PL NOUN
los fuegos artificiales

firm ADJECTIVE
▷ *see also* **firm** NOUN
1 firme (FEM firme)
□ to be firm with somebody mostrarse firme con alguien
2 duro (FEM dura)
□ a firm mattress un colchón duro

firm NOUN
▷ *see also* **firm** ADJECTIVE
la empresa

first ADJECTIVE, NOUN, ADVERB
1 primero (FEM primera)
□ for the first time por primera vez □ Rachel came first in the race. Rachel quedó primera en la carrera. □ She was the first to arrive. Fue la primera en llegar.

LANGUAGE TIP Use **primer** before a masculine singular noun.

□ my first job mi primer trabajo
■ **the first of September** el uno de septiembre
■ **at first** al principio
2 antes
□ I want to get a job, but first I have to graduate. Quiero encontrar un trabajo, pero antes tengo que acabar la carrera.
■ **first of all** ante todo

first aid NOUN
los primeros auxilios
■ **a first aid kit** un botiquín

first-class ADJECTIVE, ADVERB
1 de primera clase
□ a first-class ticket un billete de primera clase
2 de primera
□ a first-class meal una comida de primera
■ **to travel first class** viajar en primera
■ **a first-class stamp** un sello para correo urgente

DID YOU KNOW...?
In Spain there is no first-class or second-class postage. If you want your mail to arrive fast, you must have it sent express – **urgente** – from a post office.

firstly ADVERB
en primer lugar

fish NOUN
▹ *see also* **fish** VERB
1 el pez (PL los peces) *(animal)*
□ I caught three fish. Pesqué tres peces.
2 el pescado *(food)*
□ I don't like fish. No me gusta el pescado.
□ fish and chips pescado rebozado con patatas fritas

to **fish** VERB
▹ *see also* **fish** NOUN
pescar*
■ **to go fishing** ir a pescar

fisherman NOUN
el pescador
□ He's a fisherman. Es pescador.

fish fingers PL NOUN
los palitos de pescado

fishing NOUN
la pesca
□ I enjoy fishing. Me gusta la pesca.
■ **a fishing boat** un barco pesquero
■ **fishing rod** la caña de pescar

fishing tackle NOUN
los aparejos de pesca

fishmonger's NOUN
la pescadería

fish sticks PL NOUN (US)
los palitos de pescado

fish tank NOUN
el acuario

fist NOUN
el puño

fit ADJECTIVE
▹ *see also* **fit** VERB, NOUN
en forma
□ He felt relaxed and fit after his holiday. Se sentía relajado y en forma tras las vacaciones.
■ **Will he be fit to play next Saturday?** ¿Estará en condiciones de jugar el próximo sábado?

fit NOUN
▹ *see also* **fit** ADJECTIVE, VERB
■ **to have a fit** **1** *(epileptic)* sufrir un ataque de epilepsia **2** *(be angry)* ponerse hecho una furia □ My Mum will have a fit when she sees the carpet! ¡Mi madre se va a poner hecha una furia cuando vea la moqueta!

to **fit** VERB
▹ *see also* **fit** ADJECTIVE, NOUN
1 caber* *(go into a space)*
□ It's small enough to fit into your pocket. Es lo bastante pequeño como para que caber en el bolsillo.
2 encajar
□ Make sure the cork fits well into the bottle. Asegúrese de que el corcho encaja bien en la botella.
3 instalar *(install)*
□ He fitted an alarm in his car. Instaló una alarma en el coche.
4 poner* *(attach)*
□ She fitted a plug to the hair dryer. Le puso un enchufe al secador.
■ **to fit somebody** estar bien a alguien
□ These trousers don't fit me. Estos pantalones no me están bien.
■ **Does it fit?** ¿Te está bien?

to **fit in** VERB
1 encajar
□ That story doesn't fit in with what he told us. Esa historia no encaja con lo que él nos contó.
2 adaptarse
□ She fitted in well at her new school. Se adaptó bien al nuevo colegio.

fitting room NOUN
el probador (PL los probadores)

five NUMERAL
cinco
□ He's five. Tiene cinco años.

to **fix** VERB
1 arreglar
□ Can you fix my bike? ¿Me puedes arreglar la bici?
2 fijar
□ Let's fix a date for the party. Vamos a fijar una fecha para la fiesta.

fixed ADJECTIVE
fijo (FEM fija)
□ at a fixed time a una hora fija
■ **My parents have very fixed ideas.** Mis padres son de ideas fijas.

fizzy ADJECTIVE
gaseoso (FEM gaseosa)

flabby ADJECTIVE
fofo (FEM fofa)

flag NOUN
la bandera

flame NOUN
la llama

flamingo NOUN
el flamenco

flan NOUN
1 la tarta *(sweet)*
□ a raspberry flan una tarta de frambuesa
2 el pastel *(savoury)*
□ a cheese and onion flan un pastel de queso y cebolla

flannel NOUN
la toallita para lavarse *(for face)*

to **flap** VERB
■ **The bird flapped its wings.** El pájaro batió las alas.

flash NOUN
▷ *see also* **flash** VERB
el flash *(of camera)*
■ **a flash of lightning** un relámpago
■ **in a flash** en un abrir y cerrar de ojos

to **flash** VERB
▷ *see also* **flash** NOUN
■ **A lorry driver flashed him.** Un camionero le hizo señales con los faros.
■ **They flashed a torch in his face.** Le enfocaron con una linterna en la cara.

flask NOUN
el termo *(vacuum flask)*

flat ADJECTIVE
▷ *see also* **flat** NOUN
llano (FEM llana)
□ a flat surface una superficie llana
■ **flat shoes** zapatos bajos
■ **I've got a flat tyre.** Tengo una rueda desinflada.

flat NOUN
▷ *see also* **flat** ADJECTIVE
el piso (el apartamento *Latin America*)

flattered ADJECTIVE
halagado (FEM halagada)

flavour (US **flavor**) NOUN
el sabor (PL los sabores)
□ a very strong flavour un sabor muy fuerte
□ Which flavour of ice cream would you like? ¿De qué sabor quieres el helado?

flavouring (US **flavoring**) NOUN
el condimento

flea NOUN
la pulga

flew VERB ▷ *see* **fly**

flexible ADJECTIVE
flexible (FEM flexible)
□ flexible working hours un horario de trabajo flexible

to **flick** VERB
■ **She flicked the switch to turn the light on.** Le dio al interruptor para encender la luz.
■ **to flick through a book** hojear un libro

to **flicker** VERB
parpadear *(light)*

flight NOUN
el vuelo
□ What time is the flight to Paris? ¿A qué hora es el vuelo para París?
■ **a flight of stairs** un tramo de escaleras

flight attendant NOUN
el/la auxiliar de vuelo

to **fling** VERB
arrojar
□ He flung the dictionary onto the floor. Arrojó el diccionario al suelo.

to **float** VERB
flotar

flock NOUN
■ **a flock of sheep** un rebaño de ovejas
■ **a flock of birds** una bandada de pájaros

flood NOUN
▷ *see also* **flood** VERB
la inundación (PL las inundaciones)
□ The rain has caused many floods. La lluvia ha provocado muchas inundaciones.
■ **He received a flood of letters.** Recibió un aluvión de cartas.

to **flood** VERB
▷ *see also* **flood** NOUN
inundar
□ The river has flooded the village. El río ha inundado el pueblo.

flooding NOUN
la inundación

floor NOUN
1 el suelo (el piso *Latin America*)
□ a tiled floor un suelo embaldosado
■ **the dance floor** la pista de baile
2 el piso
□ the first floor el primer piso □ on the first floor en el primer piso

flop NOUN
el fracaso
□ The film was a flop. La película fue un fracaso.

floppy disk NOUN
el disquete

florist NOUN
el/la florista

flour NOUN
la harina

to **flow** VERB
fluir*
□ The river flows through the valley. El río fluye por el valle. □ Traffic is now flowing normally. El tráfico ya fluye con normalidad.
■ **Water was flowing from the pipe.** El agua brotaba de la tubería.

flower NOUN
▷ *see also* **flower** VERB
la flor (PL las flores)

to **flower** VERB
▷ *see also* **flower** NOUN
florecer*

flown VERB ▷ *see* **fly**

flu NOUN
la gripe
□ I've got flu. Tengo gripe.

fluent ADJECTIVE
■ **He speaks fluent Spanish.** Habla español con fluidez.

English-Spanish

flung VERB ▷ *see* **fling**

to **flush** VERB

■ **to flush the toilet** tirar de la cadena

flute NOUN

la flauta

fly NOUN

▷ *see also* **fly** VERB

la mosca

to **fly** VERB

▷ *see also* **fly** NOUN

volar*

□ He flew from London to Glasgow. Voló de Londres a Glasgow. □ The bird flew away. El pájaro salió volando.

foal NOUN

el potro

focus NOUN

▷ *see also* **focus** VERB

el centro

□ He was the focus of attention. Era el centro de atención.

■ **to be out of focus** estar desenfocado

to **focus** VERB

▷ *see also* **focus** NOUN

enfocar*

□ Try to focus the binoculars. Intenta enfocar los prismáticos.

■ **to focus on something** **1** *(with camera, telescope)* enfocar algo □ The cameraman focused on the bird. El cámara enfocó al pájaro. **2** *(concentrate on)* centrarse en algo

fog NOUN

la niebla

foggy ADJECTIVE

■ **It's foggy.** Hay niebla.

■ **a foggy day** un día de niebla

foil NOUN

el papel de aluminio *(kitchen foil)*

fold NOUN

▷ *see also* **fold** VERB

el pliegue

to **fold** VERB

▷ *see also* **fold** NOUN

doblar

□ He folded the newspaper in half. Dobló el periódico por la mitad.

■ **to fold one's arms** cruzarse de brazos

folder NOUN

la carpeta

folding ADJECTIVE

plegable (FEM plegable) *(bed, chair)*

to **follow** VERB

seguir*

□ You go first and I'll follow. Ve tú primero y yo te sigo. □ He followed my advice. Siguió mi consejo.

following ADJECTIVE

siguiente (FEM siguiente)

□ the following day al día siguiente

fond ADJECTIVE

■ **to be fond of somebody** tener cariño a alguien □ I'm very fond of her. Le tengo mucho cariño.

food NOUN

la comida

□ cat food comida para gatos □ We need to buy some food. Hay que comprar comida.

food processor NOUN

el robot de cocina (PL los robots de cocina)

fool NOUN

el/la idiota

foot NOUN

1 el pie *(of person)*

□ My feet are aching. Me duelen los pies.

■ **on foot** a pie

DID YOU KNOW...?
In Spain measurements are in metres and centimetres rather than feet and inches. A foot is about 30 centimetres.

□ Dave is six foot tall. Dave mide un metro ochenta.

2 la pata *(of animal)*

football NOUN

1 el fútbol

□ I like playing football. Me gusta jugar al fútbol.

■ **football boots** las botas de fútbol

2 el balón (PL los balones)

□ Paul threw the football over the fence. Paul lanzó el balón por encima de la valla.

footballer NOUN

el/la futbolista

football player NOUN

el/la futbolista

footpath NOUN

el sendero

footprint NOUN

la pisada

□ He saw some footprints in the sand. Vio algunas pisadas en la arena.

footstep NOUN

el paso

□ I can hear footsteps on the stairs. Oigo pasos en la escalera.

for PREPOSITION

LANGUAGE TIP There are three basic ways of translating 'for' into Spanish: **para, por** and **durante**. Check the boxes at the beginning of each translation to find the meaning or example you need. If you can't find it look at the phrases at the end of the entry.

1 para

LANGUAGE TIP **para** is used to indicate destination, employment, intention and purpose.

□ a present for me un regalo para mí □ the train for London el tren para Londres □ He works for the government. Trabaja para el gobierno. □ What for? ¿Para qué? □ What's it for? ¿Para qué es?

2 por

LANGUAGE TIP **por** is used to indicate reason or cause. Use it also when talking about amounts of money.

□ for fear of being criticized por temor a ser criticado □ Oxford is famous for its university. Oxford es famoso por su universidad. □ I'll do it for you. Lo haré por ti. □ I'm sorry for Steve, but it's his own fault. Lo siento por Steve, pero es culpa suya. □ I sold it for £5. Lo vendí por 5 libras. □ What did he do that for? ¿Por qué ha hecho eso?

3 durante

LANGUAGE TIP When referring to periods of time, use **durante** to refer to the future and completed actions in the past. Note that it can often be omitted, as in the next two examples.

□ She will be away for a month. Estará fuera (durante) un mes. □ He worked in Spain for two years. Trabajó (durante) dos años en España.

LANGUAGE TIP Use **hace...que** and the present to describe actions and states that started in the past and are still going on. Alternatively use the present and **desde hace**. Another option is **llevar** and an **-ando/-iendo** form.

□ He has been learning French for two years. Hace dos años que estudia francés. □ I haven't seen her for two years. No la veo desde hace dos años. □ She's been learning German for four years. Lleva cuatro años estudiando alemán.

LANGUAGE TIP See how the tenses change when talking about something that 'had' happened or 'had been' happening 'for' a time.

□ He had been learning French for two years. Hacía dos años que estudiaba francés. □ I hadn't seen her for two years. No la veía desde hacía dos años. □ She had been learning German for four years. Llevaba cuatro años estudiando alemán.

■ **There are road works for three kilometres.** Hay obras en tres kilómetros.

■ **What's the English for 'león'?** ¿Cómo se dice 'león' en inglés?

■ **It's time for lunch.** Es la hora de comer.

■ **Can you do it for tomorrow?** ¿Puedes hacerlo para mañana?

■ **Are you for or against the idea?** ¿Estás a favor o en contra de la idea?

to **forbid** VERB

prohibir*

■ **to forbid somebody to do something** prohibir a alguien que haga algo

force NOUN

▷ *see also* **force** VERB

la fuerza

□ the force of the explosion la fuerza de la explosión

■ **UN forces** las fuerzas de la ONU

■ **in force** *(law, rules)* en vigor

to **force** VERB

▷ *see also* **force** NOUN

obligar*

□ They forced him to open the safe. Le obligaron a abrir la caja fuerte.

forecast NOUN

■ **the weather forecast** el pronóstico del tiempo

foreground NOUN

el primer plano

□ in the foreground en primer plano

forehead NOUN

la frente

foreign ADJECTIVE

1 extranjero (FEM extranjera)

□ a foreign language una lengua extranjera

2 exterior (FEM exterior)

□ US foreign policy la política exterior estadounidense

foreigner NOUN

el extranjero

la extranjera

to **foresee** VERB

prever*

forest NOUN

el bosque

forever ADVERB

1 para siempre

□ He's gone forever. Se ha ido para siempre.

2 siempre

□ She's forever complaining. Siempre se está quejando.

forgave VERB ▷ *see* **forgive**

to **forge** VERB

falsificar*

□ She forged his signature. Falsificó su firma.

to **forget** VERB

olvidar

□ I've forgotten his name. He olvidado su nombre.

■ **to forget to do something** olvidarse de hacer algo □ I forgot to close the window. Me olvidé de cerrar la ventana.
■ **I'm sorry, I had completely forgotten!** ¡Lo siento, se me había olvidado por completo!
■ **Forget it!** ¡No importa!

to **forgive** VERB
perdonar
□ I forgive you. Te perdono.
■ **to forgive somebody for doing something** perdonar a alguien que haya hecho algo

forgot, forgotten VERB ▷ *see* **forget**

fork NOUN
1 el tenedor *(for eating)*
2 la horca
□ He was piling up hay with a fork. Apilaba heno con una horca.
3 la bifurcación (PL las bifurcaciones) *(in road)*

form NOUN
1 el impreso (la planilla *Latin America*)
■ **to fill in a form** rellenar un impreso
2 la forma
□ I'm against hunting in any form. Estoy en contra de cualquier forma de caza.
■ **in top form** en plena forma
■ **She's in the first form.** Está haciendo primero de secundaria.

formal ADJECTIVE
1 oficial (FEM oficial)
□ a formal occasion un acto oficial
■ **a formal dinner** una cena de gala
■ **formal clothes** la ropa de etiqueta
2 formal (FEM formal)
□ In English, 'residence' is a formal term. En inglés, 'residence' es un término formal.
■ **He's got no formal education.** No tiene formación académica.

former ADJECTIVE
antiguo (FEM antigua)

LANGUAGE TIP Put **antiguo** before the noun when translating 'former'.

□ a former pupil un antiguo alumno

formerly ADVERB
antiguamente

fort NOUN
el fuerte

forth ADVERB
■ **to go back and forth** ir de acá para allá
■ **and so forth** y demás

fortnight NOUN
■ **a fortnight** quince días □ I'm going on holiday for a fortnight. Me voy quince días de vacaciones.

fortunate ADJECTIVE
■ **He was extremely fortunate to survive.** Tuvo la gran suerte de salir vivo.
■ **It's fortunate that I remembered the map.** Menos mal que me acordé de traer el mapa.

fortunately ADVERB
afortunadamente

fortune NOUN
la fortuna
□ He made his fortune in car sales. Consiguió su fortuna con la venta de coches.
■ **Kate earns a fortune!** ¡Kate gana un dineral!
■ **to tell somebody's fortune** decir la buenaventura a alguien

forty NUMERAL
cuarenta
□ He's forty. Tiene cuarenta años.

forward ADVERB
▷ *see also* **forward** VERB
hacia delante
□ to look forward mirar hacia delante
■ **to move forward** avanzar

to **forward** VERB
▷ *see also* **forward** ADVERB
remitir *(letter)*

to **foster** VERB
acoger*
□ She has fostered more than fifteen children. Ha acogido a más de quince niños.

foster child NOUN
el niño acogido en una familia

fought VERB ▷ *see* **fight**

foul ADJECTIVE
▷ *see also* **foul** NOUN
1 horrible (FEM horrible)
□ The weather was foul. El tiempo era horrible.
2 asqueroso (FEM asquerosa)
□ It smells foul. Huele asqueroso.
■ **Brenda is in a foul mood.** Brenda está de muy mal humor.

foul NOUN
▷ *see also* **foul** ADJECTIVE
la falta *(in sports)*

found VERB ▷ *see* **find**

to **found** VERB
fundar

foundations PL NOUN
los cimientos

fountain NOUN
la fuente

fountain pen NOUN
la pluma estilográfica (la plumafuente *Latin America*)

four NUMERAL
cuatro
□ She's four. Tiene cuatro años.

fourteen NUMERAL
catorce
□ I'm fourteen. Tengo catorce años.

fourteenth ADJECTIVE
decimocuarto (FEM decimocuarta)
■ **the fourteenth floor** la planta catorce
■ **the fourteenth of July** el catorce de julio

fourth ADJECTIVE
cuarto (FEM cuarta)
□ the fourth floor el cuarto piso
■ **the fourth of July** el cuatro de julio

fox NOUN
el zorro

fragile ADJECTIVE
frágil (FEM frágil)

frame NOUN
el marco
□ a silver frame un marco de plata
■ **glasses with plastic frames** gafas con montura de plástico

France NOUN
Francia *fem*

frantic ADJECTIVE
frenético (FEM frenética)
□ There was frantic activity before the party started. Había una actividad frenética antes de empezar la fiesta. □ I was going frantic. Me estaba poniendo frenético.
■ **to be frantic with worry** estar muerto de preocupación

fraud NOUN
1 el fraude
□ He was jailed for fraud. Lo encarcelaron por fraude.
2 el impostor
la impostora
□ You're a fraud! ¡Eres un impostor!

freckles PL NOUN
las pecas

free ADJECTIVE
▷ *see also* **free** VERB
1 gratuito (FEM gratuita)
□ a free brochure un folleto gratuito
■ **You can get it for free.** Se puede conseguir gratis.
2 libre (FEM libre)
□ Is this seat free? ¿Está libre este asiento?
□ Are you free after school? ¿Estás libre después de clase?

to **free** VERB
▷ *see also* **free** ADJECTIVE
liberar

freedom NOUN
la libertad

freeway NOUN (US)
la autopista

to **freeze** VERB
1 congelar
□ She froze the rest of the raspberries. Congeló el resto de las frambuesas.
2 helarse*
□ The water had frozen. El agua se había helado.

freezer NOUN
el congelador

freezing ADJECTIVE
■ **It's freezing!** ¡Hace un frío que pela! *(informal)*
■ **I'm freezing!** ¡Me estoy congelando!
■ **three degrees below freezing** tres grados bajo cero

freight NOUN
las mercancías *(goods)*
■ **a freight train** un tren de mercancías

French ADJECTIVE
▷ *see also* **French** NOUN
francés (FEM francesa, PL franceses)

French NOUN
▷ *see also* **French** ADJECTIVE
el francés *(language)*
□ the French teacher el profesor de francés
■ **the French** los franceses

French beans PL NOUN
las judías verdes

French fries PL NOUN
las patatas fritas (las papas fritas *Latin America*)

French horn NOUN
la trompa de llaves

French loaf NOUN
la barra de pan

Frenchman NOUN
el francés (PL los franceses)

French windows PL NOUN
la puerta ventana

Frenchwoman NOUN
la francesa

frequent ADJECTIVE
frecuente (FEM frecuente)

fresh ADJECTIVE
fresco (FEM fresca)
□ I always buy fresh fish. Siempre compro pescado fresco.
■ **I need some fresh air.** Necesito tomar el aire.

to **freshen up** VERB
refrescarse*

to **fret** VERB
preocuparse

Friday NOUN
el viernes (PL los viernes)
□ I saw her on Friday. La vi el viernes.
□ every Friday todos los viernes □ last Friday el viernes pasado □ next Friday el viernes que viene □ on Fridays los viernes

fridge NOUN
la nevera (la refrigeradora *Latin America*)

fried ADJECTIVE
frito (FEM frita)
□ a fried egg un huevo frito

friend NOUN
el amigo
la amiga

friendly ADJECTIVE
simpático (FEM simpática)
□ She's really friendly. Es muy simpática.
■ **Liverpool is a friendly city.** Liverpool es una ciudad acogedora.
■ **a friendly match** un partido amistoso

friendship NOUN
la amistad

fright NOUN
el susto
□ She gave us a fright. Nos dio un susto.
□ to get a fright llevarse un susto

to **frighten** VERB
asustar
□ She was trying to frighten him. Intentaba asustarlo.
■ **Horror films frighten him.** Le dan miedo las películas de terror.

frightened ADJECTIVE
■ **to be frightened** tener miedo □ I'm frightened! ¡Tengo miedo!
■ **Anna's frightened of spiders.** A Anna le dan miedo las arañas.

frightening ADJECTIVE
aterrador (FEM aterradora)

fringe NOUN
el flequillo
□ She's got a fringe. Lleva flequillo.

Frisbee® NOUN
el disco volador

fro ADVERB
■ **to go to and fro** ir de acá para allá

frog NOUN
la rana

from PREPOSITION
1 de
□ Where do you come from? ¿De dónde eres? □ a letter from my sister una carta de mi hermana □ The hotel is one kilometre from the beach. El hotel está a un kilómetro de la playa. □ The price was reduced from £10 to £5. Rebajaron el precio de 10 a 5 libras esterlinas.
2 desde
□ Breakfast is available from 6 a.m. Se puede desayunar desde las 6 de la mañana.
□ I can't see anything from here. Desde aquí no veo nada.

LANGUAGE TIP In the following phrases **de** and **desde** are interchangeable. Use **a** to translate 'to' if you have chosen **de** and **hasta** if you have opted for **desde**.

■ **He flew from London to Bilbao.** Voló de Londres a Bilbao.
■ **from one o'clock to three** desde la una hasta las tres
■ **She works from nine to five.** Trabaja de nueve a cinco.
■ **from...onwards** a partir de... □ We'll be at home from seven o'clock onwards. Estaremos en casa a partir de las siete.

front NOUN
▷ *see also* **front** ADJECTIVE
la parte delantera
□ The switch is at the front of the vacuum cleaner. El interruptor está en la parte delantera de la aspiradora.
■ **the front of the dress** el delantero del vestido
■ **the front of the house** la fachada de la casa
■ **I was sitting in the front.** *(of car)* Yo iba sentado delante.
■ **at the front of the train** al principio del tren
■ **in front** delante □ the car in front el coche de delante
■ **in front of** delante de □ Irene sits in front of me in class. Irene se sienta delante de mí en clase.

front ADJECTIVE
▷ *see also* **front** NOUN
1 primero (FEM primera)
□ the front row la primera fila

LANGUAGE TIP Use **primer** before a masculine singular noun.

2 delantero (FEM delantera)
□ the front seats of the car los asientos delanteros del coche
■ **the front door** la puerta principal

frontier NOUN
la frontera

frost NOUN
la helada
□ There was a frost last night. Anoche cayó una helada.

frosting NOUN (US)
el glaseado *(on cake)*

frosty ADJECTIVE
■ **It's frosty today.** Hoy ha helado.

to **frown** VERB
fruncir* el ceño

frozen ADJECTIVE
congelado (FEM congelada)

fruit NOUN
la fruta
■ **fruit juice** el zumo de fruta (el jugo de fruta *Latin America*)
■ **fruit salad** la macedonia (la ensalada de frutas *Latin America*)

fruit machine NOUN
la máquina tragaperras (PL las máquinas tragaperras)

frustrated ADJECTIVE
frustrado (FEM frustrada)

to **fry** VERB
freír*

frying pan NOUN
la sartén (PL las sartenes)

fuel NOUN
el combustible
□ We've run out of fuel. Nos hemos quedado sin combustible.

to **fulfil** VERB
realizar*
□ He fulfilled his dream to visit China. Realizó su sueño de viajar a China.
■ **to fulfil a promise** cumplir una promesa

full ADJECTIVE
1 lleno (FEM llena)
□ The tank's full. El depósito está lleno.
■ **I'm full.** Estoy lleno.
■ **There was a full moon.** Había luna llena.
2 completo (FEM completa)
□ He asked for full information on the job. Solicitó información completa sobre el trabajo. □ My full name is Ian John Marr. Mi nombre completo es Ian John Marr.
■ **full board** la pensión completa
■ **at full speed** a toda velocidad

full stop NOUN
el punto *(signo de puntuación)*

full-time ADJECTIVE, ADVERB
■ **She's got a full-time job.** Tiene un trabajo de jornada completa.
■ **She works full-time.** Trabaja la jornada completa.

fully ADVERB
completamente
□ He hasn't fully recovered from his illness. No se ha recuperado completamente de su enfermedad.

fumes PL NOUN
el humo

fun ADJECTIVE
▷ *see also* **fun** NOUN
divertido (FEM divertida)
□ She's a fun person. Es una persona divertida.

fun NOUN
▷ *see also* **fun** ADJECTIVE
■ **to have fun** divertirse
■ **It's fun!** ¡Es divertido!
■ **Have fun!** ¡Que te diviertas!
■ **for fun** por gusto
■ **to make fun of somebody** reírse de alguien

funds PL NOUN
los fondos
□ to raise funds recaudar fondos

funeral NOUN
el funeral

funfair NOUN
1 la feria *(travelling fair)*
2 el parque de atracciones *(fair on permanent site)*

funny ADJECTIVE
1 gracioso (FEM graciosa)
□ a funny joke un chiste gracioso
2 raro (FEM rara)
□ There's something funny about him. Hay algo raro en él.

fur NOUN
1 la piel
■ **a fur coat** un abrigo de pieles
2 el pelaje
□ the cat's fur el pelaje del gato

furious ADJECTIVE
furioso (FEM furiosa)

furniture NOUN
los muebles
■ **a piece of furniture** un mueble

further ADVERB, ADJECTIVE
1 más lejos
□ London is further from here than Paris. Londres está más lejos de aquí que París.
■ **I can't walk any further.** No puedo andar más.
■ **How much further is it?** ¿Cuánto queda todavía?
2 más
□ Please write to us if you need any further information. No dude en escribirnos si necesita más información.

further education NOUN
la educación superior

fuse NOUN
el fusible
□ The fuse has blown. Se ha fundido el fusible.

fuss NOUN
el jaleo
□ What's all the fuss about? ¿A qué viene tanto jaleo?
■ **He's always making a fuss about nothing.** Siempre monta el número por cualquier tontería. *(informal)*

fussy ADJECTIVE
quisquilloso (FEM quisquillosa)
□ She is very fussy about her food. Es muy quisquillosa con la comida.

future NOUN
el futuro
□ What are your plans for the future? ¿Qué planes tienes para el futuro?
■ **in future** de ahora en adelante □ Be more careful in future. De ahora en adelante ten más cuidado.

Gg

to **gain** VERB
ganar
□ What do you hope to gain from this? ¿Qué esperas ganar con esto?
■ **to gain speed** adquirir velocidad
■ **to gain weight** engordar

gallery NOUN
1 el museo de arte *(state-owned)*
2 una galería de arte *(private)*

to **gamble** VERB
jugarse*
□ He gambled £100 at the casino. Se jugó 100 libras en el casino.

gambler NOUN
el jugador
la jugadora

gambling NOUN
el juego *(de azar)*

game NOUN
1 el juego
□ The children were playing a game. Los niños jugaban a un juego.
2 el partido
□ a game of football un partido de fútbol
■ **a game of cards** una partida de cartas
■ **We have games on Thursdays.** Tenemos deporte los jueves.

gang NOUN
1 la banda *(of thieves, troublemakers)*
2 la pandilla *(of friends)*

gangster NOUN
el gángster

gap NOUN
1 el hueco
□ There's a gap in the hedge. Hay un hueco en el seto.
2 el intervalo
□ a gap of four years un intervalo de cuatro años

garage NOUN
1 el garaje *(for keeping the car)*
2 el taller *(for car repairs)*

garbage NOUN
la basura
□ the garbage can el cubo de la basura
■ **That's garbage!** ¡Eso son tonterías!

garden NOUN
el jardín (PL los jardines)

gardener NOUN
el jardinero
la jardinera
□ He's a gardener. Es jardinero.

gardening NOUN
la jardinería
□ Margaret loves gardening. A Margaret le encanta la jardinería.

gardens PL NOUN
el parque

garlic NOUN
el ajo

garment NOUN
la prenda de vestir

gas NOUN
1 el gas
■ **a gas cooker** una cocina de gas
■ **a gas cylinder** una bombona de gas
■ **a gas fire** una estufa de gas
■ **a gas leak** un escape de gas
2 la gasolina (US: *petrol)*

gasoline NOUN (US)
la gasolina

gate NOUN
1 la puerta *(made of wood)*
2 la verja *(made of metal)*
■ **Please go to gate seven.** Diríjanse a la puerta siete.

gateau NOUN
la tarta

to **gather** VERB
1 reunirse*
□ We gathered around the fireplace. Nos reunimos en torno a la chimenea.
2 reunir*
□ We gathered enough firewood to last the night. Reunimos leña suficiente para toda la noche. □ to gather information reunir información
■ **to gather speed** adquirir velocidad □ The train gathered speed. El tren adquirió velocidad.

gave VERB ▷ *see* **give**

gay ADJECTIVE

gay (FEM + PL gay)

to **gaze** VERB

■ **to gaze at** mirar fijamente □ He was gazing at her. La miraba fijamente.

GCSE NOUN *(= General Certificate of Secondary Education)*

DID YOU KNOW...?
In Spain, under the reformed educational system, if you leave school at the age of 16, you get a **Título de Graduado en Educación Secundaria**.

gear NOUN
1 la marcha
□ to change gear cambiar de marcha
□ He left the car in gear. Dejó el coche con una marcha metida.
■ **in first gear** en primera
2 el equipo
□ camping gear el equipo de acampada
■ **sports gear** la ropa de deporte

gear lever NOUN
la palanca de cambio

gearshift NOUN (US)
la palanca de cambio

geese PL NOUN ▷ *see* **goose**

gel NOUN
el gel
■ **hair gel** el fijador

gem NOUN
la gema

Gemini NOUN
el Géminis *(sign)*
■ **I'm Gemini.** Soy géminis.

gender NOUN
el género *(of noun)*

general NOUN
▷ *see also* **general** ADJECTIVE
el general

general ADJECTIVE
▷ *see also* **general** NOUN
general (FEM general)
■ **in general** en general

general election NOUN
las elecciones generales

general knowledge NOUN
la cultura general

generally ADVERB
generalmente
□ I generally go shopping on Saturdays. Generalmente voy de compras los sábados.

generation NOUN
la generación (PL las generaciones)
□ the younger generation la nueva generación

generator NOUN
el generador

generous ADJECTIVE
generoso (FEM generosa)
□ That's very generous of you. Es muy generoso de tu parte.

Geneva NOUN
Ginebra *fem*

genius NOUN
el genio
□ She's a genius. Es un genio.

gentle ADJECTIVE
1 dulce (FEM dulce) *(person, voice)*
2 suave (FEM suave) *(wind, touch)*

gentleman NOUN
el caballero

gently ADVERB
1 dulcemente *(to say, smile)*
2 suavemente *(to touch)*

gents NOUN
el servicio de caballeros
□ Can you tell me where the gents is, please? ¿El servicio de caballeros, por favor?
■ **'gents'** *(on sign)* 'caballeros'

genuine ADJECTIVE
1 auténtico (FEM auténtica)
□ These are genuine diamonds. Estos son diamantes auténticos.
2 sincero (FEM sincera)
□ She's a very genuine person. Es una persona muy sincera.

geography NOUN
la geografía

gerbil NOUN
el gerbo

germ NOUN
el microbio

German ADJECTIVE
▷ *see also* **German** NOUN
alemán (FEM alemana, PL alemanes)

German NOUN
▷ *see also* **German** ADJECTIVE
1 el alemán (PL los alemanes)
la alemana *(person)*
□ the Germans los alemanes
2 el alemán *(language)*
□ our German teacher nuestro profesor de alemán

German measles NOUN
la rubéola
□ to have German measles tener rubéola

Germany NOUN
Alemania *fem*

gesture NOUN
el gesto

to **get** VERB

LANGUAGE TIP There are several ways of translating 'get'. Scan the examples to find one that is similar to what you want to say.

1 recibir *(have, receive)*
□ I got a letter from him. Recibí una carta de él.

■ **I got lots of presents.** Me hicieron muchos regalos.

2 conseguir* *(obtain)*

□ He had trouble getting a hotel room. Tuvo dificultades para conseguir una habitación de hotel.

■ **to get something for somebody** conseguir algo a alguien □ The librarian got the book for me. El bibliotecario me consiguió el libro.

■ **Jackie got good exam results.** Jackie sacó buenas notas en los exámenes.

3 ir* a buscar *(fetch)*

□ Quick, get help! ¡Rápido, ve a buscar ayuda!

4 coger* *(catch, take)*

LANGUAGE TIP Be very careful with the verb **coger**: in most of Latin America this is an extremely rude word that should be avoided. However, in Spain this verb is common and not rude at all.

□ They've got the thief. Han cogido al ladrón. (Han atrapado al ladrón. *Latin America*) □ I'm getting the bus into town. Voy a coger el autobús al centro. (Voy a tomar el autobús al centro. *Latin America*)

5 entender* *(understand)*

□ I don't get the joke. No entiendo el chiste.

6 llegar* *(arrive)*

□ He should get here soon. Debería llegar pronto. □ How do you get to the cinema? ¿Cómo se llega al cine?

■ **to get angry** enfadarse (enojarse *Latin America*)

■ **to get tired** cansarse

LANGUAGE TIP For other phrases with 'get' and an adjective, such as 'to get old, to get drunk', you should look under the word 'old', 'drunk', etc.

■ **to get something done** mandar hacer algo □ I'm getting my car fixed. He mandado arreglar el coche.

■ **I got my hair cut.** Me corté el pelo.

■ **I'll get it!** **1** *(telephone)* ¡Yo contesto! **2** *(door)* ¡Ya voy yo!

to **get away** VERB

escapar

□ One of the burglars got away. Uno de los ladrones escapó.

to **get back** VERB

1 volver*

□ What time did you get back? ¿A qué hora volvisteis?

2 recuperar

□ He got his money back. Recuperó su dinero.

to **get in** VERB

llegar*

□ What time did you get in last night? ¿A qué hora llegaste anoche?

to **get into** VERB

entrar en

□ How did you get into the house? ¿Cómo entraste en la casa?

■ **Sharon got into the car.** Sharon subió al coche.

■ **Get into bed!** ¡Métete en la cama!

to **get off** VERB

1 bajarse de

□ Isobel got off the train. Isobel se bajó del tren.

2 salir*

□ He managed to get off early from work yesterday. Logró salir de trabajar pronto ayer.

to **get on** VERB

1 subirse a

□ Phyllis got on the bus. Phyllis se subió al autobús.

2 llevarse bien

□ We got on really well. Nos llevábamos muy bien. □ He doesn't get on with his parents. No se lleva bien con sus padres.

■ **How are you getting on?** ¿Cómo te va?

to **get out** VERB

1 salir*

□ Get out! ¡Sal!

■ **She got out of the car.** Se bajó del coche.

2 sacar*

□ She got the map out. Sacó el mapa.

to **get over** VERB

1 recuperarse de

□ It took her a long time to get over the illness. Tardó mucho tiempo en recuperarse de la enfermedad.

2 superar

□ He managed to get over the problem. Logró superar el problema.

to **get together** VERB

reunirse*

□ Could we get together this evening? ¿Podemos reunirnos esta tarde?

to **get up** VERB

levantarse

□ What time do you get up? ¿A qué hora te levantas?

ghost NOUN

el fantasma

LANGUAGE TIP Although **fantasma** ends in **-a**, it is actually a masculine noun.

giant ADJECTIVE

▷ *see also* **giant** NOUN

enorme (FEM enorme)

giant NOUN
▷ *see also* **giant** ADJECTIVE
1 el gigante
2 la giganta

gift NOUN
el regalo
■ **to have a gift for something** tener dotes para algo □ **Dave's got a gift for painting.** Dave tiene dotes para la pintura.

gifted ADJECTIVE
de talento
□ **Janice is a gifted dancer.** Janice es una bailarina de talento.
■ **He's one of this country's most gifted artists.** Es uno de los artistas con más dotes de este país.

gift shop NOUN
la tienda de regalos

gigantic ADJECTIVE
gigantesco (FEM gigantesca)

gin NOUN
la ginebra

ginger NOUN
▷ *see also* **ginger** ADJECTIVE
el jengibre

ginger ADJECTIVE
▷ *see also* **ginger** NOUN
■ **She's got ginger hair.** Es pelirroja.

giraffe NOUN
la jirafa

girl NOUN
1 la niña *(young)*
□ **a five-year old girl** una niña de cinco años
□ **They've got a girl and two boys.** Tienen una niña y dos niños.
2 la chica *(older)*
□ **a sixteen-year old girl** una chica de dieciséis años

girlfriend NOUN
1 la novia
□ **Paul's girlfriend is called Janice.** La novia de Paul se llama Janice.
2 la amiga
□ **She often went out with her girlfriends.** Solía salir con sus amigas.

to **give** VERB
dar*
■ **to give something to somebody** dar algo a alguien □ **He gave me £10.** Me dio 10 libras.
■ **to give somebody a present** hacer un regalo a alguien
■ **to give way** *(in car)* ceder el paso

to **give in** VERB
rendirse*
□ **I give in!** ¡Me rindo!

to **give out** VERB
repartir
□ **He gave out the exam papers.** Repartió las hojas de examen.

to **give up** VERB
darse* por vencido
□ **I couldn't do it, so I gave up.** No podía hacerlo, así que me di por vencido.
■ **to give oneself up** entregarse □ **She gave herself up.** Se entregó.
■ **to give up doing something** dejar de hacer algo □ **He gave up smoking.** Dejó de fumar.

glad ADJECTIVE
contento (FEM contenta)
□ **She's glad she's done it.** Está contenta de haberlo hecho.

> LANGUAGE TIP **alegrarse de que** has to be followed by a verb in the subjunctive.

■ **I'm glad you're here.** Me alegro de que estés aquí.

glamorous ADJECTIVE
atractivo (FEM atractiva)

to **glance** VERB
▷ *see also* **glance** NOUN
■ **to glance at something** echar una mirada a algo □ **Peter glanced at his watch.** Peter echó una mirada al reloj.

glance NOUN
▷ *see also* **glance** VERB
la mirada
□ **We exchanged a glance.** Intercambiamos una mirada.
■ **at first glance** a primera vista

to **glare** VERB
■ **to glare at somebody** lanzar una mirada de odio a alguien □ **She glared at him.** Le lanzó una mirada de odio.

glaring ADJECTIVE
■ **a glaring mistake** un error patente

glass NOUN
1 el vaso *(without stem)*
□ **a glass of milk** un vaso de leche
2 la copa *(with stem)*
□ **a glass of champagne** una copa de champán
3 el vidrio *(substance)*
□ **a glass door** una puerta de vidrio

glasses PL NOUN
las gafas (los anteojos *Latin America*)

glider NOUN
el planeador

global ADJECTIVE
mundial (FEM mundial)
□ **on a global scale** a escala mundial
■ **a global view** una visión global

global warming NOUN
el calentamiento del planeta

globe NOUN
el globo terráqueo

gloomy ADJECTIVE
oscuro (FEM oscura)
□ He lives in a small gloomy flat. Vive en un piso pequeño y oscuro.
■ **She's been feeling very gloomy recently.** Últimamente está muy desanimada.

glorious ADJECTIVE
espléndido (FEM espléndida)

glove NOUN
el guante

glove compartment NOUN
la guantera

glue NOUN
▷ *see also* **glue** VERB
el pegamento

to **glue** VERB
▷ *see also* **glue** NOUN
pegar*
■ **to glue something together** pegar algo

GM ADJECTIVE *(= genetically-modified)*
■ **GM foods** los alimentos transgénicos

GMO NOUN *(= genetically-modified organism)*
el organismo transgénico

go NOUN
▷ *see also* **go** VERB
■ **to have a go at doing something** probar a hacer algo □ He had a go at making a cake. Probó a hacer una tarta.
■ **Whose go is it?** ¿A quién le toca?
■ **It's your go.** Te toca a ti.

to **go** VERB
▷ *see also* **go** NOUN
1 ir*
□ Where are you going? ¿Adónde vas? □ I'm going to the cinema tonight. Voy al cine esta noche.
2 irse* *(leave, go away)*
□ Where's Judy? — She's gone. ¿Dónde está Judy? — Se ha ido. □ I'm going now. Yo me voy ya. □ We went home. Nos fuimos a casa.
3 funcionar *(work)*
□ My car won't go. El coche no funciona.
■ **to go home** irse a casa
■ **to go into** entrar en □ She went into the kitchen. Entró en la cocina.
■ **to go for a walk** ir a dar un paseo
■ **How did the exam go?** ¿Cómo te fue en el examen?
■ **I'm going to do it tomorrow.** Lo voy a hacer mañana.
■ **It's going to be difficult.** Va a ser difícil.

to **go after** VERB
perseguir*
□ Quick, go after them! ¡Rápido, persíguelos!

to **go ahead** VERB
seguir* adelante
□ We'll go ahead with your suggestion. Seguiremos adelante con su propuesta.

to **go away** VERB
irse*
□ Go away! ¡Vete!

to **go back** VERB
volver*
□ We went back to the same place. Volvimos al mismo sitio. □ He's gone back home. Ha vuelto a casa.

to **go by** VERB
pasar
□ Two policemen went by. Pasaron dos policías.

to **go down** VERB
1 bajar
□ He went down the stairs. Bajó las escaleras. □ The price of computers has gone down. Ha bajado el precio de los ordenadores.
2 desinflarse
□ My airbed's gone down. Mi colchoneta se ha desinflado.
■ **My brother's gone down with flu.** Mi hermano ha pillado la gripe.

to **go for** VERB
ir* a por
□ Suddenly the dog went for me. De pronto el perro fue a por mí.
■ **Go for it!** ¡Adelante!

to **go in** VERB
entrar
□ He knocked on the door and went in. Llamó a la puerta y entró.

to **go off** VERB
1 marcharse
□ They went off after lunch. Se marcharon después de comer.
2 estallar
□ The bomb went off at 10 o'clock. La bomba estalló a las 10.
■ **The gun went off by accident.** El arma se disparó accidentalmente.
3 sonar*
□ My alarm goes off at seven. Mi despertador suena a las siete.
4 echarse a perder*
□ This milk has gone off. Esta leche se ha echado a perder.
5 apagarse*
□ All the lights went off. Se apagaron todas las luces.
■ **I've gone off that idea.** Ya no me gusta la idea.

to **go on** VERB
1 pasar
□ What's going on? ¿Qué pasa?

2 seguir*
■ **to go on doing** seguir haciendo □ He went on reading. Siguió leyendo.
3 durar
□ The concert went on until 11 o'clock at night. El concierto duró hasta las 11 de la noche.
■ **to go on at somebody** dar la lata a alguien □ They're always going on at me. Están siempre dándome la lata.
■ **Go on!** ¡Venga! □ Go on, tell me what the problem is! ¡Venga, dime cuál es el problema!

to **go out** VERB
1 salir*
□ Are you going out tonight? ¿Vas a salir esta noche? □ I went out with Steven last night. Ayer por la noche salí con Steven. □ They went out for a meal. Salieron a comer.
■ **Are you going out with him?** ¿Estás saliendo con él?
2 apagarse*
□ Suddenly the lights went out. De pronto se apagaron las luces.

to **go past** VERB
■ **to go past something** pasar por delante de algo □ He went past the shop. Pasó por delante de la tienda.

to **go round** VERB
visitar
□ We want to go round the museum today. Hoy queremos visitar el museo.
■ **I love going round the shops.** Me encanta ir de tiendas.
■ **to go round to somebody's house** ir a casa de alguien □ We're all going round to Linda's house tonight. Esta noche vamos todos a casa de Linda.
■ **There's a bug going round.** Hay un virus por ahí rondando.
■ **Is there enough food to go round?** ¿Hay comida suficiente para todos?

to **go through** VERB
1 atravesar*
□ We went through London to get to Brighton. Atravesamos Londres para llegar a Brighton.
2 pasar por
□ I know what you're going through. Sé por lo que estás pasando.
3 repasar
□ They went through the plan again. Repasaron de nuevo el plan.
4 registrar
□ Someone had gone through her things. Alguien había registrado sus cosas.

to **go up** VERB
subir
□ She went up the stairs. Subió las escaleras. □ The price has gone up. El precio ha subido.
■ **to go up in flames** arder en llamas

to **go with** VERB
pegar* con
□ Does this blouse go with that skirt? ¿Pega esta blusa con la falda?

goal NOUN
1 el gol
□ He scored the first goal. Él metió el primer gol.
2 el objetivo
□ His goal is to become the world champion. Su objetivo es ser campeón del mundo.

goalkeeper NOUN
el portero

goat NOUN
la cabra
■ **goat's cheese** el queso de cabra

god NOUN
el dios
□ I believe in God. Creo en Dios.

goddaughter NOUN
la ahijada

godfather NOUN
el padrino

godmother NOUN
la madrina

godson NOUN
el ahijado

goggles PL NOUN
las gafas protectoras (los anteojos protectores *Latin America*)

gold NOUN
el oro
□ a gold necklace un collar de oro □ the gold medal la medalla de oro

goldfish NOUN
el pez de colores (PL los peces de colores)

gold-plated ADJECTIVE
chapado en oro (FEM chapada en oro)

golf NOUN
el golf
■ **a golf club** 1 *(stick)* un palo de golf 2 *(place)* un club de golf
■ **a golf course** un campo de golf

gone VERB ▷ *see* **go**

good ADJECTIVE
1 bueno (FEM buena)
LANGUAGE TIP Use **buen** before a masculine singular noun.
□ It's a very good film. Es una película muy buena. □ a good day un buen día □ Be good! ¡Sé bueno! □ The soup is very good here. Aquí la sopa es muy buena.

English-Spanish

gg

WORD POWER
You can use a number of other words instead of **good** to mean 'great':
excellent excelente
□ an excellent book un libro excelente
fabulous fabuloso
□ a fabulous idea una idea fabulosa
fantastic fantástico
□ fantastic weather un tiempo fantástico
great estupendo
□ a great film una película estupenda

2 amable (FEM amable) *(kind)*
□ That's very good of you. Es muy amable de tu parte.
■ **They were very good to me.** Se portaron muy bien conmigo.
■ **Have a good journey!** ¡Buen viaje!
■ **Good!** ¡Bien!
■ **Good morning!** ¡Buenos días!
■ **Good afternoon!** ¡Buenas tardes!
■ **Good evening!** ¡Buenas noches!
■ **Good night!** ¡Buenas noches!
■ **I'm feeling really good today.** Hoy me siento realmente bien.
■ **to be good for somebody** hacer bien a alguien □ Vegetables are good for you. La verdura te hace bien.
■ **Jane's very good at maths.** A Jane se le dan muy bien las matemáticas.
■ **for good** definitivamente □ One day he left for good. Un día se marchó definitivamente.
■ **It's no good complaining.** De nada sirve quejarse.

goodbye EXCLAMATION
¡adiós!

Good Friday NOUN
el Viernes Santo

good-looking ADJECTIVE
guapo (FEM guapa)

good-natured ADJECTIVE
bueno (FEM buena)
LANGUAGE TIP Use **buen** before a masculine singular noun.

goods PL NOUN
los productos
□ They sell a wide range of goods. Venden una amplia gama de productos.
■ **a goods train** un tren de mercancías

goose NOUN
la oca

gooseberry NOUN
la grosella espinosa

gorgeous ADJECTIVE
1 guapísimo (FEM guapísima)
□ She's gorgeous! ¡Es guapísima!
2 estupendo (FEM estupenda)
□ The weather was gorgeous. El tiempo fue estupendo.

gorilla NOUN
el gorila
LANGUAGE TIP Although **gorila** ends in **-a**, it is actually a masculine noun.

gospel NOUN
el evangelio

gossip NOUN
▹ *see also* **gossip** VERB
1 el cotilleo
□ Tell me the gossip! ¡Cuéntame el cotilleo!
2 el/la cotilla
□ What a gossip! ¡Menudo cotilla!

to **gossip** VERB
▹ *see also* **gossip** NOUN
cotillear (comadrear *Latin America*)
□ They were always gossiping. Siempre estaban cotilleando.

got VERB
■ **to have got** *(own)* tener □ How many have you got? ¿Cuántos tienes?
■ **to have got to do something** tener que hacer algo □ I've got to tell him. Tengo que decírselo.

government NOUN
el gobierno

GP NOUN *(= General Practitioner)*
el médico de cabecera
la médica de cabecera

to **grab** VERB
agarrar
□ He grabbed my arm. Me agarró el brazo.

graceful ADJECTIVE
elegante (FEM elegante)

grade NOUN
la nota
□ He got good grades in his exams. Sacó buenas notas en los exámenes.

grade school NOUN (US)
la escuela primaria

gradual ADJECTIVE
gradual (FEM gradual)

gradually ADVERB
gradualmente

graduate NOUN
1 el licenciado (el egresado *Latin America*)
la licenciada (la egresada *Latin America*)
(from university)
2 el/la bachiller *(from US high school)*

graffiti PL NOUN
las pintadas

grain NOUN
1 el grano
□ a grain of rice un grano de arroz
2 los cereales
□ She only eats grain and pulses. Sólo come cereales y legumbres.

gram NOUN
el gramo

grammar NOUN
la gramática
□ a grammar exercise un ejercicio de gramática

grammar school NOUN
DID YOU KNOW...?
The equivalent to a grammar school in Spain is **el instituto de segunda enseñanza**.

grammatical ADJECTIVE
gramatical (FEM gramatical)

gramme NOUN
el gramo

grand ADJECTIVE
grandioso (FEM grandiosa)
□ Her house is very grand. Su casa es grandiosa.

grandchildren PL NOUN
los nietos

granddad NOUN
el abuelo

granddaughter NOUN
la nieta

grandfather NOUN
el abuelo

grandma NOUN
la abuela

grandmother NOUN
la abuela

grandpa NOUN
el abuelo

grandparents PL NOUN
los abuelos

grandson NOUN
el nieto

granny NOUN
la abuelita

grant NOUN
1 la beca *(for study)*
2 la subvención (PL las subvenciones) *(for industry, organization)*

grape NOUN
la uva

grapefruit NOUN
el pomelo

graph NOUN
el gráfico

to **grasp** VERB
agarrar

grass NOUN
1 la hierba
□ The grass is long. La hierba está alta.
2 el césped *(lawn)*
■ **'Keep off the grass'** 'Prohibido pisar el césped'
■ **to cut the grass** cortar el césped

grasshopper NOUN
el saltamontes (PL los saltamontes)

to **grate** VERB
rallar
□ grated cheese el queso rallado

grateful ADJECTIVE
agradecido (FEM agradecida)

grave NOUN
la tumba

gravel NOUN
la grava

graveyard NOUN
el cementerio

gravy NOUN
el jugo de carne

grease NOUN
1 la grasa *(in hair, on skin)*
2 el aceite *(for cars, machines)*

greasy ADJECTIVE
1 aceitoso (FEM aceitosa)
□ The food was very greasy. La comida estaba muy aceitosa.
2 graso (FEM grasa)
□ He has greasy hair. Tiene el pelo graso.

great ADJECTIVE
1 estupendo (FEM estupenda) (chévere *Latin America*)
□ That's great! ¡Estupendo!

WORD POWER
You can use a number of other words instead of **great** to mean 'good':
amazing increíble
□ amazing news una noticia increíble
marvellous estupendo
□ a marvellous idea una idea estupenda
superb magnífico
□ a superb meal una comida magnífica
wonderful maravilloso
□ a wonderful opportunity una oportunidad maravillosa

2 grande (FEM grande)
LANGUAGE TIP Use **gran** before a singular noun.
□ a great oak tree un gran roble □ a greatest hits album un disco de grandes éxitos

Great Britain NOUN
Gran Bretaña *fem*

great-grandfather NOUN
el bisabuelo

great-grandmother NOUN
la bisabuela

Greece NOUN
Grecia *fem*

greedy ADJECTIVE
1 glotón (FEM glotona, PL glotones)
□ Don't be greedy, you've already had three

English-Spanish

g

doughnuts. No seas glotón, ya te has comido tres donuts.
2 codicioso (FEM codiciosa)
□ She is greedy and selfish. Es codiciosa y egoísta.

Greek ADJECTIVE
▹ *see also* **Greek** NOUN
griego (FEM griega)

Greek NOUN
▹ *see also* **Greek** ADJECTIVE
1 el griego
la griega *(person)*
□ the Greeks los griegos
2 el griego *(language)*
□ our Greek teacher nuestro profesor de griego

green ADJECTIVE
▹ *see also* **green** NOUN
verde (FEM verde)
□ a green car un coche verde □ a green light *(at traffic lights)* un semáforo en verde
■ **green beans** las judías verdes
■ **the Green Party** el Partido Verde

green NOUN
▹ *see also* **green** ADJECTIVE
el verde
□ a dark green un verde oscuro
■ **greens** *(vegetables)* la verdura
■ **the Greens** *(party)* los verdes

greengrocer's NOUN
la verdulería

greenhouse NOUN
el invernadero
■ **the greenhouse effect** el efecto invernadero

to **greet** VERB
saludar
□ He greeted me with a kiss. Me saludó con un beso.

greetings card NOUN
la tarjeta de felicitación

grew VERB ▹ *see* **grow**

grey ADJECTIVE
gris (FEM grisa)
□ They wore grey suits. Llevaban trajes grises.
■ **He's going grey.** Le están saliendo canas.
■ **grey hair** las canas

grey-haired ADJECTIVE
canoso (FEM canosa)

grid NOUN
1 la cuadrícula *(in road, on map)*
2 la red *(of electricity)*

grief NOUN
la pena

grill NOUN
▹ *see also* **grill** VERB
1 el grill *(of cooker)*
2 la parrilla *(for barbecue)*
■ **a mixed grill** una parrillada mixta

to **grill** VERB
▹ *see also* **grill** NOUN
1 hacer* al grill *(in cooker)*
2 asar a la parrilla *(barbecue)*

grim ADJECTIVE
deprimente (FEM deprimente)
□ The outskirts of the city are very grim. Las afueras de la ciudad son muy deprimentes.

to **grin** VERB
▹ *see also* **grin** NOUN
sonreír* ampliamente
□ Dave grinned at me. Dave me sonrió ampliamente.

grin NOUN
▹ *see also* **grin** VERB
la amplia sonrisa

to **grind** VERB
1 moler* *(coffee, pepper)*
2 picar (US: *meat)*

to **grip** VERB
agarrar

grit NOUN
la gravilla

to **groan** VERB
▹ *see also* **groan** NOUN
gemir*
□ He groaned with pain. Gimió de dolor.

groan NOUN
▹ *see also* **groan** VERB
el gemido

grocer NOUN
1 el tendero
2 la tendera

groceries PL NOUN
los comestibles
■ **I'll get some groceries.** Traeré algunas provisiones.

grocer's NOUN
la tienda de ultramarinos

grocery store NOUN (US)
la tienda de ultramarinos

groom NOUN
el novio
□ the groom and his best man el novio y su padrino de boda

to **grope** VERB
■ **to grope for something** buscar algo a tientas □ He groped for the light switch. Buscó a tientas el interruptor.

gross ADJECTIVE
1 horrible (FEM horrible) *(revolting)*
■ **That's gross!** ¡Qué asco!
2 bruto (FEM bruta)
□ gross income ingresos brutos

grossly ADVERB
enormemente

□ It's grossly unfair. Es enormemente injusto.
■ **We're grossly underpaid.** Estamos tremendamente mal pagados.

ground NOUN
▷ *see also* **ground** VERB
1 el suelo
□ The ground's wet. El suelo está húmedo.
2 el campo (la cancha *Latin America*)
□ a football ground un campo de fútbol
3 el motivo
□ We've got grounds for complaint. Tenemos motivos para quejarnos.
■ **on the ground** en el suelo □ We sat on the ground. Nos sentamos en el suelo.

ground VERB ▷ *see* **grind**
▷ *see also* **ground** NOUN

ground coffee NOUN
el café molido

ground floor NOUN
la planta baja

group NOUN
el grupo

to **grow** VERB
1 crecer*
□ Haven't you grown! ¡Cómo has crecido!
2 aumentar
□ The number of unemployed has grown. Ha aumentado el número de desempleados.
3 cultivar
□ He grew vegetables in his garden. Cultivaba hortalizas en su jardín.
■ **He's grown out of his jacket.** La chaqueta se le ha quedado pequeña.
■ **to grow a beard** dejarse barba □ I'm growing a beard. Me estoy dejando barba.
■ **He grew a moustache.** Se dejó bigote.

to **grow up** VERB
criarse*
□ I grew up in Rome. Me crié en Roma.
■ **Oh, grow up!** ¡No seas crío!

to **growl** VERB
gruñir*

grown VERB ▷ *see* **grow**

growth NOUN
el crecimiento
□ economic growth crecimiento económico

grub NOUN
la manduca *(informal)*

grudge NOUN
■ **to have a grudge against somebody** guardar rencor a alguien □ He's always had a grudge against me. Siempre me ha guardado rencor.

gruesome ADJECTIVE
horroroso (FEM horrorosa)

guarantee NOUN
▷ *see also* **guarantee** VERB
la garantía
□ a five-year guarantee una garantía de cinco años □ It's still under guarantee. Todavía tiene garantía.

to **guarantee** VERB
▷ *see also* **guarantee** NOUN
garantizar*
□ I can't guarantee he'll come. No puedo garantizar que venga.

to **guard** VERB
▷ *see also* **guard** NOUN
vigilar
□ The police were guarding the entrance. La policía vigilaba la entrada.

guard NOUN
▷ *see also* **guard** VERB
1 el/la guardia *(person)*
2 el jefe de tren *(on train)*
■ **a security guard** un guarda jurado

to **guess** VERB
▷ *see also* **guess** NOUN
adivinar
□ Can you guess what it is? A ver si adivinas qué es.
■ **to guess wrong** equivocarse
■ **Guess what!** ¿Sabes qué?

guess NOUN
▷ *see also* **guess** VERB
la suposición (PL las suposiciones)
□ It's just a guess. Sólo es una suposición.
■ **Have a guess!** ¡Adivina!

guest NOUN
1 el invitado
la invitada
□ We have guests staying with us. Tenemos invitados en casa.
2 el/la huésped *(in hotel)*

guesthouse NOUN
la pensión (PL las pensiones)

guide NOUN
1 la guía
□ We bought a guide to Granada. Compramos una guía de Granada.
2 el/la guía
□ The guide showed us around the castle. El guía nos enseñó el castillo.
3 la exploradora *(girl guide)*

guidebook NOUN
la guía

guide dog NOUN
el perro lazarillo

guilty ADJECTIVE
culpable (FEM culpable)
□ She was found guilty. Fue declarada culpable. □ He felt guilty about lying to her. Se sentía culpable por haberle mentido.
■ **He has a guilty conscience.** Tiene remordimientos de conciencia.

guinea pig NOUN
el cobayo
□ She's got a guinea pig. Tiene un cobayo.

guitar NOUN
la guitarra

gum NOUN
el chicle *(chewing gum)*
■ **a piece of gum** un chicle
■ **gums** *(in mouth)* las encías

gun NOUN
1 la pistola *(small)*
2 el fusil *(rifle)*

gunpoint NOUN
■ **at gunpoint** a punta de pistola

gust NOUN
■ **a gust of wind** una ráfaga de viento

guy NOUN
el tío *(informal)*

LANGUAGE TIP The word **tío** in this sense is confined to Spain. In Latin America, the equivalent is **tipo**.
□ Who's that guy? ¿Quién es ese tío?
□ He's a nice guy. Es un tío simpático.

gym NOUN
el gimnasio
□ I go to the gym every day. Voy al gimnasio todos los días.
■ **gym classes** las clases de gimnasia

gymnast NOUN
el/la gimnasta

gymnastics NOUN
la gimnasia

gypsy NOUN
el gitano
la gitana

Hh

habit NOUN
la costumbre

to **hack** VERB
■ **to hack into a system** piratear un sistema

hacker NOUN
el pirata informático
la pirata informática

had VERB ▷ *see* **have**

haddock NOUN
el abadejo

hadn't = **had not**

hail NOUN
▷ *see also* **hail** VERB
el granizo

to **hail** VERB
▷ *see also* **hail** NOUN
granizar*

hair NOUN
el pelo
□ She's got long hair. Tiene el pelo largo.
□ I'm allergic to cat hair. Soy alérgico al pelo de los gatos.
■ **to have one's hair cut** cortarse el pelo
■ **grey hair** las canas
■ **to brush one's hair** cepillarse el pelo
■ **to wash one's hair** lavarse la cabeza

hairbrush NOUN
el cepillo *(para el pelo)*

haircut NOUN
el corte de pelo
□ You need a haircut. Necesitas un corte de pelo.
■ **to have a haircut** cortarse el pelo

hairdresser NOUN
el peluquero
la peluquera
□ He's a hairdresser. Es peluquero.
■ **at the hairdresser's** en la peluquería

hair dryer NOUN
el secador de pelo

hair gel NOUN
el fijador

hairgrip NOUN
la horquilla

hair spray NOUN
la laca

hairstyle NOUN
el peinado

hairy ADJECTIVE
peludo (FEM peluda)
□ He's very hairy. Es muy peludo.
■ **He's got hairy legs.** Tiene mucho pelo en las piernas.

half NOUN
▷ *see also* **half** ADJECTIVE
1 la mitad
□ half of the cake la mitad de la tarta
■ **to cut something in half** cortar algo por la mitad
2 el billete para niños *(ticket)*
□ One and two halves, please. Un billete normal y dos para niños, por favor.
■ **two and a half** dos y medio
■ **half a kilo** medio kilo
■ **half an hour** media hora
■ **half past ten** las diez y media

half ADJECTIVE, ADVERB
▷ *see also* **half** NOUN
medio (FEM media)
□ a half chicken medio pollo

LANGUAGE TIP When you use **medio** before an adjective, it does not change.

□ She was half asleep. Estaba medio dormida. □ They were half drunk. Estaban medio borrachos.

half-price ADJECTIVE, ADVERB
a mitad de precio
□ I bought it half-price. Lo compré a mitad de precio.

half-term NOUN
las vacaciones de mitad de trimestre

half-time NOUN
el descanso *(del partido)*

halfway ADVERB
1 a medio camino
□ Reading is halfway between Oxford and London. Reading está a medio camino entre Oxford y Londres.
2 a la mitad
□ halfway through the film a la mitad de la película

hall NOUN
1 el vestíbulo *(in house)*
2 la sala
□ a lecture hall una sala de conferencias
■ **a concert hall** un auditorio
■ **a sports hall** un gimnasio
■ **village hall** el salón de actos municipal

Hallowe'en NOUN
la víspera de Todos los Santos

hallway NOUN
el vestíbulo

halt NOUN
■ **to come to a halt** pararse

ham NOUN
el jamón (PL los jamones)

DID YOU KNOW...?
In Spain there are two basic kinds of ham in the shops: **jamón serrano**, which is cured and similar to Parma ham, and **jamón de York** or **jamón dulce**, which is boiled and similar to British ham.

hamburger NOUN
la hamburguesa

hammer NOUN
el martillo

hamster NOUN
el hámster

hand NOUN
▹ *see also* **hand** VERB
1 la mano *(of person)*
LANGUAGE TIP Although **mano** ends in **-o** it is actually a feminine noun.
2 la manecilla *(of clock)*
■ **to give someone a hand** echar una mano a alguien □ Can you give me a hand? ¿Me echas una mano?
■ **on the one hand ..., on the other hand ...** por un lado ..., por otro ...

to **hand** VERB
▹ *see also* **hand** NOUN
pasar
□ He handed me the book. Me pasó el libro.

to **hand in** VERB
entregar
□ Martin handed in his exam paper. Martin entregó su examen.

to **hand out** VERB
repartir
□ The teacher handed out the books. El profesor repartió los libros.

handbag NOUN
el bolso (la cartera *Latin America*)

handball NOUN
el balonmano

handbook NOUN
el manual

handcuffs PL NOUN
las esposas

handkerchief NOUN
el pañuelo

handle NOUN
▹ *see also* **handle** VERB
1 el picaporte *(of door)*
2 la asa *(of cup, briefcase)*
3 el mango *(of knife, saucepan)*

to **handle** VERB
▹ *see also* **handle** NOUN
1 encargarse* de
□ Kath handled the travel arrangements. Kath se encargó de organizar el viaje.
2 manejar
□ It was a difficult situation, but he handled it well. Era una situación difícil, pero él supo manejarla bien.
3 tratar
□ She's good at handling children. Sabe tratar a los niños.
■ **'handle with care'** 'frágil'

handlebars PL NOUN
el manillar

handmade ADJECTIVE
hecho a mano (FEM hecha a mano)

handsome ADJECTIVE
guapo (FEM guapa)
□ My father's very handsome. Mi padre es muy guapo.

handwriting NOUN
la letra
□ His handwriting is terrible. Tiene una letra horrible.

handy ADJECTIVE
1 práctico (FEM práctica)
□ This knife's very handy. Este cuchillo es muy práctico.
2 a mano
□ Have you got a pen handy? ¿Tienes un bolígrafo a mano?

to **hang** VERB
1 colgar*
□ Mike hung the painting on the wall. Mike colgó el cuadro en la pared. □ There was a bulb hanging from the ceiling. Una bombilla colgaba del techo.
2 ahorcar*
□ In the past criminals were hanged. Antiguamente se ahorcaba a los criminales.

to **hang around** VERB
pasar el rato
□ On Saturdays we hang around in the park. Los sábados pasamos el rato en el parque.

to **hang on** VERB
esperar
□ Hang on a minute please. Espera un momento, por favor.

to **hang up** VERB
colgar* *(clothes, phone)*
□ Don't hang up! ¡No cuelgues! □ He hung up on me. Me colgó.

hanger NOUN
la percha

hang-gliding NOUN
el ala delta

LANGUAGE TIP Although it's a feminine noun, remember that you use **el** and **un** with **ala**.

■ **to go hang-gliding** hacer ala delta

hangover NOUN
la resaca
□ I woke up with a hangover. Me desperté con resaca.

to **happen** VERB
pasar
□ What happened? ¿Qué pasó?
■ **As it happens, I do know him.** Da la casualidad de que lo conozco.
■ **Do you happen to know if she's at home?** ¿Por casualidad sabes si está en casa?

happily ADVERB
1 alegremente
□ 'Don't worry!', he said happily. '¡No te preocupes!' dijo alegremente.
2 felizmente
□ He's happily married. Está felizmente casado.
■ **And they lived happily ever after.** Y vivieron felices y comieron perdices.
3 afortunadamente
□ Happily, everything went well. Afortunadamente todo fue bien.

happiness NOUN
la felicidad

happy ADJECTIVE
feliz (FEM feliz, PL felices)
□ Janet looks happy. Janet parece feliz.

WORD POWER
You can use a number of other words instead of **happy** to mean 'glad':
cheerful alegre
□ a cheerful song una canción alegre
glad contento
□ to be glad estar contento
satisfied satisfecho
□ a satisfied customer un cliente satisfecho

■ **to be happy with something** estar contento con algo □ I'm very happy with your work. Estoy muy contento con tu trabajo.
■ **Happy birthday!** ¡Feliz cumpleaños!
■ **a happy ending** un final feliz

harbour (US **harbor**) NOUN
el puerto

hard ADJECTIVE, ADVERB
1 duro (FEM dura)
□ This cheese is very hard. Este queso está muy duro. □ to work hard trabajar duro
2 difícil (FEM difícil)
□ The exam was very hard. El examen fue muy difícil.

hard disk NOUN
el disco duro

hardly ADVERB
apenas
□ I hardly know you. Apenas te conozco.
■ **I've got hardly any money.** Casi no tengo dinero.
■ **hardly ever** casi nunca
■ **hardly anything** casi nada

hard up ADJECTIVE
■ **to be hard up** estar sin un duro (estar sin plata *Latin America*) *(informal)*

hardware NOUN
el hardware

hare NOUN
la liebre

to **harm** VERB
■ **to harm somebody** hacer daño a alguien
□ I didn't mean to harm you. No quería hacerte daño.
■ **to harm something** dañar algo
□ Chemicals harm the environment. Los productos químicos dañan el medio ambiente.

harmful ADJECTIVE
perjudicial (FEM perjudicial)
□ harmful to the environment perjudicial para el medio ambiente

harmless ADJECTIVE
inofensivo (FEM inofensiva)

harsh ADJECTIVE
1 severo (FEM severa)
□ He deserves a harsh punishment for what he did. Merece un severo castigo por lo que ha hecho.
2 áspero (FEM áspera)
□ She's got a very harsh voice. Tiene una voz muy áspera.

has VERB ▷ *see* **have**

hasn't = **has not**

hat NOUN
el sombrero

to **hate** VERB
odiar

hatred NOUN
el odio

haunted ADJECTIVE
■ **a haunted house** una casa embrujada

to have VERB

LANGUAGE TIP Use the verb **haber** to form the perfect tenses.

1 haber*

□ I've already seen that film. Ya he visto esa película. □ Has he gone? ¿Se ha ido? □ If you had phoned me I would have come around. Si me hubieras llamado habría venido.

LANGUAGE TIP If you are using 'have' in question tags to confirm a statement use **¿no?** or **¿verdad?**.

□ You've done it, haven't you? Lo has hecho, ¿verdad? □ They've arrived, haven't they? Ya han llegado, ¿no?

LANGUAGE TIP 'have' is not translated when giving simple negative or positive answers to questions.

□ Have you read that book? — Yes, I have. ¿Has leído el libro? — Sí. □ Has he told you? — No, he hasn't. ¿Te lo ha dicho? — No.

2 tener*

□ I have a terrible cold. Tengo un resfriado horrible. □ She had a baby last year. Tuvo un niño el año pasado. □ Do you have any brothers or sisters? ¿Tienes hermanos?

■ **to have to do something.** tener que hacer algo.

3 tomar

□ I'll have a coffee. Tomaré un café. □ Shall we have a drink? ¿Tomamos algo de beber?

■ **to have a shower** ducharse

■ **to have one's hair cut** cortarse el pelo

haven't = **have not**

hay NOUN

el heno

hay fever NOUN

la alergia al polen

hazelnut NOUN

la avellana

he PRONOUN

él

LANGUAGE TIP 'he' generally isn't translated unless it is emphatic.

□ He is very tall. Es muy alto.

LANGUAGE TIP Use **él** for emphasis.

□ He did it but she didn't. Él lo hizo, pero ella no.

head NOUN

▷ *see also* **head** VERB

1 la cabeza

□ Mind your head! ¡Cuidado con la cabeza! □ The wine went to my head. El vino se me subió a la cabeza. □ He lost his head and started screaming. Perdió la cabeza y empezó a gritar.

2 el director

la directora *(of school)*

3 el jefe

la jefa *(leader)*

□ a head of state un jefe de Estado

■ **I've got no head for figures.** No se me dan bien los números.

■ **Heads or tails? — Heads.** ¿Cara o cruz? — Cara.

to head VERB

▷ *see also* **head** NOUN

■ **to head for** dirigirse a □ They headed for the church. Se dirigieron a la iglesia.

headache NOUN

el dolor de cabeza

□ I've got a headache. Tengo dolor de cabeza.

headlight NOUN

el faro *(de coche)*

headline NOUN

el titular

headmaster NOUN

el director

headmistress NOUN

la directora

headphones PL NOUN

los auriculares

headquarters PL NOUN

el cuartel general *(of army)*

■ **The bank's headquarters are in London.** La oficina central del banco está en Londres.

headteacher NOUN

el director

la directora

to heal VERB

curar

health NOUN

la salud

□ She's in good health. Tiene buena salud.

healthy ADJECTIVE

sano (FEM sana)

□ She's very healthy. Es muy sana.

□ a healthy diet una dieta sana

heap NOUN

el montón (PL los montones)

to hear VERB

oír*

□ We heard the dog bark. Oímos ladrar al perro. □ She can't hear very well. No oye bien.

■ **I heard she was ill.** Me han dicho que estaba enferma.

■ **to hear about something** enterarse de algo □ I've heard about your new job. Me he enterado de que tienes un nuevo trabajo.

□ Did you hear the good news? ¿Te has enterado de la buena noticia?

■ **to hear from somebody** tener noticias de alguien □ I haven't heard from him recently. Últimamente no tengo noticias de él.

heart NOUN
el corazón (PL los corazones)
■ **hearts** *(at cards)* los corazones □ the ace of hearts el as de corazones
■ **to learn something by heart** aprenderse algo de memoria

heart attack NOUN
el infarto

heartbroken ADJECTIVE
■ **to be heartbroken** tener el corazón partido

heat NOUN
▹ *see also* **heat** VERB
el calor

to **heat** VERB
▹ *see also* **heat** NOUN
calentar*
□ Heat gently for five minutes. Caliente a fuego lento durante cinco minutos.

to **heat up** VERB
1 calentar*
□ He heated the soup up. Calentó la sopa.
2 calentarse* *(water, oven)*
□ The water is heating up. El agua se está calentando.

heater NOUN
el calentador
□ a water heater un calentador de agua
■ **an electric heater** una estufa eléctrica
■ **Could you put on the heater?** *(in car)* ¿Puedes poner la calefacción?

heather NOUN
el brezo

heating NOUN
la calefacción

heaven NOUN
el cielo
■ **to go to heaven** ir al cielo

heavily ADVERB
■ **It rained heavily in the night.** Llovió con fuerza por la noche.
■ **He's a heavily built man.** Es un hombre corpulento.
■ **He drinks heavily.** Bebe demasiado.

heavy ADJECTIVE
pesado (FEM pesada)
□ a heavy load una carga pesada
■ **This bag's very heavy.** Esta bolsa pesa mucho.
■ **heavy rain** fuerte lluvia
■ **He's a heavy drinker.** Es un bebedor empedernido.

he'd = **he would; he had**

hedge NOUN
el seto

hedgehog NOUN
el erizo

heel NOUN
1 el tacón (PL los tacones) *(of shoe)*
2 el talón (PL los talones) *(of foot)*

height NOUN
1 la estatura *(of person)*
2 la altura *(of object, mountain)*

heir NOUN
el heredero

heiress NOUN
la heredera

held VERB ▹ *see* **hold**

helicopter NOUN
el helicóptero

hell NOUN
el infierno
■ **Hell!** ¡Maldita sea!

he'll = **he will; he shall**

hello EXCLAMATION
1 ¡hola! *(when you see somebody)*
2 ¡dígame! (¡aló! *Latin America*) *(on the phone)*

helmet NOUN
el casco

to **help** VERB
▹ *see also* **help** NOUN
ayudar
□ Can you help me? ¿Puedes ayudarme?
■ **Help!** ¡Socorro!
■ **Help yourself!** ¡Sírvete!
■ **I couldn't help laughing.** No pude evitar reírme.

help NOUN
▹ *see also* **help** VERB
la ayuda
□ Do you need any help? ¿Necesitas ayuda?

helpful ADJECTIVE
útil (FEM útil)
□ He gave me some helpful advice. Me dio algunos consejos útiles.
■ **You've been very helpful!** ¡Muchas gracias por su ayuda!

hen NOUN
la gallina

her ADJECTIVE
▹ *see also* **her** PRONOUN
su (FEM su, PL sus)
□ her father su padre □ her house su casa
□ her two best friends sus dos mejores amigos □ her sisters sus hermanas

> LANGUAGE TIP 'her' is usually translated by the definite article **el/los** or **la/las** when it's clear from the sentence who the possessor is or when referring to clothing or parts of the body.

□ They stole her car. Le robaron el coche.
□ She took off her coat. Se quitó el abrigo.
□ She's washing her hair. Se está lavando la cabeza.

her PRONOUN
▹ *see also* **her** ADJECTIVE

English-Spanish

h

1 la

LANGUAGE TIP Use **la** when 'her' is the direct object of the verb in the sentence.

□ I saw her. La vi. □ Look at her! ¡Mírala!

2 le

LANGUAGE TIP Use **le** when 'her' means 'to her'.

□ I gave her a book. Le di un libro. □ You have to tell her the truth. Tienes que decirle la verdad.

3 se

LANGUAGE TIP Use **se** not **le** when 'her' is used in combination with a direct-object pronoun.

□ Give it to her. Dáselo.

4 ella

LANGUAGE TIP Use **ella** after prepositions, in comparisons, and with the verb 'to be'.

□ I'm going with her. Voy con ella. □ I'm older than her. Soy mayor que ella. □ It must be her. Debe de ser ella.

■ **She was carrying it on her.** Lo llevaba consigo.

herb NOUN

la hierba *(medicinal o aromática)*

here ADVERB

aquí

□ I live here. Vivo aquí. □ Here he is! ¡Aquí está! □ Here are the books. Aquí están los libros.

■ **Here's your coffee.** Aquí tienes el café.

■ **Have you got my pen? — Here you are.** ¿Tienes mi boli? — Aquí tienes.

■ **Here are the papers you asked for.** Aquí tienes los papeles que pediste.

hero NOUN

el héroe

heroin NOUN

la heroína

■ **a heroin addict** un heroinómano

heroine NOUN

la heroína

hers PRONOUN

1 el suyo *masc* (PL los suyos)

□ Is this her coat? — No, hers is black. ¿Es éste su abrigo? — No, el suyo es negro.

□ my parents and hers mis padres y los suyos

2 la suya *fem* (PL las suyas)

□ Is this her scarf? — No, hers is red. ¿Es ésta su bufanda? — No, la suya es roja.

□ my sisters and hers mis hermanas y las suyas

3 suyo *masc* (PL suyos)

□ Is that car hers? ¿Es suyo ese coche?

4 suya *fem* (PL suyas)

□ Is that wallet hers? ¿Es suya esa cartera?

■ **Isobel is a friend of hers.** Isobel es amiga suya.

LANGUAGE TIP Use **de ella** instead of **suyo** if you want to avoid confusion with 'his', 'theirs', etc.

□ Whose is this? — It's hers. ¿De quién es esto? — Es de ella.

herself PRONOUN

1 se *(reflexive)*

□ She's hurt herself. Se ha hecho daño.

2 sí misma *(after preposition)*

□ She talked mainly about herself. Habló principalmente de sí misma.

3 ella misma *(for emphasis)*

□ She did it herself. Lo hizo ella misma.

■ **by herself** *(alone)* sola □ She came by herself. Vino sola.

he's = **he is; he has**

to **hesitate** VERB

dudar

□ Don't hesitate to ask. No dudes en preguntar.

heterosexual ADJECTIVE

heterosexual (FEM heterosexual)

hi EXCLAMATION

¡hola!

hiccup NOUN

el hipo

□ The baby's got hiccups. El bebé tiene hipo.

to **hide** VERB

1 esconder

□ Paula hid the present. Paula escondió el regalo.

2 esconderse

□ He hid behind a bush. Se escondió detrás de un arbusto.

hide-and-seek NOUN

■ **to play hide-and-seek** jugar al escondite

hideous ADJECTIVE

horroroso (FEM horrorosa)

hi-fi NOUN

el equipo de alta fidelidad

high ADJECTIVE, ADVERB

1 alto (FEM alta)

□ The gate's too high. La verja es demasiado alta. □ Prices are higher in Germany. Los precios están más altos en Alemania. □ It's very high in fat. Tiene un alto contenido en grasas. □ The plane flew high over the mountains. El avión volaba alto sobre las montañas.

■ **How high is the wall?** ¿Cómo es de alto el muro?

■ **The wall's two metres high.** El muro tiene dos metros de altura.

2 agudo (FEM aguda)

□ She's got a very high voice. Tiene la voz muy aguda.

■ **at high speed** a gran velocidad
■ **to be high** *(on drugs)* estar colocado *(informal)*
■ **to get high** *(on drugs)* colocarse *(informal)*

higher education NOUN
la enseñanza superior

high-heeled ADJECTIVE
■ **high-heeled shoes** los zapatos de tacón alto

high jump NOUN
el salto de altura

highlight NOUN
▹ *see also* **highlight** VERB
el punto culminante
□ the highlight of the evening el punto culminante de la velada

to **highlight** VERB
▹ *see also* **highlight** NOUN
poner* de relieve

highlighter NOUN
el rotulador

high-rise NOUN
la torre de pisos

high school NOUN
el instituto (el liceo *Latin America*)

to **hijack** VERB
secuestrar

hijacker NOUN
el secuestrador
la secuestradora

hike NOUN
la caminata *(por el campo)*

hiking NOUN
■ **to go hiking** ir de excursión al campo

hilarious ADJECTIVE
graciosísimo (FEM graciosísima)

hill NOUN
1 la colina
□ a house at the top of a hill una casa en lo alto de una colina
2 la cuesta
□ I climbed the hill up to the office. Subí la cuesta hasta la oficina.

hill-walking NOUN
el senderismo
□ to go hill-walking hacer senderismo

him PRONOUN
1 lo
LANGUAGE TIP Use **lo** when 'him' is the direct object of the verb in the sentence.
□ I saw him. Lo vi. □ Look at him! ¡Míralo!
2 le
LANGUAGE TIP Use **le** when 'him' means 'to him'.
□ I gave him a book. Le di un libro. □ You have to tell him the truth. Tienes que decirle la verdad.
3 se
LANGUAGE TIP Use **se** not **le** when 'him' is used in combination with a direct-object pronoun.
□ Give it to him. Dáselo.
4 él
LANGUAGE TIP Use **él** after prepositions, in comparisons and with the verb 'to be'.
□ I'm going with him. Voy con él. □ I'm older than him. Soy mayor que él. □ It must be him. Debe de ser él.
■ **He was carrying it on him.** Lo llevaba consigo.

himself PRONOUN
1 se *(reflexive)*
□ He's hurt himself. Se ha hecho daño.
2 sí mismo *(after preposition)*
□ He talked mainly about himself. Habló principalmente de sí mismo.
3 él mismo *(for emphasis)*
□ He did it himself. Lo hizo él mismo.
■ **by himself** *(alone)* solo □ He came by himself. Vino solo.

Hindu ADJECTIVE
hindú (PL hindúes)

hint NOUN
▹ *see also* **hint** VERB
la indirecta
■ **to drop a hint** soltar una indirecta
■ **to take a hint** captar una indirecta

to **hint** VERB
▹ *see also* **hint** NOUN
insinuar*
□ He hinted that something was going on. Insinuó que estaba pasando algo.

hip NOUN
la cadera
□ She put her hands on her hips. Se puso las manos en las caderas.

hippie NOUN
el/la hippy (PL los hippies)

hippo NOUN
el hipopótamo

to **hire** VERB
▹ *see also* **hire** NOUN
1 alquilar
□ We hired a car. Alquilamos un coche.
2 contratar
□ They hired a lawyer. Contrataron a un abogado.

hire NOUN
▹ *see also* **hire** VERB
el alquiler
□ car hire el alquiler de coches
■ **'for hire'** 'se alquila'

hire car NOUN
el coche de alquiler

his ADJECTIVE
▷ *see also* **his** PRONOUN
su (FEM su, PL sus)
□ his father su padre □ his house su casa □ his two best friends sus dos mejores amigos □ his sisters sus hermanas

LANGUAGE TIP 'his' is usually translated by the definite article **el/los** or **la/las** when it's clear from the sentence who the possessor is or when referring to clothing or parts of the body.

□ They stole his car. Le robaron el coche. □ He took off his coat. Se quitó el abrigo. □ He's washing his hair. Se está lavando la cabeza.

his PRONOUN
▷ *see also* **his** ADJECTIVE
1 el suyo *masc* (PL los suyos)
□ Is this his coat? — No, his is black. ¿Es éste su abrigo? — No, el suyo es negro. □ my parents and his mis padres y los suyos
2 la suya *fem* (PL las suyas)
□ Is this his scarf? — No, his is red. ¿Es ésta su bufanda? — No, la suya es roja. □ my sisters and his mis hermanas y las suyas
3 suyo *masc* (PL suyos)
□ Is that car his? ¿Es suyo ese coche?
4 suya *fem* (PL suyas)
□ Is that wallet his? ¿Es suya esa cartera?
■ **Isobel is a friend of his.** Isobel es amiga suya.

LANGUAGE TIP Use **de él** instead of **suyo** if you want to avoid confusion with 'hers', 'theirs', etc.

□ Whose is this? — It's his. ¿De quién es esto? — Es de él.

history NOUN
la historia

to **hit** VERB
▷ *see also* **hit** NOUN
1 pegar*
□ He hit the ball. Le pegó a la bola. □ Andrew hit him. Andrew le pegó.
2 chocar* con
□ The car hit a road sign. El coche chocó con una señal de tráfico.
■ **He was hit by a car.** Le pilló un coche.
■ **to hit the target** dar en el blanco
■ **to hit it off with somebody** hacer buenas migas con alguien

hit NOUN
▷ *see also* **hit** VERB
el éxito
□ Coldplay's latest hit el último éxito de Coldplay □ The film was a massive hit. La película fue un éxito enorme.

hitch NOUN
el contratiempo
□ There's been a slight hitch. Ha habido un pequeño contratiempo.

to **hitchhike** VERB
hacer* autoestop

hitchhiker NOUN
el/la autoestopista

hitchhiking NOUN
el autoestop

hit man NOUN
el asesino a sueldo

HIV-positive ADJECTIVE
seropositivo (FEM seropositiva)

hobby NOUN
la afición (PL las aficiones)

hockey NOUN
el hockey
□ I like playing hockey. Me gusta jugar al hockey.

to **hold** VERB
1 tener*
□ He was holding her in his arms. La tenía entre sus brazos.
2 sujetar
□ Hold the ladder. Sujeta la escalera.
3 contener*
□ This bottle holds one litre. Esta botella contiene un litro.
■ **to hold a meeting** celebrar una reunión
■ **Hold the line!** *(on telephone)* ¡No cuelgue!
■ **Hold it!** ¡Espera!
■ **to get hold of something** hacerse con algo

to **hold on** VERB
1 agarrarse *(keep hold)*
□ The cliff was slippery but he managed to hold on. El acantilado se escurría, pero logró agarrarse.
■ **to hold on to something** agarrarse a algo
2 esperar *(wait)*
□ Hold on, I'm coming! ¡Espera que ya voy!
■ **Hold on!** *(on telephone)* ¡No cuelgue!

to **hold up** VERB
1 levantar
□ Peter held up his hand. Peter levantó la mano.
2 retrasar
□ We were held up by the traffic. Nos retrasamos por culpa del tráfico.
3 atracar*
□ to hold up a bank atracar un banco
■ **I was held up at the office.** Me entretuvieron en la oficina.

hold-up NOUN
1 el atraco
□ A bank clerk was injured in the hold-up.

Un empleado del banco resultó herido en el atraco.
2 el retraso
□ No-one explained the reason for the hold-up. Nadie explicó el motivo del retraso.
3 el embotellamiento
□ a hold-up on the motorway un embotellamiento en la autopista

hole NOUN
1 el agujero *(in general)*
□ a hole in the wall un agujero en la pared
2 el hoyo *(in the ground, in golf)*
□ to dig a hole cavar un hoyo

holiday NOUN
1 las vacaciones
□ the school holidays las vacaciones escolares □ on holiday de vacaciones □ to go on holiday irse de vacaciones □ to be on holiday estar de vacaciones
2 el día festivo (el día feriado *Latin America*)
□ Next Monday is a holiday. El lunes que viene es día festivo.
■ **He took a day's holiday.** Se tomó un día libre.

Holland NOUN
Holanda *fem*

hollow ADJECTIVE
hueco (FEM hueca)

holly NOUN
el acebo

holy ADJECTIVE
1 santo (FEM santa)
□ the Holy Spirit el Espíritu Santo
2 sagrado (FEM sagrada)
□ a holy place un lugar sagrado

home NOUN
▷ *see also* **home** ADVERB
la casa
□ at home en casa
■ **Make yourself at home.** Estás en tu casa.
■ **an old people's home** una residencia de ancianos

home ADVERB
▷ *see also* **home** NOUN
1 en casa
□ I'll be home at five o'clock. Estaré en casa a las cinco.
2 a casa
□ to get home llegar a casa

home address NOUN
el domicilio

homeless ADJECTIVE, NOUN
sin hogar
■ **homeless people** los sin techo

home match NOUN
el partido en casa

homeopathy NOUN
la homeopatía

home page NOUN
la página principal

homesick ADJECTIVE
■ **to be homesick** tener morriña

homework NOUN
los deberes
□ Have you done your homework? ¿Has hecho los deberes? □ my geography homework mis deberes de geografía

homosexual ADJECTIVE
homosexual (FEM homosexual)

honest ADJECTIVE
1 honrado (FEM honrada)
□ She's a very honest person. Es una persona muy honrada.
2 sincero (FEM sincera)
□ Tell me your honest opinion. Dame tu sincera opinión.
■ **To be honest, I don't like the idea.** La verdad es que no me gusta la idea.

honestly ADVERB
francamente
□ I honestly don't know. Francamente no lo sé.

honesty NOUN
la honradez

honey NOUN
la miel

honeymoon NOUN
la luna de miel
■ **to go on honeymoon** irse de luna de miel

honour (US **honor**) NOUN
el honor

hood NOUN
1 la capucha *(on coat)*
2 el capó *(US: bonnet of car)*

hook NOUN
1 el gancho
□ The jacket hung from a hook. La chaqueta estaba colgada de un gancho.
2 la alcayata
□ He hung the painting on the hook. Colgó el cuadro de la alcayata.
3 el anzuelo
□ He felt a fish pull at his hook. Notó que un pez tiraba del anzuelo.
■ **to take the phone off the hook** descolgar el teléfono

hooligan NOUN
el gamberro
la gamberra

hooray EXCLAMATION
¡hurra!

Hoover® NOUN
la aspiradora

English-Spanish

h

to **hoover** VERB
pasar la aspiradora por
□ He hoovered the lounge. Pasó la aspiradora por el salón.

to **hope** VERB
▷ *see also* **hope** NOUN
esperar
LANGUAGE TIP Use the subjunctive after **esperar que**.
□ I hope he comes. Espero que venga.
■ **I hope so.** Espero que sí.
■ **I hope not.** Espero que no.

hope NOUN
▷ *see also* **hope** VERB
la esperanza
□ to give up hope perder la esperanza

hopeful ADJECTIVE
prometedor (FEM prometedora)
□ The prospects look hopeful. Las perspectivas parecen prometedoras.
■ **He's hopeful of winning.** Tiene esperanzas de ganar.
■ **How did the interview go? — I'm hopeful.** ¿Cómo fue la entrevista? — Tengo esperanzas.
■ **We're hopeful everything will go okay.** Confiamos en que todo irá bien.

hopefully ADVERB
LANGUAGE TIP Use the subjunctive after **esperar que**.
■ **Hopefully, he'll make it in time.** Esperemos que llegue a tiempo.

hopeless ADJECTIVE
■ **She's hopeless at maths.** Es una negada para las matemáticas.

horizon NOUN
el horizonte

horizontal ADJECTIVE
horizontal (FEM horizontal)

horn NOUN
1 el claxon
□ He sounded the horn. Tocó el claxon.
2 la trompa
□ He plays the horn. Toca la trompa.
3 el cuerno (el cacho *Latin America*)
□ a bull's horns los cuernos de un toro

horoscope NOUN
el horóscopo

horrible ADJECTIVE
horrible (FEM horrible)
□ What a horrible dress! ¡Qué vestido tan horrible!

horror NOUN
el horror
□ To my horror I discovered I was locked out. Descubrí con horror que me había dejado las llaves dentro.

horror film NOUN
la película de terror

horse NOUN
el caballo

horse-racing NOUN
las carreras de caballos

horseshoe NOUN
la herradura

hose NOUN
la manguera

hosepipe NOUN
la manguera

hospital NOUN
el hospital
□ to go into hospital ingresar en el hospital

hospitality NOUN
la hospitalidad

host NOUN
el anfitrión (PL los anfitriones)
la anfitriona

hostage NOUN
el rehén (PL los rehenes)
■ **to take somebody hostage** tomar como rehén a alguien

hostile ADJECTIVE
hostil (FEM hostil)

hot ADJECTIVE
1 caliente (FEM caliente)
□ a hot bath un baño caliente
2 caluroso (FEM calurosa)
□ a hot country un país caluroso
■ **a cup of hot chocolate** una taza de chocolate
LANGUAGE TIP When you are talking about a person being hot, you use **tener calor**.
□ I'm hot. Tengo calor.
LANGUAGE TIP When you talk about the weather being hot, you use **hacer calor**.
□ It's hot today. Hoy hace calor.
3 picante (FEM picante)
□ Mexican food's too hot. La comida mejicana es demasiado picante.

hot dog NOUN
el perrito caliente

hotel NOUN
el hotel

hour NOUN
la hora
□ She always takes hours to get ready. Siempre se tira horas para arreglarse.
■ **a quarter of an hour** un cuarto de hora
■ **two and a half hours** dos horas y media
■ **half an hour** media hora

hourly ADJECTIVE, ADVERB
■ **There are hourly buses.** Hay autobuses cada hora.
■ **She's paid hourly.** Le pagan por horas.

house NOUN
la casa
□ at his house en su casa
housewife NOUN
el ama de casa (PL las amas de casa)
□ She's a housewife. Es ama de casa.
housework NOUN
las tareas de la casa
hovercraft NOUN
el aerodeslizador
how ADVERB
1 cómo
□ How are you? ¿Cómo estás?
2 qué
□ How strange! ¡Qué raro!
■ **He told them how happy he was.** Les dijo lo feliz que era.
■ **How many?** ¿Cuántos?
■ **How much?** ¿Cuánto? □ How much is it? ¿Cuánto es? □ How much sugar do you want? ¿Cuánto azúcar quieres?
■ **How old are you?** ¿Cuántos años tienes?
■ **How far is it to Edinburgh?** ¿Qué distancia hay de aquí a Edimburgo?
■ **How long have you been here?** ¿Cuánto tiempo llevas aquí?
■ **How long does it take?** ¿Cuánto se tarda?
LANGUAGE TIP Remember the accents on question and exclamation words **cómo**, **qué** and **cuánto**.
however CONJUNCTION
sin embargo
□ This, however, isn't true. Esto, sin embargo, no es cierto.
to **howl** VERB
aullar*
□ The dog howled all night. El perro estuvo aullando toda la noche. □ He howled with pain. Aullaba de dolor.
HTML NOUN
el HTML
to **hug** VERB
▷ *see also* **hug** NOUN
abrazar*
□ He hugged his daughter. Abrazó a su hija.
□ They hugged each other. Se abrazaron.
hug NOUN
▷ *see also* **hug** VERB
el abrazo
□ to give somebody a hug dar un abrazo a alguien
huge ADJECTIVE
enorme (FEM enorme)
to **hum** VERB
tararear
human ADJECTIVE
humano (FEM humana)
□ the human body el cuerpo humano □ the human race el género humano
human being NOUN
el ser humano
humble ADJECTIVE
humilde (FEM humilde)
humour (US **humor**) NOUN
el humor
■ **to have a sense of humour** tener sentido del humor
hundred NUMERAL
LANGUAGE TIP Use **cien** before nouns or before another number that is being multiplied by a hundred.
■ **a hundred** cien □ a hundred people cien personas □ a hundred thousand cien mil
LANGUAGE TIP Use **ciento** before a number that is not multiplied but simply added to a hundred.
□ a hundred and one ciento uno
LANGUAGE TIP When 'hundred' follows another number, use the compound forms, which must agreee with the noun.
□ three hundred trescientos □ five hundred people quinientas personas □ five hundred and one quinientos uno
■ **hundreds of people** cientos de personas
hung VERB ▷ *see* **hang**
Hungary NOUN
Hungría *fem*
hunger NOUN
el hambre *fem*
LANGUAGE TIP Although it's a feminine noun, remember that you use **el** and **un** with **hambre**.
hungry ADJECTIVE
■ **to be hungry** tener hambre □ I'm very hungry. Tengo mucha hambre.
to **hunt** VERB
1 cazar*
□ They hunt foxes. Cazan zorros.
2 buscar*
□ The police are hunting the killer. La policía está buscando al asesino.
■ **to go hunting** ir de caza
■ **to hunt for something** buscar algo □ I've hunted everywhere for that book. He buscado ese libro por todas partes.
hunting NOUN
la caza
□ fox-hunting la caza del zorro
hurricane NOUN
el huracán (PL los huracanes)
to **hurry** VERB
▷ *see also* **hurry** NOUN
darse* prisa (apurarse *Latin America*)
□ Hurry up! ¡Date prisa!

English-Spanish

h

■ **Sharon hurried back home.** Sharon volvió a casa a toda prisa.

hurry NOUN
▷ *see also* **hurry** VERB
■ **to be in a hurry** tener prisa (tener apuro *Latin America*)
■ **to do something in a hurry** hacer algo a toda prisa
■ **There's no hurry.** No hay prisa.

to **hurt** VERB
▷ *see also* **hurt** ADJECTIVE
1 hacer* daño a
□ You're hurting me! ¡Me haces daño!
□ Have you hurt yourself? ¿Te has hecho daño?
2 doler*
□ My leg hurts. Me duele la pierna.
■ **Hey! That hurts!** ¡Hey! ¡Que me haces daño!
3 herir*
□ His remarks really hurt me. Sus comentarios me hirieron mucho.

hurt ADJECTIVE
▷ *see also* **hurt** VERB
herido (FEM herida)
□ Is he badly hurt? ¿Está herido de gravedad? □ Luckily, nobody got hurt.
Por suerte, nadie salió herido.
■ **I was hurt by what he said.** Me hirió lo que dijo.

husband NOUN
el marido

hut NOUN
la cabaña

hymn NOUN
el himno *(religioso)*

hypermarket NOUN
el hipermercado

hyphen NOUN
el guión (PL los guiones)

Ii

I PRONOUN
yo
□ Ann and I Ann y yo
LANGUAGE TIP 'I' generally isn't translated unless it is emphatic.
□ I speak Spanish. Hablo español.
LANGUAGE TIP Use **yo** for emphasis.
□ He was frightened but I wasn't. Él estaba asustado, pero yo no.

ice NOUN
el hielo

iceberg NOUN
el iceberg (PL los icebergs)

icebox NOUN (US)
la nevera

ice cream NOUN
el helado
□ vanilla ice cream el helado de vainilla

ice cube NOUN
el cubito de hielo

ice hockey NOUN
el hockey sobre hielo
□ I like playing ice hockey. Me gusta jugar al hockey sobre hielo.

Iceland NOUN
Islandia *fem*

ice lolly NOUN
el polo

ice rink NOUN
la pista de patinaje sobre hielo

ice-skating NOUN
el patinaje sobre hielo
■ **Yesterday we went ice-skating.** Ayer fuimos a patinar sobre hielo.

icing NOUN
el glaseado *(on cake)*
■ **icing sugar** el azúcar glas

icon NOUN
el icono

ICT NOUN *(= Information and Communications Technology)*
la informática

icy ADJECTIVE
helado (FEM helada)
□ an icy wind un viento helado □ The roads are icy. Las carreteras están heladas.

I'd = **I had; I would**

idea NOUN
la idea
□ Good idea! ¡Buena idea!

ideal ADJECTIVE
ideal (FEM ideal)

identical ADJECTIVE
idéntico (FEM idéntica)

identification NOUN
la identificación (PL las identificaciones)

to **identify** VERB
identificar*

identity card NOUN
el carnet de identidad

idiot NOUN
el/la idiota

idiotic ADJECTIVE
idiota (FEM idiota)

idle ADJECTIVE
■ **It's just idle gossip.** No es más que cotilleo.
■ **I asked out of idle curiosity.** Lo pregunté por pura curiosidad.
■ **to be idle** *(worker)* estar sin trabajo

i.e. ABBREVIATION
es decir

if CONJUNCTION
si
□ You can go if you like. Puedes ir si quieres.
□ He asked me if I had eaten. Me preguntó si había comido. □ If it's fine we'll go swimming. Si hace bueno, iremos a nadar.
LANGUAGE TIP Use **si** with a past subjunctive to translate 'if' followed by a past tense when talking about conditions.
□ If you studied harder you would pass your exams. Si estudiaras más aprobarías los exámenes.
■ **if only** ojalá
LANGUAGE TIP **ojalá** has to be followed by a verb in the subjunctive.
□ If only I had more money! ¡Ojalá tuviera más dinero!
■ **if not** si no □ Are you coming? If not, I'll go with Mark. ¿Vienes? Si no, iré con Mark.

■ **if so** si es así □ Are you coming? If so, I'll wait. ¿Vienes? Si es así te espero.
■ **If I were you I would go to Spain.** Yo que tú iría a España.

ignorant ADJECTIVE
ignorante (FEM ignorante)

to **ignore** VERB
■ **to ignore something** hacer caso omiso de algo □ She ignored my advice. Hizo caso omiso de mi consejo.
■ **to ignore somebody** ignorar a alguien □ She saw me, but she ignored me. Me vió, pero me ignoró completamente.
■ **Just ignore him!** ¡No le hagas caso!

ill ADJECTIVE
enfermo (FEM enferma)
□ She was taken ill. Se puso enferma.

I'll = I will

illegal ADJECTIVE
ilegal (FEM ilegal)

illegible ADJECTIVE
ilegible (FEM ilegible)

illness NOUN
la enfermedad

illusion NOUN
la ilusión (PL las ilusiones)
□ an optical illusion una ilusión óptica
■ **He was under the illusion that he would win.** Se creía que iba a ganar.

illustration NOUN
la ilustración (PL las ilustraciones)

image NOUN
la imagen (PL las imágenes)
□ The company has changed its image. La empresa ha cambiado de imagen.

imagination NOUN
la imaginación (PL las imaginaciones)
□ She lets her imagination run away with her. Se deja llevar por su imaginación. □ It's only your imagination. Son imaginaciones tuyas.

to **imagine** VERB
imaginarse
□ You can imagine how I felt! ¡Imagínate cómo me sentí! □ Is he angry? — I imagine so! ¿Está enfadado? — ¡Me imagino que sí!

to **imitate** VERB
imitar

imitation NOUN
la imitación (PL las imitaciones)
■ **imitation leather** el cuero de imitación

immediate ADJECTIVE
inmediato (FEM inmediata)
□ We need an immediate answer. Necesitamos una respuesta inmediata.

immediately ADVERB
inmediatamente

immigrant NOUN
el/la inmigrante

immigration NOUN
la inmigración (PL las inmigraciones)

immoral ADJECTIVE
inmoral (FEM inmoral)

impartial ADJECTIVE
imparcial (FEM imparcial)

impatience NOUN
la impaciencia

impatient ADJECTIVE
impaciente (FEM impaciente)
■ **to get impatient** impacientarse
□ People are getting impatient. La gente se está impacientando.

impatiently ADVERB
con impaciencia

impersonal ADJECTIVE
impersonal (FEM impersonal)

importance NOUN
la importancia

important ADJECTIVE
importante (FEM importante)

impossible ADJECTIVE
imposible (FEM imposible)

to **impress** VERB
impresionar
□ She's trying to impress you. Está tratando de impresionarte.

impressed ADJECTIVE
impresionado (FEM impresionada)
■ **I'm very impressed!** ¡Estoy impresionado!

impression NOUN
la impresión (PL las impresiones)
□ I was under the impression that you were going out. Tenía la impresión de que te ibas.

impressive ADJECTIVE
impresionante (FEM impresionante)

to **improve** VERB
mejorar
□ They have improved the service. Han mejorado el servicio. □ The weather is improving. El tiempo está mejorando.

improvement NOUN
1 la mejora *(in situation, design)*
■ **There's been an improvement in his French.** Su francés ha mejorado.
2 la mejoría *(in health)*

in PREPOSITION, ADVERB

LANGUAGE TIP There are several ways of translating 'in'. Scan the examples to find one that is similar to what you want to say. For other expressions with 'in', see the verbs 'go', 'come', 'get', 'give', etc.

1 en
□ in the house en casa □ in my bag en mi bolsa □ in the country en el campo □ in town en la ciudad □ in Spain en España

□ in school en el colegio □ in hospital en el hospital □ in London en Londres □ in spring en primavera □ in May en Mayo □ in 1996 en mil novecientos noventa y seis □ I did it in three hours. Lo hice en tres horas. □ in French en francés □ in a loud voice en voz alta □ in good condition en buen estado

2 de

□ the best pupil in the class el mejor alumno de la clase □ at two o'clock in the afternoon a las dos de la tarde □ at six in the morning a las seis de la mañana □ the boy in the blue shirt el muchacho de la camisa azul

3 dentro de

□ I'll see you in three weeks. Te veré dentro de tres semanas. □ I'll be back in one hour. Volveré dentro de una hora.

4 por

□ I've got an exam in the morning. Tengo un examen por la mañana. □ I always feel sleepy in the afternoon. Siempre tengo sueño por la tarde.

■ **in the sun** al sol

■ **in the rain** bajo la lluvia

■ **It was written in pencil.** Estaba escrito a lápiz.

■ **in here** aquí dentro □ It's hot in here. Aquí dentro hace calor.

■ **one person in ten** una persona de cada diez

■ **to be in** *(at home, work)* estar □ He wasn't in. No estaba.

■ **in writing** por escrito

inaccurate ADJECTIVE
inexacto (FEM inexacta)

incentive NOUN
el incentivo
□ There's no incentive to work. No hay incentivo para trabajar.

inch NOUN
la pulgada

DID YOU KNOW...?
In Spain measurements are in metres and centimetres rather than feet and inches. An inch is about 2.5 centimetres.

□ 6 inches 15 centímetros

incident NOUN
el incidente

inclined ADJECTIVE
■ **to be inclined to do something** tener tendencia a hacer algo □ He's inclined to arrive late. Tiene tendencia a llegar tarde.

to **include** VERB
incluir*
□ Service is not included. El servicio no está incluido.

including PREPOSITION
■ **It will be two hundred pounds, including tax.** Son doscientas libras esterlinas con impuestos incluidos.

inclusive ADJECTIVE
■ **The inclusive price is two hundred pounds.** Son doscientas libras esterlinas con todo incluido.
■ **inclusive of VAT** con el IVA incluido

income NOUN
los ingresos
□ his main source of income su principal fuente de ingresos

income tax NOUN
el impuesto sobre la renta

incompetent ADJECTIVE
incompetente (FEM incompetente)

incomplete ADJECTIVE
incompleto (FEM incompleta)

inconvenience NOUN
la molestia
□ I don't want to cause any inconvenience. No quiero causar molestia.

inconvenient ADJECTIVE
■ **It's a bit inconvenient at the moment.** Me viene un poco mal en este momento.

incorrect ADJECTIVE
incorrecto (FEM incorrecta)

increase NOUN
▷ *see also* **increase** VERB
el aumento
□ an increase in road accidents un aumento de accidentes de tráfico

to **increase** VERB
▷ *see also* **increase** NOUN
aumentar
□ Traffic on motorways has increased. El tráfico en las autopistas ha aumentado. □ They have increased his salary. Le han aumentado el sueldo.
■ **to increase in size** aumentar de tamaño

incredible ADJECTIVE
increíble (FEM increíble)

indecisive ADJECTIVE
indeciso (FEM indecisa) *(person)*

indeed ADVERB
realmente
□ It's very hard indeed. Es realmente difícil.
■ **Know what I mean? — Indeed I do.** ¿Me comprendes? — Por supuesto que sí.
■ **Thank you very much indeed!** ¡Muchísimas gracias!

independence NOUN
la independencia

independent ADJECTIVE
independiente (FEM independiente)
■ **an independent school** un colegio privado

index NOUN
el índice alfabético *(in book)*

index finger NOUN
el dedo índice

India NOUN
la India

Indian ADJECTIVE
▷ *see also* **Indian** NOUN
indio (FEM india)

Indian NOUN
▷ *see also* **Indian** ADJECTIVE
el indio
la india
□ the Indians los indios
■ **American Indian** el indio americano (FEM la india americana)

to **indicate** VERB
1 indicar*
□ The report indicates that changes are needed. El informe indica que se necesitan cambios.
2 señalizar* *(when driving)*
□ He indicated right and turned into the Gran Vía. Señalizó hacia la derecha y torció a la Gran Vía.

indicator NOUN
el intermitente *(in car)*

indigestion NOUN
la indigestión (PL las indigestiones)
□ I've got indigestion. Tengo indigestión.

individual NOUN
el individuo

indoor ADJECTIVE
■ **an indoor swimming pool** una piscina cubierta

indoors ADVERB
dentro
□ They're indoors. Están dentro.
■ **We'd better go indoors.** Es mejor que entremos.

industrial ADJECTIVE
industrial (FEM industrial)

industrial estate NOUN
la zona industrial

industry NOUN
la industria
□ the oil industry la industria petrolífera
□ I'd like to work in industry. Me gustaría trabajar en la industria.
■ **the tourist industry** el turismo

inefficient ADJECTIVE
ineficiente (FEM ineficiente)

inevitable ADJECTIVE
inevitable (FEM inevitable)

inexpensive ADJECTIVE
económico (FEM económica)

inexperienced ADJECTIVE
inexperto (FEM inexperta)

infant school NOUN
el colegio

infection NOUN
la infección (PL las infecciones)
□ an ear infection una infección de oído

infectious ADJECTIVE
contagioso (FEM contagiosa)

infinitive NOUN
el infinitivo

infirmary NOUN
el hospital

inflatable ADJECTIVE
inflable (FEM inflable) *(mattress, dinghy)*

inflation NOUN
la inflación (PL las inflaciones)

influence NOUN
▷ *see also* **influence** VERB
la influencia
□ He's a bad influence on her. Ejerce mala influencia sobre ella.

to **influence** VERB
▷ *see also* **influence** NOUN
influenciar

influenza NOUN
la gripe
□ to have influenza tener gripe

to **inform** VERB
informar
□ Nobody informed me of the change of plan. Nadie me informó del cambio de planes.

informal ADJECTIVE
■ **informal language** el lenguaje coloquial
■ **an informal visit** una visita informal
■ **'informal dress'** 'no se requiere traje de etiqueta'

information NOUN
la información (PL las informaciones)
□ Could you give me some information about trains to Barcelona? ¿Podría darme información sobre trenes a Barcelona?
■ **a piece of information** un dato

information office NOUN
la oficina de información

information technology NOUN
la informática

infuriating ADJECTIVE
exasperante (FEM exasperante)

ingredient NOUN
el ingrediente

inhabitant NOUN
el/la habitante

to **inherit** VERB
heredar
□ She inherited her father's house. Heredó la casa de su padre.

initials PL NOUN
las iniciales
□ Her initials are CDT. Sus iniciales son CDT.

initiative NOUN
la iniciativa

to **inject** VERB
inyectar
□ They injected me with antibiotics. Me inyectaron antibióticos.

injection NOUN
la inyección (PL las inyecciones)
□ The doctor gave me an injection. El médico me puso una inyección.

to **injure** VERB
herir*
□ He injured his leg. Se hirió la pierna.

injured ADJECTIVE
herido (FEM herida)

injury NOUN
la lesión (PL las lesiones)

injury time NOUN
el tiempo de descuento

injustice NOUN
la injusticia

ink NOUN
la tinta

in-laws PL NOUN
los suegros

inn NOUN
el hostal

inner ADJECTIVE
interior (FEM interior)
■ **the inner city** los núcleos urbanos deprimidos

inner tube NOUN
la cámara de aire

innocent ADJECTIVE
inocente (FEM inocente)

inquest NOUN
la investigación judicial (PL las investigaciones judiciales)

to **inquire** VERB
■ **to inquire about something** informarse acerca de algo

inquiry NOUN
la investigación (PL las investigaciones) *(official investigation)*

inquisitive ADJECTIVE
curioso (FEM curiosa)

insane ADJECTIVE
loco (FEM loca)

inscription NOUN
la inscripción (PL las inscripciones)

insect NOUN
el insecto

insect repellent NOUN
la loción anti-insectos (PL las lociones anti-insectos)

insensitive ADJECTIVE
insensible (FEM insensible)

inside NOUN
▷ *see also* **inside** PREPOSITION, ADVERB
el interior

inside PREPOSITION, ADVERB
▷ *see also* **inside** NOUN
dentro
□ inside the house dentro de la casa □ He opened the envelope and read what was inside. Abrió el sobre y leyó lo que había dentro.
■ **Come inside!** ¡Entra!
■ **Let's go inside, it's starting to rain.** Entremos, está empezando a llover.
■ **inside out** al revés □ He put his jumper on inside out. Se puso el jersey al revés.

insincere ADJECTIVE
falso (FEM falsa)

to **insist** VERB
insistir
□ I didn't want to, but he insisted. Yo no quería, pero él insistió. □ He insisted he was innocent. Insistía en que era inocente.
■ **to insist on doing something** insistir en hacer algo □ She insisted on paying. Insistió en pagar.

inspector NOUN
el inspector
la inspectora

instalment NOUN
1 el plazo *(of payment)*
□ to pay in instalments pagar a plazos
2 el episodio *(of TV, radio serial)*
3 el fascículo *(of publication)*

instance NOUN
■ **for instance** por ejemplo

instant ADJECTIVE
▷ *see also* **instant** NOUN
inmediato (FEM inmediata)
□ It was an instant success. Fue un éxito inmediato.
■ **instant coffee** el café instantáneo

instant NOUN
▷ *see also* **instant** ADJECTIVE
el instante

instantly ADVERB
al instante

instead PREPOSITION, ADVERB
■ **instead of** en lugar de □ We played tennis instead of going swimming. Jugamos al tenis en lugar de ir a nadar. □ She went instead of Peter. En lugar de ir Peter, fue ella.
■ **The pool was closed, so we played tennis instead.** La piscina estaba cerrada, así que jugamos al tenis.

instinct NOUN
el instinto

institute NOUN
el instituto

institution NOUN
la institución (PL las instituciones)

to **instruct** VERB
■ **to instruct somebody to do something**

ordenar a alguien que haga algo

LANGUAGE TIP **ordenar que** has to be followed by a verb in the subjunctive.

□ She instructed us to wait outside. Nos ordenó que esperáramos fuera.

instructions PL NOUN
las instrucciones

instructor NOUN
el instructor
la instructora
□ skiing instructor el instructor de esquí
□ driving instructor el instructor de autoescuela

instrument NOUN
el instrumento
□ Do you play an instrument? ¿Tocas algún instrumento?

insufficient ADJECTIVE
insuficiente (FEM insuficiente)

insulin NOUN
la insulina

insult NOUN
▷ *see also* **insult** VERB
el insulto

to **insult** VERB
▷ *see also* **insult** NOUN
insultar

insurance NOUN
el seguro
□ his car insurance su seguro de automóvil
■ **an insurance policy** una póliza de seguros

intelligent ADJECTIVE
inteligente (FEM inteligente)

to **intend** VERB
■ **to intend to do something** tener la intención de hacer algo □ I intend to do languages at university. Tengo la intención de estudiar idiomas en la universidad.

intense ADJECTIVE
intenso (FEM intensa)

intensive ADJECTIVE
intensivo (FEM intensiva)

intention NOUN
la intención (PL las intenciones)

intercom NOUN
el interfono

interest NOUN
▷ *see also* **interest** VERB
1 el interés (PL los intereses)
□ to show an interest in something mostrar interés en algo
2 la afición (PL las aficiones)
□ My main interest is music. Mi mayor afición es la música.
■ **It's in your own interest to study hard.** Te conviene estudiar mucho.

to **interest** VERB
▷ *see also* **interest** NOUN
interesar
□ It doesn't interest me. No me interesa.
■ **to be interested in something** estar interesado en algo □ I'm very interested in what you're telling me. Estoy muy interesado en lo que me dices.
■ **Are you interested in politics?** ¿Te interesa la política?

interesting ADJECTIVE
interesante (FEM interesante)

interior NOUN
el interior

interior designer NOUN
el diseñador de interiores
la diseñadora de interiores

intermediate ADJECTIVE
intermedio (FEM intermedia)

internal ADJECTIVE
interno (FEM interna)

international ADJECTIVE
internacional (FEM internacional)

internet NOUN
el/la Internet
□ on the internet en Internet

internet café NOUN
el cibercafé

internet user NOUN
el/la internauta

to **interpret** VERB
hacer* de intérprete
□ Steve couldn't speak Spanish so his friend interpreted. Steve no hablaba español, así que su amigo hizo de intérprete.

interpreter NOUN
el/la intérprete

to **interrupt** VERB
interrumpir

interruption NOUN
la interrupción (PL las interrupciones)

interval NOUN
el intervalo

interview NOUN
▷ *see also* **interview** VERB
la entrevista

to **interview** VERB
▷ *see also* **interview** NOUN
entrevistar
□ I was interviewed on the radio. Me entrevistaron en la radio.

interviewer NOUN
el entrevistador
la entrevistadora

intimate ADJECTIVE
íntimo (FEM íntima)

into PREPOSITION
1 a
□ I'm going into town. Voy a la ciudad.
□ Translate it into Spanish. Tradúcelo al

español. □ He got into the car. Subió al coche.

2 en

□ to get into bed meterse en la cama □ I poured the milk into a cup. Vertí la leche en una taza. □ They divided into two groups. Se dividieron en dos grupos.

■ **to walk into a lamppost** tropezar con una farola

intranet NOUN
la intranet

to **introduce** VERB
presentar
□ He introduced me to his parents. Me presentó a sus padres.

introduction NOUN
la introducción (PL las introducciones) *(in book)*

intruder NOUN
el intruso
la intrusa

intuition NOUN
la intuición (PL las intuiciones)

to **invade** VERB
invadir

invalid NOUN
el inválido
la inválida

to **invent** VERB
inventar

invention NOUN
el invento

inventor NOUN
el inventor
la inventora

investigation NOUN
la investigación (PL las investigaciones)

investment NOUN
la inversión (PL las inversiones)

invisible ADJECTIVE
invisible (FEM invisible)

invitation NOUN
la invitación (PL las invitaciones)

to **invite** VERB
invitar
□ Michael's not invited. Michael no está invitado. □ You're invited to a party at Claire's house. Estás invitado a una fiesta en casa de Claire.

to **involve** VERB
suponer*
□ It involves a lot of work. Supone mucho trabajo.

■ **He wasn't involved in the robbery.** No estuvo implicado en el robo.

■ **She was involved in politics.** Estaba metida en política.

■ **to be involved with somebody** tener una relación con alguien □ She was involved with a married man. Tenía una relación con un hombre casado.

■ **I don't want to get involved in the argument.** No quiero meterme en la discusión.

IQ ABBREVIATION *(= intelligence quotient)*
el CI *(= el coeficiente intelectual)*

Iran NOUN
Irán *masc*

Iraq NOUN
Iraq *masc*

Ireland NOUN
Irlanda *fem*

Irish NOUN
▷ *see also* **Irish** ADJECTIVE
el irlandés *(language)*

■ **the Irish** *(people)* los irlandeses

Irish ADJECTIVE
▷ *see also* **Irish** NOUN
irlandés (FEM irlandesa, PL irlandeses)

Irishman NOUN
el irlandés (PL los irlandeses)

Irishwoman NOUN
la irlandesa

iron NOUN
▷ *see also* **iron** VERB
1 la plancha *(for clothes)*
2 el hierro *(metal)*

to **iron** VERB
▷ *see also* **iron** NOUN
planchar

ironic ADJECTIVE
irónico (FEM irónica)

ironing NOUN
■ **to do the ironing** planchar
■ **I hate ironing.** No me gusta nada planchar.

ironing board NOUN
la tabla de planchar

ironmonger's NOUN
la ferretería

irrelevant ADJECTIVE
irrelevante (FEM irrelevante)
□ That's irrelevant. Eso es irrelevante.

irresponsible ADJECTIVE
irresponsable (FEM irresponsable)
□ That was irresponsible of him. Eso fue irresponsable por su parte.

irritating ADJECTIVE
irritante (FEM irritante)

is VERB ▷ *see* **be**

Islam NOUN
el Islam

Islamic ADJECTIVE
islámico (FEM islámica)
□ Islamic law la ley islámica

island NOUN
la isla

isle NOUN
■ **the Isle of Man** la Isla de Man
■ **the Isle of Wight** la Isla de Wight

isolated ADJECTIVE
aislado (FEM aislada)

ISP NOUN *(= Internet Service Provider)*
el proveedor de servicios de Internet

Israel NOUN
Israel *masc*

issue NOUN
▷ *see also* **issue** VERB
1 el tema
LANGUAGE TIP Although **tema** ends in **-a**, it is actually a masculine noun.
□ a controversial issue un tema polémico
2 el número *(magazine)*
□ a back issue un número atrasado

to **issue** VERB
▷ *see also* **issue** NOUN
1 hacer* público
□ The minister issued a statement yesterday. El ministro hizo pública una declaración ayer.
2 proporcionar *(equipment, supplies)*

it PRONOUN
LANGUAGE TIP When 'it' is the subject of a sentence it is practically never translated.
□ Where's my book? — It's on the table. ¿Dónde está mi libro? — Está sobre la mesa. □ It's raining. Está lloviendo. □ It's six o'clock. Son las seis. □ It's Friday tomorrow. Mañana es viernes. □ It's expensive. Es caro. □ Who is it? — It's me. ¿Quién es? — Soy yo.
LANGUAGE TIP When 'it' is the direct object of the verb in a sentence, use **lo** if it stands for a masculine noun or **la** if it stands for a feminine noun.
□ There's a croissant left. Do you want it? Queda un croissant. ¿Lo quieres? □ I doubt it. Lo dudo. □ It's a good film. Have you seen it? Es una buena película. ¿La has visto?
LANGUAGE TIP Use **le** when 'it' is the indirect object of the verb in the sentence.
□ Give it another coat of paint. Dale otra mano de pintura.
LANGUAGE TIP For general concepts use the word **ello**.
□ I spoke to him about it. Hablé con él sobre ello. □ I'm against it. Estoy en contra de ello.

Italian ADJECTIVE
▷ *see also* **Italian** NOUN
italiano (FEM italiana)

Italian NOUN
▷ *see also* **Italian** ADJECTIVE
1 el italiano
la italiana *(person)*
□ the Italians los italianos
2 el italiano *(language)*

Italy NOUN
Italia *fem*

to **itch** VERB
picar*
□ It itches. Me pica. □ My head is itching. Me pica la cabeza.

itchy ADJECTIVE
■ **My head's itchy.** Me pica la cabeza.
■ **I've got an itchy nose.** Me pica la nariz.

it'd = **it had; it would**

item NOUN
1 la pieza
□ a collector's item una pieza de colección
2 el artículo
□ The first item he bought was an alarm clock. El primer artículo que compró fue un despertador.
3 la partida
□ He checked the items on his bill. Comprobó las partidas de su factura.
4 el punto
□ The next item on the agenda is... El siguiente punto del orden del día es...
■ **an item of news** una noticia

itinerary NOUN
el itinerario

it'll = **it will**

its ADJECTIVE
su (FEM su, PL sus)
□ Everything in its place. Cada cosa en su sitio.
□ It has its advantages. Tiene sus ventajas.
LANGUAGE TIP 'its' is usually translated by the definite article **el/los** or **la/las** when it's clear from the sentence who the possessor is or when referring to clothing or parts of the body.
□ The dog is losing its hair. El perro está perdiendo el pelo. □ The bird was in its cage. El pájaro estaba en la jaula.

it's = **it is; it has**

itself PRONOUN
se *(reflexive)*
□ The heating switches itself off. La calefacción se apaga sola. □ The dog scratched itself. El perro se rascó.
■ **The meal itself was tasty, though expensive.** La comida en sí estaba rica, aunque era cara.

I've = **I have**

Jj

jab NOUN
la inyección (PL las inyecciones)

jack NOUN
1 el gato
□ The jack's in the boot. El gato está en el maletero.
2 la jota *(in ordinary pack of cards)*
3 la sota *(in Spanish pack of cards)*

jacket NOUN
la chaqueta
■ **jacket potatoes** las patatas asadas con piel (las papas asadas con cáscara *Latin America*)

jackpot NOUN
el premio gordo
□ to win the jackpot sacarse el premio gordo

jail NOUN
▷ *see also* **jail** VERB
la cárcel
□ to go to jail ir a la cárcel

to jail VERB
▷ *see also* **jail** NOUN
■ **He was jailed for ten years.** Lo condenaron a diez años de cárcel.

jam NOUN
la mermelada
□ strawberry jam la mermelada de fresas
■ **a traffic jam** un atasco

jammed ADJECTIVE
atascado (FEM atascada)
□ The window's jammed. La ventana está atascada.

jam-packed ADJECTIVE
atestado (FEM atestada)
□ The room was jam-packed. La habitación estaba atestada.

janitor NOUN
el/la conserje
□ He's a janitor. Es conserje.

January NOUN
enero *masc*
□ in January en enero □ the January sales las rebajas de enero

Japan NOUN
el Japón *masc*

Japanese ADJECTIVE
▷ *see also* **Japanese** NOUN
japonés (FEM japonesa, PL japoneses)

Japanese NOUN
▷ *see also* **Japanese** ADJECTIVE
1 el japonés
la japonesa *(person)*
■ **the Japanese** los japoneses
2 el japonés *(language)*

jar NOUN
el tarro
□ a jar of honey un tarro de miel

jaundice NOUN
la ictericia
□ He's got jaundice. Tiene ictericia.

javelin NOUN
la jabalina

jaw NOUN
la mandíbula

jazz NOUN
el jazz

jealous ADJECTIVE
celoso (FEM celosa)
□ to be jealous estar celoso

jeans PL NOUN
los vaqueros
□ a pair of jeans unos vaqueros

Jehovah's Witness NOUN
el/la testigo de Jehová
□ She's a Jehovah's Witness. Es testigo de Jehová.

Jello® NOUN (US)
la gelatina

jelly NOUN
la gelatina

jellyfish NOUN
la medusa

jersey NOUN
el jersey (PL los jerseys)

Jesus NOUN
Jesús *masc*

jet NOUN
el reactor

jet lag NOUN
■ **to be suffering from jet lag** tener jet lag

jetty NOUN
el embarcadero
Jew NOUN
el judío
la judía
jewel NOUN
la joya
jeweller (US **jeweler**) NOUN
el joyero
la joyera
□ She's a jeweller. Es joyera.
jeweller's shop (US **jeweler's shop**) NOUN
la joyería
jewellery (US **jewelry**) NOUN
las joyas
Jewish ADJECTIVE
judío (FEM judía)
jigsaw NOUN
el rompecabezas (PL los rompecabezas)
job NOUN
el trabajo
□ a part-time job un trabajo de media jornada
■ **You've done a good job.** Lo has hecho muy bien.
job centre NOUN
la oficina de empleo
jobless ADJECTIVE
desempleado (FEM desempleada)
jockey NOUN
el/la jockey (PL los/las jockeys)
to **jog** VERB
hacer* footing
jogging NOUN
el footing
□ to go jogging hacer footing
john NOUN (US)
el wáter
to **join** VERB
hacerse* socio de
□ I'm going to join the ski club. Voy a hacerme socio del club de esquí.
■ **I'll join you later if I can.** Yo iré luego si puedo.
■ **If you're going for a walk, do you mind if I join you?** Si vais a dar un paseo, ¿os importa que os acompañe?
to **join in** VERB
■ **He doesn't join in with what we do.** No participa en lo que hacemos.
■ **She started singing, and the audience joined in.** Empezó a cantar, y el público se unió a ella.
joiner NOUN
el carpintero
la carpintera
□ He's a joiner. Es carpintero.
joint NOUN
1 la articulación (PL las articulaciones)
□ I've got pains in my joints. Me duelen las articulaciones.
2 el porro *(drugs: informal)*
■ **We had a joint of lamb for lunch.** Comimos asado de cordero.
joke NOUN
▷ *see also* **joke** VERB
1 la broma
□ Don't get upset, it was only a joke. No te enfades, era sólo una broma.
■ **to play a joke on somebody** gastarle una broma a alguien
2 el chiste
□ to tell a joke contar un chiste
to **joke** VERB
▷ *see also* **joke** NOUN
bromear
■ **You must be joking!** ¡Estás de broma!
jolly ADJECTIVE
alegre (FEM alegre)
Jordan NOUN
Jordania *fem*
to **jot down** VERB
apuntar
jotter NOUN
el bloc (PL los blocs)
journalism NOUN
el periodismo
journalist NOUN
el/la periodista
□ I'm a journalist. Soy periodista.
journey NOUN
el viaje
□ to go on a journey hacer un viaje
■ **The journey to school takes about half an hour.** Se tarda una media hora en ir al colegio.
joy NOUN
la alegría
joystick NOUN
el mando *(for computer games)*
judge NOUN
▷ *see also* **judge** VERB
el/la juez (PL los/las jueces)
to **judge** VERB
▷ *see also* **judge** NOUN
juzgar*
judo NOUN
el judo
□ My favourite sport is judo. Mi deporte favorito es el judo.
jug NOUN
la jarra
juggler NOUN
el/la malabarista
juice NOUN
el zumo
□ orange juice el zumo de naranja

July NOUN
julio *masc*
□ in July en julio

jumble sale NOUN
la venta de objetos usados

to **jump** VERB
saltar
□ They jumped over the wall. Saltaron el muro. □ He jumped out of the window. Saltó por la ventana. □ He jumped off the roof. Saltó del tejado.
■ **You made me jump!** ¡Qué susto me has dado!

jumper NOUN
el jersey (PL los jerseys)

junction NOUN
el cruce *(of roads)*

June NOUN
junio *masc*
□ in June en junio

jungle NOUN
la selva

junior school NOUN
el colegio

junk NOUN
los trastos viejos
□ The attic's full of junk. El desván está lleno de trastos viejos.
■ **to eat junk food** comer porquerías
■ **junk shop** la tienda de objetos usados

jury NOUN
el jurado

just ADVERB
1 justo
□ just in time justo a tiempo □ just after Christmas justo después de Navidad □ We had just enough money. Teníamos el dinero justo.
■ **He's just arrived.** Acaba de llegar.
■ **I did it just now.** Lo acabo de hacer.
■ **I'm rather busy just now.** Ahora mismo estoy bastante ocupada.
■ **I'm just coming!** ¡Ya voy!
■ **just here** aquí mismo
2 sólo
□ It's just a suggestion. Es sólo una sugerencia.
■ **I just thought that you would like it.** Yo pensé que te gustaría.
■ **Just a minute!** ¡Un momento!
■ **just about** casi □ It's just about finished. Está casi terminado.

justice NOUN
la justicia

to **justify** VERB
justificar*

Kk

kangaroo NOUN
el canguro

karate NOUN
el kárate
□ My favourite sport is karate. Mi deporte favorito es el kárate.

kebab NOUN
el pincho moruno

keen ADJECTIVE
entusiasta (FEM entusiasta)
□ a keen supporter un hincha entusiasta
■ **He doesn't seem very keen.** No parece muy entusiasmado.
■ **She's a keen student.** Es una alumna aplicada.
■ **I'm not very keen on maths.** No me gustan mucho las matemáticas.
■ **He's keen on her.** Ella le gusta.
■ **to be keen on doing something** tener ganas de hacer algo □ I'm not very keen on going. No tengo muchas ganas de ir.

to **keep** VERB
1 quedarse con
□ You can keep the watch. Puedes quedarte con el reloj.
■ **You can keep it.** Puedes quedártelo.
2 mantenerse* *(remain)*
□ to keep fit mantenerse en forma
■ **Keep still!** ¡Estáte quieto!
■ **Keep quiet!** ¡Cállate!
3 seguir*
□ Keep straight on. Siga recto.
■ **I keep forgetting my keys.** Siempre me olvido las llaves.
■ **'keep out'** 'prohibida la entrada'
■ **'keep off the grass'** 'prohibido pisar el césped'

to **keep on** VERB
continuar*
□ He kept on reading. Continuó leyendo.
■ **The car keeps on breaking down.** El coche no deja de averiarse.

to **keep up** VERB
■ **Matthew walks so fast I can't keep up.** Matthew camina tan rápido que no puedo seguirle el ritmo.

keep-fit NOUN
la gimnasia
□ I go to keep-fit classes. Voy a clases de gimnasia.

kennel NOUN
la caseta del perro *(in garden)*
■ **a kennels** una residencia canina

kept VERB ▷ *see* **keep**

kerosene NOUN (US)
el queroseno

kettle NOUN
el hervidor

key NOUN
la llave

keyboard NOUN
el teclado

keyring NOUN
el llavero

kick NOUN
▷ *see also* **kick** VERB
la patada

to **kick** VERB
▷ *see also* **kick** NOUN
■ **to kick somebody** dar una patada a alguien □ He kicked me. Me dio una patada.
■ **He kicked the ball hard.** Le dio un puntapié fuerte al balón.
■ **to kick off** *(in football)* hacer el saque inicial

kick-off NOUN
el saque inicial
■ **The kick-off is at 10 o'clock.** El partido empieza a las diez.

kid NOUN
▷ *see also* **kid** VERB
el crío
la cría *(informal)*
□ the kids los críos

to **kid** VERB
▷ *see also* **kid** NOUN
bromear
□ I'm not kidding, it's snowing. No estoy bromeando, está nevando.
■ **I'm just kidding.** Es una broma.

to **kidnap** VERB
secuestrar

kidney NOUN
el riñón (PL los riñones)
□ He's got kidney trouble. Tiene problemas de riñón. □ I don't like kidneys. No me gustan los riñones.

to **kill** VERB
matar
□ She killed her husband. Mató a su marido.
■ **to be killed** morir □ He was killed in a car accident. Murió en un accidente de coche.
■ **to kill oneself** suicidarse □ He killed himself. Se suicidó.

killer NOUN
1 el asesino
la asesina *(murderer)*
□ The police are searching for the killer. La policía está buscando al asesino.
2 el asesino a sueldo
la asesina a sueldo *(hired killer)*
■ **Meningitis can be a killer.** La meningitis puede ser mortal.

kilo NOUN
el kilo
□ at £5 a kilo a 5 libras esterlinas el kilo

kilometre (US **kilometer**) NOUN
el kilómetro

kilt NOUN
la falda escocesa

kind ADJECTIVE
▷ *see also* **kind** NOUN
amable (FEM amable)
□ to be kind to somebody ser amable con alguien
■ **Thank you for being so kind.** Gracias por su amabilidad.

kind NOUN
▷ *see also* **kind** ADJECTIVE
el tipo
□ It's a kind of sausage. Es un tipo de salchicha.

kindergarten NOUN
el jardín de infancia (PL los jardines de infancia)

kindly ADVERB
amablemente

kindness NOUN
la amabilidad

king NOUN
el rey
■ **the King and Queen** los reyes

kingdom NOUN
el reino

kiosk NOUN
el quiosco *(stall)*
■ **a telephone kiosk** una cabina telefónica

kipper NOUN
el arenque ahumado

kiss NOUN
▷ *see also* **kiss** VERB
el beso

to **kiss** VERB
▷ *see also* **kiss** NOUN
1 besar
□ He kissed her passionately. La besó apasionadamente.
2 besarse
□ They kissed. Se besaron.

kit NOUN
el equipo
□ I've forgotten my gym kit. Me he olvidado el equipo de gimnasia.
■ **a tool kit** un juego de herramientas
■ **a sewing kit** un costurero
■ **a first-aid kit** un botiquín
■ **a puncture repair kit** un juego de reparación de pinchazos
■ **a drum kit** una batería

kitchen NOUN
la cocina
□ a fitted kitchen una cocina amueblada
□ a kitchen knife un cuchillo de cocina
■ **the kitchen units** los armarios de cocina

kite NOUN
la cometa

kitten NOUN
el gatito
la gatita

knee NOUN
la rodilla
□ to be on one's knees estar de rodillas

to **kneel** VERB
arrodillarse

to **kneel down** VERB
arrodillarse

knew VERB ▷ *see* **know**

knickers PL NOUN
las bragas (los calzones *Latin America*)
□ a pair of knickers unas bragas (unos calzones *Latin America*)

knife NOUN
el cuchillo
□ a kitchen knife un cuchillo de cocina
□ a sheath knife un cuchillo de monte
■ **a penknife** una navaja

to **knit** VERB
hacer* punto (tejer *Latin America*)
□ I like knitting. Me gusta hacer punto.
■ **She is knitting a jumper.** Está haciendo un jersey a punto.

knives PL NOUN ▷ *see* **knife**

knob NOUN
1 el pomo *(on door)*
2 el dial *(on radio, TV)*

to **knock** VERB
▷ *see also* **knock** NOUN
llamar

□ Someone's knocking at the door. Alguien llama a la puerta.

■ **to knock somebody down** atropellar a alguien □ She was knocked down by a car. La atropelló un coche.

■ **to knock somebody out** **1** *(defeat)* eliminar a alguien □ They were knocked out early in the tournament. Fueron eliminados al poco de iniciarse el torneo. **2** *(stun)* dejar sin sentido a alguien □ They knocked out the watchman. Dejaron al vigilante sin sentido.

knock NOUN
▷ *see also* **knock** VERB
el golpe

knot NOUN
el nudo
□ to tie a knot in something hacer un nudo en algo

to **know** VERB

LANGUAGE TIP Use **saber** for knowing facts, **conocer** for knowing people and places.

1 saber*
□ Yes, I know. Sí, ya lo sé. □ I don't know. No sé. □ I don't know any German. No sé nada de alemán.

■ **to know that** saber que □ I didn't know that your Dad was a policeman. No sabía que tu padre era policía.

2 conocer*
□ I know her. La conozco. □ I know Paris well. Conozco bien París.

■ **to know about something** **1** *(be aware of)* estar enterado de algo □ Do you know about the meeting this afternoon? ¿Estás enterado de la reunión de esta tarde? **2** *(be knowledgeable about)* saber de algo □ He knows a lot about cars. Sabe mucho de coches. □ I don't know much about computers. No sé mucho de ordenadores.

■ **to get to know somebody** llegar a conocer a alguien

■ **How should I know?** ¿Y yo qué sé?

■ **You never know!** ¡Nunca se sabe!

know-all NOUN
el/la sabelotodo
□ He's such a know-all! ¡Es un sabelotodo!

know-how NOUN
la pericia

knowledge NOUN
el conocimiento
□ scientific knowledge el conocimiento científico

■ **my knowledge of French** mis conocimientos de francés

knowledgeable ADJECTIVE
■ **to be knowledgeable about something** saber mucho de algo

known VERB ▷ *see* **know**

Koran NOUN
el Corán

Korea NOUN
Corea *fem*

kosher ADJECTIVE
kosher (FEM + PL kosher)

Ll

lab NOUN
el laboratorio
□ a lab technician un técnico de laboratorio
label NOUN
la etiqueta
labor NOUN (US)
■ **to be in labor** estar de parto
■ **the labor market** el mercado de trabajo
■ **labor union** el sindicato
laboratory NOUN
el laboratorio
Labour NOUN
los laboristas
□ My parents vote Labour. Mis padres votan a los laboristas.
■ **the Labour Party** el Partido Laborista
labour NOUN
■ **to be in labour** estar de parto
■ **the labour market** el mercado de trabajo
labourer NOUN
el peón (PL los peones)
■ **farm labourer** el jornalero
lace NOUN
1 el cordón (PL los cordones) *(of shoe)*
2 el encaje
□ a lace collar un cuello de encaje
lack NOUN
la falta
□ He got the job, despite his lack of experience. Consiguió el empleo, a pesar de su falta de experiencia.
lacquer NOUN
la laca
lad NOUN
el muchacho
ladder NOUN
la escalera *(de mano)*
lady NOUN
la señora
■ **Ladies and gentlemen...** Damas y caballeros...
■ **the ladies'** los servicios de señoras
■ **a young lady** una señorita
ladybird NOUN
la mariquita
to **lag behind** VERB
quedarse atrás
lager NOUN
la cerveza rubia
laid VERB ▷ *see* **lay**
laid-back ADJECTIVE
relajado (FEM relajada) *(informal)*
lain VERB ▷ *see* **lie**
lake NOUN
el lago
□ Lake Michigan el Lago Michigan
lamb NOUN
el cordero
□ a lamb chop una chuleta de cordero
lame ADJECTIVE
cojo (FEM coja)
□ to be lame estar cojo □ The accident left her lame. Se quedó coja después del accidente.
■ **My pony is lame.** Mi pony cojea.
lamp NOUN
la lámpara
lamppost NOUN
la farola
lampshade NOUN
la pantalla
land NOUN
▷ *see also* **land** VERB
la tierra
□ We have a lot of land. Tenemos mucha tierra.
■ **to work on the land** trabajar la tierra
■ **a piece of land** un terreno
to **land** VERB
▷ *see also* **land** NOUN
aterrizar*
□ The plane landed at five o'clock. El avión aterrizó a las cinco.
landing NOUN
1 el aterrizaje *(of plane)*
2 el rellano *(of staircase)*
landlady NOUN
1 la casera *(of rented property)*
2 la patrona *(of pub)*
landlord NOUN
1 el casero *(of rented property)*
2 el patrón (PL los patrones) *(of pub)*

landmark NOUN
el punto de referencia
□ Big Ben is one of London's landmarks. El Big Ben es uno de los puntos de referencia de Londres.

landowner NOUN
el/la terrateniente

landscape NOUN
el paisaje

lane NOUN
1 el camino
□ a country lane un camino rural
2 el carril
□ the outside lane *(in the UK)* el carril de la derecha □ the outside lane *(on the Continent)* el carril de la izquierda

language NOUN
el idioma
LANGUAGE TIP Although **idioma** ends in **-a**, it is actually a masculine noun.
□ Greek is a difficult language. El griego es un idioma difícil.
■ **to use bad language** decir palabrotas

language laboratory NOUN
el laboratorio de idiomas

lap NOUN
la vuelta
□ I ran 10 laps. Corrí 10 vueltas.
■ **Andrew was sitting on his mother's lap.** Andrew estaba sentado en el regazo de su madre.

laptop NOUN
el (ordenador) portátil

larder NOUN
la despensa

large ADJECTIVE
grande (FEM grande)
□ a large house una casa grande □ a large dog un perro grande
LANGUAGE TIP Use **gran** before a singular noun.
□ a large number of people un gran número de personas
LANGUAGE TIP Be careful not to translate **large** by **largo**.

largely ADVERB
en gran parte

laser NOUN
el láser

lass NOUN
la muchacha

last ADJECTIVE, ADVERB
▷ *see also* **last** VERB
1 pasado (FEM pasada)
□ last Friday el viernes pasado
2 último (FEM última)
□ the last time la última vez
3 por última vez
□ I've lost my bag. — When did you last see it? He perdido el bolso. — ¿Cuándo lo viste por última vez?
4 en último lugar
□ the team which finished last el equipo que quedó en último lugar
■ **He arrived last.** Llegó el último.
■ **last night** anoche □ I got home at midnight last night. Anoche llegué a casa a medianoche. □ I couldn't sleep last night. Anoche no pude dormir.
■ **at last** por fin

to **last** VERB
▷ *see also* **last** ADJECTIVE, ADVERB
durar
□ The concert lasts two hours. El concierto dura dos horas.

lastly ADVERB
por último

late ADJECTIVE, ADVERB
tarde (FEM tarde)
□ Hurry up or you'll be late! ¡Date prisa o llegarás tarde! □ I'm often late for school. A menudo llego tarde al colegio. □ I went to bed late. Me fui a la cama tarde. □ to arrive late llegar tarde
■ **The flight will be one hour late.** El vuelo llegará con una hora de retraso.
■ **in the late afternoon** al final de la tarde
■ **in late May** a finales de mayo
■ **the late Mr Philips** el difunto Sr. Philips

lately ADVERB
últimamente
□ I haven't seen him lately. No lo he visto últimamente.

later ADVERB
más tarde
□ I'll do it later. Lo haré más tarde.
■ **See you later!** ¡Hasta luego!

latest ADJECTIVE
último (FEM última)
□ their latest album su último álbum
■ **at the latest** como muy tarde □ by 10 o'clock at the latest a las 10 como muy tarde

Latin NOUN
el latín
□ I do Latin. Estudio latín.

Latin America NOUN
América Latina *fem*

Latin American ADJECTIVE
▷ *see also* **Latin American** NOUN
latinoamericano (FEM latinoamericana)

Latin American NOUN
▷ *see also* **Latin American** ADJECTIVE
el latinoamericano
la latinoamericana

laugh NOUN

▷ *see also* **laugh** VERB
la risa
■ **It was a good laugh.** Fue muy divertido.

to **laugh** VERB
▷ *see also* **laugh** NOUN
reírse*
■ **to laugh at something** reírse de algo
□ He laughed at my accent. Se rió de mi acento.
■ **to laugh at somebody** reírse de alguien
□ They laughed at her. Se rieron de ella.

to **launch** VERB
lanzar* *(product, rocket)*

Launderette® NOUN
la lavandería automática

Laundromat® NOUN (US)
la lavandería automática

laundry NOUN
la colada
□ She does my laundry. Me hace la colada.

lavatory NOUN
el servicio

lavender NOUN
la lavanda

law NOUN
1 la ley
□ strict laws leyes severas
■ **It's against the law.** Es ilegal.
2 el derecho
□ My sister's studying law. Mi hermana estudia derecho.

lawn NOUN
el césped

lawnmower NOUN
el cortacésped

law school NOUN (US)
la facultad de derecho

lawyer NOUN
el abogado
la abogada
□ My mother's a lawyer. Mi madre es abogada.

to **lay** VERB
poner*
□ She laid the baby in his cot. Puso al bebé en la cuna. □ to lay the table poner la mesa

to **lay off** VERB
despedir*
□ My father's been laid off. Han despedido a mi padre.

lay-by NOUN
el área de descanso

LANGUAGE TIP Although it's a feminine noun, remember that you use **el** and **un** with **área**.

layer NOUN
la capa

lazy ADJECTIVE
perezoso (FEM perezosa)

lead (1) NOUN
▷ *see also* **lead** VERB
el plomo *(metal)*
□ a lead pipe una tubería de plomo

lead (2) NOUN
▷ *see also* **lead** VERB
1 el cable *(cable)*
2 la correa
□ Dogs must be kept on a lead. Los perros deben llevarse siempre sujetos con una correa.
■ **to be in the lead (2)** ir en cabeza

to **lead** VERB
▷ *see also* **lead (2)** NOUN
llevar
□ the street that leads to the station la calle que lleva a la estación □ It could lead to a civil war. Podría llevar a una guerra civil.
■ **to lead the way** ir delante

leader NOUN
el/la líder

lead singer NOUN
el/la cantante principal

leaf NOUN
la hoja

leaflet NOUN
el folleto

league NOUN
la liga
□ They are at the top of the league. Están a la cabeza de la liga.
■ **the Premier League** la primera división

leak NOUN
▷ *see also* **leak** VERB
1 el escape
□ a gas leak un escape de gas □ a leak in the pipe un escape en la tubería
2 la gotera
□ a leak in the roof una gotera en el tejado

to **leak** VERB
▷ *see also* **leak** NOUN
1 tener* un agujero *(bucket, pipe)*
2 tener* goteras *(roof)*
3 salirse* *(water, gas)*

to **lean** VERB
apoyar
□ to lean something against the wall apoyar algo contra la pared
■ **to lean on something** apoyarse en algo
□ He leant on the table. Se apoyó en la mesa.
■ **to be leaning against something** estar apoyado contra algo □ The ladder was leaning against the wall. La escalera estaba apoyada contra la pared.

to **lean forward** VERB
inclinarse hacia adelante

to **lean out** VERB
asomarse
□ She leant out of the window. Se asomó a la ventana.

to **lean over** VERB
inclinarse
□ Don't lean over too far. No te inclines demasiado.

to **leap** VERB
saltar
■ **He leapt out of his chair when his team scored.** Dio un salto de la silla cuando su equipo marcó.

leap year NOUN
el año bisiesto

to **learn** VERB
aprender
□ I'm learning to ski. Estoy aprendiendo a esquiar.

learner NOUN
■ **She's a quick learner.** Aprende con mucha rapidez.
■ **Spanish learners** los estudiantes de español

learner driver NOUN
el conductor en prácticas
la conductora en prácticas

learnt VERB ▷ *see* **learn**

least ADJECTIVE, PRONOUN, ADVERB
1 menor (FEM menor)
□ I haven't the least idea. No tengo la menor idea.
2 menos
□ Go for the ones with least fat. Escoge los que tengan menos grasa. □ the least expensive hotel el hotel menos caro □ It takes the least time. Es lo que menos tiempo lleva. □ It's the least I can do. Es lo menos que puedo hacer. □ Maths is the subject I like the least. Las matemáticas es la asignatura que menos me gusta. □ That's the least of my worries. Eso es lo que menos me preocupa.
■ **at least 1** por lo menos □ It'll cost at least £200. Costará por lo menos 200 libras esterlinas. **2** al menos □ There was a lot of damage but at least nobody was hurt. Hubo muchos daños pero al menos nadie resultó herido. □ It's very unfair, at least that's my opinion. Es muy injusto, al menos eso pienso yo.

leather NOUN
el cuero
□ a black leather jacket una chaqueta de cuero negra

leave NOUN
▷ *see also* **leave** VERB
el permiso *(from job, army)*
□ My brother is on leave for a week. Mi hermano está de permiso durante una semana.

to **leave** VERB
▷ *see also* **leave** NOUN
1 dejar
□ Don't leave your camera in the car. No dejes la cámara en el coche.
2 salir*
□ The bus leaves at eight. El autobús sale a las ocho.
3 salir* de
□ We leave London at six o'clock. Salimos de Londres a las seis.
4 irse*
□ They left yesterday. Se fueron ayer. □ She left home when she was sixteen. Se fue de casa a los dieciséis años.
■ **to leave somebody alone** dejar a alguien en paz □ Leave me alone! ¡Déjame en paz!

to **leave out** VERB
excluir*
□ Not knowing the language I felt really left out. Al no saber el idioma me sentía muy excluido.

leaves PL NOUN ▷ *see* **leaf**

Lebanon NOUN
Líbano *masc*

lecture NOUN
▷ *see also* **lecture** VERB
1 la clase *(at university)*
2 la conferencia *(public)*

to **lecture** VERB
▷ *see also* **lecture** NOUN
1 dar* clases
□ She lectures at the technical college. Da clases en la escuela politécnica.
2 sermonear
□ He's always lecturing us. Siempre nos está sermoneando.

lecturer NOUN
el profesor universitario
la profesora universitaria
■ **She's a lecturer in German.** Es profesora de alemán en la universidad.

led VERB ▷ *see* **lead**

leek NOUN
el puerro

left VERB ▷ *see* **leave**

left ADJECTIVE, ADVERB
▷ *see also* **left** NOUN
1 izquierdo (FEM izquierda)
□ my left hand mi mano izquierda
2 a la izquierda
□ Turn left at the traffic lights. Doble a la izquierda al llegar al semáforo.
■ **I haven't got any money left.** No me queda nada de dinero.

■ **Is there any ice cream left?** ¿Queda algo de helado?

left NOUN
▷ *see also* **left** ADJECTIVE
la izquierda
□ on the left a la izquierda

left-hand ADJECTIVE
■ **the left-hand side** la izquierda □ It's on the left-hand side. Está a la izquierda.

left-handed ADJECTIVE
zurdo (FEM zurda)

left-luggage office NOUN
la consigna

leg NOUN
la pierna
□ She's broken her leg. Se ha roto la pierna.
■ **a chicken leg** un muslo de pollo
■ **a leg of lamb** una pierna de cordero

legal ADJECTIVE
legal (FEM legal)

leggings NOUN
las mallas

leisure NOUN
el tiempo libre
□ What do you do in your leisure time? ¿Qué haces en tu tiempo libre?

leisure centre NOUN
el centro recreativo

lemon NOUN
el limón (PL los limones)

lemonade NOUN
la gaseosa

to **lend** VERB
prestar
□ I can lend you some money. Te puedo prestar algo de dinero.

length NOUN
la longitud
■ **It's about a metre in length.** Mide aproximadamente un metro de largo.

lens NOUN
1 la lentilla (el lente de contacto *Latin America*) *(contact lens)*
2 el cristal *(of spectacles)*
3 el objetivo *(of camera)*

Lent NOUN
la Cuaresma

lent VERB ▷ *see* **lend**

lentil NOUN
la lenteja

Leo NOUN
el Leo *(sign)*
■ **I'm Leo.** Soy leo.

leotard NOUN
el leotardo

lesbian NOUN
la lesbiana

less ADJECTIVE, PRONOUN, ADVERB
menos
□ A bit less, please. Un poco menos, por favor. □ It's less than a kilometre from here. Está a menos de un kilómetro de aquí. □ less than half menos de la mitad □ I've got less than you. Tengo menos que tú. □ It cost less than we thought. Costó menos de lo que pensábamos.
■ **less and less** cada vez menos

lesson NOUN
1 la clase
□ an English lesson una clase de inglés
□ The lessons last forty minutes. Las clases duran cuarenta minutos.
2 la lección (PL las lecciones) *(in textbook)*

to **let** VERB
1 dejar
■ **to let somebody do something** dejar a alguien hacer algo □ Let me have a look. Déjame ver.
■ **Let me go!** ¡Suéltame!
■ **to let somebody know something** informar a alguien de algo □ We must let him know that we are coming to stay. Tenemos que informarle de que venimos a quedarnos.
■ **When can you come to dinner? — I'll let you know.** ¿Cuándo puedes venir a cenar? — Ya te lo diré.
■ **to let in** dejar entrar □ They wouldn't let me in because I was under 18. No me dejaron entrar porque tenía menos de 18 años.

LANGUAGE TIP To make suggestions using 'let's', you can ask questions using **por qué no**.

□ Let's go to the cinema! ¿Por qué no vamos al cine?
■ **Let's have a break! — Yes, let's.** Vamos a descansar un poco. — ¡Buena idea!
2 alquilar
□ 'to let' 'se alquila'

to **let down** VERB
defraudar
□ I won't let you down. No te defraudaré.

letter NOUN
1 la carta
□ She wrote me a long letter. Me escribió una carta larga.
2 la letra
□ 'A' is the first letter of the alphabet. La 'a' es la primera letra del alfabeto.

letterbox NOUN
el buzón (PL los buzones)

lettuce NOUN
la lechuga

leukaemia NOUN
la leucemia

English-Spanish

l

◻ He suffers from leukaemia. Tiene leucemia.

level ADJECTIVE
▷ *see also* **level** NOUN
llano (FEM llana)
◻ a level surface una superficie llana

level NOUN
▷ *see also* **level** ADJECTIVE
el nivel
◻ The level of the river is rising. El nivel del río está subiendo.
■ **'A' levels**

DID YOU KNOW...?
Under the reformed Spanish educational system, if students stay on at school after the age of 16, they can do a two-year course – **bachillerato**. In order to get in to university, they sit an entrance exam – **la selectividad** – in the subjects they have been studying for the **bachillerato**.

level crossing NOUN
el paso a nivel

lever NOUN
la palanca

liable ADJECTIVE
■ **He's liable to panic.** Tiene tendencia a dejarse llevar por el pánico.

liar NOUN
el mentiroso
la mentirosa

liberal ADJECTIVE
liberal (FEM liberal) *(view, system)*
■ **the Liberal Democrats** los demócratas liberales

liberation NOUN
la liberación

Libra NOUN
la Libra *(sign)*
■ **I'm Libra.** Soy libra.

librarian NOUN
el bibliotecario
la bibliotecaria
◻ I'm a librarian. Soy bibliotecaria.

library NOUN
la biblioteca

LANGUAGE TIP Be careful not to translate **library** by **librería**.

Libya NOUN
Libia *fem*

licence (US **license**) NOUN
el permiso
■ **a driving licence** un carnet de conducir

to **lick** VERB
lamer

lid NOUN
la tapa

lie NOUN
▷ *see also* **lie** VERB
la mentira
■ **to tell a lie** mentir

to **lie** VERB
▷ *see also* **lie** NOUN
1 mentir*
◻ I know she's lying. Sé que está mintiendo.
◻ You lied to me! ¡Me mentiste!
2 tumbarse
◻ I lay on the floor. Me tumbé en el suelo.
■ **He was lying on the sofa.** Estaba tumbado en el sofá.

lie-in NOUN
■ **to have a lie-in** quedarse en la cama hasta tarde

lieutenant NOUN
el/la teniente

life NOUN
la vida

lifebelt NOUN
el salvavidas (PL los salvavidas)

lifeboat NOUN
el bote salvavidas (PL los botes salvavidas)

lifeguard NOUN
el/la socorrista

life jacket NOUN
el chaleco salvavidas (PL los chalecos salvavidas)

life-saving NOUN
el socorrismo
◻ I've done a course in life-saving. He hecho un curso de socorrismo.

lifestyle NOUN
el estilo de vida

to **lift** VERB
▷ *see also* **lift** NOUN
levantar
◻ It's too heavy, I can't lift it. Pesa mucho, no lo puedo levantar.

lift NOUN
▷ *see also* **lift** VERB
el ascensor
◻ The lift isn't working. El ascensor no funciona.
■ **He gave me a lift to the cinema.** Me acercó al cine en coche.
■ **Would you like a lift?** ¿Quieres que te lleve en coche?

light ADJECTIVE
▷ *see also* **light** NOUN, VERB
1 ligero (FEM ligera) *(not heavy)*
◻ a light jacket una chaqueta ligera
◻ a light meal una comida ligera
2 claro (FEM clara) *(colour)*
◻ a light blue sweater un jersey azul claro

light NOUN
▷ *see also* **light** ADJECTIVE, VERB

la luz (PL las luces)
□ He switched on the light. Encendió la luz.
□ He switched off the light. Apagó la luz.
■ **the traffic lights** el semáforo
■ **Have you got a light?** ¿Tienes fuego?

to **light** VERB
▷ *see also* **light** ADJECTIVE, NOUN
encender*

light bulb NOUN
la bombilla

lighter NOUN
el mechero

lighthouse NOUN
el faro

lightning NOUN
el relámpago
□ thunder and lightning truenos y relámpagos
□ a flash of lightning un relámpago

to **like** VERB
▷ *see also* **like** PREPOSITION

LANGUAGE TIP The most common translation for 'to like' when talking about things and activities is **gustar**. Remember that the construction is the opposite of English, with the thing you like being the subject of the sentence.

□ I don't like mustard. No me gusta la mostaza. □ Do you like apples? ¿Te gustan las manzanas? □ I like riding. Me gusta montar a caballo.
■ **I like him.** Me cae bien.
■ **I'd like...** Quería... □ I'd like this blouse in size 10, please. Quería esta blusa en la talla 10, por favor.
■ **I'd like an orange juice, please.** Un zumo de naranja, por favor.
■ **I'd like to...** Me gustaría... □ I'd like to go to China. Me gustaría ir a China.

LANGUAGE TIP To ask someone if they would like something, or like to do something, use **querer**.

□ Would you like some coffee? ¿Quieres café? □ Would you like to go for a walk? ¿Quieres ir a dar un paseo?
■ **... if you like** ... si quieres

like PREPOSITION
▷ *see also* **like** VERB
como
□ a city like Paris una ciudad como París

LANGUAGE TIP When asking questions, use **cómo** instead of **como**.

□ What was his house like? ¿Cómo era su casa?
■ **What's the weather like?** ¿Qué tiempo hace?
■ **It's a bit like salmon.** Se parece un poco al salmón.
■ **It's fine like that.** Así está bien.
■ **Do it like this.** Hazlo así.
■ **something like that** algo así

likely ADJECTIVE
probable (FEM probable)
□ That's not very likely. Es poco probable.

LANGUAGE TIP **es probable que** has to be followed by a verb in the subjunctive.

□ She's likely to come. Es probable que venga. □ She's not likely to come. Es probable que no venga.

lime NOUN
la lima *(fruit)*

limit NOUN
el límite
□ the speed limit el límite de velocidad

limousine NOUN
la limusina

to **limp** VERB
cojear

line NOUN
1 la línea
□ a straight line una línea recta □ He wrote a few lines. Escribió unas cuantas líneas.
□ to draw a line trazar una línea
2 la fila
□ a line of people una fila de gente
■ **railway line** la vía férrea
■ **Hold the line, please.** No cuelgue, por favor.
■ **It's a very bad line.** Se oye muy mal.

linen NOUN
el lino
□ a linen jacket una chaqueta de lino

liner NOUN
el transatlántico

link NOUN
▷ *see also* **link** VERB
1 la relación (PL las relaciones)
□ the link between smoking and cancer la relación entre el tabaco y el cáncer
■ **cultural links** los lazos culturales
2 el enlace *(computing)*

to **link** VERB
▷ *see also* **link** NOUN
1 asociar *(facts)*
2 conectar *(towns, terminals)*

lino NOUN
el linóleo

lion NOUN
el león (PL los leones)

lioness NOUN
la leona

lip NOUN
el labio

to **lip-read** VERB
leer* los labios

English-Spanish

l

lip salve NOUN
la crema protectora para los labios
lipstick NOUN
el lápiz de labios (PL los lápices de labios)
liqueur NOUN
el licor
liquid NOUN
el líquido
liquidizer NOUN
la licuadora
list NOUN
▷ *see also* **list** VERB
la lista
to **list** VERB
▷ *see also* **list** NOUN
1 hacer* una lista de *(in writing)*
2 enumerar *(verbally)*
to **listen** VERB
escuchar
□ Listen to this! ¡Escucha esto! □ Listen to me! ¡Escúchame!
listener NOUN
el/la oyente
lit VERB ▷ *see* **light**
liter NOUN (US)
el litro
literally ADVERB
literalmente
□ It was literally impossible to find a seat. Era literalmente imposible encontrar un asiento. □ to translate literally traducir literalmente
literature NOUN
la literatura
litre NOUN
el litro
litter NOUN
la basura
litter bin NOUN
el cubo de la basura
little ADJECTIVE, PRONOUN
pequeño (FEM pequeña)
□ a little girl una niña pequeña

> **WORD POWER**
> You can use a number of other words instead of **little** to mean 'small':
> **miniature** en miniatura
> □ a miniature doll una muñeca en miniatura
> **minute** minúsculo
> □ a minute plant una planta minúscula
> **tiny** enano
> □ a tiny garden un jardín enano

■ **a little** un poco □ How much would you like? — Just a little. ¿Cuánto quiere? — Sólo un poco.
■ **very little** muy poco □ We've got very little time. Tenemos muy poco tiempo.
■ **little by little** poco a poco
live ADJECTIVE
▷ *see also* **live** VERB
vivo (FEM viva)
□ I'm against tests on live animals. Estoy en contra de los experimentos en animales vivos.
■ **a live broadcast** una emisión en directo
■ **a live concert** un concierto en vivo
to **live** VERB
▷ *see also* **live** ADJECTIVE
vivir
□ I live with my grandmother. Vivo con mi abuela. □ Where do you live? ¿Dónde vives? □ I live in Edinburgh. Vivo en Edimburgo.
to **live together** VERB
vivir juntos
lively ADJECTIVE
■ **She's got a lively personality.** Tiene un carácter muy alegre.
liver NOUN
el hígado
lives PL NOUN ▷ *see* **life**
living NOUN
■ **to make a living** ganarse la vida
■ **What does she do for a living?** ¿A qué se dedica?
living room NOUN
la sala de estar
lizard NOUN
1 la lagartija *(small)*
2 el lagarto *(big)*
load NOUN
▷ *see also* **load** VERB
■ **loads of** *(informal)* un montón de
□ They've got loads of money. Tienen un montón de dinero.
■ **You're talking a load of rubbish!** ¡Lo que dices es una estupidez!
to **load** VERB
▷ *see also* **load** NOUN
cargar*
□ a trolley loaded with luggage un carrito cargado de equipaje
loaf NOUN
el pan
■ **a loaf of bread 1** *(French bread)* una barra de pan **2** *(baked in tin)* un pan de molde
loan NOUN
▷ *see also* **loan** VERB
el préstamo
to **loan** VERB
▷ *see also* **loan** NOUN
prestar
to **loathe** VERB
detestar

◻ I loathe her. La detesto.

loaves PL NOUN ▷ *see* **loaf**

lobster NOUN
la langosta

local ADJECTIVE
local (FEM local)
◻ the local paper el periódico local
■ **a local call** una llamada urbana

loch NOUN
el lago

lock NOUN
▷ *see also* **lock** VERB
la cerradura

to **lock** VERB
▷ *see also* **lock** NOUN
cerrar* con llave
◻ Make sure you lock your door. No te olvides de cerrar tu puerta con llave.

to **lock out** VERB
■ **The door slammed and I was locked out.** La puerta se cerró de golpe y me quedé fuera sin llaves.

locker NOUN
la taquilla
◻ left-luggage lockers las taquillas de consigna
■ **locker room** el vestuario

locket NOUN
el relicario

lodger NOUN
el inquilino
la inquilina

loft NOUN
el desván (PL los desvanes)

log NOUN
el leño

logical ADJECTIVE
lógico (FEM lógica)

to **log in** VERB
entrar en el sistema

to **log off** VERB
salir* del sistema

to **log on** VERB
entrar en el sistema

to **log out** VERB
salir* del sistema

lollipop NOUN
el pirulí (PL los pirulís)

lolly NOUN
■ **ice lolly** el polo (la paleta helada *Latin America*)

London NOUN
Londres *masc*

Londoner NOUN
el/la londinense

loneliness NOUN
la soledad

lonely ADJECTIVE
solo (FEM sola)
◻ I sometimes feel lonely. A veces me siento solo.
■ **a lonely cottage** una casita aislada

long ADJECTIVE, ADVERB
▷ *see also* **long** VERB
largo (FEM larga)
◻ She's got long hair. Tiene el pelo largo.
◻ The room is six metres long. La habitación tiene seis metros de largo.
■ **a long time** mucho tiempo ◻ It takes a long time. Lleva mucho tiempo. ◻ I've been waiting a long time. Llevo esperando mucho tiempo.
■ **How long?** *(time)* ¿Cuánto tiempo?
◻ How long have you been here? ¿Cuánto tiempo llevas aquí? ◻ How long will it take? ¿Cuánto tiempo llevará?
■ **How long is the flight?** ¿Cuánto dura el vuelo?
■ **as long as** siempre que

LANGUAGE TIP **siempre que** has to be followed by a verb in the subjunctive.

◻ I'll come as long as it's not too expensive. Iré siempre que no sea demasiado caro.

to **long** VERB
▷ *see also* **long** ADJECTIVE
■ **to long to do something** estar deseando hacer algo

long-distance ADJECTIVE
■ **a long-distance call** una llamada de larga distancia

longer ADVERB
▷ *see also* **long** ADJECTIVE
■ **They're no longer going out together.** Ya no salen juntos.
■ **I can't stand it any longer.** Ya no lo aguanto más.

long jump NOUN
el salto de longitud

loo NOUN
el wáter (el baño *Latin America*)

look NOUN
▷ *see also* **look** VERB
■ **Have a look at this!** ¡Echale una ojeada a esto!
■ **I don't like the look of it.** No me gusta nada.

to **look** VERB
▷ *see also* **look** NOUN
1 mirar
◻ Look! ¡Mira!
■ **to look at something** mirar algo ◻ Look at the picture. Mira la foto.
■ **Look out!** ¡Cuidado!
2 parecer*
◻ She looks surprised. Parece sorprendida.
■ **That cake looks nice.** Ese pastel tiene

English-Spanish

l

buena pinta.
■ **to look like somebody** parecerse a alguien □ He looks like his brother. Se parece a su hermano.
■ **What does she look like?** ¿Cómo es físicamente?

to **look after** VERB
cuidar
□ I look after my little sister. Cuido a mi hermana pequeña.

to **look for** VERB
buscar*
□ I'm looking for my passport. Estoy buscando mi pasaporte.

to **look forward to** VERB
tener* muchas ganas de
□ to look forward to doing something tener muchas ganas de hacer algo □ I'm looking forward to meeting you. Tengo muchas ganas de conocerte.
■ **I'm really looking forward to the holidays.** Estoy deseando que lleguen las vacaciones.
■ **Looking forward to hearing from you...** A la espera de sus noticias...

to **look round** VERB
1 volverse*
□ I called him and he looked round. Lo llamé y se volvió.
2 mirar
□ I'm just looking round. Sólo estoy mirando.
■ **to look round an exhibition** visitar una exposición
■ **I like looking round the shops.** Me gusta ir a ver tiendas.

to **look up** VERB
buscar*
□ If you don't know a word, look it up in the dictionary. Si no conoces una palabra, búscala en el diccionario.

loose ADJECTIVE
holgado (FEM holgada)
□ a loose shirt una camisa holgada
■ **a loose screw** un tornillo flojo
■ **loose change** dinero suelto

lord NOUN
el señor *(feudal)*
■ **the House of Lords** la Cámara de los Lores
■ **the Lord** *(God)* el Señor
■ **Good Lord!** ¡Dios mío!

lorry NOUN
el camión (PL los camiones)

lorry driver NOUN
el camionero
la camionera
□ He's a lorry driver. Es camionero.

to **lose** VERB
perder*
□ I've lost my purse. He perdido el monedero.
■ **to get lost** perderse □ I was afraid of getting lost. Tenía miedo de perderme.

loss NOUN
la pérdida

lost VERB ▷ *see* **lose**

lost ADJECTIVE
perdido (FEM perdida)

lost-and-found NOUN (US)
la oficina de objetos perdidos

lost property office NOUN
la oficina de objetos perdidos

lot NOUN
■ **a lot** mucho □ She talks a lot. Habla mucho. □ Do you like football? — Not a lot. ¿Te gusta el fútbol? — No mucho.
■ **a lot of** mucho □ I drink a lot of coffee. Bebo mucho café. □ We saw a lot of interesting things. Vimos muchas cosas interesantes. □ He's got lots of friends. Tiene muchos amigos. □ She's got lots of self-confidence. Tiene mucha confianza en sí misma.
■ **That's the lot.** Eso es todo.

lottery NOUN
la lotería
□ to win the lottery ganar la lotería

loud ADJECTIVE
fuerte (FEM fuerte)
□ The television is too loud. La televisión está muy fuerte.

loudly ADVERB
fuerte

loudspeaker NOUN
el altavoz (PL los altavoces)

lounge NOUN
la sala de estar

lousy ADJECTIVE
asqueroso (FEM asquerosa) *(informal)*
□ It was a lousy meal. Fue una comida asquerosa.
■ **I feel lousy.** Me siento fatal.

love NOUN
▷ *see also* **love** VERB
el amor
■ **to be in love** estar enamorado □ She's in love with Paul. Está enamorada de Paul.
■ **to make love** hacer el amor
■ **Give Gloria my love.** Dale recuerdos a Gloria de mi parte.
■ **Love, Rosemary.** Un abrazo, Rosemary.

to **love** VERB
▷ *see also* **love** NOUN
querer*
□ Everybody loves her. Todos la quieren.

□ I love you. Te quiero.
■ **I love chocolate.** Me encanta el chocolate.
■ **Would you like to come? — Yes, I'd love to.** ¿Te gustaría venir? — Sí, me encantaría.

lovely ADJECTIVE
1 encantador (FEM encantadora) *(person)*
□ She's a lovely person. Es una persona encantadora.
2 precioso (FEM preciosa)
□ They've got a lovely house. Tienen una casa preciosa.
■ **What a lovely surprise!** ¡Qué sorpresa tan agradable!
■ **It's a lovely day.** Hace un tiempo estupendo.
■ **Is your meal okay? — Yes, it's lovely.** ¿Está bueno? — Sí, buenísimo.
■ **Have a lovely time!** ¡Que lo paséis bien!

lover NOUN
el/la amante

low ADJECTIVE, ADVERB
bajo (FEM baja)
□ low prices los bajos precios □ That plane is flying very low. Ese avión vuela muy bajo.
□ in the low season en temporada baja

to **lower** VERB
▷ *see also* **lower** ADJECTIVE
bajar
□ He was so tall that the dentist had to lower the chair. Era tan alto que el dentista tuvo que bajar la silla.

lower ADJECTIVE
▷ *see also* **lower** VERB
inferior (FEM inferior)

low-fat ADJECTIVE
1 de bajo contenido graso *(margarine, cheese)*
2 desnatado (FEM desnatada) *(milk, yoghurt)*

loyalty NOUN
la lealtad

loyalty card NOUN
la tarjeta de cliente

luck NOUN
la suerte
□ She hasn't had much luck. No ha tenido mucha suerte.
■ **Bad luck!** ¡Mala suerte!
■ **Good luck!** ¡Suerte!

luckily ADVERB
afortunadamente

lucky ADJECTIVE
afortunado (FEM afortunada)
□ I consider myself lucky. Me considero afortunado.
■ **to be lucky** *(fortunate)* tener suerte
□ He's lucky, he's got a job. Tiene suerte de tener trabajo.
■ **That was lucky!** ¡Qué suerte!
■ **Black cats are lucky in Britain.** En Gran Bretaña los gatos negros traen buena suerte.
■ **a lucky horseshoe** una herradura de la suerte

luggage NOUN
el equipaje

lukewarm ADJECTIVE
tibio (FEM tibia)

lump NOUN
1 el trozo
□ a lump of butter un trozo de mantequilla
2 el chichón (PL los chichones) *(swelling)*
□ He's got a lump on his forehead. Tiene un chichón en la frente.

lunatic NOUN
el loco
la loca
□ He's an absolute lunatic. Está loco perdido.

lunch NOUN
el almuerzo
■ **to have lunch** almorzar □ We have lunch at half past twelve. Almorzamos a las doce y media.

luncheon voucher NOUN
el tíquet restaurante (PL los tíquets restaurante)

lung NOUN
el pulmón (PL los pulmones)
□ lung cancer el cáncer de pulmón

luscious ADJECTIVE
exquisito (FEM exquisita)

lush ADJECTIVE
exuberante (FEM exuberante)

lust NOUN
la lujuria

Luxembourg NOUN
Luxemburgo *masc*

luxurious ADJECTIVE
lujoso (FEM lujosa)

luxury NOUN
el lujo
□ It was luxury! ¡Era un lujo! □ a luxury hotel un hotel de lujo

lying VERB ▷ *see* **lie**

lyrics PL NOUN
la letra

Mm

mac NOUN
el impermeable
macaroni NOUN
los macarrones
machine NOUN
la máquina
□ It's a complicated machine. Es una máquina complicada.
■ **I put my clothes in the machine.** Puse mi ropa en la lavadora.
machine gun NOUN
la ametralladora
machinery NOUN
la maquinaria
mackerel NOUN
la caballa
mad ADJECTIVE
1 loco (FEM loca)
□ You're mad! ¡Estás loco! □ Have you gone mad? ¿Te has vuelto loco?
2 furioso (FEM furiosa)
□ She'll be mad when she finds out. Se pondrá furiosa cuando se entere.
■ **He's mad about football.** Está loco por el fútbol.
■ **She's mad about horses.** Le encantan los caballos.
madam NOUN
la señora
□ How may I help you, Madam? ¿Qué desea la señora?
made VERB ▷ *see* **make**
madly ADVERB
■ **They're madly in love.** Están locamente enamorados.
madman NOUN
el loco
madness NOUN
la locura
□ It's absolute madness. Es una locura.
magazine NOUN
la revista
magic NOUN
▷ *see also* **magic** ADJECTIVE
la magia
□ My hobby is magic. Mi hobby es la magia.
magic ADJECTIVE
▷ *see also* **magic** NOUN
mágico (FEM mágica)
□ a magic wand una varita mágica
■ **It was magic!** *(brilliant)* ¡Fue fantástico!
magician NOUN
el mago
la maga
□ There was a magician at the party. Había un mago en la fiesta.
magnet NOUN
el imán (PL los imanes)
magnificent ADJECTIVE
espléndido (FEM espléndida)
□ a magnificent view una vista espléndida
■ **It was a magnificent effort on their part.** Fue un esfuerzo extraordinario por su parte.
magnifying glass NOUN
la lupa
maid NOUN
1 la sirvienta *(servant)*
2 la camarera *(in hotel)*
■ **an old maid** *(spinster)* una solterona
maiden name NOUN
el apellido de soltera

DID YOU KNOW...?
When women marry in Spain they don't usually take the name of their husband but keep their own instead. If the couple have children they take both their father's and mother's surnames.

mail NOUN
1 el correo
■ **by mail** por correo
2 la correspondencia *(letters)*
□ We receive a lot of mail. Recibimos mucha correspondencia.
mailbox NOUN (US)
el buzón (PL los buzones)
mailing list NOUN
la lista de correo
mailman NOUN (US)
el cartero
main ADJECTIVE

principal (FEM principal)
□ the main suspect el principal sospechoso
■ **The main thing is to get it finished.** Lo principal es terminarlo.

mainly ADVERB
principalmente

main road NOUN
la carretera principal

to **maintain** VERB
mantener*
□ Teachers try hard to maintain standards. Los maestros se esfuerzan por mantener el nivel educativo. □ Old houses are expensive to maintain. Las casas viejas son costosas de mantener.

maintenance NOUN
1 el mantenimiento
□ car maintenance el mantenimiento del coche
2 la pensión alimenticia
□ £30 a week in maintenance 30 libras esterlinas a la semana en concepto de pensión alimenticia

maize NOUN
el maíz

majesty NOUN
la majestad
■ **Your Majesty** su Majestad

major ADJECTIVE
muy importante (FEM muy importante)
□ a major factor un factor muy importante
■ **Drugs are a major problem.** La droga es un grave problema.
■ **in C major** en do mayor

Majorca NOUN
Mallorca *fem*

majority NOUN
la mayoría

make NOUN
▹ *see also* **make** VERB
la marca
□ What make is it? ¿De qué marca es?

to **make** VERB
▹ *see also* **make** NOUN
1 hacer*
□ I'm going to make a cake. Voy a hacer un pastel. □ I'd like to make a phone call. Quisiera hacer una llamada. □ I make my bed every morning. Me hago la cama cada mañana. □ It's well made. Está bien hecho.
■ **She's making lunch.** Está preparando el almuerzo.
■ **Two and two make four.** Dos y dos son cuatro.
2 fabricar*
□ 'made in Spain' 'fabricado en España'
3 ganar
□ He makes a lot of money. Gana mucho dinero.
■ **to make somebody do something** hacer a alguien hacer algo □ My mother makes me eat vegetables. Mi madre me hace comer verduras.
■ **You'll have to make do with a cheaper car.** Tendrás que conformarte con un coche más barato.
■ **What time do you make it?** ¿Qué hora tienes?

to **make out** VERB
1 descifrar
□ I can't make out the address on the label. No consigo descifrar la dirección que viene en la etiqueta.
2 dar* a entender
□ They're making out it was my fault. Están dando a entender que fue culpa mía.
■ **to make a cheque out to somebody** hacer un cheque a favor de alguien

to **make up** VERB
1 componer*
□ Women make up thirty per cent of the police force. Las mujeres componen el treinta por ciento del cuerpo de policía.
2 inventarse
□ He made up the whole story. Se inventó toda la historia.
3 hacer* las paces
□ They had a quarrel, but soon made up. Riñeron, pero poco después hicieron las paces.
4 maquillarse
□ She spends hours making herself up. Pasa horas maquillándose.

maker NOUN
el/la fabricante
□ Spain's biggest car maker el mayor fabricante de automóviles de España

make-up NOUN
el maquillaje
■ **She put on her make-up.** Se maquilló.

male ADJECTIVE
▹ *see also* **male** NOUN
1 macho *(animal, plant)*
□ a male kitten un gatito macho
2 varón (PL varones) *(person)*
□ Sex: Male Sexo: Varón
■ **Most football players are male.** La mayoría de los futbolistas son hombres.
■ **a male nurse** un enfermero
■ **a male chauvinist** un machista

male NOUN
▹ *see also* **male** ADJECTIVE
el macho *(animal)*

mall NOUN
el centro comercial

mammoth ADJECTIVE

English-Spanish

m

colosal (FEM colosal) *(project, building)*
■ **a mammoth task** una obra de titanes

man NOUN
el hombre

to **manage** VERB
1 arreglárselas
□ We haven't got much money, but we manage. No tenemos mucho dinero, pero nos las arreglamos.
2 dirigir*
□ She manages a big store. Dirige una tienda grande. □ He manages our football team. Dirige nuestro equipo de fútbol.
■ **to manage to do something** conseguir hacer algo □ Luckily I managed to pass the exam. Por suerte, conseguí aprobar el examen.
■ **Can you manage a bit more?** *(food)* ¿Te pongo un poco más?
■ **Can you manage with that suitcase?** ¿Puedes con la maleta?

manageable ADJECTIVE
factible (FEM factible) *(task, goal)*

management NOUN
la dirección
□ He's responsible for the management of the project. Es responsable de la dirección del proyecto. □ management and workers la dirección y los trabajadores

manager NOUN
1 el director
la directora *(of company, department, performer)*
□ I complained to the manager. Fui a reclamar al director.
2 el/la gerente *(of restaurant, store)*
3 el entrenador
la entrenadora *(of team)*
□ the England manager el entrenador de la selección inglesa

manageress NOUN
la gerente *(of restaurant, store)*

mandarin NOUN
la mandarina

mango NOUN
el mango

maniac NOUN
el maníaco
la maníaca
■ **He drives like a maniac.** Conduce como un loco.

to **manipulate** VERB
manipular

man-made ADJECTIVE
sintético (FEM sintética) *(fibre)*

manner NOUN
la manera
□ She was behaving in an odd manner. Se comportaba de una manera extraña.
■ **He has a confident manner.** Se muestra seguro de sí mismo.

manners PL NOUN
los modales
□ Her manners are appalling. Tiene muy malos modales.
■ **good manners** la buena educación
■ **It's bad manners to speak with your mouth full.** Es de mala educación hablar con la boca llena.

manpower NOUN
la mano de obra

LANGUAGE TIP Although **mano** ends in **-o**, **mano de obra** is actually a feminine noun.

mansion NOUN
la mansión (PL las mansiones)

mantelpiece NOUN
la repisa de la chimenea

manual NOUN
el manual

to **manufacture** VERB
fabricar*

manufacturer NOUN
el/la fabricante

manure NOUN
el estiércol

manuscript NOUN
el manuscrito

many ADJECTIVE, PRONOUN
muchos (FEM muchas)
□ He hasn't got many friends. No tiene muchos amigos. □ Were there many people at the concert? — Not many. ¿Había mucha gente en el concierto? — No mucha.
■ **very many** muchos (FEM muchas)
□ I haven't got very many CDs. No tengo muchos CDs.
■ **how many?** ¿cuántos? (FEM ¿cuántas?)
□ How many hours a week do you work? ¿Cuántas horas trabajas a la semana?
■ **too many** demasiados (FEM demasiadas)
□ Sixteen people? That's too many. ¿Dieciséis personas? Son demasiadas.
■ **so many** tantos (FEM tantas)
□ He told so many lies! ¡Dijo tantas mentiras!

map NOUN
1 el mapa *(of country, region)*

LANGUAGE TIP Although **mapa** ends in **-a**, it is actually a masculine noun.

2 el plano *(of town, city)*

marathon NOUN
el maratón (PL los maratones)

marble NOUN
el mármol

□ a marble statue una estatua de mármol
■ **a marble** una canica

March NOUN
marzo *masc*
□ in March en marzo □ on 9 March el 9 de marzo

to **march** VERB
▷ *see also* **march** NOUN
desfilar
□ The troops marched past the King. Las tropas desfilaron delante del Rey.

march NOUN
▷ *see also* **march** VERB
la marcha
□ a peace march una marcha por la paz

mare NOUN
la yegua

margarine NOUN
la margarina

margin NOUN
el margen (PL los márgenes)
□ She wrote a note in the margin. Escribió una nota al margen.

marijuana NOUN
la marihuana

marital status NOUN
el estado civil

mark NOUN
▷ *see also* **mark** VERB
1 la nota
□ I get good marks for French. Saco buenas notas en francés.
2 la mancha
□ There were red marks all over his back. Tenía manchas rojas por toda la espalda.
□ You've got a mark on your shirt. Tienes una mancha en la camisa.
3 el marco *(former German currency)*
□ 30 million marks 30 millones de marcos

to **mark** VERB
▷ *see also* **mark** NOUN
1 corregir*
□ The teacher hasn't marked my homework yet. El maestro no me ha corregido los deberes todavía.
2 señalar
□ Mark its position on the map. Señala su posición en el mapa.

market NOUN
el mercado

marketing NOUN
el márketing

marmalade NOUN
la mermelada de naranja

maroon ADJECTIVE
granate (FEM + PL granate)

marriage NOUN
el matrimonio

married ADJECTIVE
casado (FEM casada)
□ They are not married. No están casados.
■ **a married couple** un matrimonio
■ **to get married** casarse

marrow NOUN
el calabacín grande (PL los calabacines grandes) *(vegetable)*
■ **bone marrow** la médula

to **marry** VERB
1 casarse
□ They married in June. Se casaron en junio.
2 casarse con
□ He wants to marry her. Quiere casarse con ella.
■ **to get married** casarse □ My brother's getting married in March. Mi hermano se casa en marzo.

marvellous (US **marvelous**) ADJECTIVE
estupendo (FEM estupenda)
□ The weather was marvellous. Hacía un tiempo estupendo. □ That's a marvellous idea! ¡Es una idea estupenda!

marzipan NOUN
el mazapán

mascara NOUN
el rímel

masculine ADJECTIVE
masculino (FEM masculina)

mashed potatoes PL NOUN
el puré de patatas (el puré de papas *Latin America*)

mask NOUN
la máscara

masked ADJECTIVE
encapuchado (FEM encapuchada) *(terrorist, attacker)*

mass NOUN
1 el montón (PL los montones)
□ a mass of books and papers un montón de libros y papeles
2 la misa
□ We go to mass on Sunday. Vamos a misa los domingos.
■ **the mass media** los medios de comunicación de masas

massage NOUN
el masaje

massive ADJECTIVE
enorme (FEM enorme)

to **master** VERB
dominar
□ Students need to master a second language. Los estudiantes tienen que dominar un segundo idioma.

masterpiece NOUN
la obra maestra (PL las obras maestras)

mat NOUN
el felpudo *(doormat)*
■ **a table mat** un mantel individual

match NOUN
▷ *see also* **match** VERB
1 el partido
□ a football match un partido de fútbol
2 la cerilla
□ a box of matches una caja de cerillas

to **match** VERB
▷ *see also* **match** NOUN
1 hacer* juego con
□ The jacket matches the trousers. La chaqueta hace juego con los pantalones.
2 hacer* juego
□ These colours don't match. Estos colores no hacen juego.

matching ADJECTIVE
a juego
□ My bedroom has matching wallpaper and curtains. Mi habitación tiene el papel y las cortinas a juego.

mate NOUN
el amigo
la amiga
□ He always goes on holiday with his mates. Siempre va de vacaciones con sus amigos.

material NOUN
1 el tejido
□ The curtains are made of a thin material. Las cortinas están hechas de un tejido fino.
2 el material
□ I'm collecting material for my project. Estoy recogiendo material para mi proyecto.

mathematics NOUN
las matemáticas

maths NOUN
las matemáticas

matron NOUN
la enfermera jefe *(in hospital)*

matter NOUN
▷ *see also* **matter** VERB
el asunto
□ It's a matter of life and death. Es un asunto de vida o muerte.
■ **What's the matter?** ¿Qué pasa?
■ **as a matter of fact** de hecho

to **matter** VERB
▷ *see also* **matter** NOUN
importar
□ I can't give you the money today. — It doesn't matter. No te puedo dar el dinero hoy. — No importa.
■ **Shall I phone today or tomorrow? — Whenever, it doesn't matter.** ¿Telefoneo hoy o mañana? — Cuando quieras, da igual.
■ **It matters a lot to me.** Significa mucho para mí.

mattress NOUN
el colchón (PL los colchones)

mature ADJECTIVE
maduro (FEM madura)

maximum NOUN
▷ *see also* **maximum** ADJECTIVE
el máximo
□ a maximum of two years in prison un máximo de dos años de cárcel

maximum ADJECTIVE
▷ *see also* **maximum** NOUN
máximo (FEM máxima)
□ The maximum speed is 100 km/h. La velocidad máxima permitida es 100km/h.

May NOUN
mayo *masc*
□ in May en mayo □ on 7 May el 7 de mayo
■ **May Day** el Primero de Mayo

may VERB
poder*
□ The police may come and catch us here. La policía puede venir y pillarnos aquí.
□ May I smoke? ¿Puedo fumar?

LANGUAGE TIP **Puede que** has to be followed by a verb in the subjunctive.

□ I may go. Puede que vaya. □ It may rain. Puede que llueva.

LANGUAGE TIP **A lo mejor** can also be used but it is a more colloquial alternative.

□ Are you going to the party? — I don't know, I may. ¿Vas a ir a la fiesta? — No sé, a lo mejor.

maybe ADVERB
a lo mejor
□ Maybe she's at home. A lo mejor está en casa. □ Maybe he'll change his mind. A lo mejor cambia de idea.

mayonnaise NOUN
la mayonesa

mayor NOUN
el alcalde
la alcaldesa

maze NOUN
el laberinto

me PRONOUN

LANGUAGE TIP Use **me** to translate 'me' when it is the direct object of the verb in the sentence, or when it means 'to me'.

me
□ Look at me! ¡Mírame! □ Could you lend me your pen? ¿Me prestas tu bolígrafo?

LANGUAGE TIP Use **yo** after the verb 'to be' and in comparisons.

□ It's me. Soy yo. □ He's older than me. Es mayor que yo.

LANGUAGE TIP Use **mí** after prepositions.

□ without me sin mí

LANGUAGE TIP Remember that 'with me' translates as **conmigo**.

□ He was with me. Estaba conmigo.

meal NOUN
la comida
■ **Enjoy your meal!** ¡Que aproveche!

mealtime NOUN
■ **at mealtimes** a las horas de comer

to mean VERB
▷ *see also* **mean** ADJECTIVE
1 significar*
□ What does 'alcalde' mean? ¿Qué significa 'alcalde'? □ I don't know what it means. No sé lo que significa.
2 querer* decir
□ That's not what I meant. Eso no es lo que quería decir.
3 referirse* a
□ Which one did he mean? ¿A cuál se refería? □ Do you mean me? ¿Te refieres a mí?
■ **to mean to do something** querer hacer algo □ I didn't mean to hurt you. No quería hacerte daño.
■ **Do you really mean it?** ¿Lo dices en serio?
■ **He means what he says.** Habla en serio.

mean ADJECTIVE
▷ *see also* **mean** VERB
1 tacaño (FEM tacaña)
□ He's too mean to buy presents. Es demasiado tacaño para comprar regalos.
2 mezquino (FEM mezquina)
□ You're being mean to me. Estás siendo mezquino conmigo.
■ **That's a really mean thing to say!** ¡Parece mentira que digas eso!

meaning NOUN
el significado

means NOUN
el medio
□ a means of transport un medio de transporte □ He'll do it by any possible means. Lo hará por todos los medios.
■ **by means of** por medio de □ They identified him by means of a photograph. Lo identificaron por medio de una clave.
■ **Can I come in? — By all means!** ¿Puedo entrar? — ¡Claro que sí!

meant VERB ▷ *see* **mean**

meanwhile ADVERB
mientras tanto

measles NOUN
el sarampión
□ I've got measles. Tengo el sarampión.

to measure VERB
medir*

meat NOUN
la carne

Mecca NOUN
La Meca

mechanic NOUN
el mecánico
la mecánica
□ He's a mechanic. Es mecánico.

mechanical ADJECTIVE
mecánico (FEM mecánica)

medal NOUN
la medalla

media PL NOUN
■ **the media** los medios de comunicación

median strip NOUN (US)
la mediana

medical ADJECTIVE
▷ *see also* **medical** NOUN
médico (FEM médica)
□ medical treatment el tratamiento médico
■ **medical insurance** el seguro médico
■ **to have medical problems** tener problemas de salud
■ **She's a medical student.** Es una estudiante de medicina.

medical NOUN
▷ *see also* **medical** ADJECTIVE
■ **He had a medical last week.** Se hizo un chequeo la semana pasada.

medicine NOUN
1 la medicina *(science)*
□ I want to study medicine. Quiero estudiar medicina.
■ **alternative medicine** la medicina alternativa
2 el medicamento *(medication)*
□ I need some medicine. Necesito un medicamento.

Mediterranean ADJECTIVE
▷ *see also* **Mediterranean** NOUN
mediterráneo (FEM mediterránea)

Mediterranean NOUN
▷ *see also* **Mediterranean** ADJECTIVE
■ **the Mediterranean** el Mediterráneo

medium ADJECTIVE
mediano (FEM mediana)
□ a man of medium height un hombre de estatura mediana

medium-sized ADJECTIVE
■ **a medium-sized town** una ciudad de tamaño mediano

to meet VERB
1 encontrarse* con *(by chance)*
□ I met Paul in town. Me encontré con Paul en el centro.
■ **We met by chance in the supermarket.**

Nos encontramos por casualidad en el supermercado.
2 reunirse* *(by arrangement)*
□ The committee met at two o'clock. El comité se reunió a las dos.
■ **Where shall we meet?** ¿Dónde quedamos?
■ **I'm going to meet my friends at the swimming pool.** He quedado con mis amigos en la piscina.
■ **I'll meet you at the station.** Te voy a buscar a la estación.
3 conocer* *(get to know)*
□ He met Tim at a party. Conoció a Tim en una fiesta.
■ **Have you met her before?** ¿La conoces?

meeting NOUN
1 el encuentro *(socially)*
□ their first meeting su primer encuentro
2 la reunión (PL las reuniones) *(for work)*
□ a business meeting una reunión de trabajo

mega ADJECTIVE
■ **He's mega rich.** *(informal)* Es super rico.

melody NOUN
la melodía

melon NOUN
el melón (PL los melones)

to **melt** VERB
1 derretir*
□ Melt 100 grams of butter in a saucepan. Derrita 100 gramos de mantequilla en una sartén.
2 derretirse*
□ The snow is melting. La nieve se está derritiendo.

member NOUN
el/la miembro
■ **'members only'** 'reservado para los socios'
■ **a Member of Parliament** un diputado (FEM una diputada)

membership NOUN
la afiliación (PL las afiliaciones) *(of party, union)*
■ **I'm going to apply for membership of the club.** Voy a solicitar el ingreso al club.

membership card NOUN
el carnet de socio (PL los carnets de socio)

memento NOUN
el recuerdo

memorial NOUN
memorial

to **memorize** VERB
memorizar*

memory NOUN
1 la memoria *(also for computer)*
□ I've got a terrible memory. Tengo una memoria espantosa.
2 el recuerdo
□ happy memories los recuerdos felices

men PL NOUN ▷ *see* **man**

to **mend** VERB
arreglar

meningitis NOUN
la meningitis
□ Her daughter's got meningitis. Su hija tiene meningitis.

mental ADJECTIVE
mental (FEM mental)
□ mental illness la enfermedad mental
■ **mental hospital** el hospital psiquiátrico

to **mention** VERB
mencionar
□ He didn't mention it to me. No me lo mencionó.
■ **I mentioned she might come later.** Dije que a lo mejor vendría más tarde.
■ **Thank you! — Don't mention it!** ¡Gracias! — ¡No hay de qué!

menu NOUN
1 la carta
□ Could I have the menu please? ¿Me trae la carta por favor?
2 el menú (PL los menús) *(on computer)*

merchant NOUN
el/la comerciante
■ **a wine merchant** un vinatero

mercy NOUN
la compasión

mere ADJECTIVE
■ **a mere five percent** sólo un cinco por ciento
■ **It's a mere formality.** No es más que una formalidad.

meringue NOUN
el merengue

merry ADJECTIVE
■ **Merry Christmas!** ¡Feliz Navidad!

merry-go-round NOUN
el tiovivo

mess NOUN
el desorden
■ **My hair's a mess today.** Hoy tengo el pelo hecho un desastre.
■ **I'll be in a mess if I fail the exam.** Voy a tener problemas si suspendo el examen.

to **mess about** VERB
■ **Yesterday I just messed about with some friends.** Ayer estuve sin hacer nada con unos amigos.
■ **Stop messing about with my computer!** ¡Deja de toquetear mi ordenador!

message NOUN
el mensaje
□ a secret message un mensaje secreto
■ **Would you like to leave him a message?**

¿Quiere dejarle un recado?

to **mess up** VERB
estropear
□ You've messed up my CDs! ¡Me has estropeado los CDs!
■ **I messed up my chemistry exam.** Metí la pata en el examen de química.

messenger NOUN
el mensajero
la mensajera

messy ADJECTIVE
desordenado (FEM desordenada)
□ Your room is really messy. Tu habitación está muy desordenada. □ She's so messy! ¡Es más desordenada!
■ **a really messy job** un trabajo muy sucio
■ **Her writing is very messy.** Tiene muy mala letra.

met VERB ▷ *see* **meet**

metal NOUN
el metal

meter NOUN
1 el contador *(for gas, electricity)*
2 el taxímetro *(for taxi)*
3 el parquímetro *(parking meter)*
4 el metro (US: *unit of measurement)*

method NOUN
el método

Methodist NOUN
el/la metodista
□ He's a Methodist. Es metodista.

metre (US **meter**) NOUN
el metro

metric ADJECTIVE
métrico (FEM métrica)

Mexico NOUN
Méjico *masc*

to **miaow** VERB
maullar*

mice PL NOUN ▷ *see* **mouse**

microchip NOUN
el microchip (PL los microchips)

microphone NOUN
el micrófono

microscope NOUN
el microscopio

microwave NOUN
el microondas (PL los microondas)

mid ADJECTIVE
■ **in mid May** a mediados de mayo
■ **He's in his mid twenties.** Tiene unos veinticinco años.

midday NOUN
el mediodía
□ at midday al mediodía

middle NOUN
▷ *see also* **middle** ADJECTIVE
el medio
□ The car was in the middle of the road. El coche estaba en medio de la carretera.
■ **in the middle of May** a mediados de mayo
■ **She was in the middle of her exams.** Estaba en plenos exámenes.

middle ADJECTIVE
▷ *see also* **middle** NOUN
del medio
□ the middle seat el asiento del medio

middle-aged ADJECTIVE
de mediana edad

Middle Ages PL NOUN
■ **the Middle Ages** la Edad Media

middle-class ADJECTIVE
de clase media

Middle East NOUN
■ **the Middle East** el Oriente Medio

middle name NOUN
el segundo nombre

midge NOUN
el mosquito

midnight NOUN
la medianoche
□ at midnight a medianoche

midwife NOUN
la comadrona
□ She's a midwife. Es comadrona.

might VERB
poder*
□ The teacher might come at any moment. El profesor podría venir en cualquier momento.

LANGUAGE TIP **Puede que** has to be followed by a verb in the subjunctive.

□ He might come later. Puede que venga más tarde. □ She might not have understood. Puede que no haya entendido.

LANGUAGE TIP **A lo mejor** can also be used but it is a more colloquial alternative.

□ We might go to Spain next year. A lo mejor vamos a España el año que viene.

migraine NOUN
la jaqueca
□ I've got a migraine. Tengo jaqueca.

mike NOUN
el micro

mild ADJECTIVE
suave (FEM suave)
□ a mild flavour un sabor suave □ The winters are quite mild. Los inviernos son bastante suaves. □ mild soap el jabón suave

mile NOUN
la milla

DID YOU KNOW...?
In Spain distances are expressed in kilometres. A mile is about 1.6 kilometres.

□ It's five miles from here. Está a unas cinco millas de aquí. □ at 50 miles per hour a 50 millas por hora
■ **We walked for miles!** ¡Caminamos kilómetros y kilómetros!

military ADJECTIVE
militar (FEM militara)

milk NOUN
▷ *see also* **milk** VERB
la leche

to **milk** VERB
▷ *see also* **milk** NOUN
ordeñar

milk chocolate NOUN
el chocolate con leche

milkman NOUN
el lechero

DID YOU KNOW...?
In Spain milk is not delivered to people's homes.

milk shake NOUN
el batido

mill NOUN
el molino *(for grain)*

millennium NOUN
el milenio

millimetre (US **millimeter**) NOUN
el milímetro

million NOUN
el millón (PL los millones)
□ two million pounds dos millones de libras esterlinas

millionaire NOUN
el millonario
la millonaria

to **mimic** VERB
imitar

mince NOUN
la carne picada (la carne molida *Latin America*)

mince pie NOUN
la empanadilla rellena de fruta picada

to **mind** VERB
▷ *see also* **mind** NOUN
1 cuidar *(look after)*
□ Could you mind the baby this afternoon? ¿Podrías cuidar al niño esta tarde? □ Could you mind my bags for a few minutes? ¿Me cuidas las bolsas un momento?
2 importar *(matter)*
□ Do you mind if I open the window? — No, I don't mind. ¿Le importa que abra la ventana? — No, no me importa.
■ **I don't mind the noise.** No me molesta el ruido.
■ **Never mind!** **1** *(don't worry)* ¡No te preocupes! **2** *(it's not important)* ¡No importa!
■ **Mind you don't fall.** Ten cuidado, no te vayas a caer.
■ **Mind the step!** ¡Cuidado con el escalón!

mind NOUN
▷ *see also* **mind** VERB
la mente
□ What have you got in mind? ¿Qué tienes en mente?
■ **I haven't made up my mind yet.** No me he decidido todavía.
■ **He's changed his mind.** Ha cambiado de idea.
■ **Are you out of your mind?** ¿Estás loco?

mine PRONOUN
▷ *see also* **mine** NOUN
1 el mío *masc* (PL los míos)
□ Is this your coat? — No, mine is black. ¿Es éste tu abrigo? — No, el mío es negro.
□ your parents and mine tus padres y los míos
2 la mía *fem* (PL las mías)
□ Is this your scarf? — No, mine is red. ¿Es ésta tu bufanda? — No, la mía es roja.
□ her sisters and mine sus hermanas y las mías
3 mío *masc* (PL míos)
□ That car is mine. Ese coche es mío.
4 mía *fem* (PL mías)
□ Sorry, that beer is mine. Disculpa, esa cerveza es mía. □ Isabel is a friend of mine. Isabel es amiga mía.

mine NOUN
▷ *see also* **mine** PRONOUN
la mina
□ a coal mine una mina de carbón □ a land mine una mina

miner NOUN
el minero
la minera
□ My father was a miner. Mi padre era minero.

mineral water NOUN
el agua mineral *fem*

LANGUAGE TIP Although it's a feminine noun, remember that you use **el** and **un** with **agua mineral**.

miniature ADJECTIVE
en miniatura

minibus NOUN
el microbús (PL los microbuses)

minicab NOUN
el taxi

Minidisc® NOUN
el minidisco

minimum NOUN
▷ *see also* **minimum** ADJECTIVE
el mínimo

minimum ADJECTIVE
▷ *see also* **minimum** NOUN
mínimo (FEM mínima)

□ The minimum age for driving is 17. La edad mínima para poder conducir es 17 años. □ minimum wage salario mínimo

miniskirt NOUN
la minifalda

minister NOUN
1 el ministro
la ministra
□ the Minister for Education el Ministro de Educación
2 el pastor
la pastora *(of church)*

ministry NOUN
el ministerio *(in politics)*

minor ADJECTIVE
secundario (FEM secundaria)
□ a minor problem un problema secundario
■ **a minor operation** una operación de poca importancia
■ **in D minor** en re menor

minority NOUN
la minoría

mint NOUN
1 el caramelo de menta *(sweet)*
2 la menta *(plant)*
□ mint sauce salsa de menta

minus PREPOSITION
menos
□ sixteen minus three dieciséis menos tres
■ **I got a B minus for my French.** Me pusieron un notable bajo en francés.
■ **minus two degrees** dos grados bajo cero

minute NOUN
▷ *see also* **minute** ADJECTIVE
el minuto
□ Wait a minute! ¡Espera un minuto!

minute ADJECTIVE
▷ *see also* **minute** NOUN
minúsculo (FEM minúscula)
□ Her flat is minute. Su apartamento es minúsculo.

miracle NOUN
el milagro

mirror NOUN
1 el espejo
□ She looked at herself in the mirror. Se miró en el espejo.
2 el retrovisor
□ She got in the car and adjusted the mirror. Entró en el coche y ajustó el retrovisor.

to **misbehave** VERB
portarse mal

mischief NOUN
■ **She's always up to mischief.** Siempre está haciendo travesuras.
■ **full of mischief** travieso

mischievous ADJECTIVE
travieso (FEM traviesa)

miser NOUN
el avaro
la avara

miserable ADJECTIVE
infeliz (FEM infeliz, PL infelices)
□ a miserable life una vida infeliz
■ **I'm feeling miserable.** Me siento deprimido.
■ **miserable weather** un tiempo deprimente

misfortune NOUN
la desgracia

mishap NOUN
el contratiempo
□ without mishap sin contratiempos

to **misjudge** VERB
juzgar* mal
□ I may have misjudged him. A lo mejor lo juzgué mal.
■ **The driver misjudged the bend.** El conductor no calculó bien la curva.

to **mislay** VERB
■ **I've mislaid my glasses.** No sé dónde he puesto las gafas.

misleading ADJECTIVE
engañoso (FEM engañosa)

Miss NOUN
1 señorita *fem*
□ Miss Peters wants to see you. La señorita Peters quiere verte.
2 Srta. *(in address)*

to **miss** VERB
perder*
□ Hurry or you'll miss the bus. Date prisa o perderás el autobús.
■ **It's too good an opportunity to miss.** Es una oportunidad demasiado buena para dejarla pasar.
■ **He missed the target.** No dio en el blanco.
■ **I miss my family.** Echo de menos a mi familia.
■ **You've missed a page.** Te has saltado una página.

missing ADJECTIVE
perdido (FEM perdida)
□ the missing link el eslabón perdido
■ **to be missing** faltar □ Two members of the group are missing. Faltan dos miembros del grupo.
■ **a missing person** una persona desaparecida

missionary NOUN
el misionero
la misionera

mist NOUN
la neblina

mistake NOUN
▷ *see also* **mistake** VERB
el error

□ There must be some mistake. Debe de haber algún error.
■ **a spelling mistake** una falta de ortografía
■ **to make a mistake** **1** *(in speaking)* cometer un error □ He makes a lot of mistakes when he speaks English. Comete muchos errores cuando habla inglés. **2** *(get mixed up)* equivocarse □ I'm sorry, I made a mistake. Lo siento, me equivoqué.
■ **by mistake** por error

to **mistake** VERB
▷ *see also* **mistake** NOUN
confundir
□ He mistook me for my sister. Me confundió con mi hermana.

mistaken ADJECTIVE
■ **to be mistaken** estar equivocado □ If you think I'm going to pay, you're mistaken. Estás equivocado si piensas que voy a pagar.

mistletoe NOUN
el muérdago

mistook VERB ▷ *see* **mistake**

mistress NOUN
1 la maestra *(in primary school)*
2 la profesora *(in secondary school)*
□ our English mistress nuestra profesora de inglés
3 la amante
□ He's got a mistress. Tiene una amante.

misty ADJECTIVE
neblinoso (FEM neblinosa)
□ a misty morning una mañana neblinosa

to **misunderstand** VERB
entender* mal
□ Sorry, I misunderstood you. Lo siento, te entendí mal.

misunderstanding NOUN
el malentendido

misunderstood VERB ▷ *see* **misunderstand**

mix NOUN
▷ *see also* **mix** VERB
la mezcla
□ The film is a mix of science fiction and comedy. La película es una mezcla de ciencia ficción y comedia.
■ **a cake mix** un preparado para pastel

to **mix** VERB
▷ *see also* **mix** NOUN
mezclar
□ Mix the flour with the sugar. Mezcle la harina con el azúcar. □ He's mixing business with pleasure. Está mezclando los negocios con el placer.
■ **I like mixing with all sorts of people.** Me gusta tratar con todo tipo de gente.
■ **He doesn't mix much.** No se relaciona mucho.

to **mix up** VERB
confundir
□ He mixed up their names. Confundió sus nombres. □ The travel agent mixed up the bookings. La agencia de viajes confundió las reservas.
■ **I'm getting mixed up.** Me estoy confundiendo.

mixed ADJECTIVE
mixto (FEM mixta)
□ a mixed salad una ensalada mixta □ a mixed school un colegio mixto
■ **I've got mixed feelings about it.** No sé qué pensar de ello.

mixer NOUN
la batidora *(for food)*

mixture NOUN
la mezcla
□ a mixture of spices una mezcla de especias

mix-up NOUN
la confusión (PL las confusiones)

MMS ABBREVIATION (= *multimedia message service*)
el MMS

to **moan** VERB
quejarse
□ She's always moaning about something. Siempre se está quejando de algo.

mobile NOUN
el móvil *(phone)*

mobile home NOUN
la caravana fija (el trailer *Latin America*)

mobile phone NOUN
el móvil

to **mock** VERB
▷ *see also* **mock** ADJECTIVE
ridiculizar*

mock ADJECTIVE
▷ *see also* **mock** VERB
■ **a mock exam** un examen de práctica

mod cons PL NOUN
■ **with all mod cons** con todas las comodidades

model NOUN
▷ *see also* **model** ADJECTIVE
1 el modelo
□ His car is the latest model. Su coche es el último modelo.
2 la maqueta
□ a model of the castle una maqueta del castillo
3 el/la modelo
□ She's a famous model. Es una modelo famosa.

model ADJECTIVE
▷ *see also* **model** NOUN
■ **a model railway** una vía férrea en miniatura
■ **a model plane** una maqueta de avión

■ **He's a model pupil.** Es un alumno modelo.

modem NOUN
el módem (PL los módems)

moderate ADJECTIVE
moderado (FEM moderada)
□ His views are quite moderate. Tiene opiniones bastante moderadas.
■ **I do a moderate amount of exercise.** Hago un poco de gimnasia.

modern ADJECTIVE
moderno (FEM moderna)

to **modernize** VERB
modernizar*

modest ADJECTIVE
modesto (FEM modesta)

to **modify** VERB
modificar*

moist ADJECTIVE
húmedo (FEM húmeda)
□ Sow the seeds in moist compost. Plantar las semillas en abono húmedo.

moisture NOUN
la humedad

moisturizer NOUN
la crema hidratante

moldy ADJECTIVE (US)
mohoso (FEM mohosa)

mole NOUN
1 el lunar
□ I've got a mole on my back. Tengo un lunar en la espalda.
2 el topo *(animal)*

moment NOUN
el momento
□ Just a moment! ¡Un momento! □ at the moment en este momento □ any moment now de un momento a otro

monarch NOUN
el/la monarca

monarchy NOUN
la monarquía

monastery NOUN
el monasterio

Monday NOUN
el lunes (PL los lunes)
□ I saw her on Monday. La vi el lunes.
□ every Monday todos los lunes □ last Monday el lunes pasado □ next Monday el lunes que viene □ on Mondays los lunes

money NOUN
el dinero
□ I need to change some money. Tengo que cambiar dinero. □ to make money ganar dinero

mongrel NOUN
el perro mestizo
■ **My dog's a mongrel.** Mi perro es mestizo.

monitor NOUN
el monitor *(on computer)*

monk NOUN
el monje

monkey NOUN
el mono
la mona

monster NOUN
el monstruo

month NOUN
el mes
□ this month este mes □ next month el mes que viene □ last month el mes pasado
□ at the end of the month a fin de mes

monthly ADJECTIVE
mensual (FEM mensual)

monument NOUN
el monumento

mood NOUN
el humor
□ to be in a good mood estar de buen humor □ to be in a bad mood estar de mal humor

moody ADJECTIVE
malhumorado (FEM malhumorada) *(in a bad mood)*
■ **to be moody** *(temperamental)* tener un humor cambiante

moon NOUN
la luna
□ There's a full moon tonight. Esta noche hay luna llena.
■ **She's over the moon about it.** Está en el séptimo cielo de contenta.

moor NOUN
▷ *see also* **moor** VERB
el páramo

to **moor** VERB
▷ *see also* **moor** NOUN
amarrar

mop NOUN
la fregona (el trapeador *Latin America*)

moped NOUN
el ciclomotor

moral NOUN
la moraleja
□ The moral of the story is... La moraleja de la historia es...
■ **morals** la moral

morale NOUN
la moral
□ Morale was at an all-time low. La moral estaba más baja que nunca.

more ADJECTIVE, PRONOUN, ADVERB
más
□ It costs a lot more. Cuesta mucho más.
□ There isn't any more. Ya no hay más.
□ A bit more? ¿Un poco más? □ Is there any

more? ¿Hay más? □ It'll take a few more days. Llevará unos cuantos días más.

■ **more than** más que

LANGUAGE TIP Use **más que** when comparing two things or people and **más de** when talking about quantities.

□ He's more intelligent than me. Es más inteligente que yo. □ I spent more than £10. Yo gasté más de 10 libras esterlinas. □ more than 20 people más de 20 personas

■ **more or less** más o menos

■ **more than ever** más que nunca

■ **more and more** cada vez más

moreover ADVERB
además

morning NOUN
la mañana
□ in the morning por la mañana □ at 7 o'clock in the morning a las 7 de la mañana □ on Saturday morning el sábado por la mañana □ tomorrow morning mañana por la mañana

■ **the morning papers** los periódicos de la mañana

Morocco NOUN
Marruecos *masc*

mortgage NOUN
la hipoteca

Moscow NOUN
Moscú *masc*

Moslem NOUN
el musulmán (PL los musulmanes)
la musulmana
□ He's a Moslem. Es musulmán.

mosque NOUN
la mezquita

mosquito NOUN
el mosquito

■ **a mosquito bite** una picadura de mosquito

most ADJECTIVE, PRONOUN, ADVERB
más
□ the thing she feared most lo que más temía □ He's the one who talks the most. Es el que más habla. □ the most expensive restaurant el restaurante más caro

■ **most of** la mayor parte de □ most of the time la mayor parte del tiempo □ I did most of the work alone. Hice la mayor parte del trabajo solo.

■ **most of them** la mayoría □ Most of them have cars. La mayoría tienen coches. □ Most people go out on Friday nights. La mayoría de la gente sale los viernes por la noche.

■ **He won the most votes.** Fue el que sacó más votos.

■ **at the most** como mucho □ two hours at the most dos horas como mucho

■ **to make the most of something** aprovechar algo al máximo □ He made the most of his holiday. Aprovechó sus vacaciones al máximo.

mostly ADVERB

■ **The teachers are mostly quite nice.** La mayoría de los profesores son bastante simpáticos.

MOT NOUN
la ITV
□ My car has failed its MOT. El coche no me ha pasado la ITV.

motel NOUN
el motel

moth NOUN
1 la mariposa nocturna
2 la polilla *(clothes moth)*

mother NOUN
la madre

■ **my mother and father** mis padres

■ **mother tongue** la lengua materna

mother-in-law NOUN
la suegra

Mother's Day NOUN
el Día de la Madre

motionless ADJECTIVE
inmóvil (FEM inmóvil)

motivated ADJECTIVE

■ **He is highly motivated.** Está muy motivado.

motivation NOUN
la motivación (PL las motivaciones)

motive NOUN
1 el motivo
□ the motive for the killing el motivo del homicidio
2 la intención (PL las intenciones)
□ for the best of motives con la mejor de las intenciones

motor NOUN
el motor

motorbike NOUN
la moto

LANGUAGE TIP Although **moto** ends in **-o**, it is actually a feminine noun.

motorboat NOUN
la lancha motora

motorcycle NOUN
la motocicleta

motorcyclist NOUN
el/la motociclista

motorist NOUN
el conductor
la conductora

motor mechanic NOUN
el mecánico
la mecánica

motor racing NOUN
las carreras de coches

motorway NOUN
la autopista
□ I had an accident on the motorway. Tuve un accidente en la autopista.

mouldy ADJECTIVE
mohoso (FEM mohosa)

mountain NOUN
la montaña
□ in the mountains en la montaña
■ **a mountain bike** una bicicleta de montaña

mountaineer NOUN
el/la alpinista

mountaineering NOUN
el alpinismo
□ I go mountaineering. Hago alpinismo.

mountainous ADJECTIVE
montañoso (FEM montañosa)

mouse NOUN
el ratón (PL los ratones) *(also for computer)*

mouse mat NOUN
la alfombrilla del ratón

mousse NOUN
1 la mousse
□ chocolate mousse la mousse de chocolate
2 la espuma *(for hair)*

moustache NOUN
el bigote
□ He's got a moustache. Tiene bigote.

mouth NOUN
la boca

mouthful NOUN
1 el bocado *(of food)*
2 el trago *(of drink)*

mouth organ NOUN
la armónica

mouthwash NOUN
el elixir bucal

move NOUN
▹ *see also* **move** VERB
1 el paso
□ That was a good move! ¡Ese fue un paso bien dado!
■ **It's your move.** Te toca jugar.
2 la mudanza
□ our move from Oxford to Luton nuestra mudanza de Oxford a Luton
■ **Get a move on!** ¡Date prisa!

to **move** VERB
▹ *see also* **move** NOUN
1 moverse*
□ Don't move! ¡No te muevas!
2 mover*
□ He can't move his arm. No puede mover el brazo.
■ **Could you move your stuff please?** ¿Podrías quitar tus cosas de aquí, por favor?
3 avanzar*
□ The car was moving very slowly. El coche avanzaba muy lentamente.
4 conmover*
□ I was very moved by the film. La película me conmovió mucho.
■ **to move house** mudarse de casa □ We're moving in July. Nos mudamos en julio.

to **move in** VERB
■ **When are the new tenants moving in?** ¿Cuándo vienen los nuevos inquilinos?

to **move over** VERB
correrse
□ Could you move over a bit, please? ¿Te podrías correr un poco, por favor?

movement NOUN
el movimiento

movie NOUN
la película
■ **the movies** el cine

moving ADJECTIVE
1 en movimiento
□ a moving bus un autobús en movimiento
2 conmovedor (FEM conmovedora)
□ a moving story una historia conmovedora

to **mow** VERB
cortar
□ I sometimes mow the lawn. A veces corto el césped.

mower NOUN
el cortacésped

mown VERB ▹ *see* **mow**

MP ABBREVIATION
el diputado
la diputada

MP3 player NOUN
el reproductor de MP3

Mr ABBREVIATION
1 señor *masc*
□ Mr Jones wants to see you. El señor Jones quiere verte.
2 Sr. *(in address)*

Mrs ABBREVIATION
1 señora *fem*
□ Mrs Philips wants to see you. La señora Philips quiere verte.
2 Sra. *(in address)*

Ms ABBREVIATION
1 señora *fem*
□ Ms Brown wants to see you. La señora Brown quiere verte.
2 Sra. *(in address)*

DID YOU KNOW...?
There isn't a direct equivalent of Ms in Spanish. If you are writing to a woman and don't know whether she is married, use **Señora**.

English-Spanish

m

much ADJECTIVE, PRONOUN, ADVERB
mucho (FEM mucha)
□ I feel much better now. Ahora me siento mucho mejor. □ I haven't got much money. No tengo mucho dinero. □ Have you got a lot of luggage? — No, not much. ¿Tienes mucho equipaje? — No, no mucho.
■ **very much** mucho □ I enjoyed myself very much. Me divertí mucho.
■ **Thank you very much.** Muchas gracias.
■ **how much?** ¿cuánto? □ How much time have you got? ¿Cuánto tiempo tienes? □ How much is it? ¿Cuánto es?
■ **too much** demasiado □ That's too much! ¡Eso es demasiado! □ They give us too much homework. Nos ponen demasiados deberes.
■ **so much** tanto □ I didn't think it would cost so much. No pensé que costaría tanto. □ I've never seen so much rain. Nunca había visto tanta lluvia.
■ **What's on TV? — Not much.** ¿Qué ponen en la tele? — Nada especial.

mud NOUN
el barro

muddle NOUN
■ **to be in a muddle** estar todo revuelto □ The photos are in a muddle. Las fotos están todas revueltas.

to **muddle up** VERB
confundir
□ He muddles me up with my sister. Me confunde con mi hermana.
■ **to get muddled up** hacerse un lío *(informal)* □ I'm getting muddled up. Me estoy haciendo un lío.

muddy ADJECTIVE
lleno de barro (FEM llena de barro)

muesli NOUN
el muesli

muffler NOUN (US)
el silenciador

mug NOUN
▹ *see also* **mug** VERB
la taza alta
□ Do you want a cup or a mug? ¿Quieres una taza normal o una taza alta?
■ **a beer mug** una jarra de cerveza

to **mug** VERB
▹ *see also* **mug** NOUN
atracar*
□ He was mugged in the city centre. Lo atracaron en el centro de la ciudad.

mugger NOUN
el atracador
la atracadora

mugging NOUN
el atraco

muggy ADJECTIVE
■ **It's muggy today.** Hoy hace bochorno.

multiple choice test NOUN
el examen tipo test

multiple sclerosis NOUN
la esclerosis múltiple
□ She's got multiple sclerosis. Tiene esclerosis múltiple.

multiplication NOUN
la multiplicación

to **multiply** VERB
multiplicar*
□ to multiply six by three multiplicar seis por tres

multi-storey car park NOUN
el aparcamiento de varias plantas

mum NOUN
mamá *fem*
□ I'll ask Mum. Le preguntaré a mamá.
□ my mum mi mamá

mummy NOUN
1 mamá *fem*
□ Mummy says I can go. Mamá dice que puedo ir.
2 la momia *(Egyptian)*

mumps NOUN
las paperas
□ My brother's got mumps. Mi hermano tiene paperas.

murder NOUN
▹ *see also* **murder** VERB
el asesinato

to **murder** VERB
▹ *see also* **murder** NOUN
asesinar
□ He was murdered. Fue asesinado.

murderer NOUN
el asesino
la asesina

muscle NOUN
el músculo

muscular ADJECTIVE
musculoso (FEM musculosa)
□ He's got muscular legs. Tiene piernas musculosas.

museum NOUN
el museo

mushroom NOUN
el champiñón (PL los champiñones)

music NOUN
la música

musical ADJECTIVE
▹ *see also* **musical** NOUN
musical (FEM musical)
■ **I'm not musical.** No tengo aptitudes para la música.

musical NOUN
▹ *see also* **musical** ADJECTIVE
el musical

music centre NOUN
el equipo de música

musician NOUN
el músico
la música
□ He's a musician. Es músico.

Muslim NOUN
el musulmán (PL musulmanes)
la musulmana
□ She's a Muslim. Es musulmana.

mussel NOUN
el mejillón (PL los mejillones)

must VERB
1 tener* que *(it's necessary)*
□ I must do it. Tengo que hacerlo. □ I must buy some presents. Tengo que comprar unos regalos. □ I really must go now. De verdad que me tengo que ir ya. □ You must come again next year. Tienes que volver el año que viene.
■ **You mustn't forget to send her a card.** No te vayas a olvidar de mandarle una tarjeta.
2 deber de *(I suppose)*
□ There must be some problem. Debe de haber algún problema. □ You must be tired. Debes de estar cansada.

mustard NOUN
la mostaza

mustn't VERB = **must not**

to **mutter** VERB
mascullar

mutton NOUN
la carne de cordero

my ADJECTIVE
mi (PL mis)
□ my father mi padre □ my house mi casa □ my two best friends mis dos mejores amigos □ my sisters mis hermanas

LANGUAGE TIP 'my' is usually translated by the definite article **el/los** or **la/las** when it's clear from the sentence who the possessor is or when referring to clothing or parts of the body.

□ They stole my car. Me robaron el coche. □ I took off my coat. Me quité el abrigo. □ I'm washing my hair. Me estoy lavando la cabeza.

myself PRONOUN
1 me *(reflexive)*
□ I've hurt myself. Me he hecho daño.
2 mí mismo (FEM mí misma) *(after preposition)*
□ I talked mainly about myself. Hablé principalmente de mí mismo.
■ **a beginner like myself** un principiante como yo
3 yo mismo (FEM yo misma) *(for emphasis)*
□ I made it myself. Lo hice yo misma.
■ **by myself** solo (FEM sola)
□ I don't like travelling by myself. No me gusta viajar solo.

mysterious ADJECTIVE
misterioso (FEM misteriosa)

mystery NOUN
el misterio
■ **a murder mystery** una novela policíaca

myth NOUN
el mito
□ a Greek myth un mito griego
□ That's a myth. *(untrue story)* Eso es un mito.

mythology NOUN
la mitología

Nn

naff ADJECTIVE
hortera (FEM hortera)

to **nag** VERB
dar* la lata
□ She's always nagging me. Siempre me está dando la lata.

nail NOUN
1 la uña
□ She bites her nails. Se muerde las uñas.
2 el clavo *(made of metal)*

nailbrush NOUN
el cepillo de uñas

nailfile NOUN
la lima para las uñas

nail scissors PL NOUN
las tijeras para las uñas

nail varnish NOUN
el esmalte de uñas
■ **nail varnish remover** el quitaesmaltes

naked ADJECTIVE
desnudo (FEM desnuda)

name NOUN
el nombre
■ **What's your name?** ¿Cómo te llamas?

nanny NOUN
la niñera *(nursemaid)*

nap NOUN
la siesta
□ She likes to have a nap in the afternoon. Le gusta echarse una siesta por la tarde.

napkin NOUN
la servilleta

nappy NOUN
el pañal

narrow ADJECTIVE
estrecho (FEM estrecha)

narrow-minded ADJECTIVE
estrecho de miras (FEM estrecho de mirasa)

nasty ADJECTIVE
1 malo (FEM mala)
□ Don't be nasty. No seas malo. □ What nasty weather! ¡Qué tiempo más malo!
LANGUAGE TIP Use **mal** before a masculine singular noun.
2 desagradable (FEM desagradable)
□ a nasty smell un olor desagradable
■ **He gave me a nasty look.** Me miró de mala manera.

nation NOUN
la nación (PL las naciones)

national ADJECTIVE
nacional (FEM nacional)

national anthem NOUN
el himno nacional

National Health Service NOUN
el servicio sanitario de la Seguridad Social

nationalism NOUN
el nacionalismo

nationalist NOUN
el/la nacionalista

nationality NOUN
la nacionalidad

national park NOUN
el parque nacional

native ADJECTIVE
natal (FEM natal)
□ my native country mi país natal
■ **his native language** su lengua materna

natural ADJECTIVE
natural (FEM natural)
□ Helping him seemed the natural thing to do. Ayudarlo parecía lo más natural.

naturalist NOUN
el/la naturalista

naturally ADVERB
naturalmente
□ Naturally, we were very disappointed. Naturalmente, estábamos muy decepcionados.

nature NOUN
la naturaleza
□ the wonders of nature las maravillas de la naturaleza
■ **It's not in his nature to behave like that.** Comportarse así no es propio de él.

naughty ADJECTIVE
travieso (FEM traviesa)
□ Naughty girl! ¡Qué traviesa!

navy NOUN
la armada
□ He's in the navy. Está en la armada.

navy-blue ADJECTIVE

azul marino (FEM + PL azul marino)
◻ a navy-blue skirt una falda azul marino

near ADJECTIVE
▹ *see also* **near** PREPOSITION, ADVERB
1 cerca (FEM cerca)
◻ It's fairly near. Está bastante cerca. ◻ My house is near enough to walk. Mi casa está muy cerca, se puede ir andando.
2 cercano (FEM cercana)
◻ Where's the nearest service station? ¿Dónde está la gasolinera más cercana?
■ **in the near future** en un futuro cercano

near PREPOSITION, ADVERB
▹ *see also* **near** ADJECTIVE
1 cerca
◻ Is there a bank near here? ¿Hay algún banco por aquí cerca?
2 cerca de
◻ I live near Liverpool. Vivo cerca de Liverpool.
■ **near to** cerca de ◻ It's very near to the school. Está muy cerca del colegio.

nearby ADJECTIVE
▹ *see also* **nearby** ADVERB
cercano (FEM cercana)
◻ a nearby village un pueblo cercano

nearby ADVERB
▹ *see also* **nearby** ADJECTIVE
cerca
◻ There's a supermarket nearby. Hay un supermercado cerca.

nearly ADVERB
casi
◻ Dinner's nearly ready. La cena está casi lista. ◻ I'm nearly fifteen. Tengo casi quince años.
■ **I nearly missed the train.** Por poco pierdo el tren.

neat ADJECTIVE
ordenado (FEM ordenada)
◻ My brother's not very neat. Mi hermano no es muy ordenado.
■ **He always looks very neat.** Siempre está muy pulcro.

neatly ADVERB
■ **neatly folded** cuidadosamente doblado
■ **neatly dressed** bien vestido

necessarily ADVERB
■ **not necessarily** no necesariamente

necessary ADJECTIVE
necesario (FEM necesaria)

necessity NOUN
la necesidad
◻ A car is a necessity, not a luxury. Un coche es una necesidad, no un lujo.

neck NOUN
el cuello
◻ a V-neck sweater un jersey de cuello en pico
■ **She had a stiff neck.** Tenía tortícolis.
■ **the back of your neck** la nuca

necklace NOUN
el collar

to **need** VERB
▹ *see also* **need** NOUN
necesitar
◻ I need a bigger size. Necesito una talla más grande. ◻ I need to change some money. Necesito cambiar dinero.
■ **You don't need to go.** No tienes por qué ir.

need NOUN
▹ *see also* **need** VERB
■ **There's no need to book.** No hace falta hacer reserva.

LANGUAGE TIP **hace falta que** has to be followed by a verb in the subjunctive.

◻ There's no need for you to do that. No hace falta que hagas eso.

needle NOUN
la aguja

negative NOUN
▹ *see also* **negative** ADJECTIVE
el negativo *(photo)*

negative ADJECTIVE
▹ *see also* **negative** NOUN
negativo (FEM negativa)
◻ He's got a very negative attitude. Tiene una actitud muy negativa.

neglected ADJECTIVE
abandonado (FEM abandonada)
◻ The garden is neglected. El jardín está abandonado.

to **negotiate** VERB
negociar

negotiations PL NOUN
las negociaciones

neighbour (US **neighbor**) NOUN
el vecino
la vecina

neighbourhood (US **neighborhood**) NOUN
el barrio

neither ADJECTIVE, CONJUNCTION, PRONOUN
1 ninguno de los dos (FEM ninguna de las dos)
◻ Carrots or peas? — Neither, thanks. ¿Zanahorias o guisantes? — Ninguno de los dos, gracias. ◻ Neither of them is coming. No viene ninguno de los dos. ◻ Neither woman looked happy. Ninguna de las dos parecía contenta.
2 tampoco
◻ I don't like him. — Neither do I! No me cae bien. — ¡A mí tampoco! ◻ I've never been to Spain. — Neither have we. No he estado nunca en España. — Nosotros tampoco.

English-Spanish

n

■ **neither...nor...** ni...ni... □ Neither Sarah nor Tamsin is coming to the party. No vienen ni Sarah ni Tamsin a la fiesta.

neon NOUN
el neón
□ a neon light una lámpara de neón

nephew NOUN
el sobrino

nerve NOUN
el nervio
□ That noise really gets on my nerves. Ese ruido me pone los nervios de punta.
■ **He's got a nerve!** ¡Qué cara tiene!
■ **I wouldn't have the nerve to do that!** ¡Yo no me atrevería a hacer eso!

nerve-racking ADJECTIVE
angustioso (FEM angustiosa)

nervous ADJECTIVE
nervioso (FEM nerviosa)
□ I bite my nails when I'm nervous. Cuando estoy nervioso me muerdo las uñas. □ I'm a bit nervous about the exams. Estoy un poco nervioso por los exámenes.

nest NOUN
el nido

Net NOUN
la Red
■ **to surf the Net** navegar por la Red

net NOUN
la red
□ a fishing net una red de pesca

netball NOUN
DID YOU KNOW...? Netball is not played in Spain.

Netherlands PL NOUN
■ **the Netherlands** los Países Bajos

network NOUN
la red

neurotic ADJECTIVE
neurótico (FEM neurótica)

never ADVERB
nunca
□ Have you ever been to Argentina? — No, never. ¿Has estado alguna vez en Argentina? — No, nunca. □ Never leave valuables in your car. No dejen nunca objetos de valor en el coche.
LANGUAGE TIP When **nunca** comes before the verb in Spanish it is not necessary to use **no** as well.
□ I never believed him. Yo nunca le creí.
■ **Never again!** ¡Nunca más!
■ **Never, ever do that again!** ¡No vuelvas a hacer eso nunca jamás!
■ **Never mind.** No importa.

new ADJECTIVE
nuevo (FEM nueva)
□ her new boyfriend su nuevo novio

newborn ADJECTIVE
■ **a newborn baby** un bebé recién nacido

newcomer NOUN
■ **They were newcomers to the area.** Eran nuevos en la zona.

news NOUN
1 las noticias
□ good news buenas noticias □ I watch the news every evening. Veo las noticias todas las noches.
■ **It was nice to have your news.** Me dio alegría saber de ti.
2 la noticia
□ That's wonderful news! ¡Qué buena noticia!
■ **an interesting piece of news** una noticia interesante

newsagent NOUN
la tienda de periódicos

newspaper NOUN
el periódico

newsreader NOUN
1 el presentador
la presentadora *(on TV)*
2 el locutor
la locutora *(on radio)*

New Year NOUN
el Año Nuevo
□ to celebrate New Year celebrar el Año Nuevo
■ **Happy New Year!** ¡Feliz Año Nuevo!
■ **New Year's Day** el día de Año Nuevo
■ **New Year's Eve** Nochevieja (la noche de Fin de Año *Latin America*)
■ **a New Year's Eve party** una fiesta de Fin de Año

New Zealand NOUN
Nueva Zelanda *fem*

New Zealander NOUN
el neozelandés (PL los neozelandeses)
la neozelandesa

next ADJECTIVE, ADVERB, PREPOSITION
1 próximo (FEM próxima)
□ next Saturday el próximo sábado □ the next time I see you la próxima vez que te vea
2 siguiente (FEM siguiente)
□ Next please! ¡El siguiente, por favor!
□ The next day we visited Gerona. Al día siguiente visitamos Gerona.
3 luego
□ What did you do next? ¿Qué hiciste luego?
■ **next to** al lado de □ next to the bank al lado del banco
■ **next door** al lado □ They live next door. Viven al lado.
■ **the next-door neighbours** los vecinos de al lado
■ **the next room** la habitación de al lado

NHS ABBREVIATION *(= National Health Service)*
el servicio sanitario de la Seguridad Social

nice ADJECTIVE
1 simpático (FEM simpática) *(friendly)*
□ Your parents are very nice. Tus padres son muy simpáticos.
2 amable (FEM amable) *(kind)*
□ She was always very nice to me. Siempre fue muy amable conmigo. □ It was nice of you to remember my birthday. Fue muy amable de tu parte que te acordaras de mi cumpleaños.
3 bonito (FEM bonita) *(pretty)*
□ That's a nice dress! ¡Qué vestido más bonito! □ Segovia is a nice town. Segovia es una ciudad bonita.

> WORD POWER
> You can use a number of other words instead of **nice** to mean 'pretty':
> **attractive** atractivo
> □ an attractive girl una chica atractiva
> **beautiful** precioso
> □ a beautiful painting un cuadro precioso
> **gorgeous** magnífico
> □ a gorgeous scarf un pañuelo magnífico
> **lovely** precioso
> □ a lovely dress un vestido precioso

4 bueno (FEM buena) *(good)*
□ This paella is very nice. Esta paella está muy buena. □ a nice cup of coffee una buena taza de café
LANGUAGE TIP Use **buen** before a masculine singular noun.
□ nice weather buen tiempo □ It's a nice day. Hace buen día.
■ **Have a nice time!** ¡Que te diviertas!

nickname NOUN
el apodo

niece NOUN
la sobrina

night NOUN
la noche
□ I want a single room for two nights. Quiero una habitación individual para dos noches.
■ **at night** por la noche
■ **Good night!** ¡Buenas noches!
■ **last night** anoche □ We went to a party last night. Anoche fuimos a una fiesta.

night club NOUN
la sala de fiestas

nightdress NOUN
el camisón (PL los camisones)

nightie NOUN
el camisón (PL los camisones)

nightlife NOUN
la vida nocturna
□ There's plenty of nightlife in Madrid. Hay mucha vida nocturna en Madrid.

nightmare NOUN
la pesadilla
□ to have nightmares tener pesadillas
□ The whole trip was a nightmare. El viaje entero fue una pesadilla.

nil NOUN
el cero
□ We won one-nil. Ganamos uno a cero.

nine NUMERAL
nueve
■ **She's nine.** Tiene nueve años.

nineteen NUMERAL
diecinueve
■ **She's nineteen.** Tiene diecinueve años.

nineteenth ADJECTIVE
decimonoveno (FEM decimonovena)
■ **the nineteenth floor** la planta diecinueve
■ **the nineteenth of March** el diecinueve de marzo

ninety NUMERAL
noventa
□ He's ninety. Tiene noventa años.

ninth ADJECTIVE
noveno (FEM novena)
□ on the ninth floor en el noveno piso
■ **on 9th August** el 9 de agosto

no ADVERB, ADJECTIVE
no
□ Are you coming? — No. ¿Vienes? — No.
□ Would you like some more? — No thank you. ¿Quieres un poco más? — No, gracias.
□ There's no hot water. No hay agua caliente.
■ **I've got no idea.** No tengo ni idea.
■ **I have no questions.** No tengo ninguna pregunta.
■ **No way!** ¡Ni hablar!
■ **'no smoking'** 'prohibido fumar'

nobody PRONOUN
nadie
□ Who's going with you? — Nobody. ¿Quién va contigo? — Nadie. □ There was nobody in the office. No había nadie en la oficina.
■ **I've got nobody to play with.** No tengo a nadie con quien jugar.
LANGUAGE TIP When 'nobody' goes before a verb in English it can be translated by either **nadie** ... or **no** ... **nadie**.
□ Nobody saw me. Nadie me vio. □ Nobody likes him. No le cae bien a nadie.

to **nod** VERB
1 asentir* con la cabeza *(in agreement)*
2 saludar con la cabeza *(as greeting)*

noise NOUN
el ruido
■ **to make a noise** hacer ruido

noisy ADJECTIVE
ruidoso (FEM ruidosa)
□ the noisiest city in the world la ciudad más ruidosa del mundo
■ **It's very noisy here.** Hay mucho ruido aquí.

to **nominate** VERB
nombrar*
□ She was nominated for the post. La nombraron para el cargo.
■ **He was nominated for an Oscar.** Le nominaron para un Oscar.

none PRONOUN

LANGUAGE TIP When 'none' refers to something you can count, such as sisters or friends, Spanish uses **ninguno** with a singular verb. When it refers to something you cannot count, such as wine, Spanish uses **nada**.

1 ninguno (FEM ninguna)
□ How many sisters have you got? — None. ¿Cuántas hermanas tienes? — Ninguna.
□ None of my friends wanted to come. Ninguno de mis amigos quiso venir.
□ There are none left. No queda ninguno.

2 nada
□ There's none left. No queda nada.

nonsense NOUN
las tonterías
□ She talks a lot of nonsense. Dice muchas tonterías.
■ **Nonsense!** ¡Tonterías!

non-smoker NOUN
el no fumador
la no fumadora
■ **He's a non-smoker.** No fuma.

non-smoking ADJECTIVE
■ **a non-smoking area** un área reservada para no fumadores

LANGUAGE TIP Although it's a feminine noun, remember that you use **el** and **un** with **área**.

■ **a non-smoking carriage** un vagón para no fumadores

non-stop ADJECTIVE, ADVERB
1 directo (FEM directa)
□ a non-stop flight un vuelo directo
■ **We flew non-stop.** Tomamos un vuelo directo.

2 sin parar
□ He talks non-stop. Habla sin parar.

noodles PL NOUN
los fideos

noon NOUN
las doce del mediodía
■ **at noon** a las doce del mediodía

no one PRONOUN
nadie
□ Who's going with you? — No one. ¿Quién va contigo? — Nadie. □ There was no one in the office. No había nadie en la oficina.
■ **I've got no one to play with.** No tengo a nadie con quien jugar.

LANGUAGE TIP When 'no one' goes before a verb in English it can be translated by either **nadie** ... or **no** ... **nadie**.

□ No one saw me. Nadie me vio. □ No one likes him. No le cae bien a nadie.

nor CONJUNCTION
tampoco
□ I didn't like the film. — Nor did I. No me gustó la película. — A mí tampoco. □ We haven't seen him. — Nor have we. No lo hemos visto. — Nosotros tampoco.
■ **neither...nor** ni...ni □ neither the cinema nor the swimming pool ni el cine ni la piscina

normal ADJECTIVE
normal (FEM normal)

normally ADVERB
1 normalmente *(usually)*
□ I normally arrive at nine o'clock. Normalmente llego a las nueve.

2 con normalidad *(as normal)*
□ Airports are working normally over Christmas. Durante las Navidades los aeropuertos funcionan con normalidad.

north NOUN
▷ *see also* **north** ADJECTIVE, ADVERB
el norte
□ in the north of Spain en el norte de España

north ADJECTIVE, ADVERB
▷ *see also* **north** NOUN
hacia el norte
□ We were travelling north. Viajábamos hacia el norte.
■ **North London** el norte de Londres
■ **north of** al norte de □ It's north of London. Está al norte de Londres.
■ **the north coast** la costa septentrional

North America NOUN
América del Norte *fem*

northbound ADJECTIVE
■ **Northbound traffic is moving very slowly.** El tráfico que se dirige hacia el norte avanza muy despacio.

northeast NOUN
el noreste
■ **in the northeast** al noreste

northern ADJECTIVE
del norte

□ Northern Europe Europa del Norte
■ **the northern part of the island** la zona norte de la isla

Northern Ireland NOUN
Irlanda del Norte *fem*

North Pole NOUN
■ **the North Pole** el Polo Norte

North Sea NOUN
■ **the North Sea** el Mar del Norte

northwest NOUN
el noroeste
■ **in the northwest** al noroeste

Norway NOUN
Noruega *fem*

Norwegian ADJECTIVE
▷ *see also* **Norwegian** NOUN
noruego (FEM noruega)

Norwegian NOUN
▷ *see also* **Norwegian** ADJECTIVE
1 el noruego
la noruega *(person)*
□ the Norwegians los noruegos
2 el noruego *(language)*

nose NOUN
la nariz (PL las narices)

nosebleed NOUN
■ **I often get nosebleeds.** Me sangra la nariz a menudo.

nosy ADJECTIVE
fisgón (FEM fisgona)

not ADVERB
no
□ I'm not sure. No estoy seguro. □ Are you coming or not? ¿Vienes o no? □ Did you like it? — Not really. ¿Te gustó? — No mucho.
■ **Thank you very much. — Not at all.** Muchas gracias. — De nada.
■ **not yet** todavía no □ They haven't arrived yet. Todavía no han llegado.

note NOUN
1 la nota
□ I'll drop her a note. Le dejaré una nota.
■ **Remember to take notes.** Acuérdate de tomar apuntes.
■ **to make a note of something** tomar nota de algo
2 el billete
□ a five pound note un billete de cinco libras

to **note down** VERB
anotar

notebook NOUN
el cuaderno

notepad NOUN
el bloc de notas (PL los blocs de notas)

notepaper NOUN
el papel de cartas

nothing NOUN
nada
□ What's wrong? — Nothing. ¿Qué pasa? — Nada. □ What are you doing tonight? — Nothing special. ¿Qué haces esta noche? — Nada especial. □ He does nothing. No hace nada.
■ **He does nothing but sleep.** No hace nada más que dormir.
■ **There's nothing to do.** No hay nada que hacer.

LANGUAGE TIP When 'nothing' goes before a verb in English it can be translated by either **nada** ... or **no** ... **nada**.

□ Nothing frightens him. Nada lo asusta.
□ Nothing will happen. No pasará nada.

notice NOUN
▷ *see also* **notice** VERB
1 el letrero *(physical object)*
□ There was a notice outside the house. Había un letrero fuera de la casa.
2 el aviso *(information)*
□ There's a notice on the board about the trip. Hay un aviso en el tablón sobre el viaje.
■ **a warning notice** un aviso
■ **He was transferred without notice.** Lo trasladaron sin previo aviso.
■ **until further notice** hasta nuevo aviso
■ **Don't take any notice of him!** ¡No le hagas caso!

LANGUAGE TIP Be careful not to translate **notice** by **noticia**.

to **notice** VERB
▷ *see also* **notice** NOUN
■ **to notice something** darse cuenta de algo □ Don't worry. He won't notice the mistake. No te preocupes. No se dará cuenta del error.

notice board NOUN
el tablón de anuncios (PL los tablones de anuncios)

nought NOUN
cero *masc*

noun NOUN
el nombre

novel NOUN
la novela

novelist NOUN
el/la novelista

November NOUN
noviembre *masc*
□ in November en noviembre □ on 7th November el 7 de noviembre

now ADVERB
ahora
□ What are you doing now? ¿Qué haces ahora?
■ **just now** en este momento □ I'm rather busy just now. En este momento estoy muy

ocupado.

■ **I did it just now.** Lo acabo de hacer.

■ **It should be ready by now.** Ya debería estar listo.

■ **from now on** de ahora en adelante

■ **now and then** de vez en cuando

nowhere ADVERB
a ninguna parte

□ Where are you going for your holidays? — Nowhere. ¿Adónde vas en vacaciones? — A ninguna parte.

■ **nowhere else** a ninguna otra parte

□ You can go to the shops but nowhere else. Puedes ir a las tiendas pero a ninguna otra parte.

■ **The children were nowhere to be seen.** No se podía ver a los niños por ninguna parte.

■ **There was nowhere to play.** No se podía jugar en ninguna parte.

nuclear ADJECTIVE
nuclear (FEM nuclear)

□ nuclear power la energía nuclear

nude NOUN
▷ *see also* **nude** ADJECTIVE

■ **in the nude** desnudo

nude ADJECTIVE
▷ *see also* **nude** NOUN
desnudo (FEM desnuda)

nudist NOUN
el/la nudista

nuisance NOUN
fastidio

□ It's a nuisance having to clean the car. Es un fastidio tener que limpiar el coche.

■ **Sorry to be a nuisance.** Siento molestarle.

■ **You're a nuisance!** ¡Eres un pesado!

numb ADJECTIVE

■ **numb with cold** helado de frío

number NOUN
el número

□ I can't read the second number. No puedo leer el segundo número. □ They live at number five. Viven en el número cinco.

□ a large number of people un gran número de gente

■ **You've got the wrong number.** Se ha equivocado de número.

■ **What's your number?** *(telephone)* ¿Cuál es tu teléfono?

number plate NOUN
la matrícula (la placa *Latin America*)

nun NOUN
la monja

nurse NOUN
el enfermero
la enfermera

■ **She's a nurse.** Es enfermera.

nursery NOUN
1 la guardería infantil *(for children)*
2 el vivero *(for plants)*

nursery school NOUN
el preescolar (guardería *Latin America*)

nursery slope NOUN
la pista para principiantes

nut NOUN
1 la almendra *(almond)*
2 el cacahuete *(peanut)*
3 la avellana *(hazelnut)*
4 la nuez (PL las nueces) *(walnut)*

■ **I don't like nuts.** No me gustan los frutos secos.

5 la tuerca *(made of metal)*

nutmeg NOUN
la nuez moscada

nutritious ADJECTIVE
nutritivo (FEM nutritiva)

nuts ADJECTIVE

■ **He's nuts.** *(informal)* Está chiflado.

nutter NOUN

■ **He's a nutter.** *(informal)* Es un chiflado.

nylon NOUN
nylon

Oo

oak NOUN
el roble
□ an oak barrel un barril de roble

oar NOUN
el remo

oats PL NOUN
la avena

obedient ADJECTIVE
obediente (FEM obediente)

to **obey** VERB
obedecer*
■ **to obey the rules** *(in game)* atenerse a las reglas del juego

object NOUN
el objeto

objection NOUN
la objeción (PL las objeciones)
□ There were no objections to the plan. No hubo objeciones al plan.

objective ADJECTIVE
objetivo (FEM objetiva)

oblong ADJECTIVE
rectangular (FEM rectangular)

oboe NOUN
el oboe

obscene ADJECTIVE
obsceno (FEM obscena)

observant ADJECTIVE
observador (FEM observadora)

to **observe** VERB
observar

obsessed ADJECTIVE
obsesionado (FEM obsesionada)
□ He's obsessed with trains. Está obsesionado con los trenes.

obsession NOUN
la obsesión (PL las obsesiones)
□ Football's an obsession of mine. El fútbol es una obsesión mía.

obsolete ADJECTIVE
obsoleto (FEM obsoleta)

obstacle NOUN
el obstáculo

obstinate ADJECTIVE
terco (FEM terca)

to **obstruct** VERB
bloquear
□ A lorry was obstructing the traffic. Un camión bloqueaba el tráfico.

to **obtain** VERB
obtener*

obvious ADJECTIVE
obvio (FEM obvia)

obviously ADVERB
claro
□ Do you want to pass the exam? — Obviously! ¿Quieres aprobar el examen? — ¡Claro! □ It was obviously impossible. Estaba claro que era imposible.
■ **Obviously not!** ¡Claro que no!

occasion NOUN
la ocasión (PL las ocasiones)
□ a special occasion una ocasión especial
■ **on several occasions** en varias ocasiones

occasionally ADVERB
de vez en cuando

occupation NOUN
el empleo

to **occupy** VERB
ocupar
□ The toilet was occupied. El lavabo estaba ocupado.

to **occur** VERB
ocurrir
□ The accident occurred yesterday. El accidente ocurrió ayer.
■ **It suddenly occurred to me that...** De repente se me ocurrió que...

ocean NOUN
el océano

o'clock ADVERB
■ **at four o'clock** a las cuatro
■ **It's one o'clock.** Es la una.
■ **It's five o'clock.** Son las cinco.

October NOUN
octubre *masc*
□ in October en octubre □ on 12 October el 12 de octubre

octopus NOUN
el pulpo

odd ADJECTIVE

1 raro (FEM rara)
□ That's odd! ¡Qué raro!
2 impar (FEM impara)
□ an odd number un número impar
■ **odd socks** calcetines desparejados

of PREPOSITION
de
□ a boy of 10 un niño de 10 años □ a kilo of oranges un kilo de naranjas □ It's made of wood. Es de madera. □ a glass of wine un vaso de vino
LANGUAGE TIP **de** + **el** changes to **del**.
□ the wheels of the car las ruedas del coche
■ **There were three of us.** Éramos tres.
■ **a friend of mine** un amigo mío
■ **That's very kind of you.** Es muy amable de su parte.

off ADJECTIVE, ADVERB, PREPOSITION
LANGUAGE TIP For other expressions with 'off', see the verbs 'get', 'take', 'turn' etc.
1 apagado (FEM apagada) *(heater, light, TV)*
□ All the lights are off. Todas las luces están apagadas.
2 cerrado (FEM cerrada) *(tap, gas)*
□ Are you sure the tap is off? ¿Seguro que el grifo está cerrado?
3 cortado (FEM cortada) *(milk)*
4 estropeado (FEM estropeada) *(meat)*
■ **to be off sick** estar ausente por enfermedad
■ **a day off** un día libre □ She took a day off work to go to the wedding. Se tomó un día libre para ir a la boda.
■ **I've got tomorrow off.** Mañana tengo el día libre.
■ **She's off school today.** Hoy no ha ido al colegio.
■ **I must be off now.** Me tengo que ir ahora.
■ **I'm off.** Me voy.
■ **The match is off.** El partido se ha suspendido.

offence (US **offense**) NOUN
el delito *(crime)*

offensive ADJECTIVE
ofensivo (FEM ofensiva)

offer NOUN
▷ *see also* **offer** VERB
1 la oferta *(of money, job)*
2 el ofrecimiento *(of help)*
■ **There was a special offer on CDs.** Los CDs estaban de oferta.

to **offer** VERB
▷ *see also* **offer** NOUN
ofrecer*
□ He offered me a cigarette. Me ofreció un cigarrillo.
■ **He offered to help me.** Se ofreció a ayudarme.

office NOUN
la oficina
■ **during office hours** en horas de oficina

officer NOUN
el/la oficial *(in the army)*

official ADJECTIVE
oficial (FEM oficial)

off-licence NOUN
la tienda de bebidas alcohólicas

off-peak ADJECTIVE
■ **off-peak calls** llamadas de tarifa reducida

offside ADJECTIVE
fuera de juego

often ADVERB
a menudo
□ It often rains. Llueve a menudo.
■ **How often do you go to the gym?** ¿Cada cuánto vas al gimnasio?

oil NOUN
▷ *see also* **oil** VERB
1 el aceite *(for lubrication, cooking)*
2 el petróleo *(crude oil)*
■ **an oil painting** una pintura al óleo

to **oil** VERB
▷ *see also* **oil** NOUN
engrasar

oil rig NOUN
la plataforma petrolífera

oil slick NOUN
la marea negra

oil well NOUN
el pozo de petróleo

ointment NOUN
la pomada

okay EXCLAMATION, ADVERB
1 de acuerdo *(more formally)*
□ Your appointment's at six o'clock. — Okay. Su cita es a las seis. — De acuerdo.
2 vale *(less formally)*
□ I'll meet you at six o'clock, okay? Te veré a las seis, ¿vale?
■ **Are you okay?** ¿Estás bien?
■ **I'll do it tomorrow, if that's okay with you.** Lo haré mañana, si te parece bien.
■ **The film was okay.** La película no estuvo mal.

old ADJECTIVE
1 viejo (FEM vieja)
□ an old house una casa vieja
■ **an old man** un viejo
LANGUAGE TIP When talking about people it is more polite to use **anciano** instead of **viejo**.
■ **old people** los ancianos
2 antiguo (FEM antigua) *(former)*

□ my old English teacher mi antiguo profesor de inglés
■ **How old are you?** ¿Cuántos años tienes?
■ **How old is the baby?** ¿Cuánto tiempo tiene el bebé?
■ **a twenty-year-old woman** una mujer de veinte años
■ **He's ten years old.** Tiene diez años.
■ **older** mayor □ my older brother mi hermano mayor □ my older sister mi hermana mayor □ She's two years older than me. Es dos años mayor que yo.
■ **I'm the oldest in the family.** Soy el mayor de la familia.

old age pensioner NOUN
el/la pensionista

old-fashioned ADJECTIVE
anticuado (FEM anticuada)
□ My parents are rather old-fashioned. Mis padres son bastante anticuados.

olive NOUN
la aceituna

olive oil NOUN
el aceite de oliva

olive tree NOUN
el olivo

Olympic ADJECTIVE
olímpico (FEM olímpica)
■ **the Olympics** las Olimpiadas

omelette NOUN
la tortilla francesa

on PREPOSITION, ADVERB
▷ *see also* **on** ADJECTIVE

LANGUAGE TIP There are several ways of translating 'on'. Scan the examples to find one that is similar to what you want to say. For other expressions with 'on', see the verbs 'go', 'put', 'turn' etc.

1 en
□ on an island en una isla □ on the wall en la pared □ It's on Channel four. Lo dan en el Canal cuatro. □ on TV en la tele □ on the 2nd floor en el segundo piso □ I go to school on my bike. Voy al colegio en bicicleta. □ We went on the train. Fuimos en tren.

2 sobre *(on top of, about)*
□ on the table sobre la mesa □ a book on Ghandi un libro sobre Ghandi

LANGUAGE TIP With days and dates, the definite article – **el, los** – is used in Spanish instead of a preposition.

□ on Friday el viernes □ on Fridays los viernes □ on 20 June el 20 de junio
■ **on the left** a la izquierda
■ **on holiday** de vacaciones
■ **It's about 10 minutes on foot.** Está a unos 10 minutos andando.
■ **She was on antibiotics for a week.** Estuvo una semana tomando antibióticos.
■ **The coffee is on the house.** Al café invita la casa.
■ **The drinks are on me.** Invito yo.
■ **What is he on about?** ¿De qué está hablando?

on ADJECTIVE
▷ *see also* **on** PREPOSITION, ADVERB

1 encendido (FEM encendida) *(heater, light, TV)*
□ I think I left the light on. Me parece que he dejado la luz encendida.

2 abierto (FEM abierta) *(tap, gas)*
□ Leave the tap on. Deja el grifo abierto.

3 en marcha
□ Is the dishwasher on? ¿Está en marcha el lavavajillas?
■ **What's on at the cinema?** ¿Qué echan en el cine?
■ **Is the party still on?** ¿Todavía se va a hacer la fiesta?
■ **I've got a lot on this weekend.** Tengo mucho que hacer este fin de semana.

once ADVERB
una vez
□ once a week una vez a la semana □ once more una vez más □ I've been to Italy once before. Ya he estado una vez en Italia.
■ **Once upon a time...** Érase una vez...
■ **once in a while** de vez en cuando
■ **once and for all** de una vez por todas
■ **at once** enseguida

one NUMERAL, PRONOUN
uno (FEM una)
□ I need a smaller one. Necesito uno más pequeño.
■ **one by one** uno a uno

LANGUAGE TIP Use **un** before a masculine noun.

□ I've got one brother and one sister. Tengo un hermano y una hermana.
■ **One never knows.** Nunca se sabe.
■ **one another** unos a otros □ They all looked at one another. Se miraron todos unos a otros.

oneself PRONOUN

1 se *(reflexive)*
□ to hurt oneself hacerse daño □ to wash oneself lavarse

2 uno mismo (FEM una misma) *(after preposition, for emphasis)*
□ It's quicker to do it oneself. Es más rápido si lo hace uno mismo.

one-way ADJECTIVE
■ **a one-way street** una calle de sentido único
■ **a one-way ticket** un billete de ida

onion NOUN
la cebolla

online ADJECTIVE
en línea

only ADVERB
▷ *see also* **only** ADJECTIVE, CONJUNCTION
sólo
□ How much was it? — Only £10. ¿Cuánto valía? — Sólo 10 libras. □ We only want to stay for one night. Sólo queremos quedarnos una noche. □ It's only a game! ¡Es sólo un juego!

only ADJECTIVE
▷ *see also* **only** ADVERB, CONJUNCTION
único (FEM única)
□ She's an only child. Es hija única.
□ Monday is the only day I'm free. El lunes es el único día que tengo libre.

only CONJUNCTION
▷ *see also* **only** ADJECTIVE, ADVERB
pero
□ I'd like the same sweater, only in black. Quería el mismo jersey, pero en negro.

onwards ADVERB
en adelante
□ from July onwards de julio en adelante

open ADJECTIVE
▷ *see also* **open** VERB
abierto (FEM abierta)
□ The shop's open on Sunday mornings. La tienda está abierta los domingos por la mañana.
■ **Are you open tomorrow?** ¿Abre mañana?
■ **in the open air** al aire libre

to **open** VERB
▷ *see also* **open** ADJECTIVE
1 abrir*
□ What time do the shops open? ¿A qué hora abren las tiendas? □ Can I open the window? ¿Puedo abrir la ventana?
2 abrirse*
□ The door opens automatically. La puerta se abre automáticamente.

opening hours PL NOUN
el horario de apertura

opera NOUN
la ópera

to **operate** VERB
operar *(machine)*
■ **to operate on someone** operar a alguien

operation NOUN
la operación (PL las operaciones)
■ **I've never had an operation.** Nunca me han operado.

operator NOUN
el operador
la operadora

opinion NOUN
la opinión (PL las opiniones)
□ in my opinion en mi opinión
■ **What's your opinion?** ¿Tú qué opinas?

opinion poll NOUN
el sondeo de opinión

opponent NOUN
el adversario
la adversaria

opportunity NOUN
la oportunidad
□ I've never had the opportunity to go to Spain. No he tenido nunca la oportunidad de ir a España.

opposed ADJECTIVE
■ **to be opposed to something** oponerse a algo □ I've always been opposed to violence. Siempre me he opuesto a la violencia.

opposing ADJECTIVE
contrario (FEM contraria)
□ the opposing team el equipo contrario

opposite ADJECTIVE, ADVERB, PREPOSITION
1 contrario (FEM contraria)
□ It's in the opposite direction. Está en dirección contraria.
2 opuesto (FEM opuesta)
□ the opposite sex el sexo opuesto
3 enfrente
□ They live opposite. Viven enfrente.
4 frente a
□ the girl sitting opposite me la chica sentada frente a mí

opposition NOUN
la oposición
□ There is a lot of opposition to the new law. Hay una fuerte oposición a la nueva ley.

optician NOUN
el óptico
la óptica
■ **He's gone to the optician's.** Ha ido a la óptica.

optimist NOUN
el/la optimista

optimistic ADJECTIVE
optimista (FEM optimista)

option NOUN
1 la opción (PL las opciones)
□ I've got no option. No tengo otra opción.
2 la asignatura optativa *(at school)*
□ I'm doing geology as my option. Tengo geología como asignatura optativa.

optional ADJECTIVE
1 optativo (FEM optativa) *(subject)*
□ Biology was optional at my school. La biología era optativa en mi colegio.
2 opcional (FEM opcional) *(feature)*
□ Fog lights are available as optional extras. Los faros antiniebla son opcionales.

or CONJUNCTION
1 o
□ Would you like tea or coffee? ¿Quieres té o café?
LANGUAGE TIP Use **u** before words beginning with **o** or **ho**.
□ six or eight seis u ocho □ men or women mujeres u hombres
■ **Hurry up or you'll miss the bus.** Date prisa, que vas a perder el autobús.
2 ni
□ I don't eat meat or fish. No como carne ni pescado. □ She can't dance or sing. No sabe bailar ni cantar.

oral ADJECTIVE
▷ *see also* **oral** NOUN
oral (FEM oral)
□ an oral exam un examen oral

oral NOUN
▷ *see also* **oral** ADJECTIVE
el examen oral (PL los exámenes orales)
□ I've got my Spanish oral soon. Tengo el examen oral de español pronto.

orange NOUN
▷ *see also* **orange** ADJECTIVE
la naranja
■ **orange juice** el zumo de naranja (el jugo de naranja *Latin America*)

orange ADJECTIVE
▷ *see also* **orange** NOUN
naranja (FEM + PL naranja)

orchard NOUN
el huerto

orchestra NOUN
la orquesta

order NOUN
▷ *see also* **order** VERB
1 el orden *(arrangement)*
□ in alphabetical order por orden alfabético
2 la orden (PL las órdenes) *(command)*
□ to obey an order obedecer una orden
■ **The waiter took our order.** El camarero tomó nota de lo que íbamos a comer.
■ **in order to** para □ He does it in order to earn money. Lo hace para ganar dinero.
■ **'out of order'** 'averiado'

to **order** VERB
▷ *see also* **order** NOUN
pedir*
□ We ordered steak and chips. Pedimos un filete con patatas fritas. □ Are you ready to order? ¿Han decidido qué van a pedir?

ordinary ADJECTIVE
normal y corriente (FEM normal y corriente)
□ He's an ordinary man. Es un hombre normal y corriente. □ an ordinary day un día normal y corriente

organ NOUN
el órgano *(instrument)*

organic ADJECTIVE
biológico (FEM biológica) *(fruit, vegetables)*

organization NOUN
la organización (PL las organizaciones)

to **organize** VERB
organizar*

origin NOUN
el origen (PL los orígenes)

original ADJECTIVE
original (FEM original)

originally ADVERB
al principio

Orkneys PL NOUN
■ **the Orkneys** las Islas Órcadas

ornament NOUN
el adorno

orphan NOUN
el huérfano
la huérfana

ostrich NOUN
el avestruz (PL los avestruces)

other ADJECTIVE, PRONOUN
otro (FEM otra)
□ Have you got these jeans in other colours? ¿Tienen estos vaqueros en otros colores?
□ on the other side of the street al otro lado de la calle
■ **the other one** el otro (FEM la otra)
□ This one? — No, the other one. ¿Éste? — No, el otro.
■ **the others** los demás (FEM las demás)
□ The others are going but I'm not. Los demás van, pero yo no.

otherwise ADVERB, CONJUNCTION
1 si no *(if not)*
□ Note down the number, otherwise you'll forget it. Apúntate el número, si no se te olvidará.
2 por lo demás *(in other ways)*
□ I'm tired, but otherwise I'm fine. Estoy cansado, pero por lo demás estoy bien.

ought VERB
LANGUAGE TIP To translate 'ought to' use the conditional of **deber**.
□ I ought to phone my parents. Debería llamar a mis padres. □ You ought not to do that. No deberías hacer eso. □ He ought to win. Debería ganar.
LANGUAGE TIP For 'ought to have' use the conditional of **deber** plus **haber** or the imperfect of **deber**.
□ You ought to have warned me. Me deberías haber avisado. □ He ought to have known. Debía saberlo.

ounce NOUN
la onza

DID YOU KNOW...? In Spain measurements are in grams and kilograms. One ounce is about 28 grams.

our ADJECTIVE
nuestro (FEM nuestra)
□ our house nuestra casa □ Our neighbours are very nice. Nuestros vecinos son muy simpáticos.

LANGUAGE TIP 'Our' is usually translated by the definite article **el/los** or **la/las** when it's clear from the sentence who the possessor is or when referring to clothing or parts of the body.

□ We took off our coats. Nos quitamos los abrigos. □ They stole our car. Nos robaron el coche.

ours PRONOUN
1 el nuestro *masc* (PL los nuestros)
□ Your car is much bigger than ours. Vuestro coche es mucho más grande que el nuestro. □ Our teachers are strict. — Ours are too. Nuestros profesores son estrictos. — Los nuestros también.
2 la nuestra *fem* (PL las nuestras)
□ Your house is very different from ours. Vuestra casa es muy distinta a la nuestra.
3 nuestro *masc* (PL nuestros)
□ Is this ours? ¿Esto es nuestro? □ a friend of ours un amigo nuestro
4 nuestra *fem* (PL nuestras)
□ Sorry, that table is ours. Disculpen, esa mesa es nuestra. □ Isabel is a close friend of ours. Isabel es muy amiga nuestra.

ourselves PRONOUN
1 nos *(reflexive)*
□ We really enjoyed ourselves. Nos divertimos mucho.
2 nosotros mismos (FEM nosotras mismas) *(after preposition, for emphasis)*
□ Let's not talk about ourselves any more. No hablemos más de nosotros mismos. □ We built our garage ourselves. Nos construimos el garaje nosotros mismos.
■ **by ourselves** solos (FEM solas)
□ We prefer to be by ourselves. Preferimos estar solos.

out PREPOSITION, ADVERB
▷ *see also* **out** ADJECTIVE

LANGUAGE TIP There are several ways of translating 'out'. Scan the examples to find one that is similar to what you want to say. For other expressions with 'out', see the verbs 'go', 'put', 'turn' etc.

nuestro
□ It's cold out. Fuera hace frío. □ It's dark out there. Está oscuro ahí fuera.
■ **She's out.** Ha salido.
■ **She's out for the afternoon.** No estará en toda la tarde.
■ **to go out** salir □ I'm going out tonight. Voy a salir esta noche.
■ **to go out with somebody** salir con alguien □ I've been going out with him for two months. Llevo dos meses saliendo con él.
■ **a night out with my friends** una noche por ahí con mis amigos
■ **'way out'** 'salida'
■ **out of town** fuera de la ciudad □ He lives out of town. Vive fuera de la ciudad.
■ **three kilometres out of town** a tres kilómetros de la ciudad
■ **to take something out of your pocket** sacar algo del bolsillo
■ **out of curiosity** por curiosidad
■ **We're out of milk.** Se nos ha acabado la leche.
■ **in nine cases out of ten** en nueve de cada diez casos

out ADJECTIVE
▷ *see also* **out** PREPOSITION, ADVERB
1 apagado (FEM apagada) *(lights, fire)*
□ All the lights are out. Todas las luces están apagadas.
2 eliminado (FEM eliminada) *(eliminated)*
■ **That's it, Liverpool are out.** Ya está, Liverpool queda eliminado.
■ **The film is now out on DVD.** La película ya ha salido en DVD.

outbreak NOUN
1 la epidemia
□ a salmonella outbreak una epidemia de salmonelosis
2 el comienzo
□ the outbreak of war el comienzo de la guerra

outcome NOUN
el resultado

outdoor ADJECTIVE
al aire libre
□ an outdoor swimming pool una piscina al aire libre

outdoors ADVERB
al aire libre

outfit NOUN
el traje
□ a cowboy outfit un traje de vaquero

outgoing ADJECTIVE
extrovertido (FEM extrovertida)

outing NOUN
la excursión (PL las excursiones)
□ to go on an outing ir de excursión

outline NOUN
1 el esquema *(summary)*

LANGUAGE TIP Although **esquema** ends in **-a**, it is actually a masculine noun.

□ This is an outline of the plan. Aquí tienen un esquema del plan.
2 el contorno *(shape)*
□ We could see the outline of the mountain. Veíamos el contorno de la montaña.

outlook NOUN
1 la actitud *(attitude)*
2 las perspectivas *(prospects)*

outrageous ADJECTIVE
1 escandaloso (FEM escandalosa) *(behaviour)*
2 exorbitante (FEM exorbitante) *(price)*
3 extravagante (FEM extravagante) *(clothes)*

outset NOUN
■ **at the outset** al principio

outside NOUN, ADJECTIVE
▷ *see also* **outside** PREPOSITION, ADVERB
1 el exterior
□ the outside of the house el exterior de la casa
2 exterior (FEM exterior)
□ the outside walls las paredes exteriores

outside PREPOSITION, ADVERB
▷ *see also* **outside** NOUN, ADJECTIVE
1 fuera
□ It's very cold outside. Hace mucho frío fuera.
2 fuera de
□ outside the school fuera del colegio
□ outside school hours fuera del horario escolar

outsize ADJECTIVE
■ **outsize clothes** ropa de tallas muy grandes

outskirts PL NOUN
las afueras
□ on the outskirts of town en las afueras de la ciudad

outstanding ADJECTIVE
excepcional (FEM excepcional)

oval ADJECTIVE
ovalado (FEM ovalada)

oven NOUN
el horno

over ADJECTIVE, ADVERB, PREPOSITION

LANGUAGE TIP When something is located over something, use **encima de**. When there is movement over something, use **por encima de**.

1 encima de
□ There's a mirror over the washbasin. Encima del lavabo hay un espejo.
2 por encima de
□ The ball went over the wall. La pelota pasó por encima de la pared.
■ **a bridge over the Thames** un puente sobre el Támesis
3 más de
□ It's over 20 kilos. Pesa más de 20 kilos.
■ **The temperature was over 30 degrees.** La temperatura superaba los 30 grados.
4 durante
□ over the holidays durante las vacaciones
□ over Christmas durante las Navidades
5 terminado (FEM terminada)
■ **I'll be happy when the exams are over.** Estaré feliz cuando se hayan terminado los exámenes.
■ **over here** aquí
■ **It's over there.** Está por allí.
■ **all over Scotland** en toda Escocia
■ **The shop is over the road.** La tienda está al otro lado de la calle.
■ **I spilled coffee over my shirt.** Me manché la camisa de café.

overall ADVERB
en general
□ Overall, we played very well. En general jugamos muy bien.

overalls PL NOUN
el mono (el overol *Latin America*) *(for work)*

overcast ADJECTIVE
cubierto (FEM cubierta)
□ The sky was overcast. El cielo estaba cubierto.

to **overcharge** VERB
cobrar de más
□ They overcharged us for the meal. Nos cobraron de más por la comida.

overcoat NOUN
el abrigo

overdone ADJECTIVE
1 recocido (FEM recocida) *(vegetables)*
2 demasiado hecho (FEM demasiado hecha) *(steak)*

overdose NOUN
la sobredosis (PL las sobredosis)

overdraft NOUN
el descubierto

to **overestimate** VERB
sobreestimar
□ We overestimated how long it would take. Sobreestimamos el tiempo que se tardaría.

overhead projector NOUN
el retroproyector

to **overlook** VERB
1 tener* vistas a
□ The hotel overlooked the beach. El hotel tenía vistas a la playa.
2 pasar por alto
□ He had overlooked one important problem. Había pasado por alto un problema importante.

overseas ADVERB
en el extranjero *(live, work)*
□ I'd like to work overseas. Me gustaría trabajar en el extranjero.

oversight NOUN
el descuido

to **oversleep** VERB
quedarse dormido
□ I overslept this morning. Me quedé dormido esta mañana.

to **overtake** VERB
adelantar (rebasar *Latin America*)

overtime NOUN
las horas extras
■ **to work overtime** trabajar horas extras

overweight ADJECTIVE
■ **to be overweight** tener exceso de peso

to **owe** VERB
deber
□ How much do I owe you? ¿Cuánto te debo?

owing to PREPOSITION
debido a
□ owing to bad weather debido al mal tiempo

owl NOUN
el búho

own ADJECTIVE, PRONOUN
▷ *see also* **own** VERB
propio (FEM propia)
□ This is my own recipe. Ésta es mi propia receta. □ I wish I had a room of my own. Me gustaría tener mi propia habitación.
■ **on his own** él solo □ on her own ella sola □ on our own nosotros solos

to **own** VERB
▷ *see also* **own** ADJECTIVE
tener*

to **own up** VERB
confesarse* culpable
■ **to own up to something** confesar algo

owner NOUN
el proprietario
la propietaria

oxygen NOUN
el oxígeno

oyster NOUN
la ostra

ozone layer NOUN
la capa de ozono

Pp

PA NOUN *(= personal assistant)*
el secretario de dirección
la secretaria de dirección
□ She's a PA. Es secretaria de dirección.
■ **the PA system** *(public address)* la megafonía

pace NOUN
el ritmo
□ the frantic pace of life in London el frenético ritmo de vida de Londres

Pacific NOUN
■ **the Pacific** el Pacífico

pacifier NOUN (US)
el chupete

to **pack** VERB
▷ *see also* **pack** NOUN
hacer* las maletas (empacar *Latin America*)
□ I'll help you pack. Te ayudaré a hacer las maletas.
■ **I've already packed my case.** Ya he hecho mi maleta.
■ **Pack it in!** ¡Vale ya!

pack NOUN
▷ *see also* **pack** VERB
el paquete
□ a pack of cigarettes un paquete de tabaco
■ **a pack of cards** una baraja

package NOUN
el paquete
■ **a package holiday** unas vacaciones organizadas

packed ADJECTIVE
abarrotado (FEM abarrotada)
□ The cinema was packed. El cine estaba abarrotado.

packed lunch NOUN
■ **I take a packed lunch to school.** Me llevo la comida al colegio.

packet NOUN
el paquete
□ a packet of cigarettes un paquete de tabaco
■ **a packet of crisps** una bolsa de patatas fritas

pad NOUN
el bloc

to **paddle** VERB
▷ *see also* **paddle** NOUN
1 chapotear *(swim)*
2 remar
□ to paddle a canoe remar en canoa

paddle NOUN
▷ *see also* **paddle** VERB
la pala
■ **to go for a paddle** mojase los pies

padlock NOUN
el candado

page NOUN
▷ *see also* **page** VERB
la página
□ on page 13 en la página 13

to **page** VERB
▷ *see also* **page** NOUN
■ **to page somebody** llamar a alguien al busca

pager NOUN
el busca

LANGUAGE TIP Although **busca** ends in **-a**, it is actually a masculine noun.

paid VERB ▷ *see* **pay**

paid ADJECTIVE
1 remunerado (FEM remunerada)
□ to do paid work realizar trabajo remunerado
2 pagado (FEM pagada)
□ three weeks' paid holiday tres semanas de vacaciones pagadas

pail NOUN
el cubo

pain NOUN
el dolor
□ a terrible pain un dolor tremendo
■ **I've got a pain in my stomach.** Me duele el estómago.
■ **She's in a lot of pain.** Tiene muchos dolores.
■ **He's a real pain.** *(informal)* Es un auténtico pelmazo.

painful ADJECTIVE

LANGUAGE TIP **doloroso** is used when talking about what causes pain, and **dolorido** for the person or thing that feels pain.

1 doloroso (FEM dolorosa)
□ a painful injury una herida dolorosa
2 dolorido (FEM dolorida)
□ Her feet were swollen and painful. Tenía los pies hinchados y doloridos.
■ **Is it painful?** ¿Te duele?

painkiller NOUN
el analgésico

paint NOUN
▹ *see also* **paint** VERB
la pintura

to **paint** VERB
▹ *see also* **paint** NOUN
pintar
□ to paint something green pintar algo de verde

paintbrush NOUN
1 el pincel *(for an artist)*
2 la brocha *(for decorating)*

painter NOUN
el pintor
la pintora
□ The painters made a real mess of the windows. Los pintores dejaron las ventanas hechas un desastre.

painting NOUN
1 el cuadro
□ a painting by Picasso un cuadro de Picasso
2 la pintura
□ My hobby is painting. Mi hobby es la pintura.

pair NOUN
el par
□ a pair of shoes un par de zapatos
■ **a pair of scissors** unas tijeras
■ **a pair of trousers** unos pantalones
■ **in pairs** por parejas

pajamas PL NOUN (US)
el pijama (el piyama *Latin America*)
□ my pajamas mi pijama
■ **a pair of pajamas** un pijama
LANGUAGE TIP Although **pijama** ends in **-a**, it is actually a masculine noun.

Pakistan NOUN
Paquistán *masc*

Pakistani ADJECTIVE
▹ *see also* **Pakistani** NOUN
paquistaní (PL paquistaníes)

Pakistani NOUN
▹ *see also* **Pakistani** ADJECTIVE
el/la paquistaní (PL los paquistaníes)

pal NOUN
el amiguete
la amigueta

palace NOUN
el palacio

pale ADJECTIVE
1 pálido (FEM pálida)
□ She still looks very pale. Está todavía muy pálida.
■ **to turn pale** ponerse pálido
2 claro (FEM clara)
□ pale green verde claro
■ **pale pink** rosa pálido
■ **pale blue** azul celeste

Palestine NOUN
Palestina *fem*

Palestinian ADJECTIVE
▹ *see also* **Palestinian** NOUN
palestino (FEM palestina)

Palestinian NOUN
▹ *see also* **Palestinian** ADJECTIVE
el palestino
la palestina

palm NOUN
la palma
□ the palm of your hand la palma de la mano
■ **a palm tree** una palmera

pamphlet NOUN
el folleto

pan NOUN
1 la cacerola *(saucepan)*
2 la sartén (PL las sartenes) *(frying pan)*

pancake NOUN
la crepe (el panqueque *Latin America*)

panic NOUN
▹ *see also* **panic** VERB
el pánico
□ The shouting caused quite a panic. El griterío provocó el pánico.

to **panic** VERB
▹ *see also* **panic** NOUN
■ **He panicked as soon as he saw the blood.** Le entró pánico en cuanto vio la sangre.
■ **Don't panic!** ¡Tranquilo!

panther NOUN
la pantera

panties PL NOUN
las bragas

pantomime NOUN
la revista musical representada en Navidad

pants PL NOUN
1 las bragas *(for women)*
2 los calzoncillos *(for men)*
3 los pantalones (US)

pantyhose PL NOUN (US)
las medias

paper NOUN
1 el papel
□ a paper bag una bolsa de papel
■ **a piece of paper** un papel (una hoja *Latin America*)
■ **an exam paper** un examen

2 el periódico
□ I saw an advert in the paper. Vi un anuncio en el periódico.

paperback NOUN
el libro de bolsillo

paper boy NOUN
el repartidor de periódicos

paper clip NOUN
el clip (PL los clips)

paper girl NOUN
la repartidora de periódicos

paper round NOUN
■ **to do a paper round** repartir los periódicos a domicilio

paperweight NOUN
el pisapapeles (PL los pisapapeles)

paperwork NOUN
el papeleo
□ I've got a lot of paperwork to do. Tengo un montón de papeleo que hacer.

parachute NOUN
el paracaídas (PL los paracaídas)

parade NOUN
el desfile

paradise NOUN
el paraíso

paraffin NOUN
el queroseno
■ **a paraffin lamp** una lámpara de petróleo

paragraph NOUN
el párrafo

parallel ADJECTIVE
paralelo (FEM paralela)

paralysed ADJECTIVE
paralizado (FEM paralizada)

paramedic NOUN
el auxiliar sanitario
la auxiliar sanitaria

parcel NOUN
el paquete

pardon NOUN
■ **Pardon?** ¿Cómo?

parents PL NOUN
los padres (los papás *Latin America*)
LANGUAGE TIP Be careful not to translate **parents** by **parientes**.

Paris NOUN
París *masc*

park NOUN
▷ *see also* **park** VERB
el parque
■ **a national park** un parque nacional
■ **a theme park** un parque temático
■ **a car park** un aparcamiento (un estacionamiento *Latin America*)

to **park** VERB
▷ *see also* **park** NOUN
aparcar*
□ Where can I park my car? ¿Dónde puedo aparcar el coche?
■ **'no parking'** 'prohibido aparcar'

parking lot NOUN (US)
el aparcamiento

parking meter NOUN
el parquímetro

parking ticket NOUN
la multa de aparcamiento

parliament NOUN
el parlamento
■ **the Spanish Parliament** las Cortes

parole NOUN
■ **on parole** en libertad condicional

parrot NOUN
el loro

parsley NOUN
el perejil

part NOUN
1 la parte
□ The first part of the play was boring. La primera parte de la obra fue aburrida.
2 el papel
□ She had a small part in the film. Tenía un pequeño papel en la película.
3 la pieza
□ spare parts piezas de repuesto
■ **to take part in something** participar en algo □ Thousands of people took part in the demonstration. Miles de personas participaron en la manifestación.

particular ADJECTIVE
1 concreto (FEM concreta) *(definite)*
□ I can't remember that particular film. No recuerdo esa película concreta.
2 especial (FEM especial) *(special)*
□ He showed a particular interest in the subject. Mostró un interés especial en el tema.
■ **in particular** en concreto □ Are you looking for anything in particular? ¿Busca algo en concreto? □ nothing in particular nada en concreto

particularly ADVERB
especialmente
□ a particularly boring lecture una clase especialmente aburrida

parting NOUN
la raya

partly ADVERB
en parte
□ It was partly my own fault. En parte fue culpa mía.

partner NOUN
1 el socio
la socia
□ He's a partner in a law firm. Es socio de un bufete de abogados.

English-Spanish

p

2 la pareja
□ That doesn't mean you don't love your partner. Eso no significa que no quieras a tu pareja. □ my dancing partner mi pareja de baile

part-time ADJECTIVE, ADVERB
a tiempo parcial
□ a part-time job un trabajo a tiempo parcial □ She works part-time. Trabaja a tiempo parcial.

party NOUN
1 la fiesta
□ a birthday party una fiesta de cumpleaños
2 el partido
□ the Conservative Party el partido conservador
3 el grupo
□ a party of tourists un grupo de turistas

pass NOUN
▷ *see also* **pass** VERB
1 el pase *(in football)*
□ a short pass un pase en corto
2 el puerto
□ The pass was blocked with snow. El puerto estaba bloqueado por la nieve.
3 el aprobado
□ She got a pass in her piano exam. Sacó un aprobado en el examen de piano.
■ **a bus pass** un abono para el autobús

to **pass** VERB
▷ *see also* **pass** NOUN
1 pasar
□ Could you pass me the salt, please? ¿Me pasas la sal, por favor? □ The time has passed quickly. El tiempo ha pasado rápido.
2 adelantar
□ We were passed by a huge lorry. Nos adelantó un camión enorme.
3 pasar por delante de
□ I pass his house on my way to school. Paso por delante de su casa de camino al colegio.
4 aprobar*
□ Did you pass? ¿Has aprobado? □ to pass an exam aprobar un examen

to **pass out** VERB
desmayarse

passage NOUN
1 el pasaje
□ Read the passage carefully. Lea el pasaje con atención.
2 el pasillo
□ a narrow passage un estrecho pasillo

passenger NOUN
el pasajero
la pasajera

passion NOUN
la pasión (PL las pasiones)
□ Football is a passion of his. El fútbol es una de sus pasiones.

passive ADJECTIVE
pasivo (FEM pasiva)
□ a passive smoker un fumador pasivo

Passover NOUN
la Pascua judía

passport NOUN
el pasaporte
□ passport control el control de pasaportes

password NOUN
la contraseña

past ADJECTIVE, ADVERB, PREPOSITION
▷ *see also* **past** NOUN
pasado (FEM pasada)
□ This past year has been very difficult. Este año pasado ha sido muy difícil.
■ **The school is 100 metres past the traffic lights.** El colegio está a unos 100 metros pasado el semáforo.
■ **to go past** pasar □ The bus went past without stopping. El autobús pasó sin parar.
■ **It's half past ten.** Son las diez y media.
■ **It's a quarter past nine.** Son las nueve y cuarto.
■ **It's ten past eight.** Son las ocho y diez.
■ **It's past midnight.** Es pasada la medianoche.

past NOUN
▷ *see also* **past** ADJECTIVE, ADVERB, PREPOSITION
el pasado
□ I try not to think of the past. Intento no pensar en el pasado.
■ **This was common in the past.** Antiguamente esto era normal.

pasta NOUN
la pasta

paste NOUN
el engrudo *(glue)*

pasteurized ADJECTIVE
pasteurizado (FEM pasteurizada)

pastime NOUN
el pasatiempo

pastry NOUN
1 la masa *(dough)*
2 el pastel *(cake)*

patch NOUN
el parche
□ a patch of material un parche de tela
■ **He's got a bald patch.** Tiene una calva incipiente.
■ **They're going through a bad patch.** Están pasando una mala racha.

patched ADJECTIVE
■ **a pair of patched jeans** unos vaqueros con remiendos

pâté NOUN
el paté

path NOUN
el sendero

pathetic ADJECTIVE
penoso (FEM penosa)
□ That was a pathetic excuse. Fue una excusa penosa.

patience NOUN
1 la paciencia
□ He hasn't got much patience. No tiene mucha paciencia.
2 el solitario *(game)*
□ She was playing patience. Estaba haciendo un solitario.

patient NOUN
▷ *see also* **patient** ADJECTIVE
el paciente
la paciente

patient ADJECTIVE
▷ *see also* **patient** NOUN
paciente (FEM paciente)

patio NOUN
el patio

patriotic ADJECTIVE
patriótico (FEM patriótica)

patrol NOUN
la patrulla
■ **to be on patrol** estar de patrulla

patrol car NOUN
el coche patrulla (PL los coches patrulla)

pattern NOUN
1 el motivo *(design)*
□ a geometric pattern un motivo geométrico
2 el patrón *(for sewing)*

pause NOUN
la pausa

pavement NOUN
la acera

paw NOUN
la pata

pay NOUN
▷ *see also* **pay** VERB
el sueldo
□ a pay rise un aumento de sueldo

to **pay** VERB
▷ *see also* **pay** NOUN
pagar*
□ They pay me more on Sundays. Me pagan más los domingos. □ Can I pay by cheque? ¿Puedo pagar con cheque?
■ **to pay money into an account** ingresar dinero en una cuenta
■ **I'll pay you back tomorrow.** Mañana te devuelvo el dinero.
■ **to pay for something** pagar algo □ I paid for my ticket. Pagué el billete.
■ **I paid £50 for it.** Me costó 50 libras.
■ **Does your current account pay interest?** ¿Le rinde intereses su cuenta corriente?
■ **to pay somebody a visit** ir a ver a alguien □ Paul paid us a visit last night. Paul vino a vernos anoche.

payable ADJECTIVE
■ **Who's the cheque payable to?** ¿A nombre de quién extiendo el cheque?

payment NOUN
el pago
□ mortgage payments los pagos de la hipoteca

payphone NOUN
el teléfono público

PC NOUN *(= personal computer)*
el PC

PE NOUN *(= physical education)*
la educación física
□ We do PE twice a week. Tenemos educación física dos veces a la semana.

pea NOUN
el guisante

peace NOUN
la paz
■ **peace talks** conversaciones de paz
■ **a peace treaty** un tratado de paz

peaceful ADJECTIVE
1 pacífico (FEM pacífica) *(non-violent)*
□ a peaceful protest una manifestación pacífica
2 apacible (FEM apacible) *(restful)*
□ a peaceful afternoon una tarde apacible

peach NOUN
el melocotón (PL los melocotones)

peacock NOUN
el pavo real

peak NOUN
1 la cumbre
□ the snow-covered peaks las cumbres nevadas
2 el apogeo
□ She's at the peak of her career. Está en el apogeo de su carrera profesional.
■ **in peak season** en temporada alta

peanut NOUN
el cacahuete (el maní *Latin America*)

peanut butter NOUN
la crema de cacahuete

pear NOUN
la pera

pearl NOUN
la perla

pebble NOUN
el guijarro

peckish ADJECTIVE
■ **to feel a bit peckish** tener un poquito de hambre

peculiar ADJECTIVE

raro (FEM rara)
□ He's a peculiar person. Es una persona rara. □ It tastes peculiar. Sabe raro.

pedal NOUN
el pedal

pedestrian NOUN
el peatón (PL los peatones)

pedestrian crossing NOUN
el paso de peatones

pedestrianized ADJECTIVE
■ **a pedestrianized street** una calle peatonal

pedestrian precinct NOUN
la zona peatonal

pedigree ADJECTIVE
de raza
□ a pedigree dog un perro de raza □ a pedigree labrador un labrador de pura raza

pee NOUN
■ **to have a pee** hacer pis

peek NOUN
■ **to have a peek at something** echar una ojeada a algo □ I had a peek at your dress and it's lovely. Le eché una ojeada a tu vestido y es muy mono.

peel NOUN
▹ *see also* **peel** VERB
la piel

to **peel** VERB
▹ *see also* **peel** NOUN
pelar
□ Shall I peel the potatoes? ¿Pelo las patatas?
■ **My nose is peeling.** Se me está pelando la nariz.

peg NOUN
1 el gancho *(for coats)*
2 la pinza *(clothes peg)*
3 la estaca *(tent peg)*

Pekinese NOUN
el pequinés (PL los pequineses)

pellet NOUN
el perdigón (PL los perdigones) *(for gun)*

pelvis NOUN
la pelvis (PL las pelvis)

pen NOUN
1 el bolígrafo *(ballpoint pen)*
2 la pluma *(fountain pen)*
3 el rotulador *(felt-tip pen)*

penalty NOUN
1 la pena
□ The penalty for this offence is life imprisonment. La pena por este delito es cadena perpetua.
■ **the death penalty** la pena de muerte
2 el penalty (PL los penaltys) *(in football)*
3 el golpe de castigo *(in rugby)*
■ **a penalty shoot-out** una tanda de penaltys

pence PL NOUN
■ **24 pence** 24 peniques

pencil NOUN
el lápiz (PL los lápices) (el lapicero *Latin America*)
■ **to write in pencil** escribir a lápiz

pencil case NOUN
el estuche

pencil sharpener NOUN
el sacapuntas (PL los sacapuntas)

penfriend NOUN
el amigo por correspondencia
la amiga por correspondencia

penguin NOUN
el pingüino

penicillin NOUN
la penicilina

penis NOUN
el pene

penitentiary NOUN (US)
la cárcel

penknife NOUN
la navaja

penny NOUN
el penique

pension NOUN
la pensión (PL las pensiones)

pensioner NOUN
el/la pensionista

pentathlon NOUN
el pentatlón

people PL NOUN
1 la gente
□ The people were nice. La gente era simpática. □ a lot of people mucha gente
2 las personas
□ six people seis personas □ several people varias personas
■ **People say that...** Dicen que...
■ **How many people are there in your family?** ¿Cuántos sois en tu familia?
■ **Spanish people** los españoles

pepper NOUN
1 la pimienta
□ Pass the pepper, please. ¿Me pasas la pimienta?
2 el pimiento (el chile *Latin America*)
□ a green pepper un pimiento verde

peppermill NOUN
el molinillo de pimienta

peppermint NOUN
el caramelo de menta
■ **peppermint chewing gum** el chicle de menta

per PREPOSITION
por
□ per person por persona □ 30 miles per hour 30 millas por hora

■ **per day** al día
■ **per week** a la semana

per cent ADVERB
por ciento
□ 50 per cent 50 por ciento

percentage NOUN
el porcentaje

percolator NOUN
la cafetera de filtro

percussion NOUN
la percusión
□ I play percussion. Toco la percusión.

perfect ADJECTIVE
perfecto (FEM perfecta)
□ Dave speaks perfect Spanish. Dave habla un español perfecto.

perfectly ADVERB
■ **You know perfectly well what happened.** Sabes perfectamente lo que ocurrió.
■ **a perfectly normal child** un niño completamente normal

to **perform** VERB
representar *(a play)*
□ to perform Hamlet representar Hamlet
■ **The team performed brilliantly.** El equipo tuvo una brillante actuación.

performance NOUN
1 el espectáculo
□ The performance lasts two hours. El espectáculo dura dos horas.
2 la interpretación (PL las interpretaciones)
□ his performance as Hamlet su interpretación de Hamlet

perfume NOUN
el perfume

perhaps ADVERB
quizás
□ Perhaps they were tired. Quizás estaban cansados.

LANGUAGE TIP Use the present subjunctive after **quizás** to refer to the future.

□ Perhaps he'll come tomorrow. Quizás venga mañana.
■ **perhaps not** quizás no

period NOUN
1 el periodo
□ for a limited period por un periodo limitado
2 la clase
□ Each period lasts forty minutes. Cada clase dura cuarenta minutos.
3 la época
□ the Victorian period la época victoriana
4 la regla
□ I'm having my period. Estoy con la regla.

perm NOUN
la permanente
□ She's got a perm. Lleva permanente.

permanent ADJECTIVE
1 permanente (FEM permanente)
□ a permanent state of tension un estado permanente de tensión
2 fijo (FEM fija)
□ a permanent job un trabajo fijo

permission NOUN
el permiso
□ Could I have permission to leave early? ¿Tengo permiso para salir antes?

permit NOUN
el permiso
□ a work permit un permiso de trabajo

Persian ADJECTIVE
■ **a Persian cat** un gato persa

persistent ADJECTIVE
persistente (FEM persistente)

person NOUN
la persona
□ She's a very nice person. Es muy buena persona.
■ **in person** en persona

personal ADJECTIVE
personal (FEM personal)
□ Those letters are personal. Son cartas personales. □ He's a personal friend of mine. Es amigo íntimo mío.

personality NOUN
la personalidad

personally ADVERB
personalmente
□ Personally I don't agree. Yo personalmente no estoy de acuerdo.
■ **I don't know him personally.** No lo conozco en persona.
■ **Don't take it personally.** No te lo tomes como algo personal.

personal stereo NOUN
el walkman®

personnel NOUN
el personal

perspiration NOUN
la transpiración

to **persuade** VERB
convencer*

LANGUAGE TIP Use the subjunctive after **convencer de que** when translating 'to persuade somebody to do something'.

■ **to persuade sb to do sth** convencer a alguien de que haga algo □ She persuaded me to go with her. Me convenció de que fuera con ella.

Peru NOUN
Perú *masc*

Peruvian ADJECTIVE
▷ *see also* **Peruvian** NOUN
peruano (FEM peruana)

English–Spanish

P

Peruvian NOUN
▷ *see also* **Peruvian** ADJECTIVE
el peruano
la peruana
pessimist NOUN
el/la pesimista
pessimistic ADJECTIVE
pesimista (FEM pesimista)
□ Don't be so pessimistic! ¡No seas tan pesimista! □ a pessimistic forecast un pronóstico pesimista
pest NOUN
el pesado
la pesada
□ He's a real pest! ¡Es un pesado!
to **pester** VERB
dar* la lata a
□ He's always pestering me. Siempre me está dando la lata.
pet NOUN
el animal doméstico
■ **Have you got a pet?** ¿Tenéis algún animal en casa?
■ **She's the teacher's pet.** Es la enchufada del profesor.
petition NOUN
la petición (PL las peticiones)
petrified ADJECTIVE
■ **She's petrified of spiders.** Las arañas le dan terror.
petrol NOUN
la gasolina
■ **unleaded petrol** gasolina sin plomo
■ **4-star petrol** gasolina súper
petrol pump NOUN
el surtidor de gasolina
petrol station NOUN
la gasolinera
petrol tank NOUN
el depósito de gasolina
phantom NOUN
el fantasma
LANGUAGE TIP Although **fantasma** ends in **-a**, it is actually a masculine noun.
pharmacy NOUN
la farmacia
DID YOU KNOW...?
Pharmacies in Spain are identified by a green cross outside the shop.
pheasant NOUN
el faisán (PL los faisanes)
philosophy NOUN
la filosofía
phobia NOUN
la fobia
phone NOUN
▷ *see also* **phone** VERB
el teléfono
■ **by phone** por teléfono
■ **to be on the phone 1** *(talking)* estar al teléfono □ She's on the phone at the moment. Ahora mismo está al teléfono.
2 *(to have a phone)* tener teléfono □ We're not on the phone. No tenemos teléfono.
■ **Can I use the phone, please?** ¿Puedo hacer una llamada?
to **phone** VERB
▷ *see also* **phone** NOUN
llamar
□ I'll phone you tomorrow. Mañana te llamo. □ Could you phone for a taxi for me, please? ¿Me puedes llamar a un taxi, por favor?
phone bill NOUN
la factura del teléfono
phone book NOUN
la guía telefónica
phone box NOUN
la cabina telefónica
phone call NOUN
la llamada de teléfono
■ **There's a phone call for you.** Tienes una llamada.
■ **to make a phone call** hacer una llamada
phonecard NOUN
la tarjeta telefónica
phone number NOUN
el número de teléfono
photo NOUN
la foto
LANGUAGE TIP Although **foto** ends in **-o**, it is actually a feminine noun.
■ **to take a photo** hacer una foto □ I took a photo of the bride and groom. Les hice una foto a los novios.
photocopier NOUN
la fotocopiadora
photocopy NOUN
▷ *see also* **photocopy** VERB
la fotocopia
to **photocopy** VERB
▷ *see also* **photocopy** NOUN
fotocopiar
photograph NOUN
▷ *see also* **photograph** VERB
la fotografía
■ **to take a photograph** hacer una fotografía □ I took a photograph of the bride and groom. Les hice una fotografía a los novios.
to **photograph** VERB
▷ *see also* **photograph** NOUN
fotografiar*
photographer NOUN
el fotógrafo

la fotógrafa
□ She's a photographer. Es fotógrafa.

photography NOUN
la fotografía
□ My hobby is photography. Mi hobby es la fotografía.

phrase NOUN
la frase

phrase book NOUN
el manual de conversación

physical ADJECTIVE
▷ *see also* **physical** NOUN
físico (FEM física)

physical NOUN (US)
▷ *see also* **physical** ADJECTIVE
el reconocimiento médico

physicist NOUN
el físico
la física
□ a nuclear physicist un físico nuclear

physics NOUN
la física
□ She teaches physics. Enseña física.

physiotherapist NOUN
el/la fisioterapeuta

physiotherapy NOUN
la fisioterapia

pianist NOUN
el/la pianista

piano NOUN
el piano
□ I play the piano. Toco el piano.

pick NOUN
▷ *see also* **pick** VERB
■ **Take your pick!** ¡Elige el que quieras!

LANGUAGE TIP Replace **el que** with **la que**, **los que** or **las que** as appropriate to agree with the thing or things you can take your pick of.

to **pick** VERB
▷ *see also* **pick** NOUN
1 elegir* *(choose)*
□ I picked the biggest piece. Elegí el trozo más grande.
2 seleccionar *(for team)*
□ I've been picked for the team. Me han seleccionado para el equipo.
3 recoger* *(fruit, flowers)*
■ **to pick on somebody** meterse con alguien □ She's always picking on me. Siempre se está metiendo conmigo.

to **pick out** VERB
escoger*
□ I like them all – it's difficult to pick one out. Todos me gustan, es difícil escoger uno.

to **pick up** VERB
1 recoger*
□ We'll come to the airport to pick you up. Iremos a recogerte al aeropuerto. □ Could you help me pick up the toys? ¿Me ayudas a recoger los juguetes?
2 aprender
□ I picked up some Spanish during my holiday. Aprendí un poco de español en las vacaciones.

pickpocket NOUN
el/la carterista

picnic NOUN
el picnic (PL los picnics)
■ **to have a picnic** irse de picnic

picture NOUN
1 la ilustración (PL las ilustraciones)
□ Children's books have lots of pictures. Los libros para niños tienen muchas ilustraciones.
2 la foto

LANGUAGE TIP Although **foto** ends in **-o**, it is actually a feminine noun.

□ My picture was in the paper. Mi foto salió en el periódico.
3 el cuadro *(painting)*
□ a picture by Picasso un cuadro de Picasso
■ **a picture of his wife** un retrato de su mujer
4 el dibujo *(drawing)*
■ **to draw a picture of something** dibujar algo
■ **to paint a picture of something** pintar algo
■ **the pictures** el cine □ Shall we go to the pictures? ¿Vamos al cine?

picture message NOUN
el mensaje con foto

picturesque ADJECTIVE
pintoresco (FEM pintoresca)

pie NOUN
1 la tarta *(sweet)*
□ an apple pie una tarta de manzana
2 el pastel *(of meat)*
□ a meat pie un pastel de carne

piece NOUN
1 el trozo
□ a piece of cake un trozo de tarta
■ **A small piece, please.** Un trocito, por favor.
2 pieza *(individual)*
□ a 500-piece jigsaw un puzzle de 500 piezas
3 pedazo *(of something larger)*
□ A piece of plaster fell from the roof. Un pedazo de yeso se cayó del tejado.
■ **a piece of furniture** un mueble
■ **a piece of advice** un consejo
■ **a 10p piece** una moneda de 10 peniques

pier NOUN
el muelle

pierced ADJECTIVE
■ **I've got pierced ears.** Tengo los agujeros hechos en las orejas.

pig NOUN
el cerdo

pigeon NOUN
la paloma

piggyback NOUN
■ **to give somebody a piggyback** llevar a alguien a cuestas

piggy bank NOUN
la hucha

pigtail NOUN
la trenza

pile NOUN
1 el montón (PL los montones) *(untidy heap)*
□ a pile of dirty laundry un montón de ropa sucia
2 la pila *(tidy stack)*
■ **Put your books in a pile on my desk.** Apilad vuestros cuadernos en mi mesa.

piles PL NOUN
las almorranas

pile-up NOUN
el accidente en cadena

pill NOUN
la píldora
■ **to be on the pill** tomar la píldora

pillar NOUN
1 el pilar

pillar box NOUN
2 el buzón (PL los buzones)

pillow NOUN
la almohada

pilot NOUN
el/la piloto
□ He's a pilot. Es piloto.

pimple NOUN
el grano

pin NOUN
el alfiler
■ **pins and needles** el hormigueo
□ I've got pins and needles. Tengo hormigueo.

PIN NOUN *(= personal identification number)*
el número secreto

pinafore NOUN
el pichi

pinball NOUN
la máquina de bolas
■ **They're playing pinball.** Juegan a la máquina.

to **pinch** VERB
1 pellizcar*
□ He pinched me! ¡Me ha pellizcado!
2 birlar* *(informal)*
□ Who's pinched my pen? ¿Quién me ha birlado el bolígrafo?

pine NOUN
el pino
□ a pine table una mesa de pino

pineapple NOUN
la piña

pink ADJECTIVE
rosa (FEM + PL rosa)

pint NOUN
la pinta

DID YOU KNOW...?
In Spain measurements are in litres and centilitres. A pint is about 0.6 litres.

■ **to have a pint** tomarse una cerveza
□ He's gone out for a pint. Ha salido a tomarse una cerveza.

pipe NOUN
1 la tubería
□ The pipes froze. Se helaron las tuberías.
2 la pipa
□ He smokes a pipe. Fuma en pipa.
■ **the pipes** la gaita □ He plays the pipes. Toca la gaita.

pirate NOUN
el/la pirata

pirated ADJECTIVE
pirata (FEM + PL pirata)
□ a pirated video un vídeo pirata

Pisces NOUN
el Piscis *(sign)*
■ **I'm Pisces.** Soy piscis.

pissed ADJECTIVE
mamado (FEM mamada) *(rude)*

pistol NOUN
la pistola

pitch NOUN
▷ *see also* **pitch** VERB
el campo (la cancha *Latin America*)
□ a football pitch un campo de fútbol

to **pitch** VERB
▷ *see also* **pitch** NOUN
montar
□ We pitched our tent near the beach. Montamos la tienda cerca de la playa.

pity NOUN
▷ *see also* **pity** VERB
la compasión
□ They showed no pity. No demostraron ninguna compasión.
■ **What a pity!** ¡Qué pena!

to **pity** VERB
▷ *see also* **pity** NOUN
compadecer*
□ I don't hate him, I pity him. No lo odio, lo compadezco.

pizza NOUN
la pizza

place NOUN
▷ *see also* **place** VERB

1 el lugar
□ It's a quiet place. Es un lugar tranquilo.
2 la plaza
□ Book your place for the trip now. Reserve ya su plaza para el viaje. □ a university place una plaza en la universidad
3 el puesto *(in sports)*
□ Britain won third place in the games. Gran Bretaña consiguió el tercer puesto en los juegos.
■ **a parking place** un sitio para aparcar
■ **to change places** cambiarse de sitio
■ **to take place** tener lugar □ Elections will take place on November 25th. Las elecciones tendrán lugar el 25 de noviembre.
■ **at your place** en tu casa □ Shall we meet at your place? ¿Nos vemos en tu casa?
■ **Do you want to come round to my place?** ¿Quieres venir a mi casa?

to place VERB
▷ *see also* **place** NOUN
colocar*
□ He placed his hand on hers. Colocó su mano sobre la de ella.

plain ADJECTIVE, ADVERB
▷ *see also* **plain** NOUN
1 liso (FEM lisa) *(not patterned)*
□ a plain tie una corbata lisa
2 sencillo (FEM sencilla) *(not fancy)*
□ a plain white blouse una blusa blanca sencilla
■ **It was plain to see.** Era obvio.

plain NOUN
▷ *see also* **plain** ADJECTIVE, ADVERB
la llanura

plain chocolate NOUN
el chocolate amargo

plait NOUN
la trenza
□ She wears her hair in plaits. Lleva trenzas.

plan NOUN
▷ *see also* **plan** VERB
1 el plan
□ What are your plans for the holidays? ¿Qué planes tienes para las vacaciones?
■ **to make plans** hacer planes
■ **Everything went according to plan.** Todo fue según lo previsto.
2 el plano
□ a plan of the campsite un plano del camping
■ **my essay plan** el esquema de mi trabajo

to plan VERB
▷ *see also* **plan** NOUN
1 planear *(make plans for)*
□ We're planning a trip to France. Estamos planeando hacer un viaje a Francia.
2 planificar* *(schedule)*
□ Plan your revision carefully. Tienes que planificar bien el repaso.
■ **to plan to do something** tener la intención de hacer algo □ I'm planning to get a job in the holidays. Tengo la intención de encontrar un trabajo para las vacaciones.

plane NOUN
el avión (PL los aviones)
□ by plane en avión

planet NOUN
el planeta

LANGUAGE TIP Although **planeta** ends in **-a**, it is actually a masculine noun.

planning NOUN
■ **The trip needs careful planning.** Hay que planear bien el viaje.
■ **family planning** la planificación familiar

plant NOUN
▷ *see also* **plant** VERB
la planta
□ I water my plants every week. Riego las plantas todas las semanas.
■ **a chemical plant** una planta química

to plant VERB
▷ *see also* **plant** NOUN
plantar
□ We planted fruit trees and vegetables. Plantamos árboles frutales y hortalizas.

plant pot NOUN
la maceta

plaque NOUN
1 la placa conmemorativa *(to famous person, event)*
2 el sarro *(on teeth)*

plaster NOUN
1 la tirita
□ Have you got a plaster, by any chance? ¿No tendrás una tirita, por casualidad?
2 la escayola
■ **Her leg's in plaster.** Lleva la pierna escayolada.

plastic NOUN
▷ *see also* **plastic** ADJECTIVE
el plástico
□ It's made of plastic. Es de plástico.

plastic ADJECTIVE
▷ *see also* **plastic** NOUN
de plástico
□ a plastic bag una bolsa de plástico

plate NOUN
el plato

platform NOUN
1 el andén (PL los andenes)
2 el estrado *(for speaker, performer)*

play NOUN
▷ *see also* **play** VERB
la obra de teatro

■ **a play by Shakespeare** una obra de Shakespeare
■ **to put on a play** montar una obra

to **play** VERB
▹ *see also* **play** NOUN
1 jugar*
□ He's playing with his friends. Está jugando con sus amigos.
2 jugar contra
□ Spain will play Scotland next month. España juega contra Escocia el mes que viene.
3 jugar a
□ Can you play pool? ¿Sabes jugar al billar americano?
4 tocar*
□ I play the guitar. Toco la guitarra. □ What sort of music do they play? ¿Qué clase de música tocan?
5 poner*
□ She's always playing that CD. Siempre está poniendo ese CD.
6 hacer* de
□ I would love to play Cleopatra. Me encantaría hacer de Cleopatra.

to **play down** VERB
quitar importancia a
□ He tried to play down his illness. Trató de quitarle importancia a su enfermedad.

player NOUN
1 el jugador
la jugadora
□ a game for four players un juego para cuatro jugadores
■ **a football player** un futbolista
2 el músico
la música *(musician)*
■ **a piano player** un pianista
■ **a saxophone player** un saxofonista

playful ADJECTIVE
juguetón (FEM juguetona)

playground NOUN
1 el patio de recreo *(at school)*
2 los columpios *(in park)*

playgroup NOUN
la guardería

playing card NOUN
el naipe

playing field NOUN
el campo de deportes (la cancha de deportes *Latin America*)

playtime NOUN
el recreo

playwright NOUN
el dramaturgo
la dramaturga

pleasant ADJECTIVE
agradable (FEM agradable)
□ We had a very pleasant evening. Pasamos una tarde muy agradable.

please EXCLAMATION
por favor
□ Two coffees, please. Dos cafés, por favor.
LANGUAGE TIP **por favor** is not as common as 'please' and can be omitted in many cases. Spanish speakers may show their politeness by their intonation, or by using **usted**.
■ **Can we have the bill please?** ¿Nos puede traer la cuenta?
■ **Please come in.** Pase.
■ **Would you please be quiet?** ¿Quieres hacer el favor de callarte?

pleased ADJECTIVE
■ **My mother's not going to be very pleased.** A mi madre no le va a hacer mucha gracia.
■ **It's beautiful: she'll be very pleased with it.** Es precioso: le va a gustar mucho.
■ **Pleased to meet you!** ¡Encantado!

pleasure NOUN
el placer
□ I read for pleasure. Leo por placer.

plenty PRONOUN
■ **Fifteen minutes is plenty.** Quince minutos es más que suficiente.
■ **I've got plenty.** Tengo de sobra.
■ **That's plenty, thanks.** Así está bien, gracias.
■ **I've got plenty to do.** Tengo un montón de cosas que hacer.
■ **plenty of** **1** *(lots of)* mucho □ He's got plenty of energy. Tiene mucha energía.
2 *(more than enough)* de sobra □ We've got plenty of time. Tenemos tiempo de sobra.

pliers NOUN
los alicates

plot NOUN
▹ *see also* **plot** VERB
1 el argumento *(of story, play)*
2 el complot (PL los complots) *(conspiracy)*
□ a plot against the president un complot contra el presidente
3 el huerto *(for vegetables)*

to **plot** VERB
▹ *see also* **plot** NOUN
conspirar

plough NOUN
▹ *see also* **plough** VERB
el arado

to **plough** VERB
▹ *see also* **plough** NOUN
arar

plug NOUN
1 el enchufe *(electrical)*
2 el tapón (PL los tapones) *(for sink)*

to **plug in** VERB

enchufar
□ Is the iron plugged in? ¿Está enchufada la plancha?

plum NOUN
la ciruela

plumber NOUN
el fontanero
la fontanera
□ He's a plumber. Es fontanero.

plump ADJECTIVE
rechoncho (FEM rechoncha)

to **plunge** VERB
zambullirse*
□ He plunged into the water. Se zambulló en el agua.

plural NOUN
el plural

plus PREPOSITION, ADJECTIVE
más (FEM más)
□ 4 plus 3 equals 7. 4 más 3 son 7.
■ **three children plus a dog** tres niños y un perro
■ **I got a B plus.** Saqué un notable alto.

p.m. ABBREVIATION
LANGUAGE TIP Use **de la tarde** if it's light and **de la noche** if it's dark.
■ **at 2 p.m.** a las dos de la tarde
■ **at 9 p.m.** a las nueve de la noche

pneumonia NOUN
la pulmonía

poached ADJECTIVE
■ **a poached egg** un huevo escalfado

pocket NOUN
el bolsillo
□ He had his hands in his pockets. Tenía las manos en los bolsillos.

pocket money NOUN
la paga
□ How much pocket money do you get? ¿Cuánto te dan de paga?

poem NOUN
el poema
LANGUAGE TIP Although **poema** ends in **-a**, it is actually a masculine noun.

poet NOUN
el poeta
la poetisa

poetry NOUN
la poesía

point NOUN
▷ *see also* **point** VERB
1 el punto
□ a point on the horizon un punto en el horizonte □ They scored five points. Sacaron cinco puntos.
2 el momento
□ At that point, we decided to leave. En aquel momento decidimos marcharnos.
3 la punta
□ a pencil with a sharp point un lápiz con la punta afilada
4 el comentario
□ He made some interesting points. Hizo algunos comentarios de interés.
■ **They were on the point of finding it.** Estaban a punto de encontrarlo.
■ **Sorry, I don't get the point.** Perdona, pero no lo entiendo.
■ **a point of view** un punto de vista
■ **That's a good point!** ¡Tiene razón!
■ **That's not the point.** Eso no tiene nada que ver.
■ **There's no point.** No tiene sentido.
□ There's no point in waiting. No tiene sentido esperar.
■ **What's the point?** ¿Para qué? □ What's the point of leaving so early? ¿Para qué salir tan pronto?
■ **Punctuality isn't my strong point.** La puntualidad no es mi fuerte.
■ **two point five (2.5)** dos coma cinco (2,5)

to **point** VERB
▷ *see also* **point** NOUN
señalar con el dedo
□ Don't point! ¡No señales con el dedo!
■ **to point at somebody** señalar a alguien con el dedo □ She pointed at Anne. Señaló a Anne con el dedo.
■ **to point a gun at somebody** apuntar a alguien con una pistola

to **point out** VERB
1 señalar
□ The guide pointed out the Alhambra to us. El guía nos señaló la Alhambra.
2 indicar*
□ I should point out that... Me gustaría indicar que...

pointless ADJECTIVE
inútil (FEM inútil)
□ It's pointless arguing. Es inútil discutir.

poison NOUN
▷ *see also* **poison** VERB
el veneno

to **poison** VERB
▷ *see also* **poison** NOUN
envenenar

poisonous ADJECTIVE
1 venenoso (FEM venenosa) *(animal, plant)*
2 tóxico (FEM tóxica) *(chemical)*
□ poisonous gases gases tóxicos

to **poke** VERB
■ **He poked me in the eye.** Me metió un dedo en el ojo.

poker NOUN
el póker
□ I play poker. Juego al póker.

English-Spanish

P

Poland NOUN
Polonia *fem*
polar bear NOUN
el oso polar
Pole NOUN
el polaco
la polaca
pole NOUN
el poste
□ a telegraph pole un poste de telégrafos
■ **a tent pole** un mástil de tienda
■ **a ski pole** un bastón de esquí
■ **the North Pole** el Polo Norte
■ **the South Pole** el Polo Sur
pole vault NOUN
■ **the pole vault** el salto con pértiga
police PL NOUN
la policía
□ We called the police. Llamamos a la policía.
police car NOUN
el coche de policía
policeman NOUN
el policía (el agente *Latin America*)
police officer NOUN
el/la agente de policía
police station NOUN
la comisaría
policewoman NOUN
la policía (la agente *Latin America*)
polio NOUN
la polio
LANGUAGE TIP Although **polio** ends in **-o**, it is actually a feminine noun.
Polish ADJECTIVE
▷ *see also* **Polish** NOUN
polaco (FEM polaca)
Polish NOUN
▷ *see also* **Polish** ADJECTIVE
el polaco *(language)*
polish NOUN
▷ *see also* **polish** VERB
1 el betún *(for shoes)*
2 la cera *(for furniture)*
to **polish** VERB
▷ *see also* **polish** NOUN
limpiar *(shoes, glass)*
■ **to polish the furniture** sacar brillo a los muebles
polite ADJECTIVE
educado (FEM educada)
□ a polite child un niño educado
■ **It's not polite to point.** Es de mala educación señalar con el dedo.
politeness NOUN
la cortesía
political ADJECTIVE
político (FEM política)
politician NOUN
el político
la política
politics NOUN
la política
□ I'm not interested in politics. No me interesa la política.
poll NOUN
el sondeo de opinión
pollen NOUN
el polen
to **pollute** VERB
contaminar
pollution NOUN
la contaminación
polo-necked sweater NOUN
el suéter de cuello alto
polo shirt NOUN
el polo
polythene bag NOUN
la bolsa de plástico
pond NOUN
1 la charca *(natural)*
2 el estanque *(artificial)*
pony NOUN
el poney
ponytail NOUN
la coleta
□ He's got a ponytail. Lleva coleta.
pony trekking NOUN
■ **to go pony trekking** ir de excursión en poney
poodle NOUN
el caniche
pool NOUN
1 el estanque *(pond)*
2 la piscina *(swimming pool)*
3 el billar americano *(game)*
■ **a pool table** una mesa de billar
■ **the pools** las quinielas □ I do the pools every week. Juego a las quinielas todas las semanas.
poor ADJECTIVE
1 pobre (FEM pobre)
LANGUAGE TIP **pobre** goes after the noun when it means that someone has not got very much money. It goes before the noun when you want to show that you feel sorry for someone.
□ a poor family una familia pobre □ Poor David, he's very unlucky! ¡Pobre David, tiene muy mala suerte!
■ **the poor** los pobres
2 malo (FEM mala)
LANGUAGE TIP Use **mal** before a masculine singular noun.
□ He's a poor actor. Es un mal actor.
□ a poor mark una mala nota

poorly ADJECTIVE
□ She's feeling a bit poorly. No se siente muy bien.
pop ADJECTIVE
pop (FEM + PL pop)
□ pop music la música pop □ a pop star una estrella pop
■ **a pop group** un grupo de música pop
to **pop in** VERB
entrar un momento
to **pop out** VERB
salir* un momento
to **pop round** VERB
■ **I'm just popping round to John's.** Voy a pasarme por casa de John.
popcorn NOUN
las palomitas de maíz
poppy NOUN
la amapola
Popsicle® NOUN (US)
el polo
popular ADJECTIVE
popular (FEM populara)
□ Football is the most popular game in this country. El fútbol es el deporte más popular de este país.
■ **She's a very popular girl.** Es una chica que cae bien a todo el mundo.
■ **This is a very popular style.** Este estilo está muy de moda.
population NOUN
la población (PL las poblaciones)
porch NOUN
el porche de entrada
pork NOUN
la carne de cerdo (la carne de puerco *Latin America*)
■ **a pork chop** una chuleta de cerdo
porn NOUN
▷ *see also* **porn** ADJECTIVE
el porno
porn ADJECTIVE
▷ *see also* **porn** NOUN
porno (FEM + PL porno)
□ a porn film una película porno
pornographic ADJECTIVE
pornográfico (FEM pornográfica)
□ a pornographic magazine una revista pornográfica
pornography NOUN
la pornografía
porridge NOUN
las gachas de avena
port NOUN
el puerto
□ a fishing port un puerto pesquero
portable NOUN
portátil
□ a portable TV un televisor portátil
porter NOUN
1 el portero
la portera *(in hotel)*
2 el mozo de equipajes
la moza de equipajes *(at station)*
portion NOUN
1 la porción (PL las porciones)
2 la ración (PL las raciones) *(of food)*
□ a large portion of chips una ración grande de patatas fritas
portrait NOUN
el retrato
Portugal NOUN
Portugal *masc*
Portuguese ADJECTIVE
▷ *see also* **Portuguese** NOUN
portugués (PL portugueses, FEM portuguesa)
Portuguese NOUN
▷ *see also* **Portuguese** ADJECTIVE
el portugués *(language)*
■ **the Portuguese** los portugueses
posh ADJECTIVE
de lujo
□ a posh car un coche de lujo
position NOUN
la posición (PL las posiciones)
□ an uncomfortable position una posición incómoda
positive ADJECTIVE
1 positivo (FEM positiva)
□ a positive attitude una actitud positiva
2 seguro (FEM segura) *(sure)*
□ I'm positive. Estoy completamente seguro.
to **possess** VERB
poseer*
□ She lost everything she possessed. Perdió todo lo que poseía.
possession NOUN
■ **Have you got all your possessions?** ¿Tienes todas tus pertenencias?
possibility NOUN
la posibilidad
□ There were several possibilities. Había varias posibilidades.
possible ADJECTIVE
posible (FEM posible)
■ **as soon as possible** lo antes posible
LANGUAGE TIP **es posible que** has to be followed by a verb in the subjunctive.
■ **It's possible that he's gone away.** Es posible que se haya ido.
possibly ADVERB
tal vez
□ Are you coming to the party? — Possibly. ¿Vas a venir a la fiesta? — Tal vez.

English-Spanish

P

■ **... if you possibly can.** ... si es que puedes.
■ **I can't possibly go.** Me es del todo imposible ir.

post NOUN
▷ *see also* **post** VERB
1 el correo
□ Has the post arrived yet? ¿Ha llegado ya el correo?
■ **by post** por correo
■ **Is there any post for me?** ¿Tengo alguna carta?
2 el poste
□ The ball hit the post. El balón dio en el poste.

to **post** VERB
▷ *see also* **post** NOUN
mandar por correo
□ You could post it. Puedes mandarlo por correo.
■ **I've got some cards to post.** Tengo que mandar algunas postales.
■ **Would you post this letter for me?** ¿Me echas esta carta al correo?

postage NOUN
el franqueo

postbox NOUN
el buzón (PL los buzones)

postcard NOUN
la postal

postcode NOUN
el código postal

poster NOUN
1 el cartel *(public)*
□ There are posters all over town. Hay carteles por toda la ciudad.
2 el póster (PL los pósters) *(personal)*
□ I've got posters on my bedrooms walls. Tengo pósters en las paredes de mi cuarto.

postman NOUN
el cartero
□ He's a postman. Es cartero.

postmark NOUN
el matasellos (PL los matasellos)

post office NOUN
la oficina de correos
□ Where's the post office, please? ¿Sabe dónde está la oficina de correos?
■ **She works for the post office.** Trabaja en correos.

to **postpone** VERB
aplazar*
□ The match has been postponed. El partido ha sido aplazado.

postwoman NOUN
la cartera
□ She's a postwoman. Es cartera.

pot NOUN
1 el tarro (el pote *Latin America*)
□ a pot of jam un tarro de mermelada
■ **a pot of paint** un bote de pintura
■ **the pots and pans** las cacerolas
2 la tetera *(teapot)*
■ **a coffeepot** una cafetera
3 la maría *(informal)*
□ to smoke pot fumar maría

potato NOUN
la patata (la papa *Latin America*)
■ **mashed potatoes** el puré de patatas ped

potential NOUN
▷ *see also* **potential** ADJECTIVE
■ **He has great potential.** Promete mucho.

potential ADJECTIVE
▷ *see also* **potential** NOUN
posible (FEM posible)
□ a potential problem un posible problema

pothole NOUN
el bache

pot plant NOUN
la planta de interior

pottery NOUN
la cerámica

pound NOUN
▷ *see also* **pound** VERB
1 la libra

> **DID YOU KNOW...?**
> In Spain measurements are in grams and kilograms. One pound is about 450 grams.

□ a pound of carrots una libra de zanahorias
2 la libra esterlina
■ **20 pounds** 20 libras
■ **a pound coin** una moneda de una libra

to **pound** VERB
▷ *see also* **pound** NOUN
latir con fuerza
□ My heart was pounding. El corazón me latía con fuerza.

to **pour** VERB
1 echar
□ She poured some water into the pan. Echó un poco de agua en la olla.
2 llover* a cántaros
□ It's pouring. Está lloviendo a cántaros.
■ **in the pouring rain** bajo una lluvia torrencial

poverty NOUN
la pobreza

powder NOUN
el polvo
■ **a fine white powder** un polvillo blanco

power NOUN
1 la corriente *(electrical)*
□ The power's off. Se ha ido la corriente.
2 la energía
□ nuclear power la energía nuclear □ solar power la energía solar

3 el poder
□ They were in power for 18 years. Estuvieron 18 años en el poder.
■ **a power point** un enchufe

power cut NOUN
el apagón (PL los apagones)

powerful ADJECTIVE
1 poderoso (FEM poderosa) *(person, organization)*
□ the most powerful country in the world el país más poderoso del mundo
2 potente (FEM potente) *(machine, substance)*
□ a powerful computer system un potente sistema informático

power station NOUN
el central eléctrica

practical ADJECTIVE
práctico (FEM práctica)
□ a practical suggestion un consejo práctico
□ She's very practical. Es muy práctica.

practically ADVERB
prácticamente
□ It's practically impossible. Es prácticamente imposible.

practice NOUN
1 la práctica
□ You'll get better with practice. Mejorarás con la práctica.
■ **in practice** en la práctica
■ **It's normal practice in our school.** Es lo normal en nuestro colegio.
2 el entrenamiento
□ football practice entrenamiento de fútbol
■ **I'm out of practice.** Estoy desentrenado.
■ **I've got to do my piano practice.** Tengo que hacer los ejercicios de piano.
■ **a medical practice** una consulta médica

to **practise** (US **practice**) VERB
1 practicar*
□ I ought to practise more. Debería practicar más. □ I practise the flute every evening. Practico flauta todas las tardes.
□ I practised my Spanish when we were on holiday. Practiqué el español cuando estuvimos de vacaciones.
2 entrenarse *(train)*
□ The team practises on Thursdays. El equipo se entrena los jueves.

practising ADJECTIVE
practicante (FEM practicante)
□ She's a practising Catholic. Es católica practicante.

to **praise** VERB
elogiar
□ Everyone praises her cooking. Todo el mundo elogia cómo cocina.

pram NOUN
el cochecito de niño

prawn NOUN
la gamba

prawn cocktail NOUN
el cóctel de gambas (el cóctel de camarón *Latin America*)

to **pray** VERB
rezar*
□ to pray for something rezar por algo

prayer NOUN
la oración (PL las oraciones)

precaution NOUN
la precaución (PL las precauciones)
■ **to take precautions** tomar precauciones

preceding ADJECTIVE
anterior (FEM anteriora)

precinct NOUN
■ **a shopping precinct** un centro comercial

precious ADJECTIVE
precioso (FEM preciosa)
□ a precious stone una piedra preciosa

precise ADJECTIVE
preciso (FEM precisa)
□ at that precise moment en aquel preciso instante
■ **to be precise** para ser exacto

precisely ADVERB
precisamente
□ That is precisely what it's meant for. Para eso precisamente está hecho.
■ **Precisely!** ¡Exactamente!
■ **at 10 a.m. precisely** a las diez en punto de la mañana

to **predict** VERB
predecir*

predictable ADJECTIVE
previsible (FEM previsible)

prefect NOUN
el monitor
la monitora *(in school)*

to **prefer** VERB
preferir*
□ Which would you prefer? ¿Tú cuál prefieres? □ I prefer chemistry to maths. Prefiero la química a las matemáticas.

preference NOUN
la preferencia

pregnant ADJECTIVE
embarazada
□ She's six months pregnant. Está embarazada de seis meses.

prehistoric ADJECTIVE
prehistórico (FEM prehistórica)

prejudice NOUN
el prejuicio
□ That's just a prejudice. Eso no es más que un prejuicio.
■ **There's a lot of racial prejudice.** Hay muchos prejuicios raciales.

prejudiced ADJECTIVE
■ **to be prejudiced against somebody** tener prejuicios contra alguien

premature ADJECTIVE
prematuro (FEM prematura)
□ a premature baby un bebé prematuro

Premier League NOUN
la primera división

premises PL NOUN
el local
□ They're moving to new premises. Se cambian de local.

premonition NOUN
el presentimiento

preoccupied ADJECTIVE
preocupado (FEM preocupada)

prep NOUN
los deberes
□ history prep los deberes de historia

to **prepare** VERB
preparar
□ He was preparing dinner. Estaba preparando la cena.
■ **to prepare for something** hacer los preparativos para algo □ We're preparing for our holiday. Estamos haciendo los preparativos para las vacaciones.

prepared ADJECTIVE
■ **to be prepared to do something** estar dispuesto a hacer algo □ I'm prepared to help you. Estoy dispuesto a ayudarte.

prep school NOUN
el colegio privado *(de enseñanza primaria)*

Presbyterian ADJECTIVE
▷ *see also* **Presbyterian** NOUN
presbiteriano (FEM presbiteriana)

Presbyterian NOUN
▷ *see also* **Presbyterian** ADJECTIVE
el presbiteriano
la presbiteriana

to **prescribe** VERB
recetar
□ The doctor prescribed a course of antibiotics for me. El doctor me recetó antibióticos.

prescription NOUN
la receta
□ a prescription for penicillin una receta de penicilina
■ **on prescription** con receta médica

presence NOUN
la presencia
■ **presence of mind** presencia de ánimo

present ADJECTIVE
▷ *see also* **present** NOUN, VERB
1 presente (FEM presente)
□ He wasn't present at the meeting. No estuvo presente en la reunión.
2 actual (FEM actual)
□ the present situation la situación actual
■ **the present tense** el presente

present NOUN
▷ *see also* **present** ADJECTIVE, VERB
1 el regalo
■ **to give somebody a present** hacer un regalo a alguien □ He gave me a lovely present. Me hizo un precioso regalo.
2 el presente
□ to live in the present vivir el presente
■ **at present** actualmente
■ **for the present** por el momento
■ **up to the present** hasta el momento presente

to **present** VERB
▷ *see also* **present** ADJECTIVE, NOUN
■ **to present somebody with something** entregar algo a alguien □ The Mayor presented the winner with a medal. El alcalde le entregó una medalla al vencedor.
■ **He agreed to present the show.** Aceptó presentar el espectáculo.

presenter NOUN
el presentador
la presentadora

presently ADVERB
1 enseguida
□ You'll feel better presently. Enseguida te sentirás mejor.
2 actualmente
□ They're presently on tour. Actualmente están de gira.

president NOUN
el presidente
la presidenta

press NOUN
▷ *see also* **press** VERB
la prensa
□ The story appeared in the press last week. La historia salió en la prensa la semana pasada.

to **press** VERB
▷ *see also* **press** NOUN
apretar*
□ Don't press too hard! ¡No aprietes muy fuerte!
■ **He pressed the accelerator.** Pisó el acelerador.

pressed ADJECTIVE
■ **We are pressed for time.** Andamos mal de tiempo.

press-up NOUN
■ **to do press-ups** hacer flexiones

pressure NOUN
la presión (PL las presiones)
■ **a pressure group** un grupo de presión
■ **to be under pressure** estar presionado
□ She was under pressure from the

management. Estaba presionada por la dirección.
■ **He's been under a lot of pressure recently.** Últimamente ha estado muy agobiado.

to **pressurize** VERB
■ **to pressurize somebody to do something** presionar a alguien para que haga algo □ My parents are pressurizing me to stay on at school. Mis padres me están presionando para que siga estudiando.

prestige NOUN
el prestigio

prestigious ADJECTIVE
prestigioso (FEM prestigiosa)

presumably ADVERB
■ **Presumably she already knows what's happened.** Supongo que ya sabe lo que ha pasado.

to **presume** VERB
suponer*
□ I presume so. Supongo que sí. □ I presume he'll come. Supongo que vendrá.

to **pretend** VERB
■ **to pretend to do something** fingir hacer algo
■ **to pretend to be asleep** hacerse el dormido

LANGUAGE TIP Be careful not to translate **to pretend** by **pretender**.

pretty ADJECTIVE, ADVERB
1 bonito (FEM bonita)
□ She wore a pretty dress. Llevaba un vestido bonito.
2 guapo (FEM guapa)
□ She's very pretty. Es muy guapa.
3 bastante
□ That film was pretty bad. La película era bastante mala.
■ **The weather was pretty awful.** Hacía un tiempo horroroso.
■ **It's pretty much the same.** Es más o menos lo mismo.

to **prevent** VERB
evitar
□ Every effort had been made to prevent the accident. Se había hecho todo lo posible para evitar el accidente.

LANGUAGE TIP **evitar que** has to be followed by a verb in the subjunctive.

■ **to prevent something happening** evitar que pase algo □ I want to prevent this happening again. Quiero evitar que esto se repita.

LANGUAGE TIP **impedir a alguien que** has to be followed by a verb in the subjunctive.

■ **to prevent somebody from doing something** impedir a alguien que haga algo □ My only thought was to prevent him from speaking. Mi única idea era impedirle que hablara.

previous ADJECTIVE
anterior (FEM anteriora)
□ the previous night la noche anterior
■ **He has no previous experience.** No tiene experiencia previa.

previously ADVERB
antes

prey NOUN
la presa
■ **a bird of prey** un ave rapaz

price NOUN
el precio
□ What price is this painting? ¿Qué precio tiene este cuadro?
■ **to go up in price** subir de precio
■ **to come down in price** bajar de precio

price list NOUN
la lista de precios

to **prick** VERB
pinchar
□ I've pricked my finger. Me he pinchado un dedo.

pride NOUN
el orgullo

priest NOUN
el sacerdote

primary school NOUN
la escuela primaria

prime minister NOUN
el primer ministro
la primera ministra

primitive ADJECTIVE
primitivo (FEM primitiva)

prince NOUN
el príncipe
□ the Prince of Wales el príncipe de Gales

princess NOUN
la princesa
□ Princess Victoria la princesa Victoria

principal ADJECTIVE
▷ *see also* **principal** NOUN
principal (FEM principal)

principal NOUN
▷ *see also* **principal** ADJECTIVE
el director
la directora

principle NOUN
el principio
□ the basic principles of physics los principios básicos de física
■ **in principle** en principio
■ **on principle** por principio

print NOUN
1 la foto

English-Spanish

p

LANGUAGE TIP Although **foto** ends in **-o**, it is actually a feminine noun.

□ colour prints fotos a color

2 la letra

□ in small print en letra pequeña

3 la huella

□ The policeman took his prints. El policía le tomó las huellas.

4 el grabado

□ a framed print un grabado enmarcado

printer NOUN
la impresora

printout NOUN
la copia impresa

priority NOUN
la prioridad

□ My family takes priority over my work. Mi familia tiene prioridad sobre mi trabajo.

prison NOUN
la cárcel

□ to send somebody to prison for 5 years condenar a alguien a 5 años de cárcel

■ **in prison** en la cárcel

prisoner NOUN

1 el preso
la presa *(in prison)*

2 el prisionero
la prisionera *(captive)*

■ **to take somebody prisoner** hacer prisionero a alguien

prison officer NOUN
el funcionario de prisiones
la funcionaria de prisiones

privacy NOUN
la intimidad

□ in privacy en la intimidad

private ADJECTIVE

1 privado (FEM privada)

□ a private school un colegio privado

■ **private life** la vida privada

■ **private property** la propiedad privada

2 particular *(for one person only)*

□ private lessons clases particulares

□ She has a private secretary. Tiene secretaria particular.

■ **a private bathroom** un baño individual

■ **'private'** *(on envelope)* 'confidencial'

■ **in private** en privado

to **privatize** VERB
privatizar*

privilege NOUN
el privilegio

prize NOUN
el premio

□ to win a prize ganar un premio

prize-giving NOUN
la entrega de premios

prizewinner NOUN
el premiado
la premiada

pro NOUN

■ **the pros and cons** los pros y los contras

probable ADJECTIVE
probable (FEM probable)

probably ADVERB
probablemente

□ He'll probably come tomorrow. Probablemente vendrá mañana.

problem NOUN
el problema

LANGUAGE TIP Although **problema** ends in **-a**, it is actually a masculine noun.

□ the drug problem el problema de la droga

■ **No problem!** **1** ¡Por supuesto! □ Can you repair it? — No problem! ¿Lo puedes arreglar? — ¡Por supuesto! **2** ¡No importa! □ I'm sorry about that — No problem! Lo siento — ¡No importa!

■ **What's the problem?** ¿Qué pasa?

proceeds PL NOUN
la recaudación

□ All proceeds will go to charity. Toda la recaudación se destinará a obras benéficas.

process NOUN
el proceso

□ the peace process el proceso de paz

■ **We're in the process of painting the kitchen.** Ahora mismo estamos pintando la cocina.

procession NOUN
la procesión (PL las procesiones)

to **produce** VERB

1 producir* *(manufacture, create)*

2 montar *(on stage)*

producer NOUN

1 el productor
la productora *(of film, record, TV programme)*

2 el director
la directora *(of play, show)*

product NOUN
el producto

production NOUN

1 la producción (PL las producciones)

□ They're increasing production of luxury models. Están aumentando la producción de modelos de lujo.

2 el montaje

□ a production of 'Hamlet' un montaje de 'Hamlet'

profession NOUN
la profesión (PL las profesiones)

professional NOUN
▷ *see also* **professional** ADJECTIVE
el/la profesional

professional ADJECTIVE
▷ *see also* **professional** NOUN
profesional (FEM profesional)
□ a professional musician un músico profesional □ a very professional piece of work un trabajo muy profesional

professionally ADVERB
■ **She sings professionally.** Es cantante profesional.

professor NOUN
el catedrático
la catedrática
LANGUAGE TIP Be careful not to translate **professor** by the Spanish word **profesor**.

profit NOUN
los beneficios
□ to make a profit sacar beneficios
□ a profit of £10,000 unos beneficios de 10.000 libras

profitable ADJECTIVE
rentable (FEM rentable)

program NOUN
▷ *see also* **program** VERB
el programa
LANGUAGE TIP Although **programa** ends in **-a**, it is actually a masculine noun.
□ a computer program un programa informático
■ **a TV program** (US) un programa de televisión

to **program** VERB
▷ *see also* **program** NOUN
programar

programme NOUN
el programa
LANGUAGE TIP Although **programa** ends in **-a**, it is actually a masculine noun.
□ a TV programme un programa de televisión

programmer NOUN
el programador
la programadora
□ She's a programmer. Es programadora.

programming NOUN
la programación

progress NOUN
el progreso
□ You're making progress! ¡Estás haciendo progresos!

to **prohibit** VERB
prohibir*
□ Smoking is prohibited. Está prohibido fumar.

project NOUN
1 el proyecto
□ an international project un proyecto internacional
2 el trabajo *(research)*
□ I'm doing a project on the greenhouse effect. Estoy haciendo un trabajo sobre el efecto invernadero.

projector NOUN
el proyector

promenade NOUN
el paseo marítimo

promise NOUN
▷ *see also* **promise** VERB
la promesa
□ He made me a promise. Me hizo una promesa.
■ **That's a promise!** ¡Lo prometo!

to **promise** VERB
▷ *see also* **promise** NOUN
prometer
□ He didn't do what he promised. No hizo lo que prometió.
■ **She promised to write.** Prometió que escribiría.
■ **I'll write, I promise!** ¡Escribiré, lo prometo!

promising ADJECTIVE
prometedor (FEM prometedora)
□ a promising tennis player un tenista prometedor

to **promote** VERB
ascender* *(employee, team)*
□ She was promoted six months later. La ascendieron seis meses después.

promotion NOUN
el ascenso

prompt ADJECTIVE, ADVERB
1 rápido (FEM rápida)
□ a prompt reply una rápida respuesta
2 puntual (FEM puntual)
□ He's always very prompt. Siempre es muy puntual.
■ **at eight o'clock prompt** a las ocho en punto

promptly ADVERB
1 puntualmente *(on time)*
□ We left promptly at seven. Nos marchamos puntualmente a las siete.
2 enseguida *(immediately)*
□ He sat down and promptly fell asleep. Se sentó y se quedó dormido enseguida.

pronoun NOUN
el pronombre

to **pronounce** VERB
pronunciar
□ How do you pronounce that word? ¿Cómo se pronuncia esa palabra?

pronunciation NOUN
la pronunciación (PL las pronunciaciones)

proof NOUN
la prueba
■ **I've got proof that he did it.** Tengo pruebas de que lo hizo.

proper ADJECTIVE
1 de verdad *(genuine)*
□ It's difficult to get a proper job. Es difícil conseguir un trabajo de verdad.
2 adecuado (FEM adecuada) *(suitable)*
□ You have to have the proper equipment. Tienes que tener el equipo adecuado.
■ **If you had come at the proper time...** Si hubieras llegado a tu hora...

properly ADVERB
correctamente
□ You're not doing it properly. No lo estás haciendo correctamente. □ Dress properly for your interview. Vaya correctamente vestido a la entrevista.

property NOUN
la propiedad
■ **'private property'** 'propiedad privada'
■ **stolen property** objetos robados

proportional ADJECTIVE
proporcional (FEM proporcional)
□ proportional representation la representación proporcional

proposal NOUN
la propuesta

to **propose** VERB
proponer*
□ I propose a new plan. Propongo un cambio de planes. □ What do you propose to do? ¿Qué te propones hacer?

LANGUAGE TIP **proponer que** has to be followed by a verb in the subjunctive.

□ He proposed that we stay at home. Propuso que nos quedáramos en casa.
■ **to propose to somebody** *(for marriage)* declararse a alguien

to **prosecute** VERB
■ **They were prosecuted for murder.** Les procesaron por asesinato.

prospect NOUN
la perspectiva
□ His future prospects are good. Tiene buenas perspectivas de futuro.

prospectus NOUN
el prospecto

prostitute NOUN
la prostituta
■ **a male prostitute** un prostituto

to **protect** VERB
proteger*

protection NOUN
la protección

protein NOUN
la proteína

protest NOUN
▷ *see also* **protest** VERB
la protesta
□ He ignored their protests. Ignoró sus protestas.
■ **a protest march** una manifestación

to **protest** VERB
▷ *see also* **protest** NOUN
protestar

Protestant NOUN
▷ *see also* **Protestant** ADJECTIVE
el/la protestante
□ I'm a Protestant. Soy protestante.

Protestant ADJECTIVE
▷ *see also* **Protestant** NOUN
protestante (FEM protestante)

protester NOUN
el/la manifestante

proud ADJECTIVE
orgulloso (FEM orgullosa)
□ Her parents are proud of her. Sus padres están orgullosos de ella.

to **prove** VERB
probar*
□ The police couldn't prove it. La policía no pudo probarlo.

proverb NOUN
el proverbio
□ a Chinese proverb un proverbio chino

to **provide** VERB
proporcionar
■ **to provide somebody with something** proporcionar algo a alguien □ They provided us with maps. Nos proporcionaron mapas.

to **provide for** VERB
mantener*
□ He can't provide for his family any more. Ya no puede mantener a su familia.

provided CONJUNCTION
siempre que

LANGUAGE TIP **siempre que** has to be followed by a verb in the subjunctive.

□ He'll play in the next match provided he's fit. Jugará el próximo partido siempre que esté en condiciones.

prowler NOUN
el merodeador
la merodeadora

prune NOUN
la ciruela pasa

to **pry** VERB
inmiscuirse*
□ He's always prying into other people's affairs. Siempre está inmiscuyéndose en asuntos ajenos.

pseudonym NOUN
el seudónimo

psychiatrist NOUN
el/la psiquiatra
psychoanalyst NOUN
el/la psicoanalista
psychological ADJECTIVE
psicológico (FEM psicológica)
psychologist NOUN
el psicólogo
la psicóloga
psychology NOUN
la psicología
PTO ABBREVIATION *(= please turn over)*
sigue
pub NOUN
el bar
public NOUN
▷ *see also* **public** ADJECTIVE
■ **the public** el público □ open to the public abierto al público
■ **in public** en público
public ADJECTIVE
▷ *see also* **public** NOUN
público (FEM pública)
■ **a public holiday** un día festivo (un día feriado *Latin America*)
■ **public opinion** la opinión pública
■ **the public address system** la megafonía
■ **to be in the public eye** ser un personaje público
publican NOUN
■ **He's a publican.** Es dueño de un pub.
publicity NOUN
la publicidad
public school NOUN
el colegio privado
public transport NOUN
el transporte público
to **publish** VERB
publicar*
publisher NOUN
1 el editor
la editora *(person)*
2 la editorial *(company)*
pudding NOUN
el postre
□ What's for pudding? ¿Qué hay de postre?
■ **rice pudding** el arroz con leche
■ **black pudding** la morcilla
puddle NOUN
el charco
puff pastry NOUN
el hojaldre
to **pull** VERB
1 tirar *(to make something move)*
□ Pull as hard as you can. Tira con todas tus fuerzas.
2 tirar de (jalar *Latin America*) *(to tug at something)*
□ She pulled my hair. Me tiró del pelo.
■ **He pulled the trigger.** Apretó el gatillo.
■ **I pulled a muscle when I was training.** Me dio un tirón mientras entrenaba.
■ **You're pulling my leg!** ¡Me estás tomando el pelo!
■ **Pull yourself together!** ¡Tranquilízate!
to **pull down** VERB
echar abajo
□ The old school was pulled down last year. El año pasado echaron abajo la vieja escuela.
to **pull out** VERB
1 sacar* *(remove)*
□ to pull a tooth out sacar una muela
2 echarse a un lado *(car)*
□ The car pulled out to overtake. El coche se echó a un lado para adelantar.
3 retirarse *(from competition)*
□ She pulled out of the tournament. Se retiró del torneo.
to **pull through** VERB
recuperarse
□ They think he'll pull through. Creen que se recuperará.
to **pull up** VERB
parar *(car)*
□ A black car pulled up beside me. Un coche negro paró a mi lado.
pullover NOUN
el jersey (PL los jerseys)
pulse NOUN
el pulso
□ The nurse took his pulse. La enfermera le tomó el pulso.
pulses PL NOUN
las legumbres
pump NOUN
▷ *see also* **pump** VERB
1 la bomba
□ a bicycle pump una bomba de bicicleta
2 la zapatilla *(de deporte)*
□ She was wearing a black leotard and black pumps. Llevaba malla y zapatillas negras.
to **pump** VERB
▷ *see also* **pump** NOUN
bombear
■ **to pump up a tyre** inflar una rueda
pumpkin NOUN
la calabaza
punch NOUN
▷ *see also* **punch** VERB
1 el puñetazo *(blow)*
2 el ponche *(drink)*
to **punch** VERB
▷ *see also* **punch** NOUN
dar* un puñetazo a
□ He punched me! ¡Me ha dado un puñetazo!

punch-up NOUN
la pelea

punctual ADJECTIVE
puntual (FEM puntual)

punctuation NOUN
la puntuación

puncture NOUN
el pinchazo
□ I had a puncture on the motorway. Tuve un pinchazo en la autopista.

to **punish** VERB
castigar*
□ They were severely punished for their disobedience. Les castigaron severamente por su desobediencia.
■ **to punish somebody for doing something** castigar a alguien por haber hecho algo

punishment NOUN
el castigo

punk NOUN
el/la punki
■ **a punk rock band** un grupo punk

pupil NOUN
el alumno
la alumna

puppet NOUN
el títere

puppy NOUN
el cachorro

to **purchase** VERB
adquirir*

pure ADJECTIVE
puro (FEM pura)
□ He's doing pure maths. Estudia matemáticas puras.

purple ADJECTIVE
morado (FEM morada)

purpose NOUN
el objetivo
□ What is the purpose of these changes? ¿Cuál es el objetivo de estos cambios?
■ **his purpose in life** su meta en la vida
■ **It's being used for military purposes.** Se está usando con fines militares.
■ **on purpose** a propósito □ He did it on purpose. Lo hizo a propósito.

to **purr** VERB
ronronear

purse NOUN
1 el monedero *(for money)*
2 el bolso (US: *handbag)*

pursuit NOUN
la actividad
□ outdoor pursuits actividades al aire libre

push NOUN
▷ *see also* **push** VERB
el empujón (PL los empujones)
■ **to give somebody a push** dar un empujón a alguien

to **push** VERB
▷ *see also* **push** NOUN
empujar
□ Don't push! ¡No empujes!
■ **to push a button** pulsar un botón
■ **to push drugs** pasar droga
■ **I'm pushed for time today.** Hoy ando fatal de tiempo.
■ **Push off!** ¡Lárgate!
■ **Don't push your luck!** ¡No tientes a la suerte!

to **push around** VERB
dar* órdenes a
□ He likes pushing people around. Le gusta dar órdenes a la gente.

to **push through** VERB
■ **I pushed my way through.** Me abrí camino a empujones.

pushchair NOUN
la silla de paseo

pusher NOUN
el camello *(of drugs)*

to **put** VERB
poner*
□ Where shall I put my things? ¿Dónde pongo mis cosas? □ Don't forget to put your name on the paper. No te olvides de poner tu nombre en la hoja.
■ **She's putting the baby to bed.** Está acostando al niño.

to **put aside** VERB
apartar
□ Can you put this aside for me till tomorrow? ¿Me lo puede apartar hasta mañana?

to **put away** VERB
1 guardar
□ Can you put the dishes away, please? ¿Guardas los platos?
2 encerrar* *(in prison)*
□ I hope they put him away for a long time. Espero que lo encierren por muchos años.

to **put back** VERB
1 poner* en su sitio *(in place)*
□ Put it back when you've finished with it. Ponlo en su sitio cuando hayas terminado.
2 aplazar* *(postpone)*
□ The meeting has been put back till 2 o'clock. La reunión ha sido aplazada hasta las 2.

to **put down** VERB
1 soltar*
□ I'll put these bags down for a minute. Voy a soltar estas bolsas un momento.
2 apuntar *(note)*
□ I've put down a few ideas. He apuntado algunas ideas.

■ to have an animal put down sacrificar a un animal □ We had to have our dog put down. Tuvimos que sacrificar a nuestro perro.

■ to put the phone down colgar

to **put forward** VERB
adelantar *(clock)*

to **put in** VERB
poner* *(install)*
□ We're going to get central heating put in. Vamos a poner calefacción central.
■ He has put in a lot of work on this project. Ha dedicado mucho trabajo a este proyecto.
■ I've put in for a new job. He solicitado otro empleo.

to **put off** VERB
1 apagar* *(light, TV)*
□ Shall I put the light off? ¿Apago la luz?
2 aplazar* *(delay)*
□ I keep putting it off. No hago más que aplazarlo.
3 distraer* *(distract)*
□ Stop putting me off! ¡Deja ya de distraerme!
4 desanimar *(discourage)*
□ He's not easily put off. No es de los que se desaniman fácilmente.

to **put on** VERB
1 ponerse* *(clothes, lipstick)*
□ I put my coat on. Me puse el abrigo.
2 poner* *(CD, DVD)*
□ Put on some music. Pon algo de música.
3 encender* *(light, TV)*
□ Shall I put the heater on? ¿Enciendo el radiador?
4 representar *(play, show)*
□ We're putting on 'Bugsy Malone'. Estamos representando 'Bugsy Malone'.
■ I'll put the potatoes on. Voy a poner a hacer las patatas.
■ to put on weight engordar □ He has put on a lot of weight. Ha engordado mucho.
■ She's not ill: she's just putting it on. No está enferma: es puro teatro.

to **put out** VERB
apagar*
□ It took them five hours to put out the fire. Tardaron cinco horas en apagar el incendio.
■ He's a bit put out that nobody came. Le sentó mal que no viniera nadie.

to **put through** VERB
poner* (comunicar* *Latin America*)
□ Can you put me through to the manager? ¿Me pone con el director? □ I'm putting you through. Le pongo.

to **put up** VERB
1 colgar* *(on wall)*
□ I'll put the poster up on my wall. Colgaré el póster en la pared.
2 montar
□ We put up our tent in a field. Montamos la tienda en un prado.
3 subir
□ They've put up the price. Han subido el precio.
■ My friend will put me up for the night. Me quedaré a dormir en casa de mi amigo.
■ to put one's hand up levantar la mano □ If you have any questions, put your hand up. Quien tenga alguna pregunta que levante la mano.
■ to put up with something aguantar algo □ I'm not going to put up with it any longer. No pienso aguantarlo más.
■ to put something up for sale poner algo en venta □ They're going to put their house up for sale. Van a poner la casa en venta.

puzzle NOUN
el rompecabezas (PL los rompecabezas)

puzzled ADJECTIVE
perplejo (FEM perpleja)
□ You look puzzled! ¡Te has quedado perplejo!

puzzling ADJECTIVE
desconcertante (FEM desconcertante)

pyjamas PL NOUN
el pijama (el piyama *Latin America*)
□ my pyjamas mi pijama
■ a pair of pyjamas un pijama
LANGUAGE TIP Although **pijama** ends in **-a**, it is actually a masculine noun.

pyramid NOUN
la pirámide

Pyrenees PL NOUN
■ the Pyrenees los Pirineos

English-Spanish

P

Qq

quaint ADJECTIVE
pintoresco (FEM pintoresca) *(house, village)*
qualification NOUN
el título
□ He left school without any qualifications. Dejó la escuela sin sacarse ningún título.
□ vocational qualifications los títulos de formación profesional □ a teaching qualification un título de profesor
qualified ADJECTIVE
1 cualificado (FEM cualificada)
□ a qualified driving instructor un profesor de autoescuela cualificado
2 titulado (FEM titulada)
□ a qualified teacher un profesor titulado
■ **She was well qualified for the position.** Estaba suficientemente capacitada para el puesto.
to **qualify** VERB
1 sacarse* el título (recibirse *Latin America*)
□ She qualified as a teacher last year. Se sacó el título de profesora el año pasado.
2 clasificarse*
□ Our team didn't qualify for the finals. Nuestro equipo no se clasificó para la final.
quality NOUN
1 la calidad
□ a good quality of life una buena calidad de vida □ good-quality paper el papel de calidad
2 la cualidad
□ She's got lots of good qualities. Tiene un montón de buenas cualidades.
quantity NOUN
la cantidad
quarantine NOUN
la cuarentena
□ in quarantine en cuarentena
quarrel NOUN
▷ *see also* **quarrel** VERB
la pelea *(discusión)*
■ **We had a quarrel.** Nos peleamos.
to **quarrel** VERB
▷ *see also* **quarrel** NOUN
pelearse *(discutir)*
quarry NOUN
la cantera *(for stone)*
quarter NOUN
el cuarto
■ **three quarters** tres cuartos
■ **a quarter of an hour** un cuarto de hora
■ **a quarter past ten** las diez y cuarto
■ **a quarter to eleven** las once menos cuarto
quarter-finals PL NOUN
los cuartos de final
quartet NOUN
el cuarteto
□ a string quartet un cuarteto de cuerda
quay NOUN
el muelle *(embarcadero)*
queasy ADJECTIVE
■ **I feel queasy.** Tengo náuseas.
queen NOUN
1 la reina
□ Queen Elizabeth la reina Isabel
2 la dama
□ the queen of hearts la dama de corazones
■ **the Queen Mother** la reina madre
query NOUN
▷ *see also* **query** VERB
la pregunta
to **query** VERB
▷ *see also* **query** NOUN
poner* en duda
□ No one queried my decision. Nadie puso en duda mi decisión.
■ **They queried the bill.** Pidieron explicaciones sobre la factura.
question NOUN
▷ *see also* **question** VERB
1 la pregunta
□ Can I ask a question? ¿Puedo hacer una pregunta?
2 la cuestión (PL las cuestiones)
□ That's a difficult question. Ésa es una cuestión complicada. □ It's just a question of... Tan sólo es cuestión de...
■ **It's out of the question.** Es imposible.
to **question** VERB
▷ *see also* **question** NOUN
interrogar*

□ He was questioned by the police. Lo interrogó la policía.

question mark NOUN
el signo de interrogación

questionnaire NOUN
el cuestionario

queue NOUN
▷ *see also* **queue** VERB
la cola
□ People were standing in a queue outside the cinema. La gente hacía cola a las puertas del cine.

to **queue** VERB
▷ *see also* **queue** NOUN
hacer* cola
□ We had to queue for tickets. Tuvimos que hacer cola para comprar los billetes.

quick ADJECTIVE, ADVERB
rápido (FEM rápida)
□ a quick lunch un almuerzo rápido □ It's quicker by train. Se va más rápido en tren.
■ **She's a quick learner.** Aprende rápido.
■ **Quick, phone the police!** ¡Rápido, llama a la policía!
■ **Be quick!** ¡Date prisa!

quickly ADVERB
rápidamente
□ It was all over very quickly. Se acabó todo muy rápidamente.

quiet ADJECTIVE
1 callado (FEM callada)
□ You're very quiet today. Estás muy callado hoy. □ She's a very quiet girl. Es una chica muy callada.
2 silencioso (FEM silenciosa)
□ The engine's very quiet. El motor es muy silencioso.
3 tranquilo (FEM tranquila)
□ a quiet little town un pueblecito tranquilo □ a quiet weekend un fin de semana tranquilo
■ **Be quiet!** ¡Cállate!
■ **Quiet!** ¡Silencio!

quietly ADVERB
1 en voz baja
□ She's dead. — He said quietly. Está muerta. — Dijo en voz baja.
2 sin hacer ruido
□ He quietly opened the door. Abrió la puerta sin hacer ruido.

quilt NOUN
el edredón (PL los edredones)

to **quit** VERB
1 dejar
□ I quit my job last week. Dejé mi trabajo la semana pasada.
2 marcharse
□ I've been given notice to quit. Me han dado el aviso para que me marche.

quite ADVERB
1 bastante
□ It's quite warm today. Hoy hace bastante calor. □ It's quite a long way. Está bastante lejos. □ I quite liked the film. La película me gustó bastante.
■ **How was the film? — Quite good.** ¿Qué tal la película? — No está mal.
2 totalmente
□ It's quite different. Es totalmente distinto. □ I quite agree with you. Estoy totalmente de acuerdo contigo.
■ **It's quite clear that this plan won't work.** Está clarísimo que este plan no va a funcionar.
■ **not quite...** no del todo... □ I'm not quite sure. No estoy del todo seguro.
■ **It's not quite the same.** No es exactamente lo mismo.
■ **quite a...** todo un □ It was quite a shock. Fue todo un susto.
■ **quite a lot** bastante □ I've been there quite a lot. He estado allí bastante. □ quite a lot of money bastante dinero □ It costs quite a lot to go abroad. Es bastante caro ir al extranjero.
■ **There were quite a few people there.** Había bastante gente allí.

quiz NOUN
el concurso *(de preguntas)*
□ a quiz show un programa concurso

quota NOUN
el cupo

quotation NOUN
la cita
□ a quotation from Shakespeare una cita de Shakespeare

quotation marks PL NOUN
las comillas

quote NOUN
▷ *see also* **quote** VERB
1 la cita
□ a Shakespeare quote una cita de Shakespeare
2 el presupuesto
□ Can you give me a quote for the work? ¿Puede darme un presupuesto por el trabajo?
■ **quotes** las comillas □ in quotes entre comillas

to **quote** VERB
▷ *see also* **quote** NOUN
citar

Rr

rabbi NOUN
el rabino
la rabina

rabbit NOUN
el conejo
■ **rabbit hutch** la conejera

rabies NOUN
la rabia
■ **a dog with rabies** un perro rabioso

race NOUN
▷ *see also* **race** VERB
1 la carrera
■ **a cycle race** una carrera ciclista
2 la raza
■ **race relations** las relaciones interraciales

to **race** VERB
▷ *see also* **race** NOUN
1 correr
□ We raced to get there on time. Corrimos para llegar allí a tiempo.
2 echarle una carrera a
□ I'll race you! ¡Te echo una carrera!

racecourse NOUN
el hipódromo

racehorse NOUN
el caballo de carreras

racer NOUN
la bicicleta de carreras

racetrack NOUN
1 el circuito *(for cars)*
2 el velódromo *(for cycles)*

racial ADJECTIVE
racial (FEM racial)
□ racial discrimination la discriminación racial

racing car NOUN
el coche de carreras

racing driver NOUN
el/la piloto de carreras

racism NOUN
el racismo

racist ADJECTIVE
▷ *see also* **racist** NOUN
racista (FEM racista)

racist NOUN
▷ *see also* **racist** ADJECTIVE
el/la racista
□ He's a racist. Es racista.

rack NOUN
el portaequipajes (PL los portaequipajes) *(for luggage)*

racket NOUN
1 la raqueta *(for sport)*
□ my tennis racket mi raqueta de tenis
2 el jaleo *(informal: noise)*
□ They're making a terrible racket. Están armando muchísimo jaleo.

racquet NOUN
la raqueta

radar NOUN
el radar

radiation NOUN
la radiación

radiator NOUN
el radiador

radio NOUN
la radio
LANGUAGE TIP Although **radio** ends in **-o**, it is actually a feminine noun.
■ **on the radio** por la radio
■ **a radio station** una emisora de radio

radioactive ADJECTIVE
radiactivo (FEM radiactiva)

radio-controlled ADJECTIVE
teledirigido (FEM teledirigida)

radish NOUN
el rábano

RAF ABBREVIATION *(= Royal Air Force)*
las fuerzas aéreas británicas
□ He's in the RAF. Está en las fuerzas aéreas británicas.

raffle NOUN
la rifa
□ a raffle ticket una papeleta de rifa

raft NOUN
la balsa

rag NOUN
el trapo
□ a piece of rag un trapo
■ **dressed in rags** cubierto de harapos

rage NOUN
rabia

□ mad with rage loco de rabia
■ **to be in a rage** estar furioso
■ **It's all the rage.** Es el último grito.

raid NOUN
▹ *see also* **raid** VERB
1 el asalto
□ a bank raid un asalto de banco
2 la redada
□ a police raid una redada policial

to **raid** VERB
▹ *see also* **raid** NOUN
1 asaltar *(bank)*
2 hacer* una redada en
□ The police raided a club in Soho. La policía hizo una redada en un club del Soho.

rail NOUN
1 la barandilla *(on stairs, bridge, balcony)*
2 el riel *(for curtains)*
■ **by rail** por ferrocarril

railcard NOUN
la tarjeta de descuento para viajes en tren

railroad NOUN (US)
el ferrocarril
■ **railroad line** la línea ferroviaria
■ **railroad station** la estación de ferrocarril

railway NOUN
el ferrocarril
■ **railway line** la línea ferroviaria
■ **railway station** la estación de ferrocarril

rain NOUN
▹ *see also* **rain** VERB
la lluvia
□ in the rain bajo la lluvia
■ **It looks like rain.** Parece que va a llover.

to **rain** VERB
▹ *see also* **rain** NOUN
llover*
□ It rains a lot here. Aquí llueve mucho.
■ **It's raining.** Está lloviendo.

rainbow NOUN
el arco iris (PL los arco iris)

raincoat NOUN
el impermeable

rainforest NOUN
la selva tropical

rainy ADJECTIVE
lluvioso (FEM lluviosa)

to **raise** VERB
1 levantar
□ He raised his hand. Levantó la mano.
2 mejorar
□ They want to raise standards in schools. Quieren mejorar el nivel escolar.
3 aumentar
□ to raise interest rates aumentar los tipos de interés
■ **to raise money** recaudar fondos
□ The school is raising money for a new gym. El colegio está recaudando fondos para un gimnasio nuevo.

raisin NOUN
la pasa

rake NOUN
el rastrillo

rally NOUN
1 la concentración (PL las concentraciones) *(of people)*
□ There was rally in Trafalgar Square. Hubo una concentración en Trafalgar Square.
2 el rally (PL los rallys) *(sport)*
□ a rally driver un piloto de rally
3 el peloteo *(in tennis)*

to **ram** VERB
embestir* contra
□ The thieves rammed a police car. Los ladrones embistieron contra un coche de la policía.

ramble NOUN
■ **to go for a ramble** *(de marcha)* ir de excursión

rambler NOUN
el/la excursionista

ramp NOUN
la rampa

ran VERB ▹ *see* **run**

ranch NOUN
el rancho

random ADJECTIVE
■ **a random selection** una selección hecha al azar
■ **at random** al azar □ We picked the number at random. Elegimos el número al azar.

rang VERB ▹ *see* **ring**

range NOUN
▹ *see also* **range** VERB
la variedad
□ There's a wide range of colours. Hay una gran variedad de colores.
■ **It's out of my price range.** Está fuera de mis posibilidades.
■ **a range of mountains** una cadena montañosa

to **range** VERB
▹ *see also* **range** NOUN
■ **to range from...to...** oscilar entre...y...
□ Temperatures in summer range from 20 to 35 degrees. En verano las temperaturas oscilan entre los 20 y los 35 grados.
■ **Tickets range from £2 to £20.** El precio de las entradas va de 2 a 20 libras esterlinas.

rank NOUN
▹ *see also* **rank** VERB
■ **a taxi rank** una parada de taxis

to **rank** VERB
▹ *see also* **rank** NOUN

■ **He's ranked third in the United States.** Está clasificado tercero en los Estados Unidos.

ransom NOUN
el rescate

rap NOUN
el rap

rape NOUN
▹ *see also* **rape** VERB
la violación (PL las violaciones)

to **rape** VERB
▹ *see also* **rape** NOUN
violar

rapist NOUN
el violador

rare ADJECTIVE
1 raro (FEM rara) *(unusual)*
2 poco hecho (FEM poco hecha) *(steak)*

rash ADJECTIVE
precipitado (FEM precipitada)

rasher NOUN
■ **a rasher of bacon** una loncha de bacon

raspberry NOUN
la frambuesa

rat NOUN
la rata

rate NOUN
▹ *see also* **rate** VERB
1 la tarifa
□ There are reduced rates for students. Hay tarifas reducidas para estudiantes.
2 el tipo
□ a high rate of interest un tipo de interés elevado
■ **the divorce rate** el porcentaje de divorcios
■ **the birth rate** la tasa de natalidad

to **rate** VERB
▹ *see also* **rate** NOUN
considerar
□ He was rated the best. Era considerado el mejor.

rather ADVERB
bastante
□ I was rather disappointed. Quedé bastante decepcionado. □ £20! That's rather a lot! ¡20 libras esterlinas! ¡Es bastante caro!
■ **rather a lot of** mucho □ I've got rather a lot of homework to do. Tengo muchos deberes que hacer.
■ **I'd rather...** Preferiría... □ Would you like a sweet? — I'd rather have an apple. ¿Quieres un caramelo? — Preferiría una manzana. □ I'd rather stay in tonight. Preferiría no salir esta noche.

LANGUAGE TIP **preferiría que** has to be followed by a verb in the subjunctive.

□ I'd rather he didn't come to the party. Preferiría que no viniera a la fiesta.
■ **rather than...** en lugar de... □ We decided to camp, rather than stay at a hotel. Decidimos acampar, en lugar de quedarnos en un hotel.

rattle NOUN
el sonajero

to **rave** VERB
poner* por las nubes
□ They raved about the film. Pusieron la película por las nubes.

raven NOUN
el cuervo

raving ADJECTIVE
■ **to be raving mad** estar loco como una cabra

raw ADJECTIVE
crudo (FEM cruda) *(food)*
■ **raw material** la materia prima

razor NOUN
la maquinilla de afeitar
■ **razor blade** la hoja de afeitar

RE ABBREVIATION *(= Religious Education)*
la religión

reach NOUN
▹ *see also* **reach** VERB
■ **out of reach** fuera del alcance □ Keep medicine out of reach of children. Guárdense los medicamentos fuera del alcance de los niños.
■ **within easy reach of** a poca distancia de □ The hotel is within easy reach of the town centre. El hotel está a poca distancia del centro de la ciudad.

to **reach** VERB
▹ *see also* **reach** NOUN
1 llegar* a
□ We reached the hotel at seven o'clock. Llegamos al hotel a las siete. □ We hope to reach the final. Esperamos llegar a la final. □ Eventually they reached a decision. Finalmente llegaron a una decisión.
2 ponerse* en contacto con *(get in touch)*
□ How can I reach you? ¿Cómo puedo ponerme en contacto contigo?

to **react** VERB
reaccionar

reaction NOUN
la reacción (PL las reacciones)

reactor NOUN
el reactor
□ a nuclear reactor un reactor nuclear

to **read** VERB
leer*
□ I don't read much. No leo mucho. □ Read the text out loud. Lee el texto en voz alta.

to **read out** VERB

leer* *(en voz alta)*
□ I was reading it out to the children. Se lo estaba leyendo a los niños.

reader NOUN
el lector
la lectora *(person)*

reading NOUN
la lectura
□ Reading is one of my hobbies. La lectura es una de mis aficiones.
■ **I like reading.** Me gusta leer.

ready ADJECTIVE
preparado (FEM preparada)
□ The meal is ready. La comida está preparada.
■ **She's nearly ready.** Está casi lista.
■ **He's always ready to help.** Siempre está dispuesto a ayudar.
■ **to get ready** prepararse
■ **to get something ready** preparar algo
□ He's getting the dinner ready. Está preparando la cena.

real ADJECTIVE
1 verdadero (FEM verdadera)
□ the real reason el verdadero motivo
□ It was a real nightmare. Fue una verdadera pesadilla.
■ **in real life** en la vida real
2 auténtico (FEM auténtica)
□ It's real leather. Es piel auténtica.

realistic ADJECTIVE
realista (FEM realista)

reality NOUN
la realidad

reality TV NOUN
la telerrealidad
■ **a reality TV show** un reality (show)

to **realize** VERB
■ **to realize that...** darse cuenta de que...
□ We realized that something was wrong. Nos dimos cuenta de que algo iba mal.

really ADVERB
de verdad
□ I'm learning German. — Really? Estoy aprendiendo alemán. — ¿De verdad?
■ **Do you really think so?** ¿Tú crees?
■ **She's really nice.** Es muy simpática.
■ **Do you want to go? — Not really.** ¿Quieres ir? — La verdad es que no.

realtor NOUN (US)
el agente inmobiliario
la agente inmobiliaria

rear ADJECTIVE
▷ *see also* **rear** NOUN
trasero (FEM trasera)
□ the rear wheel la rueda trasera

rear NOUN
▷ *see also* **rear** ADJECTIVE
la parte trasera
□ at the rear of the train en la parte trasera del tren

reason NOUN
la razón (PL las razones)
□ There's no reason to think that he's dangerous. No hay razón para pensar que es peligroso.
■ **for security reasons** por motivos de seguridad
■ **That was the main reason I went.** Fui mayormente por eso.

reasonable ADJECTIVE
1 razonable (FEM razonable)
□ Be reasonable! ¡Sé razonable!
2 bastante aceptable (FEM bastante aceptable)
□ He wrote a reasonable essay. Escribió una redacción bastante aceptable.

reasonably ADVERB
bastante
□ The team played reasonably well. El equipo jugó bastante bien.
■ **reasonably priced accommodation** alojamiento a precios razonables

to **reassure** VERB
tranquilizar*

reassuring ADJECTIVE
tranquilizador (FEM tranquilizadora)

rebellious ADJECTIVE
rebelde (FEM rebelde)

receipt NOUN
1 el ticket *(for goods bought)*
2 el recibo *(for work done)*

LANGUAGE TIP Be careful not to translate **receipt** by **receta**.

to **receive** VERB
recibir

receiver NOUN
el auricular
■ **to pick up the receiver** descolgar

recent ADJECTIVE
reciente (FEM reciente)
□ recent scientific discoveries los recientes descubrimientos científicos
■ **in recent weeks** en las últimas semanas

recently ADVERB
últimamente
□ I haven't seen him recently. No lo he visto últimamente. □ I've been doing a lot of training recently. Últimamente he estado entrenando mucho.
■ **until recently** hasta hace poco

reception NOUN
la recepción (PL las recepciones)
□ Please leave your key at reception. Por favor dejen la llave en recepción. □ The reception will be at a big hotel. La recepción tendrá lugar en un gran hotel.

receptionist NOUN
el/la recepcionista
□ She's a receptionist in a hotel. Es recepcionista en un hotel.

recession NOUN
la recesión (PL las recesiones)

recipe NOUN
la receta

to **reckon** VERB
creer*
□ What do you reckon? ¿Tú qué crees?

reclining ADJECTIVE
■ **a reclining seat** un asiento reclinable

recognizable ADJECTIVE
reconocible (FEM reconocible)

to **recognize** VERB
reconocer*

to **recommend** VERB
recomendar*
□ What do you recommend? ¿Qué me recomienda?

to **reconsider** VERB
reconsiderar

record NOUN
▷ *see also* **record** VERB
1 el récord (PL los récords) *(sport)*
2 el disco *(music)*
□ the world record el récord mundial
■ **in record time** en un tiempo récord
■ **criminal record** los antecedentes penales □ He's got a criminal record. Tiene antecedentes penales.
■ **There is no record of your booking.** No tenemos constancia de su reserva.
■ **records** los archivos □ I'll check in the records. Miraré en los archivos.

to **record** VERB
▷ *see also* **record** NOUN
grabar
□ They've just recorded their new album. Acaban de grabar su nuevo álbum.

LANGUAGE TIP Be careful not to translate **to record** by **recordar**.

recorded delivery NOUN
■ **to send something recorded delivery** enviar algo por correo certificado

recorder NOUN
la flauta dulce *(musical instrument)*
■ **video recorder** el vídeo

recording NOUN
la grabación (PL las grabaciones)

record player NOUN
el tocadiscos (PL los tocadiscos)

to **recover** VERB
recuperarse
□ He's recovering from a knee injury. Se está recuperando de una lesión de rodilla.

recovery NOUN
la mejora
■ **Best whishes for a speedy recovery!** ¡Que te mejores pronto!

rectangle NOUN
el rectángulo

rectangular ADJECTIVE
rectangular

to **recycle** VERB
reciclar

recycling NOUN
el reciclaje

red ADJECTIVE
rojo (FEM roja)
□ a red rose una rosa roja □ red meat la carne roja
■ **Gavin's got red hair.** Gavin es pelirrojo.
■ **to go through a red light** saltarse un semáforo en rojo
■ **red wine** vino tinto

Red Cross NOUN
la Cruz Roja

redcurrant NOUN
la grosella

to **redecorate** VERB
1 volver* a pintar *(with paint)*
2 volver* a empapelar *(with wallpaper)*

red-haired ADJECTIVE
pelirrojo (FEM pelirroja)

red-handed ADJECTIVE
■ **to catch somebody red-handed** coger a alguien con las manos en la masa *(Spain)* (agarrar a alguien con las manos en la masa *Latin America*)

LANGUAGE TIP Be very careful with the verb **coger**: in most of Latin America this is an extremely rude word that should be avoided. However, in Spain this verb is common and not rude at all.

redhead NOUN
el pelirrojo
la pelirroja

to **redo** VERB
rehacer*

to **reduce** VERB
reducir*
□ at a reduced price a precio reducido
■ **'reduce speed now'** 'disminuya la velocidad'

reduction NOUN
la reducción (PL las reducciones)
■ **a five per cent reduction** un descuento del cinco por ciento
■ **'huge reductions!'** '¡grandes rebajas!'

redundancy NOUN
el despido
□ a redundancy payment una indemnización por despido

redundant ADJECTIVE
■ **to be made redundant** ser despedido
reed NOUN
el junco
reel NOUN
el carrete *(of thread)*
to **refer** VERB
■ **to refer to** referirse a □ What are you referring to? ¿A qué te refieres?
referee NOUN
el árbitro
la árbitra
reference NOUN
1 la referencia
□ He made no reference to the murder. No hizo referencia al homicidio.
2 las referencias
□ Would you please give me a reference? ¿Me podría facilitar referencias?
■ **a reference book** un libro de consulta
to **refill** VERB
volver* a llenar
□ He refilled my glass. Volvió a llenarme el vaso.
refinery NOUN
la refinería
to **reflect** VERB
1 reflejar *(image)*
2 reflexionar *(think)*
reflection NOUN
el reflejo *(image)*
reflex NOUN
el reflejo
reflexive ADJECTIVE
reflexivo (FEM reflexiva)
□ a reflexive verb un verbo reflexivo
refresher course NOUN
el curso de reciclaje
refreshing ADJECTIVE
1 refrescante (FEM refrescante)
□ a refreshing drink una bebida refrescante
2 estimulante (FEM estimulante)
□ It was a refreshing change. Fue un cambio estimulante.
refreshments PL NOUN
el refrigerio
refrigerator NOUN
el frigorífico
to **refuel** VERB
repostar
□ The plane stops in Boston to refuel. El avión hace escala en Boston para repostar.
refuge NOUN
el refugio
refugee NOUN
el refugiado
la refugiada
refund NOUN
▹ *see also* **refund** VERB
el reembolso
to **refund** VERB
▹ *see also* **refund** NOUN
reembolsar
refusal NOUN
la negativa
□ her refusal to accept money su negativa a aceptar dinero
to **refuse** VERB
▹ *see also* **refuse** NOUN
negarse*
□ He refused to comment. Se negó a hacer comentarios.
refuse NOUN
▹ *see also* **refuse** VERB
la basura
■ **refuse collection** la recogida de basuras
to **regain** VERB
■ **to regain consciousness** recobrar el conocimiento
regard NOUN
▹ *see also* **regard** VERB
■ **with regard to** con respecto a
■ **Give my regards to Alice.** Dale recuerdos a Alice.
■ **'with kind regards'** 'un cordial saludo'
to **regard** VERB
▹ *see also* **regard** NOUN
■ **They regarded it as unfair.** Lo consideraron injusto.
■ **as regards...** en lo que se refiere a...
regarding PREPOSITION
referente a
□ the laws regarding the export of animals las leyes referentes a la exportación de animales
■ **Regarding John,...** En cuanto a John,...
regardless ADVERB
■ **to carry on regardless** continuar como si nada
regiment NOUN
el regimiento
region NOUN
la región (PL las regiones)
regional ADJECTIVE
regional (FEM regional)
register NOUN
▹ *see also* **register** VERB
el registro *(in hotel)*
■ **to call the register** pasar lista
to **register** VERB
▹ *see also* **register** NOUN
inscribirse* *(to enrol)*
■ **The car was registered in his wife's name.** El coche estaba matriculado a nombre de su esposa.
registered ADJECTIVE

■ **a registered letter** una carta certificada

registration NOUN
el número de matrícula
■ **Registration starts at 8.30.** La inscripción empieza a las ocho y media.

regret NOUN
▹ *see also* **regret** VERB
■ **I've got no regrets.** No me arrepiento.

to **regret** VERB
▹ *see also* **regret** NOUN
arrepentirse*
□ Try it, you won't regret it! ¡Pruébalo! ¡No te arrepentirás!
■ **to regret doing something** arrepentirse de haber hecho algo □ I regret saying that. Me arrepiento de haber dicho eso.

regular ADJECTIVE
1 regular (FEM regular)
□ at regular intervals a intervalos regulares
■ **to take regular exercise** hacer ejercicio con regularidad
2 normal (FEM normal)
□ a regular portion of fries una porción normal de patatas fritas

regularly ADVERB
con regularidad

rehearsal NOUN
el ensayo
■ **dress rehearsal** el ensayo general

to **rehearse** VERB
ensayar

reindeer NOUN
el reno

to **reject** VERB
1 rechazar* *(proposal, invitation)*
2 desechar *(idea, advice)*
■ **I applied but they rejected me.** Presenté una solicitud, pero no me aceptaron.

relapse NOUN
la recaída
□ to have a relapse tener una recaída

related ADJECTIVE
■ **We're related.** Somos parientes.
■ **Are you related to her?** ¿Eres pariente suyo?
■ **The two events are not related.** Los dos sucesos no están relacionados.

relation NOUN
1 el/la pariente
□ He's a distant relation. Es un pariente lejano mío.
2 la relación (PL las relaciones)
□ It has no relation to reality. No guarda ninguna relación con la realidad.
■ **in relation to** con relación a

relationship NOUN
la relación (PL las relaciones)
□ Their relationship is over. Su relación ha acabado. □ We have a good relationship. Tenemos una buena relación.
■ **I'm not in a relationship at the moment.** No tengo relaciones sentimentales con nadie en este momento.

relative NOUN
el/la pariente

relatively ADVERB
relativamente

to **relax** VERB
relajarse
□ I relax listening to music. Me relajo escuchando música.
■ **Relax! Everything's fine.** ¡Tranquilo! No pasa nada.

relaxation NOUN
el esparcimiento
□ I don't have much time for relaxation. No tengo muchos momentos de esparcimiento.

relaxed ADJECTIVE
relajado (FEM relajada)

relaxing ADJECTIVE
relajante (FEM relajante)
□ Having a bath is very relaxing. Darse un baño es muy relajante.
■ **I find cooking relaxing.** Cocinar me relaja.

relay NOUN
■ **a relay race** una carrera de relevos

to **release** VERB
▹ *see also* **release** NOUN
1 poner* en libertad *(prisoner)*
2 hacer* público *(report, news)*
3 sacar* a la venta *(CD, DVD)*

release NOUN
▹ *see also* **release** VERB
la puesta en libertad
□ the release of the prisoners la puesta en libertad de los presos
■ **the band's latest release** el último trabajo del grupo

relegated ADJECTIVE
■ **to be relegated** *(sport)* bajar de división

relevant ADJECTIVE
pertinente (FEM pertinente) *(documents)*
■ **That's not relevant.** Eso no viene al caso.
■ **to be relevant to something** guardar relación con algo □ Education should be relevant to real life. La educación debería guardar relación con la vida real.

reliable ADJECTIVE
fiable (FEM fiable)
□ a reliable car un coche fiable □ He's not very reliable. No es una persona muy fiable.

relief NOUN
el alivio

□ That's a relief! ¡Es un alivio! □ Much to my relief she made no objection. Para mi gran alivio, no hizo objeción alguna.

to **relieve** VERB
aliviar
□ This injection will relieve the pain. Esta inyección le aliviará el dolor.

relieved ADJECTIVE
■ **to be relieved** sentir un gran alivio
□ I was relieved to hear he was better. Sentí un gran alivio al saber que estaba mejor.

religion NOUN
la religión (PL las religiones)
□ What religion are you? ¿De qué religión eres?

religious ADJECTIVE
religioso (FEM religiosa)
□ I'm not religious. No soy religioso.

reluctant ADJECTIVE
reacio (FEM reacia)
■ **to be reluctant to do something** ser reacio a hacer algo □ They were reluctant to help us. Eran reacios a ayudarnos.

reluctantly ADVERB
de mala gana
□ She reluctantly accepted. Aceptó de mala gana.

to **rely on** VERB
confiar* en
□ I'm relying on you. Confío en ti.

to **remain** VERB
permanecer*
□ to remain silent permanecer callado

remaining ADJECTIVE
restante (FEM restante)
□ the remaining ingredients los ingredientes restantes

remains PL NOUN
los restos
□ the remains of the picnic los restos de la merienda □ human remains restos humanos
■ **Roman remains** los restos romanos

remake NOUN
la nueva versión

remark NOUN
el comentario

remarkable ADJECTIVE
extraordinario (FEM extraordinaria)

remarkably ADVERB
extraordinariamente

to **remarry** VERB
volver* a casarse
□ She remarried three years ago. Se volvió a casar hace tres años.

remedy NOUN
el remedio
□ a good remedy for a sore throat un buen remedio para el dolor de garganta

to **remember** VERB
1 acordarse*
□ I don't remember. No me acuerdo.
2 acordarse* de
□ I can't remember his name. No me acuerdo de su nombre. □ I don't remember saying that. No me acuerdo de haber dicho eso.

LANGUAGE TIP In Spanish you often say **no te olvides** – 'don't forget' – instead of 'remember'.

□ Remember your passport! ¡No te olvides del pasaporte! □ Remember to write your name on the form. No te olvides de escribir tu nombre en el impreso.

to **remind** VERB
recordar*
□ The scenery here reminds me of Scotland. Este paisaje me recuerda a Escocia.

LANGUAGE TIP When talking about reminding someone to do something, **recordar a alguien que** has to be followed by a verb in the subjunctive.

□ Remind me to speak to Daniel. Recuérdame que hable con Daniel.

remorse NOUN
el remordimiento
□ He showed no remorse. No tenía ningún remordimiento.

remote ADJECTIVE
remoto (FEM remota)
□ a remote village un pueblo remoto

remote control NOUN
el mando a distancia

removable ADJECTIVE
separable (FEM separable)

removal NOUN
la mudanza
■ **a removal van** un camión de mudanzas

to **remove** VERB
quitar
□ Please remove your bag from my seat. Por favor, quite su bolsa de mi asiento. □ Did you remove the stain? ¿Quitaste la mancha?

rendezvous NOUN
la cita

to **renew** VERB
renovar* *(passport, licence)*

renewable ADJECTIVE
renovable (FEM renovable)

to **renovate** VERB
renovar*
□ The building's been renovated. Han renovado el edificio.

renowned ADJECTIVE
renombrdo (FEM renombrda)

rent NOUN
▷ *see also* **rent** VERB
el alquiler

to **rent** VERB
▹ *see also* **rent** NOUN
alquilar
□ We rented a car. Alquilamos un coche.

rental NOUN
el alquiler
□ Car rental is included in the price. El alquiler del coche está incluído en el precio.

rental car NOUN
el coche de alquiler

to **reorganize** VERB
reorganizar*

rep NOUN *(= representative)*
el/la representante

repaid VERB ▹ *see* **repay**

to **repair** VERB
▹ *see also* **repair** NOUN
reparar
□ Can you repair this for me? ¿Me puede reparar esto? □ I got the washing machine repaired. Me repararon la lavadora.

repair NOUN
▹ *see also* **repair** VERB
la reparación (PL las reparaciones)

to **repay** VERB
devolver* *(money)*
■ **I don't know how I can ever repay you.** No sé cómo podré devolverle el favor.

repayment NOUN
el pago
□ mortgage repayments los pagos de la hipoteca

to **repeat** VERB
▹ *see also* **repeat** NOUN
repetir*

repeat NOUN
▹ *see also* **repeat** VERB
la reposición (PL las reposiciones)
□ There are too many repeats on TV. Hay demasiadas reposiciones en la tele.

repeatedly ADVERB
repetidamente

repellent NOUN
■ **insect repellent** la loción anti-insectos

repetitive ADJECTIVE
repetitivo (FEM repetitiva)

to **replace** VERB
1 sustituir*
2 cambiar *(batteries)*

replay NOUN
▹ *see also* **replay** VERB
■ **There will be a replay on Friday.** El partido se volverá a jugar el viernes.

to **replay** VERB
▹ *see also* **replay** NOUN
1 volver* a jugar *(match)*
2 volver* a poner *(track)*

replica NOUN
la réplica

reply NOUN
▹ *see also* **reply** VERB
la respuesta

to **reply** VERB
▹ *see also* **reply** NOUN
responder

report NOUN
▹ *see also* **report** VERB
1 el informe *(of event)*
2 el reportaje *(news report)*
□ a report in the paper un reportaje en el periódico
3 las notas *(at school)*
■ **I got a good report this term.** He sacado buenas notas este trimestre.

to **report** VERB
▹ *see also* **report** NOUN
1 dar* parte de
□ I reported the theft to the police. Di parte del robo a la policía.
2 presentarse
□ Report to reception when you arrive. Preséntese en recepción cuando llegue.
■ **I'll report back as soon as I hear anything.** En cuanto tenga noticias, te lo haré saber.

reporter NOUN
el/la periodista

to **represent** VERB
1 representar a *(client, country)*
2 representar *(change, achievement)*

representative ADJECTIVE
representativo (FEM representativa)

reproduction NOUN
la reproducción (PL las reproducciones)

reptile NOUN
el reptil

republic NOUN
la república

repulsive ADJECTIVE
repugnante (FEM repugnante)

reputable ADJECTIVE
acreditado (FEM acreditada)

reputation NOUN
la reputación (PL las reputaciones)

request NOUN
▹ *see also* **request** VERB
la petición (PL las peticiones)

to **request** VERB
▹ *see also* **request** NOUN
solicitar

to **require** VERB
requerir*
□ Her job requires a lot of patience. Su trabajo requiere mucha paciencia.

requirement NOUN
el requisito
□ What are the requirements for the job?

¿Cuáles son los requisitos para el puesto?
■ **entry requirements** *(for university)* los requisitos para el acceso

to **rescue** VERB
▷ *see also* **rescue** NOUN
rescatar

rescue NOUN
▷ *see also* **rescue** VERB
el rescate
□ a rescue operation una operación de rescate □ a mountain rescue team un equipo de rescate de montaña
■ **to come to somebody's rescue** ir en auxilio de alguien

research NOUN
la investigación (PL las investigaciones)
□ He's doing research. Realiza trabajos de investigación.
■ **She's doing some research in the library.** Está investigando en la biblioteca.

resemblance NOUN
el parecido

to **resent** VERB
■ **I resent being dependent on her.** Me molesta tener que depender de ella.

reservation NOUN
la reserva
□ I've got a reservation for two nights. Tengo una reserva para dos noches. □ I'd like to make a reservation for this evening. Quisiera hacer una reserva para esta tarde.
■ **I've got reservations about the idea.** Tengo mis reservas al respecto.

reserve NOUN
▷ *see also* **reserve** VERB
1 la reserva *(place)*
□ a nature reserve una reserva natural
2 el/la suplente *(person)*
□ I was reserve in the game last Saturday. Yo era suplente en el partido del sábado.

to **reserve** VERB
▷ *see also* **reserve** NOUN
reservar
□ I'd like to reserve a table for tomorrow evening. Quisiera reservar una mesa para mañana por la noche.

reserved ADJECTIVE
reservado (FEM reservada)
□ a reserved seat un asiento reservado
□ He's quite reserved. Es bastante reservado.

reservoir NOUN
el embalse

resident NOUN
el vecino
la vecina
□ local residents los vecinos del lugar

residential ADJECTIVE
residencial (FEM residencial)
□ a residential area una zona residencial

to **resign** VERB
dimitir

resistance NOUN
la resistencia

to **resit** VERB
volver* a presentarse a
□ I'm resitting the exam in December. Me vuelvo a presentar al examen en diciembre.

resolution NOUN
el propósito
□ Have you made any New Year's resolutions? ¿Has hecho algún buen propósito para el Año Nuevo?

resort NOUN
el centro turístico
□ a resort on the Costa del Sol un centro turístico en la Costa del Sol
■ **as a last resort** como último recurso

resource NOUN
el recurso

respect NOUN
▷ *see also* **respect** VERB
el respeto
■ **in some respects** en algunos aspectos

to **respect** VERB
▷ *see also* **respect** NOUN
respetar

respectable ADJECTIVE
1 respetable (FEM respetable)
□ a respectable family una familia respetable
2 decente (FEM decente)
□ My marks were quite respectable. Mis notas eran bastante decentes.

respectively ADVERB
respectivamente
□ Spain and France came third and fourth respectively. España y Francia llegaron en tercero y cuarto lugar respectivamente.

responsibility NOUN
la responsabilidad

responsible ADJECTIVE
responsable (FEM responsable)
□ You should be more responsible! ¡Deberías ser más responsable!
■ **to be responsible for something** ser responsable de algo □ He's responsible for booking the tickets. Es responsable de reservar las entradas.
■ **It's a responsible job.** Es un puesto de responsabilidad.

rest NOUN
▷ *see also* **rest** VERB
1 el descanso
□ five minutes' rest cinco minutos de descanso
■ **to have a rest** descansar □ We stopped to have a rest. Nos paramos a descansar.

English-Spanish

r

2 el resto
□ I'll do the rest. Yo haré el resto. □ the rest of the money el resto del dinero
■ **the rest of them** los demás □ The rest of them went swimming. Los demás fueron a nadar.

to **rest** VERB
▷ *see also* **rest** NOUN
1 descansar
□ She's resting in her room. Está descansando en su habitación.
■ **He has to rest his knee.** Tiene que descansar la rodilla.
2 apoyar
□ I rested my bike against the window. Apoyé la bicicleta en la ventana.

restaurant NOUN
el restaurante
□ We don't often go to restaurants. No solemos ir a restaurantes.
■ **restaurant car** el vagón restaurante

restful ADJECTIVE
plácido (FEM plácida)

restless ADJECTIVE
inquieto (FEM inquieta)

restoration NOUN
la restauración

to **restore** VERB
restaurar *(building, painting)*

to **restrict** VERB
limitar

rest room NOUN (US)
los servicios

result NOUN
el resultado
□ my exam results los resultados de mis exámenes □ The result was one-nil. El resultado fue uno a cero.

résumé NOUN (US)
el currículum vitae

to **retire** VERB
jubilarse

retired ADJECTIVE
jubilado (FEM jubilada)
□ She's retired. Está jubilada. □ a retired teacher un maestro jubilado

retirement NOUN
■ **since his retirement** desde que se jubiló

to **retrace** VERB
■ **I retraced my steps.** Volví sobre mis pasos.

return NOUN
▷ *see also* **return** VERB
1 el regreso
□ his sudden return home su repentino regreso a casa
■ **the return journey** el viaje de vuelta
■ **a return match** un partido de vuelta
2 el billete de ida y vuelta
□ A return to Bilbao, please. Un billete de ida y vuelta a Bilbao, por favor.
■ **in return** a cambio □ She helps me and I help her in return. Me ayuda y yo la ayudo a cambio.
■ **in return for** a cambio de
■ **Many happy returns!** ¡Que cumplas muchos más!

to **return** VERB
▷ *see also* **return** NOUN
1 volver*
□ I've just returned from holiday. Acabo de volver de vacaciones. □ He returned to Spain the following year. Volvió a España al año siguiente.
2 devolver*
□ She borrows my things and doesn't return them. Toma prestadas mis cosas y no las devuelve.

reunion NOUN
la reunión (PL las reuniones)
□ We had a big family reunion at Christmas. Tuvimos una gran reunión familiar en Navidad.

to **reuse** VERB
reutilizar*

to **reveal** VERB
revelar

revenge NOUN
la venganza
□ in revenge como venganza
■ **to take revenge** vengarse □ They planned to take revenge on him. Planearon vengarse de él.

to **reverse** VERB
▷ *see also* **reverse** ADJECTIVE
dar* marcha atrás *(car)*
□ He reversed without looking. Dio marcha atrás sin mirar.
■ **to reverse the charges** llamar a cobro revertido

reverse ADJECTIVE
▷ *see also* **reverse** VERB
inverso (FEM inversa)
□ in reverse order en orden inverso
■ **in reverse gear** en marcha atrás
■ **reverse charge call** llamada a cobro revertido

review NOUN
1 la revisión (PL las revisiones) *(of policy, salary)*
2 el repaso *(of subject)*

to **revise** VERB
estudiar para un examen
□ I haven't started revising yet. Todavía no he empezado a estudiar para el examen.
■ **I've revised my opinion.** He cambiado de opinión.

revision NOUN
■ **Have you done a lot of revision?** ¿Has estudiado mucho para el examen?
to **revive** VERB
resucitar
□ The nurses tried to revive him. Las enfermeras intentaron resucitarlo.
revolting ADJECTIVE
repugnante (FEM repugnante)
revolution NOUN
la revolución (PL las revoluciones)
revolutionary ADJECTIVE
revolucionario (FEM revolucionaria)
revolver NOUN
el revólver
reward NOUN
la recompensa
rewarding ADJECTIVE
gratificante (FEM gratificante)
□ a rewarding job un trabajo gratificante
to **rewind** VERB
rebobinar
□ to rewind a cassette rebobinar una cinta
rheumatism NOUN
el reumatismo
□ I've got rheumatism. Tengo reumatismo.
rhinoceros NOUN
el rinoceronte
rhubarb NOUN
el ruibarbo
rhythm NOUN
el ritmo
rib NOUN
la costilla
ribbon NOUN
la cinta
rice NOUN
el arroz
■ **rice pudding** el arroz con leche
rich ADJECTIVE
rico (FEM rica)
■ **the rich** los ricos
to **rid** VERB
■ **to get rid of** deshacerse de □ I want to get rid of some old clothes. Quiero deshacerme de algunas ropas viejas.
ridden VERB ▷ *see* **ride**
ride NOUN
▷ *see also* **ride** VERB
■ **to go for a ride 1** *(on horse)* montar a caballo **2** *(on bike)* dar un paseo en bicicleta □ We went for a bike ride. Fuimos a dar un paseo en bicicleta.
■ **It's a short bus ride to the town centre.** El centro de la ciudad queda cerca en autobús.
to **ride** VERB
▷ *see also* **ride** NOUN
montar a caballo
□ I'm learning to ride. Estoy aprendiendo a montar a caballo.
■ **to ride a bike** ir en bicicleta □ Can you ride a bike? ¿Sabes ir en bicicleta?
rider NOUN
1 el jinete
□ She's a good rider. Ella monta muy bien a caballo.
2 el/la ciclista *(cyclist)*
ridiculous ADJECTIVE
ridículo (FEM ridícula)
riding NOUN
la equitación *(as sport)*
□ a riding school una escuela de equitación
■ **to go riding** montar a caballo
rifle NOUN
el rifle
rig NOUN
■ **oil rig** la plataforma petrolífera
right ADJECTIVE, ADVERB
▷ *see also* **right** NOUN

LANGUAGE TIP There are several ways of translating 'right'. Scan the examples to find one that is similar to what you want to say.

1 correcto (FEM correcta)
□ the right answer la respuesta correcta
2 adecuado (FEM adecuada) *(place, time)*
□ We're on the right train. Estamos en el tren adecuado. □ It isn't the right size. Ésta no es la talla adecuada.
■ **Is this the right road for Ávila?** ¿Vamos bien por aquí para Ávila?
■ **to be right 1** *(person)* tener razón □ You were right! ¡Tenías razón! **2** *(statement, opinion)* ser verdad □ That's right! ¡Es verdad!
■ **Do you have the right time?** ¿Tienes hora?
3 bien
□ It's not right to behave like that. No está bien comportarse así. □ Am I pronouncing it right? ¿Lo pronuncio bien?
■ **I think you did the right thing.** Creo que hiciste bien.
4 derecho (FEM derecha) *(not left)*
□ my right hand mi mano derecha
5 a la derecha *(turn, look)*
□ Turn right at the traffic lights. Cuando llegues al semáforo dobla a la derecha.
■ **Right! Let's get started!** ¡Bueno! ¡Empecemos!
■ **right away** enseguida □ I'll do it right away. Lo haré enseguida.
right NOUN
▷ *see also* **right** ADJECTIVE
1 el derecho
□ You've got no right to do that. No tienes derecho de hacer eso.

2 la derecha

■ **on the right** a la derecha □ on the right of Mr. Yates a la derecha del Sr. Yates

■ **right of way** la prioridad □ We had right of way. Teníamos prioridad.

right-hand ADJECTIVE

■ **the right-hand side** la derecha □ It's on the right-hand side. Está a la derecha.

right-handed ADJECTIVE

diestro (FEM diestra)

rim NOUN

la montura

□ glasses with metal rims las gafas con montura metálica

ring NOUN

▷ *see also* **ring** VERB

1 el anillo

□ a gold ring un anillo de oro

■ **a wedding ring** una alianza

2 el círculo

□ to stand in a ring formar un círculo

3 el timbrazo *(at door)*

■ **After three or four rings the door was opened.** Después de tres o cuatro timbrazos la puerta se abrió.

■ **There was a ring at the door.** Se oyó el timbre de la puerta.

■ **to give somebody a ring** llamar a alguien por teléfono

to **ring** VERB

▷ *see also* **ring** NOUN

1 llamar

□ Your mother rang this morning. Tu madre llamó esta mañana.

■ **to ring somebody** llamar a alguien

2 sonar*

□ The phone's ringing. El teléfono está sonando.

■ **to ring the bell** tocar el timbre

to **ring back** VERB

volver* a llamar

□ I'll ring back later. Volveré a llamar más tarde.

to **ring up** VERB

llamar por teléfono

ring binder NOUN

la carpeta de anillas (la carpeta de anillos *Latin America*)

ring road NOUN

la carretera de circunvalación

ringtone NOUN

el tono de llamada

rink NOUN

1 la pista de hielo *(for ice-skating)*

2 la pista de patinaje *(for roller-skating)*

to **rinse** VERB

enjuagar*

riot NOUN

▷ *see also* **riot** VERB

el disturbio

to **riot** VERB

▷ *see also* **riot** NOUN

causar disturbios

to **rip** VERB

rasgar*

□ I've ripped my jeans. Me he rasgado los vaqueros. □ My shirt's ripped. Mi camisa está rasgada.

to **rip off** VERB

timar *(informal)*

□ The hotel ripped us off. En el hotel nos timaron.

to **rip up** VERB

hacer* pedazos

□ He read the note and then ripped it up. Leyó la nota y la hizo pedazos.

ripe ADJECTIVE

maduro (FEM madura)

rip-off NOUN

■ **It's a rip-off!** *(informal)* ¡Es un timo!

rise NOUN

▷ *see also* **rise** VERB

1 la subida *(in prices, temperature)*

□ a sudden rise in temperature una repentina subida de las temperaturas

2 el aumento *(pay rise)*

to **rise** VERB

▷ *see also* **rise** NOUN

1 subir *(increase)*

□ Prices are rising. Los precios están subiendo.

2 salir*

□ The sun rises early in June. En junio el sol sale temprano.

riser NOUN

■ **to be an early riser** ser madrugador

risk NOUN

▷ *see also* **risk** VERB

el riesgo

■ **to take risks** correr riesgos

■ **It's at your own risk.** Es a tu propia cuenta y riesgo.

to **risk** VERB

▷ *see also* **risk** NOUN

arriesgarse*

□ You risk getting a fine. Te arriesgas a que te multen. □ I wouldn't risk it if I were you. Yo en tu lugar no me arriesgaría.

risky ADJECTIVE

arriesgado (FEM arriesgada)

rival NOUN

▷ *see also* **rival** ADJECTIVE

el/la rival

rival ADJECTIVE

▷ *see also* **rival** NOUN

1 rival (FEM rival)

□ a rival gang una banda rival
2 competidor (FEM competidora)
□ a rival company una empresa competidora
rivalry NOUN
la rivalidad
river NOUN
el río
■ **the river Tagus** el río Tajo
Riviera NOUN
■ **the French Riviera** la Costa Azul
■ **the Italian Riviera** la Riviera
road NOUN
1 la carretera
□ There's a lot of traffic on the roads. Hay mucho tráfico en las carreteras. □ a road accident un accidente de carretera
2 la calle
□ They live across the road. Viven al otro lado de la calle.
road map NOUN
el mapa de carreteras
LANGUAGE TIP Although **mapa** ends in **-a**, it is actually a masculine noun.
road rage NOUN
la conducta agresiva al volante
road sign NOUN
la señal de tráfico
roadworks PL NOUN
las obras
□ There are roadworks on the motorway. Hay obras en la autopista.
roast ADJECTIVE
asado (FEM asada)
□ roast chicken pollo asado
■ **roast pork** el asado de cerdo
■ **roast beef** el rosbif
to **rob** VERB
■ **to rob somebody** robar a alguien □ I've been robbed. Me han robado.
■ **to rob somebody of something** robar algo a alguien □ He was robbed of his wallet. Le robaron la cartera.
■ **to rob a bank** asaltar un banco
robber NOUN
el ladrón
la ladrona
■ **a bank-robber** un asaltante de bancos (FEM una asaltante de bancos)
robbery NOUN
el robo
■ **a bank robbery** un asalto a un banco
■ **an armed robbery** un asalto a mano armada
robin NOUN
el petirrojo
robot NOUN
el robot (PL los robots)
rock NOUN
▷ *see also* **rock** VERB
1 la roca
□ They tunnelled through the rock. Abrieron un túnel a través de la roca. □ I sat on a rock. Me senté encima de una roca.
2 la piedra
□ The crowd started to throw rocks. La multitud empezó a lanzar piedras.
3 el rock
□ a rock concert un concierto de rock
■ **rock and roll** el rock and roll
■ **a stick of rock** una barra de caramelo
to **rock** VERB
▷ *see also* **rock** NOUN
1 mecer
■ **to rock a baby** *(in one's arms)* acunar a un bebé
2 sacudir
□ The explosion rocked the building. La explosión sacudió el edificio.
rocket NOUN
el cohete *(spacecraft, firework)*
rocking chair NOUN
la mecedora
rocking horse NOUN
el caballo de balancín
rod NOUN
la caña de pescar *(for fishing)*
rode VERB ▷ *see* **ride**
role NOUN
el papel
□ to play a role hacer un papel
role play NOUN
el juego de roles
□ to do a role play hacer un juego de roles
roll NOUN
▷ *see also* **roll** VERB
1 el rollo
□ a toilet roll un rollo de papel higiénico
■ **a roll of film** un carrete de fotos
2 el panecillo
□ a cheese roll un panecillo de queso
■ **Roll call is at 8.30.** Pasan lista a las ocho y media.
to **roll** VERB
▷ *see also* **roll** NOUN
rodar* *(ball, bottle)*
roller NOUN
el rulo *(for hair)*
Rollerblades® PL NOUN
los patines en línea
rollercoaster NOUN
la montaña rusa
roller skates PL NOUN
los patines de ruedas
roller-skating NOUN
el patinaje sobre ruedas

English-Spanish
r

■ **to go roller-skating** *(sobre ruedas)* ir a patinar

rolling pin NOUN
el rodillo

Roman ADJECTIVE, NOUN
romano (FEM romana)
□ the Roman empire el imperio romano
■ **the Romans** los romanos

Roman Catholic NOUN
el católico
la católica
□ He's a Roman Catholic. Es católico.

romance NOUN
1 las novelas románticas *(novels)*
□ I read a lot of romance. Leo muchas novelas románticas.
2 el romanticismo
□ the romance of Paris el romanticismo de París
■ **a holiday romance** un romance de verano

Romania NOUN
Rumania *fem*

Romanian ADJECTIVE
rumano (FEM rumana)

romantic ADJECTIVE
romántico (FEM romántica)

roof NOUN
el techo

roof rack NOUN
la baca

room NOUN
1 la habitación (PL las habitaciones)
□ She's in her room. Está en su habitación.
■ **a single room** una habitación individual
■ **a double room** una habitación doble
2 sala *(in school)*
□ the music room la sala de música
3 el espacio
□ There's no room for that box. No hay espacio para esa caja.

roommate NOUN
el compañero de cuarto
la compañera de cuarto

root NOUN
la raíz (PL las raíces)

rope NOUN
la cuerda

rose VERB ▷ *see* **rise**

rose NOUN
la rosa *(flower)*

to **rot** VERB
pudrirse*
□ The wood had started to rot. La madera había empezado a pudrirse
■ **Sugar rots your teeth.** El azúcar pica los dientes.

rotten ADJECTIVE
podrido (FEM podrida)
□ a rotten apple una manzana podrida
■ **rotten weather** un tiempo asqueroso
■ **That's a rotten thing to do!** ¡Eso está fatal!
■ **to feel rotten** sentirse fatal

rough ADJECTIVE, ADVERB
1 áspero (FEM áspera)
□ My hands are rough. Tengo las manos ásperas.
2 violento (FEM violenta)
□ Rugby's a rough sport. El rugby es un deporte violento.
3 peligroso (FEM peligrosa)
□ It's a rough area. Es una zona peligrosa.
4 agitado (FEM agitada)
□ The sea was rough. El mar estaba agitado.
5 aproximado (FEM aproximada)
□ I've got a rough idea. Tengo una idea aproximada.
■ **to feel rough** sentirse mal
■ **to sleep rough** dormir en la calle □ A lot of people sleep rough in London. Mucha gente duerme en la calle en Londres.

roughly ADVERB
aproximadamente
■ **It weighs roughly 20 kilos.** Pesa aproximadamente 20 kilos.

round ADJECTIVE, ADVERB, PREPOSITION
▷ *see also* **round** NOUN
1 redondo (FEM redonda)
□ a round table una mesa redonda
2 alrededor de
□ We were sitting round the table. Estábamos sentados alrededor de la mesa. □ She wore a scarf round her neck. Llevaba una bufanda alrededor del cuello.
■ **It's just round the corner.** Está a la vuelta de la esquina.
■ **to go round to somebody's house** ir a casa de alguien
■ **to have a look round** echar un vistazo □ We had a look round the shoe department. Echamos un vistazo a la sección de zapatos.
■ **to go round a museum** visitar un museo
■ **round here** por aquí cerca □ He lives round here. Vive aquí cerca. □ Is there a chemist's round here? ¿Hay alguna farmacia por aquí cerca?
■ **all round** por todos lados □ There were vineyards all round. Había viñedos por todos lados.
■ **all year round** todo el año
■ **round about** alrededor de □ It costs round about £100. Cuesta alrededor de 100 libras esterlinas.
■ **round about eight o'clock** hacia las ocho

round NOUN
▷ *see also* **round** ADJECTIVE, ADVERB, PREPOSITION

1 la vuelta *(of tournament)*
2 el round (PL los rounds) *(of boxing match)*
■ **a round of golf** una vuelta de golf
■ **a round of drinks** una ronda de bebidas
□ He bought them a round of drinks. Les invitó a una ronda de bebidas.
■ **I think it's my round.** Creo que me toca pagar.

roundabout NOUN
1 la rotonda *(at junction)*
2 el tiovivo *(at funfair)*

rounders SING NOUN
DID YOU KNOW...?
Rounders is not played in Spain.

round trip NOUN (US)
el viaje de ida y vuelta
■ **a round-trip ticket** un billete de ida y vuelta

route NOUN
el itinerario
□ We are planning our route. Estamos planeando el itinerario.
■ **bus route** el recorrido del autobús

routine NOUN
la rutina
□ my daily routine mi rutina diaria

row (1) NOUN
▷ *see also* **row** VERB
1 el jaleo
□ What's that terrible row? ¿Qué es ese jaleo tan tremendo?
2 la pelea
■ **to have a row** pelearse □ They've had a row. Se han peleado.

row (2) NOUN
▷ *see also* **row (2)** VERB
1 la hilera
□ a row of houses una hilera de casas
2 la fila *(of people, seats)*
□ in the front row en primera fila
■ **five times in a row** cinco veces seguidas

to **row** VERB
▷ *see also* **row (2)** NOUN
remar

rowboat NOUN (US)
la barca de remos

rowing NOUN
el remo
□ My hobby is rowing. My hobby es el remo.
■ **rowing boat** la barca de remos

royal ADJECTIVE
real (FEM real)
□ the royal family la familia real

to **rub** VERB
1 frotar *(stain)*
2 restregarse* *(part of body)*
□ Don't rub your eyes. No te restriegues los ojos.

rubber NOUN
1 la goma
□ rubber soles suelas de goma
2 la goma de borrar *(eraser)*
□ Can I borrow your rubber? ¿Me prestas la goma?
■ **a rubber band** una goma elástica

rubbish NOUN
▷ *see also* **rubbish** ADJECTIVE
1 la basura
□ When do they collect the rubbish? ¿Cuándo recogen la basura? □ They sell a lot of rubbish at the market. Venden mucha basura en el mercado.
■ **That magazine is rubbish!** *(informal)* ¡Esa revista es una porquería!
2 las estupideces
□ Don't talk rubbish! ¡No digas estupideces!
■ **That's a load of rubbish!** ¡Son puras tonterías!
■ **rubbish bin** el cubo de la basura
■ **rubbish dump** el vertedero

rubbish ADJECTIVE
▷ *see also* **rubbish** NOUN
■ **They're a rubbish team!** ¡Es un equipo que no vale nada!

rucksack NOUN
la mochila

rude ADJECTIVE
grosero (FEM grosera)
□ He was very rude to me. Fue muy grosero conmigo.
■ **It's rude to interrupt.** Es de mala educación interrumpir.
■ **a rude joke** un chiste verde
■ **a rude word** una palabrota

rug NOUN
1 la alfombra *(carpet)*
2 la manta de viaje *(travelling rug)*

rugby NOUN
el rugby
□ He enjoys playing rugby. Le gusta jugar al rugby.

ruin NOUN
▷ *see also* **ruin** VERB
la ruina
□ the ruins of the castle las ruinas del castillo
■ **in ruins** en ruinas

to **ruin** VERB
▷ *see also* **ruin** NOUN
1 estropear
□ You'll ruin your shoes. Te vas a estropear los zapatos. □ It ruined our holiday. Nos estropeó las vacaciones.
2 arruinar *(financially)*

rule NOUN
1 la regla

□ the rules of grammar las reglas de la gramática
■ **as a rule** por regla general
2 la norma
□ It's against the rules. Va en contra de las normas.

to **rule out** VERB
descartar *(possibility)*

ruler NOUN
la regla

rum NOUN
el ron

rumour (US **rumor**) NOUN
el rumor
□ It's just a rumour. Es sólo un rumor.

run NOUN
▷ *see also* **run** VERB
■ **to go for a run** salir a correr □ I go for a run every morning. Salgo a correr todas las mañanas.
■ **I did a 10-kilometre run.** Corrí 10 kilómetros.
■ **The criminals are still on the run.** Los delincuentes están todavía en fuga.
■ **in the long run** a la larga

to **run** VERB
▷ *see also* **run** NOUN
1 correr
■ **I ran five kilometres.** Corrí cinco kilómetros.
■ **to run a marathon** correr un maratón
2 dirigir*
□ He runs a large company. Dirige una gran empresa.
3 organizar*
□ They run music courses in the holidays. Organizan cursos de música en las vacaciones.
4 llevar *(by car)*
□ I can run you to the station. Te puedo llevar a la estación.
■ **Don't leave the tap running.** No dejen el grifo abierto. (No dejen la llave abierta. *Latin America*)
■ **to run a bath** llenar la bañera
■ **The buses stop running at midnight.** Los autobuses dejan de funcionar a medianoche.

to **run away** VERB
huir*
□ They ran away before the police came. Huyeron antes de que llegara la policía.

to **run out** VERB
■ **Time is running out.** Queda poco tiempo.
■ **to run out of something** quedarse sin algo □ We ran out of money. Nos quedamos sin dinero.

to **run over** VERB
atropellar
■ **to get run over** ser atropellado

rung VERB ▷ *see* **ring**

runner NOUN
el corredor
la corredora

runner beans PL NOUN
las judías verdes (las habichuelas verdes *Latin America*)

runner-up NOUN
el subcampeón (PL los subcampeones)
la subcampeona

running NOUN
el footing
■ **Running is my favourite sport.** El footing es mi deporte favorito. □ to go running hacer footing

runway NOUN
la pista de aterrizaje

rural ADJECTIVE
rural (FEM rural)

rush NOUN
▷ *see also* **rush** VERB
la prisa
□ I'm in a rush. Tengo prisa. □ There's no rush. No corre prisa.
■ **to do something in a rush** hacer algo deprisa

to **rush** VERB
▷ *see also* **rush** NOUN
1 correr
□ Everyone rushed outside. Todos corrieron hacia fuera.
2 precipitarse
□ There's no need to rush. No hay por qué precipitarse.

rush hour NOUN
la hora punta (la hora pico *Latin America*)

rusk NOUN
la galleta para bebés

Russia NOUN
la Rusia

Russian ADJECTIVE
▷ *see also* **Russian** NOUN
ruso (FEM rusa)

Russian NOUN
▷ *see also* **Russian** ADJECTIVE
1 el ruso
la rusa *(person)*
□ the Russians los rusos
2 el ruso *(language)*

rust NOUN
el óxido

rusty ADJECTIVE
oxidado (FEM oxidada)

ruthless ADJECTIVE
despiadado (FEM despiadada)

rye NOUN
el centeno
■ **rye bread** el pan de centeno

Ss

sack NOUN
▷ *see also* **sack** VERB
el saco
□ a sack of potatoes un saco de patatas
■ **to give somebody the sack** despedir a alguien
■ **He got the sack.** Lo despidieron.

to **sack** VERB
▷ *see also* **sack** NOUN
■ **to sack somebody** despedir a alguien
□ He was sacked. Lo despidieron.

sacred ADJECTIVE
sagrado (FEM sagrada)
□ sacred places lugares sagrados
■ **sacred music** música sacra

sacrifice NOUN
el sacrificio

sad ADJECTIVE
triste (FEM triste)

> **WORD POWER**
> You can use a number of other words instead of **sad** to mean 'unhappy':
> **miserable** desgraciado
> □ a miserable face una cara desgraciada
> **unhappy** infeliz
> □ an unhappy child un niño infeliz
> **upset** disgustado
> □ to be upset estar disgustado

saddle NOUN
1 la silla de montar *(for horse)*
2 el sillín *(on bike)*

saddlebag NOUN
1 la cartera *(on bike)*
2 la alforja *(for horse)*

sadly ADVERB
1 con tristeza
□ 'She's gone', he said sadly. 'Se ha ido' dijo con tristeza.
2 desgraciadamente
□ Sadly, it was too late. Desgraciadamente, era ya demasiado tarde.

safe NOUN
▷ *see also* **safe** ADJECTIVE
la caja fuerte (PL las cajas fuertes)

safe ADJECTIVE
▷ *see also* **safe** NOUN
1 seguro (FEM segura)
□ This car isn't safe. Este coche no es seguro.
2 a salvo
□ You're safe now. Ya estás a salvo.
■ **to feel safe** sentirse protegido
■ **Is the water safe to drink?** ¿Es agua potable?
■ **Don't worry, it's perfectly safe.** No te preocupes, no tiene el menor peligro.
■ **safe sex** el sexo sin riesgo

safety NOUN
la seguridad
■ **safety belt** el cinturón de seguridad
■ **safety pin** el imperdible (el seguro *Latin America*)

Sagittarius NOUN
el Sagitario *(sign)*
■ **I'm Sagittarius.** Soy sagitario.

Sahara NOUN
■ **the Sahara Desert** el Sáhara

said VERB ▷ *see* **say**

sail NOUN
▷ *see also* **sail** VERB
la vela
■ **to set sail** zarpar

to **sail** VERB
▷ *see also* **sail** NOUN
1 navegar*
□ to sail around the world dar la vuelta al mundo navegando
2 zarpar
□ The boat sails at eight o'clock. El barco zarpa a las ocho.

sailing NOUN
la vela *(sport)*
■ **to go sailing** hacer vela
■ **sailing boat** el barco de vela
■ **sailing ship** el velero

sailor NOUN
el marinero
□ He's a sailor. Es marinero.

saint NOUN
el santo
la santa

LANGUAGE TIP When used before a man's name, the word **Santo** is shortened to **San**, the exceptions being **Santo Tomás** and **Santo Domingo**.

□ Saint John San Juan

sake NOUN
■ **for the sake of argument** pongamos por caso
■ **for the sake of the children** por el bien de los niños
■ **For goodness sake!** ¡Por el amor de Dios!

salad NOUN
la ensalada
■ **salad cream** la mayonesa
■ **salad dressing** el aliño para la ensalada

salami NOUN
el salami

salary NOUN
el sueldo

sale NOUN
1 las rebajas
□ There's a sale on at Harrods. En Harrods están de rebajas. □ the January sales las rebajas de enero
2 la venta
□ Newspaper sales have fallen. Ha descendido la venta de periódicos.
■ **on sale** a la venta
■ **The house is for sale.** La casa está en venta.
■ **'for sale'** 'se vende'

sales assistant NOUN
el dependiente
la dependienta

salesman NOUN
1 el representante *(commercial)*
□ an insurance salesman un representante de seguros
2 el dependiente *(sales assistant)*
■ **a car salesman** un vendedor de coches

sales rep NOUN
el/la representante

saleswoman NOUN
1 la representante *(commercial)*
□ an insurance saleswoman una representante de seguros
2 la dependienta *(sales assistant)*

salmon NOUN
el salmón (PL los salmones)

salon NOUN
el salón (PL los salones)
□ hair salon salón de peluquería □ beauty salon salón de belleza

saloon car NOUN
el turismo

salt NOUN
la sal

salty ADJECTIVE
salado (FEM salada)

to **salute** VERB
saludar

Salvation Army NOUN
el Ejército de Salvación

same ADJECTIVE
mismo (FEM misma)
□ the same model el mismo modelo
■ **It's not the same.** No es lo mismo.
■ **They're exactly the same.** Son exactamente iguales.
■ **The house is still the same.** La casa sigue igual.

sample NOUN
la muestra
□ a free sample of perfume una muestra gratuita de perfume

sand NOUN
la arena

sandal NOUN
la sandalia
□ a pair of sandals unas sandalias

sand castle NOUN
el castillo de arena

sandwich NOUN
1 el sandwich (PL los sandwiches) *(with sliced bread)*
2 el bocadillo *(with French bread)*

sang VERB ▷ *see* **sing**

sanitary towel NOUN
la compresa

sank VERB ▷ *see* **sink**

Santa Claus NOUN
Papá Noel *masc*

sarcastic ADJECTIVE
sarcástico (FEM sarcástica)

sardine NOUN
la sardina

sat VERB ▷ *see* **sit**

satchel NOUN
la cartera

satellite NOUN
el satélite
□ by satellite vía satélite
■ **a satellite dish** una antena parabólica
■ **satellite television** la televisión vía satélite

satisfactory ADJECTIVE
satisfactorio (FEM satisfactoria)

satisfied ADJECTIVE
satisfecho (FEM satisfecha)

Saturday NOUN
el sábado (PL los sábados)
□ I saw her on Saturday. La vi el sábado.
□ every Saturday todos los sábados □ last Saturday el sábado pasado □ next Saturday el sábado que viene □ on Saturdays los sábados

■ **I've got a Saturday job.** Tengo un trabajo los sábados.

sauce NOUN
1 la salsa
□ tomato sauce salsa de tomate
2 la crema
□ chocolate sauce crema de chocolate

saucepan NOUN
el cazo

saucer NOUN
el platillo

Saudi Arabia NOUN
Arabia Saudí *fem*

sauna NOUN
la sauna

sausage NOUN
la salchicha
■ **a sausage roll** un pastelito de salchicha

to **save** VERB
1 ahorrar
□ I saved money by staying in youth hostels. Ahorré dinero yendo a albergues juveniles. □ I've saved £50 already. Ya llevo ahorradas 50 libras. □ It saved us time. Nos ahorró tiempo.
■ **We went in a taxi to save time.** Para ganar tiempo fuimos en taxi.
2 salvar
□ Doctors saved her from cancer. Los médicos la salvaron del cáncer.
■ **Luckily, all the passengers were saved.** Afortunadamente, todos los pasajeros se salvaron.
3 guardar
□ Don't forget to save your work regularly. No te olvides de guardar tu trabajo de vez en cuando.

to **save up** VERB
ahorrar
□ I'm saving up for a new bike. Estoy ahorrando para una bici nueva.

savings PL NOUN
los ahorros
□ She spent all her savings on a computer. Se gastó todos sus ahorros en un ordenador.

savoury ADJECTIVE
salado (FEM salada)
□ Is it sweet or savoury? ¿Es dulce o salado?

saw VERB ▷ *see* **see**

saw NOUN
la sierra

sax NOUN
el saxo

saxophone NOUN
el saxofón (PL los saxofones)

to **say** VERB
decir*
□ to say yes decir que sí □ What did he say? ¿Qué dijo él?
■ **Could you say that again?** ¿Podrías repetir eso?
■ **The clock said four minutes past eleven.** El reloj marcaba las once y cuatro minutos.
■ **It goes without saying that...** Ni que decir tiene que...

saying NOUN
el dicho

scale NOUN
la escala
□ a large-scale map un mapa a gran escala
■ **He underestimated the scale of the problem.** Ha subestimado la envergadura del problema.

scales PL NOUN
1 el peso *(in kitchen)*
2 la báscula *(in shop)*
■ **bathroom scales** la báscula de baño

scampi PL NOUN
las gambas rebozadas

scandal NOUN
1 el escándalo *(outrage)*
□ It caused a scandal. Causó escándalo.
2 las habladurías *(gossip)*
□ It's just scandal. No son más que habladurías.

scar NOUN
la cicatriz (PL las cicatrices)

scarce ADJECTIVE
escaso (FEM escasa)
□ scarce resources recursos escasos
■ **Jobs are scarce.** Escasean los trabajos.

scarcely ADVERB
apenas
□ I scarcely knew him. Apenas lo conocía.

scare NOUN
▷ *see also* **scare** VERB
el susto
□ We got a bit of a scare. Nos pegamos un susto.
■ **a bomb scare** una amenaza de bomba

to **scare** VERB
▷ *see also* **scare** NOUN
asustar
□ You scared me! ¡Me has asustado!

scarecrow NOUN
el espantapájaros (PL los espantapájaros)

scared ADJECTIVE
■ **to be scared** tener miedo □ Are you scared of him? ¿Le tienes miedo?
■ **I was scared stiff.** Estaba muerto de miedo.

scarf NOUN
1 la bufanda *(woollen)*
2 el pañuelo *(light)*

scary ADJECTIVE

■ **It was really scary.** Daba verdadero miedo.
■ **a scary film** una película de miedo

scene NOUN
1 la escena
□ love scenes las escenas de amor □ It was an amazing scene. Era una escena asombrosa.
2 el lugar
□ at the scene of the crime en el lugar del crimen □ The police were soon on the scene. La policía no tardó en acudir al lugar de los hechos.
■ **to make a scene** montar el número

scenery NOUN
el paisaje

scent NOUN
el perfume

schedule NOUN
el programa

LANGUAGE TIP Although **programa** ends in **-a**, it is actually a masculine noun.

□ a production schedule un programa de producción
■ **There's a tight schedule for this project.** Este proyecto tiene un calendario muy justo.
■ **a busy schedule** una agenda muy apretada
■ **on schedule** sin retraso
■ **to be behind schedule** ir con retraso

scheduled flight NOUN
el vuelo regular

scheme NOUN
el plan
□ a road-widening scheme un plan de ensanchamiento de calzadas □ a crazy scheme he dreamed up un plan descabellado que se le ocurrió

scholarship NOUN
la beca

school NOUN
1 el colegio *(for children)*
□ at school en el colegio □ to go to school ir al colegio
■ **after school** después de clase
2 la facultad *(at university)*
□ art school la facultad de bellas artes
■ **school uniform** el uniforme de colegio

schoolbook NOUN
el libro de texto

schoolboy NOUN
el colegial

schoolchildren PL NOUN
los colegiales

schoolgirl NOUN
la colegiala

science NOUN
la ciencia

science fiction NOUN
la ciencia ficción

scientific ADJECTIVE
científico (FEM científica)

scientist NOUN
el científico
la científica

scissors PL NOUN
las tijeras
□ a pair of scissors unas tijeras

to **scoff** VERB
1 mofarse
□ My friends scoffed at the idea. Mis amigos se mofaron de la idea.
2 zamparse *(informal)*
□ My brother scoffed all the sandwiches. Mi hermano se zampó todos los sandwiches.

scone NOUN
el pastel de pan

scooter NOUN
1 la Vespa® *(motorcycle)*
2 el patinete *(child's toy)*

score NOUN
▷ *see also* **score** VERB
1 la puntuación (PL las puntuaciones)
□ the highest score by an English batsman la puntuación más alta de un bateador inglés
2 el resultado
□ The score was three nil. El resultado fue de tres a cero.
■ **What's the score?** ¿Cómo van?

to **score** VERB
▷ *see also* **score** NOUN
1 marcar*
□ to score a goal marcar un gol
■ **to score a point** anotar un punto
■ **to score six out of ten** sacar una puntuación de seis sobre diez
2 llevar el tanteo
□ Who's going to score? ¿Quién va a llevar el tanteo?

Scorpio NOUN
el Escorpio *(sign)*
■ **I'm Scorpio.** Soy escorpio.

Scot NOUN
el escocés
la escocesa *(person)*

Scotch tape® NOUN (US)
el celo

Scotland NOUN
Escocia *fem*

Scots ADJECTIVE
escocés (FEM escocesa, PL escoceses)
□ a Scots accent un acento escocés

Scotsman NOUN
el escocés (PL los escoceses)

Scotswoman NOUN
la escocesa

Scottish ADJECTIVE
escocés (FEM escocesa, PL escoceses)

□ a Scottish accent un acento escocés

scout NOUN
el boy scout
la girl scout

scrambled eggs PL NOUN
los huevos revueltos

scrap NOUN
▷ *see also* **scrap** VERB
1 el trocito
□ a scrap of paper un trocito de papel
2 la pelea
□ There was a scrap outside the pub. Hubo una pelea a la salida del pub.
■ **scrap iron** la chatarra

to **scrap** VERB
▷ *see also* **scrap** NOUN
desechar
□ In the end the plan was scrapped. Al final se desechó el plan.

scrapbook NOUN
el álbum de recortes (PL los álbumes de recortes)

to **scratch** VERB
▷ *see also* **scratch** NOUN
1 rascarse* *(when itchy)*
□ Stop scratching! ¡Deja de rascarte!
2 arañar *(cut)*
□ He scratched his arm on the bushes. Se arañó el brazo con las zarzas.
3 rayar *(scrape)*
□ You'll scratch the worktop with that knife. Vas a rayar la encimera con ese cuchillo.

scratch NOUN
▷ *see also* **scratch** VERB
el arañazo *(on skin, floor)*
■ **to start from scratch** partir de cero
■ **a scratch card** una tarjeta de 'rasque y gane'

scream NOUN
▷ *see also* **scream** VERB
el grito

to **scream** VERB
▷ *see also* **scream** NOUN
gritar

screen NOUN
la pantalla *(television, cinema, computer)*

screw NOUN
el tornillo

screwdriver NOUN
el destornillador

to **scribble** VERB
garabatear

to **scrub** VERB
fregar*

sculpture NOUN
la escultura

sea NOUN
el mar
□ by sea por mar □ a house by the sea una casa junto al mar

LANGUAGE TIP The word **mar** is masculine in most cases, but in some set expressions it is feminine.

□ The fishermen put out to sea. Los pescadores se hicieron a la mar.

seafood NOUN
el marisco
□ I don't like seafood. No me gusta el marisco.
■ **a seafood restaurant** una marisquería

seagull NOUN
la gaviota

seal NOUN
▷ *see also* **seal** VERB
1 la foca *(animal)*
2 el sello *(on letter)*

to **seal** VERB
▷ *see also* **seal** NOUN
sellar

seaman NOUN
el marinero

to **search** VERB
▷ *see also* **search** NOUN
1 buscar*
□ They're searching for the missing climbers. Están buscando a los alpinistas desaparecidos.
2 registrar
□ The police searched him for drugs. La policía lo registró en busca de drogas.
■ **They searched the woods for the little girl.** Rastrearon el bosque en busca de la niña.

search NOUN
▷ *see also* **search** VERB
1 la búsqueda
□ The search was abandoned. Se abandonó la búsqueda.
■ **to go in search of** ir en busca de
2 el registro
□ a search of the building un registro del edificio

search engine NOUN
el buscador

search party NOUN
el equipo de búsqueda

seashore NOUN
la orilla del mar
□ on the seashore a la orilla del mar

seasick ADJECTIVE
■ **to be seasick** marearse en barco

seaside NOUN
la playa
■ **a seaside resort** un lugar de veraneo en la playa

season NOUN
la estación (PL las estaciones)

□ What's your favourite season? ¿Cuál es tu estación preferida?
■ **out of season** fuera de temporada
■ **during the holiday season** en la temporada de vacaciones
■ **a season ticket** un abono

seat NOUN
1 el asiento
□ I was sitting in the back seat. Yo iba sentada en el asiento trasero.
■ **Are there any seats left?** ¿Quedan localidades?
2 el escaño
□ to win a seat at the election conseguir un escaño en las elecciones

seat belt NOUN
el cinturón de seguridad (PL los cinturones de seguridad)

seaweed NOUN
el alga marina *fem*

LANGUAGE TIP Although it's a feminine noun, remember that you use **el** and **un** with **alga**.

second ADJECTIVE, ADVERB
▷ *see also* **second** NOUN
segundo (FEM segunda)
□ the second time la segunda vez
■ **to come second** llegar en segundo lugar
■ **the second of March** el dos de marzo

second NOUN
▷ *see also* **second** ADJECTIVE, ADVERB
el segundo
□ It'll only take a second. Es un segundo nada más.

secondary school NOUN
1 el instituto *(state)*
2 el colegio *(private)*

second-class ADJECTIVE, ADVERB
de segunda clase *(ticket, compartment)*
■ **to travel second class** viajar en segunda
■ **second-class postage**

DID YOU KNOW...?
In Spain there is no first-class or second-class postage. If you want your mail to arive fast, you must have it sent express – **urgente** – from a post office.

secondhand ADJECTIVE
de segunda mano

secondly ADVERB
en segundo lugar

secret ADJECTIVE
▷ *see also* **secret** NOUN
secreto (FEM secreta)
□ a secret mission una misión secreta

secret NOUN
▷ *see also* **secret** ADJECTIVE
el secreto
□ Can you keep a secret? ¿Me guardas un secreto?
■ **in secret** en secreto

secretary NOUN
el secretario
la secretaria

secretly ADVERB
en secreto

section NOUN
la sección (PL las secciones)

security NOUN
la seguridad
□ They are trying to improve airport security. Intentan mejorar las medidas de seguridad en el aeropuerto. □ They have no job security. No tienen seguridad en el empleo.
■ **security guard** el/la guarda jurado

sedan NOUN (US)
el turismo

to **see** VERB
ver*
□ I can't see. No veo nada. □ I saw him yesterday. Lo vi ayer.
■ **You need to see a doctor.** Tienes que ir a ver a un médico.
■ **See you!** ¡Hasta luego!
■ **See you soon!** ¡Hasta pronto!

seed NOUN
la semilla
□ poppy seeds semillas de amapola

to **seem** VERB
parecer*
□ She seems tired. Parece cansada. □ That seems like a good idea. Me parece una buena idea.
■ **The shop seemed to be closed.** Parecía que la tienda estaba cerrada.
■ **It seems that...** Parece que... □ It seems you have no alternative. Parece que no tienes otra opción.
■ **It seems she's getting married.** Por lo visto se casa.
■ **There seems to be a problem.** Parece que hay un problema.

seen VERB ▷ *see* **see**

seesaw NOUN
el balancín (PL los balancines)

see-through ADJECTIVE
transparente (FEM transparente)

seldom ADVERB
rara vez

to **select** VERB
seleccionar

selection NOUN
1 la selección (PL las selecciones)
□ a selection test una prueba de selección
2 el surtido
□ the widest selection on the market el más

amplio surtido del mercado

self-assured ADJECTIVE
seguro de sí mismo (FEM segura de sí misma)

self-catering ADJECTIVE
■ **self-catering apartment** el apartamento

self-centred (US **self-centered**) ADJECTIVE
egocéntrico (FEM egocéntrica)

self-confidence NOUN
la confianza en uno mismo
□ I lost all my self-confidence. Perdí toda la confianza en mí mismo.

self-conscious ADJECTIVE
1 cohibido (FEM cohibida)
□ She was really self-conscious at first. Al principio estaba muy cohibida.
2 acomplejado (FEM acomplejada)
□ She was self-conscious about her height. Estaba acomplejada por su estatura.

self-contained ADJECTIVE
independiente (FEM independiente)

self-control NOUN
el autocontrol

self-defence (US **self-defense**) NOUN
la defensa personal
□ self-defence classes clases de defensa personal
■ **She killed him in self-defence.** Lo mató en defensa propia.

self-discipline NOUN
la autodisciplina

self-employed ADJECTIVE
autónomo (FEM autónoma)
■ **to be self-employed** ser autónomo
■ **the self-employed** los trabajadores autónomos

selfish ADJECTIVE
egoísta (FEM egoísta)

self-respect NOUN
el amor propio

self-service ADJECTIVE
de autoservicio

to **sell** VERB
vender
□ He sold it to me. Me lo vendió.

to **sell off** VERB
liquidar

to **sell out** VERB
■ **The tickets sold out in three hours.** Las entradas se agotaron en tres horas.

sell-by date NOUN
la fecha de caducidad

selling price NOUN
el precio de venta

Sellotape® NOUN
el celo

semi NOUN
la casa adosada

semicircle NOUN
el semicírculo

semicolon NOUN
el punto y coma (PL los punto y coma)

semi-detached house NOUN
la casa adosada
□ We live in a semi-detached house. Vivimos en una casa adosada.
■ **a street of semi-detached houses** una calle de casas pareadas

semi-final NOUN
la semifinal

semi-skimmed milk NOUN
la leche semidesnatada

to **send** VERB
mandar
□ She sent me a birthday card. Me mandó una tarjeta de cumpleaños. □ He was sent to London. Lo mandaron a Londres.

to **send back** VERB
devolver*

to **send off** VERB
1 enviar* por correo
□ We sent off your order yesterday. Le enviamos el pedido por correo ayer.
2 expulsar
□ He was sent off. Lo expulsaron.

to **send out** VERB
enviar*

sender NOUN
el/la remitente

senior ADJECTIVE, NOUN
alto (FEM alta)
□ senior officials in the British government altos cargos del gobierno británico □ senior management los altos directivos
■ **She's five years my senior.** Es cinco años mayor que yo.
■ **senior school** el instituto de enseñanza secundaria
■ **senior pupils** los alumnos más mayores

senior citizen NOUN
la persona de la tercera edad

sensational ADJECTIVE
sensacional (FEM sensacional)

sense NOUN
el sentido
□ the five senses los cinco sentidos □ Use your common sense! ¡Usa el sentido común!
■ **It makes sense.** Tiene sentido.
■ **It doesn't make sense.** No tiene sentido.
■ **a keen sense of smell** un olfato finísimo
■ **sense of humour** sentido del humor

senseless ADJECTIVE
1 sin sentido
□ senseless violence violencia sin sentido
□ It is senseless to protest. No tiene sentido protestar.

English-Spanish

S

2 inconsciente (FEM inconsciente)
□ He was lying senseless on the floor. Yacía inconsciente en el suelo.

sensible ADJECTIVE
sensato (FEM sensata)
□ Be sensible! ¡Sé sensato! □ It would be sensible to check first. Lo más sensato sería comprobarlo antes.

LANGUAGE TIP Be careful not to translate **sensible** by the Spanish word **sensible**.

sensitive ADJECTIVE
sensible (FEM sensible)

sensuous ADJECTIVE
sensual (FEM sensual)

sent VERB ▷ *see* **send**

sentence NOUN
▷ *see also* **sentence** VERB
1 la oración (PL las oraciones)
□ What does this sentence mean? ¿Qué significa esta oración?
2 la sentencia
□ to pass sentence dictar sentencia
3 la condena
□ a sentence of 10 years una condena de 10 años
■ **the death sentence** la pena de muerte
■ **He got a life sentence.** Fue condenado a cadena perpetua.

to **sentence** VERB
▷ *see also* **sentence** NOUN
■ **to sentence somebody to life imprisonment** condenar a alguien a cadena perpetua
■ **to sentence somebody to death** condenar a muerte a alguien

sentimental ADJECTIVE
sentimental (FEM sentimental)

separate ADJECTIVE
▷ *see also* **separate** VERB
distinto (FEM distinta)
□ separate changing rooms vestuarios distintos
■ **The children have separate rooms.** Los niños tienen cada uno su habitación.
■ **I wrote it on a separate sheet.** Lo escribí en una hoja aparte.
■ **on separate occasions** en diversas ocasiones

to **separate** VERB
▷ *see also* **separate** ADJECTIVE
1 separar
□ Police moved in to separate the two groups. La policía intervino para separar a los dos grupos.
2 separarse
□ Her parents separated last year. Sus padres se separaron el año pasado.

separately ADVERB
por separado

separation NOUN
la separación (PL las separaciones)

September NOUN
septiembre *masc*
□ in September en septiembre □ on 23 September el 23 de septiembre

sequel NOUN
la continuación (PL las continuaciones)

sequence NOUN
1 la serie
□ a sequence of events una serie de acontecimientos
2 el orden (PL los órdenes)
□ in sequence en orden
3 la secuencia
□ the best sequence in the film la mejor secuencia de la película

sergeant NOUN
1 el/la sargento *(army)*
2 el/la oficial de policía *(police)*

serial NOUN
1 el serial *(on TV, radio)*
2 la novela por entregas *(in magazine)*

series NOUN
la serie

serious ADJECTIVE
1 serio (FEM seria)
□ You're looking very serious. Estás muy serio.
■ **Are you serious?** ¿Lo dices en serio?
2 grave (FEM grave)
□ a serious illness una grave enfermedad

seriously ADVERB
en serio
□ No, but seriously... No, pero ya en serio...
□ to take somebody seriously tomar en serio a alguien
■ **seriously injured** gravemente herido
■ **Seriously?** ¿De verdad?

sermon NOUN
el sermón (PL los sermones)

servant NOUN
el criado
la criada

to **serve** VERB
▷ *see also* **serve** NOUN
1 servir*
□ Dinner is served. La cena está servida.
■ **It's Murray's turn to serve.** Al servicio Murray.
■ **Are you being served?** ¿Le atienden ya?
2 cumplir
□ to serve a life sentence cumplir cadena perpetua
■ **to serve time** cumplir condena
■ **It serves you right.** Te está bien empleado.

serve NOUN
▷ *see also* **serve** VERB
el servicio

server NOUN
el servidor

to **service** VERB
▷ *see also* **service** NOUN
revisar *(car, washing machine)*

service NOUN
▷ *see also* **service** VERB
1 el servicio
□ Service is included. El servicio está incluido. □ the postal service el servicio de correos
■ **a bus service** una línea de autobús
2 la revisión (PL las revisiones)
□ The car needs a service. Al coche le hace falta una revisión.
3 el oficio religioso
□ a memorial service un oficio religioso conmemorativo
■ **the armed services** las fuerzas armadas

service area NOUN
el área de servicios *fem*
LANGUAGE TIP Although it's a feminine noun, remember that you use **el** and **un** with **área**.

service charge NOUN
el servicio
□ Service charge is included. El servicio va incluido.

serviceman NOUN
el militar

service station NOUN
la estación de servicio (PL las estaciones de servicio)

serviette NOUN
la servilleta

session NOUN
la sesión (PL las sesiones)

set NOUN
▷ *see also* **set** VERB
1 el juego *(of objects, tools)*
□ a set of keys un juego de llaves
■ **The sofa and chairs are only sold as a set.** El sofá y los sillones no se venden por separado.
2 el set (PL los sets) *(in tennis)*
□ She was leading 5–1 in the first set. Iba ganando 5 a 1 en el primer set.

to **set** VERB
▷ *see also* **set** NOUN
1 poner*
□ I set the alarm for seven o'clock. Puse el despertador a las siete.
2 establecer*
□ The world record was set last year. El récord mundial se estableció el año pasado.
3 ponerse*
□ The sun was setting. Se estaba poniendo el sol.
■ **The film is set in Morocco.** La película se desarrolla en Marruecos.
■ **to set something on fire** prender fuego a algo
■ **to set sail** zarpar
■ **to set the table** poner la mesa

to **set off** VERB
salir*
□ We set off for London at nine o'clock. Salimos para Londres a las nueve.

to **set out** VERB
salir*
□ We set out for London at nine o'clock. Salimos para Londres a las nueve.

settee NOUN
el sofá (PL los sofás)

to **settle** VERB
1 zanjar
□ That should settle the problem. Esto debería zanjar el problema.
2 pagar*
□ I'll settle the bill tomorrow. Mañana pagaré la cuenta.

to **settle down** VERB
calmarse

to **settle in** VERB
adaptarse

seven NUMERAL
siete
□ She's seven. Tiene siete años.

seventeen NUMERAL
diecisiete
□ He's seventeen. Tiene diecisiete años.

seventeenth ADJECTIVE
decimoséptimo (FEM decimoséptima)
■ **the seventeenth floor** la planta diecisiete
■ **the seventeenth of April** el diecisiete de abril

seventh ADJECTIVE
séptimo (FEM séptima)
□ the seventh floor el séptimo piso
■ **the seventh of August** el siete de agosto

seventy NUMERAL
setenta
□ She's seventy. Tiene setenta años.

several ADJECTIVE, PRONOUN
varios (FEM variosa)
□ several schools varios colegios □ several times varias veces

to **sew** VERB
coser

to **sew up** VERB
coser

English-Spanish

S

English-Spanish

sewing NOUN
la costura
□ I like sewing. Me gusta la costura.
■ **sewing machine** la máquina de coser

sewn VERB ▷ *see* **sew**

sex NOUN
el sexo
□ the opposite sex el sexo opuesto
■ **to have sex with somebody** tener relaciones sexuales con alguien
■ **sex education** la educación sexual

sexism NOUN
el sexismo

sexist ADJECTIVE
sexista (FEM sexista)

sexual ADJECTIVE
sexual (FEM sexual)
□ sexual discrimination la discriminación sexual □ sexual harassment el acoso sexual

sexuality NOUN
la sexualidad

sexy ADJECTIVE
sexy (PL sexy)

shabby ADJECTIVE
andrajoso (FEM andrajosa) *(person, clothes)*

shade NOUN
1 la sombra
□ It was 35 degrees in the shade. Hacía 35 grados a la sombra.
2 el tono
□ a beautiful shade of blue un tono de azul muy bonito

shadow NOUN
la sombra

to **shake** VERB
1 sacudir
□ She shook the rug. Sacudió la alfombra.
■ **'Shake well before use'** 'Agítese bien antes de usarse'
2 temblar*
□ He was shaking with cold. Temblaba de frío.
■ **Donald shook his head.** Donald negó con la cabeza.
■ **to shake hands with somebody** dar la mano a alguien □ They shook hands. Se dieron la mano.

shaken ADJECTIVE
afectado (FEM afectada)
□ I was feeling a bit shaken. Estaba un poco afectado.

shaky ADJECTIVE
tembloroso (FEM temblorosa) *(hand, voice)*
■ **I was feeling a bit shaky.** Estaba un poco débil.

shall VERB
■ **Shall I shut the window?** ¿Cierro la ventana?

LANGUAGE TIP **pedir que** has to be followed by a verb in the subjunctive.

■ **Shall we ask him to come with us?** ¿Le pedimos que venga con nosotros?

shallow ADJECTIVE
poco profundo (FEM poco profunda)

shambles NOUN
el desastre
□ It's a complete shambles. Es un desastre total.

shame NOUN
la vergüenza
□ I'd die of shame! ¡Me moriría de vergüenza!
■ **What a shame!** ¡Qué pena!

LANGUAGE TIP **es una pena que** has to be followed by a verb in the subjunctive.

■ **It's a shame that...** Es una pena que...
□ It's a shame he isn't here. Es una pena que no esté aquí.

shampoo NOUN
el champú (PL los champús)
□ a bottle of shampoo un bote de champú

shandy NOUN
la clara *(de cerveza con gaseosa)*

shan't = **shall not**

shape NOUN
la forma
□ in the shape of a star en forma de estrella
■ **to be in good shape** estar en buena forma

share NOUN
▷ *see also* **share** VERB
1 la acción (PL las acciones)
□ They've got shares in many companies. Tienen acciones en muchas empresas.
2 la parte
□ He refused to pay his share of the bill. Se negó a pagar su parte de la factura.

to **share** VERB
▷ *see also* **share** NOUN
compartir
□ to share a room with somebody compartir habitación con alguien

to **share out** VERB
repartir
□ They shared the sweets out among the children. Repartieron los caramelos entre los niños.

shark NOUN
el tiburón (PL los tiburones)

sharp ADJECTIVE, ADVERB
1 afilado (FEM afilada)
□ Be careful, that knife's sharp! ¡Cuidado con ese cuchillo que está afilado!
2 puntiagudo (FEM puntiaguda) *(point, spike)*
3 listo (FEM lista) *(intelligent)*

S

□ She's very sharp. Es muy lista.
■ **at two o'clock sharp** a las dos en punto

to **shave** VERB
afeitarse
□ He took a bath and shaved. Se dio un baño y se afeitó.
■ **to shave one's legs** depilarse las piernas

shaver NOUN
■ **electric shaver** la maquinilla de afeitar eléctrica

shaving cream NOUN
la crema de afeitar

shaving foam NOUN
la espuma de afeitar

she PRONOUN
ella
LANGUAGE TIP 'she' generally isn't translated unless it's emphatic.
□ She's very nice. Es muy maja.
LANGUAGE TIP Use **ella** for emphasis.
□ She did it but he didn't. Ella lo hizo, pero él no.

shed NOUN
el cobertizo

she'd = **she had; she would**

sheep NOUN
la oveja

sheepdog NOUN
el perro pastor (PL los perros pastores)

sheer ADJECTIVE
puro (FEM pura)
□ It's sheer greed. Es pura codicia.

sheet NOUN
la sábana
□ to change the sheets cambiar las sábanas
■ **a sheet of paper** una hoja de papel

shelf NOUN
1 el estante *(on wall, in shop)*
2 la parrilla *(in oven)*

shell NOUN
1 la concha (el caracol *Latin America*)
2 la cáscara *(of egg, nut)*
3 el obús (PL los obuses) *(explosive)*

she'll = **she will**

shellfish NOUN
el marisco

shell suit NOUN
el chándal de nylon (PL los chándals de nylon)

shelter NOUN
el refugio
□ a bomb shelter un refugio antiaéreo
■ **to take shelter** refugiarse

shelves PL NOUN ▷ *see* **shelf**

shepherd NOUN
el pastor

sheriff NOUN
el sheriff

sherry NOUN
el jerez

she's = **she is; she has**

shield NOUN
el escudo

shift NOUN
▷ *see also* **shift** VERB
el turno
□ the night shift el turno de noche
□ His shift starts at eight o'clock. Su turno empieza a las ocho.
■ **to do shift work** trabajar por turnos

to **shift** VERB
▷ *see also* **shift** NOUN
trasladar
□ I couldn't shift the wardrobe on my own. No podía trasladar el armario yo solo.
■ **Shift yourself!** *(informal)* ¡Quita de ahí!

shifty ADJECTIVE
sospechoso (FEM sospechosa)
□ He looked shifty. Tenía una pinta sospechosa.
■ **He has shifty eyes.** Tiene una mirada furtiva.

shin NOUN
la espinilla

to **shine** VERB
brillar
□ The sun was shining. Brillaba el sol.

shiny ADJECTIVE
brillante (FEM brillante)

ship NOUN
el barco
□ by ship en barco
■ **a merchant ship** un buque mercante

shipbuilding NOUN
la construcción naval

shipwreck NOUN
el naufragio

shipwrecked ADJECTIVE
■ **to be shipwrecked** naufragar

shipyard NOUN
el astillero

shirt NOUN
la camisa

shit EXCLAMATION
¡Mierda! *(rude)*

to **shiver** VERB
tiritar
□ to shiver with cold tiritar de frío

shock NOUN
▷ *see also* **shock** VERB
1 la conmoción (PL las conmociones)
□ The news came as a shock. La noticia causó conmoción.
2 el calambre
□ I got a shock when I touched the switch. Me dio calambre al tocar el interruptor.

to shock VERB
▷ *see also* **shock** NOUN
1 horrorizar* *(upset)*
□ They were shocked by the tragedy. Quedaron horrorizados por la tragedia.
2 escandalizar* *(scandalize)*
□ Nothing shocks me any more. Ya nada me escandaliza.

shocking ADJECTIVE
escandaloso (FEM escandalosa)
□ It's shocking! ¡Es escandaloso!

shoe NOUN
el zapato
□ a pair of shoes un par de zapatos

shoelace NOUN
el cordón (PL los cordones)

shoe polish NOUN
el betún

shoe shop NOUN
la zapatería

shone VERB ▷ *see* **shine**

shook VERB ▷ *see* **shake**

to shoot VERB
1 disparar *(fire a shot)*
□ Don't shoot! ¡No disparen!
■ **to shoot at somebody** disparar contra alguien
■ **He shot himself with a revolver.** Se pegó un tiro con un revólver.
■ **He was shot dead by the police.** Murió de un disparo de la policía.
2 fusilar *(execute)*
□ He was shot at dawn. Lo fusilaron al amanecer.
3 rodar*
□ The film was shot in Prague. La película se rodó en Praga.
4 chutar *(in football)*

shooting NOUN
1 los disparos
□ They heard shooting. Oyeron disparos.
■ **a shooting** un tiroteo
2 la caza
□ to go shooting ir de caza

shop NOUN
la tienda
□ a sports shop una tienda de deportes

shop assistant NOUN
el dependiente
la dependienta

shopkeeper NOUN
el/la comerciante *(tendero)*

shoplifting NOUN
el hurto en las tiendas

shopping NOUN
la compra
□ Can you get the shopping from the car? ¿Puedes sacar la compra del coche?
■ **to go shopping** **1** *(for food)* ir a hacer la compra **2** *(for pleasure)* ir de compras
■ **I love shopping.** Me encanta ir de compras.
■ **shopping bag** la bolsa de la compra
■ **shopping centre** el centro comercial

shop window NOUN
el escaparate

shore NOUN
la orilla
□ on the shores of the lake a orillas del lago
■ **on shore** en tierra

short ADJECTIVE
1 corto (FEM corta)
□ a short skirt una falda corta □ short hair pelo corto □ a short walk un paseo corto
□ It was a great holiday, but too short. Fueron unas vacaciones estupendas, pero demasiado cortas.
■ **a short break** un pequeño descanso
■ **a short time ago** hace poco
2 bajo (FEM baja)
□ She's quite short. Es bastante baja.
■ **to be short of something** andar escaso de algo
■ **at short notice** con poco tiempo de antelación
■ **In short, the answer is no.** En una palabra, la respuesta es no.

shortage NOUN
la escasez
□ a water shortage escasez de agua

short cut NOUN
el atajo

shorthand NOUN
la taquigrafía

shortly ADVERB
dentro de poco
□ I'll be there shortly. Estaré allí dentro de poco.
■ **She arrived shortly after midnight.** Llegó poco después de la medianoche.

shorts PL NOUN
los pantalones cortos
□ a pair of shorts unos pantalones cortos

short-sighted ADJECTIVE
miope (FEM miope)

short story NOUN
el cuento

shot VERB ▷ *see* **shoot**

shot NOUN
1 el tiro
□ to fire a shot disparar un tiro □ a shot at goal un tiro a puerta
2 la foto
LANGUAGE TIP Although **foto** ends in **-a**, it is actually a feminine noun.
□ a shot of Edinburgh castle una foto del castillo de Edimburgo

3 la inyección (PL las inyecciones) *(vaccination)*

shotgun NOUN
la escopeta

should VERB
LANGUAGE TIP When 'should' means 'ought to', use the conditional of **deber**.
deber
□ You should take more exercise. Deberías hacer más ejercicio. □ He should be there by now. Ya debería estar allí. □ That shouldn't be too hard. Eso no debería ser muy difícil.
LANGUAGE TIP **tener* que** is also a very common way to translate 'should'.
□ I should have told you before. Tendría que habértelo dicho antes.
LANGUAGE TIP When 'should' means 'would', use the conditional.
■ **I should go if I were you.** Yo que tú, iría.
■ **I should be so lucky!** ¡Ojalá!

shoulder NOUN
el hombro
□ I looked over my shoulder. Miré por encima del hombro.
■ **shoulder bag** el bolso de bandolera

shouldn't = **should not**

to **shout** VERB
▷ *see also* **shout** NOUN
gritar
□ Don't shout! ¡No grites!

shout NOUN
▷ *see also* **shout** VERB
el grito

shovel NOUN
la pala

show NOUN
▷ *see also* **show** VERB
1 el espectáculo
□ to stage a show montar un espectáculo
2 el programa
LANGUAGE TIP Although **programa** ends in **-a**, it is actually a masculine noun.
□ a radio show un programa de radio
■ **fashion show** el pase de modelos
■ **motor show** el salón del automóvil

to **show** VERB
▷ *see also* **show** NOUN
1 enseñar
■ **to show somebody something** enseñar algo a alguien □ Have I shown you my hat? ¿Te he enseñado ya mi sombrero?
2 demostrar*
□ She showed great courage. Demostró gran valentía.
■ **It shows.** Se nota. □ I've never been riding before. — It shows. Nunca había montado a caballo antes. — Se nota.

to **show off** VERB
presumir

to **show up** VERB
presentarse
□ He showed up late as usual. Se presentó tarde, como de costumbre.

shower NOUN
1 la ducha
■ **to have a shower** ducharse
2 el chubasco
□ scattered showers chubascos dispersos

showerproof ADJECTIVE
impermeable (FEM impermeable)

showing NOUN
el pase *(of a film)*
□ a private showing un pase privado

shown VERB ▷ *see* **show**

show-off NOUN
el fantasmón (PL los fantasmones)
la fantasmona

shrank VERB ▷ *see* **shrink**

to **shriek** VERB
chillar

shrimps PL NOUN
los camarones

to **shrink** VERB
encogerse* *(clothes, fabric)*

Shrove Tuesday NOUN
el martes de carnaval

to **shrug** VERB
■ **to shrug one's shoulders** encogerse de hombros

shrunk VERB ▷ *see* **shrink**

to **shudder** VERB
estremecerse*

to **shuffle** VERB
■ **to shuffle the cards** barajar las cartas

to **shut** VERB
cerrar*
□ What time do you shut? ¿A qué hora cierran? □ What time do the shops shut? ¿A qué hora cierran las tiendas?

to **shut down** VERB
cerrar*
□ The cinema shut down last year. El cine cerró el año pasado.

to **shut up** VERB
callarse
□ Shut up! ¡Cállate!

shutters PL NOUN
las contraventanas

shuttle NOUN
■ **I'll get the shuttle.** Tomaré el puente aéreo.

shuttlecock NOUN
el volante *(de bádminton)*

English-Spanish

shy ADJECTIVE
tímido (FEM tímida)

Sicily NOUN
Sicilia *fem*

sick ADJECTIVE
1 enfermo (FEM enferma)
□ She looks after her sick mother. Cuida de su madre enferma.
2 de mal gusto
□ That's really sick! ¡Eso es de muy mal gusto!
■ **to be sick** devolver (arrojar *Latin America*)
□ I was sick twice last night. Anoche devolví dos veces.
■ **I feel sick.** Tengo ganas de devolver.
■ **to be sick of something** estar harto de algo □ I'm sick of your jokes. Estoy harto de tus bromas.

sickening ADJECTIVE
repugnante (FEM repugnante)

sick leave NOUN
la baja por enfermedad

sickness NOUN
la enfermedad

sick note NOUN
1 el justificante de ausencia *(from parents)*
2 la baja médica *(from doctor)*

sick pay NOUN
la prestación por enfermedad

side NOUN
1 el lado *(of object, building, car)*
□ He was driving on the wrong side of the road. Iba por el lado contrario de la carretera.
■ **a house on the side of a mountain** una casa en la ladera de una montaña
■ **We sat side by side.** Nos sentamos uno al lado del otro.
2 el borde *(of pool, bed, road)*
□ The car was abandoned at the side of the road. El coche estaba abandonado al borde de la carretera.
■ **by the side of the lake** a la orilla del lago
3 la cara *(of paper, tape)*
□ Play side A. Pon la cara A.
4 el equipo *(team)*
□ He's on my side. Está en mi equipo.
■ **I'm on your side.** Yo estoy de tu parte.
■ **to take somebody's side** ponerse de parte de alguien
■ **to take sides** tomar partido
■ **the side entrance** la entrada lateral

sideboard NOUN
el aparador

side-effect NOUN
el efecto secundario

side street NOUN
la calle lateral

sidewalk NOUN (US)
la acera

sideways ADVERB
■ **to look sideways** mirar de reojo
■ **to move sideways** moverse de lado
■ **sideways on** de perfil

sieve NOUN
1 el colador *(for liquids)*
2 la criba *(for solids)*

sigh NOUN
▷ *see also* **sigh** VERB
el suspiro

to **sigh** VERB
▷ *see also* **sigh** NOUN
suspirar

sight NOUN
1 la vista
□ I'm losing my sight. Estoy perdiendo la vista.
■ **at first sight** a primera vista
■ **to know somebody by sight** conocer a alguien de vista
■ **in sight** a la vista
2 el espectáculo
□ It was an amazing sight. Era un espectáculo asombroso.
■ **Keep out of sight!** ¡Que no te vean!
■ **the sights** las atracciones turísticas
■ **to see the sights of London** hacer turismo por Londres

sightseeing NOUN
■ **to go sightseeing** hacer turismo

sign NOUN
▷ *see also* **sign** VERB
1 el letrero
□ There was a big sign saying 'private'. Había un gran letrero que ponía 'privado'.
2 la señal
□ She made a sign to the waiter. Le hizo una señal al camarero. □ There's no sign of improvement. No hay señales de mejoría.
■ **road sign** la señal de tráfico
■ **What sign are you?** ¿De qué signo eres?

to **sign** VERB
▷ *see also* **sign** NOUN
firmar

to **sign on** VERB
apuntarse al paro

signal NOUN
▷ *see also* **signal** VERB
la señal

to **signal** VERB
▷ *see also* **signal** NOUN
■ **to signal to somebody** hacer señas a alguien

signalman NOUN
el guardavía

S

LANGUAGE TIP Although **guardavía** ends in **-a**, it is actually a masculine noun.

signature NOUN
la firma

significance NOUN
la importancia

significant ADJECTIVE
significativo (FEM significativa)

sign language NOUN
el lenguaje por señas

signpost NOUN
la señal

silence NOUN
el silencio

silencer NOUN
el silenciador

silent ADJECTIVE
1 silencioso (FEM silenciosa) *(place)*
□ a silent room una habitación silenciosa
2 callado (FEM callada) *(person)*

silicon chip NOUN
el chip de silicio (PL los chips de silicio)

silk NOUN
la seda
□ a silk scarf un pañuelo de seda

silky ADJECTIVE
sedoso (FEM sedosa)

silly ADJECTIVE
tonto (FEM tonta)

silver NOUN
la plata
□ a silver medal una medalla de plata

similar ADJECTIVE
parecido (FEM parecida)
■ **similar to** parecido a

simple ADJECTIVE
1 sencillo (FEM sencilla)
□ It's very simple. Es muy sencillo.
2 simple (FEM simple)
□ He's a bit simple. Es un poco simple.

simply ADVERB
sencillamente

simultaneous ADJECTIVE
simultáneo (FEM simultánea)

sin NOUN
▷ *see also* **sin** VERB
el pecado

to **sin** VERB
▷ *see also* **sin** NOUN
pecar*

since PREPOSITION, ADVERB, CONJUNCTION
1 desde
□ since Christmas desde Navidad □ since then desde entonces
■ **I haven't seen him since.** Desde entonces no lo he vuelto a ver.
2 desde que
□ I haven't seen her since she left. No la he visto desde que se fue.
■ **It's a few years since I've seen them.** Hace varios años que no los veo.
3 como
□ Since you're tired, let's stay at home. Como estás cansado podemos quedarnos en casa.

sincere ADJECTIVE
sincero (FEM sincera)

sincerely ADVERB
■ **Yours sincerely...** Atentamente...

to **sing** VERB
cantar

singer NOUN
el/la cantante

singing NOUN
el canto
□ singing lessons clases de canto
■ **flamenco singing** el cante flamenco

single ADJECTIVE
▷ *see also* **single** NOUN
1 individual (FEM individual)
□ a single room una habitación individual
□ a single bed una cama individual
2 soltero (FEM soltera)
□ a single mother una madre soltera
3 solo (FEM sola)
□ She hadn't said a single word. No había dicho una sola palabra.
■ **not a single thing** nada de nada

single NOUN
▷ *see also* **single** ADJECTIVE
1 el billete de ida
2 el single
□ a CD single un single en CD

single parent NOUN
■ **She's a single parent.** Es madre soltera.
■ **a single parent family** una familia monoparental

singles PL NOUN
los individuales *(in tennis)*
□ the women's singles los individuales femeninos

singular NOUN
singular
□ in the singular en singular

sinister ADJECTIVE
siniestro (FEM siniestra)

sink NOUN
▷ *see also* **sink** VERB
1 el fregadero *(in the kitchen)*
2 el lavabo *(in the bathroom)*

to **sink** VERB
▷ *see also* **sink** NOUN
1 hundir
□ We sank the enemy's ship. Hundimos el buque enemigo.

English–Spanish

S

2 hundirse
□ The boat was sinking fast. El barco se hundía rápidamente.

sir NOUN
el señor
□ Yes sir. Sí, señor.

siren NOUN
la sirena

sister NOUN
1 la hermana
□ my little sister mi hermana pequeña
2 la enfermera jefe *(nurse)*

sister-in-law NOUN
la cuñada

to **sit** VERB
sentarse*
□ He sat in front of the TV. Se sentó frente a la tele.
■ **to be sitting** estar sentado □ He was sitting in front of the TV. Estaba sentado frente a la tele.
■ **to sit an exam** presentarse a un examen

to **sit down** VERB
sentarse*
□ He sat down at his desk. Se sentó en su escritorio.

sitcom NOUN
la telecomedia

site NOUN
1 el lugar
□ the site of the accident el lugar del accidente
2 el camping (PL los campings) *(campsite)*

sitting room NOUN
la sala de estar (PL las salas de estar)

situated ADJECTIVE
■ **to be situated...** estar situado... (estar ubicado... *Latin America*)

situation NOUN
la situación (PL las situaciones)

six NUMERAL
seis
□ He's six. Tiene seis años.

sixteen NUMERAL
dieciséis
□ He's sixteen. Tiene dieciséis años.

sixteenth ADJECTIVE
decimosexto (FEM decimosexta)
■ **the sixteenth floor** la planta dieciséis
■ **the sixteenth of August** el dieciséis de agosto

sixth ADJECTIVE
sexto (FEM sexta)
□ the sixth floor el sexto piso
■ **the sixth of August** el seis de agosto

sixty NUMERAL
sesenta
□ She's sixty. Tiene sesenta años.

size NOUN
1 el tamaño *(of object, place)*
□ plates of various sizes platos de varios tamaños

DID YOU KNOW...?
Spain uses the European system for clothing and shoe sizes.

2 la talla *(of clothing)*
□ What size do you take? ¿Qué talla usas?
3 el número *(of shoes)*
■ **I take size five.** Calzo un treinta y ocho.

to **skate** VERB
patinar

skateboard NOUN
el monopatín (PL los monopatines)

skateboarding NOUN
■ **to go skateboarding** montar en monopatín

skates PL NOUN
los patines

skating NOUN
el patinaje
□ to go skating ir a patinar
■ **skating rink** la pista de patinaje

skeleton NOUN
el esqueleto

sketch NOUN
▹ *see also* **sketch** VERB
el boceto

to **sketch** VERB
▹ *see also* **sketch** NOUN
esbozar*

to **ski** VERB
▹ *see also* **ski** NOUN
esquiar*

ski NOUN
▹ *see also* **ski** VERB
el esquí
□ a pair of skis unos esquís
■ **ski boots** las botas de esquí
■ **ski lift** el telesilla

LANGUAGE TIP Although **telesilla** ends in **-a**, it is actually a masculine noun.

■ **ski pants** los pantalones de esquí
■ **ski pole** el bastón de esquí (PL los bastones de esquí)
■ **ski resort** la estación de esquí
■ **ski slope** la pista de esquí
■ **ski suit** el traje de esquí

to **skid** VERB
patinar

skier NOUN
el esquiador
la esquiadora

skiing NOUN
el esquí
□ I love skiing. Me encanta el esquí.
■ **to go skiing** ir a esquiar
■ **to go on a skiing holiday** irse de vacaciones a esquiar

skilful ADJECTIVE
hábil (FEM hábil)

skill NOUN
la habilidad
□ It requires a lot of skill. Requiere mucha habilidad.

skilled ADJECTIVE
■ **a skilled worker** un trabajador cualificado

skimmed milk NOUN
la leche desnatada

skimpy ADJECTIVE
1 mínimo (FEM mínima) *(clothes)*
2 escaso (FEM escasa) *(meal)*

skin NOUN
la piel
■ **skin cancer** el cáncer de piel

skinhead NOUN
el/la cabeza rapada (PL los/las cabezas rapadas)

skinny ADJECTIVE
flaco (FEM flaca)

skin-tight ADJECTIVE
muy ajustado (FEM muy ajustada)

skip NOUN
▷ *see also* **skip** VERB
el contenedor de basuras

to **skip** VERB
▷ *see also* **skip** NOUN
saltarse
□ You should never skip breakfast. No debes saltarte nunca el desayuno.
■ **to skip school** hacer novillos

skirt NOUN
la falda

skittles PL NOUN
los bolos

to **skive** VERB
escaquearse *(informal)*
■ **to skive off school** hacer novillos

skull NOUN
1 la calavera *(of corpse)*
2 el cráneo *(in anatomy)*

sky NOUN
el cielo

skyscraper NOUN
el rascacielos (PL los rascacielos)

slack ADJECTIVE
1 flojo (FEM floja) *(rope)*
2 descuidado (FEM descuidada) *(person)*

to **slag off** VERB
poner* verde a *(informal)*

to **slam** VERB
cerrar* de un portazo
□ She slammed the door. Cerró la puerta de un portazo.
■ **The door slammed.** La puerta se cerró de un portazo.

slang NOUN
el argot

slap NOUN
▷ *see also* **slap** VERB
la bofetada

to **slap** VERB
▷ *see also* **slap** NOUN
dar* una bofetada a

slate NOUN
la teja de pizarra

sledge NOUN
el trineo

sledging NOUN
■ **to go sledging** ir en trineo

sleep NOUN
▷ *see also* **sleep** VERB
el sueño
□ lack of sleep falta de sueño
■ **I need some sleep.** Necesito dormir.
■ **to go to sleep** dormirse

to **sleep** VERB
▷ *see also* **sleep** NOUN
dormir*
□ I couldn't sleep last night. Anoche no podía dormir.

to **sleep around** VERB
irse* a la cama con cualquiera

to **sleep in** VERB
dormir* hasta tarde

to **sleep together** VERB
acostarse* juntos

sleeping bag NOUN
el saco de dormir

sleeping car NOUN
el coche cama (PL los coches cama)

sleeping pill NOUN
el somnífero

sleepy ADJECTIVE
■ **to feel sleepy** tener sueño
■ **a sleepy little village** un pueblecito tranquilo

sleet NOUN
▷ *see also* **sleet** VERB
la aguanieve

to **sleet** VERB
▷ *see also* **sleet** NOUN
■ **It's sleeting.** Está cayendo aguanieve.

sleeve NOUN
la manga *(of shirt, coat)*

sleigh NOUN
el trineo

slept VERB ▷ *see* **sleep**

slice NOUN
▷ *see also* **slice** VERB
1 la rebanada *(of bread)*
2 el trozo *(of cake)*
3 la rodaja *(of lemon, pineapple)*
4 la loncha *(of ham, cheese)*

to **slice** VERB
▹ *see also* **slice** NOUN
cortar

slick ADJECTIVE
impecable (FEM impecable)
□ a slick performance una actuación impecable

slide NOUN
▹ *see also* **slide** VERB
1 el tobogán (PL los toboganes) *(in playground)*
2 la diapositiva *(photo)*
3 el pasador *(hair slide)*

to **slide** VERB
▹ *see also* **slide** NOUN
deslizarse*
□ Tears were sliding down his cheeks. Las lágrimas se deslizaban por sus mejillas.
■ **She slid the door open.** Corrió la puerta.

slight ADJECTIVE
ligero (FEM ligera)
□ a slight improvement una ligera mejoría
■ **a slight problem** un pequeño problema

slightly ADVERB
ligeramente
□ They are slightly more expensive. Son ligeramente más caros.

slim ADJECTIVE
▹ *see also* **slim** VERB
delgado (FEM delgada)

to **slim** VERB
▹ *see also* **slim** ADJECTIVE
adelgazar*
□ I'm trying to slim. Estoy intentando adelgazar.
■ **I'm slimming.** Estoy a régimen.

sling NOUN
el cabestrillo
□ She had her arm in a sling. Llevaba el brazo en cabestrillo.

slip NOUN
▹ *see also* **slip** VERB
1 el desliz (PL los deslices) *(mistake)*
2 la combinación (PL las combinaciones) *(underskirt)*
■ **a slip of paper** un papelito
■ **a slip of the tongue** un lapsus

to **slip** VERB
▹ *see also* **slip** NOUN
resbalar
□ He slipped on the ice. Resbaló en el hielo.

to **slip up** VERB
equivocarse*

slipper NOUN
la zapatilla

slippery ADJECTIVE
resbaladizo (FEM resbaladiza)

slip-up NOUN
el desliz (PL los deslices)

slope NOUN
1 la cuesta *(surface)*
□ The street was on a slope. La calle era en cuesta.
2 la pendiente *(angle)*
□ a slope of 10 degrees una pendiente del 10 por ciento

sloppy ADJECTIVE
descuidado (FEM descuidada)

slot NOUN
la ranura

slot machine NOUN
1 la máquina tragaperras (PL las máquinas tragaperras) *(for gambling)*
2 la máquina expendedora *(vending machine)*

slow ADJECTIVE, ADVERB
lento (FEM lenta)
□ He's a bit slow. Es un poco lento. □ to go slow ir lento
■ **Drive slower!** ¡Conduce más despacio!
■ **My watch is slow.** Mi reloj se atrasa.

to **slow down** VERB
reducir* la velocidad
□ The car slowed down. El coche redujo la velocidad.

slowly ADVERB
lentamente

slug NOUN
la babosa

slum NOUN
el barrio bajo

slush NOUN
la nieve medio derretida

sly ADJECTIVE
astuto (FEM astuta)
□ She's very sly. Es muy astuta.
■ **a sly smile** una sonrisa maliciosa

smack NOUN
▹ *see also* **smack** VERB
el cachete

to **smack** VERB
▹ *see also* **smack** NOUN
dar* un cachete a

small ADJECTIVE
pequeño (FEM pequeña) (chico *Latin America*)
□ two small children dos niños pequeños

WORD POWER
You can use a number of other words instead of **small** to mean 'little':
miniature en miniatura
□ a miniature doll una muñeca en miniatura
minute minúsculo
□ a minute plant una planta minúscula
tiny enano
□ a tiny garden un jardín enano
■ **small change** el dinero suelto

smart ADJECTIVE
1 elegante (FEM elegante)
□ a smart navy blue suit un elegante traje azul marino
2 listo (FEM lista)
□ He thinks he's smarter than Sarah. Se cree más listo que Sarah.
smash NOUN
▷ *see also* **smash** VERB
el accidente de coche
to **smash** VERB
▷ *see also* **smash** NOUN
1 romper*
□ They smashed windows. Rompieron ventanas.
2 romperse*
□ The glass smashed into tiny pieces. El vaso se rompió en pedazos.
smashing ADJECTIVE
estupendo (FEM estupenda)
□ That's a smashing idea. Me parece una idea estupenda.
smell NOUN
▷ *see also* **smell** VERB
el olor
□ a smell of lemon un olor a limón
■ **the sense of smell** el olfato
to **smell** VERB
▷ *see also* **smell** NOUN
oler*
□ That dog smells! ¡Cómo huele ese perro!
□ I can't smell anything. No huelo nada.
■ **I can smell gas.** Me huele a gas.
■ **to smell of something** oler a algo □ It smells of petrol. Huele a gasolina.
smelly ADJECTIVE
maloliente (FEM maloliente)
□ The pub was dirty and smelly. El pub era sucio y maloliente.
■ **He's got smelly feet.** Le huelen los pies.
smile NOUN
▷ *see also* **smile** VERB
la sonrisa
to **smile** VERB
▷ *see also* **smile** NOUN
sonreír*
smoke NOUN
▷ *see also* **smoke** VERB
el humo
to **smoke** VERB
▷ *see also* **smoke** NOUN
fumar
□ I don't smoke. No fumo.
smoker NOUN
el fumador
la fumadora
smoking NOUN
■ **to stop smoking** dejar de fumar
■ **Smoking is bad for you.** Fumar es malo para la salud.
■ **'no smoking'** 'prohibido fumar'
smooth ADJECTIVE
liso (FEM lisa)
□ a smooth surface una superficie lisa
SMS ABBREVIATION (= *short message service*)
el SMS
smudge NOUN
el borrón (PL los borrones)
smug ADJECTIVE
engreído (FEM engreída)
to **smuggle** VERB
■ **to smuggle in** meter de contrabando
■ **to smuggle out** sacar de contrabando
smuggler NOUN
el/la contrabandista
smuggling NOUN
el contrabando
smutty ADJECTIVE
■ **smutty jokes** chistes verdes
snack NOUN
■ **to have a snack** picar algo
snack bar NOUN
la cafetería
snail NOUN
el caracol
snake NOUN
la serpiente
to **snap** VERB
partirse
□ The branch snapped. La rama se partió.
■ **to snap one's fingers** chasquear los dedos
snapshot NOUN
la foto *fem*
LANGUAGE TIP Although **foto** ends in **-o**, it is actually a feminine noun.
to **snarl** VERB
gruñir*
to **snatch** VERB
arrebatar
■ **to snatch something from somebody** arrebatar algo a alguien □ He snatched the keys from my hand. Me arrebató las llaves de la mano.
■ **My bag was snatched.** Me robaron el bolso.
to **sneak** VERB
■ **to sneak in** entrar a hurtadillas
■ **to sneak out** salir a hurtadillas
■ **to sneak up on somebody** acercarse sigilosamente a alguien
to **sneeze** VERB
estornudar
to **sniff** VERB
1 sorberse la nariz
□ Stop sniffing! ¡Deja de sorberte la nariz!

English-Spanish

S

2 olfatear
□ The dog sniffed my hand. El perro me olfateó la mano.
■ **to sniff glue** esnifar pegamento

snob NOUN
el/la esnob (PL los/las esnobs)

snooker NOUN
el billar

snooze NOUN
la cabezadita *(informal)*
□ to have a snooze echar una cabezadita

to **snore** VERB
roncar*

snow NOUN
▷ *see also* **snow** VERB
la nieve

to **snow** VERB
▷ *see also* **snow** NOUN
nevar*
□ It's snowing. Está nevando.

snowball NOUN
la bola de nieve

snowflake NOUN
el copo de nieve

snowman NOUN
el muñeco de nieve
□ to build a snowman hacer un muñeco de nieve

so CONJUNCTION, ADVERB
1 así que *(therefore)*
□ The shop was closed, so I went home. La tienda estaba cerrada, así que me fui a casa. □ So, have you always lived in London? Así que, ¿siempre has vivido en Londres?
■ **So what?** ¿Y qué?
2 para que *(so that)*
LANGUAGE TIP **para que** has to be followed by a verb in the subjunctive.
□ He took her upstairs so they wouldn't be overheard. La subió al piso de arriba para que nadie los oyera.
3 tan *(very, as)*
□ He was talking so fast I couldn't understand. Hablaba tan rápido que no lo entendía. □ He's like his sister but not so clever. Es como su hermana pero no tan listo.
■ **It was so heavy!** ¡Pesaba tanto!
■ **How's your father? — Not so good.** ¿Cómo está tu padre? — No muy bien.
■ **so much** tanto □ I love you so much. Te quiero tanto. □ She's got so much energy. Tiene tanta energía.
■ **so many** tantos □ I've got so many things to do today. Tengo tantas cosas que hacer hoy.
■ **That's not so.** No es así.
4 también *(also)*
■ **so do I** y yo también □ I work a lot. — So do I. Trabajo mucho. — Y yo también.
■ **I love horses. — So do I.** Me encantan los caballos. — A mí también.
■ **so have we** y nosotros también □ I've been waiting for ages! — So have we. ¡Llevo esperando un siglo! — Y nosotros también.
■ **I think so.** Creo que sí.
■ **... or so** ... o así □ at five o'clock or so a las cinco o así □ ten or so people diez personas o así

to **soak** VERB
1 poner* en remojo
□ Soak the beans for two hours. Ponga las judías en remojo dos horas.
2 empapar
□ Water had soaked his jacket. El agua le había empapado la chaqueta.

soaked ADJECTIVE
■ **to get soaked** empaparse

soaking ADJECTIVE
empapado (FEM empapada)
□ By the time we got back we were soaking. Cuando regresamos estábamos empapados.
■ **Your shoes are soaking wet.** Tienes los zapatos calados.

soap NOUN
el jabón

soap opera NOUN
la telenovela

soap powder NOUN
el detergente en polvo

to **sob** VERB
sollozar*

sober ADJECTIVE
sobrio (FEM sobria)

to **sober up** VERB
■ **He sobered up.** Se le pasó la borrachera.

soccer NOUN
el fútbol
□ to play soccer jugar al fútbol
■ **soccer player** el/la futbolista

social ADJECTIVE
social (FEM social)
□ social problems problemas sociales
■ **I have a good social life.** Tengo mucha vida social.

socialism NOUN
el socialismo

socialist ADJECTIVE, NOUN
socialista (FEM socialista)

social security NOUN
la seguridad social
■ **to be on social security** cobrar de la seguridad social

social worker NOUN
el asistente social

la asistenta social

society NOUN
1 la sociedad
□ a multi-cultural society una sociedad pluricultural
2 la asociación (PL las asociaciones)
□ a drama society una asociación de amigos del teatro

sociology NOUN
la sociología

sock NOUN
el calcetín (PL los calcetines) (la media *Latin America*)

socket NOUN
el enchufe

soda NOUN
la soda

soda pop NOUN (US)
el refresco

sofa NOUN
el sofá (PL los sofás)

soft ADJECTIVE
1 suave (FEM suave)
□ a soft towel una toalla suave
2 blando (FEM blanda)
□ The mattress is too soft. El colchón es demasiado blando.
■ **to be soft on somebody** ser blando con alguien
■ **soft cheeses** los quesos tiernos
■ **a soft drink** un refresco
■ **soft drugs** las drogas blandas
■ **soft option** la alternativa fácil

software NOUN
el software

soggy ADJECTIVE
1 revenido (FEM revenida) *(bread, biscuits)*
2 pasado (FEM pasada) *(salad)*

soil NOUN
la tierra

solar power NOUN
la energía solar

sold VERB ▷ *see* **sell**

soldier NOUN
el soldado

solicitor NOUN
1 el abogado
la abogada *(for lawsuits)*
2 el notario
la notaria *(for wills, property)*

solid ADJECTIVE
sólido (FEM sólida)
□ a solid wall un muro sólido
■ **solid gold** oro macizo
■ **for three solid hours** durante tres horas seguidas

solo NOUN
el solo
□ a guitar solo un solo de guitarra

solution NOUN
la solución (PL las soluciones)

to solve VERB
resolver*

some ADJECTIVE, PRONOUN
LANGUAGE TIP When 'some' refers to something you can't count, it usually isn't translated.
□ Would you like some bread? ¿Quieres pan? □ Have you got some mineral water? ¿Tiene agua mineral? □ Would you like some coffee? — No thanks, I've got some. ¿Quiere café? — No gracias, ya tengo.
■ **I only want some of it.** Sólo quiero un poco.
LANGUAGE TIP When 'some' refers to something you can count, use **alguno**, which is shortened to **algún** before a masculine singular noun.
□ some day algún día □ some books algunos libros □ You have to be careful with mushrooms: some are poisonous. Cuidado con las setas: algunas son venenosas.
■ **I'm going to buy some stamps. Do you want some too?** Voy a por sellos. ¿Quieres que te traiga?
■ **some day next week** un día de la semana que viene
■ **Some people say that...** Hay gente que dice que...
■ **some of them** algunos □ I only sold some of them. Sólo vendí algunos.

somebody PRONOUN
alguien
□ I need somebody to help me. Necesito que me ayude alguien.

somehow ADVERB
de alguna manera
■ **I'll do it somehow.** De alguna manera lo haré.
■ **Somehow I don't think he believed me.** Por alguna razón me parece que no me creyó.

someone PRONOUN
alguien
□ I need someone to help me. Necesito que me ayude alguien.

something PRONOUN
algo
□ something special algo especial □ Wear something warm. Ponte algo que abrigue.
■ **It cost £100, or something like that.** Costó 100 libras, o algo así.
■ **His name is Peter or something.** Se llama Peter o algo por el estilo.

sometime ADVERB
algún día

□ You must come and see us sometime. Tienes que venir a vernos algún día.

■ **sometime last month** el mes pasado

sometimes ADVERB

a veces

□ Sometimes I drink beer. A veces bebo cerveza.

somewhere ADVERB

en algún sitio

□ I left my keys somewhere. Me he dejado las llaves en algún sitio.

■ **I'd like to go on holiday, somewhere exotic.** Me gustaría irme de vacaciones, a algún sitio exótico.

son NOUN

el hijo

song NOUN

la canción (PL las canciones)

son-in-law NOUN

el yerno

soon ADVERB

pronto

□ very soon muy pronto

■ **soon afterwards** poco después

■ **as soon as possible** cuanto antes

sooner ADVERB

antes

□ Can't you come a bit sooner? ¿No puedes venir un poco antes?

■ **sooner or later** tarde o temprano

■ **the sooner the better** cuanto antes mejor

soot NOUN

el hollín

soppy ADJECTIVE

sentimentaloide (FEM sentimentaloide)

soprano NOUN

la soprano

LANGUAGE TIP Although **soprano** ends in **-o**, it is actually a feminine noun.

sore ADJECTIVE

▷ *see also* **sore** NOUN

■ **It's sore.** Me duele.

■ **I have a sore throat.** Me duele la garganta.

■ **That's a sore point.** Ése es un tema delicado.

sore NOUN

▷ *see also* **sore** ADJECTIVE

la llaga

sorry ADJECTIVE

■ **I'm sorry.** Lo siento. □ I'm very sorry. Lo siento mucho. □ I'm sorry, I haven't got any change. Lo siento, no tengo cambio.

■ **I'm sorry I'm late.** Siento llegar tarde.

■ **Sorry!** ¡Perdón!

■ **Sorry?** ¿Cómo?

■ **I'm sorry about the noise.** Perdón por el ruido.

■ **You'll be sorry!** ¡Te arrepentirás!

■ **to feel sorry for somebody** sentir pena por alguien

sort NOUN

el tipo

□ What sort of bike have you got? ¿Qué tipo de bicicleta tienes?

■ **all sorts of...** todo tipo de...

to **sort out** VERB

1 ordenar

□ Sort out all your books. Ordena todos tus libros.

2 arreglar

□ They have sorted out their problems. Han arreglado sus problemas.

so-so ADVERB

así así

□ How are you feeling? — So-so. ¿Cómo te encuentras? — Así así.

soul NOUN

1 el alma *fem*

LANGUAGE TIP Although it's a feminine noun, remember that you use **el** and **un** with **alma**.

2 el soul

□ a soul singer una cantante de soul

sound NOUN

▷ *see also* **sound** VERB, ADJECTIVE

1 el ruido

□ Don't make a sound! ¡No hagas ruido!

□ the sound of footsteps el ruido de pasos

2 el sonido

□ at the speed of sound a la velocidad del sonido

■ **Can I turn the sound down?** ¿Puedo bajar el volumen?

to **sound** VERB

▷ *see also* **sound** NOUN, ADJECTIVE

sonar*

□ That sounds interesting. Eso suena interesante.

■ **It sounds as if she's doing well at school.** Parece que le va bien en el colegio.

■ **That sounds like a good idea.** Eso me parece buena idea.

sound ADJECTIVE, ADVERB

▷ *see also* **sound** NOUN, VERB

válido (FEM válida)

□ His reasoning is perfectly sound. Su argumentación es perfectamente válida.

■ **Julian gave me some sound advice.** Julian me dio un buen consejo.

■ **sound asleep** profundamente dormido

soundtrack NOUN

la banda sonora

soup NOUN

la sopa

sour ADJECTIVE

agrio (FEM agria)

south ADJECTIVE, ADVERB

▷ *see also* **south** NOUN

1 del sur

□ a south wind un viento del sur

■ **the south coast** la costa meridional

2 hacia el sur

□ We were travelling south. Viajábamos hacia el sur.

■ **south of** al sur de □ It's south of London. Está al sur de Londres.

south NOUN

▷ *see also* **south** ADJECTIVE

el sur

□ the South of France el sur de Francia

South Africa NOUN

Sudáfrica *fem*

South America NOUN

Sudamérica *fem*

South American ADJECTIVE

▷ *see also* **South American** NOUN

sudamericano (FEM sudamericana)

South American NOUN

▷ *see also* **South American** ADJECTIVE

el sudamericano

la sudamericana

□ South Americans los sudamericanos

southbound ADJECTIVE

■ **Southbound traffic is moving very slowly.** El tráfico que se dirige hacia el sur avanza muy despacio.

southeast NOUN

el sudeste

■ **southeast England** el sudeste de Inglaterra

southern ADJECTIVE

■ **the southern hemisphere** el hemisferio sur

■ **Southern England** el sur de Inglaterra

■ **southern cuisine** la cocina sureña

South Pole NOUN

el Polo Sur

South Wales NOUN

Gales del Sur *masc*

southwest NOUN

el sudoeste

souvenir NOUN

el recuerdo

□ souvenir shop la tienda de recuerdos

soya NOUN

la soja

soy sauce NOUN

la salsa de soja

space NOUN

el espacio

□ There isn't enough space. No hay espacio suficiente. □ in space en el espacio

■ **a parking space** un sitio para aparcar

spacecraft NOUN

la nave espacial

spade NOUN

la pala

■ **spades** *(at cards)* las picas □ the ace of spades el as de picas

LANGUAGE TIP Be careful not to translate **spade** by **espada**.

Spain NOUN

España *fem*

Spaniard NOUN

el español

la española *(person)*

spaniel NOUN

el perro de aguas

Spanish ADJECTIVE

▷ *see also* **Spanish** NOUN

español (FEM española)

Spanish NOUN

▷ *see also* **Spanish** ADJECTIVE

el español

DID YOU KNOW...?

The official name for the Spanish language in Spain and Latin America is **el castellano** and is also the term many Spanish speakers prefer to use. Despite controversies, both **español** and **castellano** are perfectly acceptable.

□ Spanish lessons las clases de español

■ **the Spanish** los españoles

to **spank** VERB

zurrar

spanner NOUN

la llave inglesa

spare ADJECTIVE

▷ *see also* **spare** VERB, NOUN

1 de repuesto

□ Take a few spare batteries. Llévate unas pilas de repuesto. □ spare wheel la rueda de repuesto

2 de sobra

□ Have you got a spare pencil? ¿Tienes un lápiz de sobra?

■ **spare part** el repuesto

■ **spare room** el cuarto de los huéspedes

■ **spare time** el tiempo libre

to **spare** VERB

▷ *see also* **spare** ADJECTIVE, NOUN

■ **Can you spare a moment?** ¿Tienes un momento?

■ **I can't spare the time.** No tengo tiempo.

■ **They've got no money to spare.** No les sobra el dinero.

■ **We arrived with time to spare.** Llegamos con tiempo de sobra.

spare NOUN

▷ *see also* **spare** ADJECTIVE, VERB

■ **I've lost my key. — Have you got a spare?** He perdido la llave. — ¿Tienes una de sobra?

sparkling ADJECTIVE
con gas
□ a sparkling drink una bebida con gas
□ sparkling water agua con gas
■ **sparkling wine** vino espumoso

sparrow NOUN
el gorrión (PL los gorriones)

spat VERB ▷ *see* **spit**

to **speak** VERB
hablar
■ **Do you speak English?** ¿Hablas inglés?
□ Have you spoken to him? ¿Has hablado con él? □ She spoke to him about it. Habló de ello con él.
■ **Could I speak to Alison? — Speaking!** ¿Podría hablar con Alison? — ¡Soy yo!

to **speak up** VERB
hablar más alto
□ You'll need to speak up – we can't hear you. Habla más alto que no te oímos.

speaker NOUN
1 el altavoz (PL los altavoces) *(loudspeaker)*
2 el orador
la oradora *(at conference)*
■ **French speakers** los hablantes de francés

special ADJECTIVE
especial (FEM especial)

specialist NOUN
el/la especialista

speciality NOUN
la especialidad

to **specialize** VERB
especializarse*
□ She specialized in Russian. Se especializó en ruso.
■ **We specialize in skiing equipment.** Estamos especializados en material de esquí.

specially ADVERB
especialmente
□ It can be very cold here, specially in winter. Llega a hacer mucho frío aquí, especialmente en invierno. □ It's specially designed for teenagers. Está especialmente pensado para adolescentes. □ Do you like opera? — Not specially. ¿Te gusta la ópera? — No especialmente.

species NOUN
la especie

specific ADJECTIVE
1 específico (FEM específica)
□ certain specific issues ciertos temas específicos
2 concreto (FEM concreta)
□ Could you be more specific? ¿Podrías ser más concreto?

specifically ADVERB
1 específicamente
□ It's specifically designed for teenagers. Está específicamente pensado para adolescentes.
2 concretamente
□ in Britain, or more specifically in England en Gran Bretaña, o más concretamente en Inglaterra
■ **I specifically said that...** Especifiqué claramente que...

specs, spectacles PL NOUN
las gafas (los anteojos *Latin America*)

spectacular ADJECTIVE
espectacular (FEM espectacular)

spectator NOUN
el espectador
la espectadora

speech NOUN
el discurso
□ to make a speech dar un discurso

speechless ADJECTIVE
■ **I was speechless.** Me quedé sin habla.

speed NOUN
la velocidad
□ at top speed a toda velocidad
■ **a three-speed bike** una bicicleta de tres marchas

to **speed up** VERB
acelerar

speedboat NOUN
la lancha motora

speeding NOUN
el exceso de velocidad
□ He was fined for speeding. Lo multaron por exceso de velocidad.

speed limit NOUN
el límite de velocidad
■ **to break the speed limit** saltarse el límite de velocidad

speedometer NOUN
el velocímetro

to **spell** VERB
▷ *see also* **spell** NOUN
deletrear
□ Can you spell that please? ¿Me lo deletrea, por favor?
■ **How do you spell 'library'?** ¿Cómo se escribe 'library'?
■ **I can't spell.** Cometo faltas de ortografía.

spell NOUN
▷ *see also* **spell** VERB
el hechizo
□ to be under somebody's spell estar bajo el hechizo de alguien
■ **to cast a spell on somebody** hechizar a alguien

spelling NOUN
la ortografía
□ My spelling is terrible. Cometo muchas faltas de ortografía.
■ **a spelling mistake** una falta de ortografía

to **spend** VERB
1 gastar
□ They spend enormous amounts of money on advertising. Gastan cantidades enormes de dinero en publicidad.
2 dedicar*
□ He spends a lot of time and money on his hobbies. Dedica mucho tiempo y dinero a sus aficiones.
3 pasar
□ He spent a month in France. Pasó un mes en Francia.

spice NOUN
la especia

spicy ADJECTIVE
picante (FEM picante)

spider NOUN
la araña

to **spill** VERB
■ **You've spilled coffee on your shirt.** Se te ha caído café en la camisa.

spinach NOUN
las espinacas

spin drier NOUN
la centrifugadora

spine NOUN
la columna vertebral

spinster NOUN
la solterona

spire NOUN
la aguja

spirit NOUN
1 el espíritu
□ a youthful spirit un espíritu joven
2 el valor
□ Everyone admired her spirit. Todos admiraban su valor.
3 el brío
□ They played with great spirit. Jugaron con mucho brío.

spirits PL NOUN
los licores
□ I don't drink spirits. No bebo licores.
■ **to be in good spirits** estar de buen ánimo

spiritual ADJECTIVE
espiritual (FEM espiritual)
NOUN
▷ *see also* **spit** VERB
la saliva

to **spit** VERB
▷ *see also* **spit** NOUN
escupir

spite NOUN
▷ *see also* **spite** VERB
■ **in spite of** a pesar de
■ **out of spite** por despecho

to **spite** VERB
▷ *see also* **spite** NOUN
fastidiar
□ He just did it to spite me. Lo hizo sólo para fastidiarme.

spiteful ADJECTIVE
1 rencoroso (FEM rencorosa) *(person)*
2 malintencionado (FEM malintencionada) *(action)*

to **splash** VERB
▷ *see also* **splash** NOUN
salpicar*
□ Don't splash me! ¡No me salpiques!
■ **He splashed water on his face.** Se echó agua en la cara.

splash NOUN
▷ *see also* **splash** VERB
el chapoteo
□ I heard a splash. Oí un chapoteo.
■ **a splash of colour** una mancha de color

splendid ADJECTIVE
espléndido (FEM espléndida)

splint NOUN
la tablilla

splinter NOUN
la astilla

to **split** VERB
1 partir
□ He split the wood with an axe. Partió la madera con un hacha.
2 partirse
□ The ship hit a rock and split in two. El barco chocó con una roca y se partió en dos.
3 dividir
□ a decision that will split the party una decisión que dividirá al partido
■ **They decided to split the profits.** Decidieron repartir los beneficios.

to **split up** VERB
separarse

to **spoil** VERB
1 estropear
□ It spoiled our holiday. Nos estropeó las vacaciones.
2 mimar
□ Grandparents like to spoil their grandchildren. A los abuelos les encanta mimar a los nietos.

spoiled ADJECTIVE
mimado (FEM mimada)
□ a spoiled child un niño mimado

spoilsport NOUN
el/la aguafiestas (PL los/las aguafiestas)

spoke VERB ▷ *see* **speak**

spoke NOUN
el radio
spoken VERB ▷ *see* **speak**
spokesman NOUN
el portavoz (PL los portavoces) (el vocero *Latin America*)
spokeswoman NOUN
la portavoz (PL las portavoces) (la vocera *Latin America*)
sponge NOUN
la esponja
■ **sponge bag** la bolsa de aseo
■ **sponge cake** el bizcocho
sponsor NOUN
▷ *see also* **sponsor** VERB
el patrocinador
la patrocinadora
to **sponsor** VERB
▷ *see also* **sponsor** NOUN
patrocinar
□ The tournament was sponsored by local firms. El torneo fue patrocinado por empresas locales.
spontaneous ADJECTIVE
espontáneo (FEM espontánea)
spooky ADJECTIVE
■ **The house is really spooky at night.** La casa te pone los pelos de punta de noche.
spoon NOUN
la cuchara
spoonful NOUN
■ **a spoonful** una cucharada
sport NOUN
el deporte
■ **sports bag** la bolsa de deporte
■ **sports car** el coche deportivo
■ **sports jacket** la chaqueta de sport
sportsman NOUN
el deportista
sportswear NOUN
la ropa de deporte
sportswoman NOUN
la deportista
sporty ADJECTIVE
deportista (FEM deportista)
□ I'm not very sporty. No soy muy deportista.
spot NOUN
▷ *see also* **spot** VERB
1 la mancha
□ There's a spot on your shirt. Tienes una mancha en la camisa.
2 el lunar
□ a red dress with white spots un vestido rojo con lunares blancos
3 el grano
□ He's covered in spots. Está lleno de granos.
4 el sitio
□ It's a lovely spot for a picnic. Es un sitio precioso para un picnic.
■ **on the spot 1** en el acto □ They gave her the job on the spot. Le dieron el trabajo en el acto. **2** en el mismo sitio □ Luckily they were able to mend the car on the spot. Afortunadamente consiguieron arreglar el coche en el mismo sitio.
to **spot** VERB
▷ *see also* **spot** NOUN
notar
□ I spotted a mistake. Noté un error.
spotless ADJECTIVE
inmaculado (FEM inmaculada)
spotlight NOUN
el foco
spotty ADJECTIVE
con granos
spouse NOUN
el/la cónyuge
to **sprain** VERB
▷ *see also* **sprain** NOUN
torcerse*
□ She's sprained her ankle. Se ha torcido el tobillo.
sprain NOUN
▷ *see also* **sprain** VERB
la torcedura
spray NOUN
▷ *see also* **spray** VERB
el spray (PL los sprays) *(spray can)*
to **spray** VERB
▷ *see also* **spray** NOUN
1 rociar*
□ She sprayed perfume on my hand. Me roció perfume en la mano.
2 fumigar*
□ to spray against insects fumigar contra los insectos
■ **There was graffiti sprayed on the wall.** Había pintadas de spray en la pared.
spread NOUN
▷ *see also* **spread** VERB
■ **cheese spread** el queso para untar
■ **chocolate spread** la crema de chocolate
to **spread** VERB
▷ *see also* **spread** NOUN
1 extender*
□ She spread a towel on the sand. Extendió una toalla sobre la arena.
2 untar
□ Spread the top of the cake with whipped cream. Unte la parte superior de la tarta con nata montada.
3 propagarse*
□ The news spread rapidly. La noticia se propagó rápidamente.

to **spread out** VERB
1 dispersarse
□ The soldiers spread out across the field. Los soldados se dispersaron por el campo.
2 desplegar*
□ He spread the map out on the table. Desplegó el mapa sobre la mesa.

spreadsheet NOUN
la hoja de cálculo

spring NOUN
1 la primavera
□ in spring en primavera
2 el muelle *(metal)*
3 el manantial *(of water)*

spring-cleaning NOUN
la limpieza general

springtime NOUN
la primavera

sprinkler NOUN
el aspersor

sprint NOUN
▷ *see also* **sprint** VERB
la carrera de velocidad
■ **the women's 100 metres sprint** los cien metros lisos femeninos

to **sprint** VERB
▷ *see also* **sprint** NOUN
correr a toda velocidad
□ She sprinted for the bus. Corrió a toda velocidad para coger el autobús.

LANGUAGE TIP Be very careful with the verb **coger**: in most of Latin America this is an extremely rude word that should be avoided. However, in Spain this verb is common and not rude at all.

sprinter NOUN
el/la velocista

sprouts PL NOUN
■ **Brussels sprouts** las coles de Bruselas

spy NOUN
el/la espía

spying NOUN
el espionaje

to **squabble** VERB
reñir*
□ Stop squabbling! ¡Vale ya de reñir!

square NOUN
▷ *see also* **square** ADJECTIVE
1 el cuadrado
□ a square and a triangle un cuadrado y un triángulo
2 la plaza
□ the town square la plaza mayor

square ADJECTIVE
▷ *see also* **square** NOUN
cuadrado (FEM cuadrada)
□ two square metres dos metros cuadrados
■ **It's two metres square.** Mide dos por dos.

squash NOUN
▷ *see also* **squash** VERB
el squash *(sport)*
■ **squash court** la cancha de squash
■ **squash racket** la raqueta de squash
■ **orange squash** la naranjada
■ **lemon squash** la limonada

to **squash** VERB
▷ *see also* **squash** NOUN
aplastar
□ You're squashing me. Me estás aplastando.

to **squeak** VERB
1 chillar *(mouse, child)*
2 chirriar* *(door, wheel)*
3 crujir *(shoes)*

to **squeeze** VERB
1 exprimir
□ Squeeze two large lemons. Exprima dos limones grandes.
2 apretar*
□ She squeezed my hand. Me apretó la mano.
■ **The thieves squeezed through a tiny window.** Los ladrones se colaron por una pequeña ventana.

to **squeeze in** VERB
hacer* un hueco a
□ I can squeeze you in at two o'clock. Te puedo hacer un hueco a las dos.

squint NOUN
el estrabismo
■ **He has a squint.** Es estrábico.

squirrel NOUN
la ardilla

to **stab** VERB
apuñalar

stable NOUN
▷ *see also* **stable** ADJECTIVE
la cuadra

stable ADJECTIVE
▷ *see also* **stable** NOUN
estable (FEM estable)
□ a stable relationship una relación estable

stack NOUN
la pila
□ There were stacks of books on the table. Había pilas de libros sobre la mesa.
■ **They've got stacks of money.** Tienen cantidad de dinero.

stadium NOUN
el estadio

staff NOUN
1 el personal *(in company)*
2 el profesorado *(in school)*

stage NOUN
1 la etapa
□ in stages por etapas

■ **at this stage in the negotiations** a estas alturas de las negociaciones

2 el escenario

□ The band came on stage late. El grupo salió tarde al escenario.

■ **I always wanted to go on the stage.** Siempre quise dedicarme al teatro.

to **stagger** VERB

tambalearse

stain NOUN

▹ *see also* **stain** VERB

la mancha

to **stain** VERB

▹ *see also* **stain** NOUN

manchar

stainless steel NOUN

el acero inoxidable

stain remover NOUN

el quitamanchas (PL los quitamanchas)

stair NOUN

el escalón (PL los escalones)

staircase NOUN

la escalera

stairs PL NOUN

las escaleras

stale ADJECTIVE

■ **stale bread** el pan duro

stalemate NOUN

el punto muerto

□ to reach a stalemate llegar a un punto muerto

■ **The game ended in stalemate.** *(in chess)* La partida terminó en tablas.

stall NOUN

el puesto

□ He's got a market stall. Tiene un puesto en el mercado.

■ **the stalls** *(in theatre)* la platea

stamina NOUN

la resistencia física

stammer NOUN

el tartamudeo

■ **He's got a stammer.** Es tartamudo.

stamp NOUN

▹ *see also* **stamp** VERB

el sello (la estampilla *Latin America*)

□ My hobby is stamp collecting. Mi afición es coleccionar sellos.

■ **stamp album** el álbum de sellos (PL los álbumes de sellos)

to **stamp** VERB

▹ *see also* **stamp** NOUN

sellar

□ The file was stamped 'confidential'. El archivo iba sellado como 'confidencial'.

■ **The audience stamped their feet.** El público pateaba.

to **stand** VERB

1 estar* de pie

□ He was standing by the door. Estaba de pie junto a la puerta.

■ **What are you standing there for?** ¿Qué haces ahí de pie?

■ **They all stood when I came in.** Se pusieron de pie cuando entré.

2 soportar

□ I can't stand all this noise. No soporto todo este ruido.

to **stand for** VERB

1 significar*

□ 'EU' stands for 'European Union'. 'EU' significa 'European Union'.

2 consentir*

□ I won't stand for it any more! ¡No pienso consentirlo más!

to **stand out** VERB

destacar*

to **stand up** VERB

1 ponerse* de pie

□ I stood up and walked out. Me puse de pie y me fui.

2 estar* de pie

□ She has to stand up all day. Tiene que estar todo el día de pie.

standard ADJECTIVE

▹ *see also* **standard** NOUN

normal (FEM normal)

□ the standard procedure el procedimiento normal

■ **standard equipment** el equipamiento de serie

standard NOUN

▹ *see also* **standard** ADJECTIVE

el nivel

□ The standard is very high. El nivel es muy alto.

■ **She's got high standards.** Es muy exigente.

■ **standard of living** el nivel de vida

stand-by ticket NOUN

el billete en lista de espera

standpoint NOUN

el punto de vista

stands PL NOUN

la tribuna

stank VERB ▹ *see* **stink**

staple ADJECTIVE

básico (FEM básica)

□ their staple food su alimento básico

stapler NOUN

la grapadora

star NOUN

▹ *see also* **star** VERB

la estrella

□ a TV star una estrella de televisión

■ the stars el horóscopo

to **star** VERB

▹ *see also* **star** NOUN

■ to star in a film protagonizar una película

■ The film stars Sharon Stone. La protagonista de la película es Sharon Stone.

■ ...starring Johnny Depp ...con Johnny Depp

to **stare** VERB

mirar fijamente

□ Andy stared at him. Andy lo miraba fijamente.

stark ADVERB

■ stark naked en cueros

start NOUN

▹ *see also* **start** VERB

1 el principio

□ at the start of the film al principio de la película □ from the start desde el principio

■ for a start para empezar

■ Shall we make a start on the washing-up? ¿Nos ponemos a fregar los platos?

2 la salida *(of race)*

to **start** VERB

▹ *see also* **start** NOUN

1 empezar*

□ What time does it start? ¿A qué hora empieza?

■ to start doing something empezar a hacer algo □ I started learning Spanish two years ago. Empecé a aprender español hace dos años.

2 montar *(business, organization, campaign)*

□ He wants to start his own business. Quiere montar su propio negocio.

3 arrancar*

□ He couldn't start the car. No conseguía arrancar el coche. □ The car wouldn't start. El coche no arrancaba.

to **start off** VERB

ponerse* en camino

□ We started off first thing in the morning. Nos pusimos en camino pronto por la mañana.

starter NOUN

el primer plato *(first course)*

to **starve** VERB

morirse* de hambre

□ People are starving. La gente se muere de hambre.

■ I'm starving! ¡Me muero de hambre!

state NOUN

▹ *see also* **state** VERB

el estado

□ It's an independent state. Es un estado independiente. □ She was in a state of depression. Se encontraba en un estado de depresión.

■ He wasn't in a fit state to drive. No estaba en condiciones de conducir.

■ Tim was in a real state. Tim estaba de los nervios.

■ the States los Estados Unidos

to **state** VERB

▹ *see also* **state** NOUN

declarar

□ He stated his intention to resign. Declaró que tenía intención de dimitir.

■ Please state your name and address. Por favor indique su nombre y dirección.

stately home NOUN

la casa señorial

statement NOUN

1 la declaración (PL las declaraciones)

□ statements by witnesses las declaraciones de testigos

2 la afirmación (PL las afirmaciones)

□ Andrew now disowns the statement he made. Ahora Andrew desmiente la afirmación que hizo.

■ a bank statement un extracto de cuenta

station NOUN

la estación (PL las estaciones)

■ bus station la estación de autobuses

■ police station la comisaría

■ radio station la emisora de radio

stationer's NOUN

la papelería

station wagon NOUN (US)

la ranchera

statue NOUN

la estatua

stay NOUN

▹ *see also* **stay** VERB

la estancia

□ my stay in Spain mi estancia en España

to **stay** VERB

▹ *see also* **stay** NOUN

quedarse

□ Stay here! ¡Quédate aquí! □ I'm going to be staying with friends. Me voy a quedar en casa de unos amigos.

■ Where are you staying? In a hotel? ¿Dónde estás? ¿En un hotel?

■ to stay the night pasar la noche

■ We stayed in Belgium for a few days. Pasamos unos días en Bélgica.

to **stay in** VERB

quedarse en casa

to **stay up** VERB

quedarse levantado

□ We stayed up till midnight. Nos quedamos levantados hasta las doce.

steady ADJECTIVE

1 fijo (FEM fija)

□ a steady job un trabajo fijo

■ **a steady boyfriend** un novio formal
2 firme (FEM firme)
□ a steady hand un pulso firme
3 constante (FEM constante)
□ a steady pace un ritmo constante
■ **Steady on!** ¡Calma!

steak NOUN
el filete

to **steal** VERB
robar

steam NOUN
el vapor
□ a steam engine una máquina de vapor

steel NOUN
el acero

steep ADJECTIVE
empinado (FEM empinada)

steeple NOUN
la aguja

steering wheel NOUN
el volante

step NOUN
▹ *see also* **step** VERB
1 el paso
□ He took a step forward. Dio un paso adelante.
2 el peldaño
□ She tripped over the step. Tropezó con el peldaño.

to **step** VERB
▹ *see also* **step** NOUN
dar* un paso
□ I tried to step forward. Traté de dar un paso adelante.
■ **Step this way, please.** Pase por aquí, por favor.

stepbrother NOUN
el hermanastro

stepdaughter NOUN
la hijastra

stepfather NOUN
el padrastro

stepladder NOUN
la escalera de tijera

stepmother NOUN
la madrastra

stepsister NOUN
la hermanastra

stepson NOUN
el hijastro

stereo NOUN
el equipo de música

sterling ADJECTIVE
■ **pound sterling** la libra esterlina
■ **one hundred pounds sterling** cien libras esterlinas

stew NOUN
el estofado (el guisado *Latin America*)

steward NOUN
1 el auxiliar de vuelo *(on plane)*
2 el camarero *(on ship)*

stewardess NOUN
1 la auxiliar de vuelo *(on plane)*
2 la camarera *(on ship)*

stick NOUN
▹ *see also* **stick** VERB
el palo
■ **a walking stick** un bastón (PL unos bastones)

to **stick** VERB
▹ *see also* **stick** NOUN
1 pegar*
□ Stick the stamps on the envelope. Pegue los sellos en el sobre.
2 pegarse*
□ The rice stuck to the pan. El arroz se pegó a la olla.
3 meter
□ He picked up the papers and stuck them in his briefcase. Recogió los papeles y los metió en el maletín.
■ **I can't stick it any longer.** Ya no lo aguanto más.

to **stick out** VERB
sacar*
□ The little girl stuck out her tongue. La niña sacó la lengua.

sticker NOUN
la pegatina

stick insect NOUN
el insecto palo

sticky ADJECTIVE
1 pegajoso (FEM pegajosa)
□ to have sticky hands tener las manos pegajosas
2 adhesivo (FEM adhesiva)
□ a sticky label una etiqueta adhesiva

stiff ADJECTIVE, ADVERB
rígido (FEM rígida)
■ **to have a stiff neck** tener tortícolis
■ **to feel stiff** estar agarrotado
■ **to be bored stiff** estar aburrido como una ostra
■ **to be frozen stiff** estar tieso de frío
■ **to be scared stiff** estar muerto de miedo

still ADVERB
▹ *see also* **still** ADJECTIVE
1 todavía
□ I still haven't finished. No he terminado todavía. □ Are you still in bed? ¿Todavía estás en la cama?
■ **Do you still live in Glasgow?** ¿Sigues viviendo en Glasgow?
■ **better still** mejor aún
2 aun así *(even so)*
□ She knows I don't like it, but she still does it.

Sabe que no me gusta, pero aun así lo hace.
3 en fin *(after all)*
□ Still, it's the thought that counts. En fin, la intención es lo que cuenta.

still ADJECTIVE
▷ *see also* **still** ADVERB
quieto (FEM quieta)
□ He stood still. Se quedó quieto.
■ **Keep still!** ¡No te muevas!

sting NOUN
▷ *see also* **sting** VERB
la picadura
□ a bee sting una picadura de abeja

to **sting** VERB
▷ *see also* **sting** NOUN
picar*

stingy ADJECTIVE
tacaño (FEM tacaña)

to **stink** VERB
▷ *see also* **stink** NOUN
apestar
□ You stink of garlic! ¡Apestas al ajo!

stink NOUN
▷ *see also* **stink** VERB
el tufo
□ the stink of beer el tufo a cerveza

to **stir** VERB
agitar

to **stitch** VERB
▷ *see also* **stitch** NOUN
coser

stitch NOUN
▷ *see also* **stitch** VERB
1 la puntada *(in sewing)*
2 el punto *(in knitting, in wound)*
□ I had five stitches. Me pusieron cinco puntos.

stock NOUN
▷ *see also* **stock** VERB
1 la reserva
□ stocks of ammunition reservas de munición
2 las existencias
□ the shop's stock las existencias de la tienda
■ **Yes, we've got your size in stock.** Sí, nos quedan existencias de su número.
■ **out of stock** agotado □ I'm sorry, they're both out of stock. Lo siento, están los dos agotados.
3 el caldo
□ chicken stock caldo de pollo

to **stock** VERB
▷ *see also* **stock** NOUN
vender
□ Do you stock camping stoves? ¿Venden infiernillos?

to **stock up** VERB
abastecerse*
□ to stock up with something abastecerse de algo

stock cube NOUN
la pastilla de caldo

stocking NOUN
la media

stomach NOUN
el estómago

stone NOUN
1 la piedra
□ a stone wall un muro de piedra
2 el hueso
□ an apricot stone un hueso de albaricoque

DID YOU KNOW...?
In Spain measurements are in grams and kilograms. One stone is about 6.3 kg.

■ **I weigh eight stone.** Peso unos cincuenta kilos.

stood VERB ▷ *see* **stand**

stool NOUN
el taburete

to **stop** VERB
▷ *see also* **stop** NOUN
1 parar
□ The bus doesn't stop there. El autobús no para allí.
2 pararse
□ The music stopped. Se paró la música.
■ **This has got to stop!** ¡Esto se tiene que acabar!
■ **I think the rain's going to stop.** Creo que va a dejar de llover.
■ **to stop doing something** dejar de hacer algo □ to stop smoking dejar de fumar
3 acabar con
□ a campaign to stop whaling una campaña para acabar con la caza de ballenas

LANGUAGE TIP **impedir que** has to be followed by a verb in the subjunctive.

■ **to stop somebody doing something** impedir que alguien haga algo □ She would have liked to stop us seeing each other. Le hubiera gustado impedir que nos siguiéramos viendo.
■ **Stop!** ¡Alto!

stop NOUN
▷ *see also* **stop** VERB
la parada
□ a bus stop una parada de autobús
■ **This is my stop.** Yo me bajo aquí.

stopwatch NOUN
el cronómetro

store NOUN
▷ *see also* **store** VERB
1 la tienda
□ a furniture store una tienda de muebles

English-Spanish

S

2 el almacén (PL los almacenes)
□ a grain store un almacén de grano

to **store** VERB
▹ *see also* **store** NOUN
1 guardar
□ They store potatoes in the cellar. Guardan patatas en el sótano.
2 almacenar
□ to store information almacenar información

storey NOUN
la planta
□ a three-storey building un edificio de tres plantas

storm NOUN
la tormenta

stormy ADJECTIVE
tormentoso (FEM tormentosa)

story NOUN
1 el cuento *(tale)*
2 la historia *(account)*

stove NOUN
1 la cocina *(in kitchen)*
2 el infiernillo *(camping stove)*

straight ADJECTIVE, ADVERB
1 recto (FEM recta)
□ a straight line una línea recta
2 liso (FEM lisa)
□ straight hair pelo liso
3 heterosexual (FEM heterosexual) *(not gay)*
■ **He looked straight at me.** Me miró directamente a los ojos.
■ **straight away** enseguida
■ **I'll come straight back.** Vuelvo enseguida.
■ **Keep straight on.** Siga todo recto.

straightforward ADJECTIVE
1 sencillo (FEM sencilla)
□ It's very straightforward. Es muy sencillo.
2 sincero (FEM sincera)
□ She's very straightforward. Es muy sincera.

strain NOUN
▹ *see also* **strain** VERB
la tensión (PL las tensiones)
■ **It was a strain.** Fue muy estresante.

to **strain** VERB
▹ *see also* **strain** NOUN
■ **to strain one's eyes** forzar la vista
■ **I strained my back.** Me dio un tirón en la espalda.
■ **to strain a muscle** sufrir un tirón muscular

strained ADJECTIVE
■ **a strained muscle** una distensión muscular

stranded ADJECTIVE
■ **We were stranded on the motorway.** Nos quedamos tirados en la autopista.

strange ADJECTIVE
raro (FEM rara)
□ That's strange! ¡Qué raro!
LANGUAGE TIP **es raro que** has to be followed by a verb in the subjunctive.
□ It's strange that she doesn't talk to us anymore. Es raro que ya no nos hable.

stranger NOUN
el desconocido
la desconocida
□ Don't talk to strangers. No hables con desconocidos.
■ **I'm a stranger here.** Yo no soy de aquí.

to **strangle** VERB
estrangular

strap NOUN
1 el tirante *(of bra, dress)*
2 la correa *(of watch, camera, suitcase)*
3 el asa *fem (of bag)*
LANGUAGE TIP Although it's a feminine noun, remember that you use **el** and **un** with **asa**.

straw NOUN
1 la paja
□ a straw hat un sombrero de paja
2 la pajita
□ He was drinking his lemonade through a straw. Se bebía la gaseosa con pajita.
■ **That's the last straw!** ¡Eso es la gota que colma el vaso!

strawberry NOUN
la fresa (la frutilla *Latin America*)

stray ADJECTIVE
extraviado (FEM extraviada)
□ a stray cat un gato extraviado

stream NOUN
el riachuelo

street NOUN
la calle

streetcar NOUN (US)
el tranvía
LANGUAGE TIP Although **tranvía** ends in **-a**, it is actually a masculine noun.

streetlamp NOUN
la farola

street plan NOUN
el plano de la ciudad

streetwise ADJECTIVE
■ **to be streetwise** sabérselas todas
■ **a streetwise kid** un pillo

strength NOUN
la fuerza
□ with all his strength con todas sus fuerzas

to **stress** VERB
▹ *see also* **stress** NOUN
recalcar*
□ I would like to stress that... Me gustaría recalcar que...

stress NOUN

▷ *see also* **stress** VERB
el estrés
□ She's under a lot of stress. Está pasando mucho estrés.

to **stretch** VERB
1 estirarse
□ The dog woke up and stretched. El perro se despertó y se estiró.
■ **I went out to stretch my legs.** Salí a estirar las piernas.
■ **My jumper stretched after I washed it.** Se me dio de sí el jersey al lavarlo.
2 tender*
□ They stretched a rope between two trees. Tendieron una cuerda entre dos árboles.

stretcher NOUN
la camilla

stretchy ADJECTIVE
elástico (FEM elástica)

strict ADJECTIVE
estricto (FEM estricta)

strike NOUN
▷ *see also* **strike** VERB
la huelga
■ **to be on strike** estar en huelga
■ **to go on strike** hacer huelga

to **strike** VERB
▷ *see also* **strike** NOUN
golpear
□ She struck him across the mouth. Le golpeó en la boca.
■ **The clock struck three.** El reloj dio las tres.
■ **to strike a match** encender una cerilla

striker NOUN
1 el/la huelguista *(person on strike)*
2 el delantero
la delantera *(footballer)*

striking ADJECTIVE
1 asombroso (FEM asombrosa)
□ a striking resemblance un parecido asombroso
2 en huelga
□ striking miners mineros en huelga

string NOUN
la cuerda
■ **a piece of string** una cuerda

to **strip** VERB
▷ *see also* **strip** NOUN
desnudarse

strip NOUN
▷ *see also* **strip** VERB
la tira
■ **strip cartoon** la tira cómica (la historieta *Latin America*)

stripe NOUN
la franja

striped ADJECTIVE
a rayas
■ **a striped skirt** una falda de rayas

stripper NOUN
el/la artista de striptease

stripy ADJECTIVE
de rayas

to **stroke** VERB
▷ *see also* **stroke** NOUN
acariciar

stroke NOUN
▷ *see also* **stroke** VERB
el derrame cerebral
□ to have a stroke sufrir un derrame cerebral
■ **a stroke of luck** un golpe de suerte

stroll NOUN
■ **to go for a stroll** ir a dar un paseo

stroller NOUN (US)
la silla de paseo

strong ADJECTIVE
fuerte (FEM fuerte)

strongly ADVERB
■ **We strongly advise you to...** Te aconsejamos encarecidamente que...
■ **He smelt strongly of tobacco.** Olía mucho a tabaco.
■ **strongly built** corpulento
■ **I don't feel strongly about it.** Me da un poco igual.

struck VERB ▷ *see* **strike**

to **struggle** VERB
▷ *see also* **struggle** NOUN
forcejear
□ He struggled, but he couldn't escape. Forcejeó, pero no pudo escapar.
■ **to struggle to do something** **1** *(fight)* luchar por hacer algo □ He struggled to get custody of his daughter. Luchó por conseguir la custodia de su hija. **2** *(have difficulty)* pasar apuros para hacer algo
□ They struggle to pay their bills. Pasan apuros para pagar las facturas.

struggle NOUN
▷ *see also* **struggle** VERB
la lucha
□ a struggle for survival una lucha por la supervivencia
■ **It was a struggle.** Nos costó mucho.

stub NOUN
la colilla

stubborn ADJECTIVE
terco (FEM terca)

to **stub out** VERB
apagar*

stuck VERB ▷ *see* **stick**

stuck ADJECTIVE
atascado (FEM atascada)
□ The lid is stuck. La tapadera está atascada.

■ **to get stuck** quedarse atascado
■ **We got stuck in a traffic jam.** Nos metimos en un atasco.

stuck-up ADJECTIVE
creído (FEM creída) *(informal)*

stud NOUN
1 el pendiente *(earring)*
2 el taco *(on football boots)*

student NOUN
el/la estudiante

studio NOUN
el estudio
□ a TV studio un estudio de televisión
■ **a studio flat** un estudio

to **study** VERB
estudiar

stuff NOUN
las cosas
□ Have you got all your stuff? ¿Tienes todas tus cosas? □ There's some stuff on the table for you. En la mesa hay unas cosas para ti.
■ **I need some stuff for hay fever.** Me hace falta algo para la alergia al polen.

stuffy ADJECTIVE
■ **a stuffy room** una habitación mal ventilada
■ **It's stuffy in here.** Hay un ambiente muy cargado aquí.

to **stumble** VERB
tropezar*

stung VERB ▷ *see* **sting**

stunk VERB ▷ *see* **stink**

stunned ADJECTIVE
pasmado (FEM pasmada)
□ I was stunned. Me quedé pasmado.

stunning ADJECTIVE
pasmoso (FEM pasmosa)

stunt NOUN
■ **It's a publicity stunt.** Es un truco publicitario.

stuntman NOUN
el especialista

stupid ADJECTIVE
estúpido (FEM estúpida)

to **stutter** VERB
▷ *see also* **stutter** NOUN
tartamudear

stutter NOUN
▷ *see also* **stutter** VERB
el tartamudeo
■ **He's got a stutter.** Es tartamudo.

style NOUN
el estilo
□ That's not his style. No es su estilo.

subject NOUN
1 el tema

LANGUAGE TIP Although **tema** ends in **-a**, it is actually a masculine noun.

□ The subject of my project is the internet. El tema de mi trabajo es Internet.
2 la asignatura
□ What's your favourite subject? ¿Cuál es tu asignatura preferida?
3 el sujeto
□ 'I' is the subject in 'I love you'. 'I' es el sujeto en 'I love you'.

submarine NOUN
el submarino

subscription NOUN
la suscripción (PL las suscripciones) *(to paper, magazine)*
■ **to take out a subscription to something** suscribirse a algo

subsequently ADVERB
posteriormente

to **subsidize** VERB
subvencionar

subsidy NOUN
la subvención (PL las subvenciones)

substance NOUN
la sustancia

substitute NOUN
▷ *see also* **substitute** VERB
1 el sustituto
la sustituta *(replacement)*
2 el/la suplente *(in football, rugby)*

to **substitute** VERB
▷ *see also* **substitute** NOUN
sustituir*
□ to substitute A for B sustituir a B por A

subtitled ADJECTIVE
subtitulado (FEM subtitulada)

subtitles PL NOUN
los subtítulos
□ a Spanish film with English subtitles una película española con subtítulos en inglés

subtle ADJECTIVE
sutil (FEM sutil)

to **subtract** VERB
restar
□ to subtract 3 from 5 restar 3 a 5

suburb NOUN
el barrio residencial
□ a London suburb un barrio residencial de Londres
■ **They live in the suburbs.** Viven en las afueras.

suburban ADJECTIVE
■ **a suburban train** un tren de cercanías
■ **a suburban shopping centre** un centro comercial de las afueras

subway NOUN
1 el metro *(underground)*
2 el paso subterráneo *(underpass)*

to **succeed** VERB
1 tener* éxito

□ to succeed in business tener éxito en los negocios
2 salir* bien
□ The plan did not succeed. El plan no salió bien.
■ **to succeed in doing something** lograr hacer algo

success NOUN
el éxito
LANGUAGE TIP Be careful not to translate **success** by **suceso**.

successful ADJECTIVE
de éxito (exitoso *Latin America*)
□ a successful lawyer un abogado de éxito
■ **a successful attempt** un intento fructífero
■ **to be successful** tener éxito
■ **to be successful in doing something** lograr hacer algo

successfully ADVERB
con éxito

successive ADJECTIVE
consecutivo (FEM consecutiva)
□ He was the winner for a second successive year. Fue el ganador por segundo año consecutivo.

such ADJECTIVE, ADVERB
1 tan
□ such clever people gente tan lista □ such a long journey un viaje tan largo
2 tal (FEM tal)
□ I wouldn't dream of doing such a thing. No se me ocurriría hacer tal cosa. □ The pain was such that... El dolor era tal que...
■ **such a lot** tanto □ such a lot of work tanto trabajo □ such a long time ago hace tanto tiempo
■ **such as** como □ a hot country, such as India... un país caluroso, como la India...
■ **as such** propiamente dicho □ She's not an expert as such, but... No es una experta propiamente dicha, pero...
■ **There's no such thing.** Eso no existe. □ There's no such thing as the yeti. El yeti no existe.

such-and-such ADJECTIVE
tal (FEM tal)
□ such-and-such a place tal lugar

to **suck** VERB
chupar
■ **to suck one's thumb** chuparse el pulgar

sudden ADJECTIVE
repentino (FEM repentina)
□ a sudden change un cambio repentino
■ **all of a sudden** de repente

suddenly ADVERB
de repente

suede NOUN
el ante (la gamuza *Latin America*)
□ a suede jacket una chaqueta de ante

to **suffer** VERB
sufrir
□ She was really suffering. Sufría de verdad.
■ **to suffer from something** padecer de algo □ I suffer from hay fever. Padezco de alergia al polen.

to **suffocate** VERB
ahogarse*

sugar NOUN
el azúcar

to **suggest** VERB
1 sugerir*
LANGUAGE TIP Use the subjunctive after **sugerir que**.
□ She suggested going out for a pizza. Sugirió que saliéramos a tomar una pizza.
2 aconsejar
LANGUAGE TIP Use the subjunctive after **aconsejar que**.
□ I suggested they set off early. Yo les aconsejé que salieran pronto.
■ **What are you trying to suggest?** ¿Qué insinúas?

suggestion NOUN
la sugerencia
□ to make a suggestion hacer una sugerencia

suicide NOUN
el suicidio
■ **to commit suicide** suicidarse

suicide bomber NOUN
el/la terrorista suicida

suit NOUN
▷ *see also* **suit** VERB
1 el traje *(man's)*
2 el traje de chaqueta *(woman's)*

to **suit** VERB
▷ *see also* **suit** NOUN
1 venir* bien a
□ What time would suit you? ¿Qué hora te vendría bien?
■ **That suits me fine.** Eso me viene estupendamente.
2 sentar* bien a
□ That dress really suits you. Ese vestido te sienta la mar de bien.
■ **Suit yourself!** ¡Haz lo que te parezca!

suitable ADJECTIVE
1 conveniente (FEM conveniente)
□ a suitable time una hora conveniente
2 apropiado (FEM apropiada)
□ suitable clothing ropa apropiada

suitcase NOUN
la maleta (la valija *Latin America*)

suite NOUN
la suite
□ a suite at the Paris Hilton una suite en el Hilton de París

■ **a bedroom suite** un dormitorio completo
■ **three-piece suite** un tresillo

to **sulk** VERB
estar* de mal humor

sulky ADJECTIVE
malhumorado (FEM malhumorada)

sultana NOUN
la pasa de Esmirna

sum NOUN
la suma
□ **to do sums** hacer sumas □ **a sum of money** una suma de dinero

to **summarize** VERB
resumir

summary NOUN
el resumen (PL los resúmenes)

summer NOUN
el verano
□ **summer clothes** ropa de verano □ **the summer holidays** las vacaciones de verano
□ **a summer camp** un campamento de verano

summertime NOUN
el verano

summit NOUN
la cumbre
□ **the NATO summit** la cumbre de la OTAN
□ **the summit of Mount Everest** la cumbre del Everest

to **sum up** VERB
resumir
■ **To sum up...** Resumiendo...

sun NOUN
el sol
□ **in the sun** al sol □ **sun cream** la crema solar

to **sunbathe** VERB
tomar el sol

sunblock NOUN
la crema solar de protección total

sunburn NOUN
la quemadura

sunburnt ADJECTIVE
quemado por el sol (FEM quemado por el sol)
■ **Mind you don't get sunburnt!** ¡Cuidado de quemarte con el sol!

Sunday NOUN
el domingo (PL los domingos)
□ **I saw her on Sunday.** La vi el domingo.
□ **every Sunday** todos los domingos □ **last Sunday** el domingo pasado □ **next Sunday** el domingo que viene □ **on Sundays** los domingos

Sunday school NOUN
la catequesis

DID YOU KNOW...?
The Spanish equivalent of Sunday school takes place during the week after school rather than on a Sunday.

sunflower NOUN
el girasol
□ **sunflower seeds** pipas de girasol

sung VERB ▷ *see* **sing**

sunglasses PL NOUN
las gafas de sol

sunk VERB ▷ *see* **sink**

sunlight NOUN
la luz del sol

sunny ADJECTIVE
soleado (FEM soleada)
□ **a sunny morning** una mañana soleada
■ **It's sunny.** Hace sol.
■ **a sunny day** un día de sol

sunrise NOUN
la salida del sol

sunroof NOUN
el techo corredizo

sunscreen NOUN
el protector solar

sunset NOUN
la puesta de sol

sunshine NOUN
el sol
□ **in the sunshine** al sol

sunstroke NOUN
la insolación (PL las insolaciones)

suntan NOUN
el bronceado
■ **to get a suntan** broncearse
■ **suntan lotion** la crema bronceadora
■ **suntan oil** el aceite bronceador

super ADJECTIVE
estupendo (FEM estupenda)

superb ADJECTIVE
magnífico (FEM magnífica)

supermarket NOUN
el supermercado

supernatural ADJECTIVE
sobrenatural (FEM sobrenatural)

superstitious ADJECTIVE
supersticioso (FEM supersticiosa)

to **supervise** VERB
supervisar

supervisor NOUN
el supervisor
la supervisora

supper NOUN
la cena

supplement NOUN
el suplemento

supplies PL NOUN
las provisiones
■ **medical supplies** material médico

to **supply** VERB
▷ *see also* **supply** NOUN
suministrar
■ **to supply somebody with something**

suministrar algo a alguien □ The centre supplied us with all the equipment. El centro nos suministró todo el material.

supply NOUN
▹ *see also* **supply** VERB
el suministro
□ the water supply el suministro de agua
■ **a supply of paper** una remesa de papel

supply teacher NOUN
el profesor interino
la profesora interina

to **support** VERB
▹ *see also* **support** NOUN
1 apoyar
□ My mum has always supported me. Mi madre siempre me ha apoyado.
2 mantener*
□ She had to support five children on her own. Tenía que mantener a cinco niños ella sola.
■ **What team do you support?** ¿De qué equipo eres?
LANGUAGE TIP Be careful not to translate **to support** by **soportar**.

support NOUN
▹ *see also* **support** VERB
el apoyo

supporter NOUN
1 el/la hincha
□ a Liverpool supporter un hincha del Liverpool
2 el partidario
la partidaria
□ a supporter of the Labour Party un partidario del partido laborista

to **suppose** VERB
suponer*
□ I suppose he'll be late. Supongo que llegará tarde. □ Suppose you win the lottery... Supón que te toca la lotería...
■ **I suppose so.** Supongo que sí.
■ **You're supposed to show your passport.** Tienes que enseñar el pasaporte.
■ **You're not supposed to smoke in the toilet.** No está permitido fumar en el servicio.
■ **It's supposed to be the best hotel in the city.** Dicen que es el mejor hotel de la ciudad.

supposing CONJUNCTION
LANGUAGE TIP **suponiendo que** has to be followed by a verb in the subjunctive.
■ **Supposing you won the lottery...** Suponiendo que te tocara la lotería...

surcharge NOUN
el recargo

sure ADJECTIVE
seguro (FEM segura)
□ Are you sure? ¿Estás seguro?
■ **Sure!** ¡Claro!
■ **to make sure that...** asegurarse de que...
□ I'm going to make sure the door's locked. Voy a asegurarme de que la puerta está cerrada con llave.

surely ADVERB
■ **Surely you don't believe that?** ¿No te creerás eso, no?

surf NOUN
▹ *see also* **surf** VERB
la espuma de las olas

to **surf** VERB
▹ *see also* **surf** NOUN
hacer* surf

surface NOUN
la superficie

surfboard NOUN
la tabla de surf

surfing NOUN
el surf
□ to go surfing hacer surf

surgeon NOUN
el cirujano
la cirujana

surgery NOUN
1 el consultorio médico *(room)*
2 la cirugía *(treatment)*
■ **surgery hours** las horas de consulta

surname NOUN
el apellido

surprise NOUN
la sorpresa

surprised ADJECTIVE
■ **I was surprised to see him.** Me sorprendió verlo.
■ **I'm not surprised that ...** No me sorprende que...

surprising ADJECTIVE
sorprendente (FEM sorprendente)

to **surrender** VERB
rendirse*

to **surround** VERB
rodear
□ surrounded by trees rodeado de árboles

surroundings PL NOUN
el entorno
□ a hotel in beautiful surroundings un hotel en un hermoso entorno

survey NOUN
la encuesta
□ They did a survey of a thousand students. Hicieron una encuesta a mil estudiantes.

surveyor NOUN
1 el perito tasador
la perito tasadora *(of buildings)*
2 el agrimensor
la agrimensora *(of land)*

English-Spanish

S

survivor NOUN
el/la supervíviente
□ There were no survivors. No hubo supervivientes.

to **suspect** VERB
▷ *see also* **suspect** NOUN
sospechar

suspect NOUN
▷ *see also* **suspect** VERB
el sospechoso
la sospechosa

to **suspend** VERB
1 expulsar temporalmente *(from school)*
2 excluir* *(from team)*
3 suspender *(from job)*

suspenders PL NOUN (US: *braces*)
los tirantes

suspense NOUN
1 la incertidumbre
□ The suspense was terrible. La incertidumbre era terrible.
2 el suspense
□ a film with lots of suspense una película llena de suspense

suspension NOUN
1 la expulsión temporal *(from school)*
2 la exclusión *(from team)*
3 la suspensión *(from job)*
■ **a suspension bridge** un puente colgante

suspicious ADJECTIVE
1 receloso (FEM recelosa) *(mistrustful)*
□ He was suspicious at first. Al principio estaba receloso.
2 sospechoso (FEM sospechosa) *(suspicious-looking)*
□ a suspicious person un individuo sospechoso

to **swallow** VERB
tragar*

swam VERB ▷ *see* **swim**

swan NOUN
el cisne

to **swap** VERB
cambiar
□ to swap A for B cambiar A por B
■ **Do you want to swap?** ¿Quieres que cambiemos?

to **swat** VERB
aplastar

to **sway** VERB
balancearse

to **swear** VERB
1 jurar
□ to swear allegiance to jurar fidelidad a
2 decir* palabrotas
□ It's wrong to swear. No se deben decir palabrotas.

swearword NOUN
la palabrota

sweat NOUN
▷ *see also* **sweat** VERB
el sudor

to **sweat** VERB
▷ *see also* **sweat** NOUN
sudar

sweater NOUN
el jersey (PL los jerseys) (el suéter *Latin America*)

sweaty ADJECTIVE
1 sudoroso (FEM sudorosa) *(hands, face)*
2 sudado (FEM sudada) *(clothes)*

Swede NOUN
el sueco
la sueca *(person)*

swede NOUN
el nabo

Sweden NOUN
Suecia *fem*

Swedish ADJECTIVE, NOUN
sueco (FEM sueca)

to **sweep** VERB
barrer
□ to sweep the floor barrer el suelo

sweet NOUN
▷ *see also* **sweet** ADJECTIVE
1 el caramelo
□ a bag of sweets una bolsa de caramelos
2 el postre
□ Are you going to have a sweet? ¿Vas a tomar postre?

sweet ADJECTIVE
▷ *see also* **sweet** NOUN
1 dulce (FEM dulce)
□ a sweet wine un vino dulce
2 amable (FEM amable)
□ That was really sweet of you. Fue muy amable de tu parte.
■ **sweet and sour pork** el cerdo agridulce

sweetcorn NOUN
el maíz dulce

sweltering ADJECTIVE
■ **It was sweltering.** Hacía un calor asfixiante.

swept VERB ▷ *see* **sweep**

to **swerve** VERB
girar bruscamente
□ I swerved to avoid the cyclist. Giré bruscamente para esquivar al ciclista.

swim NOUN
▷ *see also* **swim** VERB
■ **to go for a swim** ir a nadar

to **swim** VERB
▷ *see also* **swim** NOUN
nadar
□ Can you swim? ¿Sabes nadar?

■ **She swam across the river.** Cruzó el río a nado.

swimmer NOUN
el nadador
la nadadora

swimming NOUN
la natación
□ swimming lessons clases de natación
■ **Do you like swimming?** ¿Te gusta nadar?
■ **to go swimming** ir a nadar
■ **swimming cap** el gorro de baño
■ **swimming costume** el traje de baño
■ **swimming pool** la piscina
■ **swimming trunks** el bañador

swimsuit NOUN
el traje de baño

to **swing** VERB
▷ *see also* **swing** NOUN
1 columpiarse *(on a swing)*
2 balancearse
□ Her bag swung as she walked. El bolso se balanceaba según iba andando.
■ **He was swinging on a rope.** Se balanceaba colgado de una cuerda.
3 colgar*
□ A large key swung from his belt. Le colgaba una gran llave del cinturón.
4 balancear
□ He was swinging his bag back and forth. Balanceaba la bolsa de un lado al otro.
■ **Roy swung his legs off the couch.** Con un movimiento rápido, Roy quitó las piernas del sofá.
■ **The canoe suddenly swung round.** De repente la canoa dio un viraje.

swing NOUN
▷ *see also* **swing** VERB
el columpio

Swiss ADJECTIVE, NOUN
suizo (FEM suiza)
■ **the Swiss** los suizos

switch NOUN
▷ *see also* **switch** VERB
el interruptor

to **switch** VERB
▷ *see also* **switch** NOUN
cambiar de
□ We switched partners. Cambiamos de pareja.

to **switch off** VERB
apagar* *(TV, machine, engine)*

to **switch on** VERB
encender* (prender *Latin America*)

Switzerland NOUN
Suiza *fem*

swollen ADJECTIVE
hinchado (FEM hinchada)
□ My ankle is very swollen. Tengo el tobillo muy hinchado.

to **swop** VERB
cambiar
□ to swop A for B cambiar A por B
■ **Do you want to swop?** ¿Quieres que cambiemos?

sword NOUN
la espada

swot NOUN
▷ *see also* **swot** VERB
el empollón
la empollona

to **swot** VERB
▷ *see also* **swot** NOUN
empollar
□ I'll have to swot for the maths exam. Para el examen de matemáticas me va a tocar empollar.

swum VERB ▷ *see* **swim**

swung VERB ▷ *see* **swing**

syllabus NOUN
el programa de estudios

LANGUAGE TIP Although **programa** ends in **-a**, it is actually a masculine noun.

symbol NOUN
el símbolo

sympathetic ADJECTIVE
comprensivo (FEM comprensiva)

LANGUAGE TIP Be careful not to translate **sympathetic** by **simpático**.

to **sympathize** VERB
■ **to sympathize with somebody**
1 *(feel sorry for)* compadecerse de alguien
2 *(understand)* comprender a alguien

sympathy NOUN
1 la compasión *(sorrow)*
2 la comprensión *(understanding)*

symptom NOUN
el síntoma

LANGUAGE TIP Although **síntoma** ends in **-a**, it is actually a masculine noun.

syringe NOUN
la jeringuilla

system NOUN
el sistema

LANGUAGE TIP Although **sistema** ends in **-a**, it is actually a masculine noun.

English-Spanish

S

Tt

table NOUN
la mesa
■ **to lay the table** poner la mesa
tablecloth NOUN
el mantel
tablespoon NOUN
la cuchara de servir
tablet NOUN
la pastilla
table tennis NOUN
el tenis de mesa
□ to play table tennis jugar al tenis de mesa
tabloid NOUN
■ **the tabloids** la prensa amarilla
tackle NOUN
▷ *see also* **tackle** VERB
1 la entrada *(in football)*
2 el placaje *(in rugby)*
■ **fishing tackle** el equipo de pesca
to **tackle** VERB
▷ *see also* **tackle** NOUN
■ **to tackle somebody** 1 *(in football)* entrar a alguien 2 *(in rugby)* placar a alguien
■ **to tackle a problem** abordar un problema
tact NOUN
el tacto
tactful ADJECTIVE
diplomático (FEM diplomática)
tactics PL NOUN
la táctica *sing*
tactless ADJECTIVE
poco diplomático (FEM poco diplomática)
□ He's so tactless! ¡Es tan poco diplomático!
■ **a tactless remark** un comentario con poco tacto
tadpole NOUN
el renacuajo
tag NOUN
la etiqueta *(label)*
tail NOUN
1 la cola *(of horse, bird, fish)*
2 el rabo *(of dog, bull, ox)*
■ **Heads or tails?** ¿Cara o cruz?
tailor NOUN
el sastre
□ He's a tailor. Es sastre.

to **take** VERB
1 tomar
□ Do you take sugar? ¿Tomas azúcar?
■ **He took a plate out of the cupboard.** Sacó un plato del armario.
2 llevar
□ When will you take me to London? ¿Cuándo me llevarás a Londres? □ Don't forget to take your camera. No te olvides de llevarte la cámara. □ It takes about one hour. Se tarda más o menos una hora. □ It won't take long. No tardará mucho tiempo.
■ **That takes a lot of courage.** Hace falta mucho valor para eso.
■ **It takes a lot of money to do that.** Hace falta mucho dinero para hacer eso.
3 soportar
□ He can't take being criticized. No soporta que le critiquen.
4 hacer*
□ Have you taken your driving test yet? ¿Ya has hecho el examen de conducir? □ I decided to take French instead of German. Decidí hacer francés en vez de alemán.
5 aceptar
□ We take credit cards. Aceptamos tarjetas de crédito.
to **take after** VERB
parecerse* a
□ She takes after her mother. Se parece a su madre.
to **take apart** VERB
■ **to take something apart** desmontar algo
to **take away** VERB
1 llevarse
□ They took away all his belongings. Se llevaron todas sus pertenencias.
2 quitar
□ She was afraid her children would be taken away from her. Tenía miedo de que le quitaran a los niños.
■ **hot meals to take away** platos calientes para llevar
to **take back** VERB
devolver*

□ I took it back to the shop. Lo devolví a la tienda.

■ **I take it all back!** ¡Retiro lo dicho!

to **take down** VERB

quitar

□ She took down the painting. Quitó el cuadro.

to **take in** VERB

1 comprender

□ I didn't really take it in. La verdad es que no lo comprendí.

2 engañar

□ They were taken in by his story. Se dejaron engañar por la historia que les contó.

to **take off** VERB

1 despegar*

□ The plane took off 20 minutes late. El avión despegó con 20 minutos de retraso.

2 quitar

□ Take your coat off. Quítate el abrigo.

to **take out** VERB

sacar*

□ He opened his wallet and took out some money. Abrió la cartera y sacó dinero.

■ **He took her out to the theatre.** La invitó al teatro.

to **take over** VERB

hacerse* cargo de

□ He took over the running of the company last year. Se hizo cargo del control de la empresa el año pasado.

■ **to take over from somebody 1** *(replace)* sustituir a alguien **2** *(in shift work)* relevar a alguien

takeaway NOUN

la comida para llevar *(meal)*

takeoff NOUN

el despegue *(of plane)*

talcum powder NOUN

los polvos de talco

tale NOUN

el cuento

talent NOUN

el talento

□ He's got a lot of talent. Tiene mucho talento.

■ **to have a talent for something** tener talento para algo

■ **He's got a real talent for languages.** Tiene verdadera facilidad para los idiomas.

talented ADJECTIVE

■ **She's a talented pianist.** Es una pianista de talento.

talk NOUN

▹ *see also* **talk** VERB

1 la conversación (PL las conversaciones)

□ We had a long talk about her problems. Tuvimos una larga conversación acerca de sus problemas.

■ **I had a talk with my Mum about it.** Hablé sobre eso con mi madre.

■ **to give a talk on something** dar una charla sobre algo □ She gave a talk on ancient Egypt. Dio una charla sobre el antiguo Egipto.

2 las habladurías *(gossip)*

□ It's just talk. Son sólo habladurías.

to **talk** VERB

▹ *see also* **talk** NOUN

hablar

□ What did you talk about? ¿De qué hablasteis?

■ **to talk to somebody** hablar con alguien

■ **to talk to oneself** hablar consigo mismo

■ **to talk something over with somebody** discutir algo con alguien

talkative ADJECTIVE

hablador (FEM habladora)

tall ADJECTIVE

alto (FEM alta)

■ **to be two metres tall** medir dos metros

tame ADJECTIVE

domesticado (FEM domesticada) *(animal)*

tampon NOUN

el tampón (PL los tampones)

tan NOUN

el bronceado

■ **to get a tan** broncearse

tangerine NOUN

la mandarina

tank NOUN

1 el depósito *(for water, petrol)*

2 la cisterna *(on truck)*

3 el tanque *(military)*

tanker NOUN

1 el petrolero *(ship)*

2 el camión cisterna (PL los camiones cisterna) *(truck)*

■ **an oil tanker** un petrolero

■ **a petrol tanker** un camión cisterna

tap NOUN

1 el grifo (la llave *Latin America*) *(for water)*

□ the hot tap el grifo de agua caliente

2 el golpecito *(gentle knock)*

□ I heard a tap on the window. Oí un golpecito en la ventana.

■ **There was a tap on the door.** Llamaron a la puerta.

tap-dancing NOUN

el claqué

□ I do tap-dancing. Bailo claqué.

to **tape** VERB

▹ *see also* **tape** NOUN

grabar

□ Did you tape that film last night? ¿Grabaste la película de anoche?

tape NOUN
▷ *see also* **tape** VERB
1 la cinta *(music)*
2 la cinta adhesiva *(sticky tape)*

tape measure NOUN
la cinta métrica

tape recorder NOUN
1 el casete *(large)*
2 la grabadora *(hand-held)*

target NOUN
1 la diana *(board)*
2 el objetivo *(goal)*

tart NOUN
la tarta
□ an apple tart una tarta de manzana

tartan ADJECTIVE
escocés (PL escoceses, FEM escocesa)
□ a tartan scarf una bufanda escocesa

task NOUN
la tarea

taste NOUN
▷ *see also* **taste** VERB
1 el sabor
□ It's got a really strange taste. Tiene un sabor muy extraño.
2 el gusto
□ His joke was in bad taste. Su broma fue de mal gusto.
■ **Would you like a taste?** ¿Quiere probarlo?

to **taste** VERB
▷ *see also* **taste** NOUN
probar*
□ Would you like to taste it? ¿Quiere probarlo?
■ **to taste of something** saber a algo
□ It tastes of fish. Sabe a pescado.
■ **You can taste the garlic in it.** Se le nota el sabor a ajo.

tasteful ADJECTIVE
de buen gusto

tasteless ADJECTIVE
1 soso (FEM sosa) *(food)*
2 de mal gusto *(in bad taste)*
□ a tasteless remark un comentario de mal gusto

tasty ADJECTIVE
sabroso (FEM sabrosa)

tattoo NOUN
el tatuaje

taught VERB ▷ *see* **teach**

Taurus NOUN
el Tauro *(sign)*
■ **I'm Taurus.** Soy tauro.

tax NOUN
el impuesto
■ **I pay a lot of tax.** Pago muchos impuestos.
■ **income tax** el impuesto sobre la renta

taxi NOUN
el taxi
■ **a taxi driver** un/una taxista

taxi rank NOUN
la parada de taxis

TB ABBREVIATION *(= tuberculosis)*
la tuberculosis
□ He's got TB. Tiene tuberculosis.

tea NOUN
1 té
□ Would you like some tea? ¿Te apetece un té?
■ **a cup of tea** una taza de té
2 la merienda *(afternoon tea)*
■ **to have tea** merendar □ We had tea at the Savoy. Merendamos en el Savoy.
3 la cena *(evening meal)*
■ **to have tea** cenar □ We're having sausages and beans for tea. Vamos a cenar salchichas con alubias.

tea bag NOUN
la bolsita de té

to **teach** VERB
1 enseñar
□ My sister taught me to swim. Mi hermana me enseñó a nadar.
2 dar* clases de *(subject)*
□ She teaches physics. Da clases de física.
■ **That'll teach you!** ¡Así aprenderás!

teacher NOUN
1 el profesor
la profesora *(in secondary school)*
□ a maths teacher un profesor de matemáticas □ She's a teacher. Es profesora.
2 el maestro
la maestra *(in primary school)*
□ He's a primary school teacher. Es maestro.

team NOUN
el equipo
□ a football team un equipo de fútbol

teapot NOUN
la tetera

tear NOUN
▷ *see also* **tear** VERB
la lágrima
■ **She was in tears.** Estaba llorando.

to **tear** VERB
▷ *see also* **tear** NOUN
1 romper*
□ Be careful or you'll tear the page. Ten cuidado que vas a romper la página.
■ **He tore his jacket.** Se rasgó la chaqueta.
■ **Your shirt is torn.** Tu camisa está rota.
2 romperse*
□ It won't tear, it's very strong. No se rompe, es muy resistente.

to **tear up** VERB
hacer* pedazos
□ He tore up the letter. Hizo pedazos la carta.

tear gas NOUN
el gas lacrimógeno

to **tease** VERB
1 atormentar
□ Stop teasing that poor animal! ¡Deja de atormentar al pobre animal!
2 tomar el pelo a
□ He's teasing you. Te está tomando el pelo.
■ **I was only teasing.** Lo decía en broma.

teaspoon NOUN
la cucharita

teatime NOUN
la hora de cenar *(in evening)*
□ It was nearly teatime. Era casi la hora de cenar.
■ **Teatime!** ¡A la mesa!

tea towel NOUN
el paño de cocina

technical ADJECTIVE
técnico (FEM técnica)
■ **technical college** el centro de formación profesional (la escuela politécnica *Latin America*)

technician NOUN
el técnico
la técnica

technique NOUN
la técnica

techno NOUN
el tecno

technological ADJECTIVE
tecnológico (FEM tecnológica)

technology NOUN
la tecnología

teddy bear NOUN
el osito de peluche

teenage ADJECTIVE
■ **a teenage magazine** una revista para adolescentes
■ **She has two teenage daughters.** Tiene dos hijas adolescentes.

teenager NOUN
el/la adolescente

teens PL NOUN
■ **She's in her teens.** Es adolescente.

tee-shirt NOUN
la camiseta

teeth PL NOUN ▷ *see* **tooth**

to **teethe** VERB
echar los dientes

teetotal ADJECTIVE
abstemio (FEM abstemia)

telecommunications PL NOUN
las telecomunicaciones

telephone NOUN
el teléfono
□ on the telephone al teléfono
■ **a telephone box** una cabina telefónica
■ **a telephone call** una llamada telefónica
■ **a telephone directory** una guía telefónica
■ **a telephone number** un número de teléfono

telesales NOUN
las televentas

telescope NOUN
el telescopio

television NOUN
la televisión
□ The match is on television tonight. Ponen el partido en televisión esta noche.

to **tell** VERB
decir*
■ **to tell somebody something** decir algo a alguien □ Did you tell your mother? ¿Se lo has dicho a tu madre? □ I told him I was going on holiday. Le dije que me iba de vacaciones.

LANGUAGE TIP Use the subjunctive after **decir a alguien que** when translating 'to tell somebody to do something'.

■ **to tell somebody to do something** decir a alguien que haga algo □ He told me to wait a moment. Me dijo que esperara un momento.
■ **to tell lies** decir mentiras
■ **to tell a story** contar un cuento
■ **I can't tell the difference between them.** No puedo distinguirlos.
■ **You can tell he's not serious.** Se nota que no se lo toma en serio.

to **tell off** VERB
regañar

telly NOUN *(informal)*
la tele
□ to watch telly ver la tele □ on telly en la tele

temper NOUN
el genio
□ He's got a terrible temper. Tiene muy mal genio.
■ **to be in a temper** estar de mal humor
■ **to lose one's temper** perder los estribos

temperature NOUN
la temperatura
■ **to have a temperature** tener fiebre

temple NOUN
1 el templo *(building)*
2 la sien *(on head)*

temporary ADJECTIVE
temporal (FEM temporal)

to **tempt** VERB
tentar*
□ I'm very tempted! ¡Tienta mucho!
■ **to tempt somebody to do something** tentar a alguien a hacer algo

temptation NOUN
la tentación (PL las tentaciones)

tempting ADJECTIVE
tentador (FEM tentadora)

ten NUMERAL
diez
□ She's ten. Tiene diez años.

tenant NOUN
el inquilino
la inquilina

to **tend** VERB
■ **to tend to do something** tener tendencia a hacer algo □ He tends to arrive late. Tiene tendencia a llegar tarde.

tender ADJECTIVE
tierno (FEM tierna)

tennis NOUN
el tenis
□ to play tennis jugar al tenis
■ **a tennis ball** una pelota de tenis
■ **a tennis court** una pista de tenis
■ **a tennis racket** una raqueta de tenis

tennis player NOUN
el/la tenista
□ He's a tennis player. Es tenista.

tenor NOUN
el tenor

tenpin bowling NOUN
los bolos
□ to go tenpin bowling jugar a los bolos

tense ADJECTIVE
▷ *see also* **tense** NOUN
tenso (FEM tensa)

tense NOUN
▷ *see also* **tense** ADJECTIVE
el tiempo
■ **the present tense** el presente
■ **the future tense** el futuro

tension NOUN
la tensión (PL las tensiones)

tent NOUN
la tienda de campaña
■ **a tent peg** una estaquilla
■ **a tent pole** un mástil de tienda

tenth ADJECTIVE
décimo (FEM décima)
□ the tenth floor el décimo piso
■ **the tenth of August** el diez de agosto

term NOUN
1 el trimestre *(at school)*
□ It's nearly the end of term. Ya casi es final de trimestre.
2 el plazo
□ in the long term a largo plazo
■ **to come to terms with something** aceptar algo □ He hasn't yet come to terms with his disability. Todavía no ha aceptado su invalidez.

terminal ADJECTIVE
▷ *see also* **terminal** NOUN
terminal (FEM terminal) *(illness, patient)*

terminal NOUN
▷ *see also* **terminal** ADJECTIVE
el terminal *(of computer)*
■ **airport terminal** la terminal del aeropuerto
■ **bus terminal** la terminal de autobuses
■ **oil terminal** la terminal petrolera

terminally ADVERB
■ **to be terminally ill** estar en fase terminal

terrace NOUN
1 la terraza *(patio)*
□ We were sitting on the terrace. Estábamos sentados en la terraza.
2 la hilera de casas adosadas *(row of houses)*
■ **the terraces** *(in stadium)* las gradas

terraced ADJECTIVE
■ **a terraced house** una casa adosada

terrible ADJECTIVE
espantoso (FEM espantosa)
□ This coffee is terrible. Este café es espantoso.
■ **I feel terrible.** Me siento fatal.

terrier NOUN
el/la terrier (PL los/las terriers)

terrific ADJECTIVE
estupendo (FEM estupenda) *(wonderful)*
□ That's terrific! ¡Estupendo!
■ **You look terrific!** ¡Estás guapísima!

terrified ADJECTIVE
aterrorizado (FEM aterrorizada)
□ I was terrified! ¡Estaba aterrorizado!

terrorism NOUN
el terrorismo

terrorist NOUN
el/la terrorista
■ **a terrorist attack** un atentado terrorista

test NOUN
▷ *see also* **test** VERB
1 la prueba
□ a spelling test una prueba de ortografía
□ nuclear tests pruebas nucleares
2 el análisis (PL los análisis) *(of blood, urine)*
□ a blood test un análisis de sangre
■ **an eye test** un examen de la vista
3 el examen de conducir *(driving test)*
□ He's just passed his test. Acaba de aprobar el examen de conducir.

to **test** VERB
▷ *see also* **test** NOUN
probar*

■ **to test something out** probar algo
■ **He tested us on the new vocabulary.** Nos hizo una prueba del vocabulario nuevo.
■ **She was tested for drugs.** Le hicieron la prueba antidoping.

test match NOUN
el partido internacional

test tube NOUN
la probeta

tetanus NOUN
el tétano
■ **a tetanus injection** una inyección contra el tétano

text NOUN
▹ *see also* **text** VERB
el SMS *(text message)*

to **text** VERB
▹ *see also* **text** NOUN
enviar* un SMS a
□ I'll text you when I get there. Te envío un SMS cuando llegue.

textbook NOUN
el libro de texto
□ a Spanish textbook un libro de texto de español

text message NOUN
el SMS

Thames NOUN
el Támesis

than CONJUNCTION
1 que
□ She's taller than me. Es más alta que yo.
□ I've got more CDs than tapes. Tengo más CDs que cintas.
2 de
□ more than once en más de una ocasión
□ more than 10 years más de 10 años

to **thank** VERB
dar* las gracias a
□ Don't forget to write and thank them. Acuérdate de escribirles y darles las gracias.
■ **thank you** gracias
■ **thank you very much** muchas gracias

thanks EXCLAMATION
¡Gracias!
■ **thanks to** gracias a □ Thanks to him, everything went OK. Gracias a él, todo salió bien.

that ADJECTIVE
▹ *see also* **that** PRONOUN, CONJUNCTION, ADVERB
1 ese (FEM esa)
□ that man ese hombre □ that road esa carretera

LANGUAGE TIP To refer to something more distant, use **aquel** and **aquella**.

2 aquel (FEM aquella)
□ Look at that car over there! ¡Mira aquel coche! □ THAT road there aquella carretera
■ **that one** ése (FEM ésa)
□ This man? — No, that one. ¿Este hombre? — No, ése. □ Do you like this photo? — No, I prefer that one. ¿Te gusta esta foto? — No, prefiero ésa.

LANGUAGE TIP To refer to something more distant, use **aquél** and **aquélla**.

3 aquél (FEM aquélla)
□ That one over there is cheaper. Aquél es más barato. □ Which woman? — That one over there. ¿Qué mujer? — Aquélla.

that PRONOUN
▹ *see also* **that** ADJECTIVE, CONJUNCTION, ADVERB
1 ése (FEM ésa, NEUTER eso)
□ That's impossible. Eso es imposible.
□ What's that? ¿Qué es eso?
■ **Who's that?** *(who is that man)* ¿Quién es ése?
■ **Who's that?** *(who is that woman)* ¿Quién es ésa?
■ **Who's that?** *(on the telephone)* ¿Con quién hablo?

LANGUAGE TIP To refer to something more distant, use **aquél**, **aquélla** and **aquello**.

2 aquél (FEM aquélla, NEUTER aquello)
□ That's my French teacher over there. Aquél es mi profesor de francés. □ That's my sister over by the window. Aquélla de la ventana es mi hermana. □ That was a silly thing to do. Aquello fue una tontería.
■ **Is that you?** ¿Eres tú?
3 que *(in relative clauses)*
□ the man that saw us el hombre que nos vio □ the dog that she bought el perro que ella compró □ the man that we saw el hombre que vimos

LANGUAGE TIP After a preposition **que** becomes **el que**, **la que**, **los que**, **las que** to agree with the noun.

□ the man that we spoke to el hombre con el que hablamos □ the women that she was chatting to las mujeres con las que estaba hablando

that CONJUNCTION
▹ *see also* **that** ADJECTIVE, PRONOUN, ADVERB
que
□ He thought that Henry was ill. Creía que Henry estaba enfermo. □ I know that she likes chocolate. Sé que le gusta el chocolate.

that ADVERB
▹ *see also* **that** ADJECTIVE, PRONOUN, CONJUNCTION
■ **It was that big.** Era así de grande.
■ **It's about that high.** Es más o menos así de alto.
■ **It's not that difficult.** No es tan difícil.

thatched ADJECTIVE

■ **a thatched cottage** una casita con tejado de paja

the DEFINITE ARTICLE

1 el *masc* (PL los)

□ the boy el niño □ the cars los coches

LANGUAGE TIP **a** + **el** changes to **al** and **de** + **el** changes to **del**.

□ They went to the theatre. Fueron al teatro. □ the soup of the day la sopa del día

2 la *fem* (PL las)

□ the woman la mujer □ the chairs las sillas

theatre (US **theater**) NOUN

el teatro

theft NOUN

el robo

their ADJECTIVE

su (PL sus)

□ their father su padre □ their house su casa □ their parents sus padres □ their sisters sus hermanas

LANGUAGE TIP 'Their' is usually translated by the definite article **el/los** or **la/las** when it's clear from the sentence who the possessor is, particularly when referring to clothing or parts of the body.

□ They took off their coats. Se quitaron los abrigos. □ after washing their hands después de lavarse las manos □ Someone stole their car. Alguien les robó el coche.

theirs PRONOUN

1 el suyo *masc* (PL los suyos)

□ Is this their car? — No, theirs is red. ¿Es éste su coche? — No, el suyo es rojo. □ my parents and theirs mis padres y los suyos

2 la suya *fem* (PL las suyas)

□ Is this their house? — No, theirs is white. ¿Es ésta su casa? — No, la suya es blanca. □ my sisters and theirs mis hermanas y las suyas

LANGUAGE TIP Use **de ellos** (masculine) or **de ellas** (feminine) instead of **suyo** if you want to be specific about a masculine or feminine group.

□ It's not our car, it's theirs. No es nuestro coche, es suyo. □ The suitcase is theirs. La maleta es suya. □ Whose is this? — It's theirs. ¿De quién es esto? — Es de ellos.

■ **Isobel is a friend of theirs.** Isobel es amiga suya.

them PRONOUN

1 los (FEM las)

LANGUAGE TIP Use **los** or **las** when 'them' is the direct object of the verb in the sentence.

□ I didn't know them. No los conocía. □ Have you seen my slippers? I'd left them here. ¿Has visto mis zapatillas? Las había dejado aquí. □ Look at them! ¡Míralos! □ I had to give them to her. Tuve que dárselos.

2 les

LANGUAGE TIP Use **les** when 'them' means 'to them'.

□ I gave them some brochures. Les di unos folletos. □ You have to tell them the truth. Tienes que decirles la verdad.

3 se

LANGUAGE TIP Use **se** not **les** when 'them' is used in combination with a direct-object pronoun.

□ Give it to them. Dáselo.

4 ellos (FEM ellas)

LANGUAGE TIP Use **ellos** or **ellas** after prepositions, in comparisons, and with the verb 'to be'.

□ It's for them. Es para ellos. □ My sisters didn't go. My mother stayed with them. Mis hermanas no fueron. Mi madre se quedó con ellas. □ We are older than them. Somos mayores que ellos. □ It must be them. Deben de ser ellos.

■ **They were carrying them on them.** Los llevaban consigo.

theme NOUN

el tema

LANGUAGE TIP Although **tema** ends in **-a**, it is actually a masculine noun.

theme park NOUN

el parque temático

themselves PRONOUN

1 se *(reflexive)*

□ Did they hurt themselves? ¿Se hicieron daño?

2 sí mismos (FEM sí mismas) *(after preposition)*

□ They talked mainly about themselves. Hablaron sobre todo de sí mismos.

3 ellos mismos (FEM ellas mismas) *(for emphasis)*

□ They built it themselves. Lo construyeron ellos mismos.

■ **by themselves** por sí mismos (FEM por sí mismas)

□ The girls did it all by themselves. Las chicas lo hicieron todo por sí mismas.

then ADVERB, CONJUNCTION

1 después *(next)*

□ I get dressed. Then I have breakfast. Me visto. Después desayuno.

2 pues *(in that case)*

□ My pen's run out. — Use a pencil then! Se me ha acabado el bolígrafo. — ¡Pues usa un lápiz!

3 en aquella época *(in those days)*

□ There was no electricity then. En aquella época no había electricidad.

■ **now and then** de vez en cuando □ Do you play chess? — Now and then. ¿Juegas al ajedrez? — De vez en cuando.

■ **By then it was too late.** Para entonces ya era demasiado tarde.

therapy NOUN
la terapia

there ADVERB
ahí
□ Put it there, on the table. Ponlo ahí, en la mesa.
■ **over there** allí
■ **in there** ahí dentro
■ **on there** ahí encima
■ **up there** ahí arriba
■ **down there** ahí abajo
■ **There he is!** ¡Ahí está!
■ **there is** hay □ There's a factory near my house. Hay una fábrica cerca de mi casa.
■ **there are** hay □ There are 20 children in my class. Hay 20 niños en mi clase.
■ **There has been an accident.** Ha habido un accidente.

therefore ADVERB
por lo tanto

there's = **there is; there has**

thermometer NOUN
el termómetro

Thermos® NOUN
el termo

these ADJECTIVE
▹ *see also* **these** PRONOUN
estos (FEM estas)
□ these shoes estos zapatos □ THESE shoes estos zapatos de aquí □ these houses estas casas

these PRONOUN
▹ *see also* **these** ADJECTIVE
éstos (FEM éstas)
□ I want these! ¡Quiero éstos! □ I'm looking for some sandals. — Can I try these? Quiero unas sandalias. — ¿Puedo probarme éstas?

they PRONOUN
ellos (FEM ellas)
LANGUAGE TIP 'they' generally isn't translated unless it's emphatic.
□ They're fine, thank you. Están bien, gracias.
LANGUAGE TIP Use **ellos** or **ellas** as appropriate for emphasis.
□ We went to the cinema but they didn't. Nosotros fuimos al cine pero ellos no.
□ I spoke to my sisters. THEY agree with me. Hablé con mis hermanas. Ellas estaban de acuerdo conmigo.
■ **They say that...** Dicen que... □ They say that the house is haunted. Dicen que la casa está embrujada.

they'd = **they had; they would**

they'll = **they will**

they're = **they are**

they've = **they have**

thick ADJECTIVE
1 grueso (FEM gruesa) *(wall, slice)*
□ Give him a thick slice. Dále una rebanada gruesa.
■ **The walls are one metre thick.** Las paredes tienen un metro de grosor.
2 espeso (FEM espesa) *(soup)*
□ My soup turned out too thick. La sopa me quedó demasiado espesa.
3 corto (FEM corta) *(informal: stupid)*

thief NOUN
el ladrón (PL los ladrones)
la ladrona

thigh NOUN
el muslo

thin ADJECTIVE
1 fino (FEM fina)
□ a thin slice una rebanada fina
2 delgado (FEM delgada)
□ She's very thin. Está muy delgada.

thing NOUN
la cosa
□ beautiful things cosas bonitas □ Where shall I put my things? ¿Dónde pongo mis cosas?
■ **How's things?** ¿Qué tal?
■ **What's that thing called?** ¿Cómo se llama eso?
■ **You poor thing!** ¡Pobrecito!
■ **The best thing would be to leave it.** Lo mejor sería dejarlo.

to think VERB
1 pensar*
□ What do you think about it? ¿Qué piensas? □ Think carefully before you reply. Piénsalo bien antes de responder. □ What are you thinking about? ¿En qué estás pensando?
■ **I'll think it over.** Lo pensaré.
2 creer*
□ I think you're wrong. Creo que estás equivocado.
■ **I think so.** Creo que sí.
■ **I don't think so.** Creo que no.
3 imaginar
□ Think what life would be like without cars. Imagínate cómo sería la vida sin coches.

third ADJECTIVE, ADVERB
▹ *see also* **third** NOUN
tercero (FEM tercera)
LANGUAGE TIP Use **tercer** before a masculine singular noun.
□ the third prize el tercer premio □ the third time la tercera vez □ Rachel came third in

the race. Rachel quedó la tercera en la carrera.
■ **the third of March** el tres de marzo

third NOUN
▹ *see also* **third** ADJECTIVE, ADVERB
el tercio *(fraction)*
■ **a third of the population** una tercera parte de la población

thirdly ADVERB
en tercer lugar

Third World NOUN
el Tercer Mundo

thirst NOUN
la sed

thirsty ADJECTIVE
■ **to be thirsty** tener sed

thirteen NUMERAL
trece
□ I'm thirteen. Tengo trece años.

thirteenth ADJECTIVE
decimotercero (FEM decimotercera)
■ **the thirteenth floor** la planta trece
■ **the thirteenth of January** el trece de enero

thirty NUMERAL
treinta
□ He's thirty. Tiene treinta años.

this ADJECTIVE
▹ *see also* **this** PRONOUN
este (FEM esta)
□ this boy este niño □ this road esta carretera
■ **this one** éste (FEM ésta)
□ Pass me that pen. — This one? Acércame ese bolígrafo. — ¿Éste? □ This is my room and this one's my sister's. Ésta es mi habitación y ésta es la de mi hermana.

this PRONOUN
▹ *see also* **this** ADJECTIVE
éste (FEM ésta, NEUTER esto)
□ This is my office and this is the meeting room. Éste es mi despacho y ésta es la sala de reuniones. □ What's this? ¿Qué es esto?
■ **This is my mother.** *(introduction)* Te presento a mi madre.
■ **This is Gavin speaking.** *(on the phone)* Soy Gavin.

thistle NOUN
el cardo

thorough ADJECTIVE
minucioso (FEM minuciosa)
□ a thorough check un control minucioso
■ **She's very thorough.** Es muy meticulosa.

thoroughly ADVERB
minuciosamente
□ I checked the car thoroughly. Revisé el coche minuciosamente.
■ **Mix the ingredients thoroughly.** Mézclense bien los ingredientes.
■ **I thoroughly enjoyed myself.** Me divertí muchísimo.

those ADJECTIVE
▹ *see also* **those** PRONOUN
1 esos (FEM esas)
□ those shoes esos zapatos □ those girls esas chicas

LANGUAGE TIP To refer to something more distant, use **aquellos** and **aquellas**.

2 aquellos (FEM aquellas)
□ THOSE shoes aquellos zapatos □ those houses over there aquellas casas

those PRONOUN
▹ *see also* **those** ADJECTIVE
1 ésos (FEM ésas)
□ I want those! ¡Quiero ésos!

LANGUAGE TIP To refer to something more distant, use **aquéllos**.

2 aquéllos (FEM aquéllas)
□ Ask those children. — Those over there? Pregúntales a esos niños. — ¿A aquéllos?

though CONJUNCTION, ADVERB
aunque
□ Though she was tired she stayed up late. Aunque estaba cansada, se quedó levantada hasta muy tarde.
■ **It's difficult, though, to put into practice.** Pero es difícil llevarlo a la práctica.

thought VERB ▹ *see* **think**

thought NOUN
la idea
□ I've just had a thought. Se me ocurre una idea.
■ **He kept his thoughts to himself.** No le dijo a nadie lo que pensaba.
■ **It was a nice thought, thank you.** Fue muy amable de tu parte, gracias.

thoughtful ADJECTIVE
1 pensativo (FEM pensativa) *(deep in thought)*
□ You look thoughtful. Pareces pensativo.
2 considerado (FEM considerada) *(considerate)*
□ She's very thoughtful. Es muy considerada.

thoughtless ADJECTIVE
desconsiderado (FEM desconsiderada)
□ She's very thoughtless. Es muy desconsiderada.
■ **It was thoughtless of her to mention it.** Fue una falta de consideración por su parte mencionarlo.

thousand NUMERAL
■ **a thousand** mil □ a thousand euros mil euros
■ **two thousand pounds** dos mil libras
■ **thousands of people** miles de personas

thread NOUN
el hilo

threat NOUN
la amenaza

to **threaten** VERB
amenazar*
□ He threatened me. Me amenazó.
■ to threaten to do something *(person)* amenazar con hacer algo

three NUMERAL
tres
□ She's three. Tiene tres años.

three-dimensional ADJECTIVE
tridimensional (FEM tridimensional)

threw VERB ▷ *see* **throw**

thrifty ADJECTIVE
ahorrativo (FEM ahorrativa)

thrill NOUN
la emoción (PL las emociones)
□ I remember the thrill of Christmas as a child. Recuerdo la emoción que sentía de niño en Navidades.
■ It was a great thrill to see my team win. Fue muy emocionante ver ganar a mi equipo.

thrilled ADJECTIVE
■ I was thrilled. Estaba emocionada.

thriller NOUN
1 la película de suspense (la película de misterio *Latin America*) *(film)*
2 la novela de suspense (la novela de misterio *Latin America*) *(novel)*

thrilling ADJECTIVE
emocionante (FEM emocionante)

throat NOUN
la garganta
□ I have a sore throat. Me duele la garganta.

to **throb** VERB
■ My arm's throbbing. Tengo un dolor punzante en el brazo.
■ a throbbing pain un dolor punzante

throne NOUN
el trono

through ADJECTIVE, ADVERB, PREPOSITION
1 a través de
□ to look through a telescope mirar a través de un telescopio □ I know her through my sister. La conozco a través de mi hermana.
■ I saw him through the crowd. Lo vi entre la multitud.
■ The window was dirty and I couldn't see through. La ventana estaba sucia y no podía ver nada.
2 por
□ The thief got in through the kitchen window. El ladrón entró por la ventana de la cocina. □ to go through Birmingham pasar por Birmingham □ to walk through the woods pasear por el bosque
■ to go through a tunnel atravesar un túnel
■ He went straight through to the dining room. Pasó directamente al comedor.
■ a through train un tren directo
■ 'no through road' 'calle sin salida'
■ all through the night durante toda la noche
■ from May through to September desde mayo hasta septiembre

throughout PREPOSITION
■ throughout Britain en toda Gran Bretaña
■ throughout the year durante todo el año

to **throw** VERB
tirar
□ He threw the ball to me. Me tiró la pelota.
■ to throw a party dar una fiesta
■ That really threw him. Eso lo desconcertó por completo.

to **throw away** VERB
1 tirar *(rubbish)*
2 desperdiciar *(chance)*

to **throw out** VERB
1 tirar *(throw away)*
2 echar *(person)*
□ I threw him out. Lo eché.

to **throw up** VERB
devolver*

thug NOUN
el matón (PL los matones)

thumb NOUN
el pulgar

thumb tack NOUN (US)
la chincheta

to **thump** VERB
■ to thump somebody pegar un puñetazo a alguien

thunder NOUN
los truenos

thunderstorm NOUN
la tormenta

thundery ADJECTIVE
tormentoso (FEM tormentosa)

Thursday NOUN
el jueves (PL los jueves)
□ I saw her on Thursday. La vi el jueves.
□ every Thursday todos los jueves □ last Thursday el jueves pasado □ next Thursday el jueves que viene □ on Thursdays los jueves

thyme NOUN
el tomillo

tick NOUN
▷ *see also* **tick** VERB
1 la señal
□ Place a tick in the appropriate box. Marque con una señal la casilla correspondiente.
2 el tictac

◻ The clock has a loud tick. El reloj tiene un tictac muy fuerte.
■ **in a tick** en un instante

to **tick** VERB
▹ *see also* **tick** NOUN
1 marcar*
◻ Tick the appropriate box. Marque la casilla correspondiente.
2 hacer* tictac *(clock)*

to **tick off** VERB
1 marcar* *(on form, list)*
◻ The teacher ticked the names off in the register. El profesor marcó los nombres de la lista con una señal.
2 regañar *(scold)*
◻ He was ticked off for being late. Le regañaron por llegar tarde.

ticket NOUN
1 el billete (el boleto *Latin America*) *(for bus, train, tube)*
2 el billete (el pasaje *Latin America*) *(for plane)*
3 la entrada *(for cinema, theatre, concert, museum)*
4 el ticket (PL los tickets) *(for baggage, coat, parking)*
■ **a parking ticket** *(fine)* una multa de aparcamiento

ticket inspector NOUN
el revisor (FEM la revisora)

ticket office NOUN
la taquilla

to **tickle** VERB
hacer* cosquillas a
◻ She enjoyed tickling the baby. Le gustaba hacer cosquillas al niño.

ticklish ADJECTIVE
■ **to be ticklish** tener cosquillas

tide NOUN
la marea
■ **high tide** la marea alta
■ **low tide** la marea baja

tidy ADJECTIVE
▹ *see also* **tidy** VERB
ordenado (FEM ordenada)
◻ Your room is very tidy. Tu habitación está muy ordenada. ◻ She's very tidy. Es muy ordenada.

to **tidy** VERB
▹ *see also* **tidy** ADJECTIVE
ordenar *(room)*

to **tidy up** VERB
recoger* *(toys)*
◻ Don't forget to tidy up afterwards. No os olvidéis de recoger las cosas después.

tie NOUN
▹ *see also* **tie** VERB
1 la corbata *(necktie)*
2 el empate *(in sport)*

to **tie** VERB
▹ *see also* **tie** NOUN
1 atar *(shoelaces, parcel)*
■ **to tie a knot in something** hacer un nudo en algo
2 empatar
◻ They tied three all. Empataron a tres.

to **tie up** VERB
1 atar *(person, shoelaces, parcel)*
2 atracar* *(boat)*

tiger NOUN
el tigre

tight ADJECTIVE
1 ceñido (FEM ceñida) *(fitting)*
◻ tight jeans vaqueros ceñidos
2 estrecho (FEM estrecha) *(too small)*
◻ This dress is a bit tight. Este vestido es un poco estrecho.

to **tighten** VERB
1 tensar *(rope)*
2 apretar* *(screw)*

tightly ADVERB
■ **tightly closed** fuertemente cerrado
■ **She held his hand tightly.** Le agarró la mano con fuerza.

tights PL NOUN
las medias
◻ a pair of tights unas medias

tile NOUN
1 la teja *(on roof)*
2 el azulejo *(for wall)*
3 la baldosa *(for floor)*

tiled ADJECTIVE
1 de tejas *(roof)*
2 alicatado (FEM alicatada) *(wall)*
3 de baldosas *(floor)*

till NOUN
▹ *see also* **till** PREPOSITION, CONJUNCTION
la caja

till PREPOSITION, CONJUNCTION
▹ *see also* **till** NOUN
1 hasta
◻ I waited till 10 o'clock. Esperé hasta las 10.
■ **till now** hasta ahora
■ **till then** hasta entonces
■ **It won't be ready till next week.** No estará listo hasta la semana que viene.
2 hasta que
◻ We stayed there till the doctor came. Nos quedamos allí hasta que vino el médico.

LANGUAGE TIP **hasta que** has to be followed by a verb in the subjunctive when referring to an event in the future.

◻ Don't go till I arrive. No te vayas hasta que llegue yo. ◻ Wait till I come back. Espera hasta que yo vuelva.

time NOUN

1 la hora
□ What time is it? ¿Qué hora es? □ What time do you get up? ¿A qué hora te levantas? □ It was two o'clock, Spanish time. Eran las dos, hora española.
■ **on time** a la hora □ He never arrives on time. Nunca llega a la hora.
2 el tiempo
□ I'm sorry, I haven't got time. Lo siento, no tengo tiempo. □ We waited a long time. Esperamos mucho tiempo. □ Have you lived here for a long time? ¿Hace mucho tiempo que vives aquí?
■ **from time to time** de vez en cuando
■ **in time** a tiempo □ We arrived in time for lunch. Llegamos a tiempo para el almuerzo.
■ **just in time** justo a tiempo
3 el momento
□ This isn't a good time to ask him. Éste no es buen momento para preguntarle.
■ **for the time being** por el momento
■ **in no time** en un momento □ It was ready in no time. Estuvo listo en un momento.
4 la vez (PL las veces)
□ this time esta vez □ How many times? ¿Cuántas veces?
■ **at times** a veces
■ **two at a time** de dos en dos
■ **in a week's time** dentro de una semana
■ **Come and see us any time.** Ven a vernos cuando quieras.
■ **to have a good time** pasarlo bien □ Did you have a good time? ¿Lo pasaste bien?
■ **two times two is four** dos por dos son cuatro

time bomb NOUN
la bomba de relojería

time off NOUN
el tiempo libre

timer NOUN
el reloj automático *(of video, oven)*
■ **an egg timer** reloj de arena

time-share NOUN
■ **a time-share apartment** un apartamento en multipropiedad

timetable NOUN
1 el horario *(for train, bus, school)*
2 el programa *(schedule of events)*
LANGUAGE TIP Although **programa** ends in **-a**, it is actually a masculine noun.

time zone NOUN
el huso horario

tin NOUN
1 la lata
□ a tin of beans una lata de alubias
□ a biscuit tin una lata de galletas
2 el estaño *(metal)*

tinned ADJECTIVE
enlatado (FEM enlatada) *(food)*
□ tinned products productos enlatados
■ **tinned peaches** melocotones en lata

tin opener NOUN
el abrelatas (PL los abrelatas)

tinsel NOUN
el espumillón

tinted ADJECTIVE
ahumado (FEM ahumada) *(glasses, window)*

tiny ADJECTIVE
minúsculo (FEM minúscula)

tip NOUN
▹ *see also* **tip** VERB
1 la propina *(money)*
□ to leave a tip dejar propina
2 el consejo *(advice)*
□ a useful tip un consejo práctico
3 la punta *(end)*
□ It's on the tip of my tongue. Lo tengo en la punta de la lengua.
■ **a rubbish tip** un vertedero de basuras
■ **This place is a complete tip!** ¡Esto es una pocilga!

to **tip** VERB
▹ *see also* **tip** NOUN
dar* una propina a
□ Don't forget to tip the waiter. No te olvides de darle una propina al camarero.

tiptoe NOUN
■ **on tiptoe** de puntillas

tired ADJECTIVE
cansado (FEM cansada)
□ I'm tired. Estoy cansado.
■ **to be tired of something** estar harto de algo

tiring ADJECTIVE
cansado (FEM cansada)

tissue NOUN
el Kleenex® (PL los Kleenex)

title NOUN
el título *(of novel, film)*

title role NOUN
el papel principal

to PREPOSITION
1 a
LANGUAGE TIP **a** + **el** changes to **al**.
□ to go to school ir al colegio □ to go to the doctor's ir al médico □ Let's go to Anne's house. Vamos a casa de Anne. □ to go to Portugal ir a Portugal □ I sold it to a friend. Se lo vendí a un amigo. □ the answer to the question la respuesta a la pregunta □ the train to London el tren a Londres
■ **from...to...** de...a... □ from nine o'clock to half past three de las nueve a las tres y media

English-Spanish

t

2 de
□ It's easy to do. Es fácil de hacer.
□ something to drink algo de beber □ the key to the front door la llave de la puerta principal
■ **It's difficult to say.** Es difícil saberlo.
■ **It's easy to criticize.** Criticar es muy fácil.
■ **I've never been to Valencia.** Nunca he estado en Valencia.
■ **ten to nine** las nueve menos diez
3 hasta
□ to count to ten contar hasta diez
4 para *(in order to)*
□ I did it to help you. Lo hice para ayudarte.
□ She's too young to go to school. Es muy pequeña para ir al colegio. □ ready to go listo para irse □ ready to eat listo para comer
5 con
□ to be kind to somebody ser amable con alguien □ They were very kind to me. Fueron muy amables conmigo.
■ **Give it to her!** ¡Dáselo!
■ **That's what he said to me.** Eso fue lo que me dijo.
■ **I've got things to do.** Tengo cosas que hacer.

toad NOUN
el sapo

toadstool NOUN
la seta venenosa

toast NOUN
1 el pan tostado *(bread)*
■ **a piece of toast** una tostada
2 el brindis (PL los brindis) *(speech)*
■ **to drink a toast to somebody** brindar por alguien

toaster NOUN
la tostadora

tobacco NOUN
el tabaco

tobacconist's NOUN
el estanco (la tabaquería *Latin America*)

toboggan NOUN
el trineo

tobogganing NOUN
■ **to go tobogganing** deslizarse en trineo

today ADVERB
hoy

toddler NOUN
el niño pequeño
la niña pequeña *(que empieza a caminar)*

toe NOUN
el dedo del pie (PL los dedos de los pies)
□ The dog bit my big toe. El perro me mordió el dedo gordo del pie.

toffee NOUN
el caramelo

together ADVERB
1 juntos
□ Are they still together? ¿Todavía están juntos?
2 a la vez *(at the same time)*
□ Don't all speak together! ¡No habléis todos a la vez!
■ **together with** junto con

toilet NOUN
1 los servicios *(in public place)*
2 el wáter *(in house)*

toilet paper NOUN
el papel higiénico

toiletries PL NOUN
los artículos de perfumería

toilet roll NOUN
el rollo de papel higiénico

token NOUN
■ **a gift token** un cheque-regalo (PL los cheques-regalo)

told VERB ▷ *see* **tell**

tolerant ADJECTIVE
tolerante (FEM tolerante)

toll NOUN
el peaje *(on bridge, motorway)*

tomato NOUN
el tomate
□ tomato soup sopa de tomate

tomboy NOUN
el marimacho

tomorrow ADVERB
mañana
□ tomorrow morning mañana por la mañana □ tomorrow night mañana por la noche
■ **the day after tomorrow** pasado mañana

ton NOUN
la tonelada
□ a ton of coal una tonelada de carbón
■ **That old bike weighs a ton.** Esa bici vieja pesa una tonelada.

tongue NOUN
la lengua
■ **to say something tongue in cheek** decir algo en plan de broma

tonic NOUN
la tónica
■ **a gin and tonic** un gin-tonic

tonight ADVERB
esta noche
□ Are you going out tonight? ¿Vas a salir esta noche? □ I'll sleep well tonight. Esta noche dormiré bien.

tonsillitis NOUN
la amigdalitis
□ She's got tonsillitis. Tiene amigdalitis.

tonsils PL NOUN
las amígdalas

too ADVERB
1 también *(as well)*
□ My sister came too. Mi hermana también vino.
2 demasiado *(excessively)*
□ The water's too hot. El agua está demasiado caliente. □ We arrived too late. Llegamos demasiado tarde.
■ **too much** demasiado (FEM demasiada)
□ too much noise demasiado ruido □ too much butter demasiada mantequilla □ At Christmas we always eat too much. En Navidades siempre comemos demasiado.
□ £50? — That's too much. ¿50 libras? — Eso es demasiado.
■ **too many** demasiados (FEM demasiadas)
□ too many problems demasiados problemas □ too many chairs demasiadas sillas
■ **Too bad!** *(what a pity)* ¡Qué pena!

took VERB ▷ *see* **take**

tool NOUN
la herramienta
■ **a tool box** una caja de herramientas

tooth NOUN
el diente

toothache NOUN
el dolor de muelas
□ These pills are good for toothache. Estas pastillas son buenas para el dolor de muelas.
■ **I've got toothache.** Me duele una muela.

toothbrush NOUN
el cepillo de dientes

toothpaste NOUN
el dentífrico

top NOUN
▷ *see also* **top** ADJECTIVE
1 la parte de arriba
□ at the top of the page en la parte de arriba de la página
2 la cima *(of mountain)*
3 la tapa *(of box, jar)*
4 el tapón (PL los tapones) *(of bottle)*
■ **a bikini top** la parte de arriba del bikini
■ **the top of the table** el tablero de la mesa
■ **on top of the cupboard** encima del armario
■ **There's a surcharge on top of that.** Hay un recargo, además.
■ **from top to bottom** de arriba abajo
□ I searched the house from top to bottom. Busqué en la casa de arriba abajo.

top ADJECTIVE
▷ *see also* **top** NOUN
1 de arriba *(shelf)*
□ It's on the top shelf. Está en la estantería de arriba.
■ **the top layer of skin** la capa superior de la piel
■ **the top floor** el último piso
2 eminente (FEM eminente)
□ a top surgeon un eminente cirujano
■ **a top model** una top model
■ **a top hotel** un hotel de primera
■ **He always gets top marks in French.** Siempre saca excelentes notas en francés.
■ **at top speed** a máxima velocidad

topic NOUN
el tema
LANGUAGE TIP Although **tema** ends in **-a**, it is actually a masculine noun.
□ The essay can be on any topic. La redacción puede ser sobre cualquier tema.

topical ADJECTIVE
de actualidad
□ a topical issue un tema de actualidad

topless ADJECTIVE
topless (FEM + PL topless)
■ **to go topless** ir en topless

top-secret ADJECTIVE
de alto secreto
□ top-secret documents documentos de alto secreto

torch NOUN
la linterna *(electric)*

tore, torn VERB ▷ *see* **tear**

tortoise NOUN
la tortuga

torture NOUN
▷ *see also* **torture** VERB
la tortura
□ It was pure torture. Fué una tortura.

to **torture** VERB
▷ *see also* **torture** NOUN
torturar
□ Stop torturing that poor animal! ¡Deja de torturar al pobre animal!

Tory ADJECTIVE
▷ *see also* **Tory** NOUN
conservador (FEM conservadora)
□ the Tory government el gobierno conservador

Tory NOUN
▷ *see also* **Tory** ADJECTIVE
el conservador
la conservadora
□ the Tories los conservadores

to **toss** VERB
■ **to toss pancakes** dar la vuelta a las crepes en el aire
■ **Shall we toss for it?** ¿Nos lo jugamos a cara o cruz?

total ADJECTIVE
▷ *see also* **total** NOUN
total (FEM total)

□ The total cost was very high. El coste total fue muy alto.
■ **the total amount** el total

total NOUN
▹ *see also* **total** ADJECTIVE
el total
■ **the grand total** la suma total

totally ADVERB
totalmente

touch NOUN
▹ *see also* **touch** VERB
■ **to get in touch with somebody** ponerse en contacto con alguien
■ **to keep in touch with somebody** mantenerse en contacto con alguien
■ **Keep in touch! 1** *(write)* ¡Escribe de vez en cuando! **2** *(phone)* ¡Llama de vez en cuando!
■ **to lose touch** perder el contacto
■ **to lose touch with somebody** perder el contacto con alguien

to **touch** VERB
▹ *see also* **touch** NOUN
tocar*
□ Don't touch that! ¡No toques eso!

touchdown NOUN
el aterrizaje *(of plane)*

touched ADJECTIVE
emocionado (FEM emocionada)
□ I was really touched. Estaba muy emocionada.

touching ADJECTIVE
conmovedor (FEM conmovedora)

touchline NOUN
la línea de banda

touchy ADJECTIVE
susceptible (FEM susceptible)
□ She's a bit touchy today. Hoy está un poco susceptible.

tough ADJECTIVE
1 difícil (FEM difícil)
□ It was tough, but I managed okay. Fue difícil, pero me las arreglé.
■ **It's a tough job.** Es un trabajo duro.
2 duro (FEM dura)
□ The meat is tough. La carne está dura.
3 resistente (FEM resistente)
□ tough leather gloves guantes de cuero resistentes
■ **He thinks he's a tough guy.** Le gusta hacerse el duro.
■ **Tough luck!** ¡Mala suerte!

tour NOUN
▹ *see also* **tour** VERB
1 el recorrido turístico
□ We went on a tour of the city. Hicimos un recorrido turístico por la ciudad.
■ **a package tour** un viaje organizado
■ **a bus tour** un viaje en autobús
2 la visita *(of building, exhibition)*
3 la gira
■ **to go on tour** ir de gira

to **tour** VERB
▹ *see also* **tour** NOUN
■ **Robbie Williams is touring Europe.** Robbie Williams está haciendo una gira por Europa.

tour guide NOUN
el guía turístico
la guía turística

tourism NOUN
el turismo

tourist NOUN
el/la turista
■ **tourist information office** la oficina de información y turismo

tournament NOUN
el torneo

tour operator NOUN
el operador turístico (PL los operadores turísticos)

towards PREPOSITION
hacia
□ He came towards me. Vino hacia mí.
□ my feelings towards him mis sentimientos hacia él

towel NOUN
la toalla

tower NOUN
la torre

tower block NOUN
1 el bloque de pisos *(of flats)*
2 el bloque de oficinas *(of offices)*

town NOUN
la ciudad
□ a town plan un plano de la ciudad
□ the town centre el centro de la ciudad

town hall NOUN
el ayuntamiento

tow truck NOUN (US)
la grúa

toy NOUN
el juguete
■ **a toy shop** una juguetería
■ **a toy car** un coche de juguete

trace NOUN
▹ *see also* **trace** VERB
el rastro
□ There was no trace of the robbers. No había rastro de los ladrones.

to **trace** VERB
▹ *see also* **trace** NOUN
1 trazar* *(draw)*
2 encontrar* *(locate)*

tracing paper NOUN
el papel de calco

track NOUN
1 el camino *(dirt road)*
□ a mountain track un camino de montaña
2 la vía *(railway line)*
□ A woman fell onto the tracks. Una mujer se cayó a la vía.
3 la pista *(in sport)*
□ two laps of the track dos vueltas a la pista
4 la canción (PL las canciones) *(song)*
□ This is my favourite track. Ésta es mi canción preferida.
5 la huella *(trail)*
□ They followed the tracks for miles. Siguieron las huellas durante millas.

to **track down** VERB
encontrar*
□ The police never tracked down the killer. La policía nunca encontró al asesino.

tracksuit NOUN
el chándal (PL los chándals)

tractor NOUN
el tractor

trade NOUN
el oficio
□ to learn a trade aprender un oficio

trade union NOUN
el sindicato

trade unionist NOUN
el/la sindicalista

tradition NOUN
la tradición (PL las tradiciones)

traditional ADJECTIVE
tradicional (FEM tradicional)

traffic NOUN
el tráfico
□ There was a lot of traffic. Había mucho tráfico.

traffic circle NOUN (US)
la rotonda

traffic jam NOUN
el atasco

traffic lights PL NOUN
el semáforo

traffic warden NOUN
el/la guardia de tráfico
□ I'm a traffic warden. Soy guardia de tráfico.

tragedy NOUN
la tragedia

tragic ADJECTIVE
trágico (FEM trágica)

trailer NOUN
1 el remolque *(for luggage, boat)*
2 el tráiler (PL los tráilers) *(of film)*

train NOUN
▷ *see also* **train** VERB
el tren
□ a train set un tren eléctrico

to **train** VERB
▷ *see also* **train** NOUN
entrenar
□ to train for a race entrenar para una carrera
■ **to train as a teacher** estudiar magisterio
■ **to train an animal to do something** enseñar a un animal a hacer algo

trained ADJECTIVE
cualificado (FEM cualificada) (calificado *Latin America*)
□ highly trained workers los trabajadores altamente cualificados
■ **She's a trained nurse.** Es enfermera diplomada.

trainee NOUN
el aprendiz (PL los aprendices)
la aprendiza *(apprentice)*
□ He's a trainee plumber. Es aprendiz de fontanero.
■ **She's a trainee teacher.** Es profesora de prácticas.

trainer NOUN
1 el entrenador
la entrenadora *(sports)*
2 el amaestrador
la amaestradora *(of animals)*

trainers PL NOUN
las zapatillas de deporte

training NOUN
1 la formación
□ a training course un curso de formación
2 el entrenamiento *(in sport)*
■ **He strained a muscle in training.** Se hizo un esguince entrenando.

tram NOUN
el tranvía

LANGUAGE TIP Although **tranvía** ends in **-a**, it is actually a masculine noun.

tramp NOUN
el vagabundo
la vagabunda

trampoline NOUN
la cama elástica

tranquillizer NOUN
el sedante
□ She's on tranquillizers. Está tomando sedantes.

transfer NOUN
1 la transferencia
□ a bank transfer una transferencia bancaria
2 la calcomanía *(sticker)*

transfusion NOUN
la transfusión (PL las transfusiones)

transistor NOUN
el transistor

English-Spanish

t

to **translate** VERB
traducir*
□ to translate something into English traducir algo al inglés

translation NOUN
la traducción (PL las traducciones)

translator NOUN
el traductor
la traductora
□ Anita's a translator. Anita es traductora.

transparent ADJECTIVE
transparente (FEM transparente)

transplant NOUN
el trasplante
□ a heart transplant un trasplante de corazón

transport NOUN
▷ *see also* **transport** VERB
el transporte
□ public transport el transporte público

to **transport** VERB
▷ *see also* **transport** NOUN
transportar

trap NOUN
la trampa

trash NOUN (US)
la basura
■ **the trash can** el cubo de la basura

trashy ADJECTIVE
malísimo (FEM malísima)
□ a trashy film una película malísima

traumatic ADJECTIVE
traumático (FEM traumática)
□ It was a traumatic experience. Fue una experiencia traumática.

travel NOUN
▷ *see also* **travel** VERB
■ **Air travel is relatively cheap.** Viajar en avión es relativamente barato.

to **travel** VERB
▷ *see also* **travel** NOUN
viajar
□ I prefer to travel by train. Prefiero viajar en tren.
■ **I'd like to travel round the world.** Me gustaría dar la vuelta al mundo.
■ **We travelled over 800 kilometres.** Hicimos más de 800 kilómetros.
■ **News travels fast!** ¡Las noticias vuelan!

travel agency NOUN
la agencia de viajes

travel agent NOUN
■ **She's a travel agent.** Es empleada de una agencia de viajes.

traveller (US **traveler**) NOUN
el viajero
la viajera

traveller's cheque (US **traveler's check**) NOUN
el cheque de viaje (PL los cheques de viaje)

travelling (US **traveling**) NOUN
■ **I love travelling.** Me encanta viajar.

travel sickness NOUN
el mareo

tray NOUN
la bandeja

to **tread** VERB
pisar
■ **to tread on something** pisar algo
□ He trod on her foot. Le pisó el pie.

treasure NOUN
el tesoro

treat NOUN
▷ *see also* **treat** VERB
■ **As a birthday treat, I'll take you out to dinner.** Como es tu cumpleaños, te invito a cenar.
■ **She bought a special treat for the children.** Les compró algo especial a los niños.
■ **I'm going to give myself a treat.** Me voy a dar un gusto.

to **treat** VERB
▷ *see also* **treat** NOUN
tratar
□ The hostages were well treated. Los rehenes fueron tratados bien.
■ **She was treated for a minor head wound.** La atendieron de una leve herida en la cabeza.
■ **to treat somebody to something** invitar a alguien a algo □ I'll treat you! ¡Te invito yo!

treatment NOUN
1 el tratamiento *(medical)*
□ an effective treatment for eczema un tratamiento efectivo contra el eccema
2 el trato *(of person)*
□ We don't want any special treatment. No queremos ningún trato especial.

to **treble** VERB
triplicarse*
□ The cost of living has trebled. El coste de la vida se ha triplicado.

tree NOUN
el árbol

to **tremble** VERB
temblar*

trend NOUN
1 la tendencia
□ There's a trend towards part-time employment. Existe una tendencia hacia el empleo a tiempo parcial.
2 la moda *(fashion)*
□ the latest trend la última moda

trendy ADJECTIVE
moderno (FEM moderna)

trial NOUN
el juicio *(in law)*

triangle NOUN
el triángulo

tribe NOUN
la tribu

trick NOUN
▷ *see also* **trick** VERB
1 la broma
□ to play a trick on somebody gastar una broma a alguien
2 el truco
□ It's not easy: there's a trick to it. No es fácil: tiene un truco.

to trick VERB
▷ *see also* **trick** NOUN
■ **to trick somebody** engañar a alguien

tricky ADJECTIVE
peliagudo (FEM peliaguda) *(problem)*

tricycle NOUN
el triciclo

trifle NOUN
el bizcocho borracho

to **trim** VERB
▷ *see also* **trim** NOUN
recortar

trim NOUN
▷ *see also* **trim** VERB
■ **to have a trim** cortarse las puntas

trip NOUN
▷ *see also* **trip** VERB
el viaje
□ to go on a trip ir de viaje □ Have a good trip! ¡Buen viaje!
■ **a day trip** una excursión de un día

to trip VERB
▷ *see also* **trip** NOUN
tropezarse* *(stumble)*
□ He tripped on the stairs. Se tropezó en las escaleras.

triple ADJECTIVE
triple (FEM triple)

triplets PL NOUN
los trillizos (FEM las trillizas)

trivial ADJECTIVE
insignificante (FEM insignificante)

trod, trodden VERB ▷ *see* **tread**

trolley NOUN
el carrito

trombone NOUN
el trombón (PL los trombones)

troops PL NOUN
las tropas

trophy NOUN
el trofeo

tropical ADJECTIVE
tropical (FEM tropical)

to **trot** VERB
trotar

trouble NOUN
el problema

LANGUAGE TIP Although **problema** ends in **-a**, it is actually a masculine noun.

□ The trouble is, it's too expensive. El problema es que es demasiado caro.
■ **What's the trouble?** ¿Qué pasa?
■ **to be in trouble** tener problemas
■ **stomach trouble** problemas de estómago
■ **to take a lot of trouble over something** poner mucho cuidado en algo
■ **Don't worry, it's no trouble.** No te preocupes, no importa.

troublemaker NOUN
el alborotador
la alborotadora

trousers PL NOUN
los pantalones
□ a pair of trousers unos pantalones

trout NOUN
la trucha

truant NOUN
■ **to play truant** hacer novillos

truck NOUN
el camión (PL los camiones)

truck driver NOUN
el camionero
la camionera
□ He's a truck driver. Es camionero.

true ADJECTIVE
verdadero (FEM verdadera) *(love, courage)*
■ **It's true.** Es verdad.
■ **to come true** hacerse realidad □ I hope my dream will come true. Espero que mi sueño se haga realidad.

trumpet NOUN
la trompeta

trunk NOUN
1 el tronco *(of tree)*
2 la trompa *(of elephant)*
3 el baúl *(luggage)*
4 el maletero (US: *of car*)

trunks PL NOUN
■ **swimming trunks** el traje de baño

trust NOUN
▷ *see also* **trust** VERB
la confianza
□ to have trust in somebody tener confianza en alguien

to trust VERB
▷ *see also* **trust** NOUN
■ **Don't you trust me?** ¿No tienes confianza en mí?

■ **Trust me!** ¡Confía en mí!
■ **I don't trust him.** No me fío de él.

trusting ADJECTIVE
confiado (FEM confiada)

truth NOUN
la verdad

truthful ADJECTIVE
1 sincero (FEM sincera) *(person)*
□ She's a very truthful person. Es una persona muy sincera.
2 verídico (FEM verídica) *(account)*

try NOUN
▷ *see also* **try** VERB
el intento
□ his third try su tercer intento
■ **to give something a try** intentar algo
■ **It's worth a try.** Vale la pena intentarlo.
■ **Have a try!** ¡Inténtalo!

to **try** VERB
▷ *see also* **try** NOUN
1 intentar
□ to try to do something intentar hacer algo
■ **to try again** volver a intentar
2 probar*
□ Would you like to try some? ¿Quieres probar un poco?

to **try on** VERB
probarse* *(clothes)*

to **try out** VERB
probar* *(product, machine)*

T-shirt NOUN
la camiseta

tube NOUN
el tubo
■ **the Tube** *(underground)* el Metro

tuberculosis NOUN
la tuberculosis
□ He's got tuberculosis. Tiene tuberculosis.

Tuesday NOUN
el martes (PL los martes)
□ I saw her on Tuesday. La vi el martes.
□ every Tuesday todos los martes □ last Tuesday el martes pasado □ next Tuesday el martes que viene □ on Tuesdays los martes

tug-of-war NOUN
el juego de la cuerda

tuition NOUN
las clases
□ private tuition clases particulares

tulip NOUN
el tulipán (PL los tulipanes)

tumble dryer NOUN
la secadora

tummy NOUN
la tripa *(informal)*
■ **He has tummy ache.** Le duele la tripa.

tuna NOUN
el atún (PL los atunes)

tune NOUN
la melodía *(melody)*
■ **to play in tune** tocar bien
■ **to sing out of tune** desafinar

Tunisia NOUN
Túnez *masc*

tunnel NOUN
el túnel
□ the Channel Tunnel el túnel del Canal de la Mancha

Turk NOUN
el turco
la turca
□ the Turks los turcos

turkey NOUN
el pavo

Turkey NOUN
Turquía *fem*

Turkish ADJECTIVE
▷ *see also* **Turkish** NOUN
turco (FEM turca)

Turkish NOUN
▷ *see also* **Turkish** ADJECTIVE
el turco *(language)*

turn NOUN
▷ *see also* **turn** VERB
la curva *(bend in road)*
■ **'no left turn'** 'prohibido girar a la izquierda'
■ **to take turns** turnarse
■ **It's my turn!** ¡Me toca a mí!

to **turn** VERB
▷ *see also* **turn** NOUN
1 girar
□ Turn right at the lights. Gira a la derecha al llegar al semáforo.
2 ponerse* *(become)*
□ When he's drunk he turns nasty. Cuando se emborracha se pone desagradable.
■ **The weather turned cold.** Empezó a hacer frío.
■ **to turn into something** convertirse en algo □ The holiday turned into a nightmare. Las vacaciones se convirtieron en una pesadilla.

to **turn back** VERB
volver* hacia atrás
□ We turned back. Volvimos hacia atrás.

to **turn down** VERB
1 rechazar*
□ He turned down the offer. Rechazó la oferta.
2 bajar
□ Shall I turn the heating down? ¿Bajo la calefacción?

to **turn off** VERB
1 apagar* *(light, radio)*
2 cerrar* *(tap)*

3 parar *(engine)*

to **turn on** VERB

1 encender* *(light, radio)*

2 abrir* *(tap)*

3 poner* en marcha *(engine)*

to **turn out** VERB

resultar

□ It turned out to be a mistake. Resultó ser un error. □ It turned out that she was right. Resultó que ella tenía razón.

to **turn round** VERB

1 dar* la vuelta *(car)*

2 darse* la vuelta *(person)*

to **turn up** VERB

1 aparecer*

□ She never turned up. No apareció.

□ The lost dog turned up in the next village. El perro extraviado apareció en el pueblo vecino.

2 subir

□ Could you turn up the radio? ¿Puedes subir la radio?

turning NOUN

■ **We took the wrong turning.** **1** *(in the country)* Nos equivocamos de carretera. **2** *(in the city)* Nos equivocamos de bocacalle.

turnip NOUN

el nabo

turquoise ADJECTIVE

turquesa (FEM + PL turquesa)

turtle NOUN

la tortuga de mar

tutor NOUN

el profesor particular

la profesora particular *(private teacher)*

tuxedo NOUN (US)

el esmoquin (PL los esmóquines)

TV NOUN

la tele

tweezers PL NOUN

las pinzas

□ a pair of tweezers unas pinzas

twelfth ADJECTIVE

duodécimo (FEM duodécima)

□ the twelfth floor el duodécimo piso

■ **the twelfth of August** el doce de agosto

twelve NUMERAL

doce

□ She's twelve. Tiene doce años.

■ **twelve o'clock** las doce

twentieth ADJECTIVE

vigésimo (FEM vigésima)

■ **the twentieth floor** la planta veinte

■ **the twentieth of May** el veinte de mayo

twenty NUMERAL

veinte

□ He's twenty. Tiene veinte años.

twice ADVERB

dos veces

□ He had to repeat it twice. Tuvo que repetirlo dos veces.

■ **twice as much** el doble □ He gets twice as much pocket money as me. Le dan el doble de paga que a mí.

twin NOUN

el mellizo

la melliza

□ my twin brother mi hermano mellizo

□ her twin sister su hermana melliza

■ **identical twins** gemelos

■ **a twin room** una habitación con dos camas

twinned ADJECTIVE

hermanado (FEM hermanada)

□ Nottingham is twinned with Minsk. Nottingham está hermanada con Minsk.

to **twist** VERB

1 torcer*

■ **He's twisted his ankle.** Se ha torcido el tobillo.

2 tergiversar*

□ You're twisting my words. Estás tergiversando lo que he dicho.

twit NOUN

el/la imbécil *(informal)*

two NUMERAL

dos

□ She's two. Tiene dos años.

■ **The two of them can sing.** Los dos saben cantar.

type NOUN

▷ *see also* **type** VERB

el tipo

□ What type of camera have you got? ¿Qué tipo de cámara tienes?

to **type** VERB

▷ *see also* **type** NOUN

escribir* a máquina

□ Can you type? ¿Sabes escribir a máquina?

□ to type a letter escribir una carta a máquina

typewriter NOUN

la máquina de escribir

typical ADJECTIVE

típico (FEM típica)

□ That's just typical! ¡Típico!

tyre (US **tire**) NOUN

el neumático

■ **tyre pressure** la presión de los neumáticos

Uu

UFO ABBREVIATION *(= Unidentified Flying Object)*
el OVNI *(= el Objeto Volador No Identificado)*

ugh EXCLAMATION
¡puf!

ugly ADJECTIVE
feo (FEM fea)

UK ABBREVIATION *(= United Kingdom)*
el RU *(= el Reino Unido)*

ulcer NOUN
la úlcera
■ **a mouth ulcer** una llaga en la boca

Ulster NOUN
el Ulster

ultimate ADJECTIVE
máximo (FEM máxima)
□ the ultimate challenge el máximo desafío
■ **the ultimate in luxury** el no va más del lujo

ultimately ADVERB
a fin de cuentas
□ Ultimately, it's your decision. A fin de cuentas, es tu decisión.

umbrella NOUN
el paraguas (PL los paraguas)

umpire NOUN
el árbitro
la árbitra

UN ABBREVIATION *(= United Nations)*
la ONU *(= la Organización de las Naciones Unidas)*

unable ADJECTIVE
■ **to be unable to do something** no poder hacer algo □ He was unable to come. No ha podido venir.

unacceptable ADJECTIVE
inaceptable (FEM inaceptable)

unanimous ADJECTIVE
unánime (FEM unánime)

unattended ADJECTIVE
■ **Please do not leave your luggage unattended.** Por favor, no abandonen su equipaje.

unavoidable ADJECTIVE
inevitable (FEM inevitable)

unaware ADJECTIVE
■ **I was unaware of the regulations.** Ignoraba el reglamento.
■ **She was unaware that she was being filmed.** No se había dado cuenta de que la estaban filmando.

unbearable ADJECTIVE
insoportable (FEM insoportable)

unbeatable ADJECTIVE
inmejorable (FEM inmejorable) *(quality, price)*

unbelievable ADJECTIVE
increíble (FEM increíble)

unborn ADJECTIVE
■ **the unborn child** el feto

unbreakable ADJECTIVE
irrompible (FEM irrompible)

uncanny ADJECTIVE
extraño (FEM extraña)
□ That's uncanny! ¡Es extraño!
■ **an uncanny resemblance** un asombroso parecido

uncertain ADJECTIVE
incierto (FEM incierta)
□ The future is uncertain. El futuro es incierto.
■ **to be uncertain about something** no estar seguro de algo
■ **She was uncertain how to begin.** No sabía muy bien cómo empezar.

uncivilized ADJECTIVE
poco civilizado (FEM poco civilizada)

uncle NOUN
el tío
■ **my uncle and aunt** mis tíos

uncomfortable ADJECTIVE
incómodo (FEM incómoda)

unconscious ADJECTIVE
inconsciente (FEM inconsciente)

unconventional ADJECTIVE
poco convencional (FEM poco convencional)

under PREPOSITION

LANGUAGE TIP When something is located under something, use **debajo de**. When there is movement involved, use **por debajo de**.

1 debajo de
□ The cat's under the table. El gato está debajo de la mesa. □ The tunnel goes under

the Channel. El túnel pasa por debajo del Canal.
■ **under there** ahí debajo □ What's under there? ¿Qué hay ahí debajo?
2 menos de
□ under 20 people menos de 20 personas
■ **children under 10** niños menores de 10 años

underage ADJECTIVE
■ **He's underage.** Es menor de edad.

undercover ADJECTIVE, ADVERB
secreto (FEM secreta)
□ an undercover agent un agente secreto
□ She was working undercover for the FBI. Trabajaba como agente secreto para el FBI.

to **underestimate** VERB
subestimar
□ You shouldn't underestimate her. No la subestimes.

to **undergo** VERB
someterse a *(operation)*

underground ADVERB
▷ *see also* **underground** NOUN
bajo tierra
□ Moles live underground. Los topos viven bajo tierra.

underground NOUN
▷ *see also* **underground** ADVERB
el metro
□ Is there an underground in Barcelona? ¿Hay metro en Barcelona?

to **underline** VERB
subrayar

underneath PREPOSITION, ADVERB
LANGUAGE TIP When something is located underneath something, use **debajo de**. When there is movement involved, use **por debajo de**.
1 debajo de
□ underneath the carpet debajo de la moqueta □ I got out of the car and looked underneath. Bajé del coche y miré debajo.
2 por debajo de
□ I walked underneath a ladder. Pasé por debajo de una escalera.

underpaid ADJECTIVE
mal pagado (FEM mal pagada)
□ Teachers are underpaid. Los profesores están mal pagados.

underpants PL NOUN
los calzoncillos
□ a pair of underpants unos calzoncillos

underpass NOUN
el paso subterráneo

undershirt NOUN (US)
la camiseta

underskirt NOUN
las enaguas

to **understand** VERB
entender*
□ Do you understand? ¿Entiendes? □ I don't understand the question. No entiendo la pregunta.
■ **Is that understood?** ¿Está claro?

understanding ADJECTIVE
comprensivo (FEM comprensiva)
□ She's very understanding. Es muy comprensiva.

understood VERB ▷ *see* **understand**

undertaker NOUN
el empleado de una funeraria
la empleada de una funeraria
■ **the undertaker's** la funeraria

underwater ADJECTIVE, ADVERB
1 subacuático (FEM subacuática)
□ underwater photography fotografía subacuática
2 bajo el agua
□ This sequence was filmed underwater. Esta secuencia se filmó bajo el agua.

underwear NOUN
la ropa interior

underwent VERB ▷ *see* **undergo**

to **undo** VERB
1 desabrochar *(button, blouse)*
2 desatar *(knot, parcel, shoe laces)*
3 abrir* *(zipper)*

to **undress** VERB
desnudarse *(get undressed)*
□ The doctor told me to undress. El médico me dijo que me desnudase.

uneconomic ADJECTIVE
■ **an uneconomic factory** una fábrica poco rentable
■ **It's uneconomic to put on courses for so few students.** No es rentable organizar cursos para tan pocos alumnos.

unemployed ADJECTIVE
parado (FEM parada) (desempleado *Latin America*)
■ **He's been unemployed for a year.** Lleva parado un año.
■ **the unemployed** los parados (los desempleados *Latin America*)

unemployment NOUN
el desempleo

unexpected ADJECTIVE
inesperado (FEM inesperada)
□ an unexpected visitor una visita inesperada

unexpectedly ADVERB
de improviso

unfair ADJECTIVE
injusto (FEM injusta)
□ This law is unfair to women. Esta ley es injusta para las mujeres.

unfamiliar ADJECTIVE
desconocido (FEM desconocida)
□ I heard an unfamiliar voice. Oí una voz desconocida.

unfashionable ADJECTIVE
pasado de moda (FEM pasado de moda)

unfit ADJECTIVE
■ **I'm unfit at the moment.** En este momento no estoy en forma.

to **unfold** VERB
desplegar*
□ She unfolded the map. Desplegó el mapa.

unforgettable ADJECTIVE
inolvidable (FEM inolvidable)

unfortunately ADVERB
desafortunadamente

unfriendly ADJECTIVE
antipático (FEM antipática)
□ The waiters are a bit unfriendly. Los camareros son un poco antipáticos.

ungrateful ADJECTIVE
desagradecido (FEM desagradecida)

unhappy ADJECTIVE
infeliz (FEM infeliz, PL infelices)
□ He was very unhappy as a child. De niño fue muy infeliz.
■ **to look unhappy** parecer triste

unhealthy ADJECTIVE
1 malo para la salud (FEM mala para la salud) *(food)*
2 con mala salud *(ill)*
3 malsano (FEM malsana) *(atmosphere)*

uniform NOUN
el uniforme
■ **school uniform** el uniforme de colegio

uninhabited ADJECTIVE
1 deshabitado (FEM deshabitada) *(house)*
2 despoblado (FEM despoblada) *(island)*

union NOUN
el sindicato *(trade union)*

Union Jack NOUN
la bandera del Reino Unido

unique ADJECTIVE
único (FEM única)

unit NOUN
la unidad
□ a unit of measurement una unidad de medida
■ **a kitchen unit** un módulo de cocina

United Kingdom NOUN
el Reino Unido

United Nations NOUN
las Naciones Unidas

United States NOUN
los Estados Unidos

universe NOUN
el universo

university NOUN
la universidad
□ She's at university. Está en la universidad.
□ Do you want to go to university? ¿Quieres ir a la universidad? □ Lancaster University la Universidad de Lancaster

unleaded petrol NOUN
la gasolina sin plomo

unless CONJUNCTION
a no ser que
LANGUAGE TIP **a no ser que** has to be followed by a verb in the subjunctive.
□ I won't come unless you phone me. No vendré a no ser que me llames.
■ **Unless I am mistaken, we're lost.** Si no me equivoco, estamos perdidos.

unlike PREPOSITION
a diferencia de
□ Unlike him, I really enjoy flying. A diferencia de él, a mí me encanta viajar en avión.

unlikely ADJECTIVE
poco probable (FEM poco probable)
□ That's possible, but unlikely. Es posible pero poco probable.
LANGUAGE TIP **es poco probable que** has to be followed by a verb in the subjunctive.
□ He's unlikely to come. Es poco probable que venga.

unlisted ADJECTIVE (US)
■ **an unlisted number** un número que no figura en la guía telefónica

to **unload** VERB
descargar*
□ We unloaded the furniture. Descargamos los muebles.

to **unlock** VERB
abrir*
□ He unlocked the door of the car. Abrió la puerta del coche.

unlucky ADJECTIVE
■ **to be unlucky** **1** *(be unfortunate)* tener mala suerte □ Did you win? — No, I was unlucky. ¿Ganaste? — No, tuve mala suerte.
2 *(bring bad luck)* traer mala suerte □ They say thirteen is an unlucky number. Dicen que el número trece trae mala suerte.

unmarried ADJECTIVE
soltero (FEM soltera)
□ an unmarried mother una madre soltera
■ **an unmarried couple** una pareja no casada

unnatural ADJECTIVE
poco natural (FEM poco natural)

unnecessary ADJECTIVE
innecesario (FEM innecesaria)

unofficial ADJECTIVE
no oficial (FEM no oficial)

to **unpack** VERB
deshacer*
□ I unpacked my suitcase. Deshice la maleta. □ I took my case to my room to unpack. Llevé mi maleta a mi habitación para deshacerla.
■ **I haven't unpacked my clothes yet.** Todavía no he sacado la ropa de la maleta.

unpleasant ADJECTIVE
desagradable (FEM desagradable)

to **unplug** VERB
desenchufar

unpopular ADJECTIVE
impopular (FEM impopulara)
□ It was an unpopular decision. Fue una decisión impopular.
■ **She's an unpopular child.** Tiene muy pocos amigos.

unpredictable ADJECTIVE
imprevisible (FEM imprevisible)

unreal ADJECTIVE
increíble (FEM increíble)
□ It was unreal! ¡Fue increíble!

unrealistic ADJECTIVE
poco realista (FEM poco realista)

unreasonable ADJECTIVE
poco razonable (FEM poco razonable)
□ I think her attitude is unreasonable. Creo que su actitud es poco razonable.

unreliable ADJECTIVE
poco fiable (FEM poco fiable)
□ The car was slow and unreliable. El coche era lento y poco fiable.
■ **He's completely unreliable.** Es muy informal.

to **unroll** VERB
desenrollar

unsatisfactory ADJECTIVE
insatisfactorio (FEM insatisfactoria)

to **unscrew** VERB
1 destornillar *(screw)*
2 desenroscar* *(lid)*

unshaven ADJECTIVE
sin afeitar

unskilled ADJECTIVE
■ **an unskilled worker** un trabajador no cualificado (un trabajador no calificado *Latin America*)

unstable ADJECTIVE
inestable (FEM inestable)

unsteady ADJECTIVE
1 inestable (FEM inestable) *(chair)*
2 vacilante (FEM vacilante) *(walk, voice)*
■ **He was unsteady on his feet.** Caminaba con paso vacilante.

unsuccessful ADJECTIVE
fallido (FEM fallida) *(attempt)*
■ **to be unsuccessful in doing something** no conseguir hacer algo
■ **an unsuccessful artist** un artista sin éxito

unsuitable ADJECTIVE
inapropiado (FEM inapropiada) *(clothes, equipment)*

untidy ADJECTIVE
1 desordenado (FEM desordenada) *(disorganized)*
□ Your bedroom is really untidy. Tu cuarto está muy desordenado.
2 descuidado (FEM descuidada) *(writing)*
■ **She always looks so untidy.** Siempre va tan desaliñada.

to **untie** VERB
1 deshacer* *(knot, parcel)*
2 desatar *(shoelace, animal)*

until PREPOSITION, CONJUNCTION
1 hasta
□ I waited until 10 o'clock. Esperé hasta las 10. □ It won't be ready until next week. No estará listo hasta la semana que viene.
■ **until now** hasta ahora □ It's never been a problem until now. Hasta ahora nunca ha sido un problema.
■ **until then** hasta entonces □ Until then I'd never been to Italy. Hasta entonces no había estado nunca en Italia.
2 hasta que
□ We stayed there until the doctor came. Nos quedamos allí hasta que vino el médico.
LANGUAGE TIP **hasta que** has to be followed by a verb in the subjunctive when referring to a future event.
□ Don't go until I arrive. No te vayas hasta que llegue yo. □ Wait until I come back. Espera hasta que yo vuelva.

unusual ADJECTIVE
1 poco común (FEM poco común)
□ an unusual shape una forma poco común
2 raro (FEM rara)
LANGUAGE TIP **es raro que** has to be followed by a verb in the subjunctive.
□ It's unusual to get snow at this time of year. Es raro que nieve en esta época del año.

unwilling ADJECTIVE
■ **He was unwilling to help me.** No estaba dispuesto a ayudarme.

to **unwind** VERB
relajarse *(relax)*

unwise ADJECTIVE
imprudente (FEM imprudente)
□ That was unwise of you. Lo que hiciste fue imprudente.

unwound VERB ▷ *see* **unwind**

to **unwrap** VERB
abrir*

English-Spanish

U

□ After the meal we unwrapped the presents. Después de comer abrimos los regalos.

up PREPOSITION, ADVERB

LANGUAGE TIP For other expressions with 'up', see the verbs 'come', 'put', 'turn' etc.

arriba

□ up on the hill arriba de la colina □ up here aquí arriba □ up there allí arriba

■ **up north** en el norte

■ **They live up the road.** Viven en esta calle, un poco más allá.

■ **to be up** estar levantado □ We were up at six. A las seis estábamos levantados. □ He's not up yet. Todavía no se ha levantado.

■ **What's up?** ¿Qué hay?

■ **What's up with her?** ¿Qué le pasa?

■ **to go up** subir □ The bus went up the hill. El autobús subió la colina.

■ **to go up to somebody** acercarse a alguien □ She came up to me. Se me acercó.

■ **up to** hasta □ to count up to 50 contar hasta 50 □ up to three hours hasta tres horas □ up to now hasta ahora

■ **It's up to you.** Depende de ti.

upbringing NOUN

la educación

uphill ADJECTIVE

■ **It was an uphill struggle.** Fue una tarea muy difícil.

upper ADJECTIVE

superior (FEM superior)

upright ADJECTIVE

■ **to stand upright** tenerse derecho

upset NOUN

▷ *see also* **upset** ADJECTIVE, VERB

■ **I had a stomach upset.** Tenía mal el estómago.

upset ADJECTIVE

▷ *see also* **upset** NOUN, VERB

disgustado (FEM disgustada)

□ She's still a bit upset. Todavía está un poco disgustada.

■ **Don't get upset.** No te enfades.

■ **I had an upset stomach.** Tenía mal el estómago.

to **upset** VERB

▷ *see also* **upset** NOUN, ADJECTIVE

■ **to upset somebody** disgustar a alguien

■ **Don't upset yourself.** No te enfades.

upside down ADVERB

al revés

□ The painting was hung upside down. El cuadro estaba colgado al revés.

upstairs ADVERB

arriba

□ Where's your coat? — It's upstairs. ¿Dónde está tu abrigo? — Está arriba.

■ **the people upstairs** los de arriba

■ **He went upstairs to bed.** Subió para irse a la cama.

uptight ADJECTIVE

tenso (FEM tensa)

□ She's very uptight today. Está muy tensa hoy.

up-to-date ADJECTIVE

1 moderno (FEM moderna) *(car, stereo)*

2 actualizado (FEM actualizada)

□ an up-to-date timetable un horario actualizado

■ **to bring somebody up-to-date on something** poner a alguien al corriente de algo

■ **to bring something up-to-date** actualizar algo

upwards ADVERB

hacia arriba

□ to look upwards mirar hacia arriba

urgent ADJECTIVE

urgente (FEM urgente)

urine NOUN

la orina

US ABBREVIATION *(= United States)*

los EEUU *(= los Estados Unidos)*

us PRONOUN

1 nos

LANGUAGE TIP Use **nos** to translate 'us' when it is the direct object of the verb in the sentence, or when it means 'to us'.

□ They helped us. Nos ayudaron. □ Look at us! ¡Míranos! □ They gave us some brochures. Nos dieron unos folletos.

2 nosotros (FEM nosotras)

LANGUAGE TIP Use **nosotros** or **nosotras** after prepositions, in comparisons, and with the verb 'to be'.

□ Why don't you come with us? ¿Por qué no vienes con nosotras? □ They are older than us. Son mayores que nosotros. □ It's us. Somos nosotros.

USA ABBREVIATION *(= United States of America)*

los EEUU *(= los Estados Unidos)*

use NOUN

▷ *see also* **use** VERB

el uso

■ **'directions for use'** 'modo de empleo'

■ **It's no use shouting, she's deaf.** Es inútil gritar, es sorda.

■ **It's no use, I can't do it.** No hay manera, no puedo hacerlo.

■ **to make use of something** usar algo

to **use** VERB

▷ *see also* **use** NOUN

usar

□ Can I use your phone? ¿Puedo usar tu teléfono?

■ **I used to go camping as a child.** De pequeño solía ir de acampada.

■ **I didn't use to like maths, but now I love it.** Antes no me gustaban las matemáticas, pero ahora me encantan.

■ **to be used to something** estar acostumbrado a algo □ He wasn't used to driving on the right. No estaba acostumbrado a conducir por la derecha. □ Don't worry, I'm used to it. No te preocupes, estoy acostumbrado.

■ **a used car** un coche de segunda mano

to **use up** VERB

■ **We've used up all the paint.** Hemos acabado toda la pintura.

useful ADJECTIVE

útil (FEM útil)

useless ADJECTIVE

inútil (FEM inútil)

□ a piece of useless information una información inútil

■ **You're useless!** ¡Eres un inútil!

■ **This computer is useless.** Este ordenador no sirve para nada.

■ **It's useless asking her.** No sirve de nada preguntarle.

user NOUN

el usuario

la usuaria

user-friendly ADJECTIVE

fácil de usar (FEM fácil de usar)

usual ADJECTIVE

habitual (FEM habitual)

■ **as usual** como de costumbre

usually ADVERB

normalmente

□ I usually get to school at about half past eight. Normalmente llego al colegio sobre las ocho y media.

U-turn NOUN

el cambio de sentido

■ **to do a U-turn** cambiar de sentido

■ **'No U-turns'** 'Prohibido cambiar de sentido'

Vv

vacancy NOUN
1 la vacante *(job)*
2 la habitación libre *(in hotel)*
■ **'no vacancies'** 'completo'

vacant ADJECTIVE
libre (FEM libre)
□ a vacant seat un asiento libre

vacation NOUN (US)
las vacaciones
□ to be on vacation estar de vacaciones
□ to take a vacation tomarse unas vacaciones

to **vaccinate** VERB
vacunar

to **vacuum** VERB
pasar la aspiradora
□ to vacuum the hall pasar la aspiradora por el vestíbulo

vacuum cleaner NOUN
la aspiradora

vagina NOUN
la vagina

vague ADJECTIVE
1 vago (FEM vaga)
□ I've only got a vague idea what he means. Tengo sólo una vaga idea de lo que quiere decir.
2 distraído (FEM distraída)
□ He's getting a bit vague in his old age. Se está poniendo un poco distraído en su vejez.

vain ADJECTIVE
vanidoso (FEM vanidosa)
□ He's so vain! ¡Es más vanidoso!
■ **in vain** en vano

Valentine card NOUN
la tarjeta del día de los enamorados

Valentine's Day NOUN
el día de los enamorados *(el 14 de febrero, día de San Valentín)*

valid ADJECTIVE
válido (FEM válida)
□ a valid passport un pasaporte válido
■ **This ticket is valid for three months.** Este billete tiene una validez de tres meses.

valley NOUN
el valle

valuable ADJECTIVE
1 de valor
□ a valuable painting un cuadro de valor
2 valioso (FEM valiosa)
□ valuable help una valiosa ayuda

valuables PL NOUN
los objetos de valor

value NOUN
el valor

van NOUN
la furgoneta

vandal NOUN
el vándalo

vandalism NOUN
el vandalismo

to **vandalize** VERB
destrozar*

vanilla NOUN
la vainilla
□ a vanilla ice cream un helado de vainilla

to **vanish** VERB
desaparecer*
■ **to vanish into thin air** esfumarse

variable ADJECTIVE
variable (FEM variable)

variety NOUN
la variedad

various ADJECTIVE
varios (FEM variosa)
□ We visited various villages in the area. Visitamos varias aldeas de la zona.

to **vary** VERB
variar*

vase NOUN
el jarrón (PL los jarrones)

VAT NOUN
el IVA

LANGUAGE TIP Although **IVA** ends in **-A**, it is actually a masculine noun.

VCR NOUN *(= video cassette recorder)*
el vídeo *(aparato)*

veal NOUN
la carne de ternera

vegan NOUN
el vegetariano estricto
la vegetariana estricta

vegetable NOUN
1 la verdura *(to be cooked)*
□ vegetable soup sopa de verduras
2 la hortaliza *(for salads)*
□ peppers, tomatoes and other vegetables pimientos, tomates y otras hortalizas

vegetarian NOUN
▷ *see also* **vegetarian** ADJECTIVE
el vegetariano
la vegetariana
□ I'm a vegetarian. Soy vegetariano.

vegetarian ADJECTIVE
▷ *see also* **vegetarian** NOUN
■ **vegetarian lasagne** lasaña vegetariana

vehicle NOUN
vehículo

vein NOUN
la vena

velvet NOUN
el terciopelo

vending machine NOUN
la máquina expendedora

Venetian blind NOUN
la persiana

verb NOUN
el verbo

verdict NOUN
el veredicto

vertical ADJECTIVE
vertical (FEM vertical)

vertigo NOUN
el vértigo
□ I get vertigo. Tengo vértigo.

very ADVERB
▷ *see also* **very** ADJECTIVE
muy
□ very tall muy alto
■ **It's very cold.** Hace mucho frío.
■ **not very interesting** no demasiado interesante
■ **very much** muchísimo
■ **We were thinking the very same thing.** Estábamos pensando exactamente lo mismo.

very ADJECTIVE
▷ *see also* **very** ADVERBIO
mismo (FEM misma)
□ in this very house en esta misma casa
□ That's the very book I was talking about. Ese es justamente el libro del que hablaba.
■ **The very idea!** ¡Cómo se te ocurre!

vest NOUN
1 la camiseta *(underclothing)*
2 el chaleco (US: *waistcoat)*

vet NOUN
el veterinario
la veterinaria
□ She's a vet. Es veterinaria.

via PREPOSITION
1 por
□ We drove to Lisbon via Salamanca. Fuimos a Lisboa por Salamanca.
2 vía
□ a flight via Brussels un vuelo vía Bruselas

vicar NOUN
el párroco

vice NOUN
el tornillo de banco *(tool)*

vice versa ADVERB
viceversa

vicious ADJECTIVE
1 brutal (FEM brutal)
□ a vicious attack una brutal agresión
2 feroz (FEM feroz)
□ a vicious dog un perro feroz
■ **He was a vicious man.** Era un hombre despiadado.
■ **a vicious circle** un círculo vicioso

victim NOUN
la víctima
□ He was the victim of a mugging. Fue víctima de un atraco.

victory NOUN
la victoria

to **video** VERB
▷ *see also* **video** NOUN
grabar en vídeo (grabar en video *Latin America*)
□ They videoed the whole wedding. Grabaron en vídeo toda la boda.

video NOUN
▷ *see also* **video** VERB
el vídeo (el video *Latin America*)
□ to watch a video ver un vídeo
■ **a video camera** una videocámara
■ **a video game** un videojuego
■ **a video shop** un videoclub

videophone NOUN
el videoteléfono

view NOUN
1 la vista
□ There's an amazing view. La vista es magnífica.
2 la opinión (PL las opiniones)
□ in my view en mi opinión

viewer NOUN
el telespectador
la telespectadora

viewpoint NOUN
el punto de vista

vile ADJECTIVE
repugnante (FEM repugnante)

villa NOUN
el chalet

village NOUN
1 el pueblo *(large)*

2 la aldea *(small)*

villain NOUN
1 el/la maleante *(criminal)*
2 el malo
la mala *(in film)*

vine NOUN
1 la vid *(trailing)*
2 la parra *(climbing)*

vinegar NOUN
el vinagre

vineyard NOUN
el viñedo

viola NOUN
la viola

violence NOUN
la violencia

violent ADJECTIVE
violento (FEM violenta)

violin NOUN
el violín (PL los violines)

violinist NOUN
el/la violinista

virgin NOUN
la virgen (PL las vírgenes)
□ to be a virgin ser virgen

Virgo NOUN
el Virgo *(sign)*
■ **I'm Virgo.** Soy virgo.

virtual reality NOUN
la realidad virtual

virus NOUN
el virus (PL los virus) *(also computing)*

visa NOUN
el visado (la visa *Latin America*)

visible ADJECTIVE
visible (FEM visible)

visit NOUN
▷ *see also* **visit** VERB
la visita
□ my last visit to my grandmother la última visita que le hice a mi abuela
■ **I saw him on my latest visit to Spain.** Lo vi la última vez que estuve en España.

to **visit** VERB
▷ *see also* **visit** NOUN
visitar

visitor NOUN
1 el/la visitante *(tourist)*
2 la visita *(guest)*
□ to have a visitor tener visita

visual ADJECTIVE
visual (FEM visual)

vital ADJECTIVE
vital (FEM vital)

vitamin NOUN
la vitamina

vivid ADJECTIVE
vivo (FEM viva)
□ vivid colours colores vivos
■ **to have a vivid imagination** tener una imaginación desbordante

vocabulary NOUN
el vocabulario

vocational ADJECTIVE
■ **a vocational course** un curso de formación profesional

vodka NOUN
el vodka

LANGUAGE TIP Although **vodka** ends in **-a**, it is actually a masculine noun.

voice NOUN
la voz (PL las voces)

voicemail NOUN
el buzón de voz

volcano NOUN
el volcán (PL los volcanes)

volleyball NOUN
el voleibol

volt NOUN
el voltio

voltage NOUN
el voltaje

voluntary ADJECTIVE
voluntario (FEM voluntaria)
■ **to do voluntary work** hacer voluntariado

volunteer NOUN
▷ *see also* **volunteer** VERB
el voluntario
la voluntaria

to **volunteer** VERB
▷ *see also* **volunteer** NOUN
■ **to volunteer to do something** ofrecerse a hacer algo

to **vomit** VERB
vomitar

to **vote** VERB
▷ *see also* **vote** NOUN
votar
□ Who did you vote for? ¿A quién votaste?

vote NOUN
▷ *see also* **vote** VERBO
el voto

voucher NOUN
el vale
□ a gift voucher un vale de regalo

vowel NOUN
la vocal

vulgar ADJECTIVE
vulgar (FEM vulgar)

Ww

wafer NOUN
el barquillo

wage NOUN
la paga
□ He collected his wages. Recogió la paga.

waist NOUN
la cintura

waistcoat NOUN
el chaleco

to **wait** VERB
esperar
□ I'll wait for you. Te esperaré. □ Wait a minute! ¡Espera un momento!
■ **to keep somebody waiting** hacer esperar a alguien □ They kept us waiting for hours. Nos hicieron esperar durante horas.
■ **I can't wait for the holidays.** Estoy deseando que lleguen las vacaciones.
■ **I can't wait to see him again.** Me muero de ganas de verlo otra vez.

to **wait up** VERB
esperar levantado
□ My mum always waits up till I get in. Mi madre siempre espera levantada hasta que llego.

waiter NOUN
el camarero

waiting list NOUN
la lista de espera

waiting room NOUN
la sala de espera

waitress NOUN
la camarera

to **wake up** VERB
despertarse*
□ I woke up at six o'clock. Me desperté a las seis.
■ **to wake somebody up** despertar a alguien □ Please would you wake me up at seven o'clock? ¿Podría despertarme a las siete, por favor?

Wales NOUN
Gales *masc*
■ **the Prince of Wales** el Príncipe de Gales
■ **I'm from Wales.** Soy de Gales.

to **walk** VERB
▷ *see also* **walk** NOUN
1 andar*
□ Don't walk so fast! ¡No andes tan deprisa!
□ We walked 10 kilometres. Anduvimos 10 kilómetros.
2 ir* a pie *(go on foot)*
□ Are you walking or going by bus? ¿Vas a ir a pie o en autobús?
3 pasear *(for fun)*
□ I like walking through the park. Me gusta pasear por el parque.
■ **to walk the dog** pasear al perro

walk NOUN
▷ *see also* **walk** VERB
el paseo
■ **to go for a walk** ir a pasear
■ **It's 10 minutes' walk from here.** Está a 10 minutos de aquí a pie.

walkie-talkie NOUN
el walkie-talkie

walking NOUN
el senderismo
□ I did some walking in the Alps last summer. El verano pasado hice senderismo por los Alpes.
■ **Walking is good for your health.** Andar es bueno para la salud.

walking stick NOUN
el bastón (PL los bastones)

Walkman® NOUN
el walkman®

wall NOUN
1 la pared *(of room, building)*
2 el muro *(freestanding)*
3 la muralla *(of castle, city)*

wallet NOUN
la cartera

wallpaper NOUN
el papel pintado

walnut NOUN
la nuez (PL las nueces)

to **want** VERB
querer*
□ Do you want some cake? ¿Quieres un poco de pastel?
■ **to want to do something** querer hacer

algo □ What do you want to do tomorrow? ¿Qué quieres hacer mañana?

LANGUAGE TIP **querer que** has to be followed by a verb in the subjunctive.

■ **to want somebody to do something** querer que alguien haga algo □ They want us to wait here. Quieren que esperemos aquí.

war NOUN
la guerra
■ **to be at war** estar en guerra
■ **a war memorial** un monumento a los caídos

ward NOUN
la sala *(de un hospital)*

warden NOUN
el encargado
la encargada *(of youth hostel)*

wardrobe NOUN
el armario

warehouse NOUN
el almacén (PL los almacenes)

warm ADJECTIVE
1 caliente (FEM caliente)
□ warm water agua caliente
2 caluroso (FEM calurosa)
□ a warm day un día caluroso □ a warm welcome una calurosa bienvenida
■ **warm clothing** ropa de abrigo
■ **This jumper is very warm.** Este jersey es muy calentito.
■ **He's a very warm person.** Es una persona muy afectuosa.
■ **It's warm in here.** Aquí dentro hace calor.
■ **I'm too warm.** Tengo demasiado calor.

to **warn** VERB
advertir*
□ Well, I warned you! ¡Ya te lo había advertido!

LANGUAGE TIP Use the subjunctive after **aconsejar a alguien que**.

■ **to warn somebody to do something** aconsejar a alguien que haga algo

warning NOUN
la advertencia

Warsaw NOUN
Varsovia *fem*

wart NOUN
la verruga

was VERB ▷ *see* **be**

wash NOUN
▷ *see also* **wash** VERB
■ **to have a wash** lavarse
■ **to give something a wash** lavar algo
■ **The car needs a wash.** Al coche le hace falta un lavado.

to **wash** VERB
▷ *see also* **wash** NOUN
1 lavar
□ to wash the car lavar el coche
2 lavarse *(have a wash)*
□ Every morning I get up, wash and get dressed. Todas las mañanas me levanto, me lavo y me visto.
■ **to wash one's hands** lavarse las manos
■ **to wash up** lavar los platos

washbasin NOUN
el lavabo

washcloth NOUN (US)
la toallita para lavarse

washing NOUN
la ropa lavada *(clean laundry)*
■ **to do the washing** lavar la ropa
■ **dirty washing** la ropa para lavar
■ **Have you got any washing?** ¿Tienes ropa para lavar?

washing machine NOUN
la lavadora

washing powder NOUN
el detergente

washing-up NOUN
■ **to do the washing-up** lavar los platos

washing-up liquid NOUN
el lavavajillas (PL los lavavajillas)

wasn't = **was not**

wasp NOUN
la avispa

waste NOUN
▷ *see also* **waste** VERB
1 el desperdicio
□ It's such a waste! ¡Qué desperdicio!
■ **It's a waste of time.** Es una pérdida de tiempo.
2 los residuos *pl*
□ nuclear waste residuos radioactivos

to **waste** VERB
▷ *see also* **waste** NOUN
desperdiciar *(food, space, opportunity)*
■ **to waste time** perder el tiempo
□ There's no time to waste. No hay tiempo que perder.
■ **I don't like wasting money.** No me gusta malgastar el dinero.

wastepaper basket NOUN
la papelera

watch NOUN
▷ *see also* **watch** VERB
el reloj

to **watch** VERB
▷ *see also* **watch** NOUN
1 mirar
■ **Watch me!** ¡Mírame!
2 ver*
□ to watch TV ver la tele
3 vigilar

□ The police were watching the house. La policía vigilaba la casa.

to **watch out** VERB
tener* cuidado
■ **Watch out!** ¡Cuidado!

water NOUN
▷ *see also* **water** VERB
el agua *fem*
LANGUAGE TIP Although it's a feminine noun, remember that you use **el** with **agua**.

to **water** VERB
▷ *see also* **water** NOUN
regar*
□ He was watering his tulips. Estaba regando los tulipanes.

waterfall NOUN
la cascada

watering can NOUN
la regadera

watermelon NOUN
la sandía

waterproof ADJECTIVE
impermeable (FEM impermeable)
■ **a waterproof watch** un reloj sumergible

water-skiing NOUN
el esquí acuático
□ to go water-skiing hacer esquí acuático

wave NOUN
▷ *see also* **wave** VERB
la ola

to **wave** VERB
▷ *see also* **wave** NOUN
■ **to wave to somebody 1** *(say hello)* saludar a alguien con la mano **2** *(say goodbye)* hacer adiós con la mano

wavy ADJECTIVE
ondulado (FEM ondulada)
□ He's got wavy hair. Tiene el pelo ondulado.

wax NOUN
la cera

way NOUN
1 la manera
□ She looked at me in a strange way. Me miró de manera extraña.
■ **This book tells you the right way to do it.** Este libro explica cómo hay que hacerlo.
■ **You're doing it the wrong way.** Lo estás haciendo mal.
■ **in a way...** en cierto sentido...
■ **a way of life** un estilo de vida
2 el camino *(route)*
□ I don't know the way. No sé el camino.
□ We stopped for lunch on the way. Paramos a comer en el camino.
■ **Which way is it?** ¿Por dónde es?
■ **The supermarket is this way.** El supermercado es por aquí.
■ **Do you know the way to the hotel?** ¿Sabes cómo llegar al hotel?
■ **He's on his way.** Está de camino.
■ **It's a long way.** Está lejos. □ It's a long way from the hotel. Está lejos del hotel.
■ **'way in'** 'entrada'
■ **'way out'** 'salida'
■ **by the way...** a propósito...

we PRONOUN
nosotros (FEM nosotras)
LANGUAGE TIP 'we' generally isn't translated unless it is emphatic.
□ We were in a hurry. Teníamos prisa.
LANGUAGE TIP Use **nosotros** or **nosotras** as appropriate for emphasis.
□ They went but we didn't. Ellos fueron pero nosotros no.

weak ADJECTIVE
1 débil (FEM débil)
2 poco cargado (FEM poco cargada) *(tea, coffee)*

wealthy ADJECTIVE
rico (FEM rica)

weapon NOUN
el arma *fem*
LANGUAGE TIP Although it's a feminine noun, remember that you use **el** and **un** with **arma**.

to **wear** VERB
llevar
□ She was wearing a hat. Llevaba un sombrero.
■ **She was wearing black.** Iba vestida de negro.

weather NOUN
el tiempo
□ What's the weather like? ¿Qué tiempo hace?

weather forecast NOUN
el pronóstico del tiempo

Web NOUN
■ **the Web** la Web

web browser NOUN
el navegador de Internet

webcam NOUN
la webcam

webmaster NOUN
el administrador de Web
la administradora de Web

web page NOUN
la página web

website NOUN
el sitio web

webzine NOUN
la revista electrónica

we'd = **we had; we would**

wedding NOUN
la boda

■ **wedding anniversary** el aniversario de boda
■ **wedding dress** el vestido de novia

Wednesday NOUN
el miércoles (PL los miércoles)
□ I saw her on Wednesday. La vi el miércoles. □ every Wednesday todos los miércoles □ last Wednesday el miércoles pasado □ next Wednesday el miércoles que viene □ on Wednesdays los miércoles

weed NOUN
el hierbajo
□ The garden's full of weeds. El jardín está lleno de hierbajos.

week NOUN
la semana
□ in a week's time dentro de una semana
■ **a week on Friday** el viernes de la semana que viene
■ **during the week** durante la semana

weekday NOUN
el día entre semana
LANGUAGE TIP Although **día** ends in **-a**, it is actually a masculine noun.
■ **on weekdays** los días entre semana

weekend NOUN
el fin de semana
■ **next weekend** el próximo fin de semana

to **weep** VERB
llorar

to **weigh** VERB
pesar
□ How much do you weigh? ¿Cuánto pesas?
■ **to weigh oneself** pesarse

weight NOUN
el peso
■ **to lose weight** adelgazar
■ **to put on weight** engordar

weightlifter NOUN
el levantador de pesas
la levantadora de pesas

weightlifting NOUN
el levantamiento de pesas

weird ADJECTIVE
raro (FEM rara)

welcome NOUN
▷ *see also* **welcome** VERB
la bienvenida
□ They gave her a warm welcome. Le dieron una calurosa bienvenida.
■ **Welcome!** ¡Bienvenido!
LANGUAGE TIP If you're addressing a woman remember to use the feminine form: **¡Bienvenida!** If you're addressing more than one person use the plural form **¡Bienvenidos!** or **¡Bienvenidas!**.

to **welcome** VERB
▷ *see also* **welcome** NOUN
■ **to welcome somebody** dar la bienvenida a alguien
■ **Thank you! — You're welcome!** ¡Gracias! — ¡De nada!

well ADJECTIVE, ADVERB
▷ *see also* **well** NOUN
1 bien
□ You did that really well. Lo hiciste realmente bien. □ She's doing really well at school. Le va muy bien en el colegio.
■ **to be well** estar bien □ I'm not very well at the moment. No estoy muy bien en este momento.
■ **Get well soon!** ¡Que te mejores!
■ **Well done!** ¡Muy bien!
2 bueno
□ It's enormous! Well, quite big anyway. ¡Es enorme! Bueno, digamos que bastante grande.
■ **as well** también □ We worked hard, but we had some fun as well. Trabajamos mucho, pero también nos divertimos.
■ **as well as** además de □ We went to Gerona as well as Sitges. Fuimos a Gerona, además de Sitges.

well NOUN
▷ *see also* **well** ADJECTIVE, ADVERB
el pozo

we'll = **we will**

well-behaved ADJECTIVE
■ **to be well-behaved** portarse bien

well-dressed ADJECTIVE
bien vestido (FEM bien vestida)

wellingtons PL NOUN
las botas de agua

well-known ADJECTIVE
conocido (FEM conocida)
□ a well-known film star un conocido actor de cine

well-off ADJECTIVE
adinerado (FEM adinerada)

Welsh ADJECTIVE
▷ *see also* **Welsh** NOUN
galés (FEM galesa)

Welsh NOUN
▷ *see also* **Welsh** ADJECTIVE
el galés *(language)*
■ **the Welsh** los galeses

Welshman NOUN
el galés (PL los galeses)

Welshwoman NOUN
la galesa

went VERB ▷ *see* **go**

were VERB ▷ *see* **be**

we're = **we are**

weren't = **were not**

west NOUN

▷ *see also* **west** ADJECTIVE, ADVERB
el oeste

west ADJECTIVE, ADVERB
▷ *see also* **west** NOUN
1 occidental (FEM occidental)
□ the west coast la costa occidental
■ **west of** al oeste de □ Stroud is west of Oxford. Stroud está al oeste de Oxford.
2 hacia el oeste
□ We were travelling west. Viajábamos hacia el oeste.
■ **the West Country** el sudoeste de Inglaterra

western NOUN
▷ *see also* **western** ADJECTIVE
el western

western ADJECTIVE
▷ *see also* **western** NOUN
occidental (FEM occidental)
□ the western part of the island la parte occidental de la isla
■ **Western Europe** Europa Occidental

West Indian ADJECTIVE
▷ *see also* **West Indian** NOUN
antillano (FEM antillana)
■ **She's West Indian.** Es antillana.

West Indian NOUN
▷ *see also* **West Indian** ADJECTIVE
el antillano
la antillana

West Indies PL NOUN
■ **the West Indies** las Antillas

wet ADJECTIVE
mojado (FEM mojada)
□ wet clothes ropa mojada
■ **to get wet** mojarse
■ **dripping wet** chorreando
■ **wet weather** el tiempo lluvioso
■ **It was wet all week.** Llovió toda la semana.

wetsuit NOUN
el traje de buzo

we've = **we have**

whale NOUN
la ballena

what ADJECTIVE, PRONOUN
1 qué

LANGUAGE TIP Use **qué** (with an accent) in direct and indirect questions and exclamations.

□ What subjects are you studying? ¿Qué asignaturas estudias? □ What colour is it? ¿De qué color es? □ What's the matter? ¿Qué te pasa? □ What's it for? ¿Para qué es? □ I don't know what to do. No sé qué hacer. □ What a mess! ¡Qué desorden!

LANGUAGE TIP Only translate 'what is' by **qué es** if asking for a definition or explanation.

□ What is it? ¿Qué es? □ What's a tractor, Daddy? ¿Qué es un tractor, papá? □ I asked him what DNA was. Le pregunté qué era el ADN.
2 cuál (FEM cuál, PL cuáles)

LANGUAGE TIP Translate 'what is' by **cuál es** when not asking for a definition or explanation.

□ What's the capital of Finland? ¿Cuál es la capital de Finlandia? □ What's her telephone number? ¿Cuál es su número de teléfono?
3 lo que

LANGUAGE TIP Use **lo que** (no accent) when 'what' isn't a question word.

□ I saw what happened. Vi lo que pasó. □ I heard what he said. Oí lo que dijo.
■ **What?** **1** *(what did you say?)* ¿Cómo? **2** *(shocked)* ¿Qué?
■ **What's your name?** ¿Cómo te llamas?

wheat NOUN
el trigo

wheel NOUN
la rueda
■ **steering wheel** el volante

wheelchair NOUN
la silla de ruedas

when ADVERB
▷ *see also* **when** CONJUNCTION
cuándo

LANGUAGE TIP Remember the accent on **cuándo** in direct and indirect questions.

□ When did he go? ¿Cuándo se fue? □ I asked her when the next bus was. Le pregunté cuándo salía el próximo autobús.

when CONJUNCTION
▷ *see also* **when** ADVERB
cuando
□ She was reading when I came in. Cuando entré ella estaba leyendo.

LANGUAGE TIP **cuando** has to be followed by a verb in the subjunctive when referring to an event in the future.

□ Call me when you get there. Llámame cuando llegues.

where ADVERB
▷ *see also* **where** CONJUNCTION
dónde

LANGUAGE TIP Remember the accent on **dónde** in direct and indirect questions.

□ Where do you live? ¿Dónde vives? □ Where are you from? ¿De dónde eres? □ She asked me where I had bought it. Me preguntó dónde lo había comprado.
■ **Where are you going?** ¿Adónde vas?

where CONJUNCTION
▷ *see also* **where** ADVERB
donde
□ a shop where you can buy coffee una tienda donde se puede comprar café

whether CONJUNCTION
si
□ I don't know whether to go or not. No sé si ir o no.

which ADJECTIVE, PRONOUN
1 cuál (FEM cuál, PL cuáles)
LANGUAGE TIP Remember the accent on **cuál** and **cuáles** in direct and indirect questions.
□ I know his sister. — Which one? Conozco a su hermana. — ¿A cuál? □ Which would you like? ¿Cuál quieres? □ Of the five pairs, which were sold? De los cinco pares, ¿cuáles se vendieron?
2 qué
LANGUAGE TIP Use **qué** (with an accent) before nouns.
□ Which flavour do you want? ¿Qué sabor quieres?
3 que
□ It's an illness which causes nerve damage. Es una enfermedad que daña los nervios. □ This is the skirt which Daphne gave me. Ésta es la falda que me dio Daphne. □ Our uniform, which is green, is quite nice. Nuestro uniforme, que es verde, está bastante bien.
LANGUAGE TIP After a preposition **que** becomes **el que**, **la que**, **los que**, **las que** to agree with the noun.
□ That's the film which I was telling you about. Ésa es la película de la que te hablaba.
4 lo cual
□ The cooker isn't working, which is a nuisance. La cocina no funciona, lo cual es un fastidio.

while CONJUNCTION
▷ *see also* **while** NOUN
1 mientras
□ You hold the torch while I look inside. Aguanta la linterna mientras yo miro por dentro.
2 mientras que
□ Isobel is very dynamic, while Kay is more laid-back. Isabel es muy dinámica, mientras que Kay es más tranquila.

while NOUN
▷ *see also* **while** CONJUNCTION
■ **a while** un rato □ after a while después de un rato
■ **a while ago** hace un momento □ He was here a while ago. Hace un momento estaba aquí.
■ **for a while** durante un tiempo □ I lived in London for a while. Viví en Londres durante un tiempo.
■ **quite a while** mucho tiempo □ I haven't seen him for quite a while. Hace mucho tiempo que no lo veo.

whip NOUN
▷ *see also* **whip** VERB
la fusta *(for horse)*

to **whip** VERB
▷ *see also* **whip** NOUN
1 fustigar* *(animal)*
2 azotar *(person)*
3 batir *(eggs, cream)*

whipped cream NOUN
la nata montada

whisk NOUN
el batidor

whiskers PL NOUN
los bigotes *(of animal)*

whisky NOUN
el whisky (PL los whiskys)

to **whisper** VERB
susurrar

whistle NOUN
▷ *see also* **whistle** VERB
el silbato
□ The referee blew his whistle. El árbitro tocó el silbato.

to **whistle** VERB
▷ *see also* **whistle** NOUN
1 pitar *(with a whistle)*
2 silbar *(with mouth)*

white ADJECTIVE
blanco (FEM blanca)
□ He's got white hair. Tiene el cabello blanco.
■ **white bread** el pan blanco
■ **white coffee** el café con leche
■ **a white man** un hombre blanco
■ **white people** los blancos
■ **white wine** el vino blanco

Whitsun NOUN
Pentecostés *masc*

who PRONOUN
1 quién (PL quiénes)
LANGUAGE TIP Remember the accent on **quién** and **quiénes** in direct and indirect questions.
□ Who said that? ¿Quién dijo eso? □ Who is it? ¿Quién es? □ We don't know who broke the window. No sabemos quién rompió la ventana.
2 que
□ the people who know us las personas que nos conocen
LANGUAGE TIP After a preposition **que** becomes **el que**, **la que**, **los que**, **las que** to agree with the noun.

□ the women who she was chatting with las mujeres con las que estaba hablando

LANGUAGE TIP Note that **a** + **el que** becomes **al que**.

□ the boy who I gave it to el chico al que se lo di

whole ADJECTIVE

▷ *see also* **whole** NOUN

entero (FEM entera)

□ the whole class la clase entera □ two whole days dos días enteros

■ **the whole afternoon** toda la tarde

■ **the whole world** todo el mundo

whole NOUN

▷ *see also* **whole** ADJECTIVE

■ **The whole of Wales was affected.** Todo Gales se vio afectado.

■ **on the whole** en general

wholemeal ADJECTIVE

integral (FEM integral)

□ wholemeal bread pan integral

wholewheat ADJECTIVE (US)

integral (FEM integral)

whom PRONOUN

1 quién (PL quiénes)

LANGUAGE TIP Remember the accent on **quién** and **quiénes** in direct and indirect questions.

□ With whom did you go? ¿Con quién fuiste? □ Whom did you call? ¿A quién llamaste?

2 quien

□ the man whom I saw el hombre a quien vi □ the woman to whom I spoke la mujer con quien hablé

whose ADJECTIVE

▷ *see also* **whose** PRONOUN

1 de quién (PL de quiénes) *(in questions)*

LANGUAGE TIP Remember the accent on **quién** and **quiénes** in direct and indirect questions.

□ Whose books are these? ¿De quiénes son estos libros? □ Do you know whose jacket this is? ¿Sabes de quién es esta chaqueta?

2 cuyo (FEM cuya) *(relative)*

□ the girl whose picture was in the paper la muchacha cuya foto venía en el periódico □ a neighbour whose sons go to that school un vecino cuyos hijos van a ese colegio

whose PRONOUN

▷ *see also* **whose** ADJECTIVE

de quién (PL de quiénes)

LANGUAGE TIP Remember the accent on **quién** and **quiénes** in direct and indirect questions.

□ Whose is this? ¿De quién es esto? □ I know whose they are. Yo sé de quiénes son.

why ADVERB

por qué

LANGUAGE TIP Remember to write **por qué** as two words with an accent on **qué** when translating 'why'.

□ Why did you do that? ¿Por qué hiciste eso?

■ **Why not?** ¿Por qué no?

■ **That's why he did it.** Por eso lo hizo.

wicked ADJECTIVE

1 malvado (FEM malvada) *(evil)*

2 sensacional (FEM sensacional) *(really great)*

wicket NOUN

los palos *(stumps)*

wide ADJECTIVE, ADVERB

ancho (FEM ancha)

□ a wide road una carretera ancha □ How wide is the room? — It's five metres wide. ¿Cómo es de ancha la habitación? — Tiene cinco metros de ancho.

■ **wide open** abierto de par en par □ The door was wide open. La puerta estaba abierta de par en par.

■ **wide awake** completamente despierto

widow NOUN

la viuda

□ She's a widow. Es viuda.

widower NOUN

el viudo

□ He's a widower. Es viudo.

width NOUN

la anchura

wife NOUN

la esposa

wig NOUN

la peluca

wild ADJECTIVE

1 salvaje (FEM salvaje)

□ a wild animal un animal salvaje

2 silvestre (FEM silvestre)

□ wild flowers flores silvestres

3 loco (FEM loca)

□ She's a bit wild. Es un poco loca.

wildlife NOUN

la flora y fauna

will NOUN

▷ *see also* **will** VERB

el testamento *(document)*

will VERB

▷ *see also* **will** NOUN

LANGUAGE TIP 'will' can often be translated by the present tense, as in the following examples.

□ Come on, I'll help you. Venga, te ayudo. □ We'll talk about it later. Hablamos luego. □ Will you help me? ¿Me ayudas?

LANGUAGE TIP Use **voy a**, **va a**, and so on + the infinitive to talk about plans and intentions.

□ What will you do? ¿Qué vas a hacer?

□ We'll be having lunch late. Vamos a comer tarde.

LANGUAGE TIP Use the future tense when guessing what will happen or when making a supposition.

□ It won't take long. No llevará mucho tiempo. □ We'll probably go out later. Seguramente saldremos luego. □ I'll always love you. Te querré siempre. □ That will be the postman. Será el cartero.

LANGUAGE TIP Use **querer** for 'to be willing' in emphatic requests, and invitations.

□ Tom won't help me. Tom no me quiere ayudar. □ Will you be quiet! ¿Te quieres callar? □ Will you have some tea? ¿Quieres tomar un té?

willing ADJECTIVE
■ **to be willing to do something** estar dispuesto a hacer algo

to **win** VERB
▷ *see also* **win** NOUN
ganar
□ Did you win? ¿Ganaste? □ to win a prize ganar un premio

win NOUN
▷ *see also* **win** VERB
la victoria

to **wind** VERB
▷ *see also* **wind** NOUN
enrollar *(rope, wire)*

wind NOUN
▷ *see also* **wind** VERB
el viento
■ **a wind instrument** un instrumento de viento
■ **wind power** la energía eólica

windmill NOUN
el molino de viento

window NOUN
1 la ventana *(of building)*
2 la ventanilla *(in car, train)*
■ **a shop window** un escaparate
3 el cristal *(window pane)* (el vidrio *Latin America*)
□ to break a window romper un cristal

windscreen NOUN
el parabrisas (PL los parabrisas)

windscreen wiper NOUN
el limpiaparabrisas (PL los limpiaparabrisas)

windshield NOUN (US)
el parabrisas (PL los parabrisas)

windshield wiper NOUN (US)
el limpiaparabrisas (PL los limpiaparabrisas)

windy ADJECTIVE
■ **a windy day** un día de viento
■ **Edinburgh's a very windy city.** En Edimburgo hace mucho viento.
■ **It's windy.** Hace viento.

wine NOUN
el vino
□ white wine el vino blanco □ red wine el vino tinto
■ **a wine bar** un bar especializado en vinos
■ **a wine cellar** una bodega
■ **a wine glass** una copa de vino
■ **the wine list** la carta de vinos

wing NOUN
el ala *fem*

LANGUAGE TIP Although it's a feminine noun, remember that you use **el** and **un** with **ala**.

to **wink** VERB
■ **to wink at somebody** guiñar el ojo a alguien

winner NOUN
el ganador
la ganadora

winning ADJECTIVE
vencedor (FEM vencedora)
□ the winning team el equipo vencedor
■ **the winning goal** el gol de la victoria

winter NOUN
el invierno

winter sports PL NOUN
los deportes de invierno

to **wipe** VERB
limpiar
■ **to wipe one's feet** limpiarse los zapatos
■ **to wipe one's nose** limpiarse la nariz
■ **Did you wipe up that water you spilled?** ¿Recogiste el agua que derramaste?

wire NOUN
el alambre
■ **copper wire** el hilo de cobre
■ **the telephone wire** el cable del teléfono

wisdom tooth NOUN
la muela del juicio

wise ADJECTIVE
sabio (FEM sabia)

to **wish** VERB
▷ *see also* **wish** NOUN
■ **to wish for something** desear algo
□ What more could you wish for? ¿Qué más podrías desear?
■ **to wish to do something** desear hacer algo □ I wish to make a complaint. Deseo hacer una reclamación.
■ **I wish you were here!** ¡Ojalá estuvieras aquí!
■ **I wish you'd told me!** ¡Me lo podrías haber dicho!
■ **to wish somebody happy birthday** desear a alguien un feliz cumpleaños

wish NOUN
▷ *see also* **wish** VERB

el deseo

□ to make a wish pedir un deseo

■ **'best wishes'** *(on birthday card)* 'felicidades'

■ **'with best wishes, Kathy'** 'un abrazo, Kathy'

wit NOUN
el ingenio

with PREPOSITION
1 con
□ He walks with a stick. Camina con un bastón. □ Come with me. Ven conmigo.
2 de
□ a woman with blue eyes una mujer de ojos azules □ green with envy muerto de envidia □ to shake with fear temblar de miedo □ Fill the jug with water. Llena la jarra de agua.

■ **We stayed with friends.** Nos quedamos en casa de unos amigos.

within PREPOSITION
dentro de
□ I want it back within three days. Quiero que me lo devuelvas dentro de tres días.

■ **The police arrived within minutes.** La policía llegó a los pocos minutos.

■ **The shops are within easy reach.** Las tiendas están cerca.

without PREPOSITION
sin
□ without a coat sin abrigo □ without speaking sin hablar

witness NOUN
el/la testigo
□ There were no witnesses. No había testigos.

witty ADJECTIVE
ingenioso (FEM ingeniosa)

wives PL NOUN ▷ *see* **wife**

woke up VERB ▷ *see* **wake up**

wolf NOUN
el lobo

woman NOUN
la mujer

■ **a woman doctor** una doctora

won VERB ▷ *see* **win**

to **wonder** VERB
preguntarse
□ I wonder why she said that. Me pregunto por qué dijo eso.

■ **I wonder where Caroline is.** ¿Dónde estará Caroline?

wonderful ADJECTIVE
maravilloso (FEM maravillosa)

won't = **will not**

wood NOUN
1 la madera
□ It's made of wood. Es de madera.
2 la leña *(for fire)*
3 el bosque
□ We went for a walk in the wood. Fuimos a pasear por el bosque.

wooden ADJECTIVE
de madera
□ a wooden chair una silla de madera

woodwork NOUN
la carpintería

wool NOUN
la lana
□ It's made of wool. Es de lana.

word NOUN
la palabra

■ **What's the word for 'shop' in Spanish?** ¿Cómo se dice 'shop' en español?

■ **in other words** en otras palabras

■ **to have a word with somebody** hablar con alguien □ Can I have a word with you? ¿Puedo hablar contigo?

■ **the words** *(lyrics)* la letra

word processing NOUN
el procesamiento de textos

word processor NOUN
el procesador de textos

wore VERB ▷ *see* **wear**

work NOUN
▷ *see also* **work** VERB
el trabajo
□ She's looking for work. Está buscando trabajo.

■ **It's hard work.** Es duro.

■ **at work** en el trabajo □ He's at work until five o'clock. Está en el trabajo hasta las cinco.

■ **He's off work today.** Hoy tiene el día libre.

■ **to be out of work** estar sin trabajo

to **work** VERB
▷ *see also* **work** NOUN
1 trabajar
□ She works in a shop. Trabaja en una tienda. □ to work hard trabajar mucho
2 funcionar
□ The heating isn't working. La calefacción no funciona. □ My plan worked perfectly. Mi plan funcionó a la perfección.

to **work out** VERB
1 hacer* ejercicio *(exercise)*
□ I work out twice a week. Hago ejercicio dos veces a la semana.
2 salir* *(turn out)*
□ I hope it will work out well. Espero que salga bien.
3 calcular *(calculate)*
□ I worked it out in my head. Lo calculé en mi cabeza.
4 entender* *(understand)*

English-Spanish

W

□ I just couldn't work it out. No lograba entenderlo.

■ **It works out at £10 each.** Sale a 10 libras esterlinas por persona.

worker NOUN

el trabajador

la trabajadora

□ She's a good worker. Trabaja bien.

work experience NOUN

■ **I'm going to do my work experience in a factory.** Voy a hacer las prácticas en una fábrica.

working-class ADJECTIVE

de clase obrera

□ a working-class family una familia de clase obrera

workman NOUN

el obrero

works NOUN

la fábrica

worksheet NOUN

la hoja de ejercicios

workshop NOUN

el taller

□ a drama workshop un taller de teatro

workstation NOUN

la terminal de trabajo

world NOUN

el mundo

■ **the world champion** el campeón mundial

■ **the World Cup** la Copa del Mundo

worm NOUN

el gusano

worn VERB ▷ *see* **wear**

worn ADJECTIVE

gastado (FEM gastada)

□ The carpet is a bit worn. La moqueta está un poco gastada.

■ **worn out** agotado □ We were worn out after the long walk. Estábamos agotados después de andar tanto.

worried ADJECTIVE

preocupado (FEM preocupada)

□ to be worried about something estar preocupado por algo □ to look worried parecer preocupado

to **worry** VERB

preocuparse

■ **Don't worry!** ¡No te preocupes!

worse ADJECTIVE, ADVERB

peor (FEM peora)

□ It was even worse than mine. Era incluso peor que el mío. □ I'm feeling worse. Me encuentro peor.

to **worship** VERB

adorar

worst ADJECTIVE

▷ *see also* **worst** NOUN

peor

□ the worst student in the class el peor alumno de la clase □ my worst enemy mi peor enemigo

■ **Maths is my worst subject.** Las matemáticas es la asignatura que peor se me da.

worst NOUN

▷ *see also* **worst** ADJECTIVE

■ **The worst of it is that...** Lo peor es que...

■ **at worst** en el peor de los casos

■ **if the worst comes to the worst** en el peor de los casos

worth ADJECTIVE

■ **to be worth** valer □ It's worth a lot of money. Vale mucho dinero. □ How much is it worth? ¿Cuánto vale?

■ **It's worth it.** Vale la pena.

would VERB

LANGUAGE TIP The conditional is often used to translate 'would' + verb.

□ I said I would do it. Dije que lo haría. □ If you asked him he'd do it. Si se lo pidieras, lo haría. □ If you had asked him he would have done it. Si se lo hubieras pedido, lo habría hecho.

LANGUAGE TIP When 'would you' is used to make requests, translate using **poder** in the present.

□ Would you close the door please? ¿Puedes cerrar la puerta, por favor?

■ **I'd like ... 1** Me gustaría ... □ I'd like to go to China. Me gustaría ir a China. **2** Quería ... □ I'd like three tickets please. Quería tres entradas.

■ **Would you like a biscuit?** ¿Quieres una galleta?

LANGUAGE TIP Use the subjunctive after **querer que**.

■ **Would you like me to iron your jeans for you?** ¿Quieres que te planche los pantalones?

■ **Would you like to go to the cinema?** ¿Quieres ir al cine?

wouldn't = **would not**

to **wound** VERB

▷ *see also* **wound** NOUN

herir*

□ He was wounded in the leg. Fue herido en la pierna.

wound NOUN

▷ *see also* **wound** VERB

la herida

to **wrap** VERB

envolver*

□ She's wrapping her Christmas presents. Está envolviendo los regalos de Navidad.

□ Can you wrap it for me please? ¿Me lo puede envolver en papel de regalo, por favor?

to **wrap up** VERB
1 envolver* *(parcel)*
2 abrigarse* *(put on warm clothes)*

wrapping paper NOUN
el papel de regalo

wreck NOUN
▹ *see also* **wreck** VERB
el cacharro
□ That car is a wreck! ¡Ese coche es un cacharro!
■ **After the exams I was a complete wreck.** Después de los exámenes estaba hecho polvo.

to **wreck** VERB
▹ *see also* **wreck** NOUN
1 destruir*
□ The explosion wrecked the whole house. La explosión destruyó toda la casa.
2 destrozar* *(car)*
3 echar por tierra
□ The bad weather wrecked our plans. El mal tiempo echó por tierra nuestros planes.

wreckage NOUN
1 los restos *(of vehicle)*
2 las ruinas *(of buildings)*

wrestler NOUN
el luchador
la luchadora

wrestling NOUN
la lucha libre

wrinkled ADJECTIVE
arrugado (FEM arrugada)

wrist NOUN
la muñeca

to **write** VERB
escribir*
□ to write a letter escribir una carta

to **write down** VERB
anotar
□ I wrote down her address. Anoté su dirección. □ Can you write it down for me, please? ¿Me lo puedes anotar, por favor?

writer NOUN
el escritor
la escritora

writing NOUN
la letra
□ I can't read your writing. No entiendo tu letra.
■ **in writing** por escrito

written VERB ▹ *see* **write**

wrong ADJECTIVE, ADVERB
1 incorrecto (FEM incorrecta)
□ The information they gave us was wrong. La información que nos dieron era incorrecta. □ the wrong answer la respuesta incorrecta
■ **You've got the wrong number.** Se ha equivocado de número.
2 mal
□ I think hunting is wrong. Opino que está mal cazar. □ You've done it wrong. Lo has hecho mal.
■ **to go wrong** *(plan)* ir mal □ The robbery went wrong and they got caught. El atraco fue mal y los pillaron.
■ **to be wrong** estar equivocado □ You're wrong about that. En eso estás equivocado.
■ **What's wrong?** ¿Qué pasa? □ What's wrong with her? ¿Qué le pasa?

wrote VERB ▹ *see* **write**

Xx

Xmas NOUN *(= Christmas)*
la Navidad

to **X-ray** VERB
▹ *see also* **X-ray** NOUN
hacer* una radiografía de
□ They X-rayed my arm. Me hicieron una radiografía del brazo.

X-ray NOUN
▹ *see also* **X-ray** VERB
la radiografía
□ I had an X-ray taken. Me hicieron una radiografía.

Yy

yacht NOUN
el yate

yard NOUN
1 la yarda

DID YOU KNOW...?
In Spain measurements are in metres and centimetres rather than feet and inches. A yard is about 90 cm.

2 el patio *(of school, house)*

to **yawn** VERB
bostezar*

year NOUN
el año
□ last year el año pasado
■ **to be 15 years old** tener 15 años
■ **an eight-year-old child** un niño de ocho años
■ **She's in the fifth year.** Está en quinto.

to **yell** VERB
gritar

yellow ADJECTIVE
amarillo (FEM amarilla)

yes ADVERB
sí
□ Do you like it? — Yes. ¿Te gusta? — Sí.

yesterday ADVERB
ayer
□ yesterday morning ayer por la mañana
□ all day yesterday todo el día de ayer

yet ADVERB
todavía
□ Have you eaten? — Not yet. ¿Ya has comido? — Todavía no. □ It's not finished yet. Todavía no está terminado. □ There's no news as yet. Todavía no se tienen noticias.
■ **Have you finished yet?** ¿Has terminado ya?

yob NOUN
el gamberro (el vándalo *Latin America*)

yoghurt NOUN
el yogur

yolk NOUN
la yema

you PRONOUN

LANGUAGE TIP There are formal and informal ways of saying 'you' in Spanish. As you look down the entry, choose the informal options if talking to people your own age or that you know well. Otherwise use the formal options. Note that subject pronouns are used less in Spanish – for emphasis and in comparisons.

1 tú *(informal: 1 person)*
□ What do YOU think about it? ¿Y tú qué piensas? □ She's younger than you. Es más joven que tú.
■ **You don't understand me.** No me entiendes.

2 vosotros *masc pl*
vosotras *fem pl (informal: 2 or more people)*
□ You've got kids but we haven't. Vosotros tenéis hijos pero nosotros no. □ They're younger than you. Son más jóvenes que vosotros. □ I'd like to speak to you. *(ie all female)* Quiero hablar con vosotras.
■ **How are you?** ¿Qué tal estáis?

3 usted *(formal: 1 person)*
□ They're younger than you. Son más jóvenes que usted. □ This is for you. Esto es para usted.
■ **How are you?** ¿Cómo está?

4 ustedes *(formal: 2 or more people)*

LANGUAGE TIP **ustedes** is always used in Latin America instead of **vosotros**.

□ They're younger than you. Son más jóvenes que ustedes. □ This is for you. Esto es para ustedes.
■ **How are you?** ¿Cómo están?

LANGUAGE TIP When 'you' means 'one' or 'people' in general, the impersonal **se** is often used.

□ I doubt it, but you never know. Lo dudo, pero nunca se sabe.

LANGUAGE TIP When 'you' is the object of the sentence, you have to use different forms from the ones above. See translations 5 to 10 below.

5 te *(informal: 1 person)*
□ I love you. Te quiero. □ Shall I give it to you? ¿Te lo doy?
■ **This is for you.** Esto es para ti.
■ **Can I go with you?** ¿Puedo ir contigo?
6 os *(informal: 2 or more people)*
□ I saw you. Os vi. □ I gave you the keys. Os di las llaves.
■ **I gave them to you.** Os los di.
7 lo *masc sing*
la *fem sing (formal: 1 person – direct object)*
□ May I help you? ¿Puedo ayudarlo? □ I saw you, Mrs Jones. La vi, señora Jones.
8 le *(formal: 1 person – indirect object)*
□ I gave you the keys. Le di las llaves.
LANGUAGE TIP Change **le** to **se** before another object pronoun.
■ **I gave them to you.** Se las di.
9 los *masc pl*
las *fem pl (formal: 2 or more people – direct object)*
□ May I help you? ¿Puedo ayudarlos?
10 les *pl (formal: 2 or more people – indirect object)*
LANGUAGE TIP Change **les** to **se** before another object pronoun.
□ I gave you the keys. Les di las llaves.
■ **I gave them to you.** Se las di.

young ADJECTIVE
joven (FEM joven, PL jóvenes)
■ **young people** los jóvenes
■ **He's younger than me.** Es menor que yo.
■ **my youngest brother** mi hermano pequeño

your ADJECTIVE
LANGUAGE TIP Use **tu** and **vuestro/vuestra** etc with people your own age or that you know well, and **su/sus** otherwise.
1 tu (PL tus) *(informal: 1 person)*
LANGUAGE TIP Remember there's no accent on **tu** meaning 'your'.
□ your house tu casa □ your books tus libros □ your sisters tus hermanas
2 vuestro (FEM vuestra) *(informal: 2 or more people)*
LANGUAGE TIP Remember to make **vuestro** agree with the person or thing it describes.
□ your dog vuestro perro □ These are your keys. Éstas son vuestras llaves.
3 su (PL sus) *(formal)*
LANGUAGE TIP Use **su** when talking to one person or to a group of people. **su** is used in Latin America instead of **vuestro**.
□ Can I see your passport, sir? ¿Me enseña su pasaporte, señor? □ your wife su mujer
□ your uncle and aunt sus tíos
LANGUAGE TIP Use **el, la, los, las** as appropriate with parts of the body and to translate 'your' referring to people in general.
□ Have you washed your hair? ¿Te has lavado el pelo? □ Would you like to wash your hands? ¿Queréis lavaros las manos?
■ **It's bad for your health.** Es malo para la salud.

yours PRONOUN
LANGUAGE TIP Use **tuyo/tuya** etc and **vuestro/vuestra** etc with people your own age or that you know well, and **su/sus** otherwise.
1 tuyo (FEM tuya) *(informal: 1 person)*
LANGUAGE TIP Remember to make **tuyo** agree with the person or thing it describes.
□ That's yours. Eso es tuyo. □ Is that box yours? ¿Ésa caja es tuya?
LANGUAGE TIP Add the definite article when 'yours' means 'your one' or 'your ones'.
■ **I've lost my pen. Can I use yours?** He perdido el bolígrafo. ¿Puedo usar el tuyo?
■ **These are my keys and those are yours.** Éstas son mis llaves y ésas son las tuyas.
2 vuestro (FEM vuestra) *(informal: 2 or more people)*
LANGUAGE TIP Remember to make **vuestro** agree with the person or thing it describes.
□ That's yours. Eso es vuestro.
LANGUAGE TIP Add the definite article when 'yours' means 'your one' or 'your ones'.
■ **These are my keys and those are yours.** Éstas son mis llaves y ésas son las vuestras.
3 suyo (FEM suya) *(formal)*
LANGUAGE TIP Use **suyo** in more formal situations with one person or a group of people, and remember to make it agree with the person or thing it describes. **suyo** is always used instead of **vuestro** in Latin America.
□ That's yours. Eso es suyo.
LANGUAGE TIP Add the definite article when 'yours' means 'your one' or 'your ones'.
■ **I've lost my pen. Can I use yours?** He perdido el bolígrafo. ¿Puedo usar el suyo?
■ **These are my keys and those are yours.** Éstas son mis llaves y ésas son las suyas.
■ **Yours sincerely...** Le saluda atentamente...

yourself PRONOUN

LANGUAGE TIP Use **te**, **tú mismo** and **ti mismo** when you are talking to someone of your own age or that you know well and **se** and **usted mismo** otherwise.

1 te *(reflexive)*
□ Have you hurt yourself? ¿Te has hecho daño?
2 tú mismo (FEM tú misma) *(for emphasis)*
□ Do it yourself! ¡Hazlo tú mismo!
3 ti mismo (FEM ti misma) *(after a preposition)*
□ You did it for yourself. Lo hiciste para ti mismo.
4 se *(reflexive)*
□ Have you hurt yourself? ¿Se ha hecho daño?
5 usted mismo (FEM usted misma) *(after a preposition, for emphasis)*
□ You did it for yourself. Lo hizo para usted mismo. □ Do it yourself! ¡Hágalo usted mismo!

yourselves PRONOUN

LANGUAGE TIP In Spain use **os** and **vosotros mismos** when talking to people your own age or that you know well, and **se** or **ustedes mismos** otherwise. In Latin America **se** and **ustedes mismos** replace both **os** and **vosotros mismos**.

1 os *(reflexive)*
□ Did you enjoy yourselves? ¿Os divertisteis?
2 vosotros mismos (FEM vosotras mismas) *(after a preposition, for emphasis)*
□ Did you make it yourselves? ¿Lo habéis hecho vosotros mismos?
3 se *(reflexive)*
□ Did you enjoy yourselves? ¿Se divirtieron?
4 ustedes mismos (FEM ustedes mismas) *(after a preposition, for emphasis)*
□ Did you make it yourselves? ¿Lo han hecho ustedes mismos?

youth club NOUN
el club juvenil (PL los clubs juveniles)

youth hostel NOUN
el albergue juvenil

Yugoslavia NOUN
Yugoslavia *fem*
□ in the former Yugoslavia en la antigua Yugoslavia

Zz

zany ADJECTIVE
estrafalario (FEM estrafalaria)

zebra NOUN
la cebra

zebra crossing NOUN
el paso de cebra

zero NOUN
el cero

Zimbabwe NOUN
Zimbabue *masc*

Zimmer frame® NOUN
el andador ortopédico

zip NOUN
la cremallera

zip code NOUN (US)
el código postal

zipper NOUN (US)
la cremallera

zit NOUN
el grano

zodiac NOUN
el zodíaco
□ **the signs of the zodiac** los signos del zodíaco

zone NOUN
la zona

zoo NOUN
el zoo

zoom lens NOUN
el zoom

zucchini NOUN (US)
el calabacín (PL los calabacines)